HANDBOOK OF
CLINICAL
PSYCHOLOGY

HANDBOOK OF CLINICAL PSYCHOLOGY

Volume 2   Children and Adolescents

Edited by

MICHEL HERSEN
ALAN M. GROSS

John Wiley & Sons, Inc.

Contents

PART III
Research Contributions

PART IV
Diagnosis and Evaluation

PART V
Treatment

PART VI
Special Issues

Preface

HANDBOOK OF CLINICAL PSYCHOLOGY (VOLUMES 1 AND 2)

Over the past 3 decades the field of clinical psychology has periodically been reviewed in large tomes in multiauthor editions. Indeed, the senior editor of the present work has been involved in three such projects, published in 1983, 1991, and 1998. Since publication of the last of these works there have been major developments in clinical psychology, both with adults and with children and adolescents. Some of the most interesting innovations have appeared in the areas of ethics, legal issues, professional roles, cross-cultural psychology, psychoneuroimmunology, cognitive-behavioral treatment, psychopharmacology as practiced by clinical psychologists, political issues, geropsychology, parent training, pediatric psychology, assessment of child maltreatment and its remediation, and problems in infancy. The veritable explosion of new data has been fueled by the advent of new journals in highly specialized areas, in addition to the rapid dissemination of new ideas and data rapidly presented through electronic publication.

The plethora of data is distilled into 33 chapters for Volume 1 on adults and 32 chapters for Volume 2 on children. To enable the reader to easily traverse the two volumes we decided on a parallel structure. Therefore, each of the volumes is divided into six parts (Part I: General Issues, Part II: Theoretical Models, Part III: Research Contributions, Part IV: Diagnosis and Evaluation, Part V: Treatment, and Part VI: Special Issues). In both volumes a case illustration has been included in the section on Treatment. Authors here have been encouraged, to the extent possible, to use a relatively standard format: Identifying Features of the Client, Presenting Complaints, History, Assessment, Case Conceptualization, Course of Treatment and Assessment of Progress, Complicating Factors, Managed Care Considerations, Follow-up, Treatment Implications of the Case, and Recommendations to Clinicians and Students. In the volume on children and adolescents Developmental Factors and Parental Factors are added considerations that the authors have outlined.

These two volumes were conceived with graduate students and professionals in the field in mind. We believe that the material systematically presented herein is suitable both as a general reference work and separately as a major course text for clinical psychology with adults and clinical psychology applied to children. We, of course, eagerly anticipate the comments of both professors and students.

Many individuals have been involved in the development and fruition of this two-volume work. First and foremost we thank our contributors for taking time out from their busy schedules to share their expertise with us. Second, we thank our friends at John Wiley and Sons for their appreciation of clinical psychology and the technical processing of this two-volume set. Third, once again we thank Carole Londeree for helping us to track all of the authors and manuscripts in her typical orderly and competent manner. Without her terrific help this could not have been accomplished. Finally, we thank Christopher Brown and Blake Kirschner for their wonderful technical work related to the indexes.

MICHEL HERSEN
Hillsboro, Oregon
ALAN M. GROSS
Oxford, Mississippi

Contributors

Thomas M. Achenbach, PhD
Department of Psychiatry
University of Vermont
Burlington, Vermont

Edward R. Anderson, PhD
Department of Human Ecology and
    Population Research Center
University of Texas—Austin
Austin, Texas

Courey A. Averett, BA
Department of Psychology
University of Alabama
Tuscaloosa, Alabama

Debora J. Bell, PhD
Department of Psychological Sciences
University of Missouri—Columbia
Columbia, Missouri

Leslie D. Berkelhammer, PhD
Division of Behavioral Medicine
St. Jude Children's Research Hospital
Memphis, Tennessee

Jennifer Bolden, BA
Department of Psychology
University of Central Florida
Orlando, Florida

Sarah R. Brand, BA
Department of Psychology
Emory University
Atlanta, Georgia

Sue C. Bratton, PhD
Department of Counseling and
    Higher Education
University of North Texas
Denton, Texas

Angela M. Burke, BA
Department of Psychology
Suffolk University
Boston, Massachusetts

Daniel B. Chorney, MS
Department of Psychology
West Virginia University
Morgantown, West Virginia

L. Caitlin Cook, BA
Department of Psychology
University of Nevada—Las Vegas
Las Vegas, Nevada

Lisa W. Coyne, PhD
Department of Psychology
Suffolk University
Boston, Massachusetts

Audra L. Crutchfield, MA
Department of Psychology
University of North Texas
Denton, Texas

Kristal Ehrhardt, PhD
Department of Special Education and
    Literacy Studies
Western Michigan University
Kalamazoo, Michigan

Tiffany Field, PhD
Touch Research Institutes
University of Miami School
   of Medicine
Miami, Florida

Jennifer B. Freeman, PhD
Child and Family Psychiatry
Brown Medical School and Rhode
   Island Hospital
Providence, Rhode Island

Kurt A. Freeman, PhD
Child Development and Rehabilitation
   Center
Oregon Health and Science
   University
Portland, Oregon

Patrick C. Friman, PhD, ABPP
Girls and Boys Town Outpatient
   Behavioral Pediatrics and
   Family Services
Boys Town, Nebraska, and
Department of Clinical Pediatrics
University of Nebraska Medical
   Center
Omaha, Nebraska

Jennifer M. Gillis, PhD, BCBA
Department of Psychology
Auburn University
Auburn, Alabama

Sherryl H. Goodman, PhD
Department of Psychology
Emory University
Atlanta, Georgia

Shannon M. Greene, PhD
Department of Human Ecology
   and Population Research Center
University of Texas—Austin
Austin, Texas

Amie Grills-Taquechel, PhD
Department of Psychology
University of Houston
Houston, Texas

Courtney M. Haight, MA
Department of Psychology
University of Nevada—Las
   Vegas
Las Vegas, Nevada

Grayson N. Holmbeck, PhD
Department of Psychology
Loyola University Chicago
Chicago, Illinois

Stephen D. A. Hupp, PhD
Department of Psychology
Southern Illinois University—
   Edwardsville
Edwardsville, Illinois

Ellen Jamieson, MEd
Departments of Psychiatry and
   Behavioral Neurosciences and
   Pediatrics
McMaster University
Hamilton, Ontario, Canada

Barbara Jandasek, MA
Department of Psychology
Loyola University Chicago
Chicago, Illinois

David M. Janicke, PhD
Department of Clinical and Health
   Psychology
University of Florida
Gainesville, Florida

Erin Jeffords, BA
Department of Psychology
The Citadel
Charleston, South Carolina

Jeremy D. Jewell, PhD
Clinical Child and School Psychology
   Program
Southern Illinois University—
   Edwardsville
Edwardsville, Illinois

James H. Johnson, PhD, ABPP
Department of Clinical and Health
   Psychology
University of Florida
Gainesville, Florida

Laura Johnson, PhD
Department of Psychology
University of Mississippi
University, Mississippi

Erika K. Johnson-Jimenez, PhD
Forensic Health Services
New Mexico Women's Correctional
   Facility
Grants, New Mexico

Jessica T. Kaster, PhD
Lakeland Mental Health Center, Inc.
Moorhead, Minnesota

Christopher A. Kearney, PhD
Child School Refusal and Anxiety
   Disorders Clinic and
Department of Psychology
University of Nevada—Las Vegas
Las Vegas, Nevada

Michael J. Kofler, MS
Department of Psychology
University of Central Florida
Orlando, Florida

Thomas R. Kratochwill, PhD
School Psychology Program and
   Educational and Psychological
   Training Center
University of Wisconsin—Madison
Madison, Wisconsin

Garry Landreth, EdD
Department of Counseling and Higher
   Education
University of North Texas
Denton, Texas

Eman Leung, PhD
Departments of Psychiatry and
   Behavioral Neurosciences and
   Pediatrics
University of Western Ontario
London, Ontario, Canada

Aaron M. Luebbe, MA
Department of Psychological Sciences
University of Missouri—Columbia
Columbia, Missouri

**Harriet L. MacMillan, MD,
   FRCP(C)**
Departments of Psychiatry and Behav-
   ioral Neurosciences and Pediatrics
McMaster University
Hamilton, Ontario, Canada

Jessica Madrigal-Bauguss, BA
Department of Psychology
University of North Texas
Denton, Texas

David Mark Mantell, PhD
John Jay College of Criminal Justice
University of Connecticut Medical
   School
New Britain, Connecticut

Eric J. Mash, PhD
Department of Psychology
University of Calgary
Calgary, Alberta, Canada

James P. McHale, PhD
Department of Psychology
University of South Florida—
   St. Petersburg
St. Petersburg, Florida

Raymond G. Miltenberger, PhD
Department of Child and Family
    Studies
University of South Florida
Tampa, Florida

Richard J. Morris, PhD
School Psychology Program,
    Department of Special Education,
    Rehabilitation, and School
    Psychology
University of Arizona
Tucson, Arizona

Tracy L. Morris, PhD
Department of Psychology
West Virginia University
Morgantown, West Virginia

Amy R. Murrell, PhD
Department of Psychology
University of North Texas
Denton, Texas

Douglas W. Nangle, PhD
Department of Psychology
University of Maine
Orono, Maine

Carrie Nassif, PhD
Department of Psychology
Fort Hays State University
Hays, Kansas

Thomas H. Ollendick, PhD
Department of Psychology
Virginia Polytechnic Institute and State
    University
Blacksburg, Virginia

Alan Poling, PhD
Department of Psychology
Western Michigan University
Kalamazoo, Michigan

Matthew Porritt, MA
Department of Psychology
Western Michigan University
Kalamazoo, Michigan

Mark D. Rapport, PhD
Department of Psychology
University of Central Florida
Orlando, Florida

Dee Ray, PhD
Department of Counseling and Higher
    Education
University of North Texas
Denton, Texas

Steven K. Reader, PhD
Department of Clinical and Health
    Psychology
University of Florida
Gainesville, Florida

Cara B. Reeves, PhD
College of Health Professions
Medical University of South
    Carolina
Charleston, South Carolina

David Reitman, PhD
Center for Psychological
    Studies
Nova Southeastern University
Fort Lauderdale, Florida

Michelle S. Rivera, MA
Department of Psychology
University of Maine
Orono, Maine

Mark W. Roberts, PhD
Department of Psychology
Idaho State University
Pocatello, Idaho

Joseph Robinson, BS
School Psychology Program
University of Wisconsin–
    Madison
Madison, Wisconsin

Raymond G. Romanczyk,
    PhD, BCBA
Department of Psychology
State University of New York—
    Binghamton
Binghamton, New York

Brigid M. Rose, PhD
VA Northern California
    Health Care System
Martinez, California

Sandra W. Russ, PhD
Department of Psychology
Case Western Reserve University
Cleveland, Ohio

Randall T. Salekin, PhD
Department of Psychology and
Center for the Prevention of Youth
    Behavior Problems
University of Alabama
Tuscaloosa, Alabama

Dustin E. Sarver, BA
Department of Psychology
University of Central Florida
Orlando, Florida

Stefan E. Schulenberg, PhD
Department of Psychology
University of Mississippi
University, Mississippi

Stephanie Stowman, MA
Department of Psychology
University of Nevada—Las Vegas
Las Vegas, Nevada

Kate Sullivan, MA
Department of Human Ecology
    and Population Research Center
University of Texas—Austin
Austin, Texas

Matthew J. Sullivan, PhD
Private Practice
Palo Alto, California

Cicely Taravella LaBorde, BS
Department of Psychology
University of North Texas
Denton, Texas

Lloyd A. Taylor, PhD
The Citadel
Charleston, South Carolina

Christina Tucker, BA
Department of Psychology
University of Mississippi
University, Mississippi

Adrianna Wechsler, EdM
Department of Psychology
University of Nevada—Las Vegas
Las Vegas, Nevada

Christine Wekerle, PhD
Departments of Education,
    Psychology, and Psychiatry
University of Western Ontario
London, Ontario, Canada

PART I

General Issues

CHAPTER 1

Historical Perspectives

Thomas R. Kratochwill, Richard J. Morris, and Joseph Robinson

In this chapter, we trace the historical development of the assessment and treatment of children's and adolescents' mental health issues. Although our overview is brief (see several sources for more detailed historical accounts: Doyle, 1974; Dubois, 1970; Linden & Linden, 1968; P. McReynolds, 1975), we provide some perspectives on contemporary evidence-based assessment and treatment. An examination of the historical factors in assessment and treatment is important for several reasons. First, it is important to understand that many of the contemporary issues in evidence-based practice have their origin in past practices. Second, it is important to realize that many contemporary issues are related to social or even political concerns that have their origin in the past. Third, the past has sometimes provided or even imposed a structure on assessment and treatment practices. It is important to understand this structure to understand contemporary models and the scope of psychological practices. Finally, it is important to focus on historical factors to introduce a variety of scholarly perspectives into the discussion of the issues surrounding evidence-based practice. We first review historical features of diagnosis and assessment and then turn our attention to child and adolescent therapy. However, the conceptual, theoretical, and practice issues in these domains overlap.

ASSESSMENT AND DIAGNOSIS: ANCIENT INFLUENCES

Most historical treatments of the assessment literature typically begin with a discussion of the work of Galton in England and Cattell in the United States (i.e., many books on assessment begin with this period; e.g., Sunberg, 1977). However, assessment has a much richer history, attesting to the assumption that many features of contemporary assessment actually date back to the beginnings of recorded history. L. V. McReynolds (1974) traced the historical antecedents of the current practices in assessment beginning with antiquity and extending to the second half of the twentieth century. Four phases were reviewed: antiquity, the medieval period and the Renaissance, the Age of Reason, and the period from Thomesius to Galton. We adopt this framework in this section of the chapter.

Antiquity

An examination of early assessment practices shows that there was a close interplay between the methods used and the cultural views held during that particular time.

This perspective is not unlike the contemporary views in the United States that led to the development of special education services for children (Kratochwill, Clements, & Kalymon, 2007), with its emphasis on fair assessment practices for handicapped children. It is possible that the first personality assessment procedure was based on *astrology,* and that the first psychological "test" was the horoscope. Although astrology can be regarded as invalid on scientific grounds, it did contribute to (a) the view that individual personalities represent the focus of assessment, (b) the belief that the psychological makeup of the individual is predetermined, and (c) the development of taxonomical (diagnostic) categories.

Another early assessment strategy involved physiognomy, the interpretation of an individual's character from body physique. Physiognomics, also a very limited assessment procedure, assumed a relatively fixed conception of personality but shared some methodological features with naturalistic observation, not unlike the naturalistic observations conducted using behavior modification procedures (Kazdin, 1978). L. V. McReynolds (1974) noted that the longest continued assessment technique with some claim to rationality and one that remains with us today is physiognomy. Thus, work by Mahl (1956) and Gleser, Gottshalk, and Springer (1961) on speech patterns; by Hall (1959), Eibl-Eibesfeldt (1971), and Haas (1972) on methodology of movements; of Izard (1971) and Ekman and associates (Ekman, 1973; Ekman, Friesen, & Ellsworth, 1972) on emotions and facial expressions; and of Hess and associates (Hess & Polt, 1960; Hess, Seltzer, & Schlien, 1965) on the relation of pupil size to affect can be related to earlier physiognomic conceptions (cf. L. V. McReynolds, 1974).

Developments in assessment during early times were not always limited to the area of personality assessment. For example, Civil Service examinations were used in ancient China for selection purposes. Dubois (1966, pp. 30–31) notes:

> The earliest development seems to have been a rudimentary form of proficiency testing. About the year 2200 B.C. the emperor of China is said to have examined his officials every third year.... A thousand years later in 1115 B.C., at the beginning of the Chan dynasty, formal examining procedures were established. Here the record is clear. Job sample tests were used requiring proficiency in the five basic arts: music, archery, horsemanship, writing, and arithmetic.... Knowledge of a sixth act was also required—skill in the rites and ceremonies of public and social life.

Medieval Period and the Renaissance

L. V. McReynolds (1974) notes that during this period, the acceptance of humeral psychology and physiognomic strategies of evaluating people were widespread. Generally, this period supported the recognition of the individual, and so we again see an example of cultural influences on assessment practices. In some respects this period set the occasion for what would later be a debate on research methodology, especially surrounding the use of group versus single-case research design in therapy research (Kratochwill & Levin, 1992).

Age of Reason

The Age of Reason covers the period from approximately the middle of the six-teenth century to the second half of the eighteenth. A major theme of this period was the focus on individual differences, as reflected in some important works on assess-ment: Huarte's *Tryal of Wits,* Wright's *Passions of the Minde,* and Thomesius's *New Discovery.* During this period, the recognition of individual differences prompted measurement so that an individual's sense of well-being could be more fully realized.

From Thomesius to Galton

A significant contribution to assessment during this period, particularly in the nine-teenth century, was phrenology. Phrenology bears a similarity to physiognomy, but whereas physiognomy emphasized assessment of external body features such as facial and other characteristics, phrenology emphasized the assessment of the exter-nal formations of the skull. Phrenology assumed that mental functions were based on specific processes localized in certain areas of the brain and that the intensity or magnitude of these functions was indicated in the contours and external topography of the skull (L. V. McReynolds, 1974).

Four positive contributions of phrenology that have a resemblance to contempo-rary assessment practices or activities were identified (L. V. McReynolds, 1974). First, there was an emphasis on individual differences. Second, the assessment paradigm emphasized the notions of assessor and subject, the systematic collec-tions of data during a single session, and written reports that usually included qualitative profiles. Third, the phrenological movement helped advance objectivity through blind assessment and rating scales. Fourth, phrenology contributed to the development of a primitive taxonomical system, which included affective faculties (e.g., propensities, sentiments) and intellectual faculties (e.g., perceptive, reflec-tive). This line of reasoning was likely influential in later conceptualizations of diagnostic and classification systems.

Implications

This brief historical overview of ancient influences points out that many contem-porary assessment practices have their roots deep in our past. Noteworthy is the fact that the work of the phrenologists (and later, Quetelet's work on psychological statistics) set the stage for the emergence of Galton's contributions and the subse-quent more modern era in assessment. It is interesting to speculate how some of the ancient procedures might have set the stage for child diagnoses specifically. L. V. McReynolds (1974, pp. 524–525) raises an interesting point:

> We know that such techniques as chiromancy, metaposcopy, and phrenology are in prin-ciple all totally invalid, yet I suggest that in the hands of insightful and discerning practi-tioners they may, at least on occasion, have been more valid than we suppose, even if for different reasons than their users, much less their clients imagined.

ASSESSMENT AND DIAGNOSIS: NINETEENTH-CENTURY INFLUENCES

During the nineteenth century significant developments were taking place in Western Europe and the United States that would shape the future of psychological and educational assessment (cf. Carroll, 1978; Dubois, 1970; Laosa, 1977). Specifically, events were occurring in France, Germany, England, and the United States that were to have a profound influence on assessment practices in child therapy and education.

France

Attention to two movements occurred in France that made a significant impact on the history of testing and assessment in general and child assessment in particular (Maloney & Ward, 1976). One movement, pioneered by Berhheim, Liebault, Charcot, and Freud, was focused on a new view of deviant behavior. The influence of this movement was to take abnormal behavior out of the legal or moral realm with which it had been previously associated and cast it as a psychological or psychosocial problem. This focus prompted psychological assessment rather than moral or legal sanction, as had been common prior to this period.

Also noteworthy was the movement called "the science of education." Jacques Itard, a French physician, taught Victor, the "Wild Boy of Aveyron," various skills. Many of the procedures used in Itard's work were similar to later behavior modification procedures that emphasized environmental stimulus and response changes during intervention. Itard's contributions also provided a background for Binet's work on measurement of intelligence.

Esquivol's (1722–1840) work, represented in his book *Des Maladies Mentales,* was influential in that he distinguished between "emotional disorders" and "subaverage intellect." According to his views, subaverage intelligence consists of levels of individual performance: (a) those making cries only, (b) those using monosyllables, and (c) those using short phrases but not elaborate speech. Thus, here we see the basis for an early classification scheme that could organize human behavior.

Germany

Although some of the work in France emphasized individual differences in pathology and cognitive ability, German scientists perceived individual differences as a source of measurement error. A significant contribution to the individual differences theme is found in the "Maskelyne-Kinnebrook affair." The difference between Maskelyne (the astronomer) and Kinnebrook (the assistant) in their measurement of the timing of stellar transits was later analyzed by Bessel. Bessel concluded that different persons had different transit tracking times, and that when all astronomers were checked against one standard, individual error could be calculated; thus, a sort of "personal equation" was developed (cf. Boring, 1950).

Another significant influence on assessment came from Wundt, who set up a psychological laboratory in Leipzig to study such processes as reaction time, sensation, psychophysics, and association. This work, as well as the general work occurring on measurement, was helpful to popularize the notion of measurement of differences between individuals. Some Americans who studied with Wundt were G. Stanley Hall and James McKeen Cattell. Both of these individuals were to have a large impact on future child psychological assessment.

England

The work of Charles Darwin was most influential in psychological and educational assessment, particularly through his theory of evolution presented in 1859 in *Origin of the Species*. Darwin's work emphasized that there were measurable and meaningful differences among members of each species. Galton, Darwin's half-cousin, was influential in applying evolutionary theory to humans. In his 1869 book, *Hereditary Genius,* Galton argued that genius has a tendency to run in families. He was greatly influenced by the Belgian statistician Quetelet (1770–1864), who was the first to apply the normal probability curve of Laplace and Gauss to human data. This work translated into the notion that nature's mistakes were represented as deviations from the average.

Several implications of this work for child assessment and treatment are noteworthy. First, Galton's system of classification represented a fundamental step toward the concept of standardized scores (Wiseman, 1967). Second, in the application of Quetelet's statistics, Galton demonstrated that many human variables, both physical and psychological, were distributed normally. This concept is a direct precursor to the notion of a norm and application of standardization (Laosa, 1977). Third, a major influence of this work was to establish that certain variables should be subjected to quantitative measurement. Galton's work was significant in that it encouraged other efforts in the area of measurement of individual differences in mental abilities that were considerably more sophisticated than previous efforts (Cooley & Lohnes, 1976). Finally, through the application of the normal curve, individual performance or standing could be classified as deviant or even as a mistake of nature. We know that although Galton was influenced by the phrenologists, he rejected this form of assessment. He noted in 1906, "Why capable observers should have come to such strange conclusions [can] be accounted for . . . most easily on the supposition of unconscious bias in collecting data" (quoted in Pearson, 1930, p. 577).

United States

Early work in the United States contributed to what was called the "mental testing" movement, a major part of clinical and school psychology. Cattell (1860–1944) was the first to use the term "mental test," and he is generally referred to as the father of mental testing (DuBois, 1970; Hunt, 1961). Cattell also introduced experimental psychology into the United States. A significant contribution to assessment was that he advocated testing in schools; he was also generally responsible for instigating mental testing in the United States (Boring, 1950).

In 1895, Cattell chaired the first American Psychological Association (APA) Committee on Mental and Physical Tests. Although Cattell made major changes in the nature of testing, his work was not accepted unconditionally. For example, Sharp (1899) published an article questioning the reliability of mental tests. Wissler

(1901) compared the reliability of some of Cattell's psychological measures with various measurement approaches from the physical sciences and concluded that tests used in Cattell's lab showed little correlation among themselves, did not relate to academic grades, and were unreliable (Maloney & Ward, 1976). Even Wundt was not supportive of Cattell's focus on mental measurements (Boring, 1950). Nevertheless, Cattell's work, as well as work in France, promoted the development of a movement called "differential psychology."

INTELLIGENCE TESTING MOVEMENT

Around the beginning of the twentieth century, assessment was given a new impetus through the development of differential psychology (Binet & Henri, 1895; Stern, 1900; Stern & Whipple, 1914). Stern and Whipple (1914) suggested that mental age be divided by chronological age to produce a "mental quotient," a procedure, with refinements, that evolved into the IQ concept (Laosa, 1977).

The work of Binet and his associates was quite influential, although not necessarily in the direction that Binet had envisioned or desired (Sarason, 1976; Wolf, 1973). Binet initially focused his efforts on the diagnosis of "mentally retarded" children around the late 1880s. At this time he was assisted by Theodore Simon, with whom he later worked in the development of the first formal measure of intellectual assessment for children (Wolf, 1973). Based on a study conducted for the Ministry of Public Instruction, he focused efforts on predicting which children would be unable to succeed in school (Resnick, 1982). Binet noted that performance on his scale had implications for diagnostic classification and education. Resnick (1982, p. 176) notes:

> A scale of thirty questions was developed, each of increasing difficulty. Idiots were those who could not go beyond the sixth item, and imbeciles were stymied after the twelfth. Morons were found able to deal with the first twenty-three questions. They were able to do the memory tests and arrange lines and weights in a series, but no more . . . the test . . . was designed as an examination to remove from the mainstream of schooling, and place in newly developed special classes for the retarded, those who would be unable to follow the normal prescribed curriculum. As such, it was a test for selection, removing from normal instruction those with the lowest level of ability. Binet argued, however, that the treatment the children would receive in the special classes would be more suited to their learning needs. The testing, therefore, was to promote more effective and appropriate instruction.

Interest in testing the abilities of children was at a high level during this time. This interest was prompted, in part, by the growing population of children in schools due to natural population growth and immigration and the fact that students began to stay in school longer (Chapman, Terman, & Movement, 1979). With the growing number of children in schools, it became clear that not all children could profit from regular instruction. The policies and procedures for diagnosis and assessment of children during this time set a direction that has only recently been changed with new federal regulations that has, as one focus, to reduce the emphasis on an IQ-achievement discrepancy to make a determination of disability status for children with learning problems. The new focus in assessment is called "response to intervention" and involves determining the child's response to instruction as part of the diagnostic process (Kratochwill et al., 2007).

Several American psychologists promoted Binet's work. For example, Goddard published the first revision of the Binet scale, and Terman developed the Stanford-Binet. Thereafter, the Binet scale was used to identify children who were regarded as "backwards" or "feebleminded." In 1911 the Binet scale was being used in 71 of 84 cities that administered tests to identify feebleminded children. However, the Binet scale was also being used experimentally to screen out and turn back "retarded" immigrants (Knox, 1914, as cited in Widgor & Garner, 1982).

The Stanford version of the Binet-Simon scale was originally published in 1916 by Terman; it was revised by Terman and Merrill in 1937 and 1960 and renormed in 1972 and subsequently. This translation and revision of Binet's earlier work firmly established intelligence testing in schools and clinics throughout the United States (DuBois, 1970).

Development of Group Testing

The assessment movement was given a major thrust through the development of group tests during World War I. Many assessment efforts during this time reflected a pattern of procedures similar to that used by Binet (T. E. Newland, 1977). Ebbinghaus demonstrated the feasibility of group tests, and some American psychologists (e.g., Otis, 1918; Whipple, 1910) recognized that the Binet-Simon scale could be adapted for group testing. However, there were important differences. Whereas the Binet-type items typically required a definite answer provided by the child, group tests usually called for recognition of a correct answer among several alternatives (Carroll, 1978).

A committee of the APA chaired by Robert M. Yerkes developed the Army Alpha and Army Beta group tests. The Army Beta (a nonverbal group test) was designed so as not to discriminate against illiterates and individuals speaking foreign languages. Although the impact of this development was to create a new interest in and role for testing, a review of the tests used revealed that the source of many tests was increasingly used for nonmilitary purposes (T. E. Newland, 1977).

Following the war, many clinical psychologists who were involved in wartime testing sought employment in the civilian ranks, and many became involved in the schools. Resnick (1982, p. 183) notes:

> Aiding this movement was Philander P. Clarxton, U.S. Commissioner of education, who communicated to school superintendents throughout the country about the reserve of trained people that could be tapped for the needs of the schools. He wrote enthusiastically about the "unusual opportunity for city schools to obtain the services of competent men." Among the services that they could render was "discovering defective children and children of superior intelligence."

This movement, in part, facilitated the use of group intelligence tests in the public schools for purposes of diagnosis and classification. Many of these tests were administered to identify children who could not profit from regular instruction. Although some schools had made provisions for special children, the intelligence tests formalized the decision-making process for these special services. Also, between 1919 and 1923, Terman introduced the National Intelligence Test for grades three to eight and the Terman Group Test, for grades seven to 12 and found that the schools were most receptive (Resnick, 1982). Resnick reported that the most important use of the tests was for placement of children into homogeneous groups:

> Sixty-four percent of the reporting cities used group intelligence tests for this purpose in elementary schools, 56% in junior high schools, and 41% in high schools. Enthusiasm for the use of testing systemwide for this purpose was at a high level. In 1923, Terman's group test for grades seven to thirteen sold more than a half-million copies. (pp. 184–185)

The stage for the rapid development of ability tests was also set by such psychologists as Spearman, Thorndike, and Thurstone and their respective theories of intelligence. For example, Spearman developed an elaborate theory of the organization of human abilities in which he concluded that all intellectual abilities have a common factor, g, and a number of specific factors, s, which relate uniquely to each presumed ability. Spearman's two-factor theory was the basis on which tests examining specific abilities (Edwards, 1971) rather than global scores were developed (Laosa, 1977).

Thorndike viewed intelligence as comprising a multitude of separate elements, each of which represented a specific ability. Intelligence was also perceived as having both hereditary and environmental components. Thurstone concluded that there were seven primary mental abilities (in contrast to Spearman's s and g factors) and developed the Primary Mental Abilities Test to measure each specific ability.

Intelligence tests gradually evolved into major diagnostic instruments throughout the world. Such instruments became an important diagnostic tool for identifying children with cognitive disabilities. However, not all countries accepted the use of these tests. For example, in the Soviet Union such tests were banned in 1936 by the Communist Party because they were considered methods that discriminated against the peasants and the working class in favor of the culturally advantaged (Sunberg, 1977; Wortis, 1960). As an alternative, diagnosis in the USSR was based primarily on neurophysiological evidence. The neurologist and psychophysiologist, rather than the clinical psychologist, were primarily engaged in diagnosing children with mental retardation (Dunn & Kirk, 1963).

Work in these areas, as well as other contributions prior to and during this period, led to diverse views on the nature of intelligence and its assessment. A major contribution to the testing movement was the development of the Wechsler intelligence scales. Psychologist David Wechsler developed the Wechsler Adult Intelligence Scale (WAIS) by including a group of subtests from WWI vintage that he found valuable in his work with adults. His criterion of "general adaptability" (Wechsler, 1975) was extended downward in the development of the Wechsler Intelligence Scale for Children (WISC) and the Wechsler Preschool and Primary Scale of Intelligence (WPPSI). The work of Wechsler contrasted with that of Binet. Whereas Wechsler's scales emerged from work with adults and were later developed for use with children, Binet's emerged from work with young children and later were developed for use with older children (T. E. Newland, 1977).

PERSONALITY ASSESSMENT MOVEMENT

While tests of cognitive ability were rapidly evolving during the early part of the twentieth century, tests of personality were in their infancy. Although such devices as the Woodworth Personal Data Sheet were used in the military during WWI, the personality assessment movement received increased attention through the development of projective techniques such as the Rorschach Inkblot Test and the Thematic Apperception Test (TAT).

World War II, like the first war, did much to set the stage for rapid proliferation of testing practices. Indeed, psychological testing combined with the military need for assessment was one of the primary factors leading to the development of clinical psychology as an independent specialty (Maloney & Ward, 1976).

During the period following WWII, testing practices developed dramatically. Most tests developed during this period were tied to an intrapsychic disease model or state-trait conceptualization of behavior (cf. W. Mischel, 1968). Psychoanalytic theory generally accelerated assessment procedures that would reveal unconscious processes. Assessment practices emphasized an "indirect-sign" paradigm. Assessment was indirect in that measurement of certain facets of behavior were disguised or hidden from the client (e.g., such as in the TAT). Moreover, within the context of the intrapsychic model, testing practices were said to predict certain states or traits. The clinician's task was to administer a battery of tests to a child and look for certain signs of traits or states. An example of this approach was represented in the work of Rappaport, Gill, and Schafer (1945). In their classic book, the authors demonstrated how a battery of tests (e.g., TAT, Rorschach, WAIS) could be used to diagnose deviant behavior within the intrapsychic model (in this case, the psychoanalytic model).

Similar to the sign approach was the "cookbook" method of assessment, which reached a zenith during the mid-1950s (cf. Meehl, 1956). An example of this approach is the Minnesota Multiphasic Personality Inventory (MMPI; Hathaway & McKinley, 1943). As these authors noted, one of the presumed advantages of the cookbook approach was that "it would stress representativeness of behavioral sampling, accuracy in recording and cataloguing data from research studies, and optional weighting of relevant variables and it would permit professional time and talent to be used economically" (p. 243).

Emergence of Behavior Modification and Assessment

Behavior modification (also referred to as behavior therapy) and the related assessment procedures associated with this model have made a tremendous impact on psychology and education (Kazdin, 1978; Kratochwill & Bijou, 1987). As some historical reviews illustrate (Hersen, 1976; Kazdin, 1978), behavior therapy represented a departure from traditional models of assessment and treatment of abnormal behavior, both psychological and educational. Although the history of behavior therapy cannot be traced along a single line, practice was characterized by diversity of viewpoints, a broad range of heterogeneous procedures with vastly different rationales, open debates over conceptual bases, methodological requirements, and evidence of efficacy (Kazdin & Wilson, 1978). Some reports of behavioral treatment followed Watson and Raynor's (1920) work in conditioning of fear in a child, but a significant impetus to behavioral assessment and treatment is commonly traced to the publication in 1958 of Joseph Wolpe's reciprocal inhibition therapy.

Independent of Watson's and Wolpe's work was research in the psychology of learning, in both Russia and the United States. Particularly important in learning research was operant conditioning, which Skinner brought into focus in the late 1930s (e.g., Skinner, 1938). The evolution of operant work into experimental and applied behavior analysis had an extremely important influence on the development of behavior therapy and assessment practices in general.

Although behavior therapy and assessment evolved considerably over the years, some general characteristics represented unities within the heterogeneity of evolving practice:

1. Focus upon current rather than historical determinants of behavior;
2. Emphasis on overt behavior change as the main criterion by which treatment should be evaluated;
3. Specification of treatment in objective terms so as to make replication possible;
4. Reliance upon basic research in psychology as a source of hypotheses about treatment and specific therapy techniques; and
5. Specificity in defining, treating, and measuring the target problem in therapy. (Kazdin, 1978, p. 375)

With the advent of behavior modification and its proliferation, a new assessment role also developed, particularly for clinical child and school psychologists. Behavioral assessment emphasized *repeated measurement* of some target problem prior (baseline), during, and after (follow-up) the intervention. Hersen and Bellack (1976a) noted that the psychologist's expertise in theory and application of behavioral therapy techniques (e.g., classical and operant conditioning) also enabled both an *assessment* and a *treatment* role to emerge in psychiatric settings. This focus was also to occur as a basis for the scientist-practitioner model of psychological services (Hayes, Barlow, & Nelson-Gray, 1999) and represented a strong foundation for the evidence-based treatment movement (Kratochwill & Stoiber, 2002) and what is now called response to intervention in psychological practice in schools (Brown-Chidsey & Steege, 2006; Kratochwill et al., 2007). Thus, the psychologist in various settings (e.g., clinics, hospitals, schools) became involved in direct service rather than engaged in only testing and diagnosis, although this was slower to evolve in schools. Behavior modification provided the impetus for these new roles and has continued to move practice forward in both prevention and treatment.

Developments in behavioral assessment also influenced the field of personality assessment in general. In many respects, assessment has acted as a barometer for the thinking of personality theorists. For example, a barometer of change in views about assessment has been the evolution of the title of the journal specifically devoted to assessment in professional psychology (Goldfried, 1976). The journal, founded in 1936, was initially entitled *Rorschach Research Exchange*. Other projective techniques came into existence in the assessment process, and by 1947 the journal title was changed to *Rorschach Research Exchange and Journal of Projective Techniques*. Gradually, the more objective personality assessment techniques (e.g., the MMPI) were being used, and in 1963 the title was again changed to *Journal of Projective Techniques and Personality Assessment*. Projective techniques continued to show disappointing research results, and in 1971 this may have prompted the journal's change to the title *Journal of Personality Assessment*.

Nevertheless, there remained some doubt as to whether the future direction of assessment would take a distinct behavioral orientation. Even in 1963, when the journal *Behavior, Research, and Therapy* made its appearance, the issue was raised as to whether there would be a large enough readership to justify its existence (Brady, 1976). However, as Hersen and Bellack (1976a) documented, the future looked very positive, as reflected in major journals inaugurated in the United States between 1968 and 1970 (e.g., *Journal of Applied Behavior Analysis, Behavior Therapy, Journal of Behavior Therapy and Experimental Psychiatry*). Moreover, several other behaviorally oriented journals emerged (e.g., *Cognitive Therapy and Research, Biofeedback and Self-control*), and specific journals devoted primarily to behavioral assessment (e.g., *Behavioral Assessment, Journal of Behavioral Assessment*) were formed, although they were eventually changed.

CONCEPTUAL MODELS OF HUMAN BEHAVIOR: IMPLICATIONS FOR CHILD THERAPY

An extraordinary amount of theory and research has been generated that has a bearing on child therapy (Morris & Kratochwill, in press). As a result, tremendous amounts of data have been accumulated concerning the origins, development, influences, and variations in human behavior. Nevertheless, the wealth of information has clearly not resulted in any integrated view of human performance. Indeed, the current state of knowledge generated from the various conceptual models has not only resulted in the lack of an integrated view of human functioning, but has yielded various conceptual positions that are diametrically opposed and has spawned debate in the evidence-based practice movement (Kratochwill & Shernoff, 2004).

Because our understanding of human behavior is influenced by basic assumptions concerning the "why" of behavior, assessment and treatment practices often become inextricably interwoven with the particular conceptual model of human functioning held by the psychologist. Different models, with their different perspectives on behavior, yield vastly different assessment approaches and data that are used in making decisions relative to assessment and intervention. In this section, we review some models of human behavior that influence contemporary psychological practices. The models reviewed include the medical or biogenetic model, intrapsychic disease model, psychoeducational process test-based model, and behavioral model. These various models have been discussed by others in the professional literature, and due to space limitations we are not able to discuss them in detail or cover other models (see Kratochwill & Morris, 1993, for coverage of other models). The models differ in their conceptualization of deviant behavior and assessment procedures and devices (sometimes), as well as the nature of the intervention implemented. Each model is discussed in the context of various components and considerations in its use.

Medical or Biological Model

Components

The medical model is one of the oldest approaches guiding assessment and treatment. The medical model can be applied in either a literal or a metaphorical context (Phillips, Draguns, & Bartlett, 1975). We view the model in its literal sense. That is, abnormal biological systems can be traced to some underlying biological pathology which is then treated. For example, defective hearing (symptom) may be traced to some type of infection (the cause), which may be treated with antibiotics. The prevalence of medical problems in children is actually quite high (see Bear & Minke, 2006, for an overview of various problems). A variety of health problems may be found in children in the school setting, including those children who are chronically ill and those with nutritional disorders (undernutrition, obesity), hearing and visual disorders, dental problems, disorders of bones and joints, infectious disorders, respiratory disorders, allergic disorders, urinary disorders, and drug-related problems. It seems clear that a medical model is appropriate to deal with the diversity of medical problems in the schools.

The medical model is a disease-based model. The pathology is assumed to be within the individual, although the causes may be environmental. Some theorists consider biological deviations to be the necessary and sufficient factors in the development of the pathology; others claim that chemical or neurological anomalies are the necessary but not sufficient condition for pathogenesis. Here, environmental conditions may or may not catalyze a constitutional predisposition to pathology.

Considerations

Medical model procedures are clearly justifiable when there is no basis for assuming physiological change in the organism as a result of the sociocultural environment. Controversial practices characterize medical model procedures when they are used to interpret measures of learned behavior (e.g., various forms of disruptive behavior in children, academic skill deficits). Although genetic, developmental, neurological, and biochemical factors all undoubtedly influence behavior, in reality these factors are not discrete entities. They are interwoven with one another as well as with environmental factors.

Applications of the medical model influence assessment and treatment in various ways. Organic factors may not always be the cause of an observed medical or physical problem. There is growing recognition that psychological factors may affect a physical condition and that physical symptoms may have no known organic or physiological basis. In the past, various concepts such as "psychosomatic" or "psychophysiological" have been used to describe the psychological basis for physical or somatic disorders. However, such perspectives may be of limited usefulness because they imply a simplistic relation between psychological factors and a distinct group of physical disorders when, in fact, there may be a complex interaction of biological, environmental, psychological, and social factors contributing to various physical disorders (Siegel, 1983). Long ago, Lipowski (1977, p. 234) noted:

> The concept of psychogenesis of organic disease . . . is no longer tenable and has given way to the multiplicity of all disease . . . the relative contribution of these factors [social and psychological] varies from disease to disease, from person to person, and from one episode of the same disease in the same person to another episode. . . . If the foregoing arguments are accepted then it becomes clear that to distinguish a class of disorders as "psychosomatic disorders" and to propound generalizations about psychosomatic patients is misleading and redundant. Concepts of single causes and cirilinear causal sequences for example, from psyche to soma and vise versa, are simplistic and obsolete.

The point here is that even in the treatment of physical disease, psychological factors may be involved. Exclusive reliance on medical (drug) interventions may bias treatment in the sense that psychological (or other) aspects of functioning may be ignored. Problems most often arise when behavioral measures that can be influenced by a variety of environmental circumstances are used to assess the potential organic origins of a perceived symptom. The more the individual differences observed on a behavioral measure are influenced by environmental factors, the more the measure has the potential of being biased. Such a circumstance may arise when the environmental factors that influence the measure differ across cultural groups.

Psychodynamic Model

Components

The psychodynamic model proposes that maladaptive behaviors are symptoms resulting from underlying processes analogous to disease in the literal sense. This model is sometimes labeled the medical model in psychological and psychoeducational practice. Because conceptualization and treatment of abnormal behavior initially resided largely within the domain of medicine, the medical model was extended to treatment of abnormal behavior, both medical and psychological. The historical developments of the model are not reviewed in detail here; instead, the reader is referred to several historical sources that discuss this approach (e.g., Alexander & Selesnick, 1968; Kraepelin, 1962).

The psychodynamic approach can be characterized by the following:

> (a) uses a number of procedures, (b) intended to tap various areas of psychological functioning, (c) both at a conscious and unconscious level, (d) using projective techniques as well as more objective and standardized tests, (e) in both cases, interpretation may rest on symbolic signs as well as scorable responses, (f) with the goal of describing individuals in personological rather than normative terms. (Korchin & Schuldberg, 1981, p. 1147)

As is evident in this characterization, the psychodynamic approach is aimed at providing a multifaceted description and inferences. This process is said to promote a unique and individual approach to child assessment.

The psychoanalytic model represents one example of the psychodynamic disease paradigm, as do many other dynamic models of human functioning. The dynamic approach to assessment of deviant behavior is best elucidated in the context of assumptions held about the internal dynamics of personality (W. Mischel, 1968). Traditionally, dynamic approaches inferred some underlying constructs that account for consistency in behavior. Assessment is viewed as a means of identifying some sign of these hypothetical constructs, which are of central importance in predicting behavior. This *indirect sign paradigm* in assessment (cf. W. Mischel, 1972, p. 319) includes the use of a large variety of projective tests (e.g., Rorschach, TAT, Human Figure Drawings, Sentence Completion Tests) as well as objective personality inventories (e.g., MMPI-A for adolescents, MMPI-II, California Psychological Inventory) that are still used in contemporary practice.

A second feature of the traditional psychodynamic approach is that it assumes that behavior will remain stable regardless of the specific environmental or situational context. In this regard, test content is of less concern and may even be disguised by making items ambiguous, as is true in projective testing (Goldfried & Linehan, 1977). Indeed, a particular response to a projective test is rarely examined in view of the overt qualities of the situation in which the test occurred, but rather is interpreted in the context of a complex theoretical structure.

Considerations

The dynamic approach to assessment can be criticized on several grounds. One problem is the preoccupation with historical events, often in the absence of any verifying data. The second criticism relates to the emphasis during assessment on the individual's presumed unconscious beliefs, attitudes, motivations, and so forth, as interpreted through projections. Third, behavior is assumed to be a consequence of internalized pathological features. This assumption ignores evidence showing that many behaviors are situationally specific.

The use of various psychodynamic indirect measurement procedures has direct implications for child assessment and treatment. These measures continue to be used in clinical practice despite data indicating their low predictive validity (cf. Hersen & Barlow, 1976). When these issues became important, Goldfried and Kent (1972) noted that although the interpretation of certain signs on the Bender-Gestalt test (Hutt & Briskin, 1960) had no empirical support (cf. Goldfried & Ingling, 1964; Hutt, 1968), the revised version of the Bender-Gestalt manual presumably discounted these research findings and still recommended the use of questionable interpretations. A rather extensive literature on the comprehensive (predictive) validity of indirect measurement techniques (T. Mischel, 1971; W. Mischel, 1968) suggested that the predictions made on the basis of self-reports were equal to or superior to those made on the basis of indirect measurement techniques that are interpreted and scored by clinical experts. These findings held true for a wide variety of content areas (cf. W. Mischel, 1972).

Perhaps the most important issue that has been raised over traditional dynamic assessment is its relation to treatment. A number of authors over the years have noted that there was little relation between traditional assessment and treatment (Bandura, 1969; Goldfried & Pomeranz, 1968; Kanfer & Phillips, 1970; Peterson, 1968; Stuart, 1970). Thus, although traditional dynamic assessment may lead to a diagnosis that may in turn lead to the recommendation of a particular treatment, diagnoses resulting from traditional assessment methods cannot accurately predict what particular treatment mode should be implemented (Ciminero, Calhoun, & Adams, 1977; Stuart, 1970).

Psychometric Test-Based Model

The psychometric test-based model bears similarity to the psychodynamic disease model in that underlying processes, specifically process deficits, are said to account for learning and behavior problems. In many respects, this model can be considered a part of the dynamic model; however, a psychometric approach is characterized by the use of a variety of individual and group tests to compare individuals along various trait or construct dimensions. In trait theory approaches, various personality structures are said to account for an individual's behavior (W. Mischel, 1968, 1974). Trait theorists disagreed on what traits explained certain patterns of behavior, but generally agreed that certain behaviors were consistent across time and settings and that these patterns are expressions or signs of underlying traits.

In contrast to the psychodynamic position, trait assessors traditionally placed a high premium on objective administration and scoring of tests. Attempts usually were made to establish formal reliability and validity of the various measures used. On empirical grounds, historically this statistical approach proved generally superior to the more clinical method in predicting behavior (cf. Korchin & Schuldberg, 1981), but questions have been raised over the manner in which the research reflects the reality of decision making in actual clinical practice.

Closely related to the psychometric approach is the psychoeducational process model used by many practicing school psychologists. The model can be considered analogous to the psychometric trait model in that assessment focuses on internal deficits, except its context is psychoeducational rather than personality or emotionally oriented. Because a variety of cognitive, perceptual, psycholinguistic, psychomotor, and neuropsychological processes or abilities have been cited as causes of children's academic failure, norm-referenced cognitive (e.g., WISC, McCarthy, Stanford-Binet), perceptual (Bender Visual Motor Gestalt Test, Developmental Test of Visual Perception, Developmental Test of Visual-Motor Integration), psycholinguistic (e.g., Illinois Test of Psycholinguistic Abilities), and psychomotor (e.g., Purdue Perceptual-Motor Survey) tests are used to assess these abilities.

Most of these assessment procedures follow a diagnostic-predescriptive approach. Ysseldyke and Mirkin (1982, p. 398) noted:

> All of the diagnostic-perspective approaches based on a process dysfunction viewpoint of the nature of exceptionality operate similarly. When students experience academic difficulties it is presumed that the difficulties are caused by inner process dysfunctions or

disorders. Tests are administered in an effort to identify the specific nature of the within-child disorder that is creating or contributing to learning difficulties. Disorders or deficits are test named (e.g., figure-ground deficiencies, auditory sequential memory deficits, body image problems, eye-hand coordination difficulties, visual association dysfunctions, and manual expression disorders). Specific interventions are developed to "cure" the underlying causative problems.

Considerations

There are several important implications that can be raised with regard to the assessment tactics used in the psychometric model. First, because norm-referenced devices are commonly used in the model, the clinician must assume that clients tested have background and acculturation comparable to those on whom the test was standardized (cf. Oakland & Matuszek, 1977). Yet the point was frequently raised that standardized tests are biased and unfair to individuals from cultural and socioeconomic minorities because they reflect predominantly White, middle-class values and do not reflect the experiences and the linguistic, cognitive, and other cultural values and styles of minority individuals (Laosa, 1977). For example, although the norms for some tests (e.g., some group achievement and aptitude tests, the 1972 Stanford-Binet, WISC-IV) were generally good, norming on other instruments (e.g., Illinois Test of Psycholinguistic Abilities [ITPA], Leiter International Performance Scale, Slosson Intelligence Test) was quite inadequate.

A second issue is that research examining components of reliability and validity on various process measures has not been optimistic (Salvia & Ysseldyke, 1978; Ysseldyke & Salvia, 1974). For example, several early reviews of research on the ITPA (e.g., Bateman, 1965; Buros, 1972; Sedlak & Weener, 1973) drew attention to these limitations. The magnitude of the problems of inadequate norming, inadequate or incomplete reliability data, or questionable validity was nicely represented in data presented by Salvia and Ysseldyke (1978). Clearly, the potential for biased assessment practice is high given the poor psychometric properties of these instruments.

Behavioral Model

Components

Technically, there is no one model of behavior therapy, and contemporary behavior therapy, despite commonalities, is characterized by a great deal of diversity.* Historically, the different approaches in behavior therapy include applied behavior analysis (e.g., Baer, Wolf, & Risley, 1968; Bijou, 1970), mediational stimulus-response model (e.g., Rachman, 1963; Wolpe, 1958), social learning theory (e.g., Bandura, 1969, 1977b), and cognitive-behavior modification (e.g., Meichenbaum, 1974, 1977; Mahoney, 1974; Mahoney & Arnkoff, 1978.)**

---

*A detailed account of the history of behavior modification can be found in Kazdin (1978).

**These approaches are only briefly reviewed here. The reader is referred to Kazdin and Wilson (1978) as well as original sources within each approach for a more detailed presentation. The reader is also referred to Kratochwill (1982) and Kratochwill and Bijou (1987).

Applied Behavior Analysis

This form of behavior therapy developed from the experimental analysis of behavior (cf. Day, 1976; Ferster & Skinner, 1957; Sidman, 1960; Skinner, 1945, 1953, 1957, 1969, 1974). It emphasized the analysis of the effects of independent events (variables) on the probability of specific behaviors (responses). Contemporary applied behavior analysis focuses on behaviors that are clinically or socially relevant (e.g., various social behaviors, learning disorders, mental retardation, social skills) and adheres to certain methodological criteria (e.g., experimental analysis, observer agreement on response measures, generalization of therapeutic effects).

Advocates of applied behavior analysis use a more restrictive sense of the term "behavior" than other areas represented in the field of behavior therapy: behavior as the overt activity of an organism. Internal feelings and cognitions are typically not considered a major focus for the techniques of therapy, research, and practice. However, it must be stressed that applied behavior analysis focuses on the behavior of an individual as a total functioning organism, although there is not always an attempt to observe, measure, and relate an organism's entire response taking place at one time (Bijou, 1976; Bijou & Baer, 1978).

Many intervention procedures associated with applied behavior analysis are derived from basic laboratory operant research (e.g., positive and negative reinforcement, punishment, time-out, response cost, shaping, fading stimulus control; see Bijou, 1976; Gelfand & Hartmann, 1975; Kazdin, 1980; Sulzer-Azaroff & Mayer, 1977). Assessment emphasizes the individual application of these procedures and a functional evaluation of their effectiveness (Bijou & Grimm, 1975; Emery & Marholin, 1977). Behavior analysis refers to the study of organism-environment interactions in terms of empirical concepts and laws for understanding, predicting, and controlling organism behavior and repeated measurement of well-defined and clearly observable responses (Bijou, 1976; Bijou, Peterson, & Ault, 1968; Bijou, Peterson, Harris, Allen, & Johnson, 1969).

Neobehavioristic Mediational Stimulus-Response Model

The noebehavioristic mediational stimulus-response (S-R) model is derived from the work of such learning theorists as Pavlov, Guthrie, Hull, Mower, and Miller (e.g., Eysenck, 1960, 1964; Rachman, 1963; Wolpe, 1958). These approaches are characterized by "the application of the principles of conditioning, especially classical conditioning and counter-conditioning to the treatment of abnormal behavior" (Kazdin & Wilson, 1978, p. 3). Although intervening variables and hypothetical constructs play a role in assessment and intervention, covert activities are most commonly defined in terms of a chain of S-R reactions, with cognitive formulations de-emphasized.

A number of treatment procedures such as counterconditioning and systematic desensitization have been used to treat anxiety reactions, phobic patterns, and other strong emotional disorders in children (Morris & Kratochwill, 1983; Morris, Kratochwill, Schoenfield, & Auster, in press). Systematic desensitization, based originally on the principle of reciprocal inhibition (Wolpe, 1958), has been successfully used to treat a wide range of child and adult problem behaviors (see Morris & Kratochwill, 1983; Morris et al., in press). Assessment in the mediational S-R model relies on survey schedules (e.g., fear survey schedules), self-support data, and direct measures of client behavior (as in the use of behavioral avoidance tests).

Cognitive-Behavior Therapy

A unifying characteristic of the cognitive-behavior therapy approach was an emphasis on cognitive processes and private events as mediators of behavior change (Kendall, 1981b). The source of a client's problems were said to be related to the client's own interpretations and attributions of his or her behavior, thoughts, images, self-statements, and related processes (Kazdin & Wilson, 1978). Contemporary cognitive-behavior therapy emanates from Ellis's (1962) rational-emotive therapy, Beck's cognitive therapy, and Meichenbaum's self-instructional training. Treatment strategies are quite diverse and include such techniques as problem solving, stress inoculation, self-instructional training, coping skills training, language behavior therapy, thought stopping, and attribution therapy. These techniques represent procedures not generally addressed by other behavior therapy approaches (e.g., applied behavior analysis).

Assessment in cognitive-behavior therapy tended to be quite broad-based, taking into account many different dimensions of behavior. Yet there was still an emphasis on defining the nature of the target problem, whether overt or covert. In some cases, a more traditional functional analysis of behavior, which emphasizes a careful examination of environmental antecedents and consequents as related to a certain response repertoire, was recommended (e.g., Meichenbaum, 1977).

Some specific purposes for cognitive assessment were outlined by Kendall (1981a, pp. 3–4):

1. To study the relationships among covert phenomena and their relationship to patterns of behavior and expressions of emotion.

2. To study the role of covert processes in the development of distinct psychopathologies and the behavioral patterns associated with coping.

3. To confirm the effects of treatment.

4. To check studies where cognitive factors have either been manipulated or implicated in the effects of the manipulation.

Social Learning Theory

Social learning theory is based on the original work of Bandura and his associates (e.g., Bandura, 1969, 1971, 1977b; Bandura & Walters, 1963) and has evolved considerably over time. Bandura noted that in addition to outcome expectation, a person's sense of his or her ability to perform a certain behavior mediates performance. He referred to these latter expectations as efficacy expectations or self-efficacy, and suggested that they have important implications for treatment. Psychological treatment and methods were hypothesized to produce changes in a child's expectations of self-efficacy, as in the treatment of phobic behavior. Self-efficacy was said to determine the activation and maintenance of behavior strategies for coping with anxiety-eliciting situations. Self-efficacy expectations were also said to be modified by different sources of psychological influence, including performance-based feedback (e.g., participant modeling), vicarious information (e.g., symbolic modeling), and physiological changes (e.g., traditional verbal psychotherapy; cf. Kazdin & Wilson, 1978). Intervention procedures such as symbolic modeling (e.g., Bandura, 1971), direct modeling (Bandura, 1977b; Rosenthal, 1976), and self-modeling (Brody & Brody, 1977) have been associated with the social learning theory approach. For example, modeling historically has been used to treat a variety of children's fears (e.g., animal fears, inanimate fears, dental and medical fears; Morris & Kratochwill, 1983; Morris et al., in press), socially maladjusted children (e.g., social withdrawal, aggression), distractibility, and severe deficiencies (e.g., autism, mental retardation) as well as a wide range of academic behaviors (cf. Zimmerman, 1977). In all these approaches, social learning theory stressed that human psychological functioning involved a reciprocal interaction between the individual's behavior and the environment in that a client is considered both the agent as well as the target of environmental influence, with assessment focusing on both dimensions of behavior.

Unifying Characteristics

Despite apparent diversity among the different areas within behavior therapy, several dimensions set it apart from traditional forms of psychological assessment and treatment, particularly the test-based psychometric models and psychodynamic models (Hartmann, Roper, & Bradford, 1979). Contemporary behavior therapy consists of the following characteristics:

1. A strong commitment to empirical evaluation of treatment and intervention techniques;
2. A general belief that therapeutic experiences must provide opportunities to learn adaptive or prosocial behavior;
3. Specification of treatment in operational and, hence, replicable terms, and
4. Evaluation of treatment effects through multiple-response modalities, with particular emphasis on overt behavior. (Kazdin & Hersen, 1980, p. 287)

Behavior therapy has become very diverse over time and includes a number of therapeutic strategies that were excluded from the field during the early years (e.g., rational-emotive therapy). Although these characteristics are tied to the therapeutic aspects of the behavioral approach, each can also be conceptually representative of the behavioral approach to child treatment (Bergan & Kratochwill, 1990).

HISTORICAL CONTEXT OF CHILD THERAPY

The Early Years

As we noted previously, although the study of psychological problems among adults can be traced back as far as the ancient Greeks (if not further), the study of child psychopathology represents a relatively recent phenomenon in the history of psychological treatment. The most famous early example of such study is Jean Itard's examination of and attempt to educate the Wild Boy of Aveyron beginning in 1799. However, an increased focus on problems of childhood would have to follow a greater focus on childhood as a distinct period in human development and an increased interest in the nature of psychological problems in children. The emergence of compulsory education marks an important milestone in the development of such interest, in part due to the large number of children who struggled in school.

The study of children in the United States was largely founded by G. Stanley Hall, whose work spanned 1883 through 1918 (Davidson & Benjamin, 1987). Hall focused on problems with education, and although he was not primarily concerned with psychopathology, his work helped promote a better understanding of the problems of childhood.

Clifford Beers played an important role in reversing the attitude toward the treatment of the mentally ill generally, and later this focus was applied to children. Beers became clinically depressed and suicidal as a Yale University law student. After his hospitalization, he wrote *A Mind That Found Itself* (1908), a book describing the poor treatment he received while institutionalized. The success of the book helped inform the public of the terrible conditions in state hospitals. Beers would form a number of organizations, including the Connecticut Society for Mental Hygiene (in 1908) and the National Committee for Mental Hygiene (in 1909), which promoted better conditions in state hospitals, better treatment methods, and research on the prevention and treatment of psychopathologies. This increased concern for the treatment of persons with mental illness brought about "mental hygiene" programs in schools (Morris & Kratochwill, in press-b).

Lightner Witmer is credited as the first clinical psychologist, although he had a strong interest in schools and has an APA Division 16 (School Psychology) award named after him. Witmer established the first psychological clinic in the United States, at the University of Pennsylvania, in 1896. His first client was a 14-year-old boy who had difficulty spelling (Benjamin, 2005). In the first year of the clinic's operation, Witmer and his students saw a total of 24 children between the ages of 3 and 16 years, who had such presenting problems as "learning difficulties, speech problems, and possibly chorea, hydrocephalus, and hyperactivity" (P. McReynolds, 1996, p. 238). Witmer published the first journal devoted to clinical psychology, titled *The Psychological Clinic*, in 1907 (Routh, 1996; Witmer, 1907/1996). The focus on children with problems in schools would eventually lead to the development of a specialty of psychology that involved practice in schools.

In 1909, the Cook County Juvenile Psychopathic Institute in Chicago was formed under the leadership of William Healy. The institute staff worked directly with juvenile offenders and stressed an interdisciplinary approach to studying juvenile issues (e.g., psychiatrists, psychologists, and social workers worked together on particular cases, taking into account multiple causes and perspectives). Aided by Beers's National Committee for Mental Hygiene, numerous child guidance clinics also developed across the country over the next several decades, and by 1930 there were about 500 child guidance clinics in the United States (Kanner, 1948).

Through the introduction of dynamic psychiatry and psychoanalysis during the early twentieth century, specifically the work of Sigmund Freud in Vienna and Adolph Meyer in the United States, the psychodynamic approach maintained that the origins of behavior problems lay in the past experiences (typically, childhood) of the person (Kanner, 1948), thereby turning attention to childhood. For example, with adult patients, these experiences were explored retrospectively by the psychiatrist or psychoanalyst, who attempted to draw causal relationships between these past experiences and the patients' present behavior. During the early years of the dynamic psychiatry movement, children were usually not seen in treatment by psychiatrists (Kanner, 1948). Nevertheless, the retrospective search for the relationship between early childhood events and present functioning aroused sufficient interest among professionals that some began to acquaint themselves specifically with the behavior problems of children as well as with the dynamics that contributed to their difficulties (Morris & Kratochwill, in press-a). This psychodynamic interest in children was not formally realized in the literature until the publication in 1909 of Freud's (1909/1963) detailed case of "Little Hans." Interestingly, although Freud formulated his etiological theory of phobias on the basis of Hans's symptoms and experiences, he did not treat Hans directly; Hans's father treated him under Freud's direction and supervision (Morris & Kratochwill, 1983). Although Hans's problem was treated successfully, it was not until at least 15 to 20 years later that Freudian psychoanalytic child therapy came into existence. This was largely due to the contributions and adaptations of Freud's work for children by Melanie Klein, Freud's student, and his daughter, Anna Freud, and the subsequent publication beginning in 1945 of Anna Freud's multivolume edited book series (with Hans Hartmann and Ernst Kris), *The Psychoanalytic Study of the Child*. The changes made by these women, as well as the earlier psychoanalytic therapy work with children first initiated by Hermine Hug-Hellmuth (the third woman to join Freud's Vienna Psychoanalytic Society during the 1900s), made Freud's therapeutic approach very relevant to children and contributed to its increasing popularity in the twentieth century and later influence in the development of many other forms of child and adolescent psychotherapy (Benveniste, 1998).

Some of the major methodological changes that were made for children in Freud's psychoanalysis were the substitution of play activities for the technique of free association and the use of drawings and dreams to understand a child's problems. For example, through the use of the medium of play, both Klein and Anna Freud discovered that children were able to represent to the child analyst their inner conflicts and perceptions of important relationships in their lives, as well as portray in their play their unique feelings about, perceptions of, and concerns about their various pleasurable and traumatic experiences (Morris, Li, Lizardi-Sanchez, & Morris, 2002; Warshaw, 1997).

Morris and Kratochwill (in press-b) identified some additional developments that influenced the focus of child therapy. First, as we noted previously, the intelligence testing movement had a tremendous influence on the study of children; in particular, it became possible to learn the extent to which a particular child differed from the norm in cognitive ability. It also demonstrated clearly the diversity of children in terms of their comprehension of classroom instruction (Kanner, 1948) and spawned a decade of debate on bias in testing and eventually, in the twenty-first century, federal regulations that would expand the focus of special services for children in schools (Kratochwill et al., in press).

Second, the formation of professional associations contributed to the increasing emphasis on the treatment of children. The first professional association was the Association of Medical Officers of American Institutions for Idiots and Feeble-minded Persons, founded in 1876, which evolved into the present-day American Association on Mental Retardation. Its first president was Edward Seguin. In 1892, another professional association was formed, the American Psychological Association, in which Witmer was a charter member. G. Stanley Hall was the first president of APA, and James Cattell was one of the first members of the Council (Board of Directors of APA) and the fourth president of APA. In 1922, the Council for Exceptional Children was formed; it consisted primarily of educators and other professionals, although parents were members too. The fourth early association was the American Orthopsychiatric Association, founded in 1924 and consisting primarily of psychiatrists, applied psychologists, and social workers, although educators as well as other professionals and parents were also members. Each of these groups encouraged the formulation and conduct of research with children having behavior and learning disorders, as well as the sharing of information regarding effective psychological and/or educational interventions.

Third, a treatment approach emerged that was initially much less popular than psychoanalytic child therapy. This approach was behaviorism and later became known as the behavior modification or behavior therapy movement (Kazdin, 1978; Morris, 1985). As we noted earlier, behavior modification emerged largely from the experimental psychology laboratory rather than from direct interaction with patients and was based on theories concerning how people and animals learn to behave through S-R learning and conditioning rather than through the conscious or unconscious thinking found in psychoanalytic writings. The two most famous behaviorists associated with this movement are John B. Watson (1913, 1919), often referred to as the "father of behaviorism," and B. F. Skinner (1938, 1953), the behavioral researcher and theorist who extended Watson's behaviorist views and developed a learning paradigm that Skinner referred to as "operant conditioning." The behavior modification and behavior therapy procedures that were derived from various learning theories were largely confined for many years to research settings. In fact, it was not until the mid-1960s to the late 1970s that these procedures began being applied on a regular basis in children's residential treatment settings, regular and special education classrooms, and outpatient mental health settings (Morris, 1985; Morris et al., 2002).

Developments in behavior modification set the stage for the evidence-based practice movement, when many of the procedures were implemented in research that offered strong support for effective outcomes, first with adults and eventually with children. Behaviorism also set the stage for prevention models in educational settings with particular emphasis on such models as positive behavior support, a movement with its roots in applied behavior analysis (Crone & Horner, 2003; Crone, Horner, & Hawken, 2004).

DEVELOPMENT OF THE EVIDENCE-BASED INTERVENTION AND PRACTICE MOVEMENT

As has been evident in the previous sections of this chapter, a number of different events shaped the future of psychological assessment and treatment of children. As the need for services for children and families increased, attention turned to the training of professionals in psychology. By the 1940s, considerable attention had been given to the need for a training model in clinical psychology. Up to this point, a great variety of training curricula existed in training programs, and training was often rushed and inadequate. Some programs produced statistically sophisticated therapists, and others focused on more service-oriented practice (Hayes et al., 1999). The issue had been present at least since 1918, when Leta Hollingworth argued that a training model was critical in the development of clinical psychology as a profession (Benjamin, 2005). However, there was little resolution until 1949, when 73 professionals met in Boulder, Colorado, for 15 days to discuss the training of clinical psychologists. The result became known as the scientist-practitioner model (or the Boulder model) and would profoundly influence professional psychology in subsequent years and, eventually, the evidence-based practice movement.

Training Psychologists: Advent of the Evidence-Based Practice Focus

The events leading up to the Boulder Conference were perhaps as rooted in social trends as they were in professional trends. By the 1940s, there was growing concern for mental health in the United States. The year 1944 saw written instruments and assessments used on close to 20 million persons (Reisman, 1976). World War I produced an abundance of psychological casualties for whom too few professionals could provide adequate care. In the wake of World War II, as professionals took steps to improve the quality of their care, the Veterans Administration officially declared clinical psychology a health care profession. The next major step was to improve and homogenize the training of clinical psychologists. Pressure to do so began to come from a variety of sources.

In 1941, the American Association for Applied Psychology (AAAP) endorsed a day-long conference for the development of a committee for improved training of clinical psychologists. The subsequent report, largely focused on training for the treatment of psychopathology, supported a 4-year PhD program in psychology: a year for systematic foundation in psychology, a year for psychometric and therapeutic principles and practice, a year for internship, and a final year for dissertation (Shakow, 1942). Reactions were largely positive, and the AAAP formed the Committee on Training in Clinical Psychology (CTCP). The integration of the AAAP with the APA in 1944 prevented prompt action, but the seeds were planted for the organization of professional training.

With concern for the welfare of returning soldiers, an increasing shortage of psychologists in the public, and concern over the quality of professional training, the VA and the U.S. Public Health Service (USPHS) began to commit funds for the training of clinical psychologists. In 1947, the VA and USPHS requested that the

APA assist in determining ways to train greater numbers of professional psychologists (Baker & Benjamin, 2000). The APA turned to the CTCP with four requests: recommend a clinical psychology training program, develop standards for institutions training clinical psychologists, visit and study these institutions, and maintain contact with other organizations invested in these problems (e.g., the American Orthopsychiatric Association, the National Committee for Mental Hygiene; APA, 1947). The chair of the CTCP, David Shakow, sent committee members a copy of a report titled "Graduate Internship Training in Psychology" (Shakow et al., 1945) and asked that it be critiqued. The Shakow Report, as it would become known, garnered significant support as the most comprehensive set of clinical psychology training recommendations to date.

In 1948 and 1949, the CTCP visited a number of training programs and awarded accreditation to 43 of them (APA, 1949). Although the committee was largely impressed with the efforts put forth by these programs, significant concerns were raised. First, it was contended that the focus of training was too narrow. There was certainly a social need for emphasis on psychiatric hospitals and the severely disturbed patients, but the committee argued that clinical psychologists should be trained to deal with other social issues. Second, many programs taught a variety of clinical techniques, placing limited emphasis on research methodology and theory—an issue that would become central to the Boulder Conference later that year (Baker & Benjamin, 2000).

When the Boulder Conference began, the adaptation of the scientist-practitioner model was not entirely agreed on. There was great concern that it would be difficult to train all graduate students in both research and practice. The role of research in training likely was the most difficult topic covered in the conference. However, by the end of the conference, agreement was reached among the large majority. In the most comprehensive report of the conference, titled *Training in Clinical Psychology,* Victor Raimy (1950, p. 23) reported, "The original chasm seemed to have largely disappeared and recognition of the importance of including research training in the preparation of all clinical psychologists was generally accepted." In fact, the decision to recommend training in research and practice did not require a compromise, but instead was nearly a unanimous consensus.

Recommendation for preparation in both areas rested on five major considerations. First, although most students would focus their career on either research or practice (not both), all students should be trained in both to encourage "cross fertilization and breadth of approach" (Raimy, 1950, p. 81) within the profession. That is, dual training would benefit both foci through collaboration; in addition, the study of research and practice would deter programs' tendencies to produce narrow thought processes and subsequent actions. Second, the extreme lack of dependable knowledge in the field demanded (and still demands) a need for research in clinical psychology. As Raimy reports, "Participants at the conference displayed considerable humility with respect to present techniques" (p. 80). Third, it was believed that students of clinical psychology should be capable of carrying out both roles of clinician and researcher. The number of applicants greatly surpassed the number of available positions in training programs; therefore, participants in the conference concluded that applicants should be considered for acceptance only if they showed promise in both areas of study. Fourth, it was noted that researchers would have a better knowledge of important research topics if they were directly involved with the clinical process. Fifth, services provided by clinical practice could provide financial support for research causes. This has become even truer in the current age of managed care. Increasingly, health care systems rely on evidence-based practices for success in the marketplace (Hayes et al., 1999).

The following summarizes the roles of clinical psychologists as concluded by participants at the Boulder Conference:

The basic needs of society for the services of clinical psychology are of two major kinds:

a. Professional services to:
   (1) Individuals through corrective and remedial work as well as diagnostic and therapeutic practices
   (2) Groups and social institutions needing positive mental hygiene programs in the interest of better community health
   (3) Students in training, members of other professions, and the public through systematic education and the general dissemination of information

b. Research contributions designed to:
   (1) Develop better understanding of human behavior
   (2) Improve the accuracy and reliability of diagnostic procedures
   (3) Develop more efficient methods of treatment
   (4) Develop methods of promoting mental hygiene and preventing maladjustment. (Raimy, 1950, pp. 20–21)

Though the decision to endorse the scientist-practitioner model was clear, participants recognized that there would be great difficulties involved in combining both roles. In this respect, participants in the Boulder Conference clearly anticipated the scientist-practitioner gap. A major criticism of the scientist-practitioner model developed at the Boulder Conference is its demonstrated failure to involve clinicians in research. The model has been much more universally adopted in research than in practice. The average PhD psychologist has published very few, if any, research articles.

Recent Developments in the Evidence-Based Intervention and Practice Movement

Despite great momentum in research in professional psychology, the evidence base for treatment of a variety of childhood disorders and problems lagged behind outcome research with adults. Nevertheless, as attention turned to mental health issues in children, psychologists began to review the literature on prevention and intervention (therapy) outcome research. To perform this task they needed guidelines to review the growing literature on prevention and intervention. Over the past decade criteria have been produced for developing evidence-based interventions and guidelines for how such interventions should be evaluated (see Barlow, 2004; Kratochwill & Stoiber, 2002). With pressure mounting from managed health care, governmental agencies, and professional organizations, a major task force on evidence-based interventions was formed by the APA Task Force on Promotion and Dissemination of Psychological Procedures (1995). The report stimulated considerable debate. The major controversial themes were identified: (a) The focus of research studies identified as evidence-based in the adult literature were identified as behaviorally oriented; (b) the criteria used were judged as potentially biased (e.g., methodological and statistical decision rules in the literature reviews); (c) the use of intervention manuals to standardize interventions was deemed problematic (e.g., manuals remove flexibility and adaptation to individual or group needs in psychotherapy); and (d) the generalizability of findings was deemed limited (i.e., whether and how research studies can be generalized to actual clinical practice).

Early in the evidence-based intervention movement school psychology explored evidence-based interventions and their implications for the field. Division 16 of the APA, the Society for the Study of School Psychology, and the National Association of School Psychologists supported the development of a Task Force on Evidence-Based Interventions in Schools (now co-chaired by Thomas R. Kratochwill and Kimberly Hoagwood).

The initial purpose of the School Psychology Task Force was to examine and disseminate the knowledge based on what prevention and intervention programs or approaches for children, youth, and families demonstrate empirical support for application in the school and community and to facilitate strong research methodologies, technologies, and innovations. The Task Force worked cooperatively with the APA's Division of Clinical Child and Adolescent Psychology (Division 53).

Another major direction taken in the evidence-based practice movement has involved the development of practice guidelines (White & Kratochwill, 2005). Various practice guidelines have been constructed by a variety of professional groups: the Agency for Health Care Policy and Research (AHCPR), the American Psychiatric Association, the National Institutes of Health, and the Division of Clinical Psychology (Division 12) of the APA. The AHCPR has developed guidelines for treating and diagnosing depression in primary care. The guidelines are primarily aimed at physicians and the general public. Practice guidelines of the American Academy of Child and Adolescent Psychiatry have been evolving for some time and provide a variety of foci for child intervention, including anxiety disorders, conduct disorders, and Attention-Deficit/Hyperactivity Disorder. The Division 12 Task Force (Chambless & Ollendick, 2001) provided a preliminary set of practice guidelines based on their review of empirically validated psychosocial interventions, resulting in a proposed three-category system of efficacy: well-established interventions, probably efficacious interventions, and experimental interventions (those not yet established as at least probably efficacious).

Over the past decade the Committee on Science and Practice of the Society for Clinical Psychology of APA Division 12 developed a procedural and coding manual for identification of beneficial interventions (Weisz & Hawley, 1998). The manual provided guidelines for identification, review, and coding of studies of psychological interventions for behavioral, emotional, and adjustment problems and disorders. The manual was designed to (a) identify intervention outcome studies related to the effects of psychological interventions; (b) code studies according to the committee's criteria and provide related information on characteristics of interventions in the studies that evaluate efficacy; and (c) make a determination on whether the intervention is beneficial. The procedural and coding manual extended the work of the Division 12 Task Force and the efforts of the Division 53 Task Force by clarifying what was meant by "empirically supported interventions" and expanded on a variety of published literature and the work of various committee members.

As various professional groups and researchers began to review the literature, narrative reviews and the application of meta-analysis to child psychotherapy outcome contributed to an evolving positive landscape for effective interventions (e.g., Lonigan, Elbert, & Johnson, 1998; Casey & Berman, 1985; Kazdin, Bass, Ayres, & Rodgers, 1990; Kazdin & Weisz, 2003; Weisz, Weiss, Alicke, & Klotz, 1987). Specifically, between 1952 and 1993, more than 300 research investigations of psychotherapy involving children between the ages of 2 and 18 years indicated that the intervention groups scored higher on various outcome measures than 76% to 81% of children in control groups (Casey & Berman, 1985; Kazdin, 2002). Hoagwood and Erwin (1997) conducted a 10-year research review and found that three types of interventions have empirical support: cognitive-behavior therapy, social skills training, and teacher consultation. Modest support for interventions delivered within school-based consultation occurred through traditional literature reviews (Kratochwill, Sheridan, & Van Someren, 1988; Mannino & Shore, 1975) and meta-analysis (Medway & Updyke, 1985; Sibley, 1986). Summaries of evidence-based treatments with children and adolescents can be found on a Division 53 website (www.effectivechildtherapy.org).

As the cost of treatment of adult and childhood disorders became clear, psychologists became vocal about the importance and effectiveness of prevention programs (e.g., Biglan, Mrazek, Carnine, & Flay, 2003; Coie et al., 1993; Kratochwill, Albers, & Shernoff, 2004; Nation et al., 2003; Tolan & Dodge, 2005; Weissberg, Kumpfer, & Seligman, 2003; Weisz, Sandler, Durlak, & Anton, 2005). Meta-analysis of prevention programs has also demonstrated positive outcomes (e.g., Durlak & Wells, 1997; Weisz, Jensen-Doss, & Hawley, 2006). To assist psychologists in implementing effective prevention programs, a website jointly sponsored by APA and the Society for Prevention Research presents information on over 100 reviews of prevention research on a variety of topics (www.oslc.org/spr/apa/summaries .html).

Tremendous advances have been made in the evidence-based practice area of child prevention and treatment. In recent years, several textbooks that emphasize evidence-based prevention and intervention for child and adolescent problems and disorders have appeared (see Table 1.1). The future looks very positive with regard to improving the quality of life of children and families who experience a wide range of academic and mental health concerns. To advance practice in the field, a number of issues have surfaced that have an important bearing on the future of this movement (see Kratochwill et al., in press). Although it is not possible to review these issues in great detail here, a sampling will convey the complexity of the tasks. To begin with, major concerns surround the research methods of establishing the evidence base in this area, with calls for expanding the methodologies of quantitative research and even the framework for empiricism of the movement (see Slife, Bradford, Wiggins, & Graham, 2005). Concerns have also been expressed about the

Table 1.1   Coverage and Number of Chapters of Specific Topics Addressed in Each Book on Evidence-Based Intervention

Topic	1[a]	2[b]	3[c]	4[d]	5[e]	6[f]
Treatment research methods	E	E	C	E	E	E
Developmental issues	NC	NC	C	E	E	E
Ethical issues	NC	NC	NC	E	NC	E
Assessment	NC	E	E	NC	E	E
Diversity	NC	NC	E	E	E	C
Future directions	E	E	E	E	E	C
Clinical disorders or topics						E
Adherence to medical regimens			1			E
Anxiety disorders	2	1	1	2	4	1
Attention Deficit Hyperactivity	2	1		1	1	1
Eating disorders		1		1		
Conduct Disorder, Oppositional Defiant Disorder						1
Depression	6	1	1	6	2	1
Depression	2	1		4	1	
Developmental disorders (e.g., language)		1				1
Encopresis			1			
Enuresis			1	1		
Habit disorders			1			
Obesity						
Obsessive-Compulsive Disorder				1	1	1
Pain management			1			
Pervasive developmental disorders (Autism)		1		2		1
Medical or physical conditions		1				1
Posttraumatic Stress Disorder					1	1
Prevention					4	1
Psychotic disorders		1				
School refusal						
Sleep problems			1			
Substance abuse		1				
Suicide		1				
Tourette's syndrome		1				
Somatic disorders						1
Child sexual abuse or Child maltreatment						1
Ethical and legal issues						1
Mental retardation and Intellectual disability						1
Psychopharmacology						1

Note: C = Mentioned but minimally; E = Emphasized; NC = Not covered.

[a]*Psychotherapy for Children and Adolescents: Evidence-Based Treatments and Case Examples,* by J. R. Weisz, 2004, Cambridge: Cambridge University Press.

[b]*What Works for Whom? A Critical Review of Treatments for Children and Adolescents*, by P. Fonagy, M. Target, D. Cottrell, J. Phillips, and Z. Kurtz, 2002, New York: Guilford Press.

[c]*Treatments that Work with Children: Empirically Supported Strategies for Managing Childhood Problems*, by E. R. Christophersen and S. L. Mortweet, 2003, Washington, DC: American Psychological Association.

[d]*Evidence-Based Psychotherapies for Children and Adolescents*, by A. E. Kazdin, & J. R. Weisz, (Eds.), 2003, New York: Guilford Press.

[e]*Handbook of Interventions that Work with Children and Adolescents: Prevention and Treatment,* by P. M. Barrett and T. H. Ollendick (Eds.), 2004, New York: Wiley.

[f]*The Practice of Child Therapy*, fourth edition, by R. J. Morris and T. R. Kratochwill, in press-a, Mawah, NJ: Erlbaum.

limitations of the focus of research, which traditionally has not given attention to the transportability of the prevention and intervention programs (e.g., Schoenwald & Hoagwood, 2001). Limitations of the sample of participants in evidence-based research and the need for cultural adaptations of interventions have also been noted (e.g., Bernal & Scharron-Del-Rio, 2001). In addition, limitations of outcome assessment strategies and, in particular, the arbitrary nature of the instruments used in evidence-based intervention research have been noted (see Blanton & Jaccard, 2006; Kazdin, 2006). Despite these challenges, major commitments to advance the quality of practice with a firm foundation of scientific support are in place (Frick, 2007; Kratochwill et al., in press). As the evidence-based movement progresses it will be important to consider the historical evidence and its importance in teaching us that diversity of viewpoints can best advance science and practice.

SUMMARY

Assessment and intervention for children and adolescents experiencing academic and behavior problems have come far from their ancient roots. In this chapter, we summarized the major trends and events that led to the current state of child and adolescent therapy. We began with a synopsis of progress prior to the nineteenth century, which set the stage for increasingly systematic investigations of human characteristics and behavior. This focus was exemplified by the work of Itard, Wundt, Galton, Cattell, and others. During the first half of the twentieth century, intelligence testing and personality assessment emerged as significant roles for psychologists. Methodological differentiation rapidly became an interest during World War I, and intelligence testing became important for the assessment of schoolchildren. In the second half of the twentieth century, we witnessed the rise of behavioral modification and assessment methods as greatly important in child and adolescent psychology. In particular, these assessment and intervention technologies set the stage for a scientific basis for therapy that would shape the evidence-based practice movement in psychology.

In addition to a discussion of trends and events, we described major conceptual models that have been developed and persist today, including the medical or biological model, the psychodynamic model, the psychometric test-based model, and the behavioral model. Implications for their use in current practices were discussed. We addressed the history of child therapy, from its most famous early roots to modern trends, including the emergence of the scientist-practitioner training model and the evidence-based practice movement. A brief discussion of major concerns surrounding evidence-based practice was provided. The future looks bright for the evidence-based practice movement as the complexities of selection, implementation, and sustainability of treatment technologies are being addressed in research and practice.

REFERENCES

Alexander, F. M., & Selesnick, S. T. (1968). *The history of psychiatry: An evaluation of psychiatric thought and practice from prehistoric times to the present.* New York: New American Library.

American Psychological Association, Committee of Training in Clinical Psychology. (1947). Recommended graduate training program in clinical psychology. *American Psychologist, 2,* 539–558.

American Psychological Association, Committee of Training in Clinical Psychology. (1949). Doctoral training programs in clinical psychology: 1949. *American Psychologist, 4*, 331–341.

American Psychological Association, Presidential Task Force on Evidence-Based Practice. (2006). Evidence-based practice in psychology. *American Psychologist, 61*(4), 271–285.

Baer, D. M., Wolf, M. M., & Risley, T. R. (1968). Some current dimensions of applied behavior analysis. *Journal of Applied Behavior Analysis, 1*, 91–97.

Baker, D. B., & Benjamin, L. T. (2000). The affirmation of the scientist-practitioner: A look back at Boulder. *American Psychologist, 55*(2), 241–247.

Bandura, A. (1969). *Principles of behavior modification*. New York: Holt, Rinehart and Winston.

Bandura, A. (1971). Psychotherapy based upon modeling principles. In A. E. Bergin, & S. L. Garfield (Eds.), *Handbook of psychotherapy and behavior change* (pp. 653–708). New York: Wiley.

Bandura, A. (1977a). Self-efficacy: Toward a unifying theory of behavioral change. *Psychological Review, 84*, 191–215.

Bandura, A. (1977b). *Social learning theory*. Englewood Cliffs, NJ: Prentice-Hall.

Bandura, A., & Walters, R. H. (1963). *Social learning and personality development*. New York: Holt, Rinehart and Winston.

Barlow, D. H., (2004). Psychological treatments. *American Psychologist, 59*(9), 869–878.

Barrett, P. M., & Ollendick, T. H. (Eds.). (2004). *Handbook of interventions that work with children and adolescents: Prevention and treatment*. Hoboken, NJ: Wiley.

Bateman, B. (1965). An educator's view of a diagnostic approach to learning disorders. In J. Hellmuth (Ed.), *Learning disorders* (Vol. 1, pp. 219–239). Seattle, WA: Special Child Publications.

Bear, G. G., & Minke, K. M. (Eds.). (2006). *Children's needs: Vol. III. Development, prevention, and intervention*. Bethesda, MD: National Association of School Psychologists.

Beers, C. W. (1908). *A mind that found itself*. New York: Longmans Green.

Benjamin, L. T. (2005). A history of clinical psychology as a profession in America (and a glimpse at its future). *Annual Review of Clinical Psychology, 1*, 1–30.

Benveniste, P. S. (1998). Rorschach assessment of annihilation anxiety and ego functioning. *Psychoanalytic Psychology, 15*(4), 536–566.

Bergan, J. R., & Kratochwill, T. R. (1990). *Behavioral consultation and therapy*. New York: Plenum Press.

Bernal, G., & Scharron-Del-Rio, M. R. (2001). Are empirically supported treatments valid for ethnic minorities? Toward an alternative approach for treatment research. *Cultural Diversity and Ethnic Minority Psychology, 7*(4), 328–342.

Biglan, A., Mrazek, P. J., Carnine, D., & Flay, B. R. (2003). The integration of research and practice in the prevention of youth problem behaviors. *American Psychologist, 58*(6/7), 433–440.

Bijou, S. W. (1970). What psychology has to offer education: Now. *Journal of Applied Behavior Analysis, 3*, 65–71.

Bijou, S. W. (1976). *Child development: The basic stage of early childhood*. Englewood Cliffs, NJ: Prentice-Hall.

Bijou, S. W., & Baer, S. W. (1978). *Behavior analysis of child development*. Englewood Cliffs, NJ: Prentice-Hall.

Bijou, S. W., & Grimm, J. A. (1975). Behavioral diagnosis and assessment in teaching young handicapped children. In T. Thompson, & W. S. Dockens III (Eds.), *Applications of behavior modification* (pp. 161–180). New York: Academic Press.

Bijou, S. W., Peterson, R. F., & Ault, M. H. (1968). A method to integrate descriptive and experimental field studies at the level of data and empirical concepts. *Journal of Applied Behavior Analysis, 1*, 175–191.

Bijou, S. W., Peterson, R. F., Harris, F. R., Allen, K. E., & Johnson, M. S. (1969). Methodology for experimental studies of young children in natural settings. *Psychological Record, 19*, 177–210.

Binet, A., & Henri, V. (1895). La psychologie individuelle. *Annee Psychologique 2*, 411–463.

Blanton, H., & Jaccard, J. (2006). Arbitrary metrics in psychology. *American Psychologist, 61*(1), 27–41.

Boring, E. G. (1950). *A history of experimental psychology* (2nd ed.). New York: Appleton-Century-Crofts.

Brady, J. P. (1979). Perspective on research with human subjects. *Behavior Therapists, 2*, 9–13.

Brown-Chidsey, R., & Steege, M. W. (2006). *Response to intervention: Principles and strategies for effective instruction*. New York: Guilford Press.

Buros, O. K. (Ed.). (1972). *Mental measurements yearbook*. Highland Park, NJ: Gryphon Press.

Carroll, J. B. (1978). On the theory-practice interface in the measurement of intellectual abilities. In P. Suppes (Ed.), *Impact of research on education: Some case studies* (pp. 1–105). Washington, DC: National Academy of Education.

Casey, R. J., & Berman, J. S. (1985). The outcome of psychotherapy with children. *Psychological Bulletin, 98*, 388–400.

Chambless, D. L., & Ollendick, T. H. (2001). Empirically supported psychological interventions: Controversies and evidence. *Annual Review of Psychology, 52*, 685–716.

Christophersen, E. R., & Mortweet, S. L. (2003). *Treatments that work with children: Empirically supported strategies for managing childhood problems*. Washington, DC: American Psychological Association.

Ciminero, A. R. Calhoun, K. S., & Adams, H. E. (Eds.). (1977). *Handbook of behavioral assessment*. New York: Wiley.

Coie, J. D., Watt, N. F., West, S. G., Hawkins, J. D., Asarnow, J. R., Markman, H. J., et al. (1993). The science of prevention: A conceptual framework and some directions for a national research program. *American Psychologist, 48*(10), 1013–1022.

Cooley, W. R., & Lohnes, P. R. (1976). *Evaluation research in education: Theory, principles and practice*. New York: Irving.

Crone, D. H., & Horner, R. H. (2003). *Building positive behavior support systems in schools: Functional behavioral assessment*. New York: Guilford Press.

Crone, D. H., Horner, R. H., & Hawken, L. S. (2004). *Responding to behavior problems in schools: The behavior education program*. New York: Guilford Press.

Darwin, C. (1859). *On the origin of the species by means of natural selection, or, the preservation of favoured races in the struggle for life*. London: J. Murray.

Davidson, E. S., & Benjamin, L. T. (1987). A history of the child study movement in America. In J. Glover & R. Ronning (Eds.), *Historical foundations of educational psychology* (pp. 41–60). New York: Plenum Press.

Day, W. F. (1976). Contemporary behaviorism and the concept of intention. In M. R. Jones (Ed.), *Nebraska symposium on motivation* (Vol. 23, pp. 65–131). Lincoln: University of Nebraska Press.

Doyle, I. O. (1974). Theory and practice of ability testing in ancient Greece. *Journal of the History of the Behavioral Sciences, 10*, 202–212.

Dubois, P. H. (1966). A test-dominated society: China 1115 B.C.-1905 A.D. In A. Anastasi (Ed.), *Testing problems in perspective* (pp. 29–36). Princeton, NJ: Educational Testing Service.

Dubois, P. H. (1970). *A history of psychological testing*. Boston: Allyn & Bacon.

Dunn, L. M., & Kirk, S. A. (1963). Impressions of Soviet psycho-educational service and research in mental retardation. *Exceptional Children, 35*, 5–22.

Durlak, J. A., & Wells, A. M. (1997). Primary prevention mental health programs for children and adolescents: A meta-analytic review. *American Journal of Community Psychology, 25*, 114–152.

Edwards, A. J. (1971). *Individual mental testing: Pt. I. History and theories*. Scranton, PA: Intext Educational.

Eibl-Eibesfeldt, I. (1971). *Love and hate*. New York: Holt, Rinehart and Winston.

Ekman, P. (Ed.). (1973). *Darwin and facial expression*. New York: Academic Press.

Ekman, P., Friesen, W., & Ellsworth, P. (1972). *Emotion in the human face: Guidelines for research and an integration of findings*. Oxford: Pergamon Press.

Ellis, A. (1962). *Reason and emotion in psychotherapy*. New York: Lyle Stuart.

Emery, R. E., & Marholin, D. (1977). An applied behavior analysis of delinquency: The relevancy of relevant behavior. *American Psychologist, 32*, 860–873.

Eysenck, H. J. (1960). *Behavior therapy and the neuroses*. Oxford: Pergamon Press.

Eysenck, H. J. (Ed.). (1964). *Experiments in behavior therapy*. Oxford: Pergamon Press.

Ferster, C., & Skinner, B. F. (1957). *Schedules of reinforcement*. New York: Appleton-Century-Crofts.

Fonagy, P., Target, M., Cottrell, D., Phillips, J., & Kurtz, Z. (2002). *What works for whom? A critical review of treatments for children and adolescents*. New York: Guilford Press.

Frick, P. J. (2007). Providing the evidence for evidence-based practice. *Journal of Clinical Child and Adolescent Psychology, 36*(1), 2–7.

Galton, F. (1869). *Hereditary genius: An inquiry into its laws and consequences.* London: Macmillan.

Gelfand, D. M., & Hartmann, D. P. (1975). *Child behavior analysis and therapy.* New York: Pergamon Press.

Gleser, G., Gottshalk, L. A., & Springer, K. H. (1961). An anxiety scale applicable to verbal samples. *Archives of General Psychiatry, 5*, 593–604.

Goldfried, M. R. (1976). Behavioral assessment in perspective. In J. D. Cone, & R. P. Hawkins (Eds.), *Behavioral assessment: New directions in clinical psychology* (pp. 3–22). New York: Brunner/Mazel.

Goldfried, M. R., & Ingling, J. (1964). The connotative and symbolic meaning of the Bender Gestalt. *Journal of Projective Techniques and Personality Assessment, 28*(2), 185–191.

Goldfried, M. R., & Kent, R. M. (1972). Traditional versus behavioral personality assessment: A comparison of methodological and theoretical assumptions. *Psychological Bulletin, 77*, 409–420.

Goldfried, M. R., & Linehan, M. M. (1977). Basic issues in behavioral assessment. In A. R. Ciminero K. S. Calhoun, & H. E. Adams (Eds.), *Handbook of behavioral assessment* (pp. 15–46). New York: Wiley.

Goldfried, M. R., & Pomeranz, D. M. (1968). Role of assessment in behavior modification. *Psychological Reports, 23*, 75–87.

Haas, H. (1972). *The human animal.* New York: Dell.

Hall, E. T. (1959). *The silent language.* New York: Doubleday.

Hartmann, D. P., Roper, B. L., & Bradford, D. C. (1979). Some relationships between behavioral and traditional assessment. *Journal of Behavioral Assessment, 1*, 3–21.

Hathaway, S. R., & McKinley, J. C. (1943). *The Minnesota Multiphasic Personality Inventory.* Minneapolis: University of Minnesota Press.

Hayes, S. C., Barlow, D. H., & Nelson-Gray, R. O. (1999). *The scientist practitioner: Research and accountability in the age of managed care* (2nd ed.). Needham Heights, MA: Allyn & Bacon.

Hersen, M. (1976). Historical perspectives in behavioral assessment. In M. Hersen, & A. S. Bellack (Eds.), *Behavioral assessment: A practical handbook* (pp. 1–16). New York: Pergamon Press.

Hersen, M., & Barlow, D. H. (1976). *Single case experimental designs: Strategies for studying behavior change.* New York: Pergamon Press.

Hersen, M., & Bellack, A. S. (Eds.). (1976a). *Behavioral assessment: A practical handbook.* Oxford: Pergamon Press.

Hersen, M., & Bellack, A. S. (1976b). Social skills training for chronic psychiatric patients: Rationale, research findings, and future directions. *Comprehensive Psychiatry, 17*, 559–580.

Hess, E. H., & Polt, J. M. (1960). Pupil size as related to interest value of visual stimuli. *Science, 123*, 349–350.

Hess, E. H., Seltzer, A. L., & Schlien, J. M. (1965). Pupil response of hetero and homosexual males to pictures of men and women: A pilot study. *Journal of Abnormal Psychology, 70*, 165–168.

Hoagwood, K., & Erwin, H. (1997). Effectiveness of school-based mental health services for children: A 10-year research review. *Journal of Child and Family Studies, 6*, 435–451.

Hunt, J. M. (1961). *Intelligence and experience.* New York: Ronald Press.

Hutt, M. L. (1968). *The Hutt adaptation of the Bender-Gestalt test: Revised.* New York: Grune & Stratton.

Hutt, M. L., & Briskin, G. J. (1960). *The clinical use of the revised Bender-Gestalt test.* New York: Grune & Stratton.

Izard, C. E. (1971). *The face of emotion.* New York: Appleton-Century-Crofts.

Kanfer, F. H., & Phillips, J. S. (1970). *Learning foundations of behavior therapy.* New York: Wiley.

Kanner, L. (1948). *Child psychiatry.* Springfield, IL: Charles C Thomas.

Kazdin, A. E. (1978). *History of behavior modification: Experimental foundations of contemporary research.* Baltimore: University Park Press.

Kazdin, A. E. (1980). *Behavior modification in applied settings* (Rev. ed.). Homewood, IL: Dorsey Press.

Kazdin, A. E. (2002). The state of child and adolescent psychotherapy research. *Child and Adolescent Mental Health, 7*(2), 53–59.

Kazdin, A. E. (2006). Implications for identifying evidence-based treatments. *American Psychologist, 61*(1), 42–49.

Kazdin, A. E., Bass, D., Ayers, W. A., & Rodgers, A. (1990). Empirical and clinical focus of child and adolescent psychotherapy research. *Journal of Consulting and Clinical Psychology, 58,* 729–740.

Kazdin, A. E., & Hersen, M. (1980). The current status of behavior therapy. *Behavior Modification, 4,* 283–302.

Kazdin, A. E. & Weisz, J. R. (Eds.). (2003). *Evidence-based psychotherapies for children and adolescents.* New York: Guilford Press.

Kazdin, A. E., & Wilson, G. T. (1978). *Evaluation of behavior therapy: Issues, evidence, and research strategies.* Cambridge, MA: Ballinger.

Kendall, P. C. (1981a). Assessment and cognitive-behavioral interventions: Purposes, proposals, and problems. In P. C. Kendall, & S. D. Hollon (Eds.), *Assessment strategies for cognitive behavioral interventions* (pp. 1–12). New York: Academic Press.

Kendall, P. C. (1981b). Cognitive-behavioral interventions with children. In B. B. Lahey, & A. E. Kazdin (Eds.), *Advances in clinical child psychology* (Vol. 4, pp. 53–90). New York: Plenum Press.

Knox, H. A. (1914). A scale based on the work at Ellis Island for estimating mental defect. *Journal of the American Medical Association, 62,* 741–747.

Korchin, S. J., & Schuldberg, D. (1981). The future of clinical assessment. *American Psychologist, 36,* 1147–1158.

Kraepelin, E. (1962). *One-hundred years of psychology (W. Baskin, Trans.).* New York: Citadel.

Kratochwill, T. R. (1982). Advances in behavioral assessment. In C. R. Reynolds & T. B. Gutkin (Eds.), *Handbook of school psychology* (pp. 314–350). New York: Wiley.

Kratochwill, T. R., Albers, C. A., & Shernoff, E. (2004). School-based interventions. *Child and Adolescent Psychiatric Clinics of North America, 13,* 885–903.

Kratochwill, T. R., & Alper, S., Cancelli, A. A. (1980). Nondiscriminatory assessment in psychology and education. In L. Mann & D. A. Sabatino (Eds.), *Fourth review of special education* (pp. 229–286). New York: Grune & Stratton.

Kratochwill, T. R., & Bijou, S. W. (1987). The impact of behaviorism on educational psychology. In J. A. Glover, & R. R. Ronning (Eds.), *Historical foundations of educational psychology* (pp. 131–157). New York: Plenum Press.

Kratochwill, T. R., Clements, M. A., & Kalymon, K. M. (2007). Response to intervention: Conceptual and methodological issues in implementation. In S. R. Jimmerson, M. K. Burns, & A. M. VanDerHeyeden (Eds.), *The handbook of response to intervention: The science and practice of assessment and intervention* (pp. 25–52). New York: Springer.

Kratochwill, T. R., & Levin, J. R. (1992). *Single-case research design and analysis: New directions for psychology and education.* Hillsdale, NJ: Erlbaum.

Kratochwill, T. R., & Morris, R. J. (Eds.). (1993). *Handbook of psychotherapy with children and adolescents.* Boston: Allyn & Bacon.

Kratochwill, T. R., Sheridan, S. M., & Van Someren, K. P. (1988). Research in behavioral consultation: Current status and future directions. In F. J. West (Ed.), *School consultation: Interdisciplinary perspectives on theory, research, training, and practice* (pp. 77–102). Austin, TX: Association of Educational and Psychological Consultants.

Kratochwill, T. R., & Shernoff, E. S. (2004). Evidence-based practice: Promoting evidence-based interventions in school psychology. *School Psychology Review, 33*(1), 34–48.

Kratochwill, T. R., & Stoiber, K. C. (2002). Evidence-based interventions in school psychology: Conceptual foundations of the Procedural and Coding Manual of Division 16 and the Society for the Study of School Psychology Task Force. *School Psychology Quarterly, 17*(4), 341–389.

Laosa, L. M. (1977). Nonbiased assessment of children's abilities: Historical antecedents and current issues. In T. Oakland (Ed.) *Psychological and educational assessment of minority children.* (pp.1–20). New York: Brunner/Mazel.

Linden, K. W., & Linden, J. D. (1968). *Modern mental measurement: A historical perspective.* Boston: Houghton Mifflin.

Lipowski, Z. J. (1977). Psychosomatic medicine in the seventies: An overview. *American Journal of Psychiatry, 134,* 233–244.

Lonigan, C. J., Elbert, J. C., & Johnson, S. B. (1998). Empirically supported psychosocial interventions for children: An overview. *Journal of Clinical Child Psychology, 27*(2), 138–145.

Mahl, G. F. (1956). Disturbances and silences in the patient's speech in psychotherapy. *Journal of Abnormal and Social Psychology, 52*, 1–15.

Mahoney, M. J. (1974). *Cognition and behavior modification.* Cambridge, MA: Ballinger.

Mahoney, M. J., & Arnkoff, D. (1978). Cognitive and self-control therapies. In S. L. Garfield, & A. E. Bergin (Eds.), *Handbook of psychotherapy and behavior change: An empirical analysis* (pp. 689–722). New York: Wiley.

Maloney, M. P., & Ward, M. P. (1976). *Psychological assessment: A conceptual approach.* New York: Oxford University Press.

Mannino, F. V., & Shore, M. F. (1975). The effects of consultation: A review of the literature. *American Journal of Community Psychology, 3*, 1–21.

Masling, J. (1960). The influence of situational and interpersonal variables in projective testing. *Psychological Bulletin, 57*, 65–85.

McReynolds, L. V. (1974). *Developing systematic procedures for training children's language.* Washington, DC: American Speech and Hearing Association.

McReynolds, P. (1975). Historical antecedents of personality assessment. In P. McReynolds (Ed.), *Advances in psychological assessment* (Vol. 3, pp. 477–532). San Francisco: Jossey-Bass.

McReynolds, P. (1996). Lightner Witmer: A centennial tribute. *American Psychologist, 51*, 237–240.

Medway, F. J., & Updyke, J. F. (1985). Meta-analysis of consultation outcome studies. *American Journal of Community Psychology, 13*, 489–505.

Meehl, P. (1956). Wanted: A good cookbook. *American Psychologist, 2*, 263–272.

Meichenbaum, D. H. (1974). *Cognitive behavior modification.* Morristown, NJ: General Learning Press.

Meichenbaum, D. H. (1977). *Cognitive behavior modification: An integrative approach.* New York: Plenum Press.

Mischel, T. (1971). *Cognitive development and epistemology.* New York: Academic Press.

Mischel, W. (1968). *Personality and assessment.* New York: Wiley.

Mischel, W. (1972). Direct versus indirect personality assessment: Evidence and implications. *Journal of Consulting and Clinical Psychology, 38*, 319–324.

Mischel, W. (1974). Cognitive appraisals and transformations in self-control. In B. Weiner (Ed.), *Cognitive views of human motivation* (pp. 33–49). New York: Academic Press.

Morris, R. J. (1985). *Behavior modification with exceptional children: Principles and practices.* Glenview, IL: Scott, Foresman.

Morris, R. J., & Kratochwill, T. R. (1983). *Treating children's fears and phobias: A behavioral approach.* Elmsford, NY: Pergamon Press.

Morris, R. J., & Kratochwill, T. R. (in press-a). Historical context of child therapy. In R. J. Morris, & T. R. Kratochwill (Eds.), *The practice of child therapy* (4th ed.). Mahwah, NJ: Erlbaum.

Morris, R. J., & Kratochwill, T. R. (in press-b). Historical context of child therapy. In R. J. Morris, & T. R. Kratochwill (Eds.), *The practice of child therapy* (4th ed.). Mahwah, NJ: Erlbaum.

Morris, R. J., Kratochwill, T. R., Schoenfield, G., & Auster, E. R. (in press). Childhood fears, phobias, and related anxieties. In R. J. Morris & T. R. Kratochwill (Eds.), *The practice of child therapy* (4th ed.) Mahwah, NJ: Erlbaum.

Morris, R. J., Li, H., Lizardi-Sanchez, P., & Morris, Y. P. (2002). Psychotherapy with children and adolescents. In I. Weiner (Ed.), *Comprehensive handbook of psychology: Clinical psychology* (pp. 389–405). Hoboken, NJ: Wiley.

Nation, M., Crusto, C., Wandersman, A., Kumpfer, K. L., Seybolt, D., Morrissey-Kane, E., et al. (2003). What works in prevention: Principles of effective prevention programs. *American Psychologist, 58*(6/7), 449–456.

Newland, T. E. (1977). Tested "intelligence" in children. *School Psychology Monograph, 3*, 1–44.

Oakland, T., & Matuszek, P. (1977). Using tests in nondiscriminatory assessment. In T. Oakland (Ed.), *Psychological and educational assessment of minority children* (pp. 52–69). New York: Brunner/Mazel.

Otis, A. S. (1918). An absolute point scale for the group measure of intelligence. *Journal of Educational Psychology, 9*, 238–261.

Pearson, K. (1930). *The life, letters, and labors of Francis Galton.* Cambridge, MA: Cambridge University Press.

Peterson, R. E. (1968). Predictive validity of a brief test of academic aptitude. *Educational and Psychological Measurement, 28*, 441–444.

Phillips, L., Draguns, J. G., & Bartlett, D. P. (1975). Classification of behavior disorders. In N. Hobbs (Ed.), *Issues in the classification of children* (Vol. 1, pp. 26–55). San Francisco: Jossey-Bass.

Rachman, S. (1963). Introduction to behavior therapy. *Behavior Research and Therapy, 1*, 4–15.

Raimy, V. C. (Ed.). (1950). *Training in clinical psychology*. Englewood Cliffs, NJ: Prentice-Hall.

Rappaport, D., Gill, M., & Schafer, R. (1945). *Diagnostic psychological testing*. Chicago: Year Book Medical Publishing.

Reisman, J. M. (1976). *A history of clinical psychology: Enlarged edition of the development of clinical psychology*. Oxford: Halstead Press.

Resnick, D. (1982). History of educational testing. In A. K. Widgor & W. R. Garber (Eds.), *Ability testing: Uses, consequences, and controversies* (pp. 173–194). Washington, DC: National Academy Press.

Rosenthal, T. L. (1976). Modeling therapies. In M. Hersen, R. M. Eisler, & P. M. Miller (Eds.), *Progress in behavior modification* (pp. 173–194). New York: Academic Press.

Routh, D. K. (1996). Lightner Witmer and the first 100 years of clinical psychology. *American Psychologist, 51*, 244–247.

Salvia, J., & Ysseldyke, J. E. (1978). *Assessment in special and remedial education*. Boston: Houghton-Mifflin.

Sarason, S. B. (1976). The unfortunate fate of Alfred Binet and school psychology. *Teachers College Record, 77*, 579–592.

Schoenwald, S. K., Hoagwood, K. (2001). Effectiveness, transportability, and dissemination of interventions: What matters when? *Psychiatric Services, 52*(9), 123–130.

Sedlak, R. A., & Weener, P. (1973). Review of research on the IL test of psycholinguistic abilities. In L. Mann, & D. Sabatino (Eds.), *The first review of special education* (pp. 113–163). New York: Grune & Stratton.

Shakow, D. (1942). The training of the clinical psychologist. *Journal of Consulting Psychology, 6*, 277–288.

Shakow, D., Brotemarkle, R. A., Doll, E. A., Kinder, E. F., Moore, B. V., & Smith, S. (1945). Graduate internship training in psychology: Report by the subcommittee on graduate and profession training of the American Psychological Association and the American Association for Applied Psychology. *Journal of Consulting Psychology, 9*, 243–266.

Sharp, S. E. (1899). Individual psychology: A study in psychological method. *American Journal of Psychology, 10*, 329–391.

Sibley, S. (1986). *A meta-analysis of school consultation research*. Unpublished doctoral dissertation, Texas Women's University, Denton.

Sidman, M. (1960). *Tactics of scientific research*. New York: Basic Books.

Siegel, L. J. (1983). *Psychosomatic and psychophysiological disorders*. In R. J. Morris, & T. R. Kratochwill (Eds.), *The practice of child therapy: A testbook of methods* (pp. 253–286). New York: Pergamon Press.

Skinner, B. F. (1938). *The behavior of organisms*. New York: Appleton-Century-Crofts.

Skinner, B. F. (1945). The operational analysis of psychological terms. *Psychological Review. 52,* 270–277.

Skinner, B. F. (1953). *Science and human behavior*. New York: Free Press.

Skinner, B. F. (1957). *Verbal behavior*. New York: Appleton-Century-Crofts.

Skinner, B. F. (1969). *Contingencies of reinforcement: A theoretical analysis*. New York: Appleton-Century-Crofts.

Skinner, B. F. (1974). *About behaviorism*. New York: Knopf.

Slife, B. D., Wiggins, B. J., & Graham, J. T. (2005). Avoiding an EST monopoly: Toward a pluralism of philosophies and methods. *Journal of Contemporary Psychotherapy, 35*(1), 83–97.

Stern, W. (1900). *Uber pscyhologies der individuellen differenzen: Ideen zur "Differenzellen Psychologie."* Leipzig: Barth.

Stern, W., & Whipple, G. M. (1914). *The psychological methods of testing intelligence*. Baltimore: Warwick & York.

Stuart, R. B. (1970). *Trick or treatment: How and when psychotherapy fails.* Champaign, IL: Research Press.

Sulzer-Azaroff, B., & Mayer, G. R. (1977). *Applying behavior analysis procedures with children and youth.* New York: Holt, Rinehart and Winston.

Sunberg, N. D. (1977). *Assessment of persons.* Englewood Cliffs, NJ: Prentice-Hall.

Task Force on Promotion and Dissemination of Psychological Procedures (1995). Training in and dissemination of empirically validated psychological treatments: Report and recommendations. *Clinical Psychologist, 48*, 3–23.

Tolan, P. H., & Dodge, K. A. (2005). Children's mental health as a primary care and concern: A system for comprehensive support and service. *American Psychologist, 60*(6), 601–614.

Warshaw, S. C. (1997). A psychoanalytic approach to intervention. In R. C. D'Amato, & B. A. Rothlisberg (Eds.), *Psychological perspectives on intervention* (pp. 48–68). Prospect Heights, IL: Waveland Press.

Watson, J. B. (1913). Psychology as the behaviorist views it. *Psychological Review, 20*, 158–177.

Watson, J. B. (1919). *Psychology from the standpoint of a behaviorist.* Philadelphia: Lippincott.

Watson, J. B., & Raynor, R. (1920). Conditioned emotional reactions. *Journal of Experimental Psychology, 3*, 1–14.

Wechsler, D. (1975). Intelligence defined and undefined: A relativistic appraisal. *American Psychologist, 30*, 135–139.

Weissberg, R. P., Kumpfer, K. L., & Seligman, M. E. P. (2003). Prevention that works for children and youth: An introduction. *American Psychologist, 58*(6–7), 425–432.

Weisz, J. R. (2004). *Psychotherapy for children and adolescents: Evidence-based treatments and case examples.* Cambridge: Cambridge University Press.

Weisz, J. R., & Hawley, K. M. (1998). Finding, evaluating, refining, and applying empirically supported treatments for children and adolescents. *Journal of Clinical Child Psychology, 27*, 205–215.

Weisz, J. R., Jensen-Doss, A., & Hawley, K. M. (2006). Evidence-based youth psychotherapies versus usual clinical care: A meta-analysis of direct comparisons. *American Psychologist, 61*(7), 671–689.

Weisz, J. R., Sandler, I. N., Durlak, J. A., & Anton, B. S. (2005). Promoting and protecting youth mental health through evidence-based prevention and treatment. *American Psychologist, 60*(6), 628–648.

Weisz, J. R., Weiss, B., Alicke, M. D., & Klotz, M. L. (1987). Effectiveness of psychotherapy with children and adolescents: A meta-analysis for clinicians. *Journal of Consulting and Clinical Psychology, 55*, 542–549.

Whipple, G. M. (1910). *Manual of mental and physical tests.* Baltimore: Warwick & York.

White, J. L., & Kratochwill, T. R. (2005). Practice guidelines in school psychology: Issues and directions for evidence-based interventions in practice and training. *Journal of School Psychology, 43*(2), 99–115.

Widgor, A. K. & Garner, W. R. (Eds.). (1982). *Ability testing: Uses, consequences, and controversies.* Washington, DC: National Academy Press.

Wiseman, S. (Ed.). (1967). *Intelligence and ability.* Baltimore: Penguin Books.

Wissler, C. (1901). The correlation of mental and physical tests. *Psychological Review Monograph Supplement, 3.*

Witmer, L. (1996). Clinical psychology. *American Psychologist, 51*, 248–251. (Original work published 1907).

Wolf, T. H. (1973). *Alfred Binet.* Chicago: University of Chicago Press.

Wolpe, J. (1958). *Psychotherapy by reciprocal inhibition.* Palo Alto, CA: Stanford University Press.

Wortis, J. (1960). Mental retardation in the Soviet Union. *Children, 7*, 219–222.

Ysseldyke, J. E., & Mirkin, P. K. (1982). The use of assessment information to plan instructional interventions: A review of the research. In C. R. Reynolds, & T. B. Gutkin (Eds.), *The handbook of school psychology* (pp. 395–409). New York: Wiley.

Ysseldyke, J. E., & Salvia, J. A. (1974). Diagnostic-prescriptive teaching: Two models. *Exceptional Children, 21*, 181–186.

Zimmerman, B. J. (1977). Modeling. In H. L. Hom, Jr. & P. A. Robinson (Eds.), *Psychological processes in early education* (pp. 37–70). New York: Academic Press.

CHAPTER 2

Clinical Training

Debora J. Bell and Aaron M. Luebbe

Clinical child and pediatric psychology might be considered adolescents in the field of professional psychology (Prinstein & Roberts, 2006). They have matured to the point of cohesive self-definitions that are accepted by the professional community and that guide training within the specialties. But these developments are relatively recent. Although interest in psychological treatment of youth dates back to the end of the nineteenth century, the need for specific training in child-related service provision was not vocalized until more than 50 years later, and formal initiatives to develop training standards and implement them consistently lagged even further behind. Fortunately, for both clinical child and pediatric psychology, adolescence has come with emergence of clear and complex identities that are grounded in the broad foundations of clinical psychology, integrated with related fields of human development and health psychology, and sensitive to the importance of context and diversity in addressing the needs of youth and their families. Adolescence has also come with increased autonomy and respect from the professional community, thanks to the passionate efforts of leaders in these areas. Thus, clinical child and pediatric psychology have become legitimate specialties within clinical psychology.

The current chapter focuses on issues involved in preparing aspiring psychologists for careers in clinical child psychology and pediatric psychology. We begin by highlighting some important foundational issues in general clinical psychology. We then discuss the emergence and definitions of clinical child and pediatric psychology and examine their relationship to other fields in psychology and associated disciplines. Next, we discuss training models and important components of clinical child and pediatric training at the graduate, internship, and postdoctoral levels. Finally, we address some of the current challenges in clinical psychology training, such as balancing broad and general training with more focused depth, defining and assessing professional competence, and identifying and addressing workforce issues.

GENERAL CLINICAL PSYCHOLOGY FOUNDATIONS

The birth of clinical psychology as a profession was really the birth of clinical *child* psychology, when, in 1896, Witmer established the first psychological clinic to treat youth with behavior and learning problems (Hothersall, 2004). Thus began an era in which clinical psychology began to define itself, through journals devoted to clinically relevant research and practice (e.g., *Psychological Clinic; Journal of Consulting Psychology*, now published as the *Journal of Consulting and Clinical Psychology*), establishment of psychological testing and treatment clinics (e.g., the Juvenile Psychopathic Institute in Chicago and Judge Baker Foundation in Boston), a focus on training (e.g., increased availability of textbooks, university courses, and internships; development of training standards), and establishment of professional organizations such as the American Psychological Association (APA) Section on Clinical Psychology (Edelstein & Brasted, 1991; Hothersall, 2004).

Although some of the earliest work in clinical psychology focused on youth, various social forces, notably the need to evaluate large numbers of military personnel during World Wars I and II, moved substantial focus to adults. Nonetheless, as a profession, clinical psychology did not differentiate between child- and adult-focused professionals. Indeed, the 1949 Boulder Conference on graduate training in clinical psychology, on which many of our standards of graduate education are still based, emphasized the need to avoid specialization and to focus on broad training across many age levels (Raimy, 1950).

Over the last 110-plus years, the profession of clinical psychology has grown, matured, and become increasingly complex (Prinstein & Roberts, 2006). Clinical psychologists engage in activities ranging from basic and applied research to assessment and diagnosis, prevention and intervention, consultation, teaching and training, and public policy development, in settings as diverse as universities and research institutions, medical settings, schools, businesses, and government. They address the behavioral and emotional disorders, personality disorders, physical and mental disabilities, medical issues, and environmental stresses affecting individuals from infancy to late adulthood. Thus, it is not surprising that many leaders in the field (e.g., Roberts, 2006; Tuma, 1983) have questioned the wisdom, and even the ability, of continuing to pursue the type of generalist training espoused at the Boulder Conference. In essence, it is no longer feasible (if it ever was) for clinical psychologists to master the universe of relevant literature and skills required for professional competence as generalists. This has created an interesting dilemma for the profession. On the one hand, current standards for training, as operationalized by the field's accrediting body (APA Committee on Accreditation; CoA), still call for broad and general training in clinical psychology. On the other hand, providing such generalist training by itself is increasingly likely to produce graduates who are ill prepared to make positive contributions to the profession.

So how can clinical training address the challenge of providing broad foundational education in clinical psychology without drowning students in an ever-expanding sea of knowledge? There are many possible answers to this question, and given the complexity of the issues, multiple solutions almost certainly need to be implemented. But one first step in addressing the question is to acknowledge that general training in clinical psychology does not have the same meaning that it did in 1949 and to create training environments that retain the core aspects of clinical psychology while allowing focused experience in subfields or specialty areas. Interestingly, several leaders in the field (e.g., Roberts, 2006; Roberts & Sobel, 1999; Tuma, 1983) argue that is exactly what has happened in most clinical programs, albeit somewhat covertly. Roberts and Sobel suggest that "current use of the term *clinical psychology* is today not as generally clinical as it might have been in earlier times. Today, clinical psychology typically represents only adult clinical psychology and only superficially represents a generalist clinical psychology" (p. 483). From this perspective, clinical (adult) psychology and clinical child psychology represent parallel paths to balancing the demands of breadth and focus. This *Handbook*, with separate volumes for clinical adult and clinical child psychology, overtly acknowledges the legitimacy of *broad and focused* training in adult- and child-focused clinical psychology and is an important step in advancing the field.

EMERGING CHILD CLINICAL AND PEDIATRIC IDENTITIES

During the 30 years following the Boulder Conference, several leaders in psychology education noted the existence of large numbers of unserved youth with behavioral and emotional problems or health-related issues, but a shortage of professionals with sufficient training to address the needs of these youth (Ross, 1959; Tuma, 1983; Wohlford, 1978; Wright, 1967). The fields of clinical child and pediatric psychology began to emerge, with professional organizations (e.g., APA Section on Clinical Child Psychology, now Division 53; APA Society of Pediatric Psychology, now Division 54), journals, and conferences. Graduate programs offering specialty training also started to emerge across the country, but there was little consistency in what comprised clinical child or pediatric training experiences (Roberts, Borden, Christiansen, & Lopez, 2005; Tuma, 1983). Indeed, when Tuma surveyed members of APA child, pediatric, and youth and family sections and divisions, respondents reported receiving a wide array of educational experiences to prepare them for working with youth and families, ranging from on-the-job or post-graduate training to elective coursework to more formal degree programs. Thus, leaders in clinical child and pediatric graduate training mounted several efforts to define these specialties, including training conferences, task forces, and journal sections devoted to training issues.

Hilton Head Conference

In 1985, the National Conference on Training Clinical Child Psychologists was held in Hilton Head, South Carolina. Although the need for a conference was first identified in 1977, it was almost 10 years before community need and professional training and funding priorities coalesced to allow the conference to proceed. By the time of the conference, researchers had established that the training community was falling far short of the need for well-trained clinical child psychologists, APA had recognized the need for child services and established a position in their central office to monitor child-related issues, and several child-related organizations were moving forward to establish training guidelines (Roberts, Erickson, & Tuma, 1985; Tuma, 1986). Thus, conference participants were motivated and well informed and were able to make significant progress toward addressing issues of clinical child specialty training. By the end of the 3-day conference, participants had drafted

21 recommendations, including 10 recommendations specific to graduate training, seven targeting internship, and four targeting postdoctoral training in clinical child psychology (see Table 2.1).

Interestingly, several of the graduate program recommendations focused on child-relevant training for *all* clinical psychology programs, not just those with child tracks or emphases. Specifically, the Hilton Head participants proposed that

Table 2.1   Hilton Head Recommendations: National Conference on Training Clinical Child Psychologists

Recommendations for All Clinical Training Programs
All clinical psychology programs should:
Require a course on the developmental bases of normal behavior, emphasizing a life span developmental approach.
Provide experiences with "normal" children and youth, as well as with other age groups, in diverse, "normal" settings to all graduate students.
Provide didactic and practicum training sufficient for minimal competencies in assessment, psychopathology, and intervention (e.g., treatment, consultation, prevention) with children, youth, and families.
Recommendations for Clinical Child Training Programs
Clinical child psychology programs should:
Provide didactic and practicum training sufficient for minimal competencies in assessment, psychopathology, and intervention (e.g., treatment, consultation, prevention) with adults.
Provide knowledge of and experience with children from different minority backgrounds.
Recommendations for Graduate Program Structure, Implementation, and Evaluation
APA's Committee on Accreditation should:
Ensure that accreditation site visitor teams reviewing programs that train clinical child psychologists include a member with expertise in clinical child psychology.
Clinical child psychology programs should:
Foster an appreciation of the broad and diverse contexts within which children develop and clinical child psychologists work (e.g., family, school, community).
Have at least one clinical child faculty member.
Use the Division 37 Task Force Guidelines for Training Psychologists to Work with Children, Youth and Families (Roberts, Erickson, & Tuma, 1985) as guiding principles for implementing training programs.
Endorse the Boulder scientist-practitioner model of training.
Recommendations for Internship-Level Training
Internship and graduate programs should communicate regarding:
Matching internship site characteristics with intern talents and interest and evaluating intern performance.
Development and ongoing evaluation of an individualized training plan for the intern's experience.
Child-oriented internships should:
Provide a minimum of two thirds of child-related activity training.
Within the unique constraints of the internship site, provide a broad base of experience with regard to diverse populations served (across age, gender, socioeconomic status, ethnic origin, presenting problems, theoretical orientation, and experiences).
Incorporate research into the internship by allowing time and providing role models.
Include broad-based and varied didactic and supervised training in assessment, intervention, case management, and consultation, at a minimum, including prevention if possible.
Experiences should emphasize ethical considerations and evaluation of interventions.
The Section on Clinical Child Psychology should:
Create a standing committee on internship training to expand on these recommendations.

Recommendations for Postdoctoral and Continuing Education
All clinical child psychologists should:
Participate in continuing education to stay abreast of burgeoning knowledge in assessment, consultation, and prevention relevant to clinical child psychology.
The Section on Clinical Child Psychology should:
Establish a task force to create and publish criteria for continuing education offerings relevant to clinical child psychology.
Establish a task force to conduct a survey of current postgraduate programming in clinical child psychology and establish guidelines for such programming, including specification of levels and types of supervision.
Attempt to gain representation on appropriate governance structures of APA (e.g., Education and Training Committee, subcommittees on continuing education).

From *Proceedings: Conference on Training Clinical Child Psychologists*, by J. M. Tuma (Ed.), 1985, Baton Rouge, LA: Section on Clinical Child Psychology. Adapted with permission.

all clinical programs require a course on normal life span development and provide experience with normal individuals across the life span (i.e., children, youth, adults). They also proposed that all clinical programs provide coursework and experiential training to ensure minimal competencies in psychopathology, assessment, and intervention with children, youth, and families. These recommendations speak to the importance that conference participants placed on general clinical psychology training, regardless of age-related specialization. However, with the exception of required coursework in developmental bases of behavior (a requirement for accreditation), these recommendations have not been fully embraced by many clinical programs.

Recommendations focusing on clinical child psychology graduate training emphasized similar breadth, encouraging minimal competencies in work with adults, as well as with children from diverse backgrounds and in multiple contexts. Because clinical child training was so unstandardized at that time, the Hilton Head Conference also addressed issues of program structure and evaluation. In particular, they specified that programs providing clinical child training should have at least one clinical child faculty member and that accreditation teams evaluating these programs should have at least one member with expertise in clinical child psychology. These recommendations seem fairly obvious today, but illustrate the challenge of many emerging training models: that they may be implemented or judged by people without suitable backgrounds or appreciation for the important aspects of such programs. Finally, conference participants endorsed the work of other conferences and task forces, supporting the Boulder model of scientist-practitioner training, as well as the recommendations of the Division 37 Task Force for Training Psychologists to Work with Children, Youth, and Families (Roberts et al., 1985). Although the Division 37 recommendations were endorsed as flexible guidelines for program development and clinical child programs have evolved in diverse ways, the scientist-practitioner identity remains a core aspect of clinical child psychologist training.

Recommendations regarding internship and postdoctoral training were much less developed than those for graduate training but continued to stress the importance of diverse training across ages, client demographics and presenting problems, contexts, and professional duties (e.g., assessment, intervention, consultation, research). The committee's suggestions also emphasized the role of both internship and postdoctoral fellowships as opportunities for continuing education in empirical, practical, and ethical aspects of clinical child work. Probably the most specific and unique recommendation to come out of this conference was that clinical child psychology internships should devote two thirds of the internship year to child-related experiences. Because few other specific recommendations for internship or postdoctoral training emerged from the conference, the Hilton Head conferees called for new task forces to explore clinical child internship and postdoctoral training more fully. These task forces, which would be charged with developing detailed recommendations for training experiences, emerged in the years following Hilton Head.

Post–Hilton Head: Addressing Internships and Postdoctoral Training

Between 1986 and 1988, the Section on Clinical Child Psychology commissioned two task forces to establish guidelines for clinical child psychology internships (Elbert, Abidin, Finch, Sigman, & Walker, 1988) and postdoctoral training (Ollendick, Drotar, Friedman, & Hodges, 1998). In general, these task forces reiterated the core training goals articulated at the Hilton Head Conference and subsequent internship training conferences (Belar et al., 1989). For example, they recommended that both internship and postdoctoral fellowships include opportunities to work with children, adolescents, and families across a wide range of ages (including adults), with a range of problems, from diverse backgrounds, and in diverse settings. As training experiences, both task forces also called for a range of educational activities, with internships including a combination of didactic seminars, clinical and research experiences, and supervision, and postdoctoral fellowships including approximately 50% clinical service delivery, 25% clinical research, and 25% supervision. Recommended professional activities included assessment, case conceptualization, intervention, prevention, interdisciplinary consultation, and research. The internship task force was fairly specific in the types of assessment experiences they recommended (e.g., intellectual, ability, and personality assessment, interviews, behavioral observation) and the importance of developing competencies in communicating assessment results and incorporating them into intervention planning. Both task forces emphasized that specific experiences could vary widely across training sites, and they noted the desirability of exposure to diverse treatment approaches, supervisors (including nonpsychologists), and professional experiences. They also noted the importance of addressing the increasingly complex ethical and legal issues that arise as trainees prepare for independent practice in a variety of contexts. For instance, the internship task force recommended that all interns gain awareness of the juvenile justice system, child legal rights and custody issues, and general issues in forensic psychology. In sum, these tasks forces paved the way for a sequence of training in clinical child psychology that was focused yet diverse and flexible.

Developing Pediatric Psychology Identity

At the same time that the profession was defining goals and training recommendations for clinical child psychology, psychologists who worked with children in medical settings were also defining the roles and preparation of pediatric psychologists. These early efforts did not take place in formal training conferences or task forces, but in surveys of the field and articles published largely within the pediatric psychology community. Perhaps the most common theme of training in pediatric psychology, aside from its obvious focus on integrated attention to psychological and medical health, was its variability. For example, in the late 1960s and early 1970s, Routh (1970, 1972) described pediatric psychology practicum experiences offered by some medical school departments of pediatrics. However, as Routh's surveys suggested, clinical psychology students were not necessarily the ones who took advantage of these opportunities; pediatric psychology practicum training was just as often sought by students in school, developmental, counseling, or other areas of psychology. By the 1980s, pediatric psychology training had become aligned with clinical psychology (La Greca, Stone, & Swales, 1989; Routh & La Greca, 1990). Variability in training experiences was still evident, though. La Greca and colleagues (1989; Routh & La Greca, 1990) surveyed university graduate programs that had produced at least four graduates identified as pediatric psychologists by virtue of their membership in the Society of Pediatric Psychology. Of 41 programs surveyed, over 66% provided pediatric psychology practica, but fewer than 25% offered a course on the topic. Interestingly, only 17% of programs provided both didactic and applied pediatric experience, and 27% provided neither! Routh and La Greca noted that it is conceivable that students might gain experience in pediatric psychology during graduate training through their research and then complete more formal training during internship or postdoctoral training. This is consistent with results of an earlier survey (La Greca, Stone, Drotar, & Maddux, 1988) suggesting that graduate training in clinical and developmental psychology provided the ideal foundation for later specialization in pediatric psychology. Nonetheless, pediatric psychology training at the graduate level has continued to evolve, despite the lack of formal training guidelines. It was not until the twenty-first century that such guidelines were published (Spirito et al., 2003); we discuss these guidelines in "Curriculum Domains."

CURRENT DEFINITIONS

Because the fields of clinical child and pediatric psychology are evolving, so are their definitions, varying depending on when they were written and by whom. Although definitions of clinical psychology, clinical child psychology, and pediatric psychology abound in articles and texts, perhaps the most widely accepted definitions are those adopted by the relevant divisions of the APA. These are also typically the definitions that divisions of other organizations forward to APA's Commission for the Recognition of Specialties and Proficiencies in Professional Psychology (CRSPPP) when they seek specialty status.

Clinical Child Psychology

The current definition of clinical child psychology supported by APA Division 53 Clinical Child Psychology and approved by CRSPPP (2005) states:

Clinical child psychology brings together the basic tenets of clinical psychology with a thorough background in child and family development. Clinical child psychologists conduct research and provide services aimed at understanding, preventing, and treating psychological, cognitive, emotional, developmental, behavior, and family problems of children across the age range from infancy through adolescence. Of particular importance to the Clinical Child Psychologist is an understanding of the basic psychological needs of children and how the family and other social contexts influence children's socioemotional adjustment, cognitive development, behavioral adaptation, and health status. There is an essential emphasis on a strong empirical research base recognizing the need for the documentation and further development of evidence-based assessments and treatments in clinical child and adolescent psychology.

Central to this definition are several themes. First, clinical child psychology's foundations are those of clinical psychology generally, including a focus on assessment, diagnosis, prediction, treatment, and prevention of psychopathology and adjustment problems, and an emphasis on scientifically based knowledge and application. Because the populations of interest range from infancy through adolescence, clinical child psychologists must have a thorough understanding of child and family development. Thus, the clinical child psychologist's view of pathology is based on a developmental psychopathology framework, understanding child maladjustment in the context of normal behavior and development (Rutter & Sroufe, 2000).

A second theme is the role of context in children's adjustment. Clinical child psychology explicitly emphasizes the notion that child adjustment and development do not occur in a vacuum, but in context. Understanding the relevant contexts is important for conceptualizing youths' emotional and behavioral problems, as well as for treating them effectively. To put it colloquially, contexts are usually part of the problem, and almost certainly part of the solution. Thus, for clinical child psychologists, treating children in context is both a luxury (that many clinical adult psychologists, who see individual clients during an office visit, do not have) and a necessity. As our brief definition implies, the family context has central importance in children's development and adjustment. This makes sense given that the family has typically been with the children since birth, observing and participating in their development over time and across multiple contexts. Thus, clinical child psychologists must have an understanding of family structures and systems, as well as of the personalities and issues of individuals who make up the family. How family members relate to one another regarding such issues as rules, boundaries, and values and how they share experiences and emotions influence the lessons that youth learn and carry into their relationships and roles throughout life (Minuchin, 1985). In addition, understanding family members' health and adjustment is helpful for contextualizing youth adjustment problems that may have a genetic basis (e.g., Moffitt, 2005).

Beyond the family, several other contexts are important. Schools, neighborhoods, peer groups, and religious and extracurricular organizations can have a large influence on social, emotional, cognitive, and behavioral adjustment, especially as children reach school age and adolescence and spend more time in school and peer settings (Lerner, 2006). Broader contextual factors, such as the child's culture of origin and racial/ethnic group, should also be considered (La Greca & Hughes, 1999;

Roberts, 1998). Ecological models, such as Bronfenbrenner's (Bronfenbrenner & Morris, 2006) model that considers the reciprocal interplay between a developing individual and the many environments in which he or she interacts as the determining factors in youth adjustment, are mainstays of clinical child approaches to understanding and intervening with children. Thus, for clinical child psychologists, it is routine to go beyond individual or family-focused assessment and treatment and to incorporate school, peer, and community settings in assessment, consultation, and intervention.

Finally, clinical child psychology endorses the view that psychological theory and practice are necessarily based on science, and further emphasizes that well-trained clinical child psychologists will be scientist-practitioners, integrating both science and application into their training and professional identity. The scientist-practitioner training model was endorsed at the Hilton Head Conference and continues to be considered a central aspect of clinical child psychology training (La Greca & Hughes, 1999; Tuma, 1985).

Pediatric Psychology

Pediatric psychology is defined as a subspecialty of clinical child psychology, building on clinical psychology and clinical child psychology foundations but integrating knowledge of child health issues (e.g., disease process, health promotion) and application in medical settings (Roberts, 2003; Spirito et al., 2003). Defining this field, the Society of Pediatric Psychology (APA Division 54) states:

> Society of Pediatric Psychology is dedicated to research and practice addressing the relationship between children's physical, cognitive, social, and emotional functioning and their physical well-being, including maintenance of health, promotion of positive health behaviors, and treatment of chronic or serious medical conditions. In recognition of the close interplay between children's psychological and physical health, SPP has developed liaisons with several pediatric societies and many pediatric psychologists have become experts in the behavioral and developmental aspects of acute and chronic diseases. (American Psychological Association, 2006c)

Integrating across these definitions, a picture emerges of pediatric psychology as *clinical child psychology plus*. The Society of Pediatric Psychology is rooted in clinical child psychology as opposed to health psychology, and as Spirito and colleagues (2003) note, pediatric psychology is frequently integrated with or synonymous with clinical child psychology, particularly at the graduate training stage. Pediatric psychologists share clinical child psychology's scientist-practitioner approach to understanding, assessing, and treating youth adjustment and a training focus that integrates clinical psychology foundations with a developmentally and contextually sensitive approach to assessment and treatment. Pediatric psychologists should be competent to provide general clinical child services to youth and families (Roberts & Steele, 2003; Spirito et al., 2003).

To these clinical child foundations, pediatric psychologists add didactic training and experience in issues specific to child health. Pediatric psychologists must have an understanding of disease process, including how illnesses and their treatments affect psychological and behavioral functioning, as well as of disease prevention and health promotion (Spirito et al., 2003). Research and applied activities of pediatric psychologists focus, for example, on how a healthy lifestyle can prevent conditions such as obesity and diabetes, or how chronic illness affects youths' self-concept and peer relations (Roberts, 2003). Pediatric psychologists also must master skills required for effective consultation and liaison with physicians and other professionals who address child health, as they are almost always part of an interdisciplinary team. Because of the already large demands of graduate training in clinical psychology, pediatric psychology experience often occurs primarily at the internship and postdoctoral levels (Drotar, Palermo, & Ievers-Landis, 2003; Spirito et al., 2003). Indeed, a recent Division 53 survey of clinical child and pediatric graduate programs indicated that only 3 of 45 programs that provide child-relevant training have a formal pediatric psychology track (Division of Clinical Child and Adolescent Psychology, 2006).

Relationship to Other Areas of Professional Psychology

General Clinical Psychology

As noted earlier, the scope of clinical psychology has evolved since its description at the Boulder Conference; as the knowledge base has expanded, the notion of a generalist, competent across all ages and problem areas, has become increasingly unrealistic. As Roberts (2006) suggests, few clinical training programs actually provide generalist training, but instead focus on adults. Clinical child and pediatric psychology also provide focused training on a subset of the life span. However, the core aspects of clinical psychology, including a focus on understanding, assessing, preventing, and treating maladjustment in the context of established scientific methods and broader foundations in psychology, are integral parts of training in clinical child psychology. In addition, although clinical child and pediatric training focus on children and families, they also include educational background in adult development and psychopathology and the ability to work with parents and other adults who are part of the child's life. And beyond a focus on individual clients, clinical child and pediatric psychology emphasize systems and contexts and conducting research and intervention in interdisciplinary teams.

Although clinical child and pediatric psychology are more focused than generalist clinical psychology, they could be considered broader than many clinical (adult) programs (Roberts, 2006). In their discussion of clinical training in the twenty-first century, Snyder and Elliott (2005) maintain that most clinical (adult) psychology has been characterized by a focus on individuals' weaknesses, or psychopathology. They call for clinical psychology to broaden its horizons to encompass a focus on people's strengths and to consider not just person factors, but also environmental context. Interestingly, as several authors note in their responses to Snyder and Elliott's thought-provoking article, this seems to be exactly what clinical child and pediatric psychology have been doing for years (Kendall, 2005; Roberts, 2005). Thus, clinical child and pediatric psychology training models may provide a guide for clinical adult programs that seek to broaden their perspectives to encompass client strengths and contexts.

School Psychology

School psychology shares many similarities with clinical child and pediatric psychology, including a focus on assessment, intervention, prevention, and health promotion with youth and families, a scientist-practitioner approach, and sensitivity to contextual and diversity issues in addressing youth adjustment (Reynolds & Gutkin, 1999). School psychology, however, emphasizes educational and learning processes and environments. Relevant practice may extend to learners of all ages, including adults, and often takes place in an educational setting. Assessment is frequently focused on evaluation of students' intellectual, achievement, psychological, and behavioral functioning, particularly with regard to how these areas influence learning effectiveness. Common activities of school psychologists also include consultation with parents and educators, program development and evaluation of educational programs, and advocacy for education-relevant legislation. Thus, the day-to-day activities of applied clinical child, pediatric, and school psychologists may look quite similar: involving work with children and adolescents in their relevant contexts, on issues that affect their health and adjustment, using approaches that are supported by empirical literature.

Similarities are also evident in research and academic training contexts. Like research conducted by clinical child and pediatric psychologists, school psychologists' research may examine issues such as child emotional, behavioral, and developmental disorders and health; child adjustment and health promotion; and contextual factors such as families, peer groups, schools, culture, ethnicity, and economic disadvantage. Again, the major difference is one of relative emphasis, with school psychologists more likely to research areas relevant to learning or adjustment within the learning environment. Finally, as one of the three types of accredited programs in professional psychology (along with clinical and counseling psychology), school psychology graduate program curricula include foundational training in diverse bodies of knowledge within psychology (e.g., social, cognitive, and biological bases of behavior), research methods, normal and abnormal development, and professional ethics, as well as area-specific knowledge in assessment, intervention, and prevention (APA, 2005). Like clinical child and pediatric psychologists, school psychologists complete a predoctoral internship and supervised postdoctoral experience for licensure.

TRAINING ISSUES

Training in clinical child and pediatric psychology addresses multiple purposes and, as such, serves many masters. Academically, clinical child and pediatric psychology are usually (although not always) part of psychology departments, along with other subdisciplines such as social, cognitive, developmental, experimental, and quantitative psychology. Housed within liberal arts and sciences colleges or divisions, department priorities typically involve the traditional combination of research, graduate and undergraduate teaching, and service to the campus and academic community. Professional psychology programs are somewhat unique within departments in their additional priority of training graduate students for careers in professional health service. Thus, accreditation, applied practicum and internship training, and preparation for licensure must be considered. Because accreditation provides standards for evaluating professional training programs, we discuss accreditation issues first, and then examine the context, goals, and curricula of clinical child and pediatric training programs.

Accreditation Issues

As with all professional psychology training, clinical child and pediatric psychology programs participate in the accreditation process. Accreditation is a process of voluntary self-regulation by the field, with a primary goal of protecting students and the public by ensuring that programs meet at least minimal standards of content and performance (APA, 2005). Clinical programs have been accredited since the mid-twentieth century, when the need for federally funded psychology training prompted development of a system and criteria for accreditation (Sheridan, Matarazzo, & Nelson, 1995). Since then, accreditation guidelines and procedures have undergone several revisions that reflect the evolving nature of professional psychology, and even as this chapter is being written the process is under review and modification (Schilling & Packard, 2005). General accreditation guidelines are beyond the scope of this chapter (interested readers can refer to the CoA's *Guidelines and Principles for Accreditation of Programs in Professional Psychology*, APA, 2005, as well as recent revisions to the *Policy Statements and Implementing Regulations*, APA, 2006a). Here, we focus on select issues specific to clinical child and pediatric psychology training.

As currently defined, the purpose of accreditation is to evaluate the extent to which a training program has achieved the goals and objectives of its stated training model, defined within the more broadly accepted principles of professional psychology (APA, 2005). In other words, programs must meet field-defined criteria, but beyond that are encouraged (or at least allowed) to articulate and pursue innovative training models and practices. As Roberts et al. (1998) noted, this flexibility paved the way for clinical child psychology programs to begin to define themselves more specifically than as just clinical programs and to more fully embrace the guidelines for child-focused training articulated at the Hilton Head and later conferences. As with many guidelines, standards, and rules, these accreditation guidelines are aspirational, and many would argue that they have been applied inconsistently or incompletely. This has been evident in the challenges that some clinical child programs have faced when seeking accreditation or reaccreditation. For example, Roberts (2006) notes that his clinical child training program includes formal training in adult psychopathology in order to satisfy the CoA, although he questions whether adult-focused programs receive the same level of scrutiny regarding their coverage of child psychopathology. Similar challenges likely affect other clinical child and pediatric programs, as well as the accreditation teams faced with the task of evaluating specific and varied applications of clinical psychology training goals.

Given the importance of accreditation for training programs and the time and expense involved in the process, it is easy for *Accreditation* (with a capital A) to become reified in a way that leads both training programs and accreditation committee members to forget that the process is essentially intended to serve the field rather than to define it. Whereas accreditation should promote high standards within the field and facilitate innovation and development, it is the field itself that must self-define, innovate, and evolve. Thus, continued articulation of how the fields of clinical child and pediatric psychology define optimal graduate training remains crucial for influencing future development and application of accreditation guidelines.

Academic Context

As noted, most clinical programs are housed within departments of psychology. Within the department, however, the structure of clinical child and pediatric psychology training can range from a stand-alone academic training program to a track or emphasis within a more general clinical program, to simply providing informal opportunities to gain child-specific experience. Several surveys conducted over the past 30 years have documented the diverse structures and academic settings that characterize clinical child psychology training programs (Mannarino & Fischer, 1982; Roberts, 1992; Zeman, Nangle, & Sim, 1999), and this diversity remains true today. Currently, Divisions 53 and 54 provide an online directory of programs that report providing clinical child or pediatric psychology training (Division of Clinical Child and Adolescent Psychology, 2006). Of the 45 programs listed as having child or pediatric training, only three (6.7%) report having separate clinical child training programs. Over half of the programs (24; 53%) provide formal child or pediatric tracks or specialties, but 40% (18) report providing no formal track.

Decisions about the context in which to provide clinical child and pediatric training are likely complex, encompassing philosophical, historical, and practical considerations, and an understanding of how these issues influenced training program development at each institution is obviously beyond the scope of this chapter. However, the Division 53 data do provide some suggestions of how context relates to program issues such as size of faculty and student body, course offerings, and practicum opportunities. In examining these data, it is important to remember that they represent self-reported program characteristics, and respondents may have used different definitions and counting conventions. Also, we examine descriptive data without evaluating the statistical significance of patterns. With these caveats in mind, we note several interesting findings.

Table 2.2 presents data on characteristics of programs listed in the Division 53 directory as providing clinical child and pediatric psychology training in separate programs, formal tracks, or informal opportunities. Although the separate programs tended to have a somewhat smaller overall clinical faculty than programs with or without formal tracks (approximately five versus nine clinical faculty), their child-focused faculty averaged about one more faculty member than other programs (approximately five versus four clinical child or pediatric faculty). For programs with tracks or informal child psychology training opportunities, child-focused faculty represented approximately 40% of total faculty. Similarly, child-focused students in programs with child or pediatric tracks represented just over 40% of their overall

Table 2.2   Program Characteristics for Clinical Child or Adolescent and Pediatric Psychology Training Programs (2005)

Characteristics	Type of Clinical Training Provided			
	No Formal Track or Emphasis	C or P Emphasis	Formal C or P Track	Distinct C or P Program
N	15	7	18	3
Faculty	*M (SD)*	*M (SD)*	*M (SD)*	*M (SD)*
All clinical faculty	8.93 (3.06)	8.71 (2.29)	9.83 (2.28)	5.00 (2.65)
Child clinical faculty	2.80 (1.65)	3.71 (1.55)	3.81 (1.10)	5.00 (2.65)
Pediatric faculty	0.57 (0.78)	0.57 (0.93)	0.75 (0.67)	0.67 (1.15)
Students				
All clinical students	32.33 (10.11)	43.14 (10.16)	38.18 (12.90)	31.33 (5.51)
Clinical child students	7.33 (5.08)	12.86 (5.40)	15.50 (8.17)	31.33 (5.51)
Pediatric students	1.47 (2.03)	0.57 (0.98)	2.24 (3.09)	6.00 (10.39)
Course and Opportunities				
Child clinical courses	2.60 (1.24)	3.00 (1.29)	4.28 (1.41)	9.67 (4.73)
Pediatric courses	0.27 (0.46)	0.14 (0.38)	0.56 (0.78)	1.33 (2.31)
Child practica	2.43 (1.57)	7.86 (7.86)	5.78 (5.40)	7.00 (3.61)
Pediatric practica	0.73 (1.03)	2.29 (2.14)	1.88 (2.64)	1.00 (1.73)

Note: C = Child; P = Pediatric.

student body. However, programs without formal tracks may attract fewer child-focused students, as less than 30% of their student body comprised child or pediatric psychology students. Programs overall averaged 30 to 40 clinical graduate students, but for all but the separate clinical child or pediatric programs, child-focused students were in the minority.

Course requirements and practicum opportunities varied widely, both across and within program type. Separate clinical child or pediatric programs required substantially more child-focused courses than their counterparts with tracks or informal child psychology opportunities. On average, separate programs required 11 child clinical or pediatric courses, likely because they are designing courses for their child-focused students rather than teaching some courses for students from multiple (i.e., child and adult) tracks. In contrast, child track programs required an average of approximately four child clinical or pediatric courses, and informal opportunity programs required only three such courses. There are probably benefits and costs to both approaches. For example, providing general clinical courses to adult and child track students should expose all students to broad education about issues that arise across the life span and across diverse clinical subspecialties. Unfortunately, many general courses focus primarily on adults, with perhaps 1 to 2 weeks of child-relevant material, shortchanging both child- and adult-focused students. Child-focused courses offer maximum opportunity for students to learn about the content, process, and current issues in clinical child and pediatric psychology from faculty who are expert in these areas. However, explicit attention to helping students gain exposure to adult development and psychopathology is also important. Program type seems to have important implications for practicum opportunities available to graduate students. Separate child or pediatric programs and programs with formal tracks reported having an average of eight practicum placements that focused on child or pediatric training. In contrast, programs without a formal track offered only about three child-focused practica.

Finally, across program type, clinical child training seems more extensive than pediatric psychology training. Of 24 programs that reported explicitly on the emphasis areas offered by their program or track (versus, for example, responding yes to the question about a child or pediatric track), only three reported having a pediatric track, and two of these programs also had a clinical child track. Overall, programs reported more clinical child than pediatric faculty, graduate students, courses, and practicum placements. Indeed, on average, pediatric psychology opportunities accounted for no more than 10% to 20% of child-related training opportunities. This is consistent with Spirito et al.'s (2003) statement that specialized training in pediatric psychology often does not occur until the internship or postdoctoral stage of training.

Training Goals

In preparing graduates for careers in the science and practice of clinical child and pediatric psychology, the field has emphasized several goals and competencies. For example, in the Division on Child, Family, and Youth Services (APA Division 37) training guidelines that were the basis of some of the work at the Hilton Head Conference, Roberts and colleagues (1985, p. 72) outlined four primary goals of training:

1. Training should provide at least minimal entry level skills for providing professional psychological services . . . on behalf of children, adolescents, and their mentors (e.g., parents and teachers) in a range of settings (e.g., home, school, institutions, and medical clinics). . . .

2. Training should provide the scientific basis for professional psychological applications.

3. Training should include specialized research contributing to an understanding of children, families, and psychological development, as well as in the evaluation of therapeutic interventions.

4. Child-, youth-, and family-related issues should be integrated into psychology-based courses at all levels, regardless of specialty designation.

More recently, La Greca and Hughes (1999, p. 441, Table 5) identified five competencies important for clinical child psychologists: (1) multicultural competencies; (2) delivery and evaluation of comprehensive and coordinated systems of care; (3) collaborative and interprofessional skills; (4) empirically supported assessment and treatments for promoting behavioral change in children, families, and other systems; and (5) entrepreneurial and supervisory skills. La Greca and Hughes argue that these competencies, reflecting the thinking of many educators in child-focused professional psychology, are increasingly important for effective clinical child practice in our society.

Separated by almost 15 years of developments in clinical child and pediatric psychology, these two sets of goals represent both foundational goals that are central to the definitions of clinical child and pediatric psychology as well as more progressive goals that reflect the evolution of professional psychology. In particular, the theme of empirically based assessment and intervention targeting youth in their environmental and cultural contexts has echoed throughout even the earliest definitions of the field. Likewise, the importance of an interdisciplinary perspective is one of the hallmarks of clinical child and pediatric psychology and a central goal for training and professional competence. Development of a scientist-practitioner identity is also fundamental and is reflected in the clinical child psychologist's research training as well as professional competence in evaluation of service delivery. A clinical scientist identity, based on the newer clinical science training model that emphasizes preparing students for careers that include generation, application, and dissemination of clinical science research (Academy of Psychological Clinical Science, 2007; McFall, 1991), would also be consistent with this goal.

Roberts et al.'s (1985) goal of infusing child-related issues into all clinical psychology curricula, regardless of specialty designation, underscores the importance of having a broad developmental base in all clinical psychology training. Assuming that clinical child and pediatric psychology training would of course attend to child issues, this goal seems more relevant to general or adult-focused clinical training programs. The importance of this goal for clinical child and pediatric training seems to lie primarily in its call for all clinical psychology training to view child issues as a legitimate part of broad and general training.

Some of La Greca and Hughes's (1999) competencies reflect newer or elaborated goals that have emerged in concert with changing issues and needs in society. Multicultural competence, although implicit in early definitions and goals emphasizing contextual views of child adjustment, is an explicit part of current-day competence for child psychologists. Increased attention to multicultural issues is especially important given the growing diversity of the U.S. population as well as priorities noted by APA, the CoA, and the National Institutes of Health. Finally, entrepreneurial and supervisory skills extend beyond the traditional purview of clinical psychology, but are important for preparing clinical child and pediatric psychologists for both applied and academic careers. In applied settings, these skills are important for helping clinical child psychologists function effectively as part of treatment teams that may include junior or in-training members and for maintaining fiscally viable practices. In academic settings, having faculty who have received formal training in supervision is clearly an essential component of providing high-quality practica. Entrepreneurial skills are becoming increasingly important for academics. As funding for higher education becomes tighter, universities are encouraging their faculty and departments to develop diverse sources of funding for their research and training. On the national level, psychologists are becoming increasingly active participants in legislative activity relevant to health care and education (e.g., through the APA Practice and Education Directorates, the Society for Research in Child Development's policy fellowships). To effectively influence the business and legislative sectors, convincing nonpsychologists of the importance of supporting our efforts to address child health, psychologists must speak the language of these professionals.

TRAINING CONTENT: CURRICULUM DOMAINS

As with all professional psychology programs, clinical child and pediatric psychology curricula are shaped in part by accreditation requirements for clinical programs. However, as noted earlier, accreditation requirements are designed to allow individual training programs to define their goals and methods for attaining them. So how can clinical child and pediatric programs best integrate their training goals and accreditation requirements into a curriculum that prepares competent psychologists? As several investigators have noted, this is apparently not an easy task to do well; even after definitions and goals of clinical child and pediatric psychology were developed, training programs differed widely in their curricula and did not always meet minimal training goals for these specialty areas (Roberts et al., 1998; Zeman et al., 1999).

Recent advances in professional psychology have paved the way for both greater specificity of clinical child and pediatric curricula and increased flexibility in implementation. First, starting in 1996, changes to accreditation guidelines and procedures facilitated innovation in how professional psychology programs can articulate, meet, and evaluate their training goals (Roberts et al., 1998). Second, the field has begun moving from activity-based to competency-based models of training. This is reflected in accreditation guidelines and in recent writings and conferences on professional competencies (Kaslow et al., 2004; Sumerall, Lopez, & Oehlert, 2000).

Both clinical child and pediatric specialties have articulated curriculum recommendations that fit with these developments. In 1998, Roberts and colleagues outlined a model for training clinical child psychologists based on work begun by the National Institute of Mental Health work group on improving training for child and youth service providers (Wohlford, Myers, & Callan, 1993). Roberts et al.'s training model included 11 domains of training considered important for clinical child psychologists. Several years after the clinical child training model was published, the Society of Pediatric Psychology charged a task force with developing similar guidelines for training pediatric psychologists (Spirito et al., 2003). The resulting guidelines, adapted from the clinical child model, include 12 domains of training, with 11 overlapping with the clinical child model and the final domain specific to pediatric psychology.

Although coursework is a common way to meet curricular requirements, competence in many of the domains of training requires practical experience. The clinical child and pediatric training models acknowledge this, describing student training as a three-level sequence: *exposure* to the content and processes of clinical psychology through didactic training and observation, *experience* that involves mentored practice of the relevant skill, and *expertise* that is obtained through extensive exposure and experience and enables independent practice. By the end of graduate training, students should have had at least some exposure to and experience with each domain, although they may not have expertise in any. Internship is an opportunity to gain more experience and develop expertise in some areas, and by the time students have completed postdoctoral training and are ready for licensure, they should have established sufficient expertise to support independent practice with a variety of youth and family issues. Next we outline the 12 recommended domains of clinical child and pediatric psychology training, from graduate through postdoctoral training, and offer comments about potential ways of providing didactic, applied, and research training in these domains.

Life Span Developmental Psychology

From a developmental psychopathology perspective, complete understanding of youths' adjustment problems requires an understanding of individual and contextual factors in normal development (van Eys & Dodge, 1999). At a minimum, coursework should expose students to current theory and research on life span development across social, emotional, cognitive, behavioral, and physical domains, as well as to the role of individual (e.g., sex, race) and contextual (e.g., family, peer, culture) factors in development. Practical experiences in assessment and intervention should involve youth from a variety of developmental levels and contexts, with particular emphasis on issues such as how developmental factors impact youth psychopathology and response to treatment. For pediatric psychology students, didactic and practical experiences should focus on issues relevant to child and adolescent health, such as the impact of disease process on cognitive development or the role of adolescent autonomy seeking on adherence to medical regimens. Student research should also incorporate developmental issues, addressing age, gender, and context in the specific research questions and methods, or at least conceptualizing the research from a developmentally informed perspective.

Beyond the minimum, several training programs integrate clinical child and developmental training more fully. In their survey of child-focused clinical programs, Zeman et al. (1999) found that programs characterizing themselves as clinical-developmental required more developmental courses than other programs, averaging just over five required developmental courses versus none or one course required by clinical child programs or clinical programs with a child emphasis. These programs also encourage student research mentored by developmental faculty, attendance at developmental conferences (e.g., Society for Research in Child Development, Society for Research on Adolescence), and publication in developmental as well as clinical journals. An example of a clinical child developmental program is the joint effort of the clinical and developmental programs at the University of Missouri–Columbia. Students admitted to the clinical child developmental program essentially complete requirements of both clinical and developmental training areas. Practically, this means that in addition to courses required for the clinical child program (including courses in normal development, developmental psychopathology, child assessment, child interventions, and family systems and interventions), joint program students take two additional courses in cognitive, social, and emotional development; explicitly incorporate developmental content into thesis and dissertation research and comprehensive examination; and participate in both clinical and developmental faculty labs.

Life Span Developmental Psychopathology

With foundational knowledge of normal development, students can conceptualize deviations from typical or adaptive functioning. During graduate training, courses and seminars should expose students to abnormal behavior across the life span, as well as current research on trajectories of risk and resilience. Supervised practica with various forms of psychopathology in children, adolescents, and adults allow students to gain experience conceptualizing and diagnosing psychopathology. Again, a variety of settings, including youth in clinic, family, community, school, and medical settings, give graduate students experience in incorporating context into their understanding of youth psychopathology.

Child, Adolescent, and Family Assessment

Becoming a competent clinical child or pediatric psychologist requires a thorough understanding of assessment issues, including how to evaluate the empirical foundations and utility of a variety of assessment methods, how and when to use them, and how to interpret their results for both applied and research purposes. Relevant assessments for youth go beyond tests or measures that youth complete (e.g., intelligence tests) and include evaluations of youth functioning by others (e.g., caregiver reports of adaptive functioning, school reports of academic achievement), as well as evaluations of the systems in which youth function (e.g., parent-child and parent marital relations). Assessment also goes beyond standardized tests and includes clinical conceptualizations, functional analysis, and a general hypothesis-testing framework. Both clinical work and research benefit from a scientific approach to generating questions and using appropriate assessment to address them.

Students should develop an understanding of how developmental factors such as age, sex, ethnic background, and cultural conventions can influence assessment validity, and how to conduct multimethod assessments that can maximize the strengths and contributions of the multiple methods and reporters. Finally, students should obtain experience in interpreting and disseminating assessment results and in assessment reports for clinical purposes as well as in research reports. Roberts et al. (1998) suggest a minimum of two semesters of coursework and associated practica devoted to exposing students to all relevant assessment issues and methods and allowing them to gain experience with several assessments and develop expertise with at least a few. Overall, understanding the conceptual and psychometric aspects of assessment seems most critical to competence as a clinical psychologist. If students leave graduate training with expertise in how to formulate assessment questions, design developmentally and contextually sensitive assessment plans, and integrate results from multimethod assessment, as well as exposure to the mechanics of assessment, they should be able to quickly master specific assessment tools as needed.

Intervention Strategies

Training in interventions should reflect the core values of clinical child and pediatric psychology: empirically and contextually based treatment that is developmentally and multiculturally sensitive and interdisciplinary. This is a tall order, calling for treatment that is both standardized and individualized. To be effective at delivering the standardized aspects of treatment, clinicians in training must be familiar with empirically supported treatment techniques and protocols, including how, when, and with whom to use them. For example, during graduate training, students should be exposed to many of the treatments considered well-established or probably efficacious, as defined by APA Division 12 (Division of Clinical Psychology) and Division 53 (Society of Clinical Child and Adolescent Psychology) task forces (Chambless et al., 1996, 1998; Lonigan & Elbert, 1998), including parent training and multisystemic therapy for oppositional and conduct disorders, behavioral parent training and problem-solving skills training for Attention-Deficit/Hyperactivity Disorder, interpersonal and cognitive therapy for depression, cognitive-behavioral therapy and family anxiety management for generalized and separation anxiety disorders, exposure and relaxation therapies for anxiety disorders, and behavior therapy for childhood obesity. Although exposure to some of these treatments may be limited to didactic coverage in courses or readings, experience with at least some of the treatment protocols should occur during graduate school, with additional opportunities to develop experience and expertise coming during internship and postdoctoral training.

Clearly, the list of evidence-based treatments is incomplete, and even when such treatments exist, they frequently do not have demonstrated equal applicability across multiple ages, socioeconomic groups, cultural groups, or family constellations. Thus, it is also essential for students to gain experience in how to handle situations in which there is no prescribed, empirically supported treatment. Two general approaches are valuable here. First, familiarity with the developmental and clinical literatures on the relevant treatment moderators can help guide treatment decisions. For example, clinicians might use the literature on differences in effective parenting styles across socioeconomic or racial/ethnic groups (McLoyd, 1998) to tailor family treatment for a low-income ethnic minority family. Second, using their scientist-practitioner framework, students should become expert at evaluating their treatments as they deliver them. This way, even treatments that do not have established empirical support can be appraised empirically.

Research Methods and Systems Evaluations

As noted, clinical application from a scientist-practitioner perspective includes using the empirical literature to guide treatment decisions and using empirical evaluation methods in the treatment context to assess treatment process and outcome. More broadly, advancing the literature that informs treatment, prevention, and health promotion requires sound research. Thus, students in clinical child and pediatric psychology should become proficient as both consumers and producers of applied scientific knowledge. Background in methods of conducting scientifically sound research and analyzing resulting data is an integral part of all professional psychology training. However, clinical child and pediatric training programs should ensure that methods that are especially relevant to understanding youth and families, such as longitudinal and prospective designs and hierarchical analyses that can evaluate child data in the context of schools or families, are included in child-relevant training. For pediatric psychologists, familiarity with research issues and methodologies common to medical settings is also important, including issues of health care utilization, clinical trials, and epidemiological and multisite methods. In addition, because youth work so often involves systems consultation and program development, expertise in systems and program evaluation is important for competent and marketable clinical child and pediatric psychologists. Consistent with a scientist-practitioner approach, practicum training should include opportunities to empirically evaluate treatment progress, using single-case design and other relevant methodologies. Finally, to be truly effective, research must be disseminated. Thus students should develop skills in scholarly publication and presentation and grant writing.

Although internship is acknowledged as primarily a clinical training year, continued opportunity to develop expertise in clinical research is an important part of a scientist-practitioner identity. In their recommendations for internship, Elbert et al. (1998) proposed that, at a minimum, interns be encouraged to systematically review the literature as they conceptualize cases and plan treatment. In addition, many scientist-practitioner and clinical science internships provide protected time for interns to conduct research, either independently or as part of ongoing research at the internship site. Some programs (e.g., Case Western Reserve University, Medical University of South Carolina, University of Mississippi Medical Center, Western Psychiatric Institute and Clinic) provide seminars in grant writing and funding for research and conference attendance, and may even require journal article or grant submission as part of the internship experience. Rather than distracting interns from their clinical duties, these research activities enrich interns' integration of science and application. Similarly, although a primary goal of many postdoctoral training fellowships is preparation for licensure, clinical research and development of grant writing skills can be effectively integrated into the training experience (Drotar, 1998; Ollendick et al., 1988). Often, the more research-oriented internship sites will also have postdoctoral positions in which trainees can continue the clinical and research work begun on internship.

Professional, Ethical, and Legal Issues

Working with children and adolescents comes with many unique professional, ethical, and legal issues. At the most basic level, minor youth are, in most cases, not legally in charge of their own lives. Thus, issues of who decides whether and how to pursue treatment, who receives the treatment (i.e., who is the client), and who provides the treatment must all be decided for the child. Parents are responsible for seeing that their children receive appropriate educational, medical, and psychological services, and graduate students must be aware of issues of parent informed consent, as well as how parent rights and responsibilities are influenced by divorce, abuse, and neglect. Graduate students must also know how to define the client in family treatment or school or medical consultations. In addition to identifying the client, child and pediatric work can be associated with challenges in identifying the treatment agent. In the interdisciplinary settings in which child and pediatric psychologists often work, psychologists must negotiate and define their roles on the treatment team, along with educators, health professionals, and other social service providers. In all of these tasks, the child's role as an active (albeit legally nonresponsible) participant must be appreciated. Training should address how to involve children and adolescents in assenting to, planning, conducting, and evaluating assessment and interventions, as well as how to balance legal issues with children's rights to privacy.

The types of challenges that children and adolescents face require sensitivity to specific legal and ethical issues. For example, parent divorce and custody issues, abuse and neglect, and delinquency all require familiarity with the legal system. Clinical child and pediatric psychologists should be aware of local, state, and federal laws that define abuse (e.g., the types of physical injuries or conditions that qualify) and neglect (e.g., the age at which children can be left unattended), reporting requirements, and the process by which such cases are handled in the county. Knowledge of how child truancy, other status offenses, and criminal behavior are handled is helpful in treatment of child and family treatment. Particularly by the internship and postdoctoral levels, experience with child forensic issues such as custody evaluation and expert testimony is warranted (Elbert et al., 1988). In pediatric psychology settings, graduate students should gain experience in dealing with issues such as life-threatening and terminal illness, developmental and neurological conditions, and painful medical procedures. In all of these instances, dealing with the affected youth is just one aspect of psychological care; clinicians must help youth address the challenge in the context of their ongoing development, and also help parents, siblings, and perhaps friends cope with the implications of the illness or condition.

Issues of Diversity

Given that considering youth in context is a hallmark of clinical child and pediatric psychology training, attention to the context of diversity is a natural extension of this training. During graduate training, students should gain exposure to and experience with multiple aspects of diversity, including definitions of what constitutes diversity, the influence of values and prejudice on societal and personal attitudes and behavior, and the role of diversity factors in psychological adjustment and treatment. For example, diversity should be defined broadly, to include gender and age, as well as racial/ethnic, cultural, socioeconomic, religious, sexual orientation, disability, and family constellation factors. Graduate coursework and practicum experience should expose students to information on youth with as many of these backgrounds or experiences as possible, with advanced practicum, internship, and postdoctoral training experiences selected to broaden these experiences. Issues that are important to address include the role of diversity factors in definitions of psychopathology, risk factors for certain psychological or medical conditions (e.g., conduct disorders, depression, heart disease), health care utilization and acceptability, and culturally sensitive assessment and treatment.

Class and supervision time should also be used to allow students to explore their own values and attitudes to become more effective treatment providers for diverse youth and families. Students should gain an appreciation for the balance between considering diversity factors and understanding the individual child or family. Although research may provide valuable information about diverse groups, this information may not generalize to individual cases. Additionally, a child's sex, disability status, and racial/ethnic group do not define him or her, but simply represent one aspect of the child's identity. Thus, students should remember to consider youth as individuals within the context of diversity. Finally, in addition to gaining and using information on diversity, students should use their research as an opportunity to add to the knowledge base on issues of diversity. Although psychology has made great strides in understanding male and female youth across ages and from diverse backgrounds, much remains to be done, and the scientist-practitioner and clinical science backgrounds of clinical child and pediatric psychology students places them in an ideal position to conduct clinically relevant and contextually sensitive research.

Role of Multiple Disciplines in Service Delivery Systems

As we've noted throughout this chapter, interdisciplinary work is another hallmark of clinical child and pediatric psychology. Much of working effectively within an interdisciplinary team is part of a professional issues skills set, involving mastery of how to fit into existing systems, how to divide and share tasks, and how to understand the language and approaches of multiple professions. As such, students must gain familiarity with other disciplines' approaches and contributions to child health promotion and experience in participating in interdisciplinary teams. This should include coursework in areas such as consultation, family and community psychology, and public health. Practicum experiences should allow students to observe and participate in a broad range of systems, including families, schools, social service agencies, intensive (e.g., inpatient or day) treatment programs, and medical settings. Internships are often an ideal place for trainees to gain a variety of interdisciplinary experiences, and by completion of postdoctoral training, clinical child psychologists should be able to work effectively with the full range of professionals involved in child health care.

Prevention, Family Support, and Health Promotion

A comprehensive approach to dealing with child and adolescent adjustment issues includes attending not just to diagnosed disorders, but also to factors that place youth at risk for disorder or maladjustment and factors that promote resilience and healthy adjustment. Thus, clinical child and pediatric psychologists should have a knowledge base in youth and family healthy adjustment and prevention science, as well as research and applied competence in prevention and health promotion. Such experiences can come from coursework in typical development and resilience, applied experiences in schools or primary care facilities, and interventions that focus on health promotion issues such as parent-child relationship enhancement, social skills training, healthy eating or obesity prevention, and reduction of risky sexual behavior.

Social Issues Affecting Children, Adolescents, and Families

Many of the challenges to youth adjustment are the social-environmental issues that influence children and families. Clinical child and pediatric psychologists should be aware of the sorts of social issues particularly relevant to youth, both generally and in their home communities. For example, as many as 50% of children have been exposed, either directly or indirectly (e.g., through media reports), to traumatic events such as natural disasters or violence in their homes, schools, communities, or the world (Bell & Allwood, 2007). Thus, trauma exposure is a major public health issue and one that all clinical child and pediatric psychologists will almost certainly encounter. Another important public health concern is youth access to mental health services; as many as 20% of youth are estimated to be in need of psychological services, yet only about one third of these youth receive needed services (Department of Health and Human Services, 1999). For both of these issues, clinical child and pediatric psychologists can make positive contributions in several ways, including identifying youth in need of treatment, participating in prevention programs to reduce risk for maladjustment, and participating in child advocacy efforts that can impact both individual children's lives as well as broader public policy and legislation. Involvement in Society for Research in Child Development's Office for Policy and Communications, APA's Public Interest Directorate, or state or local government can be effective ways for clinical child and pediatric psychologists to leverage their influence.

Specialty Applied Experiences

Roberts's (1998) final recommendation for clinical child training guidelines is that trainees gain applied experience in specialty practice relevant to assessment, intervention, and consultation with children, adolescents, and families. Although this is part of most of the preceding recommendations, its reiteration here emphasizes the importance of providing trainees with child-specific experience versus simply assuming that skills will generalize from adult-focused experiences. Roberts suggests that sufficient experience includes a minimum of closely supervised child practica in at least two different settings, internships that are at least half child-focused, and postdoctoral experience that provides further depth in autonomous child-related practice. Interestingly, Roberts's recommendation regarding internship is less than the two thirds child focus recommended at the Hilton Head Conference.

For the Society of Pediatric Psychology Task Force (Spirito et al., 2003), this curriculum domain centers on the importance of consultation and liaison skill development. Again, this domain underscores recommendations regarding interdisciplinary practice made throughout the Task Force's document. However, in addition to the need for pediatric psychologists to consult with parents and other professionals on child assessment and treatment, they will often serve in a training role. Specifically, pediatric psychologists should be able to educate health care professionals about principles of learning and development, psychological health (of youth and of health care professionals), and psychological research (Drotar et al., 2003; Spirito et al., 2003). This is particularly important because many psychological and behavioral issues are first raised with children's primary care physicians.

Disease Process and Medical Management

The final curriculum domain, specific to pediatric psychologists, notes the importance of understanding medical issues that they will be likely to encounter. Trainees should participate in coursework, seminars, supervision teams, and applied experiences that familiarize them with the phenomenology of relevant medical issues, as well as psychological issues related to the medical issue and its treatment (e.g., adverse behavioral effects of medical treatments). Spirito and colleagues (2003) suggest that pediatric psychology students complete practica and internship rotations in primary and specialty medical clinics in order to work directly with medical professionals and medical issues.

TRAINING OUTCOMES

There are undoubtedly many ways that successful outcomes for graduate students in clinical child and pediatric psychology can be defined. During graduate training, success can be evaluated by examining student retention, performance on program tasks (e.g., course grades, percentage of students passing comprehensive examinations), participation in professional activities such as conference presentations and publications, and more subjective issues such as personal and financial stability (e.g., the toll that graduate training takes on students' health, personal relationships, and financial debt). Postprogram outcome variables might include student program completion statistics (e.g., the likelihood that students will complete their graduate training and obtain relevant internships, the total debt load incurred to obtain the graduate degree), professional competence (e.g., number of graduates who attain licensure, diplomate status, or other demonstration of competent practice), and career tracks and success (e.g., the number of graduates who secure relevant jobs, research and mentoring productivity of graduates in academic positions, career satisfaction and longevity). Obviously, many of these outcomes are fairly subjective, multiply determined, and may not even be accessible to graduate programs. For example, the field is currently struggling with the best ways to define and assess professional competence (Kaslow et al., 2004; Roberts et al., 2005; Rodolfa, Kaslow, Stewart, Keilin, & Baker, 2005). Similarly, graduate programs are often unaware of students' personal issues unless they are clearly affecting professional functioning, and even if aware, are often in a poor position to evaluate the extent to which graduate program stresses versus other factors contributed to student health problems, relationship breakups, or decisions to leave a program or the field. Despite these limitations, however, training programs should routinely collect and evaluate data on student outcomes. At a minimum, these data are useful for the self-evaluation that programs can use to identify areas for growth (and that CoA requires). Beyond that, sharing these data with potential students and professional colleagues has the potential to improve training in the field as a whole.

For many years, the Council of University Directors of Clinical Psychology (CUDCP; the training council for scientist-practitioner and clinical science–oriented clinical doctoral programs) has supported a resolution strongly encouraging all member programs to make trainee outcome data available to the public. Programs collect and share information on program attrition, time to degree completion for graduates, and the percentage of students who obtain predoctoral internships. In addition to helping prospective graduate students evaluate training programs, these data have been useful in evaluating how clinical programs fare on these basic outcomes. For example, recent years have seen an increasing imbalance between the number of internship slots available through the Association of Psychology Postdoctoral and Internship Centers (APPIC; 2006) match system and the number of students applying for these slots, with only 77% of applicants being matched to internships on National Match Day in 2006. However, a survey of CUDCP programs indicated that 86% of students from CUDCP programs secured internships on the 2006 Match Day, and 92% of students ultimately obtained an internship through the match, internship clearinghouse, or other methods (Collins & Callahan, 2006). Although these data are not specific to clinical child or pediatric training, they do suggest that students trained in scientist-practitioner programs are faring better than the national norms.

Recently, the CoA has instituted a requirement that all accredited training programs make similar data available to the public (APA, 2006b). Specifically, beginning January 1, 2007, the CoA requires that training programs provide information on time to completion (including mean, median, and percentages of students completing the program in under 5, 6, 7, and more than 7 years), program costs (e.g., tuition, fees, any certain or possible adjustments to costs such as waivers, fellowships, or assistantships), internship placement (including APPIC match rates and overall placement rates through other methods, rates of paid and half-time internships), and attrition (i.e., the number and percentage of students who fail to complete the program for any reason). Additionally, beginning in 2008, programs will be required to report the number and percentage of graduates who have become licensed psychologists in the preceding decade.

Beyond program completion, graduates' career trajectories provide an index of training success. Given the scientist-practitioner emphasis of most clinical child and pediatric psychology programs, careers that integrate research and applied activity seem the ideal outcome, although the nature of this integration might range from jobs in academic departments or medical centers that combine research, clinical teaching and supervision, and perhaps some clinical practice, to more applied jobs in which practitioners provide evidence-based treatments, participate actively in continuing education, and perhaps provide clinical supervision to doctoral students. For clinical science programs, the desired integration is likely to emphasize research more heavily, with graduates being effective contributors to clinical science research and dissemination. Although they do not examine child-focused programs specifically, a few studies have examined clinical programs' success in placing graduates in academic department faculty positions (Ilardi, Rodriguez-Hanley, Roberts, & Seigel, 2000), graduates' research productivity once they begin their own academic careers (Roy, Roberts, & Stewart, 2006), and graduates' scores on the Examination for Professional Practice in Psychology (Yu et al., 1997). These studies provide useful information that individual programs can use to compare themselves to national norms. Interestingly, although these outcome variables all tended to relate significantly to reputation rankings such as the one published by *U.S. News and World Report*, they offer a more objective and specific way to assess training outcomes.

FUTURE CHALLENGES

Although exciting advances have shaped the growth of clinical child and pediatric psychology over the past 50 years, important challenges lie ahead as the field emerges from its adolescence into its professional adulthood. In addition, current issues that confront clinical psychology as a whole may provide distinct opportunities for leaders in child and pediatric psychology to creatively solve problems and improve training experiences for students. These challenges are the focus of several recent articles and conferences (e.g., the special issue of *Clinical Psychology: Science and Practice* on the present and future of clinical psychology; Kendall, 2006). Here, we discuss a few of these issues, include the challenges of designing curricula that balance breadth and depth, defining what it means to be a competent clinical psychologist, addressing impairment among students and faculty, and responding to dynamic market forces that shape the job outlook for clinical psychology graduates.

Broad versus Specific Training

As we discussed earlier, a central issue in the growth of clinical child and pediatric psychology has been how best to balance general (thus far primarily adult-focused) training in psychology with specialized coursework and clinical experiences that focus on child or pediatric psychology. As the field evolves in the twenty-first century, it is critical to evaluate whether broad and general training, as it is currently defined, keeps clinical psychology training stagnant. Further, we foresee attaining an appropriate balance as becoming more difficult as the technology of the field advances and expands. Clinical research is reaching deeper into existing problems and stretching into novel areas. For example, the development and validation of new assessments, preventions, and treatments translates into additional skills and educational content that students must master to be competent psychologists upon graduation.

The question remains whether specialization at the level of clinical child or pediatric psychology is appropriate and beneficial to students. Or put another way, are clinical child and pediatric psychology more of a specialty than clinical adult psychology? To date the field has taken steps to define itself as such, and many leaders in the field have embraced this definition. Yet, clinical child and pediatric psychology are not the only fields to deal with this issue. Leading clinical gerontologists, health psychologists, and clinical neuroscientists also struggle with these same training decisions (Roberts, 2006). What is potentially lost in specialization's overemphasis in one area is the scope of clinical psychology as a whole. As currently implemented by many programs, specialized child clinical or pediatric tracks often take a life span developmental and systemic approach to psychology that ensures broad training (Prinstein & Roberts, 2006; Roberts, 2006). One potential resolution to these specialization issues is to define core curricula as a set of skills that are common to all psychologists, such as training in scientific methods, data analytic techniques, and general clinical skills. In addition, training in core areas of psychology would provide content that takes a life span developmental and systemic approach. Then the focus on clinical adult or clinical child psychology would be considered at the same level in terms of specialization. This would alleviate the "adult clinical plus" model that permeates many training programs, in which students who are interested in working primarily with youth populations end up taking similar numbers of clinical classes plus additional classes or seek additional training opportunities with children (La Greca & Hughes, 1999; Roberts, 2006). Clearly, however, the significant challenge of this approach is to provide students with sufficient exposure to the burgeoning literature in important areas without extending an already lengthy training process.

Graduate students in clinical psychology fall on both sides of the argument. In a recent survey of over 1,000 graduate students in programs affiliated with the CUPCP, almost three quarters of clinical psychology graduate students report specializing within their graduate training, and over half of those who reported not specializing plan on doing so before the end of their graduate training (Luebbe, Green, & Malcolm, 2006). Further, just under 50% of those who reported specializing indicated that their specialty was a recognized or formal track within their program, and over 60% of students reported that their specialty area was a large influence on their choice of graduate programs. Interestingly, students reported specializing in a variety of ways beyond the types of populations (e.g., child) with whom they work. Students also consider themselves specializing in certain disorders, research areas, theoretical models of therapy, and specific skills such as statistics. These results suggest that graduate students want to and already are specializing during their graduate training. This makes a strong argument for officially recognizing certain specialties. Yet, these results also suggest that the word "specialty" has varied meanings, and students are finding opportunities to specialize within their current programs regardless of whether such specialties are officially recognized. Overall, designing curricula that provide broad but focused training remains a critical issue as clinical child and pediatric psychology grow.

Professional Competence

As we described, the field of clinical psychology, including its regulatory and accrediting bodies, is currently in flux as it moves away from an activity-based model of training to one that is competency-based. An ongoing challenge for training programs not only in clinical child and pediatric psychology but also clinical psychology as a whole is to continue to produce professionals who are competent to practice psychology and who are committed to a process of lifelong learning that will enable them to stay up-to-date with the best practices available. The development of training models and lists of core competencies in clinical child and pediatric psychology (e.g., La Greca & Hughes, 1999; Roberts et al., 1998; Spirito et al., 2003) are good first steps toward establishing competency-based training.

Still, several questions remain during this transition. First, how will competency be assessed? Second, *who* will be responsible for such assessments? Finally, and especially pertinent to clinical child and pediatric psychology, how will competency among specialties differ from one another regarding content of competencies, unique contexts in which competency is needed, sequence of competency development, and assessment of competency? In the future, leaders in clinical child and pediatric psychology will likely be charged not only with the task of developing novel techniques to assess competency across the span of a career, but also for conducting the necessary research showing that such assessments are reliable and valid indicators of competency (Roberts et al., 2005). For example, although the Examination for Professional Practice in Psychology provides a reliable assessment of knowledge, it does not assess other foundational competencies such as skills and attitudes. Several authors have proposed use of additional assessment techniques such as standardized patients, self-assessments, or "360 degree evaluations" (Kaslow, 2004 Roberts et al., 2005).

Recently, the field has been quite active in attempting to identify specific competencies that professional psychologists should attain across their development and exploring useful ways of assessing and documenting competence. The 2002 Competencies Conference initiated by APPIC identified several areas in which competencies should be established (Kaslow et al., 2004) and paved the way for ongoing efforts by APPIC, APA's Board of Educational Affairs, the Council of Chairs of Training Councils (a meta-organization representing the training councils in professional psychology as well as other organizations interested in training), and other training-related organizations. Hatcher and Lassiter (in press) describe the results of a multiyear practicum competencies workgroup spearheaded by the Association for Directors of Psychology Training Clinics with input from the Council of Chairs of Training Councils. With additional input from clinic and training program directors from all areas of professional psychology, the workgroup developed a document that outlines practicum competencies considered necessary at the beginning of practicum training, that develop over the course of graduate practicum, and that should be evident at the end of practicum training in order for students to be considered ready for internship. Although the document does not specify how these competencies should be assessed, training programs are already exploring creative ways of incorporating these competencies into supervisor evaluations and student self-assessments. The APA's Board of Educational Affairs is also currently active in identifying competency benchmarks for professional practice in areas such as assessment and diagnosis and multicultural competency. These efforts promise to make a substantial impact on the way professional psychologists evaluate their training efforts.

Because of the unique populations served and the varied contexts in which clinical child and pediatric psychologists work, new and specific ways to assess competency may be needed. For instance, ratings by peers or other professionals in schools, hospitals, or juvenile justice systems may complement more traditional competency assessments. In addition, as competency-based models become the norm for clinical child and pediatric training programs, it is imperative that the field as a whole also conduct an ongoing self-assessment of sorts. As the definition of a clinical child or pediatric psychologist evolves, so too must the knowledge, skills, and attitudes that compose the core competencies of these professionals. Leaders in the field must be willing to adjust and strengthen current models of training by adding new domains of competency, modifying current domains, or removing some domains altogether.

Professional Impairment

Professional competence among practicing psychologists, faculty supervisors, and students helps both to build the public's trust and to ensure its safety. Detecting and intervening with impaired professionals is therefore a vital responsibility of all clinical psychologists. Empirical studies have begun to show that graduate student impairment, whether it be lack of competence or experienced personal distress, is prevalent (e.g., Vacha-Haase, Davenport, & Kerewsky, 2004). Yet on the whole, far less has been written about this population than about interns or licensed professionals (Schwartz-Mette, in press). Further, given the vulnerability of the population with whom child and pediatric psychologists primarily work, professional competence is even more critical for students and supervisors in these fields. Also, as previously mentioned, clinical child and pediatric psychologists often work with multiple individuals in a variety of systems. This puts these students, not to mention practicing professionals, in a unique position as they potentially interact with a wider spectrum of the public than many psychologists, and as such may have to be multicompetent.

While APA ethical codes stipulate that psychologists should monitor themselves and peers for signs of impairment, graduate students may be particularly unlikely to do so for reasons associated with their professional inexperience, added stress during training, growing pains as they transition from undergraduate experiences to being a publicly recognized professional, and reservations regarding identifying impaired peers for fear of negative social consequences (Schwartz-Mette, in press). Thus, detection and appropriate intervention with impaired students often falls on the shoulders of academic training programs. Unfortunately, although both the Council on Accreditation's *Guidelines and Practices* (APA, 2005) and APA's *Ethical Principles of Psychologists and Code of Conduct* (APA, 2002) discuss impairment, neither document provides recommendations for resolving these issues. As such, most training programs are left with creating program-specific guidelines for intervening in situations in which impairment occurs, and these guidelines vary widely from program to program.

Several authors (e.g., Schwartz- Mette, in press; Vacha-Haase et al., 2004) have provided recommendations for addressing professional impairment. These include improvement of self- and peer monitoring through education about self-care and transition-related stress in graduate school, increased monitoring by clinical supervisors of students, and creation of more sensitive and open cultures in training programs. Additionally, more research is needed in the field that examines the unique issues that arise when child clinical and pediatric psychologists are impaired (e.g., prevalence of inappropriate conduct with children). Finally, training programs will need to continue to take steps toward managing students with impairments through informal (e.g., varied clinical training cases to improve competency with specific populations) and formal (e.g., required counseling for emotionally distressed students) channels.

Marketplace Developments

The exponential growth of clinical psychology over the past 100 years has not come about without some growing pains, and changing market forces have altered the job outlook for many graduates of clinical psychology training programs. In the future, clinical child and pediatric psychologists have reason to be cautious, but also optimistic. One factor that directly influences the job market for new psychologists is the ratio of qualified applicants to jobs. On the bright side, job opportunities are predicted to grow faster than average for practicing psychologists in the next 8 years, especially for clinical and school psychologists (U.S. Bureau of Labor Statistics, 2006). Despite this growth, training programs are unfortunately producing even more psychologists than there are adequate training opportunities (i.e., internships) and perhaps market demand. For example, the ratio of internship applicants to available slots decreased from 1999 to 2002 to levels close to 1:1. Yet, this ratio has risen sharply from 2003 to 2006 (APPIC, 2006). If this trend continues in a similar fashion, the market may become oversaturated with psychologists. Although the APA Office of Research collects data on employment of new graduates, no up-to-date formal workforce analysis exists. Fortunately, the Office of Research is currently pursuing such an analysis.

Positions for academic clinical child and pediatric psychologists also appear to be growing. Many departments are receiving funding for new faculty lines, and additional positions formerly occupied by retiring faculty are opening. More universities and colleges are creating interdisciplinary positions, such as developmental psychopathologist positions with dual responsibilities in clinical and developmental training areas, or have growing departments or programs in human development and family studies. Joint doctoral programs in clinical and developmental psychology, like that at the University of Missouri–Columbia described earlier, may help to expand students' marketability in the academic job market. One challenge that remains for academic psychologists deals with research funding. Unfortunately, grant funding is reliant on political factors, and despite funding levels remaining relatively stable from agencies like the National Institutes of Mental Health in the past 5 years, the competition has grown more intense and success rates for awards have decreased sharply. It is uncertain whether this trend will continue in the future.

Dynamics in the marketplace are leading many graduates of clinical training programs, including those in child and pediatric psychology, to redefine their professional roles or to enter nontraditional employment opportunities. Generally speaking, fewer clinical psychologists are working in traditional office settings seeing clients for the 50-minute hour, and this is especially true for clinical child and pediatric psychologists. In turn, training programs are challenged to keep pace with these changes by adjusting their curricula to provide relevant coursework and experiences that prepare their graduates to be competitive job applicants. However, within this trend there is reason for child and pediatric psychologists to be optimistic. Specifically, students who are trained in an ecological framework should excel in opportunities to work in a variety of settings where child clinical or pediatric psychologists traditionally have not. This will require, however, that graduates of clinical child and pediatric training programs take the lead in developing partnerships with community agencies and institutions to develop such niche positions.

SUMMARY

Although adolescents in the field of professional psychology, the future of clinical child and pediatric psychology looks promising. Defining these fields has not been an easy task, given the variety of roles, responsibilities, and endeavors undertaken by clinical child and pediatric psychologists. Further, as these definitions continue to evolve, training programs will have to modify their curricula to provide state-of-the-art instruction for their students. In this chapter, we have outlined several training models and important components of clinical child and pediatric training at the graduate, internship, and postdoctoral levels. Special attention was paid to outcomes of training, including what a competent clinical child or pediatric psychologist might look like in areas as varied as assessment and diagnosis, multiculturalism, research methods, and ethics. Such curriculum modifications are not without their challenges, and we ended this chapter with a discussion of issues that will need to be addressed both in the near future and several years down the road. Overall, training in clinical child and pediatric psychology has made considerable strides to date, and many training programs produce competent, skilled psychologists. Yet, we think it is important that leaders in clinical child and pediatric psychology not be content with the progress made thus far, but work diligently and proactively to address the challenges facing these fields.

REFERENCES

Academy of Psychological Clinical Science. (2007). *APCS mission and specific goals.* Retrieved January 5, 2007, from http://psych.arizona.edu/apcs/mission.php.

American Psychological Association. (2002). Ethical principles of psychologists and code of conduct. Retrieved September 11, 2007, from http://www.apa.org/ethics/code.html.

American Psychological Association. (2005). *Guidelines and principles for accreditation of programs in professional psychology.* New York: Author.

American Psychological Association. (2006a). *Committee on accreditation policy statements and implementing regulations.* New York: American Psychological Association.

American Psychological Association. (2006b). *Disclosure of education/training outcomes and information allowing for informed decision-making to prospective doctoral students.* Retrieved December 7, 2006, from http://www.apa.org/ed/accreditation/rev_disclosure.html.

American Psychological Association. (2006c). *Division 54: Society of Pediatric Psychology.* Retrieved December 7, 2006, from http://www.apa.org/about/division/div54.html.

Association of Psychology Postdoctoral and Internship Centers. (2006). *2006 APPIC match statistics.* Retrieved January 9, 2007, from http://www.appic.org/match/5_2_2_1_8_match_about_statistics_general_2006.html.

Belar, C. D., Bieliauskas, L. A., Larsen, K. G., Mensh, I. N., Poey, K., & Roelke, H. J. (1989). The national conference on internship training in psychology. *American Psychologist, 44*, 60–65.

Bell, D. J., & Allwood, M. (2007). Posttraumatic stress disorder. In M. Hersen, & J. C. Thomas (Eds.), *Comprehensive handbook of interviewing adults and children* (Vol. 2, pp. 172–195). Thousand Oaks, CA: Sage.

Bronfenbrenner, U., & Morris, P. A. (2006). Developmental science, developmental systems, and contemporary theories of human development. In R. M. Lerner, & W. Damon (Eds.), *Handbook of child psychology: Vol. 1. Theoretical models of human development* (6th ed., pp. 793–828). Hoboken, NJ: Wiley.

Chambless, D. L., Baker, M., Baucom, D. H., Beutler, L. E., Calhoun, K. S., Crits-Christoph, P., et al. (1998). Update on empirically validated therapies (Pt. II). *Clinical Psychologist, 51*, 3–16.

Chambless, D. L., Sanderson, W. C., Shoham, V., Bennett Johnson, S., Pope, K. S., Crits-Christoph, P., et al. (1996). An update on empirically validated therapies. *Clinical Psychologist, 49*, 5–18.

Collins, F. L., & Callahan, J. (2006). *CUDCP mini-survey: Internship match outcomes.* Retrieved January 9, 2007, from http://fp.okstate.edu/collinslab/CUDCP/Surveys/match%20survey.pdf.

Commission for Recognition of Specialties and Proficiencies in Psychology. (2005). *Archival description of clinical child psychology.* Retrieved January 3, 2007, from http://www.apa.org/crsppp/childclinic.html.

Division of Clinical Child and Adolescent Psychology. (2006). *Directory of doctoral training in clinical child/adolescent and pediatric psychology.* Retrieved December 7, 2006, from http://www.unc.edu/%7Emjp1970/Directory/index.htm.

Drotar, D. (1998). Training students for careers in medical settings: A graduate program in pediatric psychology. *Professional Psychology: Research and Practice, 29*, 402–404.

Drotar, D., Palermo, T., & Ievers-Landis, C. E. (2003). Commentary. Recommendations for the training of pediatric psychologists: Implications for postdoctoral training. *Journal of Pediatric Psychology, 28*, 109–113.

Edelstein, B. A., & Brasted, W. S. (1991). Clinical training. In M. Hersen, A. E. Kazdin, & A. S. Bellack (Eds.), *The clinical psychology handbook* (2nd ed., pp. 45–65). New York: Pergamon Press.

Elbert, J. C., Abidin, A. J., Finch, A. J., Sigman, M. D., & Walker, C. E. (1988). Guidelines for clinical child psychology internship training. *Journal of Clinical Child Psychology, 17*, 280–287.

Hatcher, R. L., & Lassiter, K. D. (in press) Initial training in professional psychology: The practicum competencies outline. *Journal of Training Education in Professional Psychology.*

Hothersall, D. (2004). *History of psychology* (4th ed.) New York: McGraw-Hill.

Ilardi, S. S., Rodriguez-Hanley, A., Roberts, M. C., & Seigel, J. (2000). On the origins of clinical psychology faculty: Who is training the trainers? *Clinical Psychology: Science and Practice, 7*, 346–354.

Kaslow, N. J., Borden, K. A., Collins, F. L., Jr., Forrest, L., Illfelder-Kaye, J., Nelson, P. D., et al. (2004). Competencies Conference: Future directions in education and credentialing in professional psychology. *Journal of Clinical Psychology, 60*, 699–712.

Kendall, P. C. (2005). Clinical psychology in the twenty-first century: The wheel remains round. *Journal of Clinical Psychology, 61*, 1083–1086.

Kendall, P. C. (2006). Editorial: Expanding the impact of clinical psychology's science and practice. *Clinical Psychology: Science and Practice, 13*, 293–294.

La Greca, A. M., & Hughes, J. N. (1999). United we stand, divided we fall: The education and training needs of clinical child psychologists. *Journal of Clinical Child Psychology, 28*, 435–447.

La Greca, A. M., Stone, W. L., & Swales, T. (1989). Pediatric psychology training: An analysis of graduate, internship, and postdoctoral programs. *Journal of Pediatric Psychology, 14*, 103–116.

Lerner, R. M. (2006). Developmental science, developmental systems, and contemporary theories of human development. In R. M. Lerner, & W. Damon (Eds.), *Handbook of child psychology: Vol. 1. Theoretical models of human development* (6th ed., pp. 1–17). Hoboken, NJ: Wiley.

Lonigan, C. L., & Elbert, J. C. (Eds.) (1998). Special issue on empirically supported psychosocial interventions for children [Special issue]. *Journal of Clinical Child Psychology*, 27.

Luebbe, A., Green, D., & Malcolm, K. (2006, January). *Student survey results: How do students view the world of "broad and general" coursework and "emphases."* Symposium conducted at the annual meeting of the Council of University Directors of Clinical Psychology, Tucson, AZ.

Mannarino, A. P., & Fischer, C. (1982). Survey of graduate training in clinical child psychology. *Journal of Clinical Child Psychology, 11*, 22–26.

McFall, R. M. (1991). Manifesto for a science of clinical psychology. *Clinical Psychologist, 44*, 75–88.

McLoyd, V. C. (1998). Socioeconomic disadvantage and child development. *American Psychologist, 53*, 185–204.

Minuchin, S. P. (1985). Families and individual development: Provocations from the field of family therapy. *Child Development, 56*, 289–302.

Moffitt, T. E. (2005). The new look of behavioral genetics in developmental psychopathology: Gene-environment interplay in antisocial behaviors. *Psychological Bulletin, 131*, 533–554.

Ollendick, T., Drotar, D., Friedman, M., & Hodges, K. (1988). Guidelines for postdoctoral training in clinical child psychology. *Journal of Clinical Child Psychology, 17*, 288–289.

Prinstein, M. J., & Roberts, M. C. (2006). The professional adolescence of clinical child and adolescent and pediatric psychology: Grown up and striving for autonomy. *Clinical Psychology: Science and Practice, 13*, 263–268.

Raimy, V. C. (1950). *Training in clinical psychology*. New York: Prentice-Hall.

Reynolds, C. R., & Gutkin, T. B. (Eds.). (1999). *The handbook of school psychology* (3rd ed.). Hoboken, NJ: Wiley.

Roberts, M. C. (1992). Vale dictum: An editor's view of the field of pediatric psychology and its journal. *Journal of Pediatric Psychology, 17*, 785–805.

Roberts, M. C. (1998). Innovations in specialty training: The clinical child psychology program at the University of Kansas. *Professional Psychology: Research and Practice, 29*, 394–397.

Roberts, M. C. (Ed.). (2003). *Handbook of pediatric psychology* (3rd ed.) New York: Guilford Press.

Roberts, M. C. (2005). Perspectives on education and training in clinical psychology: Integrating reactions. *Journal of Clinical Psychology, 61*, 1077–1082.

Roberts, M. C. (2006). Essential tension: Specialization with broad and general training in psychology. *American Psychologist, 61*, 862–870.

Roberts, M. C., Borden, K. A., Christiansen, M. D., & Lopez, S. J. (2005). Fostering a culture shift: Assessment of competence in the education and careers of professional psychologists. *Professional Psychology: Research and Practice, 36*, 355–361.

Roberts, M. C., Carlson, C., Erickson, M. T., Friedman, R. M., La Greca, A. M., Lemanek, K. L., et al. (1998). A model for training psychologists to provide services for children and adolescents. *Professional Psychology: Research and Practice, 29*, 293–299.

Roberts, M. C., Erickson, M. T., & Tuma, J. M. (1985). Addressing the needs: Guidelines for training psychologists to work with children, youth, and families. *Journal of Clinical Child Psychology, 14*, 70–79.

Roberts, M. C., & Sobel, A. B. (1999). Training in clinical child psychology: Doing it right. *Journal of Clinical Child Psychology, 28*, 482–489.

Roberts, M. C., & Steele, R. G. (2003). Predoctoral training in pediatric psychology at the University of Kansas Clinical Child Psychology Program. *Journal of Pediatric Psychology, 28*, 99–103.

Rodolfa, E. R., Kaslow, N. J., Stewart, A. E., Keilin, W. G., & Baker, J. (2005). Internship training: Do models really matter? *Professional Psychology: Research and Practice, 36*, 25–31.

Ross, A. O. (1959). *The practice of clinical child psychology*. New York: Grune & Stratton.

Routh, D. K. (1970). Psychological training in medical school departments of pediatrics: A survey. *Professional Psychology, 1*, 469–472.

Routh, D. K. (1972). Psychological training in medical school departments of pediatrics: A second look. *American Psychologist, 27*, 587–589.

Routh, D. K., & La Greca, A. M. (1990). Current status of graduate training in pediatric psychology: Results of a survey. In P. R. Magrab, & P. Wohlford (Eds.), *Improving psychological services for children and adolescents with severe mental disorders: Clinical training in psychology* (pp. 139–144). Washington, DC: American Psychological Association.

Roy, K. M., Roberts, M. C., & Stewart, P. K. (2006). Research productivity and academic lineage in clinical psychology: Who is training the faculty to do research? *Journal of Clinical Psychology, 62*, 893–905.

Rutter, M., & Sroufe, L. A. (2000). Developmental psychopathology: Concepts and challenges. *Development and Psychopathology, 12*, 265–296.

Schilling, K., & Packard, R. (2005). *The 2005 inter-organization summit on structure of the accrediting body for professional psychology: Final proposal.* Retrieved January 7, 2007, from http://www.psyaccreditationsummit.org.

Schwartz-Mette, R. (in press). Challenges in addressing graduate student impairment in academic professional psychology programs. *Ethics and Behavior.*

Sheridan, E. P., Matarazzo, J. D., & Nelson, P. D. (1995). Accreditation of psychology's graduate professional education and training programs: An historical perspective. *Professional Psychology: Research and Practice, 26*, 386–392.

Snyder, C. R., & Elliott, T. R. (2005). Twenty-first century graduate education in clinical psychology: A four level matrix model. *Journal of Clinical Psychology, 61*, 1033–1054.

Spirito, A., Brown, R. T., D'Angelo, E. J., Delamater, A. M., Rodrigue, J. R., & Siegel, L. J. (2003). Training pediatric psychologists for the 21st century. In M. C. Roberts, (Ed.), *Handbook of pediatric psychology* (3rd ed., pp. 19–31). New York: Guilford Press.

Sumerall, S. W., Lopez, S. J., & Oehlert, M. E. (2000). *Competency-based education and training in psychology: A primer.* Springfield, IL: Charles C Thomas.

Tuma, J. M. (1983). Specialty training for psychologist service providers to children? *American Psychologist, 38*, 340–342.

Tuma, J. M. (Ed.). (1985). *Proceedings: Conference on training clinical child psychologists.* Baton Rouge, LA: Section on Clinical Child Psychology.

Tuma, J. M. (1986). Clinical child psychology training: Report on the Hilton Head conference. *Journal of Clinical Child Psychology, 15*, 88–96.

U.S. Bureau of Labor Statistics. (2006). *Occupational outlook handbook (OOH), 2006–07 edition.* Retrieved January 13, 2007, from http://www.bls.gov/oco/ocos056.htm.

U.S. Department of Health and Human Services. (1999). *Mental health: A report of the surgeon general.* Rockville, MD: Author.

Vacha-Haase, T., Davenport, D. S., & Kerewsky, S. D. (2004). Problematic students: Gatekeeping practices of academic professional psychology programs. *Professional Psychology: Research and Practice, 35*, 115–122.

van Eys, P. P., & Dodge, K. A. (1999). Closing the gaps: Developmental psychopathology as a training model for clinical child psychology. *Journal of Clinical Child Psychology, 28*, 467–475.

Wohlford, P. (1978). A challenge to clinical psychology: Better training to serve children. *Journal of Clinical Child Psychology, 7*, 89–90.

Wohlford, P., Myers, H. F., & Callan, J. E. (1993). *Serving the seriously mentally ill: Public-academic linkages in services, research, and training.* Washington, DC: American Psychological Association.

Wright, L. (1967). The pediatric psychologist: A role model. *American Psychologist, 22*, 323–325.

Yu, L. M., Rinaldi, S. A., Templer, D. I., Colbert, L. A., Siscoe, K., & Van Patten, K. (1997). Scores on the Examination for Professional Practice in Psychology as a function of attributes of clinical psychology graduate programs. *Psychological Science, 8*, 347–350.

Zeman, J., Nangle, D. W., & Sim, L. (1999). Incorporating a developmental perspective in doctoral training: Survey of clinical psychology training programs and introductions to the special section. *Journal of Clinical Child Psychology, 28*, 426–434.

CHAPTER 3

Professional Practice

Daniel B. Chorney and Tracy L. Morris

The practice of professional psychology has been in existence for roughly one century. Most readers will be quite aware of the roots of clinical psychology in the independent psychiatric practice of Sigmund Freud in the late nineteenth century. Perhaps less well known, but no less pivotal, was the establishment of the world's first psychological clinic by Lightner Witmer at the University of Pennsylvania in 1896 (which specialized in the provision of services to children and their families).

Professional psychology has witnessed considerable growth over the intervening decades. In the period between World War I and World War II, the number of psychologists in the United States increased from 300 to 3,000. Prior to WWI the vast majority of psychologists were academics teaching and conducting research in colleges and universities, yet by 1930 over one third were working in applied settings (Finch & Odoroff, 1939). This proportion remains essentially the same today. Recent data indicate that of the 179,000 psychologists employed in the United States in 2004 (U.S. Department of Labor, 2006), nearly 60,000 were engaged in full-time clinical work (with an additional 18,000 engaged in some form of part-time practice; Kohout & Wicherski, 2003).

WHAT DEFINES PROFESSIONAL PRACTICE?

Professional practice is a relatively broad term used to describe all professionals within the field of psychology, not just those who choose to practice independently. Researchers, academics, clinicians—all share certain things in common that allow them to be called professionals, including, but not limited to, a shared professional code of ethics, years of graduate education in research and treatment of psychological disorders, and a license or state certification to utilize knowledge to help the public. The focus on using and evaluating empirical methods helps shape the way professional psychologists approach their work, and this rigorous training is just one aspect of what sets professional psychology apart from other helping professions (Todd & Bohart, 2003).

Professional psychologists provide a diverse range of services and skills. As Blau (1983, p. 57) points out, psychologists

> conduct a wide variety of psychotherapeutic interventions, assess intellect, aptitude, per-
> sonality, neuropsychological functioning, and marital adjustment—they design, direct,

and monitor various prevention and intervention programs ... work in many diverse medical settings utilizing uniquely psychological methods and tools that are required in health service, rarely work autonomously, and ordinarily function in psychology departments or psychology services in university clinics, hospitals, prisons, community mental health centers, agencies, courts, and treatment centers.

While many skills are shared by all professional psychologists, distinctions in preparatory work, professional roles, and skills are important to note. These differences begin in graduate training, as some psychologists are trained under the scientist-practitioner model (commonly known as the Boulder model), first outlined in 1949. This approach stresses the importance of academic research in combination with supervised clinical experience, resulting in professionals who are highly competent in the assessment, evaluation, and treatment of psychological disorders using empirical methods. As an alternative, the practitioner-scholar model places a heavy emphasis on clinical training instead of research. Although still requiring a doctoral degree, students trained under the Vail model have reduced academic research requirements and are often associated with separate schools of professional psychology rather than research universities. The two models typically provide professional psychologists with different degrees: A PhD or doctorate in philosophy is awarded upon completion of graduate work, successful defense of a research dissertation, and a year of internship at a clinical setting approved by the American Psychological Association (APA). This compares to a PhD, or doctorate in psychology, which is awarded after 4 to 6 years in a professional program where the emphasis is on clinical skills and training, a year of internship training, and research that tends to focus on more qualitative methods directly related to clinical practice. Both qualify under APA's (1987a) definition of professional psychologist: "Psychologists have a doctoral degree in psychology from an organized, sequential program in a regionally accredited university or professional school." Both models, despite their differences, allow for the ability to produce psychologists for independent practice. The Boulder model's training emphasis on the development of an evaluative attitude toward one's own and others' work is not antithetical to independent practice, and the delivery of services in the private sector by independent practitioners does not necessarily mean these psychologists are no longer critical scientists (Cantor & Moldawsky, 1985).

Professional practice is also shaped by what psychologists actually do on a day-to-day basis. The next logical question, then, is What distinguishes professional psychology from other professions? The APA (1987b, p. 2), in its Model Act for State Licensure of Psychologists, has outlined and given a definition for the role of professional psychologists, stating:

> The practice of psychology is defined as the observation, description, evaluation, interpretation, and modification of human behavior by the application of psychological principles, methods, and procedures, for the purpose of preventing or eliminating symptomatic, maladaptive, or undesired behavior and of enhancing interpersonal relationships, work and life adjustment, person effectiveness, behavioral health, and mental health. The practice of psychology includes, but is not limited to, psychological testing and the evaluation or assessment of personal characteristics, such as intelligence, personality, abilities, interests,

aptitudes, and neuropsychological functioning; counseling, psychoanalysis, psychotherapy, hypnosis, biofeedback, and behavior analysis and therapy; diagnosis and treatment of mental and emotional disorder or disability, alcoholism and substance abuse, disorders of habit or conduct, as well as of the psychological aspects of physical illness, accident, injury, or disability; and psycho-educational evaluation, therapy, remediation, and consultation. Psychological services may be rendered to individuals, families, groups, and the public.

Although a better description of how psychologists are trained, along with what skills they possess, the definition provided thus far only scrapes the surface of the many different faces, forms, and functions a professional psychologist may represent. Differences in theoretical orientation, specialization in a specific disorder, and the type of job psychologists choose all reflect what duties they will perform, how they will go about them, and with whom they will work and collaborate in daily functioning. The purpose of the present chapter is to examine in closer detail one career path a psychologist may take: private practice.

INDEPENDENT PRIVATE PRACTICE IN PSYCHOLOGY

The idea of private practice in psychology is as old as the profession itself. For many, simply saying the words aloud conjures up the image of couches and clients recollecting dreams and early childhood experiences while a therapist sits back and attempts to make sense of it all. This romantic and glorified image of the practice of psychology is easily brought to mind, yet it could not be further from the truth. Today's private practitioner lives in a world dictated by managed health care, empirically supported treatments, and constant financial uncertainty. The lure of private practice may be what motivates many people to enter the field of psychology, yet fewer and fewer psychologists are ending up in private practice. One does not have to look far for a book, article, or speech that outlines the demise of private practice in psychology. Starting up and running a business, building a referral and client base, handling an increasingly large and difficult managed care system, and dealing with legal liabilities are generally not considered reasons that people look forward to starting a private practice. Yet the profession survives. With all its limitations and challenges, the benefits of a career in private practice remain. Professional practice will inevitably remain a viable career path for many psychologists, despite the ever-changing face and demands of the profession itself.

If private practice is not meant for everyone, the question becomes For whom is it meant? In a recent survey of over 1,600 psychologists, 2% reported working full time in independent private practice. This number rises to 5% when group practice settings are included (Wicherski & Kohout, 2005). These numbers show a slight decline from the 1999 Doctorate Employment Survey (6% in total were in some form of practice). Although numbers may be declining and the environment is becoming more challenging overall, numerous advantages of establishing a private practice still exist.

RELATIVE ADVANTAGES AND DISADVANTAGES OF PRIVATE PRACTICE

As with any profession, certain qualities and individual characteristics draw people to the field of psychology. As stated earlier, a career in private practice is not for everyone, but it certainly can be rewarding for those who enjoy the benefits it has to offer. One of the most salient rewards is the notion of being your own boss. Although the same freedoms may not exist today as were available years before, establishing an independent private practice means more control over your hours, clientele, and area of specialization. For many people, the idea of going to work each day and not having to face one or multiple supervisors is a truly appealing notion.

Being your own boss brings with it a certain level of flexibility and independence, along with more responsibility. Numerous decisions must be made, such as deciding where to establish a practice (urban versus rural), what the operating hours will be (flexible and spread out or a regular 9-to-5 workday), and what types of clients you are willing to see (specialization or generalization). In addition to these important decisions, an independent private practitioner also has full control over business decisions and directs how the practice will grow (or shrink, depending on one's business skills).

With this control, the practitioner's decisions play a large role in deciding how much he or she will earn that year. Once a strong client base has been established and clients are being seen regularly, the potential for earnings increases dramatically. A key point here is that independent practice allows for the potential to earn a large salary; the median starting salary of a psychologist in independent private practice is $50,000 (this is reduced to $45,000 when in group practice), which compares to a median starting salary of $45,000 for an assistant professor on a 9-month contract (Wicherski & Kohout, 2005). Earning substantially more than this requires a large investment of time and effort (both on a daily and a long-term basis). How much is earned also will depend on what services are provided, and whether you decide to accept insurance or have a sliding scale.

Having more power over decisions and the daily running of your practice can certainly be an advantage, but it brings with it a high degree of responsibility and personal liability. As primary decision maker, the practitioner must deal with all the consequences of those decisions. Many of the advantages listed previously also have the potential to become disadvantages if not handled correctly. Independence and autonomy may be great for some, but others may require a certain level of structure and consultation in order to succeed; thus, what may be advantageous for some may be a burden for others. If one's practice is badly located, one's hours are too few or constrained, and one's area of specialization is too focused, one may soon realize how challenging private practice can be.

Financially there exists a high level of uncertainty and risk in establishing a practice, as it will take some time to develop a strong client base. Many may choose to begin in another setting and slowly build up a private practice on the side, before fully committing to such a potentially risky endeavor. As the practitioner becomes responsible for all billing, collections, insurance, and employee decisions that must be made (Barnett & Henshaw, 2003), he or she quickly realizes how important it is to be familiar with basic business principles—something many psychologists are not aware of or prepared for when entering this area. Some graduate schools are leading the way in providing courses that address the financial and business aspects of working in the field of psychology, covering aspects such as information and financial management, contract negotiation, and planning and budgeting for the future. It may be of great benefit for those interested in pursuing a career in private practice to take such business classes while in graduate school to be better prepared for the multiple financial and business responsibilities associated with working independently or as part of a private practice.

Others may experience a sense of professional isolation when practicing independently. Although this may be solved by deciding to enter into or form a group practice instead, the number of colleagues one interacts with is very limited in comparison to working in a larger institution, such as a university or medical setting. This also becomes a challenge when consultation on a case is necessary, as an independent practitioner may not have anyone to immediately turn to for advice. Such concerns may be addressed, in part, by maintaining involvement in a larger network of individuals in the same profession (state professional organizations, local treatment providers, fellow private practitioners in the area). Contact with these individuals may help ease isolation and provide a social outlet and support when necessary or desired.

When working independently it is important to remember that in many cases, one truly is working independent of others. This may require the psychologist to wear many hats, including those of accountant, public relations person, cleaning staff, insurance policy expert, receptionist, real estate agent, financial analyst, bill collector, and office manager (Vineberg, 2005). Access to clerical or support staff who can help with paperwork, correspondence, scheduling issues, and numerous other day-to-day operational tasks will affect how business is conducted in the office, as much of this work is necessary to keep a business running smoothly. All of these duties may be challenging by themselves, yet the larger burden may be the time spent ensuring that they are done correctly. Personal freedom may come at the cost of sacrificed time, and one may have to work long hours and through the weekend just to ensure that all necessary business details are covered. It may be important to remember here that these administrative duties are all above and beyond actually conducting therapy and performing one's duty as a clinical psychologist.

GROUP PRACTICE IN PSYCHOLOGY

If the disadvantages of independent private practice seem to outweigh the benefits, a viable alternative is joining or forming a group practice. Group practices can be small, composed of a few psychologists or other mental health professionals, or much larger organizations consisting of an interdisciplinary team of providers working collaboratively and sharing resources. In this manner, many of the potential downfalls of independent practice can be avoided, or at the very least reduced.

Joining a group practice allows one to experience many aspects of independent practice before actually committing to it. The daily exposure to aspects of running a business, handling client records and paperwork, and other daily activities associated with work in a practice may provide a good first step in making an informed decision as to whether a future career in independent private practice is actually desirable. By joining a group practice and getting your foot in the door, it may be easier to see if this type of work is suitable and agreeable without having to commit large amounts of time and money to opening an independent practice, only to find out it is not the best professional setting for your needs.

As mentioned earlier, a rather large financial risk accompanies a solo venture into private practice. One of the main advantages to joining a group practice is that the financial risk, investment, and capital associated with beginning a practice is distributed among group members. This may be especially appealing given recent data showing that 74% of new psychologists in practice subfields are starting their professional life with a median debt level of $67,500 (Wicherski & Kohout, 2005). As high as this seems, the level of debt grows substantially higher for those graduating with a Clinical PsyD, with a median debt level of $90,000 and 79% of new graduates reporting some level of debt. Given these numbers, and knowing that it may take a substantial amount of time before a regular client base is established and income becomes steady, it is readily apparent why the idea of sharing financial burden and risk is appealing. When joining an already established group practice, a referral base may already exist, which eliminates a large degree of work and reduces the amount of stress associated with building a clientele from scratch. Along with defraying the initial start-up costs, it may be financially beneficial overall to be in group practice. Despite the fact that generated income may need to be split among members in the group practice, this is counterbalanced by having all members of the group split the cost of expenses generated in running the practice. Everything from rental and operating fees to paying office staff can be shared, whereas an independent practitioner must pay for all of these costs without help from others. To pay for many of these expenses, a solo practitioner needs to keep overhead costs at a minimum, and often will have to perform multiple roles within the office (e.g., receptionist, therapist, and custodian). As one author puts it:

> When you consider solo versus group practice, you eventually have to ask yourself whether you want to hand over a sizable portion of your revenue to cover expenses that are paid solely by you, whether you want to minimize these expenses somewhat and add more work and headaches to your already busy schedule, or whether you want to hand over a sizable portion of your revenue to others and let them take care of the headaches so you can focus your energy on being a clinician. (Habben, 2005, p. 101)

Working alongside others in group practice eliminates the disadvantage of professional isolation and provides other benefits as well. Colleagues may help in providing knowledge and expertise on a variety of issues, including how to run a successful practice, dealing with especially difficult cases, and providing resources for referrals in the community. Colleagues also provide friendship and may help with expanding one's social and professional network. Despite working alongside others, much of the freedom of independent practice still exists, as often one can still determine to a large degree the type and amount of patients seen.

Although it may appear as though group practice solves any and all disadvantages of independent private practice, some disadvantages remain. First and foremost, the level and degree of control over decisions being made are no longer solely in one person's hands in group practice. Decisions regarding the hiring and firing of staff, the fees charged to patients, questions about referrals and providers, and all other business decisions must now be made as a group and no longer individually. To some this may seem appealing; to others this loss of independence may be enough to turn them away from group practice.

Similar to independent practice, income from group practice may be variable. Although the potential for large earnings still exists, a lot depends on the overall strength and productivity of the practice as a whole, as well as your own work. Fluctuating levels of productivity will provide varying levels of pay across time, and this may cause a high degree of frustration in anyone who prefers a steady and stable paycheck.

Another disadvantage arises primarily when one is seeking another job, as working in a group practice does not carry with it the instant credibility and respect by association as working for a university may provide (Habben, 2005). Considering the low name recognition a group practice has outside of its own community, it may be hard to communicate to a future potential employer the exact nature of work conducted, the environment and conditions, and the skills needed to work successfully in the practice being left.

PREPARING FOR LIFE IN PRIVATE PRACTICE

Perhaps one of the most difficult aspects of beginning a private practice is the transition one must make in one's sense of identity, a transition from therapist to businessperson. As an independent therapist, you are providing and selling a service: therapy. Graduate school and internships do little to prepare the training psychologist for life in private practice, and it may be difficult at first to view therapy as a marketable service provided for a consumer. One of the first questions that must be asked is What do I have to offer? The service a clinical psychologist provides is a complicated blend of the therapist's personality, character, and previous experience; the theoretical or philosophical approach and orientation he or she espouses; and the techniques and procedures used that reflect this approach (Earle & Barnes, 1999).

CHALLENGES IN STARTING AND MAINTAINING A PRACTICE

One of the first concerns in establishing a private practice is the start-up cost, which will vary immensely depending on what approach is taken and what sort of practice is wanted. Deciding to practice as part of a group may help to defer some of the initial costs, the first of which may be choosing where the practice will be and renting adequate office space. Things to consider here are the size and cost of your office space, transportation to and from your office and how accessible it is to clients, and what clientele you may draw depending on where your practice is located. The decision of where to practice also carries with it the weight of deciding where you would like to live—at least for some considerable time. Even though your skills and services may be transportable, clients are not, as they are unlikely to follow you to where you end up moving, whether that be across town or across the country.

Other initial costs include licensing fees, which will vary depending on one's state, and malpractice insurance, which will also vary depending on what coverage is desired. These fees relate to where you decide to practice, as requirements for licensing vary across the country. Substantial costs may be incurred in furnishing the office (everything from chairs to filing cabinets to children's furniture and toys), computers, assessment materials, business cards and office supplies, utilities, professional membership dues, taxes, and possibly advertising.

Of all initial start-up concerns, perhaps the most important is establishing a steady flow of referrals. This is especially difficult if one decides to enter private practice immediately after completing internship and before having a strong base of referral sources from which to draw clients. The need to begin forming professional relationships and contacts during the internship year or even earlier may be crucial to help lay the foundation for a later referral base, especially if the goal is to stay within that community. Forming ties with others in the community (schools, local pediatricians, other clinics) can help build reciprocal referral relationships and help make one's availability, services, and presence known in the area. Other mental health professionals may be vying for the same clients, making this a difficult process. Again, good business sense and a strong marketing strategy can make a substantial difference here in attracting new clients.

Numerous legal issues will inevitably arise as part of private practice, and it is imperative that all steps have been taken to prepare before the time comes. Good malpractice insurance is required, along with having a solid understanding of HIPAA regulations, licensing laws, and state regulations. Consultation with an attorney may be of great benefit as you establish your practice.

MANAGED CARE

The topic of managed care in the United States almost immediately invokes strong feelings among health care professionals, including practicing psychologists. Whether liked or not, it must be accepted at present as the medium through which a large proportion of services are delivered. The current system of managed care services can be seen positively as being a significant source of referrals for one's practice, offering clientele ranging from private direct pay to third-party payers, patients charged on a sliding scale, and pro bono cases. Unfortunately, the demand it places on both patients and providers creates an uneasy tension, ultimately changing the face of mental health treatment in ways that many psychologists find detrimental.

In a 1998 survey of almost 16,000 licensed psychologists, 4 out of 5 reported that managed care had a negative effect on their professional work, with independent practitioners and psychologists in medical settings reporting the most negative effects (Phelps, Eisman, & Kohout, 1998). Their concerns included how managed care is changing clinical practice, excess precertification requirements of managed care panels, decreases in income, and ethical dilemmas created by managed care. The authors conclude that the "marketplace-driven demands for integrated services, large and diversified group practices, and greater accountability have created obstacles and declining market opportunities that threaten the very existence of traditional psychological practice" (p. 35). Another 1998 survey (Murphy, DeBernardo, & Shoemaker, 1998) of 442 members of APA's Division 42 (Division of Independent Practice) found similar results, with only 2% of respondents reporting that managed care practices had a positive impact on quality of care. Moreover, 80% indicated that caps on the number of sessions interfered with treatment, and 84% of respondents stated that managed care companies have control over aspects of patient care and treatment that clinicians should control. Most respondents indicated that managed care had led to inappropriate treatment, insufficient treatment, or both. More specifically, they believed that overall, the number of sessions had been reduced, flexibility and room for clinical judgment had decreased, premature termination had become common, there were too many restrictions on patients served, referrals for medication had increased, use of protocols for treatment and the use of treatments outside of their primary orientation had increased, and the amount of assessment time had decreased. The negative effect of managed care on assessment is also seen in a recent survey of over 400 psychologists, in which over half reported that choice of tests, the number of tests, and the time invested in testing have been negatively impacted (Rupert & Baird, 2004). Other aspects of managed care identified as being stressful on psychologists are external constraints on services, managed care reimbursement rates, and excessive paperwork (Rupert & Baird, 2004).

Various difficulties may arise when trying to balance the needs of managed health care and the needs of patients. At times, it may be difficult to know exactly who one is working for, client or corporation. One issue that arises in independent practice is the balancing of a patient's confidentiality and privacy with the need to keep third-party providers informed about the patient's progress and need for continued treatment. In the previously mentioned study, 75% of psychologists strongly believed that contact with managed care and utilization review compromises patient confidentiality (Murphy et al., 1998). Here, as in other areas of practice affected by managed care, there appears to be a struggle between what is required by managed care and what psychologists believe is the ethical course of action. In the opinion of one practitioner, "There is nothing private about private practice, at least when it is practiced with a managed care patient. Private practice is an oxymoron in the age of managed care" (Wolf, 1999, p. 114).

Previous work has suggested that the pressures of managed care on clinicians, such as loss of autonomy, the stress of dealing with ethical dilemmas, and feelings of frustration after having treatment recommendations denied, may eventually reduce morale and increase the potential for burnout among psychologists (Kisch, 1992; Wooley, 1993). Some smaller surveys of the impact of managed care in specific states further reveal how the pressures involved with managed care may be compromising effective and ethical practice. A 1998 survey of psychologists in New Jersey (Rothbaum, Bernstein, Haller, Phelps, & Kohout, 1998) found that those with high managed care caseloads reported an increase in paperwork, a decrease in the overall number of sessions, and a drop in morale. Perhaps more important, they reported pressure to compromise quality of care and ethical principles under these circumstances. Higher proportions of managed care caseloads also have been associated with working longer hours, having more client contact, receiving less supervision, reporting more negative client behaviors, experiencing more stress, being less satisfied with income levels, and showing higher scores on emotional exhaustion (Rupert & Baird, 2004).

The implications of these findings serve to underscore the importance of preparing graduates interested in pursuing a career in private practice for the demands and ever-changing nature of managed health care in the area of mental health. Some of the major concerns and stressors indicated in the numerous surveys conducted over the past decade (i.e., dealing with paperwork, resolving ethical dilemmas related to disclosure of confidential information to third-party providers) are issues that are rarely, if ever, taught or discussed with graduate students. The increasing importance of documentation and record keeping in the field, due in large part to the increase in lawsuits and malpractice claims, also needs to be stressed to those preparing for private practice. What may be more difficult to convey is how difficult and stressful it can become for practicing professionals to stay up-to-date with their documentation and administrative duties, along with the substantial amount of time this may take. As this is generally not the reason why most practitioners go into private practice, the commitment to these side duties may become a large source of strain and frustration, and practitioners should be aware of and ready for this when entering practice.

THERAPIST BURNOUT AND IMPAIRMENT

Once in private practice, it may be difficult to ascertain exactly how much work and stress one can handle independently versus when help may be required. Multiple stressors exist in the practice of psychology, many of which can potentially cause serious distress or impairment if allowed to continue unchecked. Sherman and Thelen (1998) examined potential causes of distress and impairment for psychologists, comparing stress associated with life events and stress caused from work-related factors. The authors found that malpractice claims, changed work situations (e.g., different work responsibilities, major changes in working conditions or hours), inadequate time for all obligations, office politics, and conflicts in relationships with colleagues were all among the most distressing work-related factors in clinical practice. The greatest impairment at work was caused by malpractice claims and restrictions imposed by managed care companies. Questions have been raised as to whether psychologists can adequately perform their duties while they are distressed, and although this debate continues, research findings (Nathan, 1986) indicate high correlations between life distress and life impairment and work distress and work impairment. Distress was defined as "the interference in ability to practice therapy, which may be sparked by a variety of factors and results in a decline in therapeutic effectiveness" (p. 79). These data appear to indicate that many psychologists are not only experiencing high levels of distress, but their work, and therefore their patients, are also suffering as a consequence. The study also found that reducing the average number of client contact hours per week was not related to improvements in work distress or impairment, and that working in a private practice (versus group practice) did not appear to be related to levels of work distress, impairment, or professional satisfaction. This information may be especially salient for young professionals who are just beginning their practice, as their level of stress is likely to be high due to the inherent challenges associated with beginning a private practice in psychology.

Another potential cause of professional impairment that may be difficult for the independent practitioner to become aware of is burnout, which has three defining features: (1) emotional exhaustion, (2) depersonalization (defined as a negative and cynical attitude about one's clients), and (3) decreased sense of personal accomplishment and/or an increased likelihood of evaluating oneself and one's work negatively (Rupert & Morgan, 2005). The consequences of burnout impact both the therapist and clients, often resulting in impaired delivery and quality of services and significant stress to all individuals involved. Although research on burnout among psychologists has provided mixed results, a consistent finding is less burnout and lower levels of stress among independent practitioners when compared to agency-employed psychologists (e.g., Ackerly, Burnell, Holder, & Kurdek, 1988; Farber, 1985; Hellman and Morrison, 1987; Raquepaw and Miller, 1989; Vredenburgh, Carlozzi, & Stein, 1999). Different reasons have been hypothesized for why this finding exists, including that independent practitioners have greater control over their work activities and environment, they have fewer bureaucratic responsibilities, and they often have more say in choosing which clients they see and thus potentially see less disturbed clients. These reasons may have been true at the time these studies were conducted, but the more recent emergence of managed health care has significantly changed the environment of independent practice by reducing the amount of control and autonomy practitioners have, along with increasing financial uncertainty, creating more ethical challenges, and increasing therapist workloads. Recent studies examining burnout report similar overall rates among practitioners in comparison to studies conducted prior to the advent of managed care (Rupert & Morgan, 2005). This seems to suggest that although the health care environment may be changing in numerous ways, it does not appear to be increasing levels of burnout among practicing professionals. This does not suggest that burnout and emotional exhaustion are not serious problems faced by psychologists, as roughly 44% of respondents in the Rupert and Morgan investigation scored within the high burnout range.

Emotional exhaustion is a critical first sign of burnout. Factors related to emotional exhaustion include total hours worked, administrative and paperwork hours, managed care client percentage, negative client behaviors, and overinvolvement with clients. It is imperative that professional practitioners make efforts to safeguard their own mental health in order that they may have the energy and cognitive resources to be of maximum benefit to their clients. Potential strategies to help reduce or prevent burnout include increased self-monitoring and awareness of one's own levels of stress and symptoms of burnout, increasing one's social support network and working relationships with colleagues in the field, attending professional development workshops and seminars on prevention of burnout, and becoming involved in state or nationwide professional organizations that may provide help or support in areas causing the greatest amount of stress.

ETHICAL AND LEGAL ISSUES
IN INDEPENDENT PRACTICE

Conflict of Interest

Certain pressures exist in private practice that are unique to this setting, one of the most notable being the pressure to keep one's clients happy. This is important for a variety of reasons—not only therapeutically, but also from a business perspective. In other settings, a client's deciding to leave therapy may have detrimental effects on the progress of therapy and that client's recovery. The same is true for a client terminating therapy when seeing a private practitioner, but now there is an added financial aspect from the point of view of the therapist. An unhappy client who terminates has an immediate impact on the income of the practice, as well as having the potential to affect new referrals if that client chooses to make his or her unhappiness known to friends, family, and colleagues. The issue may be even more complex in the practice of clinical child psychology, as the client typically encompasses the family, which may include two parents (who may disagree on the course of therapy) and siblings, as well as the child or adolescent for whom the referral was initially made. As many child referrals come from school systems, the satisfaction of teachers and school counselors also may be relevant factors. Within larger organizations where financial and legal responsibilities are largely shouldered by others, the practitioner may feel more comfortable addressing clients directly than might a professional in solitary practice (Applebaum, 1992). The importance of this matter is also reflected in the kind of clients an independent practitioner chooses to accept. One survey has shown that approximately 30% of practicing psychologists have avoided taking on certain clients due to fear of being sued (Pope, Tabachnick, & Keith-Spiegel, 1987). In this case, not only is there a fear of having a client terminate prematurely with a potential loss of income, but the therapist is acting defensively and preemptively to protect his or her own interests for fear of being drawn into a lawsuit. Although such fear is understandable in some ways, this still leaves the potential client in the community without active treatment—an ethically questionable situation that may not be such a great concern for psychologists who are not acting in constant fear of litigation.

Fees

Another issue concerns decisions regarding appropriate charges for services. Managed health care and insurance complicates this matter even further, yet the basic need to set appropriate fees still exists and the practitioner is left with a difficult decision to make. With only a certain amount of time and space for clients, decisions must be made in respect to who will be seen. Will the therapist choose to see clients on a first-come-first-served basis, give preference to cases he or she finds most interesting, or accept only those who have the greatest ability to pay? Apart from client selection considerations, the dilemma about specific fees is an obvious one: Charge too little and the practice may not survive despite having many clients; charge too much and risk having too few clients to pay the bills at all. Some practitioners may consider charging clients on a sliding-scale system, where fees are based on the client's income level. However, the problem of making enough income to keep the business afloat will continue if the majority of clients are being charged the minimal fee allowed. Many clients may still not be able to pay the lowest fee allotted, leaving the therapist to decide how much time can be spent doing pro bono work. Further, regulations exist restricting differential fees for clients covered by insurance compared to those who are not covered.

The complication of reimbursement by insurance raises ethical issues for many private practitioners. In a 1987 survey of 456 practicing APA psychologists, Pope et al. found that over half the respondents reported altering an insurance diagnosis to meet insurance criteria—in other words, committing insurance fraud—either rarely (26.5%) or more frequently (35.1%). A more recent report indicates that 49% of psychologists believed other psychologists were altering patient diagnoses to help receive reimbursement, and 59% believed others were altering diagnoses to help patients get reimbursed (Murphy et al., 1998). This illegal and unethical behavior may be occurring more frequently in private practice settings, where the need to retain clients is high and oversight is low.

Termination

Similar to the dilemma of trying to keep the client happy and remain in therapy, the decision about when to terminate may cause a certain ethical conflict between client and therapist. Even if treatment goals are set out at the beginning of therapy, whether they are defined as reducing symptoms or achieving more broad life goals, the therapist is put in the difficult position of having to willingly terminate not only a client, but also a source of income for the practice. This dilemma can actually work both ways, with some therapists terminating treatment early if the client is particularly difficult or unrewarding to work with, and others prolonging therapy with clients who may have achieved all they initially set out to when entering into therapy. Again, the issue of personal needs versus client needs enters into the decision-making process while in private practice, with the potential consequences of these decisions affecting client and therapist, both monetarily and emotionally.

Leaving Practice

Psychologists choose to change their professional positions for many reasons. Whether due to financial difficulties, taking a new position elsewhere, disputes with colleagues, or simply a desire to discontinue practicing psychology, many psychologists will at one point in their career face the reality of leaving their current position or workplace. This may be an especially difficult situation for a private practitioner, who faces multiple legal and ethical dilemmas when leaving private practice. Professional ethics codes, including that of the APA (2002), discuss the importance and obligation for clinicians not to abandon their clients. As Barnett (2001, p. 183) succinctly states, "Simply leaving a practice without addressing each patient's treatment needs, arranging for a smooth transition if transfer of care is in order, or preparing patients for termination would appear contrary to the intent of relevant case law and the ethics codes of all mental health professions." Steps must be taken to ensure that the client's needs have been fully documented, met, and followed up on when a transition takes place between therapy providers. This may be especially important, not only ethically but legally, for clients who present with any sort of imminent crisis or risk. In all circumstances, it is best to anticipate and avoid potential problems with terminating or transferring clients rather than deal with the consequences of inappropriate action after the fact.

When working with other professionals, it is important to clearly outline legal responsibility prior to entering into the business relationship, seeking consultation and guidance on noncompetition clauses, record ownership, and the disposal of client records. Noncompetition clauses prohibit a departing psychologist from setting up another practice for approximately 1 to 3 years within a certain geographical area. This essentially protects a practice from a psychologist who "use[s] the practice's reputation, resources, and referral sources and then, after establishing a local reputation, leaves the practice and opens an office in the local area, taking along the patients the practice provided" (Barnett, 2001, p. 184). Record ownership generally remains with the practice and must be maintained there in accordance with state laws and ethical standards. If the client chooses to seek treatment elsewhere, copies of records can be sent to the new therapist, but the original client record with treatment reports and notes remain the property of the practice. Prior to such events, detailed plans should be made concerning the retention, storage, and potential destruction of records in accordance with state laws and regulations. Practitioners should pay special attention to the required retention times of different types of patient records, both for liability reasons and in the event a client chooses to return at a later time. This may be especially important with underage clients, whose files are required to be stored until 3 years past their age of majority. Knowledge of applicable laws and regulations is of utmost importance, as these may differ across states. Specific requirements now exist in some states outlining the proper course of action should a client's file need to be destroyed, including the notification of the former patient in writing that his or her records will be destroyed, the date of the planned record disposal, and how the record or a summary of it may be obtained prior to that date.

Rural Practice

One of the first things that one must consider in establishing a private practice is where the practice will be located. A basic distinction can be made between deciding to open a practice in an urban or a rural setting. When choosing the latter, a number of ethical issues arise specific to practicing psychology in a rural community. A recent study (Helbok, Marinelli, & Walls, 2006) found that psychologists in small towns or rural areas are significantly more likely to encounter and engage in multiple relationship behaviors and situations, have a higher degree of visibility (feeling as though they are therapists 24 hours a day, running into clients in the community, participating in events in which clients are also participating), are more likely to prepare their clients for chance encounters, and are more likely to learn information about the client from sources other than the client. A private practitioner choosing to open practice in this setting must be willing to be known as an individual and a member of the community and not just as a therapist. The alternative is to restrict one's social activities by avoiding local establishments, which may not even be a viable option in very isolated communities. Even if avoidance is a possibility, the personal toll this may take on the psychologist should be considered; therapists should not strive to isolate themselves from the community in which they live. In rural settings, clients are likely to know more about a therapist's private life and daily activities outside of practice, which may be difficult for some practitioners to accept and should be considered before choosing to operate in such settings.

Aside from operating within a small community defined by geographical and population standards, psychologists may also practice within a small community of persons who share something in common, whether that be religion, ethnicity, personal disability, sexual orientation, or a special interest. Maintaining boundaries may be difficult enough in an urban setting, but being a member of a small and visible minority group within a rural community may present even greater difficulties to the practicing psychologist. Here, where personal interests and beliefs may become known to the community, the psychologist may need to be sensitive to integrating these in the therapy setting, where a client's beliefs may be contrary to the therapist's and potentially interfere with the therapeutic relationship. Difficulties exist in striking a balance between being accepted in the community as a person and maintaining professional boundaries.

Boundaries of Competence

As mentioned previously, the financial burdens related to private practice require a certain amount of income to be maintained to keep the practice operating. This pressure, in some cases, may tempt therapists to practice outside of their boundaries of competence. This presents a complicated ethical dilemma, one where more shades of gray may exist than clear-cut answers. The APA Ethics Code (APA, 2002, p. 1063) states, "Psychologists provide services, teach, and conduct research with populations and in areas only within their boundaries of competence, based on their education, training, supervised experience, consultation, study, or professional experience." No clear definition of competence is given in the Code; however, Knapp and VandeCreek (2003, p. 49) assert that the "general rule is that psychologists can ascertain if they have become proficient in a certain area of practice after submitting their work to external feedback," although they acknowledge that this becomes difficult for practitioners to achieve once they have left their doctoral program and are practicing independently. Complicating matters further, the Ethics Code allows for provisions to this rule, whereby psychologists can provide services with different populations, techniques, areas, or technologies as long they "undertake relevant education, training, supervised experience, consultation, or study" (p. 52).

Faced with these dilemmas, it may be especially difficult for independent practitioners to know exactly when they are practicing outside of their area of competence. A balance must be struck between keeping a steady flow of new clients, being open to accepting people of varied diversity and backgrounds with different presenting problems, and ensuring that the skills necessary to treat these individuals are present and do not stretch the therapist's competency boundaries too far so that treatment itself becomes unethical, potentially causing more harm than benefit. With little or no external feedback, the independent practitioner must be able to evaluate his or her own competencies, abilities, and weaknesses and make firm decisions as to who can be seen and who would be better suited by being referred to another mental health professional.

Cultural Competency

A recent sample of professional psychologists (Hansen et al., 2006) revealed that a large proportion are practicing culturally sensitive therapy with their clients. Respecting a client's worldview and individuality, being aware of personal and societal biases (both positive and negative), establishing rapport in racially/ethnically sensitive ways, and considering the impact of race/ethnicity in diagnosis were all endorsed by at least 80% of those responding. Other areas suggest need for improvement: 50% of the sample rarely or never made efforts to improve their multicultural competencies (by creating a plan and seeking consultation or feedback), negotiating therapist-client language differences, using various resources to augment treatment (literature, translators, and indigenous healers), referring a client to a more qualified provider, and using racially/ethnically sensitive data-gathering techniques. The authors of the survey provide some hypotheses as to why these behaviors are not occurring more frequently, most notably that it may not necessarily be lack of knowledge, but rather that clinicians may be constrained by institutional or managed care mandates. Many of the behaviors listed as not being practiced would require substantial time and effort on the part of the practitioner to remedy, time and effort that may simply not be available given the stressful nature and demands of private practice. Alternatively, the authors suggest that it may be an issue of choice, as 51% of respondents indicated that they believe they were very or extremely multiculturally competent. Considering themselves experts, these practitioners may not believe they need to be any more sensitive or competent than they already are. This study further found a significant difference in what the psychologists practiced and their beliefs, indicating that they did not consistently behave in a manner congruent with what they believed is important for competent practice with a multicultural population (Hansen et al., 2006).

Given this knowledge, it is important for independent practitioners to ensure that they are continually taking steps to improve their cultural sensitivity and awareness rather than simply believing they are competent in this area. As supervision and consultation are often difficult to come by when practicing independently, practitioners should take steps to create a professional development plan that addresses any weaknesses that may detract from their ability to provide psychological services to minority groups in their community. Other behaviors that may help include "increasing the amount of culture-specific case consultations, reading relevant literature, developing a referral network of competent clinicians and translators, and learning about indigenous resources" (Hansen et al., 2006, p. 72).

SPECIAL CONSIDERATIONS WITH CHILD CLIENTS

One area of independent practice that merits further attention is that of child and adolescent populations. The number of children and adolescents with emotional and mental disorders ranges between 14% and 22% (Brandenburg, Friedman, & Silver,

1990), yet the number of private practitioners whose clinical focus is on children and adolescents remains low, and some evidence points to a national shortage of clinical child psychology specialists (Hanley, 1994; Tuma, 1989). Culbertson (1993, p. 119) states, "The United States continues to have serious deficiencies in the delivery of its mental health services for children. . . . An obvious problem is personnel shortage—there simply are not enough mental health professionals training to work with children." Overall, a need exists for greater numbers of practitioners and improved quality of mental health care for children, as the majority of the 8 million children in need of some form of mental health treatment will go unseen (Roberts, 1994).

Given this state of affairs, there is a pressing need to increase the number of graduates from clinical child psychology specialty programs. The APA defines clinical child psychology as

> a specialty of professional psychology which brings together the basic tenets of clinical psychology with a thorough background in child, adolescent and family development and developmental psychopathology. Clinical child and adolescent psychologists conduct scientific research and provide psychological services to infants, toddlers, children, and adolescents. The research and practices of Clinical Child Psychology are focused on understanding, preventing, diagnosing, and treating psychological, cognitive, emotional, developmental, behavioral, and family problems of children. Of particular importance to clinical child and adolescent psychologists is a scientific understanding of the basic psychological needs of children and adolescents and how the family and other social contexts influence socioemotional adjustment, cognitive development, behavioral adaptation, and health status of children and adolescents. . . . A defining feature of Clinical Child Psychology is the emphasis on understanding children from the perspective of both normal development and of psychopathology. Particular attention is given to specialty-specific skills for working with such diverse populations and an appreciation for those cultural, ethnic, and other diversity-related factors that must be considered in clinical practice. (APA Commission for the Recognition of Specialties and Proficiencies in Professional Psychology, 2005)

While general practitioners continue to provide a valuable service, we contend that to best meet the needs of today's youth, professionals working with substantive child or adolescent caseloads should be trained specialists.

As alluded to previously, presenting problems of children and adolescents often warrant contact with many individuals beyond the specified client. Academic performance problems and disruptive behavior in school settings are common presenting complaints. Competent assessment and intervention necessarily warrant involvement of parents as well as school personnel. Further, observations in school or home settings may be particularly advantageous. Unfortunately, independent practitioners may find it difficult to take the time for visits off-site, and equally problematic is the difficulty in obtaining reimbursement for such services. We encourage professionals to continue to lobby for appropriate funding for empirically supported assessment and intervention strategies to properly serve child and adolescent populations. In the meantime, professionals may elect to make consistent use of school-home notes and phone calls to relevant parties (see Kelly & McCain, 1995).

SUMMARY

Professional psychology has undergone significant advances since its inception. Research efforts have allowed us to continually improve our ability to accurately identify and provide treatment for those in need of services. The practice of professional psychology may be as varied as the number of individuals engaged in the pursuit. Although no single theoretical platform has been adopted, the prevailing sentiment is toward increased accountability and primary implementation of empirically supported strategies. Future efforts must be directed toward increasing the number of clinical child specialists, as the demand currently exceeds availability and the shortfall is expected to increase as the number of children and adolescents suffering from mental health problems continues to rise worldwide. In addition, we would be remiss if we did not highlight the pressing need for training in business management practices for those planning to undertake careers in independent practice. The many challenges and hours of hard work invested in a career in private practice can ultimately result in an exciting and rewarding career path, with the long-term benefit of professional independence and flexibility in one's work as a practice grows over time. Though professional psychologists are no doubt confronted with challenges on a regular basis, the vast majority report that the perceived benefits far exceed the disadvantages. For many of us, seeing just one child or adult improve, either through the efforts of our research or through direct service provision, makes all the years of training worthwhile.

REFERENCES

Ackerly, G. D., Burnell, J., Holder, D. C., & Kurdek, L. A. (1988). Burnout among licensed psychologists. *Professional Psychology: Research and Practice, 19*, 624–631.

American Psychological Association. (1987a). General guidelines for providers of psychological services. *American Psychologist, 42*, 712–723.

American Psychological Association. (1987b). Model act for state licensure of psychologists. *American Psychologist, 42*, 696–703.

American Psychological Association. (2002). Ethical principles of psychologists and code of conduct. *American Psychologist, 57*, 1060–1073.

American Psychological Association Commission for the Recognition of Specialties and Proficiencies in Professional Psychology: Archival description of clinical child psychology. (2005). Retrieved August 20, 2006, from http://www.apa.org/crsppp/childclinic.html.

Applebaum, S. A. (1992). Evils in the private practice of psychotherapy. *Bulletin of the Menninger Clinic, 56*, 141–149.

Barnett, J. E. (2001). Leaving a practice: Ethical and legal issues and dilemmas. In L. VandeCreek, S. Knapp, & T. L. Jackson (Eds.), *Innovations in clinical practice: Vol. 15. A source book* (pp. 181–188). Sarasota, FL: Professional Resource Press.

Barnett, J. E., & Henshaw, E. (2003). Training to begin a private practice. In M. J. Prinstein, & M. D. Patterson (Eds.), *The portable mentor: Expert guide to a successful career in psychology* (pp. 145–156). New York: Kluwer Academic/Plenum Press.

Blau, T. H. (1983). Roles and professional practice. In M. Hersen, A. Kazdin, & A. Bellack (Eds.), *The clinical psychology handbook* (pp. 57–62). New York: Pergamon Press.

Brandenburg, N. A., Friedman, R. M., & Silver, S. F. (1990). The epidemiology of childhood psychiatric disorders: Prevalence findings from recent studies. *Journal of the American Academy of Child and Adolescent Psychiatry, 29*, 76–83.

Cantor, D. W., & Moldawsky, S. (1985). Training for independent practice: A survey of graduate programs in clinical psychology. *Professional Psychology: Research and Practice, 16*, 768–772.

Culbertson, J. L. (1993). Clinical child psychology in the 1990's: Broadening our scope. *Journal of Clinical Child Psychology, 22*, 116–122.

Earle, R. H., & Barnes, D. J. (1999). *Independent practice for the mental health professional: Growing a private practice for the 21st century*. Philadelphia: Brunner/Mazel.

Farber, B. A. (1985). Clinical psychologists' perceptions of psychotherapeutic work. *Clinical Psychologist, 38*, 10–13.

Finch, F. H., & Odoroff, M. E. (1939). Employment trends in applied psychology. *Journal of Consulting Psychology, 3*, 118–122.

Habben, C. J. (2005). Group practice: Adapting private practice to the new marketplace. In R. D. Morgan, & T. L. Kuther (Eds.), *Life after graduate school in psychology: Insiders advice from new psychologists* (pp. 87–96). New York: Psychology Press.

Hanley, J. H. (1994). Use of bachelor-level psychology majors in the provision of mental health services to children, adolescents, and their families. *Journal of Clinical Child Psychology, 23*, 55–58.

Hansen, N. D., Randazzo, K. V., Schwartz, A., Marshall, M., Kalis, D., Frazier, R., et al. (2006). Do we practice what we preach? An exploratory survey of multicultural psychotherapy competencies. *Professional Psychology: Research and Practice, 37*, 66–74.

Helbok, C. M., Marinelli, R. P., & Walls, R. T. (2006). National survey of ethical practices across rural and urban communities. *Professional Psychology: Research and Practice, 37*, 36–44.

Hellman, I. D., & Morrison, T. L. (1987). Practice setting and type of caseload as factors in psychotherapist stress. *Psychotherapy: Theory, Research, Practice and Training, 24*, 427–433.

Kelley, M. L., & McCain, A. P. (1995). Promoting academic performance in inattentive children: The relative efficacy of school-home notes with and without response cost. *Behavior Modification, 3*, 357–375.

Kisch, J. (1992). Psychotherapy: Dilemmas of practice in managed care. *Psychotherapy in Private Practice, 11*, 33–37.

Knapp, S., & VandeCreek, L. (2003). *A guide to the 2002 revision of the American Psychological Association's ethics code*. Sarasota, FL: Professional Resource Press.

Kohout, J., & Wicherski, M. (2003). *1999 doctorate employment survey*. Washington, DC: American Psychological Association.

Murphy, M. J., DeBernardo, C. R., & Shoemaker, W. E. (1998). Impact of managed care on independent practice and professional ethics: A survey of independent practitioners. *Professional Psychology: Research and Practice, 29*, 43–51.

Nathan, P. E. (1986). Unanswered questions about distressed professionals. In R. R. Kilburg, P. E. Nathan, & R. W. Thoreson (Eds.), *Professionals in distress: Issues, syndromes, and solutions in psychology* (pp. 27–36). Washington, DC: American Psychological Association.

Phelps, R., Eisman, E. J., & Kohout, J. (1998). Psychological practice and managed care: Results of the CAPP practitioner survey. *Professional Psychology: Research and Practice, 29*, 31–36.

Pope, K. S., Tabachnick, B. G., & Keith-Spiegel, P. (1987). The beliefs and behaviors of psychologists as therapists. *American Psychologist, 42*, 993–1006.

Raquepaw, J. M., & Miller, R. S. (1989). Psychotherapist burnout: A componential analysis. *Professional Psychology: Research and Practice, 20*, 32–36.

Roberts, M. C. (1994). Models for service delivery in children's mental health: Common characteristics. *Journal of Clinical Child Psychology, 23*, 212–219.

Rothbaum, P. A., Bernstein, D. M., Haller, O., Phelps, R., & Kohout, J. (1998). New Jersey psychologists' report on managed mental health care. *Professional Psychology: Research and Practice, 29*, 37–42.

Rupert, P. A., & Baird, K. A. (2004). Managed care and the independent practice of psychology. *Professional Psychology: Research and Practice, 35*, 185–193.

Rupert, P. A., & Morgan, D. J. (2005). Work setting and burnout among professional psychologists. *Professional Psychology: Research and Practice, 36*, 544–550.

Sherman, M. D., & Thelen, M. H. (1998). Distress and professional impairment among psychologists in clinical practice. *Professional Psychology: Research and Practice, 29*, 79–85.

Todd, J., & Bohart, A. C. (2003). *Foundations of clinical and counseling psychology* (3rd ed.) Long Grove, IL: Waveland Press.

Tuma, J. M. (1989). Mental health services for children: The state of the art. *American Psychologist, 50,* 789–793.

U.S. Department of Labor, Bureau of Labor Statistics. (2006). *Occupational outlook handbook: Psychology.* Retrieved September 5, 2006, from http://www.bls.gov/oco/ocos056.htm.

Vineberg, D. (2005). Independent practice: Alive or dead? In R. D. Morgan, & T. L. Kuther (Eds.), *Life after graduate school in psychology: Insiders advice from new psychologists* (pp. 87–96). New York, NY: Psychology Press.

Vredenburgh, L. D., Carlozzi, A. F., & Stein, L. B. (1999). Burnout in counseling psychologists: Type of practice setting and patient demographics. *Counseling Psychology Quarterly, 12,* 293–302.

Wicherski, M., & Kohout, J. (2005). *2003 doctorate employment survey.* Washington, DC: American Psychological Association.

Wolf, P. (1999). "Private" practice: An oxymoron in the age of managed healthcare. In K. Weisgerber (Ed.), *The traumatic bond between the psychotherapist and managed care* (pp. 105–122). Lanham, MD: Aronson.

Wooley, S. C. (1993). Managed care and mental health: The silencing of a profession. *International Journal of Eating Disorders, 14,* 387–401.

CHAPTER 4

Ethical and Legal Issues

David Mark Mantell

This chapter is divided into two sections. The first addresses the Ethical Standards and Guidelines of the American Psychological Association (APA) and its committees as these pertain to children and adolescents. It is governed by Table 4.1, which lists the APA documents. The second section focuses on the investigative and practice guidelines published by national organizations such as the American Prosecutors Research Institute (APRI), the American Professional Society on the Abuse of Children (APSAC), and the American Academy of Child and Adolescent Psychiatry (AACAP). Comparative research reports relevant to the interface of clinical and forensic child and adolescent psychology are cited in this section. This discussion may aid the psychologist seeking to determine when a guideline assists or may compromise professional practice.

ETHICAL STANDARDS AND GUIDELINES OF THE AMERICAN PSYCHOLOGICAL ASSOCIATION

Fifteen publications of the APA that contain statements of ethical standards and policy and practice guidelines have been reviewed. Table 4.1 identifies these documents and which of these speak to children, adolescents, and their families. For a psychologist seeking guidance regarding an ethics or practice guideline issue, the document's name provides some orientation. No one guideline is an exclusive source for ethical standards and principles on a particular topic. Hence, familiarity with them all is important. Legal standards vary from state to state and are found in state statutes and case law. Both of these topics are beyond the scope of this chapter. State resources may be particularly helpful in assisting psychologists to find and apply ethical guidelines to particular cases and issues. Some state psychological associations publish a compendium of laws affecting the practice of psychology.* State licensing boards and associations may provide, on request, a listing and copy of laws defining the practice of psychology in that state. The ethics chair of the state psychological association may be of help with the same issues and also in identifying attorneys who specialize in defending psychologists in grievance and malpractice actions. Malpractice insurance carriers have an interest in assisting psychologists to practice

---

*See A Compendium of Laws Affecting the Practice of Psychology (1987) Connecticut Psychological Association.

Table 4.1   Ethical Principles, Standards, and Policies Published by the American
Psychological Association

Document Name	Applies
Ethical Principles of Psychologists and Code of Conduct (APA, 2002c)	✓
Determination and Documentation of the Need for Practice Guidelines (APA, 2005a)	
Guidelines for Psychological Practice with Older Adults (APA, 2004b)	
Record Keeping Guidelines (APA, 1993)	
Guidelines for Child Custody Evaluations in Divorce Proceedings (APA, 1994)	✓
Guidelines for Psychological Evaluations in Child Protection Matters (APA, 1999)	✓
Guidelines for Psychotherapy with Lesbian, Gay, and Bisexual Clients (APA, 2000)	✓
Guidelines on Multicultural Education, Training, Research, Practice, and Organization Change for Psychologists (APA, 2002d)	✓
Criteria for Evaluating Treatment Guidelines (APA, 2002a)	
Criteria for Practice Guideline Development and Evaluation (APA, 2002b)	
Guidelines for Providers of Psychological Services to Ethnic, Linguistic, and Culturally Diverse Populations (APA, 1990)	✓
APA Resolution on Outpatient Civil Commitment (APA, 2004a)	✓
Training Grid Outlining Best Practices for Recovery and Improved Outcomes for People with Serious Mental Illness (APA, 2005c)	
Policy Statement on Evidence-Based Practice in Psychology (APA, 2005b)	✓
Specialty Guidelines for Forensic Psychologists (1991)	✓

Note: Applies = Applies to children, adolescents, and their families.

defensively and to avoid litigation. For practicing psychologists who are insured, contacting your carrier for recommendations and for standards and case law that affect your practice can be helpful. Sometimes an attorney will offer a legal opinion.

Ethical standards and guidelines are often revised and updated. There is no one location at the APA to access all of its guidelines and statements regarding ethical conduct and professional guidelines. This also is true of the APA web page. It can be challenging to become informed and to stay abreast of national and state laws and professional standards and guidelines that effect clinical and forensic practice.

1. The Ethical Principles of Psychologists and Code of Conduct

The Ethical Principles of Psychologists and Code of Conduct (APA, 2002c) is the major ethics guideline for psychologists in the United States. It does not contain subsections that specifically refer to adolescents and children. The general principles and ethical standards apply in general to professional activity regardless of client's age. For professionals serving adolescents and children, the principles and standards are clear. It is expected that the professional will have appropriate training and experience; will be knowledgeable about assessment instruments and procedures and their strengths and limitations; will avoid multiple relationships, sexual involvement, and questionable treatments and practices; and will obtain informed consent from authorized guardians and others for professional contact with minors.

The Ethics Code applies to the activities of psychologists in their scientific, educational, and professional roles, and includes the clinical, counseling, and school practice of psychology, research, teaching, trainee supervision, and professional activities of psychologists in the public sector. The Ethics Code applies to activities in a number of contexts, including in person, postal, telephone, and Internet communications. Psychologists are advised to consider the Ethics Code of the APA as well as applicable laws and psychology board regulations and decisions. Psychologists are urged to be alert to potential conflicts between the Ethics Code, their own conscience, and state and federal law, and to seek to resolve any such conflicts in a responsible manner.

The APA Ethics Code lists five general principles that are "aspirational" in nature, that is, which have the intent to inspire psychologists to the highest ethical ideals. These aspirational principles are not meant to be a basis for imposing sanctions. The principles include striving to benefit those with whom one works; establishing relationships of trust; promoting accuracy, honesty, and truthfulness in professional conduct; recognizing that fairness and justice entitle all persons access to the benefits of psychological practice; and respecting the dignity and worth of all people as well as their rights to privacy and confidentiality. Psychologists are urged to be mindful and respectful of individual differences based on age, sex, gender identity, race, ethnicity, culture, national origin, religion, sexual orientation, disability, language, and socioeconomic status and, with these sensitivities and knowledge in mind, to strive to eliminate bias from professional practice.

Ten ethical standards are defined in the Ethics Code. These are:

1. Resolving ethical issues
2. Competence
3. Human relations
4. Privacy and confidentiality
5. Advertising and other public statements
6. Record keeping and fees
7. Education and training
8. Research and publication
9. Assessment
10. Therapy

Each of these ethical standards has a number of subsections.

Ethical Standard 1

Psychologists are required to take reasonable steps to correct or minimize the misuse or misrepresentation of their work. They are expected to abide by the law and take steps to resolve conflicts when conflicts between the law, professional practice, and other ethical standards and regulations are perceived. This includes recognizing conflicts between ethics and organizational demands and resolving them, attempting informal resolution of ethical violations with colleagues, and reporting ethical violations when professional practice has been found to cause harm or there is concern that it may do so. Psychologists are expected to cooperate with ethical investigations and proceedings, not file or encourage the filing of frivolous ethics complaints or without good cause discriminate against someone who has been the subject of an ethics complaint.

Ethical Standard 2

The ethical standard of competence requires psychologists to guide their professional practice based on the limitations of their education, training, supervised experience, consultation, study, and professional experience. Psychologists are required to obtain the training, experience, consultation, and/or supervision to ensure the competency of their professional practice according to the characteristics of the population they serve. They are expected to take "reasonable steps to ensure the competence of their work" and to protect those who receive their services. When working in a forensic role, psychologists are expected to become "reasonably familiar with the judicial or administrative rules governing their roles."

Psychologists are expected to make ongoing efforts to maintain and increase their competence, ensure that their professional practice is based on scientific principles and professional knowledge, delegate work appropriately and only when there is reason to expect it can be performed competently, and avoid the violation of ethical principles and licensure laws in such delegation.

Ethical Standard 3

Psychologists are expected to avoid unfair discrimination, sexual harassment, other forms of harassment, doing harm through professional practice, and conflicts of interest and multiple relationships. Multiple relationships that would "not be reasonably expected to cause impairment or risk exploitation or harm are not unethical." Distinguishing when a multiple relationship, a conflict of interest, and the potential for harm may or may not exist is not explained. Psychologists may want to seek peer and other consultations to clarify ambiguous situations. Psychologists are expected to avoid exploitive relationships, cooperate with other professionals, seek informed consent for their work, and clarify the implications of third-party requests for services that are court ordered or mandated. Also, the psychologist informs the recipient about the nature of the services and about limits of confidentiality. Psychologists who deliver services in an organizational setting are subject to a number of ethical standards that extend the requirements of informed consent, definition of client, issues of confidentiality, and the definition of organizational versus individual rights and responsibilities. Psychologists are expected to make reasonable efforts to plan for continuation of services when service delivery is interrupted.

Ethical Standard 4

Psychologists have an obligation to take reasonable precautions to protect confidential information developed during the course of professional practice. This includes discussing the limits of confidentiality with clients and patients, obtaining permission before recording the voice or image of a client, minimizing intrusions on privacy through professional activity, and obtaining appropriate consent for the disclosure of confidential information. Provisions are made for the disclosure of confidential information without consent. This arises in situations that are mandated by law as needed to perform professional services, to obtain appropriate professional consultation, to protect those involved from harm, and to obtain payment. Disclosure is limited "to the minimum that is necessary to achieve the purpose." Psychologists are expected to disguise the person or organization when using confidential information for public purposes (publications, lectures, etc.) unless there is written consent or legal authorization.

Ethical Standard 5

In advertising and other public statements, psychologists are required to avoid false and deceptive statements both directly and by others whom they have engaged to represent them. Psychologists adhere to the Ethics Code in media presentations and should not solicit testimonials from current therapy clients or exploit the vulnerability of persons who may be actual or potential clients for other business ventures.

Ethical Standard 6

Psychologists are expected to maintain satisfactory documentation of their professional activities and the confidentiality of records, facilitate the appropriate transfer of records, and may not withhold records that are required for emergency treatment because payment has not been received. Psychologists are expected to reach payment and billing arrangements as soon as it is feasible in a professional relationship, state fees clearly, discuss service limitation that may result from limitations in financing as soon as is feasible, inform clients of the intended use of collection agencies or other measures to collect fees, and offer an opportunity for prompt payment. Barter in return for professional services is allowed if the barter is not clinically contraindicated and the arrangement is not exploitive.

Ethical Standard 7

In education and training activities, psychologists are required to uphold APA ethical standards. In the design and delivery of education and training programs, APA standards for licensure, certification, and other goals must be met; program content must be accurately described, including specification of training goals and program completion requirements. Course content must meet ethical standards for professionalism and scientific merit. Unethical demands are not to be made on students. When therapy participation is a program or course requirement, students are allowed to select therapy from practitioners unaffiliated with the program. Here, too, dual relationships are avoided.

Ethical Standard 8

Ethical standards should be maintained in research and publication. This includes obtaining informed consent when this is required and protecting research participants from participation and nonparticipation. Conditions are specified for dispensing with informed consent requirements. These include research that would not be expected to create distress or harm, that involves the study of normal phenomena, and that offers anonymous report forms that do not place participant information or a person at risk. Excessive and inappropriate financial or other rewards for research participation should be avoided. Deception in research should also be avoided, though it can be justified under some circumstances. Psychologists must provide research participants with a debriefing opportunity and information. When they become aware that the research has harmed a participant, reasonable steps must be taken to minimize the harm. Animal research should be conducted in compliance with federal, state, and local laws and regulations and also with professional standards. Psychologists do not plagiarize or fabricate research results. Psychologists must accept publication credit only when it is deserved for work done and contributions made. The position of principal authorship is based on contribution and not status.

Ethical Standard 9

Psychologists provide opinions on the psychological characteristics of people only after proper evaluation and define factors that limit the nature and extent of their conclusions and recommendations. Sources of information are defined. Psychologists use assessment instruments with known validity and reliability for the population evaluated. Language preference and other factors are considered in assessment instrument selection. Assessment instruments are administered, scored, and adapted according to instrument and research guidelines. Informed consent is obtained for assessment and also for the use of interpreter services. This information is conveyed in the report. Issues of confidentiality are maintained. Impact assessment of interpreter involvement is included in a discussion of data limitations. Situational, personal, linguistic, and cultural characteristics of clients as well as test-taking ability are considered along with data characteristics when considering data interpretation and validity. The norms, validity, reliability, and any other special qualifications for the use of assessment and scoring services are acknowledged. Psychologists retain responsibility for test selection, scoring, and interpretation when these aspects are delegated to other persons or to an automated service. Psychologists take reasonable steps to ensure that explanation of assessment results with appropriate qualifications occurs. Test security is maintained.

Ethical Standard 10

Psychologists obtain informed consent for therapy; provide information about the course of therapy, fees, third-party involvement, and limits of confidentiality; and provide the opportunity for questioning and receiving answers. They explain the potential risks of therapy and the availability of alternative treatments and disclose therapy techniques that do not possess established results. When the therapist is a psychologist in training and is supervised, this is disclosed and the name of the supervisor is provided. When psychologists become involved in treating couples and families, the psychologist defines the professional relationship of each person, identifies which person is the client, and avoids role conflict, such as being a couples or family therapist and then a witness for one party in a divorce proceeding. Issues of confusion and conflict are also resolved in a timely fashion when deciding whether to offer services to persons receiving mental health services elsewhere. Psychologists do not provide treatment to persons with whom they have had sexual intimacy and do not have sexual intimacy with current therapy clients. Psychologists do not engage in sexual intimacy with former clients for 2 years after the termination of therapy. Even after the passage of 2 years, a psychologist may be challenged to demonstrate that a sexual involvement with a former client is consistent with the APA Ethics Code.

Therapy is terminated appropriately, such as when the service is no longer needed or is producing no benefit or when the client might be harmed by its continuation. A psychologist may terminate therapy when threatened. Psychologists provide pretermination counseling when feasible and also suggest alternative service providers as appropriate.

2. Determination and Documentation of the Need for Practice Guidelines

Determination and Documentation of the Need for Practice Guidelines (APA, 2005a) is an aspirational document in intent and references statements that are recommended for professional behavior and conduct but that are not mandatory and do not require an enforcement mechanism. Their purpose is to assist the psychologist to provide high-quality services. The Committee on Professional Practice and Standards identified a need for legal and regulatory, public benefit, and professional guidance. This document reflects the recognition that laws, court decisions, professional interaction with the legal system, and changes in regulatory and administrative systems may affect the practice of psychology. For example, *Daubert v. Merrill Dow Pharmaceuticals*, 509 U.S. 579 (1993), defines how expert opinions are to be delivered in court and evaluated there. Guidelines for Child Custody Evaluations in Divorce Proceedings (APA, 1994), Guidelines for Psychological Evaluations in Child Protection Matters (APA, 1999), and Specialty Guidelines for Forensic Psychologists (APA, 1991) are intended to assist the psychological practitioner when interacting with the legal system in the defined legal contexts. This document found that practice guidelines were needed to improve service delivery; avoid harm; meet the needs of emerging, underserved, and vulnerable client populations; and assist psychologists in responding to public policy initiatives. Psychologists may also seek guidelines for new areas of technology, for work in new contexts and emerging areas of practice with new approaches based on scientific advances, and with risk management issues.

3. The Guidelines for Psychological Practice with Older Adults

The Guidelines for Psychological Practice with Older Adults (APA, 2004b) does not apply.

4. Record Keeping Guidelines

Record Keeping Guidelines (APA, 1993) speak to an important area of psychological practice with children and adolescents. Formulated in 1993, these guidelines provide an introduction to documentation issues that receive specialized attention in later sections of this chapter, particularly in reference to forensic practice and documentation of investigatory procedures. Psychologists have many reasons for maintaining records, and the nature and extent of the documentation may vary according to the service performed. Records provide a history and offer a basis for case review, for planning, and for implementation of services. The General Guidelines for Providers of Psychological Services determined that psychologists hold widely varying rules on the wisdom of recording the content of the psychotherapeutic relationship. With respect to record keeping, a 50-state review of laws governing psychologists found substantial differences among the states on this issue. There are differing requirements in areas of professional practice between situations calling for assessment and those calling for psychotherapy.

Well-documented records may help psychologists in professional liability cases where the professional action of a psychologist is at issue.

Records include information about the nature, delivery, progress, and results of psychological services. Because of their nature, they can be reviewed and duplicated. Records of psychological services should minimally include identifying data, dates of services, types of services, fees, assessments, intervention plans, consultation, summary reports, testing reports, release of information, consent forms, and other supporting data. Psychologists are expected to maintain a reasonable degree of accurate, current, and pertinent records with sufficient detail to permit an understanding of the service by another psychologist.

Psychologists maintain the confidentiality of records, make reasonable efforts to protect against their misuse, develop reliable record keeping procedures, and strive to assure that record entries are readable and completed in a time that is proximate to the service delivery, if not simultaneous with it. Records may be maintained in a variety of formats and media. In the absence of laws and regulations to the contrary, these guidelines offer the following time periods for record maintenance:

- Complete records are maintained for a minimum of 3 years.
- Thereafter, a summary is maintained for an additional 12 years.
- If the client is a minor, the record period is extended until 3 years after the age of majority.
- A simple 7-year requirement for the retention of the complete record is preferred. The practitioner is urged to consult specialty guidelines in this regard.

5. Guidelines for Child Custody Evaluations in Divorce Proceedings

Guidelines for Child Custody Evaluations in Divorce Proceedings (APA, 1994) is one of two APA guidelines that address professional practice issues with children and their guardians and parents in legal contexts. Child custody and parenting issues arise in several legal contexts, including parental divorce, guardianship, abuse and neglect proceedings, and termination of parental rights. These guidelines were written specifically for the context of parental divorce, are aspirational in intent, are not mandatory or exhaustive, and have the stated purpose of promoting the efficiency of psychological expertise when conducting child custody evaluations. Psychologists can provide an important service to the courts and to children and families by providing "competent, objective, impartial information in assessing the best interests of the child." Psychologists performing child custody evaluations are expected to possess specialized competencies in the evaluation of adults, children, relationships, and parenting ability. Specific guidelines are discussed under three headings:

- Purpose of a Child Custody Evaluation
- Preparing for a Child Custody Evaluation
- Conducting a Child Custody Evaluation

There are 16 guidelines.

Guideline 1

The primary purpose of the evaluation is to assess the best psychological interests of the child.

Guideline 2

The child's interests and well-being are paramount.

Guideline 3

The focus of the evaluation is on parenting capacity, the psychological and developmental needs of the child, and the resulting fit. This involves focused assessment of parenting capacity in connection with the psychological characteristics and developmental needs of each involved child. Consequently, both adult and child assessments occur, and these include the assessment of the functional ability of each parent to meet the child's needs. An interactional evaluation between each adult and child also occurs.

Guideline 4

The role of the psychologist is that of a professional expert who strives to maintain an objective, impartial stance. The psychologist does not act as a judge or as an advocating attorney and remains impartial, balanced, and objective.

Guideline 5

The psychologist gains specialized competence. This includes competency in performing psychological assessments of children, adults, and families, knowledge of child and family development and child and family psychopathology, and knowledge of laws that govern divorce and custody decisions. This includes adherence to the Standards for Educational and Psychological Testing (APA, 1985). When specialized issues arise that are outside the evaluator's expertise, additional consultation and supervision should be sought.

Guideline 6

The psychologist is aware of personal and societal biases and engages in nondiscriminatory practices.

Guideline 7

The psychologist avoids multiple relationships.

Guideline 8

The scope of the evaluation is determined by the evaluator based on the nature of the referral questions. These may broaden or limit the scope of the evaluation from an entire family to a single family member. Sometimes psychologists are asked to review and critique the report of another mental health professional or serve as an expert in a specialized area of psychological knowledge.

Guideline 9

The psychologist obtains informed consent from all adult participants and, as appropriate, informs child participants. This entails informing each adult participant about the purpose, nature, and method of the evaluation, the source of the evaluation request, to whom the report will be sent, and who pays the fees. Information is given to children as is developmentally and otherwise appropriate.

Guideline 10

The psychologist informs participants about the limits of confidentiality and the disclosure of information. Participants are to be informed that they are consenting to disclosure of the evaluations' findings. It is recommended that the psychologist obtain a waiver of confidentiality from all adult participants.

Guideline 11

The psychologist uses multiple methods of data gathering: clinical interviews, observation, psychological assessments, and documentation from at least two sources about important facts. This can include the review of school, health care, and other kinds of records, and interviewing persons who know the family and who may contribute useful information. When external information is deemed significant, psychologists are urged to corroborate it by an additional source whenever possible.

Guideline 12

The psychologist neither overinterprets nor inappropriately interprets clinical or assessment data. The psychologist is urged to seek convergent validity from multiple sources of information, including interviews and test data, and to cautiously and conservatively interpret evaluation results with awareness of reliability and validity restrictions.

Guideline 13

The psychologist does not give any opinion regarding the psychological functioning of any individual he or she has not personally evaluated.

Guideline 14

Recommendations, if any, are based on what is in the psychological interests of the child. It is noted that the profession itself has not reached consensus about whether psychologists ought to make recommendations about final custody determination to the courts. When the psychologist does make a custody recommendation, this should be based on sound psychological data and reflect the child's best interests in the case at hand.

Guideline 15

The psychologist clarifies financial arrangements.

Guideline 16

The psychologist maintains written records. Reference here is made to the APA Record Keeping Guidelines (APA, 1993) and relevant statutory guidelines. Further discussion of record keeping in the particular area of investigatory interviews is found in a later section of this chapter.

6. Guidelines for Psychological Evaluations in Child Protection Matters

Guidelines for Psychological Evaluations in Child Protection Matters (APA, 1999) is the second APA guideline to address professional practice issues with children. The legal context is litigation in child abuse and neglect cases. This guideline contains useful subsections of 17 guidelines, a glossary of terms, and a bibliography of major professional publications in the field. There is also a useful listing of national information resources, including the American Academy of Pediatrics, the American Bar Association Center on Children and the Law, and the Clearinghouse on Child Abuse and Neglect Information. These guidelines were developed for psychologists conducting psychological evaluations in child protection proceedings and have the goal of promoting "proficiency in using psychological expertise."

They do not address the issues of psychologists acting in other roles, such as when serving as a therapist for an individual or family. These guidelines build on those already discussed, including Ethical Principles of Psychologists in the Code of Conduct (APA, 1992), Record Keeping Guidelines (APA, 1993), and Standards for Educational and Psychological Testing (APA, 1985).

Three stages are described for state intervention in the affairs of the parents and children in child abuse and neglect matters. In the first stage, an investigation occurs following a report of suspected child abuse and neglect. In the second stage, the state may obtain custody of a child and a rehabilitation plan may be developed. When the child cannot be returned to the family, there may be a hearing for the final disposition of the case that can include termination of parental rights. States vary in statutory and case law that applies to these matters. Psychologists may be called on to evaluate the parties and "may function as agents of the court, of a child protection agency, or of the parents." In one or in all of these roles, the psychologist may be called on to evaluate the child, the parents, the parent and child relationship, or parenting capacity; to assess specialized issues such as the impact on the child of abuse and neglect; to recommend therapeutic interventions for the parents and children; and to make predictions about future harm if the child is reconciled with the parents and if parental rights are terminated. Psychologists are urged to develop the specialized knowledge and competencies required to do this work and seek consultation as needed. There are 17 guidelines.

Guideline 1

The primary purpose of the evaluation is to provide relevant, professionally sound results or opinions in matters where a child's health and welfare may have been and/or may in the future be harmed.

Guideline 2

In child protection cases, the child's interest and well-being are paramount.

Guideline 3

The evaluation addresses the particular psychological and developmental needs of the child and/or parents that are relevant to child protection issues such as physical issues, sexual abuse, neglect, and/or serious emotional harm.

Guideline 4

The role of the psychologist conducting the evaluation is that of a professional expert who strives to maintain an unbiased, objective stance.

Guideline 5

The serious consequences of psychological assessment in child protection matters place a heavy burden on psychologists.

Guideline 6

Psychologists gain specialized competence.

Guideline 7

Psychologists are aware of personal and societal biases and engage in nondiscriminatory practice.

Guideline 8

Psychologists avoid multiple relationships.

Guideline 9

On the basis of the nature of the referral questions, the scope of the evaluation is determined by the evaluator.

Guideline 10

Psychologists performing psychological evaluations in child protection matters obtain appropriate informed consent from all adult participants and, as appropriate, inform the child participant. Psychologists need to be particularly sensitive to informed consent issues.

Guideline 11

Psychologists inform participants about the disclosure of information and limits of confidentiality.

Guideline 12

Psychologists use multiple methods of data gathering.

Guideline 13

Psychologists neither overinterpret nor inappropriately interpret clinical or assessment data.

Guideline 14

Psychologists conducting a psychological evaluation in child protection matters provide an opinion regarding the psychological functioning of an individual only after conducting an evaluation of the individual adequate to support their statements or conclusions.

Guideline 15

Recommendations, if offered, are based on whether the child's health and welfare have been and/or may be seriously harmed.

Guideline 16

Psychologists clarify financial arrangements.

Guideline 17

Psychologists maintain appropriate records.

The glossary of terms is useful for psychologists when legal issues define the professional practice context and the evidentiary standards that will be applied to psychological data and opinion. Many of the definitions contained in the glossary were taken from Working with Courts in Child Protection (National Center on Child Abuse and Neglect, 1995). Selected terms are defined (author's selection and sequence):

- *Abuse, emotional:* Also referred to as psychological maltreatment; generally defined as a repeated pattern of behavior that conveys to children that they are worthless, unwanted, or only of value in meeting another's needs; may include serious threats of physical or psychological violence.
- *Abuse, physical:* Generally defined as the suffering of a child or substantial risk that a child will imminently suffer physical harm, inflicted nonaccidentally on him or her by his or her parents or caretakers.
- *Abuse, sexual (child):* Generally defined as contacts between a child and an adult or other persons significantly older or in a position of power or control over the child, where the child is being used for sexual stimulation of the adult or other person.
- *Beyond a reasonable doubt:* Highest standard of proof used in cases where the loss of liberty interests are at stake (e.g., incarceration or loss of life). Generally defined as the highest degree of support or level of certainty (90% to 95% chance).
- *Clear and convincing:* Intermediate standard of proof used in cases where significant liberty interests are at stake (e.g., loss of parental rights, civil commitment). Generally defined as a degree of support or level of certainty (75% chance).
- *Expert witness:* An individual who by reason of education or specialized experience possesses superior knowledge of a subject about which persons having no particular training are incapable of forming an accurate opinion or deducing correct conclusions. A witness who has been qualified as an expert will be allowed (through his or her answers to questions posed) to assist the jury in understanding complicated and technical subjects not within the understanding of the average layperson. Experts are also allowed to provide testimony based on hypothetical scenarios or information and opinions that are not specifically related to the parties in a particular legal action.
- *Fact witness:* Generally defined as an individual who, by being present, personally sees or perceives a thing; a beholder, spectator, or eyewitness. One who testifies to what he or she has seen, heard, or otherwise observed regarding a circumstance, event, or occurrence as it actually took place or a physical object or appearance as it usually exists or existed. Fact witnesses are generally

not allowed to offer opinion, address issues that they do not have personal knowledge of, or respond to hypothetical situations.

- *Family preservation or reunification:* The philosophical belief of social service agencies, established in law and policy, that children and families should be maintained together if the safety of the children can be ensured.

- *Guardian ad litem:* Generally defined as an adult appointed by the court to represent and make decisions for someone (such as a minor) legally incapable of doing so on his or her own in a civil legal proceeding.

- *Maltreatment:* Generally defined as actions that are abusive, neglectful, or otherwise threatening to a child's welfare. Commonly used as a general term for child abuse and neglect.

- *Neglect:* Generally defined as an act of omission, specifically the failure of a parent or other person legally responsible for a child's welfare to provide for the child's basic needs and proper level of care with respect to food, shelter, hygiene, medical attention, or supervision. There are two types of neglect:

  1. Emotional: Generally defined as the passive or passive-aggressive inattention to a child's emotional needs, nurturing, or emotional well-being. Also referred to as psychological unavailability to a child.
  2. Physical: Generally defined as a child suffering, or at substantial risk of imminently suffering, physical harm causing disfigurement, impairment of bodily functioning, or other serious physical injury as a result of conditions created by a parent or other person legally responsible for the child's welfare or by the failure of a parent or person legally responsible for a child's welfare to adequately supervise or protect him or her.

- *Preponderance of evidence:* Lowest of the three standards of proof, and the standard applied in most civil actions; generally defined as a "probable" degree of certainty (e.g., "more likely than not," or a 51% chance).

7. Guidelines for Psychotherapy with Lesbian, Gay, and Bisexual Clients

In general, the Guidelines for Psychotherapy with Lesbian, Gay, and Bisexual Clients (APA, 2000) may be thought to apply to older adolescent and adult populations and therefore not directly applicable to the evaluation and treatment of children and adolescents in clinical and forensic contexts. Professional practice, however, indicates otherwise. Lesbian, gay, and bisexual persons are involved with children as parents, guardians, and foster parents and may individually or as couples be subject to child protection action. Children with gender identity, sexual orientation, or child abuse and neglect issues, or some combination of these, are seen in clinical and forensic evaluation cases and are often identified for specialized care. These guidelines, therefore, though not specifically addressing children and adolescents, involve populations with whom practicing psychologists are likely to have professional contact. The stated goals of these guidelines are to provide practitioners with a frame of reference for the treatment of lesbian, gay, and bisexual clients and to provide basic information and further references in the areas of assessment, intervention, identity, relationships, and the education and training of psychologists. The guidelines are organized into four sections: (1) attitudes toward homosexuality and bisexuality, (2) relationships and families, (3) issues of diversity, and (4) education. Some of the 16 guidelines are articulated.

Guideline 1

Psychologists understand that homosexuality and bisexuality are not indicative of mental illness.

Guideline 2

Psychologists are encouraged to recognize how their attitudes and knowledge about lesbian, gay, and bisexual issues may be relevant to assessment and treatment and seek consultation or make appropriate referrals when indicated.

Guideline 3

Psychologists recognize that families of lesbian, gay, and bisexual people may include people who are not legally or biologically related.

Guideline 4

Psychologists are encouraged to recognize the particular life issues or challenges that are related to multiple and often conflicting cultural norms, values, and beliefs that lesbian, gay, and bisexual members of racial and ethnic minorities face.

Guideline 5

Psychologists are encouraged to recognize the particular challenges that bisexual individuals experience.

Guideline 6

Psychologists strive to understand the special problems and risks that exist for lesbian, gay, and bisexual youth. Here it is noted that lesbian, gay, and bisexual adolescents face specialized risks, including higher rates of estrangement from their parents, rejection by their parents, and increased risks of homelessness, HIV infection, and becoming victims of violence and of attempting suicide. Gay, lesbian, and bisexual youth may have complications of adolescent development and may require specialized therapeutic strategies and a secure therapy context to address sexual orientation issues.

Guideline 7

Psychologists make reasonable efforts to familiarize themselves with relevant mental health, educational, and community resources for lesbian, gay, and bisexual people.

8. Guidelines on Multicultural Education, Training, Research, Practice, and Organizational Change for Psychologists

The increasing diversity of the American population underscores the importance of these guidelines. The four stated goals in the Guidelines on Multicultural Education, Training, Research, Practice, and Organizational Change for Psychologists (2002d) are to provide psychologists with a means of addressing multiculturalism with basic information to enhance ongoing education and broaden the purview of psychology as a profession. The guidelines address U.S. ethnic and racial minority groups as well as persons from biracial, multiethnic, and multiracial groups. The guidelines indicate that approximately one third of the American population, according to the U.S. Census Bureau 2001 data, belong to a minority group. While racial/ethnic diversity varies greatly by state, region, and urban versus rural environment, practicing psychologists are likely to encounter minority clients in their practice. This increases the "urgency for culturally responsive practices and services." Psychologists are urged to become conversant with terms of culture, race, and ethnicity. Six guidelines are defined. These encourage psychologists to develop a commitment to cultural awareness, to recognize the importance of multicultural sensitivity and responsiveness, to employ constructs of diversity in psychological education, to conduct culturally centered and ethical psychological research, to apply culturally appropriate skills in psychological practice, and to support culturally informed organizational development. In psychological assessment, this may mean determining the applicability of particular tests and measures to minority populations. For example, Grisso (1998) in "Forensic Evaluation of Juveniles" reports that no relation was found between competent versus incompetent status and gender and race. Grisso found that three causal factors were related to a clinician's conclusion about incompetence: severe mental disorder, cognitive and intellectual disabilities, and age-related characteristics. By contrast, the Wechsler Intelligence Scale for Children—Fourth Edition (Wechsler, 2004) discusses the importance of age, gender, regional, ethnic, and racial characteristics of standardization populations. The guidelines explain that cultural sensitivity means taking account of the client's cultural context, using culturally appropriate assessment tools, and using a broad array of interventions. Cases may involve unusual combinations of client characteristics with variable nationality, racial, ethnic, religious, regional, and sexual characteristics and orientations. Some persons may be in transition from one group to another. Others may be confused about their own identity and group memberships. Professional practice can lead to work with illegal aliens and requires special assistance with language issues. Critical judgment is recommended when using standardized assessment tools and methods. Knowledge of helping practices used in non-Western cultures and culture-specific therapies may be indicated for particular ethnic communities.

9. Criteria for Evaluating Treatment Guidelines

Criteria for Evaluating Treatment Guidelines (APA, 2002a) is aspirational in intent and was developed for the purpose of evaluating the guidelines of health care organizations, government agencies, and professional associations. These pertain to specific recommendations about treatments to be offered to patients. They are, therefore, patient-focused rather than practitioner-focused as are practice guidelines. The purpose of treatment guidelines is to establish the most effective treatments available, translating knowledge into clinical practice. Treatment efficacy is defined as ascertaining the effects of a given intervention as compared to an alternative intervention or with no treatment, thereby establishing the scientific basis for determining treatment benefit.

Twenty criteria are listed for the evaluation of treatment guidelines. These describe the scientific method to be used in evaluating treatment efficacy. This requires establishing the clinical utility and cost effectiveness of treatment and that guideline panels be composed by persons with a broad range of expertise.

10. Criteria for Practice Guideline Development and Evaluation

Criteria for Practice Guideline Development and Evaluation (APA, 2002b) is intended to promote quality and consistency in practice guidelines and to produce a high quality of psychological services. These guidelines are aspirational and not intended to take precedence over professional judgment. Practice guidelines consist of recommendations to professionals concerning their conduct and issues in particular areas of psychological practice.

11. Guidelines for Providers of Psychological Services to Ethnic, Linguistic, and Culturally Diverse Populations

Guidelines for Providers of Psychological Services to Ethnic, Linguistic, and Culturally Diverse Populations (APA, 1990) represents general and aspirational principles for psychologists who work with ethnic, linguistic, and culturally diverse populations. Nine guidelines are articulated. These include the recognition of research and practice issues related to the population serviced, respect for the cultural structure of the community, use of the client's language, consideration of culture in designing intervention, elimination of discriminatory practice in service delivery, and documentation of relevant cultural factors affecting the family.

12. The APA Resolution on Outpatient Civil Commitment

The APA Resolution on Outpatient Civil Commitment (APA, 2004a) addresses the increasing use of this power in courts and civil commitment venues across the country. Although this resolution does not address children and adolescents specifically, it is well known that children and juveniles are often subject to this procedure. It recognizes that persons with serious mental illness and psychological disabilities can be subject to the imposition of involuntary mental health services, including hospitalization and incarceration. There is recognition of the controversy about the legitimacy of outpatient civil commitment (OCC), how and when it should be applied, and the professional practice standards, clinical methods, and level of proof involved.

The resolution recognizes that people possess behavioral disorders severe enough to reach the point of dangerousness, that these persons and persons with serious mental illness have a right to treatment, and that psychologists often play a role in providing the functional assessments and opinions that lead to OCC. There is recognition that some populations may have a greater vulnerability to the imposition of OCC. This APA resolution states, "It is never the role of any mental health practitioner, of any discipline, acting in the role of a caregiver, to make decisions that infringe upon a person's right to consent to services." Psychologists are encouraged to promote the development of evidence-based clinical methods for determining risk and dangerousness and determining competence to make specific judgments and decisions, promote rehabilitation from serious mental illness, research alternatives to involuntary commitment, and provide professional expertise and consultation to legal and judicial authorities to ensure that legal processes and decisions are appropriately informed by scientific and clinical considerations.

13. Training Grid Outlining Best Practices for Recovery and Improved Outcomes for People with Serious Mental Illness

The Training Grid Outlining Best Practices for Recovery and Improved Outcomes for People with Serious Mental Illness (APA, 2005c) is intended to assist providers in identifying the most effective interventions and resources for advanced clinical training. This document applies to adults with serious mental illness.

14. American Psychological Association Policy Statement on Evidence-Based Practice in Psychology

The APA Policy Statement on Evidence-Based Practice in Psychology (2005b) addresses the integration of the best available research with clinical expertise and patient characteristics. The purpose is to promote effective psychological practice and enhance public health. Best research evidence relies on the use of scientific method, beginning with clinical observation and leading to randomized clinical trials. Patient groups include child, adolescent, adult, older adult, couple, family, group, organization, community, and other populations that receive psychological services.

Researchers and practitioners are encouraged to combine their efforts to improve psychological practice. Psychologists are encouraged to use their clinical expertise to conduct assessments and develop diagnostic judgments, case formulations, and treatment plans; to evaluate treatment progress; to seek additional resources when indicated; and to have a cogent rationale for clinical strategies. Psychological services are considered to be most effective when they are responsive to patient characteristics and other factors such as cultural, family, environmental, values, and treatment expectations. Some effective treatments are directed to the patient's environment, such as parents, teachers, and caregivers.

15. Specialty Guidelines for Forensic Psychologists

Specialty Guidelines for Forensic Psychologists (APA, 1991) is designed to guide forensic psychologists in monitoring their professional conduct. The goal is to improve the quality of forensic psychological services. The guidelines are aspirational. They apply to such diverse positions in forensic practice as clinical forensic examiners, psychologists employed by correctional and forensic mental health systems, researchers who offer direct testimony about the relevance of scientific data to a psycholegal issue, trial behavior consultants, and psychologists who provide professional opinions to the courts through amicus briefs or who appear as forensic experts before judicial, legislative, and administrative agencies. The guidelines amplify the Ethical Principles of Psychologists in the context of the practice of forensic psychology. The guidelines are designed to conform to state and federal laws. They specify the nature of desirable professional practice. They are not meant to apply to a psychologist who is not informed at the time of service delivery that the service would be used for forensic purposes.

Forensic psychologists have an obligation to provide services that are consistent with the highest standards of their profession. Forensic psychologists provide services only in areas of psychology in which they have specialized knowledge, skill, experience, and education. It is obligatory for forensic psychologists to inform the court about the boundaries of their competence, have a reasonable understanding of the legal and professional standards that govern psychological expertise in legal proceedings, and recognize that personal and professional relationships may be inconsistent with forensic involvement. Forensic psychologists explain their fees and their personal and professional activities that may produce a conflict of interest. They acknowledge areas of competence and limitations of competence. They do not provide services on the basis of contingent fees. Forensic psychologists are encouraged to offer a portion of their professional services on a pro bono or reduced fee basis.

Forensic psychologists inform prospective clients of their legal rights with respect to the forensic service and obtain informed consent before proceeding with the evaluation. An exception may be when the evaluation is court ordered. When the client is unwilling to proceed, the evaluation should be postponed and the psychologist should take steps to assist the client to receive legal advice regarding participation. When the client does not have the capacity to provide informed consent, the client's legal representative is informed, and if the legal representative objects to the evaluation, the forensic psychologist notifies the court that ordered the evaluation. The forensic psychologist has an obligation to inform legal authorities about any source of conflict and take reasonable steps to resolve it.

Forensic psychologists inform their clients about the limits of confidentiality. Information is released pursuant to statutory requirements, court order, or the consent of the client. Forensic psychologists document and are prepared to make available to the court all evidence that formed the basis for forensic services. They anticipate the detail and quality of documentation required by judicial scrutiny and recognize that this standard is higher than the standard for general clinical practice. Forensic psychologists also recognize that they have a special responsibility to provide the best documentation possible under the circumstances. It is understood that psychological evidence is subject to rules of discovery, disclosure, and confidentiality. The duties and obligations of forensic psychologists regarding documentation apply "from the moment they know or have a reasonable basis for knowing that their data and evidence derived from it are likely to enter into legally relevant decisions."

As an expert, the forensic psychologist actively seeks information that will test plausible rival hypotheses. Unless an individual is handling his or her representation pro se, a forensic psychologist does not provide forensic services to any party contemplating a legal proceeding prior to that person's representation by counsel. An exception to this rule is the delivery of emergency mental health services, when a failure to provide such services would pose a substantial risk of harm to the defendant or to others.

Forensic psychologists seek third-party data only with prior approval of the legal party or pursuant to a court order.

Forensic psychologists seek to obtain independent and personal verification of data relied on. An effort is made to minimize sole reliance on hearsay evidence when offering expert testimony. It is recognized that many forms of data used by forensic psychologists are hearsay; therefore, an attempt to corroborate critical data is required. When the status of the data is uncorroborated, this is acknowledged by the forensic psychologist. The forensic psychologist acknowledges information gathered by others and avoids offering information that does not directly bear on the legal purpose of the professional activity. Forensic psychologists avoid giving evidence about the psychological characteristics of a person they have not examined. When it is not possible to conduct a direct examination, the forensic psychologist explains limitations on the reliability and validity of professional products, evidence, or testimony. The forensic psychologist is mindful of the Federal Rules of Procedure, which restrict testimony by the expert based on statements made by the defendant in the course of the forensic examination.

Forensic psychologists maintain a high level of public and professional communication. This includes taking reasonable steps to correct misuse or misrepresentation of their professional services. Access to information is restricted to individuals with a legitimate professional interest in the data and steps are taken to ensure that test results are released to a qualified professional and in compliance with Principle 16 of the Standards for Educational and Psychological Testing.

A special responsibility for fairness and accuracy is a feature of forensic psychological practice. This includes a fair and accurate evaluation of the work and opinions of other experts and parties. Forensic psychologists testify fairly and avoid partisan distortion and misrepresentation and errors of commission and omission. Forensic psychologists disclose all sources of their information and which information was relied on in formulating a particular opinion. Forensic psychologists "are aware that their own professional observations, inferences, and conclusions must be distinguished from legal facts, opinions, and conclusions."

PRACTICE GUIDELINES FOR INVESTIGATIVE INTERVIEWING

The first section of this chapter reviewed the ethical standards and practice guidelines of the APA with special reference to clinical and forensic practice with children, adolescents, and their families. Now we turn to three of the more comprehensive guidelines of professional organizations which address investigative interviewing with alleged child and adolescent victims of sexual abuse. The APRI, the APSAC, and the AACAP have formally addressed the topic of investigatory interviewing guidelines and standards.

1. The American Prosecutor's Research Institute

Clearly, the most comprehensive contribution on this topic is from the APRI. Its publication, *Investigation and Prosecution of Child Abuse*, third edition (APRI, 2004), is a multidisciplinary guide for attorneys, medical professionals, and behavioral scientists involved in the investigation and prosecution of child abuse. Chapter 2, "Investigation," is of particular relevance for psychologists practicing in both clinical and forensic settings. It presents a thorough and concentrated discussion of interviewing guidelines and validation principles. Because the sponsoring organization in this case is federal in scope and extends its training and practice guidelines to all of the states, the principles contained therein can be seen as offering national guidelines in a legal context.

Interviewing the Child

The stated purpose of this section is to assist multidisciplinary interviewers and investigators, including psychologists and prosecutors, to interview children properly and to analyze the evidentiary record for completeness, accuracy, and error. Techniques for the interviewing of preschool, grade school, and adolescent children are distinguished from those used for adults. The interviewer is expected to understand the field of child abuse and the developmental capacities of children of different ages. This includes the ability to judge the quality of prior interviews conducted with all witnesses. Interviewers are expected to be thoroughly trained and to develop a protocol for conducting interviews that reflect these guidelines and that can be defended in court. It is emphasized that comfort in talking with children is required. Investigators are urged to start the interview with no assumption about whether abuse occurred or about the identity of a perpetrator or how the child might feel about the perpetrator. A stance of neutrality about the allegation is required as it has the best chance at generating the greatest amount of reliable information. Interviewers are admonished not to coerce or manipulate children or to educate them about what may have happened or how they should feel. The author refers the reader to Ceci and Bruck (1995) and Poole and Lamb (1998), who provide detailed discussions of research on investigatory error and its impact on child narration, including autobiographical event narration.

Preparing for the Interview

Preparation for the interview requires thorough review of all known information on the case. This includes police and child protection reports, medical findings, and other materials. When possible, the person who made the report, the physician who examined the child, and the parent, guardian, and therapist who may have been treating the child should all be contacted. Interested parties are cautioned not to rehearse the child prior to the forensic or clinical interview. Gathering this information in advance is seen as strengthening the interviewer's understanding of the nature of the case, or the child, and of the special issues that could affect the interview process. This discussion acknowledges that there is expert opinion that recommends "allegation-blind" interviews in which the interviewer knows nothing about the background of the child or of the allegations. This approach is recommended to neutralize interviewer expectation and to minimize leading and confirmatory errors. The work of Cantlin, Payne, and Erbaugh (1996) is referenced in this connection; they compared allegation-blind and allegation-informed structured interviews. Planning is recommended for situations in which a child may be handicapped or speaks a different language. This will necessarily involve training of the interpreter and/or a support person for the handicapped child to prepare him or her to participate in an investigative interview. Such persons should be instructed not to speak for the child and not to show reactions to what the child says. The author suggests that interpreters also be trained to give verbatim accounts and not to independently question the interviewee.

Interview Location and Circumstances

It is recommended that a neutral location be found for the investigative interview and the number of interviews be limited. Police department facilities are to be avoided as well as the presence of uniforms and weapons. The interview room should be free of distractions and furnished to help the child to feel welcome. For example, some interview rooms have child-size furniture. Anatomical drawings and dolls are not to be in view. The interview location should provide the child with a feeling of privacy. Providing a child with food during the interview should be avoided, as should the promise of a snack when the interview is over. Interviews should be scheduled at a time when the child is likely to be alert and with the least disruption to the child's daily routine.

Who Should Be Present During the Interview

It is firmly recommended that children be interviewed alone by a single adult interviewer. Only in rare circumstances should a parent of a very young child be allowed to be present during the investigative interview. Caretakers should be informed in advance that they will not be in the interview room. In rare circumstances, the sex of the interviewer may be of significance and may require rescheduling to make a child more comfortable. It is recognized that more than one interview may be necessary to receive a complete account from the child. All investigative interviews should be conducted by the same interviewer. Children should not be reinterviewed about information previously disclosed.

How to Record Information from an Interview

The APRI expresses some flexibility on this issue, recognizing that there are jurisdictions that require audiotaping or videotaping of forensic interviews with children and others that do not. The APRI notes that a videotape can be a powerful tool for demonstrating the behavior and statements of children both in the hands of the prosecution and in the hands of the defense. When taping is performed, high-quality equipment is recommended. When taping is not used, interviews are to be accurately documented. The APRI indicates that "skilled interviewers are able to fulfill both functions [interviewing and note taking]." Lamb, Orbach, Sternberg, Hershkowitz, and Horowitz (2000) demonstrate that this is not the case and that even trained forensic interviewers produce significantly incomplete and flawed "verbatim notes." Therefore, for the sake of complete documentation, Lamb et al. recommend video- and audiotaping.

Conducting the Interview

Recommended interview protocols share common features. These begin with rapport building, the interview then progressing through a series of stages. At the outset, the interviewer should help the child to feel physically comfortable. For video- or audiotaping, the child should be positioned to facilitate that recording. Although the child should be asked, "Do you know why you're here?," he or she should not be told that the parent or guardian has already informed the interviewer about the interview purpose. The child should be canvassed about his or her understanding of the purpose of the interview and the role of the interviewer. Then the child should be instructed about a few rules. The first rule is that the child should say what he or she knows but not to guess. The second rule is that the child should correct the interviewer if he or she makes a mistake. The third rule is to inform the child that if the interviewer asks a question a second time the reason is not to cause the child to give a different answer. The fourth rule is that the child should be explicitly told that he or she can answer any question with "I don't know" or "I don't remember." The fifth rule is to ask the child to report when he or she does not understand a question. The interviewer should be mindful of the child's age, developmental capacities, and attention span as well as the child's capacity to remember instructions. Open-ended questions are encouraged as the best questioning method.

Canvassing the child's capacity to differentiate between the concepts of truth and lie and telling the truth versus telling a lie is treated as optional. It is noted that younger children have difficulty with these concepts and that this procedure is essentially an attempt to assess the child's competence to take an oath. The use of this procedure is apparently widespread; it is treated as an ordinary interviewing issue by Sattler (1988) and others (APRI, 2004; APSAC, 2002; Sparta & Koocher, 2006). White and Quinn (1988, p. 274) indicate that such canvassing of children can be intimidating, confusing, and coercive. They refer to this as the "truth-lie paradigm," categorizing it as coercive in all of its forms. They note that the labeling of statements as true or untrue is the function of the judicial system. The use of this technique "signals to the child that the interviewer believes there exists a particular truth to be found." Condie (2003, p. 222) sees such questioning of a child as a "fruitless endeavor" because neither a yes nor a no answer by the child has any predictive value for the child's ability to report events accurately. Truth-lie canvassing and developmental competency assessment do not access the core testimonial issue of the child's eyewitness memory for personal experience. As such, they provide no indication of the child's capacity and willingness to provide accurate autobiographical reports.

When competency questioning is undertaken, it can begin with testing the child's capacity to give accurate and inaccurate responses to fact questions in the present. It assesses the child's developmental abilities to name colors, count, count instances of events, tell the time of day, distinguish relative positions, and so on. Questioning about autobiographical events can provide an indication of the capacity for narrative recall. The author suggests that such questioning be directed at events that lend themselves to external corroboration. Sample topics are how and with whom the child came to the interview location, what the child ate that day, and major recent and remote events in the child's life. These can be accessed with such questions as "Tell me how you got here today"; "Who brought you here today?"; "What did you eat for breakfast today?"; "Tell me some things that you did yesterday"; and "Tell me about some of the best and worst things that ever happened to you."

The third stage is the abuse inquiry. The APRI guidelines are flexible on this issue. The discussion includes the optional use of anatomical drawings to orient the child to the subject of the inquiry. The APRI notes that some interviewers, however, postpone the introduction of body drawings for a later point in an interview that has produced an abuse report and use body drawings for body identification purposes. The discussion notes that when body drawings are introduced prior to an abuse report, this procedure is open to the attack that such pictures are suggestive in and of themselves. Poole and Lamb (1998) provide a detailed discussion of the pros and cons of the use of anatomical drawings and dolls for investigative interviewing purposes. They conclude with the recommendation that the use of such explicit stimuli be postponed to the identification and validation phases of an interview and that they not be used in advance of an abuse report by the child. They point to research that shows that the use of such props increases the percentage of false reports.

The APRI states that it is important to avoid asking children to simply repeat their prior report with a question like "I want to know what you told your mom about the babysitter." A recommended alternative is "Did you tell your mom about something that happened with the babysitter?" These examples are offered to illustrate attempts to access abuse reports. The author advises that both alternatives are objectionable as they access prior reports rather than prior experience. It may be a better practice to probe the issue of prior reports after concluding the abuse interview. This allows for the chronological recapitulation of experience and the assessment of the instant eyewitness report of the child. This method attempts to minimize the compounding effect of potential contextual influences and distortions. It also allows for a distinction between the child's report to the investigator and the disclosure process itself, which is a subject of separate inquiry. The forensic interviewer should seek "investigatory independence" (White & Quinn, 1988) and avoid direct and indirect alignment with prior interviewers. When an abuse report is obtained, it can be compared to prior abuse reports. If no abuse is reported or if abuse is denied, a decision can be made to probe the causes for inconsistency of reporting.

The APRI offers a table on a continuum of question types. These range from questions that are open-ended to those that are closed-ended. Answers to open-ended questions generate more confidence than those obtained from closed-ended questions. Question types identified are general, focused, multiple choice, yes/no, and leading. The opinion is firmly stated that the most reliable information comes in response to open-ended questions. Interviewers are encouraged to avoid questions that sound accusatory, have erroneous content, and introduce elements of threat, coercion, and bribes. Putting pressure on a child to speak or to continue an interview is discouraged.

Possible Questions for the Sexual Abuse Inquiry

The APRI lists four pages of possible questions that fall into subcategories of general, penetration, erection or masturbation, ejaculation, nudity, oral contact, and pornography. There are then lists of questions about physical and sexual abuse, fears and reasons for secrecy, determining who was involved, where the abuse took place, and alternative hypothesis testing. Most of these questions are phrased in the affirmative and are therefore suitable for situations in which the possibility of abuse was previously indicated in the interview. Examples are:

- How did the touching start?
- What did his penis look like?
- What happened to his penis after he made you touch it? It is considered more appropriate in advance of an abuse report to ask questions in an open-ended interrogatory form to explore the possibility of experience that may or may not have an abusive character. Some APRI examples are:
- Have you had any touches you didn't like or that made you feel uncomfortable?
- Do you remember what you were wearing when you and . . . were playing?
- Did you see pictures/books/magazines/movies/videos at . . . ?
- What happens if you do something you're not supposed to?
- Have the police ever come to your house? Why did they come?
- Has anyone asked you to keep a secret? What was the secret?

Open-ended examples of follow-up questions are:

- Tell me about that.
- Tell me more about that.
- Do you remember more about that?

It is important to remember that requests for additional information can constitute a demand in the mind of the respondent and can cause the production of information and detail to please the questioner. Children and adolescents are rarely self-referred for investigative interviews, and most have had prior interviews by parents and others. The author advises that even general and open-ended requests for additional information be preceded by inquiry concerning the presence or absence of additional experience and knowledge. Poole and Lamb (1998) report that with additional questioning children add credible detail to both true and false reports. The risk of added detail to false reports is heightened when respondents have been exposed to misinformation in prior interviews. The well-informed investigative interview strives to offer respondents the opportunity to drop misinformation and false reports if these exist and to pursue interviewing in the least suggestive manner.

Direct questions are seen as sometimes necessary, and a distinction is made between more and less suggestive direct questioning. The example "Did something happen to your [child's word for vagina]?" is considered superior to "Did your dad do something to your [child's word for vagina]?"

Anatomical Dolls

The APRI allows for the use of anatomical dolls for demonstration purposes after an abuse report has been received. The interviewer is encouraged to use dolls that are chosen for the child and for the perpetrator, and whenever possible these dolls should be appropriate for age, sex, and race. A list of inappropriate uses of dolls includes:

- Presenting the dolls to the child unclothed.
- Encouraging play with the dolls.
- Naming the sexual parts of the doll for the child.
- Probing the doll's genitals or breasts.
- Using the dolls to demonstrate sexual behavior to the child.
- Failing to elicit a verbal description of the abuse before presenting the dolls to the child.
- Incorrectly clarifying what the child demonstrated.

The APRI advises interviewers not to ask adolescents to name body parts at the beginning of an interview and to use an anatomical doll only when this can be done in a way that is not insulting. This author advises interviewers not to introduce drawings or dolls until a verbal abuse disclosure has been made and to restrict the use of drawings and dolls to clarify important points. This admonition reflects the author's recommendation for best practice methods.

Ending the Interview

It is recommended that the interview be ended after determining that the child is no longer able to provide information. This can be preceded by such questions as "Is there anything else you want to tell me today?" and "Is there anything you want to ask me?" It is recommended that the child be thanked for participating. After the meeting with the child, it may be appropriate to meet with the parents or caregivers to provide them with information. This can include scheduling follow-up interviews, making treatment recommendations, and giving information about the investigatory and court process. Interviewers are encouraged to develop a protocol that defines the stages of the interview, including introduction, rapport building, instructions, methodology for beginning the abuse inquiry, methodology for the abuse inquiry itself, and closure.

Assessing Validity in Sexual Abuse Cases

There are 13 subsections to the validity discussion that lead to a summary of indicators of report validity in sexual abuse cases. The purpose is to determine "whether a report of sexual abuse is valid." The 13 points describe the process of evaluating the available evidence. Evidence includes eyewitness statements, confessions, medical evidence, the child's statements, emotional and behavioral characteristics of the child as seen by others, and assessment of the validity of the abuse report. No factors are thought to conclusively demonstrate the validity or invalidity of an abuse report.

1. Alternative Explanations for the Child's Statement   The investigator is required to consider alternative explanations throughout the investigation. This includes consideration of the possibility of deliberate falsehood, misinterpretation of innocent contacts, and coaching. The author adds ruling out professional error to this list of requirements. These possibilities are to be translated into active steps in document review and in investigative interviewing before the inquiry is ended.

2. Spontaneity   Spontaneous statements from children are considered more reliable as they are unlikely to be the result of prompting. The evidentiary record should be reviewed to determine whether there is reliable indication of a spontaneous disclosure by the child and which parts of the child's narration in the investigative interview possess this characteristic.

3. Consistency   Consistency of child statements in an interview and across interviews and statements is an essential feature of a validation determination. Consistency is tracked from the point of initial disclosure through all forensic interviews as well as the child's testimony in court. Consistency is tracked for core elements rather than for exact wording. The validation review should be alert to the issue of rote recital, and when this is found the record should be "scrutinized carefully for the possibility of coaching."

4. Sexual Knowledge or Behavior That Is Developmentally Unusual   This refers to the acting out of adult forms of sexuality, including sexual talk, rather than age-appropriate touching and talk about body parts, including genitalia, that may occur out of curiosity and play. Friedrich (1992) identifies explicit advanced sexual behaviors that occur with low frequency and are considered indicators for sexual abuse. These include:

- A child putting his or her mouth on another's sexual parts.
- A child asking to engage in sexual acts.
- A child masturbating with an object.
- A child inserting an object into his or her own anus or vagina.
- A child imitating intercourse.
- A child making sexual sounds.

- French kissing by a child.
- A child talking about explicit sexual acts.
- A child undressing others.
- A child asking to watch explicit sexual television or movies.
- A child using sexual words.
- A child imitating sexual acts with dolls.

Schoentjes, Deboutte, and Friedrich (1999) confirmed these data in a study of 917 2- to 12-year-old Dutch-speaking children in Belgium. More recently, however, Drach, Wientzen, and Ricci (2001) studied the utility of sexual behavior problems as diagnostic indicators of sexual abuse in a sample of 247 children evaluated for sexual abuse at a forensic child abuse evaluation clinic. It was found that non-sexually abused children were just as likely to have high scores on the Child Sexual Behavior Inventory as sexually abused children. These results suggest that the occurrence of seemingly advanced sexual behavior in relatively young children should be viewed with caution as an indicator of sexual abuse. Both the absence and the presence of advanced sexual behavior was evident in children who had been and who had not been sexually abused. This nullified the use of advanced sexual behavior as an abuse indicator.

5. Developmentally Appropriate Language   Reports about a child's disclosures and the child's interview language should be analyzed for its developmental characteristics. The interviewer is urged to adapt questions to the child's developmental language and to use the child's language during all phases of the interview. It is thought that children who have been coached or who have borrowed language from other sources for use in abuse reports may use language that is developmentally unexpected or unusual. This analysis should allow for children who have precocious language ability, who have been exposed to multiple interviews, and who may have acquired language from the offender.

6. Play and Gestures Indicative of Abuse   A suspicion of abuse may have arisen because of the observation of sexualized play. Or, after an abuse disclosure, reports may arise about previously observed sexualized play. Particularly in younger children, such play may be seen as a reenactment of an advanced sexual exposure or experience.

7. Idiosyncratic Detail   Children are considered less likely to have fabricated an abuse report that contains personalized, experiential detail. Sensory detail referencing taste, smell, touch, size, pressure, or pain, and containing mechanical descriptions is considered validating of the abuse report. Ceci and Bruck (1995), however, demonstrate that such detail can be abundantly produced by children in response to improper and suggestive interviewing. Nonetheless, an idiosyncratic report in the absence of evidence of improper questioning can be compelling. The APRI advises that this can occur when the abuse report contains "such description and detail that there can be little doubt that the child witnessed the sexual act." The child may have knowledge about a feature of the perpetrator's body such as a tattoo or knowledge of taste and texture or visual exposure to sexual activity. The child may recount highly personalized details that lend credibility to the abuse report. It is stated that "a child's total inability to furnish details that demonstrate familiarity with the sex act forced upon the child may indicate the absence of abuse."

8. Content of the Statement   The investigator is called on to consider whether the actions described make sense. This includes considering the possibility that innocent physical touches were misinterpreted as sexual and whether the progression of events fits known patterns of abuse. This can include identification of some features that have been found in validated abuse reports, including a description of multiple incidents over time, a progression of sexual activity that includes grooming, a request for secrecy, the use of power and authority to gain compliance, and attempts to cause a child to retract a complaint.

9. The Child's Manner and Emotional Response   The APRI notes that a child's emotional presentation may give a sense of whether or not an abuse account is genuine, and the investigator is called on to note all of the child's verbal and nonverbal emotions. The advantage of videotaping to capture this information is acknowledged. Hesitancy, tone of voice, and facial and bodily expressions can offer clues about fearfulness, guilt, aversion, and distaste. It is noted that the absence of emotionality does not automatically invalidate an abuse report.

10. The Existence of a Motive to Fabricate   This section states, "The assessment should consider what motives the child may have to fabricate the abuse or the motives others may have to coach a child to allege abuse." But the discussion of this topic offers little guidance about how to investigate this issue and how to translate hypotheses into investigatory procedures and questions. No specific validation procedures or questions are offered. We are cautioned that the existence of a motive is not the equivalence of a fabrication and to be alert to offenders who may attempt to confuse motive with misdeed. The author recommends that validation questions be adapted to the facts of the case and should reflect a knowledge of the complainant's personality and relationship characteristics, including his or her relationship with the accused. When the complainant's biography includes a history of lying or this issue otherwise arises (Benedek & Schetky, 1987), this issue should be explored. For younger children, the author suggests the use of questions such as:

- Is this something that really happened or is it make-believe?
- Are you saying this just to get [the accused] in trouble?
- Are you saying this because you're angry/mad at [the accused]?
- Does somebody else think this happened even though you don't?
- Are you saying this because you want to live with...?

For older children, the author recommends such questions as:

- Are you saying this to get out of the house?
- Are you saying this because [a valued person] was not being nice to you or not paying enough attention to you?
- Are you saying this to cover up because you wanted to do it (have sex)?

Other authors provide some help in identifying motives to fabricate. Kanin (1994) investigated 45 consecutive, disposed, false rape allegations over a 9-year period in a small metropolitan community that constituted 41% of the total forcible rape cases in that jurisdiction ($n = 109$). Kanin determined that the allegations appeared to serve three major functions for the complainants: providing an alibi, seeking revenge, and obtaining sympathy and attention. The sample consisted of young adults. Retrospective comparison reports with college populations produced similar results. These motives may apply differently to child and younger adolescent populations. For example, providing an alibi for consensual sexual behavior may be more applicable in an adolescent population. Seeking revenge and obtaining sympathy and attention may apply equally to child and adolescent populations that have the developmental capacity to be motivated in these ways.

Benedek and Schetky (1987) investigated child sexual abuse reports in child custody and visitation disputes. They noted that adolescents may allege sexual abuse for secondary gain because they are angry at a parent, jealous of a parent's boyfriend, or want someone excluded from the home. For younger children, they found that a history of lying, the use of rote phrases, reports from the perspective of an adult rather than from the perspective of a child, and child reports delivered only in the presence of an accusing adult were characteristics of false reports. Ash and Gyer (1991) discuss biased reporting in parents undergoing child custody evaluation. They studied 196 court-ordered child custody evaluations and found that parents give symptomatic child reports that suit litigation purposes. Everson and Boat (1989) reviewed false allegations of sexual abuse by children and adolescents in reports given to child protection workers; 88 child protection respondents who had worked on 1,249 sexual abuse cases were in the sample. The children ranged in age from preschoolers to adolescents. Child protection workers reported fewer than 2% of cases involving children under the age of 6 and 8% of those involving adolescents as cases of false report. Subsequent retraction by the child was found to be the major reason for determining an allegation to be false. Children were found to have insufficient credibility when the report itself was improbable, the details were insufficient, there were inconsistencies in the report, or there was conflicting evidence. Everson and Boat caution that obvious evidence of coercion on a child to recant should not be considered a circumstance for the invalidation of a complaint.

Jones and McGraw (1987) reviewed all reports of suspected sexual abuse made to the Denver Department of Social Services in 1983 ($n = 576$). Each report was investigated by that department and designated as either "founded" or "unfounded." Two of the evaluation categories include fictitious reports by adults and fictitious reports by children. Fictitious reports by adults included deliberate falsifications, misperceptions, and confused interpretations of nonsexual events. Fictitious reports by children included those that were falsely made and involved deliberate falsifications and misperceptions. Fictitious accounts by adults composed 5% of the sample and fictitious accounts from a child were 1% to 2%. Among the features of fictitious accounts by adults were no child reports despite careful and repeated interviewing, an ongoing custody and visitation dispute, abuse and neglect histories of alleging adults, and emotional disturbance in alleging adults that included two professionals. Among the fictitious child accounts were those from children who ranged in age from 3 to 10, and the context of all was a bitter custody or visitation dispute. The seven mothers were found to be psychiatrically disturbed. Reference is made to other studies that found a lack of detail or of accompanying emotion in fictitious reports. Reference is also made to children who had been sexually abused in the past and made an erroneous subsequent allegation of reabuse. Also noted was the absence of threats or coercive elements in the fictitious allegations.

Ceci and Bruck (1995) discuss false allegations of sexual abuse after reviewing some of the same literature. Discussing the Jones and McGraw (1987) study, they note that of the 576 cases reported that year in Denver, 23% were judged unfounded and in 24% of the cases no clear judgment could be made because of insufficient information. Six percent of the unfounded cases were considered to be deliberate or malicious and another 17% to have been wrong but made in good faith. Ceci and Bruck consider 23% of the reports to be properly categorized as false, of which 6% were deliberate lies and the other 17% baseless. Ceci and Bruck considered the Everson and Boat (1989) numbers to be underestimates. They referenced a study by Faller in 1991 that examined the reports of 136 children of divorced families referred to a project on abuse and neglect in which 35% of the reports were found to be untrue. It was noted that Faller broke down the 35% rate of unsubstantiated cases into three subgroups consisting of false allegations made (8.8%), false allegations reflecting dynamics besides divorce (11%), and false allegations arising in an atmosphere of divorce acrimony (14%). High rates of unsubstantiated sexual abuse reports are the norm, according to Besharov (1994), who studied child abuse and neglect substantiation rates in 30 states in 1986, 1987, and 1988, with rates ranging upwards of 77% in Montana in 1988 and as low as 15% in Alaska in 1986. Kuehnle and Sparta (2006) wrote of a marked nationwide decline during the 1990s of child sexual abuse reports made and in the percentage of reports that are substantiated. These statistics are a reminder to remain open-minded regarding the outcome of any particular investigation. They underscore the importance of a validation effort in every case.

Investigatory error, primarily in the form of improper questioning of alleged child victims, is the central topic of the Ceci and Bruck (1995) analysis. This topic is addressed by the APRI for the purpose of avoiding mistakes but not addressed for the purpose of identifying mistakes already made and estimating their impact. For impact assessment of professional error in the fabrication of abuse reports, we turn to other sources. Mantell (1988) based his analysis on several hundred child protection, family, and criminal court cases he evaluated. He indicates that professional error is one of several kinds of error causing false sexual abuse allegations. The impact is treated as potentially total such that an allegation can emerge from the questioning of a child without prior existence in the child's utterances or experience. The Ceci and Bruck (1995) analysis provides a full discussion of this topic and identifies categories of error sources in investigatory interviewing. Their analysis focuses on the effects of several forms of suggestive questioning, including interviewer bias, repeated questioning, negative stereotyping, the emotional tone of the interview and the effects of peer pressure, of interviews by adults of high status, of misleading information, of failure to test an alternative hypothesis, and of questioning with the request for visual imaging. This is an analysis of the confounding impact of external influence on autobiographical memory.

The *Report on Scott County Investigations* (State of Minnesota, 1985) shows the effects of repeated questioning, cross-germination (witness contagion), and private motives and pressures in generating graphically detailed false reports by teenagers and young adults of homicide and sexual abuse. This began with the interview of a 12-year-old boy who provided detailed accounts of homicides in 1984, describing seven children being stabbed, mutilated, and shot. Other children of varying ages provided reports of ritualistic torture and murder. After state authorities determined that no homicides had occurred, they turned their focus to allegations of sexual abuse and pornography. The continued interviewing of the children led to an increasingly large list of accused citizens and ultimately to the children reporting abuse by their parents. Children as old as 21 and 18 as well as 12 provided such reports. In some cases, children were interviewed together and prompted to discuss allegations in group settings.

In some respects, the 1989 edition of the APRI manual provides a more detailed account of error sources to be assessed in the validation phase of the investigation. It calls for the child to be interviewed alone, out of the presence of other adults, to make sure that the child is not "overwhelmed" or "bombed" by adult interviewers, and to assess the impact of family and support persons in providing approval and disapproval to the child witness. The interviewer is told to ask simple, direct, open-ended questions, avoid leading questions, and make sure that the information the child is giving is really coming from the child and not from other sources, such as the interviewer. Answers need to be clarified regarding their reliability. A child is never to be pressured to talk or continue an interview. If a child thinks that he or she will get into trouble for talking, the interviewer should find out with whom and for what reason. The interviewer should try to find out if any threats, promises, or rewards were offered or given to the child for talking. If the child says that no abuse occurred, the interviewer should ask the child if there is someone who thinks that something did happen. Other explanations for any behavioral or medical data that may indicate abuse should be considered. Other explanations for the child's sexual knowledge and behavior should be considered and explored. The use of nonleading questions is identified as an important assurance for the analysis of the investigatory interview that the child is using his or her own language for abuse reports. Contamination of the child witness by family members is listed as a key error source to be ruled out. Witnesses who are likely to be in contact with the child or with each other are to be told not to question or rehearse the child, not to investigate the case on their own, and not to compare notes. Members of the child's family are to be interviewed because they may be able to provide direct and indirect corroboration for the abuse report and can also provide observations of behavioral, emotional, and physical indicators of abuse as well as information about the relationship between the child and the suspect. Family members and others also should be interviewed to rule out their influence on the child to make an abuse report. Other witnesses, such as teachers, nurses, and police officers, are to be interviewed for their information. The APRI recommends a high level of care in the documentation of statements by these witnesses, including videotaping the interview.

11. The Child Corrects the Interviewer   The APRI advises that children who correct the interviewer are listening attentively and are not judged to be overly suggestible.

12. and 13. Medical and Forensic Evidence   Medical and forensic evidence are additional indicators for analysis. They are listed in the Summary of Indicators. Neither is behavioral in character, and thus they are not included in this discussion beyond noting that although both are infrequent they can be decisive in establishing that abuse occurred and in the identification of the perpetrator.

This section concludes with Table 4.2, a summary of the 13 validation indicators for sexual abuse. Table 4.2 offers a quick overview of the investigatory process and evidentiary record. It includes, as the final indicator, the nature of the alleged offender statement, if any, placing it last as an important abuse indicator. Construction of a case-specific evidentiary chart after completion of a thorough validation review offers a useful perspective on the case and can provide a basis for the development of a more thoroughly informed opinion about the strengths and weaknesses of the total evidentiary record. This can assist the development of an opinion about the completeness and reliability of the procedures used. Oftentimes, investigators are fact witnesses. They report what they have done and the results they have obtained but do not provide professional opinions about its meaning. Interviewers should remain sensitive to the nature of their role and not overstep their boundaries. Whether the interviewer considers the evidence to be strong or weak, it remains the domain of the trier of fact to determine whether or not abuse occurred. The author reminds interviewers of research by Poole and Lamb (1998) and Horner, Guyer, and Kalter (1992) that demonstrates that psychologists are not able to reliably distinguish between true and false reports of sexual abuse.

Table 4.2   Summary of Indicators of Report Validity in Sexual Abuse Cases (APRI)

 1. Medical evidence
 2. Forensic evidence
 3. The child's statement
 4. Statement spontaneity
 5. Consistency—both internally in the statement and across statements
 6. Developmentally unusual sexual knowledge/behavior
 7. Idiosyncratic detail
 8. Developmentally appropriate language
 9. Play and gestures indicative of abuse
10. The child's manner and emotional responses
11. Lack of a motive to fabricate
12. The child corrects the interviewer
13. The offender's statement

2. The American Professional Society on the Abuse of Children

The APSAC publishes seven documents that address investigatory interviewing of alleged child abuse victims:

- Practice Guidelines: Code of Ethics (APSAC, 1997a)
- Practice Guidelines: Psychosocial Evaluation of Suspected Sexual Abuse in Children, second edition (APSAC, 1997b)
- Practice Guidelines: Psychosocial Evaluation of Suspected Psychological Maltreatment in Children and Adolescents (APSAC, 1995c)
- Practice Guidelines: Photographic Documentation of Child Abuse (APSAC, 1995b)
- Practice Guidelines: Use of Anatomical Dolls in Child Sexual Abuse Assessments (APSAC, 1995d)
- Practice Guidelines: Descriptive Terminology in Child Sexual Abuse Medical Evaluations (APSAC, 1995a)
- Practice Guidelines: Investigative Interviewing in Cases of Alleged Child Abuse (APSAC, 2002)

This discussion focuses on the last of the practice guidelines, Investigative Interviewing in Cases of Alleged Child Abuse (APSAC, 2003). The content of this guideline overlaps with many aspects of the APA and APRI guidelines. This guideline opens by reminding us that "inadequate and improper interviewing can lead to errors in decision-making about child safety and criminal prosecution." The guidelines are recommended for use in conjunction with the APSAC Guidelines for the Use of Anatomical Dolls and for the Psychosocial Evaluation of Suspected Sexual Abuse in Children. Aspects of those guidelines will be discussed as well.

The stated purpose of the investigative interview is to obtain as complete and accurate a report from an alleged victim as possible. It is noted that most investigative interviews are conducted by child protective service workers and law enforcement officers and that other mental health and medical professionals may also participate in or conduct such interviews. Interviewers and investigators are expected to develop specialized knowledge. Interviews should be timed to occur as close to the event in question as is feasible and with appropriate notification of parents and guardians. A neutral environment for the interview should be selected whenever possible. Electronic recording in the forms of videotaping and audiotaping are identified as the most comprehensive and accurate method of documentation. The number of interviews should be governed by the need to gather a complete and accurate report from the child. This can often be accomplished in one interview, although some children require more than one interview. However, multiple interviews also carry risks. They have been associated with memory errors, acquiescence to interviewer expectation, and child distress. Interviewing by one interviewer is the preferable practice. The presence of additional interviewers is allowed with the recommendation that a lead interviewer be designated. Closed-circuit TV and two-way mirrors can enable other professionals to monitor the interview while remaining out of sight. Parents are not to be present during the investigative interview unless there is an exceptional circumstance. Siblings are to be interviewed separately.

Investigators are urged to practice cultural competence and to take cultural features into account during the interviewing process and also in review. Children with special needs may require accommodation.

The APSAC is concerned about interviewer bias and recommends that interviewers approach the interview with an open mind about what may have happened. The customary practice is to know the specifics of an allegation before the interview. Interviewers are reminded that the purpose of the interview is "not merely to confirm prior suspicions" but to "elicit information from the child." It is noted that in some jurisdictions there is a standard practice that the investigative interview begin with an interviewer who is blind to the allegations. Bias is seen as impairing the capacity of the interviewer to receive and to objectively interpret information and as a source for interviewer error. Negative statements about suspected abusers are one source of error and suggestion. A number of interview aids, such as anatomical dolls, anatomical drawings, and doll furniture, may be used, but the timing and manner of their use is important. Investigators are expected to have specialized knowledge about these aids. The Practice Guideline: Use of Anatomical Dolls in Child Sexual Abuse Assessments (APSAC, 1995d) essentially dismisses the concerns that the use of anatomical dolls leads to erroneous reports of sexual abuse and leaves the timing of their introduction to the judgment of the interviewer.

This position contrasts with that of Ceci and Bruck (1995), who in their own studies and the review of the literature found that with the use of anatomically detailed dolls many children made both verbal and nonverbal reports of genital touching and digital penetration though neither had occurred. Younger children were found to be more susceptible to such error. Ceci and Bruck recommend that the dolls not be used for diagnostic purposes, stating, "We have reviewed enough studies that demonstrate that this tool has the potential for serious misuse, including misdiagnosis" (p. 186). Poole and Lamb (1998) also provide a detailed discussion of the anatomical doll issue and of the research literature. They indicate that there are no standardized procedures for the use of anatomically detailed dolls in investigative interviewing and that they are not a psychological test for the diagnosis of abuse. Although the APSAC allows for them, Poole and Lamb note that the APSAC-defined preferred practice is for their use to identify body parts, to clarify previous statements, and for a demonstration by non- or low-verbal children after there is an indication of abuse activity. Sparta and Koocher (2006) appear to support the use of anatomically detailed dolls in investigative interviews without discussing the timing and manner of their use, while also noting that some researchers are concerned about the error rates associated with their use because of a reduction in the accuracy of children's reports.

The APSAC states that "research does not confirm that anatomical dolls are inherently too suggestive or sexually stimulating." The APSAC specifically recommends the use of anatomical dolls for several purposes: identification of body parts, as a visual aid for direct inquiry about the child's personal experience with private parts, and as a demonstration aid. The APSAC specifically recommends the use of dolls with preschool children, the age group in which Ceci and Bruck (1995) found the highest error rates for children's abuse reports of genital touches in pediatric examinations that did not contain such touches. Melton, Petrila, Poythress, and Slobogin (1997, p. 476) conclude that anatomical dolls are "undoubtedly the most controversial evaluation technique." They note that there is a consensus that play with anatomically detailed dolls cannot be used as a test of whether or not child maltreatment has occurred. They note that a question remains about how the dolls can be used "even as demonstration aids to clarify a child's statements" (p. 477). Ceci and Bruck indicate that jurisdictions vary dramatically in legal decisions about the use of anatomical dolls, ranging from those that ban their use entirely to others that permit children to use the dolls in court to demonstrate their own sexual abuse.

In its practice guidelines, the APSAC distinguishes anatomical drawings from anatomical dolls and provides little guidance for how anatomical drawings might be used or about their limitations. They are identified as an interview aid that can assist the child to identify names for body parts and functions and also the location of possible sexual touching or physical injuries. The author recommends the best practice approach, which is to avoid issues of suggestive questioning and reserve the use of anatomical drawings and dolls for the confirmation phase of an interview following a demonstration that their use was needed after other avenues of explanation had been exhausted (Poole & Lamb, 1998).

The APSAC recommends careful preparation for the forensic interview by developing a list of specific topics and the hypothesis to be addressed. The interviewer should appear relaxed and nonthreatening. The interview itself should be paced to mesh with the child's developmental and temperamental characteristics, and the interviewer should proceed slowly and never pressure a child to respond to questions. Especially with younger children, the interviewer should be aware of signals indicating fatigue and loss of concentration as well as the need for a break.

In regard to questioning strategies, the APSAC recommends minimizing the introduction of information to the child that might be adopted by the child in his or her report. (This is the very principle underlying objections to the use of anatomical dolls and drawings and good and bad touch instruction prior to a child abuse inquiry and an abuse report.) The use of open-ended questions is recommended. Yes/no and multiple choice questions are allowed. Yet the interviewer is encouraged to focus open-ended questions to specific topics that the child has introduced by saying "Tell me more about. . . ." In a later section, specific, closed questions such as those that have yes/no and multiple-choice formats are recommended after open-ended questioning has concluded and appears to have exhausted the information that a child can provide. When the multiple-choice format is used, the example given is, "Was he in the house, in the yard, or someplace else?" This author notes that the forced-choice format of this formulation can be reduced by including the options "I don't know" and "I don't remember" as approved alternatives and then making sure that the child has the ability and willingness to use them. It is also essential that such questioning first be clarified as relevant. This can be achieved by asking "Do you know where he was when . . . ?"

The APSAC expresses uncertainty about how to define leading and suggestive questions. White and Quinn (White and Quinn, 1988, p. 271) define a leading question according to Black's Law Dictionary, "as one which instructs the witness how to answer or puts into his mouth words to be echoed back." The suggestive question is defined as "presentation of an idea especially indirectly as through association of ideas, bringing before the mind for consideration in the nature of a hint" (p. 271). White and Quinn state that the question "Your daddy did put his finger in your vagina, didn't he?" is leading, whereas the question "Did your daddy put his finger in your vagina?" is suggestive. Others, such as the APRI, might classify the second alternative as a direct question. There would probably be unanimity about the fact that the question contains information descriptive of bodily touching and in this case of the digital penetration of the genitalia and that it is not an example of a general, open-ended question to which a child might provide a wholly spontaneous and independent response. There also can be no controversy about the fact that the question is formulated in the vocabulary of the interviewer, not the vocabulary of the child, and that its use poses the concern of the respondent acquiescing to the question with confirmation. Whenever possible, it is recommended to avoid these risks by asking questions that call on the child to independently express the substance of an idea descriptive of action and experience.

The APSAC describes the following components of investigative interviewing. It begins with the interviewer introducing himself or herself and the interviewer's role, followed by rapport building in which there is a discussion of neutral topics. Developmental screening can then occur to assess the child's ability to understand and respond to questions. The competency check may occur in jurisdictions that require an assessment of the child's understanding of the difference between the truth and a lie. This is distinguished from the assessment of the child's ability to provide information about events that are known to have occurred, such as a recent birthday party. The ground rules of the interview are then explained. The child should be told that the interview is about things that really happened, that the child will be asked many questions, and that the child cannot guess about answers and can say "I don't know" and "I don't remember." The child is encouraged to correct the interviewer when the interviewer makes a mistake. If the interviewer asks a question that is too hard or difficult for the child to talk about, the child should let the interviewer know.

The APSAC recommends that the topic of abuse be introduced in one of a number of ways:

- "I understand something may have happened to you. Tell me about it from beginning to end."
- "I understand you had to go to the doctor. Is there a reason you had to go?"

The author finds these questions problematic and recommends avoiding them. They can convey bias, expectation, and alignment of the interviewer with authority figures who may be close to the child and instructed the child about the purpose of the interview and what to say. They may convey to the child that the interviewer wants the child to repeat prior statements or the opinions of others. Getting started does not require reliance on methods that contain error and that may mislead the respondent. Alternative questions are:

- Do you know why your . . . brought you here to speak to me?
- What were you told about what we are going to do and talk about?
- How do you feel about being here?
- What would you like to do and talk about?

Situation-focused questioning is also encouraged, such as asking a child about bath time or toileting, about secrets, or about things the child doesn't like. The APSAC says that anatomical drawings and dolls are allowed at this time and are useful for the purpose of assessing the child's body knowledge, focusing the discussion on bodies and body experience, and giving the child permission to discuss sensitive topics such as private parts.

Children should be asked to provide details about concerning events. Here the APSAC recommends the use of open-ended narrative prompts, such as "Tell me more about that" and "Then what?" This actually constitutes an inversion of questioning sequence from more specific (body parts and touch experiences) to the open-ended or general questions. When abuse reports occur, the child should be encouraged to provide detailed information, contextual information, and information about abuse witnessing by other persons. The APSAC states that anatomical drawings and dolls can be useful during this phase of the interview for clarification purposes about what the child is attempting to describe. It appears that the APSAC is recommending the use of anatomical drawings and dolls for two purposes: first, to focus the child's attention on the topics of interest (to the interviewer), and second, to clarify with the child the report that has been received.

The psychologist may wonder how to start an abuse inquiry if anatomical dolls and drawings and good-touch/bad-touch clarification are not used. Opening an abuse inquiry is not difficult. Many children know why they have been brought to the interview. Often, asking about this alone is sufficient to elicit the child's report and to set the stage for the forensic interview. When the child says that he or she does not know the reason for the interview, the interviewer can inquire about who brought the child, what was discussed, and whether the person who brought the child said what the reason is. If this does not lead to mention of the forensic topic, the child can be generally canvassed about major life experiences and about relationships with people, and then ultimately about general classes of positive and negative and also body experience. This can include questioning about general safety rules when crossing the street, with hot things, with water, with dressing and undressing, with toileting, and with body touching.

The APSAC does not discuss validation procedures. The reader is referred to the APRI guidelines, Ceci and Bruck (1995), Poole and Lamb (1998), and White and Quinn (1988) for a detailed discussion of this issue.

3. Policy Statement from the American Academy of Child and Adolescent Psychiatry: Guidelines for the Clinical Evaluation of Child and Adolescent Sexual Abuse

The AACAP (1990) states that the purpose of a clinical evaluation in a child sexual abuse case is to determine whether abuse has occurred, if the child needs protection, and if the child needs treatment for medical or emotional problems. The guidelines were developed to assist clinicians performing those evaluations. The AACAP sets high standards for the qualifications of evaluators. They should possess sound knowledge of child development, family dynamics related to sexual abuse, and the effects of sexual abuse on the child. They should be trained in diagnostic evaluation of both children and adults and should be comfortable testifying in court. If not a child and adolescent psychiatrist or psychologist, clinicians performing these evaluations should be under the supervision of professionals with these qualifications. Role differentiation should occur so that the child or adolescent therapist is not the evaluator.

The child should be seen for the minimum number of times necessary to conduct the evaluation, with cross-agency sharing of information to avoid duplication and the unnecessary interviewing of the child. Optimally, evaluation teams should be formed that integrate local police and reporting agencies. Multiple interviews may be viewed by the child as a demand for more information, and the concern is specific that this alone may encourage confabulation.

The evaluation should be conducted in a relaxed environment. Comprehensive history taking is important and should include developmental history, cognitive assessment, prior history of abuse and other traumas, relative medical history, behavioral change, parental history of abuse as children, and family attitudes toward sexuality and modesty. Prior psychiatric disorders in the child or parents should be identified, and allegiances by a child to parents should be assessed.

In intrafamilial abuse, the family history and perspective of each parent should be obtained. Stressors other than sexual abuse that might account for the child's symptoms need to be identified. This can include a psychiatric assessment of each parent, particularly if there is a concern about a false allegation. This concern can arise when it is determined that the allegation is coming from a parent rather than from a child, when the parents are engaged in a dispute, and when the child is a preschooler. False allegations are seen as arising from other situations as well, such as the misinterpretation of a child's statement and the behavior of adults. Adolescents may make a false allegation because of vindictiveness or to cover up their own sexuality, and children who experienced prior sexual abuse may misinterpret or mischaracterize the behavior of an adult.

In conducting a clinical evaluation, it is required that the clinician maintain emotional neutrality, approach the case with an open mind, and seek out the unique characteristics of each case. Clinicians are urged to avoid leading and coercive questions and techniques and to allow the child to tell the story in his or her own words. The need for external corroboration distinguishes the forensic evaluation from the usual clinical evaluation; this can include the need to review medical and school reports and prior psychiatric evaluations and talking with other persons.

A number of characteristics enhance a child's credibility. These include event descriptions in the child's own language and from the child's own point of view, spontaneity, an appropriate degree of anxiety, idiosyncratic or sensorimotor detail, consistency of allegation over time, behavioral changes consistent with abuse, absence of motivation or undue influence for fabrication, and corroborating evidence.

In regard to anatomically correct dolls, AACAP states that they may be used for eliciting the child's terminology for anatomical parts and for allowing a child who cannot tell or draw what happened to demonstrate what happened. The AACAP strongly advises that dolls not be used to instruct, coach, or lead the child or as a shortcut for a more comprehensive evaluation, and that in these assessments it is not necessary to use anatomically correct dolls at all. California has barred the admissibility of evidence obtained through the use of anatomically correct dolls.

By contrast, children's drawings are seen as a helpful assessment tool. This can include spontaneous drawings or requesting a child to draw a male or female, to draw what happened and where, or to draw a picture of the alleged offender. Videotaping is encouraged. Psychological testing may be helpful but is not seen in and of itself as a method for determining whether or not sexual abuse occurred.

SUMMARY

Nine of the 15 APA publications addressing ethical standards and guidelines apply to children and adolescents. Three of the guidelines speak specifically to clinical forensic practice. Aspirational in nature, these three guidelines have much in common with one another, with APA ethical principles, and with central features of the remaining guidelines. They all call for a high level of science-based professional practice based on the principles of thoroughness and fairness. Psychologists are expected to practice and testify within the limits of their knowledge and expertise, to communicate their results and opinions clearly, to understand their role and the law when practicing in a legal context, and to avoid dual relationships, bias, and error in their work. High standards for record keeping and for the documentation of clinical and forensic work are emphasized. The increasing importance of cultural competence is the focus in several statements. Evidence-based practice is the standard. Psychologists performing child custody evaluations are expected to possess specialized competencies for the evaluation of adults, children, relationships, and parenting ability. These skills and a matching knowledge base are also expected of psychologists performing court-ordered studies in child protection matters; they are additionally expected to have a solid understanding of the field of child abuse and neglect. Psychologists do not offer opinions about persons they have not examined or about issues for which they lack clear and verifiable evidence.

The APRI has articulated the most complete statement regarding the investigative interviewing of suspected child victims of abuse concentrating on sexual abuse. The strengths and weakness of the APRI guidelines were reviewed, along with those of the APSAC and the AACAP. Whereas the APA Guidelines for Psychological Evaluations in Child Protection Matters deals with general practice issues, the APRI guidelines offer specific instruction for the forensic interviewer on how to conduct and validate an investigative interview within the larger context of a multidisciplinary forensic investigation. The strengths and weaknesses in the APRI and APSAC guidelines were identified and discussed with the help of behavioral science research. Research-based recommendations were made for alternative strategies and methods. The APRI model for a comprehensive review of the evidentiary record was presented and discussed. Unresolved and controversial issues and best practices were identified.

REFERENCES

American Academy of Child and Adolescent Psychiatry. (1990). *Guidelines for the clinical evaluation of child and adolescent sexual abuse*. Washington, DC: Author.

American Professional Society on the Abuse of Children. (1995a). *Practice guidelines: Descriptive terminology in child sexual abuse medical evaluations*. Oklahoma City, OK: Author.

American Professional Society on the Abuse of Children. (1995b). *Practice guidelines: Photographic documentation of child abuse*. Oklahoma City, OK: Author.

American Professional Society on the Abuse of Children. (1995c). *Practice guidelines: Psychosocial evaluation of suspected psychological maltreatment in children and adolescents*. Oklahoma City, OK: Author.

American Professional Society on the Abuse of Children. (1995d). *Practice guidelines: Use of anatomical dolls in child sexual abuse assessments*. Oklahoma City, OK: Author.

American Professional Society on the Abuse of Children. (1997a). *Practice guidelines: Code of ethics*. Oklahoma City, OK: Author.

American Professional Society on the Abuse of Children. (1997b). *Practice guidelines: Psychosocial evaluation of suspected sexual abuse in children* (2nd ed.). Oklahoma City, OK: Author.

American Professional Society on the Abuse of Children. (2002). *Practice guidelines: Investigative interviewing in cases of alleged child abuse*. Oklahoma City, OK: Author.

American Prosecutors Research Institute and National Center for Prosecution of Child Abuse. (1987). *Investigation and prosecution of child abuse* (2nd ed.). Alexandria, VA: Author.

American Prosecutors Research Institute and National Center for Prosecution of Child Abuse. (2004). *Investigation and prosecution of child abuse* (3rd ed.) Thousand Oaks, CA: Sage.

American Psychological Association. (1985). *Standards for educational and psychological testing*. Washington, DC: Author.

American Psychological Association. (1990). *Guidelines for providers of psychological services to ethnic, linguistic, and culturally diverse populations*. Washington, DC: APA, Office of Ethnic Minority Affairs.

American Psychological Association. (1993). Record keeping guidelines. *American Psychologist, 48*, 984–986.

American Psychological Association. (1994). Guidelines for child custody evaluations in divorce proceedings. *American Psychologist, 49*, 677–680.

American Psychological Association. (1999). Guidelines for psychological evaluations in child protection matters. *American Psychologist, 54*, 586–593.

American Psychological Association. (2000). Guidelines for psychotherapy with lesbian, gay, and bisexual clients. *American Psychologist, 55*, 1440–1451.

American Psychological Association. (2002a). Criteria for evaluating treatment guidelines. *American Psychologist, 57*, 1052–1059.

American Psychological Association. (2002b). Criteria for practice guideline development and evaluation. *American Psychologist, 57*, 1048–1051.

American Psychological Association. (2002c). Ethical principles of psychologists and code of conduct. *APA Online*. Available from www.apa.org.

American Psychological Association. (2002d). Guidelines on multicultural education, training, research, practice, and organization change for psychologists. *APA Online*. Available from www.apa.org.

American Psychological Association. (2004a). APA resolution on outpatient civil commitment. *APA Online*. Available from www.apa.org.

American Psychological Association. (2004b). Guidelines for psychological practice with older adults. *American Psychologist, 59*, 236–260.

American Psychological Association. (2005a). Determination and documentation of the need for practice guidelines. APA Online. Available from www.apa.org.

American Psychological Association. (2005b). Policy statement on evidence-based practice in psychology. *APA Online*. Available from www.apa.org.

American Psychological Association. (2005b). Policy statement on evidence-based practice in psychology. *APA Online*. Available from www.apa.org.

American Psychological Association. (2005c). Training grid outlining best practices for recovery and improved outcomes for people with serious mental illness. *APA Online*. Available from www.apa.org.

American Psychological Association. (2006). Practice directorate. *APA Online Information and Resources for Practicing Psychologists*. Retrieved February 2, 2006, from www.apa.org.

Ash, P., & Guyer, M. J. (1991). Biased reporting by parents undergoing child custody evaluations. *Journal of the American Academy of Child and Adolescent Psychiatry, 30*(6), 835–838.

Benedek, E., & Schetky, D. (1987). Clinical experience: Problems in validating allegations of sexual abuse: Pt. II. Clinical evaluation. *Journal of the American Academy of Child and Adolescent Psychiatry, 26*, 916–921.

Besharov, D. (1994). Responding to child sexual abuse: The need for a balanced approach (David and Lucile Packard Foundation). *Future of Children: Sexual Abuse of Children, 4*, 2.

Cantlin, J., Payne, G., & Erbaugh, C. (1996). Outcome-based practice: Disclosure rates of child sexual abuse comparing allegation-blind and allegation-informed structured interviews. *Child Abuse and Neglect, 20*, 1113.

Ceci, S., & Bruck, M. (1995). *Jeopardy in the courtroom: A scientific analysis of children's testimony*. Washington, DC: American Psychological Association.

Condie, L. (2003). *Parenting evaluations for the court*. New York: Kluwer Academic/Plenum Press.

Connecticut Psychological Association. (1987). A compendium of Connecticut laws affecting the practice of psychology. Hartford, CT: Author.

Drach, K. M., Wientzen, J., & Ricci, L. R. (2001). The diagnostic utility of sexual behavior problems in diagnosing sexual abuse in a forensic child abuse evaluation clinic. *Child Abuse and Neglect, 25*, 489–503.

Everson, M., & Boat, B. (1989). False allegations of sexual abuse by children and adolescents. *Journal of the American Academy of Child and Adolescent Psychiatry, 28*, 230–235.

Friedrich, W. (1992). Child sexual behavioral inventory: Normative and clinical comparisons. *Psychological Assessment, 4*(3), 303–311.

Grisso, T. (1998). *Forensic evaluation of juveniles*. Sarasota, FL: Professional Resource Exchange.

Horner, T., Guyer, M., & Kalter, N. (1992). Clinical expertise and the assessment of child sexual abuse. *Journal of the American Academy of Child and Adolescent Psychiatry, 32*, 925–933.

Jones, D., & McGraw, M. (1987). Reliable and fictitious accounts of sexual abuse in children. *Journal of Interpersonal Violence, 2*(1), 27–45.

Kanin, E. (1994). False rape allegations. *Archives of Sexual Behavior, 23*, 81–92.

Kuehnle, K., & Sparta, S. (2006). Assessing child sexual abuse allegations in a legal context. In S. Sparta, & G. Koocher (Eds.), *Forensic mental health assessment of children and adolescents*. New York: Oxford University Press.

Lamb, M., Orbach, Y., Sternberg, K., Hershkowitz, I., & Horowitz, D. (2000). Accuracy of investigators' verbatim notes of their forensic interviews with alleged child abuse victims. *Law and Human Behavior, 24*, 699–708.

Mantell, D. (1988). Clarifying erroneous child sexual abuse allegations. *American Journal of Orthopsychiatry, 58*(4), 618–621.

Melton, G., Petrila, J., Poythress, N., & Slobogin, C. (1997). *Psychological evaluations for the courts*. New York: Guilford Press.

Poole, D., & Lamb, M. (1998). *Investigative interviews of children: A guide for helping professionals*. Washington, DC: American Psychological Association.

Sattler, J. (1988). *Clinical and forensic interviewing of children and families: Guidelines for the mental health, education, pediatric and child maltreatment fields*. San Diego: Jerome M. Sattler.

Schoentjes, E., Deboutte, D., & Friedrich, W. (1999). Child Sexual Behavior Inventory: A Dutch-speaking normative sample. *Pediatrics, 104*, 885–893.

Sparta, S., & Koocher, G. (2006). *Forensic mental health assessment of children and adolescents*. New York: Oxford University Press.

Specialty Guidelines for Forensic Psychologists. (1991). *Law and Human Behavior, 15*, 655–665.

State of Minnesota. (1985). Report on the Scott County Investigations. Hubert H. Humphrey III, Attorney General, Minneapolis, MN.

Wechsler, D. (2004). *Wechsler Intelligence Scale for Children—Fourth Edition (WISC-IV)*. San Antonio, TX: Psychological Corporation.

White, S., & Quinn, K. (1988). Investigatory independence in child sexual abuse evaluations: Conceptual considerations. *Bulletin of the American Academy of the Psychiatry Law, 16*, 269–278.

CHAPTER 5

Professional Roles

James H. Johnson, David M. Janicke, and Steven K. Reader

Given that this volume of the *Handbook of Clinical Psychology* focuses on children and adolescents, it seems fitting that a chapter be devoted to a discussion of the various professional roles assumed by psychologists who work with children and youth. While these psychologists are often referred to by various labels, such as clinical child psychologists and pediatric psychologists, professionals with other backgrounds, such as school psychologists, also work with children and adolescents.

Child-oriented psychologists vary in the nature of their professional training (clinical psychology, school psychology, developmental psychology, specialty-specific training in clinical child or pediatric psychology); theoretical orientation (behavioral, cognitive-behavioral, interpersonal, psychodynamic, humanistic); the degree to which they focus on research, clinical activities, or both; the nature of the professional activities they engage in (teaching, research, assessment, therapy, consultation, advocacy); the types of child or adolescent problems they work with (mental health problems, physical health problems, school-related difficulties); and the settings in which they work (universities, medical centers, children's hospitals, pediatric clinics, private practice, mental health centers, schools). Given the diversity of training, theoretical orientation, professional activities, types of problems addressed, and settings, it should not be surprising that these professionals often function in multiple roles and engage in a range of professional activities in the context of these roles.

This topic of professional roles is of special relevance given the rapid growth of clinical child and pediatric psychology in the past 25 years and the degree to which this growth has resulted in expanded role opportunities and, in some cases, significant changes in the nature of the activities engaged in by psychologists serving children and adolescents.

ROLES AND ROLE-RELATED ACTIVITIES OF CHILD-ORIENTED PSYCHOLOGISTS

Before embarking on the task of highlighting the professional roles assumed by child-oriented psychologists, it is important to attempt to define what is meant by the term "role" and differentiate this term from the professional activities associated with these roles.

Considering several dictionary definitions, the term role, as it is used here, generally refers to a *consistent pattern of behavior* that is expected of someone based on his or her status or position in society (Merriam-Webster's New Collegiate Dictionary, 11th ed.). From this perspective, functioning in the role of a clinical child or pediatric psychologist involves engaging in a pattern of professional behavior that is consistent with one's prior training as a specific type of child health service provider. At the simplest level, the term "professional role" as applied to a clinical child psychologist can be best thought of as a general *construct* used to summarize the range of interrelated specialty-specific behaviors that are engaged in as one trained in clinical child psychology carries out his or her professional activities.

Closely associated with the term role is the pattern of specialty-specific professional activities, engaged in by the psychologist by virtue of his or her professional training, that define him or her as a specific type of health care professional. As regards the various roles of child-oriented psychologists, some function in the role of clinical child psychologist, and others function in the role of pediatric psychologist. Still others function in the role of school or applied developmental psychologist. Both clinical child and pediatric psychologists may engage in somewhat similar activities to a greater or lesser degree. For example, both may engage in assessment, intervention, consultation, research, or various other professional activities with children and families. But, while there may be some similarity in terms of the general types of activities engaged in, the roles may differ significantly in the way these activities are carried out, the problems and clinical populations dealt with, and the settings in which these professional activities take place.

As but one example, the clinical child psychologist's activities might involve an interview and administering a well-chosen selection of psychological tests to assess for the presence of Attention-Deficit/Hyperactivity Disorder (ADHD) and possible comorbid conditions (e.g., learning disability, anxiety or depressive features), collaborating with a child psychiatrist in the treatment of the child's core ADHD symptoms and using cognitive-behavioral interventions to treat the child's diagnosed anxiety or depressive disorder, in a private practice or mental health clinic setting. In contrast, a pediatric psychologist's assessment activities might entail interviews with the child and parent, consultation with the child' physician and nursing staff, and behavioral observations at meal time to determine factors contributing to a 5-year-old's frequent vomiting and failure to eat. Treatment might involve behavioral interventions designed to teach the parent how to reward successive approximations to normal eating and avoid attending to statements of stomach upset and instances of vomiting. Other interventions might involve additional forms of reinforcement for increased caloric intake, as well as other contingencies following vomiting episodes, with such treatment taking place on a pediatric floor of a university-affiliated medical center. Thus, although both may engage in similar activities (e.g., assessment, consultation, intervention), the nature of the specific activities involved may differ depending on whether the clinician is functioning in the role of clinical child or pediatric psychologist.

It should also be emphasized that child-oriented psychologists may function in roles that represent a greater or lesser degree of specificity. For example, one clinical child psychologist may engage in a wide range of child-related professional activities such as assessment, therapy, teaching, and research, and another may function more specifically in the role of child psychotherapist. Likewise, a pediatric psychologist may functional broadly in this professional role (e.g., working with children displaying both acute and chronic illnesses and engaging in a variety of child or adolescent consult-liaison activities) or may restrict his or her professional activities, as in the case of the pediatric psychologist whose work primarily involves conducting pretransplant evaluations with children and adolescents and working with children who have recently been transplanted (who may think of himself or herself as a pediatric transplant psychologist). Finally, whereas some clinical child or pediatric psychologists assume roles that involve varying levels of specialization, as described earlier, others simultaneously function in multiple professional roles (e.g., administrator *and* clinical child psychologist), each of which may vary in terms of breadth and complexity and relationship to one another.

Despite general agreement that there is an insufficient number of adequately trained child-oriented psychologists to meet the mental health needs of children, there is an increasingly large number of psychologists who, by virtue of their training and/or professional experience, currently define themselves as clinical child or pediatric psychologists and engage in a wide range of professional activities with children, youth, and families. In the sections to follow we provide an overview of the diverse range of professional activities and functions that are associated with these professional roles. This is followed by a brief commentary on the role of school psychologists, as they also often provide clinical services to children and adolescents.

CLINICAL CHILD AND ADOLESCENT PSYCHOLOGY

The area of clinical child and adolescent psychology represents a rapidly growing area of professional psychology. A capsule summary of the multiple roles and functions played by professionals working in this area can be seen in the ways this specialty has been self-defined.

The following definition of the specialty of clinical child psychology has been provided in the archival description of the specialty submitted to the Commission for the Recognition of Specialties and Proficiencies in Professional Psychology (1998), upon the formal recognition of the specialty by the American Psychological Association in 1998:

> Clinical Child Psychology is a specialty of professional psychology, which brings together the basic tenets of clinical psychology with a thorough background in child, adolescent and family development and developmental psychopathology. Clinical child and adolescent psychologists conduct scientific research and provide psychological services to infants, toddlers, children, and adolescents. The research and practices of Clinical Child Psychologists are focused on understanding, preventing, diagnosing, and treating psychological, cognitive, emotional, developmental, behavioral, and family problems of children. Of particular importance to clinical child and adolescent psychologists is a scientific understanding of the basic psychological needs of children and adolescents and how the family and other social contexts influence socioemotional adjustment, cognitive development, behavioral adaptation, and health status of children and adolescents. There is an essential

emphasis on a strong empirical research base recognizing the need for the documentation and further development of evidence-based assessments and treatments in clinical child and adolescent psychology.

Of special note in this definition is that the training of clinical child psychologists represents (or at least should represent) a blending of developmental psychology and clinical psychology in a framework that places emphasis on the developmental aspects of psychopathology, which has as its focus understanding the mechanisms of development and behavior change. Central to the focus on developmental psychopathology is the belief that the study of atypical development can add to the understanding of normal development and, conversely, that the methods and approaches used in normative developmental science can shed light on the etiology, course, and outcome of psychological disorders. It is this focus on training in child, adolescent, and family development *and* developmental psychopathology, along with the tenets of clinical psychology, that distinguishes the well-trained clinical child psychologist from the general clinical psychologists who happen to also work with children. It needs to be emphasized that clinical child psychology is more than just the knowledge of clinical psychology methods applied to children.

This definition also highlights the fact that clinical child psychologists work with a wide range of individuals, displaying a wide range of difficulties, through the application of a wide range of assessment and treatment methods. In the sections to follow we elaborate on these topics.

Populations Served

Clinical child psychologists work with children of all ages, ranging in age from infancy and childhood through the adolescent years, and their families. Nevertheless, children of some ages tend to be seen more frequently in clinical practice. For example, Tuma and Pratt (1982) found that the most common age groups seen were children between the ages of 5 and 10 (29%). The next most common age groups seen were adolescents 14 to 18 (23%), preadolescents 11 to 13 (22%), and preschoolers below 4 (13%). These child clinicians also reported seeing a significant number of adults, with 38% reporting working with patients over age 18.

Clinical child psychologists work with children who display a wide range of problems. Unlike the pediatric psychologist, who is likely to focus more on child and adolescent health-related problems, the clinical child psychologist is likely to focus more on mental health difficulties, although the distinction between the activities of clinical child and pediatric psychologists can be blurred on occasion. Problems that clinical child psychologists are often called on to assess and treat can range from easily managed problems such as bedwetting and soiling and helping parents manage a child with a difficult temperament to internalizing problems such as anxiety and depression and externalizing conditions such as Oppositional Defiant Disorder, Conduct Disorder, and ADHD. Clinical child psychologists also see children with learning disabilities, as well as those with severe psychological disorders such as mental retardation, pervasive developmental disorders, Schizophrenia, and pediatric Bipolar Disorder. Child clinicians are often called on to deal with problems that may or may not be defined in terms of a specific diagnosis. Here, examples include working with children of divorce, those who have been vicariously exposed to marital abuse, those who have experienced physical or sexual abuse, or those who have been impacted by hurricanes or other natural disasters.

Practice Settings

For those clinical child psychologists engaging in applied clinical work, practice settings include private practice, children's residential treatment centers, mental health clinics, and public health agencies, schools, medical school clinics. Those whose primary role is university teaching (often in departments of psychology) may engage in part-time clinical activities in the university setting. As will be seen later, child clinicians who are more health-oriented often practice in children's hospitals or sometimes in private practice pediatric settings.

Some figures regarding clinical practice settings have been provided by Tuma and Pratt (1982) in their survey of 358 clinical child psychologists who were members of what is now the Society of Clinical Child and Adolescent Psychology. The data provided by this survey suggest employment in a wide variety of work settings, with most respondents working in more than one setting. Most reported working in medical school settings, primarily in departments of pediatrics and psychiatry (51%). The second largest work setting was private practice (44%). Other work settings included graduate departments of psychology (21%), schools (15%), mental health centers (11%), child guidance centers (9%), children's hospitals (9%), and general hospitals (5%). A much smaller number were employed in residential and state hospitals.

More recent survey findings regarding practice settings of 162 child-oriented psychologists (including clinical child and pediatric psychologists and school psychologists) have been provided by Cashel (2002). Of these clinicians, 29% reported working in a medical center or other hospital settings. Other settings included college or university (22%), school system (17%), outpatient clinic (11%), and community mental health center (1.9%). As in the Tuma and Pratt (1982) survey, many of the respondents in this study worked in multiple settings, with approximately 31% working exclusively in private practice.

Taken together, these findings suggest that, across time, the primary practice settings of clinical child psychologists appear to be medical schools and hospitals, private practice, and university settings where the child clinician likely also plays a major role in clinical training and supervision. In other settings the numbers are considerably smaller, with surprisingly few clinical child psychologists working in community mental health centers.

Theoretical Orientations

Of interest is the theoretical orientation of clinical child psychologists, especially as this may show changes over time. This issue is of relevance to clinical practice as approaches to both assessment and treatment are usually, to some degree, tied to the theoretical orientation of the clinician. And, to the extent that the primary theoretical orientation of clinicians changes over time, this is likely to have implications both for the role functions of the clinician and for the type of training those aspiring to be clinical child psychologists will need to meet changing role functions.

Data relevant to the issue of theoretical orientation have been provided by the two surveys cited earlier. In the Tuma and Pratt (1982) survey, 28% of the 358 clinical child psychologists surveyed classified themselves as having a psychodynamic orientation, 25% described their orientation as behavioral, and 4% described their orientation as humanistic-existential; the remainder described their orientation as eclectic.

These findings regarding theoretical orientation can be contrasted with the findings 20 years later (Cashel, 2002). Here, the majority of child clinicians described themselves as cognitive-behavioral (52%), and an additional 7% described themselves as having a behavioral orientation. Thus, almost 60% of the respondents endorsed either a behavioral or cognitive-behavioral orientation. Respondents endorsing other orientations included psychodynamic (9%) and interpersonal (5%), with 25% labeling themselves eclectic.

These findings suggest that during the 20-year period between 1982 and 2002, the theoretical orientations of child clinicians have changed significantly, with a vastly increased number of clinical child psychologists now endorsing a behavioral or cognitive-behavioral theoretical framework (and presumably assessment and treatment methods based on this framework), with a concurrent reduction in clinicians claiming a psychodynamic orientation. These findings would seem to be consistent with the increasing focus on both evidence-based assessment (Kazdin, 2005; Mash & Hunsley, 2005) and evidence-based child treatment methods (Ollendick & King, 2004) that currently characterize clinical child psychology.

Role-Related Professional Activities

As suggested earlier, functioning in the role of clinical child psychologist can involve participating in an extensive array of professional activities that serve to define the specialty. Among the most prominent of these activities are assessment, treatment, and conducting research on a wide range of topics relevant to children and families. A sizable number of clinical child psychologists, especially those employed in academic settings, function as teacher and clinical supervisor, in addition to their involvement in research and perhaps part-time clinical work. A somewhat smaller but still significant number of clinical child psychologists also work in the area of prevention and engage in consultation activities. In the sections to follow we highlight the work of clinical child psychologists in a number of these areas and, where relevant, the ways these activities have changed as a function of the evolution of the specialty.

Assessment Activities

Assessment has long been a major professional activity of clinical child psychologists of various theoretical orientations, and for some practitioners, providing psychological assessments for children and adolescents is their primary professional activity. Indeed, assessment is one of the most frequently engaged in professional activities of psychologists working with children. Assessment can involve open-ended interviews, the use of intelligence tests, and the assessment of academic achievement, adaptive behavior, visual-motor functioning, as well as the use of projective tests and various questionnaires to assess personality dynamics and what are thought to be enduring personality characteristics. Assessment can also involve the use of more structured interviews to assess specific symptoms of psychopathology, the use of objective behavior problem checklists designed to assess behavioral characteristics of the child, and approaches to assess overt behaviors and the factors that elicit (antecedents) and maintain (consequences) these behaviors in the natural environment. Also commonly used are measures designed to assess aspects of parenting stress and family environment as well as other variables thought to be relevant to the functioning of the child and his or her family. Given that assessment is essential to making an accurate diagnosis of childhood problems and is usually assumed to be an essential prerequisite to the development of an appropriate treatment plan, it is not surprising that clinical child psychologists have typically devoted a significant amount of time to assessment-related activities.

It is noteworthy that the nature and, to some extent, the *type* of involvement by clinical child psychologists in assessment activities has changed over the years. For example, in the Tuma and Pratt (1982) survey, the average amount of professional time spent in assessment activities with children, adolescents, parents, and families was 28%, as compared to 41% of their time being devoted to treatment-related activities. According to the authors, assessment and treatment were the two primary professional activities engaged in by these clinical child psychologists.

These authors also provided information regarding the nature of the assessment measures used by this sample of clinical child psychologists. Here, 83% reported using intelligence tests, 54% reported using the Rorschach, 53% the Thematic Apperception Test (TAT), and 60% figure drawings. A total of 53% indicated that they used the Bender Gestalt test, 51% indicated that they used achievement tests, 18% said they used the Minnesota Multiphasic Personality Inventory (MMPI), 17% reported use of sentence completion tests, and only 13% reported the use of behavioral assessment measures. As can be seen, apart from the use of intelligence and achievement tests, the child clinicians in this survey appeared to rely heavily on the use of projective tests of various types, to the exclusion of more behaviorally oriented assessment measures.

These assessment preferences can be compared to those found by Cashel (2002), where respondents reported spending 27.3% of their time conducting psychological assessments, supporting the view that assessment continues to be a major professional activity engaged in by child-oriented clinicians. When these respondents were asked to indicate their use of various assessment measures, the Wechsler Intelligence Scale for Children was, by far, the most frequently used measure. When asked to rank other assessment approaches by order of importance, the clinical interview was ranked as most important, followed by behavioral observations, behavior ratings, self-report inventories, and, finally, projective tests (Cashel, 2002).

These findings suggest that although some clinical child psychologists still use the Rorschach, the TAT, figure drawings, and other projective approaches, the perceived value of these measures has declined, while behaviorally focused assessment measures have become increasingly more popular and appear to be more highly valued by today's clinical child psychologist. This trend parallels the increasing focus on evidence-based assessment, where the preference is not only for useful assessment methods that are supported by research findings but also for measures that are useful in monitoring treatment effectiveness (Kazdin, 2005). Not only has the focus on evidence-based practice likely had some impact on child assessment practice, but the nature of child assessment has also been impacted by managed care. Today there seems to be less of a focus on the use of standardized test batteries and more on assessment methods relevant to specific problem areas. In the Cashel (2002) survey, it was found that the utilization of many previously popular test measures such as the Rorschach and MMPI seems to have declined due to decreased reimbursement for such measures. Although assessment continues to be a major professional activity of clinical child psychologists, the nature of the assessment measures used by child clinicians today is increasingly moving away from subjective measures and projective techniques and toward more objective, behaviorally focused, and more empirically supported assessment measures.

Intervention Activities

Along with assessment, providing treatment for children, adolescents, and their families is one of the defining professional activities of clinical child psychologists. Indeed, many clinical child psychologists in private practice function primarily in the role of child and family therapist.

It can be recalled that Tuma and Pratt (1982) found that, on average, clinical child psychologists spent over 40% of their professional time engaging in treatment-related activities with children, adolescents, and families. The types of therapy engaged in included counseling with parents, play therapy, individual psychotherapy, behavior therapy, and family therapy. Not surprisingly, the type of therapy varied as a function of the child's age, with parent counseling, play therapy, and behavior therapy being used by 63%, 44%, and 36% of the therapists, respectively. With school-age children, play therapy (53%), family therapy (37%), and individual psychotherapy (35%) were the most widely used approaches, with fewer therapists endorsing parent counseling and behavior therapy (29% each). Individual psychotherapy (74%), family therapy (46%), and counseling with parents (32%) were the most widely used therapeutic approaches with adolescents.

Today, clinical child psychologists engage in a wide range of interventions with children and families. These continue to include many of the traditional approaches to child treatment described by Tuma and Pratt (1982; e.g., parent counseling, play therapy, individual psychotherapy, family therapy, behavior therapy) but with perhaps a much greater focus on behaviorally oriented parent training approaches and behavior management approaches applied in the school, community, and health care settings. Today, we also see the widespread use of more recently developed cognitive-behavioral approaches to treatment that have been found useful in dealing with children and adolescents displaying psychological difficulties such as anxiety, depression, anger management, and Obsessive-Compulsive Disorder (O'Donohue, Fisher, & Hayes, 2003), as well as multimodal interventions for children and adolescents exhibiting complex problems.

This movement toward the use of more behavioral and cognitive-behavioral child therapies appears due to two interrelated factors: the changing theoretical orientation of child-oriented clinicians and the coming of age of evidence-based treatments. As noted earlier, 25 years ago the two predominant theoretical orientations of clinical child psychologists were psychodynamic and behavioral, with somewhat more child clinicians endorsing the psychodynamic perspective and likely engaging in treatments that were in line with their orientation (Tuma & Pratt, 1982). More recent surveys suggest that almost 60% of child-oriented clinicians now define themselves as having cognitive-behavioral or behavioral orientations, with fewer than 10% identifying themselves with the psychodynamic perspective (Cashel, 2002). This represents a dramatic shift in theoretical perspective that, along with the increased focus on the development of evidence-based treatments, likely relates to the increased use of behaviorally related approaches to intervention that we see today.

Teaching and Training Activities

As was briefly noted earlier, surveys conducted 20 years apart by Tuma and Pratt (1982) and Cashel (2002) have both found that a sizable number of clinical child psychologists work in some type of academic setting. Both found that approximately 20% worked in college and university settings, often in graduate departments of psychology. Likewise, both found that many worked in medical school settings (51% in the Tuma and Pratt survey and 29% in the Cashel survey). Employment was usually in departments of pediatrics or psychiatry.

Clinical child psychologists employed in these settings are frequently involved in training of some type. In university departments of psychology, where the academic training of clinical child psychologists often takes place, teaching can take several forms. It can involve teaching basic psychology courses (e.g., introductory psychology, personality, abnormal psychology) or teaching academic courses relevant to specialty training (e.g., developmental psychology, developmental psychopathology, child assessment, child treatment, evidence-based practice). Teaching in this setting can also involve a supervisory role in the context of various clinical practica, where the primary focus is on helping the psychology trainees develop important conceptual and clinical skills. Importantly, teaching and mentoring may also take place in the context of the student's research training, which, ideally, should at some point involve research with clinical populations so the trainee can learn how clinical knowledge can inform research and how good clinical research can inform clinical practice.

For those clinical child (or pediatric) psychologists working in medical schools, teaching formal didactic courses may be less common than teaching seminars relevant to aspects of clinical practice and the clinical supervision of trainees (e.g., interns, postdoctoral fellows, psych techs). Not infrequently, psychologists working in this setting are asked to contribute to the behavioral science curriculum of medical students or to coteach courses such as "Introduction to Patient Evaluation," which are often designed to help medical students learn clinical interviewing and relationship-enhancement skills that will serve them well as professionals working with patients.

The teaching possibilities for clinical child psychologists are many. They are also important, as the quality of training that future clinical child psychology (or other) trainees receive is likely related not only to the trainees' ultimate level of professional competence but also to the quality of care that the trainees provide children and families upon completion of training.

Research Activities

Over the years, the predominant model of graduate training for clinical psychologists has been the Boulder or scientist-practitioner model (Raimy, 1950; Shakow, 1948). This model has also been repeatedly endorsed as the preferred model for training both clinical child and pediatric psychologists. As the basic premise of the scientist-practitioner model is that the clinical child psychologist should be trained as both a scientist and practitioner, it is not surprising that clinical child psychologists often adopt the roles of both researcher and practicing clinician. Although relatively few clinical child psychologists in private practice devote a significant amount of time to research, adoption of these dual roles is not at all uncommon for clinical child psychologists who work in academic or medical school settings, where they are likely to also function in the roles of teacher and supervisor.

The range of research topics addressed by clinical child psychologists is too broad to cover here but includes research related to the development and validation of assessment measures (e.g., structured and semi-structured interview measures, intelligence and achievement measures, measures of development and adaptive behavior, behavior problem checklists, personality questionnaires, computer-based assessment measures); research related to the development and documentation of the efficacy and effectiveness of various approaches to child treatment; research related to the etiology, correlates and developmental course of various types of child psychopathology; and research on factors that may place the child at risk for later psychopathology (e.g., genetic factors, difficult temperament, divorce, abuse), just to name a few areas.

One area that deserves special attention relates to efforts to identify empirically supported psychosocial treatments for children and adolescents. This work, which has a similar focus to the evidence-based practice movement in medicine (Sackett, Richardson, Rosenberg, & Haynes, 2000), resulted from the efforts of the Society of Clinical Psychology's (APA, Division 12) Task Force on Promotion and Dissemination of Psychological Procedures (Chambless, 1996; Chambless & Hollon, 1998).

This task force, which began its work in 1995, initially attempted to develop criteria for determining psychological and behavioral approaches to treatment that were well supported by research findings. Research support was to be determined by studies of treatment efficacy, with significant treatment-related change being documented in well-controlled research investigations, emphasizing internal validity. Using the criteria adopted by the task force, it was possible to categorize psychosocial treatments of various types into two efficacy-related categories: well-established treatments and probably efficacious treatments.

To qualify as a "well-established treatment," two adequately designed group studies (from different researchers), demonstrating the treatment to be significantly better than a pill placebo, psychological placebo, or other treatment or equivalent to an already established treatment were required. Alternatively, designation as a "well-established treatment" could result from a series of > 9 well-controlled, single-subject design studies that compared the experimental treatment to some other treatment. In both instances, the nature of the samples had to be adequately described and the treatment based on a treatment manual.

Treatments could qualify as "probably efficacious" based on (1) two well-controlled studies that demonstrated the treatment to be superior to a wait-list control group or (2) one or more studies that met criteria for "well-established treatments" (see previous) but conducted by the same researcher. Probably efficacious treatments could also be documented via a series (here > 3) of single-subject design studies by a single investigator that met the well-established treatment criteria. Again, treatment was to be based on a treatment manual and sample characteristics had to be clearly specified (Chambless & Hollon, 1998).

As Ollendick and King (2004) have noted, using criteria such as these, the task force was able to identify a total of 25 largely adult-focused treatments that were judged to be empirically supported to a greater or lesser degree (18 well-established treatments; 7 probably efficacious treatments). Of these, only three treatments for children were identified as well-established treatments, and one met criteria for a probably efficacious treatment. These included behaviorally oriented interventions for children with developmental delays, enuresis and encopresis, oppositional-defiant behavior (well-established treatments), and tics (probably efficacious).

Given that the initial focus of this task force was largely on adult-related treatments, the Society of Clinical Psychology and the Section on Clinical Child Psychology (Division 12; Section 1, presently Division 53 of the American Psychological Association), both subsequently developed task forces to determine empirical support for various approaches to child and adolescent treatments. The combined efforts of these two groups provided varying levels of evidence-based support for a number of additional child treatments (Lonigan, Elbert, & Johnson, 1998). Ollendick and King (2004) have also cited other attempts to delineate the degree of support available for child/adolescent treatments, using somewhat similar research criteria. Here, they cite the work of Nathan & Gorman (1998) and Roth, Fonagy, Parry, & Target (1996). Taken together, these efforts highlight a range of child treatments that have been judged as well-established or probably efficacious (Chambless & Ollendick, 2001; Ollendick & King, 2004). These treatments are listed in Tables 5.1 and 5.2.

While the information presented in Tables 5.1 and 5.2 highlights the significant advances that have been made in documenting the evidence base for a variety of approaches to child treatment, it is important to note that the treatments listed here are not likely to represent a final tally of effective psychosocial treatments for use with children and adolescents. For example, ongoing research related to the treatment of adolescent depression is providing increasing support for the role of interpersonal therapy as an evidence-based treatment for this disorder (Mufson,

Table 5.1   Examples of Well-Established Child Treatments

Problem or Disorder	Type of Treatment
Attention-Deficit/Hyperactivity Disorder	Behavioral parent training
	Classroom behavior modification
Anxiety disorders	None
Autism	None
Depression	None
Enuresis	Behavior modification
Encopresis	Behavior modification
Obsessive-Compulsive Disorder	None
Oppositional Defiant Disorder/ Conduct Disorder	Behavior parent training
	Functional family therapy
	Videotaped modeling
	Multisystemic therapy
Phobias	Graduated exposure
	Participant modeling
	Reinforced practice

From "Empirically Supported Treatments for Children and Adolescents: Advances toward Evidence-Based Practice" (p. 8), by T. H. Ollendick and N. J. King in *Handbook of Interventions that Work with Children and Adolescents: Prevention and Treatment,* P. M. Barrett and T. H. Ollendick (Eds.), 2004, Hoboken, NJ: Wiley. Adapted with permission.

Dorta, Moreau, & Weissman, 2004). Research related to the treatment of other types of child psychopathology is currently underway. As these research efforts continue, hopefully evidence will be found for the effectiveness of an even wider range of approaches that are useful in the treatment of child and adolescent problems.

Finally, although lagging behind research related to child treatment, the developing focus on evidence-based assessment (Mash & Hunsley, 2005; Kazdin, 2005) is also rapidly becoming an active area of research focus for clinical child psychologists.

Prevention Activities

Many psychologists focus on ways of treating problems already displayed by the child, adolescent, or family; the focus of other clinical child psychologists is on ways of preventing the initial development of childhood disorders (primary prevention) and/or on the early detection of problems so as to decrease the duration of the problem and minimize its effects (secondary prevention). A third form of prevention (tertiary prevention) is designed to minimize the impact of an already existing problem or disorder; in many ways, this can be equated with therapy.

Examples of primary prevention include programs designed to reduce teenage pregnancy and/or risky sexual behavior, programs designed to enhance seatbelt or car seat usage, and child-proofing homes to prevent unintentional injuries. Also included are programs designed to prevent substance abuse and family interventions to prevent child abuse in high-risk families.

Examples of secondary prevention include programs such as those designed to detect autism in very young children so that effective behavioral treatments can be used to teach social and language communication skills. Another example is the

Table 5.2   Examples of Probably Efficacious Child Treatments

Problem or Disorder	Type of Treatment
Attention-Deficit/Hyperactivity Disorder	Cognitive-behavior therapy (CBT)
Anxiety disorders	CBT
	CBT + family anxiety management
Autism	Contingency management
Depression	Behavioral self-control therapy
	Cognitive-behavioral coping skills
Enuresis	None
Encopresis	None
Obsessive-Compulsive Disorder	Exposure/response prevention
Oppositional Defiant Disorder/ Conduct Disorder	Anger control training with stress inoculation
	Anger coping therapy
	CBT
	Assertiveness training
	Delinquency prevention program
	Parent-child interaction therapy
	Problem-solving skills training
	Rational emotive therapy
	Time out + signal seat treatment
Phobias	Imaginal desensitization
	In vivo desensitization
	Live modeling
	Filmed modeling
	CBT

From "Empirically Supported Treatments for Children and Adolescents: Advances toward Evidence-Based Practice" (p. 8), by T. H. Ollendick and N. J. King, in *Handbook of Interventions that Work with Children and Adolescents: Prevention and Treatment*, P. M. Barrett and T. H. Ollendick (Eds.), 2004, Hoboken, NJ: Wiley. Adapted with permission.

Early Head Start program, which is designed to provide early education, health, and family support services for at-risk children up to age 3 from low-income families (Raikes & Love, 2002). Research has found that children benefit from this program in terms of increased cognitive development, more intellectually stimulating home environments, and the development of better paternal parenting skills (McNeil & Bernard, 2003).

Justifiably most often thought of as treatment, an excellent example of tertiary prevention is the use of parent-child interaction therapy (Brinkmeyer & Eyberg, 2003) to reduce disruptive behavior in preschool children with oppositional-defiant behavior, with the goal of preventing the long-term negative outcomes of adult antisocial behavior.

Work in the area of secondary prevention (early intervention) has been demonstrated to be of clear importance and to be of documented value in minimizing some of the negative impacts of childhood problems that, if left untreated, would likely result in negative long-term outcomes. Unfortunately, inadequate funding of primary prevention programs has left the potential value of many such programs unrealized (Boles, Mashunkashey, & Roberts, 2003). With increased levels of federal funding for the development and dissemination of such programs, work in the area of primary prevention could become a more attractive professional activity for clinical child psychologists.

The Training of Clinical Child Psychologists

Over the years there has been a dramatic increase in the number of clinical child psychology training programs, which has been prompted, in part, by the shortage of a sufficient number of adequately trained psychologists to meet the mental health needs of children (Knitzer, 1982). In the 1976–1977 edition of the American Psychological Association's *Graduate Study in Psychology,* only eight graduate programs self-identified as offering specialty training in clinical child psychology (Johnson, 2003). A survey of graduate training programs in 1982 was able to identify only 15 doctoral programs that provided clinical child specialty training (Roberts, 1982). By 1995, the Directory of Graduate Programs in Clinical Child/Pediatric Psychology (Tarnowski & Simonian, 1995) listed more than 100 programs in the United States and Canada that *self-reported* offering training in clinical child or pediatric psychology, although many of these would likely not meet strict criteria for a formal training program. Indeed, it seems likely that the number of graduate training programs offering quality specialty training in clinical child psychology is well below this number.

Given the need for *adequately trained* clinicians to meet the mental health needs of children *and* the increasing number of programs offering training in clinical child and pediatric psychology, considerable attention has been given to developing training guidelines to ensure adequate preparation of those entering the field. Over the years, three efforts in this regard are especially noteworthy.

First was the work of a task force of the APA Division of Child Youth and Family Services (Division 37), which proposed initial general guidelines (academic coursework, research experiences, and applied training in assessment and therapy) for training psychologists for working with children, youth, and families (see Roberts, Erickson, & Tuma, 1985). This work was followed by the national conference on "Training Clinical Child Psychologists," held at Hilton Head, South Carolina, in May 1985. Here, participants, who were leaders in the fields of clinical child and pediatric psychology, endorsed the general recommendations of the Division 37 Task Force and a scientist-practitioner model of training that emphasized training clinical child psychologists to function both as scientist and clinician and agreed on a range of other recommendations for clinical child training at the graduate, internship, and postdoctoral levels (Johnson & Tuma, 1986; Tuma, 1985).

A more recent attempt to integrate and elaborate on the Hilton Head conference guidelines resulted from the efforts of a National Institute of Mental Health Center for Mental Health Issues Task Force, which held a subsequent training conference at the University of Kansas in 1993. The results of these efforts, detailed by Roberts et al. (1998), represent an elaborate and well-considered framework for the professional training of individuals desiring to work with children and families. It was recommended that trainees be exposed to a wide range of didactic and applied training experiences in (a) life span developmental psychology; (b) life span developmental psychopathology; (c) child, adolescent, and family assessment;

(d) intervention strategies; (e) professional, ethical, and legal issues pertaining to children, youth, and families; (f) research methods and approaches to system evaluation; (g) issues of diversity; (h) prevention, family support, and health promotion; (i) the role of multiple disciplines and service delivery systems; (j) social issues affecting children, youth, and families; and (k) specialized applied experiences in assessment, intervention, and consultation.

These recommendations indicated that clinical training in these areas should be designed to progress sequentially from simple exposure to the development of expertise in various areas, that they should involve structured research experiences relevant to the specialty, and that internship training should build on predoctoral training and provide a foundation for postdoctoral work. This framework appears to provide an excellent foundation for clinical child specialty training. Building on these guidelines, additional training recommendations related specifically to pediatric psychology training have been outlined by Spirito et al. (2003).

A significant issue in clinical child psychology training is that, at present, there are few quality assurance mechanisms to ensure that graduate programs purporting to offer specialty training do, in fact, offer training consistent with recommendations repeatedly endorsed by professional organizations representing the specialty. This is, in part, due to the fact that historically there has been no mechanism for the accreditation of specialty programs apart from clinical, counseling, and school psychology. Thus, although graduate programs in these areas are required to conduct self-studies and meet APA Committee on Accreditation standards to initially get or maintain accreditation, there are currently no provisions to ensure that clinical training in specialty tracks (where most of clinical child training takes place) is consistent with existing specialty training guidelines. It is clear that many existing clinical child psychology training programs provide quality graduate education in this area, as evidenced by a strong clinical child training faculty, a formal sequence of required clinical child training experiences (that are consistent with specialty training guidelines), and their having a strong track record of turning out successful clinical child psychologists. Quality assurance mechanisms are necessary to ensure that all programs purporting to offer clinical child training meet these standards.

Clinical Child Psychology: Present and Future

Clinical child psychology, along with pediatric psychology, has grown rapidly over the past several decades. Since the 1960s, when the first interest groups related to clinical child psychology were organized, the field has grown in the number of professionals identified with the area and in the number of graduate programs designed to train clinical child psychologists. Likewise, as noted, the area has developed clinical training guidelines in an initial attempt to ensure that those trained in the area are trained well.

After many years of being viewed as a subspecialty of clinical psychology, clinical child psychology has now been formally recognized as a separate specialty in professional psychology, and the primary organization representing the area, the Society of Clinical Child and Adolescent Psychology, has evolved from being a section of the APA Division of Clinical Psychology to being an APA division in its own right, as has the Society of Pediatric Psychology. In the short time since its inception, research productivity of the members of the specialty has grown at an ever-increasing rate. Much of this research has been published by two journals maintained by these divisions, the *Journal of Clinical Child and Adolescent Psychology* and the *Journal of Pediatric Psychology*, which have grown from humble beginnings to currently enjoying the status of first-rate psychology journals. Cutting-edge research in the area of clinical child psychology is also regularly presented at the biannual Kansas Conference on Clinical Child and Adolescent Psychology, and current research in the area of pediatric psychology is presented at the biannual National Conference on Child Health Psychology.* The growth of the area is also highlighted by the fact that it is now possible for evidence of excellence in clinical child practice to be recognized through specialty board certification in clinical child psychology through the American Board of Clinical Child and Adolescent Psychology.

As suggested in the formal petition to the APA for specialty recognition in 1998, the area of clinical child psychology has indeed become a "well-developed, legitimate, and formally recognized area of clinical and research specialization, characterized by the development of an ever increasing body of specialized knowledge and a vibrant, diverse, and specialized area of practice" (Commission for the Recognition of Specialties and Proficiencies in Professional Psychology, 1998, p. 2). Given the rapid growth of the specialty during the past 20 to 25 years, questions arise as to where the specialty of clinical child psychology will go in the future. Here, change and advancement are likely on several fronts.

First, it seems likely that the evolving nature of the field will bring about significant changes in the practice of clinical child psychology in the years to come and result in new and different role functions for those identified with this area. As noted earlier, it appears that clinical child psychology has begun to experience a significant shift in the theoretical orientation of new clinical child psychologists coming into the field. There is clear movement toward an increasing number of practitioners with behavioral and cognitive-behavioral theoretical orientations and fewer clinical child psychologists with a predominantly psychodynamic orientation. Given this trend, in the future we will likely continue to see a de-emphasis on training in projective techniques and other more subjective assessment measures and an increased emphasis on more objective and evidence-based assessment measures. This is likely to be accompanied by a corresponding training emphasis on more evidence-based treatments for childhood disorders, which at this point seem to be interventions that are primarily behavioral or cognitive-behavioral in nature. These already evident trends in clinical training will likely also be reflected in the clinical practice of those clinical child psychologists entering the workforce.

---

*The National Conference on Clinical Child and Adolescent Psychology was founded in October 1994 by Michael Roberts and colleagues in the Clinical Child Psychology program at the University of Kansas. The National Conference on Child Health Psychology (formerly the Florida Conference on Child Health Psychology) was founded in 1988 by James H. Johnson and Suzanne Bennett Johnson and their colleagues in the Department of Clinical and Health Psychology at the University of Florida.

It is also likely that the impact of managed care will continue to influence clinical practice in terms of assessment and treatment approaches as evidence-based assessment and treatment methods are likely to become increasingly favored for reimbursement.

Consistent with these projections, it is safe to predict that the next several years will see an increased focus on clinical child psychology research related to various aspects of evidence-based practice. This will likely include expanded efforts in researching evidence-based treatments for children and adolescents, including treatments other than those based on behavioral and/or cognitive-behavioral principles, and increased research focus on evidence-based assessment as well as research on the *integration* of evidence-based assessment and evidence-based treatment methods.

As regards child and adolescent treatment we can also expect to see a significant increase in research on the effectiveness of those child treatments that have been determined to be efficacious. It is clearly important to conduct research to document significant treatment effects in the research setting; it is also essential to document the effectiveness of these treatments in applied clinical settings. This research on effectiveness is essential and will likely become a major focus of child treatment research in the near future. Related to the issue of effectiveness, one can safely predict an increasing focus on finding ways of disseminating empirically supported treatments so they are likely to be used in clinical practice as well as researching ways of individualizing manualized treatments to ensure treatment fidelity while also making them more flexible and hence more palatable to practitioners (Kendall & Beidas, 2007). Continued advances in this area of research and the increased dissemination of evidence-based approaches to treatment are likely, over time, to have a significant impact on the role functions of clinical child practitioners in terms of their increasing reliance on empirically based methods of treatment. This would be a very positive outcome for children.

The changing roles of clinical child psychologists have also been highlighted by Prinstein and Roberts (2006) who have noted that, upon completing their graduate training, new clinical child psychologists are increasingly obtaining positions in new settings such as schools, primary care, and corporations that involve new role-related activities such as consulting, public policy, program evaluation, and the supervision of nonpsychology health care professionals. Regarding this trend, Prinstein and Roberts suggest that significant modifications of professional training will likely be needed to prepare clinical child psychologists for assuming these new employment opportunities and diverse professional roles in the future.

PEDIATRIC PSYCHOLOGY

Primary to the science and practice of pediatric psychology is an emphasis on health- and illness-related issues. More specifically, "pediatric psychology is a field of science and practice that addresses a range of physical, psychological, developmental, health, and illness issues affecting children and their families" (Roberts, Mitchell, & McNeal, 2003, p. 3). This often involves working with children, and their families, who are struggling with chronic (cystic fibrosis, asthma, diabetes) or acute (enuresis, abdominal pain, headaches) health conditions. Compared to clinical child psychologists, pediatric psychologists are also more frequently involved in prevention and health promotion activities, such as promoting more healthful lifestyle behaviors and practices. Some psychologists who work with pediatric populations on health-related issues prefer to be referred to as child health psychologists. Those who differentiate between the two terms note that the term pediatric psychologist is more often associated with psychologists who focus on treatment of children with chronic health conditions, whereas child health psychologist often denotes a wider scope of practice, including work with acute and chronic health conditions, as well as general prevention and health promotion. However, for the purposes of this chapter, we use these terms interchangeably.

Practice Settings

There are a wide variety of settings in which pediatric psychologists practice their craft. The practice of pediatric psychology originated in inpatient medical centers dedicated to the treatment of disease and illness (Roberts et al., 2003). A recent survey of the members of the Society for Pediatric Psychology, Division 54 of the APA, found that pediatric psychology is still primarily a hospital-based field, with a majority (63%) of pediatric psychologists working in hospital settings (Opipari-Arrigan, Stark, & Drotar, 2006). Practice in inpatient settings often involves consultation services and treatment of children exhibiting less than optimal adjustment to illness or illness management behavior. Carter and colleagues (2003) completed a case-controlled study examining the nature of referrals to pediatric consultation and liaison service in 104 children. Reasons for referrals included problems in coping and adjustment (34.6%), medication and treatment noncompliance (30.7%), depression (29.8%), pain management (15.4%), anxiety (15.4%), illness exacerbation (14.4%), acute evaluation (13.4%), new medical diagnosis (13.4%), difficulties in parent coping (14.4%), ongoing treatment (12.5%), decision making regarding treatment (9.6%), differential diagnosis (9.6%), acting out (7.7%), general support (6.7%), and family conflict (6.5%), with many patients having multiple reasons for referral.

Hospital-based services may also involve consultation and clinical practice activities in emergency departments conducting assessments for depression or suicide risk, assessment and triage for victims of acute trauma or acute illness exacerbations, or assessment of children in acute psychosocial crisis. Medically based practice by pediatric psychologists also involves practice in medical outpatient clinics either independently or as part of multidisciplinary teams. The latter may include teams headed by pediatric subspecialties from endocrinology, pulmonology, gastroenterology, hematology, or rheumatology addressing health and coping issues related to diabetes, cystic fibrosis, asthma, inflammatory bowel disease, pediatric feeding aversion, sickle cell disease, juvenile rheumatoid arthritis, or other conditions. Pediatric psychologists also practice alongside health care professionals in primary care settings addressing acute health conditions (i.e., recurrent abdominal pain, headaches, toileting and soiling issues, sleep problems), as well as general emotional and behavior problems in children (Schroeder, 1979).

The science and practice of pediatric psychology is not limited to medical settings. Whether primarily involved in practice, training, research, or a combination of the three, pediatric psychologists also engage in role-related activities essential to the field in a variety of other settings. Whereas Opipari-Arrigan et al. (2006) found that most respondents worked in hospital settings (with about half in academic medical centers), a number of other practice settings were also noted. These included private practice (22%), academic psychology departments (5%), academic departments other than psychology (15%), mental health agencies (3%), and school systems (2%). Pediatric psychologists can also be found working or volunteering in camp settings designed for children suffering from chronic health conditions (Roberts et al., 2003). The following sections turn to the broad role and role-related activities engaged in by pediatric psychologists working in various settings.

Role-Related Professional Activities

As with clinical child psychologists, pediatric psychologists engage in a wide range of specialty-specific role-related activities. These include consultation, assessment, treatment, health promotion, promoting public health policy, training, and research. The ways pediatric psychologists carry out these activities in the context of their professional roles are detailed in the following sections.

Consultation Activities

As noted earlier, consultation is a critical role for pediatric psychologists, as our medical colleagues often represent the primary sources of patient referrals. The level of involvement between pediatric psychologists and medical colleagues during consultation may vary as a function of the case involved, the proximity of colleagues, or the presence of a formalized structure to support consultation. Consultation may be limited to brief discussions regarding general principles and strategies for dealing with children and families, provision of advice relevant to a specific case, brief involvement in assessment or development of a treatment plan, or active long-term involvement in patient treatment and case management. There are various models for the level of collaboration (Drotar, 1995; Roberts & Wright, 1982). For example, pediatric psychologists can function independently from medical colleagues (e.g., in their own outpatient clinic), providing assessment, diagnosis, and, if necessary, treatment of referred patients. Alternatively, they can function as part of a collaborative team in the assessment and treatment of children and families. This may involve working side by side with medical colleagues in multidisciplinary clinics, marked by active involvement and shared responsibility by team members leading to collaborative case conceptualization and treatment recommendations. It is within the rubric of consultations that pediatric psychologists often perform a number of functions, listed next.

Assessment Activities

As in all domains of applied clinical psychology, assessment is a central function of pediatric psychologists. In the ideal situation, most assessment leads to the development of recommendations or potential treatment options to help address areas of concern. Assessment by pediatric psychologists commonly focuses on child and family behaviors, interaction patterns, coping strategies that impact adjustment to the child's medical condition, including the challenges associated with managing the child's illness, the implications for the long-term health of the child, and social and emotional sequelae of the health condition. Common strategies to gather information include (a) structured or nonstructured interviews with children and their parents; (b) completion of self-report or parent-report questions; (c) completion of questionnaires by schoolteachers or other professionals working with the child; (d) direct observations of family interactions patterns, child social skills, or completion of illness management tasks; and (e) self-monitoring of emotions, cognitions, or behaviors.

A couple of examples may help to illustrate the assessment process. Children with cystic fibrosis are often required to engage in a variety of illness management tasks, including increased caloric intake, airway clearance (chest physiotherapy and medications to loosen mucus in the lungs), pancreatic enzyme replacement therapy, and antibiotic medications to fight bronchial infections. Adherence to these treatment tasks, whether in children with cystic fibrosis or other illness conditions, is one of the most common and challenging referrals to pediatric psychologists. Accurate assessment of the actual adherence to various treatment tasks and barriers hindering adherence (including antecedents and consequences of engaging in or not engaging in certain behaviors) are critical to developing appropriate and effective intervention plans that ultimately can impact the child's long-term physical health and quality of life. Interviews (focusing on the child, parents, the medical staff, and possible school personnel), behavioral checklists and self-report questionnaires, and written logs can be critical to documenting adherence and critical barriers. In addition, over the past 20 years electronic monitoring devices have become an invaluable tool in providing more accurate assessment of adherence to various illness management tasks. These include metered dose inhalers and medication event monitoring systems that record the date and time of vial openings and closings, as well as chest physiotherapy assistance devices, such as the Flutter or the high-frequency chest compression vest, which vibrates to loosen mucus in the lungs and can track adherence to chest physiotherapy.

Assessment may also involve evaluation of child and family functioning in anticipation of challenging future medical procedures or health issues. A common example is pretransplant evaluation of children presenting for organ transplantation. Pretransplant evaluations assess a wide variety of critical strengths, potential barriers to graft maintenance, and risk factors that may impact a child's or family's ability to follow the pre- and posttransplant treatment regimen, as well as posttransplant adjustment and coping. These include, but are not limited to, an assessment of (a) adherence to treatment regimen (taking prescribed medications, adherence to dietary recommendations), (b) understanding of the transplant process; (c) emotional coping and adjustment of child and parents or legal guardians; (d) presence of oppositional or disruptive behavior; (e) academic or social functioning; (f) social, emotional, and logistical support available to the family; (g) family communication; (h) family's ability to continue to complete daily life management tasks (grocery shopping, laundry, helping siblings with schoolwork, etc.); (i) family finances; and (j) other stressors such as additional family illness, potential job loss, and marital conflict. Accurate and reliable assessment from a multidisciplinary team is critical to establish a coherent picture of how these different areas ultimately can impact the child's and family's long-term health, quality of life, and maintenance of the graft.

Finally, assessment may involve psychoeducational assessment, including formalized measures such as the Wechsler Intelligence Scale for Children, the Stanford-Binet Intelligence Scale, or the Wechsler Individual Achievement Test to assess both cognitive functioning and academic achievement. Such testing may be advised to provide a baseline and track potential changes in cognitive functioning for children undergoing radiation or chemotherapy treatment for cancer or those who have experienced head trauma or other medical conditions that can lead to deterioration in cognitive functioning over time.

Treatment Activities

Treatment of children with acute or chronic health conditions is one of the most commonly recognized functions of pediatric psychologists. However, it is clear that treatment by pediatric psychologists (and clinical child psychologists), as well as others, does not occur in isolation. Prior to engaging in intervention efforts practitioners must travel a long road of didactic and applied clinical training to develop skills and competencies in evidence-based approaches to treatment. Moreover, prior to and throughout the course of treatment, assessment is essential to elucidate targets and pathways for change and to monitor ongoing progress. Research, either by the practitioner delivering the intervention or, more likely, by other psychologists and health care professionals, is necessary to provide data on best practices and evidence-based treatments to guide and inform intervention efforts. In fact, treatment-related research is becoming critically important, given the growing emphasis on evidence-based treatment in pediatric psychology. These treatments are highlighted by the ongoing series on empirically supported treatments in the *Journal of Pediatric Psychology*.

Potential child health-related difficulties that require intervention are numerous, but commonly involve coping and adjustment issues, adherence to treatment recommendations, or pain management. Problems of coping and adjustment may relate to death and dying, limits of daily functioning, family communication and conflict, school reentry, social interaction difficulties, or improving self-esteem. Adherence to treatment recommendations may involve increasing adherence to medication regimens, dietary recommendations (for cystic fibrosis, diabetes, inflammatory bowel disease, constipation), airway clearance (for cystic fibrosis), or increased physical activity (for obesity, Type 2 diabetes, juvenile rheumatoid arthritis). Pain management and coping with medical procedures may involve the use of diaphragmatic breathing, muscle relaxation, cognitive imagery or other active coping strategies to assist with injections, lumbar punctures, nausea associated with chemotherapy, or pain associated with sickle cell crisis or tumors. Treatment efforts often focus not only on the ill child, but also the parents and other members of the immediate and extended family, given the bidirectional influences between the child and his or her immediate family members. As with other functions performed by pediatric psychologists, collaboration with other health care and school professionals in the child's environment is essential as effective treatment often requires intervention at multiple levels in the child's environment.

Teaching and Mentoring Activities

Many pediatric psychologists spend valuable time training and mentoring the next generation of pediatric psychologists in clinical service delivery, research methodology, grant writing, and professional practice. Mentoring may involve formal and/or informal interactions of students, interns, and postdoctoral fellows. Senior faculty can also play a valuable role in the mentorship of junior colleagues and trainees. As pediatric psychologists strive to promote the value of their services to their medical colleagues and hospital administrators, education of professionals in other health care disciplines can be invaluable. This can take the form of active involvement in teaching trainees from other health care disciplines or engaging in informal teaching interactions with more senior medical colleagues (Drotar, Spirito, & Stancin, 2003; Roberts et al., 2003). This topic is reviewed in more depth later in this chapter.

Health Promotion Activities

Pediatric psychologists are becoming increasingly involved in health promotion activities such as developing and implementing lifestyle interventions to improve dietary and physical activity habits, reducing risk for childhood injuries, reducing drug and alcohol abuse, reducing tobacco use, parent training for adolescent mothers to reduce the risk for child neglect or abuse, and osteoporosis prevention. For example, Stark and colleagues (Stark, Janicke, McGrath, Mackner, & Hommel, 2005) demonstrated the effectiveness of a behavior intervention designed to improve calcium intake and bone mineral content in children with juvenile rheumatoid arthritis and inflammatory bowel disease. More recently, pediatric psychologists have ventured into the public health domain and are working to help promote public health agendas through more broad-based community initiatives (Drotar et al., 2003). There are a variety of examples of quality research in this area. One excellent example is Planet Health (Gortmaker et al., 1999), a 2-year school-based intervention that has been demonstrated to have positive effects on the weight status of middle school youth (Gortmaker et al., 1999). Another obesity prevention program is the GEMS project (Girls' Health Enrichment Multisite Studies), which is an ongoing, multisite community-based program designed to identify and implement effective obesity prevention strategies for African American girls (Rochon et al., 2003). Finally, Levy and colleagues (Levy, Brugge, Peters, Clougherty, & Saddler, 2006) have recently reported on a community-based participatory research intervention that has demonstrated reductions in respiratory symptoms of pediatric asthmatics living in public housing. These types of programs demonstrate the positive impact that innovative prevention and health promotion efforts can have on children's long-term health and quality of life.

Research Activities

As greater demands are placed on the profession to provide evidence supporting the effectiveness of psychological interventions for health-related problems and as competition for the provision of services is growing from social workers and other medical professionals, research activities are taking on greater importance for pediatric psychologists. Many of our medical colleagues have recognized what pediatric psychologists have to offer as active members of a multidisciplinary team, and subsequently are very willing to collaborate on research endeavors related to pediatric and child health psychology. One of the most important areas for future collaboration is in the area of treatment outcome research, where there has been a growing emphasis on developing evidence-based assessment and treatment methods. There is also a greater push to promote translational research and practice, to improve access to effective mental health care in diverse populations and community settings (Glasgow, Lichtenstein, & Marcus, 2003; Strauman & Merrill, 2004).

A major focus of treatment outcome research is to enhance adherence to treatment recommendations in children struggling with chronic and acute health conditions such as diabetes, cystic fibrosis, and asthma. Another common theme of current research in pediatric psychology is the identification of mediators and moderators of positive coping and adjustment in children with chronic health conditions. Finally, pediatric psychologists are at the forefront of integrating modern technology to assist in data collection and distribution of treatments for children and families, including telehealth, accelerometers to track physical activity, metered dose inhalers to track medication use, and palm pilots to assist children with accurate self-monitoring of dietary intake or physical activity.

Pediatric Psychology Compared to Clinical Child Psychology

In many ways, the field of pediatric psychology can be considered a subspecialty of clinical child psychology. Strong training in clinical child psychology is essential, but not sufficient, to function as a pediatric psychologist. Skills in assessment and intervention and knowledge of the role of developmental processes and child psychopathology are critical for pediatric and clinical child psychologists. However, there are significant differences between these disciplines. Pediatric psychologists place a much greater emphasis on medically related issues and regularly work with children and adolescents experiencing acute and chronic health conditions. Pediatric psychologists spend more time working in medical settings and collaborating with medical professionals from a variety of disciplines. As a result, they must have a greater understanding of disease processes, medical management of illness, broader health systems issues, and the referral and consultation process than clinical child psychologists.

Frequently the time allotted to pediatric psychologists to complete assessments or intervention is less than that typically allocated to clinical child psychologists (Tuma & Grabert, 1983). Children often are admitted to inpatient units for only a few days, or weeks, at a time. Many families may drive great distances for expert pediatric care. Primary care settings, another common venue for pediatric psychologists, are often fast-paced environments with a large number of patients, allowing for a limited amount of time with each family. In multidisciplinary clinics, often there is only a brief amount of time allotted to each member of the treatment team to work with a family. Moreover, whether in primary care settings, outpatient clinics, or hospital settings, pediatric psychologists may be forced to work with a child and/or family members in inpatient or exam rooms, with numerous interruptions. Given these limitations, brief, targeted, and flexible therapies that can address critical problematic behaviors or coping skills in a short period of time are often emphasized.

Training for Pediatric Psychology

As noted in the preceding sections, there are a variety of role-related professional activities and opportunities for practice open to pediatric psychologists. Not surprisingly, students pursuing a career in pediatric psychology require training to help them develop a blend of general or core skills similar to those developed through training in clinical child psychology, as well as specialized training related to the unique roles, settings, and contexts in which pediatric psychologists function. For many students, core training in child therapy and research skills comes first through coursework and in-house practicum training in graduate school. Fundamental therapy process skills and behavioral, cognitive-behavioral, interpersonal, and family systems intervention strategies form a foundation on which more specific training in pediatric psychology can build.

Regarding those elements seen as necessary for adequate training in this area, the Society of Pediatric Psychology's Task Force on Training of Pediatric Psychologists (Spirito et al., 2003) has outlined 11 domains of training that are believed to be necessary to develop the requisite knowledge and build the general and specific skills necessary for pursuing a career in pediatric psychology. These include training in the following: (a) life span developmental psychology; (b) life span developmental psychopathology; (c) child, adolescent, and family assessment; (d) child and family intervention strategies; (e) research methods and systems evaluation; (f) issues of diversity; (g) the role of multiple disciplines in service delivery systems; (h) prevention, family support, and health promotion; (i) social issues affecting children, adolescents, and families; (j) consultation and liaison roles; and (k) disease process and medical management.

One of the most salient aspects of training, unique to pediatric psychologists, is the need to have opportunities to work in interdisciplinary settings with professionals and trainees from other health professions (Spirito et al., 2003). Primary care and other outpatient clinical settings offer a fast-paced environment, where pediatric psychologists must think on their feet, remain flexible, build skills in effective but targeted brief therapy interventions, and learn to effectively communicate findings and impressions while also coordinating care with other health professionals. Given that most university academic settings have limited access to hospital-based training experiences, most in-depth hospital-based experiences usually occur during the internship and postdoctoral training experiences, although there are certainly exceptions to this rule.

Once again, the changing health care environment highlights the continuing need for additional treatment outcome research by pediatric psychologists to demonstrate the worth of our services to both patients and health care professionals. Conducting successful treatment outcome research in medical or community settings requires flexibility and teamwork, and knowledge of disease processes and medical systems, a deep respect for the issues and challenges presented to families of children struggling with acute and chronic health conditions, and research methodology considerations are critical. Almost all doctoral students in clinical psychology receive training in research methods and the evaluation of treatment outcomes. However, training students to conduct treatment outcome research studies on the scale required to support judgments of long-term efficacy and effectiveness necessitates more specialized training and experience. This may include, but are not limited to (a) training in participant recruitment and retention, (b) assessment methodology unique to specific health conditions, (c) longitudinal research design and corresponding data analytic approaches appropriate to such designs, (d) data management programs and protocol, (e) supervision and training of research team members and interventionists, (f) facilitating and maintaining collaboration with medical colleagues, (g) dissemination and translational research approaches, and (h) ethical considerations in the conduct of treatment outcome research.

Given the nature of the current health care environment with its increasing limitations on reimbursement for services provided by pediatric psychologists and the constraints on fiscal survival and success, "pediatric psychologists must be advocates not only for our services but also for the resources that support them" (Kronenberger, 2006, p. 648.). Thus, training in basic business management practices such as marketing of services, accounting, and financial management seem increasingly relevant to the ability to survive and, eventually, flourish as a profession. This may start with coursework during graduate training, but should be supplemented with seminars and hands-on practice during internship and postdoctoral training. In addition, as funding sources become more limited, training in grant writing will be beneficial for research and clinical pediatric psychologists. Again, these skills can be built through both didactic coursework and seminars, as well as hands-on experience assisting mentors with their applications or by submitting applications for their own National Research Service Awards during graduate and postdoctoral training.

Future Directions and Key Issues for Pediatric Psychologists

There are a number of key issues facing the field of pediatric psychology that will ultimately impact the direction of future practice as well as the viability of the field. Many of these issues were outlined by an expert panel of pediatric psychologists (Brown & Roberts, 2000), and some have been discussed previously in this chapter. The most important issue identified by respondents was related to potential threats to the viability of pediatric psychology. In response to this threat, there is a growing need to demonstrate the effectiveness of intervention protocols through controlled treatment outcome studies, a greater emphasis on interventions that improve health status as opposed to just coping with illness, and a greater need for research examining the cost offset associated with psychological interventions. It will also be important for pediatric psychologists to assess alternative sources of funding and reimbursement (Drotar, 2004), as many of the services provided by pediatric psychologists, such as improving adherence, adjustment to chronic illness, consultation with medical colleagues, and pain management, are not technically in the categories of the *Diagnostic and Statistical Manual of Mental Disorders.* Increasing awareness of what pediatric psychologists can do in medical settings by marketing our services to medical professionals as well as patients may help ensure the viability of pediatric psychology as a field of practice (Bradford, 2004).

Many of the populations and issues researched by pediatric psychologists involve small numbers of patients in hospital settings. As such, future research, especially treatment outcome research, will require multisite investigations to enroll adequate numbers to provide sufficient power to test study hypotheses.

Most pediatric psychologists are congregated in large academic medical centers. As a result, many people have to travel long distances for pediatric care as they do not have access to pediatric psychology services in their home town (Kronenberger, 2006). Thus, a significant opportunity for future growth of pediatric psychology lies in outpatient, primary care pediatric settings. Development and behavioral problems often first present to primary care providers, who have been referred to as the gatekeepers to the health care system. Such a setting would seem ideal for pediatric psychologists to make significant contributions to the health status and quality of life of children and families and to demonstrate their usefulness and the benefit of their services to medical colleagues. The call for pediatric psychologists to build practices in primary care settings has been echoed over the past few decades, yet few psychologists have successfully accomplished this transition. Renewed efforts in this direction could provide big dividends to pediatric psychologists and may be vital for the future of our field.

New and emerging technologies provide pediatric psychologists with a variety of opportunities to expand their service net. Genetic testing, for example, has the potential to provide families with information on the risk of children developing life-threatening diseases, chronic conditions, and development irregularities (Patenaude, 2003). There are a variety of opportunities for research to ascertain the impact of knowledge of risk on adjustment and decision making, as well as the best ways to communicate information to parents and children (Tercyak, 2003). Another emerging technology is telehealth, which provides opportunities to bring treatment to children and families in underserved areas, but expertise and research will be required to determine effective strategies to intervene using this new medium (Harper, 2003).

Prevention and health promotion are areas that hold the potential for long-term health benefits and medical cost offsets. As noted earlier, there are numerous opportunities for pediatric psychologists to make valuable contributions in these areas. Included here is work in nutrition and exercise to impact weight status and physical fitness, new and more comprehensive efforts to reduce unintentional injuries, multimodal parent training programs to reduce abuse and neglect, and approaches to osteoporosis prevention, just to name a few. Historically, reimbursement for prevention activities has been limited; however, the growing emphasis on translation and dissemination research and practice may provide more opportunities for pediatric psychologists to provide mental health services in underserved communities (Glasgow, Klesges, Dzewaltowski, Bull, & Estabrooks, 2004; Glasgow et al., 2003).

SCHOOL PSYCHOLOGY

Fagan and Wise (2000, p. 4) define a school psychologist as "a professional psychological practitioner whose general purpose is to bring a psychological perspective to bear on the problems of educators and the clients educators serve" and emphasize the "educational and psychological foundations" of the discipline. Unlike clinical child and pediatric psychology, school psychology is unique in terms of its focus on the functioning of individuals, groups, and systems in the school setting. As an area, school psychology also differs from clinical child and pediatric psychology in that the majority of practicing school psychologists have a master's or educational specialist degree rather than the doctorate, with the specialist degree being the most common. A National Association of School Psychologists membership renewal survey in 1999 found that 54% of school psychologists held a specialist degree, whereas only 26% held a doctoral degree (Fagan & Wise, 2000).

Not surprisingly, the most common setting for school psychologists is in schools, with approximately 80% of practitioners working in elementary or secondary schools. Private practice (3% to 5%) appears to be the second most common setting for school psychologists, and government agencies, community mental health centers, developmental disability centers, and universities are among some of the other work settings (Fagan & Wise, 2000). It should be noted that doctoral-level school psychologists frequently work with clinical populations outside of the school setting and engage in clinical activities similar to those performed by clinical child psychologists.

Role-Related Activities of School Psychologists

School psychologists engage in a variety of role-related professional activities, such as psychoeducational assessment, intervention, consultation, and, to a lesser degree, research and program evaluation, training, and supervision. These activities are not mutually exclusive as school psychologists often perform these activities concurrently.

Assessment Activities

School psychologists have historically spent much of their time conducting psychoeducational assessments. Indeed, Reschly (2000) has suggested that school psychologists spend approximately 50% to 55% of their time engaged in activities related to psychoeducational assessments. These assessments typically serve to gather information regarding the child's current difficulties to help plan interventions and/or provide a basis for special class placement or classroom accommodations. Presenting problems dealt with by school psychologists can relate to a range of possible areas, including academic, social, emotional, and behavioral functioning. Assessments can include multiple components, including review of school records, classroom observation, and interviews with parents, teachers, and other persons who may be able to provide information related to the child's presenting difficulties. They can also include testing of cognitive ability, academic achievement, and perceptual and motor skills, as well as the administration of standardized rating scales measuring behavior problems, personality, and adaptive functioning (Fagan & Wise, 2000). It is noteworthy that the assessment activities of school psychologists are to some degree shifting away from an emphasis on psychoeducational testing toward more functional assessments designed to generate and evaluate interventions (Reschly, 2000).

Intervention Activities

School psychologists report spending approximately 20% of their time engaged in intervention-related activities, including planning, implementation, and evaluation of interventions (Reschly, 2000). These interventions can take various forms, including both individual and group counseling and planning and implementing classroom-based intervention. Individual counseling can focus on helping children learn skills and coping strategies to deal with a range of difficulties in the areas of academic, social, emotional, and behavioral functioning. Group counseling is often used to help children learn and use adaptive skills related to peer interactions, dealing with anger, and stressful situations such as divorce or death of a parent. Classroom-based interventions can involve collaborating with the child's teacher to arrange a particular seating arrangement, selecting an appropriate classroom placement, finding additional academic supports such as tutoring, and implementing behavior management programs in the classroom.

Consultation Activities

School psychologists are reported to devote approximately 23% of their time to consultation activities (Reschly, 2000). Consultation has been viewed as a collaborative, problem-solving endeavor between school psychologists and other personnel, often teachers, to help ensure that assessment-based recommendations are implemented (Fagan & Wise, 2000). Consultation can involve multiple components, including problem identification, assessment, and intervention planning, implementation, and evaluation. It has also been conceptualized as a way to help address the potential shortage of school psychologists in the future, given the potential to impact beyond the individual. For instance, consultation with a teacher can lead to interventions that have an impact on a whole classroom, and consultation on a systemic level may have the potential to effect positive change in an entire school district. Consultation has also been viewed as a way of promoting preventive strategies by providing children with supports, increasing their subjective sense of well-being, and building competencies (Meyers, Meyers, & Grogg, 2004).

Other Role-Related Activities

Unlike clinical child and pediatric psychologists, only a small percentage of school psychologists appear to be involved in conducting applied research and program evaluation. Survey findings suggest that only about 2% of school psychologists engage in these activities (Reschly, 2000). This low number may be due in part to the fact that the large majority of school psychologists work in school settings, where research may not be supported (Fagan & Wise, 2000). Research that is conducted by school psychologists is likely most often conducted by PhD-level school psychologists who work in university settings.

Some school psychologists engage in activities related to the training of students, including teaching and supervision. School psychologists based in university settings likely engage in such roles to a significant degree, whereas school psychologists in other settings may engage in these activities on a part-time or adjunctive basis (Fagan & Wise, 2000). Other school psychologists function as administrators of psychological services or as supervisors of other school psychologists.

Factors Influencing Role-Related Activities

The amount of time school psychologists engage in various activities may be influenced by several factors. As mentioned earlier, laws and funding mechanisms can exert a significant influence. Historically, state and local education agencies have been most invested in having school psychologists conduct assessments to determine children's eligibility for special education services (Reschly, 2000).

The ratio of school psychologists to students can also influence the opportunity for school psychologists to engage in different roles. Generally, the more favorable the ratio, the more school psychologists are able to engage in activities beyond psychoeducational assessment, such as intervention and consultation (Curtis, Hunley, & Grier, 2002).

The level of training of the school psychologist is likely to be important, with doctoral-level practitioners generally being less involved in psychoeducational assessment activities and more involved in intervention, consultation, and applied research and program evaluation (Curtis et al., 2002). The availability of other providers in the setting, such as social workers and clinical psychologists, can influence the number of opportunities school psychologists have for intervention activities (Fagan & Wise, 2000).

Fagan (2002) noted that a consistent theme in the school psychology literature over the past several decades has been the call for school psychologists to expand their roles beyond assessment and become more involved in activities related to intervention and consultation. He notes that despite this consistent theme, research suggests that school psychologists continue to spend approximately half of their time involved in activities related to psychoeducational assessment, and report generally positive job satisfaction ratings.

The Expanding Role of the School Psychologist

Although the large majority of school psychologists work predominantly in school settings and spend a significant amount of time engaging in assessment-related activities, a significant number of doctoral-level school psychologists have expanded their range of clinical activities well beyond assessment and function in roles that do not differ measurably from clinical child psychologists. School psychology programs are also now providing opportunities for students pursuing doctoral training in school psychology to obtain subspecialty training in the area of pediatric school psychology. Such training is designed to prepare school psychologists to engage in health-related activities such as serving as liaisons between schools and health care agencies to address the medical, educational, psychological, and community needs of children with or at risk for emotional and behavioral disabilities. As such, doctoral-level school psychologists are becoming increasingly similar to professionals in the area of pediatric psychology in terms of role functions.

SUMMARY

As can be seen from this overview, the specialties of clinical child and pediatric psychology have grown rapidly during the past 25 to 30 years. Indeed, in a recent paper, Prinstein and Roberts (2006) characterized these specialties as currently in their "professional adolescence" and as "grown up and striving for autonomy." As these two specialties have evolved, the roles of those working in these areas have become more and more complex, with child and pediatric psychologists assuming more varied role-related activities as health care providers and taking a prominent role in research focusing on the development of evidence-based practice. While primarily working in school-related settings, doctoral-level school psychologists also often engage in clinical activities that overlap significantly with the work of both clinical child and pediatric psychologists.

REFERENCES

Boles, R. E., Mashunkashey, J. O., & Roberts, M. C. (2003). Safety and prevention. In T. H. Ollendick, & C. S. Shroeder (Eds.), *Encyclopedia of clinical child and pediatric psychology* (pp. 564–565). New York: Kluwer Academic/Plenum Press.

Bradford, W. D. (2004). Commentary from a health economist: Financing pediatric psychology: On "Buddy, can you spare a dime?" *Journal of Pediatric Psychology, 29*, 65–66.

Brinkmeyer, M., & Eyberg, S. M. (2003). Parent-child interaction therapy for oppositional children. In A. E. Kazdin, & J. R. Weisz (Eds.), *Evidence-based psychotherapies for children and adolescents* (pp. 204–223). New York: Guilford Press.

Brown, K. J., & Roberts, M. C. (2000). Future issues in pediatric psychology: Delphic survey. *Journal of Clinical Psychology in Medical Settings, 7*, 5–15.

Carter, B. D., Kronenberger, W. G., Baker, J., Grimes, L. M., Crabtree, V. M., Smith, C., et al. (2003). Inpatient pediatric consultation-liaison: A case-controlled study. *Journal of Pediatric Psychology, 28*, 423–432.

Cashel, M. L. (2002). Child and adolescent psychological assessment: Current clinical practices and the impact of managed care. *Professional Psychology: Research and Practice, 33* (5), 446–453.

Chambless, D. L. (1996). In defense of dissemination of empirically supported psychological interventions. *Clinical Psychology: Science and Practice, 3*, 230–235.

Chambless, D. L., & Hollon, S. D. (1998). Defining empirically supported therapies. *Journal of Consulting and Clinical Psychology, 66*, 7–18.

Chambless, D. L., & Ollendick, T. H. (2001). Empirically supported psychological interventions: Controversies and evidence. *Annual Review of Psychology, 52*, 685–716.

Commission for the Recognition of Specialties and Proficiencies in Professional Psychology. (1998). *Petition for the recognition of a specialty in professional psychology: Clinical child psychology* (p. 2). Retrieved February 10, 2007, from http://www.clinicalchild.com/Specialty_Links.htm.

Curtis, M. J., Hunley, S. A., & Grier, J. E. C. (2002). Relationships among the professional practices and demographic characteristics of school psychologists. *School Psychology Review, 31*, 30–42.

Drotar, D. (1995). *Consulting with pediatricians: Psychological perspectives.* New York: Plenum Press.

Drotar, D. (2004). Commentary: We can make our own dime or two, help children and their families, and advance science while doing so. *Journal of Pediatric Psychology, 29*, 61–63.

Drotar, D., Spirito, A., & Stancin, T. (2003). Professional roles and practice patterns. In M. C. Roberts (Ed.), *Handbook of pediatric psychology* (pp. 50–66). New York: Guilford Press.

Fagan, T. K. (2002). School psychology: Recent descriptions, continued expansion, and an ongoing paradox. *School Psychology Review, 31*, 5–10.

Fagan, T. K., & Wise, P. S. (2000). *School psychology: Past, present, and future* (2nd ed.). Bethesda, MD: National Association of School Psychologists.

Glasgow, R. E., Klesges, L. M., Dzewaltowski, D. A., Bull, S. S., & Estabrooks, P. (2004). The future of health behavior change research: What is needed to improve translation of research into health promotion practice? *Annals of Behavior Medicine, 27*, 3–12.

Glasgow, R. E., Lichtenstein, E., & Marcus, A. C. (2003). Why don't we see more translation of health promotion research to practice? Rethinking the efficacy-to-effectiveness transition. *American Journal of Public Health, 93*, 1261–1267.

Gortmaker, S., Peterson, K., Wiecha, J., Sobol, A., Dixit, S., Fox, M., et al. (1999). Reducing obesity via a school-based interdisciplinary intervention among youth: Planet Health. *Archives of Pediatric and Adolescent Medicine, 153*, 409–418.

Harper, D. C. (2003). Telehealth. In M. C. Roberts (Ed.), *Handbook of pediatric psychology* (pp. 735–746). New York: Guilford Press.

Johnson, J. H. (2003). Training issues. In T. H. Ollendick, & C. S. Shroeder (Eds.), *Encyclopedia of clinical child and pediatric psychology* (pp. 674–676). New York: Kluwer Academic/Plenum Press.

Johnson, J. H., & Tuma, J. M. (1986). The Hilton Head conference: Recommendations for clinical child psychology training. *Clinical Psychologist, 39*, 9–11.

Kazdin, A. E. (2005). Evidence-based assessment for children and adolescents: Issues in measurement development and clinical application. *Journal of Clinical Child and Adolescent Psychology, 34*, 548–558.

Kendall, P. C., & Beidas, R. S. (2007). Smoothing the trail for dissemination of evidence-based practices for youth: Flexibility within fidelity. *Professional Psychology: Research and Practice, 38*, 13–20.

Knitzer, J. (1982). *Unclaimed children: The failure of public responsibility to children and adolescents in need of mental health services.* Washington, DC: Children's Defense Fund.

Kronenberger, W. G. (2006). Commentary: A look at ourselves in the mirror. *Journal of Pediatric Psychology, 31*, 647–649.

Levy, J., Brugge, D., Peters, J., Clougherty, J., & Saddler, S. (2006). A community-based participatory research study of multifaceted in-home environmental interventions for pediatric asthmatics in public housing. *Social Science and Medicine, 63*, 2191–2203.

Lonigan, C. J., Elbert, J. C., & Johnson, S. B. (1998). Empirically supported psychosocial interventions for children: An overview. *Journal of Clinical Child Psychology, 27*(2), 138–145.

Mash, E. J., & Hunsley, J. (2005). Evidence-based assessment of child and adolescent disorders: Issues and challenges. *Journal of Clinical Child and Adolescent Psychology, 34*, 362–379.

McNeil, C. B., & Bernard, R. S. (2003). Early intervention. In T. H. Ollendick, & C. S. Shroeder (Eds.), *Encyclopedia of clinical child and pediatric psychology* (pp. 197–199). New York: Kluwer Academic/Plenum Press.

Meyers, J., Meyers, A. B., & Grogg, K. (2004). Prevention through consultation: A model to guide future developments in the field of school psychology. *Journal of Educational and Psychological Consultation, 15*, 257–276.

Mufson, L., Dorta, K. P., Moreau, D., & Weissman, M. M. (2004). *Interpersonal psychotherapy for depressed adolescents.* New York: Guilford Press.

Nathan, P., & Gorman, J. M. (1998). *A guide to treatments that work.* New York: Oxford University Press.

O'Donohue, W. Fisher, J. E., & Hayes, S. C. (Eds.). (2003). *Cognitive behavior therapy: Applying empirically supported techniques in your practice*. Hoboken, NJ: Wiley.

Ollendick, T. H., & King, N. J. (2004). Empirically supported treatments for children and adolescents: Advances toward evidence-based practice. In P. M. Barrett, & T. H. Ollendick (Eds.), *Handbook of interventions that work with children and adolescents: Prevention and treatment* (pp. 3–25). Hoboken, NJ: Wiley.

Opipari-Arrigan, L., Stark, L., & Drotar, D. (2006). Benchmarks for work performance of pediatric psychologists. *Journal of Pediatric Psychology, 31*, 630–642.

Patenaude, A. F. (2003). Pediatric psychology training and genetics: What will twenty-first century pediatric psychologists need to know? *Journal of Pediatric Psychology, 28*, 135–145.

Prinstein, M. J., & Roberts, M. C. (2006). The professional adolescence of clinical child and adolescent psychology and pediatric psychology: Grown up and striving for autonomy. *Clinical Psychology: Science and Practice, 13*, 263–268.

Raikes, H. H., & Love, J. M. (2002). Early Head Start: A dynamic new program for infants and toddlers and their families. *Infant Mental Health Journal, 23*(1/2), 1–13.

Raimy, V. N. (1950). *Training in clinical psychology*. New York: Prentice-Hall.

Reschly, D. J. (2000). The present and future status of school psychology in the United States. *School Psychology Review, 29*, 507–522.

Roberts, M. C. (1982). Clinical child psychology program: Where and what are they? *Journal of Clinical Child Psychology, 11*, 13–21.

Roberts, M. C., Carlson, C. I., Erickson, M. T., Friedman, R. M., LaGreca, A. M., Lemanek, K. L., et al. (1998). A model to train psychologists to provide services for children and adolescents. *Professional Psychology: Research and Practice, 29*, 293–299.

Roberts, M. C., Erickson, M. T., & Tuma, J. M. (1985). Addressing the needs: Guidelines for training psychologists to work with children, youth, and families. *Journal of Clinical Child Psychology, 14*, 70–79.

Roberts, M. C., Mitchell, M. C., & McNeal, R. (2003). The evolving field of pediatric psychology: Critical issues and future challenges. In M. C. Roberts (Ed.), *Handbook of pediatric psychology* (pp. 3–18). New York: Guilford Press.

Roberts, M. C., & Wright, L. (1982). The role of the pediatric psychologist as consultants to pediatricians. In J. M. Tuma (Ed.), *Handbook for the practice of pediatric psychology* (pp. 251–289). New York: Wiley.

Rochon, J., Klesges, R., Story, M., Robinson, T., Baranowski, T., Obarzanel, E., et al. (2003). Common design elements of the Girls Health Enrichment Multi-site Studies (GEMS). *Ethnicity and Disease, 13*, S6–S14.

Roth, A., Fonagy, P., Parry, G., & Target, M. (1996). *What works for whom? A critical review of psychotherapy research*. New York: Guilford Press.

Sackett, D., Richardson, W., Rosenberg, W., & Haynes, B. (2000). *Evidence-based medicine* (2nd ed.). London: Churchill Livingston.

Schroeder, C. S. (1979). Psychologists in a private pediatric practice. *Journal of Pediatric Psychology, 4*, 5–18.

Shakow, D. (1948). Clinical training facilities, 1948: Report of the Committee on Training in Clinical Psychology. *American Psychologist, 3*, 317–318.

Spirito, A., Brown, R. T., D'Angelo, E., Delamater, A., Rodrique, J., & Siegel, L. (2003). Society of Pediatric Psychology task force report: Recommendations for the training of pediatric psychologists. *Journal of Pediatric Psychology, 28*, 85–98.

Stark, L. J., Hommel, K., Mackner, L. M., Janicke, D. M., Davis, A. M., Pfefferkon, M., et al. (2005). Randomized trial comparing two methods of increasing dietary calcium intake in children with inflammatory bowel disease. *Journal of Pediatric Gastroenterology and Nutrition, 40*, 501–507.

Stark, L. J., Janicke, D. M., McGrath, A. M., Mackner, L. M., & Hommel, K. A. (2005). A randomized clinical trial to increase calcium intake in children with juvenile rheumatoid arthritis. *Journal of Pediatric Psychology, 30*, 377–386.

Strauman, T. J., & Merrill, K. A. (2004). The basic science/clinical science interface and treatment development. *Clinical Psychology: Science and Practice, 11*, 263–266.

Tarnowski, K., & Simonian, S. (1995). *Directory of graduate programs in clinical child and pediatric psychology*. Mahwah, NJ: Erlbaum.

Tercyak, K. P. (2003). Genetic disorders and genetic testing. In M. C. Roberts (Ed.), *Handbook of pediatric psychology* (pp. 719–734). New York: Guilford Press.

Tuma, J. M. (1985). *Proceedings: Conference on training clinical child psychologists*. Baton Rouge, LA: Section on Clinical Child Psychology.

Tuma, J. M., & Grabert, J. (1983). Internship and postdoctoral training in pediatric and clinical child psychology: A survey. *Journal of Pediatric Psychology, 8*, 245–268.

Tuma, J. M., & Pratt, J. M. (1982). Clinical child psychology practice and training: A survey. *Journal of Clinical Child Psychology, 15*, 88–96.

PART II
Theoretical Models

CHAPTER 6

Psychodynamic

Sandra W. Russ

What is the future of psychodynamic psychotherapy with children? Although psychodynamic treatment has a rich theoretical and clinical underpinning, there is a relatively small empirical base for treatment effectiveness. Because of the nature of psychodynamic treatment, it has been difficult to carry out empirical studies. These studies are beginning to occur, but there is a long way to go to catch up with cognitive-behavioral approaches. The psychodynamic approach encompasses two categories of information important to the field of child psychotherapy. One is a number of psychological constructs that provide a way of understanding child development. Many of these constructs have empirical support. The second category is a wealth of psychotherapy techniques with children that have emerged from a psychodynamic understanding of the child. Of particular importance is the use of pretend play in therapy. This chapter reviews the psychological constructs and the treatment techniques. Empirical evidence is presented as much as possible, with guidelines for future research. Implications for treatment and prevention programs are discussed.

PSYCHODYNAMIC THERAPY

The psychodynamic approach focuses on the internal world of the child (Russ, 2006). What is the child thinking and feeling, and how does he or she experience other people and their environment? A developmental perspective is used to understand underlying cognitive, affective, and interpersonal processes (Shirk & Russell, 1996). The level of development of these processes and the interaction among them largely determines the child's behavior, relationships, and internal state. The psychodynamic framework is applied to understand these internal processes and childhood disorders. This psychodynamic understanding determines the specific intervention approach and techniques to be used with a particular child.

Historically, psychodynamic approaches evolved from psychoanalytic theory and therapy. As Fonagy and Moran (1990) pointed out, many forms of psychodynamic therapies are based on the psychoanalytic conceptualization of child development. Children's play was especially important in psychoanalytic approaches in that it was used as a vehicle for communication with the therapist. Also, the therapist actively worked to establish a positive relationship with the child (Freud,

1927). Anna Freud (1966) made significant contributions to psychoanalytic theory with her work on the ego and mechanisms of defense. Melanie Klein, in a different approach, developed early concepts in object relations theory and interpersonal relations (Tyson & Tyson, 1990). Klein also utilized active interpretation of children's play. A major goal of psychoanalytic and psychodynamic therapy is to return the child to normal developmental pathways (Freud, 1965; Shirk & Russell, 1996). Psychodynamic therapy differs from psychoanalytic therapy in that it has more focused treatment goals, is less frequent and intensive, and is more flexible in terms of types of interventions used and the integration of other theoretical perspectives and techniques (Fonagy & Moran, 1990; Russ, 1998; Tuma & Russ, 1993).

In most forms of psychodynamic therapy, the therapist and child meet individually once a week for a session of 45 to 50 minutes. The basic understanding between the therapist and the child is that the therapist is there to help the child express feelings and thoughts, understand causes of behavior, and form a relationship with the therapist (Freedheim & Russ, 1992). Goals of treatment are also discussed. Play is a major tool in the therapy. Traditionally, the child has usually structured the hour, chosen the topic to discuss, chosen the toys to play with, and has determined the pace of the therapy. But as therapy has become more short term, therapists are becoming more active and directive within the psychodynamic framework in focusing on specific topics and directing the play (Russ, 2004). Also, for most child therapists, parent guidance, parent therapy, and parent education and consultation with the school are essential components to the therapy. For a review of the practical issues that arise in psychodynamic therapy and for case presentations, see Chethik (2000), Kessler (1966, 1988), and Russ (2004).

How does change occur in psychodynamic approaches? Russ and Freedheim (2001) and Russ (2004, 2006) reviewed mechanisms of change in therapy most relevant to psychodynamic approaches. Some of the mechanisms of change are similar to those of other therapy approaches. Catharsis or the release of emotion and expression of feelings is thought to be therapeutic by a number of different schools of therapy (Axline, 1947; Freud, 1965). Expression of negative feelings in particular is important for many children (Moustakas, 1953). Helping children to know that they can safely express feelings through talk or play is a major task of the therapist. The therapist labels the feeling expressed by the child or puppet, accepts the feeling, and tries to understand the feeling. Words help put the feeling into a context for the child, thus making the feeling less overwhelming.

Another mechanism of change is a corrective emotional experience. The therapist accepts the child's feelings and thoughts. Often, the child's learned expectations are not met. The relationship between the therapist and child is especially important for a corrective emotional experience to occur. For example, a child expresses angry thoughts and feelings about his or her mother. The therapist, contrary to the child's expectations, is not angry or punishing; rather, the therapist is accepting of the feelings and works to understand the reasons for the anger. After a number of these therapeutic events, a corrective emotional experience occurs (Kessler, 1966). The automatic connection between angry thoughts or feelings and anxiety or guilt gradually decreases (or extinguishes). The child then becomes more comfortable with these feelings and thoughts. In children, expression of thoughts and feelings often occurs through play. The therapist works with those expressions and, if possible, connects them to the child's daily life.

With some children, the therapist is directive and helps the child think about alternative ways of viewing a situation and generates problem-solving strategies. Role-playing and modeling of coping strategies are used by the therapist. Singer (1993) offers examples of modeling techniques during therapy. Although this mechanism of change is not often associated with psychodynamic therapy, it is frequently part of an intervention within a psychodynamic conceptualization of a case. Shapiro, Friedberg, and Bardenstein (2006) have proposed that life education also occurs in psychodynamic psychotherapy. Life education involves giving information about general human functioning. They pointed out that Anna Freud (1968) included educative components that taught adaptive skills.

The major mechanism of change associated with psychodynamic therapy is insight and the working-through process. It is this mechanism that differentiates psychodynamic therapy from other forms of interpersonal therapy. One goal of the therapist is to help the child reexperience major developmental conflicts or situational traumas in therapy. When underlying conflicts are a major issue, therapy has the goal of cognitive insight into origins of feelings and conflicts, causes of symptoms, and links between thoughts, feelings, and actions (Sandler, Kennedy, & Tyson, 1980; Shirk & Russell, 1996). Verbal labeling of unconscious impulses, conflicts, and causes of behavior helps lend higher order reasoning skills to understanding problems. Well-timed interpretations by the therapist attempt to make these links and to help the child understand the causes of his or her feelings and behavior. However, in many cases, especially with young children, cognitive insight does not occur. Rather, emotional reexperiencing, emotional working-through, and mastery of material occur and result in behavior change and changes in internal feeling states. This is an important mechanism of change and is often overlooked in the literature.

Messer and Warren (1995) stated that the goal of making the unconscious conscious needs to be modified in therapy with many children. In Erikson's (1963) concept of mastery, the child uses play to gain mastery over traumatic events and everyday conflicts. Resolving conflicts through play is part of normal child development. For normal children who are using play, cognitive insight into underlying issues does not usually occur. But the emotional processing that is occurring helps the child resolve the issues. This concept of emotional processing of negative events and traumas will be discussed further at a later point. Therapists who are using play in therapy may be helping the emotional processing occur without cognitive insight in many cases. Freedheim and Russ (1992) described the process of playing out conflict-laden content until the conflict and negative affect are resolved. The psychodynamic therapist helps guide the play, labels the feelings, describes the action, and makes interpretations to facilitate conflict resolution and the working-through process.

Another major mechanism of change with seriously emotionally disturbed children is the development of better object relations, which enables attachment and more stable day-to-day functioning. Many children have deficits in internal structures (such as internal representations) and processes that result in serious emotional disorders. Deficits in self/other differentiation and object representations and object relations can result in serious problems with self-esteem regulation, reality testing, attachment, and impulse control. In these children, there are major deficits in underlying cognitive, affective, and interpersonal processes. Psychodynamically informed structure-building approaches are based on conceptualizations by Mahler (1968) and Kohut (1977). The therapist attempts to be seen as a caring, empathic, stable, and predictable figure. Development of good object relations is a major goal of therapy with these children. Gilpin (1976) stressed that the role of the therapist is to become an internalized object for the child. The therapist serves as a stable figure who helps the child develop these ego functions as much as possible. The relationship between the therapist and the child is probably the most important aspect of the therapy in helping this process to occur. The expression of empathy by the therapist for the child's experience is an essential technique that enables the child to develop.

Different forms of psychodynamic therapy emphasize different mechanisms of change. The two major forms are insight-oriented therapy and structure-building approaches. Shapiro et al. (2006, p. 117) list four objectives for psychodynamic therapy:

1. Increased self-understanding
2. Increased acceptance of feelings and wishes
3. Replacement of (unconscious) defense mechanisms with conscious coping strategies
4. Development of realistically complex and positive schemas for relationships between self and others

Which objectives and change processes are emphasized depends on the child's particular set of problems.

Insight-Oriented Therapy

The form of therapy most closely associated with the psychodynamic approach is insight-oriented therapy; it is most appropriate for the child with anxiety and internalized conflicts (Tuma & Russ, 1993). This approach is appropriate for children who have age-appropriate ego development, show evidence of internal conflicts, can trust adults, and, for young children, can use play effectively. Insight-oriented therapy is most appropriate for children with internalizing disorders involving anxiety or depression. Children with internalizing disorders often experience internal conflicts, have good development in major areas, and have good attachment and object relations. Goals of therapy are to resolve conflicts. The major mechanism of change is insight and working through. The therapist actively interprets thoughts and feelings in play and in talk about the child's life. As mentioned earlier, often cognitive insight does not occur. Rather, the child reexperiences difficult emotions and processes these feelings and develops a better understanding of them. Through the use of play and the therapist's reflection and interpretation of thoughts and feelings, the child expresses "forbidden fantasy and feelings, works through and masters developmental problems, and resolves conflicts" (Freedheim & Russ, 1983, p. 982).

The technique of interpretation is important in facilitating insight and/or emotional reexperiencing. Shapiro et al. (2006) offer a good description of the various types of statements by the therapist that help bring new information to consciousness. They stated that interpretations are "causal explanations; they attempt to explain why the client feels, thinks, or behaves in some particular way" (p. 124).

Often, pretend play is a vehicle for the occurrence of insight and working through. The emotional resolution of conflict or trauma and negative feelings occurs in play. The play process has been thought of as a form of conflict resolution. For example, Waelder (1933) described the play process as one in which the child repeats an unpleasant experience over and over until it becomes manageable. Erikson (1963) presented the concept of mastery, in which the child uses play to gain mastery over traumatic events and everyday conflicts. During this process the therapist labels and interprets the play. The therapist will also tie the observations and interpretations to events in the child's life.

Insight and working through can be helpful for children with good internal resources who have experienced a major trauma. For example, Altschul (1988) described the use of psychoanalytic approaches in helping children to mourn the loss of a parent. Chethik (1989) discussed "focal therapy" as therapy that deals with "focal stress events" (p. 194) in the child's life. Chethik listed events such as death in the family, divorce, hospitalization, and illness as examples of specific stressors. Focal therapy focuses on the specific problem and is usually of short duration. It is a psychodynamic approach that uses insight and working through. Chethik viewed this approach as working best with children who have accomplished normal developmental tasks before the occurrence of stressful events.

Structure-Building Approaches

A second major form of psychodynamic therapy is the structure-building approach, which is used with children with deficits in object relations and interpersonal processes (Russ, 1998). For children with impaired object relations, self/other boundary disturbances, and problems distinguishing reality from fantasy, the therapist uses techniques that foster the development of object permanence, self/other differentiation, modulation of affect, and impulse control. The major mechanism of change is the development of these internal processes. The development of object relations is especially important. Mahler (1968) articulated the separation-individuation process and described the development of object constancy and object representations. Blank and Blank (1986) have pointed out that object relations plays a major role in the organization of other intrapsychic processes. Children with severely impaired object relations, such as borderline children and children with psychotic and characterological disorders, have early developmental problems in a variety of areas. Also, they tend to have severe dysfunction in the family and often a genetic predisposition.

In a structure-building approach, empathy on the part of the therapist is a much more important intervention than interpretation (Kohut & Wolfe, 1978). Kohut and

Wolfe discussed the failure of empathy from the parent that is the major issue in faulty parent-child interaction. Because of the frequency of this occurrence in the interaction between the child and parent, empathy from the therapist around the history of empathic failure becomes an important part of therapy. It is the empathy from the therapist that results in the therapist's being internalized and becoming a stable internal figure for the child. Chethik (1989) and Russ (2004) present cases of psychotherapy with borderline children. Often, help with problem solving and coping is used with these children as well. Therapy with these children is usually long term (1 to 2 years).

PSYCHODYNAMIC CONSTRUCTS

There are a number of psychodynamic constructs and hypotheses that are associated with psychodynamic theory. Research that investigates these constructs and hypotheses helps to build empirical support for psychodynamic theory. Although not directly investigating psychodynamic therapy, empirically supported constructs should guide therapy research in terns of what to focus on and what therapy techniques to emphasize. Westen (1998) reviewed the research literature and identified a number of psychodynamic constructs and propositions that have been supported. Much of the research has been carried out in cognitive, social, developmental, and personality psychology. Often, psychodynamic terminology is not used or referred to. Concepts are placed in a more contemporary cognitive-affective framework. Westen identified the following constructs and principles of psychodynamic theory that have received significant empirical support: unconscious processes, ambivalence and conflict, importance of childhood origins of personality and social dispositions, mental representations of self and others, and developmental dynamics.

Primary process thinking is another construct that has a large body of research support (Holt, 1977; Suler, 1980). Primary process thinking refers to drive-laden oral, aggressive, and libidinal material and illogical thinking related to that material (Holt, 1977). Holt described primary thought as an early, primitive system of thought that was drive-laden and not subject to rules of logic or oriented to reality. Affect and affect-laden cognition are a large component of primary process.

A large number of studies have found a relationship between access to primary process thinking and creativity, as psychoanalytic theory predicts, in adults and children (Russ, 1996; Suler, 1980). Russ has discussed these relationships within current cognitive-affective conceptualizations. The finding in a large number of studies that access to primary process thinking relates to measures of creativity supports the psychoanalytic theory that access to drive-laden thinking is important in the creative process. Repression of threatening drive-laden thoughts, images, and memories leads to a general intellectual restriction, which in turn constricts associative thinking. Access to a broad network of associations is important in most measures of creativity. Empirical support of this psychoanalytic theory is important in psychotherapy, where one goal is to help the child gain access to unconscious, repressed content so that the child can bring higher order problem-solving skills to daily problems and stressors.

Pretend play is a key resource for children. The important role of play in child development is not a concept that is unique to psychodynamic thinking. However, play has been a major technique in psychodynamic therapy and is viewed as having a central function in child development.

Pretend Play

Play has been a part of therapy with children since Melanie Klein and Anna Freud first began using play techniques in child psychotherapy in the 1930s. Currently, play is used in therapy from a variety of theoretical traditions. As of 1992, play in some form was used in child therapy by a majority of clinicians, as reported by Koocher and D'Angelo (1992).

In the child therapy literature, four broad functions of play emerge as important in therapy (Russ, 2004). First, play is a natural form of expression in children. Chethik (1989) refers to the language of play. Children use play to express feelings and thoughts. Chethik stated that play emerges from the child's internal life and reflects the child's internal world. Therefore, children use play to express affect and fantasy and, in therapy, to express troubling and conflict-laden feelings.

Second, the child uses the language of play to communicate with the therapist. By understanding these communications, the therapist develops a therapeutic relationship with the child (Chethik, 1989). The therapist actively labels, accepts, empathizes with, and interprets the play expressions, which, in turn, helps the child feel understood (Russ, 1995). These play expressions are important in enabling mechanisms of change to occur in therapy. For example, a corrective emotional experience can occur by the therapist accepting and understanding angry feelings expressed in play. Also, for many children, the feeling of empathy from the therapist around the play facilitates change in their internal representations and interpersonal functioning.

A third major function of play is as a vehicle for the occurrence of insight and working through. The emotional resolution of conflict or trauma and negative feelings is a major mechanism of change in psychodynamic child therapy. Children reexperience major developmental or situational trauma in therapy, and many of these conflicts are expressed in play. The play process itself has been thought of as a form of conflict resolution. During this process the therapist labels and interprets the play. The therapist will also tie the observations and interpretations to events in the child's life. Although there is controversy in the psychodynamic literature about how much interpretation to use (Freud, 1966; Klein, 1955), there is general agreement that working through and mastery are important mechanisms of change.

The whole area of emotion and how play helps process and regulate emotion is a key area for investigation. Shields and Cicchetti (1998) defined emotion regulation as the ability to modulate emotions and engage in an adaptive way with the environment. Mennin, Heimberg, Turk, and Fresco (2002) concluded that an emotion regulation perspective would have as goals of treatment to help individuals (a) become more comfortable with arousing emotional experience, (b) be more able to access and utilize emotional information in adaptive problem solving, and (c) be better able to modulate emotional experience and expression. Play in therapy can aid with these three processes. The insight, emotional reexperiencing, and working-through process involve some additional components. For the child who is repressing or avoiding negative affect or thoughts and images that arouse conflict, play can help the expression of that content. Although some of the negative affect (e.g., anxiety) might be extinguished after repeated play, the emotional reexperiencing and working-through process involves more than extinction of emotion. It involves building a meaningful narrative around the emotion or trauma (Gaenesbauer & Siegel, 1995). In addition, insight is applied to experiences and behaviors to which the insight pertains (Shapiro et al., 2006). Operationalizing the components of insight and working through and identifying how play facilitates this process is an important next step for research. It will also be important to identify when this type of process in therapy is important for a child, and when it is not necessary.

A fourth major function of play in therapy is to provide the child opportunities to practice with a variety of ideas, behaviors, interpersonal behaviors, and verbal expressions. Because play is occurring in a safe environment in a pretend world, with a permissive, nonjudgmental adult, the child can try out and rehearse a variety of expressions and behaviors without concern about real-life consequences. In some forms of play therapy, the therapist is quite directive in guiding the child to try new behaviors. Knell (1993) developed a cognitive-behavioral play therapy approach that actively uses modeling techniques and a variety of cognitive-behavioral techniques. Many of these can be used within a psychodynamic framework.

Although these functions of play occur in normal play situations, the therapist builds on these normal functions by enhancing the play experience. The therapist creates a safe environment, gives permission for play to occur, actively facilitates play, and labels the thoughts and feelings expressed. For the psychodynamic therapist, interpretation specifically aids conflict resolution.

For most children younger than 10 years in psychodynamic therapy, therapy is a mixture of play and talk. How play is used in psychotherapy depends on the child's ability to use play, developmental level, age, ability to verbalize, and the overall treatment approach and goals. A number of practical issues arise in using play in therapy. For suggestions about how to get the child started in using play, kinds of play materials, how much the therapist should engage in play, how much to interpret, and how much to set limits, see Chethik (1989), Singer, (1993), and Russ (2004).

RESEARCH WITH PSYCHODYNAMIC THERAPY

There has been a strong movement in the field of child psychotherapy to identify empirically supported treatments (Lonigan, Elbert, & Johnson, 1998). Most of the therapy outcome studies have been efficacy studies that are conducted under controlled conditions that involve random assignment, control groups, and single disorders. Effectiveness studies, on the other hand, are clinical utility studies that focus on treatment outcome in real-world environments. Empirically supported treatment reviews have focused on efficacy studies (Kazdin, 2000). In the child psychotherapy area, Kazdin concluded that the empirically supported treatments for children are few in number and consist mainly of cognitive-behavioral treatments.

Weisz and Weiss (1993) pointed out the low number of psychodynamic outcome studies in the literature. Psychodynamic treatments have not been investigated in the kind of controlled conditions necessary for efficacy studies. Criteria for efficacy studies include random assignment, specific child populations, use of treatment manuals, and use of multiple outcomes with blind raters.

Russ (2006) reviewed the research literature relevant to psychodynamic psychotherapy. Fonagy and Moran (1990) proposed that one reason for the paucity of research is that the rather global approach and broad goals of psychodynamic approaches do not lend themselves easily to carefully controlled outcome studies. Russ (1998) has proposed that the mechanisms of change are also broad and multiple: Therapy is individualized and the therapist is making decisions about intervention on a moment-to-moment basis. However, specificity in research is essential for the field to progress. An important conclusion from Weisz and Weiss (1993) was that studies showing positive results in psychotherapy research tend to be ones that focus on a specific problem, with careful planning of the intervention. In 1983, Freedheim and Russ stated, based on the literature to date, that therapy research needed to become very specific and investigate which specific interventions affect which cognitive, affective, and personality processes. Shirk and Russell (1996) developed a framework for conceptualizing intervention research that ties specific treatment processes to underlying cognitive, affective, and interpersonal processes within a developmental framework. They stress the importance of investigation of specific processes and change mechanisms. Psychodynamic conceptualizations such as the effect of conflict or of deficits in object relations should be testable within their framework.

There has been progress in the area of psychodynamic psychotherapy with children. Fonagy and Moran (1990) applied many of the current guidelines for psychotherapy outcome research to evaluating the effectiveness of child psychoanalysis. Their studies are models for how to investigate the efficacy of psychodynamic approaches. They have carried out different types of studies that are well suited to the psychoanalytic or psychodynamic approach. In one study (Moran & Fonagy, 1987), they used a time series analysis to study the 184 weeks of treatment of a diabetic teenager. Time series analysis investigates whether or not there is a time-bound relationship between events. A relationship was found between major themes in analysis and diabetic control. Moran and Fonagy concluded that the interpretation of conflicts in the treatment brought about an improvement in diabetic control. The improved control led to temporary increases in anxiety and guilt. The improved diabetic control appeared to increase the likelihood of manifest psychological symptomatology. This pattern fits the psychodynamic understanding of brittle diabetes.

In a second study, an inpatient program for diabetes was evaluated (Fonagy & Moran, 1990). Eleven patients received psychotherapy and medical supervision, while the comparison group received medical treatment with no psychotherapy. The analytic treatment was well defined and based on the psychoanalytic understanding of brittle diabetes as being caused by unconscious emotional factors influencing the significance of the disease or its treatment regimen. This leads to disregard for normal diabetic care. The goal of therapy was to make conscious the conflicts and anxieties that were interwoven with the diabetes treatment regimen. The treated group showed significant improvement in diabetic control. None of the untreated group showed improvement. Improvement was maintained at 1-year follow-up. Fonagy and Moran stressed the importance and feasibility of systematic and specific intervention research that investigates changes in psychic structure, such as affect regulation and empathy, as a result of psychoanalysis.

Shirk and Russell (1996) reviewed a number of research programs and measures relevant to assessing change in psychodynamic psychotherapy. Wallerstein (1988) and Kernberg (1995) have coding systems for dimensions relevant to psychodynamic treatment. The Affect in Play Scale (Russ, 1993) can be used to measure change in play processes in psychodynamic therapy.

Muratori, Picchi, Bruni, Patarnello, and Romagnoli (2003) evaluated short- and long-term effects of time-limited psychodynamic psychotherapy for children with internalizing disorders. Fifty-eight outpatient children (6 to 10 years old) who met *DSM-IV* criteria for depressive or anxiety disorder were assigned to therapy or community services. Children were assessed at baseline, 6 months, and 2-year follow-up using the Children's Global Assessment Scale (C-GAS) and Child Behavior Checklist (CBCL). Group assignment was not random. Assignment to the treatment group occurred if there was an opening; if no opening was available, the child was referred to community services. There was no significant difference at baseline between the groups on major variables. Therapy consisted of 11 sessions that followed a protocol. There were five parent-child sessions, five sessions with the child alone, and a final parent-child session. There appear to be clear guidelines about therapist intervention in each session. The treatment approach was to point out the nature of the core conflictual theme and connect it to the child's symptoms and the representational world of the parent. In the child sessions, the therapist labeled feelings and connected mental content and symptoms. Play was seen as an important part of the therapy. Therapists were trained in this approach. Their interventions were videotaped and discussed weekly to monitor adherence to the protocol.

Results revealed major improvements in the treatment group on the C-GAS and CBCL. Improvements on the C-GAS were at 6 months, and CBCL findings were at 2-year follow-up. The changes in the internalizing syndrome on the CBCL at the follow-up only is evidence for the "sleeper effect," a delayed response to the treatment. Muratori et al. (2003) concluded that changes in the shared representational world brought about by the therapy resulted in changes in parent-child interaction only after a period of time. Also, the treatment group sought mental health services less than the comparison group during the 2-year period. This study followed many methodological guidelines for adequate research design described by Weisz and Weiss (1993). The sample was relatively homogeneous (anxious and depressed); a treatment protocol was followed; and therapists were trained and monitored to make sure they adhered to the intervention techniques. In addition, there was a theoretical rationale for why this approach should affect this syndrome. This is the type of rigorous research that needs to occur in the psychodynamic area.

Trowell et al. (2002) compared psychodynamic therapy with psychoeducational topic-focused discussions for 71 girls, 6 to 14 years old, who had experienced sexual abuse. Children were randomly assigned to treatment groups and manualized treatment was used. Sessions were limited to a maximum of 30. Both treatment groups showed improvement, with the psychodynamic therapy group showing significantly more improvement on the "persistent avoidance of stimuli" measures on a PTSD scale. In a review, Ritvo (2006) pointed out that this study and the Fonagy and Moran (1990) study of children with diabetes both focused on children dealing with specific stress rather than with a clinical diagnosis. She stated that this focus on life stress is consistent with the emphasis that the psychodynamic approach places on adaptation and function rather than on clinical diagnosis per se.

We also need more studies that investigate specific mechanisms of change in therapy. A good example of the kind of study that needs to occur is that by Wiser and Goldfried (1998). Although this study was conducted with adults, it is a good model for the child area because it investigates specific types of interventions on specific processes. They investigated the effectiveness of therapeutic interventions on emotional experiencing. The expression of emotion in session has been thought to be important for different mechanisms of change to occur. An important question with adults and children is how to facilitate emotional experiencing in the session. Wiser and Goldfried coded interventions by therapists with anxious and/or depressed outpatient adults in either psychodynamic or cognitive-behavioral therapy. They found that interventions of reflections and acknowledgments, affiliative and noncontrolling interventions, and interventions highlighting nonspecific client content were associated with maintaining high emotional experiencing in both approaches (reflections were nonsignificant in the psychodynamic approach but may be significant with a larger sample size). Interestingly, no type of intervention was associated with a shift to higher emotional experiencing. Some interventions were related to shifts to low experiencing: those that were lengthy and those that were affiliative but moderately controlling. It is important to know which techniques to use to increase emotional experiencing and which to decrease emotional experiencing. Both types of interventions are therapeutic at different times with different populations. The Wiser and Goldfried study is an excellent example of the type of therapy process research that needs to be carried out with children.

Aspects of the relationship with the therapist are also important to investigate in psychodynamic therapy. Using meta-analytic procedures, Shirk and Karver (2003) reviewed associations between therapeutic relationship variables and treatment outcomes in child and adolescent therapy. Results were a modest association (.20), which was similar to that seen in adult studies. This relationship was found across diverse types and modes of child treatment.

Target (2002) reported on results from a retrospective chart study of treated children at the Anna Freud Center who were in psychodynamic or more intensive psychoanalytic treatment. Although this study was retrospective and there was no randomized design or comparison groups, the results are important and do provide guidance. Looking first at anxiety or depressive disorders, 72% of those treated for at least 6 months showed clinically significant improvement (Target & Fonagy, 1994). Phobic disorders were most likely to remit and depressive disorders least likely. Variables that identified children most likely to improve were higher IQ, younger age, longer treatment, good peer relations, poor overall adjustment of the mother, the presence of anxiety in the mother, concurrent treatment of the mother, and absence of maternal antisocial behavior.

In the chart review of disruptive disorders, improvement rates were lower than for the internalizing disorders, with one third terminating therapy prematurely. Of those who stayed in treatment, 69% were no longer diagnosable upon termination. Predictors of improvement were the presence of an anxiety disorder, absence of other disorders, younger age, intensive treatment, longer treatment, maternal anxiety disorder, treatment of the mother, and foster care for the child. Target and Fonagy (1996) concluded that psychodynamic therapy was effective with disorders involving anxiety, even when the anxiety was coupled with disruptive disorders. A different picture emerged with the disruptive (externalizing) disorders. When therapy was effective, it was when intensive treatment was used. They reported that it was the oppositional disorders that were most likely to improve and conduct disorders the least likely.

It appears that before recommending psychodynamic therapy for externalizing disorders in which anxiety is not a major factor, several issues should be considered. Cognitive-behavioral approaches have been found to be very effective for this problem. For example, parent-child interaction therapy is very effective with Oppositional Defiant Disorder (Bodiford-McNeil, Hembree-Kigin, & Eyberg, 1996). If psychodynamic therapy is recommended, two things should be kept in mind and shared with the family: (1) There is no solid empirical support for psychodynamic therapy with externalizing disorders, and (2) the intensive therapy that would be attempted is costly.

The research studies that do exist in the area support the use of psychodynamic therapy for internalizing disorders where anxiety and conflict are important factors. Shapiro et al. (2006) concluded that psychodynamic therapy's focus on play, emotion-dominated thinking, and magical fantasies makes it appropriate for young children. They concluded that no treatment approach has been proven effective for anxious children under 7 (except for simple fears and phobias) or for depression below age 9. The play intervention research that exists also supports the use of a psychodynamic conceptualization for reducing anxiety and negative affect.

Play Intervention Studies

Russ (1995, 2004) reviewed studies investigating the effect of play interventions on specific types of child problems in specific populations. I call these studies play intervention because the focus is highly specific, usually involving only a few sessions with the child. These studies have focused on reducing anxiety in children in medical settings or dealing with separation anxiety. In two different studies, puppet play reduced anxiety in children facing medical procedures when compared with a control group (Cassell, 1965; Johnson & Stockdale, 1975). Rae, Worchel, Upchurch, Sanner, and Daniel (1989) found that children in a therapeutic play group showed significantly more reduction in self-reported hospital-related fears than children in three other treatment groups. This was a well-done study that controlled for time spent with an adult, verbal support, and play activity. They concluded that fantasy activity in the play resulted in fear reduction. Milos and

Reiss (1982) found that thematic play reduced separation anxiety in preschoolers when compared with a control group. Also, the quality of play ratings were significantly negatively related to posttest anxiety. High-quality play was defined as play that showed more separation themes and attempts to resolve conflicts. They concluded that their results supported the notion that play can reduce anxiety associated with psychological problems. The results are consistent with psychodynamic theory.

A well-designed study by Barnett (1984) investigated separation anxiety. Expanding on the work of Barnett and Storm (1981), Barnett found that free play reduced distress in children following a conflict situation the first day of school. Seventy-four preschool children were observed separating from their mothers and were rated anxious or nonanxious. These two groups were further divided into a play or no-play story-listening condition. For half of the play condition, play was solitary. For the other half, peers were present. The story condition was also split into solitary and peers-present segments. Play was rated by observers and categorized into types of play. Play significantly reduced anxiety in the high-anxious group. Anxiety was measured by the Palmer Sweat Index. There was no effect for low-anxious children. For the high-anxious children, solitary play was best in reducing anxiety. High-anxious children spent more time in fantasy play than did low-anxious children, who showed more functional and manipulative play. High-anxious children also engaged more in fantasy play when no other children were present. Barnett suggested that play was used to cope with a distressing situation. The findings supported her concept that it is not social play that is essential to conflict resolution, but rather imaginative play qualities that the child introduces into playful behavior.

The results of these studies suggest that play helps children deal with fears and reduce anxiety and that something about play itself is important and serves as a vehicle for change. Both the Milos and Reiss (1982) study and the Barnett (1984) study suggest that fantasy and make-believe are involved in the reduction of anxiety. The studies effectively controlled for the variable of an attentive adult. Results also suggest that children who are already good players are more able to use play opportunities to solve problems.

These research findings are consistent with psychodynamic theoretical and clinical literature suggesting that play therapy assists children with internal conflict resolution and mastery of internal issues, as well as with external traumas and stressful life events. As a result of this conflict resolution and problem solving, anxiety is reduced. Psychodynamic approaches also suggest the use of insight, conflict-resolution approaches for children whose fantasy skills are normally developed and who can use play in therapy.

Future research should focus on the mechanisms that account for the finding that play reduces anxiety. Conceptualizations and research from other theoretical frameworks could apply to play therapy. For example, Harris (2000) views play as helping the child construct a situation model that is revisable. Children go back and forth between an imagined world and reality and develop a new cognitive appraisal of the situation. Pennebaker's work is also relevant: Adults who develop a coherent and meaningful narrative of an event through an emotional writing exercise have improved mental and physical health (Pennebaker & Graybeal, 2001). Children may be developing meaningful and coherent narratives in play therapy.

Future research should investigate techniques in therapy that facilitate play in therapy. Russ, Moore, and Pearson (2006) developed play intervention protocols that resulted in increased fantasy and imagination and affect in play in first- and second-grade children. In five 30-minute sessions with a play trainer, the child was instructed to play out various story scripts. In the affect play group, the child was asked to play out stories with different emotions and to express emotion. In the imagination play group, the child was asked to play out stories with a high fantasy content and high organization of the story. The instructions and prompts by the play trainer were standardized. The affect play group had higher scores on all play abilities when compared to a control group on the outcome play measure (Affect in Play Scale). The imagination play group had higher scores on the affect play variable. The results suggest that a brief standardized play intervention can improve play skills and increase emotional expression in play in psychotherapy. This technique could be helpful for children with constricted affect such as those with PTSD or depression. By having children make up various stories and directing them to express affect, with modeling and reinforcement by the therapist, children could increase affect expression quickly. This technique could be especially useful in time-limited therapy.

SHORT-TERM PSYCHODYNAMIC PSYCHOTHERAPY

Short-term psychotherapy (6 to 12 sessions) is a form of psychodynamic psychotherapy frequently used with children (Messer & Warren, 1995). The practical realities of HMOs and of clinical practice in general have led to briefer forms of treatment. Often, the time-limited nature of the therapy is by default, not by plan (Messer & Warren, 1995). The average number of sessions for children in outpatient therapy is 6 or fewer in private and clinical settings (Dulcan & Piercy, 1985).

There is little research or clinical theory about short-term therapy with children (Messer & Warren, 1995). A few research studies have shown that explicit time limits reduced the likelihood of premature termination (Parad & Parad, 1968), and that children in time-limited therapy showed as much improvement as those in long-term therapy (Smyrnios & Kirby, 1993). The time is right for the development of theoretically based short-term interventions for children. Messer and Warren suggest that the developmental approach utilized by psychodynamic theory provides a useful framework for short-term therapy. One can identify the developmental problems and obstacles involved in a particular case. They also stressed the use of play as a vehicle of change and, as Winnicott (1971) has said, of development. They suggest that the active interpretation of the meaning of play can help the child feel understood, which, in turn, can result in lifelong changes in self-perception and experience. In other words, the understanding of the metaphors in a child's play could give the child insight or an experience of empathy, or both. This lasting change could be accomplished in a short time.

As previously discussed, Chethik (1989) developed focal therapy to deal with specific stressful events in the child's life. Basic principles of psychodynamic therapy are applied in this short-term approach, with the basic mechanism of change being insight and working through. Chethik views this approach as working best with children who have accomplished normal developmental tasks before the stressful event occurred.

In general, brief forms of psychodynamic intervention are seen as more appropriate for the child who has accomplished the major developmental milestones. Proskauer (1969) stressed the child's ability to quickly develop a relationship with the therapist, good trusting ability, the existence of a focal dynamic issue, and flexible and adaptive defenses as criteria for short-term intervention. Messer and Warren (1995) concluded that children with less severe pathology are more responsive to brief intervention than children with chronic developmental problems. The Muratori et al. (2003) study that found that short-term intervention with anxious and depressed children was effective is consistent with this conclusion. The research and clinical literature suggest that internalizing disorders are most appropriate for brief psychodynamic intervention (Russ, 2004). The therapist is active, at times directive, and uses all mechanisms of change in the therapy. Insight and working through are essential, but modeling, rehearsal, and problem-solving strategies are also part of the therapy. Children with major deficits in object relations and those with early developmental problems need longer term structure-building approaches.

Shelby (2000) described the importance of using developmentally appropriate interventions in brief therapy with traumatized children. Working with traumatized children in Sarajevo, she used play and drawing. She described an experiential mastery technique in which children drew pictures of the thing that frightened them. Children were encouraged to verbalize their feelings about the drawing. They were also instructed to do anything they wanted to the drawing. Shelby described how this and other developmentally appropriate brief play interventions, although not empirically tested, helped a number of these traumatized children to integrate traumatic events and return to "normal developmental functioning" (p. 72).

Structured play techniques would be especially useful in short-term therapy. The MacArthur Story Stem Battery (MSSB), although designed as an assessment tool, can be used to structure the play situation. In an innovative approach, Kelsay (2002) used the MSSB to structure play therapy. The MSSB is a set of story beginnings (e.g., parents arguing over lost keys), and the child is asked to complete the story. The therapist can choose appropriate story stems tailored to the issues that the child is dealing with. This structured approach could move the therapy to central issues more quickly.

Structured play techniques have also been used with very young children. Gaensbauer and Siegel (1995) described structured play techniques with toddlers who have experienced traumatic events. They conceptualized the mechanisms of change when play is used as being similar to those in older children with PTSD. With these very young children, the therapist actively structures the play to recreate the traumatic event. Gaensbauer and Siegel outlined three purposes of structured play reenactment. First, play enables the child to organize the fragmented experiences into meaningful narratives. Second, the interpretive work by the therapist helps the child understand the personal meanings of the trauma. Third, there is desensitization of the anxiety and fear and other negative emotions associated with the trauma. They stressed that the key element that enables the child to use play adaptively, rather than in a repetitive fashion, is the "degree to which affects can be brought to the surface so the child can identify them and integrate them in more adaptive ways" (p. 297).

RESEARCH GUIDELINES

Given the results of the research in the area, research guidelines suggested by Russ (2006) that would be the most fruitful and have the most immediate impact on the field would focus on the following:

- In young children, well-controlled efficacy and effectiveness studies with anxiety disorders, PTSD, depression, and focused problems involving anxiety and conflict should be carried out with psychodynamic therapy.
- Short-term interventions should be investigated and refined.
- Mechanisms of change in therapy, especially insight and emotional working through, are needed to identify mechanisms leading to anxiety reduction and reduction of negative affect.
- Play processes and techniques that facilitate play in therapy should be researched.

Demonstration of the effectiveness of structure-building approaches with seriously emotionally disturbed children is also necessary. Because the therapy is so long term and complex with these children, single-case designs would be especially appropriate.

SUMMARY

The psychodynamic approach focuses on the internal world of the child. A developmental perspective is used to understand underlying cognitive, affective, and interpersonal processes. A psychodynamic understanding determines the specific intervention approach and techniques to be used with a particular child. The mechanisms of change most associated with psychodynamic therapy are insight, emotional reexperiencing, and working through. A key question for future research is to identify the components of these mechanisms of change. In therapy, pretend play is frequently used as a vehicle for change. There are a number of constructs in psychodynamic theory that inform therapy. Empirical support for these constructs lends support for psychodynamic therapy. Outcome research on the effectiveness of psychodynamic therapy is sparse. A few studies do offer empirical support. Research in play intervention also suggests that the use of play in therapy can reduce anxiety. Future research should focus on the use of psychodynamic therapy with internalizing disorders in young children, play facilitation techniques, short-term therapy, and the components and role of the insight and working-through process.

REFERENCES

Axline, V. (1947). *Play therapy*. Boston: Houghton Mifflin.

Barnett, I. (1984). Research note: Young children's resolution of distress through play. *Journal of Child Psychology and Psychiatry, 25*, 477–483.

Barnett, I., & Storm, B. (1981). Play, pleasure, and pain: The reduction of anxiety through play. *Leisure Science, 4*, 161–175.

Blank, R., & Blank, G. (1986). *Beyond ego psychology: Developmental object relations theory*. New York: Columbia University Press.

Bodiford-McNeil, C., Hembree-Kigin, T. L., & Eyberg, S. (1996). *Short-term play therapy for disruptive children*. King of Prussia, PA: Center for Applied Psychology.

Cassell, S. (1965). Effect of brief puppet therapy upon the emotional responses of children undergoing cardiac catheterization. *Journal of Consulting Psychology, 29*, 1–8.

Chethik, M. (1989). *Techniques of child therapy: Psychodynamic strategies*. New York: Guilford Press.

Chethik, M. (2000). *Techniques of child therapy: Psychodynamic Strategies* (2nd ed.). New York: Guilford Press.

Dulcan, M., & Piercy, P. (1985). A model of teaching and evaluating brief psychotherapy with children and their families. *Professional Psychology: Research and Practice, 16*, 689–700.

Erikson, E. H. (1963). *Childhood and society*. New York: Norton.

Fonagy, P., & Moran, G. S. (1990). Studies on the efficacy of child psychoanalysis. *Journal of Consulting and Clinical Psychology, 58*, 684–695.

Freedheim, D. K., & Russ, S. W. (1983). Psychotherapy with children. In C. E. Walker, & M. E. Roberts (Eds.), *Handbook of clinical child psychology* (pp. 978–994). New York: Wiley.

Freedheim, D. K., & Russ, S. W. (1992). Psychotherapy with children. In C. E. Walker, & M. Roberts (Eds.), *Handbook of clinical child psychology* (2nd ed., pp. 765–780). New York: Wiley.

Freud, A. (1927). Four lectures on child analysis. In *The writings of Anna Freud* (Vol. 1, pp. 3–69). New York: International Universities Press.

Freud, A. (1965). *Normality and pathology in childhood: Assessments of development*. New York: International Universities Press.

Freud, A. (1966). *The ego and the mechanisms of defense*. New York: International Universities Press.

Freud, A. (1968). Indications and contraindications for child analysis. *Psychoanalytic Study of the Child, 26*, 79–80.

Gaensbauer, T. J., & Siegel, C. H., (1995). Therapeutic approaches to posttraumatic stress disorder in infants and toddlers. *Infant Mental Health Journal, 16*, 292–305.

Gilpin, D. (1976). Psychotherapy of borderline psychotic children. *American Journal of Psychotherapy, 30*, 483–496.

Harris, P. (2000). *The work of the imagination*. Oxford: Blackwell.

Holt, R. R. (1977). A method for assessing primary process manifestations and their control in Rorschach responses. In M. Rickers-Ovsiankiina (Ed.), *Rorschach psychology* (pp. 375–420). New York: Kreiger.

Johnson, P. A., & Stockdale, D. E. (1975). Effects of puppet therapy on palmar sweating of hospitalized children. *Johns Hopkins Medical Journal, 137*, 1–5.

Kazdin, A. (2000). *Psychotherapy for children and adolescents*. New York: Oxford University Press.

Kelsay, K. (2002, October). *MacArthur Story Stem Battery as a therapeutic tool*. Paper presented at the meeting of the American Academy of Child and Adolescent Psychiatry, San Francisco.

Kernberg, P. (1995, October). *Child psychodynamic psychotherapy: Assessing the process*. Paper presented at the meeting of the American Academy of Child and Adolescent Psychiatry, New Orleans, LA.

Kessler, J. (1966). *Psychopathology of childhood*. Englewood Cliffs, NJ: Prentice-Hall.

Kessler, J. (1988). *Psychopathology of childhood* (2nd ed.). Englewood Cliffs, NJ: Prentice-Hall.

Klein, M. (1955). The psychoanalytic play technique. *American Journal of Orthopsychiatry, 25*, 223–237.

Knell, S. (1993). *Cognitive-behavioral play therapy*. Northvale, NJ: Aronson.

Kohut, H. (1977). *The restoration of the self*. New York: International Universities Press.

Kohut, H., & Wolfe, E. R. (1978). The disorders of the self and their treatment: An outline. *International Journal of Psychoanalysis, 59*, 413–424.

Koocher, G., & D'Angelo, E. J. (1992). Evolution of practice in child psychotherapy. In D. K. Freedheim (Ed.), *History of psychotherapy* (pp. 457–492). Washington, DC: American Psychological Association.

Lonigan, C., Elbert, J., & Johnson, S. (1998). Empirically supported psychosocial interventions for children: An overview. *Journal of Clinical Child Psychology, 27*, 138–145.

Mahler, M. S. (1968). *On human symbiosis and the vicissitudes of individuation*. New York: International Universities Press.

Mennin, D., Heimberg, R., Turk, C., & Fresco, D. (2002). Applying an emotion regulation framework to interactive approaches to generalized anxiety disorder. *Clinical Psychology, 19*, 85–90.

Messer, S. B., & Warren, C. S. (1995). *Models of brief psychodynamic therapy*. New York: Guilford Press.

Milos, M., & Reiss, S. (1982). Effects of three play conditions on separation anxiety in young children. *Journal of Consulting and Clinical Psychology, 50*, 389–395.

Moran, C. S., & Fonagy, P. (1987). Psychoanalysis and diabetic control: A single case study. *British Journal of Medical Psychology, 60*, 352–372.

Moustakas, C. (1953). *Children in play therapy*. New York: McGraw-Hill.

Muratori, E., Picchi, E., Bruni, C., Patarnello, M., & Romagnoli, G. (2003). A two-year follow-up of psychodynamic psychotherapy for internalizing disorders in children. *Journal of the American Academy of Child and Adolescent Psychiatry, 42*, 331–339.

Parad, L., & Parad, N. (1968). A study of crisis-oriented planned short-term treatment: Pt. 1. *Social Casework, 49*, 346–355.

Pennebaker, J. W., & Graybeal, A. (2001). Patterns of natural language use: Disclosure, personality, and social integration. *Current Directions in Psychological Science, 10*, 90–93.

Proskauer, S. (1969). Some technical issues in time-limited psychotherapy with children. *Journal of the American Academy of Child and Adolescent Psychiatry, 8*, 54–169.

Rae, W., Worchel, R., Upchurch, J., Sanner, J., & Daniel, C. (1989). The psychosocial impact of play on hospitalized children. *Journal of Pediatric Psychology, 14*, 617–627.

Ritvo, R. (2006). Is there research to support psychodynamic psychotherapy? Pt. I. *American Academy of Child and Adolescent Psychiatry News*, 262–263.

Russ, S. W. (1993). *Affect and creativity: The role of affect and play in the creative process*. Hillsdale, NJ: Erlbaum.

Russ, S. W. (1995). Play psychotherapy research: State of the science. In T. Ollendick, & R. Prinz (Eds.), *Advances in clinical child psychology* (Vol. 17, pp. 365–391). New York: Plenum Press.

Russ, S. W. (1996). Psychoanalytic theory and creativity: Cognition and affect revisited. In J. Masling, & R. Bornstein (Eds.), *Psychoanalytic perspectives on developmental psychology* (pp. 69–103). Washington, DC: APA Books.

Russ, S. W. (1998). Psychodynamically based therapies. In T. Ollendick, & M. Hersen (Eds.), *Handbook of child psychopathology* (3rd ed., pp. 537–556). New York: Plenum Press.

Russ, S. W. (2004). *Play in child development and psychotherapy: Toward empirically supported practice*. Mahwah, NJ: Erlbaum.

Russ, S. W. (2006). Psychodynamic treatments. In R. Ammerman (Ed.), *Comprehensive handbook of personality and psychopathology: Vol. 3. Child psychopathology* (pp. 425–437). Hoboken, NJ: Wiley.

Russ, S. W., & Freedheim, D. (2001). Psychotherapy with children. In C. E. Walker, & M. Roberts (Eds.), *Handbook of clinical child psychology* (3rd ed., pp. 840–859). New York: Wiley.

Russ, S. W., Moore, M., & Pearson, B. (2006). *Effects of play intervention on play skills and adaptive functioning*. Manuscript submitted for publication.

Sandler, J., Kennedy, H., & Tyson, R. L. (1980). *The technique of child psychoanalysis: Discussion with Anna Freud*. Cambridge, MA: Harvard University Press.

Shapiro, J., Friedberg, R., & Bardenstein, K. (2006). *Child and adolescent therapy: Science and art*. Hoboken, NJ: Wiley.

Shelby, J. (2000). Brief therapy with traumatized children: A developmental perspective. In A. Kaderson & C. Schaefer (Eds.), *Short-term play therapy for children* (pp. 69–104). New York: Guilford Press.

Shields, A., & Cicchetti, D. (1998). Reactive aggression among maltreated children: The contributions of attention and emotion dysregulation. *Journal of Clinical Child Psychology, 27*, 381–395.

Shirk, S. W., & Karver, M. (2003). Prediction of treatment outcome from relationship variables in child and adolescent therapy: A meta-analytic review. *Journal of Consulting and Clinical Psychology, 71*, 452–464.

Shirk, S. W., & Russell, R. (1996). *Change processes in child psychotherapy: Revitalizing treatment and research.* New York: Guilford Press.

Singer, D. (1993). *Playing for their lives.* New York: Free Press.

Smyrnios, K., & Kirby, R. L. (1993). Long-term comparison of brief versus unlimited psychodynamic treatments with children and their families. *Journal of Counseling and Clinical Psychology, 61*, 1020–1027.

Suler, J. (1980). Primary process thinking and creativity. *Psychological Bulletin, 88*, 144–165.

Target, M. (2002). The problem of outcome in child psychoanalysis: Contributions from the Anna Freud Center. In M. Leuzinger-Bohleber, & M. Target (Eds.), *Outcomes of psychoanalytic treatment* (pp. 240–251). New York: Brunner-Routledge.

Target, M., & Fonagy, P. (1994). The efficacy of psycho-analysis for children with emotional disorders. *Journal of the American Academy of Child and Adolescent Psychiatry, 33*, 361–371.

Target, M., & Fonagy, P. (1996). The psychological treatment of child and adolescent psychiatric disorders. In A. Roth Jr., & P. Fonagy (Eds.), *What works for whom?* (pp. 263–320). New York: Guilford Press.

Trowell, J., Kolvin, I., Weeramanthri, T., Sadowski, H., Berelowitz, M., Glasser, D., et al. (2002). Psychotherapy for sexually abused girls: Psychopathological outcome findings and patterns of change. *British Journal of Psychiatry, 180*, 234–247.

Tuma, J. M., & Russ, S. W. (1993). Psychoanalytic psychotherapy with children. In T. Kratochwill, & R. Morris (Eds.), *Handbook of psychotherapy with children and adolescents* (pp. 131–161). Boston: Allyn & Bacon.

Tyson, P., & Tyson, R. L. (1990). *Psychoanalytic theories of development: An integration.* New Haven, CT: Yale University Press.

Waelder, R. (1933). Psychoanalytic theory of play. *Psychoanalytic Quarterly, 2*, 208–224.

Wallerstein, R. S. (1988). Assessment of structural change in psychoanalytic therapy and research. *Journal of the American Psychoanalytic Association, 36* (Suppl.), 241–261.

Weisz, J., & Weiss, B. (1993). *Effects of psychotherapy with children and adolescents.* Beverly Hills, CA: Sage.

Westen, D. (1998). The scientific legacy of Sigmund Freud: Toward a psychodynamically informed psychological science. *Psychological Bulletin, 124*, 333–371.

Winnicott, D. W. (1971). *Playing and reality.* London: Tavistock.

Wiser, S., & Goldfried, M. (1998). Therapist interventions and client emotional experiencing in expert psychodynamic-interpersonal and cognitive-behavioral therapies. *Journal of Counseling and Clinical Psychology, 66*, 634–640.

CHAPTER 7

Family Systems

James P. McHale and Matthew J. Sullivan

This chapter provides an overview of major contributions of family systems thinking to the field of clinical psychology. Consistent with the volume's other chapters, it attends to theory, research, assessment, and treatment issues. To provide additional substance for some of the central conceptual issues advanced in this chapter, a section on treatment considerations develops a clinical case example in an outline paralleling those of other chapters covering major treatment approaches. In so doing, we strive to clarify how clinicians working from a family systems approach might work with children and families in a manner quite distinct from, though often complementary to, interventionists working from psychodynamic, behavioral, or cognitive approaches.

What our field refers to as "family systems thinking" is actually a conceptual and philosophical framework that reflects a wide array of quite different approaches and influences—indeed, there *is* no single "systems" theory. What ties together this collection of rather disparate influences and approaches is the central, guiding notion that problem behavior exhibited by a child or an adult can never be understood devoid of its relational context. Further, from a systems view, the behavioral problems evident in any individual family member are perhaps best understood as manifestations of dysfunction within the broader family unit. From this basic tenet follow distinctive lines of inquiry in research studies, and approaches in clinical formulation, assessment, and treatment, that often differ substantially from paths followed in other theoretical traditions and frameworks.

We begin this chapter with a review of some of the major assumptions of systems approaches and a brief recounting of some of the historically important forms of influence in shaping this approach to psychopathology and its treatment. We summarize roles that empirical research has played in the family systems field. From this base, we outline how family systems principles might organize clinical work with a case referred for the treatment of ostensible problems in an individual family member. We close the chapter with some reflections on the value of systems-informed approaches in clinical work.

BASIC CONCEPTS AND PRINCIPLES

Historically, the systems theory developments that inspired and were infused by early family therapies presented exciting and revolutionary challenges to the practices and theories of the times. Systems theory was held to differ from psycho-analytic approaches by emphasizing relational as opposed to intrapsychic processes, and by taking a holistic and multidirectional view of pathological behavior and its treatment (Bateson, Jackson, Haley, & Weakland, 1956; Lidz, Cornelison, Fleck, & Terry, 1957a, 1957b; Wynne, Ryckoff, Day, & Hirsch, 1958). But the sheer number of different thrusts within this emerging field and the complexity of some of the early theoretical formulations and writings meant that it would be many years before coherence in the field began to emerge. Accounts of "systems theory" and its pertinence to families and individual development often seek to trace the history of how principles governing physical systems came to be applied to social systems. In such accountings, special homage is often accorded the creative writings of von Bertanffly (1968). As Patricia Minuchin (1985) noted, however, the writings of Bateson (1972, 1979) and other family theoreticians more directly concerned with the functioning of human systems (e.g., Jackson, 1957; S. Minuchin, 1974; Watzlawick, Beavin, & Jackson, 1967) had a more formative impact on most practicing clinicians of the time. Among the most essential of systems tenets, outlined by P. Minuchin (1985) and others (e.g., Bornstein & Sawyer, 2006; Cox & Paley, 2003) are the following:

- Systems are organized wholes, and their constituting elements or subsystems are interdependent.
- Interconnected subsystems have their own integrity, are organized hierarchically, and are separated by boundaries.
- Patterns in a system are circular and not linear.
- Stable patterns are maintained over time through homeostatic processes.
- Open systems do adapt, change, reorganize, and develop.

Several important talking points follow from these central tenets. First, when clinicians consider any family system, they should find it possible to identify both a family group reality wherein patterns of organization governing the functioning of the overall unit operate as organized patterns in their own right, and a variety of subsystem realities that may or may not themselves mirror the same patterning and rules of the broader system. Most families are composed of multiple subsystems—among them, marital subsystems, parent-child subsystems, sibling subsystems, parent-grandparent and child-grandparent subsystems in multigenerational family systems, and so on. When clinicians and researchers assess family dynamics, they regularly detect logical interconnections among different subsystem levels; for example, high levels of distress in the marital subsystem typically coincide with evidence of impaired parenting of one or more children in the family (Erel & Burman, 1995). They also find that subsystem functioning both affects and is affected by broader systemic functioning, as when marital strife between a husband and wife within their dyadic marital subsystem comes to disrupt collaboration in effectively coparenting children at the family group level (Belsky, Crnic, & Gable, 1995; McHale, 1995). In other cases, such linkages are not as overt or easily detected, as when family members as a unit collude to obscure problematic alignments or abuse within a particular dyadic subsystem in the family (Wynne, 1961).

Besides these interconnections between subsystems and the functioning of the family group, the functioning of the overall unit is also properly seen as constraining and organizing interactions at all other levels. For example, in Bowen's (1978; see also Friedman, 1992) conceptualization of the family's emotional system, family members are described as having developed emotional interdependencies to the point where the emotional system through which they are connected has evolved its own principles of organization. The resulting organizational structure then comes to influence the functioning of various individuals and dyads far more than any of them alter the functioning of the full system (S. Minuchin, 1974). For example, a variety of different interaction patterns and sequences (e.g., children diffusing conflict between parents; parents exhibiting preoccupation and overprotection of children) may be seen in families whose structure is guided by the covert rule that "family members must protect one another" (see Nichols & Schwartz, 1998); although changing any particular sequence would not alter this governing structure, altering the structure would reshape interaction patterns throughout the system.

Of course, if an interventionist was successful in meaningfully changing any given aspect of a family's entrenched pattern, this would have the effect of perturbing other patterns. Such temporary ripple effects and adjustments have the potential to affect more enduring change in the problematic family pattern—but only to the extent that the short-term adjustments could be sustained. Unfortunately, supporting enduring pattern changes is very difficult, in part because systems show marked propensities for preserving equilibrium. New patterns of behavior by a child or adult that challenge established family patterns and rules are often quickly countered by adjustments elsewhere in the system that are knowingly, or unconsciously, intended to reestablish the previously enduring status quo. Said differently, because everyone's behavior has become interdependent, the family members collectively collude to maintain their existing patterns. Moreover, repetitive patterns are especially unlikely to change if they have evolved to serve some important protective function for the system as a whole (Madanes, 1981; Selvini Palazzoli, Boscolo, Cecchin, & Prata, 1978), as when a child's misbehavior deflects attention away from a more serious rift in the parents' marital relationship.

The notion of circular causality in family systems (Bateson, 1979) is also central in family systems conceptualizations. Seen as a hallmark of systems thinking that stands in contrast to the linear thinking implicit in other approaches, the principle of circular causality is that the patterns families develop are actively maintained by all of the family's participant members. Such group and subsystem reciprocity is seen as largely responsible for the enduring nature of family patterns through time. As an example, extreme emotional overinvolvement by a child's mother, to the point where she interferes with that child's own capacities for autonomous emotional regulation, is often accompanied by pronounced disengagement by the child's father (in some families, the pattern is reversed, with intense father-child involvement co-occurring with maternal disengagement). Whether fathers disengage in response to intensive maternal involvement or whether maternal overinvolvement evolves as a response to inadequate father involvement is an immaterial question; all parties (including the family's children) collude to help maintain system functioning by steadfastly keeping to the pattern that has evolved through a process of checks, balances, and recurring feedback loops.

Given these powerful corrective feedback loops self-regulating families and maintaining their enduring patterns, how do families ever change and evolve? Different theorists provide different perspectives, but most find consensus on certain points. First, all living systems do change in form (Speer, 1970). They do so in response to major and sustained perturbations either from within or from the outside that disrupt established patterns (Hoffman, 1981; Prigogine, 1973). The initial reactions of an intensively challenged system are to mobilize familiar modes of response. But as such responses fail to accommodate the new challenge, the system begins advancing previously untested, untried methods of adaptation until ultimately happening upon solutions relevant to addressing the challenge. During this period of duress, the system is in relative disarray. Indeed, it operates temporarily at a lower level of integration, as its previous modes of adaptation are abandoned in favor of newer and less refined adaptations. However, following this period of destructure and disintegration, newer structures and solutions effectively replace the old, becoming integrated into the system's patterning and modes of action. This process of disequilibration and reorganization (Block, 1982) typically eventuates in the emergence of a more complex and differentiated system, though devolution, as in the case of incestuous families, is also possible (Alexander, Sexton, & Robbins, 2002). The operating principle is that change is expectable and inevitable. In human systems this is largely because change is regularly initiated by individual development within the broader system.

Where, then, is the connection with von Bertanffly's general systems model? Extrapolating from the biological systems model, family theorists have often drawn connections to notions of systems as open, cybernetic, or closed (Bateson, 1972 1980; White, 1986, 1989). Open systems, von Bertanffly (1968) explains, have the intrinsic capacity for change, whereas change in closed (including cybernetic) systems occurs only in response to outside sources. Don Jackson (1957) was among the first to draw a parallel between closed information systems in states of homeostasis and the consistency of family disturbances and symptomatic behavior that resisted change. Appropriating the metaphor of homeostasis from general systems theory had appeal, as families stuck in recurrent maladaptive patterns could be viewed as being in a state of equilibrium, behavioral redundancy, and relationship balance. The homeostasis metaphor has remained a very influential one, though it is flawed in many ways. As Moyer (1994) has pointed out, whereas human systems are open rather than closed, theoretical concepts of cybernetics and homeostasis properly describe closed systems and hence are not truly applicable. For example, open (as opposed to cybernetic) systems are intrinsically capable of change, do possess the potential for free interchange of information, energy, or matter, and are composed of components that are simultaneously actors and acted upon (in a circular, rather than linear, dynamic).

Nonetheless, characterizations of disturbed family systems as closed, insular, and resistant (if not impermeable) to adaptive informational exchanges with the outside world have remained a recurring and robust metaphor in many clinical writings. Certainly, though, not all theorists find it necessary to invoke open-closed and cybernetic metaphors when describing closure and insularity; Bowen (1978), for example, observed simply that family members withdraw from outside relationships and insulate themselves when emotional forces within the family are in opposition and internal anxiety and tension mount. Such closed or relatively closed-off family systems are usually seen as dysfunctional when contrasted with healthier open system functioning (Olsen, Sprenkle, & Russell, 1979; Satir, 1972), though open systems too can be plagued by serious problems, such as excessive and chaotic interaction, prolonged conflict, and ambiguity (Constantine, 1983).

We now turn to several of the most influential theoretical streams and concepts emanating from the related fields of family therapy and family psychology.

Historically Important Ideas and Lines of Influence: Family Therapy and Family Psychology

The view that children's behavioral problems are inextricable from their family group context and that they are most effectively addressed through family collective approaches has been active for nearly a century. Richmond (1917), echoing practices of the social work movement of her time, posited that child adjustment problems had to be understood in their family context, advocated work with family units, and emphasized the palliative role of family cohesion. Yet even as she wrote, common practice then as now was for children's mothers (and seldom fathers) to attend such family sessions. In clinical psychology, mainstream practice did not follow suit in assuming social work's collectivist stance through most of the first half of the twentieth century, even though positions developed by Sullivan, Horney, and Fromm emphasized the interpersonal nature of psychiatric disorders. The work of these pioneering figures, however, was not truly systemic in that treatment approaches seldom moved to involve family members; such inclusion was usually construed as a violation of client confidentiality.

During the 1950s, John E. Bell, Nathan Ackerman, and a handful of other clinicians broke from these long-standing traditions and began conducting conjoint therapy when seeing problem-referred children. This significant reconceptualization of work with child cases helped catalyze the gradual spread of family-level approaches and came to spark many generative debates and discussions among clinical psychologists. Herein were the gentle beginnings of a family therapy movement, guided by the clarion call that individual psychopathology signaled dysfunctional family systems. Distressed children were said to have accepted an assignment from the family to be its "identified patient" (IP), while the child's symptomatology came to be understood as serving a "messenger" function communicating dire problems at work in the broader family system. Yet even as the IP broadcast these messages, his or her problems were also playing some functional role in protecting the family and maintaining its balance (as when redirecting parents' attention away from their own strife and onto the child's problems). Moreover, this function often eluded the conscious awareness of some or all of the family's members. Based on this premise that child behavior problems were telegraphing broader system dysfunction, family practitioners argued that it was senseless to excise a child from his or her family system to treat the child's behavior problems, and then return him or her to the very same context that had catalyzed the development and supported the maintenance of those problems to begin with. Rather, logic dictated attempting to effect change at the root source, alleviating the child's suffering by fostering meaningful change in the functioning of the child's family system.

There were many different pathways toward such ends charted by pioneers of the family therapy movement. Given space limitations, we highlight only some of the principal and most enduring contributions of various perspectives and underscore a few commonalities among approaches. However, we caution readers that by doing so we necessarily obfuscate much of the important detail and richness of theory differentiating the disparate approaches, and we recommend consulting original sources for fuller readings of theory exposition. As an orienting comment, it is probably fair to say that all of the major early schools of thought—including psychoanalytic, Bowenian, contextual, experiential, strategic, structural, communication, and behavioral therapies—shared a few things in common. All acknowledged mutual contributions by all family members to the problems they encountered, shared the therapeutic goals of helping family members assume greater responsibility and de-limit blame, and aspired to clarify and enhance intrafamily communication patterns (Kaslow, 1982; Nichols & Schwartz, 1998). How the therapies sought to do so, what each took as their point of entry, how much each privileged the intrapsychic world or privileged external interpersonal relations, and how much emphasis each gave to the role of past as opposed to contemporary, here-and-now relationships—even insofar as differing in defining who actually constituted the family (and in multigenerational and extended kin frameworks, how far this reach needed to go)—varied greatly. Yet all approaches sought essentially similar ends: greater role flexibility and adaptability, greater clarity and specificity of communications, a more equitable balance of power among the family's coparenting figures, and promotion of greater individuality and differentiation of members within a cohesive family collective. Hence family cohesion, adaptability, and communication are some of the common themes tying together different approaches (Olson, Russell, & Sprenkle, 1980).

In most accounts Ackerman, who was a psychoanalyst and child psychiatrist by training, is hailed as the pioneering figure in the family therapy movement; his early publications, *The Unity of the Family* and *Family Diagnosis: An Approach to the Preschool Child,* are counted among the field's seminal works. Perhaps the most provocative conceptual advances early on in the family therapy movement, however, emanated from work with families of young men and women diagnosed with Schizophrenia. Among the innovative clinicians bucking a therapeutic tradition of segregating schizophrenic individuals from their families when providing treatment (and involving the family members only on a need-to-know basis) was Murray Bowen, who strove to treat the schizophrenic person's entire family unit. Bowen believed that the introduction of an outside person into disturbed relational systems had the potential to modify relationships within that system, but he emphasized the importance of the therapist's keeping the intensity of therapeutic focus within the family unit rather than siphoning it into an intense transference relationship. This stance, which broke with psychoanalytic convention, was one defining feature of the Bowenian approach. Bowen's theory described how individual family members in troubled families experienced difficulty differentiating within a relatively closed-off emotional family system (in 1974, Bowen portrayed families with schizophrenic members as characterized by an "undifferentiated family ego mass"), and he was among the first family theorists to explicitly outline the role that multigenerational transmission played in family pathology. But perhaps the most central of all Bowen's many major contributions was his exposition of emotional triangles as the basic building blocks of families, and of how a third person helps to stabilize inherently unstable dyads. While similar ideas were developed by several other theorists, as outlined later, Bowen helped specify why it is that triangulation breeds stress; to the extent that one family member becomes responsible for or tries to change the relationship of two others, that person shoulders the stress for the others' relationship. Stress within emotional triangles thus came to be seen as a positional phenomenon; assuming responsibility overburdened younger, less differentiated family members, in particular, by trapping them in problematic relationships that they were ill equipped to handle (Friedman, 1992).

Elsewhere, Gregory Bateson and his colleagues in Palo Alto, California (among them Jay Haley, John Weakland, and later Don Jackson), had been developing a communication theory of Schizophrenia, from which surfaced the notions about family homeostasis discussed earlier. According to the group's double-bind theory, an individual's psychosis was understandable in the context of pathological family communication. When individuals receive contradictory messages or injunctions communicated on different (manifest content and metacommunication) levels, the theory went, they are inextricably trapped in contradictory, double-binding conundrums offering no clear channel for resolution or escape (Bateson et al., 1956). The Palo Alto group portrayed the cognitive distortions endemic to Schizophrenia as one adaptation to such insoluble double-binding communications. Despite its elegance and allure, double-bind theory as a theory for Schizophrenia did not stand up to clinical and empirical scrutiny and ultimately fell into disrepute. However, several innovative conceptualizations emanating from the group's work, including the coexistence and significance of multiple communication levels in family interactions and the notion that destructive relationship patterns endure as a result of self-regulating interactions, have had lasting impact.

As a family theory, many of the seminal ideas of the Palo Alto group, such as the double-bind notion, and Jackson's (1965) "quid pro quo," were limited in how much they could explain because they actually described dyads rather than full family systems. However, Haley developed an enduring interest in triads (which he later developed further in his writings about cross-generational coalitions and perverse triangles). This concept was influential in helping to bridge two of the more influential family systems approaches: strategic and structural family therapy (for greater historical perspective on this connection, see Nichols & Schwartz, 1998).

A third set of investigations of family dynamics in Schizophrenia that also had lasting impact in family thinking was that of the psychodynamic theorist Theodore Lidz and his colleagues (1957a, 1957b). Among Lidz's key contributions was his challenging of the blame burden that had historically been foisted exclusively upon mothers. Though he did not absolve mothers, Lidz did consider the potentially damaging role of fathering relationships in families, seeding a field now flourishing as coparenting theory (McHale et al., 2002; McHale, 2007a). Focusing on what he termed role reciprocity, Lidz outlined ways in which parents of disturbed youth had failed to achieve mutually supportive, collaborative, and coordinated parenting stances within the family. In some cases, the problem was one of marital schism, whereby parents chronically undermined one another and competed for their children's loyalties. In other families, which he characterized as showing marital skew, one of the parents held inordinate sway in the family while the other passively gave way to the domineering parent. In Lidz's published cases it was typically the father who was the one who acceded, though the dynamic could also be flipped. In both kinds of family systems, children were caught in the middle, triangulated into the problematic interadult relations.

In many of these early initiatives, there was an implicit focus on nuclear family systems and problems that eventuated when power dynamics or family roles deviated from what were seen as optimal pathways. As will be detailed shortly, some of these presumptions have been critically evaluated by contemporary family scholars, including Hare-Mustin and Leupnitz. Yet even in advance of these critiques, not all theorists and clinicians were limiting the focus of their family conceptualizations and interventions to nuclear family units; in several approaches, present-day family dynamics were framed as temporal extensions of family lineages. These multigenerational approaches, in turn, laid important foundational groundwork for contemporary approaches that view family dynamics as embedded not just within extended and historical kin relations, but also within a broader network of systems that themselves impact the family's adaptations (Henggeler & Bourdin, 1990). One example of multigenerational thinking already mentioned is Bowen's work. In contrast with seemingly related psychodynamic approaches that had long maintained that people inherit, introject, and bring forward patterns from their historical past, Bowen's perspective on multigenerational transmission was that the past never left, and that families and family emotional systems press up against and interlock daily with prior generations. Friedman (1991) captured this position's essence well in observing that for Bowen, the intergenerational evolutionary flow had more power to format the structure of relationships than did the logic of their current connections. As should be apparent, true adoption of such a framework demands a thorough rethinking of the scope of work required to dislodge a family's symptomatic patterns and sustain newer forms of functioning.

Another seminal perspective on the historical embeddedness of contemporary child and family adjustment problems is Boszormeny-Nagy's contextual family therapy. As did Bowen, Nagy emphasized the continuing powerful influence of relations with families of origin, including parents' indebtedness to their origin families (innovatively cast as a ledger of owed balances and obligations). Many of these ideas were developed in Boszormeny-Nagy and Sparks's (1973) *Invisible Loyalties: Reciprocity in Intergenerational Family Therapy,* an influential work that illustrated the ways in which origin family dynamics reach into contemporary family processes even when parents are consciously unaware of or insist on having "disowned" them. Like Bowen, Nagy emphasized the unearthing of hidden ties and loyalties and the repair of unsolved problems. Unlike Bowen (who sent families home to do such work), Nagy gathered together various members of the extended family network to address ruptured and strained relationships. The multigenerational perspective also helps to account for how it is that children in a contemporary family system come to be assigned (or to inherit) particular roles that reincarnate kindred roles that have existed in the family for generations. Attending only to the realities of the child's current-day nuclear family unit would not allow for detection of the source behind the historically entrenched family role the child has unwittingly stepped into and been expected to play.

Extended kin networks were also well attended to by the school of structural family therapy, though unlike the intergenerational approaches Salvador Minuchin's (1974) structural approach focused primarily on here-and-now family interaction and functioning. In the structural school of thought, the key core relational patterns in families are those revealed during family interactions. It would be inaccurate to imply that S. Minuchin did not give credence to the past. Rather, the structuralist perspective maintained that what is important about the past is reenacted in present transactions and is evident in current behavior. S. Minuchin, collaborating with colleagues Jay Haley (with whom he worked from 1967 to 1976), Braulio Montalvo, and Bernice Rossman, cultivated many of his seminal theses through work with low-income, inner-city families at the Child Guidance Clinic of Philadelphia; Haley later left to develop a distinctively different problem-solving therapy (see later discussion). Among the most influential core concepts contributed by structural family theory are those of family structure, boundaries, and subsystems, and in his therapeutic practice S. Minuchin worked to reconfigure nonadaptive family coalitions. He and his colleagues mapped family structure (the recurring and enduring patterns of interaction that had come to organize and structure daily family life) and then worked to foster change through techniques relying on the creation or amplification of challenges within here-and-now, ongoing family interactions. To be successful, they found it necessary to join and then work from within the family system, calling on action-oriented approaches as they worked directly with in-session enactments to help introduce, promote, and support change. By encouraging and supporting new patterns of behavior that introduced structural shifts in the family's hierarchical structure, alliance patterns, and boundary adherence, structural therapists sought to move families toward more adaptive functioning—with the identified child or adolescent client following suit. S. Minuchin and Haley each understood and respected family developmental issues as they worked to reconfigure nonadaptive family coalitions. The structural approach went further, however, to take stock of the family's entire relational field, including extended kin, other supportive figures, and helping professionals and institutions.

Perhaps most central to understanding S. Minuchin's theory are his views of hierarchy and boundaries. In structural theory, adaptive and healthy family systems are hierarchically organized, such that parents or parenting adults are clearly in charge as the system's executives. Families, as indicated earlier, can be composed of any number of different subsystems, including marital, coparenting, parent-child, and sibling subsystems. In well-functioning families, the adaptive emotional growth and development of children and other family members is contingent on the existence of appropriate boundaries between these subsystems. Conversely, when hierarchies break down, boundaries are violated, or children are triangulated into adult-adult subsystems, symptomatic behavior is far more likely. S. Minuchin outlined a number of different ways in which children can be triangulated in family systems. In some cases, parents may compete for a child's loyalty and one may succeed in establishing a coalition with the child that excludes the other parent. In other cases, parents respond to distress in their relationship by deflecting their distress and anxiety to the needs or problems of a child. This solution provides short-term relief for the adults' relational distress and can artificially bond them together, as such detouring often results in psychosomatic or other emotional problems for the pathologized child. As did many other family theorists, S. Minuchin concurred that the identified patient's symptomatology played an important role in maintaining family homeostasis, keeping the family system together, and preventing it from fragmenting (S. Minuchin, Rosman, & Baker, 1978).

There has been a fair degree of clinical and research-based support for many of these basic suppositions (Andolfi, 1978; Buchanan, Maccoby, & Dornbusch, 1991; Camara & Resnick, 1989; Johnston, Campbell, & Mayes, 1985; S. Minuchin et al., 1978; S. Minuchin, Chamberlain, & Graubard, 1967; Rosenberg, 1978), and several integrative models have been derived in recent years using classic structural family therapy as their base. These include an attachment-based family therapy promulgated by Diamond, Siqueland, and Diamond (2003); a biobehavioral family model outlined by Wood, Klebba, and Miller (2000); a multidimensional family therapy propounded by Liddle (2000); and a multisystemic family therapy model, which explicitly takes into consideration other systems in which families are embedded, advanced by Henggeler, Schoenwald, Borduin, Rowland, and Cunningham (1998).

There have been other recent and major elaborations of practice promulgated by S. Minuchin's protégés at the Philadelphia Child and Family Therapy Training Center, expanding the basics of S. Minuchin's approach rather significantly. Earlier forms of structural family therapy emphasized a relatively rapid joining of the family by a strong and directive therapist who worked first to understand and accept the family's version of reality, and then intervened actively to alter here-and-now processes. By contrast, present-day practitioners often assess far beyond here-and-now family processes in an effort to more fully understand the family in its historical and larger community context and to take stock of potentially relevant individual biological, affective, and psychological processes of family members (Jones & Lindblad-Goldberg, 2002). They rely less on appealing to the therapist's expertise in establishing a hierarchical relationship with the family and fully engage families in planning and evaluation of assessment and treatment. They attend to the creation of relationships that will promote and nurture socioemotional competencies of family members, including emotion regulation and promotion of attachment.

Jones and Lindblad-Goldberg (2002) maintain that these shifts were natural ones as greater information than was available to S. Minuchin 30 years earlier came to the fore about the particular family and parenting processes that promote or constrain socioemotional development. They also point out that with the recent shifts in practice comes a more demanding accountability, from a focus on organizational functionality as the central treatment outcome to a focus on establishment of growth-promoting practices and strength of emotional connections. For the latter to succeed, change will almost always be necessary at multiple system levels, including those beyond child and family at the child-family community interface. As Nichols and Schwartz (1998, p. 316) mused in commenting on the challenges of work with inner-city multiproblem families, "When between five to ten public agencies are involved in a family's life, and when the family is up against the crushing weight of poverty and racism, family therapy can seem quite puny. Recognizing limits has made therapists rethink their roles." We develop this systems-within-systems principle in the case example provided later in this chapter.

One other major effort from the early golden years of family therapy not yet discussed was Jay Haley's development of strategic family therapy. Following his work with the Palo Alto group and S. Minuchin, and influenced heavily by Milton Erickson's creative use of unorthodox therapeutic techniques and hypnosis to bring about rapid therapeutic change, Haley founded the Family Therapy Institute in 1976 and began offering brief problem-solving therapies. Recognizing that families in crisis sought rapid relief and seldom committed to participation in therapy for extended periods, Haley's time-compressed approach moved to initiate change in families not via insight and understanding but by the family carrying out directives prescribed by the therapist. Haley's goals were structural, and like S. Minuchin, he sought to address hierarchy and boundary problems that created and maintained problem sequences in families. Though his ideas owed in part to the cybernetic concept of positive feedback loops, Haley emphasized longer (and sometimes, much—month-long or more—longer) chains of sequence as well as chains that involved three, rather than two, people. Where he diverged from his earlier colleagues was in his calculated approach to effecting sequence and thereby system change, and in his view that family interactions could be understood as human struggles for control and power (Haley, 1976).

In strategic therapy, the therapist takes an authoritative and often manipulative stance designed to counter family resistance. Families are actively directed and maneuvered to undertake activities that amplify and exaggerate the troublesome symptoms that were actually serving as communication metaphors (see also Madanes, 1981, 1984). Strategic interventions are often subtle, usually covert, and frequently paradoxical (such as instructing families not to change and to exaggerate their disturbing symptoms). These kinds of interventions have been critiqued by many writers as both controversial and risky, not only because families inevitably deteriorated, at least temporarily, when following paradoxical directives, but also because the ultimate risk-benefit ratio and conditions for effective and safe use of paradoxical interventions were never empirically determined (Fruzzetti & Jacobson, 1991). Nonetheless, the strategic movement was one of the most active approaches on the scene during the second half of the twentieth century and gave rise to a number of creative variants (e.g., Selvini Palazzoli et al., 1978).

Prior to family therapy's embrace of multisystems thinking, most approaches had stayed squarely focused on family interiors, working with family systems as bounded entities unto themselves. As we've outlined, for some theorists this included the family's embeddedness in their multigenerational histories, and for others a lateral expansion to extended kin networks—but seldom did the views take stock of the broader organizational role of cultural attitudes and historical cohort.

This situation changed dramatically following searching critiques by Rachel Hare-Mustin (1978), Deborah Leupnitz (1988), and others who decried the gender bias inherent in the existing major schools of thought. For example, cybernetic theory, in repudiating unilateral control and power in systems (the components of which, instead, continually and circularly influenced one another in recurring feedback loops), implicitly absolved any particular system member of blame. When problems existed in a system, all of the system's components were involved and hence all could be said to bear equal responsibility. Such a posture, however, ignored the realities of the subjugation of women in a patriarchal society and effectively blamed victims in crimes against them. The implication that husbands and wives contributed equally to battering, for example, and bore equal responsibility for changing such problems reified cultural patriarchy.

Similarly, feminist writers drew attention to seldom examined historical realities driving one of the more common clinical presentations in two-parent families, in which mothers were cast as overinvolved and ineffectual and fathers as problematically underinvolved. Sadly, family therapy's seeming advance over psychodynamic theory in absolving mothers of primary blame for the child's ills (by factoring fathers into the family equation) had actually changed precious little. Mothers were still viewed negatively and pathologically, without recognition that they had been thrust by society into economically dependent, emotionally isolated, and hyper-responsible positions. Feminist therapists held that although a change of family circumstances was in order, it was not because incompetent mothers required help but because men's assumption of their responsibilities to their children would enable mothers to move out of the crazy-making situation that had been foisted upon them (McGoldrick, Anderson, & Walsh, 1989; Walters, Carter, Papp, & Silverstein, 1988).

In that systems approaches had introduced a revolutionary paradigm shift in the field of clinical psychology, it seems fitting that in closing this section we underscore how feminist theory in turn challenged existing systems beliefs. Feminist theory also had an impact on a final development highlighted here, which itself also deconstructed many of the unique expositions of earlier family theories. One critique of the early family systems work has been that its focus on cybernetics, systems, and patterns reflected a misguided search for grand theories that could explain human behavior, universal laws that could foster the understanding, diagnosis, repair, and resolution of most problems. This quest and its emphasis on the knowable and objectifiable were roundly criticized in postmodern critiques maintaining that there is no tangible reality, only the mental constructions of observers. Among the first theorists to broach this issue in family therapy were Paul Watzlawick (1984) and Lynn Hoffman (1985, 1988), who questioned the confidence and assuredness that had become such a central force in so many family therapies of the time. Collaborative approaches, such as the one introduced by Harlene Anderson (1993), followed soon thereafter, and took a position of *not* knowing in order to enable genuine conversations with families, and sticking firm to this stance rather than deftly shifting later into a position of expert. This approach, as did others, had its flaws, but it laid important groundwork for other critiques and new approaches, including narrative therapy, that were to follow.

In some ways, the essential tenets of narrative therapy threw into disarray all that family theories before it had promulgated. For decades, family therapy had stood in sharp contradistinction to psychodynamic approaches that viewed psychopathology as borne and bred within individuals; family therapy's basic tenet, as emphasized throughout this chapter, was that such problems were in interactions and relationships. But narrative theory eschewed this perspective as well, positing that problems were embedded in the stories that families lived by and that had come to organize their behavior. The focus shifted from the ways people behaved to the ways they constructed meaning. To move toward health, narrative approaches held, families needed to become aware of and discard these disempowering and self-defeating narratives they had been induced into, replacing them with alternate, health-promoting stories to govern their lives and future travels (Freedman & Combs, 1996; White, 1995). A major metaphor in such work was the externalization of problems: construing problems as forces threatening the family from the outside, rather than circulating within.

In many ways, narrative approaches incorporate very little of the systems thinking outlined throughout this chapter. Indeed, their social constructivist base deemphasizes dysfunctional family interactions and instead targets the malevolent influences of cultural biases and institutions. In so doing, narrative therapies provide a fresh, nonpathologizing view of families as capable and powerful. There is no question that their emphasis on collaboration and on expanding beyond families to frame families' problems infused creative new wisdom into the family field. It is less clear whether the accompanying wholesale rejection of systems theory by many narrative theorists was necessary. There remains relatively little evidence that any one system is inherently more or less helpful for aiding any particular problem, and there seem no inherent logical inconsistencies in retaining the valuable aspects of systems thinking while simultaneously attending to the humanizing, ethical, and empowering dimensions so celebrated in narrative frameworks (Eron & Lund, 1996). An ongoing challenge for those working in the field will be to evaluate when eclecticism in approach enhances work with families, and when it dilutes the power of particular approaches. Greater eclecticism and openness, greater collaboration with families, and refound respect for family competencies, worldviews, and inner wisdom have all enhanced modern practice, but in the end the approaches assumed by therapists are valuable only to the extent that they help effect real and meaningful change for families and family problems.

Family systems approaches and family therapy owe their place in the contemporary landscape of clinical psychology to the creativity and charismatic leadership of a relatively small group of brilliant individuals. This history has been well chronicled in a variety of sources, though this initial period of growth of the family therapy movement has been portrayed as a competitive and dogmatic one, guided by various leaders supported by groups of avid disciples emphasizing points of difference between the various approaches. As late as the 1980s, there had been relatively little integration across different approaches despite the similarities in many of the field's basic concepts. However, this circumstance has since changed. There has been a healthy and beneficial cross-pollination both across different schools of thought within family systems approaches and in integrating important conceptualizations from other fields and disciplines, including developmental psychology and individual approaches to psychotherapy.

We have attempted to highlight some of the major areas of consensus among the various approaches. The majority of contemporary approaches view and treat families as systems, attend to forces that promote stability of behavior patterns and that delimit change, emphasize the triadic nature of human relationships while also recognizing the multiple systems in which families are embedded, and appreciate in one form or another the protective function of healthy boundaries not just for individuals and subsystems, but also for the family as a cohesive entity traveling through time together. Most schools concur that family groups function best when they are cohesive; freely, openly, and directly exchange information; and attend to the different developmental needs of different family members at changing points in the family life cycle. In addition, most perspectives view families as adaptive to the extent that they can show flexibility to adapt to shifting life circumstances, solve problems effectively, include adequate hierarchical structure, and support the individual autonomy and growth of all family members.

Beyond these similarities, there remain a variety of important differences in emphasis and scope. These include whether the proper focus of conceptualization and change efforts needs to be primarily on behavior and interactions, or whether it should take account of private inner experience of family members; the extent to which change efforts are enhanced by taking stock of individual character and personality dysfunction; and the extent to which family dynamics are seen as emanating from inner turmoil as opposed to being poor adaptations to the presses of an oppressive external world and culture. There are still disputes about whether the path to health will be charted through changes in behavior, action, and interaction or whether insight is required, and whether all family members must be a part of effective family solutions or whether it is possible to affect and sustain meaningful systemic change through work with individuals and subsystems. These things said, contemporary therapies rarely adhere tenaciously to theoretical dogma, and most now benefit from the convergence of ideas and rapprochement that began during the last decade of the twentieth century.

In an era of intense scrutiny on all forms of mental health intervention, cast in the name of accountability, family systems–based approaches to mental health and treatment have been called on to prove their merit to a widening external audience. In 1998, summarizing the current state of the field, Nichols and Schwartz anticipated this emerging challenge for family scholars and practitioners as they wrote "If family problems cause psychological problems, we should be able to demonstrate it; and perhaps more important, if we say we can resolve problems with family therapy, we'll probably have to prove it" (p. 498). The burgeoning field of family psychology, outlined later in the chapter, has largely shouldered the first part of this dual charge, while assumption of the second charge has also been formally taken on, though by a relatively smaller group of active researchers whose work has largely been informing recent national policy. These developments are summarized in the next section.

RESEARCH

If not already clear, from the days of the Palo Alto group's scholarly pursuit of communication theory, research has always been central to the understanding of family systems. Over the past quarter century, however, an interesting split of sorts has occurred. The growth of a family research field has been flourishing as empirical studies of families have benefited from advances in observational and recording capacities, digitalization, statistical modeling, and other scientific technologies and breakthroughs. Concurrently, a field bearing the name of family psychology has taken firm root. It is broad in scope and has been formally recognized as a new specialty within contemporary psychology. It is represented by a flagship journal, the *Journal of Family Psychology*, which debuted in 1986 and joined *Family Process* (an outlet that has been around since 1962, when Jay Haley served as its first editor) as the major source of breaking knowledge for professionals about family systems. Yet much of the scholarly work conducted under the flag of family psychology remains unfamiliar to active family practitioners.

The lack of dialogue is unfortunate, if understandable. James Alexander, who is among the small group of family psychologists whose work is well known to national policymakers, invoked Albert Einstein in a recent publication: "Not everything that can be counted counts, and not everything that counts can be counted" (Alexander et al., 2002, p. 17). Einstein's observation captures a rather interesting paradox in the family field: On the one hand, early family therapists took pains to insist that problem sequences in families are observable, identifiable, and deeply meaningful, and yet family therapy thinking has been replete with notions that would seem to defy objectification and standard measurement. Concepts such as triangulation, boundaries, hierarchy, differentiation, legacies, family projection processes, undifferentiated ego masses, rubber fences, and the like would seem to defy objective measurement. There have been both prevailing sentiments that any reductionist objectification of such inherently fluid family processes strips them of any true meaning, and contentions that empirical research is of little creative or additive value as it typically does little more than confirm established knowledge. Perhaps of greater concern, there is the fear that in objectifying complex structures and processes, researchers run the risk of obscuring and overlooking alternative interpretive frames. Indeed, from the postmodern perspective, everything is a construction and there is no objectifiable truth.

The discussion of operationalization and standardization has sometimes become most heated and strained when the topic shifts from the valid assessment of family processes to the assessment and efficacy of family therapies. Putting aside for the moment whether it is possible to evaluate important family group processes in meaningful ways (family psychologists have made a number of important strides in this arena, summarized later), a variety of writers have advanced the position that manualized treatments, insistence on adherence to treatment protocols, and evaluation of success in terms of statistical effect sizes undermines the creativity and fluidity that have been the hallmark of family therapy since its inception (Henry, 1998). This is certainly an extreme position, and not all practitioners share this concern that the empirical movement and move to more standardized treatment regimens has a greater potential for harm than good (see, e.g., Jones & Lindblad-Goldberg, 2002).

Addressing this tension, Nichols and Schwartz (1998, p. 337) pointedly note that the research efforts of some of the major centers studying multiproblem families, including Henggeler's and Alexander's groups, Gerald Patterson's and Marion Forgatch's studies at the Oregon Social Learning Center, and major initiatives administered by Tolan and Gorman-Smith in Chicago and by Liddle and Szapocznik in Miami "provide credibility for family therapy within the larger mental health field, credibility that has been strained by the eccentric practices and unsubstantiated outcome claims" of earlier family models. Further, questioning the necessity and wisdom of casting blueprints as straitjackets, certain writers have decried the characteristically minimal dialectic between practicing family therapists and family therapy research groups. Nichols and Schwartz, for example, highlight both clinicians' ethical mandate to evaluate the efficacy of their interventions and the modern-day reality that family therapists must demonstrate the efficacy of their approaches to third-party payers. Echoing this latter point, Alexander and his colleagues (2002) noted that family-based approaches have been oddly absent from best practice lists generated by psychology's empirical treatments movement. They point out that this absence is out of keeping with accumulating empirical evidence for the effectiveness of family psychology interventions, evidence that has been gathered in research studies that have for the most part managed to sidestep the major criticisms typically levied against most other randomized clinical trial studies.

A comprehensive review of the efficacy literature generated by family psychology intervention scientists is beyond the scope of this chapter. Interested readers are referred to a comprehensive and readable volume published by the American Psychological Association, *Family Psychology: Science-Based Interventions*, edited by Liddle, Santisteban, Levant, and Bray (2002). It provides scholarly reviews and summaries of advances in family intervention research, including reviews of programs designed to enhance positive parenting practices through parent management training procedures, and other programs targeting parents' capacities for assuming responsibility (providing greater structure and closer monitoring), expressing warmth, and decreasing conflict and use of damaging disciplinary practices (e.g., Forgatch & Knutson, 2002; Liddle, 1995; Schoenwald & Henggeler, 2002; Szapocznik & Kurtines, 1989). Although initial work for some of these models was carried out in demonstration projects conducted in university settings, where conditions could be tightly controlled and titrated (e.g., Henggeler et al., 1986), there have since been concentrated efforts to render standardized family-based approaches within existing naturalistic contexts (homes, schools, community agencies, residential treatment facilities). An example of the more ambitious and intense work in this regard is multisystemic therapy provided within a family preservation model, introduced as a desirable alternative to outside-of-home placements of severely disturbed youth (Fraser, Nelson, & Rivard, 1997). In such work, outlined by Schoenwald and Henggeler (2002), anywhere from 2 to 15 hours of service per week is devoted to families over a concentrated 4- to 6-month period, with clinicians carrying low caseloads (4 to 6 families per clinician) but on call 24 hours 7 days a week.

Overall, empirically validated treatment approaches are informed by a systems perspective and by the contextual tradition of family therapy, but also focus broadly on behavioral, cognitive, and emotional transactions within the family and between the family and the influential social systems in which it resides. Such approaches generally see the focus of classic, pragmatic family therapies on intrafamilial inter-actions as insufficient to achieve and sustain meaningful gains with multiproblem youth. Most attend in one way or another to how children's intra-individual qualities (genetics, temperament) can challenge parenting systems and how social disadvan-tage, neighborhood, schools, and other contextual factors press on and interact with family processes. Many of these initiatives emphasize prevention and early identification of risk, and most are attentive to both cultural and ethic differences. Approaches vary a good deal with respect to how unabashedly they cast therapists into a role of expert educator, but all aim to affect some form of hierarchical change wherein parents assume greater responsibility for oversight and discipline of chil-dren while working to help promote greater family cohesion. Children themselves are often explicit targets of skill building as well, beyond the parenting and family work.

The other major focus of the family psychology field has been in providing evidence for ways families contribute in formative ways to the individual problems of their members. Such work often takes on a more decidedly linear focus than that endemic to cybernetic and circular perspectives, though researchers are often aware of this bias and episodically devote specific and concentrated energies to pursuing bidirectional, if not transactional, hypotheses. Again, a comprehensive review of this body of work is far beyond the scope of this chapter, but interested readers are referred to relevant overviews and contributions by P. Minuchin (1985), Cox and Paley (2003), McHale and Grolnick (2002), and Bornstein and Sawyer (2006). A special edition of the journal *Development and Psychopathology* (Davies & Cicchetti, 2004) includes a broad array of empirical papers presenting work from leading researchers involved in this area.

Much research in this tradition has been concerned with establishing and clari-fying the nature of dynamic linkages between different family subsystems. Investi-gations of couple relationships, for example, reliably tie relationship functioning to both parenting behavior and child adjustment (e.g., Hetherington, 2006; Kaczynski, Lindahl, & Malik, 2006), as would be predicted by most theoretical frameworks in the family therapy field. Studies typically document child adjustment problems in the face of destructive marital conflict (Cummings & Davies, 1994), parenting disturbances in the face of marital distress (Erel & Burman, 1995), and child dis-turbances as a consequence of insecure parent-child attachments (Arend, Gove, & Sroufe, 1979; Speltz, DeKlyen, & Greenberg, 1999; Vondra, Shaw, & Swearingen, 2001; Weiss & Seed, 2002). Studies are often quite explicit in outlining the specific nature of dynamics in families, as when mothers in marriages devoid of intimacy are at greater risk for boundary violations and seductive behavior with children (Jacobvitz, Hazen, & Curran, 2004). They substantiate the cross-generational trans-mission of relationship patterns, as when parents who deny the significance of attachment-related experiences in their own origin families parent their infants in such a way that the infants likewise end up developing avoidant patterns of attachment toward them (Steele, Steele, & Fonagy, 1996; Ward & Carlson, 1995; Zeanah, Benoit, & Barton, 1993). Such research studies are also attentive to context, as when outlining how changes in circumstances within or outside the family can alter risk trajectories (Egeland, Jacobvitz, & Sroufe, 1988).

Beginning in the mid-1990s, a new line of empirical investigations began appearing in the child and family development literature, explicitly assessing family group-level dynamics and the relationship of these whole family processes to children's adaptation (e.g., McHale & Cowan, 1996; McHale & Fivaz-Depeursinge, 1999). In particular, this work began paying explicit attention to specific coparenting dynamics in nuclear family systems, including hostility and competitiveness, alliance cohesion and support, and disconnection (Feinberg, 2003; McHale et al., 2002). A parallel line of inquiry also published during this time, fully systemic in nature, examined the development of family alliances from the prenatal period on through the toddler and preschool years (Favez et al., in press; Fivaz-Depeursinge & Corboz-Warnery, 1999). Among the most significant findings from these complementary lines of work are indications that early coparenting dynamics and family alliances can be forecast on the basis of both intrapsychic and interpersonal factors assessed during the pregnancy (McHale et al., 2004; von Klitzing, Simoni, & Burgin, 1999); coparenting processes are related to but also exert influences in the family that are independent of marital relationships and dynamics (Bearss & Eyberg, 1998; Katz & Low, 2004; McHale, 1995; Schoppe-Sullivan, Mangelsdorf, Frosch, & McHale, 2004); family alliance types consolidate early, are markedly stable through time, and affect children's social and emotional development in a host of important ways, even as early as the infant, toddler, and preschool years (Belsky, Putnam, & Crnic, 1996; Caldera & Lindsey, 2006; Fivaz-Depeursinge, Frascarolo, & Corboz-Warnery, 1996; Frosch, Mangelsdorf, & McHale, 2000; McHale, 2007b; McHale & Rasmussen, 1998); and family dynamics are sensitive to infant contributions from the very earliest months (Fivaz-Depeursinge, Favez, Lavanchy, de Noni, & Frascarolo, 2005; Fivaz-Depeursinge & Favez, 2006; McHale & Rotman, 2007). Related work has substantiated the protective effect of functional family hierarchies (Shaw, Criss, & Schonberg, 2004), and conversely, the destructive effects of family triangulation (Kerig, 1995).

These various lines of inquiry each, in their own way, have provided impetus for one form of intervention or another targeting family factors shown to increase risk. For example, if couple relationship problems before a baby's arrival are shown to foreshadow parenting and relationship problems afterward, then strengthening the couple relationship might be expected to help promote early parenting and couple adjustment (C. P. Cowan & Cowan, 1992; Shapiro & Gottman, 2005; Silliman, Stanley, Coffin, Markman, & Jordan, 2002). If maternal insensitivity places infants at risk for cultivating insecure attachments, interactive guidance and other forms of mother-infant psychotherapy targeting mothers' ability to read and respond warmly, contingently, and accurately to infants' signals may help mitigate such risk (McDonough, 1993; Robert-Tissot, Cramer, & Stern, 1996). If such reading is impeded or overwhelmed by maternal preoccupation with unresolved origin family issues, maternal representations may serve as an additional target for such interventions (Cramer, 1995; Fraiberg, 1980).

An interesting question from a systems perspective, of course, is whether long-term gains can be sustained if a single dyad in the family, be it husband-wife, mother-infant, or (as in several recent initiatives targeting father involvement; e.g., McBride & Mills, 1993) father-infant, is prioritized without parallel consideration of the ripple effects such interventions may cause throughout the family system (McHale, 2007a). Herein lies one crucial and ongoing challenge for systemically informed interventionists and clinical researchers of all sorts: establishing the extent to which an intervention with an individual or a dyad is sufficient to change a family's course, even if not all family members are the focus of intervention. Though the possibility of affecting meaningful systemic change without engaging all key players within the family would seem antithetical to most family systems theories, dyadic interventions are actually standard practice in the infant mental health field, as well as being an unfortunate reality of most community-based practice (P. A. Cowan, Cowan, Cohen, Pruett, & Pruett, in press). Hence, both basic and research efforts will continue to be crucial in helping to document the extent to which interventions seeking to effect enduring change show clinically meaningful results even without attending to all important relationships and networks in case formulations and intervention.

The vigorous dialogue about such issues that is active in family research circles exemplifies a level of inquiry and discourse healthy for all systems. For researchers, there is a never-ending revisiting and reworking of existing frameworks contingent on new data, even as certain bulwarks of the field (organizing effects of security of attachment, multirisk likelihood attendant to destructive marital conflict, and protective facets of supportive coparenting relations) provide necessary coherence. When there are episodic moves toward premature closure—some of the most vocal critiques of the movement toward empirically validated treatments have been along this line—there are corrective responses from within the research community. Episodically, someone can be counted on to stir the pot vigorously and threaten deconstruction of all held dear, as did Belsky, Campbell, Conn, and Moore, in one 1996 report failing to uncover significant stability in attachment security, either at the level of avoidance, security, and ambivalence (Mary Ainsworth's standard ABC classification rubric) or secure-insecure classifications. A more recent example involved Cook and Kenny's (2006) revisiting of data from a 1989 study by Cole and Jordan. Cole and Jordan had adapted Olson and colleagues' Cohesion and Adaptability scales on the Family Adaptability and Cohesion Evaluation Scale (FACES) instrument so that the scales' individual items reflected dyad-specific (mother-child, mother-father, father-child) rather than family-level processes. They had then asked each of the three family members to rate each of the three subsystems. Reanalyzing Cole and Jordan's data using advanced statistical analyses (EQS; Bentler, 1993), Cook and Kenny found that systematic variance at dyad subsystem levels was *rarely* significant after they took into account variance that was attributable to individuals within the family (mothers, fathers, or children). Taking the argument to its conceptual level, they speculated that in some circumstances what appears to be a systemic pattern can be as or more parsimoniously attributed to a single individual's influence, as when a father who does not like to be involved with people in general has difficulty being engaged with both his spouse and his children. Such a problem, which when framed systemically would underscore a dialectic between dyadic (marital and parent-child subsystems), could actually be traced most fundamentally to the father's personality and habits. Any empirical finding like this is clearly delimited by the fragilities of instrumentation, yet such cyclical rekindling of old debates helps keep the field and its pursuits fresh, self-evaluative, and noncomplacent.

Perhaps somewhat surprisingly, despite the many, many volumes published on measurement issues in family research (e.g., Hofferth & Casper, 2006), assessments and evaluations of families in clinical practice seldom rely on instruments developed in laboratory research. In fact, most family assessments and evaluations do not rely on standardized instruments at all. In the next section, we summarize common practices and issues in family assessment and evaluation.

ASSESSMENT AND EVALUATION

As may not be surprising given the vast array of different approaches and areas of emphasis represented by different schools of thought, no standard or universally agreed upon set of assessment practices or techniques for evaluating families has ever emerged. Many students trained in family therapy approaches are introduced to some of the innovative ways of gathering information about families, such as completing detailed genograms (McGoldrick & Gerson, 1999)—sometimes indispensable in multigenerational formulations and interventions—and some are introduced to structured checklists or inventories (which help to organize and structure behavioral therapies). But most family therapists do not define formal assessment phases during which they systematically partake in standard assessment protocols or procedures. This is certainly not to imply that assessments are not conducted or are thought of as unimportant, but only that a cataloguing of different assessment tools in this section would badly misrepresent this facet of clinical work with families. Rather, we summarize here some of the major issues attended to by most systems therapists in the early stages of working with families.

Besides explicitly seeking information and clarity during family interviews about certain critical life events (e.g., domestic violence, sexual abuse, extramarital affairs, drug and alcohol abuse), most family systems approaches give special credence to the behavioral sequences and interactions that are revealed during early contacts with families. Such interactions are thought to reveal much of what is necessary to know about family communication patterns, boundaries, rules, and hierarchies. What family members do during assessments is as important as and sometimes more important than what they say, and hence very few family assessments take place without some direct observation of the family's interaction patterns. How early assessments are conducted, how directive therapists are during initial evaluations, and what the goals of early contacts are do differ from school to school, though there are some commonalities. First, most family therapists take pains during the early stages of work with families to listen to and take stock of the family's account of the presenting problem. During this stage, each family member is usually allowed a voice, and therapists acknowledge each person's perspective on the problem. This process is usually navigated in as open-ended a way as is possible before additional detail is sought. The additional detail, when solicited, is geared to identify important details and to contextualize the problem with respect to time, place, and key players involved (including important individuals and systems outside of the immediate family). Information is also obtained about how the family has already tried to deal with the problem.

On the basis of these early assessments, interventionists are able to draw some preliminary hypotheses about structural and communication problems in families. From both session content and from observation of interaction sequences, the family hierarchy and the roles of different family members in the family's dynamics begin to become apparent. From observed family process patterns and sequences, the therapist is able to speculate about triangles, coalitions, and problematic boundaries within the system. This is particularly so when all of those principally involved in the maintenance of the problematic patterns are in attendance; understanding of family dynamics and communication patterns in families often shifts significantly when a sibling or live-in grandparent who had been absent during earlier family sessions subsequently attends a session and a different sequence pattern or alliance structure is revealed. Ultimately, however, an important aim for most therapies, not just structural approaches, is to develop an understanding of the invisible structures maintaining the referral problem.

Most therapies proceed from a general appreciation of the family life cycle and of normal family process. However, such understandings are often very global in scope and not always fully informed by contemporary developmental and family data. Most clinicians appreciate that the transition to new parenthood brings expectable strains that test the husband-wife dyad and increase risk for disengagement and/or depression by new mothers or fathers; that the early coparenting dynamic established in families often must reorganize as children move from infancy through the toddler and preschool years, since the behavioral challenges presented by mobile, verbal children introduce fresh new strain into the family system; and that adolescence requires parents to negotiate new relationships with their children to allow for greater autonomy and choice, without pulling the rug out from under them or affording too much freedom and not enough guidance. Less well understood are how normative developmental transitions are shaded by cultural expectations or by the origin family expectancies of the child's parents. For example, unlike most European and African American family systems, cosleeping and hand-feeding well through the preschool years is normative in many Asian heritage families. This cultural understanding is necessary to learn about during clinical assessments of Asian families, lest the family's parenting practices be cast as emotional overinvolvement. On a different front, cultural views of sexuality during early adolescence are also important to assess, as such views can be dramatically different in families where both parents became sexually active during their own early teens than they are in families where parents' sexual activity did not bloom until early adulthood. In research labs, developmental studies of family systems have uncovered revolutionary new data suggesting that even infants as young as 3 to 4 months are recruited into and become capable of actively shaping coparenting and family process (Fivaz-Depeursinge & Favez, 2006). Although very few families of infants this young come to the attention of family therapists because of ostensible problems in the infant, assessing a family system without including infants would be as incomplete as omitting key members from assessments of families of older children.

Beyond the assessment of families' presenting problems and the patterns sustaining them, and the cultivation of an understanding of family adaptation apropos their position in the family life cycle (informed by relevant cultural and subcultural shading), a centrally important assessment task in most modern family therapy approaches is identifying contributory roles played by systems outside the family. Although this is most acutely so in assessments completed with multiproblem families (Henggeler et al., 1998), external systems do come into play for the majority of families with children and adolescents. However, though most assessments take stock of the family's interface with other systems, the extent to which such information is formally solicited during the early phase of family evaluations differs greatly from therapy to therapy. Typically, information about significant others in the family would be explicitly pursued during questioning in the earliest contacts with families, whereas information about outside systems (schools, the mental health system, the legal system, other social agencies) would be gathered as indicated as case material was shared by the family. More than occasionally, especially in cases where there is significant involvement by systems outside the family, some contact with these systems will ultimately be indicated, though in most approaches such contacts are more likely to take place later in the course of treatment than they are during the initial family assessment phase.

Finally, it is important to emphasize that although most family therapies do not systematically evaluate the psychological functioning of each individual family member, neither do they ignore developmental problems or psychopathology in individuals when it is present. Over the long history of the family field, there have been times when such individual problems were downplayed or cast as secondary and relatively inconsequential to the more significant relationship problems that entrapped the family, though this is seldom the case any more. As outlined earlier, therapy approaches now do consider the extent to which individual biological, affective, and psychological processes of family members are relevant (Jones & Lindblad-Goldberg, 2002), as such an understanding can help, rather than obfuscate, reasons why certain families get stuck.

To illustrate some of the major concepts described in the chapter, we now turn to a case conceptualized and treated from a family systems approach. In so doing, we underscore how systemic approaches help guide both the formulation of the problem and the path toward intervention chosen in a manner that might diverge substantially from courses charted by other major theoretical approaches in this volume.

Case Illustration

The case we have chosen to illustrate family systems intervention is one involving work with the Jackson family, a married heterosexual couple and their 14-year-old son, John, the family's identified patient. John's parents describe him as having shown precipitous deterioration in many areas of functioning, citing school failure (tardies, cuts, failing grades, warnings from administration), marijuana and

(Continued)

alcohol use, and symptoms of depression (sleep disturbance, lethargy, lack of motivation, constriction of activities). For his part, John expresses anger and rejection of his mother and an alignment with his father in the marital breakdown presently occurring. John recently engaged in individual psychotherapy, though he also "forgot" several appointments. His parents were alarmed at the downward spiral in John's behavior and requested a psychiatric evaluation for medication.

John's father works as a business executive, and his mother has been a home-maker throughout the marriage. The father travels frequently and states that work has always been his primary involvement. Both parents agree that he is a good provider and concur that he has had only peripheral involvement in the domestic life of the family. Indeed, the coparenting partnership could be characterized as disconnected and skewed since John's birth. John's father took on very little of the hands-on, day-to-day work of parenting and almost always deferred to John's mother when child-related decisions had to be made. As individuals, the parents' personalities are also distinctively different. John's father impresses as low-key, intellectual, introverted, and conflict avoidant; when conflict escalates between him and his wife and/or between his wife and John, his response is typically to withdraw to his home office. By contrast, John's mother wears her emotions on her sleeve. She is extraverted and socially skilled, yet often impresses as de-pendent in her interpersonal style. The couple's long-term marriage (the first for both parents) became progressively less intimate over the years as the mother invested most of her attention in her parenting involvement with John, while the father invested in his successful career. Three years ago, the mother began an affair with a man in the community. She became increasingly preoccupied with this involvement, and as she did her parenting deteriorated. She became indul-gent and less attuned and attentive to John's needs, and not surprisingly conflict between mother and son also escalated.

Presenting Complaints

The initial telephone contact was made by the father, who wanted to come in with his son to work on his son's acting-out at home. After some inquiry as to the family situation, the family therapist convinced the father that John's mother also needed to be included in the intake session. In the initial session, where all three family members were seen, the father and son sat close together on the therapist's couch. They exchanged frequent glances throughout the session, and on a few occasions finished one another's sentences. They both also engaged in verbal attacks of the mother, who remained quiet, self-recriminatory, and tearful during the session. The father reported that he had learned of his wife's affair only recently from a friend and had immediately confronted his wife, who confirmed its 3-year duration. The father described being furious, and announced his plans to separate and divorce. He had told his wife that she could not continue to live in the family's home, and she obliged by moving to a nearby apartment. The father said he has been torn because he cannot himself assume parental responsibility for John, given his work demands, whereas John's mother, whom John won't talk to, remains completely available. The father is unequivocal in asserting that he intends to separate from his wife, but he also understands that the son and his mother need to have a relationship. He acknowledges that he has discussed the affair with John and was appalled to have discovered that John had been colluding with his mother in keeping the affair a secret. This complicity has added to John's and John's father's shared rage and contempt for the mother.

During the session, the son reported, "My life used to be great, but now it sucks. . . . I hate my mother. She had an affair with this scumbag and she made me keep it a secret from my dad for 3 years. She used to bad-mouth my dad, but now I know she was lying. I can't trust anything she says. I wish my dad would divorce her so I wouldn't have to deal with her ever again." John is vehement in his insistence that he has no desire for contact with his mother.

John's mother expresses only remorse and seems accommodating of anything that might enable John's father to reconsider staying married. She states that she now recognizes that the main reason she pursued an affair was because of the increasing loneliness and frustration she felt in her attempts to rekindle intimacy with her husband. She says that she agreed to move out of the family home voluntarily (though she hopes it is temporary) and notes that since she moved out, John's father has made some changes so as to become more available to parent their son. She adds, however, that her husband is also calling on his extended family and friends to provide coverage when he is unavailable and laments that these individuals have also been quite disparaging of her to their son. She expresses concern that John has been unsupervised for the most part after school and reports that he has regularly been having friends over to the house to party. Currently, the mother comes to the home once or twice a week, at the request of the father (and over the objection of their son) to drive the son to school and to cook meals. She seems desperate to persuade her husband to consider reconciliation, fearing that separating will only add further stress to the son.

Both parents are extremely concerned about the son's functioning and agree that addressing his deterioration is the priority over sorting out their marital issues. Because the father seems resolute in his intent to separate and divorce, the stance the family therapist elects to take in closing the intake session is that the structure of their family needs to transition to more independent parenting of the son, consistent with a postseparation shared custody arrangement. The mother was clearly devastated by the therapist's recommendation and ongoing work was necessary to help her acknowledge that this was the only viable structure that would permit the couple to quickly begin addressing their son's significant dysfunction.

Family System Assessment

In keeping with contemporary structural family frameworks, John's current symptoms were presumed to derive from the mutual influences of both individual and family system factors, as well as factors external to the family system. On an individual level, John's adjustment was hampered by several individual vulnerabilities (including the attentional deficit, the current substance abuse, and the growing depression). Each of these factors would require ongoing assessment and monitoring because John's ability to respond positively to structural systemic interventions could potentially be affected adversely by these individual-level factors. For this reason, coordination with an effective individual psychotherapy and perhaps, at some phase of the treatment, a referral for psychiatric assessment may be indicated and pursued.

With respect to the context in which John's symptoms are developing, the marital subsystem had clearly deteriorated, perhaps irrevocably. The affair, triangulating a third party into the marital relationship, compromised the marital

(Continued)

subsystem further, with the breach of trust, humiliation, and subsequent anger and contempt prompting the husband's unilateral decision to sever the marital partnership. Equally, the parental subsystem had been markedly compromised; the previous functionality of the mother's primary parental role, which had gradually deteriorated as she began neglecting domestic matters, took a further downward turn once the affair came to light because John began actively resisting her efforts to parent. While John looked to be intensely aligned with his father, the father remained substantially unavailable and was lacking in necessary parenting skills. Moreover, given the destructive conflict in the marital subsystem, the already disconnected coparenting subsystem became compromised even further.

The uncertain status of the Jackson's nuclear family given the current separation placed their family system in a family life cycle limbo. That is, it was far from clear whether the therapeutic aim should be working to restore greater functionality in the nuclear family system or working to restructure the Jacksons as a binuclear family (which would be the structural shift that would have to occur with a separation and divorce). The coparenting team's executive authority in structuring the family vis-à-vis the son had been undermined by multiple factors, including the mother's reliance on John as a confidant and the alignment John presently had with the father against John's mother. Both of these developments had disrupted the functional hierarchy in which the coparental subsystem trumped the parent-child dyadic subsystems.

Problems in the current coparenting alliance were numerous, dominated by the lack of parenting support between partners, leaving each to fly solo. For this family, the absence of a functional coparenting alliance was especially disastrous, given the father's historical absenteeism and lack of competence when he was in charge and John's newfound unwillingness to allow his mother to parent him. Successful coparenting was further compromised by ineffective child-focused communication and decision making, stemming from the adults' self-focus, hostility, and open conflict in the marriage. John's escalating symptomatology only placed added stress and pressure on this already compromised coparental subsystem. The lack of boundaries and structure (agreements and coordination about when each parent is to be parenting, if and when John's mother should and could be in the family home, who was responsible for coordinating with John's school, therapist, tutor) resulted in chaos, conflict, and further neglect of John's now considerable needs. From a family systems perspective, John's increasing symptomatology is readily cast as a response to the untenable role demanded of him in keeping his mother's affair a secret, and as a cry for help for a chaotic and disorganized family system.

This understanding of the family interior is insufficient, however. Effective family systems approaches also attend to systems outside the family currently (or anticipated to be) affecting the family system. For the Jackson family, the family therapist identified several such systems. First, there was the family's mental health care, specifically, an individual therapist whom John had been seeing. While consultation with outside therapists is often indicated in family work when such individuals are involved, it turned out to be especially pivotal in this case. There were some indications that the individual therapist may have unwittingly introduced some additional, complicating boundary problems that affected the family. By seeing John and his father conjointly but failing to involve John's mother at all in the treatment, she appeared to have unintentionally gotten entangled in the couple's marital conflict and reinforced John's alignment with his father. In their conjoint meetings, it turned out, father and son had frequently raged to the therapist about John's mother, even as the mother's phone calls to the therapist had sometimes gone unanswered for as much as a week or more, by mother's report.

To assess the role being played by the mental health system, the family therapist obtained a waiver of confidentiality to connect with John's individual therapist. Such contact was in order both to facilitate assessment of the individual therapist's perspectives and goals and to permit the family therapist to deepen her understanding of the family system so that the interventionists could try to coordinate a treatment plan together that would be working toward parallel, appropriate goals. Similarly, given John's school problems it was important to initiate contact with a relevant liaison at the school. This was essential both to better understand the nature of John's current problems at school and to permit creation of a functional coordination of home-school support for him. Finally, given the strong inkling that John's father was preparing to initiate the process of divorce, potential legal implications had to be considered so that any future involvement with the legal system could circumvent the parents' involvement in an adversarial process certain to exacerbate the family's already high level of conflict.

Case Conceptualization

For over a decade, the Jackson family had sustained a reasonably stable and functional family adaptation, although it was one characterized by a compartmentalized and skewed parenting partnership in which John's mother carried out the active parenting (cementing a strong mother-son dyadic subsystem) as the father assumed an economic provider role (functioning only marginally in both marital and father-son dyadic subsystems). This once stable structure had gradually deteriorated over time, as avoidance and alienation in the marriage ultimately precipitated the mother's undertaking of an extramarital affair. As the mother's long-standing availability and quality of parenting the son deteriorated to the point of neglect, conflict increased between the son and his mother, while the father continued to avoid involvement. Keeping the affair secret from the father (seen by many family therapists as exemplifying a pathological coalition between mother and son) had infused additional toxicity into this triadic family system. The Jackson family's dynamics are a vivid example of family subsystems mutually influencing one another, both in contributing to the escalating dysfunction of the system and in calling out for an intervention that attended to each subsystem.

John's symptoms were both a functional cry for help for his family system and a reflection of marital and parental subsystem breakdowns. The family's hierarchy and many of its boundaries (mother-son, marital-parental) had disintegrated and now needed considerable support to restructure. The limbo state of the separation and divorce decision complicated matters by impairing the Jacksons' ability to functionally respond to the family life cycle crisis. The possibility of a high-conflict custody dispute necessitated structuring any intervention to protect the family and treatment process from being cast into the legal adversarial system. The professional systems outside the family were not adequately supporting the family. Coordination was poor (as there was no functional connection with the son's school), and the son's therapist was aligned with the father.

Every individual member and every dyadic relationship subsystem in this family was showing a significant need for intervention, and the deleterious impact of each subsystem on the other (affected through the family's mutual feedback

(Continued)

loops) likewise needed to be interrupted. Given the multiple problems, a clear prioritization of need was required, and the therapist in this case chose to work from a directive, structurally based approach. The approach involved joining with the family quickly and building a collaborative working alliance by utilizing the parents' mutual concern for their son's welfare.

Complications

A number of complications became apparent only as the case progressed, introducing difficult decisions about how best to intervene. First, as already indicated, consultation with John's individual child therapist confirmed that her role in helping John process the emotional trauma of the family breakdown had been severely compromised by her unwitting but problematic entanglement in the marital conflict. Given the complications this triangulation introduced, the family therapist and John's therapist needed to process whether it would be in the Jacksons' best interests for the individual therapist to withdraw from the case and support John's engagement with a new individual therapist who specialized in high-conflict coparenting cases.

Second, the seeming inevitability of the family's move into a divorce transition led the therapist to incorporate proactive structural and psychoeducational interventions into the work. One focus of this work was on preempting new adversarial processes, inherent in the legal system, so as to keep them from infiltrating and further escalating the marital conflict and endangering the family and its members. From the outset, the family therapist also had to decide whether to advocate reconstitution of the nuclear family structure (which was the mother's clear desire) or to assist the family in restructuring to a binuclear family. Because the creation of a clear and functional structure would be the key to restoring adaptive functioning in this family, the family therapist decided to strongly advocate for disengaging the marital and parenting dyads. This stance, which prompted initial distress and resistance from John's mother, ultimately helped to enable the work of differentiating marital issues (which in a binuclear structure were not relevant targets for the therapy, except as they interfered with functional coparenting) from coparenting issues (which became the agreed-upon focus in helping the family to move toward greater functionality).

Finally, given the severity of the son's current dysfunction and the family's seeming inability to cooperate adaptively, the family therapist posed the possibility that the son may need to be placed outside the home. Individual factors such as the boy's substance use and the possibility of his school failure or dropout, complicated by the inadequate functional parental involvement and supervision, questioned whether continued in-home placement for the son would be a viable option. The out-of-home placement recommendation had not been considered by the parents, who were both resistant to the idea for multiple reasons. Their unified resistance was used to motivate all the family members to work on issues with focus and urgency.

Course of Treatment

The initial intervention occurred when the father contacted the family therapist asking to come in with the son, and the therapist insisted that the whole family come in together for the intake. The presenting problem was then reframed by the suggestion that resolution of John's symptoms needed to be addressed in the broader family system. The therapist highlighted the seriousness of the son's symptoms and used the family's immediate resistance to an outside-the-home placement to motivate the parents to prioritize the provision of better structure and support to the son and stabilize the marital and parenting subsystems. This was handled by the therapist in a directive manner, and an explicit plan was worked out with the couple to implement a binuclear family structure. The specific plan called for a nesting residential arrangement, wherein the parents shared a single apartment where first one, and then the other, resided when not parenting John. John, however, stayed in the family home with whichever parent was actively parenting. This arrangement allowed for (a) a stabilization of the basic family structure—there was no time line imposed or immediate decision called for about separation and divorce—at the same time as (b) the marital and parenting subsystems were functionally separated. Treatment was then able to progress to structuring (by creating a schedule for) the parenting time, thereby assuring that appropriate responsibility and supervision would be occurring. The boundaries between spousal issues and parenting issues were functionally reinstituted, and John's parents and the therapist mutually agreed to move spousal issues to the back burner and to focus on parenting issues as primary.

Work with the parental subsystem became the primary thrust of therapy. Disengaging the couple's focus on the marriage and keeping their energies child-focused, with exchanges taking place principally over e-mail (augmented by occasional phone contacts and in family sessions), contained their conflict and made the coparenting relationship more manageable. Sessions often clarified when spousal relationship issues were compromising coparenting, and the parents were gradually able to attain better boundaries with regard to these issues. Conjoint work with the mother and son addressed the trauma induced by the affair and the secret, working on healing the relationship breach that had occurred so that the son could gradually accept more nurturance and parenting from his mother. In the beginning, parenting time was titrated between mother and son based on the boy's tolerance of being with her. There was more variability later, depending on advances and setbacks in the mother-son reunification work, and so titration continued to be monitored in an ongoing way by the family therapist. Work with John's father addressed his need to step up and assume greater parenting responsibility, to make himself more available, and to work on his deficient parenting skills. Coparenting during these early phases was coordinated by the family therapist, with explicit focus on ongoing information exchange and active decision making about the son.

As this work began, the conversations with the boy's individual therapist commenced. It became clear rather quickly that she was aligned with the father-son coalition and that her identification with the son's rejection of the mother was especially strong. She reluctantly acknowledged that she had probably alienated the mother and possibly also compromised her primary therapeutic role by conducting conjoint parent-child work with only the father and son. However, because she was steadfast in her conviction that she would almost certainly be unable to form a working alliance with the mother, she gradually acknowledged (and helped persuade the reluctant father) that it seemed best to have the son referred to another therapist. The family therapist assisted the family with a referral to a child therapist who specialized in high-conflict cases and established a collaborative team approach with this therapist from the beginning of their involvement. The family therapist also contacted the school counselor (who had not heard from either parent) and coordinated a meeting between relevant school staff and both parents. The school counselor and parents set up a plan

(Continued)

to support the son's functioning at school, which included structures for regular feedback from the school.

Progress was soon evident in multiple parameters of this family system's functioning. John's performance at school improved, and he gradually began working through his anger toward his mother, allowing her to reconnect as his primary parent. John's mother, who had ended the affair, redoubled her attentive parenting efforts and worked diligently to prove her commitment to preserve the marriage. John's father felt content with the moratorium on pursuing separation and divorce. He willingly accepted the parent coaching that the therapist offered and soon began looking forward to and enjoying his scheduled parenting time without John's mother present. Considerable work had to be done to help John's father support the healing of the mother-son relationship, despite his own continuing anger with her. The work of coparenting continued to be effectively coordinated by the family therapist; structures for communication were put into place, parenting issues that came up were discussed and decisions made in conjoint sessions with the parents, and written documentation of specific decisions made at these meetings were provided to John's parents to reinforce these structural shifts. Responsibility and accountability were supported throughout this process, from which a functional parental hierarchy came to be established with a transformation to a more equitable and shared parenting arrangement. This arrangement was established and documented in a formal parenting plan that evolved from the treatment, so that when the father made a decision to file for divorce 6 months after the work began, the family (despite some setbacks) was ultimately able to move collaboratively with only minimal legal-adversarial involvement to a shared custody arrangement. The family therapist–child therapist team continued to support the family during this transition.

Implications of the Case

John's individual symptoms were understood as occurring in the context of this family's triadic family process. Therefore, the goals of family systems treatment were broader than immediate resolution of the identified patient's symptoms. They were focused on addressing relational processes in the marital, coparental, and parent-child subsystems and in the extrafamilial system that was impacting the family. Helping the family to functionally restructure as they negotiated a transition from nuclear family to binuclear family was a critical focus of the treatment. Work on clarifying and reinforcing functional subsystem boundaries and reestablishing the hierarchy between parents and son remained a focus throughout the treatment. Given the destructive potential of the marital breakdown, structural disengagement of the marital couple (through the nesting residential arrangement and coordination of their coparenting) was an essential intervention in this case. Similarly, assessment of and direct intervention addressing extrafamilial involvement (with the son's individual therapist and relevant school personnel) was needed to create a collaborative professional context around the family system. Psychoeducation and recommendations about more collaborative divorce processes helped the parents resist the pulls from the legal adversarial family court system to escalate their spousal conflict. As the Jackson family moved through the divorce transition, the son benefited from a more balanced, competent, shared parenting arrangement, a marked change from the almost exclusive maternal involvement that had characterized his family experience prior to the beginning of treatment.

As illustrated in earlier sections of this chapter, there are myriad ways that family therapists of different schools might have chosen to approach and formulate this case, but there would also be a number of likely commonalities. For example, most systems-oriented clinicians would have sought to observe and assess the triadic or whole family process and to evaluate problems in the family's hierarchy and boundaries during initial sessions. Most also would have looked beyond the family's interior dynamics to understand the roles being played by interrelated systems—in this case, the school, legal, and mental health systems.

The therapeutic stance and the kinds of information gathered and privileged during this process would have varied from approach to approach, of course. The approach the family therapist took in working with the family was more old school than new age, in that a clear hierarchical arrangement installing the therapist as expert was set up from the outset to help stabilize the family quickly as a number of crucial decisions were made. The therapist was quite active in proposing an appropriate course of action, rather than coaxing the family to make these decisions themselves.

Different schools may very well have attended to other aspects of the case unaddressed in the work summarized here. For example, from certain frameworks, a spotlight may have been trained on John's father's financial and executive planning power and control in the family situation and on his mother's long-standing one-down position. Or focus may have been given to the cutoff of marital intimacy John's mother felt prior to embarking on the affair and/or to her empowerment as an individual (both absent in the case formulation) in the service of supporting and sustaining postdivorce parenting adaptation. The casting of out-of-home placement as an exterior threat to the family (which thereby mobilized their cohesiveness in combating the threat) resonated well with narrative approaches. Multigenerational theorists would have sought different insights to this case, perhaps unwrapping family members' collusion with the father in denigrating the mother to her son in case formulation.

Though there would almost certainly be differences in emphasis depending on the theoretical framework, the path toward recovery for the adolescent charted by helping to restructure the family, clarify boundaries, and strengthen the co-parenting alliance was guided by a distinctively systems-driven approach. While remaining sensitive to the potential role played by intra-individual factors, the case exemplifies major ways in which therapists working from systems frameworks formulate and intervene in a manner differing in emphasis from those of other major traditions represented in this volume.

SUMMARY

Family therapy's revolutionary insight was that the problems of any given individual are a function of the whole family, and this systems viewpoint continues to guide virtually all contemporary family therapy practice. The field has undergone a dizzying number of changes in its 50-year history, and in at least certain schools of practice there have been some major breaks with long-standing traditions of focusing on interaction over cognition and on privileging relationships over individuals. Yet the hallmarks of systems approaches—thinking triadically about behavior problems, focusing on family process over content, understanding that families are open systems embedded in extrafamilial systems—remain as fresh as ever. They will undoubtedly continue to have enduring impact and, when embraced, promise to infuse critically important insights into effective clinical practice.

REFERENCES

Alexander, J. F., Sexton, T. L., & Robbins, M. S. (2002). The developmental status of family therapy in family psychology intervention science. In H. Liddle, D. Santisteban, R. Levant, & J. Bray (Eds.), *Family Psychology: Science-Based Interventions* (pp. 17–40). Washington, DC: American Psychological Association.

Anderson, H. (1993). On a roller coaster: A collaborative language systems approach to therapy. In S. Friedman (Ed.), *The new language of change* (pp. 302–322). New York: Guilford Press.

Andolfi, M. (1978). A structural approach to a family with an encopretic child. *Journal of Marital and Family Therapy, 4,* 25–29.

Arend, R., Gove, F. L., & Sroufe, L. A. (1979). Continuity of individual adaptation from infancy to kindergarten: A predictive study of ego-resiliency and curiosity in preschoolers. *Child Development, 50,* 950–959.

Bateson, G. (1972). *Steps to an ecology of mind.* New York: Ballantine Books.

Bateson, G. (1979). *Mind and nature.* New York: Dutton.

Bateson, G. (1980). *Mind and nature: A necessary unity.* New York: Bantam Books.

Bateson, G., Jackson, D. D., Haley, J., & Weakland, J. H. (1956). Towards a theory of schizophrenia. *Behavior Science, 1,* 251–264.

Bearss, K. E., & Eyberg, S. (1998). A test of the parenting alliance theory. *Early Education and Development, 9,* 179–185.

Belsky, J., Campbell, S., Cohn, J., & Moore, G. (1996). Instability of infant-parent attachment security. *Developmental Psychology, 32,* 921–924.

Belsky, J., Crnic, K., & Gable, S. (1995). The determinants of coparenting in families with toddler boys: Spousal differences and daily hassles. *Child Development, 66,* 629–642.

Belsky, J., Putnam, S., & Crnic, K. (1996). Coparenting, parenting, and early emotional development. In J. McHale, & P. Cowan (Eds.), *Understanding how family-level dynamics affect children's development: Studies of two-parent families* (pp. 45–55). San Francisco: Jossey-Bass.

Bentler, P. M. (1993). *EQS structural equations program manual.* Los Angeles: BMDP Statistical Software.

Block, J. (1982). Assimilation, accommodation, and the dynamics of personality development. *Child Development, 53,* 281–295.

Bornstein, M. H., & Sawyer, J. (2006). Family systems. In K. McCartney & D. Phillips (Eds.), *Blackwell handbook of early childhood development* (pp. 381–398). Malden, MA: Blackwell.

Boszormeny-Nagy, I., & Sparks, G. (1973). *Invisible loyalties: Reciprocity in intergenerational family therapy.* New York: Harper & Row.

Bowen, M. (1974). *Toward the differentiation of self in one's family of origin* (Georgetown Family Symposium). Washington, DC: Georgetown University Medical Center, Department of Psychiatry.

Bowen, M. (1978). *Family therapy in clinical practice.* New York: Aronson.

Buchanan, C. M., Maccoby, E. E., & Dornbusch, S. M. (1991). Caught between parents: Adolescents' experience in divorced homes. *Child Development, 62,* 1008–1029.

Caldera, Y. M., & Lindsey, E. W. (2006). Coparenting, mother-infant interaction, and infant-parent attachment relationships in two-parent families. *Journal of Family Psychology, 20,* 275–283.

Camara, K. A., & Resnick, G. (1989). Styles of conflict resolution and cooperation between divorced parents: Effects on child behavior and adjustment. *American Journal of Orthopsychiatry, 59,* 560–575.

Constantine, L. L. (1983). Dysfunction and failure in open family systems: Pt. I. Application of a unified theory. *Journal of Marriage and the Family, 45,* 725–738.

Cook, W., & Kenny, D. (2006). Examining the validity of self-report assessments of family functioning: A question of the level of analysis. *Journal of Family Psychology, 20,* 209–216.

Cowan, C. P., & Cowan, P. A. (1992). *When partners become parents: The big life change for couples.* New York: Basic Books.

Cowan, P. A., Cowan, C. P., Cohen, N., Pruett, M. K., & Pruett, K. (in press). Supporting fathers' involvement with kids. In J. D. Berrick & N. Gilbert (Eds.), *Raising children: Emerging needs, modern risks, and social responses*. Oxford: Oxford University Press.

Cox, M. J., & Paley, B. (2003). Understanding families as systems. *Current Directions in Psychological Science, 12*(5), 193–196.

Cramer, B. (1995). The child as therapist. *System Familie, 8*, 226–233.

Cummings, E. M., & Davies, P. (1994). *Children and marital conflict: The impact of family dispute and resolution*. New York: Guilford Press.

Davies, P. T., & Cicchetti, D. (Eds.). (2004). Family systems and developmental psychopathology [Special issue]. *Development and Psychopathology, 16*(3).

Diamond, G., Siqueland, L., & Diamond, G. M. (2003). Attachment-based family therapy for depressed adolescents: Programmatic treatment development. *Clinical Child and Family Psychology Review, 6*, 107–127.

Egeland, B., Jacobvitz, D., & Sroufe, L. A. (1988). Breaking the cycle of abuse. *Child Development, 59*, 1080–1088.

Erel, O., & Burman, B. (1995). Interrelatedness of marital relations and parent child relations: A meta-analytic review. *Psychological Bulletin, 118*, 108–132.

Eron. J., & Lund, T. (1996). *Narrative solutions in brief therapy*. New York: Guilford Press.

Favez, N., Frascarolo, F., Carneiro, C., Montfort, V., Corboz-Warnery, A., Fivaz-Depeursinge, E., et al. (in press). The development of the family alliance from pregnancy to toddlerhood and children outcomes at 18 months. *Infant and Child Development, 15*, 59–73.

Feinberg, M. E. (2003). The internal structure and ecological context of coparenting: A framework for research and intervention. *Parenting: Science and Practice, 3*, 95–131.

Fivaz-Depeursinge, E., & Corboz-Warnery, A. (1999). *A primary triangle: A developmental systems view of mothers, fathers, and infants*. New York: Basic Books.

Fivaz-Depeursinge, E., & Favez, N. (2006). Exploring triangulation in infancy: Two contrasted cases. *Family Process, 45*, 4–19.

Fivaz-Depeursinge, E., Favez, N., Lavanchy, C., de Noni, S., & Frascarolo, F. (2005). Four-month-olds make triangular bids to father and mother during trilogue play with still-face. *Social Development, 14*, 361–378.

Fivaz-Depeursinge, E., Frascarolo, F., & Corboz-Warnery, A. (1996). *Understanding how family-level dynamics affect children's development: Studies of two-parent families* (J. P. McHale, & P. A. Cowan, Eds.). San Francisco: Jossey-Bass.

Forgatch, M. S., & Knutson, N. M. (2002). Linking basic and applied research in a prevention science process. In H. Liddle, D. A. Santisteban, R. Levant, & J. Bray (Eds.), *Family psychology: Science-based interventions* (pp. 239–257). Washington, DC: American Psychological Association.

Fraiberg, S. (1980). *Clinical studies in infant mental health*. New York: Basic Books.

Fraser, M. W., Nelson, K. E., & Rivard, J. C. (1997). Effectiveness of family preservation services. *Social Work Research, 21*, 138–153.

Freedman, J., & Combs, G. (1996). *Narrative therapy: The social construction of preferred realities*. New York: Norton.

Friedman, E. (1991). Bowen theory and therapy. In A. S. Gurman & D. P. Kniskern (Eds.), *Handbook of family therapy*: Vol. 2 (pp. 134–170), New York: Brunner/Mazel.

Frosch, C. A., Mangelsdorf, S. C., & McHale, J. L. (2000). Marital behavior and the security of preschooler-parent attachment relationships. *Journal of Family Psychology, 14*, 144–161.

Fruzzetti, A. E., & Jacobson, N. S. (1991). Marital and family therapy. In M. Hersen, A. Kazdin, & A. Bellack (Eds.), *Clinical psychology handbook* (2nd ed., pp. 643–666). Elmsford, NY: Pergamon Press.

Haley, J. (1976). *Problem-solving therapy*. San Francisco: Jossey-Bass.

Hare-Mustin, R. T. (1978). A feminist approach to family therapy. *Family Process, 17*, 181–194.

Henggeler, S. W., & Bourdin, C. (1990). *Family therapy and beyond: A multisystemic approach to treating the behavior problems of children and adolescents*. Pacific Grove, CA: Brooks/Cole.

Henggeler, S. W., Rodick, J. D., Borduin, C. M., Hansen, C. L., Watson, S. M., & Urey, J. R. (1986). Multisystemic treatment of juvenile offenders: Effects on adolescent behavior and family interaction. *Developmental Psychology, 22*, 132–141.

Henggeler, S. W., Schoenwald, S. K., Borduin, C. M., Rowland, M. D., & Cunningham, P. B. (1998). *Multisystemic treatment of antisocial behavior in children and adolescents*. New York: Guilford Press.

Henry, P. W. (1998). Belief: The heart of healing in families and illness. *Family Journal: Counseling and Therapy for Couples and Families, 6*, 346–347.

Hetherington, E. M. (2006). The influence of conflict, marital problem solving and parenting on children's adjustment in nondivorced, divorced and remarried families. In A. Clarke-Stewart, & J. Dunn (Eds.), *Families count: Effects on child and adolescent development* (pp. 203–237). New York: Cambridge University Press.

Hofferth, S. L., & Casper, L. M. (2006). *The handbook of measurement issues in family research*. Mahwah, NJ: Erlbaum.

Hoffman, L. (1981). *Foundations of family therapy*. New York: Basic Books.

Hoffman, L. (1985). Beyond power and control: Toward a "second order" family systems therapy. *Family Systems Medicine, 3*, 381–396.

Hoffman, L. (1988). A constructivist position for family therapy. *Irish Journal of Psychology, 9*, 110–129.

Jackson, D. D. (1957). The question of family homeostasis. *Psychiatric Quarterly Supplement, 31*, 79–90.

Jackson, D. D. (1965). Family rules: Marital quid pro quo. *Archives of General Psychiatry, 12*, 589–594.

Jacobvitz, D., Hazen, N., & Curran, M. (2004). Observations of early triadic family interactions: Boundary disturbances in the family predict symptoms of depression, anxiety, and attention-deficit/hyperactivity disorder in middle childhood. *Development and Psychopathology, 16*, 577–592.

Johnston, J. R., Campbell, L. E., & Mayes, S. S. (1985). Latency children in post-separation and divorce disputes. *Journal of the American Academy of Child Psychiatry, 24*, 563–574.

Jones, C. W., & Lindblad-Goldberg, M. (2002). Ecosystemic structural family therapy. In R. F. Kaslow (Ed.), *Comprehensive handbook of psychotherapy: Vol. 3. Interpersonal/humanistic/existential* (pp. 3–33). Hoboken, NJ: Wiley.

Kaczynski, K. J., Lindahl, K. M., & Malik, N. M. (2006). Marital conflict, maternal and paternal parenting and child adjustment: A test of mediation and moderation. *Journal of Family Psychology, 20*, 199–208.

Kaslow, F. W. (1982). Portrait of the healthy couple. *Psychiatric Clinics of North America, 5*, 519–527.

Katz, L. F., & Low, S. M. (2004). Marital violence, co-parenting, and family-level processes in relation to children's adjustment. *Journal of Family Psychology, 18*, 372–382.

Kerig, P. K. (1995). Triangles in the family circle: Effects of family structure on marriage, parenting, and child adjustment. *Development and Psychopathology, 9*, 28–43.

Leupnitz, D., (1988). *The family interpreted: Psychoanalysis, feminism and family therapy*. New York: Basic Books.

Liddle, H. A. (1995). Conceptual and clinical dimensions of a multidimensional, multisystems engagement strategy in family-based adolescent treatment. *Psychotherapy: Theory, Research, Practice and Training, 32*, 39–58.

Liddle, H. A. (2000). *Multidimensional family therapy: A treatment manual*. Rockville, MD: Center for Substance Abuse Treatment.

Liddle, H. A., Santisteban, D. A., Levant, R. F., & Bray, J. H. (2002). *Family psychology: Science-based interventions*. Washington, DC: American Psychological Association.

Lidz, T., Cornelison, A. R., Fleck, S., & Terry, D. (1957a). Intrafamilial environment of schizophrenic patients: Pt. I. The father. *Psychiatry: Journal for the Study of Interpersonal Processes, 20*, 329–342.

Lidz, T., Cornelison, A. R., Fleck, S., & Terry, D. (1957b). Intrafamilial environment of schizophrenic patients: Pt. II. Marital schism and marital skew. *American Journal of Psychiatry, 114*, 241–248.

Madanes, C. (1981). *Strategic family therapy*. San Francisco: Jossey-Bass.

Madanes, C. (1984). *Behind the one-way mirror: Advances in the practice of strategic therapy*. San Francisco: Jossey-Bass.

McBride, B. A., & Mills, G. (1993). A comparison of mother and father involvement with their preschool age children. *Early Childhood Research Quarterly, 8*, 457–477.

McDonough, S. C. (1993). Interaction guidance: Understanding and treating early infant-caregiver relationship disturbances. In C. Zeanah (Ed.), *Handbook of infant mental health* (pp. 414–426). London: Guildford Press.

McGoldrick, M., Anderson, C., & Walsh, F. (1989). *Women in families: A framework for family therapy.* New York: Norton.

McGoldrick, M., & Gerson, R. (1999). *Genograms in family assessment.* New York: Norton.

McHale, J. P. (1995). Coparenting and triadic interactions during infancy: The roles of marital distress and child gender. *Developmental Psychology, 31,* 985–996.

McHale, J. P. (2007a). *Charting the bumpy road of coparenthood.* Washington, DC: Zero to Three Press.

McHale, J. P. (2007b). When infants grow up in multiperson relationship systems. *Infant Mental Health Journal, 28*(4), 1–23.

McHale, J. P., & Cowan, P. A. (1996). *Understanding how family-level dynamics affect children's development: Studies of two-parent families.* San Francisco: Jossey-Bass.

McHale, J. P., & Fivaz-Depeursinge, E. (1999). Understanding triadic and family group interactions during infancy and toddlerhood. *Clinical Child and Family Psychology Review, 2,* 107–127.

McHale, J. P., & Grolnick, W. S. (2002). *Retrospect and prospect in the psychological study of families.* Hillsdale, NJ: Erlbaum.

McHale, J. P., Kazali, C., Rotman, T., Talbot, J., Carleton, M. & Lieberson, R. (2004). The transition to coparenthood: Parents' prebirth expectations and early coparental adjustment at 3 months postpartum. *Development and Psychopathology, 16,* 711–733.

McHale, J. P., Khazan, I., Erera, P., Rotman, T., DeCourcey, W., & McConnell, M. (2002). Coparenting in diverse family systems. In M. H. Bornstein (Ed.), *Handbook of parenting: Being and becoming a parent* (2nd ed., pp. 75–107). Mahwah, NJ: Erlbaum.

McHale, J. P., & Rasmussen, J. L. (1998). Coparental and family group-level dynamics during infancy: Early family precursors of child and family functioning during preschool. *Development and Psychopathology, 10,* 39–59.

McHale, J. & Rotman, T. (2007). Is seeing believing? Expectant parents' outlooks on coparenting and later coparenting solidarity. *Infant Behavior and Development, 30,* 63–81.

Minuchin, P. (1985). Families and individual development: Provocations from the field of family therapy. *Child Development, 56,* 289–302.

Minuchin, S. (1974). *Families and family therapy.* Cambridge, MA: Harvard University Press.

Minuchin, S., Chamberlain, P., & Graubard, P. (1967). A project to teach learning skills to disturbed, delinquent children. *American Journal of Orthopsychiatry, 37,* 558–567.

Minuchin, S., Rosman, B. L., & Baker, L. (1978). *Psychosomatic families: Anorexia nervosa in context.* Cambridge, MA: Harvard University Press.

Moyer, A. (1994). Cybernetic theory does not explain family and couple process: Systems theory and dialectical metatheory. *American Journal of Family Therapy, 22,* 273–281.

Nichols, M. P., & Schwartz, R. C. (1998). *Family therapy: Concepts and methods.* Needham Heights, MA: Allyn & Bacon.

Olson, D. H., Russell, C. S., & Sprenkle, D. H. (1980). Marital and family therapy: A decade review. *Journal of Marriage and the Family, 42,* 973–993.

Olson, D. H., Sprenkle, D. H., & Russell, C. S. (1979). Circumplex model of marital and family system: Cohesion and adaptability dimensions, family types and clinical applications. *Family Process, 18,* 3–28.

Prigogine, I. (1973). *The physicist's conception of nature.* Dordrecht, The Netherlands: Reidel.

Richmond, M. E. (1917). *Social diagnosis.* New York: Russell Sage Foundation.

Robert-Tissot, C., Cramer, B., & Stern, D. N. (1996). Outcome evaluation in brief mother-infant psychotherapies: Report on 75 cases. *Infant Mental Health Journal, 17,* 97–114.

Rosenberg, J. B. (1978). Two is better than one: Use of behavioral techniques within a structural family therapy model. *Journal of Marital and Family Therapy, 4,* 31–39.

Satir, V. (1972). *Peoplemaking.* Palo Alto, CA: Science and Behavior Books.

Schoenwald, S. K., & Henggeler, S. W. (2002). *Mental health services research and family-based treatment: Bridging the gap.* Washington, DC: American Psychological Association.

Schoppe-Sullivan, S. J., Mangelsdorf, S. C., Frosch, C. A., & McHale, J. L. (2004). Associations between coparenting and marital behavior from infancy to the preschool years. *Journal of Family Psychology, 18,* 194–207.

Selvini Palazzoli, M., Boscolo, L., Cecchin, G., & Prata, G. (1978). *Paradox and counterparadox.* New York: Aronson.

Shapiro, A. F., & Gottman, J. M. (2005). Effects on marriage of a psycho-communicative-educational intervention with couples undergoing the transition to parenthood: Evaluation at 1-year post intervention. *Journal of Family Communication, 5,* 1–24.

Shaw, D. S., Criss, M. M., & Schonberg, M. A. (2004). The development of family hierarchies and their relation to children's conduct problems. *Development and Psychopathology, 9,* 28–43.

Silliman, B., Stanley, S. M., Coffin, W., Markman, H. J., & Jordan, P. L. (2002). Preventive interventions for couples. In J. Bray, R. Levant, H. Liddle, & D. Santisteban (Eds.), *Family psychology: Science-based interventions* (pp. 123–146). Washington, DC: American Psychological Association.

Speer, D. (1970). Family systems: Morphostasis and morphogenesis, or, "Is homeostasis enough?" *Family Process, 9,* 259–278.

Speltz, M. L., DeKlyen, M., & Greenberg, M. T. (1999). Attachment in boys with early onset conduct problems. *Development and Psychopathology, 11,* 269–285.

Steele, H., Steele, M., & Fonagy, P. (1996). Associations among attachment classifications of mothers, fathers, and their infants. *Child Development, 67,* 541–555.

Szapocznik, J., & Kurtines, W. M. (1989). *Breakthroughs in family therapy with drug abusing and problem youth.* New York: Springer.

von Bertanffly, L. (1968). *General systems theory.* New York: George Braziller.

Vondra, J. I., Shaw, D. S., & Swearingen, L. (2001). Attachment stability and emotional and behavioral regulation from infancy to preschool age. *Development and Psychopathology, 13,* 13–33.

von Klitzing, K., Simoni, H., & Burgin, D. (1999). Child development and early triadic relationships. *International Journal of Psycho-Analysis, 80,* 71–89.

Walters, M., Carter, B., Papp, P., & Silverstein, O. (1988). *The invisible web: Gender patterns in family relationships.* New York: Guilford Press.

Ward, M. J., & Carlson, E. A. (1995). Associations among adult attachment representations, maternal sensitivity, and infant mother attachment in a sample of adolescent mothers. *Child Development, 66,* 69–79.

Watzlawick, P. (1984). Commentary: But what about mountainous seas? *Family Process, 23,* 517–518.

Watzlawick, P., Beavin, J., & Jackson, D. (1967). *Pragmatics of human communication: A study of interactional patterns—Pathologies and paradoxes.* New York: Norton.

Weiss, S. J., & Seed, M. S. (2002). Precursors of mental health problems for low birth weight children: The salience of family environment during the first year of life. *Child Psychiatry and Human Development, 33,* 3–27.

White, M. (1986). *Anorexia nervosa: A cybernetic perspective—Eating disorders.* Gaithersburg, MD: Aspen Press.

White, M. (1989). *Selected papers.* Adelaide, Australia: Dulwich Center.

White, M. (1995). *Reauthoring lives: Interviews and essays.* Adelaide, Australia: Dulwich Center.

Wood, B. L., Klebba, K. B., & Miller, B. D. (2000). Evolving the biobehavioral family model: The fit of attachment. *Family Process, 39,* 319–344.

Wynne, L. C., (1961) The study of intrafamilial alignments and splits in exploratory family therapy. In N. W. Ackerman, F. L. Beatman, & S. N. Sherman, (Eds.), *Exploring the base for family therapy* (pp. 95–115). New York: Family Services Association.

Wynne, L. C., Ryckoff, I., Day, J., & Hirsch, S. I. (1958). Pseudo-mutuality in the family relations of schizophrenics. *Psychiatry, 21,* 205–220.

Zeanah, C. H., Benoit, D., & Barton, M. (1993). Representations of attachment in mothers and their one-year-old infants. *Journal of the American Academy of Child and Adolescent Psychiatry, 32,* 278–286.

CHAPTER 8

Applied Behavior Analysis

Amy R. Murrell, Cicely Taravella LaBorde, Audra L. Crutchfield, and
Jessica Madrigal-Bauguss

GENERAL OVERVIEW

The purpose of this chapter is to provide readers with basic information on applied
behavior analysis (ABA). Important terms used throughout the chapter are defined
first. Then, as context is highly relevant to ABA, a context for the work is provided.
This context setting is accomplished through brief discussions of the philosophy and
history associated with applied behavior analysis. Historical applications funnel to
a discussion of the current uses of ABA. Finally, ethical considerations related to
the use of ABA are covered.

Important Terms

Antecedent: A stimulus that acts as a signal or cue for future behavior either to
repeat historically reinforced behavior or to avoid historically punished behavior
(Baldwin & Baldwin, 2001).

Behavior: The organism's interaction with the environment in which there is
a change in the environment due to an overt or covert action of the organism
(Johnston & Pennypacker, 1993; Newman, Reeve, Reeve, & Ryan, 2003).

Conditioned stimulus: A stimulus that was formerly neutral that gains an ability to
elicit respondent behavior through association with an unconditioned stimulus;
was originally labeled a conditional stimulus (Newman et al., 2003).

Consequence: A stimulus that follows a behavior and results in a change in
frequency of a behavior and/or in the probability of a behavior occurring and
influences the significance of an antecedent stimulus as a cue for future behavior
(Baldwin & Baldwin, 2001).

Differential reinforcement: A procedure in which one response is reinforced and
another is extinguished; this process is involved in highly skilled and complex
behaviors such as throwing a ball (Skinner, 1953).

Discrete trial training: A procedure used to teach new skills, in which there
is a distinct block of time during which there is an instruction or prompt (an
antecedent), a measure of emitted (or nonemitted) behavior, and consequential
reinforcement (Newman et al., 2003).

Neutral stimulus: A stimulus that does not elicit a response without conditioning but can come to elicit a response after it is paired with an unconditioned stimulus and thus becomes a conditioned stimulus (Newman et al., 2003).

Operant conditioning: A procedure in which there is a behavior-environment interaction that changes the probability of a behavior (or the frequency of a behavior) occurring due to a consequence that contingently follows such behavior. This will also change the function of an antecedent consequence (Baldwin & Baldwin, 2001).

Punishment: A contingency between a behavior and a consequence that decreases the probability of that behavior occurring in the future under similar circumstances (Newman et al., 2003).

Reinforcement: A contingency between a behavior and a consequence that increases the probability of that behavior occurring in the future under similar circumstances (Baldwin & Baldwin, 2001; Leslie, 1996).

Respondent conditioning: Also known as classical conditioning or Pavlovian conditioning, a procedure in which a neutral stimulus is paired with an unconditioned stimulus and results in the neutral stimulus becoming a conditioned stimulus with the ability to elicit a response similar to that of the unconditioned stimulus with which it was paired (Newman et al., 2003).

Shaping: A process in which successively closer approximations, or variations, of a desired behavior are reinforced; learning occurs in a stepwise fashion and involves changing mastery criteria necessary to receive reinforcement so that more and more sophisticated behavior is required (Baldwin & Baldwin, 2001).

Target behavior: A behavior of interest in applied behavior analyses that can be increased or decreased depending on what is desired (Newman et al., 2003).

Unconditioned stimulus: A stimulus that elicits an innate or unlearned response, or a stimulus that leads to a response without teaching (reflex); originally called unconditional stimulus (Newman et al., 2003).

THE PHILOSOPHY OF APPLIED BEHAVIOR ANALYSIS

The Structure of Scientific Revolutions was published in 1962. In that seminal text, Thomas Kuhn wrote that it was impossible for a scientific community to conduct science without a set of foundational beliefs. Applied behavior analysis was still an emerging field in the early 1960s; however, the idea of communally shared beliefs has long been present in the philosophy underlying the work. As will become evident throughout this chapter, applied behavior analysis emphasizes not only recognition, but also explicit discussion of such a perspective.

The perspective on which applied behavior analysis is based is behaviorism. The term behaviorism can be used to refer to a philosophy of science or to a general approach to the scientific study of psychology (Lattal & Chase, 2003). At the most basic level, behaviorism refers to the idea that psychology can be explained through objective study, without making causal attributions to internal processes. There are several varieties of behaviorism and definitions of behavior, but those who subscribe to behavior analytic work, often known as radical behaviorists, define behavior as anything that an integrated organism does in relation to context.

Defining Behavior

Defining behavior has been a key charge of many philosophers and psychologists throughout history. Aristotle attempted to understand behavior. Descartes did as well; he made a link between bodily movement and mechanical, as opposed to supernatural, causes. Descartes wrote that the soul and the body were two separate entities (i.e., he described an inherent dualism). He also proposed that some behaviors were caused by the soul, whereas other (less complex) behaviors were more mechanical, or determined by biological factors. Although his dualistic and mechanistic approach is quite different from much of the thought throughout behavior analysis, Descartes's work did set the stage for others, including Pavlov, to study reflexes (Leslie & O'Reilly, 1999). Classical conditioning principles as discovered and documented by Pavlov in the early 1900s play a crucial role in the historical development and the current conduct of applied behavior analysis. Therefore, Pavlov's work is elaborated further later in this chapter. For purposes of this philosophic discussion, it is sufficient to note that Pavlov's studies on salivation in dogs led to a link between biology and observable behavior.

Materialistic Approach

The emphasis on behavior as biological opened the door to an empirical analysis of materialistic philosophy. Materialism refers to the assumption that everything is composed of physical matter, and interactions between such material result in observable behavior. All supernatural explanations are rejected from a materialistic perspective (Cziko, 2000). Although early Greek philosophers, including Leucippus and Democritus, and early Western thinkers, such as Epicurus, proposed that behavior could be explained through the combination and separation of atoms, societal pressures about religion prevented materialism from taking hold until much later. There was some advancement of materialism in the seventeenth century when Hobbes wrote of the human body as a machine and LaMettrie and d'Holbach explained learning as resulting from changes in the brain. However, it was Newton's discovery of gravity and related physical principles that allowed for matter to be examined in a systematic manner (Cziko, 2000). Thorndike's studies on instrumental learning in animals, which will be elaborated on later, followed a materialistic approach and greatly advanced behaviorism.

Selectionism

Another, related advancement in philosophical thought and the study of behavior came when Darwin's work on evolution was published. Darwin's theory allowed for behavioral observations in biological contexts (Leslie & O'Reilly, 1999). The behavior analytic approach to studying psychological events parallels selectionism, the idea that characteristics of species evolve in response to success or effectiveness (of survival and reproduction) in the environment. Behavior, like species development, is based on environmental contingencies; it is determined. Individual behavior and cultural behavior evolve in response to their effectiveness on and in context (Skinner, 1981). This emphasis on context, and behavior in interaction with context, is the reason it is so important to analyze and describe the philosophy underlying applied behavior analysis.

Contextualistic Approach

Contextualism refers to a philosophy of science that states that behavior is inseparable from the context in which it occurs. From a behavior analytic perspective, context can include the individual's learning history and internal states as well as the current physical environment. Contextualism emphasizes empiricism and experience. It is the opposite of mechanism, and involves the investigation of behavior at many levels that influence each other (Capaldi & Proctor, 1999). Contextualists believe that mechanistic attempts to study behavior lessen the quality of interpretation. Although early behaviorism was more mechanistic, and there are current behavioral works conducted from a mechanistic approach, there is wide consensus that ABA is contextualistic. One cannot perform ABA without careful consideration of context (Dougher & Hayes, 2000; Rosnow & Georgoudi, 1986). It is necessary to look at external factors that play a role in initiating and maintaining behavior.

Applied behavior analysis is built on a specific type of contextualism: functional contextualism (Biglan & Hayes, 1996). This term refers to a natural science that uses empirically based rules to predict and influence behavior with precision, scope, and depth (Biglan, 1995). From a behavior analytic perspective, prediction and influence are related to the function that is served by behavior. Related to that, causal variables are limited to those that are observable and manipulable. Given that internal variables do not meet those criteria, applied behavior analysis rejects the idea that a mind or soul causes behavior. Applied behavior analysis thus is monistic.

Pepper (1942) wrote that philosophical systems fall into one of four basic worldviews. Worldviews are characterized by root metaphors, which are how scientists attempt to understand the world, and by truth criteria, which are the measure by which analyses are evaluated. The root metaphor in functional contextualism is the act in and inseparable from its historical and current context, and the truth criterion is related to the function of the analysis. Truth depends on whether the goal is met (Biglan & Hayes, 1996). This is referred to as successful working, which was originally discussed in works on pragmatism by Pierce, Dewey, James, and Darwin. In fact, several behavior analysts have noted that contextualism and pragmatism occur symbiotically (e.g., Baer, Wolf, & Risley, 1968).

Pragmatism

Pragmatism emerged in the late nineteenth century as a mix of empiricism and psychology. More specifically, British empiricists, German Romantic idealists, Kant, Hegel, and others who worked in areas of philosophy, science, and education influenced pragmatism. Charles W. Pierce was the first in the United States to talk and write about pragmatism. He talked about making ideas clear, which was related to using operational definitions and focusing on observable units of analyses as well as using successful working as a truth criterion. This is linked to behavior analysis in that the idea is to have correspondence between the goal and outcome after the analysis is complete. John Dewey and William James both expanded on Pierce's work. James took Pierce's work, which emphasized experimental (basic) work, and applied the philosophy to concerns about human behavior (Lattal & Laipple, 2003). James's work was part of an important shift from philosophy to the real world (Baum, 1994). Thus, our discussion shifts to a focus on the development and use of behavior analytic principles in applied settings.

A BRIEF HISTORY OF APPLIED BEHAVIOR ANALYSIS

Applied behavior analysis refers to the process of utilizing the principles of behavior in an effort to improve socially important behaviors (Baer et al., 1968). Principles of behavior were discovered through the use of carefully designed experiments, which have provided general information about respondent and operant conditioning as well as more specific knowledge about reinforcement, punishment, extinction, stimulus control, and their application. These principles are utilized in techniques such as shaping, chaining, token economies, and self-management—all of which were historically designed as methods to decrease maladaptive behavior with social relevance. Applied behavior analysis as we know it today began in the 1950s. At that time, researchers first applied the behavioral principles outlined by B. F. Skinner (1938) in his seminal work, *The Behavior of Organisms,* to clinical work with humans. However, it is important to also consider those figures and events that made early contributions to the development of behavioral principles.

Sechenov

Ivan Michailovich Sechenov (1829–1905) is considered the founder of Russian physiology (Koshtoyants, 1863/1965). At a time when the philosophical and psychological establishment emphasized mind-body duality, Sechenov took a monistic and materialistic approach to the study of mental processes, which he believed could be explained physiologically (Koshtoyants, 1863/1965). In his *Reflexes of the Brain,* Sechenov (1863/1965) proposed that all forms of behavior, including thoughts, emotions, and the holding of virtuous beliefs, were reflexes of the brain. Furthermore, he emphasized the importance of using strictly objective methods in the study of mental processes, and he stressed the significance of the role of the environment in an organism's behavior. Sechenov's ideas influenced subsequent Russian physiologists, most notably Ivan Pavlov (Koshtoyants, 1863/1965).

Pavlov

Ivan Petrovich Pavlov (1849–1936) shared Sechenov's materialistic approach, viewing psychological phenomena as physiological in origin. He also adhered to stringently objective methods in his study of higher nervous system activity (Pavlov, 1927/1928). Pavlov conducted his revolutionary research over the course of 25 years, studying the gastric and salivary reflexes of dogs. His work on gastric reflexes earned him acclaim in physiology, not to mention the Nobel Prize, but it was his subsequent discovery and delineation of the principles of respondent, or classical, conditioning that made him a significant figure in psychology as well.

In the course of his research on gastric reflexes, Pavlov (1927/1928, p. 6) began to notice "psychic secretion" of saliva in his dogs. Specifically, the dogs began to salivate in the presence of external stimuli other than food (e.g., the experimenter who brought the food, the sound of the footsteps of said experimenter). Pavlov set about investigating this phenomenon in a strictly objective manner. So important to Pavlov was a precise experimental method in his studies of nervous system processes that a specially designed laboratory with a trench around the outside was constructed to ensure experimental control (Pavlov, 1927/1928). In his earliest experiments, Pavlov surgically transplanted the dog's salivary ducts to the outside of the cheek or under the chin for the purposes of observation and precise measurement. This surgical procedure made it possible to count the number of drops of saliva or measure the amount of colored fluid in a tube that was displaced by the dog's saliva. When food was presented to the dogs, they began to salivate. Pavlov considered the salivation response to food an unconditioned, or inborn, reflex that did not need to be trained, and food was considered an unconditioned stimulus. He then began preceding the presentation of food to the dogs with the sound of a beating metronome. After several trials in which the dogs heard the metronome and then received food, the sound of the metronome alone resulted in salivation. The metronome had become a conditioned stimulus, and the salivation in response to it was a conditioned response. Although at the time it was called a "conditioned reflex," today the term "reflex" is usually thought of in terms of the stimulus-response relationship. The conditioned response is a response that was previously an unlearned, or unconditioned, response to an unconditioned stimulus and is now occurring in response to a conditioned stimulus.

Pavlov (1927/1928) and his fellow researchers replicated these early experiments many times, conditioning a variety of stimuli to elicit salivation, including the buzzing of electric bells, the application of electric current, thermal stimuli, and the cessation of continuous metronome beating. In the process, Pavlov outlined several key principles:

- *Timing:* For a conditioned response to be established, the neutral stimulus must be presented such that it precedes or occurs at the same time as the unconditioned stimulus.
- *Extinction:* Repeated presentation of the conditioned stimulus without the unconditioned stimulus will result in a weakening of the conditioned response.
- *Differentiation, or discrimination:* Presentation of stimuli similar to the conditioned stimulus in the absence of the unconditioned stimulus will result in elicitation of the conditioned response only by the specific conditioned stimulus.
- *Generalization:* If discrimination training is not applied, the conditioned response may be elicited by stimuli that are similar to the conditioned stimulus even without direct pairing with the unconditioned stimulus.

Thorndike

At about the same time that Pavlov began investigating conditioned reflexes, Edward Lee Thorndike (1874–1949) was investigating other basic principles of learning in animals (Jonçich, 1968). Thorndike's work in animal, or comparative, psychology is considered part of the functionalist movement, a parent of behaviorism (O'Donnell, 1985). In his dissertation research at Columbia University, Thorndike conducted objective, methodical investigations of stimulus-response connections, or associations (Jonçich, 1968). The basic experiment consisted of placing a hungry kitten (and eventually hungry dogs and lonely chicks) in one of several puzzle boxes he designed, from which the animal could escape by actions such as pulling on the loop of a cord or pressing a lever (Thorndike, 1898). Food was placed visibly outside of the box (in the case of lonely chicks, other chicks were outside of the box), and Thorndike observed and recorded the animal's behavior and the time it took for the animal to escape the box. He plotted the time to escape over several trials on a graph and was one of the first researchers to capture evidence of learning in this way (Chance, 1999). Thorndike noted that, once the animal was successful, the time to escape generally consistently decreased with successive trials. He concluded that an association is formed between a certain situation and a certain response and that the resulting pleasure (obtaining food or company) served to strengthen this connection (Thorndike, 1898). In later works, Thorndike came to refer to this finding as the law of effect (Hearst, 1999).

Watson

If animal psychology can be thought of as a bridge between functionalism and behaviorism, John Broadus Watson (1878–1958) defiantly carried the flag of psychology across this bridge and planted it firmly on the other side. After 12 years of behavioral research with animals, Watson (1913) published "Psychology as the Behaviorist Views It," an article that called for a radically different approach to the science of psychology. He argued that psychology should abandon consciousness as its subject of study and forsake introspection as its method. Watson advocated psychology as an objective science, the goal of which would be the prediction and control of behavior through the study of observable responses to stimuli, using a precise and reproducible experimental method. The approach would be the same in studying animals and humans. Although Watson viewed the evaluation of the behavior of any species as important in its own right, he also criticized psychologists for failing to produce results that could be practically applied. Watson thus began the movement called behaviorism, which profoundly shaped psychological thought for much of the twentieth century (Bergmann, 1956).

Following his 1913 paper, Watson and others conducted behaviorist research that reflected a commitment to studying practical problems. His subsequent research on emotional responses as conditioned during childhood is a good example. In their famous experiment with 11-month-old Albert B., Watson and Rosalie Rayner (1920) endeavored to condition fear of an animal in the infant, to demonstrate that this conditioned emotional response could be transferred to similar objects, to show that the response would persist over time, and to develop a method to remove the conditioned fear reaction. In the first three endeavors, they were successful. Prior to training, Albert showed no fear response to animals and objects presented to him, including a white rat, a rabbit, a dog, masks with hair, and cotton wool. He did exhibit a fear reaction in response to the noise made by a hammer being struck against a steel bar by an examiner standing behind him. To condition the fear response to a previously neutral animal, Watson and Rayner began trials in which the presentation of a white rat to Albert was paired with the striking of the hammer on the bar behind him. Within seven pairings of the two stimuli, the fear response had been completely conditioned, and presentation of the white rat alone was sufficient to elicit crying and escape behaviors in Albert. Upon further testing, the researchers determined that the conditioned fear response had transferred (or generalized) to a rabbit, a dog, a seal fur coat, cotton wool, Watson's hair, and a Santa Claus mask. Furthermore, the fear response to such objects was still present 1 month after the trials. Watson and Rayner planned to attempt the removal of the conditioned fear response in Albert, but the infant left the hospital where the experiments were conducted before any such attempts could be made.

Four years later, however, with assistance from Watson, Mary Cover Jones successfully unconditioned an existing fear response to white rabbits and similar objects in a 2-year, 10-month-old boy named Peter (Jones, 1924). To uncondition (or recondition) Peter's fear response, Jones first presented the rabbit to Peter on several occasions with other children in the room who eagerly interacted with the rabbit. Later she began pairing the presentation of the rabbit (successively closer, at first in a cage and then out of its cage) to Peter along with food and candy. By the end of the sessions, Peter showed no fear of the rabbit or similar objects. This was a significant early application of behavioral principles to a human problem. Through the work of B. F. Skinner, such applications would become an influential force in addressing countless human difficulties.

Skinner

Burrhus Frederick Skinner (1904–1990) graduated college with a major in English. After a year and a half as a struggling writer, he took a job in a bookstore in Greenwich Village in New York (Skinner, 1976). There he read Bertrand Russell's *Philosophy* (1925) and Watson's *Behaviorism* (1924/1930). Not long after, he applied and was accepted to graduate school in psychology at Harvard. In addition to psychology courses, Skinner also took classes in physiology under the department chair William Crozier. He studied Pavlov's work, and he began conducting research in the spirit of Pavlov and Watson's stimulus-response paradigm. Specifically, Skinner began investigating eating behavior in rats, which he postulated was a series of reflexes (Vargas, 2001). However, he soon observed that not all of the rats' behaviors were elicited by stimuli. Some behaviors were, instead, controlled by the stimuli that followed them. After 8 years of methodically investigating this phenomenon, Skinner (1938) published *The Behavior of Organisms,* in which he delineated the basic principles of behavior analysis.

In the studies summarized in *The Behavior of Organisms,* Skinner (1938) examined how the likelihood of a rat's emitting a target behavior could be changed by altering the consequences (in this case, the delivery of a food pellet) of that behavior. For these experiments, he constructed an "experimental box," which included a release chamber, a food tray, a waterspout, and a small brass lever that was connected to the food-dispensing magazine and to a recording device. Skinner used white rats because they were "cheap" (p. 47) and "amazingly stable" (p. 48). He chose lever pressing as the operant of study because it was an unconditioned response that occurred spontaneously in the rats from time to time before conditioning occurred. The food pellets he made contingent on responding were Purina Dog Chow.

In a typical experiment, a hungry rat would be placed behind the release door of the experimental box for 1 to 2 minutes before the experiment began (Skinner, 1938). This was done to control for any effects of the experimenter having just handled the rat. Once the door was opened, food would periodically be dispensed into the food tray from the magazine. The lever would not be connected to the magazine during this time, because it was first important for the rat to learn to respond to the tray only when it heard the magazine and not in the absence of the sound. Once this discriminative responding was established, the lever was connected and conditioning began. Any spontaneous lever pressing would now result in a food pellet being dispensed from the magazine into the tray. Lever pressing was recorded electrically in the form of a graph, with the total number of responses plotted over time. Because Skinner was interested in rate of responding, this was calculated from the slope of the lines created on the graphs. During initial conditioning, in general only four lever presses resulting in a food pellet being released into the tray were required for the rate of responding to increase dramatically. Skinner continued these experiments, delineating principles and demonstrating that the manipulation of reinforcement contingencies could powerfully shape behavior. He labeled these principles operant conditioning (Skinner, 1938).

Classical versus Operant Conditioning

Before continuing with the history of applied behavior analysis, it is important to note similarities and differences between classical, or respondent, conditioning as first described by Pavlov (1927/1928) and operant conditioning as described by Skinner, and to outline additional principles important in operant conditioning. Whereas respondent conditioning relies on antecedent stimuli predicting the presentation of another stimulus, operant conditioning relies on the consequent stimuli that follow a behavior. In other words, a consequent stimulus contingently following a behavior changes the future probability of the behavior recurring. Such a consequent stimulus is called a reinforcer.

In a situation in which a reinforcer is presented contingent on the occurrence of a particular behavior and subsequently increases the future probability of that behavior occurring, that reinforcer is referred to as a "positive reinforcer" (Newman et al., 2003). In a situation in which a reinforcer is removed contingent on the occurrence of a particular behavior and subsequently increases the future probability of that behavior occurring, that reinforcer is referred to as a "negative reinforcer" (Newman et al., 2003). Note that in each case the reinforcers increase the future probability of a target behavior occurring. One factor that will increase the likelihood of a stimulus acting as a reinforcer is an organism's deprivation status (e.g., the longer an animal has been deprived of food, the greater the chance of food acting as a reinforcer, whereas a satiated animal's behavior may not be reinforced by food). Deprivation is an example of an establishing operation, which is a change in or characteristic of the environment that affects the power of stimuli to serve as antecedents and consequences that affect the initiation and maintenance of behavior (Newman et al., 2003).

In respondent conditioning, extinction refers to weakening of the conditioned response following presentation of the conditioned stimulus in the absence of the unconditioned stimulus (Pavlov, 1927/1928). In operant conditioning, extinction refers to a procedure or process in which the rate of a behavior of interest ultimately decreases. It involves the removal of the reinforcement contingency that produced operant conditioning, either by no longer presenting the reinforcing stimulus or by breaking the contingency that maintained the behavior of interest (Leslie, 1996, p. 57; Newman et al., 2003). In terms of behavior or process, extinction is an observed decline in the frequency of a response (Leslie, 1996).

Similar to the change in future probability of the occurrence of a target behavior (mentioned earlier in terms of reinforcement), there are also operant processes that decrease the likelihood of future behavior. As is the case with reinforcement, there are two types of punishment: positive and negative. Positive punishment is the contingent presentation of a stimulus following a particular behavior that subsequently decreases the future probability of that behavior occurring (Newman et al., 2003). Negative punishment is the contingent removal of a stimulus following a particular behavior that subsequently decreases the future probability of that behavior occurring (Newman et al., 2003). In instances of both reinforcement and punishment, positive and negative do not follow the popular connotations of "good" and "bad," but rather the presentation or removal of a stimulus, respectively. Reinforcement and punishment occur not in response to intentions, but in response to environmental contingencies that either increase or decrease the future probability of behavior, respectively (Newman et al., 2003).

The concepts of reinforcement and extinction are similar to Thorndike's instrumental behavior, but are spoken about in slightly different ways. Thorndike spoke in terms of the behavior as being influenced by pleasure or satisfaction (Leslie, 1996). Operant behavior, or more specifically, reinforcement, simply states that a reinforcer is a stimulus event that increases the probability of the behavior occurring in the future regardless of the organism's subjective evaluation (Skinner, 1953).

Operant behavior is generally thought of as voluntary behavior, and respondent behavior is thought of as involuntary behavior. Respondent behavior refers to a class of responses that are elicited by certain conditioned or unconditioned antecedent stimuli (Johnston & Pennypacker, 1993). Operants are a class of behaviors that may or may not be topographically similar and produce functionally similar consequences (Baldwin & Baldwin, 2001; Johnston & Pennypacker, 1993). The two classes of behavior are not mutually exclusive.

One way that these types of behavior overlap is that consequences can be classically conditioned. A primary, or unconditioned, reinforcer is one that is able to work effectively as a reinforcer without any prior learning or conditioning (Newman et al., 2003; Skinner, 1953). When a neutral consequence is paired with an established reinforcer, it becomes a reinforcer as well, that is then referred to as a conditioned, or secondary, reinforcer (Newman et al., 2003). One type of conditioned reinforcer is called a generalized reinforcer. A generalized reinforcer is a reinforcer that has been paired with more than one primary reinforcer and can often be exchanged for another reinforcer (Newman et al., 2003; Skinner, 1953). The benefit of a generalized reinforcer is that it has an effect on behavior despite the deprivation status of the organism. Examples of generalized reinforcers are tokens, successful control of our environment, attention, approval, affection, and the submissiveness of others (Skinner, 1953).

An area of additional overlap is that operant and respondent conditioning both affect antecedent control, albeit in different ways. An antecedent stimulus is said to have stimulus control when it reliably increases or decreases the probability of a response based on the organism's history, or experience (Baldwin & Baldwin, 2001; Leslie, 1996). Respondent conditioning involves an antecedent's ability to predict the presentation of an unconditioned stimulus. In operant conditioning, a behavior can be emitted in response to a particular antecedent stimulus but not another; these stimuli are called discriminative stimulus and S delta, respectively (Newman et al., 2003). Also in operant conditioning, one function of an antecedent is to set the occasion for an organism to repeat or avoid a past behavior that was met with reinforcement or punishment, respectively (Baldwin & Baldwin, 2001). In other words, in one situation the antecedent stimulus predicts the presence of an unconditioned stimulus (conditioned stimulus, or conditioned elicitor), and in the other case, it indicates the availability of a reinforcing or punishing consequence if a certain behavior is emitted.

Related to this issue, Skinner (1938) used the term "differentiation" to refer to operant processes, unlike Pavlov's definition, which referred to respondent responses. In *The Behavior of Organisms,* Skinner distinguished between differentiation and discrimination. Differentiation refers to distinction of the form of the response that will elicit the reinforcer from other responses in the same situation. Discrimination refers to the ability to distinguish which antecedent stimulus signals the availability of a reinforcer.

Skinner and many others continued basic laboratory research on behavioral principles (the experimental analysis of behavior) following the publication of *The Behavior of Organisms*. It became evident through such studies that reinforcement leads to maintenance of behavior, even when reinforcement is not continuous. In other words, a reinforcer does not have to immediately follow every response for behavior to be repeated (Leslie, 1996). Ferster and Skinner (1957) wrote about this phenomenon in *Schedules of Reinforcement*. The authors reported the results of comprehensive studies with pigeons, and they outlined the effect on behavior of various schedules of reinforcement. Specifically, they outlined fixed ratio (FR), fixed interval (FI), variable ratio (VR), and variable interval (VI) schedules:

- *FR:* A schedule of reinforcement in which a behavior is reinforced after a set number of responses.

- *FI:* A schedule of reinforcement in which a behavior is reinforced at the first response that occurs after a set interval of time elapses.

- *VR:* A schedule of reinforcement in which a behavior is reinforced after a variable number of responses occur that average around a value required for delivery of reinforcement.

- *VI:* A schedule of reinforcement in which a behavior is reinforced after a variable time interval elapses that averages around a value required for delivery of reinforcement.

Early Applications to Human Behavior

Ferster and Skinner's (1957) book as well as Keller and Schoenfeld's (1950) *Principles of Psychology,* which made Skinner's ideas more widely available, spurred continued *basic* research and necessitated the publishing of the *Journal of the Experimental Analysis of Behavior* (*JEAB*) in 1958 (Michael, 2004). However, it was Skinner's (1953) *Science and Human Behavior* that encouraged work in *applied* behavior analysis, or behavior modification. In this book, Skinner advocated the application of the science of behavior to human issues. He contended that human behavior could, in fact, be predicted and controlled by identifying and manipulating relevant environmental contingencies. With *Science and Human Behavior,* Skinner suggested how the basic principles outlined in *The Behavior of Organisms* apply to human individual behavior, to the behavior of groups, and to the behavior of organizations. Subsequent researchers in the 1950s and 1960s, including Skinner's students, were among the first to demonstrate that behavioral principles could indeed be applied to improving the human condition. Such effects were widely studied in work with children, adults, individuals with developmental disabilities, and individuals in mental health institutions.

During the early experiments in which Skinner outlined the importance of reinforcement, he discussed human analogues, but these plans did not come to fruition (Vargas, 2001). One very early demonstration of the principles of operant conditioning in a human was conducted by Paul R. Fuller (1949). Fuller precisely applied Skinner's methodology to operantly condition vertical right arm movements in an 18-year-old man with a severe developmental disability and limited mobility. Specifically, prior to reinforcement, he recorded the baseline rate of the participant's right-arm movements, then he reinforced the target movements with a sugar and milk solution until the rate of responding increased to desired levels, and finally he reestablished the baseline rate of responding using extinction. This experiment demonstrated that behavioral principles could indeed be applied to behavior change in humans. However, technically it was not applied behavior analysis because it did not improve a socially important behavior for the participant.

In one of the first studies that could be considered applied behavior analysis, graduate students of Skinner, Nathan Azrin and Ogden Lindsley (1956), increased cooperative behavior among children playing a game using operant conditioning techniques, without giving any instructions to cooperate. The cooperative behaviors were reinforced using jellybeans. These behaviors increased when reinforced and decreased when reinforcement was no longer given. Free operant techniques were subsequently used to decrease a variety of problematic behaviors and to increase effective behaviors in children. These techniques involve altering contingencies involving free operants, which are behaviors that can occur at any time, without any specific cue, and often occur naturally (Newman et al., 2003). Early studies showed that the application of behavioral principles was effective in decreasing, for example, thumb sucking (Baer, 1962), tantrum behavior (Williams, 1959), and enuresis (Wickes, 1958). During this time, free operant techniques were also used with children to increase imitation (Baer & Sherman, 1964), walking (Harris, Johnston, Kelley, & Wolf, 1964), and appropriate verbal responses (Hart, Allen, Buell, Harris, & Wolf, 1964). Behavioral techniques were soon applied to the classroom setting, and researchers demonstrated that disruptive behaviors could be eliminated through extinction (ignoring such behaviors maintained by attention) and that appropriate classroom behaviors could be increased using positive reinforcement (Zimmerman & Zimmerman, 1962).

With adults, early studies in applied behavior analysis included increasing personal statements of opinion through positive reinforcement (Verplanck, 1955), reducing stuttering by making the presentation of an aversive stimulus (a loud tone) contingent upon it (Flanagan, Goldiamond, & Azrin, 1958), reducing the rate of tics in a musician by removing continuous music whenever a tic occurred (Barrett, 1962), and eliminating hysterical blindness by positively reinforcing use of visual cues (Brady & Lind, 1961). Techniques utilizing the principles of operant conditioning were also shown to be successful in treating obesity (Ferster, Nurnberger, & Levitt, 1962) and marital difficulties (Goldiamond, 1965).

Much of the early work in applied behavior analysis was conducted with individuals with developmental disabilities and with individuals in residential psychiatric facilities. Early studies successfully utilized the behavioral procedures of shaping, extinction, time-out (a period of removal from opportunities for reinforcement), and differential reinforcement to reduce problematic behaviors in children with autism (Wolf, Risley, & Mees, 1964) as well as positive reinforcement to increase the behavioral repertoires of these children (Ferster & DeMyer, 1962).

Of note, the use of differential reinforcement to reduce problematic behaviors often makes use of different intermittent reinforcement schedules. In procedures such as these, the problematic behaviors are often extinguished and other (desired) behaviors are reinforced (Leslie, 1996). There are five types of differential reinforcement schedules: differential reinforcement of other behavior (DRO), differential reinforcement of incompatible behavior (DRI), differential reinforcement of alternative behavior (DRA), differential reinforcement of low rates of responding (DRL), and differential reinforcement of high rates of responding (DRH; Leslie, 1996). In a DRO, any behavior other than the problematic behavior is reinforced. In a DRI, a particular behavior that is incompatible, or mutually exclusive, with the problem behavior that is reinforced. In a DRA, reinforcement is provided for alternative behavior to the problem behavior. In the DRL procedure, reinforcement is delivered after a specific interval has passed in order to reduce the problem behavior by progressively lengthening the required interval. In opposition to this procedure, the DRH schedule delivers reinforcement only when a behavior is emitted rapidly (Baldwin & Baldwin, 2001; Leslie, 1996).

Additional early studies illustrated that parents and teachers of children with developmental disabilities such as autism and mental retardation could be trained to successfully utilize behavioral procedures to manage child behavior in the home and school settings (Bijou, Birnbrauer, Kidder, & Tague, 1966; Hawkins, Peterson, Schweid, & Bijou, 1966). In the school setting, the application of behavioral principles (including the use of secondary reinforcers such as stars or check marks that could be accumulated upon assignment completion and exchanged for other desired items) was shown to be effective, not only in eliminating inappropriate behaviors in these children, but also in facilitating learning of school subjects, including reading, writing, and arithmetic (Birnbrauer, Bijou, Wolf, & Kidder, 1965).

Behavioral principles as applied to work with residents in psychiatric institutions were effective in reducing a wide range of problematic behaviors in these settings, including vocalizations related to the experience of hallucinations (Lindsley, 1959), refusal to eat (Ayllon & Haughton, 1962), and hoarding behaviors (Ayllon, 1963). Once trained, nursing staff could effectively utilize techniques such as extinction and differential reinforcement to reduce problematic behaviors and increase adaptive behaviors in their patients, with researchers assuming a supervisory role (Ayllon & Michael, 1959).

Many of these institutional studies used various procedures to decrease or increase specific behaviors in one or two participants. Ayllon and Azrin (1965) endeavored to standardize and extend applications of behavior analysis to facilitate improvements in a wide array of behaviors in large numbers of adult patients in a psychiatric facility. Working with an entire ward population (up to 44 patients) at Anna State Hospital in Anna, Illinois, Ayllon and Azrin used a reinforcement program to increase participation and performance in ward jobs. These jobs included dietary assistant, cleaning assistant, laundry assistant, and recreational assistant. Because salient reinforcers for each patient tended to vary and many such reinforcers were impractical to deliver consistently and immediately following job participation (e.g., attention from the psychologist), the researchers used conditioned, or secondary, reinforcers in the form of specially designed tokens. Performance of each task was rewarded with a given number of tokens, which could then be exchanged in various amounts at designated times for a variety of desired reinforcers, for example, attention, privacy, and consumables. The program dramatically increased job participation and performance among patients, and it was quickly adapted for use by other professionals in facilities for children with mental retardation and juvenile offenders (Ayllon & Azrin, 1965). Programs such as this would become known as token economies (see Ayllon & Azrin, 1968).

Characteristics of Applied Behavior Analysis as Science

Several of the early endeavors in applied behavior analysis were published in *JEAB* and were collected in edited works such as *Case Studies in Behavior Modification*

(Ullmann & Krasner, 1965) and *Control of Human Behavior* (Ulrich, Stachnik, & Mabry, 1966). However, the body of applied research continued to grow and soon necessitated the publication of a counterpart to *JEAB*, the *Journal of Applied Behavior Analysis* (Risley, 2001). In the first issue in 1968, Baer et al. summarized dimensions relevant to studies in applied behavior analysis. In addition to the obvious characteristics of being "applied, behavioral, and analytic," the authors suggested that such studies should also be "technological, conceptually systematic, and effective" and "should display some generality" (p. 92). To be considered applied, studies should consider problems that are important to society and to the individual. As behavioral, the studies should precisely measure what an individual does and should include measures of reliability among those observing such behavior. Baer and colleagues suggested that in an analytic study, the experimenter must reliably demonstrate control over the behavior under study, such that the effect on behavior is replicable.

Two experimental designs that can illustrate such control are the reversal design and the multiple baseline design (Baer et al., 1968). In a reversal design, baseline levels of the target behavior are measured, then the variable of interest is applied and the target behavior is measured for change. If change occurs, the variable of interest is removed, and the target behavior is again measured. If the variable of interest was responsible for the behavior change, when it is removed the behavior change will no longer be observed. Finally, the variable of interest is reapplied, and the target behavior is measured to determine if the change recurs. If it does, there is evidence of behavioral control. When reversing a target behavior is not desired or impossible, the multiple baseline design can be used to demonstrate control (Baer et al., 1968). In this design, multiple target behaviors are identified and baseline levels are measured. A variable of interest is applied to one behavior and changes in that behavior are recorded, as well as the lack of change in the other behaviors. The variable of interest is then applied to another target behavior, and if it also changes while other behaviors go unchanged, there is evidence that this variable is successful in controlling behavior.

To be technological, Baer and colleagues (1968) suggested, the procedures used in studies in applied behavior analysis should be sufficiently described and should include specific details so that the study can be replicated. By conceptually systematic, the authors meant that such studies should include a discussion of the behavioral principles that are utilized in the procedure. With regard to effectiveness, the authors contended that studies in applied behavior analysis should strive for effects that are of sufficient size to be useful to the individual and those influenced by the individual's behavior. Finally, the authors indicated that such studies should aim for behavior change that has generality over time, across settings, and/or across similar behaviors.

Research including many of these dimensions of applied behavior analysis continued into the 1970s and 1980s, and, although work continued in educational and institutional settings, applied behavioral applications expanded into new arenas. Behavioral research provided benefits to community programs; for example, researchers used the principles of reinforcement (Kohlenberg & Phillips, 1973) and stimulus control (O'Neill, Blanck, & Joyner, 1980) to reduce littering and increase proper waste disposal. In addition, behavioral techniques were successfully used to increase use of seat belts (Geller, Paterson, & Talbott, 1982). Behavioral principles were also applied successfully to improving health-related behaviors, including increasing medical appointment keeping (Friman, Finney, Rapoff, & Christophersen, 1985) and pursuit of dental care (Reiss & Bailey, 1982), as well as facilitating healthier dietary choices (Stark, Collins, Osnes, & Stokes, 1986). Early studies in the area of sports psychology indicated that application of behavioral principles could facilitate, for example, practice attendance among athletes (McKenzie & Rushall, 1974) as well as skills acquisition in sports such as football, tennis, and gymnastics (Allison & Ayllon, 1980). Studies of applied behavior analysis were also conducted in industrial settings. Applications in the business world were effective in changing a host of work-related behaviors, including reducing tardiness (Hermann, DeMontes, Domínguez, Montes, & Hopkins, 1973) and enhancing job performance (Pierce & Risley, 1974).

In the 20 years following the first publication of the *Journal of Applied Behavior Analysis,* research in behavior analysis and modification continued to proliferate, and several additional journals were developed to publish related work, including, *Behavior Therapy* in 1970, the *Journal of Organizational Behavior Management* in 1977, and the *Behavior Analyst* in 1978 (Miltenberger, 1997). In 1987, Baer, Wolf, and Risley again examined the dimensions of applied behavior analysis. They concluded that the components applied, behavioral, analytic, conceptual, technological, effective, and capable of generalization continued to be essential in studies of applied behavior analysis. They also acknowledged that the complexity of the definitions of these terms had increased. The authors suggested that studies after 20 years and into the future may include consideration of how socially important problems are identified, more complex experimental design to take into account contextual factors, consideration of the potential for methods to be adapted to additional settings, measures of social validity, and increased focus on interventions at both the individual and system levels.

CURRENT APPLICATIONS

To implement any psychological intervention effectively, it is imperative that the clinician and treatment team first conduct a comprehensive, detailed assessment. This assessment is done to best ascertain the nature of the problem and assist in subsequent treatment planning. Although many assessment procedures are based on a conceptualization of behavior as a manifestation of an underlying disorder, behavioral assessment assumes that an individual's behavior is context-dependent. Therefore, there is recognition that behavior may not be stable across various situations; thus, behavior should be assessed in a situation-dependent manner (Galassi & Perot, 1992). Behavioral assessment utilizes an ideographic approach, focusing on addressing contingencies that directly influence an *individual's* behavior. Given the need for detailed assessment that considers individual-specific context and contingencies, applied behavior analysis includes a procedure known as functional analysis to determine the form and function of relevant behavior.

Functional Analysis of Behavior

A crucial step in applied behavior analysis is conducting the functional assessment. A functional assessment allows the practitioner to identify and describe the problem behavior and the antecedents and consequences of that behavior in the context within which it occurs. The individual performing the behavior cannot be separated from current and historical contexts.

The objective of the functional assessment, or functional case conceptualization, is to obtain data that will be used to develop an effective treatment strategy that produces the desired outcome (S. C. Hayes, Nelson, & Jarrett, 1987). This is accomplished by identifying the purpose that behavior serves and hypothesizing, based on that information, which antecedents and consequences might be manipulated to decrease maladaptive behavior and optimize positive change.

Behavior analysts differentiate between functional assessment and functional analysis. Functional assessment refers to the procedures involved in clarifying antecedents and consequences; functional analysis refers to the direct manipulation of environmental contingencies in order to observe their impact on the target behavior (Gresham, Watson, & Skinner, 2001). In more complicated cases, functional analysis may include psychotherapy that focuses on reducing aversive (or appetitive) conditioning in addition to the direct altering of environmental factors. Proper functional analysis continues throughout treatment, and plans are modified if evaluation indicates that the treatment is not effective. Thorough analysis includes consideration of respondent and operant contingencies as well as their interactions (Wilson & Murrell, 2002).

Applied Behavior Analysis for Childhood Disorders

Although there are some concerns about the traditional use of behavior analysis, myriad complex behavioral issues have been dramatically improved through the application of applied behavior analytic procedures in home, school, and primary care settings. In addition, whereas pharmacological interventions have also been shown to be helpful with childhood disorders, research suggests that a combination of pharmacological and psychosocial interventions, particularly behavioral ones, can often maximize treatment gains (Hinshaw, Klein, & Abikoff, 2002).

Concerns, Common Obstacles, and Considerations

In addition to concerns about the use of traditional behavior analysis, there are common obstacles that occur during implementation. Therefore, several factors need to be considered in design and evaluation of applied behavior analyses. Of particular importance are generalizability, ease of implementation, and experimental design.

Pelham, Wheeler, and Chronis (1998) criticized behavioral interventions by pointing out that many treatment gains that are initially shown within the therapeutic milieu fail to generalize after the intervention is completed. Therefore, it is important to use interventions outside of a laboratory setting or therapeutic environment to increase the probability of the behavior generalizing to more natural settings. To do this, it is often necessary to train others to implement an intervention.

In child cases, it is important for involved parents and teachers to be motivated and able to carry out the ABA (Kazdin, 2000; Pelham et al., 1998). To enhance treatment success outside of the therapy setting, it is therefore important to identify all factors involved in enhancing and maintaining parents' and teachers' adherence to the treatment protocol. In addition, for functional relationships between independent and dependent variables to be established, it is imperative that interventions be implemented accurately and with integrity (Gresham, Gansle, & Noell, 1993). In other words, one wants to ensure that the individuals responsible for implementing the intervention are doing so correctly and consistently.

Many assessment techniques and interventions focus on the environmental contingencies regulating the child's behavior. Allen and Warzak (2000) emphasize the importance of also examining environmental contingencies that control parent, teacher, and clinician behavior. For example, many treatments are most successful when the parents are directly involved in implementing interventions for the child. Therefore, it is also important to examine the antecedents and consequences of parental behavior. The use of idiographic assessment increases the likelihood that appropriate contingencies will be identified. Often, environmental contingencies are directly related to the parent's adherence to treatment guidelines when implementing interventions (Allen & Warzak, 2000). It should be noted that contingencies regulating teachers' and clinicians' behavior should also be considered because they, too, can influence the effectiveness of the intervention.

Another factor related to effectiveness is strength of experimental design. Many behavioral studies have failed to operationally define the independent variable (such as the intervention) and to measure the accuracy with which it is implemented (Gresham et al., 1993). These flaws in experimental design can lead to failed attempts at using and evaluating behavior analytic interventions. To make scientific advances, the independent and dependent variables must be operationally defined. This is especially important in facilitating accurate replication (Gresham et al., 1993).

When generalizability, ease of implementation, and experimental design are considered, ABA evidences great success. Behavioral principles and applied behavior analytic techniques can be successfully used with children with Autistic Disorder and other pervasive developmental disabilities, Attention-Deficit/Hyperactivity Disorder (ADHD), and pediatric medical conditions such as elimination disorders (e.g., enuresis and encopresis), sleep problems, and a variety of habit disorders (trichotillomania, thumb sucking, and hair pulling). In addition, ABA is effective in treating children with Conduct Disorder and dealing with parenting problems that result from such symptomatology. It is also successfully used to address academic issues in classroom settings, with both children and teachers. The following discussion is meant to provide a sampling of some of the ways behavioral principles and the behavior analytic process, including functional assessment of problem behaviors, are currently applied to the treatment of various clinical problems across settings.

Pervasive Developmental Disorders

Applied behavior analysis facilitates the discovery and evaluation of interventions with individuals with developmental delays, such as autism spectrum disorders and mental retardation (Frea & Vittimberga, 2000). In fact, a perusal of the current behavior analytic literature indicates that the majority of studies are being conducted with individuals with mental retardation or developmental delays (Carr, Coriaty, & Dozier, 2000; Reid, 1991).

Lovaas and colleagues (e.g., Lovaas, 1987) conducted early studies examining the impact of utilizing operant procedures to address behavioral problems in children with autism. This early work used discrete trial training to evoke and reinforce appropriate behaviors. Punishers were used to decrease inappropriate behaviors such as self-stimulatory behavior, self-injury, and incorrect vocalizations. A discrete trial is an intense, brief cycle of instruction between the instructor and the child that is used to facilitate the learning of new information and communication. One benefit of discrete trial training is that professional and trained paraprofessionals and family members can implement the procedures with the child (Smith, 2001). A typical discrete trial consists of five representative components: the cue (or discriminative stimulus), a prompt in which the instructor aids the child in responding, the actual response, a consequence, and an intertrial interval that is a brief pause before the next trial begins (Smith, 2001). In recent years, these discrete trial interventions have been modified to facilitate their use in classroom settings.

Lovaas's Young Autism Project at UCLA serves as the prototype of discrete trial training and is aimed at children under age 4. It is a time-intensive program that involves 40 hours per week of one-to-one training sessions for 3 years. It has shown success in helping children with developmental disabilities to acquire new information and new discrimination among cues.

Attention-Deficit/Hyperactivity Disorder

Direct contingency management, clinical behavior therapy, and self-management skills are three commonly used behavioral interventions for treatment of ADHD (Hinshaw et al., 2002). Contingency management procedures involve direct attempts to manipulate antecedent and reinforcement procedures to decrease problem behaviors and increase prosocial ones. Examples of contingency management procedures are time-out, in which the child is prevented from receiving reinforcement; token economy procedures; and regulating feedback from parents and/or teachers (Kronenberger & Meyer, 2001). Contingency management procedures are typically used in more professional settings, and treatment gains are often more pronounced than they are in the child's home environment (Pelham et al., 1998). Outpatient clinical behavior therapy is successful in helping parents learn to incorporate contingency management procedures in the home to facilitate treatment consistency and enhance treatment outcome (for a review, see Pelham et al., 1998).

Both direct contingency management and clinical behavior therapy place considerable demands on those implementing the programs. Self-management is a child-focused behavioral intervention for ADHD that enables the child to identify, monitor, and reinforce his or her own behaviors, thereby reducing demands on parents and teachers (Braswell & Bloomquist, 1991). Because self-management requires the child to focus on and monitor his or her own behaviors accurately in order to earn reinforcement, it not only reduces symptoms, but it also fosters independence and personal control over behavior (Barry & Messer, 2003). Self-management can be implemented in a regular classroom or at home with some initial help from the teacher or parents, respectively. This technique is very effective at increasing on-task behaviors and improving academic performance while decreasing disruptive behaviors (Barry & Messer, 2003). Due to the self-monitoring and self-evaluation components, it is likely that self-management is more appropriate for older middle school, junior high, and high school students.

Behavioral Pediatrics

Behavior problems are often seen in primary care settings, and behavior pediatrics represents the merger between applied behavior analytic principles and pediatric medicine (Blum & Friman, 2000). Behavioral pediatrics is a broad area of study that focuses on pediatric behavior problems (such as sleeping dysfunction and elimination disorders) and health (Blum & Friman, 2000). Behavioral principles are used successfully to treat elimination disorders such as enuresis and encopresis. A number of behavioral interventions have been identified and studied to treat nocturnal enuresis in children, and the most well-known and accepted practice is the urine alarm ("bell and pad") and cleanliness training intervention (see Mowrer & Mowrer, 1938, as cited in Kronenberger & Meyer, 2001, for a description). Operant theorists suggest that the success of the bell and pad intervention among children can be attributed to negative reinforcement: specifically, the absence of the alarm and having to perform cleanliness training, which includes cleaning themselves and the toilet, changing their clothes, and changing the bed linens.

Applied behavior analysis is used with children who have a variety of other pediatric conditions, including asthma (e.g., Renne & Creer, 1976), diabetes (e.g., Epstein et al., 1981), feeding disorders (e.g., Coe et al., 1997), and other medical problems. Application of behavioral principles is also effective in increasing child and parent compliance with medical procedures and treatment (see Matthews, Spieth, & Christophersen, 1995). For example, in one study, contingency management was used to increase cooperative behavior in 3- to 6-year-old children during dental work (Allen & Stokes, 1987). Escape and attention were provided when children displayed nondisruptive behaviors during successively more invasive presentations of dentistry tools. Children were also rewarded with tangible reinforcers (i.e., stickers and toys) for remaining cooperative during increasing periods of time. Physiological arousal as well as disruptive behavior decreased from baseline (Allen & Stokes, 1987).

Conduct Disorder and Parenting Problems

Behavioral therapies based on operant learning have been used to address childhood conduct problems and to enhance the child's ability to formulate appropriate solutions to problems. Brestan and Eyberg (1998) reviewed current literature in hopes of identifying effective psychosocial treatments for Conduct Disorder, Oppositional Defiant Disorder, and associated behavior problems. Despite variability in methodological rigor, the more recent and well-designed studies were shown to be effective in decreasing negative behavior. One such treatment is problem-solving skills training (PSST). This treatment, which is "probably effi-cacious," is often used to assist children in formulating prosocial responses. Games and actual social situations are used to decrease the likelihood of aggressive be-haviors (Brestan & Eyberg, 1998). Recent modifications of PSST rely heavily on applied behavior analytic principles such as shaping appropriate behavior and ex-tinguishing maladaptive responses (Kazdin, 2000).

Given the environmental contingencies that promote misconduct and possibly later antisocial behavior, PSST is often used in conjunction with parent management training (PMT; Weisz, 2004), a home-based intervention that is based on the premise that many maladaptive behaviors are due to dysfunctional parent-child interactions. Parents are taught underlying behavioral principles and skills to enhance the quality of interactions with their child, decrease problem behaviors, and facilitate adaptive behaviors. More specifically, parents are taught to implement reinforcement and punishment procedures and set appropriate rules and boundaries. In addition, the work focuses on enhancing problem-solving skills (Kazdin, 2000).

Parent-child interaction therapy (PCIT) is another evidence-based treatment de-signed to enhance interactions between parents and children and decrease parental stress (Eisenstadt, Eyberg, McNeil, Newcomb, & Funderburk, 1993). It is com-monly used with preschool children and emphasizes teaching communication skills and behavioral principles to parents to implement in play situations with their chil-dren. The parents are given feedback on their use of the skills during the ongoing session. Initially, PCIT involves a child-directed play interaction in which the child leads the activities; this is followed by the parent-led interaction in which the par-ent utilizes appropriate communication and feedback to direct the play session. Finally, appropriate discipline is taught. Sessions use positive and negative rein-forcement strategies to increase prosocial behaviors and decrease maladaptive ones (Eisenstadt et al., 1993).

Parent training programs often focus on enhanced consistency in efforts to maintain treatment gains. Most often, this work with youth and parents involves consistent application of reinforcement strategies and limited use of punishment procedures to facilitate behavior change (Thorpe & Olson, 1997). However, child-hood behavior problems are characteristic of a number of childhood disorders and are often embedded within a problematic environmental context that maintains the child's problematic behaviors and makes lasting changes difficult. Kazdin and Whitley (2003) found that an added treatment component that specifically addressed parental stress improved overall therapeutic change when used with other models (such as PSST and PMT). Similarly, Weinberg (1999) found that training programs for parents of children with ADHD enhanced parental comprehension of behavior management principles and reduced overall stress related to parenting a child with ADHD.

Classroom Settings

In addition to substantial contributions to special education, applied behavior anal-ysis is effectively used in general classroom settings. Historically, applied behavior analysis has focused on consequential procedures such as contingency management procedures using reinforcement and punishment. Due to ethical concerns, such as excessive reliance on punitive or punishment procedures, applied behavior analysis has begun to shift focus and now also includes emphasis on antecedent control (Dunlap, Kern, & Worcester, 2001).

Token economies used in the classroom setting are well-established treatments for ADHD (Pelham et al., 1998). Whole-classroom token economies to manage disruptive classroom behavior may be more practical to implement than individualized token economies (Filcheck, McNeil, Greco, & Bernard, 2004). Token economies reward children for prosocial behaviors by awarding them with secondary reinforcers, such as tokens, that can be exchanged for a more powerful reinforcer. Occasionally, tokens can be taken away from the child contingent upon maladaptive behaviors. Removing tokens from the child is called response cost (Kronenberger & Meyer, 2001). Appropriate implementation is crucial to the success of such token economies.

Implementation of an intervention is an important matter in the classroom. A study by Greenwood, Terry, Arreaga-Mayer, and Finney (1992) looked at the possible moderating role of implementation factors in students' achievement in a classwide peer tutoring program. They instructed teachers to observe and record the students' successes and failures during periods when students were responsible for tutoring peers in spelling tasks. Students who were challenged by and mastered the material received the best implementation of the program. Interaction between the students was also seen to have an effect on student performance.

To enhance student performance, Lindsley (1992) expressed a hope for classroom settings to employ a behavioral precision teaching (PT) approach instead of the traditional lecturing approach. This method intends to provide more individualized, rapid progress, using a format in which the teacher acts more as a facilitator, and the students are responsible for their progress in terms of timing performance, counting, and daily charting (Lindsley, 1992). This approach involves the utilization of repeated practice with an error-correction procedure in place, along with aims expressed in terms of fluency and monitored with the use of standard celeration charts (McDowell & Keenan, 2001). The fluency factor is an important component in PT because it takes into account both accuracy and rate of responding, with the latter shown to be more sensitive to environmental changes than percentage correct (Lindsley, 1992). The application of rate of response and cumulative recording to the classroom setting comes from a free operant conditioning background (Lindsley, 1992). The use of PT in classrooms has allowed for exponential learning gains, such as seen in Morningside Academy with gains of two to three grade-level advances per year from 1980 to 1987 (Lindsley, 1992). (See Lindsley, 1992, for a brief review of important features involved in PT.)

The use of PT procedures provides gains in fluency and endurance, or attention span, in learned material (McDowell & Keenan, 2001). McDowell and Keenan reported a case study in which the use of PT procedures with a child diagnosed with ADHD resulted in an increase in correct responding, a decrease in incorrect responding, and an increase in on-task behavior. A return to baseline procedure prior to the acquisition of goals shows a decrease in performance, whereas a return to baseline after goals are acquired shows maintenance in rate of correct responding and on-task performance (Lindsley, 1992; McDowell & Keenan, 2001).

Concern with frequency of response can be seen in other classroom procedures as well. Programmed instruction is a technique based on reinforcement contingencies in which a correct answer is contingent upon a specified preceding behavior (Kritch & Bostow, 1998). In other words, instructional material is presented in a sequence that requires successively more correct responding. Typically, students are required to fill in the blanks in lessons as they work through these programs at their own pace. They are provided feedback and the correct responses immediately after providing an answer. Kritch and Bostow conducted a study that underscores the importance of frequency in responding in programmed instruction. The authors found that students in the high-density response requirement condition (i.e., the condition that demanded frequent response) performed better on tests than students who spent equivalent time on the task without any requirement that they respond. The participants in the high-density responding group were also better able to apply the knowledge than other groups.

Despite the widespread success of behavioral interventions in the classroom, Axelrod, Moyer, and Berry (1990) indicated that many teachers fail to use behavioral interventions. Teachers are rarely taught how to implement behavioral strategies prior to entering the classroom. Axelrod and colleagues suggest that behavior analysts should focus on facilitating the accurate use of behavioral principles by individuals other than behavior analysts. One way to address this problem is to teach behavior analysis to teachers; another solution is to train clients to monitor and adapt their own behavior.

Outpatient Therapy

As mentioned, applied behavior analysis is successful in treating myriad childhood behavioral disorders, pediatric medical disorders, and accompanying parent problems. There is a recent trend, often known as clinical behavior analysis, to rely on behavior analytic principles to address more complex psychological disorders. To best understand the emergence of clinical behavior analysis, a brief history of behavior therapy is required.

The Waves of Behavior Therapy

Traditionally, behavior therapy has shown a commitment to empiricism by examining overt behaviors and modifying environmental contingencies. The goal of early behavioral treatment was to reduce problematic behaviors and/or symptoms. Less overt psychological phenomena, such as thoughts and emotions, were of little interest to early behavior therapists. This lack of interest likely resulted from difficulty in manipulation, as behavior analysis (a radical behavioral perspective) never underestimated such factors. The focus on elimination of problematic behaviors and alleviation of symptoms represents *first-order* change processes: the direct targeting of symptoms and behaviors in clinical treatment with the goal of their alleviation and/or elimination. This first wave of behavior therapy was criticized, however, for not providing an adequate account of human language and cognition (Eifert & Forsyth, 2005).

The second wave of behavior therapies sought the integration of cognitive and behavioral models to facilitate treatment development and address criticisms in the literature. The application of direct change strategies to behavior and cognition has evidenced success in the reduction of psychological symptoms (S. C. Hayes, 2004). However, although research suggests that cognitive-behavior therapy (CBT) works with a variety of disorders, dismantling studies and meta-analyses suggest that researchers do not have a comprehensive understanding of *why* it works. It appears as if CBT might not work through its proposed mechanisms (e.g., Jacobson et al., 1996). Without an understanding of the mechanisms through which a treatment works, it is less likely that researchers and practitioners will be able to effectively reach the goals of behavior analysis: to predict and control (or influence) behavior.

Given the need to address language and cognition *and* have a treatment that is closely linked to examinable and manipulable explanatory mechanisms, many clinicians and applied researchers alike have made attempts to design and utilize behavior analytic treatments that address complex phenomena. These treatments, known as the *third-wave* behavior therapies, often focus on acceptance of private psychological events (e.g., thoughts and feelings) to facilitate behavior change. Further, recent therapies have incorporated spirituality, dialectics, Eastern wisdom traditions, and interpersonal functioning and values to broaden the scope of existing treatments. Consistent with behavior analysis, third-wave therapies rely on a philosophy of contextualism and pragmatism that emphasizes the function of the behavior (what purpose it serves and whether it results in positive or negative reinforcement) rather than its form (S. C. Hayes & Bissett, 2000).

These newer approaches encourage deeper analysis of private events in both assessment and treatment phases (S. C. Hayes & Brownstein, 1986). The third wave includes such treatments as dialectical behavior therapy (Linehan, 1993), mindfulness-based cognitive therapy (Segal, Williams, & Teasdale, 2002), integrative behavioral couples therapy (Jacobson, Christenson, Prince, Cordova, & Eldridge, 2000), functional analytic psychotherapy (Kohlenberg & Tsai, 2003), and acceptance and commitment therapy (S. C. Hayes, Strosahl, & Wilson, 1999). Third-wave behavior therapists may utilize first-order change techniques in their work. However, the ultimate and overarching goal of third-wave treatments is to facilitate *second-order* change. Second-order change refers to a shift in an individual's reactions and responses to his or her problems, regardless of whether the problems are decreased or eliminated. In other words, second-order change strategies target the processes of thinking and feeling rather than the content. This shift is achieved through the use of techniques that serve two primary purposes: (1) to alter the function (or meaning) of specific behaviors through the consideration of contextual factors and (2) to expand one's behavior repertoire so that, in the presence of distressing private events, one may flexibly choose to behave in a multitude of ways (S. C. Hayes, Strosahl, Bunting, Twohig, & Wilson, 2004.)

Overview of Acceptance and Commitment Therapy and Relational Frame Theory

Acceptance and commitment therapy (ACT; S. C. Hayes et al., 1999) has been influential in the emergence of third-wave behavior therapies. The developers describe

ACT as "a therapy approach that uses acceptance and mindfulness processes, and commitment and behavior change processes, to produce greater psychological flexibility" (S. C. Hayes et al., 2004, p. 13). The two halves of this description map onto the previously mentioned purposes of second-order change techniques. Work that increases a nonjudgmental awareness of private events and their relation to an individual in the present moment (i.e., acceptance and mindfulness processes) serves to facilitate a change in function of private events. Values assessment, behavioral contracting, behavior activation, and related techniques (i.e., commitment and behavior change processes) are used to expand behavior. Depending on their pragmatic utility in the ever-changing treatment context, didactics, paradox, metaphors, and experiential exercises are used to achieve the goal of psychological and behavioral flexibility.

Acceptance and commitment therapy is widely applied behavior analysis. Like other applied behavior analytic treatments, the work draws on the philosophy of functional contextualism and pragmatism as well as the principles of conditioning. Therapy begins with a functional assessment and includes ongoing functional analysis that identifies overt problem behaviors along with antecedents and consequences. In addition, the analyses include assessment of covert events, especially values and barriers to value-consistent behavior. These barriers may include variables in the external environment and/or conditioned aversives.

Proponents of the ACT model distinguish between direct and indirect conditioning. Direct conditioning (respondent and operant learning) results from personal experience or direct sensory perception of another's experience. In contrast, indirect conditioning emerges from verbal behavior. For example, a mother may become worried that her child will die of an obscure disease that she heard about on television, though neither she nor anyone she knows has the disease. When a problematic private event has been directly conditioned, such as when a child who has been bitten by a dog is scared in the presence of dogs, an ACT therapist will do exposure as it is traditionally done (e.g., in this case, a systematic desensitization, changing environmental contingencies, to the physical presence of dogs). When psychological distress is the result of indirect learning, exposure is labeled defusion, and acceptance and mindfulness processes are targeted in treatment. The intent of traditional exposure is to reduce elicitation, arousal, or avoidance in the presence of noxious stimuli. Defusion is intended to serve a different purpose: the development of wide and flexible behavior in response to noxious stimuli.

Most often, clients will present for treatment with a desire to eliminate problems. This is consistent with the traditional exposure paradigm. However, when given a choice, many will work for the possibility of a broader life. In those cases, defusion techniques are included. From an ACT perspective, clients are repeatedly asked to choose the therapeutic direction and goals. If the client chooses to work for the possibility of a broader life, successful therapy shifts the focus from a negative reinforcement paradigm to a positive reinforcement paradigm in which the emphasis is on utilizing values to create a rich, vital, and meaningful life. This emphasis on a rich life and on values can make the difficult work of treatment feel more dignified. Values, then, can be seen as powerful conditioned reinforcers. How such positive reinforcement develops with only the possibility of broader experience can be explained by the processes associated with human language and cognition.

Acceptance and commitment therapy is based on an underlying theory of human language and cognition called relational frame theory (RFT; S. C. Hayes, Barnes-Holmes, & Roche, 2001), which is an operant account of indirect learning processes. Using traditional behavioral principles, or the principles of direct conditioning, such as generalized operants (Baer et al., 1968) and positive and negative reinforcement, RFT explains how humans derive relationships between stimulus events that have never been directly conditioned and suggests how these processes may underlie psychopathology.

Consider the following interactions as an example of how direct conditioning is related to RFT. A mother smiles and asks her child, "What am I doing?" The child responds by saying "Smiling," and the mother says, "Yes, good job! I am smiling!" The mother then frowns, asks the same question, and responds similarly when her child says, "Frowning." Thus, the child has been directly trained and reinforced for correctly answering the question "What am I doing?" Although the content changes, a generalized response develops, one in which the child's behavior of providing the corresponding label has been positively reinforced through the use of praise. The mother then says, "Show me your smile," and the child responds with a smile. The child is reinforced for discriminating smiling from other facial expressions as well as performing the act. A few years later, through similar reinforcement strategies, the child is taught that the sound *smile* goes with the letters s-m-i-l-e. Without any additional training or reinforcement, a child with typical verbal capacities will know (or derive) that the facial expression is the same as the written word.

Words then become functionally equivalent to the stimuli they represent. This indirect conditioning ability, or relational conditioning, helps us balance short- and long-term contingencies, plan for the future, and categorize and sort information. However, when these relational processes become the primary source of stimulus control, these indirect conditioning principles can reduce our contact with actual environmental contingencies. Thus, our ability to react flexibly in situations is diminished, and this contributes to psychopathology. The ACT model suggests that psychological rigidity occurs as a by-product of language and verbal behavior. More specifically, humans tend to react to verbally constructed rules as though they are true rather than as what they are: verbally constructed rules, essentially thoughts. This phenomenon is referred to as *cognitive fusion* (S. C. Hayes et al., 1999). Further, humans also engage in *experiential avoidance,* which refers to the tendency to decrease, fix, or control the form or frequency of internal events, even when doing so contributes to psychological distress (S. C. Hayes, Wilson, Gifford, Follette, & Strosahl, 1996). Experiential avoidance may be adaptive in situations that are transient and time-limited. However, when it is primarily a means of addressing problems in daily living, it can contribute to decreased quality of life (Wilson & Murrell, 2004).

Returning briefly to how ACT attempts to increase quality of life, the model includes six primary and overlapping components: acceptance, defusion, contact with the present moment, self-as-context, valuing, and committed action. *Acceptance* refers to a nonjudgmental awareness of private events, along with the recognition that struggling with the content of those events is ineffective. *Defusion* work, as previously discussed, involves assisting clients in recognizing that words, thoughts, feelings, and other such private events are not literal, real, or requiring of certain response. *Contact with the present moment* simply means that there is an ongoing effort by both the clinician and the client to remain focused on the here-and-now, as opposed to reliving the past or ruminating about the future. Although this is a process worked on in session, the skills ideally generalize to daily life. The aim of *self-as-context* is to differentiate between the content of psychological experiences and the context in which those experiences occur. In *valuing* work, clients are encouraged to identify what is important to them; therapists, along with clients, are expected to voice their values and make *committed action* to carrying out behaviors in accordance with those values.

Acceptance and Commitment Therapy with Children, Adolescents, and Families

There is growing empirical evidence to support the use of ACT with adults dealing with a variety of clinical disorders and behavioral problems (for a meta-analytic review, see S. C. Hayes, Luoma, Bond, Masuda, & Lillis, 2006). Researchers and clinicians are becoming interested in utilizing ACT for the treatment of childhood disorders as well as for the difficulties associated with parenting. Traditional ACT protocols are being modified to facilitate their applicability to children and adolescents. Such modifications in implementation include the use of more concrete language and multiple exemplars. Similarly, ACT techniques that are creative, interactive, and experiential rather than didactic or instructive are emphasized (Greco, Blackledge, Coyne, & Ehrenreich, 2005). Although treatment topics are chosen by the client, it is wise for the clinician to be aware of topics that are of typical relevance at various stages of development. For example, a clinician working with a 6-year-old should be prepared to discuss school entry difficulties. In addition, familiarity with games and television shows targeted toward young children is a plus. A clinician working with an adolescent may need to know more about current fashion trends and, more important, how the trends are related to burgeoning independence.

There are a few ACT treatment outcome studies that have been conducted with children, adolescents, and parents (for a review of current literature, see Murrell & Scherbarth, 2006). Case studies have shown promising results for youth with anorexia, anxiety, and chronic pain. One randomized clinical trial showed that ACT was more effective than medical treatment as usual for idiographic pain, and there are two ongoing randomized clinical trials that investigate the effectiveness of ACT in reducing delinquent behaviors. As with all child treatments, collateral information is often necessary while doing ACT, especially for functional analysis and other assessment. Information from parents is very important.

High levels of stress are often found among parents of children with psychological problems such as autism spectrum disorders and childhood aggression. From an ACT perspective, parenting deficits are thought to be associated with the parents' attempts to avoid painful emotions, thoughts, and experiences. Parents can make poor parenting choices to decrease their own negative psychological experiences. Consequently, this powerful motivation to avoid negative emotions may actually prohibit the development of new, more adaptive parenting skills (Coyne & Wilson, 2004). Blackledge and Hayes (2006) utilized an ACT group therapy format to address depression and stress among parents of children with autism. Significant decreases among depression levels, psychiatric symptoms, and parental stress were found at a 3-month follow-up after the group ended. Treatment consistent with ACT principles has also been effective in working with parents of aggressive children. For example, in one case study, ACT treatment components were used to facilitate more value-consistent behavior on the part of the parent (Coyne & Wilson, 2004). As a result, child misbehavior and parental stress decreased after the 3-month treatment ended.

Murrell and Scherbarth (2006) encourage use of sophisticated research methodology to determine the effectiveness of ACT with children, adolescents, and families. Specifically, they point to the need for studies with larger sample sizes and controlled designs. To date, most of the ACT studies with children and adolescents involve case studies and uncontrolled group designs. To establish ACT as a credible and empirically based approach for use with children and adolescents, more rigorous research designs are needed.

ETHICAL CONSIDERATIONS

Utilizing a new, not yet empirically supported approach like ACT comes with ethical concerns. As with many topics in psychology, there are ethical concerns about the utilization of more traditional applied behavioral analysis as well. Common misperceptions of behavior analytic procedures, particularly negative reinforcement programs, may result in ABA having a negative connotation among the general public. Misunderstandings of terminology can be easily corrected. However, the majority of concerns about the use of aversive procedures are not easily allayed, because there is not a clear-cut line of right and wrong.

Punishment: To Use or Not to Use

There is a debate over the use of aversive procedures, such as punishment, and what reasonably justifies the use of such procedures (see Axelrod, 1990, for a description). Iwata (1988) advised that behavior analysts should make attempts to refrain from the use of aversive procedures to modify behavior, as there are several negative consequences that might come from that process. One such consequence is that those who implement aversive procedures also acquire aversive properties. This could decrease demand of their services. Another possible consequence is that the addressed problems will not benefit from the use of aversive procedures. This could leave behavior analysts in the negative position of developing punishment procedures for populations that exhibit the most extreme negative behaviors. Iwata notes that aversive procedures should be utilized only as a last resort; in other words, in addressing maladaptive behavior, preference should be given first to using positive reinforcement programs.

Iwata (1987) states that the attempt to extinguish behavior can be detrimental when there is a potential of an extinction burst, a phenomenon in which behavior that is no longer reinforced increases in frequency, magnitude, and variability before it decreases (Newman et al., 2003). When the behavior in question is a life-threatening or harmful action, a temporary increase may be detrimental to the client. If unsuccessful attempts to extinguish behavior result in premature termination of the procedure, the behavior might inadvertently be reinforced at high levels (Iwata, 1987; Newman et al., 2003).

However, Iwata (1987) has also recognized the need for procedures such as punishment. Leslie (1996) suggests taking three steps when considering whether an aversive procedure should be used: First, define all involved terms; second, specify procedures to be considered; third, assess the possible consequences of the intervention, of the alternatives, and of taking no action. Leslie also stresses the need for an individualized assessment of the behavior and situation to examine important contextual aspects and the personal history of a client. General ethical principles may not be applicable because one solution will not be appropriate to all situations. There are multiple factors that should be considered in the decision of whether to use an aversive procedure. As mentioned, there is harm in failing to successfully implement an intervention. In addition, it is possible that behavioral effects such as aggression may emerge as a result of aversive procedure utilization (Leslie, 1996).

People often worry about the use of aversive procedures, yet they are already present in our natural environment (Axelrod, 1990; Leslie, 1996). The use of punishment allows for rapid response suppression (Leslie, 1996). When considering no intervention or alternatives to aversive procedures, Axelrod asks why one would want to waste a client's time with a procedure that is known to be less effective when there is a procedure available that is known to work. This is especially important when a problematic behavior could be life-threatening if allowed to continue, such as head banging or running into a busy street.

Sometimes Applied Behavior Analysis Is Painful

Sometimes punishment is necessary. Sometimes, even when punishment is not utilized, applied behavior analytic procedures can be painful. Treatment can be difficult. Another issue to consider is the balance between quality of life and the means of an intervention (L. J. Hayes & McCurry, 1990). One example is that of a cancer patient. If left untreated, the cancer may eventually be fatal. Yet while undergoing treatment, the side effects of a cure can cause an individual to be sick. The patient will need to come to a decision: to be sick now in order to feel better later, or to refuse treatment. An issue as complex as this would benefit from an empirical analysis of the phenomenon, which in turn carries its own ethical issues.

What to Do

Punishment, because it is easy and often effective, is reinforcing. Yet, there are clearly negative consequences related to its use. Some have suggested that an empirical understanding of topics such as punishment may allow us to reduce the use of such procedures. L. J. Hayes and McCurry (1990) remind us that aversive procedures serve a function for the greater good, but we cannot forget to contemplate the ends versus the means of an intervention. Finally, the complexity of these issues highlights the need for an idiographic approach.

SUMMARY

Applied behavior analysis is an area of psychological research and treatment endeavoring to use behavioral principles in an effort to improve socially important human behavior (Baer et al., 1968). Philosophically, applied behavior analysis can be seen as a materialistic, deterministic, contextual, and functional approach to science. Historically influenced by Russian physiologists, American animal psychologists, and early behaviorism's call for psychology as an objective science, applied behavior analysis was realized in the 1950s and 1960s following the work of B. F. Skinner (1938, 1953) as researchers began using the principles of operant conditioning to predict and influence human problem behavior. These early researchers applied behavioral principles and techniques, manipulating the antecedents and consequences of behavior, in the successful elimination of undesirable behaviors and the development of adaptive behaviors in schoolchildren, adults, individuals with developmental disabilities, and individuals in mental health institutions. In the 1970s and 1980s applications of behavior analysis broadened to examine and improve community programs, health-related behaviors, athletic performance, and work-related behaviors. Today, applied behavior analysis continues to be a burgeoning area of research and to offer effective, empirically supported methods of psychological treatment useful in addressing a host of human difficulties, including problems associated with ADHD, Oppositional Defiant Disorder, parenting, elimination disorders, developmental delay, and serious mental illness in home, school, and institutional settings. With the emergence of third-wave behavior therapies, techniques rooted in applied behavior analysis are being successfully extended to work in outpatient settings with individuals and couples grappling with a host of psychological difficulties.

REFERENCES

Allen, K. D., & Stokes, T. F. (1987). Use of escape and reward in the management of young children during dental treatment. *Journal of Applied Behavior Analysis, 20,* 381–390.

Allen, K. D., & Warzak, W. J. (2000). The problem of parental nonadherance in clinical behavior analysis: Effective treatment is not enough. *Journal of Applied Behavior Analysis, 33,* 373–391.

Allison, M. G., & Ayllon, T. (1980). Behavioral coaching in the development of skills in football, gymnastics, and tennis. *Journal of Applied Behavior Analysis, 13,* 297–314.

Axelrod, S. (1990). Myths that (mis)guide our profession. In A. C. Repp & N. N. Singh (Eds.), *Perspectives on the use of nonaversive and aversive interventions for persons with developmental disabilities* (pp. 59–72). Sycamore, IL: Sycamore Press.

Axelrod, S., Moyer, L., & Berry, B. (1990). Why teachers do not use behavior modification procedures. *Journal of Educational and Psychological Consultation, 1,* 309–320.

Ayllon, T. (1963). Intensive treatment of psychotic behaviour by stimulus satiation and food reinforcement. *Behaviour Research and Therapy, 1,* 53–61.

Ayllon, T., & Azrin, N. (1965). The measurement and reinforcement of behavior of psychotics. *Journal of the Experimental Analysis of Behavior, 8,* 357–383.

Ayllon, T., & Azrin, N. (1968). *The token economy: A motivational system for therapy and research.* New York: Appleton-Century-Crofts.

Ayllon, T., & Haughton, E. (1962). Control of the behavior of schizophrenic patients by food. *Journal of the Experimental Analysis of Behavior, 5,* 343–352.

Ayllon, T., & Michael, J. (1959). The psychiatric nurse as a behavioral engineer. *Journal of the Experimental Analysis of Behavior, 2,* 323–334.

Azrin, N. H., & Lindsley, O. R. (1956). The reinforcement of cooperation between children. *Journal of Abnormal and Social Psychology, 52,* 100–102.

Baer, D. M. (1962). Laboratory control of thumbsucking by withdrawal and representation of reinforcement. *Journal of the Experimental Analysis of Behavior, 5,* 525–528.

Baer, D. M., & Sherman, J. A. (1964). Reinforcement control of generalized imitation in young children. *Journal of Experimental Child Psychology, 1,* 37–49.

Baer, D. M., Wolf, M. M., & Risley, T. R. (1968). Some current dimensions of applied behavior analysis. *Journal of Applied Behavior Analysis, 1,* 91–97.

Baer, D. M., Wolf, M. M., & Risley, T. R. (1987). Some still-current dimensions of applied behavior analysis. *Journal of Applied Behavior Analysis, 20,* 313–327.

Baldwin, J. D., & Baldwin, J. I. (2001). *Behavior principles in everyday life* (4th ed.) Upper Saddle River, NJ: Prentice-Hall.

Barrett, B. H. (1962). Reduction in rate of multiple tics by free operant conditioning methods. *Journal of Nervous and Mental Diseases, 135,* 187–195.

Barry, L. M., & Messer, J. J. (2003). A practical application of self-management for students diagnosed with attention deficit/hyperactivity disorder. *Journal of Positive Behavior Interventions, 5,* 238–248.

Baum, W. M. (1994). *Understanding behaviorism: Science, behavior, and culture.* New York: Harper-Collins.

Bergmann, G. (1956). The contribution of John B. Watson. *Psychological Review, 63,* 265–276.

Biglan, A. (1995). *Changing cultural practices: A contextualist framework for intervention research.* Reno, NV: Context Press.

Biglan, A., & Hayes, S. C. (1996). Should the behavioral sciences become more pragmatic? The case for functional contextualism in research on human behavior. *Applied and Preventive Psychology: Current Scientific Perspectives, 5,* 47–57.

Bijou, S. W., Birnbrauer, J. S., Kidder, J. D., & Tague, C. (1966). Programmed instruction as an approach to the teaching of reading, writing, and arithmetic to retarded children. *Psychological Record, 16,* 505–522.

Birnbrauer, J. S., Bijou, S. W., Wolf, M. M., & Kidder, J. D. (1965). Programmed instruction in the classroom. In L. P. Ullmann & L. Krasner (Eds.), *Case studies in behavior modification* (pp. 358–363). New York: Holt, Rinehart and Winston.

Blackledge, J. T., & Hayes, S. C. (2006). Using acceptance and commitment therapy in the support of parents of children diagnosed with autism. *Child and Family Behavior Therapy, 28,* 1–18.

Blum, N. J., & Friman, P. C. (2000). Behavioral pediatrics: The confluence of applied behavior analysis and pediatric medicine. In J. Austin & J. E. Carr (Eds.), *Handbook of applied behavior analysis* (pp. 161–186). Reno, NV: Context Press.

Brady, J. P., & Lind, D. L. (1961). Experimental analysis of hysterical blindness: Operant conditioning techniques. *Archives of General Psychiatry, 4,* 331–339.

Braswell, L., & Bloomquist, M. L. (1991). *Cognitive-behavioral therapy with ADHD children: Child, family, and school interventions.* New York: Guilford Press.

Brestan, E. V., & Eyberg, S. M. (1998). Effective psychosocial treatments of conduct-disordered children and adolescents: 29 years, 82 studies, and 5,272 kids. *Journal of Clinical Child Psychology, 27,* 180–189.

Capaldi, E. J., & Proctor, R. W. (1999). *Contextualism in psychological research: A critical review.* Thousand Oaks, CA: Sage.

Carr, J. E., Coriaty, S., & Dozier, C. L. (2000). Current issues in the function-based treatment of aberrant behavior in individuals with developmental disabilities. In J. Austin & J. E. Carr (Eds.), *Handbook of applied behavior analysis* (pp. 91–112). Reno, NV: Context Press.

Chance, P. (1999). Thorndike's puzzle boxes and the origins of the experimental analysis of behavior. *Journal of the Experimental Analysis of Behavior, 72*, 433–440.

Coe, D. A., Babbitt, R. E., Williams, K. E., Hajimihalis, C., Synder, A. M., Ballard, C., et al. (1997). Use of extinction and reinforcement to increase food consumption and reduce expulsion. *Journal of Applied Behavior Analysis, 30*, 581–583.

Coyne, L. W., & Wilson, K. G. (2004). The role of cognitive fusion in impaired parenting: An RFT analysis. *International Journal of Psychology and Psychological Theory, 4*, 469–486.

Cziko, G. A. (2000). *The things we do: Using the lessons of Bernard and Darwin to understand the how and why of our behavior.* Cambridge, MA: MIT Press.

Dougher, M. J., & Hayes, S. C. (2000). Clinical behavior analysis. In M. J. Dougher (Ed.), *Clinical behavior analysis* (pp. 11–25). Reno, NV: Context Press.

Dunlap, G., Kern, L., & Worcester, J. (2001). ABA and academic instruction. *Focus on Autism and Other Developmental Disabilities, 16*, 129–136.

Eifert, G. H., & Forsyth, J. P. (2005). *Acceptance and commitment therapy for anxiety disorders: A practitioner's guide to using mindfulness, acceptance, and values-based behavior change strategies.* Oakland, CA: New Harbinger.

Eisenstadt, T. H., Eyberg, S., McNeil, C. B., Newcomb, K., & Funderburk, B. (1993). Parent-child interaction therapy with behavior problem children: Relative effectiveness of two states and overall treatment outcome. *Journal of Clinical Child Psychology, 22*, 42–51.

Epstein, L. H., Beck, S., Figueroa, J., Farkas, G., Kazdin, A. E., Daneman, D., et al. (1981). The effects of targeting improvements in urine glucose on metabolic control in children with insulin dependent diabetes. *Journal of Applied Behavior Analysis, 14*, 365–375.

Ferster, C. B., & DeMyer, M. K. (1962). A method for the experimental analysis of the behavior of autistic children. *American Journal of Orthopsychiatry, 32*, 89–98.

Ferster, C. B., Nurnberger, J. I., & Levitt, E. B. (1962). The control of eating. *Journal of Mathetics, 1*, 87–110.

Ferster, C. B., & Skinner, B. F. (1957). *Schedules of reinforcement.* Englewood Cliffs, NJ: Prentice-Hall.

Filcheck, H. A., McNeil, C. B., Greco, L. A., & Bernard, R. S. (2004). Using a whole-class token economy and coaching of teacher skills in a preschool classroom to manage disruptive behavior. *Psychology in the Schools, 41*, 351–361.

Flanagan, B., Goldiamond, I., & Azrin, N. (1958). Operant stuttering: The control of stuttering behavior through response-contingent consequences. *Journal of the Experimental Analysis of Behavior, 1*, 173–178.

Frea, W. D., & Vittimberga, G. L. (2000). Behavioral interventions for children with autism. In J. Austin & J. E. Carr (Eds.), *Handbook of applied behavior analysis* (pp. 247–274). Reno, NV: Context Press.

Friman, P. C., Finney, J. W., Rapoff, M. A., & Christophersen, E. R. (1985). Improving pediatric appointment keeping with reminders and reduced response requirement. *Journal of Applied Behavior Analysis, 18*, 315–321.

Fuller, P. R. (1949). Operant conditioning of a vegetative human organism. *American Journal of Psychology, 62*, 587–590.

Galassi, J. P., & Perot, A. R. (1992). What you should know about behavioral assessment. *Journal of Counseling and Development, 70*, 624–631.

Geller, E. S., Paterson, L., & Talbott, E. (1982). A behavioral analysis of incentive prompts for motivating seat belt use. *Journal of Applied Behavior Analysis, 15*, 403–415.

Goldiamond, I. (1965). Self-control procedures in personal behavior problems. *Psychological Reports, 17*, 851–868.

Greco, L. A., Blackledge, J. T., Coyne, L. W., & Ehrenreich, J. (2005). Integrating acceptance and mindfulness for child and adolescent anxiety disorders: Acceptance and commitment therapy as an example. In S. M. Orsillo & L. Roemer (Eds.), *Acceptance and mindfulness-based approaches to anxiety* (pp. 301–324). New York: Springer.

Greenwood, C. R., Terry, B., Arreaga-Mayer, C., & Finney, R. (1992). The classwide peer tutoring program: Implementation factors moderating students' achievement. *Journal of Applied Behavior Analysis, 25*, 101–116.

Gresham, F. M., Gansle, K. A., & Noell, G. H. (1993). Treatment integrity in applied behavior analysis with children. *Journal of Applied Behavior Analysis, 26*, 257–263.

Gresham, F. M., Watson, T. S., & Skinner, C. H. (2001). Functional behavioral assessment: Principles, procedures, and future directions. *School Psychology Review, 30,* 156–172.

Harris, F. R., Johnston, M. K., Kelley, C. S., & Wolf, M. M. (1964). Effects of positive social reinforcement on regressed crawling of a nursery school child. *Journal of Educational Psychology, 55,* 35–41.

Hart, B. M., Allen, K. E., Buell, J. S., Harris, F. R., & Wolf, M. M. (1964). Effects of social reinforcement on operant crying. *Journal of Experimental Child Psychology, 1,* 145–153.

Hawkins, R. P., Peterson, R. F., Schweid, E., & Bijou, S. W. (1966). Behavior therapy in the home: Amelioration of problem parent-child relations with the parent in a therapeutic role. *Journal of Experimental Child Psychology, 4,* 99–107.

Hayes, L. J., & McCurry, C. (1990). Moral and scientific aspects of the punishment controversy. In A. C. Repp & N. N. Singh (Eds.), *Perspectives on the use of nonaversive and aversive interventions for persons with developmental disabilities* (pp. 87–101). Sycamore, IL: Sycamore Press.

Hayes, S. C. (2004). Acceptance and commitment therapy and the new behavior therapies: Mindfulness, acceptance, and relationship. In S. C. Hayes, V. Follette, & M. Linehan (Eds.), *Mindfulness and acceptance: Expanding the cognitive-behavioral tradition* (pp. 1–29). New York: Guilford Press.

Hayes, S. C., Barnes-Holmes, D., & Roche, B. (Eds.). (2001). *Relational frame theory: A post-Skinnerian account of human language and cognition.* New York: Springer.

Hayes, S. C., & Bissett, R. T. (2000). Behavioral psychotherapy and the rise of clinical behavior analysis. In J. Austin & J. E. Carr (Eds.), *Handbook of applied behavior analysis* (pp. 231–246). Reno, NV: Context Press.

Hayes, S. C., & Brownstein, A. J. (1986). Mentalism, behavior-behavior relations and a behavior analytic view of the purposes of science. *Behavior Analyst, 9,* 175–190.

Hayes, S. C., Luoma, J., Bond, F., Masuda, A., & Lillis, J. (2006). Acceptance and commitment therapy: Model, processes, and outcomes. *Behaviour Research and Therapy, 44,* 1–25.

Hayes, S. C., Nelson, R. O., & Jarrett, R. B. (1987). The treatment utility of assessment: A functional approach to evaluating assessment quality. *American Psychologist, 42,* 963–974.

Hayes, S. C., Strosahl, K. D., Bunting, K., Twohig, M., & Wilson, K. G. (2004). What is acceptance and commitment therapy? In S. C. Hayes & K. D. Strosahl (Eds.), *Acceptance and commitment therapy: A practical guide* (pp. 3–30). New York: Springer.

Hayes, S. C., Strosahl, K. D., & Wilson, K. G. (1999). *Acceptance and commitment therapy: An experiential approach to behavior change.* New York: Guilford Press.

Hayes, S. C., Wilson, K. G., Gifford, E. V., Follette, V. M., & Strosahl, K. (1996). Experiential avoidance and behavioral disorders: A functional dimensional approach to diagnosis and treatment. *Journal of Clinical and Consulting Psychology, 64,* 1152–1168.

Hearst, E. (1999). After the puzzle boxes: Thorndike in the 20th century. *Journal of the Experimental Analysis of Behavior, 72,* 441–446.

Hermann, J. A., DeMontes, A. I., Domínguez, B., Montes, F., & Hopkins, B. L. (1973). Effects of bonuses for punctuality on the tardiness of industrial workers. *Journal of Applied Behavior Analysis, 6,* 563–570.

Hinshaw, S. P., Klein, R. G., & Abikoff, H. B. (2002). Childhood attention-deficit/hyperactivity disorder: Nonpharmacological treatments and their combination with medication. In P. E. Nathan & J. M. Gorman (Eds.), *A guide to treatments that work* (pp. 3–23). New York: Oxford University Press.

Iwata, B. A. (1987). Negative reinforcement in applied behavior analysis: An emerging technology. *Journal of Applied Behavior Analysis, 20,* 361–378.

Iwata, B. A. (1988). The development and adoption of controversial default technologies. *Behavior Analyst, 11,* 149–157.

Jacobson, N. S., Christenson, A., Prince, S. E., Cordova, J., & Eldridge, K. (2000). Integrative behavioral couple therapy: An acceptance-based, promising new treatment for couple discord. *Journal of Consulting and Clinical Psychology, 68,* 351–355.

Jacobson, N. S., Dobson, K. S., Truax, P. A., Addis, M. E., Koerner, K., Gollan, J. K., et al. (1996). A component analysis of cognitive-behavioral treatment for depression. *Journal of Consulting and Clinical Psychology, 64,* 293–304.

Johnston, J. M., & Pennypacker, H. S. (1993). *Strategies and tactics of behavioral research* (2nd ed.). Mahwah, NJ: Erlbaum.

Jonçich, G. M. (1968). *The sane positivist: A biography of Edward L. Thorndike*. Middletown, CT: Wesleyan University Press.

Jones, M. C. (1924). A laboratory study of fear: The case of Peter. *Pedagogical Seminary, 31*, 308–315.

Kazdin, A. E. (2000). *Psychotherapy for children and adolescents: Directions for research and practice*. New York: Oxford University Press.

Kazdin, A. E., & Whitley, M. K. (2003). Treatment of parental stress to enhance therapeutic change among children referred for aggressive and antisocial behavior. *Journal of Consulting and Clinical Psychology, 71*, 504–515.

Keller, F. S., & Schoenfeld, W. N. (1950). *Principles of psychology: A systematic text in the science of behavior*. New York: Appleton-Century-Crofts.

Kohlenberg, R., & Phillips, T. (1973). Reinforcement and rate of litter depositing. *Journal of Applied Behavior Analysis, 6*, 391–396.

Kohlenberg, R., & Tsai, M. (2003). *Functional analytic psychotherapy: Creating intense and curative therapeutic relationships*. New York: Springer.

Koshtoyants, K. (1965). I. M. Sechenov (1828–1905). In G. Gibbons (Ed.) & S. Belsky (Trans.), *Reflexes of the brain* (pp. 119–139). Cambridge, MA: MIT Press. (Original work published 1863).

Kritch, K. M., & Bostow, D. E. (1998). Degree of constructed-response interaction in computer-based programmed instruction. *Journal of Applied Behavior Analysis, 31*, 387–398.

Kronenberger, W. G., & Meyer, R. G. (2001). *The child-clinician's handbook* (2nd ed.). Needham Heights, MA: Allyn & Bacon.

Kuhn, T. S. (1962). *The structure of scientific revolutions*. Chicago: University of Chicago Press.

Lattal, K. A., & Chase, P. N. (2003). Themes in behavior theory and philosophy. In K. A. Lattal & P. N. Chase (Eds.), *Behavior theory and philosophy* (pp. 1–12). New York: Kluwer Academic/Plenum Press.

Lattal, K. A., & Laipple, J. S. (2003). Pragmatism and behavior analysis. In K. A. Lattal & P. N. Chase (Eds.), *Behavior theory and philosophy* (pp. 41–62). New York: Kluwer Academic/Plenum Press.

Leslie, J. C. (1996). *Principles of behavioral analysis*. New York: Harwood Academic.

Leslie, J. C., & O'Reilly, M. F. (1999). *Behavior analysis: Foundations and applications to psychology*. New York: Harwood Academic.

Lindsley, O. R. (1959). Reduction in rate of vocal psychotic symptoms by differential positive reinforcement. *Journal of the Experimental Analysis of Behavior, 2*, 269.

Lindsley, O. R. (1992). Precision teaching: Discoveries and effects. *Journal of Applied Behavior Analysis, 25*, 51–57.

Linehan, M. (1993). *Cognitive-behavioral treatment of borderline personality disorder*. New York: Guilford Press.

Lovaas, O. I. (1987). Behavioral treatment and normal educational and intellectual functioning in young autistic children. *Journal of Consulting and Clinical Psychology, 55*, 3–9.

Matthews, J. R., Spieth, L. E., & Christophersen, E. R. (1995). Behavioral compliance in a pediatric context. In M. C. Roberts (Ed.), *Handbook of pediatric psychology* (2nd ed., pp. 617–632). New York: Guilford Press.

McDowell, C., & Keenan, M. (2001). Developing fluency and endurance in a child diagnosed with attention-deficit/hyperactivity disorder. *Journal of Applied Behavior Analysis, 34*, 345–348.

McKenzie, T. L., & Rushall, B. S. (1974). Effects of self-recording on attendance and performance in a competitive swimming training environment. *Journal of Applied Behavior Analysis, 7*, 199–206.

Michael, J. L. (2004). *Concepts and principles of behavior analysis*. Kalamazoo, MI: Association for Behavior Analysis.

Miltenberger, R. G. (1997). *Behavior modification: Principles and procedures*. Pacific Grove, CA: Brooks/Cole.

Murrell, A. R., & Scherbarth, A. (2006). State of the research and literature address: ACT with children, adolescents and parents. *International Journal of Behavioral and Consultation Therapy, 2*, 531–544.

Newman, B., Reeve, K. F., Reeve, S. A., & Ryan, C. S. (2003). *Behaviorspeak: A glossary of terms in applied behavior analysis*. New York: Dove & Orca.

O'Donnell, J. M. (1985). *The origins of behaviorism: American psychology 1870–1920*. New York: New York University Press.

O'Neill, G. W., Blanck, L. S., & Joyner, M. A. (1980). The use of stimulus control over littering in a natural setting. *Journal of Applied Behavior Analysis, 13*, 379–381.

Pavlov, I. P. (1928). *Conditioned reflexes: An investigation of the cerebral cortex* (G. V. Anrep, Ed., & H. Milford, Trans.). London: Oxford University Press. (Original work published 1927).

Pelham, W. E., Wheeler, T., & Chronis, A. (1998). Empirically supported psychosocial treatments for attention-deficit/hyperactivity disorder. *Journal of Clinical Child Psychology, 27*, 190–205.

Pepper, S. C. (1942). *World hypotheses: A study in evidence*. Berkeley: University of California Press.

Pierce, C. H., & Risley, T. R. (1974). Improving job performance of neighborhood youth corps aides in an urban recreation program. *Journal of Applied Behavior Analysis, 7*, 207–215.

Reid, D. H. (1991). Technological behavior analysis and societal impact: A human services perspective. *Journal of Applied Behavior Analysis, 24*, 437–439.

Reiss, M. L., & Bailey, J. S. (1982). Visiting the dentist: A behavioral community analysis of participation in a dental health screening and referral program. *Journal of Applied Behavior Analysis, 15*, 353–362.

Renne, C. M., & Creer, T. L. (1976). Training children with asthma to use inhalation therapy equipment. *Journal of Applied Behavior Analysis, 9*, 1–11.

Risley, T. R. (2001). Do good, take data. In W. T. O'Donohue, D. A. Henderson, S. C. Hayes, J. E. Fisher, & L. J. Hayes (Eds.), *A history of the behavioral therapies: Founders' personal histories* (pp. 267–287). Reno, NV: Context Press.

Rosnow, R. L., & Georgoudi, M. (1986). *Contextualism and understanding in behavioral science: Implications for research and theory*. New York: Praeger.

Russell, B. (1925). *Philosophy*. New York: Norton.

Sechenov, I. M. (1965). *Reflexes of the brain* (G. Gibbons, Ed., S. Belsky, Trans.). Cambridge, MA: MIT Press. (Original work published 1863).

Segal, Z. V., Williams, J. M. G., & Teasdale, J. D. (2002). *Mindfulness-based cognitive therapy for depression: A new approach for preventing relapse*. New York: Guilford Press.

Skinner, B. F. (1938). *The behavior of organisms: An experimental analysis*. New York: Appleton-Century-Crofts.

Skinner, B. F. (1953). *Science and human behavior*. New York: Macmillan.

Skinner, B. F. (1976). *Particulars of my life*. New York: Knopf.

Skinner, B. F. (1981). Selection by consequences. *Science, 213*, 501–504.

Smith, T. (2001). Discrete trial training in the treatment of autism. *Focus on Autism and Other Developmental Disabilities, 16*, 86–92.

Stark, L. J., Collins, F. L., Osnes, P. G., & Stokes, T. F. (1986). Using reinforcement and cueing to increase healthy snack choices in preschoolers. *Journal of Applied Behavior Analysis, 19*, 367–379.

Thorndike, E. L. (1898). Animal intelligence: An experimental study of the associate processes in animals. *Psychological Review Monograph Supplement, 2*(4), 1–8.

Thorpe, G. L., & Olson, S. L. (1997). *Behavior therapy: Concepts, procedures and applications* (2nd ed.). Needham Heights, MA: Allyn & Bacon.

Ullmann, L. P., & Krasner, L. (Eds.). (1965). *Case studies in behavior modification*. New York: Holt, Rinehart and Winston.

Ulrich, R., Stachnik, T., & Mabry, J. (Eds.). (1966). *Control of human behavior*. Glenview, IL: Scott, Foresman.

Vargas, J. S. (2001). B. F. Skinner's contribution to therapeutic change: An agency-less contingency analysis. In W. T. O'Donohue, D. A. Henderson, S. C. Hayes, J. E. Fisher, & L. J. Hayes (Eds.), *A history of the behavioral therapies: Founders' personal histories* (pp. 59–74). Reno, NV: Context Press.

Verplanck, W. S. (1955). The control of the content of conversation: Reinforcement of statements of opinion. *Journal of Abnormal and Social Psychology, 51*, 668–676.

Watson, J. B. (1913). Psychology as the behaviorist views it. *Psychological Review, 20*, 158–177.

Watson, J. B. (1930). *Behaviorism*. New York: Norton. (Original work published 1924).

Watson, J. B., & Rayner, R. (1920). Conditioned emotional reactions. *Journal of Experimental Psychology, 3*, 1–14.

Weinberg, H. A. (1999). Parent training for attention-deficit/hyperactivity disorder: Parental and child outcome. *Journal of Clinical Psychology, 55*, 907–913.

Weisz, J. R. (2004). *Psychotherapy for children and adolescents: Evidence-based treatments and case examples*. Cambridge: Cambridge University Press.

Wickes, I. G. (1958). Treatment of persistent enuresis with the electric buzzer. *Archives of Disease in Childhood, 33*, 160–164.

Williams, C. D. (1959). The elimination of tantrum behavior by extinction procedures. *Journal of Abnormal and Social Psychology, 59*, 269.

Wilson, K. G., & Murrell, A. R. (2002). Functional analysis of behavior. In M. Hersen & W. Sledge (Eds.), *Encyclopedia of psychology* (pp. 833–839). New York: Academic Press.

Wilson, K. G., & Murrell, A. R. (2004). Values work in acceptance and commitment therapy: Setting a course for behavioral treatment. In S. C. Hayes, V. Follette, & M. Linehan (Eds.), *Mindfulness and acceptance: Expanding the cognitive-behavioral therapy* (pp. 120–151). New York: Guilford Press.

Wolf, M. M., Risley, T., & Mees, H. (1964). Application of operant conditioning procedures to the behaviour problems of an autistic child. *Behaviour Research and Therapy, 1*, 305–312.

Zimmerman, E. H., & Zimmerman, J. (1962). The alteration of behavior in a special classroom situation. *Journal of the Experimental Analysis of Behavior, 5*, 59–60.

CHAPTER 9

Cognitive-Behavioral Theory

Stephen D. A. Hupp, David Reitman, and Jeremy D. Jewell

Cognitive-behavioral therapy (CBT) continues to evolve from its early roots in behavior therapy, and it is often represented in summaries of empirically supported interventions. Since the emergence of behavior therapy in the late 1950s and early 1960s, cognitive and behavioral theories have merged to produce a theoretically complex combination of therapeutic approaches known today as CBT, though some have continued to debate the merits of adding cognitive components to the traditional behavioral model (Beidel & Turner, 1986; Reitman & Drabman, 1997). After a period of development focusing primarily on adult psychopathology, recent years have witnessed the emergence of a wide range of CBT interventions and related research for children and adolescents. Dobson and Dozois (2001, p. 4) argue that CBT interventions for children are characterized by the following assumptions: " (a) Cognitive activity affects behavior, (b) cognitive activity may be monitored and altered, and (c) behavior change may be achieved through cognitive change."

One important facet of cognitive-behavioral theory is the assumption that "cognitive activity" and "behavior" are fundamentally different. Indeed, several authors have regarded cognitive activity as a subcategory of behavior (see Watson, 1924). In this chapter, we use the term "cognitive" to represent covert behavior, including thoughts and images. We use the term "overt behavior" when it is important to distinguish it from covert behavior. In addition to the three assumptions noted by Dobson and Dozois (2001), there are other key propositions within the cognitive-behavioral framework. Namely, the environment, overt behavior, and covert behavior all influence each other. Finally, Dobson and Dozois also distinguish cognitive-behavioral therapy from "pure" forms of behavior therapy and cognitive therapy. For example, in their view, applied behavior analysis for individuals with profound mental retardation and cognitive therapy focusing completely on memories of traumatic events would be viewed as theoretically distinct.

Kendall (2006, p. 7) regards the cognitive-behavioral framework as placing "greatest emphasis on the learning process and the influence of the models in the social environment, while underscoring the centrality of the individual's mediating/information processing style and emotional experiencing." This definition includes several key components, including (a) learning from direct experience, (b) social learning, and (c) cognitive and emotional mediation. Both Kendall and

Dobson and Dozois (2001) emphasize the mediational perspective. That is, in addition to environmental influences, a person's thoughts and feelings are believed to make a unique contribution to behavioral health.

The theoretical foundation of any form of therapy is regarded as critical by some authors who argue the merits of therapeutic techniques derived from a unifying theory. Hayes, Strosahl, and Wilson (1999, pp. 13–14), for example, distinguish between *theory* and *technique* by describing theory as "statements that have broad applicability" and technique as the "practical details" of therapy. The value of a well-developed theory is the ability to adapt techniques to new problems, develop new techniques, and add coherence to applied psychology (Hayes et al., 1999). Interestingly, most of the techniques used in CBT were derived from either behavioral theories or cognitive theories but not a unified "cognitive-behavioral" theory, and many have argued for a more flexible approach to case conceptualization that incorporates elements of many theoretical perspectives (A. Lazarus, 1996).

This chapter first provides brief descriptions of behavioral and cognitive theories, followed by a discussion of the continued integration of the two theories as they relate to children and adolescents. We close with a few comments about the future of the cognitive-behavioral framework.

BEHAVIORAL THEORY

Although there were many early contributors to the development of behavioral theory, John B. Watson's (1924) *Behaviorism* represented one of the first comprehensive efforts to describe behavioral theory. Elaborating on themes first developed in his "behaviorist manifesto" (Watson, 1913), Watson (1924) argues that behaviorism ought to focus on observable phenomena rather than consciousness. Observable responses were said to include what the organism "does," including overt actions such as speaking aloud and even covert actions such as speaking to oneself (i.e., thinking). Thus, cognitions are included in Watson's account of human behavior, and in his view, thinking is subvocal speech, observable, at least in principle, to the thinker. By contrast, psychodynamic theory held that many important motivations and explanations of human behavior were subconscious, neither observable nor available for further analysis (except indirectly through dream analysis or via unconscious responses to ambiguous or neutral stimuli, etc.). Watson also emphasizes the importance of stimuli (both environmental and physiological) that elicit observable responses.

In his early writings, Watson (1924) makes several important observations. First, he describes several kinds of responses that do not appear to require conditioning. For example, following Pavlov, he observed that responses to stimuli that are essential to the survival of the species (e.g., stimuli signaling danger or the availability of food) do not require elaborate conditioning histories. That being said, Watson also gathered data suggesting that these basic behavioral repertoires could be modified by experience. Ultimately, he concludes that much human behavior is learned via classical conditioning processes. Throughout his text, Watson consistently contrasts his view of learning with the prevailing view (in the 1920s and 1930s) that heredity alone accounts for most human behavior. Watson's work with an 11-month-old infant, Albert, yielded one of the most potent examples of conditioning (Watson & Watson, 1921). Using classical conditioning procedures developed by Pavlov, Watson and Watson demonstrated that Albert showed no fear response (e.g., avoidance) to a white rat until experimenters repeatedly paired loud sounds (produced by striking a metal bar) with the introduction of the rat. After just a few pairings of the rat and sound, Albert began to show a fear response (i.e., crying and crawling away), even when the rat was presented in the absence of the sound. Albert's fear also transferred (or generalized) to similar stimuli, such as a rabbit. In other work, Watson and colleagues describe how one might use classical conditioning to alleviate fear, including (a) having other children handle the stimulus without fear and (b) deconditioning the fear by gradually presenting the feared stimulus without the accompanying aversive stimulus. These two techniques are today called participant modeling and in vivo desensitization, respectively, and both are counted among the handful of empirically supported interventions for anxiety problems (Ollendick & King, 1998). Watson and other early behaviorists went on to apply their conditioning model broadly to a wide range of human behaviors, including what they termed "emotional reactions" such as rage and love.

Over the course of the next few decades, B. F. Skinner continued to shape behavioral theory through extensive basic research and provocative theorizing about the implications of laboratory demonstrations of operant conditioning. Influenced by Thorndike's (1911) law of effect, Skinner gradually came to distinguish his work from the work of other behaviorists, including Watson. Whereas Watson tended to emphasize the stimuli that elicit responses, Skinner's work devotes greater attention to consequences of the behavioral response (see Skinner, 1953). One of the most important concepts to emerge from Thorndike's, and later, Skinner's work is the explicit recognition that under certain circumstances, humans and other organisms tend to repeat behaviors that are followed by particular events or consequences. Behavior can be strengthened through *positive reinforcement* by adding something (e.g., social, tangible, physical consequences) and can also be strengthened through *negative reinforcement,* typically by removing something aversive.

Skinner's theory also accounts for reductions in the strength of behavior. Specifically, *operant extinction* involves withholding the presentation of consequences maintaining a given behavior, whereas *negative punishment* involves reducing the frequency of behavior by the removal of a consequence following the performance of a behavior. *Positive punishment* involves weakening behavior by adding aversive stimuli contingent on the performance of a behavior. Skinner includes antecedents in his analyses of reinforcement contingencies, specifically focusing on antecedent stimuli (e.g., discriminative stimuli) that control behavioral responses because of a history of reinforcement in the presence of those stimuli. The three-term contingency describes the important relation that exists between *antecedent* stimuli, the *behavior,* and its *consequence* (i.e., the so-called A-B-Cs). Under certain circumstances, setting events that alter the discriminative functions of the antecedent stimuli are also included in the analysis (Iwata, Smith, & Michael, 2000). Ultimately, Skinner made many other important contributions to behavioral theory and applied behavior analysis, including the concepts of reinforcement schedules, shaping, fading, and functional analysis, just to name a few.

After an initial period of laboratory work with nonhumans, Skinner's students and colleagues rapidly expanded the application of learning principles utilizing laboratory methods to study, and influence, the behavior of children in child care, institutional, and educational settings (see Bijou & Baer, 1961, for an early example). Even today, the manipulation of antecedents and consequences is the basis for many empirically supported interventions for youth (Ollendick & King, 2000). Over the past few decades, applied behavior analysis has flourished, especially among individuals with developmental disabilities (see this volume's Chapter 8 for a more detailed account).

Like Watson, Skinner (1953, 1957) makes an explicit effort to address the role of cognition in his theory of human behavior. Skinner distinguishes between *private events* (e.g., thoughts, images, sensations, feelings) and *public events* (i.e., overt behavior), but does not afford private events a causal role independent of events (either contemporary or historical) occurring outside of the individual. For example, Skinner (1963, p. 953) once commented that "an adequate science of behavior must consider events taking place within the skin of the organism, not as physiological mediators of behavior, but as part of behavior itself." Put another way, Skinner considered both private events and public events to be forms of behavior that could serve as links in a "causal chain," ultimately determined by environmental factors.

In the late 1960s and early 1970s, Bandura initiated a series of studies examining the impact of social (or vicarious) learning, or what later became known as "modeling." Bandura (1974) agreed with Skinner's view that much human behavior was shaped by external consequences, but he suggests that learning would be exceptionally slow if humans were limited to learning via exposure to direct contingencies alone. Bandura (1973) argues that learning through observation is not only more efficient than direct contingency shaping; it also permits the individual to avoid aversive consequences. For example, in one of the landmark studies investigating observational learning, Bandura found that children who watched an aggressive model (i.e., live or video) demonstrated more aggressive acts with an inflatable doll than those who observed a nonaggressive model. Children observing the aggressive model also demonstrated more aggressive behavior than those who did not observe any model (see Bandura, 1973).

Although both Skinner and Bandura view verbal behavior as important to understanding behavior, Skinner (1957) emphasizes the role of the speaker and developed a fairly complex taxonomy of verbal stimuli that functioned as antecedents or consequences. Taking a different approach, Bandura places greater importance on cognitive variables (e.g., self-efficacy) and affords these variables a causal role in a wide range of human activity. Whether or not cognitions play a causal role in overt behavior continues to be debated (see Reitman & Drabman, 1997, on the relative merits of such debate).

COGNITIVE THEORY

Rational-emotive behavior therapy (REBT) was developed by Albert Ellis in the 1950s. First termed rational therapy, Ellis (1962) later adopted the name rational-emotive therapy (RET) to differentiate his theoretical approach from others sharing the same name and to distance himself from the philosophical position known as rationalism. When fellow theorists and critics pointed out that many of his therapeutic techniques were essentially compatible with behavioral theory, Ellis (1999) incorporated behavior more explicitly, changing RET to rational-emotive behavior therapy. Long regarded as an inclusive therapeutic approach (A. Lazarus, 1989), REBT liberally incorporates elements of behavioral theory and practice, thus making it difficult to distinguish many of the various techniques used in REBT from behavior therapy.

The essence of Ellis's REBT is summarized by the acronym ABCDE (Dryden & Ellis, 2001; Ellis & Bernard, 1983). In this model, "A" represents an event that *activates* specific irrational thinking (e.g., a child gets a poor grade on an assignment). "B" represents *beliefs* that are irrational and illogical (e.g., "I can't stand to get a bad grade"). "C" represents the emotional and behavioral *consequences* of irrational and illogical beliefs (e.g., sadness and withdrawal). The focus of therapy, therefore, is to intervene at the level of beliefs (B), as opposed to the particular activating event or its consequences per se. In describing persons with psychological problems, Ellis (1989, p. 217) remarked, "Their emotional problems and their behavioral dysfunctions mainly stem from their grandiose demands on themselves, on others, and on environmental conditions." The role of the therapist, therefore, is to focus on the client's irrational thinking in order to produce a widespread change in emotional and behavioral functioning. The major efforts at producing cognitive and behavioral change occur in the final two steps of the model, where "D" represents the therapist *disputing* irrational thinking and beliefs (in conjunction with other REBT techniques) and "E" represents the healthier, more *effective,* state of emotional, behavioral, and cognitive functioning.

Although much of his theory places prime importance on a universally held irrational belief system, the REBT model reflects Ellis's (1962) view that all human existence consists of the primary domains of thought, emotion, and overt behavior. Ellis and Bernard (1983, p. 9) stated that people "almost never experience *pure* thoughts, feelings, or actions." Therefore, although Ellis suggests that cognitions can elicit behavioral and emotional consequences, he emphasizes that thoughts, emotions, and overt behavior are part of a holistic process in which no single domain determines activity in other domains.

Ellis contrasts REBT with humanistic models that emphasize the importance of unconditional support of the client as the primary goal in therapy. He argues that although the client should be valued, the dysfunctional thoughts and overt behavior of the client should be vigorously challenged (Ellis, 1962). In fact, Ellis is known for his often confrontational approach to therapy. Early critics of his theory questioned his forceful challenges to the client's irrational thinking, but Ellis argued that such efforts were necessary to maximize the effectiveness of therapy.

Aaron T. Beck is another highly influential figure in the history of CBT. Developing his theory independently of Ellis, A. Beck (1963) was one of the first researchers to offer a detailed account of the role of cognition in psychopathology. In one of his earliest works, he describes a pattern of cognitive distortions and themes in his adult patients with depression, and concludes that the actual source of his patients' depressed mood was distorted and irrational thinking (A. Beck, 1963). For example, he observed that many patients perceived themselves "as incapable, incompetent, and helpless," regardless of their actual life circumstances (p. 327). In addition to having negative views of themselves, other common negative beliefs encompassed aspects of the future and the world. Collectively, these negative beliefs about the self, future, and world became known as the "cognitive triad" (DeRubeis, Tang, & Beck, 2001).

In his original formulation of the theory, A. Beck (1963) refutes the idea that mental health problems such as depression are driven by the affect experienced by the patient. Rather, he suggests that the affective, behavioral, and social facets of depression result from distorted thinking. Through interviews and extensive clinical experience with depressed patients, he began to notice certain patterns of cognitive distortions. Some of the most common forms of depressive cognitions were arbitrary inference, selective abstraction, overgeneralization, and exaggeration (A. Beck, 1963). For example, selective abstraction refers to the tendency for some persons to attend to only negative facets of a particular situation and neglect other details (A. Beck, Rush, Shaw, & Emery, 1979). In the case of depression, a person may recall a past conversation, focusing only on perceived subtle criticisms, while ignoring complimentary information.

A. Beck (A. Beck et al., 1979) has also described people with depression as shifting cognitively from "mature" thinking to more "primitive" thinking, which in turn leads to negative affective consequences. Mature thinking is characterized by reflection and insight that allows the individual to form a multidimensional, changeable, and relatively nonjudgmental self-concept. On the other hand, primitive thinking is absolute and global, leading the person to view themselves as unchangeable and fundamentally flawed (A. Beck et al., 1979). Early work by A. Beck (1963) focuses on depression, but he later suggests that cognitive theory could be applied to other disorders such as externalizing problems and anxiety (A. Beck, 1999; A. Beck, Emery, & Greenberg, 2005). Additionally, although cognitive theory focuses primarily on cognition, A. Beck and others have argued that the relation of cognition and affect may be complex (see Kohlenberg & Tsai, 1991). In any event, both Ellis and A. Beck were united in their hope that the explicit focus on cognitions would promote more efficient alleviation of negative affect (A. Beck et al., 1979).

A. Beck's (A. Beck et al., 1979) early work implies that there are different levels of belief, and his theory has evolved to incorporate these observations. For example, Judith Beck (1995) describes three levels of belief: automatic thoughts, intermediate beliefs, and core beliefs. *Automatic thoughts* are situation-specific and idiosyncratic (e.g., "I'm going to fail this test"). *Intermediate beliefs* are essentially rules or assumptions that a person applies to his or her life (e.g., "Things never work out for me"). Finally, *core beliefs* are both global and fixed (e.g., "I am a failure"). In this theory, automatic thoughts and intermediate beliefs are considered to be a reflection of a related core belief. Thus, the ultimate goal of treatment for a particular disorder is to modify irrational thinking at the level of the core belief, although treatment often begins with related automatic thoughts and intermediate beliefs.

Both Ellis and A. Beck have acknowledged the importance of reciprocal relations between cognition, the social environment, and overt behavior. For example, if the host of a holiday party excuses herself to greet other guests, a person prone to depression and/or social anxiety may react with (a) the automatic thought "She thinks I'm boring," (b) the intermediate belief "Nobody wants to talk to a person like me," and (c) withdrawal from further social interaction. The withdrawal response may then prompt others to avoid the individual in that social situation. Consequently, the individual's intermediate belief (i.e., "Nobody wants to talk to me") may be supported by his or her subsequent experience at the party. Interestingly, the depressed or anxious individual is also likely to discount evidence contrary to the distorted hypotheses, reasoning "People only spoke to me because I was standing near the bar" and so forth. This sequence of events illustrates the reciprocal nature of individual cognition, overt behavior, and social conditioning that can maintain distorted thinking (A. Beck et al., 1979).

Although both Ellis and A. Beck postulate that irrational thinking maintains maladaptive behaviors, neither regards irrational thinking as the ultimate cause of psychopathology. Rather, both point to biological and environmental influences as important factors in the development of irrational thinking (A. Beck et al., 1979; Bernard & DiGiuseppe, 1989). According to A. Beck et al., a person's genetics and childhood environment may initiate a pattern of irrational thinking, which then leads to, and maintains, maladaptive behaviors and psychopathology. A. Beck suggests that most people lead life governed by rational thinking. However, irrational thoughts formed early in life could be triggered at some point by environmental stress, allowing for a shift from a pattern of rational thinking to irrational thinking.

The term cognitive-behavioral therapy is often used to refer specifically to the combination of A. Beck's cognitive techniques with other behavioral techniques. At other times, CBT is used as a generic term to refer to all manner of cognitive and behavior therapy blends. Although admitting many similarities, Ellis (1980; Ellis & Bernard, 1983) distinguishes between REBT and CBT. For example, Ellis states that CBT tends to focus more on cognitive change as it affects behavior, whereas REBT is primarily concerned with cognitive change as it leads to both emotional change and a broader change in one's philosophy of life, thus ostensibly affecting one's ability to cope with future problematic situations. Additionally, Ellis suggests that CBT focuses more on situation-specific cognitions and behaviors, and REBT addresses more global, irrational thinking and beliefs.

Most cognitive therapists began their work focused on problems confronted by adults in outpatient psychotherapy, so it is only recently that CBT has begun to formulate a coherent theoretical model to guide work with children. Ellis and Bernard (1983) were among the first to discuss the application of cognitive therapies to children and adolescents. Specifically, they noted that "although preferential RET is highly suitable for many bright adolescents, it may require too much philosophical analysis and more of an application of rigorous scientific method than many average youngsters, not to mention most younger children, are capable of fulfilling" (p. 8). Thus, children and many adolescents may benefit more from behavioral techniques and cognitive techniques that address situation-specific cognitions rather than belief systems.

A. Beck has written little on the subject of applying cognitive theory to children and adolescents. For example, a description of manualized cognitive therapy treatment for adolescents who have attempted suicide seems more or less consistent with adult CBT as it progresses from the first session to termination, with no discussion of changes necessary to the therapy due to the developmental stage of adolescence (Henriques, Beck, & Brown, 2003). Recently, a few researchers have begun to examine the applicability of cognitive therapy to young children and adolescents. Specifically, Doherr, Reynolds, Wetherly, and Evans (2005) describe two studies that experimentally examined the ability of young children (5 to 7 years old) to complete cognitive tasks that would be required for cognitive therapy. Their findings indicate that, for the most part, the 5- to 7-year-olds possessed the cognitive abilities necessary to participate in cognitive therapy, although materials used for this therapy required alteration. For example, cognitive-behavioral therapy with adults often involves the use of a dysfunctional thought record in which clients record situations, automatic thoughts, and rational responses (J. Beck, 1995); some children may be able to talk about these concepts but would have difficulty writing them down independently.

At this time, the existing literature on adapting cognitive techniques for children is limited, and researchers and clinicians attempting to apply cognitive techniques to children rely on many theoretical and practical assumptions that were developed through research with adults (Derisley, 2004). On the other hand, many empirically supported interventions for youth (Ollendick & King, 2000) have been influenced by Ellis and A. Beck. Perhaps most important, changes in children's negative self-talk seem to mediate treatment outcome (Treadwell & Kendall, 1996). In the next section we present a brief review of CBT models developed more explicitly for children or that emerged based on work with child and adolescent populations.

FURTHER INTEGRATION OF BEHAVIORAL AND COGNITIVE THEORIES

While many theorists in the 1970s debated the strengths and weaknesses of the behavioral and cognitive models, some argued for an integrationist perspective including both theories. Cognitive therapists included many behavioral techniques, and some behaviorists focused more on covert behavior. These integrationist approaches ultimately had an important influence on the development of CBT interventions for children and adolescents.

Many of the integrated theories have been included under the broad label of "self-management" and include a variety of behavioral and cognitive approaches. Though sometimes referring to specific techniques, when the term self-management is used broadly, it implies that the person's behavior is partly controlled by external and internal stimuli and that the person is capable of manipulating those external and internal stimuli to achieve long-term goals (Rokke & Rehm, 2001). Thus, the derived self-management (or self-control) therapies focus on teaching learning and cognitive principles to clients so that they can apply them in their own lives. Self-management techniques therefore include monitoring one's own overt and covert behavior (i.e., self-monitoring), efforts to alter or change one's own external and internal antecedents to behavior (i.e., stimulus control), and the application of both external and internal consequences to one's own behavior (i.e., self-reward and self-punishment; Mahoney & Arnkoff, 1978). Some self-management theorists place greater emphasis on adults (e.g., Goldfried, Decenteceo, & Weinberg, 1974); others focus more on children (Bandura, 1973; Meichenbaum, 1977). Theories of self-efficacy, problem solving, and self-instruction all fit within the self-management model.

Bandura (1997) first significantly influenced behavioral theory by adding social learning; he later continued to shape cognitive-behavioral theory with his self-efficacy model, which places primary importance on the beliefs of the individual. Although Bandura's writings are generally supportive of Skinner's behavioral theory, he suggests that earlier behavioral theories are incomplete, rather than inaccurate. For example, Bandura's research demonstrates that the consequences that follow a model's behavior play an important role in the behavior of the observer. That is, modeling is often more powerful when the model receives a reward, and Bandura (1977a) suggests that this increases the observers' expectations that reinforcers would likely follow their behavior as well. Indeed, basic research has shown that an individual's beliefs about a given reinforcement schedule could prove a more powerful predictor of behavior than the actual reinforcement schedule itself (Baron, Kaufman, & Stauber, 1969). As a result, social learning theory has increasingly emphasized the importance of cognition in predicting behavior. In particular, Bandura's recent work focuses on outcome expectations and self-efficacy. Outcome expectations are a person's predictions about future consequences, and self-efficacy describes the "beliefs in one's capabilities to organize and execute the courses of action required to produce given attainments" (Bandura, 1977b, p. 3). Bandura (1977b) describes four primary ways to develop self-efficacy; that is, self-efficacy develops when (1) mastery experiences result in the individual successfully obtaining a reinforcer, (2) social modeling involves observing others having success, (3) social persuasion is used to enhance the individuals' belief that they too can be successful, and (4) people are taught to read their own physical and emotional states and use these as a guide to success. Reflecting his greater emphasis on the role of cognitions in influencing behavior, Bandura (2004) now uses the term "social cognitive theory" to describe his theoretical model.

Cognitive problem solving is another model that emerged from the integrationist perspective. D'Zurilla and Goldfried (1971) present problem solving as the "self-directed cognitive-behavioral process by which a person attempts to identify or discover effective or adaptive solutions for specific problems encountered in everyday living" (D'Zurilla & Nezu, 2001, p. 212). D'Zurilla and Nezu draw largely from the work of R. Lazarus (1966; R. Lazarus & Folkman, 1984) in developing their "coping" or problem-solving model. In this model, stress is defined as a relationship between a person and the environment in which the person's coping skills are strained. Specific stressors include life's major problems as well as daily hassles. D'Zurilla and Nezu distinguish between two types of coping responses. *Problem-focused* coping responses are used to change something about a situation (e.g., communication style) and are best employed when the person has some control over the problem situation. On the other hand, *emotion-focused* coping responses are an attempt by the person to change his or her own emotional response (e.g., relaxation techniques to decrease anxiety or anger) and are best used when the person does not have control over the problem situation.

Problem solving involves first identifying a situation requiring a coping response and then generating an adaptive cognitive coping response, a behavioral coping response, or both (D'Zurilla & Nezu, 2001). D'Zurilla and Nezu also distinguish between being *oriented* to a problem and then *solving* the problem. That is, before one can start generating effective solutions, one must (a) recognize that there is a problem, (b) attribute the problem to normal life rather than an internal stable deficiency, (c) see the problem as significant to one's well-being, (d) be willing to put time and effort into solving the problem, and (e) have high self-efficacy and an expectancy for change. Evidently, their problem-solving model was influenced by Bandura's work. Actually solving problems includes several components as well: (a) formulating the problem, (b) generating several possible solutions, (c) choosing the best solution, (d) implementing the solution, and (e) evaluating the solution's effectiveness. Interestingly, formulation of the problem might include cognitive and/or behavioral influences, and the solutions might be cognitive and/or behavioral in nature.

Meichenbaum (1977) offers yet another integrationist perspective, and he explicitly positioned his book *Cognitive-Behavior Modification* as an attempt to "bridge the gap" between behavior therapy and the cognitively focused therapies of Ellis and A. Beck. Meichenbaum also cites Luria (1959, 1961) and Vygotsky (1962) as important influences on his approach. Based on Luria and Vygotsky, Meichenbaum argues that the behavior of young children is first directed by their parents' verbal behavior. Children then begin to direct their own behavior through overt speech, and finally, inner speech is developed to direct their own behavior. Meichenbaum adds that once a child becomes proficient at a task, the inner speech for that task is no longer emitted. Thus, he hypothesized that maladaptive child behavior is partly the result of deficits in inner speech. For example, Meichenbaum theorizes that children with high rates of impulsive behavior have deficits in producing and effectively using inner speech. His theoretical focus on the progression of inner speech development was the impetus for the development of self-instruction training, which he applied to children with high rates of impulsive and hyperactive behavior. Self-instruction training assumes that children may have a deficit in that they do not produce enough effective inner speech to direct their behavior.

Meichenbaum was influenced by both social learning theory and the problem-solving model. Following from research suggesting that children imitate their parents' verbal reasoning (Maccoby, 1968), Meichenbaum extends Bandura's social learning theory (which focuses on modeling overt behaviors) to modeling inner speech, a form of covert behavior. Thus, self-instruction training first uses "cognitive modeling," in which adults model the use of problem-solving skills by talking aloud while performing a task. Using this technique, the adult verbally models defining the problem, focusing attention on task requirements, and providing self-praise and corrective feedback. The second step is for the child to perform the task while being instructed by the adult. The next steps involve the child imitating the adult with overt speech, then later with whispered speech, and finally with inner speech. Meichenbaum (1977) also discusses integrating behavioral components, such as employing external reinforcers in addition to the use of self-praise.

Meichenbaum (1977) offers some important distinctions between his theory and those offered by Ellis and A. Beck. Specifically, he suggests that Ellis and A. Beck place a greater emphasis on the *presence* of maladaptive thoughts, and Meichenbaum places a greater emphasis on the *absence* of adaptive thoughts. He uses impulsive behavior as a prime example, arguing that it is not the presence of maladaptive thoughts that is problematic per se, but the absence of adaptive thoughts prior to impulsive behavior. Meichenbaum also suggests that some maladaptive thinking is normal, but that it is the degree of adaptive thinking that distinguishes normal functioning from abnormal functioning. Kendall and Hollon (1979) suggest that this distinction is the cognitive equivalent of behavioral excesses and behavioral deficits, and more recently, Kendall (2000) has used the terms "cognitive distortions" and "cognitive deficiencies" to explore this issue. Practically, this distinction suggests that for some problems maladaptive thoughts need to be directly challenged, whereas for other problems the focus of therapy should be on teaching more adaptive thoughts.

Meichenbaum's (1977, 1985) integrative theory also led to the development of stress inoculation training, another cognitive-behavioral approach to therapy. Stress inoculation training includes self-instruction training but incorporates additional components. The label "stress inoculation" is an analogy to medical inoculation, which builds antibodies to prevent diseases. In stress inoculation therapy, the concept is to build coping skills (i.e., "psychological antibodies") to prevent psychological problems (Meichenbaum, 1985). Meichenbaum gives credit to other investigators for independently developing similar ideas. For example, he cites Goldfried et al. (1974) as integrating Ellis's RET with behavioral theory. Overall, coping skill-based therapies involve teaching clients both more adaptive social behavior and cognitive coping skills. In the case of anxiety, a client is taught physiological relaxation (e.g., deep breathing and muscle relaxation) and adaptive self-statements. Clients first practice using these skills in a nonstressful situation (i.e., a therapy session) before deploying the skills in a more stressful situation.

Commenting on the diverse integrationist approaches to CBT that were emerging in the late 1970s, Mahoney and Arnkoff (1978) categorized cognitive-behavioral interventions as falling into three categories: cognitive restructuring, coping skills, and problem solving. The *cognitive restructuring* category includes the work of Ellis and A. Beck. In these therapies, maladaptive thinking is considered to be the primary cause of distress for the person. Cognitive restructuring therapies often use some behavioral techniques and carefully monitor the effects of treatment; however, the ultimate goal is to replace the person's maladaptive cognitions (internal problems) with more adaptive cognitions. The *coping skills* category includes Meichenbaum's stress inoculation therapy and other therapies that focus more on adapting to external challenges by increasing coping skills. Thus, though these therapies also address cognitions, successful therapy is determined by changes in behavioral responses rather than cognitive ones. Finally, the *problem-solving* category is perhaps the broadest in scope. These therapies focus on teaching the person a general strategy for identifying problems and generating solutions. Thus, the focus for any given problem could be cognitive, behavioral, or both, and the range of possible solutions could include making changes to cognitions, overt behaviors, and/or the environment. Clearly, many empirically supported interventions with youth have been directly influenced by the work of cognitive-behavioral therapists with an integrationist perspective.

APPLYING THE COGNITIVE-BEHAVIORAL FRAMEWORK TO YOUTH

Cognitive-behavioral theory was largely developed by clinical researchers working with adult populations, and in recent years discussion has revolved around the extent to which the CBT framework applies to work with children and adolescents. Braswell and Kendall (2001) highlighted the importance of cognitive development in child CBT. Specifically, children's memory, attention, verbal expression, comprehension, and conceptual reasoning all might affect their response to treatment. Adaptation of CBT for children and adolescents would seem to minimally require that they be capable of sharing private events with the therapist and able to distinguish rational and irrational thoughts. To the extent that the child or adolescent is unable or unwilling to perform these tasks, the role that cognitive interventions such as cognitive restructuring can play in the therapy will be limited.

Another point of departure for adult and child CBT is that collaterals (e.g., parents and teachers) are unlikely to be directly involved in therapy for adults. Also, children rarely seek out therapy themselves, making the process of gaining their trust and engaging them in the therapeutic process especially challenging. Recognizing the importance of client motivation for treatment, Braswell and Kendall (2001) note that the manner in which CBT is presented must be altered to maximize the likelihood of positive therapy outcomes. Specifically, "a therapist must be able to teach in a playful manner and play in a way that teaches" (p. 250). To compensate for both limited cognitive capacity and motivation, Braswell and Kendall recommend greater emphasis on the incorporation of play (e.g., games, puppets), more role-plays, and the use of visual aids to supplement language-based aspects of therapy. For example, whereas adults often rate their fear on a 0 to 100 scale, in child CBT for anxiety children report on fears by choosing from an array of pictures (e.g., a row of faces depicting progressively greater fear). Some therapists use cartoon characters with thought bubbles as a tool in sharing thoughts.

Cognitive-behavioral therapy with children typically incorporates the four major components of behavioral skills training—modeling, instructions, rehearsal, and feedback (Miltenberger, 2004)—as well as manipulation of behavioral contingencies. The focus on behavioral skills training is to replace an undesirable behavior with a desirable behavior. That is, the goal is to teach the learner what to do in addition to what not to do. *Modeling* includes showing the learner how to perform a behavior, and examples include modeling behaviors for children (e.g., how to share) as well as modeling behaviors for their parents (e.g., how to use time-out). *Instructions* describe the desired behavior to the learner; examples include verbal instructions as well as written instructions. *Rehearsal* provides the learner with several opportunities to practice the desired behavior in front of the therapist.

Finally, the therapist provides *feedback* based on rehearsal, which includes praise and positively valenced critiques of the rehearsal. Thus, in the feedback component, behavioral contingencies are used to shape the learner's behavior, and the learner's behavior is ideally reinforced within the context of the role-play. Behavioral contingencies are employed outside of the therapy setting to increase generalization. Consistent with Bandura's (1974a) social learning theory, behavioral skills training increases self-efficacy through mastery experiences, social modeling, social persuasion, and sometimes through changing internal physical and emotional states.

Since their inception, behavioral and cognitive theories have drawn on other theoretical traditions. For example, the cognitive-behavioral framework is particularly compatible with *ecological systems theory* (Bronfenbrenner, 2005). The ecological systems perspective considers both characteristics of the individual and those of the family, school, and community; CBT is being increasingly used in schools (Mennuti, Freeman, & Christner, 2006). Importantly, both ecological systems theory and the cognitive-behavioral framework acknowledge that genetics and other biological influences play a role in the development of psychopathology. However, it is often difficult to determine the degree of bidirectional influence on behavior stemming from environmental and biological factors and, further, to distinguish normal behavioral variation from deviant developmental trajectories (Jensen, Knapp, & Mrazek, 2006).

In the following subsections, we discuss the application of cognitive-behavioral theory to specific problems for youth defined by the *Diagnostic and Statistical Manual of Mental Disorders,* fourth edition, text revision (*DSM-IV-TR;* American Psychiatric Association, 2000). Although our focus is on depression, anxiety, conduct problems, attention problems, and parenting stress, the cognitive-behavioral framework has also been successfully applied to many other problems affecting youth, including eating disorders and obesity (Wilfley, Passi, Cooperberg, & Stein, 2006), abuse (Deblinger, Behl, & Glickman, 2006), academic problems (Harris & Graham, 1996), and chronic pain (Masek, Russo, & Varni, 1984).

Depression

Cognitive-behavioral theorists have offered several accounts of potential etiological factors involved in youth depression (i.e., Major Depressive Disorder and Dysthymic Disorder). Lewinsohn (1974) hypothesizes that a lack of positive reinforcement could lead to depression. Some research has supported the notion that children with depression lack the social skills needed to obtain social reinforcement (Rudolph & Clark, 2001). Stressful life events (e.g., hospitalization, moving) have also been implicated in the development of depression among adolescents (Lewinsohn, Allen, Seeley, & Gotlib, 1999; Seligman, 1975). For example, in a study of over 1,500 adolescents, Lewinsohn et al. found that three or more stressful life events in the previous year appear to be the threshold for making predictions about the onset of a first depressive episode. Interestingly, recurrent depressive episodes could not be predicted using this threshold.

Consistent with a more cognitive (mediational) account of adolescent depression, experiencing several stressful life events could influence depression through the development of a depressive attributional style (Seligman, 1975). Interestingly, negative attributional style does not predict depression when a high number of life stressors are present, but it does predict depression when there are lower levels of stress (Lewinsohn, Joiner, & Rohde, 2001). In a meta-analysis of 28 studies involving youth, depressive symptoms were correlated with internal (i.e., blame oneself), stable (i.e., not changeable), and global (i.e., applies to everything) attributions for *negative* life events and external, unstable, and specific attributions for *positive* life events (Gladstone & Kaslow, 1995). The influence of maladaptive thinking as a contributor to child and adolescent depression has also received support in the literature. Negative self-appraisals have been found to be predictive of depressive symptoms in children in sixth and seventh grade (Hoffman, Cole, Martin, Tram, & Seroczynski, 2000), but the study did not distinguish between cognitive distortions and potentially accurate negative self-statements. In another study, children with depression rated their own social status lower than peers rated them (Rudolph & Clark, 2001). Furthermore, McGrath and Repetti (2002) studied fourth- through sixth-grade students and found that depressive symptoms were predictive of later cognitive distortions; however, cognitive distortions were not predictive of an increase in depressive symptoms over 3 years. This study suggests that cognitive distortions may play a greater role in the maintenance of depression in children than in the development of depression.

The cognitive-behavioral framework allows for parental influence on the development of childhood depression. For example, recent research suggests that childhood depression is associated with family conflict (Pilowsky, Wickramaratne, Nomura, & Weissman, 2006). Also, though the study was correlational, parents of youth with depression appear to provide less praise and are more critical than parents of nondepressed youth (Puig-Antich et al., 1993). Meichenbaum's theory of cognitive modeling suggests a possible mechanism for the transmittal of negative self-appraisal. For example, a parent's critical statement "You are lazy" may later be covertly modeled "I am lazy."

Anxiety

As noted previously, Watson (1924) was among the first to examine how children's fears could be acquired through classical conditioning. According to Mowrer's (1939) two-factor theory, once acquired, fear-related behaviors can be maintained through negative reinforcement (e.g., through escape or avoidance behaviors). Following Bandura's social learning theory, Rachman (1991) notes that fears can develop both by watching other people engage in fearful behavior and by receiving other fear-provoking information through language. A. Beck's (A. Beck et al., 2005) theory of cognitive distortions was originally developed for depression but has been extended to anxiety disorders as well.

DSM-IV-TR anxiety-related problems that have been diagnosed among children and adolescents include Separation Anxiety Disorder, Panic, Agoraphobia, Specific Phobia, Social Phobia, Obsessive-Compulsive Disorder, Posttraumatic Stress Disorder, and Generalized Anxiety Disorder. With the exception of Separation Anxiety Disorder, the diagnostic criteria applied to adult anxiety problems and those applied to child anxiety problems are nearly identical. Lang's (1968) tripartite model of anxiety is among the most influential of the cognitive-behavioral theories of anxiety and is composed of physiological (i.e., activation of the sympathetic nervous system), behavioral (e.g., fight-or-flight responses), and cognitive (i.e., fear-related speech) dimensions. More recently, a fourth dimension, emotional responding, has been explored (Southam-Gerow & Kendall, 2002). These four response dimensions are considered to be common to all of the anxiety disorders.

Research indicates that anxious children view ambiguous situations as more threatening than nonanxious children (Barrett, Rapee, Dadds, & Ryan, 1996). Barrett et al. also reported that parents play a significant role in children's anxiety. Specifically, like their children, parents of anxious children also interpret ambiguous situations as more threatening than do parents of nonanxious children. Furthermore, after anxious children had a chance to converse with their parents following an ambiguously threatening situation, the children's choice of avoidant behavior increased. The authors suggest that parents modeled anxious coping and reinforced anxious behavior by offering reassurance following avoidant responding.

Cognitive-behavioral approaches to child and adolescent anxiety have been designed to address concerns at each level of the model (Kendall & Suveg, 2006). For example, at the physiological level, children may learn relaxation techniques (e.g., diaphragmatic breathing, muscle relaxation, visual imagery). Cognitive rumination may be addressed by teaching children how to generate rational coping responses to cognitive distortions. At the behavioral level, the majority of treatment alternatives for anxiety continue to emphasize the role of exposure-based techniques such as systematic desensitization. Most recently, CBT researchers have begun to emphasize the role of the social environment in maintaining social anxiety. Thus, parents and teachers and other important influences (e.g., siblings, peers) on the child have been more aggressively recruited to participate in treatment. For example, in some cases, it has been suggested that to maximize the power of modeling and social reinforcement, parents must first be taught to manage their own anxiety before treatment for their child is initiated (Silverman & Kurtines, 1996).

Conduct Problems

As with internalizing problems, both environmental and cognitive variables are hypothesized to play a key role in the development of externalizing problems such as Conduct Disorder and Oppositional Defiant Disorder. Drawing both on Bandura's social learning theory and Skinner's operant model, Gerald Patterson's (Granic & Patterson, 2006) coercion model has been shown to account for significant variance in the development and maintenance of externalizing problems. According to the coercion model, parents may accidentally teach their children to exhibit externalizing problems. The cycle begins with parent demands for compliance. Children typically respond to requests for compliance with relatively mild coercive behavior (e.g., whining, aggression). For the coercive process to advance, parents then withdraw demands contingent on the child's aversive behaviors. Interestingly, both the child's behavior (via withdrawal of the demand) and the parent's permissive behavior (via the child's withdrawal of aversive behavior) are negatively reinforced. As a result, the child becomes more likely to use coercive behavior in the future, and the parent is more likely to give in. The development of this pattern of behavior is deemed the "coercive cycle" or "coercion trap" and, if unabated, is hypothesized to lead to antisocial behavior.

Cognitions are believed by many to play an important role in externalizing problems. For example, in addition to studying anxiety in children, Barrett et al. (1996) also investigated oppositional behavior, with similar results. That is, consistent with Dodge (1986), children categorized in the oppositional group interpreted ambiguous situations as more threatening than did children in a control group. In fact, the differences observed in the oppositional group were even greater than the differences observed in the anxious group. Although the anxious and oppositional groups each viewed the situation as threatening, the groups differed in their choice of responses to the situation. As might be expected, the anxious group chose generally avoidant responses, and the oppositional group chose aggressive responses. As in the anxious group, parents of oppositional children viewed the ambiguous situation as more threatening than parents in the control group. Remarkably, parent-child discussions following the first exposure to the ambiguous stimulus also increased the likelihood of an aggressive child response.

Attention Problems

Kendall's (2000) distinction between cognitive distortions and cognitive deficiencies is relevant to both internalizing and externalizing problems; however, the distinction is perhaps most relevant to Attention-Deficit/Hyperactivity Disorder (ADHD). That is, researchers tend to characterize ADHD as a problem of cognitive deficiency rather than a problem of cognitive distortion, thus potentially rendering the disorder more difficult to treat (Barkley, 1997; Hinshaw, 2006). Indeed, cognitive-behavioral interventions for ADHD have generally been regarded as less effective than interventions for anxiety, depression, and conduct problems. Current state-of-the-art treatment for many children diagnosed with ADHD is a combination of stimulant medication and behavioral interventions in the classroom and at home (MTA Cooperative Group, 2004).

Despite their apparent utility for other problems affecting youth, CBT interventions for ADHD have received only inconsistent support (Pelham, Wheeler, & Chronis, 1998). On the other hand, some authors have claimed some success in shifting the control of behavior from external consequences to internal ones. As noted previously, Meichenbaum (1977) presented self-instructional training as one promising alternative. Some research has even supported using CBT procedures with preschoolers labeled impulsive, and treatment gains have sometimes generalized to the classroom (e.g., Bryant & Budd, 1982). However, little research has been conducted on self-instructional training as a treatment option for ADHD.

Because approximately 50% of children with ADHD also have significant social problems (Pelham & Bender, 1982), social skills training has become increasingly popular with this population (Hupp, Reitman, Northup, O'Callaghan, & LeBlanc, 2002; Pfiffner & McBurnett, 1997). Indeed, it is well known that effective social skills training should incorporate elements of behavioral therapy such as teaching problem-solving skills in social contexts (Barkley, Edwards, Laneri, Fletcher, & Metevia, 2001; Fenstermacher, Olympia, & Sheridan, 2006). By and large, the effectiveness of such efforts in improving short-term outcomes for children diagnosed with ADHD is promising (see Pfiffner & McBurnett, 1997) but remains speculative over the long term.

Parenting and Parenting Stress

Cognitive-behavioral therapy has the potential to affect parents in at least four ways. First, CBT teaches parents how to more effectively manipulate antecedents and consequences associated with their child's problem behavior. Second, CBT often employs parents as models for desirable, adaptive behaviors. Third, CBT may address the parent's own psychopathology (e.g., depression, anger). Fourth, beyond simply addressing the need for some parents to obtain treatment of their own psychopathology, CBT has begun to focus more attention on the role of parenting stress. Specifically, researchers have become interested in how stress may influence parental perceptions of the child. The first three issues have been discussed in previous sections; we now examine how the cognitive-behavioral framework may be applied to parent perceptions of child behavior.

Cognitive-behavioral theorists have recently begun to examine the extent to which parenting behavior may be influenced by parental attributions about child behavior (Anastopolous & Farley, 2003; Sanders, Cann, & Markie-Dadds, 2003). In an experimental manipulation of parents' attributions, Slep and O'Leary (1998) randomly assigned 40 mothers to one of two conditions. In one condition, the mothers were given feedback that their child was primarily responsible for his or her own disruptive behavior (i.e., child-responsible group). In the other condition, parents were told that their child's disruptive behavior was developmentally appropriate (i.e., child-*not*-responsible group). This feedback was actually not based on anything other than random assignment, though parents were told it was based on a previous interview. During observations of a parent-child interaction that followed the bogus feedback, mothers in the child-responsible group demonstrated significantly more harsh parenting behaviors than parents in the child-not-responsible group. Thus, experimentally manipulated parenting attributions played a significant role in the parent's behavior. This line of research has now led to the development of child abuse prevention programs that incorporate components targeting parental attributions for change (Sanders et al., 2004).

SUMMARY

Cognitive-behavioral theory has been described as a big tent with room for many complementary (and some competing) theories. Cognitive-behavioral therapists can choose from an increasingly large number of intervention options, but there are at least three major unifying factors underlying CBT for children and adolescents. Although these factors are not uniformly characteristic of all research and theory in CBT, these general principles continue to offer guidance concerning the future path that CBT research and practice may take. First, CBT for children should emphasize the development of a collaborative relationship between the therapist and the client (or family) as well as a focus on the response of the individual to treatment. Second, consistent with the view offered by Wolpe (1993) and other CBT founders, empirical data should serve as the basis for future modifications of CBT theory and practice (Reitman & Drabman, 1997). The development of manualized and, more recently, modularized treatment approaches are recent changes in practice that were driven by empirical data suggesting that the treatment outcomes could be enhanced with improvements in treatment integrity. Third, CBT therapists emphasize the importance of client activity outside of the therapy room, including homework exercises between sessions, self-monitoring, and a variety of other techniques that ensure that improvements are noted in session ultimately result in meaningful change (i.e., change that generalizes and can be maintained over time; see Stokes & Baer, 1977).

Despite the development of manualized treatments for children and adolescents, no two children, parents, or families that participate in CBT will have the same therapeutic experience. Moreover, as noted previously, treatment targets and developmental considerations may dictate the use of procedures that emphasize or de-emphasize the inclusion of cognitive variables. For some youth, overt behavioral problems may be the only focus of intervention, whereas other youth might be more likely to benefit from a therapeutic approach emphasizing cognitions. Also, as noted by Kendall (2000), cognitive-behavioral therapists may focus on cognitive distortions or cognitive deficiencies.

Nor is it presently necessary to make a hard choice between CBT approaches based on their overt and covert characteristics. Overt and covert approaches can certainly be used in a complementary fashion. For example, Mennuti, Christner, and Freeman (2006) recently enumerated common CBT procedures based on this overt-covert dimension. Drawing on their work, we have drafted a similar table (see Table 9.1) that more directly contrasts the overt behavioral technique with its covert counterpart. Though not comprehensive, this table provides a useful index of common cognitive techniques and nicely summarizes the therapeutic tools available to contemporary cognitive-behavioral therapists.

Table 9.1 Examples of Techniques Used in Cognitive-Behavioral Therapy

Overt Behavior Techniques	Covert Behavior Techniques
Self-monitoring	Thought record
Participant modeling	Cognitive modeling
Social skills training	Self-instructions
Competing response training	Rational responses
Positive activity scheduling	Increasing positive thoughts
Tokens and reinforcers	Self-praise
Role-playing	Mental rehearsal
Behavioral experiments	Socratic questioning
Progressive muscle relaxation	Visual imagery
Exposure to external stimuli	Exposure to internal stimuli

As can be seen in Table 9.1, monitoring can be employed to track either overt or covert behavior. Similarly, the covert counterpart to participant modeling is Meichenbaum's cognitive modeling. Social skills training is commonly used to overcome social deficits, and self-instruction training can be used to deal with cognitive deficits. Competing behavioral responses can be generated for overt or covert behavior (e.g., irrational thoughts). Increases in positive reinforcement theoretically can be achieved through positive activity scheduling (see Lewinsohn et al., 1999) or techniques aimed at increasing positive thoughts (see Henriques et al., 2003, for an example called the Hope Kit). Additionally, as seen at the bottom of Table 9.1, anxiety treatments may involve exposure to overt or covert (e.g., imaginal) stimuli. For example, a "worry chair" (e.g., making oneself worry for a set amount of time each day) is designed to expose a client with Generalized Anxiety Disorder to covert stimuli (e.g., worry), and interoceptive exposure (e.g., intentionally making oneself dizzy) is designed to produce covert exposure to panic symptoms (see Barlow, 2002, for a detailed account).

The last pairing in Table 9.1 hints at the newest theoretical wrinkle in the cognitive-behavioral framework. Specifically, Hayes (2004) describes "three waves" of behavior therapy. The first wave was heavily influenced by the work of Watson and Skinner. As shortcomings of the first wave became apparent, a second wave emerged. Influenced largely by Ellis and A. Beck, this second wave is sometimes referred to as the "cognitive revolution." Mahoney and Arnkoff (1978) summarized such innovations during this time as cognitive restructuring, coping skills, and problem solving as part of the behavior therapy tradition. The third wave of behavior therapy is thus characterized as a response to the shortcomings of the second wave. For example, Hayes (2004, p. 645) argues that it is "possible to alter the function of thoughts without first altering their form." Hayes goes on to present alternatives to directly attempting to modify cognitive distortions. These most recent additions to the CBT model are presently referred to as acceptance- or mindfulness-based therapies, and they incorporate principles borrowed from theology, Middle Eastern philosophy, and meditation.

One of the best known of the acceptance-based approaches is acceptance and commitment therapy (ACT; Hayes et al., 1999). In ACT, clients are instructed to learn to accept their cognitive distortions and emotional reactions without having to avoid or change them. Clients are taught to simply observe cognitions and, further, that the only cognitive change that is needed is to accept the fact that it is okay to have cognitive distortions and intense emotions. Similar therapies are mindfulness-based cognitive therapy (Teasdale et al., 2002) and dialectical behavior therapy (Linehan, 1993). Although acceptance- and mindfulness-based therapies are relatively new, early research appears encouraging (Hayes, Masuda, Bissett, Luoma, & Guerrero, 2004). Very little research has been devoted to ACT for youth, but a few case examples have yielded promising results (Heffner, Sperry, Eifert, & Detweiler, 2002; Wicksell, Dahl, Magnusson, & Olsson, 2005; see also Greco, Blackledge, Coyne, & Ehrenreich, 2005; Murrell, Coyne, & Wilson, 2004). As with other innovations within the cognitive-behavioral framework, ACT does not diminish the value of the other cognitive-behavioral techniques. Rather, it appears to offer yet another treatment alternative.

Throughout this chapter, CBT has been discussed primarily in the context of individual or single-family psychotherapy; however, cognitive and behavioral techniques hold significant promise for group therapy. In fact, CBT for adolescent depression may be enhanced by group social support (see Clarke, DeBar, & Lewinsohn, 2003). Because CBT is suitable for group administration it may also prove useful when incorporated into prevention programs. There are several forms of prevention: indicated, selective, universal, and health promotion models (Weisz, Sandler, Durlak, & Anton, 2005). Indicated prevention is intended to address the needs of individuals with significant symptoms that fall short of diagnosis. Selective prevention programs are for groups of individuals who share risk factors for developing problems (e.g., exposure to a traumatic event). Universal prevention programs are designed to limit the effects of potential risk factors for all youth (e.g., everyone in a school district), without specifically identifying individuals with certain risk factors. Finally, recent trends in the prevention literature point toward a health promotion focus that emphasizes building competencies within an entire population rather than focusing on risk reduction. An evidence base is quickly emerging for cognitive-behavioral prevention and health promotion programs at all four levels (Weisz et al., 2005).

In a recent symposium of former presidents of the Association for Behavioral and Cognitive Therapies (ABCT;* Albano, 2006), a number of topics relevant to the development of CBT were discussed, and two issues were central to this chapter and the future of CBT for children and adolescents. The first issue concerns core principles. Specifically, other than empiricism, are there any remaining core principles associated with CBT? If the answer is no, then theoretical considerations must always take a backseat to what works. Indeed, many early behavior therapists seemed to suggest that data should trump theory in behavior therapy, and that no aspect of the therapeutic model was to be regarded as sacred (see Reitman & Drabman, 1997). Nevertheless, in the symposium, Ollendick (2006) noted that he was initially drawn to the behavioral approach by something akin to core principles, specifically, its emphasis on functional assessment and idiographic case analysis. Wilson (2006) suggested that the validity of core theoretical principles should be subjected to rigorous analysis in dismantling studies, and he noted the substantive contributions made by Jacobson and Rachman in challenging the status quo via such an approach.

A second major issue discussed in the symposium concerned how best to go about exporting or disseminating behavioral work. Heimberg (2006) pointed out that many clients still do not benefit from cognitive-behavioral therapy and warned against complacency. Wilson (2006) suggested that efforts to disseminate existing treatment packages were unlikely to be successful without the elucidation of simpler, universal change principles underlying CBT. Interestingly, there were different ideas presented regarding how to best refine CBT. On the one hand, some viewed the future as requiring more sophisticated studies (with greater numbers of

---

*Reflecting a greater emphasis on cognitions, the association changed its name from Association for the Advancement of Behavior Therapy to Association for Behavioral and Cognitive Therapies in 2005.

participants) examining the mediators and moderators of treatment outcome; others thought more progress could be made by returning to idiographic approaches (to better understand change mechanisms at the level of the individual). Ultimately, this collection of ABCT past presidents suggested that much progress had been made on both theoretical and practical levels, yet there was broad consensus that much remained to be done.

REFERENCES

Albano, A. M. (Moderator). (2006, November). *The evolution of cognitive behavioral treatment and assessment*. Panel discussion given at the 40th annual meeting of the Association for Behavioral and Cognitive Therapies, Chicago.

American Psychiatric Association. (2000). *Diagnostic and statistical manual of mental disorders* (4th ed., text rev.). Washington, DC: Author.

Anastopolous, A. D., & Farley, S. E. (2003). A cognitive-behavioral training program for parents of children with attention-deficit/hyperactivity disorder. In A. E. Kazdin, & J. R. Weisz (Eds.), *Evidence-based psychotherapies for children and adolescents* (pp. 187–203). New York: Guilford Press.

Bandura, A. (1973). *Aggression: A social learning analysis*. Englewood Cliffs, NJ: Prentice-Hall.

Bandura, A. (1974). Behavior theory and the models of man. *American Psychologist, 29*, 859–869.

Bandura, A. (1977a). Self-efficacy: Toward a unifying theory of behavioral change. *Psychological Review, 84*, 191–215.

Bandura, A. (1977b). *Social learning theory*. Englewood Cliffs, NJ: Prentice-Hall.

Bandura, A. (1997). *Self-efficacy: The exercise of control*. New York: Freeman.

Bandura, A. (2004). Health promotion by social cognitive means. *Health Education and Behavior, 31*, 143–164.

Barkley, R. A. (1997). *ADHD and the nature of self-control*. New York: Guilford Press.

Barkley, R. A., Edwards, G., Laneri, M., Fletcher, K., & Metevia, L. (2001). The efficacy of problem-solving communication training alone, behavior management training alone, and their combination for parent-adolescent conflict in teenagers with ADHD and ODD. *Journal of Consulting and Clinical Psychology, 69*, 926–941.

Barlow, D. H. (2002). *Anxiety and its disorders: The nature and treatment of anxiety and panic* (2nd ed.). New York: Guilford Press.

Baron, A., Kaufman, A., & Stauber, K. A. (1969). Effects of instructions and reinforcement-feedback on human operant behavior maintained by fixed-interval reinforcement. *Journal of the Experimental Analysis of Behavior, 12*, 701–712.

Barrett, P. M., Rapee, R. M., Dadds, M. M., & Ryan, S. M. (1996). Family enhancement of cognitive style in anxious and aggressive children. *Journal of Abnormal Child Psychology, 24*, 187–203.

Beck, A. T. (1963). Thinking and depression: Pt. 1. Idiosyncratic content and cognitive distortions. *Archives of General Psychiatry, 9*, 324–333.

Beck, A. T. (1999). *Prisoners of hate: The cognitive basis of anger, hostility, and violence*. New York: HarperCollins.

Beck, A. T., Emery, G., & Greenberg, R. L. (2005). *Anxiety disorders and phobias: A cognitive perspective*. New York: Basic Books.

Beck, A. T., Rush, A. J., Shaw, B. F., & Emery, G. (1979). *Cognitive therapy of depression*. New York: Guilford Press.

Beck, J. S. (1995). *Cognitive therapy: Basics and beyond*. New York: Guilford Press.

Beidel, D. C., & Turner, S. M. (1986). A critique of the theoretical basis of cognitive-behavioral theories and therapy. *Clinical Psychology Review, 6*, 177–197.

Bernard, M. E., & DiGiuseppe, R. (1989). Rational-emotive therapy today. In M. E. Bernard, & R. DiGiuseppe (Eds.), *Inside rational-emotive therapy: A critical appraisal of the theory and therapy of Albert Ellis* (pp. 1–7). San Diego, CA: Academic Press.

Bijou, S. W., & Baer, D. M. (1961). *Child development: Vol. 1. A systematic and empirical theory*. East Norwalk, CT: Appleton-Century-Crofts.

Braswell, L., & Kendall, P. C. (2001). Cognitive-behavioral therapy with youth. In K. S. Dobson (Ed.), *Handbook of cognitive-behavioral therapies* (2nd ed., pp. 246–294). New York: Guilford Press.

Bronfenbrenner, U. (2005). *Making human beings human.* Thousand Oaks, CA: Sage.

Bryant, L. E., & Budd, K. S. (1982). Self-instruction training to increase independent work performance in preschoolers. *Journal of Applied Behavior Analysis, 15,* 259–271.

Clarke, G. N., DeBar, L. L., & Lewinsohn, P. M. (2003). Cognitive-behavioral group treatment for adolescent depression. In A. E. Kazdin, & J. R. Weisz (Eds.), *Evidence-based psychotherapies for children and adolescents* (pp. 120–134). New York: Guilford Press.

Deblinger, E., Behl, L. E., & Glickman, A. R. (2006). Treating children who have experienced sexual abuse. In P. C. Kendall (Ed.), *Child and adolescent therapy: Cognitive-behavioral procedures* (3rd ed., pp. 383–416). New York: Guilford Press.

Derisley, J. (2004). Cognitive therapy for children, young people, and families: Considering service provision. *Child and Adolescent Mental Health, 9,* 15–20.

DeRubeis, R. J., Tang, T. Z., & Beck, A. T. (2001). Cognitive therapy. In K. S. Dobson (Ed.), *Handbook of cognitive-behavioral therapies* (2nd ed., pp. 349–392). New York: Guilford Press.

Dobson, K. S., & Dozois, D. J. A. (2001). Historical and philosophical bases of the cognitive-behavioral therapies. In K. S. Dobson (Ed.), *Handbook of cognitive-behavioral therapies* (2nd ed., pp. 3–39). New York: Guilford Press.

Dodge, K. A. (1986). A social information processing model of social competence in children. In M. Perlmutter (Ed.), *Cognitive perspectives on children's social and behavioral development* (pp. 77–126). Hillsdale, NJ: Erlbaum.

Doherr, L., Reynolds, S., Wetherly, J., & Evans, E. (2005). Young children's ability to engage in cognitive therapy tasks: Associations with age and educational experience. *Behavioural and Cognitive Psychotherapy, 33,* 201–215.

Dryden, W., & Ellis, A. (2001). Rational emotive behavioral therapy. In K. S. Dobson (Ed.), *Handbook of cognitive-behavioral therapies* (2nd ed., pp. 295–348). New York: Guilford Press.

D'Zurilla, T. J., & Goldfried, M. R. (1971). Problem solving and behavior modification. *Journal of Abnormal Psychology, 78,* 107–126.

D'Zurilla, T. J., & Nezu, A. M. (2001). Problem-solving therapies. In K. S. Dobson (Ed.), *Handbook of cognitive-behavioral therapies* (2nd ed., pp. 211–245). New York: Guilford Press.

Ellis, A. (1962). *Reason and emotion in psychotherapy.* New York: Lyle Stuart.

Ellis, A. (1980). Rational emotive therapy and cognitive behavior therapy: Similarities and differences. *Cognitive Therapy and Research, 4,* 325–340.

Ellis, A. (1989). Comments on my critics. In M. E. Bernard & R. DiGiuseppe (Eds.), *Inside rational-emotive therapy: A critical appraisal of the theory and therapy of Albert Ellis* (pp. 199–233). San Diego, CA: Academic Press.

Ellis, A. (1999). Why rational emotive therapy to rational-emotive behavior therapy? *Psychotherapy: Theory, Research, Practice and Training, 36,* 154–159.

Ellis, A., & Bernard, M. (1983). An overview of rational-emotive approaches to the problems of childhood. In A. Ellis & M. E. Bernard (Eds.), *Rational-emotive approaches to the problems of childhood* (pp. 3–44). New York: Plenum Press.

Fenstermacher, K., Olympia, D., & Sheridan, S. M. (2006). Effectiveness of a computer-facilitated, interactive social skills training program for boys with attention-deficit/hyperactivity disorder. *School Psychology Quarterly, 21,* 197–224.

Gladstone, T. R. G., & Kaslow, N. J. (1995). Depression and attributions in children and adolescents: A meta-analytic review. *Journal of Abnormal Child Psychology, 23,* 597–606.

Goldfried, M., Decenteceo, E., & Weinberg, L. (1974). Systematic rational restructuring as a self-control technique. *Behavior Therapy, 5,* 247–254.

Granic, I., & Patterson, G. R. (2006). Toward a comprehensive model of antisocial development: A dynamic systems approach. *Psychological Review, 113,* 101–131.

Greco, L. A., Blackledge, J. T., Coyne, L. W., & Ehrenreich, J. T. (2005). Integrating acceptance and mindfulness into treatments for child and adolescent anxiety disorders: Acceptance and commitment therapy as an example. In S. M. Orsillo, & L. Roemer (Eds.), *Acceptance and mindfulness-based approaches to anxiety: Conceptualization and treatment* (pp. 301–324). New York: Springer.

Harris, K., & Graham, S. (1996). *Making the writing process work: Strategies for composition and self-regulation.* Cambridge, MA: Brookline Books.

Hayes, S. C. (2004). Acceptance and commitment therapy, relational frame theory, and the third wave of behavioral and cognitive therapies. *Behavior Therapy, 35,* 639–665.

Hayes, S. C., Masuda, A., Bissett, R., Luoma, J., & Guerrero, L. F. (2004). DBT, FAP, and ACT: How empirically supported are the new behavior therapy technologies? *Behavior Therapy, 35,* 35–54.

Hayes, S. C., Strosahl, K. D., & Wilson, K. G. (1999). *Acceptance and commitment therapy: An experiential approach to behavior change.* New York: Guilford Press.

Heffner, M., Sperry, J., Eifert, G. H., & Detweiler, M. (2002). Acceptance and commitment therapy in the treatment of an adolescent female with anorexia nervosa: A case example. *Cognitive and Behavioral Practice, 9,* 232–236.

Heimberg, R. G. (Panelist). (2006, November). *The evolution of cognitive behavioral treatment and assessment* (A.M. Albano, moderator). Panel discussion given at the 40th annual meeting of the Association for Behavioral and Cognitive Therapies, Chicago.

Henriques, G., Beck, A., & Brown, G. (2003). Cognitive therapy for adolescent and young adult suicide attempters. *American Behavioral Scientist, 46,* 1258–1268.

Hinshaw, S. P. (2006). Treatment for children and adolescents with attention-deficit/hyperactivity disorder. In P. C. Kendall (Ed.), *Child and adolescent therapy: Cognitive-behavioral procedures* (3rd ed., pp. 82–113). New York: Guilford Press.

Hoffman, K. B., Cole, D. A., Martin, J. M., Tram, J., & Seroczynski, A. D. (2000). Are the discrepancies between self- and others' appraisals of competence predictive or reflective of depressive symptoms in children and adolescents: Pt. II. A longitudinal study. *Journal of Abnormal Psychology, 109,* 651–662.

Hupp, S. D. A., Reitman, D., Northup, J., O'Callaghan, P., & LeBlanc, M. (2002). The effects of delayed rewards, tokens, and stimulant medication on sportsmanlike behavior with ADHD-diagnosed children. *Behavior Modification, 26,* 148–162.

Iwata, B. A., Smith, R. G., & Michael, J. L. (2000). Current research on the influence of establishing operations on behavior in applied settings. *Journal of Applied Behavior Analysis, 33,* 411–418.

Jensen, P. S., Knapp, P., & Mrazek, D. A. (2006). *Toward a new diagnostic system for child psychopathology: Moving beyond the DSM.* New York: Guilford Press.

Kendall, P. C. (2000). Guiding theory for therapy with children and adolescents. In P. C. Kendall, (Ed.), *Child and adolescent therapy: Cognitive-behavioral procedures* (2nd ed., pp. 3–27). New York: Guilford Press.

Kendall, P. C. (2006). Guiding theory for therapy with children and adolescents. In P. C. Kendall (Ed.), *Child and adolescent therapy: Cognitive-behavioral procedures* (3rd ed., pp. 3–32). New York: Guilford Press.

Kendall, P. C., & Hollon, S. D. (1979). Cognitive-behavioral interventions: Overview and current status. In P. C. Kendall, S. D. Hollon, (Eds.), *Cognitive-behavioral interventions: Theory, research, and practice* (pp. 1–9). New York: Academic Press.

Kendall, P. C., & Suveg, C. (2006). Treating anxiety disorders in youth. In P. C. Kendall (Ed.), *Child and adolescent therapy: Cognitive-behavioral procedures* (3rd ed., pp. 322–355). New York: Guilford Press.

Kohlenberg, R. J., & Tsai, M. (1991). *Functional analytic psychotherapy: Creating intense and therapeutic relationships.* New York: Plenum Press.

Lang, P. (1968). Fear reduction and fear behavior: Problems in treating a construct. In J. M. Shlien (Ed.), *Research in psychotherapy* (pp. 90–102). Washington, DC: American Psychological Association.

Lazarus, A. A. (1989). The practice of rational-emotive therapy. In M. E. Bernard, & R. DiGiuseppe (Eds.), *Inside rational-emotive therapy: A critical appraisal of the theory and therapy of Albert Ellis* (pp. 95–112). San Diego, CA: Academic Press.

Lazarus, A. A. (1996). Some reflections after 40 years of trying to be an effective psychotherapist. *Psychotherapy: Theory, Research, Practice and Training, 33,* 142–145.

Lazarus, R. S. (1966). *Psychological stress and the coping process.* New York: McGraw-Hill.

Lazarus, R. S., & Folkman, S. (1984). *Stress, appraisal, and coping.* New York: Springer.

Lewinsohn, P. M. (1974). A behavioral approach to depression. In R. J. Friedman, & M. M. Katz (Eds.), *The psychology of depression: Contemporary theory and research* (pp. 157–185). Washington, DC: Winston-Wiley.

Lewinsohn, P. M., Allen, N. B., Seeley, J. R., & Gotlib, I. H. (1999). First onset versus recurrence of depression: Differential processes of psychosocial risk. *Journal of Abnormal Psychology, 108*, 483–489.

Lewinsohn, P. M., Joiner, T. E., Jr., & Rohde, P. (2001). Evaluation of cognitive diathesis-stress models in predicting major depressive disorder in adolescents. *Journal of Abnormal Psychology, 110*, 203–215.

Linehan, M. M. (1993). *Cognitive-behavioral treatment of borderline personality disorder.* New York: Guilford Press.

Luria, A. (1959). The directive function of speech in development. *Word, 18*, 341–352.

Luria, A. (1961). *The role of speech in the regulation of normal and abnormal behaviors.* New York: Liveright.

Maccoby, E. (1968) The development of moral values and behavior in children. In J. Clausen (Ed.), *Socialization and society* (pp. 227–269). Boston: Little, Brown.

Mahoney, M. J., & Arnkoff, D. (1978). Cognitive and self-control strategies. In S. L. Garfield & A. E. Bergin (Eds.), *Handbook of psychotherapy and behavior change: An empirical analysis* (2nd ed., pp. 689–722). New York: Wiley.

Masek, B., Russo, D. C., & Varni, J. W. (1984). Behavioral approaches to the management of chronic pain in children. *Pediatric Clinics of North America, 31*, 1113–1131.

McGrath, E. P., & Repetti, R. L. (2002). A longitudinal study of children's depressive symptoms, self perceptions, and cognitive distortions about the self. *Journal of Abnormal Psychology, 111*, 77–87.

Meichenbaum, D. (1977). *Cognitive-behavior modification.* New York: Plenum Press.

Meichenbaum, D. (1985). *Stress inoculation training.* New York: Pergamon Press.

Mennuti, R. B., Christner, R. W., & Freeman, A. (2006). An introduction to a school-based cognitive-behavioral framework. In R. B. Mennuti, A. Freeman, & R. W. Christner (Eds.), *Cognitive-behavioral interventions in educational settings: A handbook for practice* (pp. 3–19). New York: Routledge.

Mennuti, R. B., Freeman, A., & Christner, R. W. (Eds.). (2006). *Cognitive-behavioral interventions in educational settings: A handbook for practice.* New York: Routledge.

Miltenberger, R. G. (2004). Behavior modification: Principles and procedures (3rd ed.) Belmont, CA: Wadsworth/Thomson Learning.

Mowrer, O. H. (1939). A stimulus-response analysis of anxiety and its role as a reinforcing agent. *Psychological Review, 46*, 553–565.

MTA Cooperative Group. (2004). National Institute of Mental Health Multimodal Treatment Study of ADHD follow-up: 24-month outcomes of treatment strategies for attention-deficit/hyperactivity disorder. *Pediatrics, 113*, 754–761.

Murrell, A. R., Coyne, L. W., & Wilson, K. G. (2004). ACT with children, adolescents, & their parents. In S. C. Hayes, & K. Strosahl, (Eds.), *Acceptance and commitment therapy: A clinician's guide* (pp. 249–273). New York: Springer Press.

Ollendick, T. H. (Panelist). (2006, November). *The evolution of cognitive behavioral treatment and assessment* (A.M. Albano, moderator). Panel discussion given at the 40th annual meeting of the Association for Behavioral and Cognitive Therapies, Chicago.

Ollendick, T. H., & King, N. J. (1998). Empirically supported treatments for children with phobic and anxiety disorders: Current status. *Journal of Clinical Child Psychology, 27*, 156–167.

Ollendick, T. H., & King, N. J. (2000). Empirically supported treatments for children and adolescents. In P. C. Kendall (Ed.), *Child and adolescent therapy: Cognitive-behavioral procedures* (2nd ed., pp. 386–425). New York: Guilford Press.

Pelham, W. E., & Bender, M. E. (1982). Peer relationships in hyperactive children: Description and treatment. *Advances in Learning and Behavioral Disabilities, 1*, 365–436.

Pelham, W. E., Wheeler, T., & Chronis, A., (1998). Empirically-supported psychosocial treatments for attention-deficit/hyperactivity disorder. *Journal of Clinical Child Psychology, 27*, 190–205.

Pfiffner, L. J., & McBurnett, K. (1997). Social skills training with parent generalization: Treatment effects for children with attention-deficit/hyperactivity disorder. *Journal of Consulting and Clinical Psychology, 65*, 749–757.

Pilowsky, D. J., Wickramaratne, P., Nomura, Y., & Weissman, M. M. (2006). Family discord, parental depression, and psychopathology in offspring: 20-year follow-up. *Journal of the American Academy of Child and Adolescent Psychiatry, 45*, 452–460.

Puig-Antich, J., Kaufman, J., Ryan, N. D., Williamson, D. E., Dahl, R. E., Lukens, E., et al. (1993). The psychosocial functioning and family environment of depressed adolescents. *Journal of the American Academy of Child and Adolescent Psychiatry, 32*, 244–253.

Rachman, S. (1991). Neo-conditioning and the classical theory of fear acquisition. *Clinical Psychology Review, 11*, 155–173.

Reitman, D., & Drabman, R. S. (1997). The value of recognizing our differences and promoting healthy competition: The cognitive-behavioral debate. *Behavior Therapy, 28*, 419–429.

Rokke, P. D., & Rehm, L. P. (2001). Self-management therapies. In K. S. Dobson (Ed.), *Handbook of cognitive-behavioral therapies* (2nd ed., pp. 173–210). New York: Guilford Press.

Rudolph, K. D., & Clark, A. G. (2001). Conceptions of relationships in children with depressive and aggressive symptoms: Social-cognitive distortion or reality? *Journal of Abnormal Child Psychology, 29*, 41–56.

Sanders, M. R., Cann, W., & Markie-Dadds, C. (2003). The triple P-positive parenting program: A universal population-level approach to the prevention of child abuse. *Child Abuse Review, 12*, 155–171.

Sanders, M. R., Pidgeon, A. M., Gravestock, F., Connors, M. D., Brown, S., & Young, R. W. (2004). Does parental attributional retraining and anger management enhance the effects of the triple P-positive parenting program with parents at risk of child maltreatment? *Behavior Therapy, 35*, 513–535.

Seligman, M. E. P. (1975). *Helplessness: On depression, development, and death.* New York: Freeman.

Silverman, W. K., & Kurtines, W. M. (1996). *Anxiety and phobic disorders: A pragmatic approach.* New York: Plenum Press.

Skinner, B. F. (1953). *Science and human behavior.* New York: Free Press.

Skinner, B. F. (1957). *Verbal behavior.* New York: Appleton-Century-Crofts.

Skinner, B. F. (1963). Behaviorism at fifty. *Science, 140*, 951–958.

Slep, A. M., & O'Leary, S. G. (1998). The effects of maternal attributions on parenting: An experimental analysis. *Journal of Family Psychology, 12*, 234–243.

Southam-Gerow, M. A., & Kendall, P. C. (2002). Emotion regulation and understanding: Implications for child psychopathology and therapy. *Clinical Psychology Review, 22*, 189–222.

Stokes, T. F., & Baer, D. M. (1977). An implicit technology of generalization. *Journal of Applied Behavior Analysis, 10*, 349–367.

Teasdale, J. D., Moore, R. G., Hayhurst, H., Pope, M., Williams, S., & Segal, Z. V. (2002). Metacognitive awareness and prevention of relapse in depression: Empirical evidence. *Journal of Consulting and Clinical Psychology, 70*, 275–287.

Thorndike, E. L. (1911). *Animal intelligence: Experimental studies.* Lewiston, NY: Macmillan.

Treadwell, K. R. H., & Kendall, P. C. (1996). Self-talk in anxiety-disordered youth: States of mind, content specificity, and treatment outcome. *Journal of Consulting and Clinical Psychology, 63*, 560–568.

Vygotsky, L. (1962). *Thought and language.* New York: Wiley.

Watson, J. B. (1913). Psychology as a behaviorist views it. *Psychological Review, 20*, 158–177.

Watson, J. B. (1924). *Behaviorism.* New York: People's Institute.

Watson, J. B., & Watson, R. R. (1921). Studies in infant psychology. *Scientific Monthly, 13*, 493–515.

Weisz, J. R., Sandler, I. N., Durlak, J. A., & Anton, B. S. (2005). Promoting and protecting youth mental health through evidence-based prevention and treatment. *American Psychologist, 60*, 628–648.

Wicksell, R. K., Dahl, J., Magnusson, B., & Olsson, G. L. (2005). Using acceptance and commitment therapy in the rehabilitation of an adolescent female with chronic pain: A case example. *Cognitive and Behavioral Practice, 12*, 415–423.

Wilfley, D. E., Passi, V. A., Cooperberg, J., & Stein, R. I. (2006). Cognitive-behavioral therapy for youth with eating disorders and obesity. In P. C. Kendall (Ed.), *Child and adolescent therapy: Cognitive-behavioral procedures* (3rd ed., pp. 322–355). New York: Guilford Press.

Wilson, G. T. (Panelist). (2006, November). *The evolution of cognitive behavioral treatment and assessment* (A.M. Albano, moderator). Panel discussion given at the 40th annual meeting of the Association for Behavioral and Cognitive Therapies, Chicago.

Wolpe, J. (1993). The cognitivist oversell and comments on symposium contributions. *Journal of Behavior Therapy and Experimental Psychiatry, 24*, 141–147.

PART III

Research Contributions

CHAPTER 10

Statistical Considerations: Moderators and Mediators

Barbara Jandasek, Grayson N. Holmbeck, and Brigid M. Rose

In recent years, researchers who study pediatric populations have begun to posit complex theoretical models to explain developmental and psychological phenomena of interest. These models include longitudinal developmental pathways, risk and protective factors, and cognitive appraisal and coping processes (Thompson & Gustafson, 1996). This increase in theoretical complexity has necessitated an increase in terminological sophistication and the use of multivariate statistical strategies. Research based on mediational and moderational models has emerged as a critical method for testing competing theories about developmental pathways and other concepts central to clinical child and pediatric psychology. This chapter represents a compilation of the authors' previous works regarding mediation and moderation (Holmbeck, 1997, 2002; Rose, Holmbeck, Coakley, & Franks, 2004).

Specifically, the goal of this chapter is to provide an overview of mediators and moderators and their application to both research and practice in clinical child and pediatric psychology. First, definitions of each term and applied examples are provided, including more complex uses of these terms (e.g., moderated mediation, mediated moderation) and common definitional inconsistencies found in the literature. Next, statistical strategies used to evaluate mediator and moderator effects are reviewed (i.e., multiple regression and structural equation modeling techniques), including a presentation of strengths and limitations, common statistical inconsistencies, and applied statistical examples. Third, mediator and moderator effects in longitudinal research, intervention and outcome studies, and the study of risk and protective factors are discussed. Finally, we provide recommendations for applying mediational and moderational research to clinical practice.

Completion of this manuscript was supported by research grants from the National Institute of Child Health and Human Development (NICHD, R01-HD048629) and the March of Dimes Birth Defects Foundation (MOD; 12-FY-04-47).

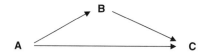

Figure 10.1   Mediated relationship among variables (A = Predictor; B = Mediator; C = Criterion/outcome).

DEFINITIONAL ISSUES

What Is a Mediator?

A mediator is an explanatory link in the relationship between two other variables (Figure 10.1; see Table 10.1 for definitions of all important terms). Often a mediator variable is conceptualized as the mechanism through which one variable (i.e., the predictor) influences another variable (i.e., the criterion; Baron & Kenny, 1986; Holmbeck, 1997, 2002). In other words, a mediator specifies how (or the mechanism by which) a given effect occurs (Baron & Kenny, 1986; James & Brett, 1984). Other terminology, such as *indirect effect* and *surrogate* or *intermediate endpoint effect,* is sometimes used interchangeably with mediation (MacKinnon, Lockwood, Hoffman, West, & Sheets, 2002), although these terms may not be conceptually identical (Holmbeck, 2002).

Suppose, hypothetically, that a researcher finds that parental intrusiveness is negatively associated with child adherence to a medical regimen. Although interesting, this finding does not tell us very much about processes that underlie the relationship between intrusiveness and adherence. By testing for mediational effects, a researcher can explore whether a third variable (e.g., child independence) might account for or explain the relationship between these variables. Continuing with the example, suppose that child independence mediates the

Table 10.1   Definition of Terms

Term	Definition
Mediator	The variable or mechanism by which a predictor influences an outcome variable (Figure 10.1).
Moderator	A variable that influences the strength or direction of a relationship between a predictor and an outcome (Figure 10.2).
Moderated mediation	A mediational model is significant only at certain levels of a moderator variable (Figure 10.3).
Mediated moderation	A moderational (or interaction) effect is mediated by another variable (Figure 10.4).
Protective factor	A variable that decreases the likelihood of a negative outcome under adverse conditions (Figure 10.7).
Resource factor	A variable that positively influences outcome, regardless of the presence of adversity (Figure 10.7).
Vulnerability factor	A variable that increases the likelihood of a poor outcome under adverse conditions (Figure 10.8).
Risk factor	A variable that negatively influences outcome regardless of the presence of adversity (Figure 10.8).

relationship between intrusiveness and adherence (more intrusive parenting $\rightarrow$ less child independence $\rightarrow$ less medical adherence). That is, parental intrusiveness impacts negatively on level of child independence, which in turn contributes to poor medical adherence (see Holmbeck, Shapera, & Hommeyer, 2002, for a similar example). In intervention studies, mediator effects may describe critical components of an intervention through which therapeutic change occurs (MacKinnon, Krull, & Lockwood, 2000, see later in chapter for more detail).

It is critical to note that a mediational model is, by its nature, a causal model. In other words, a mediational hypothesis is appropriate when one seeks to explain the causal process, or mechanism, by which an independent variable impacts a dependent variable (MacKinnon et al., 2000). Even if one's data do not permit causal conclusions (e.g., the data are cross-sectional and nonexperimental), the theory that underlies such a model is still inherently causal because it suggests a direction of influence.

One additional clarification about mediator variables is warranted. Typically, mediator mechanisms are proposed only after a significant association between the independent variable and the dependent variable has been fairly well established in the literature (i.e., indicating that there is, in fact, an effect to mediate). In other words, one does not typically begin study in a new research area by proposing mediational models. Such models are usually a natural extension of a well-established body of literature. Continuing with the earlier example, if one was interested in examining variables that mediate the link between parental intrusiveness and child medical adherence, one would want to be very confident that this link would be significant in one's own data set based on past research conducted on the variables.

What Is a Moderator?

Unlike a mediator, a moderator is a variable that influences the strength or the direction of a relationship between a predictor variable and a criterion variable (Figure 10.2). In other words, moderation describes an interaction effect whereby the impact of the independent variable on the dependent variable varies as a function of the level, or value, of the moderator variable. Moderator variables are frequently described as individual (e.g., sex, coping) or contextual (e.g., social support, family environment) characteristics (Grant et al., 2006). Suppose a researcher finds that familial stress is negatively associated with child psychological adjustment. Although this finding may be of interest to the researcher, it may be that the effect becomes more or less robust in the presence of other contextual variables. In fact, the researcher may develop specific theories about conditions that determine

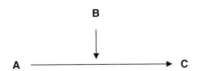

Figure 10.2   Moderated relationship among variables (A = Predictor; B = Moderator; C = Criterion/outcome).

the strength of the relationship between stress and adjustment. For example, the strength or the direction of the relationship between stress and adjustment may depend on the type of coping used by the family. That is, a significant association may emerge *only* when a child copes in a maladaptive manner. By testing coping style as a moderator of the relationship between stress and outcome, the researcher can specify certain conditions under which family stress predicts child adjustment. Such findings would likely have implications for future interventions.

Diagrammatic Distinction between Mediators and Moderators

Mediators and moderators can also be differentiated diagrammatically (see Figures 10.1 and 10.2; Baron & Kenny, 1986; J. Cohen & Cohen, 1983). A mediator (B; top of Figure 10.1) falls in the causal pathway between two variables (A and C in Figure 10.1; James & Brett, 1984). That is, if A is significantly associated with C, and A influences B, and B influences C, then B is a mediating variable between A and C. On the other hand, if A is expected to be related to C, but only under certain conditions of B, then B is a moderator variable. The moderator (B) can be drawn to indicate that it has an impact on the relationship between A and C (see Figure 10.2). Although some variables are more likely to be moderators than mediators (e.g., gender), some variables could serve either function—depending on the conceptual model under investigation (for examples where "coping strategies" were tested as both mediators and moderators in competing models, see Lewis & Kliewer, 1996; Sandler, Tein, & West, 1994). Moreover, both moderators and mediators can be specified within the same model (e.g., moderated mediation; James & Brett, 1984; for examples of this strategy, see Holmbeck, 1996; Simons, Lorenz, Wu, & Conger, 1993).

Applied Examples of Mediation and Moderation

An example will illustrate the distinction between moderated and mediated effects. This example is based on Kaczynski, Lindahl, Malik, and Laurenceau's (2006) study of marital conflict, parenting, and child adjustment. The authors hypothesized that maternal and paternal parenting would function as a mediator between marital functioning and adjustment difficulties (i.e., internalizing and externalizing symptoms) in children. In other words, marital conflict was expected to negatively impact the quality of parenting, which, in turn, would increase child maladjustment. Additionally, the authors tested a moderational effect: that parent gender would impact the nature of the relationship between marital conflict and disrupted parenting behavior. Specifically, this relationship was expected to be stronger for fathers than for mothers. Their findings fully supported the hypothesized mediational model. The moderational model was found to be valid as well, but only for families of boys.

As noted, the same variable can serve as either a mediator or a moderator (or both), depending on the research question. For example, Quittner (1992) provided a useful example of how a single construct (i.e., social support) could potentially serve as either a mediator *or* a moderator. She proposed two competing theoretical models in an attempt to study the role of social support in the relationship between parenting-related stress and psychological distress in parents of children with hearing impairment and seizure disorder. She reasoned that parenting stress is more likely to have adverse effects on adjustment when parents have low levels of social support (i.e., social support is a moderator). On the other hand, it could also be that parenting stress undermines one's ability to garner social support, which in turn impacts on parental adjustment (i.e., social support is a mediator).

In her analyses, Quittner (1992) found that the relationship between parental stress and psychological distress did not vary as a function of level of social support. That is, social support did not *moderate* or alter the strength or direction of the relationship between parental stress and psychological distress. Having ruled out social support as a possible moderator, she tested social support as a mediator. Initially, she found that parenting stress (the predictor) was significantly associated with psychological distress (the outcome). Parenting stress was also a significant predictor of social support (mediator). Specifically, parents who experienced more stress tended to have fewer social contacts and to perceive themselves as less supported. Moreover, Quittner found a significant relationship between social support (the mediator) and psychological distress (the outcome), such that lower levels of social support were associated with higher distress ratings. When she tested the relationship between parental stress and psychological distress in the presence of this mediator, the strength of this previously significant relationship dropped significantly. She was able to conclude that the relationship between stress and psychological functioning was mediated by social support (parenting stress → social support → psychological distress) and that reduced social support may be one mechanism by which parental stress is linked with parental psychological distress.

Complex Models: Moderated Mediation and Mediated Moderation

Other types of theoretical models can be proposed that include both mediational and moderational effects. For example, with a moderated mediational model (Figure 10.3), a researcher can test whether a mediational model is significant only at certain levels of a moderator variable. Building on the earlier mediational example (i.e., parental intrusiveness → child independence → medical adherence), we might hypothesize that the entire mediational relationship will hold for only one gender and not the other. If this were found to be the case, this mediational model would be moderated by gender (i.e., moderated mediation). Similarly, mediated moderation is possible (Figure 10.4). For example, suppose that the association between intrusiveness and adherence is moderated by child gender (i.e., intrusiveness ×

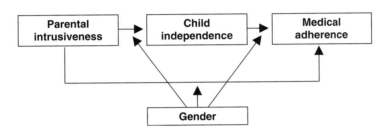

Figure 10.3   Moderated mediation.

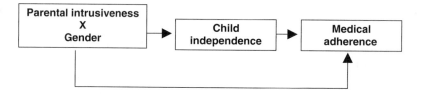

Figure 10.4   Mediated moderation.

gender → medical adherence; see later discussion regarding statistical methods for testing moderator effects as interaction terms). The investigator may then be interested in determining the mediational processes (e.g., child independence) that account for this significant moderational effect. One then tests whether the significant interaction (moderational) effect is mediated by child independence. Although statistically similar, it is important to note that moderated mediation and mediated moderation are not equivalent hypotheses when viewed conceptually. The former is based on the notion that an entire mediational model is significant only at certain levels of a moderator. The latter is based on the notion that a significant moderational effect is mediated by some variable of interest. The reader is referred to Muller and colleagues' (Mulleret, Judd, & Yzerbyt, 2005) article for a more detailed discussion regarding definitional issues and analytical procedures for mediated moderation and moderated mediation.

Common Definitional Inconsistencies

A lack of conceptual and statistical clarity in the study of mediated and moderated effects has become particularly prevalent in mental health literatures where investigators seek to examine factors that mediate or moderate associations between selected predictors and adjustment outcomes. In the child clinical and pediatric psychology literatures, for example, models of predictor-adjustment relationships have become quite complex (e.g., Grych & Fincham, 1990; Thompson, Gil, Burbach, Keith, & Kinney, 1993). Investigators working in these areas have found it necessary to invoke conceptual models that include mediated and moderated effects. Despite the appearance of several useful discussions of differences between mediated and moderated effects (e.g., Aldwin, 1994; Baron & Kenny, 1986; James & Brett, 1984), there continue to be inconsistencies in the use of these terms. More specifically, several types of definitional problems occur with some regularity: (a) vague or interchangeable use of the terms, (b) inconsistencies between terminology and the underlying conceptualization of the variables employed, and (c) a mismatch between written text and diagrammatic figures (see Holmbeck, 1997, for examples).

One concerning issue is that definitions used in the literature are not always consistent, in that they do not adhere to established statistical definitions (see Baron & Kenny, 1986) or the necessary A → B → C causal relationship. Although it is not the case that all investigators must adhere to the same definitions of all terms, it is likely that progress in the field will be hampered if the same term is used in different ways by different scholars. Research studies also often confuse or inappropriately interchange the terms "mediation" and "moderation" (Holmbeck, 1997). Baron and Kenny provide some examples of this problem from the social psychology literature. For example, some research has referred to variables such as age of onset and socioeconomic status (SES) as mediators. However, it is likely that the effect described is moderational in nature. For example, variables such as age of onset and SES presumably dictate conditions under which a stressor is (or is not) associated with problematic outcomes (i.e., these variables are more likely to serve a moderational than a mediational role). Studies sometimes refer erroneously to an interaction effect as a mediation effect (Holmbeck, 1997). The opposite problem is also possible, where authors describe a moderational effect as mediation without making a clear case for how their variables could serve a mediational function. To be considered a mediational effect, the conceptual relationships between the variables of interest must adhere to a mediational model (A → B → C).

One potential cause for confusion regarding mediational models lies in the distinction between *temporal* and *causal* models (Holmbeck, 1997). For example, variables such as coping and appraisal are often misrepresented as mediators. This error is likely attributable to the use of models illustrating *temporal* pathways (see Thompson & Gustafson, 1996, for several examples of temporally oriented models). For example, one might provide a flowchart whereby a stressor is followed *in time* by various coping processes that are, in turn, followed by changes in psychosocial adjustment (i.e., stressor → coping → adjustment). Flowcharts like these are temporal (rather than mediational) in nature because they specify a time-based sequence of events rather than a causal sequence of events. For example, this type of model could illustrate how a stressor, a coping process, and changes in psychosocial adjustment are all placed *in time* relative to each other. The model becomes causal (and mediational) only if the investigator posits causal associations among the variables. The model just discussed would become mediational if the investigator hypothesized that the stressor actually impacted on or changed the way a person copes (e.g., the stressor causes a person to use more avoidance coping), which, in turn, impacted on subsequent levels of adjustment. Because researchers do not usually expect a stressor to influence or cause changes in the style with which a person copes, coping is not usually viewed as a mediational variable (although it *is* often viewed as a moderational variable).

Frequently, terminological, conceptual, and statistical errors are all present in the same study, such as when investigators conceptualize a variable as a moderator (e.g., coping strategies are hypothesized to serve a protective or buffering function), use the term mediator (rather than moderator) to describe the impact of the variable, provide a figure where the variable is presented as a mediator (rather than as a moderator), and conduct statistical analyses that test neither mediation nor moderation. When such a mismatch between terminology, theory, figures, and statistical analyses exists, findings become particularly difficult to interpret.

STATISTICAL STRATEGIES

Now that the conceptual differences between mediators and moderators have been clarified and their potential application within research has been addressed, the next portion of the chapter is devoted to a more complete discussion of how mediational and moderational effects are tested statistically. For a more detailed overview of statistical methods and post-hoc probing (introduced later), as well as Statistical Package for the Social Sciences (SPSS) syntax, the reader is referred to relevant papers by Holmbeck (1997, 2002). This chapter focuses primarily on two types of statistical strategies: multiple regression (as suggested by Baron & Kenny, 1986, and as used by several investigators) and structural equation modeling (SEM; see Tabachnick & Fidell, 2007, for a relatively straightforward discussion; also see Bollen, 1989; Byrne, 1994; Hoyle, 1995; Jaccard & Wan, 1996; Joreskog and Yang, 1996; Mueller, 1996). Although SEM is often considered the preferred method because of the information it provides on the degree of fit for the entire model after controlling for measurement error (Peyrot, 1996), proper use of regression techniques can also provide meaningful tests of hypotheses. Moreover, for investigators working in areas of study where sample Ns are often relatively small, such as pediatric psychology, use of regression techniques (as opposed to SEM) may be necessary because of power considerations (see Tabachnick & Fidell, 2007, for a discussion of sample size and SEM).

Statistical Approaches for Testing Mediation

This section addresses mediational analyses. Techniques utilizing both regression and SEM are presented, with a focus on the importance of evaluating the potency of a mediator. Criticisms of and alternatives to common approaches used in testing mediation are discussed, followed by an applied statistical example.

Regression Approach to Testing Mediated Effects

According to Baron and Kenny (1986), four conditions must be met for a variable to be considered a mediator: (1) The predictor, A, must be significantly associated with the hypothesized mediator, B (letters refer to variables in Figure 10.1); (2) the predictor, A, must be significantly associated with the dependent measure, C; (3) the mediator, B, must be significantly associated with the dependent variable, C, after controlling for the effect of A; and (4) the impact of the predictor, A, on the dependent measure, C, is less after controlling for the mediator, B. A corollary of the second condition is that there first has to be a significant relationship between the predictor and the dependent variable for a mediator to serve its mediating role. In other words, if A and C are not significantly associated, there is no significant effect to mediate. Such a bivariate association between A and C is not required in the case of moderated effects (nor is it required in the case on an indirect effect, as discussed later).

These four conditions can be tested with three multiple regression analyses (see Eckenrode, Rowe, Laird, & Brathwaite, 1995, for an example that includes figures as well as a complete explanation of this data analytic strategy). This strategy is similar to that employed when conducting a path analysis (J. Cohen & Cohen, 1983; Nie, Hull, Jenkins, Steinbrenner, & Bent, 1975). The significance of the A → B path (condition 1 above) is examined in the first regression, after controlling for any covariates. The significance of the A → C path (condition 2) is examined in the second regression. Finally, A and C are employed as simultaneous predictors in the third equation, where C is the dependent variable. Baron and Kenny (1986) recommend using simultaneous entry (rather than hierarchical entry) in this third equation so that the effect of B on C is examined after controlling for A, and the effect of A on C is examined after controlling for B (borrowing from path analytic methodology; Nie et al., 1975). The significance of the B $\rightarrow$ C path in this third equation is a test of condition 3. The relative effect of A on C in this equation (when B is controlled), in comparison to the effect of A on C in the second equation (when B is not controlled), is the test of condition 4. Specifically, A should be less highly associated with C in the third equation than was the case in the second equation (see later discussion for a more detailed example). In other words, one is interested in determining whether the predictor $\rightarrow$ outcome effect is less after controlling for the mediator. The question that arises in this type of analysis is How much reduction in the total effect is necessary to claim the presence of mediation? The degree to which the effect is reduced is an indicator of the potency of the mediator. As Baron and Kenny discuss, it would be unusual in psychology for this A $\rightarrow$ C effect to be reduced from significance to zero.

In the past, some researchers have reported whether the predictor $\rightarrow$ outcome effect drops from significance (e.g., $p < .05$) to nonsignificance (e.g., $p > .05$) after the mediator is introduced into the model. This strategy is flawed, however, because a drop from significance to nonsignificance may occur, for example, when a regression coefficient drops from .28 to .27 but may not occur when the coefficient drops from .75 to .35 (Holmbeck, 2002). In other words, it is possible that significant mediation *has not* occurred when the test of the predictor $\rightarrow$ outcome effect drops from significance to nonsignificance after taking the mediator into account. On the other hand, it is also possible that significant mediation *has* occurred even when the statistical test of the predictor $\rightarrow$ outcome effect continues to be significant after taking the mediator into account. Clearly, a test is needed for the significance of this drop. This significance in the drop of the total effect on inclusion of the mediator in the model is computed using the Sobel test (Sobel, 1988).

Failure to test the significance of a mediated effect is likely to lead to false conclusions. One risks both false-positive and false-negative conclusions when one fails to test the significance of a mediated effect (Holmbeck, 2002). Suppose one tests the utility of a mediational model and seeks to determine whether the significance of the total effect drops to nonsignificance after the mediator is taken into account. Also suppose that this "drop to nonsignificance" criterion is used as the basis for whether significant mediation has taken place. If an initial total effect was just below the $p < .05$ threshold of significance (e.g., $p = .049$) and then dropped so that the significance level was now just above the $p < .05$ threshold (e.g., $p = .061$), one might conclude that significant mediation has occurred. Upon further analysis (using the strategy employed here), however, one may find that this represents a false-positive conclusion. On the other hand, if the original total effect was well under the significance threshold (e.g., $p = .001$) and remained under the threshold (e.g., $p = .040$) after accounting for the mediator, one might conclude that no mediation occurred (which would likely be a false-negative conclusion). Indeed, analyses using the Sobel equation may reveal that significant mediation had occurred in this latter case. As noted earlier, the "drop to nonsignificance" criterion is flawed. It is also worth mentioning that there may be other reasons for false-negative conclusions (i.e., Type II errors). For example, there may be limited power to detect an effect, or the measures may be weak (e.g., they may have low reliability).

The reader is referred to an article by Sobel (1988, p. 56) that includes a complete explanation of how to apply the significance test and compute confidence intervals for the indirect effect (for empirical examples, see also Colder, Chassin, Stice, & Curran, 1997; Ireys, Werthamer-Larsson, Kolodner, & Gross, 1994; Lustig, Ireys, Sills, & Walsh, 1996). Holmbeck (2002) provides a detailed explanation, in addition to a computational example. Finally, an interactive website is available that conducts the Sobel test (with significance tests) if path coefficients and standard errors are entered (www.psych.ku.edu/preacher/sobel/sobel.htm).

Structural Equation Modeling Approach to Testing Mediated Effects

The SEM strategy is often preferred when the investigator has more than one measured variable for each of the constructs (or latent variables) assessed. Assuming there is a latent predictor variable (A), a hypothesized latent mediator variable (B), and a latent outcome variable (C), one would first assess the fit of the direct effect (A → C) model (Hoyle & Smith, 1994). Assuming an adequate fit, the investigator then tests the fit of the overall A → B → C model. Assuming the overall model provides an adequate fit, the A → B and B → C path coefficients are examined. At this point, the A → C, A → B, and B → C paths (as well as the A → B → C model) should all be significant (which is analogous to the regression strategy discussed earlier).

The final step in assessing whether there is a mediational effect is to assess the fit of the A → B → C model under two conditions (where the first condition is nested within the second): (1) when the A → C path is constrained to 0, and (2) when the A → C path is not constrained. One then examines whether the second model provides a significant improvement in fit over the first model. As noted earlier, improvement in fit is assessed with a significance test based on the difference between the two model chi-squares. If there is a mediational effect, the addition of the A → C path to the constrained model should not improve the fit. In other words, the previously significant A → C path is reduced to nonsignificance (i.e., it does not improve the fit of the model) when the mediator is taken into account (which is again analogous to the regression approach).

An additional consideration in using SEM to test for mediational effects is the important distinction between *indirect* and *mediated* effects. In this case, we define an indirect effect as a mediational effect where the A → C path is not significant (i.e., there is no effect to mediate, and only the A → B and B → C paths are significant). An example is used to highlight this distinction. Capaldi, Crosby, and Clark (1996) recently conducted a longitudinal study using structural equation modeling, where they concluded that the effect of aggression in the family of origin on aggression in young adult intimate relationships was mediated by the level of boys' antisocial behaviors during adolescence. On the other hand, Capaldi and her colleagues appear to have found that the direct path between the predictor and the criterion was not significant even though the predictor-mediator and mediator-criterion paths were significant. Although there appears to be evidence for an indirect effect between predictor and criterion, the findings suggest that the mediator does not (and cannot) significantly account for the predictor-criterion relationship (because there was not a significant relationship between predictor and criterion in the first place; Hoyle & Smith, 1994). Thus, Capaldi et al.'s findings fit the criteria for an indirect effect but do not fit the criteria for a mediated effect (as they have been defined here). In the case of such an indirect effect, one must be conservative when discussing interpretations of links between predictor and criterion because one cannot claim that the predictor and the criterion are significantly associated.

Criticisms and Alternative Approaches for Testing Mediation

MacKinnon (MacKinnon et al., 2002; see David MacKinnon's website: www. public.asu.edu/~davidpm/ripl/mediate.htm) has argued recently that the regression approach to testing mediation may be overly conservative, with low power and inaccurate Type I error rates. In addition, MacKinnon and colleagues (2002, p. 87) criticize the Baron and Kenny (1986) approach, commenting that it does "not provide the full set of conditions for the strong inference of a causal effect of the independent variable on the dependent variable through the intervening variable." He and others are currently considering alternative methods in testing the significance of indirect effects (MacKinnon et al., 2002; Shrout & Bolger, 2002; also see David Kenny's website: http://davidakenny.net/cm/mediate.htm).

Some statisticians have argued that the Baron and Kenny (1986) approach, although appropriate in some cases, is overused (Spencer, Zanna, & Fong, 2005). These authors articulate several disadvantages of this approach, including that it (a) requires that the constructs of interest be easily measurable and that their measurement not interfere with the underlying processes (e.g., avoidance of priming effects); (b) relies on correlational, as opposed to causal, evidence; and (c) must adhere to statistical assumptions of multiple regression, which can, at times, be difficult to fulfill. Consideration of experimental designs to support mediational effects is suggested as an alternative to more traditional approaches, especially in cases where the constructs, or processes of interest, are easily manipulated.

Applied Statistical Example of Mediation

In a study of parental overprotection and adjustment in children with spina bifida, Holmbeck and colleagues (Holmbeck, Johnson, et al., 2002) found that parents of children with spina bifida tended to be more overprotective than parents of typically developing comparison children. The authors reasoned that group-related differences in the children's cognitive ability might explain or mediate the observed group differences in parenting style because developmental and intellectual delays might elicit more protective behavior from their parents. Specifically, it was hypothesized that level of cognitive functioning would mediate the relationship between group status and parental overprotective behavior (Figure 10.5).

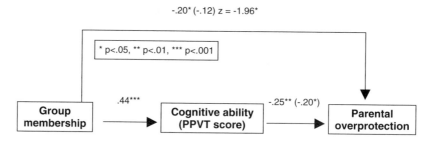

Figure 10.5 Mediational model: Cognitive ability as a mediator of the relationship between group status (spina bifida versus comparison sample) and parental overprotection.

As discussed previously, a mediational model is supported when four statistical criteria are met: (1) The predictor variable is significantly associated with the criterion outcome variable; (2) the predictor variable is significantly associated with the mediator; (3) the mediator is significantly associated with the outcome variable, after controlling for the predictor; and (4) the previously significant predictor → outcome relationship is significantly diminished when effects of the mediator are controlled (Barron & Kenny, 1986; Holmbeck, 1997). These four conditions can be tested with three regression equations (with steps 3 and 4 being tested with a single regression analysis; Holmbeck, 1997, 2002).

In the current example, the first step involved demonstrating that the predictor variable, group status (i.e., spina bifida versus comparison sample), was significantly associated with the outcome variable, overprotection. If the predictor and outcome variables were not found to be significantly associated, there would be no effect to mediate and further testing would not be necessary. In support of their hypothesis, Holmbeck and colleagues (Holmbeck et al., Holmbeck, Johnson, et al., 2002) found that group status significantly predicted parental overprotection, as measured by self-report questionnaires and observer ratings, so they proceeded to test condition 2 (the relationship between the predictor and the mediator). As expected, the second regression showed that the predictor variable (group status) was significantly associated with cognitive ability (as measured by the Peabody Picture Vocabulary Test—Revised; PPVT-R; Dunn & Dunn, 1981), thus supporting the second criterion for mediation.

Regarding the third and fourth mediational criteria, it was necessary to show that PPVT scores significantly predicted parental overprotection when group status was held constant (condition 3) and that the strength of the group status → overprotection effect dropped significantly when the mediator was controlled (condition 4). This was achieved by using simultaneous entry (rather than hierarchical entry) to enter group status and PPVT scores as predictors with parental overprotection as the dependent variable. The results of the analyses provided the information necessary to confirm the mediational effect. First, it was observed that the mediator (PPVT) was a significant predictor of overprotection, with group status controlled (condition 3). Second, in support of condition 4, it was shown that the relationship between group status and overprotection dropped significantly in this last analysis (when PPVT scores were controlled), as compared with the strength of the relationship observed in the first regression model (when PPVT scores were not controlled). The significance of the drop was tested using Sobel's equation (Figure 10.5; Holmbeck, 2002; Sobel, 1988). This suggests that the mediator (PPVT score) accounted for a significant portion of the variance in the relationship between the predictor (group status) and the outcome (overprotection).

Statistical Approaches for Testing Moderation

Although statistical approaches used to test moderational effects primarily rely on both regression and SEM, this section focuses on regression. The use of various SEM techniques to evaluate moderation has demonstrated significant progress in the past several years, and a discussion of these approaches is, therefore, beyond the scope of this chapter. The reader should be aware that analytic strategies utilizing SEM may be advantageous when one has multiple indicators for the latent variables under investigation. Additionally, SEM analyses are generally less vulnerable to measurement error compared to those utilizing regression (Jaccard & Wan, 1995; Peyrot, 1996; Ping, 1996). For more information regarding SEM approaches used to test moderation, the reader is referred to articles by Moulder and Algina (2002) and Schumaker (2002).

Regression Approach to Testing Moderated Effects

Although the manner in which moderators are tested statistically varies somewhat depending on whether the predictor and/or moderator are continuous or dichotomous (Baron & Kenny, 1986; Mason Tu, & Cauce, 1996), the general strategy is the same regardless of the nature of the variables involved. As noted earlier, a moderator effect is an interaction effect. The preferred strategy is to use the variables in their continuous form (if they are not dichotomies) and employ multiple regression techniques (J. Cohen & Cohen, 1983; S. Cohen & Wills, 1985; Jaccard, Turrisi, & Wan, 1990; James & Brett, 1984; Mason et al., 1996).

The predictor and moderator main effects (and any covariates, if applicable) are entered into the regression equation first, followed by the interaction of the predictor and the moderator (e.g., Fuhrman & Holmbeck, 1995). Depending on the investigator's conceptual framework, the main effects can be entered in a hierarchical, stepwise, or simultaneous fashion (J. Cohen & Cohen, 1983). For example, in analyses involving marital conflict as a predictor and family structure as a moderator, marital conflict and family structure could be entered in any order or simultaneously. The interaction term is represented by the product of the two main effects (e.g., marital conflict × family structure) and "only becomes the interaction when its constituent elements are partialled" (J. Cohen & Cohen, 1983, p. 305; also see Aiken & West, 1991; Evans, 1991; Friedrich, 1982; Holmbeck, 1989). Thus, although the main effects may be entered in any order, they must be entered prior to the interaction term for the product of these two terms to represent the interaction when it enters the equation.

Given the manner in which the interaction is computed, the main effects (i.e., the predictor and the moderator) will be highly correlated with the interaction term, which can produce "ill-conditioning" error messages when using some statistical software packages. To eliminate problematic multicollinearity effects between first-order terms (i.e., the independent variable and the moderator) and the higher order terms (i.e., the interaction terms), Aiken and West (1991) recommend that the independent variable and the moderator be "centered" prior to testing the significance of the interaction term. To center a variable, scores are put into deviation score form by simply subtracting the sample mean from all individuals' scores on the variable, thus producing a revised sample mean of zero. Such transformations have no impact on the level of significance of the interaction terms or the simple slopes of any plotted regression lines (see Holmbeck, 2002).

Post-Hoc Probing of Moderational Effects

Failure to conduct post-hoc probing with moderational effects may lead to false conclusions. When one tests for the presence of a moderational effect with multiple regression, one examines whether an interaction between two variables (one independent variable and a moderator) is a significant predictor of an outcome variable, after controlling for the effect of the two predictors. The presence of a significant interaction tells us that there is significant moderation (i.e., that the association between the predictor and the outcome is significantly different across levels of the moderator or that the association is conditional on values of the moderator), but tells us little about the specific conditions that dictate whether or not the predictor is significantly related to the outcome.

For example, if one was interested in whether the association between a parenting variable (e.g., father psychological control; Holmbeck, Shapera, et al., 2002) and an outcome (e.g., school grades) is moderated by group status (e.g., spina bifida versus an able-bodied comparison sample), one would test the interaction of psychological control and group as a predictor of school grades after controlling for the parenting and group main effects. If the interaction is significant, this tells us that the slope of the regression line (i.e., simple slope) that represents the association between parenting and grades for the spina bifida sample is significantly different from the slope for the comparison sample. Unfortunately, the significance of the interaction effect does *not* tell us whether either of the simple slopes is significantly different from zero. In other words, we do not know, based on the initial significant interaction effect, whether the relationship between parenting and grades is significant for the spina bifida sample, the comparison sample, or both samples. Post-hoc probing of the interaction effect via computation of the simple slopes with statistical tests is necessary to gain this information (see Holmbeck, 2002, for computational examples). Additionally, such information also facilitates the plotting of regression lines in figure form.

If an investigator is examining moderational effects by testing the significance of interaction terms, it is likely that the investigator has hypothesized previously that the impact of a predictor on an outcome is conditional on the level of a moderator variable. Suppose one has predicted that "A" will be related to "B" for males, but not for females. A significant "A × gender" interaction effect only tells you that A is related to B differentially as a function of gender; unfortunately, this statistical test does not answer the research question of interest. Only the post-hoc probing procedure will tell you if A is significantly associated with B for males, but not for females. In the past, some investigators have merely plotted significant interaction effects and interpreted the significance of regression line slopes based on visual inspection, without conducting post-hoc probes. This strategy is likely to lead to false-positive results; one may be more likely to conclude that a slope is significantly different from zero based on eyeballing than via statistical tests. Thus, post-hoc probing is a critical step in the evaluation of a moderator effect.

One might also be tempted to employ post-hoc probing strategies that differ from those suggested here. For example, if one has isolated a significant interaction effect between a dichotomous variable and a continuous variable, one might choose to examine the bivariate correlation between the continuous predictor and the outcome at each level of the dichotomous moderator. Similarly, if one had found an interaction between two continuous variables, one might be tempted to examine the bivariate correlation between one of the continuous predictors and the outcome at high and low levels (usually based on a median split) of the other continuous variable.

Although this bivariate correlation approach is superior to doing no post-hoc probing, this strategy is less desirable for several reasons. First, the bivariate correlation strategy does not provide the investigator with a regression equation. Without such an equation, the plotting of findings is not a straightforward task. Second, when one generates regression line equations with slopes and intercepts, the slope is in the same metric as the outcome. Given the slope, one is able to determine the increase (or decrease) that will occur in the value of the outcome as a function of a 1 unit increase (or decrease) in the predictor (at a particular level of the moderator). Third, by computing the regression equations one can determine mathematically where the regression lines cross (see Aiken & West, 1991, pp. 23–24), which may be of practical or theoretical interest. Finally, the post-hoc strategy discussed here allows for greater flexibility in computing and plotting regression lines. In the case of an interaction between two continuous variables, one can use the $+ 1\ SD$ convention *or* a variety of other values. When using the bivariate correlation strategy, one typically uses only the median split approach. An additional drawback of the median split strategy is that it yields a correlation for a fairly diverse subsample of participants (i.e., the association between the predictor and the outcome for all individuals above or below the median on the continuous moderator). The post-hoc strategy discussed in this chapter allows one to examine associations between predictor and outcome at any possible value of the moderator.

Applied Statistical Example of Moderation

The following example demonstrates how a moderational effect can be tested using multiple regression analyses. In a conference presentation drawn from the data set described earlier, the authors investigated the moderational influence of cognitive ability on the longitudinal relationship between early parental psychological control and adjustment in children with spina bifida 2 years later (Rose, Buck, Hagstrom, Skelnik, & Stafiej, 2002). Psychological control, or the use of guilt induction and coercive behavior as methods of influencing a child's behavior, has been shown to have detrimental effects on child adjustment in many developmental contexts.

However, it was hypothesized that psychological control might be less harmful in the context of spina bifida because children with greater physical and/or cognitive impairment tend to spend more time at home with their family and tend to be more dependent on their parents for assistance with basic needs. As a result, it is possible that they are less distressed by more intense parental involvement. Moreover, the authors predicted that intellectual ability (as approximated by PPVT score) would moderate the relationship between psychological control and adjustment, such that psychological control would be less strongly predictive of psychological maladjustment (as measured by the Children's Depression Inventory, CDI; Kovacs, 1992) in children who were more cognitively impaired. At the most complex level, it was hypothesized that associations between psychological control and adjustment would be the least strong among those with spina bifida *and* those with low IQ and most strong among those in an able-bodied comparison sample *and* those with high IQ. Thus, 3-way interactions (i.e., moderated moderation) among psychological control, group status, and PPVT scores were tested.

To demonstrate a moderational effect using multiple regression, the main effects and interaction effects of the predictor variables (i.e., group, psychological control, PPVT score) on the dependent variable (CDI score) were analyzed. Before the regression analyses were run, all continuous predictor variables (e.g., IQ) were centered around zero to prevent multicollinearity among the predictors and the interaction terms in the equation and to allow for proper testing of simple slopes. To do this, each predictor variable was transformed by subtracting the sample mean for that variable from all individual scores. Dichotomous variables (e.g., group) were recoded as 0 or 1. To allow for the testing of interaction terms, new variables were created consisting of all possible 2-way and 3-way products of the centered and/or dichotomous predictor variables. These new variables were then tested as interaction terms in the regression analyses.

Once these steps were complete, all predictor variables (i.e., group, psychological control, and PPVT) were entered in the first step of the regression equation to test for main effects. All possible 2-way products of the predictors (i.e., group $\times$ psychological control, group $\times$ PPVT, psychological control $\times$ PPVT) were entered on the second step. Finally, to test the 3-way interaction (in this case, group $\times$ psychological control $\times$ PPVT), all possible 3-way products of the predictors were entered in the third step.

In the current example, contrary to expectations, there were no significant 2-way interactions between PPVT and psychological control. In other words, PPVT did not appear to moderate the relationship between parental psychological control and child depression across the entire sample. The other 2-way interactions were also nonsignificant. However, there was a significant 3-way interaction (group $\times$ PPVT $\times$ psychological control), indicating that there was a significant difference in the interactions among the predictor variables (PPVT $\times$ psychological control) for the two groups. Once significant interactions were identified, simple regression slopes representing the predictor $\rightarrow$ outcome relationship at high and low levels of the two moderator variables were plotted and tested for significance.

Probing of the 3-way interaction revealed that the interaction between psychological control and PPVT in the prediction of depression varied by subsample.

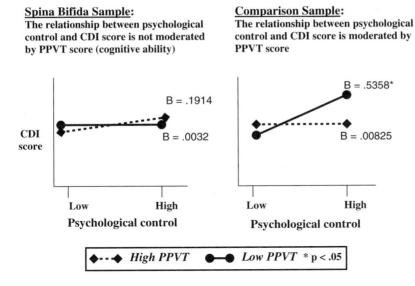

Spina Bifida Sample:
The relationship between psychological control and CDI score is not moderated by PPVT score (cognitive ability)

Comparison Sample:
The relationship between psychological control and CDI score is moderated by PPVT score

Figure 10.6   Three-way moderational model: In children with spina bifida there was no relationship between parental psychological control and child depressive symptoms. However, in the comparison sample, the relationship between psychological control and depressive symptoms was moderated by cognitive ability of the child (i.e., the relationship was significantly positive among children with relatively low PPVT-R scores).

Among children with spina bifida, the association between psychological control and depression was not significantly moderated by PPVT (Figure 10.6). In fact, psychological control and depression were not significantly related in this condition. However, among children in the comparison sample, the interaction between psychological control and PPVT was significant (Figure 10.6). Consistent with the hypotheses, PPVT scores appeared to influence or moderate the relationship between psychological control and depression in this group. On the other hand, and contrary to the hypotheses, tests of the simple slopes at two levels of the moderator (high PPVT and low PPVT) showed that there was a significant positive relationship between psychological control and depression among children with *low* PPVT scores. Among children with *higher* PPVT scores, the relationship between psychological control and depression was nonsignificant. Thus, it was concluded that the effects of psychological control on depression were moderated by condition status (i.e., psychological control was not associated with depression in children with spina bifida) and by level of intellectual functioning (among comparison children, higher intellectual ability appeared to protect against the effects of psychological control on depression).

Common Statistical Inconsistencies

In addition to the challenges already mentioned regarding inconsistent use of definitional terms in the literature, problems involving statistical testing of mediation and moderation also appear. These concerns fall into three general categories:

(1) use of data analytic procedures that fail to test for mediated and moderated effects when one of these effects is hypothesized, (2) a mismatch between terminology and statistical analyses (mediation is hypothesized, but moderation is tested), and (3) a lack of clarity in discussing implications of statistical results. These challenges often result in varying and discrepant interpretations of findings (see Holmbeck, 1997, for a detailed discussion and examples).

Inappropriate application of statistical strategies often occurs when a variable is included in a model that represents a response to another variable in the model. This issue is likely related to the use of temporal flowcharts that are subsequently interpreted as mediational models (see earlier discussion regarding diagrammatic inconsistencies). Variables such as coping strategies, cognitive appraisals, and causal attributions cannot exist in isolation; they exist only in relation to variables that have preceded them (e.g., marital conflict, a chronic illness). One cannot exhibit a coping strategy in response to marital conflict, for example, if there is no marital conflict in the first place. Some have also argued that such response variables are the mechanism through which the independent variable influences the dependent variable and are therefore best thought of as mediators. In many investigations, such variables are included in a box which is placed, connected by arrows, between antecedent (e.g., stress) and outcome (e.g., adjustment) variables.

Investigators who employ variables such as coping strategies and cognitive appraisals as mediators rarely provide a complete rationale for how these variables could serve a mediational function (as has been defined in this chapter). To do so, they would need to select a specific coping strategy (e.g., denial) and propose how such a coping strategy is expected to be employed with greater (or lesser) frequency when there are higher (or lower) levels of some illness parameter (e.g., severity of illness; Frese, 1986; A → B in Figure 10.1). They would also need to propose that higher (or lower) rates of certain maternal adjustment outcomes are expected when this particular coping strategy is employed with greater (or lesser) frequency (B → C in Figure 10.1). Finally, they would need to propose that the illness parameters are expected to be associated with the maternal adjustment outcomes (A → C in Figure 10.1).

RESEARCH APPLICATIONS IN CLINICAL CHILD PSYCHOLOGY

Now that mediators and moderators have been defined and differentiated and statistical approaches have been discussed, the next portion of this chapter focuses on the relevance and importance of mediator and moderator analyses in clinical child and pediatric psychology research. Interestingly, the study of mediators and moderators can be applied to a wide range of research questions. Specifically, mediational and moderational processes can be proposed in correlational and regression-oriented predictive utility studies, group differences research, longitudinal investigations, complex model testing (with structural equation modeling), studies of interventions including randomized clinical trials, and temporal relationship models in which "What precedes what?" questions are of interest. In this section, we discuss the application of mediation and moderation across three types of research studies: longitudinal studies, risk and protective factor research, and intervention trials.

Longitudinal Research

Longitudinal mediational analyses allow researchers to test specific causal theories about time-ordered relationships among variables and the particular mechanism or pathway by which a relationship occurs. Such analyses differ from standard mediational analyses only insofar as they include variables gathered at different points in time. For example, information gathered using longitudinal data can advance what is known about the development of health behaviors, psychopathology, and problem behavior by allowing researchers to test the degree to which more immediate or proximal etiological factors can explain links between more remote or distal risk factors and adjustment, thereby contributing to intervention and prevention efforts (Weisz & Hawley, 2002). Furthermore, longitudinal analyses allow for a life span developmental perspective, which is helpful in understanding variability in adjustment trajectories (Cicchetti & Rogosch, 2002). In recent years, longitudinal mediational analyses have been used creatively to explain developmental pathways to resilience or maladjustment, beginning in early childhood and continuing through late adolescence (Masten et al., 1999). Knowledge of high-risk time points or critical transitional periods in child development may also facilitate the development of more effective treatments and interventions (a point discussed in more detail later; Weisz & Hawley, 2002).

Unlike research that is based solely on cross-sectional data, the use of mediational models with multiple data points enables the researcher to clarify the temporal sequencing of causal processes by ruling out bidirectional pathways (Holmbeck, 1997). Continuing with the mediational example discussed earlier, an investigator can propose a longitudinal hypothesis by arguing that high levels of parental intrusiveness are likely to be associated with *subsequent* decreases in child independence. The researcher might also hypothesize that low levels of child independence are likely to be associated with *subsequent* decreases in medical adherence. Longitudinal data would not only permit an examination of these hypotheses but would also allow the investigator to rule out the possibility that lower levels of child independence or lower levels of adherence are associated with *subsequent* increases in parental intrusiveness (an equally plausible scenario with a causal direction opposite from that proposed in the original model). Such hypotheses could not be tested with cross-sectional data.

At a minimum, two data points are needed to begin testing causal time-ordered mediational hypotheses (although three or more are preferred; Cole & Maxwell, 2003). To test the predictor → mediator link, initial Time 1 data are used for the predictor and Time 2 data are used for the mediator *after* controlling for Time 1 mediator data. More generally, partialing out the Time 1 dependent variable data from the Time 2 dependent variable data essentially converts the Time 2 dependent measure into a residual change variable. That is, a given participant's residual score represents the change in rank for this participant (relative to the other participants in the sample) on the dependent measure between Time 1 and Time 2. Similarly, when examining the mediator → outcome link, initial Time 1 data are used for the mediator and Time 2 data are used for the criterion outcome, after controlling for the Time 1 data on the criterion outcome (Cole & Maxwell, 2003). One continues in this way when testing all pathways in the mediational model. It is important to note that if one has 3 waves of data, one could use Time 1 data for the predictor, Time 2 data for the mediator (controlling for Time 1 mediator data), and Time 3 data for the criterion outcome (controlling for Time 2 criterion outcome data).

Latent growth curve modeling is another statistical method by which to evaluate mediational processes using longitudinal data. Cheong, MacKinnon, and Khoo (2003) describe this type of mediational analysis as measuring two distinct parallel processes: (1) *growth* in the mediator and (2) concurrent *growth* in the outcome variable. This approach builds on the traditional A → B → C mediational model, in that the independent variable affects the growth (or trajectory) of the mediator, which in turn impacts the growth (or trajectory) of the outcome variable. In their study, Cheong and colleagues evaluated the effects of a prevention program geared toward reducing drug use and improving health behaviors among high school football players. Their results supported a longitudinal mediational model; exposure to the prevention program was found to increase perceived importance of team leaders over time, which, in turn, resulted in improvement in nutrition behaviors over time. Although this approach requires large sample sizes and multiple data points, it holds several advantages: It (a) allows for individual differences in development, (b) measures the impact of change in the mediator on *change* in the outcome, and (c) is able to model various trajectory shapes, including curvilinear trajectories (Cheong et al., 2003).

Longitudinal data can also be useful for testing moderator effects within a longitudinal or developmental framework. Using Cole and Maxwell's (2003) approach described earlier, it is necessary to control for earlier levels of the outcome variable when testing the relationship between a predictor (or a predictor-moderator interaction) and a later outcome. MacKinnon and Lockwood (2003) describe longitudinal moderational analyses that parallel Cheong and colleagues' (2003) approach to longitudinal mediation. These authors utilize growth modeling techniques to capture moderational effects on trajectories of change, or growth, over time. For example, one could test whether the impact of peer relationships on growth in deviant behavior during adolescence varies based on ethnicity.

Risk and Protective Factor Research

The study of risk and protective factors often implies mediational and moderational processes. Generally, research on risk and protective factors is focused on understanding the adjustment of youth who are exposed to varying levels of adversity. There is evidence that both contextual factors (e.g., SES, family-level functioning, peer relationships) and developmental variables (e.g., cognitive skills, autonomy development) can significantly influence outcomes for individuals living under adverse conditions, and thus serve a moderational role (Coaklay, Holmbeck, Friedman, Greenley, & Thill, 2002; Holmbeck et al., 2003; Holmes, Yu, & Frentz, 1999; Masten et al., 1999; Rutter, 1990). Risk and protective processes have been

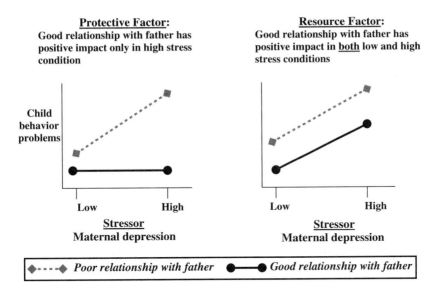

Figure 10.7   Factors associated with favorable outcomes: Protective and resource factors.

explored in the study of resilience, a term used with increasing frequency. Re-silience refers to the process by which youth successfully navigate stressful sit-uations or adversity and attain developmentally relevant competencies (Masten, 2001). Appropriate application of the terms commonly used to identify processes that influence the adjustment of youth exposed to adversity is necessary to pro-mote terminological consistency. Thus, a brief description of several terms, and their relevance to moderational analyses, is presented using hypothetical examples (presented in Figures 10.7 and 10.8).

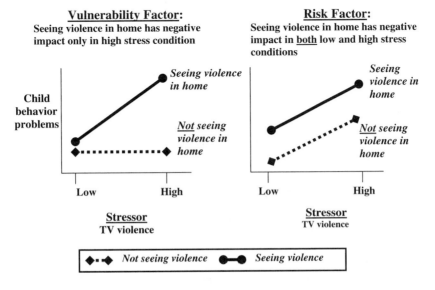

Figure 10.8   Factors associated with unfavorable outcomes: Vulnerability and risk factors.

Protective versus Resource Factors

A protective factor either ameliorates negative outcomes or promotes adaptive functioning. To isolate a true protective factor, however, there must be a particular stressor that influences the sample under investigation. The protective factor serves its protective role only in the context of adversity; a protective factor does not operate in low adversity conditions.

Protective factors are contrasted with resource factors. Specifically, a factor that has a positive impact on the sample *regardless* of the presence or absence of a stressor is a resource factor (Rutter, 1990). For example, if a positive father-child relationship reduces behavior problems only in children of depressed mothers, but has no impact for children of nondepressed mothers, then the father-child relationship would be conceptualized as a protective factor (Figure 10.7). However, if the positive father-child relationship reduces behavior problems in all children, regardless of mother's level of depression, then it would be conceptualized as a resource factor (Figure 10.7; Rutter, 1990). A model may also identify a positive father-child relationship as both a protective and a resource factor if it reduces behavior problems in children who have depressed mothers *more* than in children who have nondepressed mothers, but if it also produces a significant reduction in behavior problems for all children, regardless of level of maternal depression. It is important to note that a protective factor represents a moderational effect (see the statistically significant interaction effect in Figure 10.7), whereas a resource factor represents an additive effect. Statistically, a resource factor emerges as two main effects.

Risk versus Vulnerability Factors

Risk and vulnerability factors operate in much the same way as resource and protective factors, but in the opposite direction (Figure 10.8). A vulnerability factor is a moderator that increases the chances for maladaptive outcomes in the presence of adversity (Rutter, 1990). Similar to a protective factor, a vulnerability factor operates only in the context of adversity. By contrast, a variable that negatively influences outcome regardless of the presence or absence of adversity is a risk factor (Rutter, 1990). For example, witnessing violence in the home environment is conceptualized as a vulnerability factor if it only increases behavior problems in children who are also exposed to a stressor, such as viewing extensive violence on television (Figure 10.8). A vulnerability factor is a moderator and is demonstrated statistically with a significant interaction effect. Witnessing violence in the home can be conceptualized as a risk factor if it results in an increase in child behavior problems for all children, regardless of the amount of TV violence witnessed. As with resource factors, a risk factor represents an additive effect (i.e., two main effects). A model may also identify a factor as being both a risk and a vulnerability factor if it increases the chance of a maladaptive outcome in samples with and without exposure to a stressor, but increases the chances for maladaptive functioning significantly more in the sample with the stressor.

To summarize, if a factor significantly promotes or impairs the chances of attaining adaptive outcomes in the face of a stressor, then it operates via protective or vulnerability mechanisms, respectively. In these cases, the factor serves a moderational role. However, if a factor significantly promotes or impairs the chance of attaining adaptive outcomes without differentiating between the presence or absence of a stressor, then it is conceptualized as operating via resource or risk mechanisms, respectively. Given that new research in the field has found that predictor → outcome effects may be moderated by developmental and contextual factors, there is an impetus for investigating these mechanisms at a more process-oriented level.

Intervention and Prevention Research

Research that involves a randomly assigned intervention as the predictor variable provides a particularly powerful design for drawing conclusions about causal mediational relationships (Clingempeel & Henggeler, 2002; Howe, Reiss, & Yuh, 2002). These types of models have three important strengths. First, significant mediational models that involve interventions inform us about the mechanisms through which treatments have their impact (Kraemer, Wilson, Fiarburn, & Agras, 2002; Rutter, Pickles, Murray, & Eaves, 2001; Weersing & Weisz, 2002). Simply put, with such models one is able to ask *how and why* an intervention or prevention program works (Kraemer et al., 2002; MacKinnon & Lockwood, 2003).

Second, as noted by Collins, Maccoby, Steinberg, Hetherington, and Bornstein (2000), if a manipulated variable (i.e., the randomly assigned intervention) is associated with change in the mediator, which is in turn associated with change in the outcome, there is significant support for the hypothesis that the mediator is a *causal* mechanism. One is more justified in invoking causal language when examining mediational models in which the predictor is manipulated than in mediational models in which no variables are directly manipulated.

Third, when one isolates a significant mediational process, one has learned that the mediator may play a role in the maintenance of the outcome (e.g., problem behavior). In this way, knowledge about mediational processes in the context of randomized clinical trials (RCTs) informs us about etiological theories of disorders (Kraemer et al., 2002). It is also important to note that when examining mediational processes in RCTs, one must demonstrate (via the research design and the timing of the data collections) that changes in the mediator *precede* changes in the treatment outcome (Kraemer, Stice, Kazdin, Offord, & Kupfer, 2001).

As an example of this strategy, Forgatch and DeGarmo (1999) examined the effectiveness of a parenting-training program for a large sample of divorcing mothers with sons. They also examined several parenting practices as mediators of the relationship between the intervention and child adjustment (see Figure 10.9 for an example of this type of model). Compared to mothers in the control sample, mothers in the intervention sample showed improvement in parenting practices. Improvements in parenting practices were linked with improvements in child adjustment (although, interestingly, the intervention did not have a direct effect on child outcome). As indicated in Figure 10.9, such models not only allow one to test potential mediators within an experimental design, but they also allow one to examine the differential utility of different mediators. In other words, one can determine which mediator best accounts for the effectiveness of a given treatment.

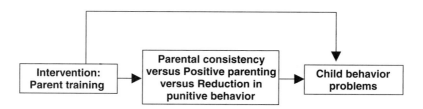

Figure 10.9   Mediators in intervention research: Parenting behaviors as mediators of the relationship between parent training (intervention) and child behavior (outcome).

At a more complex level of analysis, one could posit moderated mediational models. Such a model would not only suggest processes by which a treatment has an effect (i.e., a mediational process) but also which subsamples demonstrate the mediated treatment effects. Findings based on such complex models would provide important information that could be applied to modify the intervention so that it targets relevant mediational processes for specific subgroups of treatment participants.

Kraemer and colleagues (2002) have distinguished between moderators and mediators in the context of RCTs. According to these authors, a moderator is present prior to treatment and a mediator occurs during the treatment process. For example, a moderator might be a pretreatment characteristic of the individual (e.g., gender, IQ, initial severity of symptoms) or a contextual treatment variable (e.g., the setting of the treatment, of the level of exposure to the intervention). A mediator, on the other hand, is a variable that is expected to change as a result of treatment (e.g., parenting behaviors). In other words, while mediators inform *how* and *why* change occurs, moderators provide information regarding *for whom* the intervention or prevention is effective (MacKinnon & Lockwood, 2003). Given these definitions in the context of RCTs, Kraemer and colleagues maintain that the same variable cannot be both a moderator and a mediator (because of their differential temporal relationship to the treatment).

The ability of mediators and moderators to elucidate the impact of an intervention emphasizes the need to hypothesize and measure potential mediational and moderational effects. Unfortunately, although program effects are frequently reported, mediators and moderators of treatment often remain unspecified (MacKinnon & Lockwood, 2003; Weersing & Weisz, 2002). Measurement of potential mediators not only helps us to understand how and why an intervention program is successful, but also illuminates why certain programs may fail. In addition, evaluation of treatment mediators and moderators may facilitate informed modification of intervention efforts and improved cost-effectiveness of services (MacKinnon & Lockwood, 2003).

Research Findings and Future Directions

Grant and colleagues (2006) recently conducted a review of literature investigating mediational or moderational effects in the context of the relationship between stressors and child or adolescent adjustment. Their paper highlights several important overall findings and challenges, as well as future directions for research incorporating mediation and moderation.

Examination of past moderational research revealed that demographic variables, such as age, sex, and ethnicity, were most frequently analyzed, with relatively few studies focusing on the role of cognition, competencies, and coping. Although age, sex, and ethnicity were not consistently significant across studies, significant findings did reveal some interesting patterns. For instance, it appears that for younger children, symptoms, as reported by parents, may be more strongly associated with stressors, whereas self-report may be more strongly related for adolescents. In terms of gender, girls may be more likely to develop internalizing symptoms in response to a stressor, whereas boys may be more prone to externalizing symptoms. Finally, associations between stressors and maladjustment may be stronger for White youth than for youth of other ethnicities. The moderational role of cognition was consistently supported, especially in the development of depressive symptoms. In terms of individual protective factors, academic competence appears to function as a buffer more consistently than social competence and coping. Finally, social support may protect against negative effects associated with exposure to violence and abuse.

The authors point to several challenges that permeate moderational research. First, inclusion of moderators in analyses frequently lacked theory. That is, analysis of potential moderators largely consisted of non-hypothesis-driven inclusion of demographic variables, with sparse research devoted to theory-based moderator variables, such as cognition. Second, measures and definitions of potential moderators were inconsistent, precluding generalization across findings. Finally, assessment of environmental moderators overrelied on use of child report, which can be problematic given possible common source variance and confounding with other child characteristics (e.g., competence).

In contrast to moderational studies, research studies investigating mediational effects were, for the most part, theory-driven. Although some evidence of statistical inconsistencies and use of inappropriate statistical analyses was found, sophistication of analyses appeared to increase over time. Across studies, family process (e.g., parenting behavior) emerged as a consistent mediator in the relationship between stressors and psychosocial adjustment. The authors noted that the majority of mediational research utilized multiple regression or SEM to analyze mediational effects. Weaknesses of mediational research included an overreliance on cross-sectional data and a failure to test competing mediational models.

This review indicates several future directions for mediation and moderation research in the area of clinical child and adolescent psychology. First, routine incorporation of conceptual models and theory grounded in developmental psychopathology would strengthen research pertaining to moderation. Second, utilization of consistent measures and definitions of moderator variables, such as coping, would promote cross-generalization across studies. Third, research would benefit from inclusion of other sources and methodologies in assessing environmental context beyond child report, such as observational measures and parent report. Fourth, longitudinal data are needed to explore mediational and moderational variables that impact on developmental phenomena. Fifth, recent criticisms of the multiple regression approach for analyzing mediation encourage exploration of newer statistical methodology based on recent recommendations (e.g., Cheong et al., 2003; Cole & Maxwell, 2003; MacKinnon et al., 2002; Shrout & Bolger, 2002). Finally, mediation research should incorporate tests of competing mediational and integrative models investigating how family, child, and environmental variables operate in conjunction with each other (i.e., mediated moderation and moderated mediation).

IMPLICATIONS OF RESEARCH FOR CLINICAL PRACTICE

Now that the applications of mediational and moderational analyses in the field of research have been reviewed, it may be helpful to address briefly the relevance of this type of research to clinical practice. This chapter has reviewed the utility of mediational and moderational research for a variety of purposes: confirming or refuting theories about developmental pathways, identifying circumstances that promote or inhibit successful adaptation to chronic healthy or life stressors, and identifying specific mechanisms associated with positive outcomes following a therapeutic or clinical intervention. These accomplishments are important not only for the researcher, but also for the clinician seeking empirically validated prevention or intervention techniques.

For example, suppose that a clinician is treating a young child with a chronic illness (such as diabetes). The child lives with a single parent who is suffering from Major Depressive Disorder and is unable to provide consistent care. Mediational and moderational research can be of use to a clinician treating a child living under these circumstances. First, mediational research involving random assignment to intervention conditions can provide information about the relative efficacy of various treatments or combinations of treatments (e.g., medication, dietary changes, exercise, and all possible combinations of these). Mediational research can also clarify which specific aspects of traditionally accepted treatments are most responsible for observed changes, so that unnecessary components of the treatment may be eliminated. Mediational research such as this allows the clinician to make more informed decisions about treatment (e.g., which treatment is best, based on the means by which the treatment is shown to operate) and also provides information about critical points for intervention in a child's development.

Moderational research is also readily applicable to the clinical setting. First, it can clarify whether a treatment is equally effective when applied in the presence of various demographic, genetic, and environmental factors (e.g., child gender, family medical history, level of parental involvement). For example, perhaps a treatment found to be most effective in a sample of children in a rural setting is not very effective when applied to children living in an urban area. Or perhaps risk and protective factor research suggests that an intervention is beneficial only under particular conditions or circumstances. By considering these issues, moderational research fine-tunes the conclusions drawn from typical intervention studies. Through awareness of the variables that moderate the appropriateness of a given treatment, a clinician can tailor interventions to the individual rather than providing a "one size fits all" treatment.

SUMMARY

In this chapter, we provided definitions of mediated and moderated effects, reviewed statistical approaches, and discussed how such effects can be examined in longitudinal, intervention, and risk and protective factor research. The need for consistency in the use and analysis of mediation and moderation in the child clinical and pediatric psychology literatures was highlighted. It is recommended that care be taken in discussing these processes and that investigators be clear about what statistical approaches are appropriate for a given hypothesis. Because research in pediatric and child clinical psychology has important treatment, prevention, and public policy implications, appropriate modeling and statistical techniques are needed to move the field toward greater understanding. Additionally, this research could benefit from (a) greater inclusion of theory and complex models, (b) consistency in definitions and measures of mediational and moderational constructs, (c) integration of multiple methods and sources to assess environmental variables, (d) use of longitudinal data, (e) exploration of newer statistical methodologies, and (f) generation and testing of complex models.

To conclude, we provide a list of important concepts pertaining to mediational and moderational research. This list, which incorporates the major points of this chapter, is intended to serve as a guide and inspiration for future mediational and moderational research:

- If a researcher is interested in examining a relationship between two variables, the use of mediational and moderational models can lead to deeper and more comprehensive knowledge about the relationship by providing information about the conditions under which the two variables will be associated (moderation) and also about the intervening processes that help to explain the association (mediation).

- The same variable can either mediate *or* moderate a relationship between a predictor and an outcome, depending on the nature of the research question and the role the variable is thought to play in the relationship.

- Mediational models are usually proposed after an association between predictor and criterion variables is well established in the literature. If there is no established relationship, one may be better served by first examining associations among the predictor and criterion variables.

- Mediational models are causal models that illustrate a pathway of influence among variables. In this chapter, we distinguished between causal and temporal models.

- Risk, protective, vulnerability, and resource factors can all be identified and illustrated with the use of a moderational model.

- Mediational models are particularly informative and compelling when they are tested with longitudinal data and/or when they are tested in a randomized clinical treatment research design.

- The statistical strategies used to test mediational and moderational effects are distinct. The models differ both conceptually and statistically.

- In choosing a statistical approach for testing mediation and moderation, one should take into account the nature of one's data (e.g., sample size), as well as the strengths and weaknesses of each approach.

- Post-hoc probing is necessary to understand the nature of mediational and moderational effects.

- It is possible to propose complex theoretical models that include mediated moderation and moderated mediation.

- Mediational and moderational models are useful not only to researchers. Because they can provide information about developmental pathways and conditions affecting treatment efficacy, these models can be useful to clinicians as well.

- With the use of mediational and moderational models, researchers can test competing theories about relationships among variables of interest. By directly testing two or more alternative models, a researcher can determine statistically which theoretical model best captures or explains observed relations among the variables of interest.

As has been emphasized throughout this chapter, attention to mediation and moderation has great potential to enrich the field of clinical child and pediatric psychology. It is hoped that this chapter will encourage more widespread and accurate use of these concepts and techniques to enhance the scientific contribution of research.

REFERENCES

Aiken, L. S., & West, S. G. (1991). *Multiple regression: Testing and interpreting interactions.* Newbury Park, CA: Sage.

Aldwin, C. M. (1994). *Stress, coping, and development: An integrative perspective.* New York: Guilford Press.

Baron, R. M., & Kenny, D. A. (1986). The moderator-mediator variable distinction in social psychological research: Conceptual, strategic, and statistical considerations. *Journal of Personality and Social Psychology, 51,* 1173–1182.

Bollen, K. A. (1989). *Structural equations with latent variables.* New York: Wiley.

Byrne, B. M. (1994). *Structural equation modeling with EQS and EQS/Windows: Basic concepts, applications, and programming.* Thousand Oaks, CA: Sage.

Capaldi, D. M., Crosby, L., & Clark, S. (1996, March). *The prediction of aggression in young adult intimate relationships from aggression in the family of origin: A mediational model.* Paper presented at the meeting of the Society for Research on Adolescence, Boston.

Cheong, J., MacKinnon, D. P., & Khoo, S. T. (2003). Investigation of mediational processes using parallel process latent growth curve modeling. *Structural Equation Modeling, 10,* 238–262.

Cicchetti, D., & Rogosch, F. A. (2002). A developmental psychopathology perspective on adolescence. *Journal of Consulting and Clinical Psychology, 70,* 6–20.

Clingempeel, W. G., & Henggeler, S. W. (2002). Randomized clinical trials, developmental theory, and antisocial youths: Guidelines for research. *Development and Psychopathology, 14,* 695–711.

Coakley, R. M., Holmbeck, G. H., Friedman, D., Greenley, R. N., & Thill, A. W. (2002). A longitudinal study of pubertal timing, parent-child conflict, and cohesion in families of young adolescents with spina bifida. *Journal of Pediatric Psychology, 27,* 461–473.

Cohen, J., & Cohen, P. (1983). *Applied multiple regression/correlation analysis for the behavior sciences* (2nd ed.). Hillsdale, NJ: Erlbaum.

Cohen, S., & Wills, T. A. (1985). Stress, social support, and the buffering hypothesis. *Psychological Bulletin, 98*, 310–357.

Colder, C. R., Chassin, L., Stice, E. M., & Curran, P. J. (1997). Alcohol expectancies as potential mediators of parent alcoholism effects on the development of adolescent heavy drinking. *Journal of Research on Adolescence, 7*, 349–374.

Cole, D. A., & Maxwell, S. E. (2003). Testing mediational models with longitudinal data: Myths and tips in the use of structural equation modeling. *Journal of Abnormal Psychology, 112*, 558–577.

Collins, W. A., Maccoby, E. E., Steinberg, L., Hetherington, E. M., & Bornstein, M. H. (2000). Contemporary research on parenting: The case for nature and nurture. *American Psychologist, 55*, 218–232.

Dunn, L. M., & Dunn, L. M. (1981). *Peabody Picture Vocabulary Test—Revised*. Circle Pines, MN: American Guidance Service.

Eckenrode, J., Rowe, E., Laird, M., & Brathwaite, J. (1995). Mobility as a mediator of the effects of child maltreatment on academic performance. *Child Development, 66*, 1130–1142.

Evans, M. G. (1991). The problem of analyzing multiplicative composites: Interactions revisited. *American Psychologist, 46*, 6–15.

Forgatch, M. S., & DeGarmo, D. S. (1999). Parenting through change: An effective prevention program for single mothers. *Journal of Consulting and Clinical Psychology, 67*, 711–724.

Frese, M. (1986). Coping as a moderator and mediator between stress at work and psychosomatic complaints. In M. H. Appley, & R. Trumball (Eds.), *Dynamics of stress: Physiological, psychological, and social perspectives* (pp. 183–206). New York: Plenum Press.

Friedrich, R. J. (1982). In defense of multiplicative terms in multiple regression equations. *American Journal of Political Science, 26*, 797–833.

Fuhrman, T., & Holmbeck, G. N. (1995). A contextual-moderator analysis of emotional autonomy and adjustment in adolescence. *Child Development, 66*, 793–811.

Grant, K. E., Compas, B. E., Thurm, A. E., McMahon, S. D., Gipson, P. Y., Campbell, A. J., et al. (2006). Stressors and child and adolescent psychopathology: Evidence of moderating and mediating effects. *Clinical Psychology Review, 26*, 257–283.

Grych, J. H., & Fincham, F. D. (1990). Marital conflict and children's adjustment: A cognitive-contextual framework. *Psychological Bulletin, 108*, 267–290.

Holmbeck, G. N. (1989). Masculinity, femininity, and multiple regression: Comment on Zeldow, Daugherty, and Clark's "Masculinity, femininity, and psychosocial adjustment in medical students: A 2-year follow-up." *Journal of Personality Assessment, 53*, 583–599.

Holmbeck, G. N. (1996). A model of family relational transformations during the transition to adolescence: Parent-adolescent conflict and adaptation. In J. A. Graber, J. Brooks-Gunn, & A. C. Petersen (Eds.), *Transitions through adolescence: Interpersonal domains and context* (pp. 167–199). Mahwah, NJ: Erlbaum.

Holmbeck, G. N. (1997). Toward terminological, conceptual, and statistical clarity in the study of mediators and moderators: Examples from the child-clinical and pediatric psychology literatures. *Journal of Consulting and Clinical Psychology, 65*, 599–610.

Holmbeck, G. N. (2002). Post-hoc probing of significant moderational and mediational effects in studies of pediatric populations. *Journal of Pediatric Psychology, 27*, 87–96.

Holmbeck, G. N., Johnson, S. Z., Wills, K. E., McKernon, W., Rolewick, S., & Skubic, T. (2002). Observed and perceived parental overprotection in relation to psychosocial adjustment in preadolescents with a physical disability: The mediational role of behavioral autonomy. *Journal of Consulting and Clinical Psychology, 70*, 96–110.

Holmbeck, G. N., Shapera, W. E., & Hommeyer, J. S. (2002). Observed and perceived parenting behaviors and psychosocial adjustment in pre-adolescents with spina bifida. In B. K. Barber (Ed.), *Parental psychological control of children and adolescents* (pp. 191–234). Washington, DC: American Psychological Association.

Holmbeck, G. N., Westhoven, V. C., Shapera, W., Bowers, R., Gruse, C., Nikolopoulos, T., et al. (2003). A multimethod, multi-informant, and multidimensional perspective on psychosocial adjustment in preadolescents with spina bifida. *Journal of Consulting and Clinical Psychology, 71*, 782–796.

Holmes, C. S., Yu, Z., & Frentz, J. (1999). Chronic and discrete stress as predictors of children's adjustment. *Journal of Consulting and Clinical Psychology, 67*, 411–419.

Howe, G. W., Reiss, D., & Yuh, J. (2002). Can prevention trials test theories of etiology? *Development and Psychopathology, 14*, 673–694.

Hoyle, R. H. (Ed.). (1995). *Structural equation modeling: Concepts, issues, and applications.* Thousand Oaks, CA: Sage.

Hoyle, R. H., & Smith, G. T. (1994). Formulating clinical research hypotheses as structural equation models: A conceptual overview. *Journal of Consulting and Clinical Psychology, 62*, 429–440.

Ireys, H. T., Werthamer-Larsson, L. A., Kolodner, K. B., & Gross, S. S. (1994). Mental health of young adults with chronic illness: The mediating effect of perceived impact. *Journal of Pediatric Psychology, 19*, 205–222.

Jaccard, J., Turrisi, R., & Wan, C. K. (1990). *Interaction effects in multiple regression.* Newbury Park, CA: Sage.

Jaccard, J., & Wan, C. K. (1995). Measurement error in the analysis of interaction effects between continuous predictors using multiple regression: Multiple indicator and structural equation approaches. *Psychological Bulletin, 117*, 348–357.

Jaccard, J., & Wan, C. K. (1996). *LISREL approaches to interaction effects in multiple regression.* Thousand Oaks, CA: Sage

James, L. R., & Brett, J. M. (1984). Mediators, moderators, and tests for mediation. *Journal of Applied Psychology, 69*, 307–321.

Joreskog, K., & Yang, F. (1996). Nonlinear structural equation models: The Kenny-Judd model with interaction effects. In G. Marcoulides, & R. Schumaker (Eds.), *Advanced structural equation modeling* (pp. 57–88). Hillsdale, NJ: Erlbaum.

Kaczynski, K. J., Lindahl, K. M., Malik, N. M., & Laurenceau, J. (2006). Marital conflict, maternal and paternal parenting, and child adjustment: A test of mediation and moderation. *Journal of Family Psychology, 20*, 199–208.

Kovacs, M. (1992). *Children's Depression Inventory manual.* North Tonawanda, NY: Multi-Health Systems.

Kraemer, H. C., Stice, E., Kazdin, A., Offord, D., & Kupfer, D. (2001). How do risk factors work together? Mediators, moderators, and independent, overlapping, and proxy risk factors. *American Journal of Psychiatry, 158*, 848–856.

Kraemer, H. C., Wilson, T., Fiarburn, C. G., & Agras, W. S. (2002). Mediators and moderators of treatment effects in randomized clinical trials. *Archives of General Psychiatry, 59*, 877–883.

Lewis, H. A., & Kliewer, W. (1996). Hope, coping, and adjustment among children with sickle cell disease: Tests of mediator and moderator models. *Journal of Pediatric Psychology, 21*, 25–41.

Lustig, J. L., Ireys, H. T., Sills, E. M., & Walsh, B. B. (1996). Mental health of mothers of children with juvenile rheumatoid arthritis: Appraisal as a mediator. *Journal of Pediatric Psychology, 21*, 719–733.

MacKinnon, D. P., Krull, J. L., & Lockwood, C. M. (2000). Equivalence of the mediation, confounding, and suppression effect. *Prevention Science, 1*, 173–181.

MacKinnon, D. P., & Lockwood, C. M. (2003). Advances in statistical methods for substance abuse prevention research. *Prevention Science, 4*, 155–171.

MacKinnon, D. P., Lockwood, C. M., Hoffman, J. M., West, S. G., & Sheets, V. (2002). A comparison of methods to test mediation and other intervening variable effects. *Psychological Methods, 7*, 83–104.

Mason, C. A., Tu, S., & Cauce, A. M. (1996). Assessing moderator variables: Two computer simulation studies. *Educational and Psychological Measurement, 56*, 45–62.

Masten, A. S. (2001). Ordinary magic: Resilience processes in development. *American Psychologist, 56*, 227–238.

Masten, A. S., Hubbard, J. J., Gest, S. D., Tellegen, A., Garmezy, N., & Ramirez, M. (1999). Competence in the context of adversity: Pathways to resilience and maladaptation from childhood to late adolescence. *Development and Psychopathology, 11*, 143–169.

Moulder, B. C., & Algina, J. (2002). Comparison of methods for estimating and testing latent variable interactions. *Structural Equation Modeling, 9*, 1–19.

Mueller, R. O. (1996). *Basic principles of structural equation modeling: An introduction to LISREL and EQS.* New York: Springer

Muller, D., Judd, C. M., & Yzerbyt, V. Y. (2005). When moderation is mediated and mediation is moderated. *Journal of Personality and Social Psychology, 89*, 852–863.

Nie, N. M., Hull, C. H., Jenkins, J. G., Steinbrenner, K., & Bent, D. H. (1975). *SPSS: Statistical package for the social sciences* (2nd ed.). New York: McGraw-Hill.

Peyrot, M. (1996). Causal analysis: Theory and application. *Journal of Pediatric Psychology, 21*, 3–24.

Ping, R. A. (1996). Latent variable interaction and quadratic effect estimation: A two-step technique using structural equation analysis. *Psychological Bulletin, 119*, 166–175.

Quittner, A. L. (1992). Re-examining research on stress and social support: The importance of contextual factors. In A. M. La Greca, L. J. Siegel, J. L. Wallander, & C. E. Walker (Eds.), *Stress and coping in child health* (pp. 85–115). New York: Guilford Press.

Rose, B. M., Buck, C., Hagstrom, J., Skelnik, N., & Stafiej, S. (2002, April). *Cognitive functioning as a moderator of the relationship between parenting and adjustment in children with spina bifida.* Poster presented at the biennial meetings of the Society for Research on Adolescence, New Orleans, LA.

Rose, B. M., Holmbeck, G. N., Coakley, R. M., & Franks, E. A. (2004). Mediator and moderator effects in developmental and behavioral pediatric research. *Developmental and Behavioral Pediatrics, 25*, 58–67.

Rutter, M. (1990). Psychosocial resilience and protective mechanisms. In J. Rolf, A. S. Masten, D. Cicchetti, K. H. Nuechterlein, & S. Weintraub (Eds.), *Risk and protective factors in the development of psychopathology* (pp. 181–214). New York: Cambridge University Press.

Rutter, M., Pickles, A., Murray, R., & Eaves, L. (2001). Testing hypotheses on specific environmental causal effects on behavior. *Psychology Bulletin, 127*, 291–324.

Sandler, I. N., Tein, J. Y., & West, S. G. (1994). Coping, stress, and the psychological symptoms of children of divorce: A cross-sectional and longitudinal study. *Child Development, 65*, 1744–1763.

Schumaker, R. E. (2002). Latent variable interaction modeling. *Structural Equation Modeling, 9*, 40–54.

Shrout, P. E., & Bolger, N. (2002). Mediation in experimental and nonexperimental studies: New procedures and recommendations. *Psychological Methods, 7*, 422–445.

Simons, R. L., Lorenz, F. O., Wu, C. I., & Conger, R. D. (1993). Social network and marital support as mediators and moderators of the impact of stress and depression on parental behavior. *Developmental Psychology, 29*, 368–381.

Sobel, M. E. (1988) Direct and indirect effect in linear structural equation models. In J. S. Long (Ed.), *Common problems/proper solutions: Avoiding error in quantitative research* (pp. 46–64). Beverly Hills, Ca: Sage.

Spencer, S. J., Zanna, M. P., & Fong, G. T. (2005). Establishing a causal chain: Why experiments are often more effective than mediational analyses in examining psychological processes. *Journal of Personality and Social Psychology, 89*, 845–851.

Tabachnick, B. G., & Fidell, L. S. (2007). *Using multivariate statistics* (5th ed.) Boston: Allyn & Bacon.

Thompson, R. J., Gil, K. M., Burbach, D. J., Keith, B. R., & Kinney, T. R. (1993). Role of child and maternal processes in the psychological adjustment of children with sickle cell disease. *Journal of Consulting and Clinical Psychology, 61*, 468–474.

Thompson, R. J., & Gustafson, K. E. (1996). *Adaptation to chronic childhood illness.* Washington, DC: American Psychological Association.

Weersing, V. R., & Weisz, J. R. (2002). Mechanisms of action in youth psychotherapy. *Journal of Child Psychology and Psychiatry and Allied Disciplines, 43*, 3–29.

Weisz, J. R., & Hawley, K. M. (2002). Developmental factors in the treatment of adolescents. *Journal of Consulting and Clinical Psychology, 70*, 21–43.

CHAPTER 11

Single-Case Research Designs

Kurt A. Freeman and Eric J. Mash

Clinical child and adolescent psychology concerns itself with the assessment and treatment of abnormal behavior or psychopathology. Most branches of contemporary clinical psychology are firmly grounded in the scientific method or empirical approach to studying psychopathology and methods of its amelioration. This is affirmed by the adoption of the Boulder model of training by most clinical psychology doctoral training programs (though the development and growth of professional schools of psychology arguably have detracted from this emphasis), which espouses integration of scientific methods with clinical practice. For years, there has been concern about the disconnect between clinical psychology training in the scientist-practitioner model and real-world clinical practice (Hayes, Barlow, & Nelson-Gray, 1999). However, many argue that instead of abandoning training in research methods, the mandate remains to identify methods of bridging the gap between scientific endeavors and clinical practice through the identification of research methods and evidence-based practices applicable to clinical settings (Gelso, 2006; Hayes et al., 1999; Weisz, 2004; Weisz, Jensen-Doss, & Hawley, 2006).

Scientific inquiry assists in understanding the cause-effect relationships between various life events and situations and the clinical phenomena with which clients present. Such an understanding can be developed either via group or single-subject design methodologies, depending on the particular questions of interest and constraints present. In fact, though there are misunderstandings about each approach (e.g., Aeschleman, 1991) and some suggest or imply that one approach may be better than the other (Bailey & Burch, 2002; Gliner, Morgan, & Harmon, 2000), no one type of design is inherently better and each addresses important questions about clinical phenomena of interest.

Since the early days of the behavioral sciences there has been some debate regarding the most appropriate approach to scientific inquiry (Leary, 2001). Today most researchers in the behavioral sciences, including those in clinical child and adolescent psychology, take a nomothetic approach. This involves studying larger groups of individuals to identify general principles and broadly applicable generalizations (Blampied, 2001). Based on this perspective, using group designs (both between- and within-group designs) is most appropriate. They can assist with answering questions such as the percentage of individuals who respond a particular way given certain conditions (e.g., the percentage of youth with depressed mood who respond to cognitive-behavior therapy) and the association between variables (e.g., child age or gender and treatment outcome). Others, however, have argued that the idiographic approach must be included to ensure that behavioral processes are understood at the level of the individual (for discussion, see Blampied, 2001; Leary, 2001). Idiographic research, therefore, focuses on describing, examining, and comparing the performance of an individual against his or her own performance at different times or in different situations, and thus typically involves single-case research designs. The current chapter focuses on the latter designs.

The primary goal of this chapter is to provide a discussion of single-case designs (SCDs). Specifically, an introduction to the various SCDs currently in use is described in terms of the processes involved in their use, as well as the benefits and weaknesses of each. Although some have argued that SCDs are most appropriate for testing the relation between particular variables of interest and targeted behavioral patterns because one can experimentally demonstrate a cause-effect relationship (e.g., Bailey & Burch, 2002), we intend to provide no judgment as to whether group or single-subject designs should be given greater value. In fact, the American Psychological Association's task force charged with determining guidelines for classifying empirical support for psychological treatments indicated that either can be an appropriate method for determining whether an intervention is efficacious (Chambless et al., 1996; Task Force on Promotion and Dissemination of Psychological Procedures, 1995), an issue that is discussed more thoroughly in a later section. Instead, our focus is on developing a better understanding of SCDs. We emphasize how SCDs are useful in clinically oriented research, but are also applicable to clinical practice.

CHARACTERISTICS OF SINGLE-CASE RESEARCH DESIGNS

When evaluated from a group design perspective, SCDs may be considered limited in scope and application, or even meaningless. For example, some have argued that SCDs are limited in terms of internal and external validity (Aeschleman, 1991). However, such concerns are grounded in the group design perspective of scientific inquiry, and taking such an approach may be misleading (Hillard, 1993). To appreciate the complexity and utility of the various single-subject designs, one needs to understand their fundamental premises and characteristics.

Repeated Observation of Phenomena of Interest

Single-case designs share in common repeated observation of the phenomena of interest across time under standard conditions (Holcombe, Wolery, & Gast, 1994). Specifically, measurement of the dependent variable occurs multiple times, across at least two separate conditions, which are usually referred to as *baseline* and *intervention*. Such a method of data collection is based on the perspective that determining whether the dependent variable differs from one condition to the next in a meaningful way requires multiple data points within each condition. Doing so allows the researcher to investigate whether desired trends in the data are evident (see "Visual Inspection" section) and protects against making assumptions about differences that may be spurious or the result of natural variation in the dependent variable of interest.

Often in research, the dependent measure utilized is some form of observable behavioral phenomenon (e.g., aggressive behavior of a young child, out-of-seat behavior of a child with Attention-Deficit/Hyperactivity Disorder, duration of crying by a depressed adolescent). However, there is nothing inherent in SCDs that requires the dependent variable be of such form. End products (e.g., weekly weight loss for overweight children), scores on questionnaires (e.g., obtained scores on the Children's Depression Inventory), or subjective ratings (e.g., measurements of anxiety using the Subjective Units of Distress Scale) can be obtained repeatedly in SCD research, allowing for inferences regarding the impact of the independent variable on measures of outcome. Multiple examples abound regarding the use of various types of dependent measures in a single-subject research paradigm (e.g., Glicksohn, Gvirtsman, & Offer, 1997; Nugent, 1992).

In clinical practice, repeated observation can serve an important role in the therapeutic process. Specifically, if the clinician and/or client gathers data in a systematic and repeated manner, decisions can be made regarding whether to alter interventions when monitoring suggests a lack of progress. How one goes about making changes in clinical interventions will determine whether the practitioner adheres to methods that retain sufficient experimental rigor so as to empirically demonstrate causal relations between changes in the dependent and independent variables. However, because the goal of most clinical endeavors is not to demonstrate experimental control but to document change in the clinical phenomena of interest, such violations may be less important than when engaged in research practices.

Participants as Their Own Experimental Controls

Similar to what occurs in within-subjects group designs, participants serve as their own controls in SCDs. However, there is an avoidance of aggregating obtained data across cases with SCDs. Instead, they are based primarily on demonstrating experimental control through replication of the impact of an independent variable on a case-by-case basis. The main analytic process used to determine experimental control involves comparing an individual's behavior across experimental conditions, rather than comparing across individuals. This is viewed as the relevant comparison, because the real question is whether an individual's behavior has changed as a result of treatment relative to pretreatment behavioral presentation (Morgan & Morgan, 2001). For instance, a child psychologist is more concerned with whether depressive symptoms of an adolescent client have changed as a result of therapy relative to preintervention level of symptoms rather than whether the client's symptoms changed relative to a statistically derived group mean. Note that intrasubject comparison across experimental conditions as an empirical test of the effect of the independent variable on the symptoms of interest is different from completing a normative assessment (i.e., comparing a particular individual's performance or behavioral level to normative data) to determine if a person's current level of functioning is within normal limits. This latter practice is often an important issue clinically and has some relevance to determining whether changes observed are clinically significant or meaningful (Atkins, Bedics, McGlinchey, & Beauchaine, 2005).

Given the focus on intrasubject variability as the primary issue of importance, SCDs are particularly relevant for psychotherapy research (Hayes et al., 1999; Hilliard, 1993; Lundervold & Bellwood, 2000; Morgan & Morgan, 2001). Typically, psychotherapy involves repeated interactions between the therapist and the client (e.g., child, adolescent, family) as a means of producing change. Further, there is usually a period of assessment in which the therapist learns about the client's presenting problems (analogous to baseline in research scenarios) and then treatment, during which the therapist creates conditions in an effort to produce change in the client's presenting problem. Like the SCD, psychotherapy as a process allows for comparison across conditions.

Replication of the Experimental Effect

Experimental replication of observed effects is one of the primary principles of scientific inquiry (Morgan & Morgan, 2001). Through replication, scientists are able to provide information about the reliability of observed effects, as well as to self-correct when initial findings are not consistently obtained. Unfortunately, replication studies are lacking in the behavioral sciences, including clinical child and adolescent psychology. This is likely due to a host of reasons, an important one being the energy and expense of replicating studies that rely on large groups of participants.

A hallmark of experimentally sound SCDs (i.e., those that allow for a determination of the functional relation between the independent variable and changes in dependent variables) is replication. That is, SCDs set as the standard repeated demonstration of the impact of the independent variable as the measure of experimental control. Support for the interpretation of the independent variable (e.g., training parents in methods of giving clear instructions to their children) as the cause of the change in the dependent variable (e.g., rate of child compliance to adult instructions) increases each time one demonstrates that the latter changes as a function of a change in the former. Because of this, each participant in single-subject research is repeatedly exposed to baseline and treatment conditions. This is in stark contrast to the most common group design used in psychological research, the between-groups design. In the between-groups design, the experimenter compares the aggregate level of the dependent variables across at least two groups: the comparison group, which is not exposed to the independent variable, and the treatment group, which is. In such a design, the experimenter rarely introduces, withdraws, and reintroduces the independent variable while obtaining measurement of the dependent variable across conditions. Instead, there is reliance on statistical analysis to determine whether the obtained difference would occur by chance versus as a result of the treatment.

Replication occurs across participants as well. The nomenclature describing SCDs implies that only one participant is involved (e.g., single-subject design, n of 1 designs). However, most research using these designs involves multiple participants (Horner et al., 2005; Leary, 2001), though there is no gold standard for the number of individuals who should be included in a single study to allow for adequate assessment of intervention effects across individuals. Each time an intervention effect is observed with a different participant, confidence that the independent variable is responsible for the change increases. Thus, when there is a small effect, researchers strive to have more participants to increase confidence in interpretation of the source of the effect. The number of participants needed may be fewer if the effect is large.

There are instances in which repeatedly introducing and removing an intervention is impractical or unethical. For instance, one may implement an intervention focused on skills acquisition (e.g., teaching a child with an intellectual disability how to tie his shoes). In this instance, maintenance of the behavior is probable even if intervention is withdrawn because of the naturally rewarding properties of engaging in the behavior. In other words, once one has mastered the skill of tying one's shoes, the skill may not return to baseline levels when the intervention used to establish that skill is removed. When the intervention is designed to address a serious or threatening behavior (e.g., suicidal self-harm behavior), removing an effective intervention may be considered unethical. In these instances, researchers will rely on SCDs that more heavily focus on intersubject replication and, in some cases, cross-situational replication as a means of investigating experimental control of the independent variable on changes observed in the dependent variable (see "Multiple Baseline Designs" section).

Changing One Variable at a Time

Another essential tenet of SCDs is that only one variable should be altered at a time when moving from one phase of the experiment to the next (Barlow & Hersen, 1984; Hersen, 1982). For example, if a researcher is determining effective interventions for treating nocturnal enuresis, he or she would want to introduce only one intervention (e.g., the urine alarm) at the start of the treatment phase. If more than one variable is changed, it is impossible to determine which variable is producing change in the dependent variable. Using two strategies, such as decreasing evening fluid intake *and* introducing a particular behavioral intervention (e.g., the urine alarm) at the same time, would result in a situation in which it would be impossible to determine which produced any noted improvements that occur. Thus, unless the investigator is actually evaluating an intervention with multiple components (see later discussion), standard practice is to hold all variables constant except for one independent variable as the investigation moves from the baseline to the treatment phase.

Although the general guideline is to change only one variable at a time as one moves from baseline to treatment, as with any rule there are exceptions. Specifically, if a researcher is interested in the combined effect of several independent variables, as is often the case with many empirically supported interventions (Kazdin & Weisz, 2003; Mash & Barkley, 2006), it is acceptable to change more than one variable. For example, Freeman and Piazza (1998) were interested in the effects of a combined intervention for treating food refusal (i.e., stimulus fading, escape extinction, and reinforcement) and therefore introduced several strategies as a package intervention.

In this way, the authors were able to determine the impact of the combined treatment on the targeted behavior. It should be noted, however, that if investigators are using such an approach to experimentally demonstrate control over the dependent variable, all independent variables should be introduced simultaneously, rather than progressively. In this way, the package intervention essentially becomes one independent variable. Although by using a package treatment it is impossible to determine which component of the intervention is producing the change, or whether it is the components in concert, such an approach allows one to determine if the combined intervention impacts the dependent variable.

Utilizing a package intervention is becoming more common as psychotherapies become increasingly manualized (Drozd & Goldfried, 1996; Scaturo, 2005). Thus, at first glance, using SCDs to empirically test the effect of manualized interventions with different client populations or clinical settings seems reasonable. Theoretically this is true, but there are some challenges to testing manualized psychotherapies using SCDs. Specifically, manualized treatments typically involve multiple components that are applied in a sequential, versus simultaneous, fashion. For example, popular manuals to guide parent management training for young children with disruptive behavior disorders typically start by training parents in various positive parenting practices (e.g., use of labeled praise, token systems), followed by discipline strategies (e.g., time-out, response cost). Because of this, using relevant components of SCDs (e.g., repeated measurement) may be useful for documenting clinical outcome but may not be appropriate for empirically demonstrating cause-effect relations. Of course, if the package intervention is implemented such that all components are introduced simultaneously, one can systematically withdraw components of treatment over time to evaluate which components are essential (Kazdin, 2003; see also Jones, 1993).

Graphical Representation and Visual Analysis of Data

Data presentation and analysis differ markedly between SCDs and group designs. The most obvious difference is that data are presented for individual participants rather than as a summarized group aggregate. Additionally, information is typically presented in real-time, graphical representation, allowing the researcher to easily examine the data. Data are represented in the manner that most accurately captures the variable of interest (e.g., frequency per observation, duration of the behavior), typically with each data point representing one observation period (e.g., 1 day, one class period, one session).

Although data gathered using SCDs can be subjected to statistical analysis (for attention to this issue, see Parker et al., 2005; Todman & Dugard, 2001; see also Perone, 1999, for argument for experimental control versus statistical control), traditionally analysis involves visual inspection of data attending to level, trend, and variability within and across phases (Horner et al., 2005; Kazdin, 2003). *Level* refers to mean performance within a condition or phase; *trend* refers to the rate of increase or decrease in the hypothetical best-fit line of the variable being measured within a phase, or slope; *variability* refers to the amount that data vary around the mean or slope within a phase. Hayes and colleagues (1999) suggest that *course is* also an important consideration when analyzing data gathered via SCDs. They define course as a more flexible method of investigating trend, allowing for a determination of whether data follow a linear or curvilinear pattern. Finally, latency to change in the dependent variable after changes in the independent variable is also important for understanding the impact of the latter on the former (Kazdin, 2003). Specifically, the closer in time between the introduction of the treatment and the change in the dependent variable, the more confident one is in the source of the change. By attending to each of these variables while visually inspecting data obtained, one can make determinations about the reliability and consistency of the intervention effect.

Compared against statistical analysis of data, visual inspection focuses much more heavily on clinical significance than statistical significance (Kazdin, 2003; Zhan & Ottenbacher, 2001). In clinical psychology, there has been increasing focus on clinical significance of intervention effectiveness versus simply statistical significance. Clinical significance refers to value or meaningful difference that an intervention has on a person's functioning or everyday life (Kazdin, 1999). Criteria have been suggested regarding how to determine clinical significance when using group designs (e.g., Jacobson, Roberts, Berns, & McClinchey, 1999; Jacobson & Truax, 1991), and some researchers argue that to determine clinical significance one must analyze the data at the level of the individual (Jacobson & Truax, 1991).

Single-case designs are well suited for attention to clinical significance of intervention effects. Because analysis relies on visual inspection, emphasis is placed on ensuring that there is a large effect present to say with confidence that the independent variable produced a meaningful change in the dependent variables. That is, to trip the belief operant that there is an effect present, single-subject researchers demand notable changes in dependent variables from baseline to intervention phases. Of course, for clinical purposes, there still may be valid reasons to complete norm-based assessment using standardized instruments to determine whether the change altered behaviors of interest so that they are now within typical or nonclinical limits (Hartmann, Roper, & Bradford, 1979).

VALIDITY AND SINGLE-CASE DESIGNS

Paramount to any research methodology is the ability to adequately address issues of internal and external validity. Without careful attention to these variables, obtained findings have little scientific meaning and thus are not helpful to the scientific or practitioner community. *Internal validity* refers to the extent to which one can say with confidence that a change in the dependent variable is the result of the independent variable. Multiple threats to internal validity exist and must be accounted for in order for research findings to be interpretable. A complete discussion of the factors that may threaten the internal validity of research findings is beyond the scope of this chapter. For a more in-depth discussion of these issues, readers are referred to Campbell and Stanley (1966), Scotti, Morris, and Cohen (2003), and Shadish, Cook, and Campbell (2001).

When using group designs, one of the primary methods for controlling for threats to internal validity is through random assignment of participants to experimental groups (e.g., treatment, no treatment). Though some have argued for the use of randomization procedures in SCDs (e.g., Edgington, 2007), such a practice is not typical. Instead, SCDs adequately address threats to internal validity in several critical ways through other processes. For example, through use of repeated measurement of behavior across time, repeated demonstrations of the impact of independent variables, and intra- and interparticipant comparison, they control for threats such as maturation and history effects. Extraneous variables that threaten internal validity are assumed to be constant across baseline and treatment conditions, and thus any notable differences across the conditions can be attributed to the independent variable. How this is controlled for depends on the type of SCD used. Additionally, because data analysis involves frequent plotting and visual inspection of data, researchers using SCDs have the ability to observe whether aberrant or unusual patterns of behavior emerge during the course of an experiment and can go about searching for (and potentially controlling) the source of variability accounting for those patterns (Morgan & Morgan, 2001; Perone, 1999).

External validity relates to generality of findings and thus refers to the ability to extrapolate findings observed with participants from a particular study to a larger group of individuals who are similar on characteristics considered important. External validity of findings obtained using SCDs is enhanced with each replication of intervention effect across participants, settings, or conditions and/or different measures of the same independent variable (Horner et al., 2005). Thus, SCDs address external validity through two types of replication: direct and systematic replication (Sidman, 1960). Direct replication is accomplished by demonstrating the impact of the independent variable across participants with similar characteristics. As the number of replications of the impact increases across participants, the extent of generality is identified (McReynolds & Thompson, 1986). Systematic replication (i.e., varying some aspect of the original experimental conditions) is also used to address external validity. Thus, using SCDs to demonstrate replication of treatment effects across clinical disorders, settings, clinicians, and so forth allows for the assessment of the extent to which the findings are externally valid.

CHOOSING A BASELINE

With few exceptions, the experimenter utilizing an SCD initiates the process by completing a period of observations of the dependent variable as it occurs in the absence of the independent variable. Conventionally, this first phase is referred to as the *baseline* and is labeled with an "A" when representing the data on a graph. The data pattern that emerges during this phase of the research serves as the point of comparison for patterns of data during other (often intervention) conditions. Thus, careful attention to the patterns that develop during baseline data collection is important, with particular attention to level and trend (Bailey & Burch, 2002; Kazdin, 2003).

In basic research, investigators are typically concerned with establishing baseline responding under tightly controlled conditions that produce patterns of data with little variability (e.g., Perone, 1991; Sidman, 1960). In contrast, applied researchers usually collect baseline data during naturally occurring conditions

(Barlow & Hersen, 1984; Hersen, 1982). Rather than creating the baseline conditions, the applied researcher often simply documents the occurrence of the dependent variable in the typical environment. Thus, obtaining the level of control over the environment necessary to produce data with minimal fluctuation can be difficult. Further, applied researchers, because they are often working with human participants who may be experiencing significant distress, may not have the luxury of continuing baseline observations until a narrowly defined pattern of data emerges. As such, the definition of "stability" or "pattern" is typically viewed differently when in the applied context. This is not to suggest that applied researchers should not be vigilant in minimizing or eliminating variability in data patterns due to measurement errors or other extraneous variables that are controllable (and for which control is warranted). Rather, the point is that the acceptable amount of control, and thus the amount of variability, differs considerably across basic and applied research environments. The remaining discussion focuses on issues primarily relevant to applied research situations.

When conducting baseline observations, applied researchers and clinicians are interested in gathering a sample of the dependent variable sufficient to serve as a standard against which to compare patterns of data produced during other conditions. To date, there remains no definitive criterion for the right length of baseline. The most important consideration when determining whether one's baseline observation period is adequate is that of consistency in data patterns, which then allows one to predict future data patterns in the absence of any change to experimental conditions (Kazdin, 2003). Once a pattern of consistency in the desired direction has developed (e.g., the baseline pattern is increasing if one expects the independent variable to produce decreases), one can introduce the independent variable and obtain interpretable findings. It is conventional to consider a minimum of three data points as sufficient for determining whether consistency or pattern exists (Barlow & Hersen, 1984). However, one can easily find published examples of single-subject research baseline periods that include fewer or greater numbers of baseline observations. Thus, although most single-subject researchers strive for a minimum of three baseline data points, the ultimate criterion of being able to adequately assess the impact of the independent variable prevails.

Although various combinations and permutations could occur, several basic baseline patterns have been described (Barlow & Hersen, 1984; Hersen, 1982). Each has particular implications for the interpretation of the impact of the independent variable on the dependent variable. Figure 11.1 (top graph) depicts a stable baseline using a 6-point baseline observation period with hypothetical data. Here there is minimal variation with no significant increasing or decreasing trends across observations. Introducing the independent variable following this baseline period would result in unambiguous interpretation of its effect, easily determining whether there is no change (i.e., pattern remains the same during treatment), improvements (i.e., data patterns either increased or decreased, depending on the goal of the intervention), or worsening (i.e., again, data patterns either increased or decreased, depending on the goal of intervention).

The second general pattern of baseline is a worsening of the problem (i.e., increasing or decreasing trend). Take, for example, a situation in which a researcher

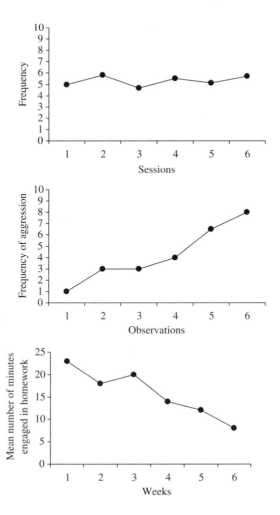

Figure 11.1   The stable baseline: hypothetical data demonstrating slight but negligible variation in data patterns (top graph). The increasing or decreasing baseline: hypothetical data on aggressive acts demonstrating an increasing baseline (middle graph) and hypothetical data on the number of minutes per evening spent engaging in homework (bottom graph), both representing worsening baseline trends.

is measuring the rate of aggressive acts displayed by a youth at recess (see Figure 11.1, middle graph). An increasing baseline pattern would document more frequent occurrence of the aggressive acts as baseline continued, suggesting that the behavior is worsening over time. Alternately, Figure 11.1 (bottom graph) depicts a decreasing trend in the mean number of minutes spent completing homework per evening across successive weeks, which is also indicative of a worsening of the problem during baseline. Both baselines are acceptable patterns for treatment comparison because meaningful interpretations of the impact of the independent variable can be made. Specifically, if the independent variable produces a reversed pattern of data (i.e., decrease in the number of aggressive acts or increase in minutes spent on homework), then the original pattern serves as an adequate comparison. An increasing or decreasing baseline trend becomes problematic, however, when

the independent variable does not produce a reversal in the direction of the behavior pattern. Specifically, such trends may mask whether an intervention has a
detrimental effect, such as a worsening of the problem (Hersen, 1982). However,
if there were a marked shift in the slope of the data (significantly steeper in either
direction), one would be able to determine that the independent variable was having
an adverse impact on the dependent measure.

In contrast to increasing or decreasing trends that represent a worsening in the
dependent measure, the same data patterns that indicate improvements are troublesome as baseline patterns. Returning to the previous examples, one would not want
a baseline that indicates a decreasing trend in aggressive acts or an increasing trend
in number of minutes spent engaged in homework. These patterns are problematic as points of comparison because one could not determine whether continued
improvements following the start of treatment are the result of naturally occurring
factors (i.e., those that resulted in the initial improvement) or of the treatment.

The fourth pattern is the variable baseline (see Figure 11.2), which can be relatively common in applied research given difficulties in establishing tight experimental control over environmental variables. Although one could aggregate the
data in a manner that minimizes the variability (e.g., by averaging the data collected over two sessions), this simply masks the variability and does not alter the
basic pattern. Sidman (1960) recommended that, when a researcher is faced with
such a pattern in baseline data, he or she should seek out and eliminate the extraneous factors that produce such variability. However, as has already been mentioned,
this may be difficult or excessively time consuming for the applied researcher.

The utility of the variable baseline as a point of comparison depends on the impact
of the independent variable. If the treatment produces a decrease in the variability
of the data pattern *and* a change in the desired direction, then it is appropriate
to conclude that the treatment had the desired impact. However, if variability is
reduced, but the problem remains at unacceptable levels, then interpretation of
the independent variable as useful would not be warranted. In this latter situation,
although the dependent measure is impacted by the independent variable, the impact
is not in the desired direction. Thus, one would not want to retain the treatment.

Another pattern of baseline is the variable-stable baseline. Here, the pattern is
initially variable, but then becomes stable. Such a pattern may be achieved by

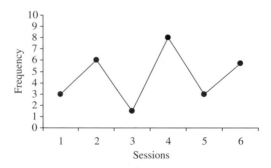

Figure 11.2   The variable baseline.

extending the baseline observation period for sufficient length so as to have the dependent measure come under the control of the baseline conditions. Such an approach might be warranted, for instance, if baseline conditions are novel to the participant. Because the independent variable is introduced following a period of stability, interpretation of its impact is the same as with the stable baseline: unambiguous. However, although perhaps the ideal scenario when initially obtaining variable data, practical and/or ethical constraints may limit the applied researcher's ability to extend the baseline to a sufficient length to establish stability (e.g., as in the case of a brief inpatient hospitalization, or when the dependent measure is severe self-injurious behavior).

The stable-variable baseline presents particular challenges as a point of comparison. Although unstable patterns of baseline data are not in and of themselves problematic, the stable-variable pattern suggests the influence of extraneous variables introduced after the initiation of baseline measurement. This may make it difficult to evaluate the impact of treatment as the extraneous variable may interfere with the independent variable. In these instances, attempts to seek out and control (or at least identify and describe) these outside influences are important.

SPECIFIC SINGLE-CASE DESIGNS

Now that defining characteristics of SCDs and issues related to evaluating baseline data patterns have been presented, the discussion is extended to encompass methods of introducing the independent variable to allow for appropriate comparisons. Specifically, defining features of commonly used SCDs are described.

Exploratory or Quasi-experimental Designs

There are times when it is not necessary or is impractical to utilize rigorous experimental SCDs when attempting to gather useful information about clinical phenomena of interest. Clinical psychology, as well as many other fields, is replete with many examples of interesting anecdotal descriptions of unique cases or systematic yet nonscientific observations of unusual phenomena. Gathering information using *exploratory* methods contributes to our understanding of phenomena of interest and often serves as the impetus for more in-depth and thorough analysis. In this section, we review two types of SCDs that allow for exploration of phenomena of interest without applying rigorous experimental criteria.

The Case Study

A case study is the "detailed study of a single individual, group, or event" (Leary, 2001, p. 321). The field of clinical psychology abounds with case studies of interesting, unique, and challenging clinical cases. In fact, early endeavors in this field to more rigorously analyze variables contributing to clinical phenomena relied heavily on the in-depth analysis of individual clients (Bailey & Burch, 2002). Even today, there are peer-reviewed journals devoted to publishing case studies based on psychotherapeutic work (e.g., *Clinical Case Studies*), a testament to the fact that there is much to be learned about the clinical phenomena experienced by our clients and the experience of attempting to address those problems by presenting descriptive, typically qualitative summaries of observations and client reports.

Although case studies lack attention to systematic or replicable collection of information and are without controls to threats to validity, they have several beneficial characteristics (Kazdin, 2003). They serve as a source for information and ideas about clinical problems, as well as a source for developing therapy techniques. Further, they can be a beneficial way of studying phenomena of interest that are rare. A well-documented case study can also be used to challenge principles or practices that are considered well established by describing how they did not appear to apply to a given individual. Thus, though case studies are not experimental in nature, they play an important role in clinical psychology.

The Simple A-B Design

As was previously mentioned, the hallmarks of SCDs include repeated observation of the behavior of interest across time and systematic changes in independent variables. The least complex SCD utilized to accomplish these goals is the A-B design. With this design, the experimenter collects measures of the dependent variable during baseline and then again during the treatment condition. Thus, the effect of the independent variable is demonstrated once. The A-B design moves beyond the clinical case study in regard to experimental rigor because of its reliance on repeated and systematic collection of data on the dependent variable of interest.

However, in consideration with other SCDs, the simple A-B design lacks experimental rigor. Specifically, inclusion of only one phase of each of the components (i.e., baseline and treatment) decreases the ability to adequately assess experimental control or internal validity. Theoretically, it is possible that a change in an extraneous variable affecting the individual occurred concurrently with introduction of treatment. If or when this occurs, making inferences about the impact of the independent variable separate from the impact of the extraneous variable is impossible. Take a situation in which a clinician is working with an adolescent experiencing depressive symptoms. Suppose, after gathering baseline data on daily subjective assessment of mood, the clinician initiates behavioral activation strategies. Coinciding with this, the adolescent's family also initiates services with a psychiatrist, who prescribes a medication. If subjective ratings of mood change, the clinician will be unable to determine whether this change is due to the behavioral activation strategies, the medication, or a combination of both. Several other threats to internal validity (e.g., maturation, instrument decay, statistical regression to the mean) are also not well accounted for by the simple A-B design.

Despite limitations in the ability to make definitive conclusions about the causal role of independent variables using the A-B design, it can be useful given certain circumstances, and it offers advantages over the uncontrolled case study methodology. Specifically, for problems that have been resistant to change for significant periods of time, noticeable improvements observed during the B phase offer some support for the intervention as the causal mechanism. Further, the A-B design is appropriate when practical or ethical limitations decrease one's ability to remove the intervention as a means of demonstrating experimental control (e.g., treating severe, life-threatening behavior). In these situations, the scientist-practitioner is at least gathering data to document whether change is occurring, regardless of whether effects can be fully ascribed to the specified intervention. Finally, for practitioners, reliance on A-B designs can be an important component of documenting that change occurred in a client's presenting problems, even if methodological weaknesses prevent making strong statements about the source of the change. Use of this design may be particularly valid for practitioners when they are implementing empirically supported interventions that have been previously evaluated via more rigorous methods and when one is primarily interested in documenting change rather than determining the source of change, a process referred to as Level II research (Hawkins & Matthews, 1999).

Classic Single-Case Withdrawal Designs

One of the most common categories of SCDs used in research involves systematically and repeatedly introducing and withdrawing an intervention and documenting the impact of those changes on the dependent variable of interest. This group of designs has been referred to as equivalent time-samples designs (Campbell & Stanley, 1966), withdrawal designs, and reversal designs (Kazdin, 2001). In this section, we describe common designs that are the result of permutations of the basic procedure of introducing and withdrawing intervention.

The A-B-A Design

The A-B-A design corrects the primary limitation of the A-B design by including a return to the original baseline conditions. This serves as a means of confirming experimental control over the dependent measure by allowing for repeated demonstration of experimental effect. If the dependent measure returns to a pattern that is similar to the original baseline, then stronger assumptions about the causal role of the independent variable can be made. In contrast to the A-B design, one is less concerned that some extraneous variables coincided with the introduction of the treatment phase. Although this may happen once, the possibility of another change in extraneous variables occurring at precisely the same time that the intervention is both introduced and withdrawn is so remote that it does not constitute a realistic threat to internal validity.

Although the A-B-A design corrects for problems of the simple A-B design, it has limitations. Most important for the clinical researcher, completing an investigation while the participant is exposed to baseline conditions is problematic. Let us return to the example of the adolescent client with depressive symptoms. Assume that an A-B-A design was used in which the B phase consisted of effective use of behavioral activation strategies. Ending the investigation while the participant is exposed to baseline conditions would be problematic if those conditions produced a return in data patterns similar to the original baseline. In this example, the client would be left to deal with his or her problems without the aid of intervention. Although perhaps not required to demonstrate experimental control, clinically and ethically it would seem prudent to reintroduce the intervention so as to address the presenting complaint.

The A-B-A-B Design

By introducing an additional treatment phase, the investigator creates the A-B-A-B design. This design controls for the limitation of the A-B-A design and is more methodologically rigorous due to the fact that three opportunities occur to compare the behavior patterns during baseline and treatment conditions (i.e., A to B, B to A, and A to B).

To illustrate the A-B-A-B design, consider Friman et al. (1999), who investigated the impact of an intervention for bedtime behavior problems exhibited by two children, ages 3 and 10 years. Both children exhibited bedtime problems in the form of calling out from their bedroom and leaving their room after their parents had put them to bed. Baseline data were collected across 15 days, during which time the parents were instructed to respond to the bedtime problems as they would typically. Treatment began on the 16th day and involved parents providing each child with a "bedtime pass" good for one free trip outside of the room past bedtime (e.g., get a drink of water, get another hug). Once the pass was used, it was relinquished to the parents, and no further trips were allowed. The pass was returned to the child on the subsequent night. During intervention, the parents were instructed to ignore all crying and to simply physically guide the child back into his room if he were to leave without the use of the pass.

Results of the experimental analysis are presented in Figure 11.3. Somewhat variable but increasing trends are noted in the dependent measure for both participants during the initial baseline. Following introduction of the intervention, a marked decrease in the targeted behavior occurred, to zero for the 10-year-old participant. Thus, it was demonstrated quite clearly with both participants that the behavior changed in the desired direction during the initial intervention phase. This is tempered slightly, however, with the 3-year-old participant. For him, as intervention continued the behavior problems began to increase again after the initial decrease. Reintroduction of the baseline conditions (i.e., withdrawal of the bedtime pass) resulted in the increased occurrence of the bedtime behavior problems, which decreased to zero for both participants upon the readministration of the intervention. Obtaining zero rates of behavior with the 3-year-old participant during the second intervention phase adds strength to the determination of experimental control given the initial variability in the first intervention phase.

The B-A-B Design

Although single-subject research typically starts with an initial baseline period, there may be instances in which this is not feasible. For example, perhaps the investigator is able to gather data only after some form of intervention is put into place. Or perhaps a participant's behavior problems are so severe that intervention is needed immediately. In either case, it is possible to use the B-A-B design. Although not as complete as the A-B-A-B design (because it does not allow for as many repeated comparisons of the experimental effect), it is more advantageous than the A-B-A design because it ends on a treatment phase (Hersen, 1982).

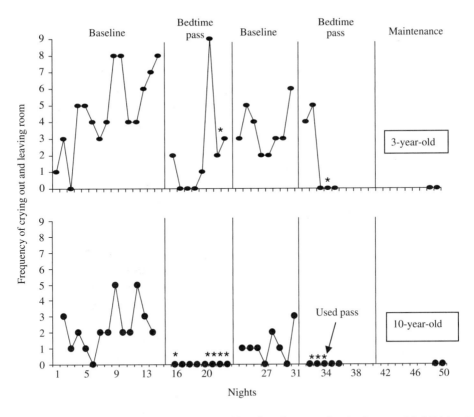

Figure 11.3 Nightly frequency of crying and leaving the room for the 3-year-old child (top) and the 10-year-old child (bottom). Asterisks indicate use of the pass. *Source:* "The Bedtime Pass: An Approach to Bedtime Crying and Leaving the Room," by P. C. Friman et al., 1999, *Archives of Pediatric and Adolescent Medicine, 153,* pp. 1027–1029, figure 1. Copyright 1999 by *Archives of Pediatric and Adolescent Medicine.* Reprinted with permission.

Variations of the Withdrawal Designs

The underlying strategy employed to demonstrate functional control using the various withdrawal designs (e.g., A-B-A, B-A-B)—the repeated introduction and withdrawal of the intervention—allows for various extensions of the basic designs. Thus, perhaps endless permutations or formations of the basic components of the designs can be created to address particular questions of interest. Several examples of such designs are considered next, although the list is not meant to be exhaustive.

A-B-A-B-A-B Design

The basic components of the A-B-A design can be extended, resulting in multiple withdrawals and administrations of the independent variable (e.g., the A-B-A-B-A-B design). Using such a design adds further support for the demonstration of functional control of the independent variable over the dependent variable. By demonstrating multiple times that the data patterns change in the expected direction when the treatment is added and withdrawn, the researcher can be more confident that the effect is due to the particular treatment variables. Although this might not be necessary when the treatment effect is large (i.e., when there is a significant difference in the data pattern between baseline and treatment conditions), repeatedly demonstrating the desired effect may be necessary when the effect is small (i.e., when the difference between the two conditions is small). Observing minimal or moderate changes multiple times may provide more convincing evidence that the independent variable is producing the impact, above and beyond natural variability.

A-B-A-C-A-C Design

Introducing a condition in which the effects of a second independent variable are assessed, as with the A-B-A-C-A-C design, also can extend the basic A-B-A design. In such a design, the investigator compares the impact of treatment conditions B and C on the dependent variable. However, with such a design, one is not able to compare the *relative* effects of the different independent variables because they are confounded by the extraneous variable of time (Hersen, 1982). Further, order effects may confound the findings. Perhaps the conditions present in C have an impact only after the participant is exposed to the conditions present in B. With such a design, one is unable to determine whether this is the case, and thus there is a threat to the internal validity of the study. If completing intersubject comparisons, one can control for this by using a counterbalancing technique (i.e., participants 1 and 3 are exposed to the conditions in the following order: A-B-A-C-A-C, whereas participants 2 and 4 are exposed to them in the following order: A-C-A-B-A-B). By using counterbalancing, the researcher is able to determine whether the independent variables produce similar effects regardless of order of presentation. Thus, if all participants respond to condition C in similar ways regardless of when they were exposed to this condition, then one has greater confidence in the effect of C alone.

Interaction Designs

As stated earlier, single-subject research typically involves a change in only one variable at a time across conditions. This rule can be applied in a way that allows the investigator to evaluate the combined effects of multiple independent variables by using a withdrawal design. Specifically, by introducing a condition in which two independent variables are present, it becomes possible to assess the impact of the combined intervention relative to a single intervention. In some situations, a particular treatment may produce minimal impact or may produce an impact that is less than that which is desired. By extending the basic components of the A-B-A design, one can assess the impact of adding additional treatment components.

Assume, for example, that a researcher is interested in treating teen smoking. Figure 11.4 shows hypothetical data in this scenario. After establishing a baseline of the number of cigarettes smoked per day, the impact of a reinforcement-based treatment is evaluated. As is shown, although the number of cigarettes smoked decreases somewhat, the desired goal of zero cigarettes smoked is not achieved. Thus, the investigator adds an additional component to the intervention, the use of a nicotine patch. This results in a condition labeled "BC" because it involves

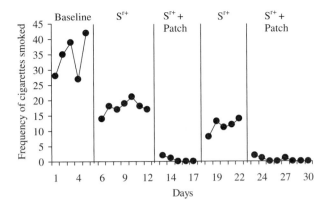

Figure 11.4   Number of cigarettes smoked per day. Hypothetical data of the assessment of interventions for teen smoking.

both components (i.e., reinforcement + nicotine patch). As shown in Figure 11.4, the combined intervention results in decreases in the dependent variable to zero. When the investigator withdraws the nicotine patch, the data patterns return to being similar to the original treatment phase. Finally, the combined intervention is reintroduced, resulting in the elimination of smoking. As illustrated, it is possible to demonstrate the impact of the combined intervention with such a design. Put another way, one is able to investigate the relative impact of condition C over condition B. The number of combinations is theoretically endless, potentially resulting in conditions such as BCD, BCDE, and so forth.

STAGE-PROCESS DESIGNS

Although the withdrawal designs have proven remarkably useful in scientific inquiry, partly because of the flexibility in applying the basic concepts of repeated observations and replication of experimental effect in multiple ways, there are situations in which their use is not appropriate. Withdrawal designs may be considered inappropriate due to a variety of reasons (e.g., ethical, practical). As mentioned earlier, withdrawal of a treatment may be unethical if the behavior problem is severe or life threatening. Also, it may not be possible to withdraw or remove certain therapeutic strategies. For example, once instructions have been given to a participant, it is impossible to remove them. Although the researcher could stop giving them in a particular condition, the fact that the instructions were given earlier could result in a change that is not removable. As another example, if the intervention results in behavior that is supported beyond the treatment conditions, then withdrawal of the intervention may have no impact on the behavior. For instance, if a clinician teaches someone to be appropriately assertive, the reactions of others may maintain use of assertive behavior regardless of whether the clinician removes the intervention. In this scenario, the lack of a return to baseline data patterns might suggest a lack of functional control of the independent variable. However, such is likely not the case; instead, other controlling variables continue to maintain the behavior patterns in the absence of the intervention. Because of these limitations, various other SCDs are used. These include the multi-elements design, multiple baseline designs, and changing criterion designs.

The Multi-Elements Design

The multi-elements design (also referred to as the simultaneous treatment design or the alternating treatments design) differs from other SCDs in that multiple conditions (i.e., baseline and treatment conditions, two or more treatment conditions) are conducted in rapid succession, with the order of presentation typically determined through random selection, and compared against each other (Miltenberger, 2001). For example, perhaps baseline conditions are in effect on one day, treatment conditions the next, and so forth. Thus, unlike withdrawal designs, the effects of the different experimental conditions are evaluated across the same time frame. This helps eliminate the possibility of extraneous influences on the dependent variable during only one experimental condition. In other words, any extraneous variable is going to impact the dependent variable during all conditions because they are occurring essentially in conjunction. One is able to rule out the extraneous influence as the cause of any differences noted across conditions.

With the multi-elements design, often there are three phases: baseline, comparison (rapid alternation between two or more conditions), and the use of the effective intervention (Holcombe et al., 1994). In some situations, however, the baseline might not be necessary. This may be particularly true if one of the comparison conditions is a baseline condition. One treatment condition is judged to be superior if it produces data patterns in the expected direction at a level that is greater than other conditions. Another component of the multi-elements design is that an equal number of sessions of each condition should be conducted. To ensure discriminated responding across conditions, researchers often pair separate but salient stimuli with each condition. This design may be particularly useful if the investigator is comparing interventions that have an immediate effect, and when the dependent measure is particularly sensitive to changes in stimulus conditions (i.e., reversible; Holcombe et al., 1994).

The multi-elements design can be used to compare a variety of different variables of interest. For example, the design can be used to compare different assessment conditions, such as in functional analysis research (e.g., Anderson, Freeman, & Scotti, 1999). In addition, this design can be used to compare a treatment condition to baseline (e.g., Freeman & Piazza, 1998) or to compare multiple treatments (e.g., Kahng, Iwata, DeLeon, & Wallace, 2000). Such an approach allows the investigator to assess which intervention may prove to be the most effective in changing the targeted dependent variable. The benefit of such a design over other designs is the ability to make such treatment comparisons in a relatively short amount of time.

Multiple Baseline Designs

There are three types of multiple baseline designs: (1) multiple baseline across behaviors, (2) multiple baseline across persons, and (3) multiple baseline across settings (or situations; Hersen, 1982; Miltenberger, 2001). With the multiple baseline design across behaviors, the impact of an intervention across different behaviors emitted by the same person is evaluated. As such, this is a within-subjects design. The intervention is applied sequentially to the different (presumably) independent behaviors. An example is evaluating the use of a particular reward strategy in affecting a child completing chores, cleaning his room, and completing his homework. The second design—multiple baseline across persons—involves the evaluation of the impact of a particular intervention across at least two individuals *matched* according to relevant variables who are presumed to be exposed to identical (or at least markedly similar) environments. For example, the investigator may compare an intervention across two students who attend math class with a particular teacher, one who attends in the morning and one who attends in the afternoon. Finally, with the multiple baseline across settings design, a particular intervention is applied sequentially to a single participant or group of participants across independent environments (e.g., home and school).

Technically, there must be at least two separate dimensions (i.e., behaviors, settings, or persons) present to utilize a multiple baseline design, although convention suggests a minimum of three or more. Multiple baseline designs are characterized by the presence of only two conditions: baseline and treatment. However, unlike the simple A-B design, treatment is introduced in such a way that one is able to evaluate experimental control of the independent variable. Specifically, the baseline condition is extended for increasing lengths of time as the intervention is introduced with the other dependent variables. Thus, these designs are particularly useful for studying irreversible effects because replication is achieved without withdrawal and reintroduction of the independent variable (Perone, 1991).

An assumption underlying the multiple baseline designs is that the dependent measures (i.e., behaviors, persons, settings) are functionally independent. If this is the case, a change in one dependent variable as a result of the independent variable should not produce changes in the other dependent variables. Treatment effects, therefore, are inferred when the dependent measure changes only when the intervention is applied to it. Variables still exposed to baseline conditions should show little to no change when the treatment is introduced with the other dependent variables. In this way, the multiple baseline designs are weaker than other designs (Barlow & Hersen, 1984; Hersen, 1982). Specifically, experimental control is inferred based on the comparison of nontreated dependent variables as compared to the treated variables, as well as the replication of the effect across behaviors, persons, or settings.

If the dependent variables are not functionally independent (i.e., treatment with one variable produces changes in the other variables), then the ability to establish experimental control is compromised. Determining a priori whether dependent variables are independent can be difficult, however. Take, for example, a situation in which the dependent measures are three problematic behaviors of a student in a classroom (i.e., talking out of turn, throwing spit wads, getting out of seat without permission). As an intervention, the investigator instructs the teacher to respond in a particular way to the behaviors (e.g., differential reinforcement of competing behavior) and evaluates the impact of the intervention using a multiple baseline design. The student may well learn to change each of the behaviors simply by exposure to the treatment for one behavior (e.g., differential reinforcement when the student talks out of turn affects other behaviors). As this example illustrates, as an artifact of the lack of independence, intervention with one dependent variable may produce changes in the other variables, resulting in the *inability to demonstrate* experimental control. This is problematic because the intervention may be the controlling variable in this situation, but this cannot be demonstrated in a convincing manner.

Kazdin and Kopel (1975) provided three recommendations for addressing problems of dependence across dependent variables. First, they recommend selecting dependent measures that are as topographically distinct as possible as a means of increasing the likelihood that they are independent. However, such an approach still relies on successful guessing, as topographically distinct behaviors may still be functionally related. Second, they suggest that investigators utilize four or more baselines as compared to two or three. They argue that, by increasing the number of baselines, one is increasing the likelihood of selecting measures that are independent. However, as pointed out by Hersen (1982; Barlow & Hersen, 1984), the probability of interdependence may be enhanced with a larger number of dependent variables. Third, Kazdin and Kopel recommend that, when faced with the occurrence of dependence across variables, the investigator withdraw and then reintroduce the independent variable. By doing so, it may be possible to demonstrate adequate experimental control. Although the investigator originally may have selected the multiple baseline design to avoid using a withdrawal design, this may be necessary to adequately demonstrate control.

To a certain extent, there are competing clinical and research goals when considering multiple baseline designs. From a research standpoint, the goal is to identify target dependent variables that are less likely to be influenced by changes in other targeted dependent variables. However, clinically, one is often interested in designing interventions that not only address targeted behavior patterns, but are also likely to produce change that generalizes to other relevant behaviors or contexts. For instance, a therapist working with an adolescent with social anxiety is likely interested in implementing interventions that address anxious responding not only in the classroom setting, but also in the lunchroom, during extracurricular activities, and elsewhere. The clinical goal is to teach skills that will generalize to relevant contexts. Of course, whether generalization happens naturally (e.g., teaching use of relaxation skills in the classroom results in the person also using those skills in the lunchroom) or must be programmed explicitly (e.g., prompting the adolescent to use skills across settings) will be determined only as one progresses.

Nonconcurrent Multiple Baseline Design

The presumption of the multiple baseline designs is that the measurement of the different dependent variables occurs simultaneously. In this way, the designs control for threats to internal validity such as history effects. However, there may be situations in which it is particularly difficult to simultaneously observe multiple individuals who meet the specified criteria, thus limiting one's ability to utilize the multiple baseline across persons design. This may be particularly true in applied or clinical research (Hayes, 1985). In such situations, it may be possible to utilize the nonconcurrent multiple baseline design, originally described by Watson and Workman (1981).

With the nonconcurrent multiple baseline across persons design, each baseline length is predetermined (e.g., 3, 6, 9 days). Then, when a participant with the requisite features is available, he or she is exposed to a randomly selected baseline period. From this point, the methodology is conducted in the same manner as the simple A-B design: baseline observations are conducted for the predetermined length, followed by the application of treatment. In this way, baseline and treatment data are obtained from multiple participants, allowing for adequate between-persons comparisons. If a participant fails to display an acceptable baseline pattern, that individual is dropped from the investigation, although his or her eventual reaction to treatment may still be useful as a replication (Watson & Workman, 1981).

Some (e.g., Harris & Jenson, 1985a, 1985b) have argued that the nonconcurrent multiple baseline design across persons is equivalent to a series of A-B designs with replication. This nomenclature has been recommended because multiple baseline designs rely on simultaneous data collection as a means of demonstrating adequate control over threats to internal validity. As described earlier, by showing that the change in the dependent variable occurs only when the treatment is introduced, the investigator has confidence in the causal relationship. This is strengthened when data with several individuals are collected simultaneously because the design controls for history effects. Harris and Jenson argued that the nonconcurrent multiple baseline design does not control for such effects because the data are not collected across individuals simultaneously; thus, the individual is not exposed to the same environment.

By varying the length of baseline, however, the nonconcurrent multiple baseline design does control for threats to internal validity (Hayes, 1985; Mansell, 1982). Specifically, each time the investigator demonstrates that the dependent measure changes when the treatment is introduced, regardless of the length of baseline, the likelihood that an extraneous variable produced the change for each participant is greatly reduced. Further, by using increasing lengths of baseline, the researcher controls for the possibility that the exposure to baseline conditions naturally produces changes in the dependent measure. Thus, although generally considered one of the weaker SCDs, the nonconcurrent multiple baseline across persons design can serve as a useful methodology if other factors limit the ability to utilize a more stringent design.

Changing Criterion Design

The changing criterion design shares features with both the simple A-B design and the alternating treatments design (Hersen, 1982; Miltenberger, 2001). Specifically, this design is characterized by the presence of only one baseline and one treatment phase. However, what differentiates this design from the A-B design is that the treatment condition is defined by the sequential introduction of different performance goals. In other words, the treatment phase is applied until the targeted dependent variable achieves a specified level of performance. At that time, the goal (i.e., criterion) of performance is altered, and the intervention continues until the behavior again achieves the desired level. Changes in the criterion occur until the dependent measure is occurring at the desired terminal level. As such, the changing criterion design is particularly well suited for situations in which the investigator is interested in evaluating shaping programs that are expected to result in increases or decreases in the dependent measure (e.g., decreased cigarette smoking, increased level of exercise; Hersen, 1982). Evaluation of the intervention as the causal agent occurs through two comparisons: between the occurrence of the dependent measure during baseline and during treatment, and between the occurrence of the dependent measure across the different levels of the intervention. If the dependent variable changes in the desired direction only when the criterion changes, then the investigator can have confidence in the controlling nature of the independent variable.

SINGLE-CASE DESIGNS AND EMPIRICALLY SUPPORTED TREATMENT

In 1993, the Division of Clinical Psychology of the American Psychological Association (APA) initiated efforts to define the criteria for determining whether treatments for clinical problems are adequately supported by empirical evidence. The task force charged with this assignment, now referred to as the Committee on Science and Practice (CSP), issued their first report in 1995 (Task Force, 1995), with updates offered in the following years by the committee (Chambless et al., 1996) and independently by members of the committee (Chambless & Hollon, 1998). The CSP provided guidelines or decision rules for defining empirically supported treatments (EST), as well as a list of psychotherapies meeting those criteria at the time. Establishing a process for determining whether an intervention approach is scientifically grounded, as well as a list of ESTs, has been viewed by many as important for promoting evidence-based practice within the fields of psychotherapy and clinical psychology (Herbert & Gaudiano, 2005), though others have questioned both the exercise and the criteria offered (for a summary, see Beutler, 1998).

The importance of evidence-based practice (a broader term used in other disciplines such as medicine and special education) has increased over the years and is now influenced by multiple sources. For instance, increasingly insurance companies are looking to providers to utilize therapies with known efficacy (Hayes et al., 1999; Morgan & Morgan, 2001). Additionally, certain federal initiatives and funding agencies are increasingly giving funding priority to proposed studies that utilize research methods to determine effectiveness of interventions (Horner et al., 2005; McDonald & O'Neill, 2003). Currently, many fields, including clinical psychology, tout between-group designs as the most scientifically rigorous method of determining effectiveness, with randomized clinical trials seen as the gold standard. However, SCDs can play an important role in determining empirical evidence for effectiveness.

The CSP (Task Force, 1995; Chambless et al., 1996) as well as modifications made since (Chambless & Hollon, 1998) provide guidelines for determining whether an intervention is "well established" or "probably efficacious." Initial CSP statements (Chambless et al., 1996; Task Force, 1995) included guidelines for determining whether an intervention was empirically supported using either group or single-subject designs. Regarding the latter, they recommended considering an intervention's efficacy to be well established if a large series of studies using SCDs demonstrate intervention effects, and the intervention to be considered probably efficacious if a small series of studies supported the intervention. Chambless et al. specified that the series of studies needed to include nine or more participants total to be considered a large series.

Horner and colleagues (2005) provided greater specificity regarding how SCDs may be used to determine empirical evidence for interventions or practices. Though their discussion occurs in the context of educational practices, it has relevance for clinical child and adolescent psychology. Specifically, they provide five standards that must be met for SCDs to demonstrate evidence of efficacy for a practice (e.g., intervention, strategy, approach):

> (a) The practice is operationally defined; (b) the context in which the practice is to be tested is defined; (c) the practice is implemented with fidelity; (d) results from single subject research document the practice to be functionally related to change in dependent measures; and (e) the experimental effects are replicated across a sufficient number of studies, researchers, and participants to allow confidence in the findings. (pp. 175–176)

They elaborate on these standards, providing important information regarding suggested guidelines for ensuring that each is met. In particular, they suggest more rigorous criteria for the number of studies and participants using SCDs than the CSP guidelines. Specifically, they recommend that, for an intervention or practice to be considered efficacious, there be a minimum number of five studies using SCDs, that the studies be conducted by at least three different researchers or research teams, and that the number of participants included in those five studies total at least 20. Adherence to these criteria ensures that the effect of the independent variable on the dependent variable has been repeated multiple times by several researchers, increasing the internal and external validity of findings (Horner et al., 2005).

SUMMARY

An overview of the basic characteristics of various single-subject research designs has been provided, based in the context of clinical child and adolescent psychology. Single-case designs are distinguished from group design approaches to scientific inquiry by several features, including repeated observation of the dependent variable, replication of treatment effects, intrasubject and intersubject comparisons, visual analysis of individual participant data, and systematic manipulation of independent variables. Further, direct and systematic replications are used to establish the generality of the findings. Together, these features allow the investigator to guard against, or to detect when present, threats to internal and external validity. Thus, their use in psychological and psychotherapy research can allow investigators to answer questions of interest in a manner that meets the requirements of the scientific method (Hayes et al., 1999; Hilliard, 1993; Morgan & Morgan, 2001).

A particular strength of SCDs is their flexibility, allowing an investigator to change the purpose of the study when warranted as the investigation progresses (Barlow & Hersen, 1984; Holcombe et al., 1994). In fact, some have argued that the defining features of SCDs allow researchers to be more intimately involved with their subject matter as compared to group designs (e.g., Perone, 1999). Assume, for example, that baseline data are variable. Rather than simply moving to the treatment phase in which the impact of a particular intervention is assessed, the investigator may wish to determine the source of the variability (Sidman, 1960). In this way, the investigation becomes an extended assessment that involves the identification of extraneous variables affecting the dependent variable. Once this is done, the researcher may wish to introduce a treatment (which, consequently, may be more effective now that sources of variability have been identified and can be accounted for).

Or perhaps the researcher was initially interested in the impact of a particular intervention on the dependent variable. For instance, perhaps a researcher is investigating the impact of time-out as an intervention for a noncompliant child using an A-B-A-B withdrawal design. Baseline data are collected on the rate of compliance per day. Then use of time-out as a consequence for noncompliance is introduced, which produces no change in the occurrence of the noncompliance. If this were a group design comparing the effects of time-out on noncompliance against either no treatment or an alternative treatment, the investigator would need to continue to utilize the exact procedures across all participants to assure experimental integrity, or consider the research unacceptable and stop the experiment altogether. With the SCDs, however, the investigator can extend the original lack of findings by evaluating another treatment (e.g., praise for compliance). Specifically, if there is no difference in the occurrence of the dependent variable between the initial baseline and treatment phases (A and B phases), it would be appropriate to introduce the second intervention (C phase) without returning to the original baseline conditions. If this produced an effect, withdrawal of the intervention would involve a return to the B phase. In other words, because data patterns do not differ between A and B, it is possible to use B as the comparison against patterns during the C phase. Thus, SCDs may be more economical than group designs in that they are malleable and changeable based on the data obtained.

In this way, single-subject designs are useful not only in the context of psychological research, but also in the context of demonstrating the effectiveness of clinical interventions (Hayes et al., 1999; Hilliard, 1993; Kazdin, 2003). Psychotherapy as a process involves, first, hypothesis building (i.e., developing reasonable explanations for the client's current conditions) and, second, hypothesis testing (i.e., assessing the effectiveness of an intervention expected to be effective based on the original hypothesis). Initial interventions may not be effective, and thus clinicians may experiment with others until improvements are noted. The flexibility of SCDs can allow clinicians to collect data and manipulate variables in a way that allows for adequate demonstration of therapeutic outcome as a result of specific interventions. Therefore, their use in psychotherapy can facilitate a clinician truly operating as a scientist-practitioner.

Multiple investigations have demonstrated that most graduates of clinical psychology programs, including those who come from scientist-practitioner programs, are involved in clinical endeavors rather than research pursuits (for review, see Gelso, 2006). As such, increased emphasis on training in empirical designs that have relevance for clinical settings seems prudent; in fact, cases for such an emphasis have been made (Blampied, 1999; Hayes et al., 1999). As Hayes and colleagues noted, one of the major challenges in fostering greater connection between practice and scientific inquiry has been the lack of research designs appropriate for clinical settings. Single-case designs seem to have several distinct advantages over group designs in relation to conducting research in applied settings (e.g., applied at the individual level, more malleable so as to be responsive to information learned through the process); thus, they seem to have a greater probability of being incorporated into clinical practice.

Rigorously applying SCDs to clinical practice presents challenges, however. Specifically, as articulated at various places throughout this chapter, the requirements needed to experimentally demonstrate that changes in the dependent variable are the result of an intervention using SCDs can be at odds with the realities of clinical practice. A fundamental issue is identifying the variables (e.g., context, type of behavior, question being asked, population being served, resources available) for deciding which SCD is most appropriate for use in a particular clinical context for a specific purpose. For instance, if a treatment has already been established as evidence-based, then a simple A-B design may be appropriate as a mechanism of monitoring change. Further, reporting to the scientific community multiple applications of an intervention's effects using simple A-B designs will help support clinical application of the intervention that was originally tested in highly controlled conditions. On the other hand, because many interventions (including those identified as empirically supported according to APA criteria) have not been subjected to effectiveness trials or used with special populations (e.g., rare disorders, with individuals with comorbid disorders), use of SCDs provides an opportunity to establish effectiveness of the treatment in a clinical context and with variations of client characteristics that were not included in randomized clinical trials. One can envision a multistage process in which SCDs are initially used in clinical contexts to establish treatments as evidence-based; following this, treatments can be used more clinically in a single-case decision-making framework that meets certain purposes (e.g., case formulation, treatment design, monitoring progress) but that would not require withdrawal or multiple baseline designs, in part because the intervention had been established as effective in previous research.

The issue of how to successfully incorporate SCDs into clinical practice is complex, and full attention to it is beyond the scope of this chapter. We raise the issue here to encourage people to consider how to integrate SCDs into clinical practice, and how the pursuit of doing so is beneficial for not only clinicians and their clients (e.g., through documentation of change, better informed decision making) but also for the research community (e.g., by verifying previous outcomes with unique populations, by raising additional questions to be addressed through more comprehensive or precise research).

Single-case designs have critical underlying assumptions and basic characteristics that separate them from group designs, while still ensuring that data are collected and analyzed in an experimentally rigorous manner. Single-case designs are typically aligned with operant traditions of behavioral psychology, in particular Skinnerian radical behaviorism and the applied branch of this science, given ardent endorsements by critical leaders in this field (Sidman, 1960; Skinner, 1974).

However, as has been noted (e.g., Hayes, 1981), these designs are largely theory-free and can be useful for any investigator (whether a researcher or a practitioner) who gathers time-series data in a systematic fashion. Thus, regardless of theoretical premise of a given researcher or practitioner, SCDs may be appropriate for determining causal or functional relations between changes in the dependent variable and introduction of the independent variable. This is not to suggest that solid training in the philosophical and theoretical context in which these designs were developed is not important (Blampied, 1999), but instead to support their broad utility in the diverse field of clinical child psychology. Further, their utility is exemplified by the fact that there are frequently calls for more single-subject research in various fields of psychology and beyond (e.g., Cook, 1996; Hrycaiko & Martin, 1996; Lundervold & Bellwood, 2000). Not only are SCDs useful for explicit research purposes, but they can also be used to assist practitioners in determining the impact of their efforts. Because of this, understanding SCDs is important for both researchers and clinicians alike.

REFERENCES

Aeschleman, S. R. (1991). Single-subject research designs: Some misconceptions. *Rehabilitation Psychology, 36*, 43–49.

Anderson, C. M., Freeman, K. A., & Scotti, J. R. (1999). Evaluation of the generalizability (reliability and validity) of analog functional assessment methodology. *Behavior Therapy, 30*, 21–30.

Atkins, D. C., Bedics, J. D., McGlinchey, J. B., & Beauchaine, T. P. (2005). Assessing clinical significance: Does it matter which method we use? *Journal of Consulting and Clinical Psychology, 73*, 982–989.

Bailey, J. S., & Burch, M. R. (2002). *Research methods in applied behavior analysis.* Thousand Oaks, CA: Sage.

Barlow, D., & Hersen, M. (1984). *Single case experimental designs: Strategies for studying behavior change* (2nd ed.). Elmsford, NY: Pergamon Press.

Beutler, L. E. (1998). Identifying empirically supported treatments: What if we didn't? *Journal of Consulting and Clinical Psychology, 66*, 113–120.

Blampied, N. M. (1999). A legacy neglected: Restating the case for single-case research in cognitive-behaviour therapy. *Behaviour Change, 16*, 89–104.

Blampied, N. M. (2001). The third way: Single-case research, training, and practice in clinical psychology. *Australian Psychologist, 36*, 157–163.

Campbell, D. T., & Stanley, J. C. (1966). *Experimental and quasi-experimental designs for research and teaching.* Chicago: Rand McNally.

Chambless, D. L., & Hollon, S. D. (1998). Defining empirically supported therapies. *Journal of Consulting and Clinical Psychology, 66*, 7–18.

Chambless, D. L., Sanderson, W. C., Shoham, V., Johnson, S. B., Pope, K. S., Crits-Christoph, P., et al. (1996). An update on empirically validated therapies. *Clinical Psychologist, 49*, 5–14.

Cook, D. J. (1996). Randomized trials in single subjects: The N of 1 study. *Psychopharmacology Bulletin, 32*, 363–367.

Drozd, J. F., & Goldfried, M. R. (1996). A critical evaluation of the state-of-the-art in psychotherapy outcome research. *Psychotherapy: Theory, Research, Practice and Training, 33*, 171–180.

Edgington, E. S. (2007). *Randomization tests* (4th ed.) Boca Raton, FL: Taylor & Francis.

Freeman, K. A., & Piazza, C. C. (1998). Combining stimulus fading, reinforcement, and extinction to treat food refusal. *Journal of Applied Behavior Analysis, 31*, 691–694.

Friman, P. C., Hoff, K. E., Schnoes, C., Freeman, K. A., Woods, D. W., & Blum, N. (1999). The bedtime pass: An approach to bedtime crying and leaving the room. *Archives of Pediatric and Adolescent Medicine, 153*, 1027–1029.

Gelso, C. J. (2006, August). On the making of a scientist-practitioner: A theory of research training in professional psychology [Special volume]. *Training and Education in Professional Psychology, 1,* 3–16.

Glicksohn, J., Gvirtsman, D., & Offer, S. (1997). The compensatory nature of mood: A single-subject time-series approach. *Imagination, Cognition and Personality, 15,* 385–396.

Gliner, J. A., Morgan, G. A., & Harmon, R. J. (2000). Single-subject designs. *Journal of the American Academy of Child and Adolescent Psychiatry, 39,* 1327–1329.

Harris, F. N., & Jenson, W. R. (1985a). AB designs with replication: A reply to Hayes. *Behavioral Assessment, 7,* 133–135.

Harris, F. N., & Jenson, W. R. (1985b). Comparisons of multiple-baseline across persons designs and AB designs with replication: Issues and confusions. *Behavioral Assessment, 7,* 121–127.

Hartmann, D. P., Roper, B. L., & Bradford, D. C. (1979). Some relationships between behavioral and traditional assessment. *Journal of Behavioral Assessment, 1,* 3–21.

Hawkins, R. P., & Mathews, J. R. (1999). Frequent monitoring of clinical outcomes: Research and accountability for clinical practice. *Education and Treatment of Children, 22,* 117–135.

Hayes, S. C. (1981). Single case experimental design and empirical clinical practice. *Journal of Consulting and Clinical Psychology, 49,* 193–211.

Hayes, S. C. (1985). Natural multiple baselines across persons: A reply to Harris and Jenson. *Behavioral Assessment, 7,* 129–132.

Hayes, S. C., Barlow, D. H., & Nelson-Gray, R. O. (1999). *The scientist practitioner: Research and accountability in the age of managed care.* Boston: Allyn & Bacon.

Herbert, J. D., & Gaudiano, B. A. (2005). Moving from empirically supported treatment lists to practice guidelines in psychotherapy: The role of the placebo concept. *Journal of Clinical Psychology, 61,* 893–908.

Hersen, M. (1982). Single-case experimental designs. In A. S. Bellack M. Hersen & A. E. Kazdin (Eds.), *International handbook of behavior modification and therapy.* (pp. 167–203). New York: Plenum Press.

Hillard, R. B. (1993). Single-case methodology in psychotherapy process and outcome research. *Journal of Consulting and Clinical Psychology, 61,* 373–380.

Holcombe, A., Wolery, M., & Gast, D. L. (1994). Comparative single-subject research: Descriptions of designs and discussions of problems. *Topics in Early Childhood Special Education, 14,* 119–145.

Horner, R. H., Carr, E. G., Halle, J., McGee, G., Odom, S., & Wolery, S. (2005). The use of single-subject research to identify evidence-based practice in special education. *Exceptional Children, 71,* 165–179.

Hrycaiko, D., & Martin, G. L. (1996). Applied research studies with single-subject designs: Why so few? *Journal of Applied Sports Psychology, 8,* 183–199.

Jacobson, N. S., Roberts, L. J., Berns, S. B., & McClinchey, J. B. (1999). Methods for defining and determining the clinical significance of treatment effects: Description, application, and alternatives. *Journal of Consulting and Clinical Psychology, 67,* 300–307.

Jacobson, N. S., & Truax, P. (1991). Clinical significance: A statistical approach to defining meaningful change in psychotherapy research. *Journal of Consulting and Clinical Psychology, 59,* 12–19.

Jones, E. E. (Ed.). (1993). Special section: Single-case research in psychotherapy. *Journal of Consulting and Clinical Psychology, 61,* 371–430.

Kahng, S., Iwata, B. A., DeLeon, I. G., & Wallace, M. D. (2000). A comparison of procedures for programming noncontingent reinforcement schedules. *Journal of Applied Behavior Analysis, 33,* 223–231.

Kazdin, A. E. (1999). Clinical significance: Measuring whether interventions make a difference. In A. E. Kazdin (Ed.), *Methodological issues and strategies in clinical research* (3rd ed. pp. 691–710). Washington, DC: American Psychological Association.

Kazdin, A. E. (2001). *Behavior modification in applied settings* (6th ed.). Belmont, CA: Wadsworth/ Thomson Learning.

Kazdin, A. E. (2003). *Research design in clinical psychology* (4th ed.) Boston: Allyn & Bacon.

Kazdin, A. E., & Kopel, S. A. (1975). On resolving ambiguities of the multiple-baseline design: Problems and recommendations. *Behavior Therapy, 6,* 601–608.

Kazdin, A. E., & Weisz, J. R. (Eds.). (2003). *Evidence-based psychotherapies for children and adolescents.* New York: Guilford Press.

Leary, M. R. (2001). *Introduction to behavioral research methods.* Boston: Allyn & Bacon.

Lundervold, D. A., & Bellwood, M. F. (2000). The best kept secret in counseling: Single-case (N = 1) experimental designs. *Journal of Counseling and Development, 78,* 92–102.

Mansell, J. (1982). Repeated direct replication of AB designs. *Journal of Behavior Therapy and Experimental Psychiatry, 13,* 261.

Mash, E. J., & Barkley, R. A. (Eds.). (2006). *Treatment of childhood disorders* (3rd ed.) New York: Guilford Press.

McDonald, J., & O'Neill, R. (2003). A perspective on single/within subject research methods and "scientifically based research." *Research and Practice for Persons with Severe Disabilities, 28,* 138–142.

McReynolds, L. V., & Thompson, C. K. (1986). Flexibility of single-subject experimental designs: Pt. I. Review of the basics of single-subject designs. *Journal of Speech and Hearing Disorders, 51,* 194–203.

Miltenberger, R. G. (2001). *Behavior modification: Principles and procedures.* Belmont, CA: Wadsworth/ Thomson Learning.

Morgan, D. L., & Morgan, R. K. (2001). Single-participant research design: Bridging science to managed care. *American Psychologist, 56,* 119–127.

Nugent, W. R. (1992). The affective impact of a clinical social worker's interviewing style: A series of single-case experiments. *Research on Social Work Practice, 2,* 6–27.

Parker, R. I., Brossart, D. F., Vannest, K. J., Long, J. R., Garcia De-Alba, R., Baugh, F. G., et al. (2005). Effect sizes in single case research: How large is large? *School Psychology Review, 34,* 116–132.

Perone, M. (1991). Experimental design in the analysis of free-operant behavior. In I. H. Iversen, & K. A. Lattal (Eds.), *Experimental analysis of behavior* (Pt. I, pp. 135–171). Amsterdam: Elsevier Science.

Perone, M. (1999). Statistical inference in behavior analysis: Experimental control is better. *Behavior Analyst, 22,* 109–116.

Scaturo, D. J. (2005). *Clinical dilemmas in psychotherapy: A transtheoretical approach to psychotherapy integration.* Washington, DC: American Psychological Association.

Scotti, J. R., Morris, T. L., & Cohen, S. H. (2003). Validity: Making inferences from research outcomes. In J. C. Thomas & M. Hersen (Eds.), *Understanding research in clinical and counseling psychology* (pp. 97–129). Mahwah, NJ: Erlbaum.

Shadish, W. R., Cook, T. D., & Campbell, D. T. (2001). *Experimental and quasiexperimental designs for generalized causal inference.* New York: Houghton Mifflin.

Sidman, M. (1960). *Tactics of scientific research.* Boston: Authors Cooperative.

Skinner, B. F. (1974). *About behaviorism.* New York: Knopf.

Task Force on Promotion and Dissemination of Psychological Procedures, (1995). Training in and dissemination of empirically-validated treatments: Report and recommendations. *Clinical Psychologist, 48,* 3–23.

Todman, J. B., & Dugard, P. (2001). *Single-case and small-n experimental designs: A practical guide to randomization tests.* Mahwah, NJ: Erlbaum.

Watson, P. J., & Workman, E. A. (1981). The non-concurrent multiple-baseline across-individuals design: An extension of the traditional multiple-baseline design. *Journal of Behavior Therapy and Experimental Psychiatry, 12,* 257–259.

Weisz, J. R. (2004). *Psychotherapy for children and adolescents: Evidence-based treatments and case examples.* Cambridge: Cambridge University Press.

Weisz, J. R., Jensen-Doss, & Hawley, K. M. (2006). Evidence-based youth psychotherapies versus usual clinical care: A meta-analysis of direct comparisons. *American Psychologist, 61,* 671–689.

Zhan, S., & Ottenbacher, K. J. (2001). Single subject research designs for disability research. *Disability and Rehabilitation, 23,* 1–8.

CHAPTER 12

Personality in Childhood and Adolescence

Randall T. Salekin and Courey A. Averett

There has been a great deal of research on the personality characteristics of youth over the past 3 decades. In part, this blossoming of research has stemmed from the availability of models of general personality theories and the broadening of research within the adult literature on general personality. Much more research is being conducted on children and adolescents, and there has been a greater emphasis in better understanding the etiology, general structure, and stability of personality of youth and its connection to psychopathology. This area of study is somewhat controversial, as noted by the current nomenclature's lack of formal acknowledgment of personality and personality disorders in children and adolescence. However, our current nomenclature does suggest that personality disorders can be recognized in childhood and adolescence, and the research has been advancing to show that there are likely broad identifiable personality traits in children and adolescents.

The purpose of this chapter is to review aspects of research on early emerging individual differences during the years from infancy through late adolescence. First, we provide a general description of temperament and personality and discuss how the two have been conceptualized over time. In this section of the chapter we also discuss the potential links between temperament and personality and examine whether the two might be one and the same. Second, we describe what is known about the structure of personality in children and adolescents. We discuss four primary models of general personality developed over the past several decades and attempt to integrate the competing models. Third, we review the stability of childhood personality over time. We examine the data on personality models, showing the existence of both stability and change across major age groups. Fourth, and importantly, we explain some of the potential processes involved in continuity and change. Research examples of several processes are provided to shed light on this important issue. In this section of the chapter we also discuss Thomas and Chess's (e.g., Thomas & Chess, 1977; Thomas, Chess, & Birch, 1968; Thomas, Chess, Birch, Hertzig, & Korn, 1963) notion of the "goodness of fit" between the child's temperament and personality and his or her predominant environment. Fifth, we discuss childhood personality and its connection to both positive (adaptive) and negative (psychopathology) outcomes. This section of the chapter is important if

We would like to thank Rebecca Shiner, Jennifer Tackett, and Robert Krueger for their guidance.

we are to better understand how normal personality traits can lead to meaningful and fulfilling lives, and it also sheds light on how certain personality traits might be linked to psychopathology. Finally, we look at the *Diagnostic and Statistical Manual of Mental Disorders*, fourth edition, text revision (*DSM-IV;* American Psychiatric Association, 2000) model of pathology and its application to personality problems in youth. There is not an easy alliance between general models of personality and the *DSM-IV* categories of pathology, although researchers are beginning to bridge these gaps. The chapter concludes with suggestions for future research in this area, highlighting the exciting research on the near horizon for examining personality in children and adolescents as it relates to both positive and negative outcomes.

DESCRIPTION OF PERSONALITY IN CHILDREN AND ADOLESCENTS

Few would argue that children differ in their personalities. Some children are outgoing and exuberant, whereas others are more quiet and reserved. Some are irritable and emotionally labile; others show equanimity from an early age. Some are aggressive and others are gentle. These individual differences, although observed by parents, peers, teachers, and psychologists in everyday life, are not always easily described in research and clinical practice (Caspi & Shiner, in press; Shiner, 2006).

Traditionally, personality has been viewed as a stable and enduring set of characteristics that affects one's perceptions of oneself, others, and the world. The *DSM-IV* defines personality traits as "enduring patterns of perceiving, relating to, and thinking about the environment and oneself that are exhibited in a wide range of social and personal contexts" (American Psychiatric Association, 2000, p. 630). A personality disorder, in turn, is defined as an enduring pattern of inner experience and behavior that has deviated markedly from the expectations of the individual's culture, is pervasive and inflexible, has an onset in adolescence or adulthood, is stable over time, is evident across a broad range of personal and social situations, and leads to distress and impairment (p. 630).

Although there have been numerous studies of personality in adult samples, there has been limited research in the direct emergence or development of child personality and the concomitant problems that can stem from personality (Bernstein, Cohen, Velez, Schwab-Stone, Siever, & Shinsato, 1993). There is also little information on change or stability in childhood and adolescent personality. Part of the concern, when thinking about personality in children and adolescents is a general uneasiness that the identification of traits (or disorder) suggest little opportunity for change. Some scientists and clinicians believe that personality has not yet crystallized in children or adolescents; in this case, the existence of personality and/or personality disorder makes little conceptual sense. Others (e.g., Shapiro, 1990) question only whether general personality can be identified and personality disorders diagnosed before adolescence, when adultlike identity is thought to coalesce (Blos, 1967; Erikson, 1968). This is a nontrait and nondevelopmental approach because it does not consider the process by which, at each phase of development, an age-appropriate identity and personality exist and continue to form. However, researchers have noted that ignoring the existence of a general blueprint for personality and the developmental line of the structuring of identity and personality means ignoring the ways personality development can occur across time but also how it might be positively or adversely affected at any age (Roberts & Wood, 2006; Shiner, 2006; Tackett, 2006).

BRIEF HISTORY OF THE STUDY OF PERSONALITY IN CHILDREN AND ADOLESCENTS

Individual differences in infants and children have focused on temperament and personality. The scientific study of early temperament can be traced to the seminal work of Thomas and Chess, who initiated the New York Longitudinal Study to study the significance of biologically based temperament in infancy and childhood (Thomas, Chess, Birch, Hertzig, & Korn, 1963). Thomas and Chess viewed temperament as a style of behavior and abilities. Their work challenged the way social development was studied at the time because they emphasized the two-way interaction of biology and environment in shaping children's outcomes. Prior to this view, many researchers and clinicians viewed child personality and outcome as being influenced almost exclusively by rearing environments. Thus, the work of Thomas and Chess was an important step in research because it suggested that there are preexisting personality styles from which individuals then operate.

Temperament has been defined differently by different researchers, and the link between temperament and personality is not fully understood (Frick, 2004). There are a variety of points of view on this topic: (a) that temperament is different from personality, (b) that temperament is linked to certain personality traits, and (c) that temperament is personality. Developmental and child psychologists traditionally describe stable and observable differences in young children by relying on temperamental constructs such as negative emotionality (Thomas & Chess, 1977) or emotionality (Buss & Plomin, 1984), sociability (Buss & Plomin, 1984) or surgency (Rothbart & Derryberry, 1981), task persistence (Thomas & Chess, 1977) or effortful control (Rothbart & Derryberry, 1981), and activity level (Buss & Plomin, 1984; Goldsmith & Campos, 1982; Putnam, Ellis, & Rothbart, 2001; Thomas & Chess, 1977). Researchers assume that temperament differences are expressions of neurobiological mechanisms that have a strong genetic basis (Mervielde, De Clercq, De Fruyt, & Van Leeuwen, 2005). In contrast, personality traits are mainly used to chart stable latent differences in adults, presumed to be partly influenced by temperament and interaction with the environment. According to this model, temperament can be considered a direct precursor to personality and, thus, is the earliest expression of individual difference.

Temperament is thought to be most directly observable during infancy and toddlerhood (Goldsmith et al., 1987) and to make up the entirety of personality during these early years (Caspi & Shiner, in press; Shiner & Caspi, 2003). It is thought that as children develop, early temperament traits develop into broader, more inclusive higher order personality traits as well as increasingly differentiated lower order traits (Buss & Finn, 1987; Caspi, Roberts, & Shiner, 2005; Caspi & Shiner, in press; Lahey, 2004; Rothbart & Ahadi, 1994; Shiner, 1998). Specifically, personality develops as children progress through various cognitive and emotional stages that increasingly allow them to interact with, experience, and respond to the world in more complex ways (Caspi, 2000; Roberts & Wood, 2006; Rothbart & Ahadi, 1994). Thus, the structure of personality may change as children gain new skills (e.g., motor or language), gain the capacity to regulate emotions, and develop a sense of self (Roberst & Wood, 2006; Rothbart & Ahadi, 1994; Shiner, 1998, 2006; Shiner, Masten, & Tellegen, 2002). However, despite growing consensus that temperament traits make up the core of later personality, a clear understanding of the developmental relationship between temperament and personality is lacking (Halverson et al., 2003; Shiner & Caspi, 2003). This model is not embraced by all researchers, and the idea of temperament as "style" has been critiqued as vague and unnecessarily narrow. In fact, there are a variety of definitions of the term temperament (see Table 12.1), and some researchers claim that behavioral styles even early on are both biologically and environmentally influenced (see Frick, 2004; Plomin & Daniels, 1984), raising the question of whether the distinction between temperament and personality is necessary.

The resurgence of trait psychology, and especially the preponderance of the five-factor model (FFM; Digman, 1990), challenged both the viewpoint that personality could not be assessed in youth and that it could not also be considered a biologically based constellation of differences in youth. To elaborate on this point, personality psychologists have made several key and compelling arguments about the applicability of personality to children and adolescents. First, personality psychologists tend to agree that five broad dimensions—neuroticism, extraversion, openness, agreeableness, and conscientiousness—can be considered the basic dimensions underlying adult personality. Personality psychologists interested in the developmental antecedents of this FFM later showed that these five dimensions are also applicable to individual differences in children and adolescents (Digman, 1963; Digman & Inouye, 1986; Goldberg, 1993; John, Caspi, Robins, Moffitt, & Stouthamer-Loeber, 1994; Kohnstamm, Halverson, Mervielde, & Havill, 1998;

Table 12.1   Definitions of Temperament

Source	Definition
Buss (1995)	"Inherited personality traits that appear during the first two years of life and endure as basic components of personality." (p. 49)
Goldsmith (1996)	"Individual differences aspect of emotionality apparent early in development." (p. 221)
Kagan & Snidman (1991)	"Initial, inherited profiles that develop into different envelopes of psychological outcomes." (p. 856)
Rothbart & Derryberry (1981)	"Individual differences in reactivity and regulation assumed to have a constitutional basis." (p. 40)
Thomas & Chess (1977)	"The constellation of behaviors exhibited at any one age-period [and] are the result of all the influences, past and present, which shape and modify behaviors in a constantly evolving interactive process." (p. 171)

Note: Frick (2004) identified these definitions with the exception of Thomas and Chess earlier and also outlined specific dimensions of temperament.

Lamb, Chuang, Wessels, Broberg, & Hwang, 2002). In a key study, John et al. introduced the basic personality dimensions to developmental psychologists and demonstrated that the "little five" predict externalizing problem behavior in children.

McCrae and his colleagues (McCrae et al., 2000) cogently argued against the artificial distinction between temperamental constructs and personality traits, noting there are strong empirical and conceptual links between the domains of temperament and personality. The defining characteristics of temperament variables also apply to traits, including genetic basis, early observability, and pervasive impact on a range of behaviors (McCrae & Costa, 1997). In the past decade, behavior genetic studies have consistently documented the strong genetic basis of FFM traits (Jang, McCrae, Angleitner, Riemann, & Livesley, 1998), with heritability estimates ranging from .40 to .60 depending on the trait and method used for indexing the trait. McCrae and Costa (1996) conceptualized the FFM dimensions as basic tendencies shaping interactions with the environment, resulting in characteristic (mal)adaptations such as interests, values, and attitudes but also problem behavior and psychopathology. In another key study, Mervielde et al. (2005) compared the major models of temperament with the FFM and showed similarities and conceptual overlap between them. Frick (2004) commented that much of the work on temperament, personality, and psychopathology has been separated largely by discipline boundaries, which may account for differences in the terminology but not necessarily differences in the underlying concepts. Caspi et al. (2005) recently concluded that temperament and personality increasingly appear to be more alike than different.

Despite differences in terminology and perhaps conceptual differences, it has been suggested that the field of temperament and childhood personality needs a unifying framework to allow organization and integration of empirical findings and to facilitate communication among researchers within the field, as well as with researchers in clinical, developmental, and personality psychology subdisciplines (Frick, 2004; Halverson et al., 2003; Lonigan, Vasey, Phillips, & Hazen, 2004; Shiner & Caspi, 2003).

The popularity of the FFM in adult personality research has contributed to the growing body of literature documenting investigations of the five-factor structure in children and adolescents (e.g., Caspi & Shiner, in press; Digman, 1990; Graziano & Ward, 1992; John et al., 1994; Lamb et al., 2002; Martin, Wisenbaker, & Huttunen, 1994; Widiger & Trull, 2007). These studies tend to find evidence for the five-factor structure, although there is some evidence to suggest that openness to experience may not emerge until adolescence (Lamb et al., 2002). Halverson et al. (2003) in a novel study used a bottom-up approach to the structural debate by attempting to construct a cross-cultural, cross-age measure of childhood personality. These researchers collected parental descriptors of children (ages 3 to 12) across eight countries and, using a combination of rational (sorting done by focus groups) and factor analytic techniques, derived a somewhat new model of childhood personality. The resulting model consisted of a five-factor structure, although openness to experience was linked to only a single intellect scale, which reflects characteristics such as precociousness, intelligence, and speediness in comprehension. Overall, the authors concluded that results of their effort produced a preliminary comprehensive taxonomy of childhood personality.

Shiner and Caspi (2003) also proposed a preliminary comprehensive taxonomy for childhood personality, which the authors recently extended (Caspi et al., 2005; Caspi & Shiner, 2006). They based their proposed taxonomy on a review of the literature on childhood and adolescent personality and also integrated existing and emerging work on the structure of personality. They initially defined a classification system consisting of four superordinate traits and 11 lower level traits, recently extending the taxonomy to include a fifth higher order trait (Caspi et al., 2005; Caspi & Shiner, 2006). The higher order traits mapped onto the five factors in the Big 5. They noted that questions remain over whether the fifth factor in the FFM, openness to experience, has a direct analogue in childhood (Shiner, 2006) or whether it emerges later in development (Caspi & Shiner, 2006). These two recent attempts to provide a preliminary classification system for childhood and adolescent personality virtually agreed on the relevant higher order traits. This convergence on the superordinate structure is particularly compelling given the different research approaches used to construct the two taxonomies.

Taken together, these studies provide a good starting point for discussing childhood personality within a comprehensive framework. Moreover, the framework put forth will allow for greater communication in the area of childhood personality, as well as linking areas of childhood and adult personality (Caspi & Shiner, 2006). These findings suggest that many researchers believe that the FFM should be chief in both child and adult research investigations, although we believe that it is also critical to reevaluate and revise theories as new evidence arises. Although the childhood measures have been developed from both bottom-up and top-down perspectives, we briefly review the adult models of personality and attempt to integrate the research on these models to better inform the models that have resulted for child and adolescent samples.

GENERAL MODELS OF PERSONALITY

Researchers (Watson, Kotov, & Gamez, 2006; Widiger & Trull, 2007) have noted that there are superordinate factors to the structure of human personality in adulthood, and the field is somewhat divided between two or three prominent models of personality. Watson et al. asked the question, If there is a stable factor structure for adult and child personality, why are there so many different models? These authors noted that despite a variety of models and some disagreement, these models are closely related or converge, and it has been shown that they can be easily integrated with each other (see Clark & Watson, 1999; Markon, Krueger, & Watson, 2005; Watson, Clark, & Harkness, 1994). We discuss each of these basic models of personality in turn. Then we show how the three major models can be integrated, drawing on the work of Clark and Watson (1999; see also Watson, Kotov, & Gamez, 2006).

The Big 5 Factors of Personality

The Big 5 factor model of personality developed out of a number of attempts to understand the lexicon or natural language of trait descriptors (John & Srivastava,

1999; McCrae et al., 2000). Factor analytic studies of these descriptors consistently revealed five broad factors: extraversion, agreeableness, conscientiousness, neuroticism, and openness to experience (or imagination, intellect, or culture). This structure has been shown to be robust, with the same five factors emerging in both self- and peer ratings (McCrae & Costa, 1987), in analyses of both children and adults (Digman, 1997), and across a wide variety of languages and cultures (McCrae & Costa, 1997).

The Big 3 Factors of Personality

The Big 3 factor structure of personality is based on a smaller set of superordinate factors: negative emotionality (paralleling neuroticism), positive emotionality (paralleling extraversion), and disinhibition versus constraint (paralleling conscientiousness; Clark & Watson, 1999; Markon et al., 2005). This structural format emerged from the seminal and pioneering work of Eysenck (Eysenck, 1997) and his colleagues. Eysenck originally created an influential two-factor model consisting of neuroticism and extraversion. Subsequent analyses led to the identification of a third broad dimension, labeled psychoticism. Although thus titled, this third dimension is better viewed as assessing individual differences in disinhibition versus constraint (Watson & Clark, 1993).

Other theorists subsequently posited similar three-factor models. For instance, Tellegen (1985) proposed a structure consisting of negative emotionality (paralleling neuroticism), positive emotionality (cf. extraversion), and constraint (which is strongly negatively correlated with psychoticism). Watson and Clark (1993) delineated a similar model, with factors named negative temperament, positive temperament, and disinhibition (versus constraint), respectively. In his reformulation of the California Psychological Inventory, Gough (1987) introduced the higher order "vectors" of self-realization, internality, and norm-favoring, which represent the low ends of neuroticism, extraversion, and psychoticism, respectively.

The Interpersonal Circumplex Model of Personality

Based on the work of Sullivan and Leary (Leary, 1957; Sullivan, 1953; Wiggins & Broughton, 1985; Wiggins & Pincus, 1989, 1994) proposed that personality was made up of octants: assured-dominant (PA), arrogant-calculating (BC), cold-hearted (DE), aloof-introverted (FG), unassured-submissive (HI), unassuming ingenuous (JK), warm-agreeable (LM), and gregarious-extraverted (NO). There exists considerable empirical literature on the correlates of the interpersonal circumplex model (e.g., Kiesler, 1996; Plutchik & Conte, 1997; Wiggins, Trapnell, & Phillips, 1988). Accordingly, the interpersonal circumplex model provides elements from a model of general personality and attempts to map the interpersonal circumplex onto Big 5 factor models that are generally well understood and are delineated in further detail next.

Integrating the Big 3, Big 5, and Interpersonal Circumplex Models of Personality

The accumulating data establish that the Big 5 model essentially represents an expanded and more differential version of the Big 3 (Markon et al., 2005; Rothbart,

Ahadi, Hershey, & Fisher, 2001; Watson, 2005). Most notably, the neuroticism and extraversion dimensions of the Big 5 essentially are equivalent to the negative emotionality and positive emotionality factors, respectively, of the Big 3. Thus, negative emotionality and positive emotionality are common to both models and constitute what Watson et al. (2006) refer to as the basic Big Two of personality. Moreover, the disinhibition versus constraint dimension of the Big 3 is a mixture of (low) conscientiousness and agreeableness. More specifically, according to Watson et al. (2006), disinhibited individuals tend to be impulsive, reckless, and irresponsible (i.e., low conscientiousness), as well as uncooperative, unsympathetic, and manipulative (i.e., low agreeableness). Finally, openness is strongly associated to the Big 3, although it does show a moderate positive association with positive emotionality (Digman, 1997; Markon et al., 2005). The interpersonal circumplex also maps onto the Big 5; many believe this personality framework taps two higher order dimensions, dominance and love. Dominance is most closely linked to extraversion and love is most closely linked to agreeableness and possibly openness (McCrae & Costa, 1989). Putting these data together, Clark and Watson (1999) noted that one can transform the Big 3 into the Big 5 by (a) decomposing disinhibition versus constraint into agreeableness and conscientiousness and (b) incorporating the additional dimension of openness. In addition the interpersonal circumplex can be subsumed under this broader umbrella of personality components and traits. Not surprisingly, of the somewhat varying models of personality in research, the FFM or Big 5 model of personality appears to subsume the others and thus is the most commonly used measure of personality traits.

It is important to note that some researchers have found flaws with this model. Specifically, although the Big 5 is the most common model, Block (1996, 2001) argued that the word "approach" might be more applicable than "model," since there is such an array of models that have not converged as of yet. He claimed that there are deficiencies in the FFM becoming the general perspective on personality, and pointed to the absence of an overall explanation for the five-factor approach. Others (Briggs, 1989) have voiced similar concerns, stating that there is no theoretical explanation for why these five dimensions were more coherent than other models' dimensions. On the other hand, no one has offered an explanation as to why this model is an invalid system of measure.

It is probably safe to say that the general consensus among researchers is that this model can be useful in describing the personality structure from which variant patterns can develop, thus forming the uniqueness of personality of an individual. Although it has shown reliable results when viewing adult differences, there have been limited findings with regard to children and the FFM. This could be for a number of reasons. For instance, there could be concerns about the reliability of self-reports and developmental and maturity levels, as well as diverging ideas about the age at which personality begins to develop from baseline attachments. In addition to these factors, reliability of parent reports of young children, or semantics, could have limited the degree to which research is conducted with children and the Big 5.

However limited, the FFM is increasingly credited with being one of the best currently available models for the study of personality, and research has been aiming to find a universality of personality as well as using it to track the development of personality. Yamagata et al. (2006) conducted a study with 1,200 twins from Canada, Germany, and Japan to determine if the FFM identifies general personality structure that can be considered universal across cultures. These researchers found a significant congruence across genetic and environmental factors in relation to the FFM across all three countries, therefore providing a basic, universal genetic component in addition to the environmental factors involved in personality development.

A study by McCrae et al. (2002) examined changes in personality during adolescence, using the FFM to directly compare the adolescent results to the adult scores. They argue that adult personality measures can be meaningful when used with adolescent samples, as demonstrated by De Fruyt, Mervielde, Hoekstra, and Rolland (2000) and Parker and Stumpf (1998). Parker and Stumpf measured a sample of intellectually gifted adolescents and found that self- and parent reports were valid and reliable and yielded the same factor structure seen in adults. It is possible that psychologists underestimate the capacity of adolescents to relate to the adult personality items. Not only do adolescents understand the factors in the adult measure, but the factors seem to easily describe personality among adolescents when personality is evaluated by a variety of sources, including parents, teachers, and other adult observers. McCrae et al. (1999; see also McCrae et al., 2002) focused on the personality changes that occur during adolescence and used the FFM to examine each specific factor of neuroticism, extraversion, openness, agreeableness, and conscientiousness, predicting that adolescents would exhibit high neuroticism and extraversion and low agreeableness and conscientiousness. Although only moderate correlations were found with regard to high neuroticism, openness was also moderately elevated in adolescence. However, De Fruyt (De Fruyt et al., 2000) has noted that there is a need for continuity in measures. More specifically, it is possible that if there were a child version of the FFM the correlations may be stronger (or weaker). Either way, more research about the transition between childhood temperament and developmental maturity and later personality development should be examined not only with the FFM, but with other, equally strong measures of personality, such as the three, four, six or seven-factor models. We elaborate on this point next.

ASSESSING PERSONALITY AT A YOUNG AGE

A comprehensive assessment of age-specific indicators of traits is crucial to studying personality at a young age, especially in development. Different approaches have been adopted to assess FFM dimensions in children and adolescents, and as mentioned, work in this area is still in its infancy. Often, FFM measures—initially developed for adults—are downwardly extended and used to describe differences in younger age groups (see, e.g., studies using the Neuroticism Extraversion Openness Personality Inventory—Revised [NEO-PI-R] to assess adolescents' personality: De Clercq & De Fruyt, 2003; De Fruyt, Mervielde, Hoekstra, & Rolland, 2000; Goldberg, 2001; McCrae et al., 2002). Other studies adapted the phrasing of personality items for younger age groups (e.g., the junior version of Eysenck's Personality Questionnaire measure; Eysenck, 1963; Eysenck, Makaremi, & Barrett, 1994) to be more developmentally appropriate. However, it can be argued that these downwardly extended measures are probably not ideal for fine-grained assessment of childhood and adolescent personality differences and especially not to index developmental change (De Clercq, De Fruyt, & Van Leeuwen, 2004). Therefore, according to De Clercq and De Fruyt an alternative approach that is more sensitive to subtle personality differences and developmental status at a variety of ages should be developed on the basis of the full range of personality differences observable prior to adulthood.

De Fruyt and his colleagues (De Fruyt et al., 2000; Slotboom, Havill, Pavlopoulos, & De Fruyt, 1998) have offered several suggestions for research and tool development in this area. Specifically, the lexical approach to personality description provides a convincing justification for the development of a comprehensive child and adolescent personality taxonomy. Mervielde and De Fruyt (1999) adopted this approach to construct such a taxonomy for classification of a large pool of parental personality descriptions in Flemish children between 6 and 13 years old (Kohnstamm et al., 1998). These authors subsequently developed the Hierarchical Personality Inventory for Children (HiPIC), representing the content of parental descriptions in short sentence items referring to concrete and observable behavior. The HiPIC can be considered a lexically based measure of the active parental vocabulary, in contrast to the NEO-PI-R, in which the facets are not derived empirically but are selected after a careful search of the adult personality literature. The HiPIC items span five broad domains: extraversion, benevolence, conscientiousness, emotional instability or neuroticism, and imagination. Some domain labels differ from the lexical adult Big 5 (Goldberg, 1993), although there is quite a bit of overlap in the content. It is beyond the scope of this chapter to cover comprehensively the measures used to assess the Big 5, but it should be noted that age-specific measures ought to undergo development and be tested. Researchers and clinicians alike are referred to Caspi and Shiner (2006) for a review of the existing measures, which might serve as a starting point for the development of newer measures with a developmentally sensitive theoretical framework. We comment on some important developmental factors that are likely to have an impact on personality development when considering the interaction between biology and environment and the two-way interplay that can lead to various outcomes for children and adolescents.

PERSONALITY DEVELOPMENT IN CHILDREN AND ADOLESCENCE

Developmental theories conceive a number of child and adolescent cognitive developments as well as puberty as important stages for social and personality development (Roberts & Wood, 2006), involving changing social interactions with parents and peers and increasing societal influences (e.g., Crick & Dodge, 1994; Roberts & Wood, 2006). Of course, we are increasingly aware that development occurs across the life span and that we are in the midst of development at any given age and developmental period. Nonetheless, the importance of adolescence as a key transitional phase has been acknowledged by a number of prominent theorists and researchers. Adolescence was acknowledged by Erikson (1950, 1968) as a critical stage in our development. Erikson considered adolescence a second individuation stage in which change is likely. Similarly, behavioral theories (Robin & Foster,

1989) emphasize that during adolescence, learning processes and contingencies are embedded in novel social networks and environments, including changing peer groups. In addition, organismic theories such as Piaget's (1983) theory of cognitive development and subsequent brain architecture suggest that newly acquired cognitive structures influence the way children and adolescents interact with their environment.

Personality theories such as Cloninger's (Cloninger, Svrakic, & Przybeck, 1993) theory of character development discern qualitatively different life strategies that an individual has to master before a more advanced developmental phase or level can be met. These theories emphasize developmental discontinuities, but it remains to be established whether these discontinuities reflect changes in basic tendencies or whether they are restricted to changing characteristic adaptations (McCrae & Costa, 1996; Shiner & Caspi, 2003). The demonstration of different forms of stability across the FFM trait hierarchy in childhood and adolescence would underscore McCrae and Costa's five-factor theory and therefore requires that the previously reviewed theories of personality development account not only for trait change but also for trait stability. We agree that there are some reasons to believe that personality would be stable across the life span; however, there are also compelling reasons with respect to maturation to expect both stability and change and that there would be a variety of outcomes for youth (both positive and negative) even if they manifested similar constellations of traits (e.g., extraversion and openness).

During the past several decades, research has uncovered considerable knowledge about the child's developing personality, including the emergence of a sense of identity, affect modulation, thinking style, and relationship with the external word (Mroczek & Little, 2006). With respect to the development of a sense of self, for example, it has been found that recognition of oneself by name in a mirror occurs by 3 years of age; a sense of shame, implying self-consciousness, emerges before 2 years of age (Lewis, 1993). Another example is empathy; a basic component of interpersonal functioning because of its role in the relationship between self and others, empathy develops in early childhood (Hoffman, 1977), evidencing clear signs by 2 years of age (see Salekin, 2006). These factors could also impact the development of personality in that youth might evaluate their basic personality characteristics and start to shape the various outcomes that result from their general personality makeup. Therefore, another component of developmental status and maturity—thinking style and the presence of a concrete operational reasoning system (Piaget, 1950)—is apparent by middle childhood and persists into adulthood. Differences in style of reasoning could impact the eventual outcome for youth. All these developmental considerations need a point of reference. That is, we need to know how stable personality is across childhood and adolescence and, more generally, across the life span.

Stability of Personality across Time: Continuity and Change

In the past decade, there has been a wealth of studies on personality continuity that were recently summarized in two meta-analyses of longitudinal data on differential (Roberts & DelVecchio, 2000) and mean-level (Roberts, Walton, & Viechtbauer,

2006) continuity. Differential continuity describes the degree to which the relative differences among individuals remain stable across time. Mean-level stability refers to the extent to which personality scores change over time. Longitudinal designs are required to investigate differential stability, looking at trait correlations across time. Mean-level stability can be studied with the use of longitudinal data (Roberts, Walton, Viechtbauer, 2006). Moreover, mean trait scores from cross-sectional age cohorts are useful for mean-level stability comparisons (McCrae et al., 1999).

Roberts and DelVecchio (2000) recently conducted a meta-analysis of differential stability and examined whether and when stability peaks during the life course, challenging Costa and McCrae's (1994; McCrae & Costa, 1984, 1990) claim that personality is "set like plaster" after the age of 30. They analyzed 3,217 test-retest correlation coefficients from 152 longitudinal studies and demonstrated an increase in stability from .31 during childhood to .54 in young adulthood, rising to .64 by age 30, with the highest stability of .74 observed between the ages of 50 and 70 years. These data suggest that personality is less stable during the preadult years; however, there was still a considerable amount of stability.

McCrae and colleagues (2002) examined both mean-level and differential changes during adolescence in self-descriptions using the NEO-PI-R, including an analysis of continuity at the level of the individual. These researchers found that mean-level personality scores for extraversion, agreeableness, and conscientiousness were stable between the ages of 12 and 18; however, neuroticism appeared to increase in girls and openness increased in boys and girls. A 4-year longitudinal study of intellectually gifted students showed a considerable degree of rank-order instability across the two assessment points. Stability coefficients for boys across a 4-year interval ranged from .31 (agreeableness) to .49 (conscientiousness) and for girls from .30 (neuroticism) to .63 (conscientiousness). Individual-level continuity analyses relying on the reliable change index (Jacobson & Truax, 1991) indicated that about 60% of the sample did not change over the 4-year interval for each of the FFM dimensions. A similar analysis for college-aged individuals (Robins, Fraley, Roberts, & Trzesniewski, 2001) showed that almost 80% were stable on each of the FFM dimensions, again suggesting that differential stability is somewhat lower during adolescence.

The meta-analysis of Roberts et al. (2006) on mean-level change during adolescence (10 to 18 years) showed a small increase for openness ($d = .23$) and a significant increase for social dominance ($d = .20$). No significant mean-level changes were reported for social vitality, agreeableness, and conscientiousness during adolescence. Studies examining stability of personality prototype classification using three personality profiles (resilient, undercontrolled, and overcontrolled children), provided partial evidence of ipsative stability (De Fruyt, Mervielde, & Van Leeuwen, 2002). However, according to De Fruyt et al., it was unclear whether the instability to prototype classification for some individuals should be attributed to real developmental change measurement error or the procedure to derive prototypes.

Taken together, these important studies and others (Funder, Parke, Tomlinson-Keasey, & Widaman, 1993; Graziano, 2003; Halverson, Kohnstamm, & Martin, 1994; Mroczek & Little, 2006) lead to two general conclusions. First, the level of personality continuity in childhood and adolescence is higher than often expected (e.g., compared with young adulthood; Roberts et al., 2006). Second, personality change occurs further into adulthood than one might expect. Caspi and colleagues (2005) argued in this respect that personality trait development is not a continuity-versus-change proposition, but that continuity and change coexist. These authors concluded that the major challenge for developmental theories will be to account not only for trait continuity but also for trait changes. We return to this point later in the chapter when we cover contextual factors and what Thomas and Chess (1977) and recently Shiner (2006) have referred to as "goodness of fit."

PERSONALITY AND LIFE OUTCOMES

The importance of studying personality is that certain traits will be able to forecast certain outcomes for children and adolescents. Quite often in psychology and psychiatry, the fields have focused on the negative aspects of personality; this is particularly apparent in the *DSM-IV* and its successive versions, which have focused on personality disorder. Fortunately, there is also a movement in the field to focus on positive and healthy outcomes for children and adolescents. This section of the chapter highlights some previous work in the area of child and adolescent personality that has emphasized both positive and negative outcomes (Caspi & Bem, 1990; Caspi & Shiner, 2006; Rothbart & Bates, 1998; Shiner, 2006; Shiner & Caspi, 2003). Specifically, we focus on positive outcomes such as academic achievement, social competence with peers, rule-abiding conduct, the development of romantic relationships, and work competence in order to build on Shiner's and others work in this area (Funder et al., 1993; Masten et al., 1995; Shiner, 2006). With respect to negative outcomes, this section covers children's internalizing and externalizing behaviors. Taken together, the studies reviewed in this section point to two important conclusions: Children's traits are differentially linked with specific outcome, and these patterns are often replicated across studies, and there is convincing evidence for the consequential nature of children's individual differences or personality (Shiner, 2006). Typically, the prediction afforded by children's temperament and personality traits is modest in size. We take each of the Big 5 dimensions and tie each to positive and negative outcomes to build on Shiner's work in this area (2006). Although we do not examine personality disorders as conceptualized in the *DSM-IV,* we provide a road map for how this approach might allow for further study of *DSM-IV* disorders (see Table 12.2).

Extraversion: Negative and Positive Outcomes

It has been noted that children's differences in extraversion predict a complex set of outcomes (Shiner, 2006). There are some positive outcomes associated with extraversion. Shiner has noted that for some children extraversion is associated with positive and meaningful peer relations concurrently and across time into late adolescence and early adulthood. Moreover, extraversion predicts positive changes in social competence across time (Shiner, 2000; Shiner, Masten, & Roberts, 2003). Similarly, extraversion in early adolescence predicts growth in perceived social

Table 12.2 Outcomes Associated with Each Big 5 Factor Trait

Trait	Positive Outcome	Negative Outcome
Extraversion	Social competence Promotes good health	Antisocial behavior Callousness
Neuroticism	Conscience development Guilt when expected	Poor relationships Relationship conflict Relationship abuse Relationship dissolution Less competent parenting Risk for unemployment
Conscientiousness	School adjustment Educational achievement Occupational attainment Job performance	Obsessive
Agreeableness	Social competence Positive parenting Responsible parenting	
Openness	Exploring Friendliness Academic achievement	Exposure to risks

Note: This table is intended to be illustrative and not an exhaustive list of positive and negative outcomes.

support from early adolescence to late adolescence (Asendorpf & van Aken, 2003a, 2003b). Extraverted children are more likely than introverted children to have a life history of stable, high-quality romantic relationships by age 30 (Shiner, 2006; Shiner et al., 2003). Childhood extraversion is associated with lower levels of later internalizing symptoms (Chen et al., 2002).

Although being extraverted has some positive aspects to it, research has shown that some of the outcomes for those scoring high on extraversion measures are negative and may even point to certain types of pathology. For instance, a wide variety of studies have linked early signs of extraversion to heightened risk of externalizing symptoms and aggression (Chen et al., 2002; Frick & Scheffield-Morris, 2004; Huey & Weisz, 1997; Markey, Markey, & Tinsley, 2004). As Shiner (2006) indicated, the mechanisms for why extraverted children are more likely than introverted children to develop antisocial behavior are not yet clear; they may have stronger impulses that they must learn to regulate, or they may be more likely to engage in antisocial behavior with peers. Outcomes of shyness and inhibition essentially parallel those found with low extraversion, including lower social support (Newman, Caspi, Moffitt, & Silva, 1997) and higher rates of anxiety symptoms (Kagan, Snidman, Zentner, & Peterson, 1999). Socially inhibited and/or shy boys may experience more negative life outcomes than shy girls. According to Caspi and his colleagues (Caspi, Bem, & Elder, 1989; see also Gest, 1997), this might be because shyness is more socially sanctioned for girls than for boys.

Neuroticism: Negative and Positive Outcomes

Neuroticism and the broader negative emotionality trait are associated with negative outcomes in a variety of areas. Children high on negative emotionality are at risk for a wide variety of social difficulties (see Eisenberg, Fabes, Guthrie, & Reiser, 2000; see also Shiner, 1998 and Muris, Schmidt, Merckelbach, & Schouten, 2001). Negative emotionality in children predicts both internalizing and externalizing psychopathology, suggesting a broad bandwidth of psychopathology (Lengua, 2002; Rothbart & Bates, 1998). Caspi and Shiner (2006; Shiner, 2006) have noted that it is important to consider the outcomes for anxiety and fear separately from the outcomes of irritability given that there is some heterogeneity in the neuroticism concept. According to these authors, this is important because in some cases, the lower order traits predict similar outcomes but may do so for quite different reasons. For example, they note that higher anxiety or fear and higher irritability both predict greater social difficulties (Asendorpf & van Aken, 2003a, 2003b; Eisenberg, Pidada, & Liew, 2001) and lower occupational attainment in adulthood (Caspi et al., 1989; Judge, Higgins, Thoresen, & Barrick, 1999). Yet, anxiety and fear may cause such difficulties as preventing children from fully participating in social and work spheres, whereas children's irritability may exert its effects through alienating other youths. Importantly, in other cases, these two components of negative emotionality may predict different outcomes altogether. For example, anxiety and fear are associated with greater risk for internalizing symptoms, and irritability with greater risk for externalizing symptoms (Rothbart & Bates, 1998; Shiner, 2006).

Although high negative emotionality spans a broad range of negative outcomes, it is equally important to recognize that higher fearfulness may promote positive outcomes for some children. For example, more fearful children experience greater guilt when they believe they have done something wrong, and this guilt proneness in turn appears to mediate the association between children's level of fear and their later compliance with rules (Kochanska, Gross, Linn, & Nichols, 2002). These findings are consistent with research documenting that childhood fearfulness protects against the development of externalizing behavior problems, including aggression (Raine, Reynolds, Venables, Mednick, & Farrington, 1998). These findings have also been linked to conscience development and the possibility of protecting against psychopathy-like traits in youth (Salekin, 2006). Like high extraversion, high fear predicts a complex mixture of both positive and negative outcomes.

Conscientiousness: Negative and Positive Outcomes

There is little to chart the negative outcomes for being conscientious. It might be that extreme forms of conscientiousness lead to obsessiveness and perhaps other forms of anxiety, but to our knowledge there are no data to support this supposition. Rather, scientific work on children's conscientiousness documents what might be considered somewhat obvious findings. That is, greater self-control appears to promote many good outcomes (Shiner, 2006). First, children's attention, self-control, and carefulness predict later academic achievement, even when controlling for earlier measurement of academic ability and IQ (Martin, Olejnik, & Gaddis, 1994; Shiner, 2000; Shiner et al., 2003). Childhood conscientiousness predicts positive changes in academic achievement from childhood to adulthood (Shiner, 2000; Shiner et al., 2003). These positive changes continue into adulthood, resulting in happiness and well-being in other areas. Specifically, conscientiousness in adolescence forecasts adult career success in terms of both income and occupational status. Conscientiousness also predicts job satisfaction (Judge et al., 1999). Children's attention and self-control, regardless of the method of indexing these traits, also appear to promote the development of rule-abiding behavior rather than externalizing, antisocial behavior (Shiner, 2006). Put another way, children who are impulsive, inattentive, or careless are at risk for developing externalizing behaviors (Ackerman, Brown, & Izard, 2003; Olson, Schilling, & Bates, 1999; Shiner, 2000, 2006). Again, it is important to note that these links between early self-control and lower risk of externalizing problems may be mediated in part by more self-controlled children's tendencies to develop a stronger conscience (Kochanska & Knaack, 2003; Salekin, 2006). Finally, components of conscientiousness in childhood, including effortful attention, self-control, and carefulness, have predicted children's concurrent and later social competence with peers in several studies (Lamb et al., 2002; Hawley, 2006; Shiner, 2000).

Agreeableness: Negative and Positive Outcomes

Similar to conscientiousness, childhood agreeableness has few known negative outcomes, but instead points to many different positive life outcomes (Graziano & Eisenberg, 1997). With respect to negative outcomes, high compliance, an aspect of agreeableness, could be problematic for children and may be a particular risk factor for negative outcomes for girls (Pulkkinen, 2002). Although there are few data on the negative outcomes for agreeableness, it will be important for future work to address whether extremely high agreeableness poses adaptive risks for children.

Greater childhood agreeableness is associated with better peer relationships concurrently and across time (Graziano, Jensen-Campbell, & Finch, 1997; Shiner, 2000, 2006). However, some authors have noted that the name of this trait is somewhat misleading if it suggests that its importance is confined to interpersonal relationships. Childhood agreeableness is also linked to greater academic attainment and a reduced risk of externalizing behaviors and delinquency (Laursen, Pulkkinen, & Adams, 2002; Shiner, 2000, 2006; Shiner et al., 2003). In one longitudinal study, childhood agreeableness predicted positive work competence 20 years later, when childhood academic achievement and IQ were controlled (Shiner et al., 2003).

As noted previously, agreeableness has some heterogeneity to its lower order traits, and the components of this higher order trait include at least two major lower order traits: prosocial tendencies and antagonism (which includes aggressiveness). Findings for children's prosocial tendencies parallel those for agreeableness. For example, a stronger prosocial orientation in childhood predicts positive social adjustment and academic achievement. Moreover, and relatedly, a stronger prosocial orientation predicts fewer externalizing behaviors over time (Chen, Li, Li, Li, & Liu, 2000). Alternately, findings for antagonism and aggression typically are like those found for low agreeableness. More antagonistic, aggressive children are at risk for a number of negative outcomes, including academic failure, peer rejection, job difficulties and unemployment, and later conflictual romantic relationships (Kokko

& Pulkkinen, 2000; Moffitt & Caspi, 1998; Rubin, Bukowski, & Parker, 1998; Shiner, 2006). Boys who are chronically aggressive are at a heightened risk of serious delinquency and even violence (Nagin & Tremblay, 1999).

Thus, the traits underlying both conscientiousness and agreeableness promote positive adaptation in many different domains, and there are not a lot of data to suggest negative outcomes. As noted, these two higher order traits appear to share a common core of behavioral constraint or self-control, with conscientiousness focused on task-related behavior and agreeableness focused on interpersonal behavior, which may account for their concomitant positive outcomes. It is interesting to note, however, that the positive outcomes of conscientiousness are not restricted to the domains of achieving and striving. Nor should it be interpreted that the positive outcomes of agreeableness are limited to interpersonal domains. Rather, there is more likely a greater array of positive benefits that stem from each higher order construct. More detailed research on how highly conscientious and agreeable children approach a variety of situations will help shed light on why the two traits share such similar positive outcome profiles.

Openness to Experience: Negative and Positive Outcomes

Few studies have shown negative outcomes for the openness to experience construct. However, it is possible that being too open could leave one slightly more vulnerable. Research is needed in this area to determine if there are some negative aspects associated with extreme levels of openness. For the most part, research on the links between openness to experience and intellect shows positive outcomes. However, research in this area is more limited than for the other four higher order traits; yet, the findings generally are consistent. Openness to experience has been shown to have concurrent relations with academic achievement in samples of school-age children and young adolescents (Graziano et al., 1997; John et al., 1994; Measelle, Ablow, Cowan, & Cowan, 1998). Moreover, the size of the correlation varies from modest to strong, and this difference in magnitude could stem from the differences in trait descriptors for this dimension across indexes, with some emphasizing intellectual characteristics and others less broadly covering this aspect of the higher order trait (Shiner, 2006). Because openness and intellect in childhood are moderately associated with IQ or other measures of intellectual ability (Lamb et al., 2002), it is not clear to what extent these traits predict academic achievement; thus, these traits differ from the other Big 5 traits in that they may show more narrowly focused importance for adaptation (Caspi & Shiner, 2006; Shiner, 2006).

MODELS OF PERSONALITY AND THEIR CONNECTION TO PSYCHOPATHOLOGY

One of the questions that has fueled scholarly and popular interest in temperament is whether children with particular temperaments are at a greater risk for negative outcomes, including psychopathology. Much of the early interest in temperament traits was initiated by Thomas and Chess (1977), who suggested that early individual differences could set off a chain of transactions between the child and the environment that could ultimately end with clinical disorders. The previous section highlighted general negative and positive outcomes associated with each of the Big 5 personality factors; this section focuses more specifically on the connection between the five factors and psychopathology.

Shiner and Caspi (2003) noted that although individual differences in personality shape individuals' adaptation over time, childhood personality also plays a key role in the development of psychopathology. Much of the current research on personality and psychopathology simply documents correlations between temperament or personality traits and aspects of psychopathology, without articulating how the two domains may be connected (Caspi & Shiner, 2006; Hoyle, 2000; Maziade et al., 1990; Rothbart & Bates, 1998). Shiner and Caspi (2003) and more recently Tackett (2006) present conceptual models of the possible associations between personality and psychopathology in childhood and adolescence. These childhood models have parallels to those developed by Clark, Watson, and Mineka (1994) and Widiger, Verheul, and van den Brink (1999). The models posit several different links to pathology. First, these authors all suggest that psychopathology may represent the extreme end of a continuously distributed personality trait or cluster of traits (this is also referred to as the spectrum model). Second, personality may set in motion processes that cause the development of psychopathology (referred to as the vulnerability model). Third, personality may protect against the development of psychopathology in the face of stress and adversity (referred to as the resilience model). Fourth, personality may influence the form and prognosis of a disorder, even if the personality trait is not a component or cause of the disorder (referred to as the pathoplastic model). Fifth, psychopathology may influence the course of personality development itself (referred to as the scar model; Shiner & Caspi, 2003; Tackett, 2006; see Table 12.3).

Over the past 2 decades, a growing body of research has attempted to explain the nature of these relationships (for reviews, see Krueger & Tackett, 2003; Widiger & Clark, 2000; Widiger et al., 1999), building on current research investigating the etiology and structure of both personality and psychopathology. However, this work has primarily focused on adult populations, despite the growing evidence of robust associations between personality traits and mental disorders in children and adolescents. Tackett (2006) has argued that to promote understanding and further investigation of the relationship between personality and psychopathology, existing work with children and adolescents must be integrated into research on adults to create a broader developmental picture.

Table 12.3   Models Depicting the Connection between Personality and Pathology

Model Name	Path (or Relation) to Pathology
Spectrum	Pathology is an extreme form of personality (viewed along a continuum).
Vulnerability	Personality sets in motion and is the cause of pathology.
Resilience	Personality may protect against or buffer against pathology.
Pathoplastic	Personality may influence the form of the disorder even if it is not the cause.
Scar	Pathology affects personality change.

Evidence for each of these models is limited in part because the study designs needed to detect the hypothesized relations are complex and time consuming. Nonetheless, there is some emerging research in this area. For instance, the one longitudinal study found that childhood antisocial behavior problems predicted an increase in neuroticism, or negative emotionality, in adulthood even after controlling for the level of neuroticism in childhood (Shiner et al., 2002); this model provides some support for the scar model, which suggests that childhood psychopathology may cause changes in personality later in life. However, without a measurement of personality before the onset of Axis I pathology, one cannot infer whether these changes in personality traits were a result of the Axis I disorder (Tackett, 2006).

There is also some evidence for the pathoplasty model. One area of study has concentrated on comorbidity between anxiety disorders and Conduct Disorder (CD) in children. This literature has largely found that disruptive children with high levels of inhibition or shyness, which would be related to the higher order factor of neuroticism, have less severe manifestations of CD and better prognosis compared to those with low levels of inhibition (Kerr, Tremblay, Pagani, & Vitaro, 1997; Walker et al., 1991). The bulk of research evidence to date appears to back the vulnerability and dimensional models.

The vulnerability model splits childhood pathology into externalizing and internalizing disorders. Several types of childhood and adolescent problem behaviors are typically categorized as externalizing pathology, such as Oppositional Defiant Disorder (ODD), Conduct Disorder, Attention-Deficit/Hyperactivity Disorder, and substance use. Disorders characterized by antisocial behaviors, such as ODD and CD, have received the greatest attention from the vulnerability perspective. In general, this literature has primarily identified conscientiousness and neuroticism as potentially relevant personality risk factors for the development of later psychopathology.

A number of studies have found that characteristics related to impulsivity (which has been related to low conscientiousness) were significantly related to antisocial behaviors throughout childhood (Hirshfeld et al., 1992; Raine et al., 1998; Tremblay, Pihl, Vitaro, & Dobkin, 1994) and adolescence (Lynam et al., 2000; Salekin, Lesitico, Trobst, Schrum, & Lochman, 2005). Some longitudinal studies that followed individuals into adulthood have also shown strong relationships between early characteristics of impulsivity and later antisocial behaviors. This finding has been substantiated by studies with measurements of impulsivity in adolescence (Sigvardsson, Bohman, & Cloninger, 1987; White, Bates, & Buyske, 2001), middle childhood (Farrington & West, 1993), and as early as 3 years of age (Caspi, 2000; Caspi, Moffitt, Newman, & Silva, 1996; Henry, Caspi, Moffitt, & Silva, 1996). In addition to the aforementioned findings related to low conscientiousness, early observations of negative emotions have been connected with antisocial behaviors in middle childhood (Renken, Egeland, Marvinney, Mangelsdorf, & Sroufe, 1989). Augmenting this work on general antisocial behavior, other lines of research have focused on relationships across time between personality traits and specific subtypes of antisocial behavior (Lynam, 1996; Moffitt, 1993; Moffitt, Caspi, Dickson, Silva, & Stanton, 1996; Salekin, 2006; White et al., 2001). Another strand of research has measured personality traits related to the construct of psychopathy, such as callousness and impulsiveness, and found them to predict antisocial behavior across childhood (Lynam, 2006; Lynam et al., 2005; Salekin, 2006; Salekin & Frick, 2005; Salekin et al., 2005; Salekin, Neumann, Leistico, DiCicco, & Duros, 2004; Tremblay et al., 1994).

A larger body of work has demonstrated that measures of disinhibition predict externalizing pathology in early and middle childhood (Caspi, Henry, McGee, Moffitt, & Silva, 1995; Eisenberg et al., 2000 2004; Mun, Fitzgerald, Von Eye, Puttler, & Zucker, 2001; Rende, 1993; Rubin, Burgess, Dwyer, & Hastings, 2003; Silverman & Ragusa, 1992) and later into adolescence (Olson et al. 1999). Related to these results, other studies have reported that high levels of inhibition predicted lower levels of externalizing psychopathology in childhood and adolescence (Schwartz, Snidman, & Kagan, 1996; Sigvardsson et al., 1987; Tremblay et al., 1994).

Another major domain of disorders, typically referred to as internalizing pathology, consists primarily of problems with anxiety and depression. One personality construct that has received a great deal of attention regarding its connection with anxiety disorders is often called behavioral disinhibition (BI; Tackett notes that this is typically described as a temperament). In the context of personality, BI would represent a combination of high neuroticism and extraversion. Having said this, a substantial literature has reported a relation between BI and later internalizing problems (see Hirschfeld-Becker et al., 2003). Indices of BI in toddlerhood and early childhood predicted anxiety disorder in early middle childhood (Biederman et al., 1993, 1990; Hirschfeld et al., 1992; Rosenbaum et al., 1993) and adolescence (Hayward, Killen, Kraemer, & Taylor, 1998; Schwartz, Snidman, & Kagan, 1999).

A smaller set of studies has examined the links between personality characteristics and depression. These studies suggest that traits reflecting extreme inhibition in early childhood predict depression in adulthood and may show a significant relation with suicide attempts when combined with traits marking low conscientiousness (Caspi, 2000; Caspi et al., 1996). Another study reported that high levels of neuroticism and high levels of novelty seeking in adolescence predicted later suicidal behavior (Fergusson, Beautrais, & Horwood, 2003). Although the dimensional models are also very compelling, we do not cover them in as great of detail in this chapter. The essence of this model is that personality is pathology when the personality is extreme. One example of this is the work of Lynam (2006) and Salekin (2006), who have examined the extreme form of some personality traits that could in fact be psychopathy. They have found a potential connection between personality and externalizing disorders. The dominant model linking internalizing disorders to personality traits is the tripartite model, which has recently been applied to children (Clark & Watson, 1991; Clark et al., 1994).

In summary, the research on the connection between personality and pathology provides preliminary support for both vulnerability and spectrum approaches to conceptualizing the personality-psychopathology relationship in children and adolescents, with the vulnerability, or risk factor, approach receiving the greatest research attention. Specifically, neuroticism and conscientiousness have been implicated as particularly relevant in the development of later psychopathology. The resilience or protective factor model also has support (Chiccetti & Luthar, 1990). There is less support for alternative conceptualizations, such as the scar and pathoplasty models, due to the lack of research. Although the spectrum model has not been a driving hypothesis to the extent that the vulnerability model has, it is difficult to disentangle evidence for these two approaches. Indeed, research supporting a vulnerability explanation for the personality-psychopathology relationship may also support a dimensional conceptualization, and these two approaches may ultimately work in concert to provide the best explanation. More direct tests of the scar, pathoplasty, and spectrum models will help elucidate a comprehensive approach to conceptualizing the personality-psychopathology relationship. Ultimately, we may find that all models are necessary to create such a comprehensive picture, possibly differing for various types of psychopathology or various individuals (Tackett, 2006).

CONNECTIONS BETWEEN BIG 5 AND THE *DIAGNOSTIC AND STATISTICAL MANUAL*

Some researchers have argued that the personality superfactors are too broad to capture all the interesting variation in children's personality, and distinctions at the level of more specific, lower order traits are necessary (McAdams, 1992; Tackett, 2006). Such is the case, for example, if using structural models of personality traits to distinguish between different personality disorders (Lynam & Widiger, 2001; Widiger, Trull, Clarkin, Sanderson, & Costa, 2002); recent work suggests that categorical personality disorders are distinguished by particular patterns of dimensional lower order personality traits, as shown earlier. The advantage of broad, higher order superfactors is their substantial bandwidth; the disadvantage is their low fidelity (Robins, John, & Caspi, 1994). There is much to learn from studying variation at different levels of the personality trait hierarchy, but this does not obviate the need to understand how different levels are associated hierarchically to each other.

The connection between the Big 5 and *DSM-IV* disorders is not all that well known. Research appears to be progressing along independent lines with little integration of the two (e.g., Brent, Zelenak, Buckstein, & Brown, 1990), similar to the problems with the research on temperament and personality (Bernstein, Cohen, Skodol, Bezirganian, & Brook, 1996). Although there is some connection between Axis I childhood pathology and the Big 5 (e.g., the connection between CD and neuroticism), much less has been conducted on the *DSM-IV* personality disorders themselves. Some have argued that the impact of *DSM* personality disorders on functioning can be as profound for a young person as for an adult (Kernberg, Weiner, & Bardenstein, 2000). For example, some preliminary research indicates that suicide is more likely for adolescents diagnosed with impulsive, dramatic, Avoidant or Dependent Personality Disorder (Brent et al., 1994), and suicidal behavior is more severe in older adolescents and young adults who have both Borderline Personality Disorder and depression (Friedman, 1982). Researchers should attempt to make connections between *DSM* disorders and the Big 5 and eventually integrate the models and then possibly tie the personality concepts to the *DSM-IV* Axis I disorders (see Table 12.4). Some significant strides have been made in this regard (see Krueger, 1999; Krueger, McGue, & Iacono, 2001; Tackett & Krueger, 2006).

Table 12.4   Connecting the Big 5 to Specific Childhood Disorders

Externalizing (high extraversion, low conscientiousness, and low agreeableness)	Internalizing (high neuroticism, low extraversion, high conscientiousness, low agreeableness)
Oppositional Defiant Disorder	Separation anxiety
Conduct Disorder	Depression
Attention-Deficit/Hyperactivity Disorder	Generalized anxiety
Substance abuse	Obsessive-Compulsive Disorder
	Eating disorders

Processes Underlying Continuity and Change in Personality Development

As noted in the preceding sections, children's early temperament and personality traits show both substantial continuity and change (Shiner, 2006). By the preschool years, individual differences are moderately stable. Children's individual differences moderately predict many aspects of development, including both positive and negative outcomes. Thus, early temperament and personality traits meaningfully predict later personality and life outcomes for some children (including both positive and negative outcomes, including psychopathology), but other children appear to undergo significant change over time. As Shiner points out, this finding regarding stability and change requires explanation: What is the process that underlies both the stability and the change? In part, the answer lies in contextual factors. This issue is hardly new, as Thomas and Chess (Thomas et al., 1963) raised the question of explaining continuity and change in their early theoretical work on temperament. Specifically, they argued that each early temperamental trait could yield a variety of subsequent outcomes, depending on the goodness of fit between the child's temperament and the context in which the child flourished, languished, or simply did okay. For example, some infants with a difficult temperament may continue to exhibit irritable, hard-to-manage behavior as children, whereas other infants with similarly challenging early temperaments may learn to manage their intense negative emotions if their parents can successfully adapt their parental style, and subsequently lead successful and happy lives. This means that a variety of intervening processes can play important roles in determining the eventual outcomes of children's early individual differences. These differences may promote personality continuity by shaping children's experience and engagement with their environment.

Caspi and Shiner (Caspi & Shiner, in press; Shiner & Caspi, 2003) compellingly cover the processes that facilitate stability. Briefly, these authors talk about elaboration, which could lead to further solidifying of a given personality style. According to these authors, the process of elaboration may involve at least six processes, thought to develop at different stages of development. The first of these processes starts in the first few months of life and includes learning processes and environmental elicitation. In early to middle childhood, after the emergence of necessary cognitive functions, the second set of processes—environmental construal and social comparison processes—may influence personality development.

Third, in late childhood and adolescence, environmental selection and manipulation emerge. These processes come online once the self-regulatory functions have developed. Shiner and Caspi describe these six processes through which endogenous biological and experiential learning sources of influence may serve to elaborate an initial disposition over time so that it increasingly organizes thought, emotion, and action. The theoretical models are in place; research is now needed on each of these processes in relation to different temperament and personality traits.

Other processes promoting continuity and change range from genetic or biological processes to more broad, contextual processes involving classrooms and neighborhoods (Kagan, 1998; Shiner, 2006). Genetic influences may play a role in shaping the continuity versus discontinuity of early individual differences. The MacArthur Longitudinal Twin Study (Saudino & Cherny, 2001) showed that for all of the traits except shyness, twins' stability in temperament—in terms of activity, task orientation, affect-extraversion, shyness at home, and behavioral inhibition in the lab—was derived from genetic influences; for shyness, both genetic and shared (familywide) environmental factors contributed to stability. On the other hand, sources of change varied for the traits; changes in shyness across time derived from both shared and nonshared (child-specific) environmental influences, whereas change in affect-extraversion was due to nonshared environmental influences only. These results fit well with other research on children and adults suggesting that, whereas personality stability appears to be due to genetic factors, change is due to environmental influences (Saudino & Plomin, 1996). Research in this area is preliminary. The Louisville Twin Study has found evidence for genetic influences on change in temperament in the first 4 years of life (Loehlin, 1992), but clearly, more work is needed to establish more definitively the genetic influences on change in children's individual differences, particularly focusing on both positive and negative outcomes.

Another factor that could be related to stability and change may have to do with the permutations of traits and other characteristics that accompany personality. Shiner (2006) has referred to these factors as intrapersonal factors. The point here is that the mix or makeup of children's characteristics is another source of stability and change. Allport's (1937, p. 48) classic definition of personality assumes the importance of intra-individual psychological organization: "Personality is the dynamic organization within the individual of those psychophysical systems that determine his unique adjustment to his environment." Researchers have recently attempted to understand how this "dynamic organization within the individual" may shape the stability and change in youths' personalities. These types of intra-individual characteristics have been investigated as potential moderators of personality stability and change and include other personality traits, IQ, and adaptation.

To elaborate on this point, Eisenberg and colleagues (2000) demonstrated that children's negative emotionality often moderates the links between aspects of conscientiousness and children's social behavior, such that children with poor attentional and behavioral control have poorer quality social functioning when they are also high on negative emotionality. In addition, poor self-control is particularly associated with later externalizing, antisocial behavior for children with higher levels of negative emotionality (Henry et al., 1996). Second, and importantly, children's intelligence may moderate the stability and outcomes of their personalities. Brighter children may find it easier to handle challenging aspects of their personalities. For example, a longitudinal study of children from age 4 to age 10 demonstrated that IQ predicted the stability and change in behavioral inhibition or shyness. This study found that more intelligent children became increasingly less inhibited over the 6-year span (Asendorpf, 1994). Third, children's relative success or failure in important developmental domains (e.g., academic achievement, social competence with peers) may influence personality development. Research previously reviewed makes clear that childhood personality shapes later adaptation in work, school, and relationships (Shiner, 2006). It is true that the converse can occur, whereby life adaptation may influence children's typical ways of feeling, thinking, and behaving (Shiner & Masten, 2002; Shiner et al., 2002). Clearly, in the future it will be important to examine the patterning of children's individual differences in personality, IQ, and adaptation in order to understand the circumstances leading to stability versus change (Shiner, 2006).

Other factors impacting personality development are parenting, neighborhood context, schools, and the like. As noted previously, Thomas and Chess's (Thomas et al., 1963) early work on temperament highlighted the potential role of family environment in moderating the outcomes of children's early individual differences. This idea was at the core of their goodness-of-fit model of personality development. Recent research has shown several replicable patterns of interactions between childhood temperament and parenting in the prediction of a variety of outcomes (Bates & McFadyen-Ketchum, 2000; Gallagher, 2002; Hawley, 2003; Putnam, Sanson, & Rothbart, 2002). In a handful of studies, it has been found that parenting practices moderate the links between temperament and later externalizing problems. Specifically, when children are high on irritability or score low on agreeableness, several maternal parenting variables predict higher externalizing behaviors. These predictor variables include unskilled disciplining tactics, negativity toward the child, and a lack of monitoring and control over the child (Bates, Pettit, Dodge, & Ridge, 1998; Belsky, Hsieh, & Crnic, 1998; Hagekull & Bohlin, 2003; Rubin et al., 2003; Shiner, 2006; Stoolmiller, 2001). Some research has shown that parenting affects attachment, which impacts emotion regulation and developing extraversion (Sroufe, Carlson, Levy, & Egeland, 1999). Attachment was also found to predict neuroticism and openness (Hagekull & Bohlin, 2003). It appears that skillful, warm parenting may protect highly negative and hard-to-manage children from developing externalizing problems. These findings are similar to those noted by Dishion and Patterson (2006). Because it is possible that genetic factors can account for the covariance of children's temperaments and family variables, future work on goodness of fit and contextual factors should utilize genetically informative research designs (Caspi & Shiner, 2005; Shiner, 2006).

Another source of children's personality continuity and change involves the broader context in which children develop, including the neighborhoods in which they grow and the schools they attend. Children's school environments, peer relationships, and neighborhoods could all have important impacts on whether children's personalities remain stable and whether their personalities lead to either poor or good outcomes (Shiner, 2006). Although these broad contextual factors have received less research attention than more proximal family processes, a number of recent studies have found evidence of moderating effects of children's contexts on their personality development (Chang, 2003; Dodge et al., 2003; Gazelle & Ladd, 2003). These studies suggest that peer relations, teacher warmth, and neighborhood warmth, safety and stability moderate the links between poor self-control and criminal involvement. Impulsive youth in better-off neighborhoods or who remain in school show less criminal behavior than similarly impulsive youth who live in poor neighborhoods or who drop out of school prematurely (Henry, Caspi, Moffitt, Harrington, & Silva, 1999; Lynam et al., 2000). Taken together, these studies provide clues that broader contexts are, in fact, important moderators and help chart the course of personality development.

CONCLUDING COMMENTS

Despite substantial progress in the decades since Thomas and Chess's (Thomas et al., 1963) classic work on temperament, some aspects of childhood personality development remain quite limited. Great strides have been made with respect to better understanding the connection between temperament and personality. In addition, the higher order structure of personality appears to be gaining further resolution. Yet, although these aspects of personality development have made remarkable progress, some of the same old debates continue to arise in personality research, particularly as it applies to children and adolescents. These include whether it is developmentally appropriate to look for and examine personality in children, and whether it should be assessed in child samples. Much of the concern has to do with whether personality is stable across the life span. Shiner and Caspi (2005) have argued that it is not an either/or argument with regard to stability, but rather both stability and change occur, and the process that underlies that change requires much greater understanding. This does not negate the importance of studying and using the concepts of personality with children and adolescents. The research cited in this chapter shows that not assessing personality means not understanding it. Along with these concerns, the connection between personality and psychopathology is not well understood. Importantly, Caspi and Shiner and Tackett (2006) have pointed the way to some important methods and research designs to advance our understanding of personality as it relates to positive and pathological outcomes in children and adolescents.

Although significant strides have been made in the area of personality in children and adolescents, this chapter signals the need for study in several other areas. The following are suggestions for potentially productive avenues of work on early personality structure that stem from the already important work conducted on children and adolescents. The research reviewed in this chapter leads to some natural conclusions and may provide a road map for where we need to go with personality investigations. These suggestions have in mind the goal of examining the long-term outcomes of childhood personality and the process shaping personality continuity and change from childhood to adulthood. One area of research that is needed is to continue to work on measures that are developmentally appropriate for children and adolescents. Although some work has been done in this area (De Fruyt et al.,

2006), efforts that focus on bottom-up approaches might be informative. As noted by Caspi et al. (2005), the field could benefit from continued creative measures of individual differences and an openness to the need to refine measures. Relatedly, another area of importance for research studies is to continue to examine the higher order structure of personality in children, particularly the structure of individual differences from the very earliest ages (infancy through to age 7 or 8). Shiner (2006) has noted that this is a particularly important area of study because the developmental changes during this period are rapid and sweeping. This chapter also signals the need for future research to specify lower order traits that can be identified in children. Many lower order traits examined in adults may prove to exist in children (e.g., integrity, talent, unconventionality).

Aside from structural issues, much more work is needed on the developmental mechanisms (or processes) at work. Although many of the findings on the long-term outcomes of children's personalities are robust and consistent, future work should examine the pathways linking personality and positive outcomes (Shiner & Masten, 2002). Scientists need to understand more about the mediating processes (Funder, 2001). As Shiner (2006) noted, many studies linking early personality with later outcomes span long periods of time. It could be very informative to also use more short-term longitudinal studies to provide an up-close glimpse of the processes at work. An avenue of research that needs work is the study of the genetic, intra-individual, family, neighborhood, and other contextual factors promoting personality continuity and change in children. Again, it will be important to explore the processes that actually mediate stability and change. Finally, much more research is needed to model the relation between personality and psychopathology. Caspi and Shiner (2005) and Tackett (2006) have provided explicit models for how these relations could be tested, and their guidelines offer a very good starting point.

Discoveries in all these areas may lead to interventions to help children with challenging temperaments or personality styles. Research is also likely to help us understand the features in children and adolescents that promote healthy development and well-being. Future work may serve to enrich understanding of how resilience emerges across development. Each of these avenues of research, and each of these research aims, will be very informative for intervention programs designed to help youth grow and flourish.

SUMMARY

This chapter reviewed research on the development of personality in children and adolescents. It covered the differences between the terms temperament and personality and examined the structure of personality in children and adolescents. An important aspect of studying personality is examining how stable it is across time. This chapter shows that personality is stable but that it also changes across time, even well into adulthood. This chapter also examined both the positive and negative outcomes associated with each of the Big Five dimensions. In addition, this chapter examined the connection between personality and psychopathology. Finally, the current chapter points to directions for future research that could shed light on the development of personality across the life span.

REFERENCES

Ackerman, B. P., Brown, E., & Izard, C. E. (2003). Continuity and change in levels of externalizing behavior in school children from economically disadvantaged families. *Child Development, 74*, 694–709.

Allport, G. W. (1937). *Personality: A psychological interpretation.* New York: Henry Holt.

American Psychiatric Association, (2000). *Diagnostic and statistical manual of mental health disorders* (4th ed., text rev.). Washington, DC: Author.

Asendorpf, J. B. (1994). The malleability of behavior inhibition: A study of individual developmental functions. *Developmental Psychology, 30*, 912–919.

Asendorpf, J. B., & van Aken, M. A. G. (2003a). Personality-relationship transaction in adolescence: Core versus surface personality characteristics. *Journal of Personality, 71*, 629–666.

Asendorpf, J. B., & van Aken, M. A. G. (2003b). Validity of Big Five personality judgments in childhood: A 9 year longitudinal study. *European Journal of Personality, 17*, 1–17.

Bates, J. E., & McFadyen-Ketchum, S. (2000). Temperament and parent-child relations as interacting factors in children's behavioral adjustment. In V. J. Molfese & D. L. Molfese (Eds.), *Temperament and personality development across the life span* (pp. 141–176). Mahwah, NJ: Erlbaum.

Bates, J. E., Pettit, G. S., Dodge, K. A., & Ridge, B. (1998). Interaction of temperamental resistance to control and restrictive parenting in the development of externalizing behavior. *Developmental Psychology, 34*, 982–995.

Belsky, J., Hsieh, K., & Crnic, K. (1998). Mothering, fathering, and infant negativity as antecedents of boys' externalizing problems and inhibition at age 3: Differential susceptibility to rearing influence? *Development and Psychopathology, 10*, 301–319.

Bernstein, D. P., Cohen, P., Skodol, A., Bezirganian, S., & Brook, J. S. (1996). Childhood antecedents of adolescent personality disorders. *Psychiatry, 153*, 7.

Bernstein, D. P., Cohen, P., Velez, N., Schwab-Stone, M., Siever, L., & Shinsato, L. (1993). Prevalence and stability of the DSM-III personality disorders in a community-based survey of adolescents. *American Journal of Psychiatry, 150*, 1237–1243.

Biederman, J., Rosenbaum, J. F., Bolduc-Murphy, E. A., Faraone, S. V., Chaloff, J., Hirshfeld, D. R., et al. (1993). A three-year follow-up of children with and without behavioral inhibition. *Journal of the American Academy of Child and Adolescent Psychiatry, 32*, 814–821.

Block, J. (1996). Some jangly remarks on Baumeister and Heatherton. *Psychological Inquiry, 7*, 28–32.

Block, J. (2001). Millennial contrarianism: The five-factor approach to personality description 5 years later. *Journal of Research in Personality, 35*, 98–107.

Blos, P. (1967). The second individuation process of adolescence. *The Psychoanalytic Study of the Child, 22*, 162–186.

Brent, D. A., Johnson, B., Perper, J., Connolly, J., Bridge, J., Bartle, S., et al. (1994). Personality disorder, personality traits, impulsive violence, and completed suicide in adolescents. *Journal of the American Academy of Child and Adolescent Psychiatry, 33*, 1080–1086.

Brent, D. A., Zelenak, J. P., Buckstein, O., & Brown, R. V. (1990). Reliability and validity of the Structured Interview of Personality Disorders in Adolescents. *Journal of the American Academy of Child and Adolescent Psychiatry, 29*, 349–354.

Briggs, S. R. (1989). The optimal level of measurement of personality constructs. In D. M. Buss & N. Canto (Eds.), *Personality psychology: Recent trends and emerging directions* (pp. 246–260). New York: Springer-Verlag.

Buss, A. H. (1995). *Personality, temperament, social behavior, and self.* Boston, MA: Allyn & Bacon.

Buss, A. H., & Finn, S. E. (1987). Classification of personality traits. *Journal of Personality and Social Psychology, 52*, 432–444.

Buss, A. H., & Plomin, R. (1984). *Temperament: Early developing personality traits.* Hillsdale, NJ: Erlbaum.

Caspi, A. (2000). The child is the father of the man: Personality continuity from childhood to adulthood. *Journal of Personality and Social Psychology, 78*, 158–172.

Caspi, A., & Bem, D. (1990). Personality continuity and change across the life course. In L. Pervin (Ed.), *Handbook of personality: Theory and research* (pp. 549–575). New York: Guilford Press.

Caspi, A., Bem, D. J., & Elder, G. H. (1989). Continuities and consequences of interactional styles across the life course. *Journal of Personality, 57*, 375–406.

Caspi, A., Henry, B., McGee, R. O., Moffitt, T. E., & Silva, P. A. (1995). Temperamental origins of child and adolescent behavior problems: From age 3 to age fifteen. *Child Development, 66,* 55–68.

Caspi, A., Moffitt, T. E., Newman, J. P., & Silva, P. A. (1996). Behavioral observations at age 3 predict adult psychiatric disorders: Longitudinal evidence from a birth cohort. *Archives of General Psychiatry, 53,* 1033–1039.

Caspi, A., Roberts, B. W., & Shiner, R. L. (2005). Personality development: Stability and change. *Annual Review of Psychology, 56,* 453–484.

Caspi, A., & Shiner, R. L. (2006). Personality development. In W. Damon & R. Lerner (Series Eds.) & N. Eisenberg (Vol. Ed.), *Handbook of child psychology: Vol. 3. Social, emotional, and personality development* (6th ed., pp. 300–365). Hoboken, NJ: Wiley.

Caspi, A., & Shiner, R. L. (in press). Temperament and personality. In M. Rutter, D. Bishop, D. Pine, S. Scott, J. Stevenson, E. Taylor, & A. Thapar (Eds.), *Rutter's child and adolescent psychiatry* (5th ed.). London: Blackwell.

Chang, L. (2003). Variable effects of children's aggression, social withdrawal, and prosocial leadership as functions of teacher beliefs and behaviors. *Child Development, 74,* 535–548.

Chen, X., Li, D., Li, Z., Li, B., & Liu, M. (2000). Sociable and prosocial dimensions of social competence in Chinese children: Common and unique contributions to social, academic, and psychological adjustment. *Developmental Psychology, 36,* 302–314.

Chen, X., Liu, M., Rubin, K. H., Cen, G., Gao, X., & Li, D. (2002). Sociability and prosocial orientation as predictors of youth adjustment: A 7-year longitudinal study in a Chinese sample. *International Journal of Behavioral Development, 26,* 128–136.

Clark, L. A., & Watson, D. (1999). Temperament: A new paradigm for trait psychology. In L. A. Pervin & O. P. John (Eds.), *Handbook of personality: Theory and research* (2nd ed. pp. 399–423). New York: Guilford Press.

Clark, L. A., Watson, D., & Mineka, S. (1994). Temperament, personality, and the mood and anxiety disorders. *Journal of Abnormal Psychology, 103,* 103–116.

Cloninger, C. R., Svakic, D. M., & Przybeck, T. R. (1993). A psychobiological model of temperament and character. *Archives of General Psychiatry, 39,* 1242–1247.

Costa, P. T., & McCrae, R. R. (1994). Stability and change in personality from adolescence through adulthood. In C. F. Halverson & G. A. Kohnstamm (Eds.), *The developing structure of temperament and personality from infancy to adulthood* (pp. 139–150). Hillside, NJ: Erlbaum.

Costa, P. T., & McCrae, R. R. (1997). Set like plaster? Evidence for the stability of adult personality. In T. F. Heatherton and J. L. Weinberger (Eds.), *Can personality change?* (pp. 21–40). Washington, DC: American Psychological Association

Crick, N. R., & Dodge, K. A. (1994). A review and reformulation of social information processing mechanisms in children's social adjustment. *Psychological Bulletin, 115,* 74–101.

De Clercq, B., & De Fruyt, F. (2003). Personality disorder symptomatology in adolescence: A five-factor model perspective. *Journal of Personality Disorders, 17,* 269–292.

De Clercq, B., De Fruyt, F., & Van Leeuwen, K. (2004). A "little five" lexically-based perspective on personality disorder symptoms in adolescence. *Journal of Personality Disorders, 18,* 479–499.

De Fruyt, F., Bartels, M., Van Leeuwen, K. G., De Clercq, B., Decuyper, M., & Mervielde, I. (2006). Five types of personality continuity in childhood and adolescence. *Journal of Personality and Social Psychology, 91,* 538–552.

De Fruyt, F., Mervielde, I., Hoekstra, H., & Rolland, J. (2000). Assessing adolescents' personality with the NEO-PI-R. *Assessment, 7,* 329–346.

De Fruyt, F., Mervielde, I., & Van Leeuwen, K. (2002). The consistency of personality type classification across samples and five factor measures. *European Journal of Personality, 16,* 57–72.

Digman, J. M. (1963). Principal dimensions of child personality as inferred from teacher's judgments. *Child Development, 34,* 43–60.

Digman, J. M. (1990). Personality structure: Emergence of the Five-Factor Model. *Annual Review of Psychology, 41,* 417–440.

Digman, J. M. (1997). Higher-order factors of the Big Five. *Journal of Personality and Social Psychology, 73,* 1246–1256.

Digman, J. M., & Inouye, J. (1986). Further specification of the five robust factors of personality. *Journal of Personality and Social Psychology, 71,* 341–351.

Dishion, T. J., & Patterson, G. R. (2006). The development and ecology of antisocial behavior in children and adolescents. In D. Cicchetti, & D. J. Cohen (Eds.), *Developmental psychopathology* (Vol 3, pp. 503–541). Hoboken, NJ: Wiley.

Dodge, K. A., Lansford, J. E., Burks, V. S., Bates, J. E., Pettit, G. S., Fontaine, R., et al. (2003). Peer rejection and social information-processing factors in the development of aggressive behavior problems in children. *Child Development, 74*, 374–393.

Eisenberg, N., Fabes, R. A., Guthrie, I. K., & Reiser, M. (2000). Dispositional emotionality and regulation: Their role in predicting quality of social functioning. *Journal of Personality and Social Psychology, 78*, 136–157.

Eisenberg, N., Pidada, S., & Liew, J. (2001). The relations of regulation and negative emotionality to Indonesian children's social functioning. *Child Development, 72*, 1747–1763.

Eisenberg, N., Spinrad, T., Fabes, R., Reiser, M., Cumberland, A., Shepard, S., et al. (2004). The relations of effortful control and impulsivity to children's resiliency and adjustment. *Child Development, 75*, 25–46.

Erikson, E. H. (1950). *Childhood and society*. New York: Norton.

Erikson, E. H. (1968). *Identity: Youth and crisis*. New York: Norton.

Eysenck, S. B. G. (1963). *Junior Eysenck Personality Inventory*. San Diego, CA: Educational and Industrial Testing Service and Human Services.

Eysenck, H. J. (1997). Personality and experimental psychology: The unification of psychology and the possibility of a paradigm. *Journal of Personality and Social Psychology, 73*, 1224–1237.

Eysenck, S. B. G., Makaremi, A., & Barrett, P. T. (1994). A cross-cultural study of personality—Iranian and English children. *Personality and Individual Differences, 16*, 203–210.

Farrington, D. P., West, D. J. (1993). Criminal, penal and life histories of chronic offenders: Risk and protective factors and early identification. *Criminal Behaviour and Mental Health, 3*, 492–523.

Fergusson, D. M., Beautrais, A., & Horwood, L. J. (2003). Vulnerability and resiliency to suicidal behaviors in young people. *Psychological Medicine, 33*, 61–73.

Frick, P. J. (2004). Integrating research on temperament and psychopathology: Its pitfalls and promise. *Journal of Clinical Child and Adolescent Psychology, 33*, 2–7.

Frick, P. J., & Scheffield-Morris, A. (2004). Temperament and developmental pathways to conduct disorder. *Journal of Clinical Child and Adolescent Psychology, 33*, 54–68.

Friedman, R. (1982). DSM-III and affective pathology in hospitalized adolescents. *Journal of Nervous and Mental Diseases, 170*, 511–521.

Funder, D. C. (2001). Personality. *Annual Review of Psychology, 52*, 197–221.

Funder, D. C., Parke, R. D., Tomlinson-Keasey, C., & Widaman, K. (Eds.). (1993). *Studying lives through time: Personality and development*. Washington, DC: American Psychological Association.

Gallagher, K. C. (2002). Does child temperament moderate the influence of parenting on adjustment? *Developmental Review, 22*, 623–643.

Gazelle, H., & Ladd, G. W. (2003). Anxious solitude and peer exclusion: A diathesis-stress model of internalizing trajectories in childhood. *Child Development, 74*, 257–278.

Gest, S. D. (1997). Behavioral inhibition: Stability and associations with adaptation from childhood to early adulthood. *Journal of Personality and Social Psychology, 72*, 467–475.

Goldberg, L. R. (1993). The structure of phenotypic personality traits. *American Psychologist, 48*, 26–34.

Goldberg, L. R. (2001). Analyses of Digman's child-personality data: Derivation of Big Five factor scores from each of six samples. *Journal of Personality, 69*, 709–743.

Goldsmith, H. H., (1996). Studying temperament via construction of the Toddler Behavior Assessment Questionnaire. *Child Development, 67*, 218–235.

Goldsmith, H. H., Buss, A., Plomin, R., Rothbart, M. K., Thomas, A., Chess, S., et al. (1987). Roundtable: What is temperament? *Child Development, 58*, 505–529.

Goldsmith, H. H., Campos, J. J., (1982). Toward a theory of infant temperament. In R. N. Emde & R. J. Harmon (Eds.), *The development of attachment and affiliative systems* (pp. 161–193). New York: Plenum Press.

Gough, H. G. (1987). *The California Personality Inventory administrator's guide*. Palo Alto, CA: Consulting Psychological Press.

Graziano, W. G. (2003). Personality development: An introduction toward process approaches to long-term stability and change in persons. *Journal of Personality, 71*, 893–903.

Graziano, W. G., & Eisenberg, N. (1997). Agreeableness: A dimension of personality. In R. Hogan J. Johnson & S. Briggs (Eds.), *Handbook of personality psychology* (pp. 795–824). San Diego: Academic Press.

Graziano, W. G., Jensen-Campbell, L. A., & Finch, J. F. (1997). The self as a mediator between personality and adjustment. *Journal of Personality and Social Psychology, 73*, 392–404.

Graziano, W. G., & Ward, D. (1992). Probing the big five in adolescence: Personality and adjustment during a developmental transition. *Journal of Personality, 60*, 425–439.

Hagekull, B., & Bohlin, G. (2003). Early temperament and attachment as predictors of the five factor model of personality. *Attachment and Human Development, 5*, 2–18.

Halverson, C. F., Havill, V. L., Deal, J., Baker, S. R., Victor, J. B., Pavlopoulos, V., et al. (2003). Personality structure as derived from parental ratings of free descriptions of children: The inventory of child individual differences. *Journal of Personality, 71*, 995–1026.

Halverson, C. F., Kohnstamm, G. A., & Martin, R. P. (Eds.). (1994). *The developing structure of temperament and personality from infancy to adulthood*. Hillsdale, NJ: Erlbaum.

Hawley, P. H. (2003). Prosocial and coercive configurations of resource control in early adolescence: A case for the well-adapted Machiavellian. *Merrill-Palmer Quarterly, 49*, 279–309.

Haywood, C., Killen, J., Kraemer, K., & Taylor, C. (1998). Linking self-reported childhood behavioral inhibition to adolescent social phobia. *Journal of the American Academy of Child and Adolescent Psychiatry, 37*, 1308–1316.

Henry, B., Caspi, A., Moffitt, T. E., Harrington H., & Silva, P. A. (1999). Staying in school protects boys with poor self-regulation in childhood from later crime: A longitudinal study. *International Journal of Behavioral Development, 23*, 1049–1073.

Henry, B., Caspi, A., Moffitt, T. E., & Silva, P. A. (1996). Temperamental and familial predictors of violent and nonviolent criminal convictions: Age 3 to age 18. *Developmental Psychology, 32*, 614–623.

Hirshfeld, D. R., Rosenbaum, J. F., Biederman, J., Bolduc, E. A., Faraone, S. V., Snidman, N., et al. (1992). Stable behavioral inhibition and its association with anxiety disorder. *Journal of the American Academy of Child and Adolescent Psychiatry, 31*, 103–111.

Hirshfeld-Becker, D. R., Biederman, J. Callharp, S., Rosenbaum, E. D., Faraone, S. V., & Rosenbaum, J. F. (2003). Behavioral inhibition and disinhibition as hypothesized precursors to psychopathology: Implications for pediatric bipolar disorder. *Biological Psychiatry, 53*, 985–999.

Hoffman, M. (1977). Empathy, its development and pre-social implications. *Nebraska Symposium on Motivation, 25*, 169–217.

Hoyle, R. H. (2000). Personality processes and problem behaviors. *Journal of Personality, 68*, 953–966.

Huey, S. J., & Weisz, J. R. (1997). Ego control, ego resiliency, and the five-factor model as predictors of behavioral and emotional problems in clinic-referred children and adolescents. *Journal of Abnormal Psychology, 106*, 404–415.

Jacobson, N. S., & Truax, P. (1991). Clinical significance: A statistical approach to defining meaningful change in psychotherapy research. *Journal of Consulting and Clinical Psychology, 59*, 12–19.

Jang, K. L., McCrae, P. T., Angleitner, A., Riemann, R., & Livesley, J. W. (1998). Heritability of the facet level traits in a cross-cultural twin sample: Support for a hierarchical model of personality. *Journal of Personality and Social Psychology, 74*, 1556–1565.

John, O. P., Caspi, A., Robins, R. W., Moffitt, T. E., & Stouthamer-Loeber, M. (1994). The "little five": Exploring the nomological network of the five-factor model of personality in adolescent boys. *Child Development, 65*, 160–178.

John, O. P., & Srivastava, S. (1999). The Big Five trait taxonomy: History, measurement, and theoretical perspectives. In L. A. Pervin, & O. P. John (Eds.), *Handbook of personality: Theory and research* (2nd ed., pp. 102–138). New York: Guilford Press.

Judge, T. A., Higgins, C. A., Thoresen, C. J., & Barrick, M. R. (1999). The Big Five personality traits, general mental ability, and career success across the life span. *Personnel Psychology, 52*, 621–652.

Kagan, J. (1998). Biology and the child. In W. Damon, (Series Ed.) & N. Eisenberg, (Vol. Ed.), *Handbook of child psychology: Vol. 3. Social, emotional, and personality development* (5th ed., pp. 177–235). New York: Wiley.

Kagan, J., & Snidman, N. (1991). Temperamental factors in human development. *American Psychologist, 46*, 856–862.

Kagan, J., Snidman, N., Zentner, M., & Peterson, E. (1999). Infant temperament and anxious symptoms in school age children. *Development and Psychopathology, 11*, 209–224.

Kernberg, P. F., Weiner, A. S., & Bardenstein, K. K. (2000). *Personality disorders in children and adolescents.* New York: Basic Books.

Kiesler, D. J. (1996). *Contemporary interpersonal theory and research: Personality, psychopathology, and psychotherapy.* New York: Wiley.

Kochanska, G., Gross, J. N., Linn, M., & Nichols, K. E. (2002). Guilt in young children: Development, determinants, and relations with a broader system of standards. *Child Development, 73*, 461–482.

Kochanska, G., & Knaack, A. (2003). Effortful control as a personality characteristic of young children: Antecedents, correlates, and consequences. *Journal of Personality, 71*, 1087–1112.

Kohnstamm, G. A., Halverson, C. F., Mervielde, I., & Havill, V. (1998). *Parental descriptions of child personality: Developmental antecedents of the Big Five?* Mahwah, NJ: Erlbaum.

Kokko, K., & Pulkkinen, L. (2000). Aggression in childhood and long-term unemployment in adulthood: A cycle of maladaptation and some protective factors. *Developmental Psychology, 36*, 463–472.

Krueger, R. F. (1999). Personality traits in late adolescence predict mental disorders in early adulthood: A prospective-epidemiological study. *Journal of Personality, 67*, 39–65.

Krueger, R. F., McGue, M., & Iacono, W. G. (2001). The higher-order structure of common DSM mental disorder: Internalization, externalization, and their connection to personality. *Personality and Individual Differences, 30*, 1245–1259.

Kreuger, R. F., & Tackett, J. L. (2003). Personality and psychopthology: Working toward the bigger picture. *Journal of Personality Disorders, 17*, 107–119.

Lahey, B. B. (2004). Commentary: Role of temperament in developmental models of psychopathology. *Journal of Clinical Child and Adolescent Psychology, 33*, 88–93.

Lamb, M. E., Chuang, S. S., Wessels, H., Broberg, A. G., & Hwang, C. P. (2002). Emergence and construct validation of the Big Five factors in early childhood: A longitudinal analysis of their ontogeny in Sweden. *Child Development, 73*, 1517–1524.

Laursen, B., Pulkkinen, L., & Adams, R. (2002). The antecedents and correlates of agreeableness in adulthood. *Developmental Psychology, 38*, 591–603.

Leary, T. (1957). *Interpersonal diagnosis of personality.* New York: Roland.

Lengua, L. J. (2002). The contribution of emotionality and self-regulation to the understanding of children's responses to multiple risk. *Child Development, 73*, 144–161.

Lewis, M. (1993). The emergence of human emotions. In M. Lewis & J. Haviland (Eds.), *Handbook of emotions* (pp. 265–280) New York: Guilford.

Loehlin, J. C. (1992). *Genes and environment in personality development.* Newbury Park, CA: Sage.

Lonigan, C. J., Vasey, M. W., Phillips, B. M., & Hazen, R. A. (2004). Temperament, anxiety, and processing of threat-relevant stimuli. *Journal of Clinical Child and Adolescent Psychology, 33*, 8–20.

Lynam, D. R. (1996). The early identification of chronic offenders: Who is the fledgling psychopath? *Psychological Bulletin, 120*, 209–234.

Lynam, D. R., Caspi, A., Moffitt, T. E., Raine, A., Loeber, R., & Stouthamer-Loeber, M. (2005). Adolescent psychopathy and the Big Five: Results from two samples. *Journal of Abnormal Child Psychology, 33*, 431–443.

Lynam, D. R., Caspi, A., Moffitt, T. E., Wikstrom, P. H., Loeber, R., & Novak, S. (2000). The interaction between impulsivity and neighborhood context on offending: The effects of impulsivity are stronger in poorer neighborhoods. *Journal of Abnormal Psychology, 109*, 563–574.

Markey, P. M., Markey, C. N., & Tinsley, B. J. (2004). Children's behavioral manifestations of the five-factor model of personality. *Personality and Social Psychology Bulletin, 30*, 423–432.

Markon, K. E., Krueger, R. F., & Watson, D. (2005). Delineating the structure of normal and abnormal personality: An integrative hierarchical approach. *Journal of Personality and Social Psychology, 88*, 139–157.

Martin, R. P., Olejnik, S., & Gaddis, L. (1994). Is temperament an important contributor to schooling outcomes in elementary school? Modeling effects of temperament and scholastic ability on academic achievement. In W. B. Carey, & S. C. McDevitt (Eds.), *Prevention and early intervention: Individual differences as risk factors for the mental health of children: A festschrift for Stella Chess and Alexander Thomas* (pp. 59–68). New York: Brunner/Mazel.

Martin, R. P., Wisenbaker, J., & Huttunen, M. (1994). Review of factor analytic studies of temperament measures based on the Thomas-Chess structural model: Implications for the Big Five. In C. F. Halverson, G. A. Kohnstamm, & R. P. Martin (Eds.), *The developing structure of temperament and personality from infancy to adulthood* (pp. 157–172). Hillsdale, NJ: Erlbaum.

Masten, A. S., Coatsworth, J. D., Neemann, J., Gest, S. D., Tellegen, A., & Garmezy, N. (1995). The structure and coherence of competence from childhood through adolescence. *Child Development, 66,* 1635–1659.

Maziade, M., Caron, C., Cote, R., Merette, C., Bernier, H., Laplante, B., et al. (1990). Psychiatric status of adolescents who had extreme temperaments at age 7. *American Journal of Psychiatry, 147,* 1531–1536.

McCrae, R. R., & Costa, P. T. (1984). *Emerging lives, enduring dispositions: Personality in adulthood.* Boston, MA: Little Brown.

McCrae, R. R., & Costa, P. T. (1987). Validation of the five-factor model of personality across instruments and observers. *Journal of Personality and Social Psychology, 52,* 81–90.

McCrae, R. R., & Costa, P. T. (1989). The structure of interpersonal traits: Wiggins' circumplex and the five factor model. *Journal of Personality and Social Psychology, 56,* 586–595.

McCrae, R. R., & Costa, P. T. (1996). Toward a new generation of personality theories: Theoretical contexts for the five-factor model. In J. S. Wiggins, (Eds.), *The five-factor model of personality: Theoretical perspectives* (pp. 51–87). New York: Guilford Press.

McCrae, R. R., & Costa, P. T. (1997). Personality trait structure as human universal. *American Psychologist, 52,* 509–516.

McCrae, R. R., Costa, P. T., de Lima, M. P., Simoes, A., Ostendorf, F., Angleitner, A., et al. (1999). Age differences in personality across the adult life span: Parallels in five cultures. *Developmental Psychology, 35,* 466–477.

McCrae, R. R., Costa, P. T., Ostendorf, F., Angleitner, A., Hrebickova, M., Avia, M. D., et al. (2000). Nature over nurture: Temperament, personality, and life span development. *Journal of Personality and Social Psychology, 78,* 173–186.

McCrae, R. R., Costa, P. T., Terracio, A., De Fruyt, F., Mervielde, I., Parker, W. D., et al. (2002). Personality trait development from age 12 to age 18: Longitudinal, cross-sectional, and cross-cultural analyses. *Journal of Personality and Social Psychology, 83,* 1456–1468.

Measelle, J. R., Ablow, J. C., Cowan, P. A., & Cowan, C. P., (1998). Assessing young children's views of their academic, social, and emotional lives: An evaluation of the self-perception scales of the Berkeley puppet interview. *Child Development, 69,* 1556–1576.

Mervielde, I., De Clercq, B., De Fruyt, F., & Van Leeuwen, K., (2005). Temperament, personality, and developmental psychopathology as childhood antecedents of personality disorders. *Journal of Personality Disorders, 19,* 171–201.

Mervielde, I., & De Fruyt, F. (1999). Construction of the Hierarchical Personality Inventory for Children (HPIC). In I. Mervielde, I. Deary, F. De Fruyt, & F. Ostendorf (Eds.), *Personality psychology in Europe: Proceedings of the Eighth European conference on personality* (pp. 107–127). The Netherlands: Tilburg University Press.

Moffitt, T. E. (1993). Adolescence-limited and life-course persistent antisocial behavior: A developmental taxonomy. *Psychological Review, 100,* 674–701.

Moffitt, T. E., & Caspi, A. (1998). Implications of violence between intimate partners for child psychologists and psychiatrists. *Journal of Child Psychology and Psychiatry, 39,* 137–144.

Moffitt, T. E., Caspi, A., Dickson, N., Silva, P., & Stanton, W. (1996). Childhood-onset versus adolescent-onset antisocial conduct problems in males: Natural history from ages 3 to 18 years. *Development and Psychopathology, 8,* 399–424.

Mroczek, D. K., & Little, T. (2006). *Handbook of personality development.* Mahwah, NJ: Erlbaum.

Muris, P., Schmidt, H., Merckelbach, H., & Schouten, E. (2001). The structure of negative emotions in adolescents. *Journal of Abnormal Child Psychology, 29,* 331–337.

Nagin, D., & Tremblay, R. E. (1999). Trajectories of boys' physical aggression, opposition, and hyperactivity on the path to physically violent and nonviolent juvenile delinquency. *Child Development, 70,* 1181–1196.

Newman, D. L., Caspi, A., Moffitt, T. E., & Silva, P. A. (1997). Antecedents of adult interpersonal functioning: Effects of individual differences in age 3 temperament. *Developmental Psychology, 33,* 206–217.

Olson, S. L., Schilling, E. M., & Bates, J. E. (1999). Measurement of impulsivity: Construct coherence, longitudinal stability, and relationship with externalizing problems in middle childhood and adolescence. *Journal of Abnormal Child Psychology, 27*, 151–165.

Parker, W. D., & Stumpf, H. (1998). A validation of the five-factor model of personality in academically talented youth across observers and instruments. *Personality and Individual Differences, 25*, 1005–1025.

Piaget, J. (1950). *The psychology of intelligence*. New York: Harcourt.

Piaget, J. (1983). Piaget's theory. In P. H. Mussen (Ed.), *Handbook of child psychology: History, theory, and methods* (pp. 103–128). New York: Wiley.

Plomin, R., & Daniels, D. (1984). The interaction between temperament and environment. *Merrill-Palmer Quarterly, 30*, 149–162.

Plutchik, R., & Conte, H. R. (1997). *Circumplex models of personality and emotions*. Washington, DC: American Psychological Association.

Pulkkinen, L. (2002). Social development and its risk factors. In C. von Hofsten, & L. Backman (Eds.), *Psychology at the turn of the millennium: Vol. 2. Social, developmental, and clinical perspectives* (pp. 53–76). New York: Taylor & Francis.

Putnam, S. P., Ellis, L. K., & Rothbart, M. K. (2001). The structure of temperament from infancy through adolescence. In A. Eliasz, & A. Angleitner, (Eds.), *Advances in research on temperament* (pp. 165–182). Miami, FL: Pabst Science.

Putnam, S. P., Sanson, A. V., & Rothbart, M. K. (2002). Child temperament and parenting. In M. H. Bornstein, (Ed.), *Handbook of parenting: Vol. 1. Children and parenting* (2nd ed., pp. 255–277). Mahwah, NJ: Erlbaum.

Raine, A., Reynolds, C., Venables, P. H., Mednick, S. A., & Farrington, D. P. (1998). Fearlessness, stimulation-seeking, and large body size at age 3 years as early predispositions to childhood aggression at age 11 years. *Archives of General Psychiatry, 55*, 745–751.

Rende, R. (1993). Longitudinal relations between temperament traits and behavioral syndromes in middle childhood. *Journal of the American Academy of Child and Adolescent Psychiatry, 32*, 287–290.

Renken, B., Egeland, B., Marvinney, D., Mangelsdorf, S., & Sroufe, L. A. (1989). Early childhood antecedents of aggression and passive withdrawal in early elementary school. *Journal of Personality, 57*, 257–281.

Roberts, B. W., & DelVecchio, W. F. (2000). The rank-order consistency of personality traits from childhood to old age: A quantitative review of longitudinal studies. *Psychological Bulletin, 126*, 3–25.

Roberts, B. W., Walton, K., & Viechtbauer, W. (2006). Patterns of mean-level change in personality traits across the life-course: A meta-analysis of longitudinal studies, *Psychological Bulletin, 132*, 1–25.

Roberts, B. W., & Wood, D. (2006). Personality development in the context of the neo-socioanalytic model of personality. In D. K. Mroczek, & T. D. Little, (Eds.), *Handbook of personality development* (pp. 11–39). Mahwah, NJ: Erlbaum.

Robin, A. L., & Foster, S. L. (1989). *Negotiating parent-adolescent conflict: A behavioral-family systems approach*. New York: Guilford Press.

Robins, R. W., Fraley, R. C., Roberts, B. W., & Trzesniewski, K. H. (2001). A longitudinal study of personality change in young adulthood. *Journal of Personality, 69*, 617–640.

Rothbart, M. K., & Ahadi, S. A. (1994). Temperament and development of personality. *Journal of Abnormal Psychology, 103*, 55–66.

Rothbart, M. K., Ahadi, S. A., Hershey, K. L., & Fisher, P. (2001). Investigations of temperament at 3 to 7 years: The Children's Behavior Questionnaire. *Child Development, 72*, 1394–1408.

Rothbart, M. K., & Bates, J. E. (1998). Temperament. In W. Damon (Series Ed.) & N. Eisenberg (Vol. Ed.), *Handbook of child psychology: Vol. 3. Social, emotional, and personality development* (5th ed., pp. 105–176). New York: Wiley.

Rothbart, M. K., & Derryberry, D. (1981). Development of individual differences in temperament. In M. E. Lamb, & A. L. Brown (Eds.), *Advances in developmental psychology* (Vol. 1, pp. 37–86). Hillsdale, NJ: Erlbaum.

Rubin, K. H., Bukowski, W., & Parker, J. G. (1998). Peer interactions, relationships, and groups. In W. Damon (Series Ed.) & N. Eisenberg (Vol. Ed.), *Handbook of child psychology: Vol. 3. Social, emotional, and personality development* (5th ed., pp. 619–700). New York: Wiley.

Rubin, K. H., Burgess, K. B., Dwyer, K. M., & Hastings, P. D. (2003). Predicting preschoolers' externalizing behaviors from toddler temperament, conflict, and maternal negativity. *Developmental Psychology, 39*, 164–176.

Salekin, R. T., (2006). Psychopathy in children and adolescents: Key issues in conceptualization and assessment. In C. J. Patrick (Eds.), *Handbook of psychopathy* (pp. 389–414). New York: Guilford Press.

Salekin, R. T., & Frick, P. J. (2005). Psychopathy in children and adolescents: The need for a developmental perspective. *Journal of Abnormal Child Psychology, 33*, 403–409.

Salekin, R. T., Lesitico, A. -M. R., Trobst, K. K., Schrum, C. L., & Lochman, J. E. (2005). Adolescent psychopathy and personality theory: The interpersonal circumplex—Expanding evidence of a nomological net. *Journal of Abnormal Child Psychology, 33*, 445–460.

Salekin, R. T., Neumann, C. S., Leistico, A. R., DiCicco, T. M., & Duros, R. L. (2004). Psychopathy and comorbidity in a young offender sample: Taking a closer look at psychopathy's potential importance over disruptive behavior disorders. *Journal of Abnormal Psychology, 113*, 416–427.

Saudino, K. J., & Cherny, S. S. (2001). Sources of continuity and change in observed temperament. In R. N. Emde & J. K. Hewitt (Eds.), *Infancy to early childhood: Genetic and environmental influences on developmental change* (pp. 89–110). New York: Oxford University Press.

Saudino, K. J., & Plomin, R. (1996). Personality and behavior genetics: Where have we been and where are we going? *Journal of Research in Personality, 30*, 335–347.

Schwartz, C. E., Snidman, N., & Kagan, J. (1996). Early childhood temperament as a determinant of externalizing behavior in adolescence. *Development and Psychopathology, 8*, 527–537.

Shapiro, T. (1990). Debate orum-resolved: Borderline personality disorder exists in children under twelve. *Journal of the American Academy of Child and Adolescent Psychiatry, 29*, 478–483.

Shiner, R. L. (1998). How shall we speak of children's personalities in middle childhood? A preliminary taxonomy. *Psychological Bulletin, 124*, 308–332.

Shiner, R. L. (2000). Linking childhood personality with adaptation: Evidence for continuity and change across time into late adolescence. *Journal of Personality and Social Psychology, 78*, 310–325.

Shiner, R. L. (2006). Temperament and personality in childhood. In D. K. Mroczek & T. D. Little (Eds.), *Handbook of personality development* (pp. 213–230). Mahwah, NJ: Erlbaum.

Shiner, R. L., & Caspi, A. (2003). Personality differences in childhood and adolescence: Measurement, development, and consequences. *Journal of Child Psychology and Psychiatry, 44*, 2–32.

Shiner, R. L., & Masten, A. S. (2002). Transactional links between personality and adaptation from childhood through adulthood. *Journal of Research in Personality, 36*, 580–588.

Shiner, R. L., Masten, A. S., & Roberts, J. M. (2003). Childhood personality foreshadows adult personality and life outcomes two decades later. *Journal of Personality, 71*, 1145–1170.

Shiner, R. L., Masten, A. S., & Tellegen, A. (2002). A developmental perspective on personality in emerging adulthood: Childhood antecedents and concurrent adaptation. *Journal of Personality and Social Psychology, 83*, 1165–1177.

Sigvardsson, S., Bohman, M., & Cloninger, C. R. (1987). Structure and stability of childhood personality: Prediction of later social adjustment. *Journal of Child Psychology and Psychiatry, 28*, 929–946.

Silverman, I., & Ragusa, D. (1992). A short-term longitudinal study of the early development of self-regulation. *Journal of Abnormal Child Psychology, 20*, 415–435.

Slotboom, A. -M., Havill, V. L., Pavlopoulos, V., & De Fruyt, F. (1998). Developmental changes in personality descriptions of children: A cross-national comparison of parental descriptions of children. In G. A. Kohnstamm, C. F. Halverson, I. Mervielde, & V. L. Havill (Eds.), *Parental descriptions of child personality: Developmental antecedents of the Big Five?* (pp. 127–153). Mahwah, NJ: Erlbaum.

Sroufe, L. A., Carlson, E. A., Levy, A. K., & Egeland, B. (1999). Implications of attachment theory for developmental psychopathology. *Development and Psychopathology, 11*, 1–13.

Stoolmiller, M. (2001). Synergistic interaction of child manageability problems and parent-discipline tactics in predicting future growth in externalizing behavior for boys. *Developmental Psychology, 37*, 814–825.

Sullivan, H. S. (1953). *The interpersonal theory of psychiatry*. New York: Norton Press.

Tackett, J. L. (2006). Evaluating models of the personality-psychopathology relationship in children and adolescents. *Clinical Psychology Review, 26*, 548–599.

Thomas, A., & Chess, S. (1977). *Temperament and development*. New York: Brunner/Mazel.

Thomas, A., Chess, S., & Birch, H. (1968). *Temperament and behavior disorders in children*. New York: New York University Press.

Thomas, A., Chess, S., Birch, H., Hertzig, M., & Korn, S. (1963). *Behavioral individuality in early childhood*. New York: New York University Press.

Trapnell, P., & Wiggins, J. S. (1991). Extension of the Interpersonal Adjective Scales to the big five dimensions of personality. *Journal of Personality and Social Psychology, 59*, 781–790.

Tremblay, R. E., Pihl, R. O., Vitaro, F., & Dobkin, P. L. (1994). Predicting early onset of male antisocial behavior from preschool behavior. *Archives of General Psychiatry, 51*, 732–739.

Walker, J. L., Lahey, B. B., Russo, M. F., Frick, P. J., Christ, M. A. G., McBurnett, K., et al. (1991). Anxiety, inhibition, and conduct disorder in children: Part I. Relation to social impairment. *Journal of the American Academy of Child and Adolescent Psychiatry, 30*, 187–191.

Watson, D., & Clark, L. A. (1993). Behavioral disinhibition versus constraint: A dispositional perspective. In D. M. Wegner & J. W. Pennebaker (Eds.), *Handbook of mental control*. Englewood Cliffs, NJ: Prentice Hall.

Watson, D., Clark, L. A., & Harkness, A. R., (1994). Structures of personality and their relevance to psychopathology. *Journal of Abnormal Psychology, 103*, 18–31.

Watson, D., Kotov, R. & Gamez, W. (2006). Basic dimensions of temperament in relation to personality and psychopathology. In R. F. Krueger & J. L. Tackett (Eds.), *Personality and psychopathology* (pp. 7–38). New York: Guilford Press.

White, H. R., Bates, M. E., & Buyske, S. (2001). Adolescent-limited versus persistent delinquency: Extending Moffitt's hypothesis into adulthood. *Journal of Abnormal Psychology, 110*, 600–609.

Widiger, T. A., & Clark, L. A. (2000). Toward DSM-V and the classification of psychopathology. *Psychological Bulletin, 126*, 946–963.

Widiger, T. A., & Trull, T. J. (2007). Plate tectonics in the classification of personality disorder: Shifting to a dimensional model. *American Psychologist, 62*, 71–83.

Widiger, T. A., Trull, T. J., Clarkin, J. F., Sanderson, C., & Costa, P. T. (2002). A description of the DSM-IV personality disorders with the five factor model of personality. In P. T. Costa & T. A. Widiger (Eds.), *Personality disorders and the five factor model of personality* (2nd ed., pp. 89–99). Washington, DC: American Psychological Association.

Widiger, T. A., Verheul, R., & van den Brink, W. (1999). Personality and psychopathology. In L. A. Pervin & O. P. John (Eds.), *Handbook of personality: Theory and research* (2nd ed., pp. 347–366). New York: Guilford Press.

Wiggins, J. S., & Broughton, R. (1985). The interpersonal circle: A structural model for the integratrion of personality research. In R. Hogan & W. H. Jones (Eds.), *Perspectives in personality: A research annual* (Vol. 1, pp. 1–47). Greenwich, CT: JAI Press.

Wiggins, J. S., & Pincus, A. L. (1989). Conceptions of personality disorders and dimensions of personality. *Psychological Assessment, 1*, 305–316.

Wiggins, J. S., & Pincus, A. L. (1994). Personality structure and the structure of personality disorders. In P. T. Costa, & T. A. Widiger (Eds.), *Personality disorders and the five factor model of personality* (pp. 73–93). Washington, DC: American Psychological Association.

Wiggins, J. S., Trapnell, P., & Phillips, N. (1988). Psychometric and geometric characteristics of the revised Interpersonal Adjective Scale (IAS-R). *Mutivariate Behavioral Research, 23*, 517–530.

Yamagata, S., Ando, J., Yoshimura, K., Ostendorf, F., Rainer, R., Spinath, F., et al. (2006). Is the genetic structure of human personality universal? A cross-cultural twin study from North America, Europe, and Asia. *Journal of Personality and Social Psychology, 90*, 987–998.

CHAPTER 13

Treatment Research

Mark D. Rapport, Michael J. Kofler, Jennifer Bolden, and Dustin E. Sarver

This chapter provides a broad overview of principles, practices, and issues related to planning, conducting, and evaluating treatment research with children. We begin by discussing relevant issues, considerations, and obstacles in conducting child research. These include developmental considerations, measurement issues, informed consent, and confidentiality. The ensuing sections recapitulate the evolving debate concerning clinical efficacy and clinical effectiveness, and the evolution of empirically supported treatments (ESTs) for children. Methodological approaches that address the selection and evaluation of outcome measures appropriate for children—including the clinical significance of findings—are highlighted afterward. The last two sections provide broad coverage of research designs frequently used in child research and discuss factors relevant to identifying a research sample, including sample size and power.

MEASUREMENT ISSUES AND DEVELOPMENTAL CONSIDERATIONS

Measurement Issues

Conducting research with children requires broad knowledge of measurement issues related to maturation, selection of dependent measures, and the degree to which informants (parents, teachers, observers) agree with one another when providing information about children's behavior. This is due to several factors. Children's behavior is qualitatively different from that of adults and thus requires special consideration with respect to measurement and observation. Extrapolating adult measures for use in child research—by changing wording, modifying administration procedures, and making other adjustments—frequently fails to capture the intended underlying construct. Childhood behavior problems typically entail a broad range of symptoms, and these difficulties can affect functioning in multiple situations and settings. Observations of core and secondary symptoms may consequently vary significantly depending on setting and task demands. For example, children with Attention-Deficit/Hyperactivity Disorder (ADHD) typically experience chronic behavioral and academic difficulties at home and at school, and there is generally good agreement among observers. In contrast, children with internalizing disorders are frequently underrecognized until daily functioning is sufficiently impaired to render their suffering more transparent. Multiproblem and multisituation assessment and analysis are thus the rule rather than the exception in child research.

Finally, children's rapidly emerging and changing verbal and cognitive abilities require careful consideration for research studies in which children are asked questions about themselves, others, and internal (e.g., mood/affect, anxiety, concentration) or external (e.g., activity level, impulsiveness) states. This consideration is complicated by extant research demonstrating differences among raters (e.g., parents, teachers, and trained observers), across settings (e.g., home and school), and for different types of behavior problems, as discussed later in the chapter.

Developmental Considerations

Treatment research with children is an intriguing but complicated domain of clinical psychology due to developmental factors that play a key role in our understanding of and assessing maladaptive behavior. For example, many behaviors associated with or mistaken as maladjustment and emotional disturbance are relatively common during childhood. Estimated prevalence rates based on parent reports indicate that fears and worries (43%), temper tantrums (80%), bedwetting (17%), and restlessness (30%) occur frequently in 6- to 12-year-old children (Lapouse & Monk, 1959) but do not necessarily portend later psychological dysfunction. In a similar vein, most children exhibit stranger anxiety around 8 months of age that mirrors their ability to discriminate a familiar face from an unfamiliar face. Separation anxiety becomes evident shortly after stranger anxiety begins, characterized by distress and an inability to be readily comforted by others in the absence of the child's parents or primary care providers. This is a normal response pattern in very young children, whereas excessive anxiety concerning separation from major attachment figures in later years accompanied by other behaviors—such as reluctance to attend school, unrealistic worry that an untoward calamitous event will separate the child from his or her parents, and somatic complaints—may signal the onset of a clinical disorder. Oppositional behavior is a normal developmental phenomenon in 18- to 36-month-old children; however, its persistence and accompaniment by other behavior problems is considered maladaptive in later years.

Behavioral and emotional problems evident in less severe forms during different developmental stages frequently represent normal developmental progressions in children, whereas their persistence may predict developing psychopathology. Consider the heterotypic continuity of ADHD symptoms as an example. Symptoms of ADHD arise early in childhood; however, their presence does not necessarily portend a persistent pattern of ADHD beyond 3 years of age in an estimated 50% to 90% of children so characterized (Palfrey, Levine, Walker, & Sullivan, 1985). Continuation of early ADHD-like symptoms to 4 years of age, however, is highly predictive of clinical hyperactivity at 9 years of age (Campbell, 1990). Thus, the early onset, degree, and persistence of symptoms past 4 years of age is highly predictive of a clinical diagnosis (indicating continuing and worsening impairment) and continuing difficulties throughout adolescence and early adulthood.

Other problem behaviors show clear developmental trends and are not considered maladaptive until late childhood. Lying and destructiveness are common exemplars. An estimated 50% of boys and girls engage in lying by age 6, based on parent report. Frequency of lying decreases to approximately 25% and 13% by age 7 in boys and girls, respectively, and continues to follow a downward trend as a function of increasing age in most children. Destructive behavior shows a similar developmental trend, peaking at 3 and 5 years of age in girls and boys, respectively, with a clear downward trend for both sexes through age 13 (MacFarlane, Allen, & Honzik, 1954).

Some maladaptive behaviors remain stable over time in terms of their frequency, but change with respect to topography or form. The manifestation of childhood aggression is a good example. Threatening, pushing, and shoving in young children frequently evolve into verbal and physical assault in older children, who continue to manifest aggressive behavior (Dishion & Patterson, 2006).

The foregoing examples inform us that many problematic behaviors in children will diminish or remit over the course of normal development and may not be appropriate or high priorities for intervention unless the behavior is sufficiently impairing and more rapidly alleviated by clinical treatment. They also highlight the importance of understanding the typical frequency and topography with which specific behavioral and emotional problems occur in children, and how base rates change over the course of development. Failure to appreciate and control for these variables may inadvertently result in attributing change to treatment rather than maturation or other historical events. Study design must also plan for possible topographical changes in maladaptive behavior if outcome assessment spans several years (e.g., in some cross-sectional and longitudinal studies). This may necessitate using different age norms or even different measurement instruments, which introduces unwanted error into the protocol.

A different set of developmental considerations comes into play when research studies require investigators to assign children to groups based on the presence or absence of a clinical disorder. Structured or semi-structured clinical interviews, coupled with other instruments and measures, are characteristically used to render a clinical diagnosis for purposes of group assignment (for reviews, see Orvaschel, 2006; Rapport, Timko, & Wolfe, 2006). Skilled interviewers have little difficulty interviewing adult informants, whereas interviewing children about their emotional state can be extremely difficult, and at times impractical, depending on developmental factors. Children's emotional development significantly affects their ability to respond to clinical interview questions about themselves and how they feel. The ability to label emotions and talk to others about feelings develops by about 2 years of age, and children have a reasonably well-developed range of emotional displays and labels by school age. Children can report changes in positive emotions before negative ones, but most experience difficulty describing variability in negative emotions until late childhood or early adolescence. Conscious awareness of and the ability to report on emotions as a state or system is not fully developed until middle or late adolescence (Haviland-Jones, Gebelt, & Stapley, 1997).

MEASURING AND ASSESSING CHILDREN'S BEHAVIOR

Informant Ratings of Children's Behavior

Behavior checklists and rating scales play a prominent role in child research. They serve as an important source of information concerning a child's behavior in different settings, how others judge behavior, and the extent to which behavior deviates from age- and gender-related norms. Information gleaned from rating scales contributes to the diagnostic process, and several scales serve as treatment efficacy measures.

Standardized scales are available that provide broad (e.g., internalizing, externalizing behavior problems) and narrow (e.g., measures of particular clinical disorders or states such as depression) indices of behavior, as well as for particular constructs (e.g., self-esteem, perceived competence) and other types of functioning (e.g., classroom performance, adaptive behavior, peer perceptions). Incorporating rating scales in research necessitates examination of the scale's psychometric properties (i.e., whether the instrument provides valid and reliable information with respect to what it purports to measure), general knowledge concerning the degree to which different informants can be counted on to provide valid information about a child's behavior, and factors that influence informant ratings. A judicious review of an instrument's psychometric properties is a necessary first step in constructing a research protocol. This is accomplished by checking with the publisher or author of the instrument, conducting a literature search of the instrument's psychometric properties, and researching specialty texts that cover tests and rating scales (e.g., *The Fifteenth Mental Measurements Yearbook,* edited by Plake, Impara, & Spies, 2003).

Extant research examining the degree to which raters agree concerning the presence of behavior problems reveals several, relatively consistent trends. In general, informants who interact with the child in the same environment (e.g., parents) tend to show better agreement in their reports of behavior than those who interact with the child in different environments (e.g., parents versus teachers versus mental health workers; Achenbach, McConaughy, & Howell, 1987). Agreement between parents, however, is less than ideal, as highlighted in a recent meta-analytic review (Duhig, Renk, Epstein, & Phares, 2000). Correspondence between mother and father ratings of children's behavior problems varied depending on the category of problem behaviors examined. For example, mean correspondence between parents for internalizing behavior problems was .45 as opposed to .63 and .70 for externalizing and total behavior problem scores, respectively—perhaps because externalizing behavior problems are easier to judge and/or more consistent across situations or settings (Achenbach et al., 1987; Walker & Bracken, 1996). Although a correlation of .45 is considered a moderate level of agreement between raters, it nevertheless indicates that only 20% ($.45^2$) of the variability in one parent's ratings can be explained (predicted) by the variability in the other parent's ratings. Higher correspondence between parents was reported for adolescents than for younger children when examining both internalizing and externalizing behavior problems, and the family's socioeconomic status appears to exert small but significant effects on parent ratings. Agreement among raters also varies for clinical and nonclinical samples, is more variable for particular types of behavior and emotional problems, and is unacceptably low when comparing children's self-ratings to adult ratings (Achenbach et al., 1987).

The foregoing summary indicates that parents and teachers can be relied on to provide reasonably reliable ratings of children's behavior in the context in which they observe children for broad indices of behavior problems such as internalizing and externalizing behavior problems. Diminished correspondence between informants is evident, however, for ratings of more discrete types of behavior problems, when informant ratings are based on different settings, and when comparing children's own ratings to those of adults. Investigators need to consider these issues during the research design stage and minimize error variance by utilizing a multitrait, multimethod approach. This approach recognizes the undesirable shared overlap (variance) among similar measures and raters of specific constructs and behaviors and informs the investigator how to maximize the unique contribution of measures relevant to the variables studied (cf. Burns & Haynes, 2006, for a review).

Measurement Limitations

Limitations common to most rating scales include their reliance on subjective judgments and multiple threats to internal validity. These include halo effects, response bias, intensity and immediacy effects, and rater expectation bias (Harris & Lahey, 1982; McClellen & Werry, 2000). The underlying assumptions that Likert rating formats reflect interval-level measurement (i.e., that the unit of measure between 2 and 4 is identical to the difference between 1 and 3, and that these behavioral units are consistent across scales) and that all behavioral and emotional problems should be equally weighted (count the same when endorsed at the same level) represent additional psychometric challenges to clinical rating scales. For example, two children could receive identical Conduct Disorder rating scale scores, yet be dramatically different with respect to behavioral disturbance. One child might receive four 2-point ratings (indicating the highest level of severity or frequency) for items such as lying, stealing, cursing, and truancy, whereas the other child receives four 2-point ratings for breaking and entering, rape, firearm violation, and physical aggressiveness. Their total scores would be identical, yet the second child's symptoms are clearly more serious than the former's. Other factors, such as the presence of psychopathology among informants, the informant's experience with children, and other demand characteristics, represent additional challenges to clinical child rating scales.

Several desirable psychometric properties have not been thoroughly established for many child rating scales. For example, scale validity is usually accomplished by demonstrating that scores derived from one instrument correlate with those derived from an already established scale of the same latent variable, or by demonstrating that children known to be highly active (e.g., ADHD) score significantly higher than normal peers on the scale. Most scales meet at least one of these two criteria. Extant research, however, reveals that even when scale scores are correlated, they may be unrelated to objective measures of the same trait (e.g., Rapoport, Abramson,

Alexander, & Lott, 1971; Stevens, Kupst, Suran, & Schulman, 1978). For example, when measured by step counter, nearly 64% of children rated as clinically hyperactive were less active than the most active child rated as being normal by the teacher (Tryon & Pinto, 1994). Collectively, these shortcomings limit the interpretability and usefulness of activity rating scales.

The diagnostic utility of most rating scales is unknown; however, this situation has improved considerably over the past several years. Four metrics address this concern: sensitivity, specificity, positive predictive power (PPP), and negative predictive power (NPP). Sensitivity and specificity indicate the proportion of the group with a target diagnosis who test positive and negative on a measure, respectively. These two indices are useful for examining the overall classification accuracy of rating scales and other instruments, but are not particularly valuable to clinicians who are unaware of a child's diagnostic standing prior to referral. The statistics most relevant for this purpose are PPP and NPP. As it applies to rating scale utility, PPP indicates the conditional probability that a child exceeding a rating scale cutoff score meets criteria for a particular diagnosis such as ADHD (i.e., the ratio of true positive cases to all test positives). In contrast, NPP indicates the conditional probability that a child who doesn't exceed an established cutoff score will not meet criteria for a particular clinical diagnosis (i.e., the ratio of true negative cases to all test negatives). High values (e.g., >.80) for all four indices are desirable.

Finally, it is becoming increasingly common for investigators to create specific measures for assessing outcome by borrowing from measures with established psychometric properties and reconfiguring them for the study. For example, items contained in adult rating scales may be reworded and rekeyed (i.e., changed from a 1–5 to a 1–3 metric scale) before administering them to children. Others borrow from different scales that reflect a similar latent construct (e.g., anxiety) and combine or select specific items thought to better reflect the construct. These well-intentioned efforts ignore the backbone of psychological measurement: psychometric theory. Altering a measure, no matter how strong its existing psychometric properties, requires the investigator to reestablish its psychometric properties with the intended population (e.g., children) before using it in research. The researcher must also consider relevant developmental phenomena when reconfiguring rating scales and other questionnaire instruments. For instance, young children are unable to describe variability in negative emotions until late childhood or early adolescence, and usually cannot reliably discriminate between behavioral descriptions on a 5-point frequency or severity scale.

Interview Measures of Children's Behavior

Conducting detailed clinical interviews with children and their caregivers is a common method for screening participants, determining group assignment, and obtaining study data for child research investigations. Structured and semi-structured clinical interviews provide unique information beyond the data gained from rating scales and currently represent the only assessment option that allows clinicians to probe for the onset, course, and duration of endorsed symptoms—a necessity for differential diagnosis. As a result, they are considered the gold standard for assessment and diagnosis. The distinction between structured and semi-structured interviews lies in the degree of freedom granted to the clinician to stray from a given script and ask open-ended, probing questions in response to symptom endorsements made by the interviewee. As a general rule of thumb, semi-structured interviews evoke more detailed information concerning presenting symptomatology owing to the extensive probing and clarification permitted (e.g., by asking for examples) but require greater clinical acumen and training.

The development of structured and semi-structured interviews represents the recognition of both the questionable reliability and validity of unaided clinical interviews and the frequent disagreement between parent and child reports of symptom endorsement and severity. Structured and semi-structured clinical interviews result in decreased error compared to unstructured clinical interviews arising from both internal (e.g., differential training level of clinicians, clinician biases) and external (e.g., discrepancies between informants) sources. The interviews typically require between 1 and 2 hours to complete, depending on a range of factors. These include the clinician's experience, the informant's ability to remain focused and recall historical information, and the severity, range, and duration of presenting problems (Table 13.1). The time investment limits their practicality for repeated use (e.g., for assessing treatment effects). Financial investment varies significantly across interview schedules. Some are free and available online (e.g., Schedule for Affective Disorders and Schizophrenia for School-Age Children [K-SADS]), whereas others have an initial cost of $600 in addition to $2,000 fixed training costs (e.g., Child and Adolescent Psychiatric Assessment [CAPA]). All but one of the semi-structured interviews covers all major *DSM-IV* diagnoses for school-age children through age 18. Some of the semi-structured interviews provide separate versions for parents, children, and adolescents. None of the available semi-structured interviews includes teacher versions. Clinicians must use other instruments to obtain school-related information for purposes of establishing impairment across multiple settings.

Strong convergent and discriminant validity is reported for most of the available semi-structured interviews, and test-retest reliability suggests stability of diagnosis over 1 to 3 years in clinical samples (Pelham, Fabiano, & Massetti, 2005). High sensitivity and specificity are typically reported for the semi-structured interviews, with only limited information available pertaining to PPP and NPP. The lack of PPP and NPP metrics is due in part to the use of semi-structured clinical interviews as the gold standard from which the predictive power of other measures (e.g., rating scales) is established.

The CAPA appears to be the most extensively developed of the clinical interviews, but it requires up to 2 weeks of classroom instruction and an additional 1 to 2 weeks of practice to acquire the necessary certification (Angold & Costello, 2000). This training is estimated to cost $600, and there is an additional fixed cost of $2,000, which may limit widespread usage among clinicians, especially when schedules such as the K-SADS demonstrate adequate reliability and validity and are available online at no cost. The CAPA, however, may be superior to other available schedules due to several excellent features. The instrument provides for an intensity rating that varies by three symptom groupings: intrapsychic phenomena

Table 13.1 Clinical Child Diagnostic Interviews

Measures	Age Range	Time (min)	Test-Retest (Kappa)	Symptom History	Disorders Considered	Scoring Format	Instrument Cost ($)	Training Required
Structured Interviews								
Diagnostic Interview Schedule for Children IV (DISC-IV)	6–17 (P) 9–17 (C)	90–120 (P) 45–90 (C)	0.79 (P) 0.42 (C)	4 weeks/ 12 months	All major Dx	Y/N	150– 2,000	2–3 day training module
Diagnostic Interview for Children and Adolescents IV (DICA-IV)	6–17	60–120	NR (P) 0.32 (C) 0.59 (A)	4 weeks/ 12 months	All major Dx	Y/N	1,000	2–4 weeks
Children's Interview for Psychiatric Syndromes (CHiPS)	6–18	40	0.4	NR	All major Dx	Y/N	115	NDR
Semi-structured Interviews								
Schedule for Affective Disorders and Schizophrenia for School-Age Children (K-SADS)	6–17	30–90	0.63	6 months/ lifetime	All major Dx	0–3	Free online	CTR
Semi-structured Clinical Interview for Children and Adolescents (SCICA)	13–18	60–90	0.57 (AP Scale)	NR	Does not correspond with *DSM-IV*		110–295 25 for 50	NDR
Child and Adolescent Psychiatric Assessment (CAPA)	9–17	20–210 $M = 66$ (P) 22–150 $M = 59$ (C)	NR for ADHD 0.55 for CD	3 months	All major Dx	0–3	600 + 2,000 Fixed Costs	BA
Interview Schedule for Children and Adolescents (ISCA)	8–17	120–150 (P) 45–90 (C)	Between 0.64–1.0	NR	All major Dx	0–3		CTR

Notes: Properties are equivalent for parent and child/adolescent version unless otherwise indicated.
A = Adolescent; AP = Attention Problems; BA = Bachelor's level training; C = Child; CTR = Clinical training required; Dx = Diagnosis; NDR = No degree requirements; NR = Not reported; P = Parent.

such as worrying, qualitatively different symptoms such as psychosis, and conduct disturbances. Training and coding are based on a detailed glossary, and thoroughly investigated symptoms are matched to appropriate glossary definitions and levels of severity. Formal rules are provided for the use of screening, mandatory, and discretionary questions.

The Diagnostic Interview for Children and Adolescents, *DSM-IV* edition (DISC-IV), provides separate versions for children (ages 6 to 12) and adolescents (13 to 18) based on field testing of interview questions with different age, gender, and racial groups. Two to 4 weeks of training at a cost of approximately $1,000 are required to reach the desired level of competence. The duration of training is based on clinician experience and includes topics such as age-appropriate probe questions and maintaining a child's interest through techniques such as tone of voice and appropriate nonverbal gestures. Reliability estimates corroborate research findings indicating that children are less reliable reporters of externalizing symptoms but more reliable reporters on internalizing symptoms relative to their parents. Computer versions are available, but initial research suggests poor reliability compared to the standard interview format.

The K-SADS is currently the most widely used semi-structured clinical interview. The Present-Lifetime (PL) version collects information from the parent regarding both current symptomatology as well as symptomatology at its most frequent and severe levels in the past. A separate interview is conducted with the child, and a third pair of ratings is generated based on integration of the parent and child reports with historical information and other data (e.g., rating scales). The K-SADS-PL focuses on chronology, treatment, impairment, and severity of symptoms. The initial screening interview consists of 82 items covering all major *DSM-IV* diagnostic categories. Cutoff scores are used to determine the need to administer the in-depth supplementary sections available for each diagnostic category, thus shortening administration time by allowing the clinician to skip supplementary sections based on negative endorsement of key screening questions. Interrater reliability estimates for the K-SADS are among the highest of any of the semi-structured clinical interviews. Extensive knowledge of diagnostic and symptom subtleties is required owing to lack of formal training requirements, and clinicians must use their judgment to interject noncued verbal probes to clarify informant responses and elicit examples of problematic behavioral and emotional symptoms.

Observational Measures of Children's Behavior

Behavioral observation is a time-consuming but valuable approach for obtaining detailed information about children and the environments in which they learn, play, and interact with others. It refers to a process in which observers record motor, verbal, and interactive behaviors of children using carefully defined operational criteria as opposed to evaluative judgments (e.g., rating scales) or mechanically activated devices (e.g., movement monitors, physiological monitoring). As such, many consider it the sine qua non of child assessment. An advantage of using behavioral observations is that the technique is virtually unrestricted with respect to context. Observations can be conducted in naturalistic settings (e.g., to record classroom, playground, or bus riding behavior), analogue settings (e.g., a clinic room furnished to resemble a classroom), or specialty clinics (e.g., to assess parent-child interactions as part of a treatment program for children with Conduct Disorder, to assist a diagnostic evaluation for autism).

Numerous observational coding schemas are available for research purposes. Some permit coding of a wide range of behaviors (e.g., parent-child interactions, general classroom deportment) and are best suited for particular settings (e.g., home or classroom observations). Others permit highly refined and detailed observation, recording, and measurement of more discrete types of behavior (e.g., gross motor activity). Assessing interobserver agreement is nearly always required for research studies and involves pretraining on the selected coding schema and arranging for multiple observers to code the targeted behaviors simultaneously while in the setting or based on taped recordings. Detailed information concerning how to select particular stimuli, responses, and specific recording techniques; how to operationalize particular types, forms, and classes of behavior; and how to calculate interobserver reliability is readily available in classic texts on child behavior assessment (Kazdin, 1982; Ollendick & Hersen, 1998).

Direct observations represent the gold standard for experimental and outcome research for many investigators, but their use in clinical assessment is limited by several factors. No two research teams or commercially available observation systems define behaviors in exactly the same way, and research indicates that differences in observational schema can produce widely discrepant results in collected data (see Kofler, Rapport, & Alderson, in press, for a meta-analytic review).

Commercially available observation systems shown in Table 13.2 are available for school-age children and typically require between 10 and 30 minutes of observation. Multiple observation days are required to produce representative and reliable data; however, some systems offer software versions of their product, allowing researchers to record behavior directly onto a personal digital assistant (PDA) or laptop computer.

Direct observations are commonly used in school and institutional settings that require a formal functional analysis to determine whether antecedent and consequential stimuli or events contribute to a child's maladaptive behavior. These specialized assessments are typically conducted by highly trained school psychologists and individuals specializing in applied behavior analysis.

Although direct observations by independent observers can provide more objective and valid data than any of the other assessment methods discussed here, their relatively high temporal cost, coupled with the general lack of norms, suggests that their usefulness for assessment and group assignment may be limited to situations where large discrepancies exist among informant reports.

An alternative and less costly procedure for obtaining information relevant to children's classroom functioning is to ask classroom teachers to answer specific questions about a child's day or to save work samples. For example, desk checks ("Is the child prepared for class?"), teacher records of verbally intrusive behavior, and the percentage of daily academic assignments completed correctly appear to be useful for discriminating between children with and without ADHD (Pelham

Table 13.2   Mechanical and Observational Assessment Tools

Instrument/ Distributor	Age Range	Recording Length	Norms	Software Available	Cost
Mechanical					
Actigraphs Ambulatory Monitoring MiniMitter MTI, Inc.	Any	22 days per 32 kilobytes of memory	N	Y	Starter: $1,000+ (with necessary software and reader interface); $500–$2,000 for each additional actigraph
Actometers[a] Model 108 Engineering Department Times Industries Waterbury, CT 06720	Any	Variable	N	Y[b]	*NR*
Pedometers (available at sporting goods stores) Stand-alone with data downloadable to PC	Any	Range: 99,999 steps (~5.25 miles) to 1,000 miles	N	N Y	$10–$40 $125–$400+
Direct Observations					
ADHD BCS Barkley, 1990	*NR*	15 min.	N	N	*NR*
AET-SSBD Sopris West	School age	15 min.	Y	N	Kit: $108 (includes all three parts of SSBD)
ADHD-SOC Checkmate Plus, Ltd.	School age	16 min.	N	N	Kit: $25
BASC-2 SOS AGS, Inc.	School age	15 min.	N	Y	25 forms @ $33
BOSS Harcourt Assessment	School age	15 min.	N	Y	Kit: $120
COC Abikoff, 1977/1980	School age	32 min.	N	N	NR
DOF ASEBA	5–14	10 min.	Y	Y	50 forms @ $25
SECOS Saudargas, 1997	Grades 1–5	20 min.	Y	N	
Noldus Observer Noldus Information Technology	Any	Variable	N	Y	Observer Basic 5.0 $1,795 Observer Video Pro 5.0 $5,850

Notes: AET-SSBD = Academic Engaged Time Code of the SSBD; BCS = Behavior Coding System; BOSS = Behavioral Observation of Students in Schools; COC = Classroom Observation Code; DOF = Direct Observation Form; NR = not reported; SECOS = State-Event Classroom Observation System; SOC = School Observation Code; SOS = Student Observation System.

[a]Many studies report either using the Kaulins & Willis actometers (no longer manufactured) or enlisting a jeweler to modify a self-winding wristwatch as described by Schulman & Reisman (1959).

[b]Eaton, McKeen, & Saudino (1996) provide SAS syntax for performing group-level data analysis based on actometer readings.

et al., 2005). These methods have the potential for objectivity that characterizes the independent observation methodologies but await critical evaluation to determine their utility for rendering diagnostic judgments at the individual level.

Potential Obstacles to Conducting Research with Children

Knowledge of regulatory statutes, the role and function of institutional review boards (IRBs), and general procedures for ensuring and obtaining informed consent is essential for conducting research with children. Detailed information concerning procedures and regulatory statutes related to studies involving children can be obtained from the Department of Health and Human Services website (www.nihtraining.com/ohsrsite/guidelines/guidelines.html). These regulations provide the minimum standards for protecting human subjects, particularly under the subpart D section, which includes detailed information concerning the involvement of children in research.

Regulations require the *assent* of the child or minor and the permission or *consent* of the parents or legally authorized guardian when children are involved in research. Assent is a child's affirmative agreement to participate in research. The standard for assent is the ability to understand, to some degree, the purpose of the research and what will happen if one participates.

Consent refers to the permission or agreement of parents or guardian to the participation of their child or ward in research. There are two forms of parental consent. *Passive* parental consent is a procedure that requires parents to respond only if they *do not* want their child to participate in a research project. *Active* parental consent requires the parent to return a signed consent form indicating whether or not they are willing to allow their child to participate. The latter method is recommended, although many researchers prefer the passive consent procedure because of the larger participant pool typically achieved. As a general rule for research involving minimal risk, it is sufficient to obtain informed consent from one parent.

Informed consent consists of three primary elements: knowledge, volition, and competency. Parents or guardians of children must be knowledgeable about all aspects of a study, which includes a thorough description of the facts, plausible risks, and potential sources of discomfort associated with an experimental study that may affect their decision to permit their child to participate. This information must be presented to the child's parents or legal guardian in an understandable fashion, followed by an opportunity for them to ask questions and clarify any issues that might not be thoroughly understood.

Volition refers to the process in which participants (or, in the case of minor children, their parents or guardian) agree to participate in a study free of coercion or threat. Subjects (or, in the case of minor children, their parents or guardian) must be able to decline or withdraw from participating at any time preceding or during an experiment without penalty, and should be informed of this provision (i.e., participation must be entirely voluntary).

Ensuring competency in child research typically entails the parents' or guardian's ability to render an educated decision and give consent for their child to participate based on thorough knowledge and understanding of the study.

A consent form signed by the parents or guardian of children indicates their willingness to have their child participate in the study based on an informed decision. These forms traditionally undergo formal review by an IRB or agency committee that evaluates the research proposal, consent procedures, and the form itself. Consent forms vary by design, but must contain a thorough description of the study, inherent and potential risks and benefits, procedures, and issues concerning confidentiality and how the study data may be used. Components of an informed consent form are described in Table 13.3.

Institutional review boards serve to assess the risks, possible benefits, and discomforts associated with a research project. Before beginning a project, an appropriate IRB committee must consider and formally approve all research proposals. University-based projects will typically be reviewed by the institution's IRB panel, and additional approvals may need to be obtained from other agency boards (e.g., hospitals, school systems, National Institute of Mental Health), depending on the selection of participants and whether the project is funded or sponsored by private or federal agencies. Many universities and research centers currently mandate

Table 13.3 Components of Informed Consent Forms

Section of the Form	Purpose and Contents
Overview	Presentation of the goals of the study, why this is conducted, who is responsible for the study and its execution.
Description of procedures	Clarification of the experimental conditions, assessment procedures, requirements of the subjects.
Risks and inconveniences	Statement of any physical and psychological risks and an estimate of their likelihood. Inconveniences and demands to be placed on the subjects (e.g., how many sessions, requests to do anything, contact at home).
Benefits	A statement of what the subjects can reasonably hope to gain from participation, including psychological, physical, and monetary benefits.
Costs and economic considerations	Charges to the subjects (e.g., in treatment) and payment (e.g., for participation or completing various forms).
Confidentiality	Assurances that the information is confidential and will only be seen by people who need to do so for the purposes of research (e.g., scoring and data analysis), procedures to assure confidentiality (e.g., removal of names from forms, storage of data). Also, caveats are included here if it is possible that sensitive information (e.g., psychiatric information, criminal activity) can be subpoenaed.
Alternative treatments	In an intervention study, alternatives available to the client before or during participation are outlined.
Voluntary participation	A statement that the subject is willing to participate and can say no now or later without penalty of any kind.
Questions and further information	A statement that the subject is encouraged to ask questions at any time and can contact an individual (or individuals) (listed by name and phone number) who is available for such contacts.
Signature lines	A place for the subject as well as the experimenter to sign.

Source: Clinical Psychotherapy: Developing and Identifying Effective Treatments, by A. E. Kazdin, 1988, New York: Pergamon Press. Reprinted with permission from Allyn & Bacon and the author.

that all persons involved in the conduct of research—from the investigators to the research assistants—take a specific training course and pass an exam concerning the ethical and appropriate conduct of research. Several of these are offered online (e.g., www6.miami.edu/citireg/), and results are forwarded to the host university's IRB as a precondition for conducting research.

CHILD RESEARCH SETTINGS

General Dimensions

A research study may be conducted in a laboratory (e.g., clinic, university laboratory) or an applied setting (e.g., school, home, hospital, community mental health center). The advantage of most laboratory settings is that they typically allow for maximal control over the experiment. Their most apparent disadvantage is that the nature of the setting is usually quite different from most real-life situations, which calls into question the generality of results. The advantage of applied settings is that they frequently represent real-life situations or environments, which allows for greater generalization of results. Their most obvious disadvantage is that they usually afford less control than a laboratory setting. Typically, one thinks of true experimental and quasi-experimental designs as taking place in a laboratory setting and observational designs as taking place in an applied setting. This is because the researcher attempts to exert a high degree of control in true and quasi-experimental designs, whereas few or no controls over extraneous variables are implemented in observational designs. True or quasi-experiments, however, can be conducted in applied settings, and observational studies can occur in a laboratory setting. Single-case research designs are used in both settings.

Gaining Access to Educational Settings

Conducting research in applied settings such as a school involves striking a balance between maintaining the requisite degree of scientific rigor and respecting the mission and structure of the educational setting. Research protocols must be planned such that disruption of the school or classroom routine is minimized. The investigator must be mindful that in the educational setting, classes (as opposed to individuals) are frequently the units of analysis. For protocols involving individual administration, pulling a child from some class periods (e.g., recreational reading) may be less disruptive than others (e.g., small group science activity) for the class as a whole and the child in particular. Moreover, schools may be especially protective of certain groups of students, such as children with developmental disabilities or behavioral/emotional problems. Conducting research in educational settings consequently requires careful planning and organization to maintain scientific rigor and accommodate the structure of the school. The ensuing discussion is particularly relevant for group studies in which a large sample of participants is required.

Subject recruitment is a necessary first step for most research projects, and schools are a logical source for studies involving children. The choice of school depends on a number of factors, which vary in degree of relevance depending on the focus of the investigation. Among the factors to consider are the socioeconomic status of the community served by the school and the ethnic distribution of the school's population of students. For investigations involving multiple groups, the number of students enrolled in the school becomes an important consideration, in light of the power needs of the study's design to detect group differences.

Gaining access to research participants involves a stepwise progression to enhance the likelihood of a proposal's acceptance by educational institutions. Prior to contacting schools, it behooves the investigator to obtain endorsements from related agencies and the district superintendent of education—this smoothes the way to the engagement phase of decision making for the school principal. Subsequent contact with the principal should first be handled formally through an individually addressed letter that briefly explains the importance and nature of the study and mentions the endorsements received, followed by a telephone call approximately 1 week later to secure an appointment for a meeting.

Prior to contacting schools, the investigator must prepare to address any questions or concerns that may be forthcoming. Petosa and Goodman (1991) outline five phases of decision making that school officials undergo and discuss them in relation to decisions surrounding research proposals. In the *legitimacy phase,* the credibility of the investigator and the relevance of the study are of central concern. Representatives of the research project who contact the school should be prepared to address questions concerning the expertise and affiliation of the chief investigator, the source of funding for the project, and the project's relevance for the education and welfare of children or the community at large. In the second, *information-seeking phase,* the concerns of school officials involve the impact of the project on the day-to-day operation of the school. The investigator should consider the timing of the data collection with the school's schedule in mind. For example, the weeks preceding the winter holiday break and the end of the school year are often hectic for school personnel. Other times of the year, depending on the school system, are largely devoted to mandated standardized achievement testing. School officials will also wish to know the specific requirements of the project to gauge its impact on the school's mission and function. The investigator should be prepared to address questions pertaining to the measures to be administered, the class time required for participation in the project, the costs of participation accruing to the school (e.g., the extent of involvement of school staff), and the resources that will be available to the school (e.g., teacher training and curricular materials). During this phase, school officials will also be vigilant of any potential controversy that may arise due to the study's methodology, including parent objections to particular rating scales or survey questions and the potential for wasted classroom learning time.

In the ensuing *expression of limitations phase,* education officials are likely to express concerns over idiosyncratic situational factors that may pose obstacles to the school's participation in the project. The resourceful investigator should prepare to address concerns over issues of *fit* between the study's requirements and the school's structure, without undermining the integrity of the research project. If the investigator is successful, all parties enter the *engagement phase* of mutual problem solving, in which various ways of increasing the feasibility of the study are considered, such as finding the optimal dates and times and allocating physical space for data collection.

In the final, *commitment phase,* all parties make specific plans for the school's participation in the research project. Olds and Symons (1990) recommend presenting a *data collection participation form* for the principal's signature to secure the school's commitment. The initial start date for the study should be made far enough in advance to allow the school time to block the dates set aside for the data collection in its master calendar and to disseminate the information to parents and school staff. At least 1 week prior to the agreed-upon date for data collection, a follow-up reminder to the school should be made by telephone. At that time, information concerning any changes in the school's normal schedule or routine—such as assemblies or field trips—made subsequent to the meeting with the principal should be solicited.

The foregoing information and sequence of steps pertains primarily to school-wide and classroom studies but is also applicable to conducting single-case research. Because single-case research impacts a classroom rather than a school, the key contact becomes the teacher and, as a courtesy, the principal, rather than the district superintendent. The decision-making process on the part of school personnel remains the same, however, and the investigator should follow the same suggestions for proactive planning and organization.

Additional considerations are warranted once project personnel are in the school to facilitate school support and cooperation. Gaining and maintaining the support of school personnel depend on the behavior and professionalism of research associates. These individuals need to be visible but unobtrusive, professional in appearance and demeanor, friendly and polite without exception, and respectful of school policies, procedures, and personnel. Research associates must be mindful of the school's mission to educate children in a safe environment and, from the outset, solicit information from school staff about such routine procedures as signing in and out upon entering and leaving the campus and whether identification badges are required. Most important, researchers should adhere to the original contract as agreed to by the school principal and refrain from such deviations as adding measures, collecting data on other dates, and attempting to deliver any intervention not previously agreed upon.

The research design and methodology are of prime concern to the investigator, but respect for the mission and structure of the educational setting is equally important. Demonstrating respect by minimizing disruption of daily operations increases the likelihood that the research proposal will be approved and ensures that the data collection process will run as smoothly as possible. Moreover, following through with promised benefits after the data have been collected represents a sound investment, as the school may be amenable to participation in future research projects. One means of accomplishing this is to volunteer to provide a teacher workshop that includes summarizing the study's results.

Clinic and Laboratory Investigations

Clinic- and laboratory-based investigations provide researchers with unique opportunities to manipulate carefully designed independent variables and observe their effects on dependent variables. These types of studies tend to have unparalleled heuristic value and frequently test predictions stemming from extant models of child psychopathology. For example, a recent model of ADHD hypothesized a causal relationship between working memory and activity level in children (Rapport, Chung, Shore, & Isaacs, 2001; Rapport, Kofler, Alderson, & Raiker, in press) and challenged the notion that hyperactivity represents a ubiquitous deficit unrelated to task and setting demands (Porrino et al., 1983). Testing predictions stemming from the working memory model would be difficult to accomplish in a typical classroom for a variety of reasons. Measuring classroom activity level by utilizing actigraphs or behavioral observations does not represent a serious obstacle; however, introducing working memory tasks at varying degrees of difficulty in a counterbalanced manner to specific children and appropriate controls might prove impractical, if not unfeasible. Moreover, obtaining appropriate control over ambient noise levels (including ongoing student conversations or comments), lighting, chair type and placement, distractions, movement, and other setting characteristics is necessary to ensure that changes in the dependent variable (e.g., activity level) are due to differences in working memory demands (e.g., manipulating stimulus set size) rather than extraneous factors. The research clinic provides an ideal setting for these types of investigations.

Research clinics also enable investigators to scrutinize a vast array of personal and interpersonal processes by means of analogue investigations. These studies establish pseudo-situations that mimic important aspects of a child's life, either at home (e.g., asking parents to interact with their children following specific guidelines) or at school (e.g., having children attend a simulated classroom). Results of these studies often have important diagnostic and treatment implications. For example, observations of children with autism interacting with their parents in an analogue setting reveals a high degree of diagnostic sensitivity based on the child's reciprocal social interaction, play, stereotypic behaviors, gesturing, and communication (Filipek, Accardo, & Baranek, 1999). Teaching parents more adaptive ways to interact with their children in analogue settings has also shown exceptional promise for reducing Oppositional Defiant Disorder (Reid, Webster-Stratton, & Hammond, 2003).

CLINICAL EFFICACY, CLINICAL EFFECTIVENESS, AND EMPIRICALLY SUPPORTED THERAPIES

Overview

The terms *clinical efficacy* and *clinical effectiveness* emerged in response to calls for increased use of empirically validated treatments for individuals suffering from mental health problems. Debate evolved between research centers demonstrating that particular treatments resulted in significant client improvement following prescribed protocols, and the failure to find similar levels of improvement in applied settings such as community mental health centers. Hypothesized variables contributing to the lack of generalization of treatment effects across settings included differences in therapist training and orientation, use of manualized therapies to minimize therapist influences and maximize treatment integrity, and the extensive oversight and supervision typically found in research centers. The essential concern was that treatments developed and tested in highly controlled settings were not enjoying the same level of success in applied settings.

Clinical Efficacy

The term clinical efficacy was coined to reflect the situation in which a particular treatment has proven useful and beneficial in treating psychological problems in children through controlled research. For example, Stein and colleagues (Stein, Jayxoc, & Kataoka, 2003) found that children treated with cognitive-behavior therapy for 10 weeks experienced significantly fewer symptoms associated with Posttraumatic Stress Disorder and depression, as well as improved psychosocial functioning and classroom behavior, relative to a 3-month wait-list control group in a randomized clinical trial.

Additional conditions are required to satisfy the recommended criteria for establishing clinical efficacy. The therapy must be significantly superior to no treatment, placebo, or an alternative treatment, or equivalent to a treatment already established as efficacious. These comparisons must be accomplished in the context of a randomized controlled trial, equivalent time-samples design, or controlled single-subject experimental design, and replicated by an independent research team.

Empirically Supported Treatments

Psychological therapies meeting clinical efficacy criteria are considered empirically supported treatments. Empirically supported treatments are psychological treatments proven effective for specific populations through controlled research (Chambless & Hollon, 1998). Meta-analytic reviews attest to the clinical efficacy of many therapies for children by computing and analyzing effect size estimates across studies. Thus, studies rather than subjects become the focus of analysis, and an overall effect size based on reviewed studies provides compelling evidence of the magnitude of the difference (in standard deviation units) between treatment and nontreatment groups. For those unfamiliar with meta-analysis, effect size estimates are calculated based on recommended formulas (Hedges, 1982) and involve subtracting treatment means from control group means and dividing by the pooled standard deviation of the two groups. The result is a number that reflects the difference between the two groups—for example, before and after therapy—in standard deviation units. Thus, an effect size of 1.2 indicates that the treated children are 1.2 standard deviations higher on a particular measure (e.g., in social competence) relative to the untreated group. Larger effect sizes are usually desirable and indicate greater mean differences in outcome measures between the treated and untreated or comparison groups.

Effect size metrics reported in meta-analyses can also be related back to a central clinical question. For example, Kofler et al. (in press) examined how often children with ADHD were on-task relative to control children in regular classroom environments. They used best case estimation to determine the magnitude of on-task deficits after accounting for significant moderators and obtained an effect size of 1.40. This effect size was translated onto the control group distribution to estimate actual percentage rates, and revealed that children with ADHD were on-task an average of 74.7% compared to 87.9% for typically developing children.

Some of the published criteria for establishing a therapeutic intervention as an EST are dubious. For example, the superiority of the intervention must be demonstrated in at least two independent research settings *or* with a sample size of three or more subjects for single-subject design experiments also in at least two independent research settings. This means that a treatment can be considered clinically efficacious based on results from only six children—a rather weak case for suggesting that treatment effects are likely to generalize to other children with similar difficulties and in similar settings. The moniker *possibly efficacious* reflects the situation in which a single, well-controlled study supports the treatment's efficacy, highlighting the critical need for replication.

Clinical Effectiveness

In contrast to clinical efficacy, clinical effectiveness addresses whether the treatment is useful in applied clinical settings, that is, its clinical utility. The distinction between the two terms reflects the frequent failure to replicate treatment effects produced in highly controlled research environments—such as university- or hospital-based research clinics—in regular psychological service delivery systems such as community mental health centers and private practice settings. Variables likely to contribute to a treatment's lack of utility in applied settings, despite proving successful in controlled settings, are reviewed elsewhere (Chambless & Hollon, 1998; Kazdin, 1988). In response to these criticisms, several researchers have attempted to establish clinical effectiveness in applied settings; however, traditional design controls (e.g., random assignment to groups, nontherapeutic waiting-list groups) are certain obstacles to these efforts.

Relevant Issues

Determining whether a treatment or intervention is effective is not as straightforward as it may seem. Effectiveness varies significantly based on the type of measure (self-report, standardized rating scale, direct observation, clinical interview, objective measure such as an actigraph), the source of measurement (child self-ratings, teachers, parents, therapists), and the area of functioning assessed (e.g., social deportment versus academic functioning).

Many measures—and particularly rating scales—currently used in research studies have inadequate measurement units, insufficient psychometric properties, and lack age and sex norms. As an example, none of the available child activity level rating scales has a standard unit of measurement—that is, a meaningful unit of activity or movement that is equivalent within and across measures and raters. Accurately defining activity level is severely compromised as a result and leaves us in the uncomfortable position of describing differences and changes in children's activity level by referring back to the scales used to initially quantify the behavior. The moderate correlations reported between activity rating scales only partially mitigates this concern when contrasted with correlations between rating scales and objective measures of children's activity level. For example, correlations between activity rating scales and actigraphs are generally between .32 and .58. These values indicate that 66% to 91% of the variability in activity rating scale scores is not linearly related to variability in actigraph scores in the same children measured at the same time. This finding probably reflects the fact that children's activity rating scales tend to reflect other aspects of behavior and not just activity level. The wording of most scale items and reliance on factor analytic scale construction methodology contribute to this phenomenon because descriptions of activity level may correlate highly, but usually reflect a broader range of behavior than just movement.

STATISTICALLY AND CLINICALLY SIGNIFICANT CHANGES

Overview

The importance of changes that occur following an intervention can be quantified in three ways. The first and most common approach is statistical significance testing, which examines group differences and estimates the reliability of change. Statistical significance testing calculates how certain we are that changes from pre- to posttest are robust—for example, not due to other factors such as measurement error. It does not tell us, however, about the magnitude of this change or its impact on children's lives. Effect size and correlational approaches can provide meaningful estimates of the magnitude of change, but these estimates do not necessarily have clinical or practical significance. Clinical significance refers to the practicality of an intervention—whether or not it makes a meaningful difference in the daily lives of children or those who interact with the child.

Intuitively, larger effects are more likely to be clinically relevant. The magnitude of effect, however, is not necessarily related to clinical significance. Kazdin (2004) has argued that an intervention can be clinically significant—or insignificant—with large, small, or no changes from pre- to posttest. As examples, he offers the possibility that a large but clinically insignificant effect may be obtained on a cognitive or laboratory task that has little to do with daily living. Likewise, a clinically significant finding of no change may occur when symptom deterioration was expected. The impetus of these examples is to demonstrate that a measure's ecological validity—its relevance to real life—must be considered when selecting measures used to test clinical significance.

Evaluating Clinical Significance

Several methods currently are used to evaluate clinical significance (Kazdin, 2004). Subjective evaluation methods rely on the judgments of the child or relevant others and ask whether they can discern meaningful improvement in their daily lives. Measures of social impact may also inform clinical significance, for example, whether there was a change in arrest record frequency, days worked, or missed school days. Absolute change methods are interested in determining whether a problem or symptom has been eliminated, or whether the child continues to meet diagnostic criteria for a psychiatric disorder.

The most common type of clinical significance testing is the *comparison method*, which asks whether members of the treatment group are distinguishable from

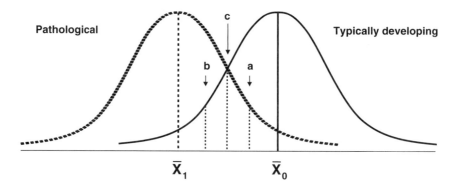

Figure 13.1 Clinical significance cutoff scores based on different criteria.

members of a typically developing (normal control) comparison group after treatment. Comparisons can be made to normative data or to a normal control group. Several commercially and freely available rating scales and direct observation systems provide standard scores based on normative data from nationwide community samples. Clinical significance may be demonstrated when a child changes from the clinical (usually 1.5 or 2 *SD* above the mean) to the normal (usually less than 1.5 *SD* above the mean) range following treatment. Comparison with rating scale norms is potentially problematic, however, due to different assessment conditions (Kazdin, 2004). For example, norms are typically based on a single test administration, whereas treatment outcomes are based on multiple administrations. Comparison with results from a concurrently collected normal control group is preferred.

Absolute change and two normal comparison, cutoff criterion methods are shown in Figure 13.1. X_0 represents the mean of the control group; X_1 represents the pathological group pretreatment mean. Three distinct cutoff scores have been proposed for determining clinical significance. The first (a) represents an absolute change method; the other two (b and c) estimate *normalization:* clinical significance in relation to a normal control group. Some argue that clinically significant improvement has occurred if a child's posttest functioning is (a) outside the range of the pathological group, defined as 2 standard deviations above the pathological control group pretreatment mean. Others argue that the child must fall (b) within the range of the normal population as defined by a score within 2 standard deviations of the normal group mean. A third proposal represents a compromise between these two options, defining normalization as occurring when a child is functioning (c) closer to the mean of the normal group than the pathological group.

In practice, children are classified as deteriorated, unchanged, improved, or normalized. The first three are determined by creating a confidence interval around the children's pretreatment score.* Children falling within the confidence interval are considered unchanged; those falling outside of it are labeled deteriorated

---

*Estimated true score is used if regression to the mean is considered a threat. See Speer (1992) for a discussion and simple method for determining whether regression to the mean is likely affecting posttreatment scores.

or improved. For example, children with a score of X_0 at pretreatment would be considered improved if they scored at or above cutoff score *a* in Figure 13.1. Children who improved and exceeded the predetermined cutoff score (*b* or *c*; see Figure 13.1) are considered normalized.

The difference between statistical and clinical significance is illustrated in the following example. Rapport, Denney, DuPaul, and Gardner (1994) evaluated the effectiveness of methylphenidate (Ritalin) on the classroom performance of children with ADHD. They used three outcome measures: teacher ratings of children's classroom deportment, academic efficiency scores (percentage of assigned class work completed correctly), and observed rates of on-task behavior in the classroom. Traditional significance tests revealed that all three outcome measures were significantly improved as a function of medication. Were these changes meaningful? Rapport and colleagues used the Jacobson and Truax (1991) model, correcting for regression to the mean as recommended by Speer (1992). As depicted in Figure 13.2, they found that between 50% and 78% of children were normalized, meaning that they were functioning within the normal control group range. Interestingly, although statistical significance was demonstrated for all three outcome variables, the rates of improvement or normalization were quite different. Most noticeable is the difference between teacher ratings of behavior, with 94% of ADHD children rated as improved or normalized, and actual classroom academic assignments completed correctly, with only 53% of ADHD children improved or normalized. Their findings also illustrate the importance of selecting relevant outcome

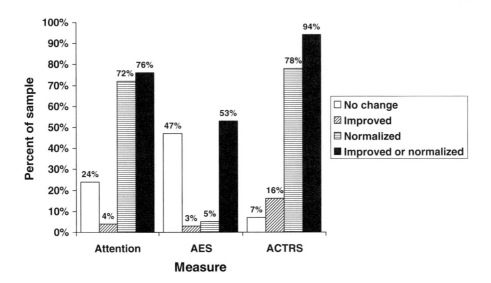

Figure 13.2 Clinical status of the group (*n* = 76) collapsed across methylphenidate dose conditions for three classroom measures. AES = Academic Efficiency Score; ACTRS = Abbreviated Conners Teacher Rating Scale. *Source:* "Attention Deficit Disorder and Methylphenidate: Normalization Rates, Clinical Effectiveness, and Response Prediction in 76 Children," by M. D. Rapport, C. Denney, G. J. DuPaul, and M. J. Gardner, 1994, *Journal of the American Academy of Child and Adolescent Psychiatry, 33*(6), pp. 882–893. Reprinted with permission.

measures. Teachers rated 94% of ADHD children as improving significantly when taking medication. When looking at their schoolwork, however, only 53% made actual improvements compared to their pretreatment performance. In most situations, when relevant outcome measures are used, statistical significance will be a necessary but not sufficient condition for clinical significance. Likewise, large effects may be more likely to be clinically significant effects. The presence of one or both of these conditions, however, does not demonstrate clinical significance.

In summary, clinical significance testing operates at the individual rather than group level. Beyond statistically reliable group differences, it is interested in the practical effects of an intervention—whether treatment makes a noticeable difference in the day-to-day lives of the clients we serve. Clinical significance can be defined subjectively by asking children about changes in their behavior, socially by comparing impact measures (e.g., school absences or test scores), or statistically using absolute and normative comparisons.

RESEARCH METHODS

Research *methodology* refers to the principles, practices, and procedures that direct research, whereas research *design* refers to the organized plan used to examine questions of interest. Both aspects represent important knowledge that guide the planning, implementation, and analysis of a research project.

Selection of Measures

Relationship between and among Variables

Selection of measures will depend on your specific research question as well as the level of understanding you wish to accomplish with respect to the phenomenon studied. For example, research may focus on examining *correlates,* or relationships between or among variables without consideration of time sequence or causality. Other studies may focus on identifying *risk factors,* or characteristics that precede and increase the likelihood of some event, outcome, or behavior pattern that may be modifiable. *Marker variables*—characteristics that precede and increase the likelihood of some event or behavior, but are not modifiable or have no effect on the outcome if modified—may be the focus of other investigations. Other measures will be more appropriate for questions concerning *treatment outcome* or *prevention* in children (for a detailed discussion, see Kazdin, 1999). Establishing causal factors, wherein one variable precedes and influences some other variable, represents the purest form of research if one embraces prediction of human behavior as the sine qua non of research.

Studying variables (*moderators*) that influence the direction, magnitude, and nature of a relationship between or among variables represents important avenues for clinical research, particularly when *protective factors* (a special case of moderator variables) can be identified that reduce the likelihood of an undesirable outcome. Researchers examine moderator variables when they suspect that the relationship among variables may differ because of the influence of some other variable. For example, if the relationship between type of aggressive behavior and a diagnosis of

Conduct Disorder is different for boys and girls, sex may be considered a moderator variable. Several moderating variables may be important to examine in research with children, including age, sex, ethnicity, height, weight, and motivation.

Once a causal relationship is established in the literature, researchers may wish to focus on explaining the process or mechanism by which the process evolves (*mediator variables* such as psychological or biological mechanisms). In this situation, a previously unconsidered variable is hypothesized to intercede between two related variables and reflects an indirect effect of one variable on another. For example, Rapport, Scanlan, and Denney (1999) found that the relationship between children's early attention problems and later scholastic achievement was mediated by differences in working memory.

In summary, a correlational relationship represents the most basic level of understanding between or among variables. A deeper level of understanding is achieved if it can be determined that one or more variables preceded the occurrence of other variables in time. To establish a causal linkage, investigators must provide evidence of a correlation and ordered temporal relationship between or among variables, complemented by three additional considerations: Other influences must be ruled out as possible explanations for the findings; the findings must be replicable across different samples from the same population; and a valid explanation concerning the mechanisms and processes through which the causal variables operate and are related to outcome variables must be explicated.

Types of Dependent Measures

The foregoing summary suggests that researchers need to consider the level of understanding they wish to achieve with respect to their research topic before selecting particular measures. Selection of measures will depend on a host of factors (e.g., availability of instruments or instrumentation, time constraints, costs) and can include a wide range of instruments and techniques. Popular exemplars include self-report inventories, behavior rating scales completed by others, and physiological instrumentation. Consultation of specialty texts on child assessment is advised for those interested in reviewing the broad range of instruments and techniques available (e.g., see Mash & Terdal, 1997; Hersen, 2006; and current volume).

Innovative measures can be created to assess discrete incidences (e.g., stereotypic movement, drooling) or categories of behavior (e.g., bizarre speech) but must meet expected standards of psychometric rigor (e.g., interrater reliability, validity). Computerized assessment is commonly used to assess important constructs such as vigilance (e.g., continuous performance tasks) and behavioral inhibition (e.g., stop-signal paradigm) in children. Incorporating current or archival indices of target behaviors or latent constructs reflects an additional method of data collection available to child researchers. For example, Fergusson and Horwood (1995) used arrest records as an index of later delinquency in children with early conduct problems and ADHD. Duration of hospital stay, school attendance, earned grades, completed academic assignments, and retention rates are other common examples of measures with high face validity used by researchers.

As a general rule of thumb, try to incorporate multiple indices of behavior that have strong psychometric properties. That is, select instruments, indices, or observations that provide valid and reliable measures of both the specific behaviors of interest as well as other potentially related areas of functioning. Doing so demonstrates that identified behavior problems or changes in behavior are not confined to a particular type of instrument or recording procedure and permits measurement of corresponding improvement in other domains related to the child's functioning. For example, designing a treatment outcome study to improve a child's academic performance in the classroom may result in corresponding improvement in the child's attention and classroom behavior. In such cases, teacher rating scales coupled with direct observational recording procedures that measure domains other than just academic performance are needed to document the broader spectrum of treatment gains related to the independent variable. Including collateral measures that reflect areas not expected to change (unless the researcher is expecting a generalized treatment effect) or undesirable change is necessary in some research protocols. The former provides evidence for discriminate validity (e.g., only the targeted area changes with the introduction of the independent variable), whereas the latter addresses the possibility of emergent symptoms or undesirable change due to the intervention.

Studies of specific clinical groups (e.g., ADHD, childhood depression), learning problems (e.g., academic deficits), or maladaptive behavior (e.g., peer aggression) may require measures different from those used to evaluate change due to intervention. For example, structured or semi-structured clinical interviews complemented by specific rating scales are traditionally used to define, classify, or describe children with a particular clinical disorder (i.e., serve as grouping variables), whereas other instruments, observations, or ratings may be used to measure change associated with intervention (i.e., serve as dependent variables). Therapy effects are strongest for outcome measures that match the problems targeted in treatment rather than through nonspecific or artifactual effects (Weisz, Weiss, Han, Granger, & Morton, 1995).

RESEARCH DESIGNS

Single-Subject Research Designs

Single-case research designs are valuable methodological tools used to evaluate different types of research questions involving individuals and groups. Consider some of the important scientific discoveries in psychology over the years. Single-case research was the principal paradigm in Wundt's (1832 to 1920) investigations of sensation and perception, Ebbinghaus's (1850 to 1909) studies of human memory, Pavlov's (1849 to 1936) classic experiments in respondent conditioning, and B. F. Skinner's (1904 to 1990) research in operant conditioning. These designs are particularly relevant to understanding children and the environments in which they live, where changes in everyday life may be of greater importance than obtaining a statistically significant change between groups (i.e., greater clinical relevance). Experimentation at the level of the individual case study may also provide greater insights with respect to understanding therapeutic change.

In contrast to the heavy reliance on established psychometric techniques and instruments required by between-group research, single-case methodology begins with identifying the focus of investigation (i.e., designating target behaviors) and proceeds to selecting potential strategies of assessment. When deciding on target behaviors, try to select observable behaviors and environment events as opposed to covert behaviors such as thoughts and ideas or hypothetical constructs such as anxiety and self-concept. Doing so will facilitate objective measurement and agreement between observers. Definitions should be written with absolute clarity to avoid ambiguity, and the boundaries of the defined target behavior must be clearly specified to minimize inference concerning whether a particular behavior qualifies as an occurrence or a nonoccurrence. On the surface, this may appear to be an easy task, but consider selecting classroom attentiveness ("on-task" in educational parlance) as a target behavior. Should off-task or inattentive behavior be recorded if a child is gazing up at the ceiling while working on a math assignment? Perhaps the child was thinking about the problem at hand or performing mental arithmetic. Are children permitted to ask peers for assistance when working on a problem, or allowed to leave their seat to sharpen a pencil during an academic work period? Does a momentary glance away from one's work count as off-task behavior? These and other definitional parameters must be decided and agreed upon, and preferably subjected to extensive pilot testing, prior to beginning formal observation and data collection. Once established, clear definitions of target behaviors will permit the recording of reliable baseline data and, in turn, serve as the traditional yardstick by which change is measured.

Assessing Behavior

Assessment of behavior can be accomplished in many different ways and will depend on what is being assessed and which method of recording best suits the needs of the researcher. The most commonly used methods of assessment include using frequency measures, classifying responses into discrete categories, counting the number of children or events, and measuring behavior based on discrete units of time.

Frequency counts are used when dealing with discrete behaviors that require a relatively constant time interval to perform. The first criterion enables observers to know when a designated behavior begins and ends, whereas the second permits recorded behavior to be treated as similar units for purposes of comparison. Consider the situation in which a researcher records the frequency with which a child speaks out of turn in a classroom. The child may blurt out an answer on one occasion and on another may turn and talk with a peer for 10 minutes or longer. Clearly, the two incidents are not comparable, and an alternative assessment method such as time interval recording should be considered. For situations in which frequency measures are taken for different periods of time (e.g., 20 minutes on day 1 and 40 minutes on day 2), calculate the frequency per minute or response rate by dividing the frequency of responses by the number of minutes observed each day. This metric, frequency per minute or response rate, will yield data that are comparable for different durations of observation.

Discrete categorization is used in situations in which behavior is best defined by categorical assignment. Commonly used categories include appropriate–not appropriate (e.g., social interactions between children), complete–not complete (e.g., classroom assignments), and discrete behaviors that form a functional (e.g., getting dressed in the morning, wherein each article of clothing counts as a discrete behavior) or correlated but unrelated (e.g., performing household chores) response chain.

Counting children is often used to assess the effectiveness of an intervention program. Examples include counting the number of children who perform a designated target behavior while on a school field trip, or calculating the percentage of children who complete their daily academic assignments in a classroom each morning. Contingencies can be introduced subsequently to reinforce daily academic assignment completion rates, for example, by scheduling in-class free time if at least 80% of the class meets the established criterion or for children who independently complete the assigned work.

Interval recording is used in situations in which the researcher wishes to obtain a representative sample of a target behavior during particular times of the day. Common examples of appropriate child behaviors include staying in one's seat during an academic work period, appropriate talk with peers, and paying attention. A block of time (e.g., a 30-minute daily or every other day observation period) is divided into a series of shorter intervals (e.g., 15-second observation blocks followed by 5-second recording blocks), and the target behavior is recorded as occurring or not occurring during each 15-second observation interval. This example would yield three observation blocks per minute and 90 intervals of recorded behavior per day. Variations of the interval recording method are common (e.g., time sampling) and might involve brief observations of a target behavior throughout the day rather than being confined to a single block of time.

Recording *duration* is another time-based method for observing behavior and is more appropriate for recording behaviors that are continuous rather than discrete acts. Common examples include observing ongoing social interactions between or among children or the total time required to complete an academic assignment. In these cases, the total duration or time interval that the behavior is performed serves as the dependent variable. An interesting but infrequently used variation of the duration method involves recording elapsed time before a particular behavior is performed (i.e., response latency). An example is to record how long a child takes to perform a particular behavior or chain of behaviors following adult instruction. Contingencies might be established subsequently based on the child's compliance within an increasingly shorter time interval over several days or weeks.

Design Types

The essence of single-subject research lies in its ability to demonstrate experimental control of an independent variable (IV) over one or more dependent variables (DV) by means of shrewd design and graphical illustration. Although statistical procedures exist that can be used to assess outcome effects associated with single-subject case studies, the more traditional means of demonstrating experimental control is to provide a compelling visual (graphical) illustration that even a Doubting Thomas would acknowledge as evidence. To convince the scientific audience, an IV is introduced using a variety of design options such that its effects on the DV are systematically produced, reproduced, and/or eliminated, as in a carefully choreographed dance. Detailed descriptions of specific types of single-subject designs are provided in this volume (see Chapter 11).

Group Experimental Designs

Overview

Despite the numerous benefits associated with single-subject design methodology, the fact remains that an overwhelming majority of studies in psychology involve the comparison of groups, not individuals. Group designs are conventionally classified as true experimental designs, quasi-experimental designs, and observational designs, and may be used in a variety of contexts.

A true experimental design is a design in which the researcher manipulates one or more independent variables and measures one or more dependent variables. The researcher chooses what independent variables to manipulate, how they are manipulated (e.g., which levels to include), and what dependent variables to measure, based on the nature of the research question. For example, a researcher might be interested in determining what type of therapy works best for children with school phobia. Therefore, the research question has determined that the independent variable is *type of therapy* and the dependent variable is *school phobia*. Now, the researcher must decide whether any other independent or dependent variables should be included in the study and operationally define the independent variable(s) and the dependent variable(s).

Operationally defining independent variables refers to deciding what the levels should consist of, whereas operationally defining dependent variables refers to deciding exactly how to measure them. For example, the researcher needs to decide what levels of therapy to include (e.g., behavior therapy, cognitive therapy, cognitive-behavior therapy), whether or not to include a control group (condition), and how to measure school phobia. In the context of a between-subject design, a control group is a randomly assigned group that receives either no experimental treatment or a substitute for the experimental treatment. In the context of a within-subject design, a control condition is a condition (administered to all participants) in which either no experimental treatment or a substitute for the experimental treatment is administered. Control conditions (groups) are sometimes needed to control for nonspecific treatment effects (e.g., some children might believe that simply taking a pill helps because it's "medicine").

A quasi-experimental design is a design that is set up to emulate a true experimental design but includes one or more independent variables that cannot be manipulated by the researcher (often referred to as quasi-independent variables). These include variables such as sex, ethnicity, height, and weight, or clinical diagnoses such as ADHD or Reading Disorder. Another reason for the inability to manipulate certain variables may be due to ethical reasons such as substance abuse, smoking, exposure to harmful toxins, and cancer. The limitation to quasi-experimental designs is the inability to express a causal relationship for quasi-independent variables.

Nonspecific Treatment Effects

Nonspecific treatment effects are any effects brought about by the experiment besides the treatment, such as being aware of what the experiment is about, contact with the experimenter, and discussing the experiment with other people. Nonspecific treatment effects are basically extraneous (nuisance) variables related to participants' perceptions concerning the experiment. Related to nonspecific treatment effects are placebo effects, in which participants improve simply because they believe that they are receiving treatment. If a control condition (group) is included, it is important that there are no other differences between the control condition and the experimental conditions except for an absence or substitute for the experimental treatment. Any other differences would introduce extraneous (nuisance) variables. Control conditions are necessary only when there is concern that nonspecific treatment effects may have an effect on the results. Nonspecific treatment effects are possible only if the participants' perceptions about the experiment can have an effect on the results. There are many situations in which participants' perceptions cannot have an effect on the results. For example, if a researcher is interested in studying what type of teaching method works best for teaching mathematics to third-grade children, a control condition consisting of teaching no mathematics would be benighted. Conversely, a child with social phobia may believe that taking a pill provides him with the necessary confidence to complete an in vivo exposure protocol.

There are three main classes of experimental designs: the between-subject design, the within-subject design, and the mixed-subject design, each with multiple variations possible.

Between-Subject Designs

The between-subject design is a design in which participants are randomly assigned to different treatment groups (levels of the independent variable) and each treatment group receives a different experimental condition. For example, in a single-factor experiment (an experiment with only one IV) examining two methods for teaching science to third-grade children (Technique 1 and Technique 2), half of the students would be randomly assigned to receive Technique 1 and half to receive Technique 2.

In a factorial experiment—an experiment with more than one independent variable—examining different methods for teaching science to third-grade children (Technique 1 and Technique 2) and the mode of presentation (teacher versus computer), one fourth of the students would be randomly assigned to receive Technique 1 via computer, one fourth to receive Technique 1 via teacher, one fourth to receive Technique 2 via computer, and one fourth to receive Technique 2 via teacher.

Advantages of the between-subject design as compared to the within-subject design include no carryover effects and no order or sequence effects. Disadvantages of the between-subject design include the fact that many more participants are required than for the within-subject design, and the between-subject design yields less power than the within-subject design.

Ideally, there are an equal number of participants in each of the different treatment groups and assignment to the different treatment groups is random. Random assignment to treatment conditions simply means that each participant has an equal probability of being assigned to any given treatment group. Both ideals, equal number of participants per treatment group and random assignment to treatment groups, may not be possible for a given study. In the case of an equal number of participants per treatment group, the total number of participants may not be equally divisible among the various treatment groups or some participants may drop out of the study or miss the day that data are collected. In the case of random assignment of participants to the different treatment groups, this may not be possible. As in the example concerning methods of teaching science, it might be difficult to randomly assign half of each class to receive a different teaching method. The teacher cannot very well teach half of her class at a time, and even if he or she could, this would introduce the confound of which method is taught first. Both problems (unequal sample size and nonrandom assignment) can frequently be handled statistically. It is important, however, to take into account both unequal sample size and nonrandom assignment when analyzing data (i.e., one should not ignore them and analyze the data as if there were equal sample size and random assignment).

Another important issue is the loss of participants from the experiment, referred to as *attrition*. If the loss of participants is random (e.g., roughly an equal number of participants dropped out of each of the experimental groups), there is no problem and certain statistical techniques may be used to correct the situation. If, however, the loss of participants is not random but due to some aspect of particular treatment conditions (e.g., almost every participant who dropped out was in one particular treatment condition), then little can be done to salvage the experiment other than conducting a post-hoc test to determine whether attrition significantly biased one group relative to the other. For example, one may need to demonstrate that children with the most deviant scores did not drop out of one of the two groups receiving treatment, or that noncompleters were not significantly different on particular measures relative to completers.

As an additional note, the problems associated with randomly assigning some children within a given classroom to receive one level of the independent variable (treatment) and other children from the same classroom to receive other levels of the independent variable is not uncommon to research conducted in school settings (or even clinic or hospital settings). For example, it may not be possible for the teacher to teach some students using one teaching method and the other students using different teaching methods. When it is not possible to randomly assign children from the same class to different levels of the independent variable, an alternative is to randomly assign different classrooms to the different levels of the independent variable. This type of design is called a *hierarchical design* and requires special analysis. In a hierarchical design, the levels of at least one independent variable are nested under the levels of another independent variable, and the remaining independent variables are fully crossed. For example, if each level of IV 2 (e.g.,

Table 13.4   Hierarchical Design

	Technique 1		Technique 2
Classroom 1 Classroom 2		Classroom 3 Classroom 4	

classrooms) appears with only one level of IV 1 (e.g., teaching method), then IV 2 (classrooms) is said to be nested under IV 1 (teaching method). Examining two different methods for teaching science to third-grade children, two third-grade classes could be randomly assigned to receive Technique 1 and two third-grade classes could be randomly assigned to receive Technique 2. The design for this model is diagramed in Table 13.4.

The separate columns for Technique 1 and Technique 2 indicate that the model is not fully crossed, as classrooms (1, 2, 3, 4) are nested under techniques (1, 2). In this experiment, the independent variable *classroom* (classrooms 1, 2, 3, 4) is an extraneous (nuisance) variable. It is included in the design and analysis because it might have an effect on the dependent variable, and including it allows its effects to be isolated. If a hierarchical design is used, it is incorrect to analyze the data as if students were randomly assigned to each level of the independent variable (e.g., teaching method). There are additional complications that may arise when employing a hierarchical design, for example, when the levels of the nested variable (classroom) cannot be randomly assigned to the levels of the variable it is nested under (teaching method). Hierarchical designs are considered balanced if they satisfy two criteria. First, there must be an equal number of participants in each treatment combination (e.g., students in each class for each teaching method). Second, there must be an equal number of levels of the nested variable under each level of the other independent variable (e.g., two classes under each level of treatment method). If these criteria are not satisfied, the model is considered unbalanced and more complicated to analyze than balanced designs.

Within-Subject Designs

Every participant receives every treatment condition (levels of the independent variables) in a within-subject design. In the single-factor experiment on teaching techniques, every participant would receive Technique A and Technique B. In the factorial experiment involving teaching technique and mode of presentation, every participant would receive Technique A via computer, Technique A via teacher, Technique B via computer, and Technique B via teacher. A within-subject design may have children participating in the different levels of the independent variable simultaneously, or children may complete one level of the independent variable before participating in the next level. When participants must complete one level of the independent variable before participating in the next level, this is commonly referred to as a *crossover design.*

Within-subject designs present some special problems, including carryover effects, order effects, and sequence effects. Because participants receive every treatment condition, the effects of one treatment condition may carry over to the next treatment condition. For example, once children are exposed to a particular reading method, they may be irreversibly changed. The investigator cannot simply cross them over into an alternative method and assume that nothing has been gained during the earlier experience. The order in which the treatment conditions are presented to the participants may also have an effect on the results. Finally, the sequence in which the treatment conditions are presented may have an effect. For example, in a study of perceived heaviness of objects, whether someone lifted a 10 pound object and then a 20 pound object or lifted a 20 pound object and then a 10 pound object would have an effect on the perceived heaviness of each object. Order and sequence effects may sound similar; however, order effects refer to the ordinal position in which the condition is presented in (e.g., first, second, third). Sequence effects, in contrast, have to do with which treatment follows which other treatment. As an example, consider the two sequences A—B—C and C—B—A. In both sequences, B has the same ordinal position (second). However, in the first case B follows A and in the second case B follows C; therefore, the sequence is different. Counterbalancing procedures are frequently used to control for problems related to carryover effects, order effects, and sequence effects.

Counterbalancing means that participants are exposed to the different treatment conditions in different orders. Ideally, one or more participants could be exposed to every possible order of treatment conditions. This is not possible with more than a few treatment conditions, as the number of possible orders increases rapidly (number of possible orders equals $n!$, such that three treatment conditions produces six possible orders: $3 \times 2 \times 1$). When the number of possible orders is too great, only a subset may be used. One method of obtaining a subset of the possible orders of treatment conditions is to simply randomly select a subset of the possible orders. This may pose a problem, however, because if the order or the sequence of treatment conditions has an effect on the dependent variable, random selection of treatment orders will not control for these effects.

Another method that not only controls for the order effect of treatment conditions but also allows for the order effect to be analyzed separately is the Latin square design. The Latin square design has as many orders represented as there are treatment conditions. Therefore, if there are four treatment conditions (Rx = treatment), four orders (indicated by uppercase letters A, B, C, D) would be represented as depicted in Table 13.5. Next, a random selection procedure is invoked to determine which of the four treatments corresponds to which letter (i.e., the order treatments will be administered). For example, if it was randomly determined that A = Treatment 3, B = Treatment 1, C = Treatment 4, and D = Treatment 2, then the matrix is designed as in Table 13.5.

Table 13.5 Simple Latin Square Design

A = Rx 3	B = Rx 1	C = Rx 4	D = Rx 2
B = Rx 1	C = Rx 4	D = Rx 2	A = Rx 3
C = Rx 4	D = Rx 2	A = Rx 3	B = Rx 1
D = Rx 2	A = Rx 3	B = Rx 1	C = Rx 4

Table 13.6   Balanced Latin Square Design

A = Rx 3	B = Rx 1	C = Rx 4	D = Rx 2
B = Rx 1	D = Rx 2	A = Rx 3	C = Rx 4
C = Rx 4	A = Rx 3	D = Rx 2	B = Rx 1
D = Rx 2	C = Rx 4	B = Rx 1	A = Rx 3

The Latin square design ensures that every treatment condition appears in every possible order (first, second, third, etc.). Therefore, if the order in which participants experience the different treatment conditions has an effect on the dependent variable, the Latin square design will cancel out that effect. The Latin square design also allows for the comparison of the different treatment orders (by including order as another independent variable) to determine whether there is a significant difference between the different orders. As mentioned earlier, in some situations both *order* and *sequence* may have an effect on the dependent variables. The balanced Latin square design controls for the effects of order and sequence effects and allows these differences to be compared. It ensures that treatment condition appears in every possible order (first, second, third, etc.) and that each treatment condition is preceded and followed by every other treatment condition exactly once (e.g., Rx 1 is preceded once by Rx 2, Rx 3, and Rx 4), as depicted in Table 13.6.

As a result, if order or sequence of treatment conditions affects the dependent variable, the balanced Latin square design will cancel out these effects. This design also allows for the comparison of the different treatment orders and sequences (taken together, not separately) to determine whether there is a significant difference between them. In Table 13.6, the rows indicate the order in which treatments will be assigned, and the columns indicate the sequence in which treatments will be received. As in the simple Latin square design, a random selection procedure is invoked to determine which treatment is assigned to which letter.

Mixed-Subject Designs

The mixed-subject design is a design in which one or more independent variables are between-subject variables (e.g., different participants randomly assigned to different levels of the independent variables) and one or more independent variables are within-subject variables (e.g., all participants receive all levels of the independent variables). For example, in the experiment involving teaching technique and mode of presentation, every participant would receive Technique A and Technique B (teaching technique is a within-subject variable), and half of the subjects would be taught by a computer and half would be taught by a teacher (mode of presentation is a between-subject variable). All of the issues discussed concerning between-subject designs and within-subject designs apply to mixed-subject designs.

Extraneous Variables

A major advantage of true experimental designs is that they are the only method that allow causal relationships among variables to be proven, which includes ruling out outside or extraneous influences. Thus, it is important to use a design in which nothing else differs between the experimental groups except for the experimental conditions (levels of the independent variable). Any other differences besides the treatment conditions (called extraneous or nuisance variables) can call into question the causal inference.

Extraneous variables can sometimes affect all treatment conditions equally, either weakening or strengthening their effects. For example, in the study comparing teaching technique and mode of presentation for schoolchildren, if the treatment conditions were administered immediately following recess, it is possible that participants would be too wound up to pay attention, thus weakening the effects of all of the treatment conditions. When an extraneous variable varies systematically with the different treatment conditions, it is referred to as a *confounding variable* and poses an even greater danger to the interpretation of the results. When a confounding variable is present, any changes in the dependent variable cannot be attributed to the treatment condition with absolute certainty. Using our teacher study example, if everyone receiving Technique A via teacher had one teacher and everyone receiving Technique B via teacher had a different teacher, it could not be determined whether the different technique or the different teacher was responsible for any differences found in the dependent variable. Thus, it is important to keep everything constrained equally across the different treatment levels except for the treatment itself. This is not always possible, especially when conducting research in school and clinic settings. It does not necessarily invalidate the study to have extraneous or confounding variables present; however, it does limit the degree of causality that you can attribute to your treatment conditions.

Correlational Designs

In observational designs, the researcher simply measures variables as they occur naturally in the environment, which limits the degree to which causality can be inferred. Many observational studies, however, are conducted to examine whether a relationship exists between two or more variables or to predict certain variables (criterion variables) from other variables (predictor variables). Observing behavior and recording predictor and criterion variables is another method used in observational studies. For example, a researcher could observe children in the classroom and record the number of times they raise their hands to answer questions and the frequency of praise they receive from the teacher. Alternatively, observational studies may rely on self-report methods such as teacher or parent questionnaires that measure the variables of interest. Observational studies may also be conducted by obtaining ratings about children by people who know them, such as parents, teachers, or peers, or use combinations of these techniques.

Longitudinal and Cross-Sectional Designs

Overview

Longitudinal designs involve measuring participants repeatedly over an extended period of time, perhaps years or even decades. Cross-sectional designs and longitudinal designs are ways of obtaining different types of information. Cross-sectional designs are best used for answering questions concerning how a treatment works at one point in time. Longitudinal designs are best used for answering questions concerning developmental change. For this reason, they can be especially informative when studying children because of their rapid developmental changes. Cross-sectional designs may be set up to assess different age groups simultaneously (e.g., children at ages 2, 6, 10, 14, 18), which would answer questions concerning possible age differences. However, it is possible that differences may exist between children of different age groups at a single point in time because they have different histories (cohort effects). Therefore, the children who are 2 years of age at the same point in time as other children who are 14 years of age might not display the same characteristics when they become 14 years of age. Longitudinal designs involve examining the long-term effects of some event or intervention. An additional advantage to longitudinal designs is that because information is collected with measures repeated at multiple time periods, error variance is reduced, often allowing for the detection of small behavior changes. Additionally, participants are compared to themselves at different points in time.

Potential Limitations

Disadvantages of longitudinal designs are mostly tied to the length of time required and the inherent cost associated with the study. Because the data are collected over long time periods, procedures and measures may become outdated and new procedures and measures may be developed. This leads to a major quandary: Should the outdated procedures and/or measures be continued so that differences may be compared across time, or should the new procedures and/or measures be adopted because they are better? One possible solution is to continue using the old procedures and/or measures to ensure accurate comparison and to adopt new procedures and/or measures as they are developed. Participant attrition is also a major problem with longitudinal designs because it is quite possible that the group that remains at the end of the study is not representative of those who dropped out along the way. Additionally, participant attrition increases the probability of a Type II error (failing to find a treatment effect when one exists) and decreases the generality of the results. Another problem is the potential confound between the effects of personal age and the effects of historical period (e.g., children growing up during a particular decade may be exposed to environmental or other events such as war that younger cohorts are not exposed to).

PARTICIPANT DEMOGRAPHICS AND SAMPLING

Identifying a Population of Interest

After formulating a research question and establishing a basic design, the next step is to consider how best to define and describe the population of interest. Review recent articles in credible journals to gain an understanding of how others have accomplished this task. For example, most research studies dealing with children contain basic sociodemographic information, such as children's age and grade (mean and *SD*), estimated level of intelligence, family socioeconomic status, sex, and ethnicity.

This information is included for other participants (e.g., parents) when relevant to the study (e.g., when studying parental attitudes toward medication compliance in children).

Detailed information is also included relevant to identifying, categorizing, or describing the population of interest. This may involve (a) a clear description of how a diagnosis is ascertained (e.g., using structured or semi-structured clinical interviews combined with using rating scale cutoff scores), (b) how a group is identified (e.g., a learning disability discrepancy formula), or (c) describing the characteristics of a select group of children (e.g., children attending a special education classroom). The use of diagnostic monikers (e.g., ADHD, Social Phobia) for identifying research samples is conventionally based on instruments with acceptable psychometric properties. This approach usually entails the administration of a structured or semi-structured clinical interview coupled with parent and teacher rating scales. Inclusion criteria for a particular diagnostic group is typically based on meeting *DSM-IV* criteria for the disorder in addition to exceeding an identified cutoff score, such as 2 standard deviations above the mean or the scale's identified range for clinical diagnosis. Exclusion criteria vary according to the research question posed. For example, a researcher studying children with learning disabilities may wish to exclude children with ADHD to determine how well an innovative intervention works with reading disabled children independent of ADHD. Conversely, a different research team investigating whether working memory deficits are unique to language-impaired children as opposed to a more generalized deficiency associated with psychiatric disability (e.g., common to many childhood disorders) may wish to include children with and without comorbid ADHD.

Alternative methods for identifying research samples are available, depending on the nature of the investigation. For example, children with poorly developed social skills who do not meet diagnostic criteria for a clinical disorder may nevertheless benefit from a social skills training program. Specific measures of social skill deficits, such as parent-teacher ratings and even direct observations, can be used if they reliably identify the sample.

Sampling

As a general guideline, researchers must sufficiently describe characteristics of their sample that might affect the generalizability of findings as discussed earlier and determine how best to obtain the research sample from the targeted population. This is particularly important for group designs but also applies to single-subject designs.

There are two classes of samples, *probability* and *nonprobability* samples. Probability samples are samples in which every member of the population has a known probability of being selected for inclusion, whereas nonprobability samples are samples in which the probability of being selected for inclusion is unknown.

Four well-known types of probability samples are *simple random samples, stratified random samples, systematic samples,* and *cluster samples.* A simple random sample is one in which every member of the population has an equal probability of being selected, whereas a stratified random sample is a random sample in which the proportion of certain characteristics in the population (e.g., race, ethnicity, culture, sex, age, education, income, SES) are matched in the sample. For example, if sex is considered important to a study and the population under study consists of 58% boys and 42% girls, the sample reflects these same proportions. Samples may also be stratified on several different characteristics simultaneously. For the sample to be a stratified random sample, sampling would be random within each characteristic considered important to the study.

A systematic sample is a sample selected in a nonrandom fashion. For example, if 10% of the child population is to be included in the sample, then every 10th child would be chosen for inclusion.

A cluster sample is a sample in which clusters (groups) are randomly selected rather than individuals. For example, if researchers are interested in sampling grade school children, they would start with a list of grade schools and randomly select which schools to include. Within each school, you could include all of the students, randomly select students for inclusion, or randomly select additional clusters (e.g., grade levels).

The most commonly used types of nonprobability samples include the *convenience sample,* the *stratified convenience sample,* and the *snowball sample*. A convenience sample is a sample of participants that is convenient for the researcher to obtain (e.g., college undergraduates, hospital patients, child referrals to a university-based specialty clinic). A stratified convenience sample is the same as a stratified random sample, except that the participants are selected for convenience rather than randomly. A snowball sample is a sample that is created by having the initial participants (e.g., children's parents) suggest additional possible participants; these additional participants suggest additional possible participants, and so on. Because researchers do not typically have access to the entire population they wish to study, most studies use nonprobability samples.

Sample Size and Power

An important issue concerning samples is determining how many participants should be included. The main issue concerning sample size is that you want to recruit a sufficient number of participants to have a powerful test, but not more than you need, as this can be costly and time consuming. *Power* refers to the probability of finding a significant treatment effect when one truly exists (probability of rejecting a false null hypothesis). Power can be increased by setting alpha equal to 0.05 rather than 0.01, increasing the size of the treatment effect (increasing the between-condition or group variation), or reducing the error (reducing the within-condition or group variation). One method of reducing the within-condition variation (error) is to increase the number of participants. As sample size increases, within-group variation (error) decreases.

Convention generally holds that .80 is the minimum acceptable level of power. This means that if there truly is a treatment effect, your statistical test has an 80% probability of finding that treatment effect (rejecting the null hypothesis). Before you conduct an experiment, you should do a power analysis to determine how many subjects are needed to achieve (at least) 80% power. Conducting a power analysis requires the researcher to make several educated guesses concerning the data (e.g., size of treatment effect and the population standard deviation). Specialty texts (see Cohen, 1988) and software (GPower: www.psycho.uni-duesseldorf.de/abteilungen/aap/gpower3/) for computing a power analysis are readily available. Researchers recognize that a certain degree of controversy exists concerning hypothesis testing, because with a large enough sample, even trivial treatment effects may be statistically significant. For this reason, researchers should specify the minimum interesting treatment effect (i.e., the minimum effect that would be of interest) to be found with 80% power before conducting a power analysis.

SUMMARY

Conducting research with children is a multifaceted enterprise that requires broad knowledge of research methods, research design, psychometric theory, statistics, and child development, coupled with a healthy dose of curiosity and tenacity. Textbooks and coursework are useful resources for novice researchers, but there is no substitution for working in an active research laboratory under the guidance of an accomplished mentor.

REFERENCES

Achenbach, T. M., McConaughy, S. H., & Howell, C. T. (1987). Child/adolescent behavioural and emotional problems: Implications of cross-informant correlations for situational specificity. *Psychological Bulletin, 101*(2), 213–232.

Angold, A., & Costello, E. J. (2000). The Child and Adolescent Psychiatric Assessment (CAPA). *Journal of the American Academy of Child and Adolescent Psychiatry, 39*(1), 39–48.

Burns, L. G., & Haynes, S. N. (2006). Clinical psychology: Construct validation with multiple sources of information and multiple settings. In M. Eid & E. S Diener (Eds.), *Handbook of multimethod measurement in psychology* (pp. 401–418). Washington, DC: American Psychological Association.

Campbell, S. B. (1990). *Behavioral problems in preschoolers: Clinical and developmental issues.* New York: Guilford Press.

Chambless, D. L., & Hollon, S. D. (1998). Defining empirically supported therapies. *Journal of Consulting and Clinical Psychology, 66*(1), 7–18.

Cohen, J. (1988). *Statistical power analysis for the behavioral sciences* (2nd ed.). New York: Erlbaum.

Dishion, T. J., & Patterson, G. R. (2006). The development and ecology of antisocial behavior in children and adolescents. In D. Cicchetti & D. J. Cohen (Eds.), *Developmental psychopathology: Vol. 3. Risk, disorder, and adaptation* (2nd ed., pp. 503–431). Hoboken, NJ: Wiley.

Duhig, A. M., Renk, K., Epstein, M. K. & Phares, V. (2000). Interparental agreement on internalizing, externalizing, and total behavior problems: A meta-analysis. *Clinical Psychology: Science and Practice, 7*(4), 435–453.

Fergusson, D. M., & Horwood, L. J. (1995). Early disruptive behavior, IQ, and later school achievement and delinquent behavior. *Journal of Abnormal Child Psychology, 23*(2), 183–199.

Filipek, P. A., Accardo, P. J., & Baranek, G. T. (1999). The screening and diagnosis of autistic spectrum disorders. *Journal of Autism and Developmental Disorders, 29*(6), 439–484.

Harris, F. C., & Lahey, B. B. (1982). Recording system bias in direct observational methodology: A review of critical analysis of factors causing inaccurate coding behavior. *Clinical Psychological Review, 2*(4), 539–556.

Haviland-Jones, J., Gebelt, J. L., & Stapley, J. C. (1997). The questions of development in emotion. In P. Salovey & D. J. Sluyter (Eds.), *Emotional development and emotional intelligence: Educational implications* (pp. 233–256). New York: Basic Books.

Hedges, L. V. (1982). Estimation of effect size from a series of independent experiments. *Psychological Bulletin, 92*(2), 490–499.

Hersen, M. (2006). *Clinician's handbook of child behavioral assessment.* San Diego, CA: Academic Press.

Jacobson, N. S., & Truax, P. (1991). Clinical significance: A statistical approach to defining meaningful change in psychotherapy research. *Journal of Consulting and Clinical Psychology, 59*(1), 12–19.

Kazdin, A. E. (1982). *Single-case research designs: Methods for clinical and applied settings.* New York: Oxford University Press.

Kazdin, A. E. (1988). *Clinical psychotherapy: Developing and identifying effective treatments.* New York: Pergamon Press.

Kazdin, A. E. (1999). Current (lack of) status of theory in child and adolescent psychotherapy research. *Journal of Clinical Child Psychology, 28*(4), 533–543.

Kazdin, A. E. (2004). Clinical significance: Measuring whether interventions make a difference. In A. E. Kazdin (Ed.), *Methodological issues and strategies in clinical research* (3rd ed., pp. 691–710). Washington, DC: American Psychological Association.

Kofler, M. J., Rapport, M. D., & Alderson, R. M. (in press). Classroom observation of ADHD and comparison children: A meta-analytic review. *Journal of Child Psychology and Psychiatry.*

Lapouse, R., & Monk, M. A. (1959). Fears and worries in a representative sample of children. *American Journal of Orthopsychiatry, 29,* 803–818.

MacFarlane, J. W., Allen, L., & Honzik, M. P. (1954). *A developmental study of the behavioral problems of normal children between 21 months and 14 years.* Berkeley: University of California Press.

Mash, E. J., & Terdal, L. G. (1997). *Assessment of childhood disorders* (3rd ed.) New York: Guilford Press.

McClellan, J. M., & Werry, J. S. (2000). Research psychiatric diagnostic interviews for children and adolescents. *Journal of the American Academy of Child and Adolescent Psychiatry, 39*(1), 19–27.

Olds, R. S., & Symons, C. W. (1990). Recommendations for obtaining cooperation to conduct school-based research. *Journal of School Health, 60*(3), 96–98.

Ollendick, T. H., & Hersen, M. (1998). *Handbook of child psychopathology* (3rd ed.) New York: Plenum Press.

Orvaschel, H. (2006). Structured and semistructured interviews. In M. S Hersen (Ed.), *Clinician's handbook of child behavioral assessment* (pp. 159-179). San Diego, CA: Academic Press.

Palfrey, J. S., Levine, M. D., Walker, D. K. & Sullivan, M. (1985). The emergence of attention deficits in early childhood: A prospective study. *Behavioral Pediatrics, 6*(6), 339–348.

Pelham, W. E., Fabiano, G. A., & Massetti, G. M. (2005). Evidence-based assessment of attention-deficit/hyperactivity disorder in children and adolescents. *Journal of Clinical Child and Adolescent Psychology, 34*(3), 449–476.

Petosa, R., & Goodman, R. M. (1991). Recruitment and retention of schools participating in school health research. *Journal of School Health, 61*(10), 426–429.

Plake, B. S. Impara, J. C. & Spies, R. A. (Eds.). (2003). *The fifteenth mental measurements yearbook.* Lincoln, NE: Buros Institute of Mental Measurements.

Porrino, L. J., Rapoport, J. L., Behar, D., Sceery, W., Ismond, D. R., & Bunney, W. E. (1983). A naturalistic assessment of the motor activity of hyperactive boys: Pt. I. Comparison with normal controls. *Archives of General Psychiatry, 40*(6), 681–687.

Rapoport, J., Abramson, A., Alexander, D., & Lott, I. (1971). Playroom observations of hyperactive children on medication. *Journal of the American Academy of Child and Adolescent Psychiatry, 10*(3), 524–534.

Rapport, M. D., Chung, K., Shore, G., & Isaacs, P. (2001). A conceptual model of child psychopathology: Implications for understanding attention deficit hyperactivity disorder and treatment efficacy. *Journal of Clinical Child Psychology, 30*(1), 48–58.

Rapport, M. D., Denney, C., DuPaul, G. J., & Gardner, M. J. (1994). Attention deficit disorder and methylphenidate: Normalization rates, clinical effectiveness, and response prediction in 76 children. *Journal of the American Academy of Child and Adolescent Psychiatry, 33*(6), 882–893.

Rapport, M. D., Kofler, M., Alderson, M., & Raiker, J.(in press). Attention-deficit/hyperactivity disorder. In M. Hersen, & D. Reitman (Eds.), *Handbook of psychological assessment, case conceptualization and treatment: Vol. 2 Children and adolescents.* Hoboken, NJ: Wiley.

Rapport, M. D., Scanlan, S. W., & Denney, C. B. (1999). Attention-deficit/hyperactivity disorder and scholastic achievement: A model of dual developmental pathways. *Journal of Child Psychology and Psychiatry, 40*(8), 1169–1183.

Rapport, M. D., Timko, T. M., & Wolfe, R. (2006). Attention-deficit/hyperactivity disorder. In M. Hersen (Ed.), *Clinician's handbook of child behavioral assessment* (pp. 401–435). San Diego, CA: Academic Press.

Reid, J. M., Webster-Stratton, C., & Hammond, M. (2003). Follow-up of children who received the Incredible Years intervention for oppositional-defiant disorder: Maintenance and prediction of 2-year outcome. *Behavior Therapy, 34*(4), 471–491.

Speer, D. C. (1992). Clinically significant change: Jacobson and Truax (1991) revisited. *Journal of Consulting and Clinical Psychology, 60*(3), 402–408.

Stein, B. D., Jayxoc, L. H., & Kataoka, S. H. (2003). A mental health intervention for schoolchildren exposed to violence: A randomized controlled trail. *Journal of the American Medical Association, 290*(5), 603–611.

Stevens, T. M., Kupst, M. J., Suran, B. G., & Schulman, J. L. (1978). Activity level: A comparison between actometer scores and observer ratings. *Journal of Abnormal Child Psychology, 6*(2), 163–173.

Tryon, W. W., & Pinto, L. P. (1994). Comparing activity measurement and ratings. *Behavior Modification, 18*(3), 251–261.

Walker, K. C., & Bracken, B. A. (1996). Inter-parent agreement on four preschool behavior rating scales: Effects of parent and child gender. *Psychology in the Schools, 33*(4), 273–281.

Weisz, J. R., Weiss, B., Han, S. S., Granger, D. A., & Morton, T. (1995). Effects of psychotherapy with children and adolescents revisited: A meta-analysis of treatment outcome studies. *Psychological Bulletin, 117*(3), 450–468.

PART IV
Diagnosis and Evaluation

CHAPTER 14

Assessment, Diagnosis, Nosology, and Taxonomy of Child and Adolescent Psychopathology

Thomas M. Achenbach

This chapter addresses a host of interrelated issues that are especially salient for those who work with children. (For brevity, I use "children" to include "adolescents.") These issues are also becoming increasingly salient for those who work with adults, so much so that they are shaping drafts of the forthcoming fifth edition of the American Psychiatric Association's *Diagnostic and Statistical Manual of Mental Disorders* (*DSM-V*). The issues are organized in terms of four interrelated aspects of what can be understood as continuous processes. These four aspects are assessment, diagnosis, nosology, and taxonomy.

In clinical services, assessment is often viewed as an initial step that then leads to diagnosis. Diagnosis, in turn, is shaped by nosologies (classifications of diseases) that specify the criteria for the disorders to be diagnosed. And taxonomies systematically represent similarities and differences among the phenomena to be distinguished from one another in terms of taxonomic constructs. Assessment data are essential for diagnosis, nosology, and taxonomy. However, the data sought and the procedures for seeking the data are shaped by diagnostic, nosological, and taxonomic concepts and criteria. Figure 14.1 illustrates the continuous process that includes assessment, diagnosis, nosology, and taxonomy. Although everyday clinical services focus primarily on assessment and diagnosis, these enterprises are ultimately structured according to nosological and taxonomic systems. Multiinformant, multicultural, and multitaxonomic perspectives are needed to take account of variations in the phenomena to be distinguished and in the models for representing the phenomena.

The clinical phenomena on which this chapter focuses include behavioral, emotional, social, and thought problems occurring between the ages of 18 months and 18 years with sufficient severity to warrant the term "psychopathology" and a likely need for professional help. The chapter does not focus on problems that result primarily from severe mental retardation or known physical abnormalities. The prospects for significant changes in the *DSM-V* argue for viewing existing *DSM* diagnostic criteria and categories as provisional and subject to change, despite their current influence on practice and reimbursement. Consequently, the *DSM* nosology

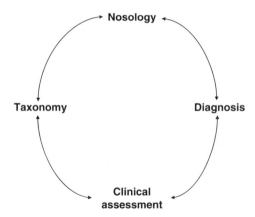

Figure 14.1 Schematic relations among assessment, diagnosis, nosology, and taxonomy.

is viewed as but one way to represent psychopathology rather than as embodying immutable truths concerning disorders and how to identify them. The *International Classification of Disease,* tenth edition (*ICD-10;* World Health Organization, 1992) provides a different nosology for representing psychopathology in terms of diagnostic categories, but it, too, is being revised. Continuing research on these and other ways of representing psychopathology is needed to optimize relations between clinical practice and advances in scientific findings.

CLINICAL ASSESSMENT

Clinical assessment refers to procedures for identifying the distinguishing features of problems, disorders, or cases, as well as relevant strengths. Many tests, questionnaires, inventories, interviews, and other procedures have been developed for the clinical assessment of children. Some assessment procedures, such as projective tests and unstructured clinical interviews, tend to be highly inferential. In using these assessment procedures, the practitioner makes inferences from responses to stimuli and questions in order to construct idiographic representations of the individual being assessed. Less inferential assessment procedures obtain responses whose meanings are more nomothetic. In other words, they are used to determine individuals' standing on scales or to place them in diagnostic categories, rather than to yield idiographic representations on the basis of the practitioner's interpretations. Assessment procedures also differ with respect to whether data obtained for individuals are judged in relation to norms versus nonnormed decision rules, such as those provided in the *DSM*.

Assessment procedures have long been used in clinical evaluations of children. However, the particular procedures, objectives, and types of conclusions have varied widely. In response to massive efforts to advance evidence-based treatment (EBT), Mash and Hunsley (2005) have argued for greater attention to what they call "evidence-based assessment" (EBA) as a necessary component of scientific support for clinical practice. Considering the flood of publications on EBT, it is surprising how little attention has been paid to obtaining assessment data with which to choose the most appropriate treatment. Much of the EBT literature appears to assume that practitioners automatically know what should be treated and need only apply the appropriate EBT. The lack of explicit attention to systematically using assessment to determine what should be treated may reflect the fact that participants in EBT trials are often recruited on the basis of a priori definitions of the problems to be treated. Consequently, children are admitted to EBT trials if they are deemed to have the target disorder. However, criteria for recruiting participants for EBT trials may not be readily translatable into practical assessment procedures for helping clinicians decide which EBT to use with each client.

Mash and Hunsley (2005) have done a great service by calling attention to the failure of EBT to include generalizable assessment procedures. Nevertheless, their use of the term "evidence" may be somewhat ambiguous in "evidence-based assessment." In EBT, "evidence" appropriately refers to the informational basis for concluding that a particular kind of treatment is worthwhile. However, when applied to assessment, "evidence" is the *product* of the assessment process as well as the informational basis for deeming the assessment process to be worthwhile. In other words, assessment should *obtain evidence* on which to base choices of treatment, to judge the progress of treatment, and to evaluate the outcomes of treatment. Because assessment should serve these functions by empirically obtaining appropriate information about the case being assessed, I use EBA to stand for "empirically based assessment." This in no way weakens Mash and Hunsley's argument that EBT cannot stand alone without EBA. My own way of emphasizing their point is to observe that, "without EBA, EBT may be like a magnificent house with no foundation" (Achenbach, 2005, p. 547).

Obtaining Assessment Data on Children

Every individual differs from every other individual in countless ways. Consequently, no clinical assessment procedure can identify everything that is unique about each child and about the family members who are also important parts of each child's case. To focus on the subset of characteristics deemed most relevant to clinical decision making, assessment instruments are typically designed to obtain data according to particular diagnostic, nosological, and/or taxonomic models, as outlined in the following sections.

Diagnostically Based Assessment Instruments

Assessment instruments designed to make diagnoses include interviews consisting of questions about whether criteria for particular diagnoses are met. Several standardized interviews for making *DSM* diagnoses of children have been published. *ICD-10* diagnoses can also be made from some of the interviews, but most focus mainly on *DSM* diagnoses. Some diagnostic interviews, such as the Diagnostic Interview Schedule for Children (DISC; Shaffer, Fisher, Lucas, Dulcan, & Schwab-Stone, 2000), are highly structured in that they use precisely scripted questions to obtain yes-or-no answers as to whether each criterion is met for particular *DSM* diagnostic categories. Other diagnostic interviews, such as the Schedule for Affective Disorders and Schizophrenia for School-Age Children (K-SADS; Ambrosini, 2000), are semi-structured in that interviewers are free to adapt the questions according to their clinical judgment.

In addition to ranging from highly structured to semi-structured, diagnostic interviews also vary in the degree to which conclusions are based only on the *respondent's* endorsement or denial of each *DSM* criterion versus being based on the *interviewer's judgment* of whether each criterion is met. The DISC is an example of a respondent-based interview, whereas the Child and Adolescent Psychiatric Assessment (Angold & Costello, 2000) is an example of an interviewer-based interview that requires interviewers to decide whether each *DSM* criterion is met.

When the first standardized *DSM* diagnostic interviews for children were developed in the 1980s, it was discovered that children's replies to interview questions often differed greatly from what parents and others reported about the children (Costello, Edelbrock, Kalas, Kessler, & Klaric, 1982; Herjanic & Reich, 1982). Consequently, parent versions of the interviews have been developed, and child versions have come to be used primarily with preadolescents and adolescents, rather than with younger children. However, even when restricted to preadolescents and adolescents, *DSM* diagnoses made from child interviews do not agree well with *DSM* diagnoses made from interviews with the children's parents. For example, in the massive Methods for Epidemiology of Child and Adolescent Disorders (MECA) Study of 1,283 9- to 18-year-olds, the mean kappa was .12 for agreement between diagnoses made from DISC interviews with children and their parents (P. Jensen et al., 1999). To provide some perspective on the meaning of the kappa statistic, Jacob Cohen (1960), the inventor of kappa, showed that the magnitude of kappa approximates the phi coefficient, which is the Pearson r scored from 2×2 tables (e.g., tables displaying relations between yes-versus-no categorizations of diagnoses made from child and parent interviews). Low agreement between parent and child reports of psychopathology is by no means limited to DISC interviews, as meta-analyses have yielded a mean r of only .25 between reports of child psychopathology by children and their parents, averaged across many instruments (Achenbach, McConaughy, & Howell, 1987).

In addition to interviews, another approach to assessing children in terms of *DSM* diagnoses is via questionnaires for rating *DSM* symptom criteria. An example is the ADHD Rating Scale IV, which consists of the *Diagnostic and Statistical Manual of Mental Disorders,* fourth edition (*DSM-IV;* American Psychiatric Association, 1994) symptom criteria for the inattentive and hyperactive impulsive types of Attention-Deficit/Hyperactivity Disorder (ADHD; DuPaul, Power, Anastopoulos, & Reid, 1998). Parent and teacher versions are available, on which each item is rated 0 to 3.

An example of a questionnaire for rating a broader range of *DSM* diagnostic categories is the Adolescent Symptom Inventory 4 (ASI-4; Gadow & Sprafkin, 1998). Parents and teachers rate symptoms for several *DSM-IV* diagnoses on 0 to 3 scales. A parallel self-rating questionnaire, the Youth Inventory-4 (YI-4; Gadow & Sprafkin, 1999), includes many of the same symptoms as the ASI-4.

Empirically Based Assessment Instruments

A key difference between the *DSM*-based instruments and what are here called empirically based instruments can be described in terms of their top-down versus bottom-up approaches. The *DSM*-based instruments are top-down in the sense that they start from the diagnostic categories and criteria that are listed in the *DSM*. The *DSM*-based assessment instruments are then constructed by wording the diagnostic criteria as questions that are either answered in interviews or are rated on questionnaires. The data sought with the *DSM*-based instruments are thus entirely shaped by the *DSM* nosology. Equally important, the conclusions drawn from assessment with these instruments are yes-versus-no judgments of whether criteria for particular *DSM* diagnoses are met.

By contrast, the empirically based instruments are bottom-up in the sense that their development starts with a large pool of assessment items that are chosen for their potential ability to identify children who are likely to need help for psychopathology. The items are pilot-tested by having them rated by appropriate respondents, such as parents, teachers, and children. Items that survive pilot testing are then used to assess large general population and clinical samples to determine how well they discriminate between children who have been referred for mental health services and demographically similar children who have not been referred for such services. Items that are found to be easily understood by the respondents, to be appropriately distributed, and to significantly discriminate between clinically referred and nonreferred children then become candidates for the scales of the assessment instruments. Items scored for large samples of children are subjected to statistical analyses, such as exploratory and confirmatory factor analyses (EFA and CFA), to identify sets (syndromes) of problems that tend to co-occur. The generalizability of the statistically derived syndromes is tested by performing similar analyses of items rated for children of each gender and different ages, by different informants, and in different cultures. These steps are outlined in Table 14.1.

Table 14.1 Developing Empirically Based Instruments for Assessing Child Psychopathology

1. Assemble pool of items that describe children's problems.
2. Formulate instructions and rating scales appropriate for the informants (e.g., parents, teachers, children).
3. Pilot-test and revise instruments based on informants' responses.
4. Use instruments to assess large clinical and epidemiological samples.
5. Do statistical analyses to identify syndromes of co-occurring problems.
6. Construct scales and profiles for scoring syndromes from the assessment forms.
7. Construct norms based on scores obtained by samples that are representative of relevant populations.
8. Test reliability and other psychometric properties.
9. Test validity in relation to external criteria.
10. Test replicability of syndrome structure in multiple cultures.

From *Multicultural Understanding of Child and Adolescent Psychopathology: Implications for Mental Health Assessment,* by T. M. Achenbach and L. A. Rescorla, 2007b, New York: Guilford Press. Adapted with permission.

Some of the steps required to develop empirically based instruments and scales for scoring them have been followed in the development of many instruments. For example, factor analyses were used in the development of some scales scored from the Behavior Assessment System for Children (Reynolds & Kamphaus, 2004). However, the results of the factor analyses were overridden when they contradicted the authors' judgments of what the scales and their constituent items should look like.

For another instrument, the Strengths and Difficulties Questionnaire (SDQ; Goodman, 1997), a priori scales were constructed and factor analyses were subsequently performed to see whether the obtained factors would match the scales (e.g., Dickey & Blumberg, 2004; Goodman, 2001; Koskelainen, Sourander, & Vauras, 2001; Muris, Meesters, Eijkelenboom, & Vincken, 2004; Rønning, Handegaard, Sourander, & Mørch, 2004). The factor analytic results varied considerably, perhaps owing at least partly to variations in methodology, samples, and criteria for determining whether the factors matched the SDQ scales.

Two families of widely used instruments have been developed according to steps like those outlined in Table 14.1. C. Keith Conners (1997, 2001) has developed a family of instruments primarily for assessing ADHD and related problems. The items comprising the instruments are rated on 0-1-2-3 scales by parents (Conners Parent Rating Scale—Revised; CPRS-R), teachers (Conners Teacher Rating Scale—Revised; CTRS-R), and youths (Conners-Wells Adolescent Self-Report Scale). The item pools and scales differ across the three instruments.

The CPRS-R and CTRS-R are scored for ages 3 to 17 and have been used much more widely than the youth form. The CPRS-R and CTRS-R both have factor-analytically derived scales designated as follows: Oppositional, Cognitive Problems/Inattention, Hyperactivity, Anxious-Shy, Perfectionism, and Social Problems. The CPRS-R is also scored on a scale designated as Psychosomatic, which cannot be scored from the CTRS-R because it lacks somatic items. Although the main scales were derived and then replicated by using factor analysis, items were eliminated if they lacked "conceptual coherence" with the factor on which they loaded (Conners, Sitarenios, Parker, & Epstein, 1998, p. 282). The CPRS-R and CTRS-R also have scales that paraphrase the *DSM-IV* symptom criteria for ADHD.

A family of instruments developed according to all the steps outlined in Table 14.1 includes the Child Behavior Checklist for Ages 6 to 18 (CBCL/6–18), Teacher's Report Form (TRF), and Youth Self-Report (YSR; Achenbach & Rescorla, 2001). Together with interview and observational instruments covering these ages, plus other instruments for ages 1.5 to 5, 18 to 59, and 60 to 90+, the CBCL/6–18, TRF, and YSR are components of the Achenbach System of Empirically Based Assessment (ASEBA; Achenbach & Rescorla, 2004; Rescorla & Achenbach, 2004). In addition to the factor-analytically derived scales, ASEBA instruments also have *DSM*-oriented scales comprising items identified by international experts as being very consistent with *DSM* diagnostic categories, as well as scales for assessing strengths. The problem items of most ASEBA instruments are rated 0 = not true, 1 = somewhat or sometimes true, and 2 = very true or often true.

As noted earlier, correlations between parents' and children's reports of child psychopathology are quite modest, as indicated by an *r* of only .25 in meta-analyses

(Achenbach et al., 1987). This low level of agreement means that parent reports and self-reports cannot be substituted for one another. Furthermore, agreement between adults who play different roles with respect to the children they rate is also modest, with meta-analyses yielding a mean r of only .28 between reports by parents versus teachers versus mental health workers versus observers. The rs averaged .60 between pairs of adults who play similar roles with respect to the children they rate (pairs of parents, teachers, mental health workers, observers). However, even these higher correlations do not indicate enough agreement to enable reports by any one informant to routinely serve as proxies for reports by other informants who play similar roles with respect to the children.

Although the meta-analytic findings were published in 1987, cross-informant agreement continues to be quite modest. As noted by De Los Reyes and Kazdin (2005, p. 483), the modest cross-informant agreement reported in the 1987 meta-analyses "has come to be one of the most robust findings in clinical child research: Different informants' (e.g., parents, children, teachers) ratings of social, emotional, or behavior problems in children are discrepant." Moreover, cross-informant discrepancies are not restricted to ratings of childhood problems. Meta-analyses of correlations between self-reports and others' reports of adult psychopathology have yielded mean rs of .43 for internalizing problems (depression, anxiety, somatic complaints) and .44 for externalizing problems (aggressive and rule-breaking behavior) when the probands and informants completed parallel instruments (Achenbach, Krukowski, Dumenci, & Ivanova, 2005). When probands and informants completed different instruments, the mean r was only .30. The fundamental fact is that agreement between different people's reports of psychopathology is simply too low to allow data from any single person to serve as a gold standard. Consequently, assessment, diagnosis, nosology, and taxonomy must all take account of the differences between the pictures obtained from different people.

The ASEBA instruments are designed to explicitly compare and contrast data from different informants. For preschoolers, the Child Behavior Checklist for Ages 1.5 to 5 (CBCL/1.5–5) is designed to be filled out by parent figures, and the Caregiver-Teacher Report Form (C-TRF) is designed to be filled out by day care providers and preschool teachers (Achenbach & Rescorla, 2000). These forms are scored on parallel syndrome scales that were derived from EFA and CFA of large general population and clinical samples. The scoring software provides profiles of scores and systematic comparisons of ratings by up to eight informants, as illustrated in Figures 14.2 and 14.3.

For school-age children, the scoring software compares scores from up to eight CBCL/6–18, TRF, and YSR forms. Furthermore, to take account of multicultural variations in norms, the scoring software enables users to display scale scores in relation to percentiles and T scores based on normative data obtained in many different societies (Achenbach & Rescorla, 2007a). For example, if a child lives in a society where problem scores tend to be relatively low, the user can elect to display the child's scale scores in relation to norms based on data from low-scoring societies. On the other hand, if a child comes from a low-scoring society but currently resides in a society where scores tend to be relatively high, the user can elect to display the child's scale scores in relation to norms for high-scoring

CBCL/1.5-5 - Syndrome Scale Scores for Boys

ID: S65432-001
Name: Kenny K. Randall

Gender: Male
Age: 30 months

Date Filled: 01/12/2000   Clinician: Dr. Winter
Birth Date: 07/10/1997   Verified: Yes

Informat: Amy Randall
Relationship: Mother

	Internalizing					Externalizing	
	Emotionally Reactive	Anxious/ Depressed	Somatic Complaints	Withdrawn	Sleep Problems	Attention Problems	Aggressive Behavior
Total Score	8	4	4	10	6	4	9
T Score	69-B	56	62	82-C	62	57	51
Percentile	97	73	89	>97	89	76	54

Emotionally Reactive	Anxious/Depressed	Somatic Complaints	Withdrawn	Sleep Problems	Attention Problems	Aggressive Behavior
2 21.DistChange	0 10.Dependent	0 1.AchesPains	1 2.ActsYoung	0 22.NotSleepAlone	0 5.Concentrate	1 8.Can'tWait
1 46.Twitching	0 33.FeelingsHurt	1 7.ThingsOut	0 4.AvoidaEye	0 38.SleepProb	0 6.Can'tSitStill	0 15.Defiant
1 51.ShowsPanic	0 37.UpsetBySep	0 12.Constipated	2 23.NoAnswer	0 48.Nightmares	0 56.Clumsy	1 16.Demanding
0 79.RapidShifts	1 43.LookUnhappy	0 19.Diarrhea	0 62.RefusesActive	1 64.ResistsBed	2 59.ShiftsQuickly	0 18.DestroyOther
1 82.MoodChange	2 47.Nervous	2 24.NotEat	1 67.UnRespAffect	2 74.SleepLess	2 95.Wanders	0 20.Disobedient
2 82.Sulks	0 68.SelfConse	0 39.Headaches	2 70.LittleAffect	2 84.TalkInSleep		0 27.NoGuilt
1 92.UpsetByNew	1 87.Fearful	0 45.Nausea	2 71.Little Intrest	2 94.WakesOften		2 29.Frustrated
0 97.Whining	0 90.Sad	0 52.PainfulBM	1 98.Withdrawn			0 35.Fights
0 99.Worries		0 78.Stomachaches				0 40.HitsOther
		1 86.TooNeat				2 42.HurtsAccident
		0 93.Vomiting				0 44.AngryMoods
						0 53.Attacks
						0 58.Punishment
						0 66.Screams
						1 69.Selfish
						1 81.Stubborn
						1 85.Temper
						0 88.Uncooperative
						0 96.WantAttention

Copyright 2000 T. Achenbach & L. Rescorla   B = Borderline clinical range; C = Clinical range; Broken lines = Borderline clinical range

Figure 14.2   Profile of empirically based syndrome scores for a 30-month-old boy rated by his mother on the CBCL/1.5–5. (Names are fictitious.) Source: *Manual for the ASEBA Preschool Forms and Profiles*, by T. M. Achenbach and L. A. Rescorla, 2000, Burlington: University of Vermont, Research Center for Children, Youth, and Families. Reprinted with permission.

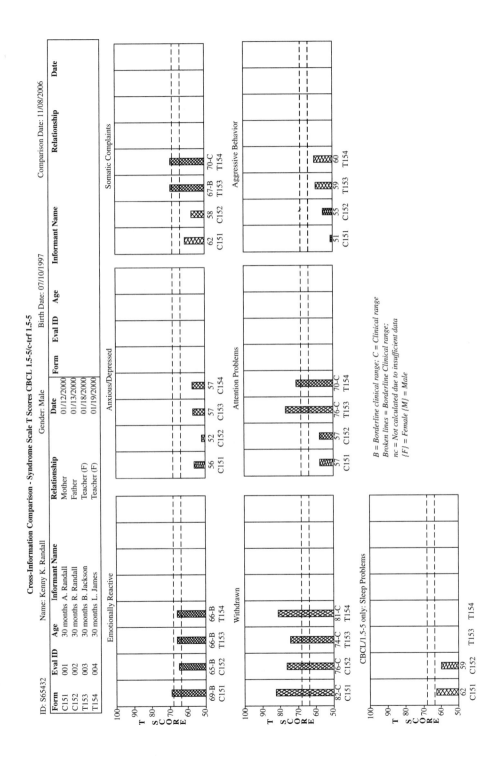

Figure 14.3 Cross-informant comparisons of syndrome scores for a 30-month-old boy rated on the CBCL/1.5–5 by his mother and father and on the C-TRF by two preschool teachers. (Names are fictitious.) *Source: Manual for the ASEBA Preschool Forms and Profiles*, by T. M. Achenbach and L. A. Rescorla, 2000, Burlington: University of Vermont, Research Center for Children, Youth, and Families. Reprinted with permission.

437

societies but can also display the child's scale scores in relation to norms for low-scoring societies like the child's home society. In this way, the user can determine whether the child's scores are clinically deviant according to both sets of norms, one set of norms, or neither set of norms. And, because the child's scale scores can be displayed for parent, teacher, and self-ratings, the user can compare scores obtained from each informant to whichever set of norms the user deems appropriate. Translations of ASEBA forms in more than 80 languages facilitate multicultural applications (Bérubé & Achenbach, 2008).

Obtaining Assessment Data on Parent Figures

Clinical assessment of children typically involves parent figures, including biological, adoptive, and stepparents. Parent figures may also include relatives, such as grandparents, aunts, uncles, and older siblings, and unrelated caregivers, such as foster parents, group home parents, the boyfriend or girlfriend of a child's parent, and child care workers. Parent figures (hereafter collectively designated as "parents") often instigate clinical assessment or seek it in response to urging by school, medical, welfare, or law enforcement personnel. Parents are key sources of information about children's functioning, are apt to affect children's problems and strengths, and are often pivotal in determining what will be done to help children.

Because child clinical cases typically need to be conceptualized in relation to parents, assessment of parents is a key component of the process of deciding how a child's problems should be viewed. When evaluating a child, mental health practitioners usually interview parents to learn about the background of the referral, to form impressions of the parents, and to discuss options. Parents may also be asked to complete instruments for assessing their child, such as *DSM*-based interviews, empirically based rating forms, and questionnaires focused on particular referral problems, such as ADHD, anxiety, or depression.

Because parents' reports and discrepancies between parents' reports are apt to be shaped by characteristics of the parents, it is helpful to illuminate these characteristics by assessing parents with instruments that parallel those for assessing their children. Although *DSM*-based interviews are typically too costly and intrusive to administer to parents, self-administered empirically based adult assessment instruments are available that parallel the ASEBA instruments for children (Achenbach & Rescorla, 2003).

The ASEBA adult instruments include parallel self- and other-report forms that tap adult versions of many of the strengths, problems, and scales that are scored from the child instruments, plus characteristics that are more specific to adults. To take account of differences between reports of adults' functioning by themselves and by others, the scoring software for the adult instruments can compare scores obtained from self-reports by each parent about himself or herself and reports by the parent's partner or someone else who knows the parent. Because the self- and other-report forms can each be completed in about 15 minutes at home, in a waiting room, or on the Internet, no professional time is needed to obtain the assessment data.

The profiles and comparisons of self- and other-reports can help the practitioner see relations between these different pictures of the parents' functioning and what the parents report about the child who is being evaluated. This approach enables the practitioner to efficiently document parental characteristics relevant to understanding children who are being assessed. The practitioner may also elect to show the parents the profiles obtained from the self- and other-reports to highlight similarities and differences in how their functioning is perceived. Viewing the profiles and cross-informant comparisons can teach parents about differences between perceptions of functioning and may motivate them to change their own behavior.

CLINICAL DIAGNOSIS

Since the publication of *DSM-III* (American Psychiatric Association, 1980), diagnosis has become an increasingly central focus of mental health services, training, research, and reimbursement. The introduction of explicit diagnostic criteria and fixed decision rules in *DSM-III* probably contributed to the ascendance of diagnosis. It was hoped that the change from inferential narratives in *DSM-II* (American Psychiatric Association, 1968) would produce more reliable diagnoses, etiological discoveries, and prescriptive treatments. Although the more explicit diagnostic criteria have led to much more detailed documentation of problems, the hopes for greater reliability of *DSM-III* diagnoses than achieved for *DSM-II* diagnoses were not realized for childhood disorders (Mattison, Cantwell, Russell, & Will, 1979; Mezzich, Mezzich, & Coffman, 1985). Furthermore, the hopes for etiological discoveries and for treatment specificity based on *DSM* diagnoses have not been realized either (Kupfer, First, & Regier, 2002; Rounsaville et al., 2002).

Although the term "diagnosis" may imply authoritative identification of a particular disorder, the Greek roots of *dia* = "apart" and *gignoskein* = "to know" pertain to distinguishing a particular condition from other conditions. In other words, diagnoses involve distinguishing among a variety of possibilities rather than simply identifying a condition whose identity can be understood without reference to similarities and differences between it and other conditions. Accordingly, the meaning of each possible diagnosis depends on how it is differentiated from other diagnoses within a system of diagnoses. The assessment data on which diagnoses are based must therefore ultimately be linked to a system that distinguishes among the phenomena that different diagnoses are supposed to represent. However, to clarify the relations between assessment and diagnosis and the nosological and taxonomic systems to which they should ultimately be linked, it is important to distinguish among the different meanings of diagnosis that sometimes confuse efforts to advance knowledge of child psychopathology. At least three meanings of diagnosis need to be distinguished, as outlined in the following sections.

Diagnostic Processes

Diagnostic processes consist of gathering data with which to make formal diagnoses and diagnostic formulations. Diagnostic processes can be thought of as constituting that portion of assessment that is directed toward making formal diagnoses and diagnostic formulations. Although assessment thus includes diagnostic processes, it is not necessarily limited to diagnostic processes because it may include obtaining data on strengths, problems, and other variables that are not included in diagnostic criteria. However, assessment that is focused only on determining whether diagnostic criteria are met, such as *DSM*-based interviews, can be viewed as limited to diagnostic processes.

Formal Diagnoses

Formal diagnoses are made by determining the category of a nosology to which a case belongs. Diagnosis in this sense is what a leading psychiatric diagnostician called "the medical term for classification" (Guze, 1978, p. 53). When it is determined that a child meets criteria for a category of a nosology, such as *DSM* or *ICD*, this determination constitutes a formal diagnosis of the child, that is, a matching of the child's problems to a category of a nosology.

Diagnostic Formulations

Diagnostic formulations involve putting together various kinds of information about a case into a comprehensive picture of the case. For children, the information may include developmental history, family dynamics, physical liabilities, stressors, formal diagnoses, and prospects for change. In clinical practice, the diagnostic formulation may say more about the child's needs and the indications for particular treatments than formal diagnoses do.

To prevent undue reverence for diagnosis from clouding our thinking about relations among assessment, diagnosis, nosology, and taxonomy, it is important to be clear that the *DSM* and *ICD* consist of formal diagnoses but do not specify either diagnostic processes or diagnostic formulations. Although the *DSM* has been said to provide "operational definitions" for diagnoses (Rapoport & Ismond, 1996, p. 13), it does not in fact specify assessment operations (i.e., diagnostic processes) for most childhood disorders. About the only operationalized diagnostic criteria specified by *DSM-IV* are "an IQ of approximately 70 or below on an individually administered IQ test" (American Psychiatric Association, 2000, p. 49) as a criterion for mental retardation, plus low performance on relevant tests for learning disorders (Widiger & Clark, 2000). Thus, although diagnostic processes and formulations are certainly essential clinical activities, they are not within the purview of the *DSM* or *ICD* nosologies. Instead, these nosologies are classifications of formal diagnoses, as addressed in the following sections.

NOSOLOGICAL CATEGORIES

The *DSM* and *ICD* are nosologies, that is, systems for classifying diseases (called "disorders" in the *DSM*). They provide criteria for defining categories of disorders and for distinguishing particular disorders from other disorders. Since the publication of *DSM-III* (American Psychiatric Association, 1980), the *DSM* has included explicit criteria for each disorder and has specified fixed decision rules for determining whether a child has a particular disorder. Each criterion must be judged in a yes-or-no fashion as either being met or not met. The *DSM* provides guidelines for describing some disorders as mild, moderate, or severe, but if the required number of criteria is not met, the disorder is deemed absent. Conversely, if the required number of criteria is met, the disorder is deemed present. The standard version of *ICD-10* (World Health Organization, 1992) does not provide such explicit diagnostic criteria or fixed rules for formal diagnoses, although a little-used research version of *ICD-10* does provide explicit criteria (World Health Organization, 1993).

Challenges of Comorbidity

Since the advent of explicit diagnostic criteria in *DSM-III,* numerous studies have found that many children qualify for multiple diagnoses. Termed "comorbidity," the tendency for disorders to co-occur could be very informative. For example, if many children diagnosed as having Disorder A are also diagnosed as having Disorder B, this could suggest that one of the disorders causes the other or that both disorders have a common cause. Comorbidity between Disorder A and Disorder B could also suggest that having one disorder makes a child more vulnerable to the other disorder, perhaps as a consequence of weakened resistance or of adverse effects of treatment for the initial disorder. However, because the *DSM* does not have well-validated markers for distinguishing each childhood disorder from each other disorder, it is also possible that apparent comorbidity between disorders reflects a lack of clear boundaries between them (Achenbach, 1991; Caron & Rutter, 1991). In other words, the diagnostic criteria for different nosological categories may not accurately represent truly different disorders. Nosologies may thus imply distinctions between disorders without evidence for true differences between the disorders.

As an example of a possible "distinction without a difference," two studies found that 96% of boys who met *DSM-III* criteria for Conduct Disorder (CD) also met criteria for Oppositional Defiant Disorder (ODD; Faraone, Biederman, Keenan, & Tsuang, 1991; Walker et al., 1991). Furthermore, field trials for the *Diagnostic and Statistical Manual of Mental Disorders,* third edition, revised (*DSM-III-R;* American Psychiatric Association, 1987) found that 84% of clinically referred children who met criteria for CD also met criteria for ODD (Spitzer, Davies, & Barkley, 1990). These findings certainly suggest that the nosological distinction between CD and ODD did not reflect two truly different disorders.

Unidirectional versus Bidirectional Comorbidity

Computing comorbidity in the other direction, that is, as the percentage of children diagnosed with ODD who were also diagnosed with CD, might yield a different picture. For example, if the proportion of children diagnosed with ODD were much greater than the proportion diagnosed with CD, the percentage of those diagnosed with ODD who had comorbid CD would be lower than the percentage of children diagnosed with CD who had comorbid ODD. Thus, if 200 children in a sample are diagnosed with ODD but only 100 are diagnosed with CD, the percentage of children who have ODD and also have CD could not exceed 50%. However, if all 100 of the children diagnosed with CD were among the 200 diagnosed with ODD, 100% of the children with CD would have comorbid ODD.

To avoid the misleading results of unidirectional computations of comorbidity rates, McConaughy and Achenbach (1994) recommended that comorbidity be computed as the mean of the comorbidities obtained by computing comorbidity in each of the two possible directions. Computing comorbidity bidirectionally in our hypothetical example would yield 100 CD/200 ODD = 50% + 100 ODD/100CD = 100%, for a bidirectional comorbidity of 50% + 100%/2 = 75%. Unfortunately, many studies of comorbidity fail to do this.

Although unidirectional computation of comorbidity makes it difficult to draw generalizable conclusions about precise rates of comorbidity, it is certainly clear that comorbidity rates have remained high even after *DSM* criteria were modified to reduce the amazingly high rates found for diagnoses such as CD and ODD (e.g., Angold, Costello, & Erkanli, 1999). In addition to high comorbidity between particular pairs of formal diagnoses, high comorbidity is also evident in findings that large proportions of children qualify for multiple diagnoses in community samples (e.g., Bird, Gould, & Staghezza, 1993) and clinical samples (e.g., A. Jensen & Weisz, 2002). In other words, children who have enough problems of a particular type to qualify for a diagnosis often have enough other kinds of problems to qualify for additional diagnoses as well.

Implications of Comorbidity

What are the implications of the high comorbidity rates found for formal diagnoses? As indicated by the 96% comorbidity found between CD and ODD in two studies, some comorbidity rates are so high that they raise questions about whether nosological distinctions between formal diagnostic categories accurately reflect true differences between disorders. If the different nosological categories do not in fact discriminate between different disorders, then comorbidity may be an artifact of having multiple categories for the same disorders.

The criteria for ODD and CD were changed from *DSM-III* to *DSM-III-R* to *DSM-IV* to reduce the overlap between these two diagnostic categories. However, it may still be an open question as to whether there is a meaningful difference between ODD, designated in *DSM-IV* as "[a] pattern of negativistic, hostile, and defiant behavior," and CD, designated as "[a] repetitive and persistent pattern of behavior in which the basic rights of others or major age-appropriate societal norms or rules are violated" (American Psychiatric Association, 2000, pp. 98, 102). Furthermore, the 15 criterial symptoms for CD are grouped into subcategories designated "aggression to people and animals," "destruction of property," "deceitfulness or theft," and "serious violations of rules." Because only 3 of the 15 criterial symptoms need to be judged present to warrant a diagnosis of CD, some children who qualify may have three aggressive symptoms, whereas others may have three rule-violating symptoms, and still others may have three deceitful symptoms or various combinations of aggressive, destructive, deceitful, and rule-violating symptoms. Consequently, diagnoses of CD may include very different patterns of behavior problems, some of which overlap considerably with ODD criteria, whereas others do not. Although changes in criteria since *DSM-III* may have reduced comorbidity between formal diagnoses of ODD and CD, overlaps between ODD kinds of problems and particular subsets of CD problems may still artifactually contribute to apparent comorbidity.

Another implication of high comorbidity rates is that multiple diagnoses can greatly complicate use of treatments that are designed for particular disorders. For example, suppose that Treatment X has been found effective with children who were selected for having Disorder A. Does this mean that Treatment X should also be used for children who have Disorder B and Disorder C, as well as Disorder A? Even if the answer is yes, should additional Treatments Y and Z be used because they have found been effective with Disorders B and C?

If formal diagnoses of behavioral, emotional, social, and thought problems validly discriminate between disorders that are as distinct as physical diseases such as cancer, measles, and diphtheria, it would make sense to use multiple specific treatments for children who qualify for multiple diagnoses. However, because neither physical etiologies nor other physical abnormalities have been identified as underlying nosological categories for children's behavioral, emotional, social, or thought problems, treatments cannot be aimed at different physical abnormalities marked by different formal diagnoses. Instead, treatments are aimed at altering behaviors, feelings, and thoughts that may overlap among nosological categories. Consequently, research is needed not only on the effectiveness of specific treatments for specific diagnoses but also on the effectiveness of treatment for the many children who qualify for multiple diagnoses.

A related implication of comorbidity is that children who qualify for multiple diagnoses supposedly have multiple disorders. If such children in fact have multiple disorders, it could be hypothesized that they would have worse outcomes than children who have only one diagnosis. Doss and Weisz (2006) tested this hypothesis by analyzing the effects of initial severity on particular empirically based syndromes versus the effects of multiple syndrome deviance on treatment outcomes. They found that initial severity (high scores) on particular syndromes had much larger effects on outcomes than did deviance on multiple syndromes. Although these analyses did not directly test the effects of comorbidity among categorical diagnoses, such tests may be quite impractical, as discussed in the section on taxonomy.

New Directions in Nosology

A major thrust in planning for *DSM-V* involves possible quantification of at least some aspects of the diagnostic criteria (Helzer, Kraemer, Krueger, Wittchen & Regier, in press). Although quantified diagnostic criteria are often referred to as "dimensions," dimensions are not the only relevant forms of quantification. Consequently, I use the more comprehensive term "quantitative" to include dimensional as well as other quantitative approaches. Quantitative approaches have long been advanced for nosologies of personality disorders (Trull & Durrett, 2005), which primarily concern adult psychopathology. Quantitative approaches to nosologies of other adult disorders have also been proposed (Krueger & Markon, 2006). As will be evident in the section on taxonomic systems, quantitative approaches to child psychopathology have spawned extensive taxonomic research on psychopathology, including groupings compatible with existing categorical nosologies.

Although categorical and quantitative approaches are often assumed to be incompatible with one another, Kraemer (in press) has pointed out that each categorical diagnosis in the *DSM* nosology can be viewed as representing two (binary) values on a dimension. The two values are positive (the proband is deemed to have the disorder) versus negative (the proband is deemed free of the disorder). Most *DSM* diagnoses are specified in terms of a list of criterial symptoms and a cut point on the symptom list for distinguishing between positive and negative values (i.e., diagnosis present versus absent). The number of symptoms deemed present thus constitutes a score that ranges from 0 to N with N being the total number of symptoms on the list.

Kraemer (in press) argues that dichotomization is especially detrimental when, as is usually the case, there is no strong empirical basis for choosing cut points to discriminate between those who truly do versus do not have a particular disorder. To illustrate the detrimental effects of dichotomization, Kraemer cites studies of genetic influences on psychopathology, where unrealistically large samples are needed to detect genetic effects when the phenotypic characteristics are dichotomized rather than quantified. Kraemer also cites examples of research on treatment in which quantification of outcome measures revealed significant differences between the effects of different treatment conditions that were not detected when the same measures were analyzed dichotomously.

Although it has been argued that clinicians need categorical diagnoses (e.g., First, 2005), Kraemer (in press) provides examples of clinical diagnoses of hypertension, diabetes, and cancer that all involve quantitative specifications. She argues that the increasing importance of genetic, imaging, and biochemical data for research, training, and treatment related to psychopathology makes it essential to quantify aspects of the *DSM-V,* rather than deferring quantification to some unspecified future date, as was done when quantification of previous editions of the *DSM* was proposed. Preparations for the next edition of the *ICD* also include possibilities for quantification.

TAXONOMIC CONSTRUCTS

As discussed in the preceding section, nosologies are classifications of disorders. Like many classifications, they are constructed for the convenience of users. Accordingly, nosological categories may be constructed according to a variety of procedures and principles that are not necessarily consistent among all the categories. In a general medical nosology, for example, categories of bone fractures may be organized quite differently from categories of infectious diseases, cancers, and cardiac disorders.

Within the *DSM* and *ICD* nosologies, categories for disorders defined mainly in terms of behavioral and emotional problems are organized very differently from categories for mental retardation, learning disabilities, and dementias. Rather than being based directly on scientific principles or research findings, the *DSM* and *ICD* nosological categories were constructed mainly on the basis of negotiations among various stakeholders. A key consideration was whether the nosologies would be useful to clinicians, third-party payers, and those responsible for health care records. Maintenance of continuity with previous editions of the nosologies was also an important objective.

The Nature of Taxonomies

Taxonomies are classification systems that are intended to capture intrinsic distinguishing features of the phenomena that are classified (Gove, 1971). Consequently, all taxonomies are classification systems, but classifications that do not apply scientific principles to distinctions among the classified phenomena are not taxonomies.

One view of taxonomies is that they should arrange entities into "natural categories on the basis of key features they share" (Millon, 1991, p. 246). Consistent with this view, it has been hoped that a taxonomy of psychopathology would "carve nature at its joints" (Kendell, 2002, p. 7). The goal of basing taxonomies on natural categories that carve nature at its joints is inspired largely by taxonomies of plant and animal species that are thought to distinguish among "natural kinds," each of which is inherently different from other natural kinds. However, no particular criteria have been found to consistently distinguish among species or even to provide an overarching definition of what "species" means. Consequently, biological species are now viewed as taxonomic constructs, rather than as embodying categories that are inherent in nature (Levin, 1979; Mayr, 1987). Considering that even taxonomies of biological species thus consist of constructs, current concepts of psychopathology are certainly unlikely to embody natural categories. Because it seems unrealistic to expect current concepts of psychopathology to yield taxonomies of natural kinds, Zachar (2000, p. 167) has argued that taxonomic constructs should be based on "patterns (of psychopathology) that can be identified with varying levels of reliability and validity."

If we acknowledge that natural taxonomic categories of psychopathology are unlikely to be discovered in the near future (if ever), it may be more realistic to consider multiple ways of taxonomically organizing data on psychopathology. This means that we should compare and contrast different ways of taxonomically organizing data on psychopathology. To avoid reifying any single set of taxonomic constructs, it may be helpful to view data on child psychopathology from multiple taxonomic perspectives. Considering the differences typically found between reports by different informants, it is also essential that taxonomic constructs take account of multi-informant variations. And because the patterning and prevalence of problems may differ among cultural groups, taxonomic constructs should take account of multicultural variations.

Nosologically Based Taxonomic Constructs

Although nosologies are classifications constructed for the convenience of users, it is assumed that each of their categories represents a particular type of disorder. In effect, each category represents a taxonomic construct that is defined in terms of the diagnostic criteria for the category. For example, the diagnostic criteria for CD define a taxonomic construct that is assumed to be different from the taxonomic constructs of ODD and ADHD. As illustrated in Figure 14.4, the approach to defining these taxonomic constructs can be described as top-down because it

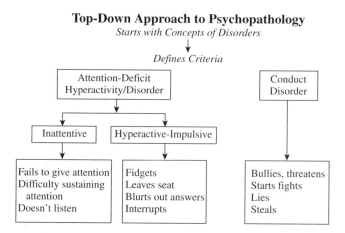

Figure 14.4 The top-down approach to defining taxonomic constructs. *Source: Multicultural Understanding of Child and Adolescent Psychopathology: Implications for Mental Health Assessment,* by T. M. Achenbach and L. A. Rescorla, 2007b, New York: Guilford Press. Reprinted with permission.

starts with a concept of a nosological category that is negotiated by the formulators of the nosology. The formulators of the nosology then work downward from the concept of the category to diagnostic criteria for determining which children fit the category.

Operationalizing Nosologically Based Criteria

Although diagnostic criteria have been made explicit in *DSM-III, DSM-III-R,* and *DSM-IV,* they are not specified in terms of operations for assessing individual children to determine which criteria are met. Instead, separate assessment procedures must be used to operationalize the diagnostic criteria to determine which children meet criteria for which diagnoses. Standardized diagnostic interviews, such as the DISC (Shaffer et al., 2000) and K-SADS (Ambrosini, 2000), and *DSM* rating forms, such as the ADHD Rating Scale-IV (DuPaul et al., 1998) and the YI-4 (Gadow & Sprafkin, 1999), operationalize criteria for those nosological categories that are based primarily on behavioral, emotional, social, and thought problems. However, each operationalization may yield different conclusions about which children meet criteria for which categories. For example, a mean kappa of only .03 was found for agreement between "definite" *DSM* diagnoses made from the DISC administered to mothers and their children versus the K-SADS administered to the same mothers and children (P. Cohen, O'Connor, Lewis, Velez, & Malachowski, 1987). When the diagnostic criteria were relaxed to include agreement between "possible" diagnoses, the mean kappa rose to only .14. Thus, even when criteria were operationalized by means of two of the most thoroughly researched and widely used interviews, the interviews failed to agree on their assignments of individual children to *DSM* categories. Furthermore, meta-analyses have yielded a mean kappa of only .15 between *DSM* diagnoses of children made from standardized interviews, including the DISC and K-SADS, and diagnoses made from clinical evaluations of the children (Rettew, Doyle, Achenbach, Dumenci, & Ivanova, 2006).

DuPaul et al. (1998) reported point-biserial correlations averaging .31 between various combinations of *DSM* ADHD diagnoses and scores from the ADHD Rating Scale-IV completed by parents and teachers. When Gadow et al. (2002) selected the highest point-biserial correlations between 11- to 18-year-olds' self-ratings on YI-4 scales and *DSM* diagnoses in the youths' clinic charts, they found a mean correlation of .25 for diagnoses of ADHD, ODD, CD, depressive disorders, and anxiety disorders. Although not quite as low as the kappas, these modest correlations further indicate that major challenges remain for operationalizing the nosological taxonomic constructs.

Empirically Based Taxonomic Constructs

Empirically based assessment instruments were presented earlier in the chapter. Some of these instruments were explicitly designed to obtain data from which taxonomic constructs could be derived. For example, development of the CBCL/6–18, TRF, and YSR started with diverse assessment items that were then culled, revised, and augmented on the basis of extensive pilot testing. Subsequently, EFA and CFA were used to derive syndromes of co-occurring problems (Achenbach & Rescorla, 2001). The statistically derived syndromes serve as taxonomic constructs, where "constructs" are defined as "objects of thought constituted by the ordering or systematic uniting of experiential elements" (Gove, 1971, p. 489).

Although parent, teacher, and self-ratings differed with respect to some specific items, as well as with respect to the raters' perspectives, EFA and CFA identified eight similar syndromes in ratings by all three kinds of informants. The items common to the syndromes derived from the CBCL/6–18, TRF, and YSR define "cross-informant" syndrome constructs. Individuals' ratings of a particular child on the specific items composing the CBCL/6–18, TRF, and YSR versions of the syndromes operationalize the cross-informant syndrome constructs in ways that reflect variations in the raters' perceptions of the child. The cross-informant correlations between ratings on virtually all instruments, including the empirically based instruments, are inevitably limited by factors such as differences in the informants' roles (e.g., mother versus father versus math teacher versus history teacher versus self), knowledge and memory of the child's behavior, interpretations of assessment items, and candor. Because the empirically based approach derives syndromes statistically from data on large samples of real children, this approach to taxonomy can be described as working from the bottom up, as illustrated in Figure 14.5.

Relations between Nosologically Based and Empirically Based Taxonomic Constructs

Despite differences in their origins, some of the nosological categories include criterial symptoms analogous to the problem items comprising some of the empirically based syndromes. As an example, many of the criterial symptoms for ADHD have counterparts among the problem items that comprise the empirically based

Bottom-Up Approach to Psychopathology

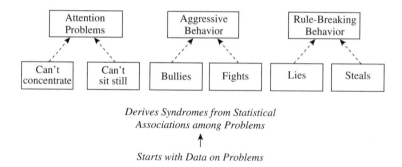

*Derives Syndromes from Statistical
Associations among Problems*

↑

Starts with Data on Problems

Figure 14.5   The bottom-up approach to defining taxonomic constructs. *Source: Multicultural Understanding of Child and Adolescent Psychopathology: Implications for Mental Health Assessment,* by T. M. Achenbach and L. A. Rescorla, 2007b, New York: Guilford Press. Reprinted with permission.

attention problems syndrome. On the other hand, some nosological categories group criterial symptoms differently than the empirically based syndromes group the corresponding problem items. For example, the nosological category of CD includes both overtly aggressive symptoms and nonaggressive rule-breaking symptoms. By contrast, factor analyses of the CBCL/6–18, TRF, and YSR, as well as of other instruments (Quay, 1986), have yielded separate syndromes of overtly aggressive versus rule-breaking behavior. Conversely, criterial symptoms for depression and anxiety are grouped in separate nosological categories, whereas factor analyses of the CBCL/6–18, TRF, and YSR, as well as other instruments (Achenbach & Rescorla, 2003), have yielded a syndrome that includes both depressive and anxiety problems.

Despite differences between the ways particular kinds of problems are partitioned, as well as differences between the categorical nosological criteria versus the quantification of items and syndromes, multiple studies have reported significant associations between *DSM* diagnoses and scores on empirically based syndromes (e.g., Bird, Gould, Rubio-Stipec, Staghezza, & Canino, 1991; Graetz, Sawyer, Hazell, Arney, & Baghurst, 2001; Steinhausen, Metzke, Meier, & Kannenberg, 1997; Verhulst, van der Ende, Ferdinand, & Kasius, 1997).

To facilitate cross-walks between nosological and empirically based approaches to taxonomy of child psychopathology, a top-down "expert judgment" approach has been used to construct *DSM*-oriented scales from the same pools of items that were factor analyzed to identify syndromes. This has been done for preschoolers, school-age children, adults, and the elderly (Achenbach, Dumenci, & Rescorla, 2003; Achenbach, Newhouse, & Rescorla, 2004; Achenbach & Rescorla, 2003). The *DSM*-oriented scales were constructed by having expert psychiatrists and psychologists from many cultural backgrounds identify problem items that they judged to be very consistent with particular *DSM-IV* categories. For nosological categories for which enough items were identified by a substantial majority of experts, the items were used to construct *DSM*-oriented scales. Like the empirically based syndromes, the *DSM*-oriented scales are displayed on profiles in relation to age-, gender-, and informant-specific norms.

Multi-informant Perspectives

Previous sections have summarized findings of low to moderate levels of agreement between reports of psychopathology by different informants. Each informant may contribute clinically valuable information about a child's functioning and how it is perceived by the informant. The differences among the informants' reports are as valuable as the similarities for indicating the possible situational specificity versus cross-situational consistency of a child's problems. Differences among informants' reports may also reveal outlier informants whose perceptions of the child are idiosyncratic enough to warrant exploration of the informant's interactions with the child. Such findings may warrant interventions that focus on a particular informant or on the informant's interactions with the child.

To help clinicians efficiently document and compare reports by multiple informants, software is available that displays *DSM*-oriented scale scores, as well as syndrome scores obtained from any combination of up to eight forms (Achenbach & Rescorla, 2007a). As illustrated in Figure 14.6, bar graphs indicate standard scores (*T* scores) on each *DSM*-oriented scale in relation to norms for peers of the child's age and gender, as rated by different kinds of informants, such as parents, teachers, and children themselves. In each bar graph, the broken lines demarcate a borderline clinical range. Scores beneath the bottom broken line are in the normal range, whereas scores above the top broken line are in the clinical range. By looking at the bar graphs, the clinician can quickly identify clinically elevated scores and can also identify similarities and differences among informants' reports. If nosologically based taxonomic constructs are quantified, as exemplified by the *DSM*-oriented scales and as proposed for *DSM-V* (Helzer et al., in press), scores on such constructs can also be used for systematic cross-informant comparisons.

Multicultural Perspectives

Today's clinical caseloads include people from many different backgrounds. Native-born minority groups and immigrants from other regions and countries may need to be evaluated in relation to norms different from those of the majority groups in the societies where they are being clinically evaluated (Achenbach & Rescorla, 2007b). Before considering norms for different groups, it is important to determine whether particular taxonomic constructs are appropriate for representing psychopathology among different cultural groups. The multicultural generalizability of the statistically derived syndromes of the ASEBA instruments has been tested by performing CFA on large samples of parents' ratings of their children in 30 societies, teachers' ratings of their students in 20 societies, and youths' self-ratings in 23 societies (Ivanova, Achenbach, Dumenci, et al., 2007; Ivanova, Achenbach, Rescorla, Dumenci, Almqvist, Bathiche, et al., 2007; Ivanova, Achenbach, Rescorla, Dumenci, Almqvist, Bilenberg, et al., 2007). The societies differed in many ways from the United States, where the syndromes were originally derived. Examples of societies that differed in geographical region, language, ethnicity, religion, and

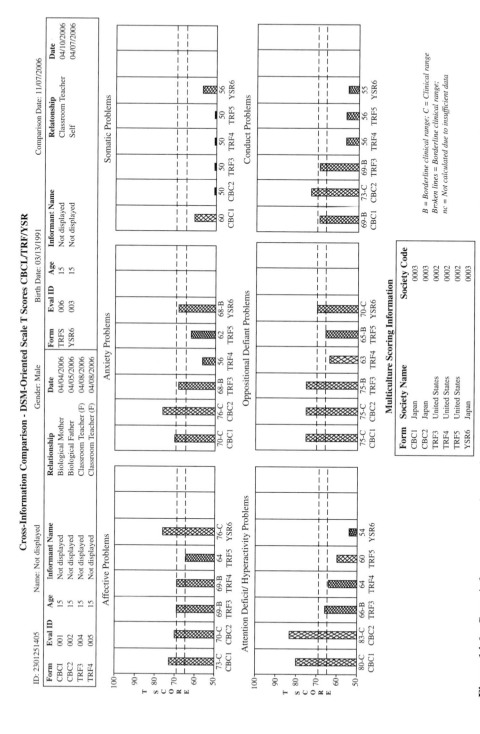

Figure 14.6 Cross-informant comparisons of *DSM*-oriented scale scores using Japanese norms for parents' ratings (designated as CBC) and youth's self-ratings (designated as YSR) and U.S. norms for teachers' ratings (designated as TRF). *Source: Multicultural Supplement to the Manual for the ASEBA School-Age Forms and Profiles*, by T. M. Achenbach and L. A. Rescorla, 2007a, Burlington: University of Vermont, Research Center for Children, Youth, and Families. Reprinted with permission.

political systems are Iran, China, Japan, Thailand, Korea, Ethiopia, Lebanon, Russia, and Turkey. Societies from the Caribbean and from western, eastern, northern, and southern Europe were also included.

To the surprise of the researchers, the syndromes derived primarily from U.S. samples were found to fit the data for all the other societies. The taxonomic constructs embodied by the statistically derived syndromes thus represent patterns of parent, teacher, and self-ratings of behavioral, emotional, social, and thought problems for at least this large array of very diverse societies. At this writing, no multicultural studies have tested taxonomic constructs embodied in the *DSM* or *ICD* nosologies for children's disorders.

The multicultural CFA support for the statistically derived syndromes justifies use of the syndromes for assessing children from many societies. However, this does not necessarily mean that the distributions of scale scores are similar enough to justify use of the same norms for different societies. The distributions of scale scores have been statistically compared for the United States and all the societies that were included in the CFA tests of the statistically derived syndromes (Rescorla et al., 2007, 2007a, 2007b). A great deal of overlap was found between the distributions of problem scores from all societies and the mean total problems scores from most societies were clustered within a narrow range. However, some societies had mean total problems scores that were low or high enough to warrant separate norms.

To take account of the relatively low scores, one set of norms was constructed by averaging the scores for societies whose mean total problems scores were more than 1 standard deviation below the mean of all the societies (called the "omnicultural mean"; Ellis & Kimmel, 1992). Another set of norms was constructed by averaging the scores for societies whose mean total problems scores were more than 1 standard deviation above the omnicultural mean. A third set of norms, for the middle scoring societies, consists of norms for U.S. samples, which are about in the middle of the middle group and which have been used in many clinical and research applications.

When evaluating individual children, clinicians can elect to have the children's syndrome and *DSM*-oriented scale scores displayed on profiles and cross-informant bar graphs in relation to norms for the low-scoring, middle-scoring, or high-scoring societies. The clinician can also choose to have percentiles and *T* scores from the low-, middle-, or high-scoring societies displayed. Equally important, the clinician can see how the child's scale scores compare with different sets of norms. This is especially useful for immigrant children and for children whose parents and/or teachers have very different cultural backgrounds.

As an example, for the cross-informant comparisons shown in Figure 14.6, the clinician elected to have the parents' CBCL/6–18 scale scores displayed in relation to norms for the high-scoring societies, because the parents had emigrated from a high-scoring society, maintained its customs, still spoke its language, and completed a translation of the CBCL/6–18 in that society's language. Because their child attended a mainstream school in the host society where TRF scores were in the middle-norm group, the clinician elected to have the TRF scale scores displayed in relation to the middle norms. Because YSR scores in the youth's home culture were in the high-norm group, the clinician elected to have the YSR scale scores displayed in relation to the high norms. However, because the host society's YSR scores were in the middle-norm group, the clinician subsequently had the cross-informant comparisons displayed again with the youth's YSR scores displayed in relation to the middle norms. This enabled the clinician to see whether any scales would be clinically elevated that had not been clinically elevated in relation to the high norms. Note that all scales in the cross-informant comparisons are displayed in terms of T scores, but the user decides whether to display scores for each informant in relation to T scores based on the low-scoring, middle-scoring, or high-scoring societies.

Implications for Clinical Practice

Taxonomic constructs may seem irrelevant to clinical practice. However, they provide foundations for assessment, diagnosis, nosology, and treatment. Nosological categories such as ADHD, ODD, CD, Major Depressive Disorder, and Generalized Anxiety Disorder shape many aspects of clinical practice. Although such categories may seem to have an intrinsic reality, changes in the categories from one edition to another edition of a nosology, the lack of operational definitions, poor agreement among "gold standard" diagnostic procedures, and high comorbidity indicate that current nosological categories cannot be equated with categorically distinct disorders. Instead, the categories can be viewed as representing implicit taxonomic constructs. As such, they should be subjected to comparisons with alternative taxonomic constructs. For child psychopathology, statistically derived syndromes offer one alternative set of taxonomic constructs for which there is considerable empirical support. Options for scoring both statistically derived syndromes and *DSM*-oriented scales from the same sets of parent, teacher, and self-ratings can help clinicians view children's problems from both taxonomic perspectives. Multi-informant and multicultural comparisons of both kinds of scales further enhance opportunities for flexibly adapting clinical assessment to the needs of children from diverse backgrounds, as seen from different informants' perspectives.

SUMMARY

Assessment, diagnosis, nosology, and taxonomy can be understood as interdependent aspects of continuous processes. This chapter focused on these processes as they pertain to behavioral, emotional, social, and thought problems occurring between the ages of 18 months and 18 years with sufficient severity to warrant the term "psychopathology" and a likely need for professional help.

Clinical assessment refers to procedures for identifying the distinguishing features of problems, disorders, or cases, as well as relevant strengths. Some assessment instruments are designed to determine whether children meet criteria for *DSM* diagnoses, whereas other instruments assess broader spectra of functioning. Evidence- (or empirically) based assessment is necessary for appropriate applications of evidence-based treatment and other clinical services. Comprehensive clinical assessment of children should include assessment of parent figures.

Diagnosis has become a primary focus of clinical services since the *DSM-III* introduced explicit diagnostic criteria. Confusion often arises from failure to distinguish clearly among diagnostic processes, formal diagnoses, and diagnostic formulations. Most relevant to nosology and taxonomy, formal diagnoses are made by determining how a case should be categorized.

Nosologies such as the *DSM* and the *ICD* are systems for classifying diseases (or disorders). Since the introduction of explicit diagnostic criteria by *DSM-III*, many children have been found to meet criteria for multiple diagnoses. Although comorbid diagnoses may provide useful information, the implications of comorbidity have been clouded by failure to compute it bidirectionally and by rates of comorbidity between some diagnoses that are so high as to cast doubt on whether they really represent different disorders. Quantitative approaches that are being advocated for *DSM-V* could help to alleviate problems arising from excess comorbidity among diagnoses as well as to bring diagnoses more in tune with advances in genetics, imaging, and biochemistry.

Taxonomic constructs may seem irrelevant to clinical practice, but they provide foundations for assessment, diagnosis, nosology, and treatment. The lack of known natural categories for psychopathology means that we should think in terms of multiple ways of taxonomically organizing data on psychopathology to avoid reifying any single set of taxonomic constructs. Nosological categories can be viewed as taxonomic constructs, although criteria for the constructs must be operationalized in a top-down process of developing assessment procedures such as diagnostic interviews. However, even the most thoroughly researched and widely used diagnostic interviews have yielded negligible agreement for child diagnoses made from other diagnostic interviews and from clinical evaluations.

Empirically based taxonomic constructs have been derived from statistical analyses of data obtained with empirically based assessment instruments. The generalizability of the syndromes derived from this bottom-up process has been supported by CFA of large samples from many societies.

There are important points of contact between nosologically based and empirically based taxonomic constructs. Both kinds of constructs have been operationalized via a common pool of assessment items. For both kinds of constructs, assessment data from multiple informants and normative data from multiple cultures are needed for clinical research and practice in the twenty-first century.

REFERENCES

Achenbach, T. M. (1991). "Comorbidity" in child and adolescent psychiatry: Categorical and quantitative perspectives. *Journal of Child and Adolescent Psychopharmacology, 1*, 271–278.

Achenbach, T. M. (2005). Advancing assessment of children and adolescents: Commentary on evidence-based assessment of child and adolescent disorders. *Journal of Clinical Child and Adolescent Psychology, 34*, 541–547.

Achenbach, T. M., Dumenci, L., & Rescorla, L. A. (2003). DSM-oriented and empirically based approaches to constructing scales from the same item pools. *Journal of Clinical Child and Adolescent Psychology, 32*, 328–340.

Achenbach, T. M., Krukowski, R. A., Dumenci, L., & Ivanova, M. Y. (2005). Assessment of adult psychopathology: Meta-analyses and implications of cross-informant correlations. *Psychological Bulletin, 131*, 361–382.

Achenbach, T. M., McConaughy, S. H., & Howell, C. T. (1987). Child/adolescent behavioral and emotional problems: Implications of cross-informant correlations for situational specificity. *Psychological Bulletin, 101*, 213–232.

Achenbach, T. M., Newhouse, P. A., & Rescorla, L. A. (2004). *Manual for the ASEBA older adult forms and profiles*. Burlington: University of Vermont, Research Center for Children, Youth, and Families.

Achenbach, T. M., & Rescorla, L. A. (2000). *Manual for the ASEBA preschool forms and profiles*. Burlington: University of Vermont, Research Center for Children, Youth, and Families.

Achenbach, T. M., & Rescorla, L. A. (2001). *Manual for the ASEBA school-age forms and profiles*. Burlington: University of Vermont, Research Center for Children, Youth, and Families.

Achenbach, T. M., & Rescorla, L. A. (2003). *Manual for the ASEBA adult forms and profiles*. Burlington: University of Vermont, Research Center for Children, Youth, and Families.

Achenbach, T. M., & Rescorla, L. A. (2004). The Achenbach System of Empirically Based Assessment (ASEBA) for ages 1.5 to 18 years. In M. R. Maruish (Ed.), *The use of psychological testing for treatment planning and outcomes assessment* (3rd ed., Vol. 2, pp. 179–213). Mahwah, NJ: Erlbaum.

Achenbach, T. M., & Rescorla, L. A. (2007a). *Multicultural supplement to the Manual for the ASEBA School-Age Forms and Profiles*. Burlington: University of Vermont, Research Center for Children, Youth, and Families.

Achenbach, T. M., & Rescorla, L. A. (2007b). *Multicultural understanding of child and adolescent psychopathology: Implications for mental health assessment*. New York: Guilford Press.

Ambrosini, P. J. (2000). Historical development and present status of the Schedule for Affective Disorders and Schizophrenia for School-Age Children (K-SADS). *Journal of the American Academy of Child and Adolescent Psychiatry, 39*, 49–58.

American Psychiatric Association. (1968). *Diagnostic and statistical manual of mental disorders* (2nd ed.). Washington, DC: Author.

American Psychiatric Association. (1980). *Diagnostic and statistical manual of mental disorders* (3rd ed.) Washington, DC: Author.

American Psychiatric Association. (1987). *Diagnostic and statistical manual of mental disorders* (3rd ed., rev.). Washington, DC: Author.

American Psychiatric Association. (1994). *Diagnostic and statistical manual of mental disorders* (4th ed.) Washington, DC: Author.

American Psychiatric Association. (2000). *Diagnostic and statistical manual of mental disorders* (4th ed., text rev.). Washington, DC: Author.

Angold, A., & Costello, E. J. (2000). The Child and Adolescent Psychiatric Assessment (CAPA). *Journal of the American Academy of Child and Adolescent Psychiatry, 39*, 39–48.

Angold, A., Costello, E. J., & Erkanli, A. (1999). *Comorbidity. Journal of Child Psychology and Psychiatry 40*, 57–87.

Bérubé, R. L., & Achenbach, T. M. (2008). *Bibliography of published studies using the Achenbach System of Empirically Based Assessment (ASEBA): 2008 edition*. Burlington: University of Vermont, Research Center for Children, Youth, and Families.

Bird, H. R., Gould, M. S., Rubio-Stipec, M., Staghezza, B. M., & Canino, G. (1991). Screening for childhood psychopathology in the community using the Child Behavior Checklist. *Journal of the American Academy of Child and Adolescent Psychiatry, 30*, 116–123.

Bird, H. R., Gould, M. S., & Staghezza, B. M. (1993). Patterns of diagnostic comorbidity in a community sample of children aged 9 through 16 years. *Journal of the American Academy of Child and Adolescent Psychiatry, 32*, 361–368.

Caron, C., & Rutter, M. (1991). Comorbidity in child psychopathology: Concepts, issues, and research strategies. *Journal of Child Psychology and Psychiatry, 32*, 1063–1080.

Cohen, J. (1960). A coefficient of agreement for nominal scales. *Educational and Psychological Measurement, 20*, 37–46.

Cohen, P., O'Connor, P., Lewis, S., Velez, C. N., & Malachowski, B., (1987). Comparison of DISC and K-SADS-P interviews of an epidemiological sample of children. *Journal of the American Academy of Child and Adolescent Psychiatry, 26*, 662–667.

Conners, C. K. (1997). *Conners' Rating Scales—Revised technical manual*. North Tonawanda, NY: Multi-Health Systems.

Conners, C. K. (2001). *Conners' Rating Scales—Revised technical manual*. North Tonawanda, NY: Multi-Health Systems.

Conners, C. K., Sitarenios, G., Parker, J. D. A., & Epstein, J. N. (1998). Revision and restandardization of the Conners Teacher Rating Scale (CTRS-R): Factor structure, reliability, and criterion validity. *Journal of Abnormal Child Psychology, 26*, 279–291.

Costello, A., Edelbrock, C., Kalas, R., Kessler, M., & Klaric, S. A. (1982). *Diagnostic Interview Schedule for Children (DISC)* (Contract No. RFP-DB-81-0027). Bethesda, MD: National Institute of Mental Health.

De Los Reyes, A., & Kazdin, A.E. (2005). Informant discrepancies in the assessment of childhood psychopathology: A critical review, theoretical framework, and recommendations for further study. *Psychological Bulletin, 131*, 483–509.

Dickey, W. C., & Blumberg, S. J. (2004). Revisiting the factor structure of the Strengths and Difficulties Questionnaire: United States, 2001. *Journal of the American Academy of Child and Adolescent Psychiatry, 43*, 1159–1167.

Doss, A. J., & Weisz, J. R. (2006). Syndrome co-occurrence and treatment outcomes in youth mental health clinics. *Journal of Consulting and Clinical Psychology, 74*, 416–425.

DuPaul, G. J., Power, T. J., Anastopoulos, A. D., & Reid, R. (1998). *ADHD Rating Scale-IV: Checklists, norms, and clinical interpretation.* New York: Guilford Press.

Ellis, B. B., & Kimmel, H. D., (1992). Identification of unique cultural response patterns by means of item response theory. *Journal of Applied Psychology, 77*, 177–184.

Faraone, S. V., Biederman, J., Keenan, K., & Tsuang, M. T. (1991). A family genetic study of girls with DSM-III attention deficit disorder. *American Journal of Psychiatry, 148*, 112–117.

First, M. R. (2005). Clinical utility: A prerequisite for the adoption of a dimensional approach in DSM. *Journal of Abnormal Psychology, 114*, 560–564.

Gadow, K. D., & Sprafkin, J. (1998). *Adolescent Symptom Inventory-4 norms manual.* Stony Brook, NY: Checkmate Plus.

Gadow, K. D., & Sprafkin, J. (1999). *Youth's Inventory-4 manual.* Stony Brook, NY: Checkmate Plus.

Gadow, K. D., Sprafkin, J., Carlson, G. A., Schneider, J., Nolan, E. E., Mattison, R. E., et al. (2002). A DSM-IV referenced, adolescent self-report rating scale. *Journal of the American Academy of Child and Adolescent Psychiatry, 41*, 671–679.

Goodman, R. (1997). The Strengths and Difficulties Questionnaire: A research note. *Journal of Child Psychology and Psychiatry, 38*, 581–586.

Goodman, R. (2001). Psychometric properties of the Strengths and Difficulties Questionnaire. *Journal of the American Academy of Child and Adolescent Psychiatry, 40*, 1337–1345.

Gove, P. (Ed.). (1971). *Webster's third new international dictionary of the English language.* Springfield, MA: Merriam-Webster.

Graetz, B. W., Sawyer, M. G., Hazell, P. L., Arney, F., & Baghurst, P. (2001). Validity of DSM-IV ADHD subtypes in a nationally representative sample of Australian children and adolescents. *Journal of the American Academy of Child and Adolescent Psychiatry, 40*, 1410–1417.

Guze, S. (1978). Validating criteria for psychiatric diagnosis: The Washington University approach. In M. S. Akiskal & W. L. Webb (Eds.), *Psychiatric diagnosis: Exploration of biological predictors* (pp. 49–59). New York: Spectrum.

Helzer, J. E. Kraemer, H. C. Krueger, R. F. Wittchen, H.-U. & Regier, D. A. (Eds.). (in press). *Dimensional approaches in diagnostic classification: Refining the research agenda for DSM-V.* Washington, DC: American Psychiatric Association.

Herjanic, B., & Reich, W. (1982). Development of a structured psychiatric interview for children: Agreement between child and parent on individual symptoms. *Journal of Abnormal Child Psychology, 10*, 307–324.

Ivanova, M. Y., Achenbach, T. M., Dumenci, L., Rescorla, L. A., Almqvist, F., Weintraub, S., et al. (2007). Testing the 8-syndrome structure of the CBCL in 30 societies. *Journal of Clinical Child and Adolescent Psychology, 36*, 405–417.

Ivanova, M. Y., Achenbach, T. M., Rescorla, L. A., Dumenci, L., Almqvist, F., Bathiche, M., et al. (2007). Testing the Teacher's Report Form syndromes in 20 societies. *School Psychology Review, 36*, 468–483.

Ivanova, M. Y., Achenbach, T. M., Rescorla, L. A., Dumenci, L., Almqvist, F., Bilenberg, F., et al. (2007). The generalizability of the Youth Self-Report syndrome structure in 23 societies. *Journal of Consulting and Clinical Psychology, 75*, 729–738.

Jensen, A. L., & Weisz, J. R. (2002). Assessing match and mismatch between practitioner-generated and standardized interview-generated diagnoses for clinic-referred children and adolescents. *Journal of Consulting and Clinical Psychology, 70*, 158–168.

Jensen, P. S., Rubio-Stipec, M., Canino, G., Bird, H. R., Dulcan, M. K., Schwab-Stone, M. E., et al. (1999). Parent and child contributions to diagnosis of mental disorder: Are both informants always necessary? *Journal of the American Academy of Child and Adolescent Psychiatry, 38*, 1569–1579.

Kendell, R. E. (2002). Five criteria for an improved taxonomy of mental disorders. In J. E. Helzer & J. J. Hudziak (Eds.), *Defining psychopathology in the 21st century: DSM-V and beyond* (pp. 3–17). Washington, DC: American Psychiatric Press.

Koskelainen, M., Sourander, A., & Vauras, M. (2001). Self-reported strengths and difficulties in a community sample of Finnish adolescents. *European Child and Adolescent Psychiatry, 10*, 180–185.

Kraemer, H. C. (in press). DSM categories and dimensions in clinical and research contexts. In J. E. Helzer, H. C. Kraemer, R. F. Krueger, H.-U. Wittchen, & D. A. Regier (Eds.), *Dimensional approaches in diagnostic classification: Refining the research agenda for DSM-V*. Washington, DC: American Psychological Association.

Krueger, R. F., & Markon, K. E. (2006). Understanding psychopathology: Melding behavior genetics, personality, and quantitative psychology to develop an empirically based model. *Current Directions in Psychological Science, 15*, 113–117.

Kupfer, D. J., First, M. B., & Regier, D. E. (2002). Introduction. In D. J. Kupfer, M.B. First, & D. E. Regier (Eds.), *A research agenda for DSM-IV* (pp. xv–xxiii). Washington, DC: American Psychiatric Association.

Levin, D. A. (1979). The nature of plant species. *Science, 204*, 381–384.

Mash, E. J., & Hunsley, J. (2005). Evidence-based assessment of child and adolescent disorders: Issues and challenges. *Journal of Clinical Child and Adolescent Psychology, 34*, 362–379.

Mattison, R., Cantwell, D. P., Russell, A. T., & Will, L. (1979). A comparison of DSM-II and DSM-III in the diagnosis of childhood psychiatric disorders. *Archives of General Psychiatry, 36*, 1217–1222.

Mayr, E. (1987). The ontological status of species: Scientific progress and philosophical terminology. Species concepts and their application. *Biology and Philosophy, 2*, 145–166.

McConaughy, S. H., & Achenbach, T. M. (1994). Comorbidity of empirically based syndromes in matched general population and clinical samples. *Journal of Child Psychology and Psychiatry, 35*, 1141–1157.

Mezzich, A. C., Mezzich, J. E., & Coffman, G. A. (1985). Reliability of DSM-III vs. DSM-II in child psychopathology. *Journal of the American Academy of Child Psychiatry, 24*, 273–280.

Millon, T. (1991). Classification in psychopathology: Rationale, alternatives, and standards. *Journal of Abnormal Psychology, 100*, 245–261.

Muris, P., Meesters, C., Eijkelenboom, A., & Vincken, M. (2004). The self-report version of the Strengths and Difficulties Questionnaire: Its psychometric properties in 8- to 13-year-old non-clinical children. *British Journal of Clinical Psychology, 43*, 437–448.

Quay, H. C. (1986). Classification. In H. C. Quay, & J. S. Werry (Eds.), *Psychopathological disorders of childhood* (3rd ed., pp. 1–34). New York: Wiley.

Rapoport, J., & Ismond, D. R. (1996). *DSM-IV training guide for diagnosis of childhood disorders*. New York: Brunner/Mazel.

Rescorla, L. A., & Achenbach, T. M. (2004). The Achenbach System of Empirically Based Assessment (ASEBA) for ages 18 to 90+ years. In M. R. Maruish (Ed.), *The use of psychological testing for treatment planning and outcomes assessment* (3rd ed., Vol. 3, pp. 115–152). Mahwah, NJ: Erlbaum.

Rescorla, L. A., Achenbach, T. M., Ginzburg, S., Ivanova, M. Y., Dumenci, L., Almqvist, F., et al. (2007). Consistency of teacher-reported problems for students in 21 countries. *School Psychology Review, 36*, 91–110.

Rescorla, L. A., Achenbach, T. M., Ivanova, M. Y., Dumenci, L., Almqvist, F., Bilenberg, N., et al. (2007a). Behavioral and emotional problems reported by parents of children ages 6 to 16 in 31 societies. *Journal of Emotional and Behavioral Disorders, 15*, 130–142.

Rescorla, L. A., Achenbach, T. M., Ivanova, M. Y., Dumenci, L., Almqvist, F., Bilenberg, N., et al. (2007b). Epidemiological comparisons of problems and positive qualities reported by adolescents in 24 countries. *Journal of Consulting and Clinical Psychology, 75*, 351–358.

Rettew, D. C., Doyle, A. C., Achenbach, T. M., Dumenci, L., & Ivanova, M. Y. (2006). Meta-analyses of diagnostic agreement between clinical evaluations and standardized diagnostic interviews. *Comprehensive Psychiatry*. Manuscript submitted for publication.

Reynolds, C. R., & Kamphaus, R. W. (2004). *BASC-2 Behavior Assessment System for Children manual* (2nd ed.). Circle Pine, MN: AGS.

Rønning, J. A., Handegaard, B. H., Sourander, A., & Mørch, W-T. (2004). The Strengths and Difficulties Self-Report Questionnaire as a screening instrument in Norwegian community samples. *European Child and Adolescent Psychiatry, 13*, 73–82.

Rounsaville, B. J., Alarcon, R. D., Andrews, G., Jackson, J. S., Kendell, R. E., & Kendler, K., (2002). Basic nomenclature issues for DSM-V. In D. J. Kupfer, M. B. First, & D. E. Regier (Eds.), *A research agenda for DSM-V* (pp. 1–29). Washington, DC: American Psychiatric Association.

Shaffer, D., Fisher, P., Lucas, C. P., Dulcan, M. K., & Schwab-Stone, M. E. (2000). NIMH Diagnostic Interview Schedule for Children Version IV (NIMH DISC-IV): Description, differences from previous versions, and reliability of some common diagnoses. *Journal of the American Academy of Child and Adolescent Psychiatry, 39*, 28–38.

Spitzer, R. L., Davies, M., & Barkley, R. A. (1990). The DSM-III-R field trial of disruptive behavior disorders. *Journal of the American Academy of Child and Adolescent Psychiatry, 29*, 690–697.

Steinhausen, H. C., Metzke, C. W., Meier, M., & Kannenberg, R. (1997). Behavioral and emotional problems reported by parents for ages 6 to 17 in a Swiss epidemiological study. *European Child and Adolescent Psychiatry, 6*, 136–141.

Trull, T. J., & Durrett, C. A. (2005). Categorical and dimensional models of personality disorder. *Annual Review of Clinical Psychology, 1*, 355–380.

Verhulst, F. C., van der Ende, J., Ferdinand, R. F., & Kasius, M. C., (1997). The prevalence of DSM-III-R diagnoses in a national sample of Dutch adolescents. *Archives of General Psychiatry, 54*, 329–336.

Walker, J. L., Lahey, B. B., Russo, M. F., Frick, P. J., Christ, M. A. G., McBurnett, K., et al. (1991). Anxiety, inhibition, and conduct disorder in children: Pt. I. Relations to social impairment. *Journal of the American Academy of Child and Adolescent Psychiatry, 30*, 187–191.

Widiger, T. A., & Clark, L. A. (2000). Toward DSM-V and the classification of psychopathology. *Psychological Bulletin, 126*, 946–963.

World Health Organization. (1992). *Mental disorders: Glossary and guide to their classification in accordance with the tenth revision of the international classification of diseases* (10th ed.) Geneva, Switzerland: Author.

World Health Organization. (1993). *The ICD-10 classification of mental and behavioral disorders: Diagnostic criteria for research*. Geneva, Switzerland: Author.

Zachar, P. (2000). Psychiatric disorders are not natural kinds. *Philosophy, Psychiatry, and Psychology, 7*, 167–182.

CHAPTER 15

Diagnostic Interviewing

Amie Grills-Taquechel and Thomas H. Ollendick

It is well recognized by those involved in children's mental health that proper assessment and diagnosis of the diverse childhood psychopathologies are critical undertakings. The importance of these issues has been reflected in the numerous changes and developmental adaptations made to the *Diagnostic and Statistical Manual of Mental Disorders* (*DSM*). The criteria provided in the *DSM* are considered the basis for all major psychiatric diagnoses and constitute the necessary requirements for reimbursement or coverage by major health management organizations. Over the past 25 years, the *DSM* has undergone several changes specific to childhood disorders. In so doing, the *DSM* has begun to recognize that children are not miniature adults and that the identification of various disorders in childhood requires developmental adaptations (Ollendick & Hersen, 1983, 1989, 1998). For example, with the third revision of the *DSM,* a section specific to disorders that are usually first diagnosed in infancy, childhood, or adolescence was introduced. In addition, with each revision to the *DSM,* increasingly more diagnostic criteria that incorporate developmental considerations have been put forth. To illustrate, in the current *DSM-IV* (American Psychiatric Association, 1994, pp. 416–417), the diagnostic criteria for Social Phobia provide the following distinctions for children:

> (A) In children, there may be evidence of the capacity for age-appropriate social relationships with familiar people and the anxiety must occur in peer settings, not just in interactions with adults; (B) In children, the anxiety may be expressed by crying, tantrums, freezing, or shrinking from social situations with unfamiliar people; (C) In children, this feature (i.e., recognition of the fear as excessive or unreasonable) may be absent; and (F) In individuals under age 18 years, the duration is at least 6 months.

Similar modifications have been made to other psychiatric disorders to make them more applicable to children and adolescents for whom separate categories do not exist.

Increased attention to the issue of proper evaluation of child psychopathology has also been reflected in the actual role of children in the assessment and diagnostic process. In the past, parents were thought to be the best informants regarding

---

This chapter was funded in part by National Institute of Mental Health Grant R0151308 to Thomas H. Ollendick.

a child's behavior and were, therefore, the only ones included in the assessment process (Loeber, Green, & Lahey, 1990; Rutter & Graham, 1968; Rutter, Tizard, & Whitmore, 1970; Williams, McGee, Anderson, & Silva, 1989). Any information collected from or reported by the child was considered secondary to the parents' reports. Reliance on parental report was primarily based on the assumption that children lacked the cognitive sophistication to respond appropriately in an interview format. For example, researchers reported concern that children would be inattentive to the assessment process, lack insight regarding their feelings, and be unable to accurately describe their own behaviors and symptoms (Edelbrock & Costello, 1990; Herjanic, Herjanic, Brown, & Wheatt, 1975; Schwab-Stone, Fallon, Briggs, & Crowther, 1994). Thus, the amount of credence placed on the child's report was minimal, and parents were considered the experts regarding the child's outward behaviors as well as their internal thoughts and feelings.

This view changed dramatically following seminal studies by Lapouse and Monk (1958), who included mothers and their children in the interview process, and Rutter, Graham, and colleagues (Rutter & Graham, 1968; Rutter et al., 1970; Rutter, Tizard, Yule, Graham, & Kingsley, 1977; Rutter, Tizard, Yule, Graham, & Whitmore, 1976), who designed and psychometrically validated the first structured interview procedures for children. The consideration of the child as a separate and valuable respondent by these researchers as well as their careful evaluation of the interview process paved the way for today's inclusion of multiple informants in clinical interview procedures. Currently, most researchers and clinicians consider a child assessment incomplete if information from numerous sources (e.g., teachers, parents, doctors), including the child, is not obtained (Ollendick & Hersen, 1984, 1993). Thus, children are now viewed as reliable, valid, and valuable informants regarding their subjective thoughts, behaviors, and emotions (Chambers et al., 1985; Edelbrock, Costello, Dulcan, Kalas, & Conover, 1985; Herjanic et al., 1975; Hodges, McKnew, Cytryn, Stern, & Kline, 1982; Kazdin, French, & Unis, 1983; Moretti, Fine, Haley, & Marriage, 1985; Verhulst, Althaus, & Berden, 1987). Consequently, companion diagnostic interviews for children and their parents have been developed (and revised) in line with the changes in the *DSM*. To demonstrate their psychometric soundness (e.g., reliability, validity, clinical utility), careful evaluations have been conducted with both the child and parent diagnostic interviews.

In general, "reliability refers to the consistency of measurements," whereas "the validity of a test refers to the extent to which a test measures what it is supposed to measure, and therefore the appropriateness with which inferences can be made on the basis of the test results" (Sattler, 1988, pp. 25, 30). Although a measure can be reliable while lacking validity, both of these psychometric features are necessary to proclaim an interview psychometrically sound.*

---

*The kappa statistic (i.e., κ) is commonly used in studies that assess reliability with dichotomous data. The kappa is a correlational statistic that corrects for chance and ranges from -1.00 (total disagreement) to 1.00 (pure agreement). Although the kappa statistic evaluates agreement beyond the level of chance, it is also sensitive to base rates, resulting in lower κs for less prevalent symptoms or disorders. Interpretations vary, but typically $\kappa s < .40$ are considered poor, $\kappa s = .40$ to .70 are considered acceptable, and $\kappa s > .70$ are considered good or excellent.

Important distinctions in the literature regarding reliability are those among different indices of interrater, test-retest, and multiple-informant agreement. *Interrater agreement* refers to the amount of consensus between two observers of the same child or of the same child's behaviors at the same point in time and in the same setting. With the diagnostic interviews, this is usually accomplished in one of two ways: live observation with simultaneous coding or video or audiotape recordings that are coded following the diagnostic interview. In general, interrater reliability tends to be high and is frequently higher than the other two types of reliability. *Test-retest reliability*, also called within-informant reliability, refers to the amount of consistency, or agreement, found regarding the same measure of behavior over time. In diagnostic interviews, this type of reliability customarily examines the level of symptom or diagnostic agreement *in the same informant* from one assessment time to another. *Multiple-informant agreement*, on the other hand, concerns the consensus of ratings made regarding a particular child *by different individuals* (e.g., parent-child, parent-teacher). Although discrepancies can affect all types of reliability, research findings suggest that more pronounced differences are found with multiple informants. That is, in contrast to generally acceptable levels of interrater and test-retest agreement, multiple-informant reliability studies have consistently yielded poor results. This has been so for child behavior rating scales as well as diagnostic interviews (cf. Achenbach, Dumenci, & Rescorla, 2002; Achenbach, McConaughy, & Howell, 1987; Grills & Ollendick, 2002).

In general, *validity* refers to how well a test measures what it is supposed to measure. Common types of validity examined include content, criterion-related, and construct validity. *Content validity* refers to the degree to which questions in the interview represent all aspects of the disorder and cannot be examined with traditional statistical procedures. Basically, it refers to the extent to which the diagnostic interview taps the various symptoms of a given disorder. *Criterion-related validity*, on the other hand, concerns the degree to which a measure like a diagnostic interview predicts an outcome on another measure such as adjustment, and is typically separated into concurrent (i.e., both measures obtained at the same time) and predictive (i.e., one measure obtained prior to the other) validity categories. Finally, *construct validity* measures how effectively the information obtained from the interview agrees with the theoretical construct being investigated (i.e., depression). Construct validity is typically determined via positive correlations with established measures of the construct under investigations (convergent validity) and nonsignificant associations with measures previously established to measure theoretically diverse constructs (divergent validity).

Establishing the validity of psychiatric diagnoses based on diagnostic interviews is frequently problematic because no gold standard exists with which to compare the findings. Consider the validity of diagnostic interviews and less structured and more traditional clinical interviews. Without a definitive comparison or standard, it cannot be determined whether it is the diagnostic interview or the clinical interview that is more accurate. Indeed, there are myriad factors that could influence either indicator, for example, the need for clinicians to obtain a diagnosis in order to receive insurance reimbursement or the inability of structured diagnostic interviews to allow for additional inquiry of symptoms (see A. Jensen & Weisz, 2002, for further discussion of factors that could affect each). Moreover, very few studies have been conducted with regard to the validity of diagnostic interviews, and oftentimes estimates of validity are put together based on various methodological designs. For example, examination of content validity cannot be statistically evaluated, and yet the face validity of structured interviews is typically considered certain as items are derived from the *DSM* diagnostic criteria. A bit of circular reasoning is involved with such conclusions.

Criterion-related validity of the concurrent type is also difficult to determine. These findings are troubling as agreement between diagnoses generated by diagnostic interviews and real-world clinicians is often poor (cf. A. Jensen & Weisz, 2002), despite the use of varied methodologies and interviews. For example, A. Jensen and Weisz examined diagnostic interview diagnoses and diagnoses determined at community health clinics and found agreement not significantly better than chance for most individual disorders (e.g., Dysthymic Disorder) and broad categories of those disorders (e.g., mood disorders). Similarly, Lewczyk, Garland, Hurlburt, Gearity, and Hough (2003) found poor agreement with diagnostic interviews and diagnoses generated by a multidisciplinary team that included diverse mental health practitioners, including a child psychiatrist, a child psychologist, and a social worker. Overall, studies have shown poor validity when diagnoses obtained from diagnostic interviews are compared to clinician diagnoses at outpatient clinics (e.g., Ezpeleta, de la Osa, Doménech, Navarro, & Losilla, 1997), inpatient clinics (Pellegrino, Singh, & Carmanico, 1999; Vitello, Malone, Buschle, & Delaney, 1990), and on admission (Weinstein, Stone, Noam, & Grimes, 1989) and discharge (Aronen, Noam, & Weinstein, 1993; Welner, Reich, Herjanic, Jung, & Amado, 1987) from both of these settings.

Predictive validity has been demonstrated in only a few studies. For example, ratings of disruptive behavior disorders on diagnostic interviews and later problematic behaviors (e.g., delinquency, oppositional behavior) have been demonstrated (Jewell, Handwerk, Almquist, & Lucas, 2004). Furthermore, significantly better predictive validity (over a 6-month period) was found for child reports of Conduct Disorder on diagnostic interviews than for children who received diagnoses only from clinicians (and not reported by themselves) and a control group of children for whom no reports of externalizing problems were reported.

With regard to construct validity, diagnoses derived from diagnostic interviews are used to validate information obtained from rating scales, self-report instruments, and behavioral observations. In addition, some research has examined this process in reverse; that is, questionnaires and rating scales have been used as the criterion, and diagnoses obtained from diagnostic interviews have been examined in relation to these measures. For example, empirical research has confirmed the validity of diagnoses formulated using the child and parent versions of the Anxiety Disorders Interview Schedule (see later discussion) by showing that scores on child and parent rating scales converge in expected ways with diagnoses (e.g., Weems, Silverman, Saavedra, Pina, & Lumpkin, 1999; Wood, Piacentini, Bergman, McCracken, & Barrios, 2002). Wood et al. evaluated the validity of Anxiety Disorders Interview Schedule: Child and Parent Versions (ADIS-C/P) diagnoses of Social

Phobia, Separation Anxiety Disorder, Generalized Anxiety Disorder, and Panic Disorder in children and adolescents referred to an outpatient anxiety disorders clinic. In addition to youth and parents being administered their respective versions of the ADIS interviews, they were administered the Multidimensional Anxiety Scale for Children (MASC; March, Parker, Sullivan, Stallings, & Conners, 1997). Strong correspondence was found between ADIS-C/P diagnoses and empirically derived MASC factor scores corresponding to each of these diagnoses and disorders, with the exception of Generalized Anxiety Disorder. For example, MASC social anxiety factor scores, but no other factor scores, were significantly elevated for children meeting *DSM-IV* criteria for Social Phobia on the ADIS-C/P. Despite these positive findings, there is a need for research that evaluates the validity of diagnoses formulated with interview schedules beyond looking at diagnoses' convergence and divergence with questionnaire data (Jarrett, Wolff, & Ollendick, 2007). Ideally, other markers, including what have come to be known as endophenotypes, could be used for this purpose.

In addition to establishing the correct diagnosis, diagnostic interviews are also frequently used for case conceptualization and treatment planning purposes (Silverman & Ollendick, in press). Such purposes refer to the clinical utility of the instrument being used. Diagnoses themselves yield powerful information about treatment targets and potential treatment plans. For example, the anxiety and worry of Generalized Anxiety Disorder (GAD) is associated with one or more of the following six *DSM-IV* symptoms: being restless, being easily fatigued, having difficulty concentrating, being irritable, having muscle tension, and having difficulty falling or staying asleep. Any one or more of these problems (i.e., target symptoms) could lead to highly specific treatment plans designed to address them. This approach to prescriptive interventions is illustrated in the early work of Eisen and Silverman (1993, 1998) and is captured well in a recent book on modularized treatment by Chorpita (2007). In an early study, Eisen and Silverman (1993) showed that cognitive-behavior therapy was most effective for children with overanxious disorder (the *DSM-III-R* precursor to GAD) when they were matched with specific symptoms. For example, children with primary symptoms of worry and obsessions responded more favorably to cognitive therapy, whereas children with primary symptoms of somatic complaints responded more favorably to relaxation training aimed at dealing with physiological and somatic complaints. This early study was replicated in a second study by Eisen and Silverman (1998), in which these authors again showed that although both treatments were generally effective, only the prescriptive treatments produced sufficient improvements for the treated children to meet exacting positive end-state functioning criteria. Similar effects of matching were shown by Ollendick, Hagopian, and Huntzinger (1991) with separation anxious children and by Ollendick (1995) with adolescents with Panic Disorder and Agoraphobia. Thus, in these studies, treatments were shown to be maximally effective when they were closely matched with the symptom presentation of the individual child or adolescent. That is, specific diagnoses when supplemented with symptom profiles led to superior outcomes.

Likewise, diagnostic interviews have been used for treatment evaluation purposes. For example, in treatment outcome studies, 100% of youth necessarily meet diagnostic criteria at pretreatment. In evaluating treatment outcome, of interest is the diagnostic recovery rate at posttreatment and follow-up; most studies report 60% to 80% of participants as recovered and no longer meeting diagnostic criteria at posttreatment and follow-up. As such, diagnostic interviews are extremely useful and provide one of the most rigorous ways of determining treatment outcomes and providing an evidence base for various treatment interventions (Ollendick, King, & Chorpita, 2006).

Finally, before proceeding to a review of specific diagnostic interviews, brief mention should be made of what has come to be called the treatment utility (a form of clinical utility) of measures such as diagnostic interviews. As we have noted, if one wishes to use the treatment that possesses the most research evidence for a given disorder, it is important to first have *confidence* (i.e., have reliable and valid information) that the youth or groups of youths with whom one is working are in fact accurately diagnosed with the disorder under study, rather than some other clinical disorder. Second, it is important to have confidence about the *specific* type(s) of disorder that the youth is diagnosed with. For example, with the anxiety disorders, it is crucial to know the exact disorder so that appropriate exposure tasks can be assigned in and out of the treatment sessions (e.g., expose the child to social evaluative situations if the child has a Social Phobia; to separation situations if the child has Separation Anxiety Disorder). However, as Nelson-Gray (2003) has pointed out, empirical verification of treatment utility is yet to be demonstrated. That is, it has not been empirically tested whether different outcomes result for children who have received diagnoses assigned with a diagnostic interview schedule and are given an intervention versus a group of children who have *not* been given a diagnostic interview schedule and receive the same treatment. Although such may be so, it seems to us that starting an intervention without this information would be premature.

As is evident, a host of issues surrounding diagnostic interviews exist, including their reliability, validity, and clinical utility. Although many questions remain about the psychometric properties of these interviews, much progress has been made. A number of reliable, valid, and clinically useful interviews have been developed, a topic to which we next turn our attention.

DIAGNOSTIC INTERVIEWS

Generally speaking, diagnostic interviews are considered to be a formal and full examination of a particular problem area or areas. There are several expectations imposed on these interviews: (a) They are psychometrically sound measurements, (b) they have specific rules regarding the content and order of the questions and topics being addressed (e.g., asking whether depressed mood is present prior to asking the possible effects of the depressed mood) as well as the manner of recording responses, and (c) some degree of structure is imposed with regard to final diagnostic decisions (Weiss, 1993). The degree of correspondence with these specifications appears to be directly related to the amount of structure imposed by the interview. Various descriptions have been applied to distinguish among diagnostic interviews, with the most common distinction pertaining to the structure (semi- or highly structured) of the interview. Specifically, distinctions have been made among unstructured, semi-structured, and highly structured interviews.

Unstructured interviews give complete discretion to the interviewer as to what, when, and how questions will be asked and recorded. Although these interviews typically contain questions pertaining to the child's history (e.g., medical, psychological, developmental, academic, social), presenting problems (e.g., antecedents, behaviors, consequences), environmental contexts (e.g., home and family, school), and treatments (i.e., past and present), there are no set procedures used across clinicians. Semi-structured interviews also tend to allow leeway for the interviewer regarding the order in which questions are asked, the manner in which the questions are phrased, and the way responses are recorded. Emphasis is placed on obtaining consistent and reliable information; thus extensive training is generally required for administration of these interviews to ensure that clinical discretion will be applied judiciously. Highly structured interviews, on the other hand, are more restrictive in the amount of freedom allotted to the interviewer. With these interviews, it is generally expected that examiners ask all questions in the same manner and order, as well as record all responses in a prespecified manner. Clinical judgment is reduced with highly structured interviews, such that specific and/or extensive training is not required for their administration. In fact, highly structured interviews are commonly administered by laypersons (e.g., individuals without a formal degree in psychology, psychiatry, or social work), and several have been converted to computer-based formats (e.g., Diagnostic Interview Schedule for Children [DISC], Diagnostic Interview for Children and Adolescents [DICA]; see later discussion). Although highly structured formats allow for more confidence in the exactness of the interview's administration and perhaps more reliable findings, the rigidity of the interview may also make it seem impersonal, hinder the establishment of rapport, and interfere with reliability and validity by not providing the interviewee the opportunity to report all difficulties or to explore them in full depth. As a result, the use of highly structured interviews may result in unanswered questions for the clinician that might have been addressed in a less structured format (e.g., knowing a child feels sad most days does not answer questions of potential precipitants, etiological factors, responses by others in the child's environment).

In addition to differentiations based on interview structure, a variety of descriptors have been used in the literature (i.e., respondent-based versus interviewer-based, glossary-driven versus clinician-driven). Nevertheless, each of these distinctions concerns the degree of latitude allotted the interviewer, as well as the type of research with which the interview was designed to be used. Initially, highly structured interviews were used for epidemiological research, and semi-structured interviews were used in clinical research and randomized controlled trials. However, currently these distinctions seem less meaningful, with all research teams but that of the DISC considering their interviews semi-structured and some creating separate epidemiological and clinical interview versions (e.g., Schedule for Affective Disorders and Schizophrenia for School-Age Children [K-SADS]; see later discussion).

For the most part, the format of companion parent and child interviews is similar; each contains (a) an introductory section designed to help build rapport with the informant (e.g., demographics, school, free time activities) and elicit initial information regarding presenting problems; (b) symptom-specific modules (e.g., mood disorders) that usually begin with screener questions and determine whether to skip or continue with follow-up questions (i.e., regarding frequency, intensity, duration, and interference); and (c) the determination of diagnostic presence or absence based on algorithms or clinical judgments. Several of the most commonly utilized diagnostic interviews are discussed next, with general psychometric information provided. Overall, acceptable test-retest and interrater reliability coefficients have been reported for each of these interviews; however, findings for multiple-informant reliability have been more varied (cf. Grills & Ollendick, 2002), with little data published on the validity of these instruments.

The Anxiety Disorders Interview Schedule for Children for DSM-IV: Child and Parent Versions

The ADIS-CP for *DSM-IV* (Silverman & Albano, 1996; Silverman, Saavedra, & Pina, 2001) is a downward extension of the adult Anxiety Disorders Interview Schedule for *DSM-IV* (Brown, Di Nardo, & Barlow, 1994) and is most detailed in its coverage of the anxiety disorders, relative to the other interview schedules. The ADIS for *DSM-IV:* C/P and its previous *DSM-III* and *DSM-III-R* versions (Silverman, 1991) have been used most frequently in the youth anxiety disorders research literature, including randomized clinical trials. The ADIS for *DSM-IV:* C/P contains a series of modules that cover all the anxiety disorders described in *DSM-IV,* as well as sections that cover the most prevalent disorders of childhood and adolescence (e.g., Attention-Deficit/Hyperactivity Disorder [ADHD], depressive disorders) and screening questions for most other disorders (e.g., eating disorders, enuresis). Additional questions are included that allow interviewers to obtain information about the history of the problem as well as situational and youth cognitive factors influencing anxiety. In addition, the ADIS for *DSM-IV:* C/P contains clinician severity rating scales that assess for degree of impairment or interference in youth functioning associated with the specific anxiety disorder endorsed by the youth and parent, respectively. Specifically, based on the information obtained from the child and parent versions of the interview, interviewers assign the degree of distress and interference associated with each disorder (0 = None to 8 = Very severely disturbing/impairing) with respect to the youth's peer relationships, school work, family life, and personal distress. Each module in the interview also contains questions that allow interviewers to assign 0 to 8 ratings on the youth's fear and avoidance of diverse situations relevant to a particular disorder (e.g., Social Phobia). Similar to the adult ADIS, clinician severity ratings of 4 (definitely disturbing/impairing) or higher are viewed as clinical diagnoses, and those less than 4 are viewed as subclinical or subthreshold.

Acceptable test-retest reliability (7 to 14 days) estimates have been reported for the ADIS for *DSM-IV* Child (aged 7 to 16; $\kappa = .61$ to .80), Parent ($\kappa = .65$ to 1.00), and combined ($\kappa = .62$ to 1.00) diagnoses (Silverman et al., 2001). Likewise, interrater agreement for earlier versions of the ADIS have generally fallen within the acceptable to excellent range for videotape ($\kappa = .45$ to .82; Rapee, Barrett, Dadds, & Evans, 1994) and live observer (.35 to 1.00; Silverman & Nelles, 1988) paradigms. In contrast, findings for multiple-informant reliability have been poor for both the most recent and earlier versions of the ADIS (Grills & Ollendick, 2003; Rapee et al., 1994).

Schedule for Affective Disorders and Schizophrenia for School-Age Children

There are currently several different forms of the K-SADS, all of which include corresponding parent and child (ages 6 to 18) versions. The three most current (*DSM-IV* applicable) and researched are Present state (P-IVR; Ambrosini & Dixon, 1996); Epidemiological (E-Version 5; Orvaschel, 1995); and Present/Lifetime (P/L; Kaufman et al., 1997). Each version of the K-SADS has undergone extensive revisions, which have been detailed elsewhere (see Ambrosini, 2000; Kaufman et al., 1997). Although the primary focus is affective disorders, these three K-SADS versions also assess for several additional disorders (see Table 15.1). The primary difference among these versions is the diagnostic time frame; that is, the K-SADS-P-IVR assesses disorders from the current episode (within the week preceding the interview) as well as from the past 12 months, whereas the K-SADS-E and P/L diagnose current and lifetime disorders (with a focus on the most severe past episode). In all cases, the interviews are conducted with the parent or primary guardian first, and the same interviewer then administers the corresponding version to the child. Information is gathered regarding the child's current symptoms, as well as from when the informant considered the symptoms worst during the specified time frame (i.e., past 12 months or lifetime). Discrepancies in reports of observable behaviors are addressed in a joint parent/child interview prior to the clinician's final ratings. Finally, based on all of the information obtained (e.g., parent, child, schools, charts), the clinician determines summary severity scores for each symptom and makes a diagnosis using accompanying criteria checklists. Research diagnostic criteria (RDC) are used whenever possible, with *DSM* diagnostic criteria used for those disorders not covered by RDC.

Using varied approaches (i.e., videotape, audiotape, live or joint observation), acceptable interrater reliability has been reported for the most recent (K-SADS-P IV, $\kappa = .80$ to 1.00) and earlier (K-SADS-P IIIR, $\kappa = .46$ to .91; K-SADS-E, $\kappa = .51$ to .77; Ambrosini, 2000; Ambrosini, Metz, Prabucki, & Lee, 1989) K-SADS versions. Likewise, test-retest studies have generally revealed adequate reliability coefficients for the K-SADS (P-IIIR, $\kappa = .46$ to .91; E, $\kappa = 1.00$ major depression past episode; P/L, .55 to 1.00). Despite these, agreement between parent and child reports on earlier versions of the KSADS, administered by the same interviewer, has varied greatly ($\kappa = -08$ to .96, Chambers et al., 1985: $\kappa = -.07$ to .52, Angold et al., 1987; $\kappa = .05$ to .66, Hodges, McKnew, Burbach, & Roebuck, 1987), and information on the most recent K-SADS is not currently available. In addition to these reliability estimates, predictive and construct validity have been demonstrated for the K-SADS interviews (see Ambrosini, 2000; Ambrosini et al., 1989).

Diagnostic Interview for Children and Adolescents

The DICA (Reich, 1998) is a semi-structured instrument, with parent and companion child (ages 6 to 12) and adolescent (ages 13 to 18) versions. The most recent revision of the DICA corresponds with the latest revisions to the *DSM* (*III-R, IV*) and is relatively unique in that it examines lifetime diagnoses (cf. Reich, 2000; Rourke & Reich, 2004). In addition to diagnostic sections (see Table 15.1), the DICA includes questions about psychosocial stressors, risk and protective factors, and perinatal, delivery, and early child development (parent interview only). Following completion of the interview, the interviewer pursues problematic areas which are then resolved by consultation with the DICA manual and/or discussion with more experienced clinicians or primary investigators. There are also more structured versions of the DICA, specifically a computerized version, which can be administered by a trained interviewer or completed by the informant alone.

Table 15.1   Summary of Diagnoses Possible with the Structured Interviews Reviewed

Diagnoses	K-SADS-P IV, -E, -P/L	ADIS-IV	DISC-IV	DICA
Major Depressive Disorder	Y	Y	Y	Y
Dysthymic Disorder	Y	Y	Y	Y
Bipolar Disorder	Y	N	N	N
Mania	Y	N	Y	Y
Hypomania	Y	N	Y	Y
Cyclothymia	Y	N	N	N
Anorexia Nervosa	Y	Y (screens for)	Y	Y
Bulimia Nervosa	Y	Y (screens for)	Y	Y
Enuresis	Y (E, P/L, only)	Y (parent version)	Y	N
Encopresis	Y (E, P/L, only)	N	Y	N
Tic disorders	Y (E, P/L, only)	N	Y	Y
Schizophrenia	Y	N	Y	N
Schizoaffective Disorder	Y	N	N	N
Generalized Anxiety Disorder	Y	Y	Y	Y
Separation Anxiety Disorder	Y	Y	Y	Y
Obsessive-Compulsive Disorder	Y	Y	Y	Y
Simple Phobia	Y	Y	Y	Y
Social Phobia	Y	Y	Y	Y
Agoraphobia	Y	Y	Y	N
Panic Disorder	Y	Y	Y	Y
Posttraumatic Stress Disorder	Y	Y	Y	Y
Oppositional Defiant Disorder	Y	Y (parent version)	Y	Y
Attention-Deficit/ Hyperactivity Disorder	Y	Y	Y	Y
Conduct Disorder	Y	Y (parent version)	Y	Y
Substance disorders	Y	Y	Y	Y
Personality disorders	Y	N	N	N

Generally acceptable 1-week test-retest reliability for the current DICA version has been reported for the adolescent ($\kappa = .59$ to $.92$) and child ($\kappa = .32$ to $.65$) versions. Examinations of earlier DICA versions revealed poor parent-child agreement for most diagnoses ($\kappa = .00$ to $.58$, Reich, Herjanic, Welner, & Gandhy, 1982; $\kappa = .00$ to $.35$, Brunshaw & Szatmari, 1988; $\kappa = .11$ to $.42$, Sylvester, Hyde, & Reichler, 1987; $\kappa = -.05$ to $.68$, Boyle et al., 1993). In addition, at the symptom level, Herjanic and Reich (1982) found kappa coefficients ranging from $.00$ to $.87$; however, coefficients for only 16 of the 185 questions examined obtained acceptable status. A notable exception was found by Welner and colleagues (1987; $\kappa = .49$ to .80) through inclusion of probable cases of parent-child agreement (i.e., one symptom lacking or duration uncertain). Test-retest and multiple-informant agreement for the current DICA were not found.

The Diagnostic Interview Schedule for Children

The only interview considered highly structured, the DISC was originally designed for epidemiological surveys of children that were conducted by laypersons. The most recent revision (DISC-IV; Shaffer, Fisher, Lucas, Dulcan, & Schwab-Stone, 2000) contains criteria for disorders that can be diagnosed in children and adolescents using either the *DSM-IV* or *ICD-10* (see Table 15.1). Interviewers are trained to read questions exactly as written, with the majority of responses requested in a yes/no format. The DISC-IV inquires first about symptoms from the past 12 months. If the informant responds positively to this initial inquiry, information regarding symptoms from the past 4 weeks is obtained. The DISC is scored using a computer program (SAS) and algorithms that match *DSM-IV* (or *ICD-10*) criteria. In addition to the paper version, the DISC has computerized (C-DISC-4.0), Spanish, Present State, Teacher, Voice, Young Adult, and Quick versions (cf. Shaffer et al., 2000) and is considered the most highly researched and utilized of the parent/child companion interviews (A. Jensen & Weisz, 2002).

The DISC-IV diagnostic scales have evidenced generally acceptable test-retest reliability for parent ($\kappa = .43$ to $.96$) and combined parent/child ($\kappa = .48$ to $.86$) versions, with slightly less reliable findings for the child version ($\kappa = .25$ to $.92$, Fisher et al., 1997). Similar test-retest reliability rates were found for prior DISC versions in community and clinical samples (P. Jensen et al., 1995; Schwab-Stone et al., 1996). In addition, excellent interrater reliability has been reported for earlier versions of the DISC (Shaffer, Schwab-Stone, Fisher, & Cohen, 1993). Recent examinations of parent-child agreement have found poor reliability with the DISC-IV ($\kappa = -.08$ to $.25$, Crowley, Mikulich, Ehlers, Whitmore, & MacDonald, 2001; P. Jensen et al., 1999).

To summarize, several well-researched semi- or highly structured interviews exist for researchers and clinicians. As shown in Table 15.1, the majority of these interviews cover basic *DSM-IV* diagnoses for childhood disorders, with some focused more on specific areas than others (e.g., the ADIS and anxiety disorders versus the K-SADS and depressive disorders). In addition to procedural differences (e.g., level of structure, computer administration capability, same versus different interviewer for parent and child components) among these interviews, several have also been adapted for use in multiple languages. For example, in addition to the standard English versions, there are currently Chinese (Ho et al., 2005), French (Breton, Bergeron, Valla, Berthiaume, & St. Georges, 1998), and Zhosa versions of the DISC, as well as a Greek version of the K-SADS (Kolaitis, Korpa, Kolvin, & Tsiantis, 2003). Therefore, although specific cases where the primary focus of study (e.g., epidemiological studies) or presenting problem (e.g., a disorder not assessed by all interviews, such as Bipolar Disorder) guides the choice of diagnostic interview, given the similarities among interviews, most often the clinician's or researcher's discretion or preference guides this decision. In fact, Hodges (1994) suggested that there is not one best interview, but that researchers and clinicians should determine which interview to use based on the sample and focus of their endeavor. Finally, it is important to note that the previously described interviews do not represent an exhaustive list of those available. Additional commonly utilized interviews are the Child Assessment Schedule (Hodges, Kline, Stern, Cytryn, & McKnew, 1982) and the Child and Adolescent Psychiatric Assessment (Angold, Prendergast, Cox, & Harrington, 1995), among others.

LINGERING ISSUES INVOLVED WITH DIAGNOSTIC INTERVIEWS

One of the most consistently raised difficulties involved in using parent-child diagnostic interviews concerns the discordant reports received. That is, symptom and diagnostic agreement within and across informants is generally poor—a finding that has led several researchers to examine potential factors that may influence multiple informants' reports and thus contribute understanding to the discrepancies found (cf. Grills & Ollendick, 2003). In general, these variables can be described in terms of whether they pertain to the interviewee, the interviewer, or the interview itself.

Beginning at the *interviewer* level, establishment of rapport is an important aspect of any clinical relationship. Although diagnostic interviews attempt to incorporate rapport-building strategies (e.g., beginning with general information), the lengthy interview format likely impedes rapport, in the traditional sense, from being fully developed (LaGreca & Stone, 1992; Verhulst et al., 1987). Individuals who have not established rapport with the interviewer may not feel comfortable disclosing diagnostic information, requesting clarification, or stopping the interview (Breton et al., 1995), thus potentially affecting the reliability and validity of the reports obtained. Unfortunately, this is likely often the case, as clinicians and researchers tend to use diagnostic interviews early in the assessment process to probe for areas of concern. In addition, despite requiring specific training in their administration, individual and across-site differences and errors likely remain. Furthermore, differences in clinician experience levels may affect interviews, as one with more experience may complete the interview in a more timely, fluid, and comprehensive manner. This latter issue would be particularly relevant for semi-structured diagnostic interviews (e.g., ADIS), as there is more clinical probing and leeway permitted with these instruments. An additional source of confounding can occur when the same interviewer administers both interviews. For instance, information from the first interview may alter the interviewer's opinions and subsequently the style (nonverbal cues) and emphasis given to probing certain domains as well as the recording of responses in the second interview. With multiple informants, joint meetings may be held to resolve discrepant reports; however, the clinician cannot be sure that the final consensus accurately represents both informants' opinions or the concession of one of them (Angold et al., 1987; Sylvester et al., 1987).

Interview methodological problems are another area of concern for researchers. For example, it has been suggested that the sequence of disorder presentation in the interviews may affect informants' reports. Sylvester et al. (1987) noted that questions regarding externalizing disorders are asked first with the DICA and that this may influence parents' reports by focusing them on these outward behaviors. Thus, later questions about internalizing symptoms may be overshadowed by this earlier focus (Sylvester et al., 1987). This notion was recently supported by findings of order effects in the total number of symptoms endorsed, impairment ratings, and diagnostic criteria met for both parent and child reports on the DISC (P. Jensen et al., 1999). In contrast, the ADIS requests information on all anxiety-related symptoms early in the interview, with externalizing disorders probed later. Comparison of these measures and order effects may prove another area important for future studies. Similarly, parent-child concordance may be affected by differences in the informants' emotional state at the time of the interview. To illustrate, parents may overemphasize behavioral problems if the child was behaving especially poorly earlier that day or in the waiting room. They may also overemphasize behavioral problems if they themselves are having a difficult day or are under stress of one type or another. For children, poor reliability may be a reflection of their desire to quickly complete an interview (e.g., by saying no to all the probes) or impatience or boredom with the interview process (Edelbrock et al., 1985; P. Jensen et al., 1995; Reich, 2000). Potential differences concerning the degree of structure (semi- versus highly) imposed by interviews has also been reported. Whereas semi-structured interviews may lead to improved reliability over highly structured interviews (i.e., DISC) by allowing for more clinical probing (Verhulst et al., 107), highly structured interviews may limit confounding characteristics (e.g., interviewer experience, differences in probing across administrations). Thus, it is not surprising that studies conducted for the various interviews have revealed similar findings regardless of the degree of structure associated with the interview (Grills & Ollendick, 2003). It is important to note that these clinical interviews must be considered in the context of the diagnostic system on which they are based. If diagnostic criteria are not presented in a manner that allows for their adequate assessment, this will be reflected in the interviews as well. Furthermore, if the boundaries between normal and pathological child disorders are unclear, assessment strategies will also likely produce blurred and discrepant results. Thus, reliability and validity problems on multiple interviews may speak to the need for further alterations or amendments to the diagnostic system itself.

The most attention has clearly been devoted to *interviewee* (parent and child) characteristics proposed to affect agreement, including those particular to children and/or parents. For example, it is often presumed that younger children will evidence less agreement with their parents due to factors (e.g., verbal, cognitive, memory, and attentional) related to their ability to understand and describe their feelings and behaviors (Breton et al., 1995; Edelbrock et al., 1985; Rapee et al., 1994; Schwab-Stone et al., 1994). Several researchers have indicated that structured interviews may require information that is too complex or beyond the cognitive capabilities of young children (Breton et al., 1995; Brunshaw & Szatmari, 1988; Edelbrock et al., 1985; Ezpeleta et al., 1997; Herjanic & Reich, 1982; Piacentini et al., 1993; Schwab-Stone et al., 1994; Valla, Bergeron, Berube, Gaudet, & St Georges, 1994; Welner et al., 1987; Young, O'Brien, Gutterman, & Cohen, 1987). Indeed, the majority of research studies have found improved ratings within (i.e., test-retest) and across (e.g., parent/child, clinician/child) informants for older children regardless of the interview used (Edelbrock, Costello, Dulcan, Conover, & Kalas, 1986; Edelbrock et al., 1985; Ezpeleta et al., 1997; Grills & Ollendick, 2002; P. Jensen et al., 1999; Rapee et al., 1994; Reich et al., 1982; Silverman & Eisen, 1992; Verhulst et al., 107). It appears that both the wording (e.g., length, vague concepts such as "most" and "fair," number of concepts included in the question) and types (e.g., yes/no versus open-ended, duration, age of onset, clustering, frequency, concrete information versus comparative judgments) of questions included in these interviews can be problematic. Concerns like these have been supported by studies revealing low overall understanding of concepts (16% to 56%) and time dimensions (24% to 30%) of DISC questions when children (ages 9 to 11) were asked to explain their answers (Breton et al., 1995). Likewise, Perez, Ezpeleta, Domenech, and de la Osa (1998) reported that the most reliable questions on the DICA-R were those containing no time concepts, clustering of symptoms, or impairment ratings and no peer comparisons or subjective judgments, externalizing (versus internalizing) content, and shorter duration (for younger children, but not adolescents). Although not all researchers have found support for age differences on the reliability of interviews (Angold et al., 1987; Boyle et al., 1993; Briggs-Gowan, Carter, & Schwab-Stone, 1996; Earls, Smith, Reich, & Jung, 1988; Perez et al., 1998; Thompson, Merritt, Keith, Murphy, & Johndrow, 1993), a higher minimal age for structured interviewing has been proposed by some (e.g., age 10+ for the DISC; Edelbrock et al., 1985; Schwab-Stone et al., 1994). Importantly, studies in this area also demonstrate aspects of potential revision for child structured interviews. For example, it may be helpful for interviewers to use multiple examples, visual aids, and explanations to ensure children's comprehension.

Interestingly, the child's age may also influence parent reports, as older children typically spend more time outside the home (e.g., with friends, in extracurricular activities), potentially decreasing parents' knowledge of their child's behaviors (Edelbrock et al., 1985). Although this notion has not been well-studied, it certainly remains an important consideration and further supports the need for both adolescent and parent reports.

Motives may also influence reliability. For example, symptoms may be overreported to gain services for a child that the parent feels are necessary to obtain. In addition, parent-child concordance may be disrupted if children intentionally hide information from their parents (e.g., drug use, truancy; Edelbrock et al., 1985), perhaps to avoid negative consequences (e.g., punishment, forced treatment) resulting from disclosure. Alternatively, children may attempt to conceal emotional problems while in the presence of others, such as their peers or the clinician, to portray a positive image of themselves (DiBartolo, Albano, Barlow, & Heimberg, 1998; Grills & Ollendick, 2003; P. Jensen, Traylor, Xenakis, & Davis, 1988; Silverman & Rabian, 1995; Stavrakaki, Vargo, Roberts, & Boodoosingh, 1987). Similarly, parents may underreport symptoms in an attempt to conceal the child's behavioral problems (Crowley et al., 2001; Victor, Halverson, & Wampler, 1988), perhaps to prevent stigma or conceal family problems (e.g., marital conflicts). These social desirability concerns could then lead to the appearance of overreporting on the part of another informant. Social desirability may also influence concordance within or across informants if disagreeing with others or one's own earlier report is perceived as being viewed unfavorably.

Another commonly discussed area concerns the type of disorder on which the informants are reporting. That is, externalizing (e.g., hyperactivity, aggression), as compared to internalizing (e.g., anxiety, depression), symptoms are generally considered easier to observe and to report on by others, resulting in increased diagnostic agreement. Likewise, the severity of the disorder may influence reliability, perhaps through relation with more open dialogue about problems, more pronounced or observable symptoms, or less reliable answers (Cohen, O'Connor, Lewis, Velez, & Malachowski, 1987; Perez et al., 1998). Whereas findings with the various diagnostic interviews support the former proposal, such that increased reliability is often found for externalizing behaviors (Bidault et al., 1995; Chambers et al., 1985; Costello & Edelbrock, 1985; Edelbrock et al., 1986; Ezpeleta et al., 1997; Herjanic & Reich, 1982; Hodges, Gordon, & Lennon, 1990; P. Jensen et al., 1988; Kolko & Kazdin, 1993; Orvaschel, Weissman, Padian, & Lowe, 1981; Silverman & Eisen, 1992), the influence of disorder severity does not appear to be supported by multiple-informant reliability studies (e.g., Angold et al., 1987; Grills & Ollendick, 2003). Likewise, there remains debate as to whether parental psychopathology contributes to decreased interview reliability, perhaps due to greater sensitivity to their children's symptoms, misinterpreting of their child's behaviors, or projection of their own symptoms onto the child (Angold et al., 1987; Breslau, Davis, & Prabucki, 1988; Briggs-Gowan et al., 1996; Fergusson, Lynskey, & Horwood, 1993; P. Jensen et al., 1988; Kashani, Orvaschel, Burk, & Reid, 1985; Kolko & Kazdin, 1993; Miles et al., 1998; Moretti et al., 1985; Rapee et al., 1994). Poor family communication (Bidault-Russell et al., 1995) and family conflict or stress may also influence reliability. For example, children and parents from families characterized by high conflict have been found to evidence poorer agreement on the ADIS (Grills & Ollendick, 2003).

Although gender is also commonly examined, Klein (1991) has argued that there are no theoretical grounds on which to expect gender differences to occur. Indeed, findings for gender differences have been exceedingly mixed, and review of studies reporting them reveals generally few and small differences (cf. Grills & Ollendick, 2003). Furthermore, there remain myriad potential factors that have not yet been well examined for their influence on the reliability and validity of reports on clinical interviews (e.g., ethnicity, socioeconomic status). Although determining the role of these variables awaits future research, it seems likely that similar findings to those already described will result. That is, despite some trends regarding particular interviewee characteristics, findings have not been particularly robust for any one area.

In sum, various interviewer, interviewee, and interview characteristics may influence the reliability and validity of clinical interviews. Future research should attempt to clarify the role of these characteristics to limit additional variance that may be introduced through them. The most robust findings appear to be related to children's comprehension of the interview itself.

Several procedures have been proposed to manage discordant findings with interviews: (a) basing diagnostic decisions on just one of the reports (Silverman et al., 2001) or only when both reports agree, (b) following specific guidelines for the consideration of each report (e.g., rules of evidence, P. Jensen et al., 1999; Shaffer et al., 2000), and (c) applying rules for how reports should be combined (e.g., ADIS Composite Diagnoses; Silverman & Albano, 1996; "or" rules; Bird, Gould, & Staghezza, 1992). Applying rules for combining reports appears most advantageous as this allows discrepancies to be interpreted as informative, not problematic (Boyle et al., 1996; Schwab-Stone et al., 1996). That is, parent and child reports should not be viewed as interchangeable, but complementary.

In light of these findings, the general consensus in the youth assessment area (Silverman & Ollendick, 2005, in press) is that parents and children should both be involved in the assessment of youth symptoms and diagnoses. One is not necessarily more right or wrong than the other. By carefully considering each source's information, there is increased likelihood that no child or adolescent is denied services (Comer & Kendall, 2004; Foley et al., 2005). De Los Reyes and Kazdin (2005), in a comprehensive review of the informant discrepancy literature in clinical child and adolescent psychology, further proposed that in addition to obtaining information of youths' problems from multiple informants, efforts should be made to collect information from these informants about their perceptions of why the youth is exhibiting these problems, as well as their perceptions of the desired treatment of the youth for these problems. De Los Reyes and Kazdin further discussed how gathering this type of information can serve as the basis for an assessment model that can guide research and clinical practice to help explain informant discrepancies in clinical child and adolescent research.

SUMMARY

A host of issues surrounding diagnostic interviews exist, including their reliability, validity, and clinical utility. Although many questions remain about the psychometric properties of these interviews, much progress has been made and a number of reliable, valid, and clinically useful interviews have been developed and are in wide use today. These interviews vary along a number of lines, including the amount and extent of structure embedded in them (unstructured, semi-structured, and highly structured). The semi-structured and the highly structured interviews enjoy the best psychometric properties. It is also evident that a number of complications can arise when using diagnostic interviews during the assessment process. For example, it is a common practice in the assessment of children to include multiple informants since it is believed that adults alone cannot provide all of the information that is needed concerning the child's behavior. However, inclusion of multiple informants also creates a dilemma, as disagreements commonly occur. A number of potential variables related to the interviewer, the interviewee, and the interview itself have been considered in terms of their influence on the reliability, validity, and clinical utility of these instruments. However, few, if any, clear or consistent patterns have emerged. It seems likely that there is a complex interaction among the various factors that cannot be ignored and that will require additional research. Nonetheless, diagnostic interviews represent one of the most reliable, valid, and clinically useful instruments for diagnosis, treatment planning, and treatment evaluation. They are an indispensable part of our clinical armamentarium.

REFERENCES

Achenbach, T. M., Dumenci, L., & Rescorla, L. A. (2002). Ten-year comparisons of problems and competencies for national samples of youth: Self, parent, and teacher reports. *Journal of Emotional and Behavioral Disorders, 10*, 194–203.

Achenbach, T. M., McConaughy, S. H., & Howell, C. T. (1987). Child/adolescent behavioral and emotional problems: Implications of cross-informant correlations for situational specificity. *Psychological Bulletin, 101*, 213–232.

Ambrosini, P. J. (2000). Historical development and present status of the Schedule for Affective Disorders and Schizophrenia for School-Age Children (K-SADS). *Journal of the American Academy of Child and Adolescent Psychiatry, 39*, 49–58.

Ambrosini, P. J., & Dixon, J. F. (1996). *Schedule for Affective Disorders and Schizophrenia for School-Age Children (K-SADS-IVR) present state and epidemiological version.* Philadelphia: Medical College of Pennsylvania and Hahneman University.

Ambrosini, P. J., Metz, C., Prabucki, K., & Lee, J. (1989). Videotape reliability of the third revised edition of the K-SADS. *Journal of the American Academy of Child and Adolescent Psychiatry, 28*, 723–728.

American Psychiatric Association. (1994). *Diagnostic and statistical manual of mental disorders* (4th ed.) Washington, DC: Author.

Angold, A., Prendergast, M., Cox, A., & Harrington, R. (1995). The Child and Adolescent Psychiatric Assessment (CAPA). *Psychological Medicine, 25*(4), 739–753.

Angold, A., Weissman, M. M., John, K., Merikangas, K. R., Prusoff, B. A., Wickramaratne, P., et al. (1987). Parent and child reports of depressive symptoms in children at low and high risk for depression. *Journal of Child Psychology and Psychiatry, 28*, 901–915.

Aronen, E., Noam, G., & Weinstein, S. (1993). Structured diagnostic interviews and clinicians' discharge diagnoses in hospitalized adolescents. *Journal of the American Academy of Child and Adolescent Psychiatry, 32*(3), 674–681.

Bidault-Russell, M., Reich, W., Cottler, L. B., Robins, L. N., Compton, W. M., & Mattison, R. E. (1995). The Diagnostic Interview Schedule for Children (PC-DISC v.3.0): Parents and adolescents suggest reasons for expecting discrepant answers. *Journal of Abnormal Child Psychology, 23*, 641–659.

Bird, H. R., Gould, M. S., & Staghezza, B. (1992). Aggregating data from multiple informants in child psychiatry epidemiological research. *Journal of the American Academy of Child and Adolescent Psychiatry, 31*, 78–85.

Boyle, M. H., Offord, D. R., Racine, Y., Sanford, M., Szatmari, P., Fleming, J. E., et al. (1993). Evaluation of the Diagnostic Interview for Children and Adolescents for use in general population samples. *Journal of Abnormal Child Psychology, 21*, 663–681.

Boyle, M. H., Offord, D. R., Racine, Y. A., Szatmari, P., Sanford, M., & Fleming, J. E. (1996). Interviews versus checklists: Adequacy for classifying childhood psychiatric disorder based on adolescent reports. *International Journal of Methods in Psychiatric Research, 6*, 309–319.

Breslau, N., Davis, G. C., & Prabucki, K. (1988). Depressed mothers as informants in family history research: Are they accurate? *Psychiatry Research, 24*, 345–359.

Breton, J., Bergeron, L., Valla, J., Berthiaume, C., & St. Georges, M. (1998). Diagnostic Interview Schedule for Children (DISC-2.25) in Quebec: Reliability findings in light of the MECA Study. *Journal of the American Academy of Child and Adolescent Psychiatry, 37*(11), 1167–1174.

Breton, J., Bergeron, L., Valla, J., Lepine, S., Houde, L., & Gaudet, N. (1995). Do children aged 9 through 11 years understand the DISC version 2.25 questions? *Journal of the American Academy of Child and Adolescent Psychiatry, 34*, 946–956.

Briggs-Gowan, M. J., Carter, A. S., & Schwab-Stone, M. (1996). Discrepancies among mother, child, and teacher reports: Examining the contributions of maternal depression and anxiety. *Journal of Abnormal Child Psychology, 24*, 749–765.

Brown, T. A., Di Nardo, P., & Barlow, D. H. (1994). *Anxiety Disorders Interview Schedule, lifetime version.* New York: Oxford University Press.

Brunshaw, J. M., Szatmari, P. (1988). The agreement between behaviour checklists and structured psychiatric interviews for children. *Canadian Journal of Psychiatry, 33*, 474–481.

Chambers, W. J., Puig-Antich, J., Hirsch, M., Paez, P., Ambrosini, P. J., Tabrizi, M. A., et al. (1985). The assessment of affective disorders in children and adolescents by semistructured interview: Test-retest reliability of the Schedule for Affective Disorders and Schizophrenia for School-Age Children, present episode version. *Archives of General Psychiatry, 42*, 696–702.

Chorpita, B. F. (2007). *Modular cognitive-behavioral therapy for childhood anxiety disorders.* New York: Guilford Press.

Cohen, P., O'Connor, P., Lewis, S., Velez, C. N., & Malachowski, B. (1987). Comparison of DISC and K-SADS-P interviews of an epidemiological sample of children. *Journal of the American Academy of Child and Adolescent Psychiatry, 26*, 662–667.

Comer, J. S., & Kendall, P. C. (2004). A symptom-level examination of parent-child agreement in the diagnosis of anxious youth. *Journal of the American Academy of Child and Adolescent Psychiatry, 43*, 878–886.

Costello, E. J., & Edelbrock, C. S. (1985). Detection of psychiatric disorders in pediatric primary care: A preliminary report. *Journal of the American Academy of Child Psychiatry, 24*, 771–774.

Crowley, T. J., Mikulich, S. K., Ehlers, K. M., Whitmore, E. A., & MacDonald, M. J. (2001). Validity of structured clinical evaluations in adolescents with conduct and substance problems. *Journal of the American Academy of Child and Adolescent Psychiatry, 40*, 265–273.

De Los Reyes, A., & Kazdin, A. E. (2005). Informant discrepancies in the assessment of childhood psychopathology: A critical review, theoretical framework, and recommendations for further study. *Psychological Bulletin, 131*, 483–509.

DiBartolo, P. M., Albano, A. M., Barlow, D. H., & Heimberg, R. G. (1998). Cross-informant agreement in the assessment of social phobia in youth. *Journal of Abnormal Child Psychology, 26*, 213–220.

Earls, F., Smith, E., Reich, W., & Jung, K. G. (1988). Investigating psychopathological consequences of a disaster in children: A pilot study incorporating a structured diagnostic interview. *Journal of the American Academy of Child and Adolescent Psychiatry, 27*, 90–95.

Edelbrock, C., & Costello, A. J. (1990). Structured interviews for children and adolescents. In G. Goldstein & M. Hersen (Eds.), *Handbook of psychological assessment: Vol. 131. Pergamon general psychology series* (pp. 308–323). New York: Pergamon Press.

Edelbrock, C., Costello, A. J., Dulcan, M. K., Conover, N. C., & Kalas, R. (1986). Parent-child agreement on child psychiatric symptoms assessed via structured interview. *Journal of Child Psychology and Psychiatry, 27*, 181–190.

Edelbrock, C., Costello, A. J., Dulcan, M. K., Kalas, R., & Conover, N. C. (1985). Age differences in the reliability of the psychiatric interview of the child. *Child Development, 56*, 265–275.

Eisen, A. R., & Silverman, W. K. (1993). Should I relax or change my thoughts? A preliminary study of the treatment of overanxious disorder in children. *Journal of Cognitive Psychotherapy, 7*, 265–280.

Eisen, A. R., & Silverman, W. K. (1998). Prescriptive treatment for generalized anxiety disorder in children. *Behavior Therapy, 29*, 105–121.

Ezpeleta, L., de la Osa, N., Doménech, J. M., Navarro, J. B., & Losilla, J. M. (1997). Diagnostic agreement between clinicians and the Diagnostic Interview for Children and Adolescents—DICA-R—in an outpatient sample. *Journal of Child Psychology and Psychiatry and Allied Disciplines, 38*, 431–440.

Fergusson, D. M., Lynskey, M. T., & Horwood, L. J. (1993). The effect of maternal depression on maternal ratings of child behavior. *Journal of Abnormal Child Psychology, 21*, 245–269.

Fisher, P. W., Shaffer, D., Piacentini, J. C., Lapkin, J., Kafantaris, V., Leonard, H., et al. (1997). Sensitivity of the Diagnostic Interview Schedule for Children, 2nd ed. (DISC-2.1) for specific diagnoses of children and adolescents. *Journal of the American Academy of Child and Adolescent Psychiatry, 32*, 666–673.

Foley, D. L., Rutter, M., Angold, A., Pickles, A., Maes, H. M., Silberg, J. L., et al. (2005). Making sense of informant disagreement for overanxious disorder. *Journal of Anxiety Disorders, 19*, 193–210.

Grills, A. E., & Ollendick, T. H. (2002). Issues in parent-child agreement: The case of structured diagnostic interviews. *Clinical Child and Family Psychology Review, 5*, 57–83.

Grills, A. E., & Ollendick, T. H. (2003). Multiple informant agreement and the Anxiety Disorders Interview Schedule for parents and children. *Journal of the American Academy of Child and Adolescent Psychiatry, 42*, 30–40.

Herjanic, B., Herjanic, M., Brown, F., & Wheatt, T. (1975). Are children reliable reporters? *Journal of Abnormal Child Psychology, 3*, 41–48.

Herjanic, B., & Reich, W. (1982). Development of a structured psychiatric interview for children: Agreement between child and parent on individual symptoms. *Journal of Abnormal Child Psychology, 10*, 307–324.

Ho, T., Leung, P., Lee, C., Tang, C., Hung, S., Kwong, S., et al. (2005). Test-retest reliability of the Chinese version of the Diagnostic Interview Schedule for Children—Version 4 (DISC-IV). *Journal of Child Psychology and Psychiatry, 46*(10), 1135–1138.

Hodges, K. (1994). Debate and argument. Reply to David Shaffer: Structured interviews for assessing children. *Journal of Child Psychology and Psychiatry and Allied Disciplines, 35*, 785–787.

Hodges, K., Gordon, Y., & Lennon, M. P. (1990). Parent-child agreement on symptoms assessed via a clinical research interview for children: The Child Assessment Schedule (CAS). *Journal of Child Psychology and Psychiatry, 31*, 427–436.

Hodges, K., Kline, J., Stern, L., Cytryn, L., & McKnew, D. (1982). The development of a child assessment interview for research and clinical use. *Journal of Abnormal Child Psychology, 10*(2), 173–189.

Hodges, K., McKnew, D., Burbach, D. J., & Roebuck, L. (1987). Diagnostic concordance between the Child Assessment Schedule (CAS) and the Schedule for Affective Disorders and Schizophrenia for School-Age Children (K-SADS) in an outpatient sample using lay interviewers. *Journal of the American Academy of Child and Adolescent Psychiatry, 26*, 654–661.

Hodges, K., McKnew, D., Cytryn, L., Stern, L., & Kline, J. (1982). The Child Assessment Schedule (CAS) diagnostic interview: A report on reliability and validity. *Journal of the American Academy of Child and Adolescent Psychiatry, 21*, 468–473.

Jarrett, M. A., Wolff, J. C., & Ollendick, T. H. (2007). Concurrent validity and informant agreement of the ADHD Module of the Anxiety Disorders Interview Schedule for DSM IV. *Journal of Psychopathology and Behavioral Assessment, 29*, 159–168.

Jensen, A., & Weisz, J. (2002). Assessing match and mismatch between practitioner-generated and standardized interview-generated diagnoses for clinic-referred children and adolescents. *Journal of Consulting and Clinical Psychology, 70*(1), 158–168.

Jensen, P., Roper, M., Fisher, P., Piacentini, J., Canino, G., Richters, J., et al. (1995). Test-retest reliability of the Diagnostic Interview Schedule for Children (DISC 2.1): Parent, child, and combined algorithms. *Archives of General Psychiatry, 52*, 61–71.

Jensen, P., Rubio-Stipec, M., Canino, G., Bird, H. R., Dulcan, M. K., Schwab-Stone, M. E., et al. (1999). Parent and child contributions to diagnosis of mental disorder: Are both informants always necessary? *Journal of the American Academy of Child and Adolescent Psychiatry, 38*, 1569–1579.

Jensen, P., Traylor, J., Xenakis, S. N., & Davis, H. (1988). Child psychopathology rating scales and interrater agreement: Pt. I. Parents' gender and psychiatric symptoms. *Journal of the American Academy of Child and Adolescent Psychiatry, 27*, 442–450.

Jewell, J., Handwerk, M., Almquist, J., & Lucas, C. (2004). Comparing the validity of clinician-generated diagnosis of conduct disorder to the Diagnostic Interview Schedule for Children. *Journal of Clinical Child and Adolescent Psychology, 33*(3), 536–546.

Kashani, J. H., Orvaschel, H., Burk, J. P., & Reid, J. C. (1985). Informant variance: The issue of parent-child disagreement. *Journal of the American Academy of Child and Adolescent Psychiatry, 24*, 437–441.

Kaufman, J., Birmaher, B., Brent, D., Rao, U., Flynn, C., Moreci, P., et al. (1997). Schedule for Affective Disorders and Schizophrenia for School-Age Children—Present and Lifetime version (K-SADS-PL):

Initial reliability and validity data. *Journal of the American Academy of Child and Adolescent Psychiatry, 36*, 980–988.

Kazdin, A. E., French, N. H., & Unis, A. S. (1983). Child, mother, and father evaluations of depression in psychiatric inpatient children. *Journal of Abnormal Child Psychology, 11*, 167–180.

Klein, R. G. (1991). Parent-child agreement in clinical assessment of anxiety and other psychopathology: A review. *Journal of Anxiety Disorders, 5*, 187–198.

Kolaitis, G., Korpa, T., Kolvin, I., & Tsiantis, J. (2003). Schedule for Affective Disorders and Schizophrenia for School-Age Children—Present episode (K-SADS-P): A pilot inter-rater reliability study for Greek children and adolescents. *European Psychiatry, 18* (7), 374–375.

Kolko, D. J., & Kazdin, A. E. (1993). Emotional/behavioral problems in clinic and nonclinic children: Correspondence among child, parent, and teacher reports. *Journal of Child Psychology and Psychiatry, 34*, 991–1006.

LaGreca, A. M., & Stone, W. L. (1992). Assessing children through interviews and behavioral observations. In C. E. Walker, & M. C. Roberts (Eds.), *Handbook of clinical child psychology* (2nd ed., pp. 63–83). New York: Wiley Interscience.

Lapouse, R., & Monk, M. A. (1958). An epidemiologic study of behavior characteristics of children. *American Journal of Public Health, 48*, 1134–1144.

Lewczyk, C., Garland, A., Hurlburt, M., Gearity, J., & Hough, R. (2003). Comparing DISC-IV and clinician diagnoses among youths receiving public mental health services. *Journal of the American Academy of Child and Adolescent Psychiatry, 42*(3), 349–356.

Loeber, R., Green, S. M., & Lahey, B. B. (1990). Mental health professionals' perception of the utility of children, mothers, and teachers as informants on childhood psychopathology. *Journal of Clinical Child Psychology, 19*, 136–143.

March, J. S., Parker, J. D. A., Sullivan, K., Stallings, P., & Conners, C. K. (1997). The Multidimensional Anxiety Scale for Children (MASC): Factor structure, reliability, and validity. *Journal of the American Academy of Child and Adolescent Psychiatry, 36*, 554–565.

Miles, D. R., Stallings, M. C., Young, S. E., Hewitt, J. K., Crowley, T. J., & Fulker, D. W. (1998). A family history and direct interview study of familial aggregation of substance abuse: The adolescent substance abuse study. *Drug and Alcohol Dependence, 49*, 105–114.

Moretti, M. M., Fine, S., Haley, G., & Marriage, K. (1985). Childhood and adolescent depression: Child-report versus parent-report information. *Journal of the American Academy of Child Psychiatry, 24*, 298–302.

Nelson-Gray, R. (2003). Treatment utility of psychological assessment. *Psychological Assessment, 15*(4), 521–531.

Ollendick, T. H. (1995). Cognitive-behavioral treatment of panic disorder with agoraphobia in adolescents: A multiple baseline design analysis. *Behavior Therapy, 26*, 517–531.

Ollendick, T. H., Hagopian, L., & Huntzinger, R. (1991). Cognitive-behavior therapy with nighttime fearful children. *Journal of Behavior Therapy and Experimental Psychiatry, 22*(2), 113–121.

Ollendick, T. H., & Hersen, M. (Eds.). (1983). *Handbook of child psychopathology.* New York: Plenum Press.

Ollendick, T. H., & Hersen, M. (Eds.). (1984). *Child behavioral assessment: Principles and procedures.* New York: Pergamon Press.

Ollendick, T. H., & Hersen, M. (Eds.). (1989). *Handbook of child psychopathology* (2nd ed.). New York: Plenum Press.

Ollendick, T. H., & Hersen, M. (Eds.). (1993). *Handbook of child and adolescent assessment.* Boston: Allyn & Bacon.

Ollendick, T. H., & Hersen, M. (Eds.). (1998). *Handbook of child psychopathology* (3rd ed.) New York: Plenum Press.

Ollendick, T. H., King, N., & Chorpita, B. (2006). Empirically supported treatments for children and adolescents. In P. C. Kendall (Ed.), *Child and adolescent therapy: Cognitive-behavioral procedures* (3rd ed., pp. 492–520). New York: Guilford Press.

Orvaschel, H. (1995). *Schedule for Affective Disorders and Schizophrenia for School-Age Children Epidemiologic Version-5.* Ft. Lauderdale, FL: Nova Southeastern University, Center for Psychological Studies.

Orvaschel, H., Weissman, M. M., Padian, N., & Lowe, T. L. (1981). Assessing psychopathology in children of psychiatrically disturbed parents. *Journal of the American Academy of Child Psychiatry, 20*, 112–122.

Pellegrino, J., Singh, N., & Carmanico, S. (1999). Concordance among three diagnostic procedures for identifying depression in children and adolescents with EBD. *Journal of Emotional and Behavioral Disorders, 7*(2), 118–127.

Perez, R. G., Ezpeleta, L. A., Domenech, J. M., & de la Osa, N. C. (1998). Characteristics of the subject and interview influencing the test-retest reliability of the Diagnostic Interview for Children and Adolescents—Revised. *Journal of Child Psychology and Psychiatry, 39*, 963–972.

Piacentini, J., Shaffer, D., Fisher, P., Schwab-Stone, M., Davies, M., & Gioia, P. (1993). The Diagnostic Interview Schedule for Children—Revised version (DISC-R): Pt. III. Concurrent criterion validity. *Journal of the American Academy of Child and Adolescent Psychiatry, 32*, 658–665.

Rapee, R. M., Barrett, P. M., Dadds, M. R., & Evans, L. (1994). Reliability of the DSM-III-R childhood and anxiety disorders using structured interview: Interrater and parent-child agreement. *Journal of the American Academy of Child and Adolescent Psychiatry, 33*, 984–992.

Reich, W. (1998). *The Diagnostic Interview for Children and Adolescents (DICA): DSM-IV version.* St. Louis, MO: Washington University School of Medicine.

Reich, W. (2000). Diagnostic Interview for Children and Adolescents (DICA). *Journal of the American Academy of Child and Adolescent Psychiatry, 39*, 59–66.

Reich, W., Herjanic, B., Welner, Z., Gandhy, P. R. (1982). Development of a structured psychiatric interview for children: Agreement on diagnosis comparing child and parent interviews. *Journal of Abnormal Child Psychology, 10*, 325–336.

Rourke, K., & Reich, W. (2004). The Diagnostic Interview for Children and Adolescents (DICA). In M. Hersen, & G. Goldstein (Eds.), *Comprehensive handbook of psychological assessment: Vol. 2. Personality assessment* (pp. 271–280). Hoboken, NJ: Wiley.

Rutter, M., & Graham, P. (1968). The reliability and validity of the psychiatric assessment of the child: Pt. I. Interview with the child. *British Journal of Psychiatry, 114*, 563–579.

Rutter, M., Tizard, J., & Whitmore, K. (1970). *Education, health, and behavior.* London: Longmans.

Rutter, M., Tizard, J., Yule, W., Graham, P., & Kingsley, W. (1977). Isle of Wight studies 1964–1974. In S. Chess & A. Thomas (Eds.), *Annual progress in child psychiatry and child development* (pp. 359–392). New York: Brunner/Mazel.

Rutter, M., Tizard, J., Yule, W., Graham, P., & Whitmore, K. (1976). Isle of Wight studies 1964–1974. *Psychological Medicine, 6*, 313–332.

Sattler, J. M. (1988). *Assessment in children.* San Diego, CA: Jerome Sattler.

Schwab-Stone, M., Fallon, T., Briggs, M., & Crowther, B. (1994). Reliability of diagnostic reporting for children aged 6-11years: A test-retest study of the Diagnostic Interview Schedule for Children—Revised. *American Journal of Psychiatry, 151*, 1048–1054.

Schwab-Stone, M., Shaffer, D., Dulcan, M. K., Jensen, P. S., Fisher, P., Bird, H. R., et al. (1996). Criterion validity of the NIMH Diagnostic Interview Schedule for Children Version 2.3 (DISC-2.3). *Journal of the American Academy of Child and Adolescent Psychiatry, 35*, 878–888.

Shaffer, D., Fisher, P., Lucas, C. P., Dulcan, M. K., & Schwab-Stone, M. E. (2000). NIMH Diagnostic Interview Schedule for Children Version IV (NIMH DISC-IV): Description, differences from previous versions, and reliability of some common diagnoses. *Journal of the American Academy of Child and Adolescent Psychiatry, 39*, 28–38.

Shaffer, D., Schwab-Stone, M., Fisher, P., & Cohen, P. (1993). The Diagnostic Interview Schedule for Children—Revised version (DISC-R): Pt. I. Preparation, field testing, interrater reliability, and acceptability. *Journal of the American Academy of Child and Adolescent Psychiatry, 32*(3), 643–650.

Silverman, W. K. (1991). Diagnostic reliability of anxiety disorders in children using structured interviews. *Journal of Anxiety Disorders, 5*, 105–124.

Silverman, W. K., & Albano, A. M. (1996). *Anxiety Disorders Interview Schedule, Parent/Child version.* New York: Oxford University Press.

Silverman, W. K., & Eisen, A. R. (1992). Age differences in the reliability of parent and child reports of child anxious symptomatology using a structured interview. *Journal of the American Academy of Child and Adolescent Psychiatry, 31*, 117–124.

Silverman, W. K., & Nelles, W. B. (1988). The Anxiety Disorders Interview Schedule for Children. *Journal of the American Academy of Child and Adolescent Psychiatry, 27*, 772–778.

Silverman, W. K., & Ollendick, T. H. (2005). Evidence-based assessment of anxiety and its disorders in children and adolescents. *Journal of Clinical Child and Adolescent Psychology, 34*, 380–411.

Silverman, W. K., & Ollendick, T. H. (in press). Assessment of child and adolescent anxiety disorders. In J. Hunsley & E. Mash (Eds.), *A guide to assessments that work*. New York: Oxford University Press.

Silverman, W. K., & Rabian, B. (1995). Test-retest reliability of the DSM-III-R childhood anxiety disorders symptoms using the Anxiety Disorders Interview Schedule for children. *Journal of Anxiety Disorders, 9*, 139–150.

Silverman, W. K., Saavedra, L. M., & Pina, A. A. (2001). Test-retest reliability of anxiety symptoms and diagnoses with the Anxiety Disorders Interview Schedule for DSM-IV: Child and Parent versions. *Journal of the American Academy of Child and Adolescent Psychiatry, 40*, 937–944.

Stavrakaki, C., Vargo, B., Roberts, N., & Boodoosingh, L. (1987). Concordance among sources of information for ratings of anxiety and depression in children. *Journal of the American Academy of Child and Adolescent Psychiatry, 26*, 733–737.

Sylvester, C. E., Hyde, T. S., & Reichler, R. J. (1987). The Diagnostic Interview for Children and Personality Inventory for Children in studies of children at risk for anxiety disorders or depression. *Journal of the American Academy of Child and Adolescent Psychiatry, 26*, 668–675.

Thompson, R. J., Merritt, K. A., Keith, B. R., Murphy, L. B., & Johndrow, D. A. (1993). Mother-child agreement on the Child Assessment Schedule with nonreferred children: A research note. *Journal of Child Psychology and Psychiatry and Allied Disciplines, 34*, 813–820.

Valla, J. P., Bergeron, L., Berube, H., Gaudet, N., & St. Georges, M. (1994). A structured pictoral questionnaire to assess DSM-III-R based diagnoses in children (6-11years): Development, validity, and reliability. *Journal of Abnormal Child Psychology, 22*, 403–423.

Verhulst, F. C., Althaus, M., & Berden G. F. (1987). The Child Assessment Schedule: Parent-child agreement and validity measures. *Journal of Child Psychology and Psychiatry and Allied Disciplines, 28*, 455–466.

Victor, J. B., Halverson, C. F., & Wampler, K. S. (1988). Family-school context: Parent and teacher agreement on child temperament. *Journal of Consulting and Clinical Psychology, 56*, 573–577.

Vitello, B., Malone, R., Buschle, P., & Delaney, M. (1990). Reliability of DSM-III diagnoses of hospitalized children. *Hospital and Community Psychiatry, 41*(1), 63–67.

Weems, C., Silverman, W., Saavedra, L., Pina, A., & Lumpkin, P. (1999). The discrimination of children's phobias using the revised Fear Survey Schedule for Children. *Journal of Child Psychology and Psychiatry, 40*(6), 941–952.

Weinstein, S., Stone, K., Noam, G., & Grimes, K. (1989). Comparison of DISC with clinicians' DSM-III diagnoses in psychiatric inpatients. *Journal of the American Academy of Child and Adolescent Psychiatry, 28*(1), 53–60.

Weiss, D. S. (1993). Structured clinical interview techniques. In J. P. Wilson & R. Beverley (Eds.), *International handbook of traumatic stress syndromes* (pp. 179–187). New York: Plenum Press.

Welner, Z., Reich, W., Herjanic, B., Jung, K. G., & Amado, H. (1987). Reliability, validity, and parent child agreement studies of the Diagnostic Interview for Children and Adolescents (DICA). *Journal of the American Academy of Child and Adolescent Psychiatry, 26*, 649–653.

Williams, S., McGee, R., Anderson, J., & Silva, P. A. (1989). The structure and correlates of self-reported symptoms in 11-year old children. *Journal of Abnormal Child Psychology, 17*, 55–71.

Wood, J., Piacentini, J., Bergman, R., McCracken, J., & Barrios, V. (2002). Concurrent validity of the anxiety disorders section of the Anxiety Disorders Interview Schedule for DSM-IV: Child and Parent versions. *Journal of Clinical Child and Adolescent Psychology, 31*(3), 335–342.

Young, J. G., O'Brien, J. D., Gutterman, E. M., & Cohen, P. (1987). Research on the clinical interview. *Journal of the American Academy of Child and Adolescent Psychiatry, 30*, 613–620.

CHAPTER 16

Intellectual Assessment

Lloyd A. Taylor, Cara B. Reeves and Erin Jeffords

The practice of estimating intellectual abilities dates back to the beginnings of scientific thought. Greek philosophers and modern-day psychologists alike have attempted to understand the nature of human intelligence and to devise methods by which to measure intellectual capabilities. These intellectual assessments often play important roles in diagnoses of learning disabilities, academic placement, occupational selection, and medical treatment plans. Additionally, intellectual assessments routinely have a significant role in the conceptualization of neurocognitive sequelae following traumatic injuries. Thus, the methods by which we estimate intellectual functioning, and the scientific integrity of these assessment tools, are critical to our practice as psychologists.

The goals of this chapter are to provide an overview of the history of intellectual assessment and common definitions of intelligence. We additionally review traditional intellectual assessment tools, as well as more recent additions to the intellectual assessment arsenal. We discuss the impact of intellectual assessment in the context of psychoeducational assessments and review legislation related to intellectual assessment in the context of educational settings. Finally, we provide two clinical case examples to reiterate the role of cognitive assessment in clinical practice.

HISTORY OF INTELLECTUAL ASSESSMENT

We begin our discussion of intellectual assessment with a review of historical perspectives. This vantage point is critical because little can be understood devoid of knowledge of its history.

Speculations into the nature of human intelligence can be traced back to the Greek philosopher Plato (ca. 428/427–348/347 B.C.E.) who referred to *reason* as the highest functioning part of the soul. Since that time, philosophers and scientists have engaged in dialogue pertaining to the nature of cognitive processing and intelligent behavior. Beginning in the sixteenth century, attempts were made to differentiate mental deficiencies from mental illness. Prominent philosophers and psychologists involved in this work include Jean Esquirol, Sir Francis Galton, Alfred Binet, and James Cattell.

Jean Etienne Esquirol

Jean Esquirol (1772–1840) was among the first scientists to differentiate mental deficiency, or "idiocy," from mental illness (Sattler, 2001). He regarded mental deficiency as a condition in which the intellectual facilities are not fully developed whereas mental illness involved the loss of functioning once possessed by the afflicted individual (Zusne, 1957). To differentiate these groups, Esquirol developed the first rudimentary test of cognitive functioning, in which he used a language criterion to determine mental retardation.

Sir Francis Galton

Sir Francis Galton (1822–1911) is commonly referred to as the founder of the testing movement (Kail & Pellegrino, 1985; Sattler, 2001). A diversified scholar, Galton's published work significantly contributed to the fields of geography, biology, psychology, and criminology. However, he is most highly recognized for his contributions to the field of behavioral genetics (Clayes, 2001). Greatly influenced by his cousin, Charles Darwin, Galton focused much of his work on the heritability of mental functioning. In his published work, Galton theorized that superior mental functioning was passed genetically from parent to offspring and used the bell-shape curve to describe differences in intellectual functioning (Sattler, 2001; Seligman, 2002). Additionally, Galton developed the statistical concepts of *regression to the mean* and *correlation,* which allowed for the empirical study of heritability of traits over time and among family members. His significant contributions to the fields of behavioral genetics and psychology paved the way for future statisticians and psychometricians, and his statistical concepts are still used as the gold standard in test construction and validation (Bynum, 2002).

Alfred Binet

While Esquirol developed the first crude measure of cognitive functioning, Alfred Binet (1857–1911) is credited with developing the first practical test of intelligence (Kail & Pellegrino, 1985; Sattler, 2001). In 1904, Binet was commissioned by the French government to develop an instrument that identified mentally retarded children in need of alternative education. In collaboration with his student, Theodore Simon, Binet created an intelligence test that consisted of 30 subtests measuring a broad range of cognitive abilities, including language skills, abstract reasoning, and memory functioning (Siegler, 1992). This test, commonly referred to as the 1905 Scale, compared the testing subject's performance to a chronological cohort deemed by their teachers to be of average intellectual functioning. The scale was revised in 1908 and adapted to English by Lewis Terman of Stanford University in 1916. Terman's adaptation, referred to as the Stanford-Binet, included culturally appropriate items and reported the child's level of performance in terms of an intelligence quotient (IQ) consisting of the child's mental age divided by chronological age multiplied by 100.

Although the Binet-Simon scale was created as a diagnostic instrument, Binet was equally interested in developing a theory of intelligence (Kail & Pellegrino,

1985). In fact, his definition of intelligence as consisting of complex cognitive processes including abstract reasoning, memory and comprehension greatly influenced the design of the Binet-Simon testing instrument. However, the practical demands of creating and maintaining the Binet-Simon scales overshadowed his pursuits in intelligence theory, thus marking a division in psychometrics between those scientists most interested in theory and those most interested in diagnostic measurement. The theory versus measurement discourse continues among psychologists.

James McKeen Cattell

James McKeen Cattell (1860–1944) was the first American psychologist to emphasize the study of individual differences and cognitive functioning (Kail & Pellegrino, 1985; Sattler, 2001). Cattell is often remembered for his work on theories of personality and bringing an empirical and scientific perspective to theories of personality. Rather than following in the footsteps of his predecessors and focusing on the specific *outcome* of his research, Cattell was more concerned with the *process* of research and shifting psychology to an empirical science based on observable behavior and subjected to statistical analysis. He believed that sensory, perceptual, and motor processes were the fundamental elements of cognitive functioning and, consequently, sought to measure these phenomena in the tests he designed. In his work, he attempted to use *mental tests,* a term he coined, to predict college success. Although the measures he used did not correlate well with educational achievement, Cattell was among the first scientists to empirically study cognitive functioning.

DEFINITIONS OF INTELLIGENCE

We now turn our attention to commonly employed definitions of intelligence. There are basically two main approaches utilized to understand and define intelligence. *Factor analytic theories* involve understanding intelligence by examining patterns of individual differences on assessments and then attempting to describe these patterns based on statistical principles. Theorists embracing this paradigm include Charles Spearman, Philip Vernon, Lewis Thurston, and Raymond Cattell.

Alternatively, *information-processing theories* describe the *components* of intelligent thought that translates external stimuli into an internal concept leading to an appropriate behavioral response. Theorists in this camp include psychologists such as Joseph Campione, Ann Brown and John Borkowski, and Robert Sternberg.

Factor Analytic Theories

Throughout the twentieth century, the factor analytic approach has dominated intelligence theory, research, and practice. Scientists adopting this approach attempt to understand intelligence by examining patterns of individual differences on tests measuring various cognitive skills such as vocabulary, general knowledge, visual-spatial processing, abstract reasoning, and arithmetic. These theories, also known as psychometric theories, statistically analyze test performance to identify the basic units, or *factors,* of intelligence. Although providing insight into the structure of intelligence, there is much debate regarding whether intelligence represents a global, general ability or multiple abilities. The following section presents theories supporting a general factor of intelligence as well as those supporting a multifactor approach.

Spearman's Two-Factor Theory

Charles E. Spearman (1863–1945) was a prominent British psychologist best known for his statistical contributions to the study of intelligence (Kail & Pellegrino, 1985; Sattler, 2001). In his landmark 1904 publication, Spearman (1904a) introduced the statistical concept of factor analysis in an effort to measure factors associated with general intelligence. More specifically, he examined patterns of correlations among IQ subtest scores to look for consistency of performance with the reasoning that if intelligence is global, there would be a high degree of association among subtests. Once correcting for subtest attenuation (for more information, see Williams, Zimmerman, Zumbo, & Ross, 2003), Spearman found evidence in support of a two-factor theory of intelligence in which a general factor, or *g*, superseded more specific factors, or *s*. According to this theory, the *g-factor* accounts for complex cognitive processes such as deductive and analytic reasoning. It is available to the same individual across different intellectual acts and explains consistency in performance across these acts. In contrast, the *s-factors* account for more rudimentary mental processes, including processing speed, recognition, and recall. They are unique to the intelligent act and individuals can exhibit strengths and weaknesses across factors.

Vernon's Hierarchical Group Factor Theory

Heavily influenced by Spearman's work, Philip E. Vernon (1905–1987) adopted a factor analytic approach to intelligence. At the top of his hierarchical model was Spearman's *g*, which accounted for the largest source of variance in intelligence (Kail & Pellegrino, 1985; Sattler, 2001). Underlying *g* were two major group factors: verbal-educational ability (v:ed) and practical-spatial-mechanical abilities (k:m). These major group factors were subdivided into minor group factors, which were further decomposed into several more basic factors. For example, *k:m* subsumed more specific abilities such as spatial, mechanical, and physical abilities. Spatial ability, which was a minor group factor, could then be broken down into three specific factors: spatial orientation (i.e., ability to orient oneself in space relative to environmental markers), spatial relations (i.e., mental rotation of objects), and spatial visualization (i.e., complex mental manipulation of objects). Similar to Spearman's theory, Vernon believed that factors at the top of the hierarchy were more general abilities that affected a wider range of intelligent behaviors, and those at the bottom of the hierarchy involved skills unique to a specific act.

Thurstone's Theory of Primary Mental Abilities

Lewis L. Thurstone (1887–1955) was an established statistician, psychometrician, and intelligence theorist. Among his many contributions to the field of psychology was the development of a new method of factor analysis that allowed for the exploration of multiple latent factors within a set of variables (Sattler, 2001). The use of this new analytic method challenged Spearman's theory of a unified intelligence in support of seven primary mental abilities: word fluency, verbal comprehension, spatial visualization, number facility, associative memory, reasoning, and perceptual speed (Thurstone, 1938). Moreover, Thurstone found that people with similar IQ scores often displayed vastly different profiles on the primary mental abilities, which he felt further substantiated his claim of multiple intelligence factors. Later studies conducted on a more heterogeneous group of people, however, found fewer discrepancies in primary mental abilities and, instead, supported the notion of a unitary intelligence. Thurstone conceded a statistical compromise that accounted for the presence of both a general factor and the seven primary mental abilities.

The Cattell-Horn Theory of Fluid and Crystallized Intelligence

Among many accomplishments, Raymond Bernard Cattell (1905–1998) is widely recognized for his contribution to intelligence theory. Along with his student, John Horn, Cattell proposed a model of intelligence describing general intelligence as a conglomeration of different abilities falling into two categories: fluid abilities (Gf) and crystallized abilities (Gc) (Horn & Cattell, 1966). Fluid abilities include novel problem-solving skills and the ability to think and act quickly. They are innate abilities that are free from education and acculturation. Examples of fluid abilities include spatial reasoning and symbolic classification. Fluid abilities have been shown to peak during adolescence and then gradually decline as the individual progresses into adulthood. They are more susceptible to brain injury and physiological degeneration than crystallized abilities. In contrast, crystallized abilities include acquired knowledge and skills that are the direct result of education, personal motivation, and culture. They develop throughout adulthood and are less susceptible to physiological degeneration. Examples of crystallized intelligence include general information and language skills.

Information Processing

Whereas the psychometric approach to intelligence focused on factor *structure,* the information-processing approach to intelligence is concerned with the *processes* involved in intelligent acts. Information processing theories elaborate on the structure of intelligence by describing the internal workings of intelligent thought and how it results in behavioral output. Rather than studying *factors,* information-processing theorists describe the *components* of intelligent thought that translates external stimuli into an internal concept and designates appropriate behavioral responses.

Campione, Brown, and Borkowski's Theory

In 1978, Joseph Campione and Ann Brown proposed an information-processing theory of intelligence that was later expanded on by John Borkowski (1985). The theory describes intelligence as consisting of both an architectural system, which describes the structure of cognition, and an executive system, which describes the processes involved in intellectual thought. Of particular importance to the model were the executive skills of metacognition, which are skills used to monitor and regulate cognitive processes. The metacognitive skills utilized in intelligent thinking include (a) *planning* steps in problem solving, (b) *monitoring* effectiveness of the steps, (c) *revising* steps as needed, and (d) *evaluating* the efficacy of the problem-solving steps. An example of a metacognition is the selection of a rehearsal strategy to learn a word list or telephone number.

Sternberg's Triarchic Theory

Robert J. Sternberg (1985) proposed a triarchic theory of intelligence in which he divided intelligence into three different information-processing components. *Metacomponents* are higher order components that, much like Campione's metacognitive skills, are used to monitor and regulate cognitive processes. They involve the ability to recognize a problem as it arises, select a lower order strategy to correct the problem, monitor the efficacy of the strategy, and evaluate the outcome of the solution. *Performance components* are lower order components used to execute a solution to an identified problem, such as inferring the relationship between two objects. *Knowledge-acquisition components* are involved in learning new information and storing and retaining the information in long-term memory. Three knowledge-acquisition components involved in cognitive processing are (1) selective encoding, which involves distinguishing relevant from irrelevant information; (2) selective combinations, which is the process by which previously encoded information is combined in a new way that maximizes interconnectedness; and (3) selective comparison, in which the previously encoded and connected information is related to information stored in memory.

COMMONLY EMPLOYED MEASURES OF INTELLIGENCE

The impact of theory on the development of intellectual assessment tools cannot be overemphasized. Theories of intelligence have played an important role in the development of many of the traditional and more recent tools designed to measure intellectual abilities. Although many theorists focused mainly on the development and study of their unique theoretical assumptions regarding intelligence, their work has been instrumental to assessment tools that have been generated to measure intellectual capabilities. This section reviews traditional and more recent intellectual assessment tools, highlighting the theoretical basis of each measure where applicable.

Traditional Measures of Intelligence

Traditional measures of intellectual assessment include the Stanford-Binet Intelligence Scale, Wechsler Scales of Intelligence, and the Woodcock-Johnson Test of Cognitive Functioning.

Stanford-Binet

The Stanford-Binet Scale was developed to provide a global estimate of intellectual functioning in children. The most recent version, the Stanford-Binet Intelligence

Scales, 5th edition, was released in 1986 and incorporates into its arsenal of subtests a measure of working memory, which has been shown to relate to reading and math achievement (Johnson & D'Amato, 2004). The Stanford-Binet typically takes 45 to 75 minutes to administer and covers a wide age range (2 to 85 years).

The Full-Scale IQ score is based on the administration of 10 subtests and provides a global measure of cognitive ability (Johnson & D'Amato, 2004). The test battery includes two index scores: Verbal and Nonverbal IQ. The Verbal index requires the examinee to speak, read, and comprehend age-appropriate language. The Nonverbal index requires minimal language and, instead, emphasizes the use of fine motor coordination to maneuver toys and puzzle pieces and point to correct answers. The subtests on the Stanford-Binet measure concepts of fluid reasoning, knowledge, quantitative reasoning, visual-spatial processing, and working memory.

The Stanford-Binet has numerous strengths. For example, it has an expansive age range (2 to 85) and can be used in assessing a variety of disorders where verbal ability is limited (e.g., autism, hearing impairments, limited English-speaking skills). Internal consistency reliability is considered to be good, ranging from .95 to .98 for IQ scores; criterion validity using the individuals tested on the SB4 and SB5 was high ($r = .90$; Kush, 2004).

In spite of these strengths, the Stanford-Binet has been criticized for being racially and culturally biased, although efforts have been made to standardize recent editions on more heterogeneous populations. The Stanford-Binet was further criticized for its emphasis on speed, causing older adult test takers to be penalized for protracted test completion. As such, Binet's mental age norms were thought to be inadequate when applied to adult populations. Furthermore, historically, the Binet scales did not consider the deterioration of intellectual ability that coincides with aging.

Wechsler Intelligence Scales

David Wechsler is best known for his development of a widely used series of intelligence tests, including the Wechsler Preschool and Primary Scale of Intelligence, the Wechsler Intelligence Scales for Children, the Wechsler Adult Intelligence Scales, and the Wechsler Abbreviated Scale of Intelligence. Although a student of Spearman, Wechsler believed that the concept of general g was too narrow to adequately describe intellectual functioning. Rather, it was best described in terms of both verbal and nonverbal abilities. As a result, the Wechsler scales consist of several subsets designed to assess abilities within the domains of verbal and nonverbal intelligence, although an estimate of global cognitive functioning is additionally provided. The Wechsler scales have undergone numerous revisions and updates (approximately every 10 years) and are among the most widely used assessment instruments for intellectual functioning across the life span.

Strengths of the Wechsler scales include an adequate standardization sample and good satisfactory reliability and validity. The ability to estimate scores on other Wechsler scales is another advantage for both screening and reevaluation purposes (Keith, 2004).

In spite of efforts to improve on the original Binet scales, the first Wechsler scales were not without flaws. One criticism was the inaccuracy in population representation. The first Wechsler scale's normative sample was insufficient, comprising 1,081 Whites from the eastern United States (Kaplan & Saccuzzo, 2005). Not only was this sample underrepresentative of the country's various regions, but it was racially and ethnically restricted as well.

Woodcock Johnson Scales

The Woodcock Johnson scales are based on the Cattell-Horn-Carroll (CHC) theory of cognitive abilities, a derivative of Spearman's *g* (Kaufman & Lichtenberger, 2006). As previously mentioned, Spearman's theory states that a single *g* sufficiently describes cognitive abilities. This is in contrast to the Wechsler scales, which describe intelligence in terms of abilities across multiple domains, including verbal and performance capabilities.

The Woodcock Johnson scales consist of two separate batteries measuring cognitive ability and achievement. The WJ III cognitive battery consists of 10 subtests (e.g., Verbal Comprehension, Auditory Working Memory) and the extended form consisting of 10 additional subtests (e.g., Picture Recognition, Decision Speed). The cognitive battery provides two indices of general intelligence: a GIA score (general intellectual ability) and a BIA score (brief intellectual ability). The GIA is considered to be a highly reliable score, with the highest median reliability coefficient across ages of.97 on the standard battery (Sandoval, 2004). The BIA score is obtained by administering three subtests only and has a high reliability coefficient of.95 (Cizek, 2004).

The Woodcock Johnson scales have numerous strengths. Construct validity using factor analysis shows the 7-factor CHC cognitive model is more closely linked than any of the other six models frequently used in deriving cognitive batteries; however, more data on validity would be useful (Sandoval, 2004). The split-half method was used in computing reliability for a coefficient of.80 for 38 tests and greater than.90 for 11 tests (Sandoval, 2004). The WJ-III software, manuals, and test materials are impressively modern, but hand scoring is cumbersome. Another advantage of the WJ-III is that the user can administer only selected subtests that can be individually tailored to meet specific testing requirements of individual subjects without sacrificing validity. Extended subtests are available to acquire additional information (Sandoval, 2004).

Recent Measures of Intellectual Functioning

Recently, a number of psychologists have developed assessment tools in attempts to address shortcomings of more traditional measures. Specifically, these assessments have sought to demonstrate applicability across diverse populations, incorporate developmental and educational perspectives into the assessments, and provide a method to assess intellectual functioning among nonverbal and non-English-speaking clients. These assessments include the Kaufman Adolescent and Adult Intelligence Test, the Differential Abilities Scales, and the Test of Nonverbal Intelligence.

Kaufman Adolescent and Adult Intelligence Test

The Kaufman Adolescent and Adult Intelligence Test (KAIT), one of the newest measures of cognitive functioning, was derived from Horn and Cattell's theory of fluid (Gf) and crystallized (Gc) intelligence, Luria's definition of planning ability, and the formal operational stage of development in Piaget's theory (Kaufman & Lichtenberger, 2006). It is a standardized measure of old (crystallized) and new (fluid) learning which can be consolidated into the construct of general intelligence. The core battery consists of Definitions, Auditory Comprehension, Double Meanings, Rebus Learning, Logical Steps, and Mystery Codes (Kaufman & Lichtenberger, 2006).

The KAIT contains a Gf scale and a Gc scale. The Gf scale measures one's adaptability and flexibility when solving both verbal and nonverbal new problems. The Gc scale measures acquired facts, problem-solving ability, and concepts using stimuli dependent on schooling, acculturation, and verbal conceptual development for success, and a composite IQ score.

The strengths of the KAIT include its ease in administration, scoring, and manipulation (Flanagan, 2004). The KAIT yields high test-retest reliability coefficients, ranging from .87 to .97 (Flanagan, 2004). This test also exhibits high construct validity for Caucasian, African American, and Hispanic populations (Flanagan, 2004). It seems to be an adequate assessment of fluid ability and is stimulating to examinees (Flanagan, 2004).

A weakness of the KAIT is that the guiding theory of fluid and crystallized intelligence was included after the test had been standardized and, therefore, raises the question regarding the theoretical basis for the development of the test (Keith, 2004).

Differential Abilities Scale

The Differential Abilities Scale (DAS) was originally developed from the British Ability Scales (Aylward, 2004). The DAS consists of 17 cognitive and three achievement subtests and assesses individuals from 2 years, 6 months to 17 years, 11 months. The cognitive battery generates a General Conceptual Ability score, and the three achievement subtests yield measures of math, spelling, and reading. Internal consistency reliability coefficients of the DAS (based on item-response theory) ranged from .70 to .92 on individual subtests (Aylward, 2004). Correlations with the DAS and other cognitive measures are high (Reinehr, 2004).

The strengths of the DAS include the test's incorporation of a developmental and educational perspective and practicality in evaluating children suspected of having developmental delays, hearing or language difficulties, mild mental retardation, and learning disabilities (Aylward, 2004). The DAS includes special education categories in its normative sample. The chief limitation is the complexity in administration, scoring, and interpretation (Reinehr, 2004). The record form is a lengthy 22 pages and the summary page requires a 12-step process to complete (Reinehr, 2004). Additionally, the manual suggests that administration can be completed in less than $1\frac{1}{2}$ hours, yet this is difficult at best (Reinehr, 2004).

Test of Nonverbal Intelligence

The Test of Nonverbal Intelligence (TONI) was developed to evaluate aptitude intelligence, abstract reasoning, and problem solving in a nonverbal format. Nonverbal tests are useful to the mental health and education fields in that they allow for differential diagnoses, treatment, and placement recommendations. The TONI is brief, taking only 15 to 20 minutes to administer, and is a substitute intelligence measure for those who do not speak English or suffer from sensory deficits (Atlas, 2004). The TONI's Intelligence score was created from the Ravens Progressive Matrices Test (Atlas, 2004). It is used primarily in testing non-English-speaking, learning-disabled, emotionally disturbed, gifted, dyslexic, and ADHD populations (Atlas, 2004). Although the TONI is a popular instrument for nonverbal assessments, it has low concurrent validity, ranging from.53 to.63 (DeMauro, 2004).

PSYCHOEDUCATIONAL ISSUES RELATED TO INTELLIGENCE TESTING

There are numerous issues related to the use of intellectual assessments and testing in formal educational settings. Children are routinely placed in classrooms (either gifted classrooms or classrooms designed to provide children school-based interventions for learning difficulties) based on the outcomes of routine psychoeducational evaluations. Currently, approximately 5% of children attending public schools are diagnosed as having learning disabilities (LD), diagnoses that are routinely based on a discrepancy between intellectual abilities and academic achievement. Typically, these evaluations are conducted by clinical psychologists or school psychologists and frequently include assessment of intellectual functioning, along with achievement-based assessment measures. Intellectual assessments routinely serve as the benchmark for competence and capability.

All children suspected of having handicaps or disabilities impacting school-based performance must be identified and classified accordingly. A multidisciplinary team often is involved with this identification and typically includes a clinical and/or school psychologist, special education teacher with expertise in the area of the suspected disability, the regular education teacher, the parents, and sometimes the student. The team is formed to evaluate whether or not a student meets criteria for a disability using behavioral observations, a review of educational records, additional testing, and any other information necessary to determine eligibility for accommodations (McIntosh & Decker, 2005). Educational testing assesses the domains of intelligence and achievement, which have been established as substantially related (McIntosh & Decker, 2005). To evaluate learning disabilities, initial screening measures are administered to determine if the discrepancy between IQ and achievement meet state guidelines for qualification. To meet inclusion criteria for a learning disability, there must be a substantial difference between expected ability (estimated by intelligence tests) and actual academic performance (Gordan, Lewandowski, & Keiser, 1999). Thus, the role of accurate intellectual assessment is paramount in the determination of learning difficulties.

Outcomes from psychoeducational assessments often lead to specific accommodations for school-based interventions. The intent of these school-based interventions is to increase the likelihood that the student will be able to achieve academically at a level commensurate with his or her intellectual abilities. Obviously, the importance of the validity of the assessments utilized and the interventions subsequently employed is paramount. The significance of these assessments has led to the establishment of specific legislation aimed at increasing the likelihood that accommodations are employed and routinely monitored.

This section reviews the major legal issues related to utilization of intellectual assessments as a component of psychoeducational testing. Specifically, we provide an overview of 504 plans and individualized educational planning. In the general context of the discussion of intellectual assessment, this overview is important because intellectual abilities routinely serve as the starting point for assessment of learning disabilities (and, thus, psychoeducational accommodations).

504 Plan

Section 504 of the Rehabilitation Act of 1973 (34 CFR §104.3j; Rehabilitation Act, 1973) and the Americans with Disabilities Act (ADA) of 1990 (ADA; PL 101-336, 1990) were designed to protect the civil rights of students with disabilities and provide protection against discrimination for those with disabilities. Section 504 defines a disability as substantially limiting one or more major life activities, and this limitation is determined by comparing the individual's performance to the average performance of the general population (Smith, 2001). This definition includes the prevention of any form of discrimination against individuals who are otherwise qualified or capable with the exception of their disability limitations (Smith, 2001).

Section 504 applies to all entities that receive federal funding, but there is no federal funding attached to compliance with Section 504. The ADA applies to almost every entity in the United States, with the exception of churches and private clubs (Smith, 2001). If an individual is protected under the IDEA, that individual is also protected under Section 504. However, if an individual qualifies for services under Section 504, that individual may not necessarily qualify for services under IDEA (McIntosh & Decker, 2005). The basic requirements of Section 504 are nondiscrimination, equal access to free appropriate public education, and participation opportunity in the same academic and extracurricular activities as all other students (Smith, 2001). Section 504 plans may be implemented at any level of education (i.e., kindergarten through 12th grade, as well as at the collegiate level).

Under Section 504, "A qualified [college] student with a disability is one who is able to meet a program's admission, academic, and technical standards either with or without accommodation" (Thomas, 2000, p. 250). If a postsecondary institution receives federal aid of any sort, it is mandated to comply with Section 504. This compliance is verified by filing a document stating that the college does not discriminate based on disability, providing such a notice to recipients of the program, identifying an employee to coordinate efforts to comply, conducting an evaluation of programs, and adopting grievance procedures (Thomas, 2000).

During the preadmission process, colleges are prohibited from requesting information regarding disabilities; yet postadmission inquiries can be made confidentially to determine adequate accommodations (Thomas, 2000).

In determining whether a student is qualified under Section 504, any criteria that may adversely impact the admission of a student with a disability, such as first-year grades, must be excluded from admission requirements. Any admission test used to evaluate a student's performance must be designed to accommodate those with disabilities (Thomas, 2000). Accommodations are necessary only for students with appropriate documentation and should not result in the fundamental alteration of academic standards (Thomas, 2000). Once a student with a disability has been admitted and a review of his or her qualifications is conducted, assessment of that student's ability given the requested accommodations is necessary (Thomas, 2000). The caveat with accommodations is that they should not allow a student with a disability an unfair advantage over those students without disabilities (Thomas, 2000).

Individualized Education Plan

The IDEA mandates that all children, regardless of exceptionality, be entitled to free and appropriate public education in the least restrictive environment. Per the least restrictive environment clause, it is initially assumed that children with specific learning disabilities and/or behavior difficulties may be educated in the regular classroom with the help of supplementary aids and services. The IDEA further requires that each state develop and implement a plan for special education services, as outlined in an individualized education Program (Jacob & Hartshorne, 2003).

Typically, following a psychoeducational evaluation that includes an intellectual assessment, a multidisciplinary team is formed to develop and implement the individualized education program (IEP). A growing trend is including the student in his or her IEP meeting (Arndt, Konrad, & Test, 2006).

The IEP includes the student's present level of performance, defined as both academic achievement and functional performance. The annual goals are outlined to monitor progress in the general education curriculum, and the individualized education program must be reviewed, and if necessary revised, annually (Gartin & Murdick, 2005). Quarterly reports or other periodic reports are required to monitor a student's progress toward annual goals. To meet these goals, the IEP contains a description of the services to be offered and the extent to which the individual participates in general education with his or her peers. In compliance with state and district wide assessments, the IEP must include a statement regarding the appropriate accommodations to measure the student's academic achievement and functional performance. Finally, the IEP must specify a target start date for services to be provided.

CULTURAL ISSUES RELATED TO INTELLIGENCE TESTING

The number of children in the United States whose primary language is not English continues to grow; this trend has been apparent for the past two decades (Lam, 1993). This enormous growth of children in the United States whose primary language is not English and who vary in their rates of acculturation has occurred at a time when public schools are placing increasing emphasis on the use of standardized tests and intellectual assessments to make placement decisions (Lam, 1993). In 1991, Torres reported that approximately 5 million students were inappropriately (because of their unique cultural background) administered standardized assessments in U.S. school systems. Obviously, that number has likely risen since 1991.

There are inherent problems related to the validity and reliability of intellectual assessments and standardized tests administered to individuals whose background differs from that of the normative population. As Lam (1993) discusses, legal cases aimed at challenging the validity of placement decisions based on standardized tests administered to non-English-speaking or diverse populations have led to mixed decisions.

Lam (1993) provides an excellent review of examiner and test-taker concerns related to administration of standardized tests to students whose primary language is not English. He describes five basic assumptions that clinicians should be mindful of when administering standardized assessments (e.g., the aforementioned intellectual assessments) to these children. First, the test-takers need to be able to follow the direction of the tests and have no linguistic barriers that limit their performance. Second, the test selected should have appropriate content and be consistent with the unique training the child has received prior to testing. In other words, the test administered (especially in the case of standardized achievement tests) should accurately reflect the child's exposure and past curricula. Third, the test-takers should have a previous history of taking standardized tests and some familiarity with this process in order for the results to be considered accurate reflections of their true abilities. Fourth, motivation plays an important factor in the validity of the results. A child who has a long-standing history of academic failure and/or difficulties attributable to cultural and language barriers may not be properly motivated to perform on standardized tests. The examiner should be aware of the impact of this lack of motivation on the interpretability of the results. Five, the examiner needs to be aware of any adverse reactions the test-taker may have to being assessed. Cultural barriers, language barriers, and past history of academic failures and struggles may lead to anxiety that impacts overall performance. While this type of anxiety can be found among the normative population, it has the potential to lead to greater difficulty among a non-English-speaking population. It is critically important that examiners take into account the test-taker's cultural background, specifically language barriers and previous educational curricula, when interpreting the results of standardized tests routinely used in the school setting. At a minimum, results should always be interpreted cautiously and judiciously.

CLINICAL APPLICATION

In an attempt to demonstrate the importance of intellectual assessment in the context of academic settings and medical treatment planning, two clinical case studies are reviewed next. The first case involves a 16-year-old, Caucasian American male referred for psychoeducational assessment following multiple academic failures at the college level. The second case involves a 10-year-old, African American male referred for academic difficulties following treatment for a pediatric brain tumor.

Case Illustration

C.R. was referred for a psychoeducational evaluation to assess for a specific learning disorder. According to his parents' report, he experienced difficulty learning foreign languages and failed several foreign-language classes in high school. C.R. reported difficulty remembering and pronouncing words and that spelling [was] always difficult for him. At the time of the referral, C.R. was required to take 2 years of foreign-language classes as a requirement for high school graduation. There was no history of psychiatric disorders or attention problems.

Cognitive testing revealed that C.R.'s overall ability fell within the average range, with little discrepancy between his verbal and nonverbal abilities. This pattern suggested that he performed equally well on verbal and performance-based tasks. On achievement testing, C.R. performed at a level commensurate with his academic history and estimated cognitive ability on tasks related to reading comprehension, pseudo-word decoding, numerical operations, math reasoning, and listening comprehension. However, his achievement scores for spelling and written expression were drastically lower than expected based on his educational background. Thus, he was generally achieving academically at a level consistent with his estimated cognitive functioning except for tasks involving written expression and word reading. This pattern suggested the presence of a learning disorder. More specifically, the discrepancy between his IQ and achievement test scores met criteria for the diagnosis of Disorder of Written Expression. Because academic curricula, including foreign languages and literature classes, rely heavily on written expression, C.R.'s difficulty in this domain was interpreted to negatively impact his academic performance in this content area and special classroom and curriculum accommodations were recommended to provide him with the optimal learning environment.

Case Illustration

C.T. was referred for a psychological evaluation by his mother for academic difficulties. At the time of testing, he was 5 years posttreatment (tumor resection, radiation, chemotherapy) for a pediatric brain tumor, with no signs of progressive disease. Although historically a good student, C.T. began to exhibit academic problems 2 years prior to the referral. More specifically, his mother reported that C.T. would "study for a test and know the material, but forget it" when he took the exam. This pattern resulted in a significant decline in his academic performance, with grades plummeting from primarily B's to mostly D's and F's. His mother reported that it appeared to take him longer to read than other children his age and that he had a hard time focusing while studying. C.T. indicated that he, also, felt it took him longer to read, but if given the time he could process the information. C.T. stated that he knew "the information, but when it [was] time for the test [he forgot] it all." To study, C.T. reported that he read the material several times and then tested himself on the material. Furthermore, he indicated that his difficulty seemed to be global and was not specific to one particular subject. He reported no sleep difficulties prior to a test

(Continued)

and no sudden change in appetite. He indicated that although he got nervous before a test (i.e., worried about not performing well, sweaty hands), he "never panicked" and did not feel that his nervousness interfered with his performance. Thus, his academic difficulties were not likely the result of test or performance anxiety. There was no reported family history of substance abuse, learning disorders, psychiatric disorders, or attention problems. He exhibited no significant behavior problems and denied the use of alcohol or drugs. Baseline testing (prior to diagnosis) indicated superior intellectual functioning.

C.T. was administered a comprehensive psychoeducational test battery to determine the nature of his recent academic declines. This battery included, among other instruments, the Wechsler Intelligence Scale for Children, Fourth Edition (WISC-IV) and the Wechsler Individual Achievement Test. Results of the WISC-IV indicated that C.T.'s Full-Scale IQ score was in the average range. Although consistent with scores of peers his age, his score was significantly below baseline testing and suggested a decline in intellectual functioning. Moreover, his verbal working memory index and processing speed fell within the low average range. Although these scores were not significantly lower than those of peers his age, the pattern showed a trend toward deficient memory functioning and processing speed in that the scores were two thirds of a standard deviation below average performance. The results from this achievement test suggested that C.T. performed at a level consistent with or better than his estimated cognitive ability on all academic tasks; thus, there was no evidence of a specific learning disorder.

Taken collectively, the pattern of results indicated a significant decline in cognitive functioning that was likely attributed to problems with memory and processing speed. This pattern is consistent with the cognitive late effects observed among pediatric cancer survivors. Thus, his academic difficulties were interpreted to be the result of cognitive late effects secondary to the disease process itself and/or aggressive treatment protocols (tumor resection, radiation). C.T. was diagnosed with Cognitive Disorder NOS and appropriate treatment recommendations were made.

The significance of intellectual assessment in both of these clinical cases is apparent. Accurate intellectual assessment assisted with the case conceptualization and, ultimately, the treatment planning for both clients. In the case of C.R., estimated intellectual abilities provided the basis to demonstrate a discrepancy between aptitude and achievement necessary for a diagnosis of Disorder of Written Expression and appropriate accommodations at school. In the case of C.T., declining intellectual functioning along with deficient memory and processing speed led to an efficacious treatment plan for treatment-related cognitive deficits and baseline to measure longitudinal changes postinjury.

SUMMARY

Intellectual assessment has a long-standing history in the disciplines of philosophy and psychology. Numerous theorists have developed theories of intelligence that have sought to best describe overall intellectual abilities of clients and patients.

Factor analytic theories attempt to understand intellectual functioning by examining patterns of individual differences on tests of cognitive skills. Information-processing theories of intelligence focus on the processes believed to be involved in intellectual activities by attempting to describe the internal workings of intelligent thought. Theories of intelligence have impacted both the definitions of intellectual functioning and the assessment tools utilized to measure intellectual abilities.

Intellectual assessments are clinically important for a variety of reasons. These measures routinely serve as the starting point of psychoeducational evaluations for learning disabilities. Baseline estimates of intellectual functioning are commonly utilized to demonstrate discrepancies between achievement (academic) and ability (intellectual prowess) necessary for the diagnosis of learning disabilities.

Intellectual assessments are also important in the classification of employees and in the context of military service. Assessment utilizing intelligence tests, specifically crystallized versus fluid intelligence, provides important diagnostic information for professionals working with patients who have suffered brain injuries and/or insults.

As a result of these multifaceted applications of intellectual assessments, it is important for the practitioner to remain abreast of novel and innovative approaches to assess intellectual abilities. It is equally important to remain mindful of the shortcomings of these assessment tools in light of their numerous ramifications, especially with respect to cultural biases that may be present. Finally, it is imperative that practitioners utilizing intellectual assessment tools accurately convey findings to clients and patients in such a manner that the information is easily understood.

REFERENCES

American with Disabilities Act. (1990). 42 U.S.C.A. Sections 12101-12213.

Arndt, S. A., Konrad, M., & Test, D. W. (2006). Effects of the self directed IEP on student participation in planning meetings. *Remedial and Special Education, 27*, 194–207.

Atlas, J. A. (2004). Review of the Test of Nonverbal Intelligence. *Mental Measurement Yearbook*. Retrieved September15, 2006, from http://search.ebscohost.com/login.aspx?direct=true&db=loh&AN=14072077&site=ehost-live.

Aylward, G. P. (2004). Review of the Differential Ability Scales. *Mental Measurement Yearbook*. Retrieved September15, 2006, from http://search.ebscohost.com/login.aspx?direct=true&db=loh&AN=11010989&site=ehost-live.

Borkowski, J. G. (1985). Signs of intelligence: Strategy generalization and metacognition. In S. Yussen's (Ed.), *Development of reflection in children* (pp. 105–144). San Diego, CA: Academic Press.

Campione, J. C., & Brown, A. L. (1978). Toward a theory of intelligence: Contributions from research with retarded children. *Intelligence, 2*, 279–304.

Cizek, G. J. (2004). Review of the Woodcock-Johnson (r) III. *Mental Measurement Yearbook*. Retrieved September 15, 2006, from http://search.ebscohost.com/login.aspx?direct=true&db=loh&AN=16073134&site=ehost-live.

Clayes, G. (2001). Introducing Francis Galton, "Kantsaywhere" and "The donoghues of dunno weir." *Utopian Studies, 12* (2), 188–190.

DeMauro, G. E. (2004). Review of the Test of Nonverbal Intelligence. *Mental Measurement Yearbook*. Retrieved September 15, 2006, from http://search.ebscohost.com/login.aspx?direct=true&db=loh&AN=14072077&site=ehost-live.

Flanagan, D. P. (2004). Review of Kaufman Adolescent and Adult Intelligence Test. *Mental Measurement Yearbook*. Retrieved September 15, 2006, from http://search.ebscohost.com/login.aspx?direct=true&db=loh&AN=12071370&site=ehost-live.

Galton, F. (1869/1892/1962). *Hereditary genius: An inquiry into its laws and consequences.* London: Macmillan/Fontana.

Gartin, B. C., & Murdick, N. L. (2005). IDEA 2004: The IEP. *Remedial and Special Education, 26*(6), 327–331.

Gordon, M., Lewandowski, L., & Keiser, S. (1999). The LD label for relatively well-functioning students: A critical analysis. *Journal of Learning Disabilities, 32,* 485–490.

Horn, J. L., & Cattell, R. B. (1966). Refinement and test of the theory of fluid and crystallized general intelligences. *Journal of Educational Psychology, 57,* 253–270.

Jacob, S., & Hartshorne, T. S. (2003). *Ethics and law for school psychologists* (4th ed.) Hoboken, NJ: Wiley.

Johnson, J. A., & D'Amato, R. C. (2004). Review of the Stanford-Binet Intelligence Scales. *Mental Measurement Yearbook.* Retrieved September 15, 2006, from http://search.ebscohost.com/login.aspx?direct=true&db=loh&AN=17073217&site=ehost-live.

Kail, R., & Pellegrino, J. W. (1985). *Human intelligence: Perspectives and prospects.* New York: W.H. Freeman.

Kaplan, R. M., & Saccuzzo, D. B. (2005). The Wechsler Intelligence Scales: WAIS-III, WISC-IV, and WPPSI-III. In *Psychological testing: Principles, applications, and issues* (pp. 254–277). Belmont, CA: Thomson Wadsworth.

Kaufman, A. S., & Lichtenberger, E. O. (2006). *Assessing adolescent and adult intelligence.* Hoboken, NJ: Wiley.

Keith, T. Z. (2004). Review of the Wechsler Abbreviated Scale of Intelligence. *Mental Measurement Yearbook.* Retrieved September 14, 2006, from http://search.ebscohost.com/login.aspx?direct=true&db=loh&AN=14072466&site=ehost-live.

Kush, J. C. (2004). Review of the Stanford-Binet Intelligence Scales. *Mental Measurement Yearbook.* Retrieved September 15, 2006, from http://search.ebscohost.com/login.aspx?direct=true&db=loh&AN=17073217&site=ehost-live.

Lam, T. C. (1993). Testability: A critical issue in testing language minority students with standardized tests. *Measurement and Evaluation of Counseling and Development, 56* (3), 179–191.

McIntosh, D. E., & Decker, S. L. (2005). Understanding and evaluating special education, IDEA, ADA, NCLB, and Section 504 in school neuropsychology. In R. C. D'Amato, E. Fletcher-Jansen, & C. R. Reynolds (Eds.), *Handbook of school neuropsychology* (pp. 365–382). Hoboken, NJ: Wiley.

Rehabilitation Act of 1973, 29 U.S.C. 794.

Reinehr, R. C. (2004). Review of the Differential Ability Scales. *Mental Measurement Yearbook.* Retrieved September 15, 2006, from http://search.ebscohost.com/login.aspx?direct=true&db=loh&AN=11010989&site=ehost-live.

Sandoval, J. (2004). Review of the Woodcock-Johnson (r) III. *Mental Measurement Yearbook.* Retrieved September 15, 2006, from http://search.ebscohost.com/login.aspx?direct=true&db=loh&AN=16073134&site=ehost-live.

Sattler, J. M. (2001). *Assessment of children: Cognitive applications.* San Diego, CA: Author.

Seligman, D. (2002). Good breeding. *National Review, 54*(1), 53–54.

Siegler, R. S. (1992). The other Alfred Binet. *Developmental Psychology, 28,* 179–190.

Smith, T. E. C. (2001). Section 504, the ADA and public schools. *Remedial and Special Education, 22,* 335–343.

Spearman, C. (1904a). General intelligence objectively determined and measured. *American Journal of Psychology, 15,* 201–293.

Sternberg, R. J. (1985). Cognitive approaches to intelligence. In B. B. Wolman (Ed.), *Handbook of intelligence: Theories, measurement, and applications.* New York: Wiley.

Thomas, S. B. (2000). College students and disability law. *Journal of Special Education, 33,* 248–257.

Thurstone, L. L. (1938). *Primary mental abilities.* Chicago: University of Chicago Press.

Torres, J. (1991). Equity in education and the language minority student. *Forum, 14*(4), 1–3.

Williams, R. H., Zimmerman, D. W., Zumbo, B. D., & Ross, E. (2003). Charles Spearman: British behavioral scientist. *Human Nature Review, 3,* 114–118.

Zusne, L. (1957). *Names in the history of psychology.* New York: Wiley.

CHAPTER 17

Pediatric Neuropsychological Evaluation

Leslie D. Berkelhammer

"Left brained, right brained—I call that bird brained." Nearly 20 years ago, this was the opening sentence in the first lecture of my first neuropsychology professor, Ursula Kirk, EdD, at Teachers College of Columbia University. With characteristic dry wit, she encouraged us to think critically at a time when hemispheric special-ization was all the rage. Neuropsychology is no longer the black box it once was and appreciation of brain-behavior relationships is more commonplace. Advances in our understanding of cognitive neuroscience, genetics, neuroimaging, and med-ical technology have enhanced neuropsychological research and clinical practice. Perhaps the challenge before today's researchers, clinicians, and students is best phrased by the late Ray Mulhern, PhD, of St. Jude Children's Research Hospital, who exhorted, "Don't think—know." Integration and consolidation of interdisci-plinary findings in design research and clinical protocols is essential to advance the field and to gain recognition of the unique contributions of neuropsychologists working collaboratively with multidisciplinary colleagues in an academic medical setting.

DEFINITION OF A CLINICAL NEUROPSYCHOLOGIST

Clinical neuropsychology is a specialty formally recognized by the American Psy-chological Association, Canadian Psychological Association, and many other in-ternational bodies. In 1989, Division 40 of the APA first published the definition of a clinical neuropsychologist. The Houston Conference on Specialty Education and Training in Clinical Neuropsychology, held in 1997, formalized the programmatic and competency-based components of an integrated scientist-practitioner model for specialty training in clinical neuropsychology. The Houston Conference defined a clinical neuropsychologist as

> a professional psychologist trained in the science of brain-behavior relationships who specializes in the application of assessment and intervention principles based on the sci-entific study of human behavior across the life span as it relates to normal and abnormal functioning of the central nervous system.

In 2001, the National Academy of Neuropsychology updated the 1989 APA Division 40 definition with wording consistent with that of the Houston Conference. The

NAN definition further delineated the methods of a clinical neuropsychologist as one who

> uses psychological, neurological, cognitive, behavioral, and physiological principles, techniques and tests to evaluate patients' neurocognitive, behavioral, and emotional strengths and weaknesses and their relationship to normal and abnormal central nervous system functioning. The clinical neuropsychologist uses this information and information provided by other medical/health care providers to identify and diagnose neurobehavioral disorders, and plan and implement intervention strategies.

SCOPE OF PRACTICE

Some neuropsychologists are primarily clinicians or researchers; others combine these roles. Both those in academic medical centers and those in practice settings provide opportunities for training and mentorship. Professional organizations serve the interests of their constituents. The four primary professional organizations are the International Neuropsychological Society, the National Academy of Neuropsychology, Division 40 of the APA, and the Society for Neuroscience. A web-based, interactive database of programs offering training in clinical neuropsychology at the graduate, internship, and postdoctoral levels was recently added to the Division 40 website (www.apa.div40.org).

The Web has made access to information easier while also raising the bar for expectations of immediate responses and professional exposure. Many consumers of neuropsychological services now seek information on providers via the Internet that was previously based on a trusted referral. For professionals and future practitioners, opportunities for self-education are easily accessed on the Web, particularly for neuroanatomy tutorials and interactive brain atlases (e.g., www.digitalanatomist.com). Listservs such as the Pediatric Neuropsychology and Women in Neuropsychology listservs are useful resources for a wide audience, with discussions about particular cases, diseases and disorders, practice issues, and career development.

HYPOTHESIS-DRIVEN ASSESSMENT

Neuropsychological assessment is a hypothesis-driven assessment of higher brain functions resulting in an integrative analysis of findings in the context of a neurodevelopmental-systems approach and detailing recommendations for addressing the presenting problems as well as those that may be revealed in the course of the evaluation. Whether a neuropsychological test is conducted to profile the strengths and weaknesses of an individual or a population, the potential for changing how others view the presenting problem or research question is considerable. At an individual level, neuropsychological testing samples multiple cognitive domains and contextualizes findings within a neurodevelopmental approach. Indeed, skilled clinicians are able to translate test results into meaningful relevance for parents and educators such that the feedback session serves as a therapeutic intervention. Families and educators often change their perspective of the child and

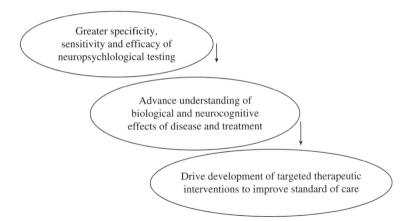

Figure 17.1   An integrative model of neuropsychological evaluation, treatment, and research.

reset expectations for parenting and teaching demands based on this more informed view. Further, the feedback session allows the child to gain a better understanding of his or her ability profile (Roman, 2004). Within and across groups, analysis of performance via empirical research affords opportunity to advance understanding of biological and neurocognitive effects of disease and treatment. Thus, neuropsychological data of individual and group performance drive development of targeted therapeutic interventions and have potential to improve standards of care (see Figure 17.1).

Pediatric or child neuropsychology is the evaluation, treatment, investigation, and teaching of brain-behavior relationships in children with a neurological, medical, or psychiatric disorder that negatively affects cognitive, psychological, and/or behavioral functioning. At its core, pediatric neuropsychology examines neurodevelopmental factors and the effects of disability, disease, and trauma in comparison to typical development and premorbid baseline abilities. In this chapter, I share with you some of my thoughts about child neuropsychological assessment. I describe the development of the discipline, distinguish pediatric neuropsychology from other child psychology specialties, and offer clinical tools for practice.

A NEURODEVELOPMENTAL APPROACH

The neuropsychologist approaches the testing session with an informed plan, based on a thorough review of the child's medical and school records, to test hypotheses regarding underlying neurological and developmental factors contributing to the child's presenting problem. It's not enough to simply document that the child's reading comprehension is at the 76th percentile compared to same-age peers. Rather, analysis of the subcomponents and reasons for the deficits as well as recommendations for accommodations and strategies for compensatory methods must be delineated within a brain-behavior and developmental-systems approach.

Bernstein (2000, p. 434) describes her neurodevelopmental model in terms of an interaction effect between the variables of brain, context, and development: "The clinical assessment is not just a tally of skills made in a vacuum; it is a principled undertaking in the context of a theory of the organism." Neuropsychological testing is a dynamic (nonstatic) environment wherein the examiner, examinee, and examination are influenced by those same three factors (Bernstein, Kammerer, Prather, & Rey-Casserly, 1998).

Analogous to brain maturation and child developmental theory, the specialty of pediatric neuropsychology has evolved from infancy through childhood. The work of Bernstein and colleagues suggests the coming of age of child neuropsychological assessment. In essence, they have extended Kaplan's pioneering principle of the process approach inherent in clinical assessment of an individual to a more global view of the systems in which the particular child has lived, lives, and will live. Importantly, findings must take into account the four overlapping systems in which the child is affected and affects: medical, school, family, and community.

Levine (1991) has facilitated cross-talk among educators and more neuropsychologically based professionals interested in the interface of developmental pediatrics, neuropsychology, and pedagogy. He describes eight neurodevelopmental constructs (attention, temporal sequential ordering, spatial ordering, memory, language, neuromotor functions, social cognition, and higher order cognition) and their applications to specific curriculum objectives, instructional strategies, and accommodations for learning.

INDICATIONS FOR NEUROPSYCHOLOGICAL EVALUATION

A neuropsychological evaluation is indicated in cases in which brain-based impairment in thinking or behavior is suspected. Examples of relevant conditions include cognitive changes associated with medical conditions (e.g., childhood cancers, sickle cell disease, hematological disorders, HIV/AIDS, epilepsy) or medical treatments (e.g., brain surgery, radiation, chemotherapy, shunt placement, bone marrow transplantation, certain medicines) and brain injury, including stroke. Specific areas of difficulty may include language problems, memory difficulties, organizational problems, emotional difficulties, or behavior problems. Evaluation may be needed to characterize initial functioning and monitor change in children with potentially unstable conditions (e.g., children undergoing treatments with known cognitive risks, children at risk for stroke, children with a history of seizure), make a diagnosis, update academic or vocational plans, or assess for psychosocial problems related to a medical condition. A neuropsychological evaluation is particularly useful for tracking progress in rehabilitation after brain injury or neurological disease. Neuropsychological evaluations may confirm or clarify a diagnosis, identify changes in functioning since prior examinations, provide a profile of strengths and weaknesses to guide rehabilitation or educational or vocational services, identify beneficial compensatory strategies, or result in referrals to other specialists (e.g., educators, neurologists, psychologists, psychiatrists, social workers, vocational counselors).

SHARED VARIANCE AMONG CHILD PSYCHOLOGY SPECIALTIES

Neuropsychology is "the study, evaluation, and treatment of known and suspected brain disorders using the methods of psychology," according to the definition posted on the National Academy of Neuropsychology (NAN) website. By comparison, the American Psychological Association (APA) website posts definitions for clinical and pediatric psychology:

> The field of clinical psychology integrates science, theory, and practice to understand, predict, and alleviate maladjustment, disability, and discomfort as well as to promote human adaptation, adjustment, and personal development. Clinical Psychology focuses on the intellectual, emotional, biological, psychological, social, and behavioral aspects of human functioning across the life span, in varying cultures, and at all socioeconomic levels.

Finally, "Pediatric psychology is an interdisciplinary field addressing physical, cognitive, social, and emotional functioning and development as it relates to health and illness issues in children, adolescents, and their families."

Neuropsychological evaluations may include some of the same tests as those used to conduct a psychoeducational evaluation. However, a noticeable difference will be evident in the breadth and depth of skills measured and interpretation in relationship to brain processes. Neuropsychological assessment is not about the tests. It's about the dynamic testing environment and the theoretical approach of the professional who interprets the findings and ensures that a qualitative analysis of the child's performance is every bit as important as the quantitative results.

Commonalities and differences exist across specialties in child psychology. Pediatric neuropsychology incorporates elements of clinical, school, counseling, and organizational psychology. Pediatric neuropsychologists must be well versed in developmental psychopathology, knowledgeable about pedagogy and school systems, familiar with counseling principles, and informed about organizational behavior when rendering feedback and conducting cognitive rehabilitation to both the child and the family.

QUANTITATIVE AND QUALITATIVE DESCRIPTION OF GLOBAL AND SPECIFIC FUNCTIONS

A neuropsychological assessment provides quantitative and qualitative data on the domains of intelligence, attention, executive functions, language, learning and memory (verbal and nonverbal), visual-spatial, motor, behavioral, psychological, adaptive, and academic skills. However, select areas will be emphasized over others, based on the reasons for referral and data that emerge during the evaluation. The clinical interview is the foundation for the evaluation as it sets the tone for the patient and allows the examiner a period of focused data gathering on which to refine the preliminary testing. The Pediatric Neuropsychology Questionnaire (Baron, Fennell, & Voeller, 1995) is a particularly useful structured interview.

Components of the evaluation include the following: presenting problems and reasons for referral; relevant developmental, family, medical, educational, and psychosocial history; an integrative assessment and analysis of cognitive domains and skills within and across domains; comparison of the student's performance to same-age peers for normative comparison; description of the individual's relative strengths and weaknesses; specific recommendation for intervention; and prognosis, given all these considerations taken together.

Assessment of global cognitive abilities, or general g, should allow for comparison of verbal and nonverbal skills as well as analysis of specific subtests and the underlying skills presumed to be measured. Evaluation of attention and concentration abilities should compare auditory versus visual attentional skills, attention span, sustained and divided attention, and processing of simple versus complex information. Executive functions influence the expression within multiple domains and are particularly reliant on the connectivity of neural systems. Throughout the evaluation, task analysis of ability to prioritize, plan, sequence, analyze, reason, and make decisions should be prominent.

Language assessment should explore components such as expressive and receptive abilities, comprehension, verbal fluency, repetition, naming, speech production, conversational speech, organization of verbal output, and pragmatics (e.g., prosody, rambling speech, and nonverbal aspects of speech: eye contact, turn-taking, gestures, interpersonal space). Similarly, information processing should examine auditory versus visual abilities, response speed, and the relative pacing of simple versus complex information. Learning and memory assessment should also be multimodal and quantify functioning visual, verbal, auditory, tactile, and motor skills. There are several well-normed measures that allow the neuropsychologist to analyze which component of memory is problematic for the individual being examined: encoding versus retrieval. Recommendations should account for intra-individual performance in short- versus long-term memory and for simple versus complex information for both verbal and visual-spatial material.

Evaluation of current levels of academic achievement compared to peers is an integral part of the neuropsychological evaluation. Again, the goal should not be limited to mere reporting of ability levels in the core areas of mathematics, reading, spelling, and written expression. Instead, data-driven conclusions about the neuropsychological underpinnings of these expressed deficits should be offered. Recommendations to maximize strengths and minimize weaknesses should also be considered along the same lines. In sum, neuropsychological findings should inform opinions about the *goodness of fit* between the child and his or her learning environment.

Psychological, social-emotional, behavioral, and adaptive functions should be assessed. Recommendations for interventions and skill building should be grounded in an integrated understanding of the child's neuropsychological abilities. For example, the child with Attention-Deficit/Hyperactivity Disorder may require social skills training and cognitive rehabilitation to compensate for deficient frontal feedback loops that limit awareness of his or her effect on others. Temperament, or the biological bases of personality, seems to be underexamined by neuropsychologists, although there appears to be some common ground with child neuropsychology.

NEUROPSYCHOLOGICAL REPORT

The neuropsychological report is an important document. Often, there are multiple consumers of the report, each interpreting the information from the viewpoint of his or her respective disciplines (e.g., physician, educator, coach, and parent). Yet, each of these consumers relies on the information in the report to get a sense of the child's abilities under ideal conditions and to extrapolate to the situation in which the consumer of the report interacts with the child. Accordingly, the report should contain an integrated analysis of the child's cognitive abilities, academic achievement, and psychological functioning. The neuropsychologist should provide quantitative and qualitative data to elucidate multiple factors contributing to the presenting problems, including relevant neurological, medical, and developmental issues. Thus, the report is often a critical tool in decisions regarding school planning, educational program placement, medical care, and treatment monitoring.

By any measure, evaluation is an expensive procedure. Cognitive screening may be appropriate to prioritize those in need of a more comprehensive evaluation, estimate restricted functions, and generate epidemiological data. Regardless of the comprehensiveness of the testing, documentation of the child's strengths and weaknesses, comparison to age-level expectations, recommendations for instruction and curriculum, accommodations to optimize learning and development, and identification of children in need of additional services is expected.

COGNITIVE REHABILITATION

The emergence and development of the subspecialty of cognitive rehabilitation is a logical progression from the discipline's early emphasis on testing and test development (Sohlberg & Mateer, 2001). Cognitive rehabilitation is a subspecialty that employs functional activities to a systematic application of remediation strategies designed to ameliorate impaired brain functions after injury based on a thorough evaluation of the patient's acquired deficits and residual strengths. Treatment goals include strengthening premorbid adaptive skills and behaviors, establishing new patterns of cognition via compensatory strategies for impaired neurological systems, establishing new patterns via external compensatory supports, and adapting to reduced levels of ability. Learning therapy to improve acquired cognitive deficits by instruction and rehearsal of compensatory strategies with environmental modifications can have a profound difference on quality of life following injury or disease. Butler and colleagues (Butler & Copeland, 2002; Butler & Mulhern, 2005) have demonstrated the efficacy of cognitive rehabilitation in children treated for cancer. Moreover, evidence-based outcomes have been demonstrated on functional magnetic resonance imaging studies (Ogg, Zou, White, et al., 2002; Laatsch, Thulborn, Krisky, Shobat, & Sweeney, 2004).

FUTURE DIRECTIONS

As understanding of the biological basis of behavior and cognition become more important, and there are medical or biological treatments to be applied, the only method of functionally monitoring such treatment is neuropsychological assessment. We need to be at the forefront of working with those who are devising treatments for diseases caused by both innate and acquired injuries to monitor functional outcomes of both biological and behavioral treatments.

—Elsa Shapiro

Historically, neuropsychologists have relied heavily on their expertise in assessment and test development to thoroughly document the cognitive and psychological strengths and weaknesses of the patient. Over time, demand for shorter test batteries, multidisciplinary treatment team involvement, and application of test findings to cognitive rehabilitation, forensics, and policy development has emerged. I have long posed a challenge to myself and colleagues with a two-word question: "So what?" That is, although quantification of an individual's neuropsychological profile in comparison to normally developing peers on standardized measures is important, relevance to the varied environments in which children operate is critical.

These are, indeed, exciting times for those who conduct neuropsychological assessment, treatment, and research and train the next generation of clinicians and researchers. Opportunities to incorporate neuropsychological theory and novel applications in forensic settings, day treatment programs, and automated environments push the envelope. Virtual reality applications to neuropsychological assessment and cognitive rehabilitation of acquired brain injury and neurological disorders are poised to further the field as we move beyond assessment and toward evidence-based outcomes (Schultheis, Himelstein, & Rizzo, 2002). Building on the well-received text, *Neuropsychological Evaluation of the Child*, Baron (2004) describes the growth and development of pediatric neuropsychology in the context of maturation of the field, development of cognitive rehabilitation models applied to a range of disorders, and increased cross-fertilization from allied health, psychology, neuroscience, and neuroradiology (Baron, in press).

I have included several clinical forms and a sample neuropsychological report in six appendixes. Appendix 1 is a disease-specific clinical intake form with content customized to known areas of cognitive vulnerability and contact information for the multidisciplinary team serving this group of patients. Appendix 2 is a test results summary grid provided by my colleague Jordi Bernabeu, PhD, of the La Fe Hospital in Valencia, Spain. He has found it helpful to explain test results to persons unfamiliar with specific tests using a common metric of z-scores with domains color-coded across multiple measures. I believe that we sometimes overestimate the readability of our reports. Even with tables embedded in the report to render scores into more meaningful functional categories, the consumer—multidisciplinary treatment team providers, parents, and educators—may not easily appreciate the psychometrics of reported data. Appendix 3 is a 24-hour preliminary feedback form on which test abbreviations and relevant scores can be entered by domain and categorical outcome. I have found this form helpful in rapidly communicating with the referral source. Appendix 4 is a preferred tests form, with measures grouped by domain and presented in a check box format to aid the examiner before and during the testing session. Given the proliferation of commercially available tests, the list is not exhaustive; it reflects my own selection biases. Appendix 5 is a recommendations form letter, summarizing medical background and specific accommodations to be implemented in the school setting. Appendix 6 is a neuropsychological sample report.

SUMMARY

In this chapter, child neuropsychological evaluation was defined as a hypothesis-driven assessment of higher brain functions. Indications for and components of neuropsychological testing were defined. The importance of the neuropsychological report as a descriptive analysis of cognitive, psychological, and behavioral strengths and weaknesses, contextualized within a neurodevelopmental-systems framework, was explored. Professional qualifications, scope of practice, and differences between select child psychology specialties were described. Progress and future directions for the field of pediatric neuropsychology were discussed.

An integrated model of neuropsychological testing, treatment, and research was presented. Greater specificity, sensitivity, and efficacy of neuropsychological assessment was proposed as a means to advance understanding of the biological and neurocognitive effects of disease and treatment. In turn, these refinements were proposed as a catalyst to drive development of targeted therapeutic interventions and yield improvement in standards of care. As a specialty area of practice, research, and teaching, the field of neuropsychology has a bright future. Creative and well-trained neuropsychologists will, most certainly, further established lines of research and explore new applications with an increased reliance on emerging biotechnology.

REFERENCES

Baron, I. S. (2004). *Neuropsychological evaluation of the child*. New York: Oxford University Press.

Baron, I. S. (in press). Growth and development of pediatric neuropsychology. In J. Morgan & J. Ricker (Eds.), *Textbook of clinical neuropsychology*. New York: Psychology Press.

Baron, I. S., Fennell, E. B., & Voeller, K. S. (1995). *Pediatric neuropsychology in the medical setting*. New York: Oxford University Press.

Bernabeu, J., Cañete, A., Fournier, C., López-Luengo, B., Barahona, A., Grau, C., et al. (2003). Evaluacion y rehabilitacion neuropsicologica en oncologia pediatrica. *Psicooncologia, 1*, 117–134.

Bernstein, J. H., Kammerer, B., Prather, P., & Rey-Casserly, C. (1998). Developmental neuropsychological assessment. In G. P. Koocher, J. C. Norcross, & S. S. Hill, Jr. (Eds.), *Psychologists' desk reference*. New York: Oxford University Press.

Butler, R. W., & Copeland, D. R. (2002). Attentional processes and their remediation in children treated for cancer: A literature review and the development of a therapeutic approach. *Journal of the International Neuropsychological Society, 8*, 115–124.

Butler, R. W., & Mulhern, R. K. (2005). Neurocognitive interventions for children and adolescents surviving cancer. *Journal of Pediatric Psychology, 30*, 65–78.

Hannay, H. J., Bieliauskas, L., Crosson, B. A., Hammeke, T. A., Hamsher, K. D., & Koffler, S. (1998). Proceedings of the Houston conference on specialty education and training in clinical neuropsychology. *Archives of Clinical Neuropsychology, 13*, 157–250.

Hunter, S., & Donders, J. (2007). *Pediatric neuropsychological intervention*. New York: Cambridge University Press.

Laatsch, L. K., Thulborn, K. R., Krisky, C. M., Shobat, D. M., & Sweeney, J. A. (2004). Investigating the neurobiological basis of cognitive rehabilitation therapy with fMRI. *Brain Injury, 18*, 957–974.

Levine, M. D. (1991). The subspecialty of developmental-behavioral pediatrics: Presidential address. *Journal of Developmental Behavioral Pediatrics, 12*(1), 1–3.

Ogg, R., Zou, P., White, H., et al. (2002). Attention deficits in survivors of childhood cancer: An fMRI study. *Journal of the International Neuropsychological Society, 8*, 494–495.

Roman, M. J. (2004). Child neuropsychological assessment. In M. Rizzo, & P. J. Eslinger (Eds.), *Principles and practice of behavioral neurology and neuropsychology*. Philadelphia: Saunders.

Schultheis, M. T., Himelstein, J., & Rizzo, A. A. (2002). Virtual reality and neuropsychology: Upgrading the current tools. *Journal of Head Trauma Rehabilitation, 17*(5), 378–394.

Sohlberg, M. M., & Mateer, C. A. (2001). *Cognitive rehabilitation: An integrative neuropsychological approach*. New York: Guilford Press.

APPENDIX 1: CLINICAL REFERRAL FORM

CONFIDENTIAL
CLINICAL REFERRAL FORM
Sickle Cell Disease

Name: _____ MRN #: _____

Date of Testing: _____ Date of Birth: _____ Age: _____

Grade: _____ School: _____

Referring Physician: _____

SCD Genotype: ☐ HbSS   ☐ HbSC   ☐ HbSβ° thalassemia

                      ☐ HbSβ± thalassemia   ☐ HbSβ+ thalassemia

Therapy: ☐ None ☐ Chronic Transfusion ☐ Hydroxyurea ☐ Transplantation

Education: ☐ Retained _____ ☐ Sp. Ed. _____

Psychiatric: ☐ Diagnosis _____ ☐ Medication _____

              ☐ Psychotherapy _____ ☐ Pica   ☐ Sleep Disorder

TCD: ☐ Normal   ☐ Conditional ☐ Abnormal

MRI: ☐ Infarct _____   ☐ Other _____

Presenting Problem(s) & Reason for Referral:

Evaluate:

☐ Intelligence
☐ Attention   ☐ Processing Speed
☐ Executive Functions
    ☐ Working Memory   ☐ Cognitive Flexibility   ☐ Planning and Organization
    ☐ Fluency   ☐ Task Initiation   ☐ Task Persistence
☐ Learning and Memory
☐ Language
☐ Visual-Spatial
☐ Motor
☐ Psychosocial   ☐ Behavioral / Adaptive   ☐ Pain / Coping
☐ Academic Achievement
    ☐ Reading   ☐ Math   ☐ Writing   ☐ Spelling

CONTACT INFORMATION FOR SCD TEAM

                                              Phone   Page

Neuropsychologist

Nurse Case Managers *Infant & Toddler (0–4 years)*

                            School-Age (5–13 years)

                     Teen (13–18 years)

                     Hydroxyurea (all ages)

Educators

Social Worker

Physicians

APPENDIX 2: TEST RESULTS SUMMARY GRID

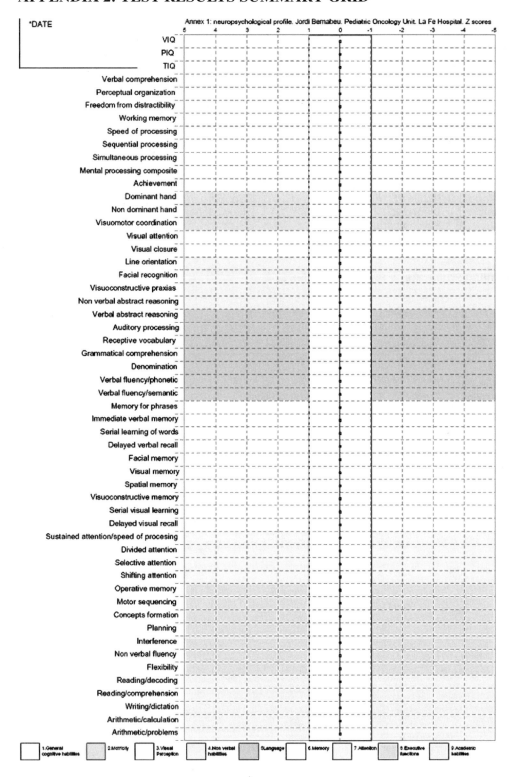

APPENDIX 3: 24-HOUR PRELIMINARY FEEDBACK FORM

CONFIDENTIAL
PRELIMINARY RESULTS OF NEUROPSYCHOLOGICAL TESTING
Feedback provided within 24 hours as professional courtesy. Report to follow within 30 days.

Name: _____   **Medical Record #:** _____
Date of Birth: _____   **Date of Testing:** _____
Age: _____   **Grade:** _____
Examiner: _____   **Supervising Neuropsychologist:** _____
Diagnosis: _____   **Referring Physician:** _____
Reason for Referral:

_____
_____

	Impaired	Borderline	Below Average	Average	Above Average	Superior	Very Superior	Not Tested
Intelligence								
Attention & Executive								
Learning & Memory								
Language								
Visual-Spatial & Motor								
Psychosocial, Behavioral & Adaptive								
Academics								

IMPRESSIONS:

_____   _____
Neuropsychology Fellow   Licensed Neuropsychologist

APPENDIX 4: PREFERRED TESTS FORM

CONFIDENTIAL
PREFERRED TESTS FORM

Please evaluate this patient's skills within the following domains and, if indicated, using the tests indicated. It is understood that clinical judgment may require changes to this plan.

NAME: _____ MEDICAL RECORD #: _____

DATE OF TESTING: _____ DATE OF BIRTH: _____

AGE: _____ GRADE: _____ SCHOOL: _____

DIAGNOSIS: _____ MEDICATION: _____

REFERRAL QUESTION: _____

BEHAVIORAL OBSERVATIONS: _____

_____

_____

_____

_____

☐ **Intellect and Global Cognitive**
  ☐ Bayley Scales of Infant and Toddler Development, Third Edition (Bayley-III)
  ☐ Bayley-III Screening Test
  ☐ Bracken Basic Concept Scale, Third Edition: Receptive (BBCS-3:R)
  ☐ Differential Abilities Scale (DAS)
  ☐ Kaufman Assessment Battery for Children, Second Edition (KABC-II)
  ☐ Kaufman Brief Intelligence Test, Second Edition (KBIT-2)
  ☐ McCarthy Scales of Children's Abilities
  ☐ McCarthy Screening Test (MST)
  ☐ Miller Assessment for Preschoolers (MAP)
  ☐ Mullen Scales of Early Learning
  ☐ NEPSY-II: A Developmental Neuropsychological Assessment, Second Edition (NEPSY-II)
  ☐ Raven's Progressive Matrices
  ☐ Stanford-Binet Intelligence Scales, Fifth Edition (SB-V)
  ☐ Universal Nonverbal Intelligence Test (UNIT)
  ☐ Wechsler Preschool and Primary Scale of Intelligence, Third Edition (WPPSI-III)
  ☐ Wechsler Intelligence Scale for Children, Fourth Edition (WISC-IV)
  ☐ Wechsler Intelligence Scale for Children, Fourth Edition, Integrated (WISC-IV-Integrated)
  ☐ Wechsler Abbreviated Scale of Intelligence (WASI)
  ☐ Wechsler Adult Intelligence Scale, Third Edition (WAIS-III)
  ☐ Woodcock-Johnson Tests of Cognitive Abilities, Third Edition (WJ-III COG)

☐ **Academic**
  ☐ Gray Oral Reading Test, Fourth Edition (GORT-4)
  ☐ Kaufman Test of Educational Achievement, Second Edition (KTEA-II)
  ☐ School Motivation and Learning Strategies Inventory (SMALSI)
  ☐ Wechsler Individual Achievement Test, Second Edition (WIAT-II)
  ☐ Woodcock-Johnson Tests of Achievement, Third Edition (WJ-III ACH)

☐ **Attention and Executive Function**
  ☐ Behavior Rating Inventory of Executive Function (BRIEF)
  ☐ Conners' Continuous Performance Test II, Version 5 (CPT II)
  ☐ Delis-Kaplan Executive Function System (D-KEFS)
  ☐ Clock Drawing
  ☐ Test of Variables of Attention (TOVA)
  ☐ Test of Everyday Attention in Children (TEA-Ch)
  ☐ Wisconsin Card Sort Test: Computer Version 4 (WCST: CV4)

☐ **Learning and Memory**
  ☐ California Verbal Learning Test, Children's Version (CVLT-C)
  ☐ California Verbal Learning Test, Second Edition (CVLT-II)
  ☐ Children's Memory Scale (CMS)
  ☐ Rey-Osterreith Complex Figure Test
  ☐ Wechsler Memory Scale, Third Edition (WMS-III)
  ☐ Wide Range Assessment of Memory and Learning, Second Edition (WRAML-2)

☐ **Language**
  ☐ Clinical Evaluation of Language Fundamentals, Fourth Edition (CELF-IV)
  ☐ Controlled Oral Word Association (COWA) / Verbal Fluency
  ☐ Expressive One-Word Picture Vocabulary Test, 2000 Edition (EOWPVT-2000)
  ☐ Comprehensive Test of Phonological Processing (CTOPP)
  ☐ Peabody Picture Vocabulary Test, Third Edition (PPVT-III)
  ☐ Receptive One-Word Picture Vocabulary Test (ROWVT-2000)
  ☐ Test of Written Language, Third Edition (TOWL-3)
  ☐ Writing Sample: ☐ Cookie Theft Test   ☐ TOWL-3   ☐ WIAT-II
  ☐ Test of Word Reading Efficiency (TOWRE)

☐ **Visual-Spatial and Motor**
  ☐ Beery-Buktenica Developmental Test of Visual Motor Integration, Fifth Edition (Beery VMI)
  ☐ Finger Tapping Test
  ☐ Grooved Pegboard Test
  ☐ Hooper Visual Organization Test
  ☐ Judgment of Line Orientation, Short Form (JLO-S)
  ☐ Luria Sequential Hand Movements
  ☐ Wide Range Assessment of Visual-Motor Abilities (WRAVMA)

☐ **Psychosocial, Behavioral, and Adaptive**
  ☐ Adaptive Behavior Assessment System, Second Edition (ABAS-Second Edition)
  ☐ Behavior Assessment Scale for Children, Second Edition (BASC-2)
  ☐ Parenting Relationship Questionnaire (PRQ)
  ☐ Vineland Adaptive Behavior Scales, Interview Edition, Survey Form (VABS)
  ☐ Visual Analog Mood Scale (VAMS)
  ☐ PedsQL
  ☐ Pain Rating Scales (Faces)
  ☐ Sickle Cell Self-Efficacy Scale: Adolescent Version (SCSES-A)

APPENDIX 5: RECOMMENDATIONS FORM LETTER

[Letterhead]

[Director of Special Education]
[School or District]
[City, State Zip Code]

RE: **Patient Name & Medical Record Number**

Dear [Director of Special Education]:
[Full Name (Nickname)] completed a neuropsychological evaluation on [date(s)]. Recommendations and accommodations are summarized below. If you have any questions, please do not hesitate to contact me at [phone]. Respectfully,

[Signature & Title]

MEDICAL BACKGROUND
Diagnosis:
Treatment:
Vision Impairment ☐ Yes ☐ No
Hearing Impairment ☐ Yes ☐ No
Gross/Fine Motor Impairment ☐ Yes ☐ No
Speech Impairment ☐ Yes ☐ No
Assistive Device(s):

RECOMMENDATIONS
Due to the diagnosis, results of neuropsychological testing, and the educational impact of diagnosis and treatment, [Name] meets criteria to receive special education services and accommodations under the category [classification] as per [federal law #]. Specific recommendations are as follows:
☐ Regular classroom with accommodations
☐ Resource room for the following subjects: _____
☐ Self-contained classroom   ☐ Full-time aide   ☐ Part-time aide
☐ Abbreviated school day   ☐ Part-time school attendance/part-time homebound

Instructional Strategies
☐ Review, preview, and summarize new material
☐ Specific, immediate, and frequent feedback
☐ Notebook color coded to textbook color
☐ Neuropage or other electronic prompting device
☐ Copy of material to be copied from book or board
☐ Copy of best notes in an anonymous manner
☐ Study guide
☐ Review assignment 1:1 to ensure understanding
☐ Modify assignment format (photo essay or skit)
☐ Other:

Classroom Modifications
☐ Preferential seating
☐ Second set of books
☐ Assignment book or Electronic organizer
☐ Abbreviated assignments, reduced homework
☐ Extended time to complete assignment
☐ Elevator or extra time to navigate hallway
☐ Color coded map of school
☐ Adaptive P.E.
☐ Other:

Testing and Grading Accommodations
☐ Extended time for testing
☐ Extended time to complete assignments
☐ Modify test format (word bank, multiple choice)
☐ Extra grade opportunities (redo items)
☐ Oral testing
☐ Portfolio-based assessment
☐ Quiet environment with few distractions to take tests
☐ Modified grading scale

☐ Read aloud/sign for internal instructions
☐ Read aloud/sign for test items
☐ Use of calculator
☐ Talking or electronic device with Braille display
☐ Word processor w/ or w/o talk-text technology
☐ Reads into auditory recorder and plays back
☐ Other:

APPENDIX 6: SAMPLE NEUROPSYCHOLOGICAL REPORT

CONFIDENTIAL
NEUROPSYCHOLOGICAL REPORT

KEISHA ST. JUDE
Dates of Testing: 7/14 and 27/2005
Dates of Feedback: 9/12/05 (mother, legal guardian)
                              9/21/05 (grandmother, durable power of attorney for health care decisions)
Date of Birth: 5/20/1988

REASON FOR EVALUATION: Keisha is a 17 year, 2 month old African American young woman with HbSS sickle cell anemia (SCA), status post cerebral vascular accident (CVA) at age 6 years old, who was referred by _____, MD for a comprehensive neuropsychological evaluation. A neuropsychological evaluation has not previously been conducted. The purpose of this neuropsychological evaluation was to evaluate her intelligence, attention, executive function, memory, language, behavioral, and psychosocial abilities for educational, vocational, and treatment planning.

BACKGROUND INFORMATION: Keisha had a documented CVA (stroke) in 1994 at age 6 with reported symptoms of slurred speech and weakness in her right hand and leg. Of note, Keisha and her mother reported a 2nd possible neurological event approximately 3 years ago which was previously not known to the treatment team prior to the clinical interview conducted as part of this neuropsychological evaluation. Symptoms of slurred speech, "eyes looking funny", weakness, and "not feeling good" were reported. Allegedly, the emergency room physicians in her home state determined that Keisha had an "allergic reaction" despite her mother reportedly stating that Keisha has a prior history of stroke secondary to SCA and denial of any known source for the "allergic reaction". It has been years since Keisha's last brain MRI and an updated MRI is pending.

Keisha's primary caretaker has been her maternal grandmother for most of Keisha's formative years. Keisha's biological mother, with whom she currently resides, remains her legal guardian but has awarded durable power of attorney for health care decisions to the grandmother. Keisha returned to Memphis to live with her mother and four younger half-siblings, reportedly, to remove her from school problems and the influence of negative peers as she had acquired a considerable history of multiple fights and association with delinquent peers.

Keisha and her mother denied basic knowledge of the effect of stroke on her cognitive and academic abilities. They also denied understanding of the importance of hydration and Desferal for iron overload due to chronic red blood cell transfusions. These medical and SCA management issues have been discussed at length on multiple occasions and by multiple providers with Keisha, her mother, and grandmother.

Keisha disclosed a prior episode of suicidal ideation with plan approximately one year ago (cutting wrists), which was previously unknown to the treatment team and grandmother. It was during a low point in her life at the time when she relocated to her current residence, thus being "made" to leave her boyfriend and grandmother. At the time, Keisha reportedly discussed her feelings with a trusted aunt who provided comfort and agreed not to tell anyone about Keisha's suicidal ideation with plan. Keisha denies current suicidal ideation or plan. She contracted to tell her grandmother or other responsible adult if she has suicidal ideation in the future. Grandmother was advised to ensure Keisha's immediate safety if suicidal ideation or plan were to become known.

There is a history of receiving special education services while in the 5th and 6th grades. However, Keisha and her mother have reportedly refused special education since the 7th grade. Keisha was retained in the 9th grade and is not currently receiving special education services in her current 9th grade placement. She enjoys gym and science. Keisha's career aspiration is to become a nurse.

BEHAVIORAL OBSERVATIONS: Keisha was accompanied by her mother to the first testing session and her grandmother to the next session. Initially, Keisha showed a defensive, passive response style and seemed somewhat despondent. However, she responded well to support with open communication and warmed to the examiner and the testing experience. On the second and third visits, Keisha smiled broadly upon greeting this examiner and seemed attentive and cooperative. Overall, Keisha presented as a very likeable young lady who demonstrated good effort on testing, although she lacked confidence in her performance and seemed to have limited ability to appreciate how her past choices have contributed to her current difficulties. Keisha tolerated participation well. Results are considered valid.

PROCEDURES:
Behavioral Observations
Clinical Interview with Keisha, mother, and grandmother
School consultation with two of Keisha's teachers
Wechsler Abbreviated Scale of Intelligence (WASI)
Tests of Variables of Attention (TOVA)
Wide Range Assessment of Memory and Learning-Second Edition (WRAML-2):
    Story and Design Memory subtests
Rey-Osterreith Complex Figure Test
Woodcock-Johnson Tests of Achievement-Third Edition (WJ-III):
    Word Attack, Reading Fluency, Calculation, and Spelling subtests
Wechsler Individual Achievement Test: Written Expression subtest
Behavior Assessment System for Children (BASC): Self-Report, Parent, and Teacher Forms
Childhood Depression Inventory: Short Form (CDI-S)
Feedback session with Keisha & her grandmother (9/12/05)
Feedback session with Keisha & her mother (9/14/05)

CPT CODE 96117, Neuropsychological Testing
Billable hours = 12 (7 hours testing; 5 hours scoring, interpretation, and documentation)

RESULTS:
<u>Intelligence</u>: Intellectual functioning fell within the lowest end of the *Borderline* range for verbal and *Impaired* range for nonverbal abilities, as measured on the Wechsler Abbreviated Scale of Intelligence (WASI) (VIQ=70, 2nd percentile; PIQ=54, <1st percentile). The WASI is an abbreviated test of general cognitive abilities, comprised of 4 subtests measuring verbal (i.e., word knowledge and verbal reasoning) and nonverbal (i.e., pattern analysis and nonverbal problem solving) skills compared to same-age peers. There was a significant difference between her obtained verbal and performance score. Therefore, the full scale IQ is not reported. The discrepancy is attributable to her T-score of 35 on the Similarities subtest as compared to T-scores of 20, 21, and 20 on the Vocabulary, Block Design, and Matrix Reasoning subtests, respectively. That is, the Similarities subtest requires associative reasoning to compare how two objects or concepts are alike. In contrast, on subtests requiring higher level language and conceptual reasoning skills, Keisha consistently performed three standard deviations below the mean. Qualitatively, Keisha's performance on a subtest of word knowledge was notable for her concrete responses and simple word associations. On a task of nonverbal problem solving, she demonstrated good task persistence, although an efficient trial and error approach lacking a systematic plan.

Attention and Executive Function: Keisha performed within the *Impaired* range on measures of attention and executive function. On a computerized test of visual attention, the Test of Variables of Attention (TOVA), Keisha demonstrated significant difficulty maintaining her attention after 5 to 6 minutes of a low-response (boring) task. Similarly, verbal and nonverbal subtests of the WASI requiring higher level conceptual reasoning were *Impaired* (i.e., Block Design=21 T-score, Similarities=35 T-score, and Matrix Reasoning=20 T-score). Further, Keisha's ability to analyze and copy a complex visual-spatial design indicated *Impaired* ability to integrate and synthesize the component parts into an integrated whole figure (Rey-Osterreith Complex Figure: Copy=9 of 36 raw score).

Learning and Memory: Learning and memory for language presented in context (i.e. 2 paragraph-length oral stories) was *Average* on the Wide Range Assessment of Memory and Learning, Second Edition (WRAML-2: Story Memory: Immediate recall=10 scaled score, Delayed Free Recall=9 scaled score). Cueing, using a multiple choice recognition format, was helpful (Delayed Recognition Recall=11 scaled score). Visual spatial learning and memory of simple to moderately complex designs was *Below Average* (WRAML-2: Design Memory= 7 scaled score). In contrast to her recall for verbal material, cueing was not helpful on the delayed visual-spatial recognition recall on which her performance declined to the *Borderline* range (WRAML-2: Delayed Recognition Recall=5 scaled score). It may be that Keisha's impaired sustained attention and decision-making abilities may have negatively influenced her demonstrated visual-spatial recall abilities. On a more complex task, copy and recall of the Rey-Osterreith Complex Figure was *Impaired* (Copy=9 raw score, Immediate recall=8.5 raw score, Delayed recall=7 raw score of 36 points, respectively). Despite several attempts at the copy task, she was unable to integrate the component parts. However, Keisha was able to retain the information initially acquired. This suggests that Keisha's deficiency in this area may be due to difficulty with visual-spatial analysis and integration rather than a memory problem.

Language: Possible expressive and receptive language problems were suggested. Qualitative analysis of Keisha's conversational speech was remarkable for sparse output, misarticulation, and word substitutions. For example, Keisha substituted the word "summer" for "day" in recalling the target phrase of the "hottest day in July". On several occasions, Keisha requested repetition of the target words. Her responses seemed to indicate that she did not hear the ending of select words presented in isolation. The possibility of an auditory processing deficit was discussed with Keisha who agreed that she often has difficulty understanding the speech and language of others. She agreed that her misunderstanding of language frequently results in miscommunication impacting socialization and school. Keisha reported that she sometimes studies material presented orally, only to get a poor test grade due to having learned erroneous information.

Academic: Tests of academic achievement were administered. Keisha's performance on both the Wechsler Individual Achievement Test, Second Edition (WIAT-II) and Woodcock-Johnson Tests of Achievement, Third Edition (WJ-III) fell within the *Impaired* range relative to same-age peers in reading, math, and spelling. Reading comprehension and speed on short passages was *Impaired* on the WIAT-II (Reading Comprehension=46 standard score, Reading Speed=4th quartile). The following subtest age- and grade-equivalent scores are reported for the WJ-III:

WJ-III Subtests	Age-Equivalent	Grade-Equivalent
Word Attack	7-7	2.1
Reading Fluency	10-1	4.7
Calculation	9-8	4.1
Spelling	13-3	7.1

Qualitatively, Keisha demonstrated some understanding of elementary rules of phonics, although she was inconsistent in her application of select rules. She was able to demonstrate accurate ability to read for understanding on simple sentences requiring basic reflective thought and judgment of everyday events. It may be that residual effect of Keisha's stroke sometimes causes her to misinterpret the visual code essential for reading and application of rules of sound to symbol associations. Further, it may be that increased complexity of the task contributes to performance declines.

In terms of mathematical skills, Keisha was able to add, subtract, multiply, and divide single-digit problems. She was able to subtract two-digit numbers that did not require "borrowing", add a three-column straight addition problem, and sometimes multiply a two-digit number by a one-digit number. Keisha was observed to count on her fingers for single-digit arithmetic problems. She lacked automaticity for basic multiplication problems. For example, although Keisha was able to correctly mentally multiply 8×5, she required considerable time and effort to produce the correct response. Keisha remarked that she "goes through the times table" in her head to arrive at most answers on multiplication problems.

Written expression, although well below age- and grade-level expectations, was notable for the suggestion of functional writing skills. Keisha responded well to structure and support. Spontaneously, Keisha wrote the following to the scenario of the WIAT-II: "I am writing to the editor of the newspaper informing them why uniform is a bad opinion. First, everybody have on the same color everyday and the staff have a problem finding out who we are when we be in the cafeteria." Examiner prompting resulted in Keisha adding: "I think that uniforms are hot because most of the time there is no air on in the building and we can't be in the uniform all the time." Examiner encouragement yielded additional information: "A reason uniforms are good is because some kids can't afford cloths like everybody else. And they need to wear uniform because their parents can't afford those expenise cloths or shoes."

In clinical interview, Keisha remarked that it is often difficult for her to demonstrate what she knows and particularly difficult to elaborate on her thoughts in writing. Keisha agreed that she tends to exert less effort on academics because of repeated failure experiences and frustration with her lack of abilities. Moreover, attempts to work independently without adequate academic support for her efforts have not been positive and are, therefore, avoided. Keisha added that she enjoys reading, if the material is at her level.

Psychosocial and Behavioral: In clinical interview, Keisha acknowledged a prior history of suicidal ideation with plan (see Background Information section) but denies current suicidal ideation or plan and contracted to tell grandmother or another responsible adult if suicidal ideation or plan should return. Other significant psychosocial and behavioral concerns were reported, including current gang association and ongoing issues with anger control and poor interpersonal relations. Keisha acknowledged that she now has a reputation as a "fighter" and that it is difficult for her to change this expected pattern of behavior, even though she verbalized desire to change. Keisha reports that there have been times when she has been "provoked" into a fight and has not seen an alternative acceptable behavior. For example, a boy reportedly poured chocolate milk on her jacket. In another circumstance, Keisha fought to defend the honor of her stepfather subsequent to peer teasing. Of note, Keisha endorsed desire to "drop out" of school, which was new information to her mother and grandmother. Risk for school failure is assessed as extremely high.

School consultation with Keisha's English teacher was remarkable for her commitment to Keisha's success and her concern about Keisha's psychosocial problems. The teacher described that Keisha's behavior and attitude has improved following a recent intervention. That is, the teacher approached Keisha after she noted that Keisha seemed to be having difficulty with a female classmate. The teacher spoke privately with Keisha and presented her with a supportive challenge: "You're not going to let somebody else bring you down are you?" Since that time, the girls have not bothered each other in the classroom and Keisha's efforts in class seem considerably more appropriate.

The Behavior Assessment System for Children (BASC) was administered to Keisha, her grandmother, and her teacher. Responses of Keisha's grandmother, who has been her primary caretaker for many years, indicated clinically significant problems in several areas. Of note, Keisha's grandmother endorsed critical items of concern that Keisha sometimes says that she wants to kill herself, die, or wishes she were dead and often threatens to hurt others. The following T-score, percentile, and descriptive ratings are provided:

	T-Score	%ile	Rating
Conduct Problems	70	95	Mild
Anxiety	77	98	Mild
Depression	88	99	Moderate
Hyperactivity	66	93	At-Risk
Attention Problems	68	95	At-Risk
Withdrawal	64	91	At-Risk
Leadership	26	1	Mild
Social Skills	30	3	Mild
Externalizing Problems Composite	74	97	Mild
Internalizing Problems Composite	81	99	Moderate
Behavioral Symptoms Index	80	99	Moderate

Similarly, Keisha's English teacher indicated problems of clinical significance in the following areas:

	T-Score	%ile	Rating
Anxiety	77	99	Mild
Learning Problems	75	98	Mild
Withdrawal	81	99	Mild

In contrast, Keisha's responses on the BASC: Self-Report Form failed to indicate any problems of clinical significance and her response pattern fell within the *Caution* range, suggesting lack of forthrightness in her responses. However, Keisha did endorse critical items of "I can't seem to control what happens to me", "Nobody ever listens to me", and "I get into fights at school." Similarly, Keisha's responses to the Childhood Depression Inventory: Short Form (CDI-S) failed to indicate problems of significance. It may be that Keisha's responses underestimated her true feelings. Indeed, she cried during the initial feedback session and acknowledged that her mood is frequently sad, which she tends to mask with anger/socially-acting out behaviors and that she is frequently upset about her school failure. Keisha, her mother, and grandmother are in agreement that counseling, which has been strongly and repeatedly recommended by the SCA treatment team at the hospital, seems well indicated and may be helpful. However, the family has had difficulty following through on prior recommendations for counseling.

DSM-IV DIAGNOSES:

294.9	**Cognitive Disorder NOS; status post cerebral vascular accident (CVA)**
296.3x	**Major Depressive Disorder, Recurrent**
312.82	**Conduct Disorder, Adolescent-Onset Type**

SUMMARY: Keisha is a 17 year, 2 month old African-American female with HbSS sickle cell anemia who is status post cerebral vascular accident (CVA) approximately eleven years ago. She was retained in the 9th grade and is currently receiving special education services in high school. Clinical interview revealed a possible second CVA, previously unknown, that was allegedly diagnosed as an "allergic reaction" by emergency room physicians in Arkansas approximately three years ago. An updated MRI is scheduled for 9/21/2006.

Results of this comprehensive neuropsychological evaluation revealed *Impaired* cognitive abilities (WASI: VIQ=70, 2nd percentile, *Borderline*, PIQ=54, 0.1 percentile, *Impaired*). Significant deficits in attention and executive function were indicated. Keisha was unable to sustain her attention for more than 6 minutes on a low-response (boring) task. On verbal and nonverbal tasks requiring high-level conceptual reasoning, Keisha's performance was deficient compared to same-age peers. Learning and memory for language presented in context, such as stories, was *Average*. However, visual-spatial learning and memory for simple to moderately complex designs was *Below Average* and dropped to *Impaired* with increased complexity of the material. Cueing was mildly helpful for verbal but not for nonverbal information. Possible deficits in expressive and receptive language functions were suggested. Academic achievement was approximately 8 years below age-level expectations in reading and math compared to approximately 4 years below age-level expectations in spelling.

Significant problems in psychosocial and behavioral functioning were reported by multiple informants at home, school, and with peers. Specifically, Keisha in addition to her mother, grandmother, and teachers described problems of clinical significance in the areas of anxiety, depression, hyperactivity, inattention, withdrawal, leadership, social skills, learning, and behavior. Ongoing problems of clinical significance were reported for physical aggression to peers and gang involvement. There is a reported history of suicidal ideation with active plan, approximately one year ago, which Keisha confided in a trusted aunt. Current suicidal ideation and/or plan were denied. Keisha contracted to immediately seek out a responsible adult if suicidal ideation and/or plan should occur in the future. Despite these difficulties, Keisha presents as a likeable young woman who seems distressed about her school failure yet lacks understanding as to how to alter her current maladaptive academic and psychosocial behaviors. Risk for school failure and drop out are assessed as extremely high. Keisha's knowledge and age-appropriate responsibility for medical management of her sickle cell anemia is well below expectations. Without significant intervention, the prognosis for this young lady is not positive.

RECOMMENDATIONS:
1. Continued consultation with the Director of the STAR Program at SJCRH, to further consider educational advocacy and vocational planning is strongly recommended. A highly structured academic program, with appropriate support and objectively rendered consequences, is strongly recommended. Teachers will need to become aware of Keisha's true cognitive abilities so as to structure expectations appropriately. It should be noted that Keisha seems to respond well to praise, reinforcement, and reward. Keisha should be encouraged to pursue her vocational aspirations at a level commensurate with her abilities and interests. Educators with the STAR Program were informed of the results of this evaluation.

2. Immediate need for counseling continues to be strongly recommended, particularly given newly disclosed report of a prior history of suicidal ideation with a plan. Current suicidal ideation and/or plan was denied. However, Keisha presented as tearful and fragile when discussing this history and her current psychological state. Continued assistance to the family in following through with this prior recommendation for counseling is of high priority. The LCSW was informed about these results. The family was informed and appeared to understand that if Keisha becomes suicidal in the future, they should take her to the emergency room to ensure safety. Keisha contracted for safety and agreed to inform her mother, grandmother, or other responsible adult if she were to become suicidal in the future. Keisha's current gang association and extremely high risk for school failure and "drop out" were discussed at length with Keisha and her mother and grandmother. This was allegedly new information to the mother and grandmother.

3.   Recommendation for a speech/language evaluation is made. Of note, there were times when Keisha did not seem to hear the ending of select words, despite repetition. She reports and demonstrates considerable difficulty elaborating on her thoughts in both oral and written language. This relative weakness may be a reflection of her global cognitive abilities. However, additional evaluation seems warranted and may help elucidate findings and contribute to educational and vocational planning.

4.   Educational recommendations for additional time on tests and assignments, reduced homework load, and ability to complete written assignments in alternative formats are suggested. For example, portfolio-based assessment and independent learning projects that allow a creative and hands-on demonstration of her knowledge should be encouraged.

5.   Opportunities for appropriate and supervised peer socialization are strongly recommended. Participation in the Adolescent Support Group for teens with sickle cell anemia continues to be recommended. In the past, Keisha has declined participation in this group. Of note, in the interview, she expressed interest in attending the group. This information was communicated to the Teen Clinic Nurse Coordinator and Social Worker who co-lead the monthly Teen Group. Efforts will again be initiated to encourage Keisha to participate in the Teen Group. Also, Keisha's English teacher, Ms. Smith, described two positive peer socialization clubs available at school. She agreed to, again, encourage Keisha to consider participation.

6.   Keisha, her mother, and grandmother were informed of the results of this neuropsychological evaluation and appeared to agree with and understand the findings. It was a pleasure to evaluate Keisha and to work collaboratively with her mother, grandmother, and school-based professionals. If there are additional questions, please do not hesitate to contact me at 901-495-5040.

Leslie Berkelhammer, Ph.D.
Chief Neuropsychologist, Sickle Cell Program
St. Jude Children's Research Hospital

cc: Mother (legal guardian)
       Grandmother (durable power of attorney for health care decisions)
       Relevant providers on the sickle cell disease multidisciplinary treatment team

CHAPTER 18

Assessment of Psychopathology

Stefan E. Schulenberg, Jessica T. Kaster, Carrie Nassif, and
Erika K. Johnson-Jimenez

INTRODUCTION

Psychological assessment has long been a core aspect in the training and practice
of applied psychologists, with trends over time characterized by remarkable consistency (Archer, Maruish, Imhof, & Piotrowski, 1991; Archer & Newsom, 2000;
Camara, Nathan, & Puente, 2000; Cashel, 2002; Watkins, Campbell, Nieberding,
& Hallmark, 1995). Applied psychology includes such fields as clinical psychology, counseling psychology, school psychology, and neuropsychology. Assessment
comprises many areas (e.g., personality, behavior, intelligence) and is conducted
in many professional contexts (e.g., inpatient, outpatient, forensic, medical, educational and occupational settings). For clinicians who work directly with consumers
in applied settings, some spend a significant portion of professional time conducting assessments, with the remainder of time divided among other activities, such as
therapy, research, teaching, supervision, consultation, and administration (Archer
& Newsom, 2000; Cashel, 2002; Watkins et al., 1995). Assessment of personality and psychopathology is common, particularly among clinical psychologists
(Camara et al., 2000). As for youth assessment, testing is a major aspect of psychological services that is experiencing swift expansion in measure development,
with a concomitant challenge for clinicians to keep up with this growth (Geffken, Keeley, Kellison, Storch, & Rodrigue, 2006; Kamphaus, Petoskey, & Rowe,
2000).

The purpose of this chapter is to discuss issues in the assessment of personality in older children and adolescents, with particular regard for the evaluation of
psychopathology. A comprehensive approach to youth clinical assessment is presented, including a discussion of the referral questions, informed consent and assent,
rapport, clinical and collateral interviews and collateral records, test and measure
selection, cognitive and achievement testing, self-reports via objective personality inventories, and behavioral rating scales (completed by youths, their parents,
and their teachers) and observations. The controversy surrounding projective techniques is addressed, followed by a discussion of report writing and feedback. Potential complicating factors to conducting comprehensive assessments are outlined, as
well as suggestions for developing assessment competency. The perspective of the
authors is that of clinical psychology; however, the chapter has relevance to other

applied fields of psychology. Although a number of areas are discussed, the major focus is on how each area contributes to the understanding of psychopathology, and therefore greatest attention is paid to personality and behavioral assessment, where behavior is viewed as an external manifestation of personality.

THE IMPORTANCE OF IDENTIFYING PSYCHOPATHOLOGY IN OLDER CHILDREN AND ADOLESCENTS

Clinicians frequently are called on to assess disruptions in personality and behavior for a variety of referral questions, such as accurate diagnostic classification and assisting in psychological care and treatment monitoring. Given the variety of problems with which youths present, be they internalizing (depression, anxiety) or externalizing (Attention-Deficit/Hyperactivity Disorder or ADHD, Conduct Disorder), early intervention, accurate diagnosis, and congruence between consumer abilities and resources and treatment recommendations are critical. Kasen, Cohen, Skodol, Johnson, and Brook (1999) hypothesized that experiencing any disorder is disruptive to the general developmental process, but especially so with regard to social and interpersonal skills. A delay or lack of resolution of these developmental tasks would logically manifest in a higher risk of subsequent disturbed personality functioning. Additionally, Ramklint, von Knorring, von Knorring, and Ekselius (2003) found that the presence of a Major Depressive Disorder, disruptive disorder, and substance use disorder in childhood or adolescence each independently increases the odds of personality disorders in adulthood. Finally, youths with Conduct Disorder appear to be at increased risk for developing Antisocial Personality Disorder in adulthood, the connection of which is made in the *Diagnostic and Statistical Manual of Mental Disorders,* fourth edition, text revision (*DSM-IV-TR;* American Psychiatric Association, 2000; Kimonis & Frick, 2006).

Comprehensive assessment of psychopathology can aid the clinician in demarcating the line between adaptive and maladaptive functioning, accurately identifying problematic symptoms and behaviors, and developing a thorough and appropriate treatment strategy that is tailored to the unique attributes of the youth. Are the behaviors or symptoms extreme variations of otherwise normal development (and likely to be transient)? Or are the symptoms or behaviors no longer within the acceptable range and indicative of a potentially severe or chronic pathological syndrome that is causing impairment in functioning? Assessment is well suited to providing illumination to such important questions.

ASSESSING PSYCHOPATHOLOGY IN OLDER CHILDREN AND ADOLESCENTS

Clarifying the Referral Questions

Prior to beginning the assessment, it is necessary to clarify the referral questions and establish a collaborative working relationship with the consumer (Brenner, 2003; Harvey, 2006; Schroeder & Gordon, 2005; Snyder, Ritschel, Rand, & Berg, 2006). What is it that the referral source (e.g., parents or legal guardians) wishes to learn about the youth's functioning? Working with the referral source throughout the evaluation is integral to conducting quality psychological assessments, in selecting the tests that are most appropriate to answering the referral questions effectively, and in tailoring the report to the referral questions (Brenner, 2003; Michaels, 2006; Snyder et al., 2006). With well-defined referral questions that take into account areas of difficulty and strength, clinicians can shape the evaluation and the report to the unique needs of the individual. Vague referral questions result in less precise evaluations, despite the efforts of clinicians to determine what problems may be evident. In many cases, the referral source will be a parent requesting assistance with better understanding a child's functioning or current problems. However, referral sources may also involve physicians, other mental health professionals, schools, or the courts.

Informed Consent and Assent

A variety of issues must be covered to obtain informed consent (American Psychological Association, 2002; Urbina, 2004). What purpose does the evaluation serve? How will the results be used? Who will receive a copy of the results? Will verbal feedback be available given the context of the assessment? Are the consumers apprised of the nature of confidentiality and the limits thereof? It is also important to determine the extent of the information requested to guard the youth's privacy. For instance, a clinical or forensic evaluation will contain more personal data than an evaluation conducted during a school-based assessment. When conducting assessments with older children and adolescents, informed consent must be obtained from the parent or legal guardian, and obtaining assent from the youth being tested is highly important to facilitate cooperation and build rapport.

Assent entails the explanation of the nature and purpose of the evaluation in language appropriate for the youth's developmental level. What is the youth's understanding as to why he or she is being assessed? Obtaining assent is an intricate and evolving issue, as it is unclear at what age a child may make an informed decision. Although offering a youth the opportunity to assent can be an affirming, rapport-building action on the part of the clinician, the question arises as to whether a youth with serious emotional problems referred by his or her parents should be able to refuse (Merrell, 2003). Depending on the maturity of the child, it is helpful to discuss the pros and cons of compliance, how the information will be used, the limits of confidentiality, and the like, offering youths the opportunity to have their questions answered.

Establishing Rapport

Through the clarification of the referral questions and by working with youths (assent) and their parents or legal guardians (informed consent), the chances that rapport will be healthy are enhanced significantly. The importance of finding ways to encourage youths and their parents to devote themselves throughout the assessment process cannot be overstated. Absence of rapport can negatively influence the evaluation to the extent that the results may be invalid, and it is necessary to prepare individuals and encourage them to be personally invested to do their best on measures of ability and to respond frankly on personality instruments (Urbina, 2004). To build rapport with children, the examiner should be flexible and patient and possess an understanding of youth development; in addition, discussing topics familiar to youths, such as movies, sports, or computers, may be of assistance (Morrison & Anders, 1999).

As for adolescents, these youths often present difficulties for clinicians due to response styles characterized by resistance or denial (McCann, 1998). For instance, when adolescents are asked to complete the Minnesota Multiphasic Personality Inventory—Adolescent (MMPI-A) as a part of an assessment battery, they are essentially being asked to complete a long, exam-like questionnaire, which results in the possibility that they will not give their best effort (Archer & Krishnamurthy, 2002). Here we return to the issue of assent. It is important that the purpose of testing and the use of the results be explained (adolescents should be made aware that total confidentiality cannot be provided given their status as a minor), with opportunities for questions to be asked and answered, and with a clear indication that feedback of the results will be provided; such efforts demonstrate respect and create opportunities for youths to become involved (Archer, 2005; Archer & Krishnamurthy, 2002). It has been suggested that a firm, task-oriented approach may be helpful to solicit participation that will lead to meaningful results (Archer, 2005; Archer & Krishnamurthy, 2002). Other ways of increasing rapport include noting where restrooms and drinking fountains are, praising effort during testing, and offering adequate breaks (Archer & Krishnamurthy, 2002).

Conducting Interviews: Considering the Cultural Context

Adolescence is a time of transition, of expanding cognitive, physical, social, and personality development. The perceived and actual number of stressors experienced varies from youth to youth and is moderated by a diverse array of variables (e.g., coping skills, acculturative stress), and thus there may be a high level of variation when considering individual development.

For psychopathology to be accurately identified and understood, it must be assessed not only in the developmental context, but in the context of culture, gender, language, and socioeconomic status as well (Achenbach & Rescorla, 2007; Jones et al., 2001; Kuperminc & Brookmeyer, 2006; Leong, Levy, Gee, & Johnson, 2007). From culture to culture there may be different emphases on the importance of some personality traits being expressed over others, how youths should be socialized and values transferred, and how normal and unusual behaviors are defined. Thus, a behavior that is problematic in one cultural context may not be problematic in another. Clinicians also need to be aware that variations within cultures (from individual to individual) are just as significant as variations across cultures (Achenbach & Rescorla, 2007; Jones et al., 2001; Leong et al., 2007).

Cultural variables that clinicians should consider include acculturation, racial/ethnic identity, and minority status stress, all of which can significantly impact the results obtained and interpretations made in an assessment (Jones et al., 2001; Leong et al., 2007; Strack, Dunaway, & Schulenberg, in press). A variety of measures are available to assess these constructs; however, they are not used routinely in clinical practice. Further research and developmental efforts must be undertaken with individuals of varied ages and backgrounds, and especially with youths, so that at some future point clinicians will be able to routinely and systematically measure these variables as part of a larger assessment battery when clinically indicated.

Another way that these variables may be examined is through clinical interviews. What values are important to the family? How strongly does the youth identify with his or her cultural background, and how does this affect his or her worldview? What communication style is most comfortable to the youth and his or her family? What is the family's perspective on mental illness, assessment, and mental health treatment? If there is a previous history of mental health assessment or intervention, this should be determined to assess the potential impact on the youth and his or her family. In the case of multicultural assessments, this may be of particular relevance given that some individuals may have had negative experiences that could influence the current assessment, and those with limited experience could be influenced by their expectations about what will happen (Allen, 2002; Strack et al., in press). These circumstances reflect on the importance of rapport and informed consent with parents or legal guardians and assent with youths.

Clinical Interviews: Selecting a Format

There are a variety of kinds of interviews that can be conducted, generally falling under the categories of unstructured, structured, and semi-structured. Unstructured interviews consist of open-ended questions that allow the interviewee to talk with little guidance from the examiner. Strengths of unstructured interviews are flexibility and facilitation of rapport (Schroeder & Gordon, 2005; Wiger & Huntley, 2002). Although follow-up information can be gathered based on what is learned during the interview, the content and quality of the information gathered, as well as the diagnoses assigned, may be substantially influenced by the training, experience, and perspective of the interviewer (Wiger & Huntley, 2002).

Structured interviews (increased exactitude, less flexibility) increase the psychometric properties of the data gathering process (Faul & Gross, 2006; Karg & Wiens, 2005; Wiger & Huntley, 2002). Questions are asked to determine the presence or absence of clinical symptoms and minimize the role of interviewer bias. Often there are versions for children and parents available. Structured interviews use the same questions across interviewees to maximize the chances that diagnostic areas are not overlooked, and they may help uncover problematic areas not identified in other sources (such as collateral records); however, although structured interviews tend to result in increased precision, the rigid format may interfere with rapport and the collecting of data not included on the interview form (Wiger & Huntley, 2002).

Semi-structured interviewing, a combination of the unstructured and structured approaches, is often used by clinicians to account for diagnostic precision and the uniqueness of the interviewee (Wiger & Huntley, 2002). It consists of a more guided approach, but also allows for following leads and inquiring further about information gathered. The interviewer decides which areas need to be addressed, such as school, home, friends, behavior, and history of the problem. While it is generally the case that a semi-structured approach is useful in terms of collecting data and meeting the needs of the interviewee, clinicians themselves must be flexible in terms of their own style to account for important moderating factors (e.g., culture). There are numerous sources available for information on formal structured and semi-structured interviews (e.g., Loney & Frick, 2003; Orvaschel, 2006; Rourke & Reich, 2004; Shaffer, Fisher, & Lucas, 2004). The remainder of this discussion focuses on the standard clinical interview, in which a clinician probes a variety of symptom constellations and areas, using flexibility as necessary to evaluate for diagnoses and also to collect information relevant to understanding the youth's unique attributes. We begin with the parent or legal guardian interview.

Interviews with Parents or Legal Guardians

When conducting interviews, the clinician should be collecting data in such a way as to understand what events are occurring in the youth's life, when symptoms manifested themselves, whether there is an external cause evident, and whether symptoms wax and wane in accordance with certain events. Depth of understanding of contextual factors and how they intertwine with symptoms, coupled with an understanding of the youth's unique patterns of strength, will afford the clinician greater opportunities to discern whether a diagnosis is warranted, as well as to plan appropriate intervention, if needed.

When interviewing parents or legal guardians it is important that they feel comfortable and that the examiner is in tune with their concerns. It is ideal to interview both parents; however, this may not be possible given family dynamics (e.g., work schedule conflict, divorce). Interviews with parents or legal guardians offer a great deal of information about the youth's history and current functioning. In addition to providing information, parents can be brought on board early in the process, which can be beneficial when it is time to present and work on treatment interventions (Schroeder & Gordon, 2005).

Data to be gathered during an interview generally includes duration, frequency, and severity of youth behaviors and symptoms. Interviewing the child or adolescent independently, as well as together with parents or legal guardians, can yield information as well as family dynamics. Various symptom constellations should be addressed, whether or not they appear as part of the presenting complaint, to clarify the diagnostic picture. Other information to be gathered includes behavioral observations, developmental history (e.g., meeting of developmental milestones), family physical and mental health history, social history (e.g., friendships, relationships with siblings), losses in the family, and medical (e.g., injuries, medication allergies) and mental health (e.g., previous diagnoses, treatment) histories. Data should also be collected on the child's or adolescent's educational and cultural background, as well as occupational history in the case of some older adolescents. The interviewer can also inquire about parenting style, approach to discipline, the youth's behavior at home, and youth strengths. Focusing on these and related areas has been described to varying degrees in a number of sources (e.g., Merrell, 2003; Schroeder & Gordon, 2002 2005; Snyder et al., 2006). Finally, it is important to convey to parents the idea that positive action may be taken, and if additional data are needed it is paramount to explain the rationale and methods consistent with the collaborative approach (Schroeder & Gordon, 2005).

Interviews with Older Children and Adolescents

With regard to conducting interviews with youths, behavioral observation and life history data are quite important to the overall quality of the assessment and should not be disregarded in favor of interviews with parents or legal guardians. Rather, a clinician may gather relevant information from parents or legal guardians and the youth being evaluated. Clinicians interviewing youths should expect to see variations based on such variables as development, education, and culture.

School-age children (ages 6 to 12) typically think in factual, literal, and rigid terms (they are able to consider some, but not all, eventualities) and are likely to participate little in discussions characterized as abstract or involving feelings and attitudes (Gudas & Sattler, 2006). Children may be concerned with how well they are doing on psychological tests and with pleasing the interviewer and/or deferring to the wishes of their parents, legal guardians, or other authority figures. Rapport building with youths is needed to account for such potential complicating factors.

Adolescents, in comparison to school-age children, think less concretely and are able to consider a substantially wider range of alternatives and to test hypotheses (Gudas & Sattler, 2006). They are able to report on symptoms and to consider elements of time and place; however, although they can think with increasing abstraction, problems with risk taking and invincibility may be evident (Gudas & Sattler, 2006). Their peer group tends to take on more influence in the determination of behavior, a role that typically was previously held by parents or legal guardians. Although this differentiation is often regarded as a part of developing into independent adulthood, it has specific implications during the interview. Adolescents tend to be more concerned about how they fit in and how they will be judged by others than with reporting how they actually experience things. They may be actively searching for an identity, including how they relate to ascribed gender and cultural roles. The adolescent interviewee may present at once as being genuinely both naive and blasé. Having an approachable yet frank presence can help foster a vitally important sense of acceptance and build rapport necessary to facilitate the interview.

As with older children, adolescents are capable of providing information useful to skilled clinicians. It is important for youths to know that their views are important to the clinician, and for the clinician such data are imperative in the process of developing and refining clinical hypotheses. In interviews of youths, especially adolescents, it is important to establish confidentiality and the limits thereof. With regard to interview content, it is important to assess such areas as drug and alcohol use, behaviors harmful to self or others, and sexual activity (Wiger & Huntley, 2002), in addition to the other areas outlined earlier.

Collateral Interviews

With appropriate consent, discussion with other relevant individuals, such as extended family members, teachers, and case managers, may provide important contextual data about the youth's functioning across multiple settings. Information from as many sources as are reasonable will improve the ability of the interviewer to gain a comprehensive picture of the youth (Boggs, Griffin, & Gross, 2003). Such interview data may also be combined with behavior rating scales (discussed later) to enhance the clinical picture. For additional information on interviewing techniques and procedures as they relate to both clinical and collateral interviews, an array of sources is available (Groth-Marnat, 2003; Merrell, 2003; Morrison & Anders, 1999; Sattler & Hoge, 2006; Sharp, Reeves, & Gross, 2006; Wiger & Huntley, 2002).

Review of Collateral Records

The review of collateral records is of importance in improving the quality of psychological assessments. Are there certain medical or physical conditions that have a bearing on the current presentation? Are school records available that reveal academic performance or behavioral problems? In the case of adolescents in particular, if they are demonstrating behaviors that bring them into contact with the law, are police records available? Having access to collateral data is critical to understanding context, as a basis to facilitate discussion with the youth and his or her parents or legal guardians, and as a comparison with test data. Collateral records aid the clinician in establishing the youth's history, facilitating an individualized case conceptualization for the presenting complaints.

Selecting Tests and Measures for the Evaluation

There is a distinction between testing and assessment. A test is standardized, reliable, valid, and clinically useful (Hunsley, Lee, & Wood, 2003), whereas assessment involves the integration of data from multiple sources, such as tests (e.g., Wechsler Intelligence Scale for Children, fourth edition [WISC-IV]) and nontests (e.g., collateral records). Psychometric properties of a test may vary depending on the individual being tested (based on cultural or socioeconomic factors), the context (a test may be psychometrically sound for one clinical purpose but not another), and the composition of the test (tests with multiple subscales will have different psychometric properties for each scale). In a survey of psychologists who work with adolescents, Archer and Newsom (2000) learned of an array of factors relevant to instrument selection, including soundness of psychometric properties, relationship between the instrument and the referral question, the relevance of the generated data for treatment planning, provision of comprehensive information pertinent to psychopathology and diagnosis, and simplicity of scoring and administration.

As for a practical example of how tests may be selected, consider a relatively common referral question: "My teenage son is getting into fights in school, he's struggling academically, and he is having trouble paying attention to his teachers. What's wrong? Does he have ADHD?" An assessment battery may be composed of interviews with the youth and his parents; collateral interviews (e.g., with a teacher); a review of collateral records (e.g., report cards and other school records); intelligence and achievement testing (e.g., WISC-IV, Wechsler Individual Achievement Test, second edition [WIAT-II]); a continuous performance test to assess for difficulties with attention; self, parent, and teacher ratings (e.g., Behavior Assessment

System for Children, second edition [BASC-2]); and additional measures of functioning as needed (e.g., MMPI-A, Children's Depression Inventory [CDI]). Why such a comprehensive battery? Because ADHD is comorbid with learning disorders, externalizing behavior disorders such as Oppositional Defiant Disorder and Conduct Disorder, and internalizing disorders such as depressive and anxiety disorders (Sattler, Weyandt, & Willis, 2006). A thorough assessment facilitates a detailed diagnostic formulation. As a case in point, inattentiveness may be taken for ADHD, when in some cases it may be related to depression or anxiety. Aggression could be part of a larger constellation of symptoms meeting criteria for a diagnosis such as Conduct Disorder. A partial assessment may miss the mark.

Another consideration for clinicians when selecting a test is the degree of fit between the test and the language and cultural background of the respondent (Butcher & Pope, 2006; Flores & Obasi, 2003). This means determining that the norms, standardization, reliability, and validity are acceptable for the individual being evaluated and that the instrument is in the person's preferred language, all of which are necessary to minimize erroneous clinical interpretations (Flores & Obasi, 2003; Jones et al., 2001; Leong et al., 2007; Strack et al., in press). It is heartening that in recent years additional attention has been paid to multicultural issues in assessment (both within the United States and internationally), and this emphasis will likely continue; however, it is disheartening that empirical research continues to lag behind the need (Leong et al., 2007; Strack et al., in press; Wood, Garb, Lilienfeld, & Nezworski, 2002).

Cognitive and Achievement Testing: Clues to Personality Style?

In addition to clinical and collateral interviews and collateral records reviews, cognitive and achievement testing may reveal clues about personality functioning that may be evaluated using more systematic, standardized, and comprehensive methods. Of the intelligence tests used, the Wechsler scales are among the most commonly employed by clinicians and are quite common in adolescent and child batteries specifically (Archer & Newsom, 2000; Camara et al., 2000; Cashel, 2002; Kamphaus et al., 2000). The current edition of the Wechsler scales appropriate for older children and most adolescents is the WISC-IV (Wechsler, 2003).

Why mention a cognitive test in a chapter on assessment of psychopathology in older children and adolescents? As many clinicians know, behavioral observations are a heavily emphasized part of clinical assessments, and observing a youth's performance on the WISC-IV, and on achievement tests such as the WIAT-II (The Psychological Corporation, 2002), may reveal hypotheses about how the youth interacts with his or her world that may be examined subsequently through other methods. Looking at the WISC-IV specifically, a variety of tasks are asked of the youth, including those that tap performance-oriented abilities (e.g., Block Design) and verbal-oriented abilities (e.g., Comprehension). The administration of each subtest yields behavioral observation information for the clinician. For example, as noted by Sattler and Dumont (2004), during Block Design, where the task involves the examinee putting together blocks to match a series of designs, a number of hypotheses about performance may be generated. Is the youth deliberate or impulsive? Does the youth persist in the task or give up easily? Fumbling too much may be indicative of anxiety, youths very slow in their work may be experiencing boredom, and youths who constantly check their work may be insecure (Sattler & Dumont, 2004).

Observations similar to these may be collected throughout a test such as the WISC-IV and also may be made in the area of achievement testing. In the case of the WIAT-II, what is the youth's attitude toward perceived success and perceived failure? Does the youth show resilience or quickly give up? How does the youth respond to the praising of effort? Such clinical observations and interpretive hypotheses are valued by many clinicians as a means to better understand the functioning of youths, but clinicians must exercise caution in relying on behavioral observations in isolation or otherwise placing too much emphasis on them. Intelligence and achievement tests are not standardized for these purposes, and interpreting clinical observations appropriately can be difficult, as there are many reasons why a youth may respond in a certain way in a certain context. Also, there is no guarantee that informal observations or interpretations relating to personality style will translate to the youth's typical environments. There is a danger for clinicians to form erroneous impressions early and stay with them. Multiple and appropriate standardized sources of data should be considered, and systematic evaluation of disconfirming data should be undertaken, prior to arriving at a diagnostic formulation.

Objective Comprehensive Measures of Psychopathology

Objective instruments of personality and psychopathology are typified by standardization and norms, as well as straightforward items, response format (e.g., true-false), and scoring (Segal & Coolidge, 2004; Urbina, 2004). As compared to specific domain measures (discussed later), comprehensive measures tend to be characterized by several hundred items and require added time to administer; however, they tend to have better norms and a wider range of applications and generate many scores (Hogan, 2007). Comprehensive measures are often desired in clinical assessments given the thorough data they provide across a range of domains. These data are generally useful for hypothesis testing and treatment planning. Commonly used comprehensive measures in youth assessments are the MMPI-A and the Millon Adolescent Clinical Inventory (MACI; Archer & Newsom, 2000; Cashel, 2002), both of which are considered to be effective tools (Groth-Marnat, 2003).

The Minnesota Multiphasic Personality Inventory—Adolescent

The MMPI-A (Butcher et al., 1992) is composed of 478 true-false items, is based on a large and diverse normative sample, and is used in a variety of settings to assess emotional functioning and/or refine clinical hypotheses in adolescents between the ages of 14 and 18 (Archer & Newsom, 2000; Baer & Rinaldo, 2004; Butcher & Pope, 2006; Graham, 2006). The normative sample consisted of 805 males and 815 females, and data on a clinical sample were also gathered (420 boys, 293 girls; Baer & Rinaldo, 2004). The MMPI-A contains a number of validity scales to detect random or unusual responding, and its many clinical (e.g., Depression, Psychasthenia, Psychopathic Deviate), content (e.g., School Problems, Conduct Problems), and supplementary scales (e.g., Alcohol-Drug Problem Acknowledgment, Alcohol-Drug Problem Proneness) provide the clinician with a wealth of potentially useful data.

Raw scores are translated into T scores (uniform or linear translation, depending on the scale), and though there is no clear cutoff for scale elevations, scores as low as 60 to 64 possibly have interpretive significance (Baer & Rinaldo, 2004; Butcher & Pope, 2006; Graham, 2006). Interpretation is undertaken knowing the larger context of the adolescent's life history and presenting problems, proceeding with an examination of the MMPI-A's validity scales; if the profile is valid, the clinical scales are interpreted, with content and supplementary scales aiding in the refinement of clinical hypotheses (Baer & Rinaldo, 2004; Butcher & Pope, 2006). Thus, although the MMPI-A yields many data regarding an adolescent's personality functioning, clinicians must be aware of the psychometric properties of the many validity, clinical, content, and supplementary scales. For further information regarding developmental, psychometric, and interpretive considerations, numerous resources are available (e.g., Archer, 2005; Archer & Krishnamurthy, 2002; Archer, Krishnamurthy, & Stredny, 2007; Archer, Zoby, & Stredny, 2006; Butcher & Williams, 2000; Frick & Kamphaus, 2001).

There are a variety of positive aspects to using the MMPI-A, including provision of comprehensive information, useful adolescent-related material and norms, simplicity of administration, and research support with a wide variety of clinical populations (Archer & Newsom, 2000; Butcher & Pope, 2006). The measure is available in a standardized recorded version, it has been translated into Spanish with adolescent norms available for Spanish-speaking youths in the United States, and a variety of translations are available in languages such as Arabic, Chinese, Korean, and Hebrew, to name a few (Butcher & Pope, 2006).

Negative aspects of using the MMPI-A include the length of the measure and the test-like demands placed on the examinee, a demanding reading level for many adolescents (about seventh grade), time demands (administration, scoring, interpretation), and cost when considering the context of a managed care environment (Archer & Newsom, 2000). Additionally, Frick and Kamphaus (2001) criticized the MMPI-A's normative sample for undersampling Hispanic youths and 18-year-olds. Finally, although some multicultural studies have been conducted (e.g., Cashel, Rogers, Sewell, & Holliman, 1998; Gumbiner, 1998; Negy, Leal-Puente, Trainor, & Carlson, 1997), Baer and Rinaldo's (2004) review noted that in some cases there were no differences between racial/ethnic groups studied, but that when differences were found it was difficult to determine what the findings meant, or whether the differences were clinically meaningful. More multicultural research is needed (Gómez, Johnson, Davis, & Velásquez, 2000; Leong et al., 2007).

The Millon Adolescent Clinical Inventory

The MACI (Millon, Millon, & Davis, 1993) is a 160-item, true-false, self-report instrument based on the theory of personality and psychopathology put forth by Millon (Millon & Grossman, 2005; Tringone, 2002; Tringone, Millon, & Kamp, 2007). It is composed of 31 scales across four domains: Personality Patterns, Expressed Concerns, Clinical Syndromes, and Reliability and Modifying Indices (Millon &

Grossman, 2005; Tringone, 2002; Tringone et al., 2007). The MACI requires approximately a sixth-grade reading level and is useful for evaluating areas of concern, difficulties with personality styles, and psychopathology with adolescents ranging in age from 13 to 19 (Millon & Grossman, 2005; Tringone, 2002; Tringone et al., 2007). The measure has four separate norm tables (13- to 15-year-old males and females and 16- to 19-year-old males and females) seen in clinical settings, with the overall norm group consisting of over 1,000 adolescents from the United States and Canada (McCann, 2006; Tringone, 2002; Tringone et al., 2007).

Item development comprised a three-stage process: theoretical-substantive, internal-structural, and external-criterion (Millon & Grossman, 2005; Tringone, 2002; Tringone et al., 2007). The MACI utilizes base rate scores (BR), as opposed to T scores, where BR cutoff scores of 85 and 75 indicate trait prominence and presence of a trait, respectively (McCann, 2006; Millon & Grossman, 2005). Interpretation occurs in the context of the youth's history and involves systematic review and subsequent integration of the Modifying Indices (validity indicators), Personality Patterns (e.g., Inhibited, Unruly, Oppositional), Expressed Concerns (e.g., Sexual Discomfort, Social Insensitivity, Family Discord), and Clinical Syndromes (e.g., Substance-Abuse Proneness, Delinquent Predisposition, Anxious Feelings, Depressive Affect; McCann, 2006; Millon & Grossman, 2005; Tringone, 2002). The Expressed Concerns scales target areas that may be problematic to troubled youths, while elevations on the Personality Patterns and Clinical Syndromes scales signify psychopathology necessitating professional intervention (Millon & Grossman, 2005; Tringone, 2002). For more information on developmental, psychometric, and interpretive considerations, a variety of sources are available (e.g., McCann, 1999, 2006; Meagher, Grossman, & Millon, 2004; Pinto & Grilo, 2004; Tringone, 2002; Tringone et al., 2007).

The MACI may be useful in some clinical situations, such as when distortions in personality development appear to be evident, so long as such use is supported by the empirical literature and data are not used in isolation. Proponents of the MACI note that its advantages include its multistage construction, brevity, design for use with adolescent clinical populations (tapping both Axis I and Axis II symptoms), inclusion of Modifying Indices, and theoretical basis (Millon & Grossman, 2005; Tringone, 2002; Tringone et al., 2007). Noted disadvantages include a sixth-grade reading level being necessary (audiocassette administration is available for clients who speak English and Spanish), and more severe types of psychopathology such as thought and psychotic disorders, bipolar disorders, and paranoid ideation are not directly measured (McCann, 2006; Millon & Grossman, 2005; Tringone, 2002; Tringone et al., 2007). Moreover, few multicultural studies involving the MACI have appeared in the literature (for examples with Mexican American youths, see Blumentritt, Angle, & Brown, 2004; Blumentritt & Wilson VanVoorhis, 2004).

Objective Specific Domain Measures of Psychopathology

The MMPI-A and the MACI cast a broad net, assessing many different kinds of behavioral and emotional difficulties. Other measures assess specific constructs and therefore tend to have fewer items (faster administration times), yield fewer scores (perhaps a single score), and have norms and applications that are more limited

(Hogan, 2007). Specific domain instruments are often desirable to clinicians given their focus on a specific problem and the ease with which they may be combined with other data, such as comprehensive objective measures and interview data. Specific domain measures straddle many clinical areas, commonly depression and anxiety. Although a comprehensive review is not possible in a single chapter, we mention a few measures prior to discussing a recent constellation of specific domain measures that appears promising pending future research.

One of the most popular specific domain measures is the CDI (Kovacs, 1992). The CDI may be used with youths between the ages of 7 and 17. It includes 27 items of depressive symptoms with a choice of three response options (0, 1, or 2). Scores are summed, with higher scores considered to be more symptomatic. Raw scores are converted to T scores to yield a global score and five subscales: Negative Mood, Interpersonal Problems, Ineffectiveness, Anhedonia, and Negative Self-Esteem. The CDI is generally considered to be reliable (Campbell, 2006b; Merrell, 2003). However, given mixed discriminant validity support, and because it is more an indicator of distress as opposed to a diagnostic indicator, it should not be used in isolation (Fristad, Emery, & Beck, 1997; Schroeder & Gordon, 2002). This is excellent advice for any instrument, especially those of the specific domain variety. Sitarenios and Stein (2004) review the CDI's psychometric characteristics.

Additional self-report measures of depression include the Reynolds Child Depression Scale (RCDS; Reynolds, 1989) and the Reynolds Adolescent Depression Scale, second edition (RADS-2; Reynolds, 2002). The 30-item RCDS covers ages 8 to 13 years and is considered to thoroughly assess symptoms of depression, with good psychometric properties and adequate norms (Merrill, 2003; Reynolds, 2006; Schroeder & Gordon, 2002). The RADS-2 contains 30 items utilizing a 4-point response format and is used with youths between the ages of 11 and 20 (Campbell, 2006b; Reynolds, 2004, 2006). It yields T scores with a mean of 50 and a standard deviation of 10 and includes four factorially derived subscales in addition to the total score: Dysphoric Mood, Anhedonia/Negative Affect, Negative Self-Evaluation, and Somatic Complaints (Campbell, 2006b; Reynolds, 2004, 2006).

As for the measurement of anxiety, one self-report measure that has been receiving increasing attention is the Multidimensional Anxiety Scale for Children (MASC; March, 1997), which assesses anxiety in youths ages 8 to 19 years. The MASC's 39-item, 4-point response format yields T scores and is composed of a Total Anxiety score, Inconsistency Index, and Anxiety Disorder Index, as well as four factor scores: Physical Symptoms, Harm Avoidance, Social Anxiety, and Separation/Panic (Campbell, 2006a; Schroeder & Gordon, 2002). In reviews of the MASC, authors have noted the measure's reliability (particularly the internal consistency of the Total Anxiety score), convergent and discriminant validity support, and apparent utility in distinguishing youths with and without anxiety disorders (Campbell, 2006a; Schroeder & Gordon, 2002; Woodruff-Borden & Leyfer, 2006).

Beck Youth Inventories for Children and Adolescents, Second Edition

The Beck Youth Inventories for Children and Adolescents (BYI-II; Beck, Beck, Jolly, & Steer, 2005) are a recently available group of specific domain measures.

The original Beck Youth Inventories for Emotional and Social Impairment (Beck, Beck, & Jolly, 2001) were composed of five separate 20-item scales (Anxiety, Depression, Disruptive Behavior, Anger, and Self-Concept) that could be used separately or in combination with youths ages 7 to 14 (Beck et al., 2001; Bose-Deakins & Floyd, 2004; Steer, Kumar, Beck, & Beck, 2001). The scales appear to be internally consistent for clinical screening purposes, with growing evidence for convergent validity (Beck et al., 2001; Bose-Deakins & Floyd, 2004; Steer et al., 2001). However, Bose-Deakins and Floyd noted the need for additional discriminant validity data.

Given that the BYI-II was recently published, limited research is available beyond the manual at this time. The BYI-II continues the format of the original (second-grade reading level, five inventories of 20 questions each that may be used separately or in combination) with an expanded age range (7 to 18). Although initial psychometric properties appear promising, additional psychometric data are needed. Although the Anger, Anxiety, Depression, and Disruptive Behavior scales assess potentially problematic areas, it is noteworthy that the Self-Concept scale assesses positive attributes such as self-worth and may be one means of evaluating a youth's strengths. Considering that there are many specific domain measures available to assess personality and psychopathology in youths, it will be intriguing to see where these measures will eventually fit.

Behavior Rating Scales

Behavior rating scales are increasing in availability and popularity among clinicians (Archer & Newsom, 2000; Cashel, 2002; Kamphaus et al., 2000). They are advantageous in terms of their ease of use with a variety of respondents (youths, parents, teachers), cost effectiveness, and coverage of a wide variety of clinical domains such as ADHD and other disruptive behavior disorders (Elliot, Busse, & Gresham, 1993; Kamphaus et al., 2000; Piacentini, 1993). They are useful in providing data about low-frequency behaviors (e.g., assaults) that direct observation sessions may miss, assessing youths who are unwilling or unable to provide information about themselves, and accessing data in youths' typical environments, such as school and home settings, by those who know them well (Merrell, 2003). Potential disadvantages include their being subject to the perceptions of raters (e.g., response biases) and that they tend to focus on current functioning with little guidance as to etiology or intervention strategies (Elliot et al., 1993; Frick & Kamphaus, 2001; Merrell, 2003; Piacentini, 1993).

Rating scale systems frequently used by clinicians are the BASC, currently revised as the BASC-2, the Child Behavior Checklist (part of the Achenbach System of Empirically Based Assessment, or ASEBA), and the Conners Rating Scales (Archer & Newsom, 2000; Cashel, 2002; Kamphaus et al., 2000). For recent reviews of the ASEBA, see Achenbach (2007) and Achenbach and Rescorla (2006); for the Conners Rating Scales—Revised, see Kollins, Epstein, and Conners (2004). The rest of this discussion focuses on the most recently revised of these major rating systems, the BASC-2.

The BASC-2 (Reynolds & Kamphaus, 2004; see also Kamphaus, VanDeventer, Brueggemann, & Barry, 2007) contains separate rating forms for teachers, parents, and youths. The various 100- to 139-item Teacher Rating Scales (TRS) assess adaptive and problematic behaviors evidenced by the youth in the school setting, with the specific form used depending on the child's age (ages 2 to 5, 6 to 11, and 12 to 21). Clinical scales include Aggression, Anxiety, Atypicality, Depression, and Attention Problems. Adaptive scales include Adaptability and Functional Communication. The 134- to 160-item Parent Rating Scales (PRS; ages 2 to 5, 6 to 11, and 12 to 21) prompt parents to provide data on adaptive and problematic behaviors in the home and community. The 139- to 185-item Self-Report of Personality (SRP) forms provide information on the youth's perception of his or her functioning (child, ages 8 to 11; adolescent, ages 12 to 21; college, ages 18 to 25). Clinical scales include Attention Problems, Anxiety, Depression, Hyperactivity, Sense of Inadequacy, and Social Stress, and adaptive scales include Self-Reliance, Self-Esteem, Relations with Parents, and Interpersonal Problems. In general, there are many similarities across forms in terms of clinical and adaptive scales, item content, and composite scores, although there are some variations based on the age of the respondent and the rater (Kamphaus et al., 2007). Raw scores are converted to norm-referenced T scores to facilitate interpretation, and each of the sets of forms contains scales to evaluate the quality of obtained data (validity and response set indicators; Kamphaus et al., 2007). The BASC-2 also contains a Structured Developmental History (a data gathering tool) and a Student Observation System (a classroom observation method based on momentary time sampling).

With regard to how a rating system such as the BASC-2 may be used in a psychological evaluation, BASC-2 forms may be used to gather self-reports of youths (SRP), their parents or legal guardians (PRS), and their teachers (TRS). Such ratings generally provide psychometrically sound data to accompany clinical and collateral interviews. When feasible and depending on the clinical context, separate ratings may be sought from each parent, and if the youth has multiple teachers, more than one rater may be requested. Thus, rating scale data could be collected from three to five people (youth, one to two parents or legal guardians, one to two teachers) to get a better idea as to behaviors and symptoms that are considered problematic, to what degree, and in what context. Problems may be occurring at home and not in school, or vice versa; problems may be seen with one parent and not another, or with one teacher but not another. Such differences could be related to the clinical presentation or the environment, which has both diagnostic and treatment implications.

Behavioral Observations in Different Settings

As part of a multifaceted assessment, behavioral observations in the school, home, and other germane settings may be helpful in facilitating the development of a comprehensive picture of the context of the youth's behavior and how he or she interacts with others. Observations may take on a variety of forms, ranging from time-limited and informal to time-involved and intensely structured (Gudas & Sattler, 2006; Winsor, 2003). Although observations may be a rich source of data that enhance the assessment, similar to interviews the quality of the data is largely dependent on the skill and objectivity of the observer and on the recording system that is employed (Urbina, 2004; Winsor, 2003).

The school is one environment where observations are typically conducted. The observation of older children (as opposed to adolescents, where observation tends to be more intrusive) in their school environment may be undertaken with the permission of the parents or legal guardians, the school, and teachers. With regard to aid in hypothesis generation, is the child inadvertently being reinforced for negative behaviors by the attention of a teacher? Are there alternative behavioral strategies that may be implemented by teachers to reinforce the child for more adaptive behaviors? Collecting behavioral observations may be helpful in certain cases, but they are somewhat limited by factors such as reactivity (behavior change in response to being evaluated) and the lack of ability to monitor internal affective states (Franz & Gross, 1998; Merrell, 2003; Tryon, 1998; Winsor, 2003). Direct observations in the schools are also substantially limited by the amount of time involved. Clinicians working under time constraints at community mental health centers, for example, may be hard-pressed to conduct observations of behaviors for this reason. For further information on direct observations, such as defining target behaviors, and the different forms of coding procedures (e.g., event recording, duration recording, time sampling) and observation systems, many references are available (e.g., Merrell, 2003; Miltenberger, 2001; Tryon, 1998; Winsor, 2003).

PROJECTIVE TECHNIQUES: A PSYCHOMETRIC CONTROVERSY

Projective techniques have been, and continue to be, an enduring aspect of the training and practice of the clinician (Camara et al., 2000; Hogan, 2007; Watkins et al., 1995), and they are commonly employed with children and adolescents (Archer & Newsom, 2000; Cashel, 2002). Projective techniques rely on vague stimuli and a free-response format. The idea is that with freedom to answer, the person's deep-seated personality characteristics will shape the response, revealing important information about underlying desires, motivations, perceptions, and so on (Hogan, 2007; Segal & Coolidge, 2004; Urbina, 2004). Examples of popular projective techniques are the Rorschach, the Thematic Apperception Test (TAT), the Children's Apperception Test, sentence completion forms, and projective drawings such as Human Figure Drawings, House-Tree-Person, and the Kinetic Family Drawing (Hogan, 2007; Urbina, 2004; Watkins et al., 1995).

On the Controversial Nature of Projective Techniques

Some have called into question the psychometric relevance of projective techniques to assessment and diagnosis, noting that they are not science but pseudo-science, and that in the rare cases where they are useful they do not appear to add much beyond other methods, such as interviews and objective inventories (Hunsley et al., 2003; Lilienfeld, Wood, & Garb, 2001). Another criticism centers on the lack of standardization among many of the techniques and the question of how well clinicians adhere to procedures with the techniques that are standardized (Hunsley et al., 2003). Standardization is necessary to counter problems with subjectivity in administration, scoring, and interpretation. Despite such criticisms, projective techniques continue to be used with great frequency. Proponents argue that they are a source of insight beyond what objective inventories can provide, that they assess personality at a deeper level. Another justification is that they may be useful as a means to settle in to the assessment, perhaps as an "ice-breaker" (Hogan, 2007, p. 522).

Projective Drawings

Projective drawings may be popular for their rapport-building capabilities or as a means of facilitating discussion, because youths often enjoy such activities (Cashel, 2002; Hunsley et al., 2003). Some clinicians use projective drawings to get a sense of the youth. Others use specifics of the drawing, or signs, to make diagnostic inferences about personality and psychopathology (Lilienfeld et al., 2001). The validity of using signs is quite limited (Lally, 2001; Lilienfeld et al., 2001), and the diagnostic relevance of projective drawings to assessments has often been questioned (e.g., Motta, Little, & Tobin, 1993; Palmer et al., 2000; Stawar & Stawar, 1989). Some have argued that they should not be used in personality assessments given their psychometric and diagnostic shortcomings and considering the lack of scientific data on the variability of drawings by age, gender, and interest in the task (Hunsley et al., 2003; Motta et al., 1993). Such data are lacking with regard to multicultural variations in drawings as well.

With regard to formal scoring systems, some clinicians use them, but it does not seem to be a common practice. Structured scoring systems may fare better given the integration of multiple pieces of data (Lilienfeld et al., 2001). However, even the utility of one of the most recent attempts to establish a psychometrically sound, structured scoring system, the Draw-a-Person: Screening Procedure for Emotional Disturbance (Naglieri, McNeish, & Bardos, 1991), has been criticized as flawed, with poor validity and limited peer-reviewed, published data available (Lally, 2001; Motta et al., 1993). Others indicate that the psychometric success of such systems is "modest" (Hogan, 2007, p. 542), or holds "very limited promise" (Hunsley et al., 2003, p. 65). Ultimately, although some use projective drawings as a means of communicating with young clients and in establishing rapport, clinicians must exercise due caution given that the nature of the task pulls for impressionistic interpretation.

Sentence Completion Techniques

Sentence completion techniques also enjoy widespread use, as is evident from surveys of clinical assessment practices. They are not one technique, but rather a group of forms with similar formats, where the respondent completes a series of sentence fragments, or stems, the process of which is thought to reveal something about certain aspects of personality style (Hogan, 2007; Holaday, Smith, & Sherry, 2000; Rogers, Bishop, & Lane, 2003). Given the variety of sentence completion techniques available, clinicians may not be aware which form is best for which client, the psychometric properties behind the form, or even the name of the form they are using (Holaday et al., 2000; Rogers et al., 2003). There is also some evidence that clinicians tend to use these measures informally, without recognized scoring procedures (Holaday et al., 2000). Interpreting sentence completion techniques through impressionistic methods, that is, based on clinical intuition, without a standardized and psychometrically sound scoring system, will leave clinicians susceptible to errors in decision making.

Storytelling Techniques

The Thematic Apperception Test (Murray, 1943) consists of 31 cards, where the goal is to solicit a narration from the respondent as to the content of the card. Through the narration the respondent is thought to reveal underlying attitudes, drives, and the like, and cards may be selected based on whether the respondent is male or female, a youth or an adult (Hunsley et al., 2003). A major problem with the TAT is standardization, as examiners select different sets of cards (different cards, different numbers of cards, and/or different orders of cards) for use with different examinees (Groth-Marnat, 2003; Hunsley et al., 2003; Lilienfeld et al., 2001). Each set of cards results in a different technique, and psychometric properties need to be established for each set. This property of the TAT also makes the evaluation of research difficult, as studies do not always report the combination of cards that were used. Although some scoring systems are available, there is currently no widely used, well-validated administration and scoring system for the TAT. Thus, those who use it in formal assessments risk misdiagnosis due to reliance on impressionistic interpretation (Hunsley et al., 2003; Lilienfeld et al., 2001). Finally, although a number of derivatives of the TAT have been developed for a variety of populations (e.g., the Children's Apperception Test; Bellak, 1954; see also Bellak & Abrams, 1997), the same caveats apply to the use of any narrative technique with regard to the importance of norms and standardized administration and scoring procedures in generating interpretations that are empirically supported as accurate and clinically useful.

The Rorschach

The Rorschach consists of 10 inkblots (one inkblot per card), and respondents reveal the way they perceive their world through their verbal responses to each card (Ritzler, 2005; Urbina, 2004). There are a variety of coding and scoring systems for the Rorschach; Exner's Comprehensive System (CS; Exner, 2001, 2003) is the most popular (Ritzler, 2005; Weiner, 2005). There are Rorschach proponents (e.g., Ritzler, 2005; Weiner, 2003, 2005), but there are those who raise serious psychometric criticisms. For example, it has been argued that the Rorschach's CS norms may result in erroneous clinical impressions (i.e., respondents may look like they have more pathology than they do or have psychopathology when they do not) and that there is a lack of data and inconsistent psychometric support for many of the CS scores (Garb, Wood, & Lilienfeld, 2005; Hunsley et al., 2003; Lilienfeld et al., 2001; Wood et al., 2002; Wood, Nezworski, Lilienfeld, & Garb, 2003). Psychometric data must be established for each Rorschach score, which is quite a daunting task given the number of variables that make up the CS system. Psychometric properties will differ from variable to variable.

Some uses have been acknowledged even by critics of the method, as in the case of the Rorschach's apparent ability to assist in the evaluation of thought disorders (Garb et al., 2005; Hunsley et al., 2003; Wood et al., 2003). Beyond these rare points of consensus, however, the discussion is polarized, with impassioned debates characterized by point/counterpoint arguments appearing in various professional journals in recent years. The debate will likely continue for some time and is quite relevant to the assessment of older children and adolescents. It is not uncommon to find those who describe or otherwise support the use of the Rorschach with youths (e.g., Erdberg, 2007; Weiner, 2003, 2005). However, Wood et al. warn that the technique may overpathologize children, which may result in harm due to the possibility of inaccurate conclusions being drawn and a resulting incongruence of fit between the youth and recommended treatment options (Garb et al., 2005; Lilienfeld et al., 2001; Wood et al., 2003).

Projective Techniques: The Bottom Line

Clinicians are advised to carefully consider the arguments and data when selecting measures for formal clinical evaluations. Instruments incorporated into a psychological assessment battery should be selected with the referral questions in mind; be standardized and psychometrically sound with regard to norms, administration, scoring, and interpretive procedures; possess utility for the intended clinical purpose; and be appropriate for the context and the person being evaluated. Clinicians must make their own decisions whether to include projective techniques and be prepared to justify them based on these considerations. Lilienfeld et al. (2001) warn clinicians against the use of projective techniques, except in the rare cases where the merit of scoring and interpretation has been supported. For research-based guidelines on incorporating projective techniques into clinical practice, the reader is referred to Garb, Wood, Lilienfeld, and Nezworski (2002). As for the future of projective techniques, it is important for those who advocate their use to decide on standardized procedures (norms, administration, scoring, and interpretation) so that evaluation of their psychometric properties may take place through well-designed research studies (Hunsley et al., 2003).

THE PSYCHOLOGICAL REPORT: ENHANCING WRITTEN COMMUNICATION

In general, a good psychological report is one that explains the nature of the referral, documents observations of the person's behavior, lists the instruments and techniques used in the assessment and the dates employed, notes reliability and validity issues pertaining to the assessment, clearly and adequately explains results, offers diagnostic impressions, contains a summary and recommendations, and is signed with adequate credentials evident (Braaten, 2007; Brenner, 2003; Groth-Marnat & Horvath, 2006; Harvey, 1997, 2006; Koocher, 2005). The content of the report should be tailored to the individual (Groth-Marnat & Horvath, 2006), and the pros and cons of diagnosis should be considered. When an integrated assessment supports the presence of a diagnosis, clinicians should make diagnostic distinctions that are appropriate, while also considering the diagnosis that is the least stigmatizing. A diagnosis may be helpful in fostering the implementation of services, as well as respecting the consumer's right to knowledge; however, less severe diagnoses may be associated with less stigmatization and emotional distress, and with youths there is the added danger of others reviewing the report, with certain elements being integrated into other documents and becoming part of the youth's records (Michaels, 2006). Although there are numerous variables to consider when writing a psychological report, a few important points are delineated here relating to inclusion of client strengths, improving readability, and using computerized interpretative narratives. For further general information on report writing, the reader is referred to Groth-Marnat (2003); Lichtenberger, Mather, Kaufman, and Kaufman (2004); and Sattler and Hoge (2006).

Inclusion of Strengths

Personal (e.g., good social skills) and environmental (e.g., solid social network) strengths should be highlighted, as often evaluations remain deficit-oriented and general (Brenner, 2003; Groth-Marnat & Horvath, 2006; Snyder et al., 2006). A separate section on strengths could be included in the psychological report (Groth-Marnat & Horvath, 2006; Snyder et al., 2006), or the material could be integrated into the narrative of the report and become a focal point of the feedback session. Focusing on an individual's assets is perhaps one means of alleviating stigmatization and emotional distress (Michaels, 2006), as well as empowering a youth to make adaptive and effective choices. Incorporating client strengths is a challenge given that it is more labor-intensive during the assessment and report writing phases; however, it results in a more thorough and appropriate case conceptualization (Snyder et al., 2006).

Improving Readability

Psychological reports need to be geared toward the consumer to be of utility (Brenner, 2003; Harvey, 2006). Reports are read by a variety of individuals with varied academic backgrounds, such as psychologists, educators, court employees, and, increasingly, clients and parents of youths (Groth-Marnat & Horvath, 2006; Harvey, 1997, 2006; Snyder et al., 2006). A major problem is that reports continue to be written at a level that is difficult for consumers to understand (Groth-Marnat & Horvath, 2006; Harvey, 1997, 2006), and use of technical terms may result in the misinterpretation of information, which is potentially harmful to the consumer (Michaels, 2006). To increase the readability of psychological reports, difficult and technical words, wordiness, passive verbs, and acronyms should be minimized (avoided if possible), sentences should be shortened, and subheadings employed (Brenner, 2003; Groth-Marnat & Horvath, 2006; Harvey, 1997, 2006). These efforts are critical to writing clear, consumer-oriented reports, although additional report writing time is required, which may be an added stressor for clinicians working in environments characterized by time constraints (Harvey, 2006).

Computerized Interpretive Narratives

Computerized interpretive narratives are often available with the computer scoring packages of personality instruments such as the MMPI-A and the MACI. These computerized narratives must be carefully tailored to the individual being assessed to combat interpretations and language that are hard to understand, lengthiness, and incorrect hypotheses and recommendations (Harvey, 2006). They should also be viewed as one source of data, confirmed by other sources (Michaels, 2006). Clinicians should be thorough consumers of the quality (e.g., validity) of the computerized interpretive packages that they use (Butcher, 2003; Garb, 2000; Snyder, 2000), as clinicians retain responsibility for the applicability of computerized interpretations and the content eventually included in the written psychological report (American Educational Research Association, American Psychological Association, & National Council on Measurement in Education, 1999; American Psychological Association, 2002; Association of State and Provincial Psychology Boards, 2001; Groth-Marnat & Horvath, 2006; Schulenberg & Yutrzenka, 2004).

THE FEEDBACK SESSION: ENHANCING ORAL COMMUNICATION

Conducting feedback sessions is important for cultivating relationships with consumers of assessment services (Brenner, 2003). Feedback sessions afford additional opportunities for clinicians to clarify hypotheses, refine the precision of their reports, work to ensure that the content of the report is understood, and emphasize the importance of following recommendations (Brenner, 2003; Harvey, 2006; Snyder et al., 2006). When communicating assessment results, clinicians are advised to tailor feedback to the educational level of the intended recipient and to be sensitive to cultural issues related to diagnosis and treatment. Communicating in clearly understandable language may be difficult, however, as many terms commonly used by professionals have different meanings from professional to professional, and therefore feedback provided to consumers may be substantially different based on the clinician providing the interpretations (and also by the consumers receiving feedback, who may be relying on their own definitions; Harvey, 2006).

Consumers should feel that they have been heard, that they are a part of the process, and that they have opportunities to pose questions, have concerns addressed, and comment on recommendations (Braaten, 2007; Brenner, 2003; Harvey, 2006; Snyder et al., 2006). Comments from parents or legal guardians and the youth being assessed can encourage the clinician to clarify the findings, particularly if there is a discrepancy between the test results and other data (e.g., collateral information). As for recommendations, they should be presented in a clear, straightforward, and convincing manner, relate to the referral questions, and take into account cultural variables, community resources, client strengths, and the ability of individuals (e.g., parents, teachers) to carry them out (Brenner, 2003; Gudas & Sattler, 2006; Harvey, 2006; Jones et al., 2001; Snyder et al., 2006). Explanation of recommendations is particularly important, as there may be a variety of barriers to implementing them (e.g., transportation, cultural differences; Geffken et al., 2006; Jones et al., 2001).

Potential barriers to following through with recommendations may be examined, and the clinician may problem-solve with consumers to minimize treatment non-adherence (see Geffken et al., 2006, for a discussion of recommendation follow-through).

Parents or legal guardians whose youths are undergoing psychological evaluations typically want to know if there is something "wrong," and they may experience anxiety at the prospect of the evaluation results and have questions about the testing and the implications of the findings. Parents or legal guardians may feel defensive regarding their youth's presenting problems (Lichtenberger et al., 2004), and some may need to be referred for treatment for their own psychological problems. The emotional responses of the parents or legal guardians should be addressed; however, the focus of the feedback session should remain on the youth (Braaten, 2007). Thus, clinicians must work to strike a delicate balance between providing information that is nonjudgmental and supportive, yet is accurate to the situation (Braaten, 2007; Lichtenberger et al., 2004). Starting the feedback session with positive comments about the youth, reiterating these positives throughout the evaluation, focusing on how parents or legal guardians can help their child, and conveying a sense of hope are generally useful strategies (Braaten, 2007).

A more complicated question is when and how to provide personality assessment feedback to the youths themselves. What age is appropriate for youths to hear this type of information? Could this information be detrimental? Young children who are able to read should not review their personality descriptions; however, it is appropriate to provide them with verbal feedback consistent with their developmental level (Lichtenberger et al., 2004). Older children and adolescents may be involved in feedback to the degree possible given a variety of variables, such as their developmental level, parental wishes, and the nature of the feedback. Focusing on a youth's strengths provides a critical starting point on which to build. Involving them in the assessment early on by building good rapport can be helpful later in involving them in the feedback session. Adolescents in particular may be interested in obtaining answers to their questions, and in some cases it is useful to provide feedback to the youth on an individual basis, as well as to the youth and his or her family together (Lichtenberger et al., 2004). Assessment and feedback should provide supportive and tactful illumination on areas of concern, identifying ways that youths may navigate their environments with greater effectiveness.

PSYCHOLOGICAL ASSESSMENT WITH YOUTHS: COMPLICATING FACTORS

Thus far we have presented a thorough model for the assessment of psychopathology in youths. Although the model presented is comprehensive, it should be noted that many clinicians work in different environments or under circumstances that complicate the thorough assessment of psychopathology. We now turn to a discussion of complicating factors: the forensic environment, mental retardation and developmental disabilities, and managed care.

The Forensic Environment

Increasingly, clinicians are conducting psychological assessments in juvenile forensic settings. To be effective working in the forensic environment, clinicians must be able to work with youths, families, attorneys, and legal officials, as well as understand the differences between clinical and forensic roles. Clinical roles tend to be supportive, whereas forensic roles tend to be more neutral. Additional intricacies relate to the referral questions, informed consent and assent, limitations of confidentiality, identifying who exactly is the client, establishing the role of the evaluator, and determining the content and length of the psychological report, as well as who will receive feedback and how feedback will be conducted (e.g., Ackerman, 2006; Butcher & Pope, 2006; Gudas & Sattler, 2006; Koocher, 2006). Is the client an attorney, a youth's parents, or a court? Does the referral relate to a specific legal issue, and if so, how is the assessment of personality relevant? The answers to such questions are important, as they have a bearing on how forensic interviews are conducted to a degree that requires specialized training (Gudas & Sattler, 2006).

With regard to the selection of measures appropriate to the clinical or forensic task at hand, specific guidelines are available (Butcher & Pope, 2006; Heilbrun, 1992), and clinicians should be prepared to justify their decisions (Gudas & Sattler, 2006; Koocher, 2006). In addition, given the forensic nature of the evaluation, the concern that adolescents may malinger is prominent (Butcher & Pope, 2006; McCann, 1998; Steffen & Ackerman, 1999). One means of countering this problem is by using objective personality inventories with validity indicators to aid in the identification of unusual response styles. As part of a comprehensive battery of assessment tools, the MMPI-A has some effectiveness in this regard (Butcher & Pope, 2006; McCann, 1998), and the MACI's utility is also viewed as promising (McCann, 1998, 2006). Thus, both the MMPI-A and the MACI are potentially useful in juvenile forensic settings (e.g., Archer et al., 2006; Butcher & Pope, 2006; McCann, 2006).

Working with Youths with Mental Retardation or Developmental Disabilities

Another issue that may arise is the assessment of psychopathology in youths with mental retardation or developmental disabilities (MR/DD). In an article focusing on working in a high-management group home setting with youths with MR/DD and who also demonstrated sexual offending behaviors, Schulenberg (2003) noted the impossibilities inherent in assessing these youths with self-report measures such as the MMPI-A and the MACI given the reading difficulties with this population. However, the potential assessment utility of having others complete standardized behavior rating scales in this context was noted.

Managed Care

In their review, Wood et al. (2002) noted the apparent impact of managed care on assessment practices, with psychologists facing increasing accountability to justify the utility, cost-effectiveness, and incremental validity of their services. In Cashel's (2002) survey, although the overall impact of managed care on test and technique utilization was minimal, the largest and most noticeable declines in reported test usage were with measures such as the WISC, Rorschach, TAT, and MMPI-A. Similar findings were noted in Archer and Newsom's (2000) survey, with clinicians reporting less use of several measures as a result of managed care limitations, including the Rorschach, the TAT, the Wechsler scales, and the MMPI-A. For some clinicians, managed care may result in reduced activity in the area of psychological assessment, with fewer measures included in the battery (making batteries less comprehensive) and with diminished reimbursement (Archer & Newsom, 2000). With specific regard to the continued use of projective measures, although they continue to be popular among clinicians, it is possible that they may experience an eventual decline in the area of youth assessment. If such a decline were to occur, it could be due to the psychometric criticisms that have been raised, the increased use of behavior rating scales, and/or managed care (Archer & Newsom, 2000; Cashel, 2002; Groth-Marnat, 2003; Kamphaus et al., 2000).

SUMMARY

Delineating a specific standard for youth assessments is difficult given that they are conducted in a variety of environments (Palmiter, 2004). Our approach in this chapter was to paint a broad stroke with regard to major issues in the assessment of psychopathology in youths. In doing so a variety of issues were covered, beginning with the referral questions, informed consent and assent, rapport building, and measure selection, and continuing with clinical and collateral interviews, review of collateral records, and intelligence and achievement testing. The objective assessment of personality, as well as the psychometric controversy surrounding the use of projective techniques, was also discussed, and the potential utility of behavior ratings scales (administered to youths, their parents, and their teachers) and behavioral observations were underscored. Finally, issues in report writing and feedback were outlined, followed by complicating factors to the assessment process. Given space limitations, it was beyond our scope to provide an in-depth view of each area. For example, despite the emphasis on the importance of psychometric properties, a thorough treatment of each instrument discussed simply was not possible, nor was it possible to discuss all of the numerous measures available in a given area despite clinical popularity or psychometric support in certain circumstances.

To make sense of the wide array of instruments available, clinicians must be trained in test construction and psychometrics. They should be aware of the psychometric pros and cons of their tools and their applicability to the diagnostic question in the specific context of the assessment.

In addition to psychometrics, to competently conduct personality assessments with youths, clinicians must understand relevant developmental, environmental, personality, psychopathological, diagnostic, ethical, and multicultural variables. Assessments should be thorough, taking into account multiple sources of data through a variety of means, to generate hypotheses about a youth's functioning and to arrive at a precise and comprehensive case formulation. Thorough training in the administration, scoring, and interpretation of psychological tests, as well as strength identification, integration of findings, development of individualized recommendations, and constructive methods of report writing and feedback provision is also necessary. These recommendations are consistent with other sources denoting standards for assessment competency (e.g., Krishnamurthy et al., 2004). For additional information on ethical and professional standards in assessment, see the publications by the American Educational Research Association, American Psychological Association, and National Council on Measurement in Education (1999); the American Psychological Association (1991, 1993, 2002); and the Association of State and Provincial Psychology Boards (2001). For those looking for additional information on psychometric properties of instruments useful in the personality and psychopathological assessment of older children and adolescents, beyond consulting the respective manuals, the *Mental Measurements Yearbook* (www.unl.edu/buros/), a comprehensive database for psychometric reviews of a variety of measures, is a useful place to begin. In addition, readers should consult the respective chapters, texts, and empirical articles that continue to increase in availability.

REFERENCES

Achenbach, T. M. (2007). Applications of the Achenbach System of Empirically Based Assessment to children, adolescents, and their parents. In S. R. Smith, & L. Handler (Eds.), *The clinical assessment of children and adolescents: A practitioner's handbook* (pp. 327–344). Mahwah, NJ: Erlbaum.

Achenbach, T. M., & Rescorla, L. A. (2006). The Achenbach System of Empirically Based Assessment. In R. P. Archer (Ed.), *Forensic uses of clinical assessment instruments* (pp. 229–262). Mahwah, NJ: Erlbaum.

Achenbach, T. M., & Rescorla, L. A. (2007). *Multicultural understanding of child and adolescent psychopathology: Implications for mental health assessment*. New York: Guilford Press.

Ackerman, M. J. (2006). Forensic report writing. *Journal of Clinical Psychology, 62*, 59–72.

Allen, J. (2002). Assessment training for practice in American Indian and Alaska Native settings. *Journal of Personality Assessment, 79*, 216–225.

American Educational Research Association, American Psychological Association, & National Council on Measurement in Education. (1999). *Standards for educational and psychological testing*. Washington, DC: Author.

American Psychiatric Association. (2000). *Diagnostic and statistical manual of mental disorders* (4th ed., text rev.). Washington, DC: Author.

American Psychological Association. (1991). Specialty guidelines for forensic psychologists. *Law and Human Behavior, 15*, 655–665.

American Psychological Association. (1993). Guidelines for providers of psychological services to ethnic, linguistic, and culturally diverse populations. *American Psychologist, 48*, 45–48.

American Psychological Association. (2002). *Ethical principles of psychologists and code of conduct*. Washington, DC: Author.

Archer, R. P. (2005). *MMPI-A: Assessing adolescent psychopathology* (3rd ed.). Mahwah, NJ: Erlbaum.

Archer, R. P., & Krishnamurthy, R. (2002). *Essentials of MMPI-A assessment*. Hoboken, NJ: Wiley.

Archer, R. P., Krishnamurthy, R., & Stredny, R. V. (2007). The Minnesota Multiphasic Personality Inventory—Adolescent. In S. R. Smith, & L. Handler (Eds.), *The clinical assessment of children and adolescents: A practitioner's handbook* (pp. 237–266). Mahwah, NJ: Erlbaum.

Archer, R. P., Maruish, M., Imhof, E. A., & Piotrowski, C. (1991). Psychological test usage with adolescent clients: 1990 survey findings. *Professional Psychology: Research and Practice, 22*, 247–252.

Archer, R. P., & Newsom, C. R. (2000). Psychological test usage with adolescent clients: Survey update. *Assessment, 7*, 227–235.

Archer, R. P., Zoby, M., & Stredny, R. V. (2006). The Minnesota Multiphasic Personality Inventory—Adolescent. In R. P. Archer (Ed.), *Forensic uses of clinical assessment instruments* (pp. 57–87). Mahwah, NJ: Erlbaum.

Association of State and Provincial Psychology Boards. (2001). *ASPPB code of conduct*. Montgomery, AL: Author.

Baer, R. A., & Rinaldo, J. C. (2004). The Minnesota Multiphasic Personality Inventory—Adolescent (MMPI-A). In M. Hersen, (Editor-in-chief) & M. J. Hilsenroth, & D. L. Segal (Vol. Eds.), *Comprehensive handbook of psychological assessment: Vol. 2. Personality assessment* (pp. 213–223). Hoboken, NJ: Wiley.

Beck, J. S., Beck, A. T., & Jolly, J. (2001). *Beck Youth Inventories of Emotional and Social Impairment manual*. San Antonio, TX: Psychological Corporation.

Beck, J. S., Beck, A. T., Jolly, J. B., & Steer, R. A. (2005). *Beck Youth Inventories for Children and Adolescents manual* (2nd ed.). San Antonio, TX: Harcourt Assessment.

Bellak, L. (1954). *The Thematic Apperception Test and the Children's Apperception Test in clinical use*. New York: Grune, & Stratton.

Bellak, L., & Abrams, D. M. (1997). *The T.A.T., C.A.T., and the S.A.T. in clinical use* (6th ed.). Boston: Allyn & Bacon.

Blumentritt, T. L., Angle, R. L., & Brown, J. M. (2004). MACI personality patterns and DSM-IV symptomology in a sample of troubled Mexican-American adolescents. *Journal of Child and Family Studies, 13*, 163–178.

Blumentritt, T. L., & Wilson VanVoorhis, C. R. (2004). The Millon Adolescent Clinical Inventory: Is it valid and reliable for Mexican American youth? *Journal of Personality Assessment, 83*, 64–74.

Boggs, K. M., Griffin, R. S., & Gross, A. M. (2003). Diagnostic interviewing of children. In M. Hersen, & S. Turner (Eds.), *Diagnostic interviewing* (3rd ed., pp. 393–413). New York: Kluwer Academic/Plenum Press.

Bose-Deakins, J. E., & Floyd, R. G. (2004). A review of the Beck Youth Inventories of Emotional and Social Impairment. *Journal of School Psychology, 42*, 333–340.

Braaten, E. B. (2007). Personality assessment feedback with parents. In S. R. Smith, & L. Handler (Eds.), *The clinical assessment of children and adolescents: A practitioner's handbook* (pp. 73–83). Mahwah, NJ: Erlbaum.

Brenner, E. (2003). Consumer-focused psychological assessment. *Professional Psychology: Research and Practice, 34*, 240–247.

Butcher, J. N. (2003). Computerized psychological assessment. In J. R. Graham, & J. A. Naglieri (Eds.), *Handbook of psychology: Assessment psychology* (pp. 141–163). Hoboken, NJ: Wiley.

Butcher, J. N., & Pope, K. S. (2006). The MMPI-A in forensic assessment. In S. N. Sparta, & G. P. Koocher (Eds.), *Forensic mental health assessment of children and adolescents* (pp. 401–411). New York: Oxford University Press.

Butcher, J. N., & Williams, C. L. (2000). *Essentials of MMPI-2 and MMPI-A interpretation* (2nd ed.). Minneapolis: University of Minnesota Press.

Butcher, J. N., Williams, C. L., Graham, J. R., Archer, R. P., Tellegen, A., Ben-Porath, Y. S., et al. (1992). *Minnesota Multiphasic Personality Inventory—Adolescent (MMPI-A): Manual for administration, scoring, and interpretation*. Minneapolis: University of Minnesota Press.

Camara, W. J., Nathan, J. S., & Puente, A. E. (2000). Psychological test usage: Implications in professional psychology. *Professional Psychology: Research and Practice, 31*, 141–154.

Campbell, J. M. (2006a). Anxiety disorders. In R. W. Kamphaus, & J. M. Campbell (Eds.), *Psychodiagnostic assessment of children: Dimensional and categorical approaches* (pp. 211–244). Hoboken, NJ: Wiley.

Campbell, J. M. (2006b). Depressive disorders. In R. W. Kamphaus, & J. M. Campbell (Eds.), *Psychodiagnostic assessment of children: Dimensional and categorical approaches* (pp. 169–209). Hoboken, NJ: Wiley.

Cashel, M. L. (2002). Child and adolescent psychological assessment: Current clinical practices and the impact of managed care. *Professional Psychology: Research and Practice, 33*, 446–453.

Cashel, M. L., Rogers, R., Sewell, K. W., & Holliman, N. G. (1998). Preliminary validation of the MMPI-A for a male delinquent sample: An investigation of clinical correlates and discriminative validity. *Journal of Personality Assessment, 71*, 46–69.

Elliot, S. N., Busse, R. T., & Gresham, F. M. (1993). Behavior rating scales: Issues of use and development. *School Psychology Review, 22*, 313–321.

Erdberg, P. (2007). Using the Rorschach with children. In S. R. Smith, & L. Handler (Eds.), *The clinical assessment of children and adolescents: A practitioner's handbook* (pp. 139–147). Mahwah, NJ: Erlbaum.

Exner, J. E. (2001). *A Rorschach workbook for the Comprehensive System* (5th ed.). Asheville, NC: Rorschach Workshops.

Exner, J. E. (2003). *The Rorschach—A Comprehensive System: Vol. 1. Basic foundations and principles of interpretation* (4th ed.). Hoboken, NJ: Wiley.

Faul, L. A., & Gross, A. M. (2006). Diagnosis and classification. In M. Hersen, & J. C. Thomas, (Editors-in-Chief) & R. T. Ammerman (Vol. Ed.), *Comprehensive handbook of personality and psychopathology: Vol. 3. Child psychopathology* (pp. 3–15). Hoboken, NJ: Wiley.

Flores, L. Y., & Obasi, E. M. (2003). Positive psychological assessment in an increasingly diverse world. In S. J. Lopez, & C. R. Snyder (Eds.), *Positive psychological assessment: A handbook of models and measures* (pp. 41–54). Washington, DC: American Psychological Association.

Franz, D., & Gross, A. M. (1998). Assessment of child behavior problems: Externalizing disorders. In A. S. Bellack, & M. Hersen (Eds.), *Behavioral assessment: A practical handbook* (4th ed., pp. 361–377). Boston: Allyn & Bacon.

Frick, P. J., & Kamphaus, R. W. (2001). Standardized rating scales in the assessment of children's behavioral and emotional problems. In C. E. Walker, & M. C. Roberts (Eds.), *Handbook of clinical child psychology* (3rd ed., pp. 190–204). Hoboken, NJ: Wiley.

Fristad, M. A., Emery, B. L., & Beck, S. J. (1997). Use and abuse of the Children's Depression Inventory. *Journal of Consulting and Clinical Psychology, 65*, 699–702.

Garb, H. N. (2000). Computers will become increasingly important for psychological assessment: Not that there's anything wrong with that! *Psychological Assessment, 12*, 31–39.

Garb, H. N., Wood, J. M., & Lilienfeld, S. O. (2005). Rorschach assessment: Questions and reservations. In G. P. Koocher, J. C. Norcross, & S. S. Hill (Eds.), *Psychologists' desk reference* (2nd ed., pp. 169–172). New York: Oxford University Press.

Garb, H. N., Wood, J. M., Lilienfeld, S. O., & Nezworski, M. T. (2002). Effective use of projective techniques in clinical practice: Let the data help with selection and interpretation. *Professional Psychology: Research and Practice, 33*, 454–463.

Geffken, G. R., Keeley, M. L., Kellison, I., Storch, E. A., & Rodrigue, J. R. (2006). Parental adherence to child psychologists' recommendations from psychological testing. *Professional Psychology: Research and Practice, 37*, 499–505.

Gómez, F. C., Johnson, R., Davis, Q., & Velásquez, R. J. (2000). MMPI-A performance of African and Mexican American adolescent first-time offenders. *Psychological Reports, 87*, 309–314.

Graham, J. R. (2006). *MMPI-2: Assessing personality and psychopathology* (4th ed.). New York: Oxford University Press.

Groth-Marnat, G. (2003). *Handbook of psychological assessment* (4th ed.). Hoboken, NJ: Wiley.

Groth-Marnat, G., & Horvath, L. S. (2006). The psychological report: A review of current controversies. *Journal of Clinical Psychology, 62*, 73–81.

Gudas, L. S., & Sattler, J. M. (2006). Forensic interviewing of children and adolescents. In S. N. Sparta, & G. P. Koocher (Eds.), *Forensic mental health assessment of children and adolescents* (pp. 115–128). New York: Oxford University Press.

Gumbiner, J. (1998). MMPI-A profiles of Hispanic adolescents. *Psychological Reports, 82*, 659–672.

Harvey, V. S. (1997). Improving readability of psychological reports. *Professional Psychology: Research and Practice, 28*, 271–274.

Harvey, V. S. (2006). Variables affecting the clarity of psychological reports. *Journal of Clinical Psychology, 62*, 5–18.

Heilbrun, K. (1992). The role of psychological testing in forensic assessment. *Law and Human Behavior, 16*, 257–272.

Hogan, T. P. (2007). *Psychological testing: A practical introduction* (2nd ed.). Hoboken, NJ: Wiley.

Holaday, M., Smith, D. A., & Sherry, A. (2000). Sentence completion tests: A review of the literature and results of a survey of members of the Society for Personality Assessment. *Journal of Personality Assessment, 74*, 371–383.

Hunsley, J., Lee, C. M., & Wood, J. M. (2003). Controversial and questionable assessment techniques. In S. O. Lilienfeld, S. J. Lynn, & J. M. Lohr (Eds.), *Science and pseudoscience in clinical psychology* (pp. 39–76). New York: Guilford Press.

Jones, R. T., Kephart, C., Langley, A. K., Parker, M. N., Shenoy, U., & Weeks, C. (2001). Cultural and ethnic diversity issues in clinical child psychology. In C. E. Walker, & M. C. Roberts (Eds.), *Handbook of clinical child psychology* (3rd ed., pp. 955–973). Hoboken, NJ: Wiley.

Kamphaus, R. W., Petoskey, M. D., & Rowe, E. W. (2000). Current trends in psychological testing of children. *Professional Psychology: Research and Practice, 31*, 155–164.

Kamphaus, R. W., VanDeventer, M. C., Brueggemann, A., & Barry, M. (2007). Behavior Assessment System for Children—Second Edition. In S. R. Smith, & L. Handler (Eds.), *The clinical assessment of children and adolescents: A practitioner's handbook* (pp. 311–326). Mahwah, NJ: Erlbaum.

Karg, R. S., & Wiens, A. N. (2005). Improving diagnostic and clinical interviewing. In G. P. Koocher, J. C. Norcross, & S. S. Hill (Eds.), *Psychologists' desk reference* (2nd ed., pp. 13–16). New York: Oxford University Press.

Kasen, S., Cohen, P., Skodol, A. E., Johnson, J. G., & Brook, J. S., (1999). Influence of child and adolescent psychiatric disorders on young adult personality disorder. *American Journal of Psychiatry, 156*, 1529–1535.

Kimonis, E. R., & Frick, P. J. (2006). Conduct disorder. In M. Hersen, & J. C. Thomas, (Editors-in-Chief) & R. T. Ammerman (Vol. Ed.), *Comprehensive handbook of personality and psychopathology: Vol. 3. Child psychopathology* (pp. 299–315). Hoboken, NJ: Wiley.

Kollins, S. H., Epstein, J. N., & Conners, C. K. (2004). Conners' Rating Scales—Revised. In M. E. Maruish (Ed.), *The use of psychological testing for treatment planning and outcomes assessment: Vol. 2. Instruments for children and adolescents* (3rd ed., pp. 215-233). Mahwah, NJ: Erlbaum.

Koocher, G. P. (2005). Assessing the quality of a psychological testing report. In G. P. Koocher, J. C. Norcross, & S. S. Hill (Eds.), *Psychologists' desk reference* (2nd ed., pp. 117–119). New York: Oxford University Press.

Koocher, G. P. (2006). Ethical issues in forensic assessment of children and adolescents. In S. N. Sparta, & G. P. Koocher (Eds.), *Forensic mental health assessment of children and adolescents* (pp. 46–63). New York: Oxford University Press.

Kovacs, M. (1992). *Children's Depression Inventory manual*. North Tonawanda, NY: Multi-Health Systems.

Krishnamurthy, R., VandeCreek, L., Kaslow, N. J., Tazeau, Y. N., Miville, M. L., Kerns, R., et al. (2004). Achieving competency in psychological assessment: Directions for education and training. *Journal of Clinical Psychology, 60*, 725–739.

Kuperminc, G. P., & Brookmeyer, K. A. (2006). Developmental psychopathology. In M. Hersen, & J. C. Thomas, (Editors-in-Chief) & R. T. Ammerman (Vol. Ed.), *Comprehensive handbook of personality and psychopathology: Vol. 3. Child psychopathology* (pp. 100–113). Hoboken, NJ: Wiley.

Lally, S. J. (2001). Should Human Figure Drawings be admitted into court? *Journal of Personality Assessment, 76*, 135–149.

Leong, F. T. L., Levy, J. J., Gee, C. B., & Johnson, J. (2007). Clinical assessment of ethnic minority children and adolescents. In S. R. Smith, & L. Handler (Eds.), *The clinical assessment of children and adolescents: A practitioner's handbook* (pp. 545–574). Mahwah, NJ: Erlbaum.

Lichtenberger, E. O., Mather, N., Kaufman, N. L., & Kaufman, A. S. (2004). *Essentials of assessment report writing*. Hoboken, NJ: Wiley.

Lilienfeld, S. O., Wood, J. M., & Garb, H. N. (2001). What's wrong with this picture? *Scientific American, 284*, 80–87.

Loney, B. R., & Frick, P. J. (2003). Structured diagnostic interviewing. In C. R. Reynolds, & R. W. Kamphaus (Eds.), *Handbook of psychological and educational assessment of children: Personality, behavior, and context* (2nd ed., pp. 235–247). New York: Guilford Press.

March, J. S. (1997). *Multidimensional Anxiety Scale for Children*. North Tonawanda, NY: Multi-Health Systems.

McCann, J. T. (1998). *Malingering and deception in adolescents: Assessing credibility in clinical and forensic settings*. Washington, DC: American Psychological Association.

McCann, J. T. (1999). *Assessing adolescents with the MACI: Using the Millon Adolescent Clinical Inventory*. Hoboken, NJ: Wiley.

McCann, J. T. (2006). Measuring adolescent personality and psychopathology with the Millon Adolescent Clinical Inventory (MACI). In S. N. Sparta, & G. P. Koocher (Eds.), *Forensic mental health assessment of children and adolescents* (pp. 424–439). New York: Oxford University Press.

Meagher, S. E., Grossman, S. D., & Millon, T. (2004). Studying outcomes in adolescents: The Millon Adolescent Clinical Inventory (MACI) and Millon Adolescent Personality Inventory (MAPI). In M. E. Maruish (Ed.), *The use of psychological testing for treatment planning and outcomes assessment: Vol. 2. Instruments for children and adolescents* (3rd ed., pp. 123–139). Mahwah, NJ: Erlbaum.

Merrell, K. W. (2003). *Behavioral, social, and emotional assessment of children and adolescents* (2nd ed.). Mahwah, NJ: Erlbaum.

Michaels, M. H. (2006). Ethical considerations in writing psychological assessment reports. *Journal of Clinical Psychology, 62,* 47–58.

Millon, T., & Grossman, S. D. (2005). Millon Adolescent Clinical Inventory (MACI). In G. P. Koocher, J. C. Norcross, & S. S. Hill (Eds.), *Psychologists' desk reference* (2nd ed., pp. 159–165). New York: Oxford University Press.

Millon, T., Millon, C., & Davis, R. (1993). *Millon Adolescent Clinical Inventory (MACI) manual.* Minneapolis: National Computer Systems.

Miltenberger, R. G. (2001). *Behavior modification: Principles and procedures* (2nd ed.). Belmont, CA: Wadsworth/Thomson Learning.

Morrison, J., & Anders, T. F. (1999). *Interviewing children and adolescents: Skills and strategies for effective DSM-IV diagnosis.* New York: Guilford Press.

Motta, R. W., Little, S. G., & Tobin, M. I. (1993). The use and abuse of Human Figure Drawings. *School Psychology Quarterly, 8,* 162–169.

Murray, H. A. (1943). *Thematic Apperception Test.* Cambridge, MA: Harvard University Press.

Naglieri, J. A., McNeish, T. J., & Bardos, A. N. (1991). *Draw a Person: Screening Procedure for Emotional Disturbance.* Austin, TX: ProEd.

Negy, C., Leal-Puente, L., Trainor, D. J., & Carlson, R. (1997). Mexican American adolescents' performance on the MMPI-A. *Journal of Personality Assessment, 69,* 205–214.

Orvaschel, H. (2006). Structured and semistructured interviews. In M. Hersen, (Ed.), *Clinician's handbook of child behavioral assessment* (pp. 159–179). San Diego, CA: Academic Press.

Palmer, L., Farrar, A. R., Valle, M., Ghahary, N., Panella, M., & DeGraw, D. (2000). An investigation of the clinical use of the House-Tree-Person projective drawings in the psychological evaluation of child sexual abuse. *Child Maltreatment, 5,* 169–175.

Palmiter, D. J. (2004). A survey of the assessment practices of child and adolescent clinicians. *American Journal of Orthopsychiatry, 74,* 122–128.

Piacentini, J. (1993). Checklists and rating scales. In T. H. Ollendick, & M. Hersen (Eds.), *Handbook of child and adolescent assessment* (pp. 82–97). Boston: Allyn & Bacon.

Pinto, M., & Grilo, C. M. (2004). Reliability, diagnostic efficiency, and validity of the Millon Adolescent Clinical Inventory: Examination of selected scales in psychiatrically hospitalized adolescents. *Behaviour Research and Therapy, 42,* 1505–1519.

Psychological Corporation. (2002). *Wechsler Individual Achievement Test* (2nd ed.). San Antonio, TX: Author.

Ramklint, M., von Knorring, A. L., von Knorring, L., & Ekselius, L. (2003). Child and adolescent psychiatric disorders predicting adult personality disorder: A follow-up study. *Nordic Journal of Psychiatry, 57,* 23–28.

Reynolds, C. R., & Kamphaus, R. W. (2004). *Behavior Assessment System for Children manual* (2nd ed.). Circle Pines, MN: American Guidance Service.

Reynolds, W. M. (1989). *Reynolds Child Depression Scale: Professional manual.* Odessa, FL: Psychological Assessment Resources.

Reynolds, W. M. (2002). *Reynolds Adolescent Depression Scale: Professional manual* (2nd ed.). Odessa, FL: Psychological Assessment Resources.

Reynolds, W. M. (2004). The Reynolds Adolescent Depression Scale—Second Edition (RADS-2). In M. Hersen, (Editor-in-Chief) & M. J. Hilsenroth, & D. L. Segal (Vol. Eds.), *Comprehensive handbook of psychological assessment: Vol. 2. Personality assessment* (pp. 224–236). Hoboken, NJ: Wiley.

Reynolds, W. M. (2006). Depression. In M. Hersen (Ed.), *Clinician's handbook of child behavioral assessment* (pp. 291–311). San Diego, CA: Academic Press.

Ritzler, B. A. (2005). Thumbnail guide to the Rorschach method. In G. P. Koocher, J. C. Norcross, & S. S. Hill (Eds.), *Psychologists' desk reference* (2nd ed., pp. 166–168). New York: Oxford University Press.

Rogers, K. E., Bishop, J., & Lane, R. C. (2003). Considerations for the use of sentence completion tests. *Journal of Contemporary Psychotherapy, 33*, 235–242.

Rourke, K. M., & Reich, W. (2004). The Diagnostic Interview for Children and Adolescents (DICA). In M. Hersen, (Editor-in-Chief) & M. J. Hilsenroth, & D. L. Segal (Vol. Eds.), *Comprehensive handbook of psychological assessment: Vol. 2. Personality assessment* (pp. 271–280). Hoboken, NJ: Wiley.

Sattler, J. M., & Dumont, R. (2004). *Assessment of children: WISC-IV and WPPSI-III supplement.* San Diego, CA: Jerome Sattler.

Sattler, J. M., & Hoge, R. D. (2006). *Assessment of children: Behavioral, social, and clinical foundations* (5th ed.). San Diego, CA: Jerome Sattler.

Sattler, J. M., Weyandt, L., & Willis, J. O. (2006). Attention-Deficit/Hyperactivity Disorder. In J. M. Sattler, & R. D. Hoge (Eds.), *Assessment of children: Behavioral, social, and clinical foundations* (5th ed., pp. 374–389). San Diego, CA: Jerome Sattler.

Schroeder, C. S., & Gordon, B. N. (2002). *Assessment and treatment of childhood problems: A clinician's guide* (2nd ed.). New York: Guilford Press.

Schroeder, C. S., & Gordon, B. N. (2005). Interviewing parents. In G. P. Koocher, J. C. Norcross, & S. S. Hill (Eds.), *Psychologists' desk reference* (2nd ed., pp. 55–60). New York: Oxford University Press.

Schulenberg, S. E. (2003). Use of Logotherapy's Mountain Range Exercise with male adolescents with mental retardation/developmental disabilities and sexual behavior problems. *Journal of Contemporary Psychotherapy, 33*, 219–234.

Schulenberg, S. E., & Yutrzenka, B. A. (2004). Ethical issues in the use of computerized assessment. *Computers in Human Behavior, 20*, 477–490.

Segal, D. L., & Coolidge, F. L. (2004). Objective assessment of personality and psychopathology: An overview. In M. Hersen, (Editor-in-Chief) & M. J. Hilsenroth, & D. L. Segal (Vol. Eds.), *Comprehensive handbook of psychological assessment: Vol. 2. Personality assessment* (pp. 3–13). Hoboken, NJ: Wiley.

Shaffer, D., Fisher, P., & Lucas, C. (2004). The Diagnostic Interview Schedule for Children (DISC). In M. Hersen, (Editor-in-Chief) & M. J. Hilsenroth, & D. L. Segal (Vol. Eds.), *Comprehensive handbook of psychological assessment: Vol. 2. Personality assessment* (pp. 256–270). Hoboken, NJ: Wiley.

Sharp, W. G., Reeves, C. B., & Gross, A. M. (2006). Behavioral interviewing of parents. In M. Hersen (Ed.), *Clinician's handbook of child behavioral assessment* (pp. 103–124). San Diego, CA: Academic Press.

Sitarenios, G., & Stein, S. (2004). Use of the Children's Depression Inventory. In M. E. Maruish (Ed.), *The use of psychological testing for treatment planning and outcomes assessment: Vol. 2. Instruments for children and adolescents* (3rd ed., pp. 1–37). Mahwah, NJ: Erlbaum.

Snyder, C. R., Ritschel, L. A., Rand, K. L., & Berg, C. J. (2006). Balancing psychological assessments: Including strengths and hope in client reports. *Journal of Clinical Psychology, 62*, 33–46.

Snyder, D. K. (2000). Computer-assisted judgment: Defining strengths and liabilities. *Psychological Assessment, 12*, 52–60.

Stawar, T. L., & Stawar, D. E. (1989). Kinetic Family Drawings and MMPI diagnostic indicators in adolescent psychiatric inpatients. *Psychological Reports, 65*, 143–146.

Steer, R. A., Kumar, G., Beck, J. S., & Beck, A. T. (2001). Evidence for the construct validities of the Beck Youth Inventories with child psychiatric outpatients. *Psychological Reports, 89*, 559–565.

Steffen, L., & Ackerman, M. (1999). Essentials of juvenile assessment. In M. J. Ackerman (Ed.), *Essentials of forensic psychological assessment* (pp. 165–207). Hoboken, NJ: Wiley.

Strack, K. M., Dunaway, M. H., & Schulenberg, S. E. (in press). On the multicultural utility of the 16PF and the CPI-434 in the United States. In L. A. Suzuki, J. G. Ponterotto, & P. J. Meller (Eds.), *Handbook of multicultural assessment* (3rd ed.). San Francisco: Jossey-Bass.

Tringone, R. (2002). Essentials of MACI assessment. In S. Strack (Ed.), *Essentials of Millon inventories assessment* (2nd ed., pp. 106–174). Hoboken, NJ: Wiley.

Tringone, R., Millon, T., & Kamp, J. (2007). Clinical utility of two child-oriented inventories: The Millon Pre-Adolescent Clinical Inventory and the Millon Adolescent Clinical Inventory. In S. R. Smith, & L. Handler (Eds.), *The clinical assessment of children and adolescents: A practitioner's handbook* (pp. 267–287). Mahwah, NJ: Erlbaum.

Tryon, W. W. (1998). *Behavioral observation.* In A. S. Bellack, & M. Hersen (Eds.), *Behavioral assessment: A practical handbook* (4th ed., pp. 79–103). Boston: Allyn & Bacon.

Urbina, S. (2004). *Essentials of psychological testing*. Hoboken, NJ: Wiley.

Watkins, C. E., Campbell, V. L., Nieberding, R., & Hallmark, R. (1995). Contemporary practice of psychological assessment by clinical psychologists. *Professional Psychology: Research and Practice, 26*, 54–60.

Wechsler, D. (2003). *Wechsler Intelligence Scale for Children: Administration and scoring manual* (4th ed.). San Antonio, TX: Psychological Corporation.

Weiner, I. B. (2003). *Principles of Rorschach interpretation* (2nd ed.). Mahwah, NJ: Erlbaum.

Weiner, I. B. (2005). Rorschach assessment: Scientific status and clinical utility. In G. P. Koocher, J. C. Norcross, & S. S. Hill (Eds.), *Psychologists' desk reference* (2nd ed., pp. 173–177). New York: Oxford University Press.

Wiger, D. E., & Huntley, D. K. (2002). *Essentials of interviewing*. Hoboken, NJ: Wiley.

Winsor, A. P. (2003). Direct behavioral observation for classrooms. In C. R. Reynolds, & R. W. Kamphaus (Eds.), *Handbook of psychological and educational assessment of children: Personality, behavior, and context* (2nd ed., pp. 248–255). New York: Guilford Press.

Wood, J. M., Garb, H. N., Lilienfeld, S. O., & Nezworski, M. T. (2002). Clinical assessment. *Annual Review of Psychology, 53*, 519–543.

Wood, J. M., Nezworski, M. T., Lilienfeld, S. O., & Garb, H. N. (2003). *What's wrong with the Rorschach? Science confronts the controversial inkblot test*. San Francisco: Jossey-Bass.

Woodruff-Borden, J., & Leyfer, O. T. (2006). Anxiety and fear. In M. Hersen (Ed.), *Clinician's handbook of child behavioral assessment* (pp. 267–289). San Diego, CA: Academic Press.

CHAPTER 19

Behavioral Assessment

Christopher A. Kearney, L. Caitlin Cook, Adrianna Wechsler, Courtney M. Haight, and Stephanie Stowman

One of the most important approaches to evaluating children and adolescents is behavioral assessment. No single definition of behavioral assessment exists, but the approach is often thought of as a problem-solving-oriented means of gathering information about current, observable behavior and what maintains behavior over time. Behavioral assessment is an idiographic approach involving detailed evaluations of specific behavior to develop a prescriptive treatment plan. A prescriptive treatment plan is one tailored to the individual needs of a given child. Although behavioral assessors derive from different traditions within psychology and other professions, the overarching goal of designing a customized treatment regimen for a particular child has remained largely unchanged over time (Mash & Terdal, 1997).

Behavioral assessment methods focus on *forms* of behavior that can be clearly defined and monitored. Examples include aggression in the form of slapping a classmate and fear in the form of avoiding a large dog. Frequency, duration, intensity, and other topographies of behavior may be assessed as well. Behavioral assessment methods also focus on *functions* of behavior, or antecedents and rewarding consequences that maintain behavior. Examples include teacher attention after slapping a classmate and reduction of unpleasant physical sensations after avoiding a large dog.

Behavioral assessment has been differentiated from global or traditional forms of assessment in several ways (Reitman, 2006). First, behavioral assessment emphasizes current, contextual factors in a child's life that are well defined and observable. Global forms of assessment such as intelligence and personality tests are designed to obtain information about general characteristics of a child such as problem-solving ability or psychological discomfort. In contrast, methods of behavioral assessment are designed to garner information about *molecular* characteristics of a child, such as length of attention when listening to a teacher command and amount of time spent in school.

Second, behavioral assessment emphasizes instability of behavior across settings. Global forms of assessment assume a more trait-like approach to behavior, wherein a child's cardinal characteristics, such as extraversion, will largely determine actions across settings. In contrast, behavioral assessors assume a child's behavior to be more situation-specific. A child may, for example, be relatively gregarious and talkative with family members at home but somewhat inhibited and soft-spoken in peer-based social situations.

Third, behavioral assessment emphasizes multiple samplings of behavior to understand a child's actions. Global forms of assessment such as achievement tests are often given once to obtain information about general characteristics of a child, such as academic status. In contrast, behavioral assessors employ *ongoing* techniques, such as daily logbooks, to examine patterns of actions across settings and over time. In related fashion, behavioral assessment relies less on historical factors and more on present aspects of behavior and commonly involves multiple sources of information.

Fourth, behavioral assessment emphasizes direct, on-site methods such as behavioral observation and self-monitoring to gather information about specific aspects of a child's behavior. Global forms of assessment include more circuitous analyses of a child's behavior, such as a neuropsychological test in an office setting to indirectly assess brain dysfunction. In contrast, behavioral assessors actively evaluate a child's behavior in direct, natural environments such as home, school, playground, and social events.

Finally, behavioral assessment may be more appropriate for children with diverse ethnic backgrounds compared to traditional assessment. Because behavioral assessment emphasizes concrete and proximal influences on behavior, such as learning processes, the process may be freer of cultural bias compared to standardized tests. In addition, behavioral assessment techniques can be quite useful for identifying different behaviors across different cultural contexts (Castillo, Quintana, & Zamarripa, 2000; Suzuki, Alexander, Lin, & Duffy, 2006).

This chapter covers a central model of behavioral assessment, functional analysis, in addition to specific techniques endemic to the model. These techniques include interview, analogue assessment, behavioral observation, rating scales, self-monitoring, sociometric assessment, physiological assessment, and activity measures.

FUNCTIONAL ANALYSIS

A central model of behavioral assessment is functional analysis, defined as examining and manipulating antecedents and consequences of a behavior of interest to provide information about the relationship of these events to the behavior (McComas, Hoch, & Mace, 2000). Functional analysis is often linked to terms such as functional assessment and descriptive and experimental functional analysis. *Functional assessment* is a broader term that refers to developing general hypotheses about the function of problem behavior (Gresham & Lambros, 1998). A clinician addressing a child with temper tantrums in public, for example, might develop a hypothesis that the behavior is driven by attention and tangible rewards from parents. In this case, the child's parents may be inadvertently rewarding the tantrums by quickly attending and providing candy to quash the behavior.

Functional assessment typically consists of descriptive and experimental functional analysis. *Descriptive functional analysis* refers to indirect methods of gaining information about the relationship of a behavior to antecedent and consequent events. Typical methods of assessment in descriptive functional analysis are interviews, rating scales, review of records, self-monitoring, and naturalistic observations. *Experimental functional analysis* refers to direct methods of gaining information about the relationship of a behavior to antecedent and consequent events. Experimental functional analysis involves standardized procedures to identify key maintaining variables of behavior and rule out competing explanations for why behavior continues to occur (Mace, 1994).

Functional analysis has been a key staple for assessing and treating developmental and disruptive behavior disorders in youth. Functional analysis is typically utilized for externalizing problems such as self-injurious behavior, aggression, tantrums, property destruction, and pica (Hanley, Iwata, & McCord, 2003). Functional analysts typically assess maintaining variables of behavior, such as sensory reinforcement, escape from aversive situations, attention, and tangible rewards. However, functional assessment may be broadened to include other contextual variables that trigger and reinforce behavior. Such assessment usually leads to effective treatments; such as training persons with developmental disorders to communicate desires more effectively so maladaptive behavior is not necessary (Durand & Merges, 2001).

Two examples of functional assessment using descriptive and experimental procedures are presented here. Field and colleagues (Field, Nash, Handwerk, & Friman, 2004) evaluated a 12-year-old male with disruptive behavior that included noncompliance and other misbehaviors in a residential group home. Noncompliance was defined as opposition to commands, rules, or stated expectations within the home. Descriptive functional analysis to garner hypotheses about the boy's behavior was conducted via teacher interviews, case file review, behavioral observations, and an interview with the boy. These data led the authors to hypothesize that attention was largely responsible for noncompliance. Specifically, attention typically followed noncompliance, and the boy often escalated noncompliance to force attention from others.

Experimental functional analysis then consisted of a reversal design that alternated two treatments. Standard treatment within the group home, which consisted of token economy and teacher interactions, was compared to modified treatment involving increased positive teacher interactions with the boy. Modified treatment led to a substantial decrease in noncompliance, thus supporting the original hypothesis that the misbehavior was reinforced by attention. In this case, the experimental functional analysis assessment strategy also consisted of effective intervention.

Kearney designed a functional assessment model for school refusal behavior, a behavior with many internalizing components. In this model, youths are thought to refuse school for one or more of several reasons: to avoid school-based stimuli that provoke negative affectivity, to escape aversive social and/or evaluative situations, to pursue attention from significant others, and to pursue tangible rewards outside of school. Descriptive functional analysis consists of a structured diagnostic interview, in-session behavioral observations, and a rating scale (School Refusal Assessment Scale—Revised) that measures relative influence of each of the four hypothesized functions of school refusal behavior (Kearney, 2002, 2006).

Procedures for experimental functional analysis include establishing parameters for a child's school day that best predict attendance and nonattendance (Kearney & Albano, 2007). If a child were suspected of refusing school to escape an aversive evaluative situation, such as tests, then the child's attendance could be evaluated on typical school days and days when the child is exempted from tests. Similarly, if a child were suspected of refusing school for tangible rewards outside of school, then attendance could be compared for typical school days and days when parents provide substantial tangible reinforcement for being in class. A functional assessment approach has been shown to be effective for predicting which prescriptive treatment strategy is best for youths who refuse school for different functions (Chorpita, Albano, Heimberg, & Barlow, 1996; Kearney, Pursell, & Alvarez, 2001; Kearney & Silverman, 1999).

The remaining portion of the chapter focuses on methods of behavioral assessment with children that may be used within a functional analytic model. These methods include interviews, analogue assessment, behavioral observation, rating scales, self-monitoring, sociometric assessment, physiological assessment, and activity measures.

BEHAVIORAL ASSESSMENT MEASURES

Interviews

Interviews with children and parents are the most common form of assessment used by mental health professionals. Although many professionals use unstructured interviews, clinicians and others who emphasize behavioral assessment tend to utilize structured interviews that are psychometrically stronger. In the area of behavioral assessment, structured interviews may be diagnostic or functional in nature. Structured diagnostic interviews are typically linked to *DSM* criteria for mental disorders (American Psychiatric Association, 2000). The interviews are designed to provide detailed information about the form of a child's mental disorder and help an assessor derive a formal diagnosis.

Diagnostic interviewing is discussed in more length in another chapter of this volume, but a brief list of measures is presented here:

- Anxiety Disorders Interview Schedule for DSM-IV: Child and Parent Versions (Silverman & Albano, 1996)
- Child and Adolescent Psychiatric Assessment (Angold & Costello, 2000)
- Child Assessment Schedule (Hodges, McKnew, Cytryn, Stern, & Kline, 1982)
- Children's Interview for Psychiatric Syndromes (Weller, Weller, Fristad, Rooney, & Schecter, 2000)
- Diagnostic Interview for Children and Adolescents (Welner, Reich, Herjanic, Jung, & Amado, 1987)
- Interview Schedule for Children (Kovacs, 1985)
- National Institute of Mental Health Diagnostic Interview for Children (Shaffer et al., 1996)

- Schedule for Affective Disorders and Schizophrenia for School-Age Children: Present and Lifetime Version (Kaufman et al., 1997)

Each of these interviews has demonstrated good reliability and validity. Though most cover externalizing disorders in youth in great detail, less attention has been paid historically to internalizing problems. However, the Anxiety Disorders Interview Schedule for DSM-IV: Child and Parent Versions (ADIS: C/P) has been recognized as the gold standard for assessing anxiety-related disorders in youth. In addition, the interview contains sections for other internalizing disorders, such as depression, as well as sections for externalizing, eating, developmental, and psychotic disorders. A section for school refusal behavior is also available and concentrates on yes/no questions regarding whether a child has problems attending school, whether a child is nervous when attending school, whether a child is upset about performing poorly in school, and whether a child has been medicated for nonattendance.

Structured diagnostic interviews have strengthened the child assessment process and are commonly used to steer treatment and evaluate outcome. Problems with these interviews have been noted, however. First, the interviews provide an overall view of a child's difficulty but may not provide specific information necessary for developing a detailed treatment plan. Second, the interviews are not particularly sensitive to developmental or cultural differences. An older adolescent with Attention-Deficit/Hyperactivity Disorder (ADHD), for example, is likely to present with different symptoms than a younger child with the disorder. In related fashion, a Hispanic child and a European American child may differ with respect to symptoms of Separation Anxiety Disorder. Third, the interviews are not generally designed for ongoing use or for multiple sources of information. A snapshot of a child's behavior is obtained, but behavioral changes that occur over time may not be examined (Kearney, 2005).

Interviews within a behavioral assessment paradigm may also be functional in nature and help address problems of structured diagnostic interviews. These interviews may be unstructured or structured, but more specifically concentrate on operationally defined forms of behavior and what maintains behavior over time. These interviews can be shaped in various ways to accommodate different developmental levels and can provide detailed information to help a clinician form a unique treatment plan.

Behavioral and functional interviews may be given to gather multiple sources of information; a sample excerpt with a parent is presented here. Contrast these questions with the general yes/no questions for the ADIS: C/P:

Therapist: What specifically does Brian do on the playground before school?

Parent: He just won't go into school.

Therapist: Okay, what does he say and do during that time?

Parent: He cries, clings to my leg, and sometimes tries to run away. When the teacher comes out to line everybody up for school, he runs behind me and holds tight.

Therapist: Does he do this every day?

Parent: No, not every day, but I notice it's worse on Mondays and Tuesdays or after a long break from school.

Therapist: How do you and the teacher react when Brian does this? What specifically do you and she do?

Parent: I try to comfort and reassure him as much as possible, giving him a lot of hugs even as the other kids are going into the school. The teacher tells Brian to come into the school but has to deal with the other kids, so she often leaves me and Brian behind.

Therapist: Does the extra attention and reassurance you give Brian help him go to class?

Parent: No, he just clings more and cries and I feel so bad that I just take him home.

Note that these questions are very specific about one episode of school refusal behavior. Questions surround the form of Brian's particular behaviors, when the behaviors occur, and what reinforcer (attention, in this case) might be maintaining the behavior. These kinds of questions can be asked of different people and at various times during the assessment and treatment process. The questions can also be tailored to the developmental level of a child. If Brian were an older child, for example, questions about his cognitions prior to entry into school might be particularly salient.

Behavioral and functional interviews are flexible enough to cover a wide range of material relevant to a particular case, especially the following topics:

- Specific behavioral, cognitive, and physiological aspects of a child's difficulty
- Effects of misbehavior on a child's and family's daily functioning
- Current life stressors
- Contextual or distal variables or risk factors that might influence a child's behavior, such as family dynamics, marital conflict or divorce, poor financial and social support, maltreatment, school-based threats, temperament, and physical and medical status
- Antecedents and consequences pertaining to specific episodes of misbehavior, such as sensory reinforcement, negative reinforcement, attention seeking, and pursuit of tangible rewards
- Child's skill levels in various areas, such as social, verbal, and academic
- Pertinent cultural variables such as language differences, normative behaviors for a particular culture, and perspectives on child misbehavior

Behavioral and functional interviews can be more structured as well. A good example is the Functional Diagnostic Profile modified for youths with selective mutism by Schill and colleagues (Schill, Kratochwill, & Gardner, 1996). The assessment protocol initially consisted of soliciting general information about a particular child with selective mutism to derive hypotheses about the function of the child's behavior. In this case, several hypotheses were formed. The child's mutism was thought to be potentially related to several conditions: (a) escaping aversive requests, directives, or task demands; (b) avoiding attention from unfamiliar others; and (c) deriving attention from familiar others. Following this assessment process, the researchers engaged in analogue assessment to experimentally support these hypotheses and design individualized treatment that eventually led to increased verbalizations. A greater explication of analogue assessment is described next.

Analogue Assessment

Analogue assessment refers to behavioral observations typically conducted in a controlled setting, such as a therapist's office or research laboratory (Barkley, 1991). The observations are often done within a behavioral assessment paradigm to confirm hypotheses about the function of behavior. The premise behind analogue assessment is that a child's behavior in the contrived setting will mirror behavior in the child's natural environment. In the case presented by Schill and colleagues (1996), the child's mutism was explored under several conditions: allowing the child to escape a demand, asking the child to read before others, and providing positive reinforcers for speech such as play and parent praise. The child's responses under this set conditions helped the researchers confirm expectations about what maintained selective mutism.

A popular form of analogue assessment is a *behavioral assessment test* or *behavioral avoidance test,* in which a child role-plays a given situation or performs in some way before others. Behavioral assessment tests are commonly used to evaluate anxiety- and fear-based behavior in children. Among children with Social Phobia, for example, behavioral assessment tests may include conversing with others, writing or solving problems before others, speaking before others, reading a story aloud before others, and taking tests, such as subsections of an intelligence or achievement test (Beidel, 1991; Beidel, Turner, & Morris, 1999).

Behavioral assessment or avoidance tests may be used as well for youths who fear specific stimuli. A test in this situation might involve asking a child to approach a feared animal as close as possible, or spend as much time as possible in school. As a child approaches a feared stimulus, ratings of discomfort may be solicited and distance to the stimulus can be measured. Behavioral assessment or avoidance tests have been used to evaluate youth phobic of dogs, snakes, water, blood, heights, medical procedures, strangers, school-related events, and darkness, among other stimuli (Barrios & Hartmann, 1997).

Behavioral assessment tests have also been used to evaluate externalizing behavior problems in children. Children with ADHD, for example, have been subjected to controlled observations of their behavior in playrooms divided into grids to measure excess movement across the grids. Analogue classrooms with desks have also been used to measure attention problems, out-of-seat behavior, and inappropriate vocalizations. Analogue assessment procedures can help evaluate social skills, aggression, noncompliance, and academic behaviors such as completing worksheets (Barkley, 1991, 1997; Elliot & Gresham, 1991; Gable, Hendrickson, & Sasso, 1995; M. A. Roberts, 1990). Parent-adolescent conflict and interpersonal problem solving may be evaluated in this manner as well (Goldstein, 1999; Robin & Foster, 1989).

Traditional analogue assessments are common but inconsistent methods for evaluating children's behavior. The assessments have several advantages, including control of stimulus conditions, practicality, cost-effectiveness, and evaluation of multiple motor and other behaviors at one time. However, the assessments have variable test-retest reliability and construct validity because they have not been well standardized (Mori & Armendariz, 2001).

An increasingly popular form of analogue assessment among adults is *virtual reality assessment,* which involves placing a person in a digitally created environment that mimics a particular setting and allows for interaction within that setting. A person afraid of heights, for example, may interact in virtual scenes involving progressively higher places. The assessment can thus be conducted quite confidentially, can be manipulated to include many different contexts, and is amenable to examining different response systems at one time. Virtual reality assessment for children remains largely in development, with particular focuses on eating disorders, Social Phobia, ADHD, learning difficulties, and pain (Lannen, Brown, & Powell, 2002; Riva, Wiederhold, & Molinari, 1998; Rizzo et al., 2006).

Behavioral Observation

Analogue assessments are contrived observations often preferred because of their practicality. Direct naturalistic observations, however, represent the purest form of behavioral assessment and functional analysis. Analogue assessments often target a specific area of interest, such as approach toward a feared stimulus, whereas direct naturalistic observations usually involve a much wider range of target behaviors and contextual variables.

Behavioral observations typically concentrate on specific topographies of overt behaviors. The process typically begins by defining a behavior of interest in operational terms. Aggression, for example, may be operationally defined as a slap to the head of a classmate or verbal insult given to a sibling. In related fashion, aspects of a certain behavior may be observed and recorded. Behavior may be recorded with respect to intensity, duration, frequency, and latency. A rater may record the length of time between a teacher's command and a child's compliance. Behavior accuracy, such as number of mistakes on a spelling test, can be assessed as well.

Behavioral observations also include contextual variables or events that surround and influence behavior. Many researchers observe and code valence, which may involve classifying a behavior into positive, negative, neutral, and other categories. In addition, key antecedents and consequences to behavior are commonly observed for purposes of functional analysis. A child who slaps a classmate may do so with an angry facial expression (negative valence) immediately after a frustrating test (antecedent) and prior to a harsh teacher reprimand and attention from classmates (consequences; Watson & Steege, 2003).

Direct observation can involve simple systems of narrative recording as well as more complex research-based observational systems. Narrative recording involves simple written accounts of behavior as it transpires, though more sophisticated accounts may include recording topographies such as frequency and intensity. Raters who are observing and interacting with a child simultaneously may find it difficult to maintain an ongoing log of transpired behavior, so interval recording is common. In this system, a rater may simply record the presence or absence of a behavior in blocks of time, such as every 20 seconds or 5 minutes (Skinner, Rhymer, & McDaniel, 2000).

Behavioral observations in research settings typically involve greater complexity. Many have been designed to evaluate youths with disruptive behavior disorders because of the overt nature of problems such as noncompliance. Some of these observational systems are highly contrived and qualify more as analogue assessments. These often involve analyses of free play, parent-directed play, and parent-directed chores (M. W. Roberts, 2001). Research-based observation systems for more naturally occurring behavioral phenomena have also been designed, however. These most prominently include systems for evaluating children's social and coping skills, play, and parent-adolescent communications (Anderson, Moore, Godfrey, & Fletcher-Flinn, 2004; Margolin et al., 1998; Pellegrini, 2001; Pretzlik & Sylva, 1999).

Whether simple or more complex behavioral observations are used, a key goal is to derive interrater reliability or consistency of ratings across two or more observers. At a basic level, interrater reliability can be calculated as the number of agreements divided by the number of agreements plus the number of disagreements times 100. Thus, 12 agreements and 3 disagreements would result in interrater reliability of 80%. At more complex levels, interrater reliability can be calculated in several ways, though a predominant way is Cohen's kappa.

Direct observations of behavior carry several strong advantages. Observations can supply a plethora of data regarding forms and functions of behavior and are often essential components of a detailed assessment plan for complex behaviors. In addition, observations in natural settings have high external validity. Observations can supply data about the molecular characteristics of a given behavior, such as a child's problem-solving method when completing a math worksheet or subtle changes in tone during parent-adolescent communications. Knowledge about these molecular characteristics is often invaluable for designing an individualized treatment plan.

A primary disadvantage to behavioral observation is that covert or low-frequency behaviors are not amenable to the process. Behavioral observation is not particularly useful for assessing internal mood states, visceral responses, or secretive behaviors. In addition, behavioral observations are subject to reactivity and other demand characteristics that could bias the assessment process. Observer drift, where raters deviate from the original operational definition of a targeted behavior, can reduce validity of the process as well. Finally, behavioral observations require substantial time, effort, training, and, ideally, multiple raters. As such, observations are not as practical or cost-effective as rating scales, which are described next.

Rating Scales

A particularly well-developed area of behavioral assessment for children is rating scales. *Rating scales* or questionnaires are instruments wherein children and significant others endorse the presence or absence of various physiological, cognitive, and behavioral symptoms. Rating scales have several strong advantages, including ease of use, good reliability and validity, excellent coverage of many topics, sensitivity to treatment effects, standardization, and extension to multiple sources of information, such as parents and teachers. In addition, rating scales are good for assessing low-frequency behavior and behavior not amenable to direct observation, such as internalizing constructs of worry or sadness.

Rating scales also have several disadvantages, however. A key problem is rater bias, especially among parents and teachers, who may rate a child more negatively or positively than is actually the case. Measurement error is endemic to rating scales as well, and can come from variance in behavior across time as well as variable rater, setting, and instrument characteristics. In addition, rating scales have poor applicability to very young children and correlate inconsistently with real-life behavior. Developmental differences between children and adolescents are often not fully considered. Finally, rating scales provide summaries of perceptions of behavior rather than direct measures of actual behavior (Merrell, 2000; Myers & Winters, 2002a).

A full explication of all rating scales in all areas of child functioning is beyond the scope of this chapter, but a summary is presented here of the major rating scales available for children, parents, and teachers. Measures were chosen based on their psychometric strength, widespread use in the field, and applicability to designing an individualized treatment plan for a child. In addition, only the most prevalent areas of mental disorder among children and adolescents are covered here: anxiety, depression, ADHD and other disruptive behavior disorders, and developmental disorders. Primary measures in other areas are listed as well.

Anxiety Disorders

Anxiety disorders are the most common mental disorders in children, and research into the assessment and treatment of these problems has burgeoned in the past 2 decades. Because anxiety is largely an internalizing problem, the development and use of rating scales has become widespread in this area. Developers of anxiety rating scales must naturally contend with a phenomenon that changes quickly over time, but several scales appear to have excellent psychometric strength (Kearney & Bensaheb, 2007; Myers & Winters, 2002b).

Rating scales for anxiety disorders may be divided into traditional measures that assess broad swaths of anxiety and more recent measures that specifically target more narrow types of anxiety. Traditional child self-report measures include the Revised Children's Manifest Anxiety Scale (RCMAS), State-Trait Anxiety Inventory for Children (STAIC), and Fear Survey Schedule for Children—Revised (FSSC-R). The RCMAS measures physiological anxiety symptoms, worry and oversensitivity, and fear and concentration. The STAI-C assesses situation-specific and global anxiety. The FSSC-R contains subscales for fear of failure and criticism, injury and small animals, danger and death, medical topics, and a category of unknown fears (Ollendick, 1983; C. Reynolds & Richmond, 1985; Spielberger, 1973). Recent measures of general anxiety constructs include the Multidimensional Anxiety Scale for Children, which measures social anxiety, separation anxiety and panic, physical anxiety, and harm avoidance, and the Screen for Child Anxiety Related Emotional Disorders, which measures somatic and panic symptoms, general and separation anxiety, and school and social phobias (Birmaher et al., 1999; March, 1997).

Though useful, traditional measures of anxiety are gradually becoming replaced by more specific measures that cover particular aspects of anxiety. With respect to social anxiety, for example, the Social Anxiety Scale for Children—Revised (SASC-R) and Social Phobia Anxiety Inventory for Children (SPAI-C) are most common (Beidel, Turner, & Morris, 1995; La Greca & Stone, 1993). These measures cover fear of negative evaluation and social avoidance and distress (SASC-R) as well as assertiveness and concerns about social encounters and public performance (SPAI-C).

With respect to Obsessive-Compulsive Disorder, the Leyton Obsessional Inventory—Child Version is a brief rating scale for compulsions, obsessions and incompleteness, and cleanliness (Bamber, Tamplin, Park, Kyte, & Goodyer, 2002). Finally, the Trauma Symptom Checklist for Children is useful for measuring children's reactions to trauma and the Child PTSD Symptom Scale is useful for measuring criteria necessary for a diagnosis of Posttraumatic Stress Disorder (Briere, 1996; Foa, Johnson, Feeny, & Treadwell, 2001).

Depression

Depression is a highly prevalent disorder among youth in general and adolescents in particular. The most robust and common child self-report measure of depression is the Children's Depression Inventory (CDI), which purportedly measures symptoms of negative mood, interpersonal problems, ineffectiveness, anhedonia, and negative self-esteem (Kovacs, 1992). Factor analysis of the measure, however, has yielded constructs for dysphoria-sadness, social self-esteem, and oppositional-misbehavior (D. Cole, Hoffman, Tram, & Maxwell, 2000). The CDI has been used extensively to assess youths with depression, to distinguish depressed youths from other populations, and to examine developmental, psychological, and ethnic differences in children and adolescents. Another common child self-report measure of depression is the Reynolds Child (and Adolescent) Depression Scales, which are based on *DSM* criteria (W. Reynolds & Mazza, 1998).

Internalizing problems of childhood, which include anxiety and depression, can also be measured via parent and teacher ratings. The most common measures for doing so are the Child Behavior Checklist (CBCL), Teacher Report Form (TRF), Conners Rating Scales—Revised (CRS-R), and Child Symptom Inventory 4 (CSI-4; Achenbach & Rescorla, 2001; Conners, 1997; Sprafkin, Gadow, Salisbury, Schneider, & Loney, 2002). The CBCL and TRF have an Anxious/Depressed subscale. The CRS-R has subscales for Anxious-Shy and Perfectionism, and the CSI-4 has subscales related to generalized, separation, and social anxiety.

Attention-Deficit/Hyperactivity Disorder

In contrast to anxiety and depressive problems, externalizing problems of childhood are more commonly rated by parents and teachers. A popular rating scale for

ADHD is the ADHD Rating Scale IV, which measures symptoms of hyperactivity-impulsivity and inattention in home and school settings. The scale is linked to *DSM-IV* criteria and can successfully distinguish youths with and without ADHD (DuPaul, Power, Anastopoulos, & Reid, 1998). Related measures include the ADHD Symptoms Rating Scale and Attention Deficit Disorders Evaluation Scale, second edition (Holland, Gimpel, & Merrell, 2001; McCarney, 1995). In addition, the Strengths and Weaknesses of ADHD Symptoms and Normal Behavior has been designed as a dimensional measure of ADHD symptoms. Items are presented in Likert-scale format so raters can judge the strength of certain symptoms such as inattention (Collett, Ohan, & Myers, 2003).

General rating scales such as the CBCL, TRF, and CRS-R are also commonly used to assess symptoms of ADHD. The CBCL and TRF have a subscale for Attention Problems, and the CRS-R has several ADHD subscales for Cognitive Problems/Inattention, Hyperactivity, and an ADHD index. The CSI-4 is useful for examining symptoms of ADHD across settings. The Conners ADHD/DSM-IV Scales may also be used to assess more specific symptoms of ADHD, such as trouble concentrating and difficulty playing quietly (Conners, 1999). Finally, the Behavior Assessment System for Children, second edition (BASC-2) allows for parent and teacher ratings of many different behaviors from the preschool period to adolescence. Relevant subscales regarding ADHD include Attention Problems and Hyperactivity (C. Reynolds & Kamphaus, 1998).

Other Disruptive Behavior Disorders

General scales for ADHD also contain subscales relevant to other disruptive behavior disorders such as Oppositional Defiant and Conduct Disorder. The CBCL and TRF contain subscales for Rule-breaking and Aggressive Behavior, the CRS-R contains an Oppositional subscale, the CSI-4 contains subscales for Oppositional Defiant and Conduct Disorder, and the BASC-2 contains subscales for Aggression and Conduct Problems.

Measures more specifically designed for oppositional and conduct problems have also been developed. The Eyberg Child Behavior Inventory (parent) and Sutter-Eyberg Student Behavior Inventory—Revised (teacher) evaluate the number of difficult behavior problems and the frequency with which they occur (Eyberg & Pincus, 1999). The ACQ Behavior Checklist is an amalgam of items from the CBCL, Conners parent scale, and Quay-Peterson Revised Behavior Problem Checklist that assesses aggressive and delinquent behavior (Achenbach, Howell, Quay, & Conners, 1991; Quay & Peterson, 1996). Finally, the Conduct Disorder Scale contains ratings and yes/no questions regarding key aspects of oppositional and conduct problems such as argumentativeness and cruelty to others (Gilliam, 2002).

Developmental Disorders

Rating scales for developmental disorders such as autism and mental retardation have also been widely developed in recent years. These scales are typically completed by clinicians or teachers. A popular one for autism is the Childhood Autism Rating Scale, which solicits ratings for difficulty relating to people, odd body movements, intense reactions to change, and verbal and nonverbal communication (Schopler, Reichler, & Renner, 1988). In addition, the Autism Screening Instrument for Educational Planning 2 (ASIEP-2) assesses for sensory, relating, body concept, language, and social self-help behaviors. The Autism Behavior Checklist is part of the ASIEP-2 and can be completed by parents and teachers (Krug, Arick, & Almond, 1995). Other prominent measures include the Gilliam Asperger's Disorder Scale, Gilliam Autism Rating Scale, second edition, and the Social Communication Questionnaire (Gilliam, 2001, 2006; Rutter, Bailey, & Lord, 2003).

Clinician-administered rating scales are commonly used to assess adaptive behavior in youths with mental retardation. A predominant measure is the Vineland Adaptive Behavior Scales, second edition, which assesses communication, daily living skills, socialization, motor skills, and maladaptive behavior (Sparrow, Cicchetti, & Balla, 2005). In addition, the American Association on Mental Retardation's AAMR Adaptive Behavior Scale—School (second edition) includes domains of independent functioning, physical development, economic activity, language development, prevocational and vocational activity, numbers and time, self-direction, responsibility, socialization, and maladaptive behavior (Nihira, Leland, & Lambert, 1993). Other prominent measures in this area include the Adaptive Behavior Assessment System (second edition) and Scales of Independent Behavior—Revised (Bruininks, Woodcock, Weatherman, & Hill, 1996; Harrison & Oakland, 2003).

Other Disorders

A full explication of all rating scales for all other disorders and problems that apply to children and adolescents is beyond the scope of this chapter, but some prominent ones are listed here:

- Adolescent Substance Abuse Screening Inventory (Miller, 2001)
- Dyslexia Screening Instrument (Coon, Waguespack, & Polk, 1994)
- Eating Attitudes Test (Foreyt & Mikhail, 1997)
- Pediatric Pain Questionnaire (Varni, Thompson, & Hanson, 1987)
- Scales of Social Competence and School Adjustment (Walker & McConnell, 1995)

Self-Monitoring

Self-monitoring refers to observing and recording one's own behavior as well as antecedents and consequences to the behavior. At a basic level, self-monitoring involves asking a child to record whether a specific behavior occurred or did not occur during a certain time period. A child may, for example, record whether he or she fully completed homework during a prescribed evening time. Or a child may record the number of hours spent in school per day. In addition, a child may record events just prior to and following a behavior, such as parent prompts to do homework and playing with friends after school. Recordings are typically done in paper-and-pencil fashion but can be done via self-analysis of audiotaping or videotaping.

Self-monitoring is utilized within a behavioral assessment paradigm for several reasons. First, self-monitoring is intricately linked to self-regulation, as people more aware of their own behavior often become better at controlling the behavior. This is especially true of excess maladaptive behavior; the more one self-monitors and becomes aware of excess maladaptive behavior, the less one tends to engage in the behavior. Self-monitoring is often linked to self-regulation processes of goal setting, self-evaluation, and self-reinforcement to reduce maladaptive behavior (Agran & Wehmeyer, 2006).

A salient example is habit reversal training to treat Trichotillomania (compulsive hair pulling) in children. One component of habit reversal training for this population is awareness training in which a child is instructed to increase attention toward subtle movements that eventually lead to hair pulling. Awareness training may be supplemented with self-monitoring and other behavioral assessment measures to modify behavior associated with less conscious thought (Azrin, Nunn, & Frantz, 1980; Romaniuk, Miltenberger, & Deaver, 2003).

Second, self-monitoring is important for educating youths about a targeted behavior. For example, psychoeducation for anxious children includes a detailed explication of the three response systems of anxiety: physiological, cognitive, and behavioral. A clinician treating an anxious child may ask him or her to provide daily ratings of physiological distress as well as lists of problematic thoughts and avoided situations. These personal examples are then used to explain how one anxiety response system leads to another. In one case, for example, a child's aversive physiological symptoms may lead to worry about harm from the symptoms and subsequent avoidance of a certain situation (Kearney & Albano, 2007).

Third, self-monitoring is important for assessing treatment outcome. Global measures of behavior are not particularly sensitive to treatment changes over time, but measures such as daily ratings of distress, hours spent in school, frequency of aggressive acts, and words spoken audibly can provide much more information about patterns of behavior change across time (Kearney & Silverman, 1999). Finally, self-monitoring may be useful for assessing secretive behaviors and helps alleviate pressure on others, such as teachers, to supply data for behavioral analysis.

Basic self-monitoring, such as recording the presence or absence of a behavior, may be more appropriate for younger children, those with a singular, primary behavior problem, and those who need initial training in how to self-monitor behavior. More sophisticated self-monitoring strategies can involve recording multiple behaviors, providing ratings of severity and intensity of the behaviors, and rating internal sensations or mood states. Children and adolescents are generally considered to be the best reporters of their own internal mood states, so self-monitoring is particularly relevant to youths with anxiety and depressive disorders. However, self-monitoring has also been used to assess aggression, socially appropriate behavior, and academic tasks such as paying attention, staying seated, and completing work problems accurately (C. Cole, Marder, & McCann, 2000).

Formal methods of self-monitoring have been developed for anxious children (Beidel, Neal, & Lederer, 1991). These methods involve daily diaries in which children list anxiety-provoking situations, time and setting of the situations, and responses to the situations. Children may also be asked to endorse an illustration that best represents how they felt in a given situation and to rate their level of avoidance, physical symptoms, and coping skills. Daily diaries such as these have adequate reliability, but a key problem is that children are not typically compliant with the task, nor do they tend to engage in the task for more than 2 weeks (Beidel et al., 1999). In addition, the quality and accuracy of self-monitoring data may be questionable given children's limited cognitive development, distractibility, and lack of cooperation.

To address these concerns, clinicians should carefully tailor self-monitoring to the individual needs of a given child, simplify the procedure as much as possible, provide detailed training on how to engage in self-monitoring, link incentives and negative consequences to compliance and noncompliance, and ask parents and others to closely supervise self-monitoring without unduly influencing a child's responses. In addition, child self-monitoring may be supplemented with reports from informed others such as parents and teachers to assess accuracy (C. Cole et al., 2000).

Sociometric Assessment

Sociometric assessment refers to measures of children's social relationships and standing among peers. Sociometric assessment is important for identifying children with poor social competence who may be at risk for emotional, behavioral, and academic problems. This assessment approach is also used to identify children with exceptional social skills and who have particularly good social standing within a peer group. In many cases, sociometric assessment is conducted in school settings such as classrooms or play areas. Procedures for sociometric assessment include peer nominations, rating scales, and rankings.

Peer nominations typically involve asking children to privately identify or sort peers or classmates along certain dimensions. In many cases, a simple listing is provided of names of children a child most and least likes to play with. Although younger children are often asked to nominate three classmates for a given question, older children and adolescents may provide longer lists. Peer nominations are usually scored by dividing the total number of nominations by the total number of raters.

From Chan and Mpofu (2001), the following questions are often asked as part of a peer nomination sociometric procedure:

- What three classmates do you like the best?
- What three classmates do you like the least?
- Which three people do you admire most in your class?
- Which three people do you respect most among your classmates?
- What three people would you wish to be like in your class?
- Which of your classmates try hard and get good grades?
- Which of your classmates do not try hard and get poor grades?
- Which of your classmates get angry much of the time?
- Which of your classmates is most cooperative?

- Which of your classmates is a good leader?
- Which of your classmates start fights or become disruptive in class?

Peer nominations have been used to classify children into social groups. Children who receive many positive peer nominations tend to be popular or socially accepted, and those who receive many negative peer nominations tend to be rejected. Neglected or isolated students generally receive no peer nominations of any sort, though controversial students are linked to many positive and negative peer nominations (Elksnin & Elksnin, 1997; Terry & Coie, 1991). In addition, peer nominations may be helpful for identifying children with Social Phobia who engage in avoidant self-isolation (Kearney, 2005).

Peer nominations have several advantages, including ease of use, portability, and linkage to social groupings that have good psychometric stability. Peer nominations also have disadvantages, however. First, only those children actually nominated by peers are available for analysis. As such, some students may be mistakenly classified as isolated and a full examination of a classroom's social dynamics may be impaired. Second, peer nominations may work less well in racially diverse classrooms where student groups may not readily interact (Chan & Mpofu, 2001).

An alternative to peer nominations is peer ratings, in which all children in a classroom or social setting rate all other peers in that setting. Ratings may be linked to the questions listed earlier for peer nominations, such as rating a particular child on a 1 to 5 Likert-type scale where 1 = not at all liked and 5 = very much liked. Ratings can also be obtained for traits such as cheerfulness, humorousness, and disruptiveness. In many cases, children are presented with a grid that lists names of relevant peers as well as spaces for ratings. Peer ratings are then averaged for each child. Peer sociometric ratings can also be supplemented by teacher ratings (Hintze, Stoner, & Bull, 2000).

A key advantage of peer ratings over peer nominations is that data for all children in a particular setting may be obtained. In addition, ratings are more amenable to psychometric analysis and have been shown to be reliable and valid measures. The dimensional aspect of peer ratings allows for a better way of assessing social acceptance of a particular child. A downside of peer ratings is they may be less useful than nominations for categorizing a child's social status. Also, younger children may have difficulty understanding a rating system; in this case, peer nominations and ratings may be integrated, or a simpler rating scale may be used (Chan & Mpofu, 2001).

Sociometric assessment also includes rankings whereby all children are ranked by all other children in a particular social setting. In this way, all children are included in the assessment process and ratings are unnecessary. Rankings may come from teachers and other knowledgeable adults as well. Rankings may involve comparison to a standard for a particular characteristic, such as likeability, or comparison against all other peers. Rankings could also be made for each possible peer pair, such as student A, B, C, and so on versus all other students. Unfortunately, rankings require substantial effort on the part of a clinician and raters, and so are rarely used except in conjunction with other sociometric techniques (Mpofu, Carney, & Lambert, 2006).

Physiological Assessment

Physiological assessment, sometimes referred to as *psychophysiological assessment,* includes measures designed to directly evaluate the relationship between physiological processes and thoughts, emotions, and behavior. Physiological assessment concentrates on motor and visceral responses that underscore higher order cognitive processes and behavior to increase the psychometric strength of other forms of behavioral assessment. Physiological assessment with children remains less well-developed than other forms of behavioral assessment, especially with respect to traditional measures such as electrocardiogram for changes in heart rate and electroencephalogram for changes in brain wave activity. With newer techniques such as functional magnetic resonance imaging, however, physiological assessment is rapidly becoming a dominant force.

Traditional physiological assessment primarily includes heart rate, blood pressure, and measures of skin conductance and resistance, perspiration, and muscle tension. Heart rate, blood pressure, and vasomotor activity (constriction and dilation of blood vessels) have been commonly measured via electrocardiogram, a device that records electrical activity of the heart. However, simple pulse rate and systolic/diastolic values are often obtained without formal use of an electrocardiogram (Chakrabarti & Stuart, 2005; King, 1994).

Skin conductance and resistance are measured via electrodermal devices; electrodes are placed on a person's palm, middle and index fingers, or wrist and forearm. An electrical signal is introduced and the device measures the length of time necessary for the signal to travel from one electrode to another. Greater conductance or less resistance to the signal generally indicates greater autonomic arousal. In related fashion, perspiration may be measured by the number of active sweat glands in a certain skin area, often the palm (palmar sweat index), by means of a plastic impression method. Muscle tension is typically assessed via electromyogram, a device that measures muscle contraction and atonia (Kohler & Schuschel, 1994; Latzman, Knutson, & Fowles, 2006; Tedroff, Knutson, & Soderberg, 2006).

These traditional physiological measures have been prominently used to study children with anxiety disorders, with variable results. Children with anxiety disorders generally show increased heart rate, perspiration, and muscle tension. However, these increases are not consistently found, nor are they always maintained over time (Beidel, 1991; Schniering, Hudson, & Rapee, 2000; Turner, Beidel, & Epstein, 1991). With respect to externalizing behavior problems, low resting and task-related electrodermal activity has been associated with psychopathy and conduct problems. Low resting heart rate and high heart rate reactivity have been associated with aggression and conduct problems (Lorber, 2004).

These traditional forms of physiological assessment are gradually giving way to more advanced techniques. These include electroencephalograph, computerized axial tomography, magnetic resonance imaging, functional magnetic resonance imaging, and positron emission tomography. The electroencephalograph traditionally involved multiple electrodes placed on a person's head to measure brain wave activity and evoked response potentials, but more contemporary devices involve elaborate and less intrusive head covers that contain high-density electrodes. Brain wave measurement has been particularly salient with respect to child sleep problems, learning disorders, ADHD, and seizure disorder (Collins & Rourke, 2003; Kuntsi, McLoughlin, & Asherson, 2006; Tay et al., 2006).

Neuroimaging methods now produce computer-generated pictures of specific brain sections. Computerized axial tomography is used to assess structural abnormalities of the brain such as tumors or enlarged ventricles potentially related to mental disorder. Iodine is injected and brain tissue density is assessed by detecting the amount of radioactivity from X-rays that penetrate the tissue. Magnetic resonance imaging produces higher quality brain images without radiation by having a person lie in a large cylindrical magnet as radio waves are beamed through the magnetic field. Functional magnetic resonance imaging is a more advanced technique, whereby brain images are taken rapidly to assess metabolic changes in the brain.

Positron emission tomography is an invasive procedure whereby radioactive molecules are injected into the bloodstream and emit positrons that collide with electrons. The resulting light particles emitted from the skull are utilized by a computer to construct a full image of the brain. Neuroimaging techniques have received greater attention in the child literature, particularly with respect to major problems such as traumatic brain injury, Schizophrenia, autism, mood disorders, ADHD, and learning disorders (Ernst & Rumsey, 2000).

Physiological assessment with children may also include biochemical assessment, such as analysis of metabolites for neurotransmitters or toxicology examinations. Although much basic information about child behavior may be obtained from physiological assessment, key disadvantages include its prohibitive cost and need for technical expertise. In addition, physiological assessment has long been criticized for providing information not particularly useful for developing an individualized treatment plan. An exception may be biofeedback, where children are provided feedback regarding internal responses and trained to regulate them to help reduce problems such as hyperventilation and accelerated heart rate (Hirshberg, Chiu, & Frazier, 2005).

Other Areas

Behavioral assessment for children can consist of other measures as well. Children's activity levels, for example, can be measured via behavioral observation or rating scales, but objective *activity measures* include the following:

- Pedometer, a device that records steps taken while walking
- Accelerometer, an electronic device that measures accelerations produced by body movement
- Actometer, a modified watch that records frequency of movement

These measures are commonly used to assess youths with ADHD but can also be useful for evaluating inactivity from a developmental disorder or sedentary lifestyle (Rapport, Kofler, & Himmerich, 2006; Sirard & Pate, 2001).

Behavioral assessment can also include review of archival or record data. Case history files, academic and school attendance records, medical and psychiatric reports, completed written or oral schoolwork, report cards, and audiotapes and videotapes can be useful sources of information. A particularly innovative use of archival data has involved analysis of home movies of youngsters very early in life to identify emerging patterns of developmental disorders such as autism (Werner & Dawson, 2005).

Behavioral assessment also includes methods of evaluating cognitions more specifically than the rating scales described earlier. *Thought listing,* for example, requires a child to maintain a written log of thoughts before, during, and after a critical event such as an oral presentation. Thought listing may be done in naturalistic settings such as a classroom, but many children have difficulty identifying or listing their thoughts in these situations. In research settings, therefore, thought listing is sometimes utilized as part of a behavioral assessment test where a child engages in a task while videotaped. The clinician and child can then review the videotape and the child can recall various cognitions during certain segments (Kendall & Chansky, 1991; Spence, Donovan, & Brechman-Toussaint, 1999).

An alternative method is a *think-aloud procedure,* in which a child is asked to verbalize thoughts and emotions before, during, and after a behavioral assessment test. Solicited thoughts and emotions can then be categorized with respect to content and valence, such as positive, negative, or neutral. Unfortunately, this procedure is highly subject to reactivity and the information received may not be useful for developing a treatment plan. As such, researchers have modified the think-aloud procedure to focus on simple ratings of distress or perceived threat as well as open-ended questions about a child's cognitions, the responses from which are then coded (Bogels & Zigterman, 2000; Chansky & Kendall, 1997).

SUMMARY

Behavioral assessment is a problem-solving-oriented means of gathering information about current, observable behavior and what maintains that behavior over time. Methods of behavioral assessment include interviews, analogue assessments, behavioral observation, rating scales, self-monitoring, sociometric assessment, physiological assessment, and activity and other measures. A central model of behavioral assessment is functional analysis, or examining and manipulating antecedents and consequences of a behavior to provide information about the relationship of these events to the behavior. Methods of behavioral assessment emphasize molecular aspects of behavior, situation-specific behavior, and ongoing sampling of overt and current behavior in multiple contexts and from multiple sources of information. Behavioral assessment is thus a key aspect of evaluating children with myriad behavior problems and mental disorders.

REFERENCES

Achenbach, T. M., Howell, C. T., Quay, H. C., & Conners, C. K. (1991). National survey of problems and competencies among 4- to 16-year-olds. *Monographs of the Society for Research in Child Development, 56*(3, Serial No. 225).

Achenbach, T. M., & Rescorla, L. A. (2001). *Manual for the ASEBA school-age forms and profiles.* Burlington: University of Vermont Research Center for Children, Youth, and Families.

Agran, M., & Wehmeyer, M. L. (2006). Child self-regulation. In M. Hersen (Ed.), *Clinician's handbook of child behavioral assessment* (pp. 181–199). New York: Elsevier.

American Psychiatric Association. (2000). *Diagnostic and statistical manual of mental disorders* (4th ed., text rev.). Washington, DC: Author.

Anderson, A., Moore, D. W., Godfrey, R., & Fletcher-Flinn, C. M. (2004). Social skills assessment of children with autism in free-play situations. *Autism, 8*, 369–385.

Angold, A., & Costello, E. J. (2000). The Child and Adolescent Psychiatric Assessment (CAPA). *Journal of the American Academy of Child and Adolescent Psychiatry, 39*, 39–48.

Azrin, N. H., Nunn, R. G., & Frantz, S. E. (1980). Treatment of hairpulling (trichotillomania): A comparative study of habit reversal and negative practice training. *Journal of Behavior Therapy and Experimental Psychiatry, 11*, 13–20.

Bamber, D., Tamplin, A., Park, R. J., Kyte, Z. A., & Goodyer, I. M. (2002). Development of a short Leyton Obsessional Inventory for children and adolescents. *Journal of the American Academy of Child and Adolescent Psychiatry, 41*, 1246–1252.

Barkley, R. A. (1991). The ecological validity of laboratory and analogue assessment methods of ADHD symptoms. *Journal of Abnormal Child Psychology, 19*, 149–178.

Barkley, R. A. (1997). *Defiant children: A clinician's manual for assessment and parent training* (2nd ed.). New York: Guilford Press.

Barrios, B. A., & Hartmann, D. P. (1997). Fears and anxieties. In E. J. Mash, & L. G. Terdal (Eds.), *Assessment of childhood disorders* (3rd ed., pp. 230–327). New York: Guilford Press.

Beidel, D. C. (1991). Social phobia and overanxious disorder in school age children. *Journal of the American Academy of Child and Adolescent Psychiatry, 30*, 545–552.

Beidel, D. C., Neal, A. M., & Lederer, A. S. (1991). The feasibility and validity of a daily diary for the assessment of anxiety in children. *Behavior Therapy, 22*, 505–517.

Beidel, D. C., Turner, S. M., & Morris, T. L. (1995). A new inventory to assess childhood social anxiety and phobia: The Social Phobia and Anxiety Inventory for Children. *Psychological Assessment, 7*, 73–79.

Beidel, D. C., Turner, S. M., & Morris, T. L. (1999). Psychopathology of childhood social phobia. *Journal of the American Academy of Child and Adolescent Psychiatry, 38*, 643–650.

Birmaher, B., Brent, D. A., Chiappetta, L., Bridge, J., Monga, S., & Baugher, M. (1999). Psychometric properties of the Screen for Child Anxiety Related Emotional Disorders (SCARED): A replication study. *Journal of the American Academy of Child and Adolescent Psychiatry, 38*, 1230–1236.

Bogels, S. M., & Zigterman, D. (2000). Dysfunctional cognitions in children with social phobia, separation anxiety disorder, and generalized anxiety disorder. *Journal of Abnormal Child Psychology, 28*, 205–211.

Briere, J. (1996). *Trauma Symptom Checklist for Children (TSCC): Professional manual.* Lutz, FL: Psychological Assessment Resources.

Bruininks, R. H., Woodcock, R. W., Weatherman, R. F., & Hill, B. K. (1996). *Scales of Independent Behavior—Revised.* Itasca, IL: Riverside.

Castillo, E. M., Quintana, S. M., & Zamarripa, M. X. (2000). Cultural and linguistic issues. In E. S. Shapiro, & T. R. Kratochwill (Eds.), *Conducting school-based assessments of child and adolescent behavior* (pp. 274–308). New York: Guilford Press.

Chakrabarti, S., & Stuart, A. G. (2005). Understanding cardiac arrhythmias. *Archives of Disease in Childhood, 90*, 1086–1090.

Chan, S.-Y., & Mpofu, E. (2001). Children's peer status in school settings: Current and prospective assessment procedures. *School Psychology International, 22*, 43–52.

Chansky, T. E., & Kendall, P. C. (1997). Social expectancies and self-perceptions in anxiety-disordered children. *Journal of Anxiety Disorders, 11*, 347–363.

Chorpita, B. F., Albano, A. M., Heimberg, R. G., & Barlow, D. H. (1996). A systematic replication of the prescriptive treatment of school refusal behavior in a single subject. *Journal of Behavior Therapy and Experimental Psychiatry, 27*, 281–290.

Cole, C. L., Marder, T., & McCann, L. (2000). Self-monitoring. In E. S. Shapiro, & T. R. Kratochwill (Eds.), *Conducting school-based assessments of child and adolescent behavior* (pp. 121–149). New York: Guilford Press.

Cole, D. A., Hoffman, K., Tram, J. M., & Maxwell, S. E. (2000). Structural differences in parent and child reports of children's symptoms of depression and anxiety. *Psychological Assessment, 12*, 174–185.

Collett, B. R., Ohan, J. L., & Myers, K. M. (2003). Ten-year review of rating scales: Pt. V. Scales assessing attention-deficit hyperactivity disorder. *Journal of the American Academy of Child and Adolescent Psychiatry, 42*, 1015–1037.

Collins, D. W., & Rourke, B. P. (2003). Learning-disabled brains: A review of the literature. *Journal of Clinical and Experimental Neuropsychology, 25*, 1011–1034.

Conners, C. K. (1997). *Conners Rating Scales—Revised*. North Tonawanda, NY: Multi-Health Systems.

Conners, C. K. (1999). *Conners ADHD/DSM-IV Scales*. North Tonawanda, NY: Multi-Health Systems.

Coon, K. B., Waguespack, M. M., & Polk, M. J. (1994). *Dyslexia screening instrument*. San Antonio, TX: Psychological Corporation.

DuPaul, G. J., Power, T. J., Anastopoulos, A. D., & Reid, R. (1998). *ADHD Rating Scale-IV: Checklists, norms, and clinical interpretation*. New York: Guilford Press.

Durand, V. M., & Merges, E. (2001). Functional communication training: A contemporary behavior analytic intervention for problem behaviors. *Focus on Autism and Other Developmental Disabilities, 16*, 110–119.

Elksnin, L. K., & Elksnin, N. (1997). Issues in the assessment of children's social skills. *Diagnostique, 22*, 75–86.

Elliot, S. N., & Gresham, F. M. (1991). *Social skills intervention guide: Practical strategies for social skills training*. Circle Pines, MN: American Guidance Services.

Ernst, M., & Rumsey, J. M. (Eds.). (2000). *Functional imaging in child psychiatry*. Cambridge: Cambridge University Press.

Eyberg, S. M., & Pincus, D. (1999). *Eyberg Child Behavior Inventory and Sutter-Eyberg Behavior Inventory—Revised: Professional manual*. Odessa, FL: Psychological Assessment Resources.

Field, C. E., Nash, H. M., Handwerk, M. L., & Friman, P. C. (2004). Using functional assessment and experimental functional analysis to individualize treatment for adolescents in a residential care setting. *Clinical Case Studies, 3*, 25–36.

Foa, E. B., Johnson, K. M., Feeny, N. C., & Treadwell, K. R. H. (2001). The Child PTSD Symptom Scale: A preliminary examination of its psychometric properties. *Journal of Clinical Child Psychology, 30*, 376–384.

Foreyt, J. P., & Mikhail, C. (1997). Anorexia nervosa and bulimia nervosa. In E. J. Mash, & L. G. Terdal (Eds.), *Assessment of childhood disorders* (3rd ed., pp. 683–716). New York: Guilford Press.

Gable, R. A., Hendrickson, J. M., & Sasso, G. M. (1995). Toward a more functional analysis of aggression. *Education and Treatment of Children, 18*, 226–242.

Gilliam, J. E. (2001). *Gilliam Asperger's Disorder Scale*. Austin, TX: ProEd.

Gilliam, J. E. (2002). *Conduct Disorder Scale*. Austin, TX: ProEd.

Gilliam, J. E. (2006). *GARS-2: Gilliam Autism Rating Scale: 2nd ed. Examiner's manual*. Los Angeles: Western Psychological Services.

Goldstein, A. P. (1999). *The PREPARE curriculum: Teaching prosocial competencies* (Rev. ed.). Champaign, IL: Research Press.

Gresham, F. M., & Lambros, K. M. (1998). Behavioral and functional assessment. In T. S. Watson, & F. M. Gresham (Eds.), *Handbook of child behavior therapy* (pp. 3–22). New York: Plenum Press.

Hanley, G. P., Iwata, B. A., & McCord, B. E. (2003). Functional analysis of problem behavior: An overview. *Journal of Applied Behavior Analysis, 36*, 147–185.

Harrison, P. L., & Oakland, T. (2003). *Adaptive behavior assessment system* (2nd ed.). San Antonio, TX: Psychological Corporation.

Hintze, J. M., Stoner, G., & Bull, M. H. (2000). Analogue assessment: Emotional/behavioral problems. In E. S. Shapiro, & T. R. Kratochwill (Eds.), *Conducting school-based assessments of child and adolescent behavior* (pp. 55–77). New York: Guilford Press.

Hirshberg, L. M., Chiu, S., & Frazier, J. A. (2005). Emerging brain-based interventions for children and adolescents: Overview and clinical perspective. *Child and Adolescent Psychiatric Clinics of North America, 14*, 1–19.

Hodges, K., McKnew, D., Cytryn, L., Stern, L., & Kline, J. (1982). The Child Assessment Schedule (CAS) Diagnostic Interview: A report on reliability and validity. *Journal of the American Academy of Child and Adolescent Psychiatry, 21*, 468–473.

Holland, M. L., Gimpel, G. A., & Merrell, K. W. (2001). *ADHD Symptoms Rating Scale manual*. Wilmington, DE: Wide Range.

Kaufman, J., Birmaher, B., Brent, D., Rao, U., Flynn, C., Moreci, P., et al. (1997). Schedule for Affective Disorders and Schizophrenia for School-Age Children—Present and Lifetime Version (K-SADS-PL): Initial reliability and validity data. *Journal of the American Academy of Child and Adolescent Psychiatry, 36,* 980–988.

Kearney, C. A. (2002). Identifying the function of school refusal behavior: A revision of the School Refusal Assessment Scale. *Journal of Psychopathology and Behavioral Assessment, 24,* 235–245.

Kearney, C. A. (2005). *Social anxiety and social phobia in youth: Characteristics, assessment, and psychological treatment*. New York: Springer.

Kearney, C. A. (2006). Confirmatory factor analysis of the School Refusal Assessment Scale—Revised: Child and parent versions. *Journal of Psychopathology and Behavioral Assessment, 28,* 139–144.

Kearney, C. A., & Albano, A. M. (2007). *When children refuse school: A cognitive-behavioral therapy approach—Therapist's guide* (2nd ed.). New York: Oxford University Press.

Kearney, C. A., & Bensaheb, A. (2007). Anxiety disorders. In S. R. Smith, & L. Handler (Eds.), *The clinical assessment of children and adolescents: A practitioner's guide* (pp. 467–483). Mahwah, NJ: Erlbaum.

Kearney, C. A., Pursell, C., & Alvarez, K. (2001). Treatment of school refusal behavior in children with mixed functional profiles. *Cognitive and Behavioral Practice, 8,* 3–11.

Kearney, C. A., & Silverman, W. K. (1999). Functionally-based prescriptive and nonprescriptive treatment for children and adolescents with school refusal behavior. *Behavior Therapy, 30,* 673–695.

Kendall, P. C., & Chansky, T. E. (1991). Considering cognition in anxiety-disordered children. *Journal of Anxiety Disorders, 5,* 167–185.

King, N. J. (1994). Physiological assessment. In T. H. Ollendick, N. J. King, & W. Yule (Eds.), *International handbook of phobic and anxiety disorders in children and adolescents* (pp. 365–379). New York: Plenum Press.

Kohler, T., & Schuschel, I. (1994). Changes in the number of active sweat glands (Palmar Sweat Index, PSI) during a distressing film. *Biological Psychiatry, 37,* 133–145.

Kovacs, M. (1985). The Interview Schedule for Children (ISC). *Psychopharmacology Bulletin, 21,* 991–994.

Kovacs, M. (1992). *Children's Depression Inventory manual*. North Tonawanda, NY: Multi-Health Systems.

Krug, D., Arick, J., & Almond, P. (1995). *Autism Screening Instrument for Educational Planning (ASIEP-2)*. Austin, TX: ProEd.

Kuntsi, J., McLoughlin, G., & Asherson, P. (2006). Attention deficit hyperactivity disorder. *Neuromolecular Medicine, 8,* 461–484.

La Greca, A. M., & Stone, W. L. (1993). Social Anxiety Scale for Children—Revised: Factor structure and concurrent validity. *Journal of Clinical Child Psychology, 22,* 17–27.

Lannen, T., Brown, D., & Powell, H. (2002). Control of virtual environments for young people with learning difficulties. *Disability and Rehabilitation, 24,* 578–586.

Latzman, R. D., Knutson, J. F., & Fowles, D. C. (2006). Schedule-induced electrodermal responding in children. *Psychophysiology, 43,* 623–632.

Lorber, M. F. (2004). Psychophysiology of aggression, psychopathy, and conduct problems: A meta-analysis *Psychological Bulletin, 130,* 531–552.

Mace, F. C. (1994). The significance and future of functional analysis methodologies. *Journal of Applied Behavior Analysis, 27,* 385–392.

March, J. (1997) *Multidimensional Anxiety Scale for Children*. North Tonawanda, NY: Multi-Health Systems.

Margolin, G., Oliver, P. H., Gordis, E. B., O'Hearn, H. G., Medina, A. M., Ghosh, C. M., et al. (1998). The nuts and bolts of behavioral observation of marital and family interaction. *Clinical Child and Family Psychology Review, 1,* 195–213.

Mash, E. J., & Terdal, L. G. (1997). Assessment of child and family disturbance: A behavioral-systems approach. In E. J. Mash, & L. G. Terdal (Eds.), *Assessment of childhood disorders* (3rd ed., pp. 3–68). New York: Guilford Press.

McCarney, S. B. (1995) *The Attention Deficit Disorders Evaluation Scale, home version, technical manual* (2nd ed.). Columbia, MO: Hawthorne Educational Service.

McComas, J. J., Hoch, H., & Mace, F. C. (2000). Functional analysis. In E. S. Shapiro, & T. R. Kratochwill (Eds.), *Conducting school-based assessments of child and adolescent behavior* (pp. 78–120). New York: Guilford Press.

Merrell, K. W. (2000). Informant report: Rating scale measures. In E. S. Shapiro, & T. R. Kratochwill (Eds.), *Conducting school-based assessments of child and adolescent behavior* (pp. 203–234). New York: Guilford Press.

Miller, G. A. (2001). *Adolescent SASSI-A2 Substance Abuse Subtle Screening Inventory*. Springville, IN: SASSI Institute.

Mori, L. T., & Armendariz, G. M. (2001). Analogue assessment of child behavior problems. *Psychological Assessment, 13*, 36–45.

Mpofu, E., Carney, J., & Lambert, M. C. (2006). Peer sociometric assessment. In M. Hersen (Ed.), *Clinician's handbook of child behavioral assessment* (pp. 233–263). New York: Elsevier.

Myers, K., & Winters, N. C. (2002a). Ten-year review of rating scales: Pt. I. Overview of scale functioning, psychometric properties, and selection. *Journal of the American Academy of Child and Adolescent Psychiatry, 41*, 114–122.

Myers, K., & Winters, N. C. (2002b). Ten-year review of rating scales: Pt. II. Scales for internalizing disorders. *Journal of the American Academy of Child and Adolescent Psychiatry, 41*, 634–659.

Nihira, K., Leland, H., & Lambert, N. (1993). *AAMR Adaptive Behavior Scale—Residential and Community* (2nd ed.). Austin, TX: ProEd.

Ollendick, T. H. (1983). Reliability and validity of the Revised Fear Survey Schedule for Children (FSSC-R). *Behaviour Research and Therapy, 21*, 685–692.

Pellegrini, A. D. (2001). Practitioner review: The role of direct observation in the assessment of young children. *Journal of Child Psychology and Psychiatry, 42*, 861–869.

Pretzlik, U., & Sylva, K. (1999). Paediatric patients' distress and coping: An observational measure. *Archives of Disease in Childhood, 81*, 528–530.

Quay, H. C., & Peterson, D. R. (1996). *Revised Behavior Problem Checklist: PAR edition*. Odessa, FL: Psychological Assessment Resources.

Rapport, M. D., Kofler, M. J., & Himmerich, C. (2006). Activity measurement. In M. Hersen (Ed.), *Clinician's handbook of child behavioral assessment* (pp. 125–157). New York: Elsevier.

Reitman, D. (2006). Overview of behavioral assessment with children. In M. Hersen (Ed.), *Clinician's handbook of child behavioral assessment* (pp. 3–24). New York: Elsevier.

Reynolds, C. R., & Kamphaus, R. W. (1998). *Behavior Assessment System for Children manual* (2nd ed.). Circle Pines, MN: American Guidance Service.

Reynolds, C. R., & Richmond, B. O. (1985). *Revised Children's Manifest Anxiety Scale manual*. Los Angeles: Western Psychological Services.

Reynolds, W. M., & Mazza, J. J. (1998). Reliability and validity of the Reynolds Adolescent Depression Scale with young adolescents. *Journal of School Psychology, 36*, 295–312.

Riva, G., Wiederhold, B. K., & Molinari, E. (Eds.). (1998). *Virtual environments in clinical psychology and neuroscience: Methods and techniques in advanced patient-therapist interaction*. Amsterdam, The Netherlands: IOS Press.

Rizzo, A. A., Bowerly, T., Buckwalter, J. G., Klimchuk, D., Mitura, R., & Parsons, T. D. (2006). A virtual reality scenario for all seasons: The virtual classroom. *CNS Spectrums, 11*, 35–44.

Roberts, M. A. (1990). A behavior observation method for differentiating hyperactive and aggressive boys. *Journal of Abnormal Child Psychology, 18*, 131–142.

Roberts, M. W. (2001). Clinic observations of structured parent-child interaction designed to evaluate externalizing disorders. *Psychological Assessment, 13*, 46–58.

Robin, A. L., & Foster, S. L. (1989). *Negotiating parent-adolescent conflict: A behavioral-family systems approach*. New York: Guilford Press.

Romaniuk, C., Miltenberger, R. G., & Deaver, C. (2003). Long-term maintenance following habit reversal and adjunct treatment for trichotillomania. *Child and Family Behavior Therapy, 25*, 45–59.

Rutter, M., Bailey, A., & Lord, C. (2003). *SCQ: The Social Communication Questionnaire manual*. Los Angeles: Western Psychological Services.

Schill, M. T., Kratochwill, T. R., & Gardner, W. I. (1996). An assessment protocol for selective mutism: Analogue assessment using parents as facilitators. *Journal of School Psychology, 34*, 1–21.

Schniering, C. A., Hudson, J. L., & Rapee, R. M. (2000). Issues in the diagnosis and assessment of anxiety disorders in children and adolescents. *Clinical Psychology Review, 20*, 453–478.

Schopler, E., Reichler, R., & Renner, C. (1988). *The Childhood Autism Rating Scale (CARS)*. Los Angeles: Western Psychological Services.

Shaffer, D., Fisher, P., Dulcan, M. K., Davies, M., Piacentini, J., Schwab-Stone, M. E., et al. (1996). The NIMH Diagnostic Interview for Children version 2.3 (DISC-2.3): Description, acceptability, prevalence rates, and performance in the MECA study. *Journal of the American Academy of Child and Adolescent Psychiatry, 35*, 865–877.

Silverman, W. K., & Albano, A. M. (1996). *The Anxiety Disorders Interview Schedule for Children for DSM-IV, child and parent versions*. San Antonio, TX: Psychological Corporation.

Sirard, J. R., & Pate, R. R. (2001). Physical activity assessment in children and adolescents. *Sports Medicine, 31*, 439–454.

Skinner, C. H., Rhymer, K. N., & McDaniel, E. C. (2000). Naturalistic direct observation in educational settings. In E. S. Shapiro, & T. R. Kratochwill (Eds.), *Conducting school-based assessments of child and adolescent behavior* (pp. 21–54). New York: Guilford Press.

Sparrow, S. S., Cicchetti, D., & Balla, D. A. (2005). *Vineland Adaptive Behavior Scales: Vineland II* (2nd ed.). Bloomington, MN: Pearson.

Spence, S. H., Donovan, C., & Brechman-Toussaint, M. (1999). Social skills, social outcomes, and cognitive features of childhood social phobia. *Journal of Abnormal Psychology, 108*, 211–221.

Spielberger, C. D. (1973). *Manual for the State-Trait Anxiety Inventory for Children*. Palo Alto, CA: Consulting Psychologists Press.

Sprafkin, J., Gadow, K. D., Salisbury, H., Schneider, J., & Loney, J. (2002). Further evidence of reliability and validity of the Child Symptom Inventory-4: Parent checklist in clinically referred boys. *Journal of Clinical Child and Adolescent Psychology, 31*, 513–524.

Suzuki, L. A., Alexander, C. M., Lin, P.-Y., & Duffy, K. M. (2006). Psychopathology in the schools: Multicultural factors that impact assessment and intervention. *Psychology in the Schools, 43*, 429–438.

Tay, S. K., Hirsch, L. J., Leary, L., Jette, N., Wittman, J., & Akman, C. I. (2006). Nonconvulsive status epilepticus in children: Clinical and EEG characteristics. *Epilepsia, 47*, 1504–1509.

Tedroff, K., Knutson, L. M., & Soderberg, G. L. (2006). Synergistic muscle activation during maximum voluntary contractions in children with and without spastic cerebral palsy. *Developmental Medicine and Child Neurology, 48*, 789–796.

Terry, R., & Coie, J. D. (1991). A comparison of methods for defining sociometric status among children. *Developmental Psychology, 27*, 867–880.

Turner, S. M., Beidel, D. C., & Epstein, L. H. (1991). Vulnerability and risk for anxiety disorders. *Journal of Anxiety Disorders, 5*, 151–166.

Varni, J. W., Thompson, K. L., & Hanson, V. (1987). The Varni/Thompson Pediatric Pain Questionnaire: Pt. I. Chronic musculoskeletal pain in juvenile rheumatoid arthritis. *Pain, 28*, 27–38.

Walker, H. M., & McConnell, S. R. (1995). *Walker-McConnell Scale of Social Competence and School Adjustment: Elementary version*. San Diego, CA: Singular.

Watson, T. S., & Steege, M. W. (2003). *Conducting school-based functional behavioral assessments*. New York: Guilford Press.

Weller, E. B., Weller, R. A., Fristad, M. A., Rooney, M. T., & Schecter, J. (2000). Children's Interview for Psychiatric Syndromes (ChIPS). *Journal of the American Academy of Child and Adolescent Psychiatry, 39*, 76–84.

Welner, Z., Reich, W., Herjanic, B., Jung, K. G., & Amado, H. (1987). Reliability, validity, and parent-child agreement studies of the Diagnostic Interview for Children and Adolescents (DICA). *Journal of the American Academy of Child and Adolescent Psychiatry, 26*, 649–653.

Werner, E., & Dawson, G. (2005). Validation of the phenomenon of autistic regression using home videotapes. *Archives of General Psychiatry, 62*, 889–895.

PART V

Treatment

CHAPTER 20

Play Therapy

Sue C. Bratton, Dee Ray, and Garry Landreth

Identifying early mental health interventions tailored to the maturational needs of children is a growing concern in the United States (New Freedom Commission on Mental Health, 2003). Increases in societal problems that directly involve and impact young children has focused greater attention on this issue. The most recent U.S. surgeon general's report on mental health described the shortage of appropriate services for children as a major health crisis and estimated that, although at least 1 in 10 of all children suffer from emotional and behavioral problems severe enough to impair normal functioning, fewer than half receive treatment (U.S. Public Health Service, 2000). Thus, providing families with greater access to interventions that are responsive to the distinct needs of young children is critical, not only to diminish unnecessary suffering, but to prevent the development of more serious impairment across the life span.

Play therapy is founded on the principle that children must be approached and understood from a developmental perspective. Children are not miniature adults, and just as their world is a world of concrete realities, so too their means of communicating their world is on a child's level through play (Landreth & Bratton, 1998). Play is to the child what verbalization is to the adult. Play provides a developmentally responsive means for expressing thoughts and feelings, exploring relationships, making sense of experiences, disclosing wishes, and developing coping strategies (Landreth, 2002).

Although play therapy has been a treatment of choice for children since the early 1900s, the formation of the Association for Play Therapy (APT) in 1982 established play therapy as a specialized treatment modality within the field of mental health. The Association's influence, along with an increase in university-based play therapy training programs, provided the momentum for the substantial growth of the field over the past 25 years. Today, play therapy is widely used among clinicians to successfully treat a range of emotional and behavioral problems (Bratton & Ray, 2000, 2002). According to APT's web site (2006), approximately 5,000 mental health professionals identify themselves as play therapists. The growing interest in the field is also evident in the more than 3,500 play therapy publications describing its use, rationale, and efficacy, the majority of which were produced after 1980 (Center for Play Therapy, 2006).

RATIONALE FOR PLAY THERAPY

Play has long been considered significant in children's lives. As early as the eighteenth century Rousseau (1762, 1930) acknowledged the importance of observing children's play as a means of understanding them; however, it was not until the early twentieth century that the symbolic function of play was recognized. Froebel (1903) proposed that children's play has a conscious and unconscious purpose and thus is meaningful and important. More recently, the value of play has been recognized by early childhood experts as the way children learn about themselves, others, and their world as they try to organize and make sense of their experiences. Frank (1982) suggested that play is the way children learn what no one can teach them.

Play has been used by child therapists since the early twentieth century to provide children with a medium for self-expression. Most children below the age of 11 lack a fully developed capacity for abstract thought, which is a prerequisite to meaningful verbal expression and understanding of complex issues, motives, and feelings (Piaget, 1962). The child's world is one of concrete realities; thus, children must be afforded a concrete means of expressing their perception of self, others, and the world. Children can more meaningfully express their inner world through the symbolic representation provided by toys, with toys and play materials serving as their language. Although children often use play to directly express their experiences, in play therapy it is the symbolic function of play that is most significant. Sometimes children's symbolization of their experiences is quite apparent; at other times the connection may seem rather remote. Regardless, children use symbolic play to develop mastery and a sense of control over their world as they reenact their experiences directly in the safety of the therapeutic milieu.

In play therapy, then, play is viewed as the vehicle for communication between child and therapist on the assumption that the child will use play materials to directly or symbolically act out feelings, thoughts, and experiences that the child is not able to express meaningfully through words alone (Axline, 1947; Kottman, 2001; Landreth, 2002; O'Connor, 2001; Schaefer, 2001). Play allows children to bridge the chasm between their experiences and understanding, thereby providing the means for insight, learning, problem solving, coping, and mastery. In play therapy, regardless of the reason for referral, the therapist has the opportunity to enter into and experience the child's world and actively deal with the issues that brought the child to therapy. Axline described this process as one in which the child has the opportunity to play out feelings as they emerge, getting them out in the open, and either learning to appropriately control them or abandon them.

DEVELOPMENT OF PLAY THERAPY

As early as the eighteenth century play was recognized as essential to children's healthy development, but it was not until the early twentieth century that play was introduced into a therapeutic setting. The use of play in therapy originated with the classical child analysis case of Little Hans by Sigmund Freud. Freud saw Hans only once for a brief visit and conducted treatment by advising Hans father of ways to respond, with suggestions based on the father's notes about Hans play.

Generally acknowledged as the originators of play therapy, Anna Freud (1928) and Melanie Klein (1932) used play as a substitute for verbalized free association in their efforts to apply analytic techniques to their work with children. David Levy's (1939) development of release play therapy, along with the structured approach of Gove Hambidge (1955), marked the next advance in the field. In these two approaches play materials were structured by the therapist to induce catharsis; this is in contrast to psychoanalytic methods, in which the analyst made no attempt to direct the child's play.

Virginia Axline (1947) was the first to apply nondirective therapeutic principles in play therapy based on her trust in children's capacity to resolve their own problems through their play. Her work and writings in the late 1940s and 1950s, including her accounting of play therapy with Dibs (Axline, 1964), heralded perhaps the most significant development in the field of play therapy and popularized play therapy as a psychotherapeutic treatment modality for children. Building on Axline's work, Haim Ginott (1961), Clark Moustakas (1953), Louise Guerney (1983), and Garry Landreth (1991, 2002) contributed significantly to the widespread acceptance and practice of what is now more commonly referred to as child-centered play therapy (CCPT). Landreth (1991, 2002) provides an in-depth description of the principles and procedures of CCPT.

The development of filial therapy by Bernard and Louise Guerney in the early 1960s marked a significant and innovative development in the field of play therapy. The Guerneys were the first to develop a model for training and supervising parents in client-centered play therapy methods to use with their own children (Guerney, 2000). Since the late 1980s the use of filial therapy by practitioners has increased tremendously. Guerney (2000) credited this growth, in part, to the efforts of Landreth (1991, 2002) and his protégés. Building on the work of the Guerneys, Landreth developed a more condensed, 10-session parent training format based on his experience that time and financial constraints often hindered parents' participation. Landreth and Bratton (2005) formalized the 10-session training format in a text, *Child Parent Relationship Therapy (CPRT): A 10-Session Filial Therapy Model*. Grounded in the principles and procedures of child-centered play therapy, the CPRT parent training model emphasizes a balance of didactic and supervision experiences in a 2-hour weekly support group format and requires parents to conduct weekly, videotaped play sessions at home. The CPRT protocol was recently manualized by Bratton, Landreth, Kellam, and Blackard (2006), allowing for replication of the model. Although originally conceived as a group model for training parents, filial therapy has also been successfully adapted for individual parents and couples (VanFleet, 1994) and for training teachers, mentors and other paraprofessionals who play a significant role in children's lives (L. Jones, Rhine, & Bratton, 2002; Morrison, 2006; White, Flynt, & Draper, 1997).

The field of play therapy grew dramatically during the 1980s and 1990s as various theorists, academicians, and practitioners developed specific play therapy approaches based on their theoretical views and personal experiences with children, including gestalt play therapy (Oaklander, 1994), Jungian play therapy (Allan, 1997), Adlerian play therapy (Kottman, 1995), developmental play therapy (Brody, 1997), cognitive-behavioral play therapy (Knell, 1997), ecosystemic play therapy

(O'Connor, 2000), and prescriptive play therapy (Schaefer, 2001), to name a few. The sheer number of contributors to the development of this discipline prevents mentioning each.

Play therapy has grown over its 100-year history to include a variety of theoretical schools of thought. Although they may differ in their approach, they all embrace the therapeutic and developmental properties of play: "to help [children] prevent or resolve psychosocial difficulties and achieve optimal growth and development" (APT, 2001, p. 20). It would be impossible to describe all the various theoretical approaches to play therapy within the scope of this chapter; thus, in the practice and case study sections, we focus on the principles and procedures of the play therapy approach with the longest history of use and the strongest base of research support, CCPT.

RESEARCH IN PLAY THERAPY

Identifying mental health interventions that are effective for young children is a critical need for the twenty-first century (U.S. Public Health Service, 2000). In spite of play therapy's growing popularity among clinicians, the scientific community has been slower to embrace this modality as an empirically sound intervention. Scientifically proving the effectiveness of any therapeutic intervention is essential to its widespread acceptance and use. Although the field of play therapy has a history of over 60 years of continuous research, historically play therapy studies have been hindered by inadequate research design, most notably the lack of a control group and small sample sizes. More current research has utilized well-designed methodologies and supports the use of play therapy as an effective treatment that is responsive to children's unique developmental needs.

Play therapy research dates back to the 1940s, demonstrating one of the longest histories of research of any psychological intervention. In 1942, Dulsky attempted to study the relationship between intellect and emotional problems. He inadvertently established the effect of nondirective play therapy, which was to improve social and emotional adjustments, yet no improvement was shown on intellect. Although the research demonstrated a positive effect, several flaws in the research are noted, including a lack of control or comparison group, and insufficient description of treatment and participants. Since Dulsky's 1942 study, an approximate count of play therapy research, excluding filial therapy research, includes 103 studies, of which 71 were published in professional journals and 32 remained in dissertation form. The majority of play therapy studies demonstrate some positive effect of play therapy on the participants.

An examination of the play therapy research focused on filial therapy modality reveals 37 studies using a pre-post control group design, 27 of which were published in professional journals. Of the 37 filial therapy outcome studies, 27 utilized the 10-session CPRT model (Landreth & Bratton, 2005), originally introduced by Landreth (1991). Of the 27 studies examining the effects of the 10-session model, 24 were conducted under the supervision of the CPRT authors to ensure treatment integrity. Videotaped and live supervision was used to assure adherence to the procedures originally developed by Landreth and recently formalized in a published treatment manual (Bratton et al., 2006). A detailed summary of filial therapy research from 1967 to 2005 can be found in Landreth and Bratton. For the purpose of this chapter, we focus our discussion on research examining the effects of play therapy conducted directly by professionals.

Current Play Therapy Research

Since 1990, 36 (27 published) research studies on the impact of play therapy have been conducted. These recent studies have demonstrated the positive impact of play therapy on general behavioral problems (Raman & Kapur, 1999; Shashi, Kapur, & Subbakrishna, 1999), externalizing behavioral problems (Flahive & Ray, in press; Garza & Bratton, 2005; Karcher & Lewis, 2002; Kot, Landreth, & Giordano, 1998; Schumann, 2005), internalizing problems (Packman & Bratton, 2003), self-efficacy (Fall, Balvanz, Johnson, & Nelson, 1999), self-concept (Kot et al., 1998; Post, 1999), anxiety (Baggerly, 2004; Shen, 2002), depression (Baggerly, 2004), speech problems (Danger & Landreth, 2005), and diabetes treatment compliance (E. Jones & Landreth, 2002).

Meta-Analytic Research on Play Therapy

LeBlanc and Ritchie (1999) published the initial results of their meta-analysis of play therapy outcomes summarizing the results of 42 controlled studies, with an effect size of .66 standard deviation. The researchers further detailed their study in a later publication citing that benefits of play therapy appear to increase with the inclusion of parents and optimal treatment duration (LeBlanc & Ritchie, 2001). Using Cohen's (1988) guidelines for interpretation of effect size, .66 denotes a moderate treatment effect, similar to effect sizes (ES) found in other child psychotherapy meta-analyses (Casey & Berman, 1985, ES = .71; Weisz, Weiss, Han, Granger, & Morton, 1995, ES = .71).

Bratton, Ray, Rhine, and Jones (2005) conducted the largest meta-analysis on play therapy outcome research. This meta-analysis reviewed 180 documents that appeared to measure the effectiveness of play therapy from 1942 to 2000. Based on stringent criteria for inclusion—use of a controlled research design, sufficient data for computing effect size, and the identification by the author of a labeled "play therapy" intervention—93 studies were included in the final calculation of effect size. The overall effect size was calculated at .80 standard deviation, interpreted as a large effect, indicating that children receiving play therapy interventions performed .80 standard deviation above children who did not receive play therapy. LeBlanc and Ritchie (2001) and Bratton et al. (2005) included filial therapy research in their definitions of play therapy. Filial therapy is a parental intervention based on CCPT.

Bratton et al. (2005) coded specific characteristics of play therapy that impacted or had no impact on play therapy outcome. Effect sizes for humanistic (ES = .92) and nonhumanistic (ES = .71) play therapy interventions were considered to be effective regardless of theoretical approach. However, the effect size reported for the humanistic approach was in the large effect category, whereas the ES for the nonhumanistic approach was in the moderate category. This difference in effect may be attributed to a larger number of calculated humanistic studies ($n = 73$)

compared to nonhumanistic studies ($n = 12$). When play therapy was delivered by a parent (ES = 1.15), the effect size was much larger than when delivered by a mental health professional (ES = .72), indicating the importance of involving parents in treatment to increase the chances of a successful outcome. This finding was similar to the conclusions of LeBlanc and Ritchie (2001), who reported parent involvement as a predictor of play therapy outcome. Treatment duration was also a factor in the success of play therapy. Optimal treatment effects were obtained in 35 to 40 sessions. However, many studies with fewer than 14 sessions also produced medium and large effect sizes. Age and gender were not found to be significant factors from which to predict the effects of play therapy; play therapy appeared to be equally effective across age and gender. An effect size was not calculated for ethnicity due to the lack of specificity in the reporting of ethnicity in individual studies. In addressing presenting problems, the researchers encountered difficulty distinguishing specific diagnoses and symptoms due to the variation among the studies. However, 24 studies were coded as investigating internalizing problems; analysis revealed an effect size of .81. An effect size of .78 was calculated for the 17 studies coded as examining the effects of play therapy on externalizing problems. For the 16 studies that addressed a combination of internalizing and externalizing problems, the effect size was .93. These results indicated that play therapy had a moderate to large beneficial effect for internalizing, externalizing, and combined problem types.

Individual Study Research on Play Therapy

Ray (2006) highlighted specific empirical studies that support the use of CCPT with children with behavioral and emotional challenges. The following studies are the most recent supportive research on CCPT that were identified as adhering to current experimental rigor. Kot et al. (1998) found that among child witnesses of domestic violence between the ages of 4 and 10 years, children who participated in 12 CCPT sessions scored significantly higher on self-concept than children who did not receive play therapy. Their mothers further reported significantly fewer externalizing behavior problems and total behavioral problems than mothers of children who did not receive play therapy. Among Hispanic children identified by parents or teachers as demonstrating behavioral problems at school, parents reported that those children who participated in 15 CCPT sessions demonstrated significantly fewer externalizing problems than children who participated in a small group curriculum-based guidance program, with the greatest improvement in conduct problems (Garza & Bratton, 2005). The children who participated in CCPT also demonstrated moderate improvements in internalizing problems. Flahive and Ray (in press) found that, compared to the control group, after 10 sessions of a child-centered approach to sand tray therapy for preadolescents in upper elementary school, teachers reported that the students significantly improved in their internalizing and externalizing problem behaviors, and parents reported improvement in children's externalizing problem behaviors. In this study, the wait-list control group continued to experience increased behavioral problems, both internalizing and externalizing.

Fall et al. (1999) and Post (1999) found that children who participated in CCPT demonstrated statistically significantly greater self-efficacy and self-esteem over their peers who did not participate in play therapy. Shen (2002) explored the effect of CCPT on Chinese children who experienced a devastating earthquake in Taiwan. Children who participated in 10 group sessions of CCPT demonstrated a significant decrease in anxiety and suicide risk compared to children who did not participate in play therapy. E. Jones and Landreth (2002) examined the efficacy of 12 sessions of intensive individual play therapy sessions on anxiety levels and medical compliance of 30 insulin-dependent children, ages 7 to 11 years. Compared with the control group children who attended the same camp, the 15 experimental group children demonstrated significant improvement in medical compliance (giving shots, following diet, etc.), when measured immediately following camp and at a 3-month follow-up. These are just a few examples of recent research conducted on CCPT that support the validity of the intervention in helping to reduce childhood problems and improve emotional conditions.

Historical Play Therapy Studies

The focus on these exemplary play therapy research studies by no means devalues the significant contribution that many other historical play therapy studies have made to the field. A rich history of play therapy efficacy has been established in the areas of hospitalized children with symptoms of anxiety (Cassell, 1965; Clatworthy, 1981; Johnson & Stockdale, 1975; Rae, Worchel, Upchurch, Sanner, & Daniel, 1989), self-concept (Crow, 1990; Gould, 1980; House, 1970; Perez, 1987), social adjustment (Cox, 1953; Oualline, 1976; Pelham, 1972; Thombs & Muro, 1973), and behavioral difficulties (Brandt, 2001; Gaulden, 1975; Hannah, 1986; Quayle, 1991). Detailed accounts of these studies can be found in the compilation of play therapy research summarized in Bratton and Ray (2000).

PLAY THERAPY IN PRACTICE

As stated earlier, the scope of this chapter prevents a description of the practice of play therapy from all theoretical viewpoints. Although the various play therapy approaches may differ philosophically and technically, they are alike in their use of the therapeutic and developmental properties of play to help children benefit from treatment. In this section, we focus on the principles and procedures of CCPT. Of the many well-established play therapy schools of thought, CCPT has the longest history of use, the strongest research support, and, according to a survey of APT members (Lambert et al., 2005), the largest number of followers.

Role of Therapist and the Therapeutic Relationship

The goal of child-centered play therapy is to establish conditions so that the child can experience growth and integration. Raskin and Rogers (2005) postulated that if the therapist is successful in conveying genuineness, unconditional positive regard, and empathy, then the child will respond with a changed personality organization.

Child-centered play therapists believe that a child client's experience in the counseling relationship is the factor that is most meaningful and helpful in creating lasting, positive change.

Given the opportunity, children will play out their feelings and needs in a manner or process of expression that is similar for adults. Although the dynamics of expression and the vehicle for communication are different for children, the expressions (fear, satisfaction, anger, happiness, frustration, contentment) are similar to those of adults. Children may have considerable difficulty describing what they feel or how their experiences have affected them. If permitted, however, in the presence of a caring, sensitive, and empathetic adult, they will reveal inner feelings through the toys and materials they choose, what they do with and to the materials, and the stories they act out. Children's play is meaningful and significant to them, for through their play they extend themselves into areas they have difficulty entering verbally.

Because the child's world is a world of action and activity, play therapy provides the therapist with an opportunity to enter the child's world. The child is not restricted to discussing what happened; rather, the child lives out at the moment of play the past experience and associated feelings. If the reason the child was referred to the therapist is aggressive behavior, the medium of play gives the therapist an opportunity to experience the aggressive behavior firsthand as the child attempts to break toys or to shoot the therapist with a dart gun, while also allowing the child opportunities to learn self-control by responding with appropriate therapeutic limit-setting procedures.

Axline (1947) identified eight basic principles that guide the therapist in child-centered play therapy. These basic principles are consistent with a person-centered philosophy of working with children by emphasizing the primacy of the counseling relationship. These principles insist that the therapist (1) must develop a warm, friendly relationship with the child; (2) accepts the child unconditionally, without wishing the child were different in some way; (3) establishes a feeling of permissiveness in the relationship so that the child feels free to express himself or herself; (4) recognizes and reflects the feelings of the child to create understanding for the child; (5) respects the child's innate ability to solve his or her own problems and offers the child the opportunity to take responsibility for his or her own behavior; (6) does not attempt to direct the child's actions or conversation, but allows the child to lead the way; (7) recognizes the gradual nature of the child's process and does not try to rush counseling; and (8) establishes only those limitations that are necessary to anchor the child's experience in counseling to the world of reality.

Without the presence of play materials, the therapist could only talk with the child about the aggressive behavior the child exhibited yesterday or in the past weeks. In play therapy, whatever the reason for referral, the therapist has the opportunity to experience and actively deal with that problem in the immediacy of the child's experiencing.

How Play Therapy Facilitates Change in Children

Play therapy assists children's development by helping them learn to know and accept themselves. Most of what is learned in the play therapy relationship is not cognitive learning, but experiential, intuitive learning about the self that occurs over the course of therapy. Landreth (2002) described the following learning experiences:

- *Children learn to respect themselves.* The play therapist maintains and communicates constant regard and respect for children regardless of their behavior, whether they are playing passively, acting out aggression, or being whiny and insisting on help with even the simplest tasks. Children sense the therapist's respect, feel respected, and, because of the absence of evaluation and an ever present acceptance, they internalize the respect. Once children have respect for themselves, they learn to respect others.

- *Children learn that their feelings are acceptable.* By playing out their feelings in the presence of an adult who understands and accepts even the intensity of their feelings, children learn that all of their feelings are acceptable. As children begin to experience that their feelings are acceptable, they begin to be more open in expressing them.

- *Children learn to express their feelings responsibly.* Once children have expressed their feelings openly and been accepted, those feelings lose their intensity and can more easily be controlled appropriately. This is a freeing process for children to experience in that they are free to go beyond those feelings.

- *Children learn to assume responsibility for themselves.* In the natural process of development, children strive toward independence and self-reliance but often are thwarted in their efforts by adults who, although well intentioned, take charge by doing things for them and thus deprive children of opportunities to experience how being responsible for themselves feels. In the play therapy relationship, the therapist believes in children's ability to be resourceful and so resists doing anything that would deprive children of the opportunity to discover their own strength. As the therapist allows children to struggle to do things for themselves, they discover what that responsibility feels like.

- *Children learn to be creative and resourceful in confronting problems.* When children are allowed to figure out things for themselves, to derive their own solutions to problems, and to complete their own tasks, their own creative resources are released. With increasing frequency, children will tackle their own problems and experience the satisfaction of doing things all by themselves. Although children may at first resist the opportunity to solve their own problems, the creative tendency of the self will come forth in response to the therapist's patience.

- *Children learn self-control and self-direction.* If no opportunities are available to experience being in control, learning self-control and self-direction is not possible. Although this principle seems simplistically obvious, the absence of opportunities like this in children's lives is conspicuous when one takes the time to carefully observe children's interactions with significant adults. Unlike most other adults in children's lives, the play therapist does not make decisions for children or try to control them either directly or subtly. Limits on children's behavior in the playroom are verbalized in such a way that children are allowed to control their own behavior. Because control is not applied externally, children are able to make their own decisions.

- *Children gradually learn, at a feeling level, to accept themselves.* As children experience being accepted just as they are with no conditional expectations from the therapist, they gradually, and in sometimes imperceptible ways, begin to accept themselves as worthwhile. This is both a direct and an indirect process of communication and learning about self. Acceptance is an attitudinal message communicated verbally and nonverbally by all that the therapist is and does. The children first feel acceptance and then know it by being accepted nonjudgmentally for who they are, just as they are, with no desire that they be different. This increased self-acceptance is a major contributing factor to the development of a positive self-concept.

- *Children learn to make choices and to be responsible for their choices.* Life entails a never-ending series of choices. How can children learn how to make a choice if they are not afforded the opportunity of making choices, of being indecisive, of struggling, of wanting to avoid, of feeling incapable, of being anxious, and of feeling apprehensive that their choice will be unacceptable to others? Therefore, the therapist avoids making even simple choices for children.

Structuring the Relationship and Play Sessions

Beginning the Relationship

For most children, the therapeutic relationship is like no other they have experienced, one in which they are fully accepted and valued for who they are. The play therapist maintains and communicates a constant regard and respect for children. The structuring of the relationship begins with the initial interactions between therapist and child in the waiting room. The therapist's task is to give full attention to the child, communicating the child's importance. (*Note: Prior to the initial meeting with the child, the therapist has met with the parents without the child present to fully focus on the parents' needs and concerns, gather background history, and inform parents of what to expect.*)

In the initial meeting between therapist and child, the therapist should crouch down, make eye contact, and greet the child. Following a short introduction, the therapist can say, "We can go to the playroom now. Your mom (or the person who brought child) will wait here, so she will be here when we come back from the playroom." The play therapy relationship is further structured by how the therapist introduces the child to the playroom. Verbal communication should be kept to a minimum at this point. No amount of words will convey to the child that this is a safe place. The child learns this through experience. The therapist should choose words carefully to communicate to the child freedom, self-direction, and the parameters of the relationship. The therapist might say something such as "Sarah, this is our playroom, and this is a place where you can play with the toys in a lot of the ways you would like to." This statement conveys responsibility for direction, freeing the child. Boundaries on this freedom are conveyed by the words "in a lot of the ways," which in effect communicates limits on behavior. The playroom is not a place of complete freedom where children can do anything they want.

Playroom and Materials

Landreth (2002) suggested that the dimensions of a playroom be 12 by 15 feet. However, an open space of almost any size will suffice. In school buildings, we have used janitorial closets, old book rooms, and portable buildings for a playroom. If a therapist is very limited on space, he or she can develop a traveling playroom by maintaining a box or bag of materials that can be used in an office or conference room.

Because toys and materials are part of the communicative process for children, careful attention must be given to the selection of appropriate items. The rule is selection rather than accumulation. Play areas and playrooms containing an assortment of randomly acquired toys and materials often resemble a junk room and doom the play therapy process to failure. Toys and materials should be carefully selected for (a) the contribution they make to the accomplishment of the objective of play therapy and (b) the extent to which they are consistent with the rationale for play therapy. Not all play materials automatically encourage the expression of children's needs, feelings, and experiences. Because toys and materials are used by the child in the act of play to communicate a personal world to the counselor, toys should reflect the cultural experiences of children. Landreth (2002) suggested that toys and materials should be selected with the following goals in mind:

- Establishment of a positive relationship with the child.
- Expression of a wide range of feelings.
- Exploration of real life experiences.
- Testing of limits.
- Development of a positive image.
- Development of self-understanding.
- Opportunity to redirect behaviors unacceptable to others.

The following toys and materials are recommended because they can encourage a wide range of expressions and can be easily transported in a tote bag or stored out of the way in a corner or in a closet. They can be grouped into three broad categories:

1. Real-life toys, such as a doll (small size with soft body); a bendable doll family; a small cardboard box with rooms indicated by strips of tape or felt pen marker (could double as container for materials); doll house furniture (cost will probably necessitate purchase of plastic furniture and thus set limits on how it is used); a nursing bottle (plastic); two play dishes and cups (plastic or tin); spoons (avoid forks because of sharp points); a small car; a small airplane; and a telephone.

2. Acting-out or aggressive release toys, such as handcuffs (spring-release type without key because of possible embarrassment if child cannot get them off), a dart gun, toy soldiers (30-count size is sufficient because of the difficulty of picking up more than that), a pounding bench, and a rubber knife.

3. Toys for creative expression and emotional release, such as crayons (8-count size to avoid too many choices; break some in half and peel paper off to convey that it is not necessary to be neat and precise); newsprint; blunt scissors; pipe cleaners; popsicle sticks; Play-doh (place it in small plastic container to keep it pliable; the top of the cardboard Play-doh can may fray and allow air to enter can); hand puppets; a small plain mask (Lone Ranger type); a Nerf ball (a rubber ball bounces too much); Gumby (bendable, nondescript figure); scotch tape; nontoxic glue or paste; and an empty vegetable can (doubles as container for toy soldiers).

An inflatable punching toy (Bobo) is desirable if the room allows. Additional toys and materials can be added by counselors who have a permanent place for play therapy. Landreth (2002) provided a complete list of play materials in a fully equipped play therapy room. Highly structured materials and electronic toys should generally be avoided because they may interfere with rather than facilitate children's expressions. Because toys are the child's words, they should be in good condition.

Facilitative Responses

The following therapist skills are considered to be essential to the child-centered play therapy process. These are specific skills expected to be demonstrated in most play therapy sessions. The extent to which they will be used depends on the therapist's intuitive understanding of the child's needs in the immediacy of the session.

Nonverbal Skills

Play therapy is heavily reliant on nonverbal skills. Because play therapists believe that play is the language of children, the verbal world becomes less important in a play therapy session. Nonverbal skills are critical to any person-centered approach, but especially to play therapy. Nonverbal skills are demonstrated when the therapist leans toward the child and is physically directed toward the child at all times, showing keen interest in the child throughout the session. As with counseling adults, the therapist should strive to be congruent with how the child expresses himself or herself. The therapist should not only match the level of affect displayed by the child but should also convey a sense of genuineness. The skill of matching verbal response with nonverbal response is representative of the therapist's level of genuineness with the child. Mental health professionals who are new to play therapy often find this skill challenging, as they are not yet comfortable with responding to children's nonverbal play. Just as the therapist would not flatly respond, "You're happy that you got that to stick" (after the child looks over with a big smile after finally getting the dart to stick on the wall after 10 unsuccessful attempts), the therapist should avoid being so animated that he or she overwhelms the child. Again, congruence and genuineness are the key.

Verbal Skills

How the therapist verbally responds to the child is almost as impactful as the words chosen. Effective delivery of responses includes a focus on succinct, interactive responses and rate of responses. Because play therapy is offered to young children and because play therapy recognizes the limited language ability of these children, the importance of short therapeutic responses is key. Lengthy responses quickly lose the child's interest, confuse the child, and often convey a lack of understanding on the part of the therapist. Therapists match their level of interaction to that of the child. If the child is quiet and reserved, the play therapist will slow his or her responses; if the child is highly interactive and talkative, the play therapist will match this level of energy with an increased number of responses.

Child-centered play therapy verbal responses can be structured into categories that help facilitate growth in the child. The following are several relevant categories of verbal responses. Therapist responses should reflect the developmental level of the child; responses to a 3-year-old and an 8-year-old should be different. The examples that follow are appropriate for most young children.

Reflecting Nonverbal Play Behavior: Tracking   The therapist tracks or reflects the nonverbal content of the child's play behavior simply by stating what he or she observes. Reflecting the child's nonverbal behavior allows the child to know that the therapist is interested and accepting of the child. It also helps the therapist immerse himself or herself into the child's world. Examples of tracking behavior are "Hmm, you're not sure what you want to play with" (as a child walks around, briefly touching several different toys) or "You decided to play with that" (as the child picks up the plastic horse and puts in the sandbox).

Reflecting Content   Reflecting verbal content in play therapy is identical to reflecting content in talk therapy. To reflect content, the play therapist paraphrases the verbal interaction of the child. Reflecting content validates the children's perceptions of their experience and helps to clarify their understanding of themselves (Landreth, 2002). An example of reflecting content is "You know a lot about dinosaurs" (after the child shares detailed information on dinosaurs).

Reflecting Feeling   Reflecting feeling is the verbal response to emotions expressed by children in play therapy. The reflection of feeling can sometimes be threatening to a child and should be presented carefully. Reflecting feeling helps a child become aware of emotions, thereby leading to the appropriate acceptance and expression of such emotions. Examples of reflecting feeling are "You are really angry with that guy" (after the child throws the big elephant across the room, saying, "He stepped on everyone. I hate him") and "You're frustrated that it's not working out the way you wanted" (when the child tries unsuccessfully to cut a heart design out of paper and then crumples it up). As stated previously, therapist nonverbals and intonation of voice are as important, if not more so, as the words used.

Facilitating Decision Making and Returning Responsibility   One of the play therapist's goals is to help children experience a sense of their own capability and to take responsibility for their expression of capability. Responses that facilitate decision making or return responsibility help children experience themselves as able and empowered. Examples of responses that facilitate decision making or return responsibility are "In here, you can decide what color you want it to be" or "In here, that's up to you" (when the child wants to draw a picture and asks, "What color of paper should I use?") and "Show me what you want me to do" (when, without making an attempt, the child points to her wet painting on the easel and asks, "Can you take this off for me?"). The latter response allows the therapist to see if the child already knows how to use the clips holding the paper to the easel or is quite capable of doing so once she tries. Many children come to play therapy with little experience of figuring things out for themselves. In their experience, adults have all the answers, so there is no point in their trying. The rule of thumb in play therapy is to never do for a child what the child can do for himself or herself (Landreth, 2002).

Facilitating Creativity and Spontaneity   Helping children experience their own sense of creativity and freedom is another benefit of play therapy. Acceptance and encouragement of creativity sends a message to children that they are unique and special in their own way. Experiencing the freedom of expression allows them to develop flexibility in thought and action. Examples of responses that facilitate creativity or spontaneity are "You can make whatever you want" (when the child picks up craft material sticks and asks, "What do I make with these?") and "You've got a lot of ideas about want you want to make today" (when the child moves from making one craft project to another in play session).

Esteem Building and Encouraging   Encouraging children to feel better about themselves and their abilities is a constant objective for the play therapist. The use of esteem-building statements works to help children experience themselves as capable. Examples of esteem-building and encouraging responses are "You're trying lots of different ideas. You're not giving up" (when the child has trouble getting the glue bottle open and tries several different solutions) and "You did it" or "You kept at it until you found a way" (when the child tries and tries to reach the top shelf, and after a few attempts, succeeds).

Facilitating Relationship   Because the therapeutic relationship serves as a model for all intimate relationships, the play therapist seeks to respond to any attempt by the child to address the relationship. Relational responses help the child learn effective communication patterns and express the therapist's care for the child. Examples of responses that facilitate the relationship are "You're wondering what I think about that" (when the child is drawing a picture and stops to look up at the therapist but says nothing) and "You want us to look just alike" (when the child puts a hat on the therapist and says, "Now yours is like mine") and "You're mad at me, because I wouldn't do what you wanted" (after the therapist declines to eat the sand given by the child, and the child responds, "You're no fun, I don't want to come here anymore"). Relationship responses should always include a reference to the child and a reference to oneself as therapist.

Limit Setting   In an attempt to provide an environment for a child that allows self-direction and self-responsibility, minimal limits are established in child-centered play therapy. The goal is to help the child move toward the ability to self-limit. Typically, limits are set when children attempt to damage themselves, another person, and certain expensive or irreplaceable toys or if their behavior impedes counselor acceptance.

Landreth (2002) proposed a specific method for setting limits in play therapy. This method has been widely adopted by play therapists, regardless of theoretical orientation, as the initial response to setting a limit in the playroom. The A-C-T model of limit-setting is Acknowledge the feeling, Communicate the limit, and Target an alternative. In this model, the play therapist first recognizes and addresses the child's feelings in the moment: "You're really excited about your project." Then the therapist sets a short, concrete, definitive limit: "But it's not for stapling to the walls." Finally, the therapist provides an alternative to the action: "You can tape it to the walls." When children have directed energy in the moment, it is important to provide them an alternative for that energy so that they do not feel the need to act on impulse. Although there are other methods for setting limits, the A-C-T model is short, direct, and works effectively.

Involving Parents as Partners in the Therapeutic Process

Prior to the first play session, the play therapist should meet with the parents without the child present. The content and length of the initial parent meeting will vary with the therapist's theoretical and personal approach to involving parents in their child's therapy and the importance placed on intake assessment. The therapist's primary task during this session is to form a connection with the parents, focusing entirely on the parents' needs and concerns and conveying to them their importance in their child's therapy. The initial parent consultation provides the play therapist with the opportunity to inform parents what they need to know about play therapy and what to expect during the process. During this initial session, the therapist will explain the play therapy process to the parents, including the description of the playroom, how the therapist responds to the child, and how the process is helpful to the child. The therapist will also want to inquire about special considerations for the child that would impact the therapeutic process. For example, some young children have a history of difficulty separating from their parents. It is helpful to know that information prior to the child's first visit for play therapy so the therapist can discuss possible options with the parents and coach them on how to respond if the child clings to them.

The therapist will also take this opportunity to convey the importance of confidentiality. Although, in most states, children do not have the legal right to confidentiality, the play therapist emphasizes the need for children to experience confidentiality of specific actions and words in the playroom. In play therapy, it is expected that parents will not observe their children's play so that the child can feel free to fully express thoughts, feelings, and actions. In the first consultation, the therapist will also review the importance of attendance, indicating that sporadic participation in play therapy interferes with progress.

Finally, the play therapist highlights the need for a final session if the parents decide to prematurely terminate therapy. Often, when parents decide to terminate therapy without the support of the therapist, the process is abrupt and disconcerting to the child. A final session allows children to experience a positive end to a relationship that has been important to them. Play therapists approach the initial consultation with an attitude of relational alignment. For parents to invest in the therapeutic process, they need to feel that the play therapist is understanding and accepting of their plight. An initial consultation is not a time for education and instruction, which can quickly become overwhelming and feel judgmental to the parents.

The play therapy process encourages consistent contact with parents on an individual basis for subsequent consultations. Meeting with parents on a regular basis (at least monthly) from 30 minutes to an hour allows the play therapist to develop a relationship with the parents that will, consequently, support the child's progress. The length and frequency of parent meetings is determined by the unique needs of each family. In continuing consultations, therapists typically check with the parents about new events at home and school. To keep parents involved in their child's play therapy and help them develop a better understanding of their child, the play therapist will discuss play themes exhibited by the child during play and discuss the relevance to the child's home and school life. For example, a therapist may share that the child in play therapy seems to exhibit a significant need for power and control and responds well to choice giving by the therapist. After helping the parents better understand the child, a therapist may then teach a short concept. Using the example just given, the play therapist may follow the explanation of the theme with teaching how choice giving works and then practicing with the parents. Common skills for play therapists to teach parents are choice giving, encouragement, reflection of feeling, problem-solving techniques, returning responsibility to the child, and limit setting (Bratton et al., 2006).

Facilitating consistent consultations with parents encourages continuation of the child's therapy, improves in parenting skills, and fosters better systemic relationships within the therapeutic context. For some children who are experiencing significant difficulties at school, similar consultations with an invested teacher can be helpful and provide greater consistency in how significant adults respond to the child.

In addition, the use of CCPT principles, including involving parents more fully in their child's therapy through filial therapy training, can impact the family system by encouraging the adults in the system to make use of CCPT's relational principles, thereby creating a safer, more enhancing environment for children. The scope of this chapter prevents a detailed description of filial therapy procedures. Landreth and Bratton (2005) provide a comprehensive description of their 10-session filial therapy model based on CCPT principles and skills.

Group Play Therapy Applications

The skills used in child-centered individual play therapy are the same skills used in child-centered group play therapy. As in individual play therapy, a child-centered play therapist recognizes the group members' ability to develop their own potential to move in a positive direction (Landreth & Sweeney, 1999). Ginott (1961) recognized a child's "social hunger" as a need to interact and develop relationships with other children. Group play therapy feeds this social hunger by placing children together in an environment that provides for freedom of expression and understanding of multiple worldviews. A child's appropriateness for a referral to group play therapy is dependent on developmental readiness and presenting concerns (Landreth & Sweeney, 1999). White and Flynt (1999) advocated the use of child-centered group play therapy due to its focus on developmental appropriateness, variation of function (applicable for preventive, remedial, or crisis intervention counseling), vicarious learning and cathartic effect, positive socialization, and growth through insight.

The practicality of using child-centered group play therapy is limited by space and scheduling. In response to this limitation, the play therapist may be able to serve only two to three children in a group setting. This number allows for comfortable movement in the space, while still providing the benefits of a social environment.

Multicultural Applications

Play therapy, including filial therapy, has been used as an effective treatment modality for children across cultures (Bratton et al., 2005; Landreth & Bratton, 2005). Because of the acceptance of the child as a holistic organism, negating any preconceived labels or designations, child-centered play therapists have the opportunity to serve all children while embracing their cultural and ethnic backgrounds. As the play therapist seeks to fully know and understand each child, it is imperative that the therapist recognizes the significance of the child's culture and is open to learning about the child's and family's unique social and cultural environment. Person-centered philosophy is sometimes criticized for its individual focus that potentially ignores the contextual nature of some cultures (Kirschenbaum, 2004). However, a well-trained child-centered play therapist will recognize the impact of culture and embrace the culture as well as embracing the individual. Because toys and materials are used by the child to communicate a personal world to the counselor, toys should reflect the cultural experiences of the child.

Therapist Training

Mental health professionals who practice play therapy should have specific training in child development, as well as didactic training and supervised experience in play therapy theories and procedures. Children are not miniature adults. Because talk therapy may not be developmentally appropriate, they require an alternative form of communication. Thus, those who provide therapy for children require specialized training. All too often, graduate students receive no training to counsel children and then are assigned to an internship setting that requires them to work exclusively with children. Many universities do not have specific play therapy training; however, play therapy training and supervision is widely available through conferences and workshops. To find training near you, check with the Association for Play Therapy (www.a4pt.org) and the Center for Play Therapy (www.centerforplaytherapy.com).

Case Illustration

The following case provides a glimpse into the process of play therapy with a young child with a history of multiple interpersonal traumas. The child participated in play therapy and filial therapy with the first author for a total of 55 sessions over a 20-month period using CCPT procedures presented in the practice section. My initial objective was to establish a therapeutic relationship in which the child would feel secure and safe enough to explore all his experiences, including those that in the past had been too threatening to admit to awareness. Axline (1947) described the optimal play therapy climate as "good growing ground," where the child can fully experience all aspects of self and realize potential for growth. Specifically, this case illustration shows the child's movement toward trusting primary adults in his life, integration of his early experiences into his self-concept, and increased levels of self-acceptance and self-regulation. Regular parent consultation and filial therapy training were important components of treatment. As part of the filial therapy training, parents participated in 16 supervised play sessions with their child during the treatment period. Identifying information has been changed to protect the child and his family.

Identifying Features of the Client

Dom, an approximately 6-year-old male of Chinese descent, was referred to play therapy by his adoptive parents, both of whom are of Anglo descent. He was adopted at the age of approximately 4 years of age. Prior to then, he lived at an orphanage in China. According to sketchy records, he was abandoned at the orphanage when he was approximately 1 year old by a neighbor and given the name Dom.

At the time of intake, Dom had recently decided he wanted to be called Andy. He was living in the southwestern region of the United States with his adoptive parents, Carol and Tom; a 14-year-old stepsister, Ann (biological child of parents); and a 7-year-old stepbrother, Chris, also adopted from China when Andy was 5½ years of age. His mother was 45 years old and employed as a teacher in the private school that Andy and Chris attended. Andy's father, also 45 years old, was employed as a sales professional and traveled several days a week. The parents shared similar values and traditional Protestant beliefs. Both were actively involved in their children's extracurricular activities.

Presenting Complaints

During a phone consultation with Andy's mother, she reported concerns about his mood swings, violent outbursts, running away, stealing (at home), and refusing to let her leave home without him. Secondary concerns included eating and sleeping difficulties, gender identity issues, and possible sexual abuse from when he lived in the orphanage. She further disclosed that Andy had been diagnosed by the school psychologist with Reactive Attachment Disorder and that he was receiving special education services for a learning disability and speech and language delays. Carol's stress was obvious in her voice. I immediately scheduled her and her husband for an intake and initial parent consultation, emphasizing the importance of both of them attending. I allotted 2 hours to permit sufficient time to focus on Carol's and Tom's needs as parents of this child and to help them feel supported, while also allowing them time to tell Andy's story, a story that appeared to be rather complicated for such a short life.

Although both Tom and Carol attended the initial intake session, the following information, unless otherwise specified, was reported by Andy's mother. Intake was conducted 1 week after Andy's sixth birthday, during the summer after he had completed kindergarten. Carol began by relaying her concerns almost verbatim to her phone report, with Tom nodding but not adding anything. When asked what they enjoyed most about Andy, Carol described Andy as charming, adding, "He is very affectionate and funny and loves to cuddle." However, she quickly refocused on her concern about his episodes of sudden violent outbursts that she described as "coming out of nowhere." She reported that Andy purposely damaged things during his violent outbursts, adding that he had put holes in the wall and broken windows in their home. She reported that when he was in a "rage," she physically restrained him until he calmed down, adding that Andy generally wanted her to continue to hold him and "cuddle" after an episode.

Carol expressed a high level of frustration about not being able to leave the house without Andy. When she tried, he would chase the car until she came back. At the time of intake, she had resigned to not leaving him except at school and to occasionally try to run an errand after he was asleep. Because Carol was employed as a reading specialist at Andy's school, administrators allowed him to come to her classroom when his teacher determined that he needed his mother. Both boys came to her classroom after school while she completed her workday. When I inquired about when she had any time to herself, she joked, "Only in the bathroom . . . and even then, not always!" Although she did not complain during the intake, my impression of Carol was that she was highly stressed in her role as parent and feeling resentful.

Carol and Tom both expressed their alarm that Andy had lately begun stealing from them. When confronted, he would first deny that he took anything, and then immediately tell Carol where she "might find it." Andy's speech delay, possible learning problems, and eating and sleeping problems were briefly discussed, but those issues were not at the top of their list of current concerns.

When asked about Andy's adjustment to his adoption experience and his new family, Carol stated that he had adjusted well to their family, and Tom agreed. She reported that he refused to discuss that he was adopted or that he had lived anywhere other than with them, adding, "Andy tells people that he was born in my [Carol's] tummy." Andy acknowledged the difference in his skin color by telling Carol that she needed to "get a tan like mine." Carol found this humorous and endearing. She believed that he had blocked out all his early memories from the orphanage. Tom said little during the intake, other than that he agreed with Carol's report. Tom acknowledged that Andy is more of a problem for Carol than for him and that Andy was much closer to Carol than to him. Tom acknowledged that because he traveled several days a week, he had much less responsibility for caretaking of Andy and Chris. Tom reported that although Andy seemed to obey him better than Carol, Andy would not stay with him without Carol present.

(Continued)

Tom explained that Carol was generally the one who restrained Andy when he was out of control, because he was afraid that he would hurt Andy.

Socially, Andy was described by his parents and teacher as "acting younger than his age." He enjoyed playing with a few younger children; however, his preference was to play at home with his mother. The decision had been made that Andy would repeat kindergarten in the fall with the same teacher.

Carol's and Tom's responses on the Child Behavior Checklist (CBCL) administered at intake supported their worries about Andy's behavior at home and his performance at school. Carol's scores on the CBCL (reported in Table 20.1) fell in the clinical range in several areas. Tom's responses on the CBCL revealed a pattern of concern similar to Carol's, but showed a lesser degree of concern. A psychiatric referral for Andy was briefly discussed, but Tom and Carol were adamantly opposed to medication as a treatment option.

Table 20.1   Carol's Scores on the Child Behavior Checklist

Elements	*5 months Prior	July Pretreatment	December 5 month	May 9 month	August 12 month	December 16 month	April 20 month
Total problems	64C	65C	61B	59	59	60	58
Externalizing problems	69C	72C	67C	63B	62B	62B	60B
Syndrome scales							
Aggressive behavior	71C	72C	69B	65B	63	64	62
Rule-breaking behavior	70C	73C	65B	60	60	65B	62
Thought problems	66B	65B	58	57	58	61	58
Social problems	70C	68B	60	63	60	61	59
DSM-oriented scales							
Conduct problems	72C	73C	66B	64	63	64	63
Oppositional defiant	68B	71C	64	62	61	60	58
Affective problems	70C	70C	65B	64	61	61	60
Competency scale scores							
School	27C	24C	27C	29C	35B	30C	31B

Note: Only CBCL scales that were elevated at pretreatment intake are included.
B = Borderline clinical range; C = Clinical range.
*Administration by school psychologist 5 months prior to intake.

Carol and Tom seemed to recognize that Andy's behavior stemmed from his early experiences and genuinely wanted to understand how to help him. During this initial consultation, I believed that I had forged a strong connection with Andy's parents and that they would be active partners in the therapeutic process. We discussed what they could expect during the process of play therapy and the important role that they would play in Andy's treatment. I reviewed *What Parents and Children Need to Know about Play Therapy* (Center for Play Therapy, 1998) and gave them a copy to take home. Because Andy was genuinely remorseful after he calmed down after his violent outbursts, and Carol had already been responding by saying, "I know you don't like it when you feel this way," we mutually decided that the next time he had an episode, she would take that opportunity to explain about coming to play therapy and how it could help Andy. Because of Carol's worries regarding Andy's inability to separate from her, we decided that the three of us would meet together for Andy's first introduction to the playroom and me.

Developmental History

Very little is known about Andy's developmental history prior to adoption at age 4. His birth date and exact age were unknown, and his adoptive parents had no pictures of him until he was about 3 years old. Sketchy orphanage records revealed that when Andy was a small baby, his birth mother abruptly abandoned him with a neighbor under the pretense of running an errand, and that the neighbor kept him for an unspecified length of time prior to leaving him at the orphanage at what officials guessed to be around the age of 1 year. Andy was initially abandoned at the orphanage with no information, and these brief details were later reported by the neighbor. The orphanage staff guessed at his age based on this limited information and gave him a birth date of July 1.

Orphanage records stated that Andy never talked but that he was a very affectionate and loving baby and child. His developmental milestones were not recorded, but he was mostly toilet-trained at the time of adoption. His gross motor skills and coordination were reported by his adoptive parents to be above average. When Carol and Tom first met Andy in the orphanage they noticed that he appeared cross-eyed but that he was able to focus when they came close to him. Andy had just turned 4 years of age in July when Carol and Tom brought him from China to join their family in the United States. A checkup by the family pediatrician determined that Andy's eye condition was so severe that he could see very little and only from very close up. After being in the United States a little over 1 week, he underwent major eye surgery. Carol recalled the week directly after surgery as very stressful for Andy and for her. As part of his eye treatment, Andy wore glasses with a very strong correction.

Within a month of his arrival, 4-year-old Andy was enrolled in the prekindergarten program at Carol's school. He was described as "extremely affectionate, clingy, and shy" and as "not wanting to be away from Carol...ever!" At the age of 5, Andy was enrolled in kindergarten at the same school. During his second year with Carol and Tom, Andy began exhibiting some anger outbursts and uncontrollable crying, but not to the current extent. Because of his immaturity, Andy was scheduled to repeat kindergarten. As noted earlier, he had recently requested that everyone call him Andy, saying that Dom was a stupid name (his official American name was Andy Dom Smith).

Parental Factors and Family Dynamics

Tom and Carol had been married for 18 years at the time of intake and reported satisfaction with their marriage and lifestyle. Neither reported any remarkable history. Neither set of grandparents lived close, so the family had little contact with them other than an annual summer vacation at the beach with Carol's parents. Tom and Carol reported no more than the usual problems in rearing their

(Continued)

14-year-old daughter, Ann, whom they described as loving but stubborn and strong-willed as a child. Both parents stated that they felt closer to Andy than to Chris (who had been recently diagnosed with Fetal Alcohol Syndrome), adding that Ann and Andy also enjoyed a close relationship. Ann appeared to assume a significant amount of responsibility in helping with Andy and his brother, including discipline. Family church activities were important, although more so to Carol. Carol was the primary disciplinarian; however, she reported, "When Tom speaks the children tend to listen to him more than they do to me." She also noted that when Tom got involved in discipline it was when "he has had enough," typically when Andy and Chris are fighting and their behavior and emotions are out of control. Andy tended to be the catalyst for most fights and enjoyed being "the boss." The brothers reportedly played together fairly well because Chris would generally go along with what Andy wanted to do.

In later consultations with Carol, she disclosed feeling overwhelmed with the role of primary caretaking, and that she did not feel supported by Tom. Carol's self-report was supported by her scores on the Parenting Stress Index (PSI; Abidin, 1983), reported in Table 20.2.

Table 20.2   Parent Stress Index: Percentile Rankings for Carol's Scores

Elements	July Pretreatment (%)	December 5 month (%)	May 9 month (%)	August 12 month (%)	December 16 month (%)	May 20 month (%)
Total stress	85	83	75	50	65	55
Child domain	96	93	80	55	75	60
Adaptability	99+	98	85	55	80	70
Reinforces parent	90	80	80	55	80	55
Demandingness	85	90	65	65	75	55
Mood	85	85	60	50	60	60
Acceptability	85	90	50	50	60	40
Parent domain						
Isolation	90	85	80	70	80	70
Attachment	85	80	75	65	75	50
Spouse	85	85	80	70	80	70

Note: Scores at or above 85% are considered high. Only those scales that were elevated at time of intake are included.

Assessment

Information was gathered through interviews, informal observation, and formal assessment. Andy presented as a much smaller than average (by American norms) 6-year-old male who had just completed public school kindergarten. Formal assessment by the school district 5 months prior to his referral for play therapy confirmed significant language delays and revealed cognitive delays in several areas. However, the school psychologist determined that intelligence test results could not be considered reliable due to his significant receptive and expressive language delay. The CBCL (Achenbach, 2001) was also administered as part of the school's assessment battery. Carol's scores indicated clinical levels of concern regarding Andy's externalizing behaviors. In addition, Andy had been diagnosed by the school psychologist with Reactive Attachment Disorder (American Psychiatric Association, 1994). Carol and Tom's description of Andy's current behavior and early history were consistent with diagnostic criteria for this disorder, particularly Andy's ambivalent and contradictory approach/avoidance response to Carol and, to a lesser degree, his excessive familiarity with relative strangers. It made sense that Andy's early history placed him at risk for difficulties in developing appropriate and stable attachments.

I administered the CBCL (Achenbach, 2001) and the PSI (Abidin, 1983) to Tom and Carol. Carol's elevated scores on the CBCL were consistent with her self-report at intake and similar to, although slightly higher than, her report at the time of the school administration 5 months prior. Carol reported clinical levels of concern in Externalizing and Total Problems, School Competency, and several subscales. Her scores are shown in Table 20.1. Tom's scores on the CBCL reflected a similar pattern of behavioral concern, but at consistently lower levels than Carol. Carol's scores on the PSI were higher than what I expected based on her initial verbal report and, as shown in Table 20.2, indicate high levels of Total Stress and high levels of stress related to the Child Domain. Tom did not complete the PSI during intake. The CBCL and PSI were administered approximately every 4 months for the duration of play therapy to provide a measure of treatment outcome. Although both parents were asked to complete both instruments at each point of measurement, only Carol complied. Tables 20.1 and 20.2 show CBCL and PSI results at time of assessment, along with results from repeated measurements of the PSI and CBCL over the treatment period.

Informal assessment supported the school's findings regarding Andy's significant expressive and receptive language deficits. Immature social-emotional behavior was noted by parents and confirmed through informal observation over the first several weeks of therapy. Consistent with parent report, Andy's motor skills and coordination were observed to be very well developed for his age. Because he was receiving special education services for a learning disability and speech and language delays, and because the school recommended retesting after 1 year, no further testing was done at time of intake.

Case Conceptualization

My understanding of Andy and his treatment needs was based more on what I believe all children need rather than on the facts presented during intake. Andy needed to experience a secure and consistent relationship, both in play therapy and within his family, in which he could fully experience all aspects of self and become the person he was meant to be. That does not mean that I view all children the same, nor does that mean that the background history and information presented by Carol and Tom were not useful. It provided me with a context for understanding Andy's experiences played out in therapy as well as an understanding of the child's system, including sources of support to tap into and elements within the system that were likely hindering Andy's optimal growth.

Andy was displaying many of the symptoms one would expect from a child with his history: hypervigilance to noise (exacerbated by his inability to see much during the first 4 years of his life), difficulty going to sleep and staying asleep, eating difficulties (refusing to eat much, but wanting to save the food for later), inappropriate affection with relative strangers, and incessant fear that his adoptive mother would leave him. Andy's early experiences were characterized by a series of abandonment and loss of primary caregivers—first his mother, then the neighbor who cared for him for several months, then caregivers that came and left in the orphanage—and the loss of his cultural identity and the only home Andy could remember in his young life. That these experiences likely occurred

(Continued)

during the time in his development when separation anxiety was at its peak confirmed for Andy that his fears were real: his significant caregivers (mother, neighbor) left and did not come back. These early traumatic events likely compounded the impact of his hospitalization shortly after he arrived in the United States and his brief but traumatic separation from his new mother.

Based on Andy's behavior as reported by his parents, and consistent with my experiences of Andy as we began our relationship, I guessed that his early attachment experiences had been inconsistent; sometimes his needs had been responded to and his cries had been soothed, and other times they had not. He seemed to view the world as sometimes safe and secure and sometimes unpredictable and scary. These inconsistent early experiences with primary caregivers seemed to have resulted in two internalized and contradictory messages: (1) "I cannot depend on you. I must not be worthy of being loved and cared for. I have to take care of myself. I don't need you," and (2) "I need you, but I don't trust you. I cannot let you out of my sight, because you might not come back when I need you. I have to make you like me so you will not want to leave me." Thus, Andy approached relationships with ambiguity, which was very puzzling to Tom, and even more so to Carol, who felt rejected and confused when Andy pushed her away. I knew that helping Carol to understand that Andy's contradictory approach/avoidance response to her was "normal" given his history would be a top priority as we began therapy.

I believed that a significant factor in Andy's progress would revolve around helping Carol and Tom better understand how Andy's previous experiences impacted his current functioning. As they began to see the relationship between his early experiences, his unmet needs, and the resulting behavior that he chose to get his needs met, I believed that they would be able to accept him more fully. Several events from Andy's early experiences seemed particularly salient to his current functioning, as evidenced by his repeatedly playing out related themes. Because Andy was able to symbolically, and at times quite literally, express his world to me through play therapy, I was able to help Carol and Tom better understand Andy's needs and how they could meet them. This type of collaborative feedback proved particularly helpful to Carol.

A wise mentor once told me that if I focus too much on the problem I will lose sight of the child. With a case as complicated as this one proved to be, I had to be vigilant to not let that happen. My primary objective would be to first establish a consistent relationship in which Andy would feel secure and safe enough to explore all his experiences, including those in the past that were too threatening to admit to awareness. I would need to be patient in developing this kind of relationship with Andy, whose experience had taught him that relationships were not consistent, safe, or secure. It was my job to provide him with a corrective experience, an experience in which he would come to perceive me as an adult who was trustworthy, consistent, and predictable, one who would not leave him prematurely. An additional objective was for Andy to experience our relationship as unconditional, one in which he did not have to earn my approval or acceptance by impressing me or being overtly affectionate (his mode of connecting when we first began our relationship). My hope was that as Andy experienced unconditional acceptance in our relationship, he would begin to alter his self-perception of "damaged . . . no good," not worthy of love, to one of "lovable" and worthy of positive regard. Through these experiences, I hoped that Andy would form new perceptions of his world as safe and predictable. I believed that by providing Andy with this kind of experience he would be ready for the most critical therapeutic task of all, to experience this kind of relationship with his adoptive parents. I believed that as Andy grew to allow himself to fully experience his parents' love for him, he would no longer feel the need to push them away for fear that they would eventually leave him.

Andy's current family situation was a significant strength, a strength that I would build on during his therapy. Carol and Tom seemed amenable to participating in additional parent or family therapy services that might be recommended as an adjunct to play therapy. Although there were parenting strategies that I believed would help Carol and Tom to respond more effectively to Andy's needs, their interactions did not appear to be contributing to Andy's difficulties in any significant way. As is true for most parents and caregivers of children who have experienced trauma, I believed that Tom and Carol would benefit from direction and support regarding how to talk to Andy about his early experiences, particularly his complicated adoption story. Andy's refusal to stay with Tom was an issue that we would focus on to provide Carol with some relief and hopefully reduce her level of stress related to parenting Andy.

Helping Andy's parents learn how to establish a healthy attachment with their son would be critical to his healing; therefore, I planned to incorporate CPRT into our overall treatment plan. Additional goals that would be addressed through CPRT were (a) fostering greater understanding of Andy and his experiences, (b) normalizing Carol and Tom's understanding and response to Andy's behavior problems, (c) enhancing parent-child attunement through creating mutually enjoyable and developmentally responsive interactions, and (d) strengthening parenting skills and confidence in responding to Andy's unique and challenging needs. However, my first priority in our parent consults was to address several safety issues around Andy's violent outbursts and to help Carol become more attuned to what precipitated the events as well as develop strategies that she could implement to prevent or de-escalate the situation. One strategy that I expected would be useful was helping Carol identify times throughout the day when she could initiate holding Andy close in a loving and playful manner, rather than waiting for him to get his "holding" needs met during the aftermath of his "rages."

Course of Treatment and Assessment of Progress
Andy's mother brought him to therapy and participated in regular parent consultation. Andy attended 55 play therapy sessions, approximately 45 minutes in length, over a 20-month period. I saw Andy weekly for the first 15 weeks of treatment and after that an average of 3 times per month with the exception of summer. I met with Carol every 2 to 3 weeks to provide support and help her develop a better understanding of Andy by describing themes I observed in his play, the connection between his play and his early experiences, and how these themes were relevant to his behavior at home and school. I also used this opportunity to introduce brief CPRT parenting skills that I believed Carol could implement successfully, including reflecting feelings (particularly anger), limit setting, and choice giving (Bratton et al., 2006). Carol competed a weekly parent report form during each session while Andy was in play therapy

(Continued)

to keep me informed of any changes or significant events at home or school over the past week, as well as to rate Andy's behavior and mood compared to the week before. This was a very effective communication tool for Carol and me, providing an efficient means for us to stay connected on the weeks that we didn't formally meet.

As therapy progressed, I suggested many strategies that Carol and Tom could implement at home to promote the work being done in play therapy. They also participated in intensive filial therapy training using the CPRT protocol (Bratton et al., 2006), meeting 2 times per week over 6 weeks in the summer, when they both had breaks from teaching. During that time Andy participated in 10 supervised play sessions with his father, and Carol conducted play sessions with Chris. In the final phase of counseling, Carol participated in 6 additional weeks of supervised filial play sessions with Andy.

The playroom where Andy and I met was a fully equipped playroom similar to Landreth's (2002) description. I made sure there were baby dolls and doll figures with varying skin tones, including dolls representative of Andy's ethnicity. Andy was immediately drawn to a Native American baby doll with thick, short black hair that he initially decided was a girl. As Carol was not aware of any particular toys that Andy had played with in the orphanage, the only other culturally responsive toys included were musical instruments, food items, and eating utensils.

During a brief meeting with Andy and his mother prior to his first play therapy session, I introduced Andy to the playroom, saying, "Andy, this is the playroom where we will come each week. In here you can play with the toys in lots of the ways that you'd like," and then I allowed him time to explore. I bent down to be on his level and inquired if there was anything he wanted to ask or know more about. When he shook his head, I asked him if his mother had told him why they were here today. He informed me (with very limited English), as he looked at his mother, "Get mad and break things." I responded to let him know that lots of kids come here for the same reason, and added that this was a special place where he could play and talk about things that bothered him. Andy looked up at me and smiled, and although he didn't let go of his mother's hand, I believed that in those brief moments we had made a tentative connection. I ended the initial meeting by loaning Andy and Carol a child's storybook on play therapy to read together to help Andy feel more secure about coming to play therapy. I followed up with a phone call to Carol to discuss her concern that Andy would not separate from her and go to the playroom with me in the upcoming week and to formulate a plan for how we would respond if that occurred.

Andy was sitting in his mother's lap when I greeted him in the waiting room to take him to the playroom for our first session. I noted that he seemed a little anxious. I leaned down and made eye contact and said, "Hi, Andy. Hi, Carol. Andy, remember I showed you and your mom the playroom last week? It's time for us to go back to the playroom and play" (I slowly stood up). As if on cue (and following the instructions I had given her during intake), Carol stated, "Andy, I'll be right here waiting for you when you get through playing!" He smiled up at me, but then hesitated and looked at his mother. I quickly added, "You can choose: Should we run to the playroom or walk?" His face lit up, and he jumped up and said "Run!" as he took off down the hall with me running behind him trying to catch up. That started a weekly ritual of Andy running to beat me to the playroom. Although I gave Andy the choice of running or walking to the playroom to take his focus off separating from his mother, I was surprised he went so easily. Based on Carol's report of his extreme difficulty leaving her, I had prepared her for the eventuality of coming to the playroom with us for at least the first week. (As Andy and I ran to the playroom, I was thinking to myself that this child has more resiliency than his mother gives him credit for!) As we entered the playroom, I reminded Andy, "You can play with the toys in lots of the ways you'd like to. We will have 45 minutes to play, and then it will be time to go back to the waiting room where your mom is."

Andy's first four sessions were characterized by his need to win my approval and affection by impressing me, playing close to me, and by overt demonstrations of affection, which included touching me, patting my head, and putting his face right up next to mine. Based on his early history, it was not a surprise that he acted overly familiar with me. I knew that no amount of words would convince Andy that I already accepted him without condition—that he did not need to win my acceptance and approval. He would have to experience my acceptance firsthand before he could come to see himself as acceptable. During the fourth session, he used the flashlight to connect with me in a playful way by turning off the light in the room, then coming close to me and shining the flashlight so we could see each other's faces, saying, "You see me; I see you." I responded in kind, "I see you; you see me." He enjoyed repeating this over and over, often moving his face closer and farther away and giggling, but without trying to touch me. He seemed to have discovered a safe and fun way to connect with me.

Andy's expressive language was very underdeveloped and his speech was often difficult to understand. Many of his interactions with me consisted of one- to two-word utterances. Among his favorites were "Hey!"; "No good"; "Bad"; "What?"; "What that?"; and later, an exclaimed "Yes!" to show pride in his accomplishments. Nevertheless, he managed to communicate his world to me quite eloquently through his play. As might be expected from a traumatized child, Andy was initially hypervigilant to every noise he heard in and outside of the playroom. These disruptions made it difficult for him to focus. It was no wonder that learning was so difficult for him!

In the beginning phase of developing our relationship, Andy worked hard to gain my approval by showing me he was strong and could do difficult things, including hammering nails, lifting the sandbox and other heavy objects in the playroom, and climbing to the top of the shelves. After he successfully completed these tasks, he would often make a "muscle" with his arm to show me how strong he was. One of the first ways that he chose to impress me with his strength and ability was hammering nails into the log stump in the playroom. Because the log and hammer were next to where I usually sat, this also allowed him to remain very close to me. During our third session, as he stood by me and looked around the room, he kept glancing over at the log and hammer. I reflected, "Looks like you're wondering about that." Andy looked at me and said, "Dangerous" (obviously a response he had heard from adults). I reflected his concern, "You think maybe that would be dangerous to play with," and he shook his head no, as if to say he did not think it was dangerous. I responded, "You're not sure.

(Continued)

Well, in here it's up to you to decide if you want to play with that," letting him know that he was free to decide what to play with, just as adult clients are free to talk about what they want to talk about. Andy looked at me and looked at the log wistfully, letting me know he really would like to play with it. I reflected, "Looks like you're thinking you might like to try it out. There are some safety glasses on the hook." Andy immediately picked up the hammer and a nail and exclaimed a word I did not understand, but his actions and affect clearly communicated what he was trying to say. I replied, "You decided you want to hammer!" This brief interaction revealed Andy's struggle between his internal motivation and desire, wanting to hammer, and the external message he had received from adults that hammers are dangerous. Because I was able to respond to his internal world, he became more focused in his play and his anxiety was reduced. After he carefully hammered the first nail in, he looked at me and exclaimed, "Look!" I leaned over to look closely at his work and reflected his obvious excitement: "You wanted me to see. You got it all the way in!" He proceeded to hammer in several more nails with strength and precision and looked up at me and showed me the muscle in his arm, to which I replied, "You're really strong." He nodded his head in agreement. Then I understood better what the hammering was all about and added, "It took a lot of strength to get those nails all the way in." Although hammering initially served as an activity that Andy chose to gain my admiration, later this activity served other important functions, including demonstrating competency and expression of anger. *(A note of caution: because children can accidentally injure themselves with a hammer, I always sit close by when a child chooses this activity.)*

The fifth session marked a shift in Andy's play. He was now feeling safe enough to leave my side and explore the playroom. He delighted in his discovery of a western-type hat that had a whistle attached by a string and proceeded to spend a considerable amount of time exploring the toys on the shelves and happily blowing the whistle. He noticed the baby bottle for the first time and filled it with water from the sink, sucking contentedly on it for approximately the last third of our session while he continued to wear the hat. When I told Andy that we had 5 minutes left to play, he went to the sandbox, climbed in, lay back against the edge, and sucked on the bottle with a glazed look on his face. When I announced that our time was up, he shook his head with the bottle still in his mouth, letting me know that he wasn't ready to leave. I was patient and restated the limit as I leaned down to his level and made eye contact and reflected his desire to stay longer: "Andy, I know that you'd like to stay longer, but our time is up for today. You can drink some more from the bottle next week." I repeated similar statements three more times, letting him know I understood it was hard to leave when he was enjoying himself. Still he shook his head and remained in the sandbox. Ordinarily, I would tell my students that this is a time when you need to be more firm in your tone of voice, but I sensed that there was something different about this experience. I realized in that moment that I wished that Andy didn't have to leave either. I understood that the sucking was serving a very important function for him, but that it was also important that he experience the consistency and predictability of our time together. I bent down even closer to him and said, "Andy, I wish we didn't have to leave either, but we do. It's time for us to go back to the waiting room where Mom is." Focusing my responses on our relationship, rather than on Andy's behavior, seemed to be what he needed—a lesson that I shared with Carol in our next parent consultation. This brief but powerful interaction with Andy reminded me how important it is for me to trust my experience with children—that when I do, they let me know what they need from me.

Our next several sessions together were characterized by Andy's fascination with the whistle and the bottle (although his sucking was less intense), while continuing to show me how strong and competent he was at hammering. Blowing the whistle seemed to be serving an important expressive function for Andy. During session 7, as he happily blew to his own beat while he played, he suddenly stopped and looked at me, saying "Take whistle home?" Then he added, "Please . . . I bring back next time." For a brief moment as I looked into his pleading eyes, I almost gave in; however, I knew that this, too, was part of the consistency and predictability of the play therapy experience that Andy needed so desperately to experience. Instead, I let him know that I understood how much he wished that he could take it home and explained the playroom rule: "All the toys are for staying here in the playroom, but it will be here for you to play with next week." He seemed to be considering the rule, but stopped playing with the whistle. (Because of Andy's delay in language development, I sometimes wondered how much he understood.) A few minutes later I told Andy that we had 5 minutes left (a time when he often introduced significant play themes or play sequences). He began to paint for the first time, painting all the colors on top of each other to make a blob of brownish-black. The following brief interaction seemed to reveal Andy's inner conflict between his own wishes and needs and trying to please others, especially "Mommy."

Andy: Mommy be mad (as he began to use his hands to smear the paint).

S: You're worried that Mommy will be mad.

Andy: Messy (as he went to the sink and washed the paint off hurriedly).

S: You're worried that Mom wouldn't like it if you got messy. But before I could get the words out, he began to take his shoes off and looked over at me to see what I thought (as if to ask my approval).

S: Looks like you're not sure if that's okay. In here you can decide if you want to take your shoes off or leave them on. (Andy takes both shoes off.) You decided you wanted them off. (I responded to his internal desire.)

Andy went back to the paints and picked up the paint brush and looked at me and said something I did not understand as he proceeded to paint one hand and then the other, then sat down and began to paint the bottom of his feet, enjoying the feel of the brush (much like the sensorimotor play of a younger child).

Andy: Tickles (a big smile on his face).

S: You like how that feels.

S: Andy, we have 1 minute left to play, then it's time to wash up to go home. (I was careful to make sure that we washed all the paint off his feet and hands before we went back to the waiting room to prevent potential guilt feelings that Andy might experience if Carol reacted adversely to a "messy Andy.")

(Continued)

In our next parent consultation, I reminded Carol of the importance of Andy's wearing old clothes to play therapy so that he could get messy if he needed to, and we discussed what making "messes" might symbolize for him.

For the next 2 sessions, Andy repeated this ambivalent play theme of "Mommy be mad" and "Not supposed to get messy" and the obvious joy of getting messy, smearing paint on the paper and painting his hands and feet. My responses followed a similar pattern, reflecting that he was concerned about what his mom would think, but focusing on his enjoyment of the experience and always making sure he was returned to his mother mostly clean. Andy's play seemed to reflect his continued internal struggle between perceived external demands of pleasing others (hypervigilance), including an awareness that his "out-of-control" behavior was unacceptable ("not okay to be messy"), and his internal need to express all aspects of self, even the "messy and chaotic."

Andy reveled in his newfound freedom in the playroom. As he experienced the safety and freedom to fully express himself, his play became more focused and meaningful. It was during this phase of play therapy that he began to display more of his conflicted and difficult feelings, most notably his sense of being damaged or "no good." He would inspect all the toys, and any that had the slightest flaw or did not seem to work properly were deemed "no good" and thrown away. During this period, he would sometimes mumble "No good" up to two dozen times in a session.

During our parent consult in week 9, Carol announced that Andy's "stealing" was now happening at school as well as at home. It was obvious from Andy's play ("Mommy be mad") that he perceived that Carol was angry and upset with him, although she denied it initially. On the surface Carol was trying to appear understanding, but underneath her façade she was embarrassed and upset with Andy. Her response seemed exacerbated by the fact that she taught at the same school and was concerned about what her colleagues would think. I helped her understand that Andy was picking up on her underlying feelings, even though she was not directly expressing them to him. We again discussed Andy's hypersensitivity to nonverbals. This problem was significantly impacting Carol's acceptance of Andy; thus we needed to actively address possible solutions.

My first priority was to help Carol and others to reframe how they viewed Andy's behavior. It seemed obvious that Andy's stealing, as described by Carol, was not malicious. Thus I asked Carol to use the term "taking things that belong to others" instead of "stealing" when talking to Andy (and others) about his behavior. Although I could have made guesses about several possible underlying reasons why Andy was taking things that did not belong to him, the explanation that seemed to help Carol and others normalize Andy's actions was that this behavior could best be understood as a function of a significant developmental delay (one of many regressed behaviors he demonstrated). I explained to Carol that her description of the events and Andy's response when confronted were consistent with what one would expect from much younger children who simply see something they want or need and take it. I reminded her of a toddler's worldview: "If I want it, it's mine!" She agreed that if Andy were 2 years old she would not see his behavior as stealing. Carol and I devised a plan for how to respond to Andy at home and at school if and when he initiated this behavior again. Carol and I talked with Andy's teacher at school to discuss the plan, and Carol also elicited school administrators' help. We all approached this as if Andy's behavior was a function of development and that it was our job as adults to help further his development by helping him learn the concept of ownership and people's related feelings about their property. Andy's parents and the school were instrumental in helping Andy move through this phase over the next several weeks. This is just one example of many instances in which they proved to be incredible allies throughout the therapeutic process!

Andy's play during the next several weeks could best be described as disorganized and chaotic. This relatively short phase was marked by the most intensely negative affect during our time together. Themes of "bad boy" and "no good" persisted. He began to actively deal with the issue of stealing. For the next 4 weeks he was focused on trying to figure out a way to take the whistle from the playroom. Each week he would retrieve the hat with whistle from the shelf, take it behind the puppet theater, cut the string to get the whistle off, and then try to figure out how to take it out without my knowing. He was generally agitated and often unfocused in his play once he had the whistle cut off. The first time he hid the whistle under the beanbag chair behind the puppet theater. He kept asking me how much time we had left and for the first time wanted to leave early. After I stated that there were 5 minutes left, he went behind the theater and put the whistle in his pocket and then came over to me and pulled it out and showed me "his whistle" that he had "brought from home." I responded that it looked just like the one we had in the playroom. At first he tried to convince me that it was his and then said, "Just kidding," and put it back on the shelf. I let him know that I understood how much he liked the whistle and wished that he had one like it.

During the next 2 sessions his level of agitation was at an all-time high. In each session, Andy immediately took the hat and whistle behind the theater, cut the whistle off, and stuffed it in his pocket. His play was highly disorganized and he was clearly distressed. (I was having difficulty being with him in this experience and found myself wanting to rescue him. I had to work very hard to not let my need to protect Andy from these difficult feelings interfere with his need to work through them in his own way. I found myself needing to seek peer supervision over the next few weeks to process my own feelings and avoid imposing my needs onto Andy.) During session 13, with the whistle already pocketed, Andy spent 15 minutes throwing toys, repeating, "No good, no good." I reflected, "Nothing seems to be going right today." He seemed to calm down for a moment, and with less intensity than before, he hit himself in the head (with his hand) and said, "Stupid." I went over to him and reflected, "Andy, I know you're upset about something, but you're not for hitting." He paused and looked up at me and quietly said, "I want to go." I knew it was important to maintain the structure and consistency of our time together, so I held firm and replied with all the empathy I was feeling for this little boy, "Andy, I know that you're having a hard time in the playroom today, but we have 20 minutes left and then it will be time to go." He insisted, "I don't want to play anymore." I replied softly, "That's up to you.... You can choose to play or not to play in the 20 minutes that we have left." He did not try to leave, but every few minutes he looked at the clock and asked me how much time we had left. When I told him we had 1 minute left, he went straight to the door with obvious relief. At this point, he still had the whistle in his pocket. As he got to the door, I gently responded, "Andy, I think maybe you put the whistle in your pocket

(Continued)

when you were playing with it earlier. Remember, the toys are for staying in the playroom." First he shook his head no. "Maybe you should check to make sure." He put his hand in his pocket and said, "I forgot," and pulled out the whistle and handed to me. As I put it back on the shelf I reminded him that "it will be right here for you next week." (I tried to remember each week to check the playroom in advance to make sure I kept my promise.) The next session followed a similar pattern; however, Andy was noticeably less agitated, and when it was time to leave he pulled the whistle out of his pocket without any prompting and said, "Oh yeah," and handed it to me matter-of-factly.

The change in Andy's affect in our next session was remarkable. He was very excited to see me and ran straight to find the hat and whistle and put it on his head. It was the first time in 5 weeks that he had not cut the string and hidden the whistle. He put the hat on and marched around the room happily blowing the whistle (very free), all the while sucking on the baby bottle for the first time since he became preoccupied with the whistle. He spent the majority of the session with the whistle in one hand and the bottle in the other, much of the time marching to a beat of suck-suck—whistle-whistle. Whereas his play over the past 4 weeks was constricted, agitated, and chaotic, his play this week was spontaneous and joyful. It was during the last 5 minutes of this session that Andy first introduced the "spinning game," his name for a game he devised that involved his directing me to spin him around while he sat in the swivel chair that I normally sat in. There were several variations of this game, but they all had in common a theme of mother-baby play. Little did I know just how important this game would become!

This tumultuous phase in Andy's play seemed to represent his struggle for self-regulation as he internalized the concept that the whistle was not his and that although he wanted it, he could now choose to play with it and give it back (just as outside of the session, he was struggling with understanding this concept on a larger scale). The combined impact of his being able to play out his struggles in the safety of the playroom with me as a supportive witness to his expression of difficult feelings, and his parents' and teacher's changed attitude and response to his behavior at home and school resulted in an almost complete halt in the stealing behavior. Carol reported that Andy was no longer taking things at school and that he had mostly stopped this behavior at home. Her scores on the CBCL and PSI completed after session 15 supported her verbal report of Andy's improvement in this area as well as in the frequency and intensity of his anger outbursts.

Andy's play over the next 10 sessions was characterized by greater spontaneity in self-expression and increased positive affect. For a child that had begun therapy being so hypersensitive to what he needed to be in order to win others' approval, this movement was just what I had hoped for. During this time, he found the baby dolphin and chose it to become a central figure in his play. He often carried "Baby" around while he played or gave it to me to hold. He determined that the dolphin was male and was especially gentle with it. Andy continued the spinning game, which became increasingly more intimate. He would often lie in the chair and suck from the bottle, gazing at me and sometimes giggling while he directed me to spin him around and around.

It was also during this time that he introduced his favorite game, "hide-and-find." With the exception of a few breaks, this was a game that Andy delighted in up until our termination, sometimes spending over half of our session in this activity. From the first time he introduced this activity, with "Close eyes, I hide," I sensed that this game was very important to him. I wanted to play my part just the way he needed me to; thus I inquired, "How will I know when you're ready?" Andy said, as if it were obvious, "Count to 10," and after I did, "Find me!" he yelled. I slowly began to look for him. (I was wondering to myself, Does he need me to find him easily or take a long time? Because of his abandonment issues, I believed that how I responded to my task of finding him was vital.) In a soft voice, I asked, "Are you going to be easy to find or hard to find?" Andy paused a minute and said, "Hard!" So I began a long search around the room, amplifying my movements and efforts to find him, often exclaiming variations of "I bet you're over here.... Hmm, not here ... You hid really well.... I wonder where you are?" When he would giggle, I would reflect, "I hear something. You must be over there." Each time we played this out, no matter whether he chose to be easy to find or hard to find, he always gave me clues to let me know when he was ready to be found. We were in synch with each other; I knew when and how he needed me to respond. Again, Andy had chosen a playful and safe way to deepen our relationship and work through his early experiences of what I guessed to be an inconsistent response to his nurturing needs. He was learning that I could be trusted to consistently respond to what he needed. Through this experience and his experience of being with a loving family, I hoped that Andy would begin to see the world as secure and predictable—a place where he could depend on adults to keep him safe and respond appropriately to his needs.

Andy was clearly working on attachment and trust issues that I believed could be more effectively addressed by involving Carol and Tom in his play therapy. We discussed starting CPRT training in the near future so that Andy could play out his attachment needs with his parents. We agreed that Andy was making good progress, including a reduction in his violent outbursts, a marked decrease in stealing, and fewer sleep problems. We tentatively discussed ending therapy by the end of the school year.

During this time, Carol reported that Andy was showing more interest in what he was like as a baby. When he saw babies on television, he would ask, "Did I look like that?" When he saw pictures of babies, he would ask, "Was that me?" Once again, I recommended that Carol help Andy make an adoption scrapbook to help him understand his adoption story, and we practiced how she could explain events to him in appropriate words (suggestions that Carol continued to resist; it was, after all, a difficult story to explain). However, as a result of our discussions, Carol and Tom came up with a remarkable plan. They had arranged for a 17-year-old exchange student from China to live with them for the next academic school year. Because of Andy's increased interest in adoption issues and Tom's work schedule which prevented him from starting the CPRT and filial training, we decided to continue play therapy until the end of the school year and begin CPRT the first week in June, when his schedule allowed him to travel less.

Sessions 25 through 28 marked the introduction of another significant play theme, although I had no idea what it meant at the time. Andy's play was highly

(Continued)

organized and purposeful. He clearly had a plan in mind. He began to use the dress-up clothes trunk as an important part of his play, first by taking everything out and trying on most of the clothes to see how he looked. He would often dress up both of us so that we looked similar and exclaim, "I girl like you!" I was a bit puzzled by what this meant for Andy, but he took great delight in this activity. However, what puzzled me most was that he ended this play sequence each week with a ritual of putting the lit flashlight in the trunk, along with the baby dolphin, and closing the lid. Before he left the playroom, he would open the lid to make sure the light was still on. He seemed to gain a great deal of satisfaction from his play during these weeks. Although at this point I did not comprehend the meaning his play held, I conveyed my understanding that it was important to him.

By this time, school was out and Andy had successfully completed his second year of kindergarten. Carol's scores on the CBCL and PSI (Table 20.1 and 20.2) reflected her weekly reports and comments regarding Andy's improved behavior, most notably in the areas of sleep, stealing, and anger outbursts.

In keeping with our plan, Carol and Tom began intensive CPRT training twice a week, following the treatment protocol outlined by Bratton et al. (2006). We had 6 weeks before they and their family would be going on vacation. During that time I did not see Andy in play therapy, because he was coming to the clinic twice a week to have play sessions with his dad as part of the CPRT and filial therapy training. Carol conducted her play sessions with Andy's stepbrother, Chris. Carol and Tom and I decided that this was a good opportunity to focus on helping Andy develop a closer bond with Tom, in hopes of relieving Carol of her full-time parenting role. Andy played out some of the same themes with his dad that he played with me, particularly doctoring the baby and sucking from the baby bottle. I had prepared Tom for the possibility that Andy might want to suck from the bottle, but Tom struggled to accept that behavior from his now almost 7-year-old son. He understood that it was important to Andy and that he should be accepting, but as he said, "That's easier said than done." We role-played how Tom could respond in a way that would convey his acceptance and encourage Andy to involve him in his play, but what seemed to help most was asking Tom to remember when Anne (his 14-year-old biological daughter) was a baby and how he had enjoyed holding her close and giving her a bottle. Andy had not had the opportunity to have that experience with him or Carol (and maybe not with anyone).

Both Tom and Carol were motivated students and became fairly proficient in demonstrating the CCPT play skills taught in CPRT. Each session began with a review of skills, role-play, and questions, immediately followed by Tom and Carol taking turns conducting play sessions with their respective child of focus, while I supervised through the two-way mirror. After both parents had conducted a play session, I met briefly with them to give feedback and to process their play sessions. I focused primarily on helping them better understand what Andy and Chris were communicating through their play. The children were supervised by clinic staff when they were not participating in play sessions. During this time, both Tom and Carol reported that this was the least stressful time since they had adopted both boys. They agreed to continue their weekly play sessions while they were on their monthlong vacation at the beach. Because Andy seemed to be actively addressing his attachment needs, we decided that I would see

Andy for at least one more month after they returned to allow for appropriate termination of our relationship.

Andy and I resumed play therapy 2 weeks before he would start first grade and the week before Dong, the exchange student, arrived from China. I had not seen Andy in 5 weeks and had not had a play session with him in 11 weeks. Carol completed the fourth measurement of the CBCL and PSI to assess progress over the summer months, when the only treatment provided had been CPRT (and going to the beach for a month!).

Andy was very excited to see me and pulled me down the hall running. He ran ahead and when I entered the room, he was inside the trunk covered with clothes. He delighted in jumping up and yelling, "Boo!" Andy's play seemed to pick up where he had left off, with a fascination for the dress-up clothes and the trunk. With 5 minutes left, I guessed that he had something important in mind as he blocked the door and taped it so "we can't get out." He quickly threw the rest of the clothes from the trunk and climbed inside, trying several different positions to see how he could make himself fit. Then he climbed in again and curled up in a distinctly fetal position and told me he wanted me to close the lid. I clarified that he would let me know when I should open it. He told me he would knock, and he demonstrated that he would knock three times. He replayed this scenario three more times, staying inside only a few seconds each time. He obviously had something else in mind, as he very purposefully retrieved the flashlight from its spot on the shelf to take it with him inside the trunk. He turned on the light and curled into a little ball and told me to shut the lid "all the way." This time he stayed for almost a minute, although it seemed like several minutes to me. I glanced at my watch and noted that we had 1 minute left and bent down and whispered into the trunk, "Andy, we have 1 minute left." He immediately knocked on the lid to let me know he was ready to come out and ran over to get the baby dolphin and the baby bottle of juice. He carefully laid them inside the trunk on a soft piece of fabric, along with the lit flashlight and shut the lid. Again, I had no idea what all of this meant for Andy, only that he was working hard and had a definite plan in mind, one that he first conceived of 12 weeks ago!

Following this session, Carol and I met for our regular consultation. She looked more relaxed than I had ever seen her. She discussed Dong's arrival from China in the coming week and how excited Andy was that he and Dong would be sharing a room. Then Carol said, "I just remembered what I wanted to tell you. Andy said the strangest thing to me this week. He asked me if he had a flashlight when he was in his mommy's tummy." (By now, Andy was able to acknowledge that he came from someone else's tummy—not Carol's.) Carol disclosed that Andy had continued to be preoccupied with babies over the summer. He loved to watch shows on cable television that showed babies being born and persistently asked, "Was that me?" They had recently purchased *The Miracle of Life,* which was now Andy's favorite movie. Now, Andy's flashlight-in-the-trunk play made perfect sense: He was trying to make sense of where he came from, quite literally! Carol's scores on the fourth measure of the CBCL and PSI in August reflected her self-report of "how relaxing and uneventful" the summer had been. The CPRT filial training, 1 month at the beach, and continuing the home play sessions seemed to be just what the doctor ordered for this family.

(Continued)

"I got new big brother!" Andy exclaimed when I greeted him the next week. He was obviously excited, and much of his play revolved around his "new big brother." He played inside of the trunk again with the baby dolphin and the flashlight, but with less intensity. He did not ask me to close the lid. This was the end of Andy's important in-the-trunk play until our closing session. In the next 5 sessions, his play was primarily focused on issues related to attachment and mastery. His play showed increased levels of reciprocity and sharing. He continued to suck the bottle, but with much less intensity (his sucking need seemed to have decreased in response to the play sessions with his mom and dad over the summer). We spent extended periods of time playing the spinning game, which had become increasingly more intimate, sometimes with the light off and sometimes with Andy directing me to shine the flashlight under my chin or his so we could see each other. He delighted in inventing several variations of baby-like games in which he directed me to touch and count his fingers and toes while I spun him around. During this time, he also began to express negative feelings toward me directly. One day I was 15 minutes late for a session and he wouldn't look at me as we walked to the playroom (no running today!). When we entered the playroom, he looked at me and then kicked the inflatable bop bag. I reflected, "Seems like you might be mad that I was late. It's okay to tell me that you're mad." Andy shook his head slightly as if to say he was not mad. It seemed important to help him understand that it is okay for people to get mad at each other and that our relationship could recover. I bent down to Andy and gently said, "You were expecting me to be here today when I was supposed to, and I wasn't. I'm sorry" (something I should have said earlier).

Dong's arrival seemed an impetus for Andy to more directly address issues around the orphanage, his adoption, and cultural identity. Themes of attachment, trust, and mothers and babies (often looking for each other) continued over the next 15 weeks. His play became more complex and imaginative. During this time he often had difficulty leaving the playroom. Carol and I discussed the importance of Andy's play themes and his need for the safety of the play therapy relationship to play out and express these confusing experiences. We decided he should continue in play therapy.

Session 36 marked Andy's first attempts to play out what seemed to be experiences that were directly related to his abandonment by his birth mother and his orphanage experience. The baby dolphin had long been a favorite and a meaningful toy for him. I already sensed that he used the dolphin to represent himself. (Andy had previously identified it as a baby and as a male during in-the-trunk play.) He took the baby dolphin and for the first time buried it deep in the sand. He abruptly left it there and began to hammer nails in the log for the first time in several weeks. I saw this behavior as a "play disruption," a sudden shift from play that seems to hold specific meaning for the child in response to anxiety or discomfort (Findling, Bratton, & Hensen, 2006). Dealing with traumatic material can be retraumatizing; thus it was important for Andy to approach this at his own pace. Later he went back to the sandbox and looked at me and said, shaking his head, "Don't know where he is." I simply reflected, "Not sure where he is," not knowing who it was that didn't know where the baby was. I waited patiently to see if a story would unfold. Andy found the large dolphin (which I interpreted as a mother or caregiver figure) and a few other caregiver-figure animals (a seal, a walrus, and a polar bear) off the shelf and placed them carefully in the sandbox. He again abruptly went back to hammering (an activity that he had long ago mastered). After I announced that we had 5 minutes left, Andy went to the sandbox and hurriedly moved the "mother" animals all around on top of the sand as if they were all looking for the baby, then had the large dolphin dig down and find the baby and exclaim, "There he is!" He then took the little dolphin and made it flip up in the air as if it were jumping out of water. I reflected, "It looks like he's happy that they found him." (Inside, I was struggling with staying with Andy's expression of wanting his mother to find him and knowing that that will not happen. My need to try to protect him from being hurt had surfaced again.) I wondered if Andy's play represented wishful thinking that he could go back and find his mom (or remembered "mother figure"), like Dong would go back to his family in China at the end of the year.

From the beginning of Dong's stay Carol and I had discussed the importance of helping Andy understand that Dong would be going back to China at the end of the school year. Because of Andy's thematic play, I made a note to further discuss these issues with Carol, along with adding more facts to his adoption story. I also found a child's book on adoption that more closely mirrored Andy's own experience than the books that Carol had been able to find. *We Adopted You, Benjamen Koo* (Girard, 1989) became a favorite of Andy's; he could relate to the boy, whose skin color was different from his parents', who did not know his real birthday or name, and who would probably "never know his birth mother."

Using animals rather than people figures to make sense of his adoption experience seemed to provide Andy with the safety and distance he needed. On two occasions he initiated brief play with mother dolls with two different skin colors, but both times he abandoned the play. Over the next several weeks Andy was preoccupied with babies and mothers. In our clinic playrooms, we have several sets of animal families grouped together. He readily identified the "babies" and separated them from the mother-figures, devising various scenarios of what happened next. Often he would place the babies across the room from the mothers, sometimes out of sight behind the puppet theater. My responses mirrored his actions; sometimes the babies could not find the mothers and sometimes the mothers could not find the babies. In Andy's play there were always more babies than mothers, which seemed to reflect his orphanage experience. Another theme that emerged was that the baby dolphin began to receive better care than the other babies; the others often were thrown down from the shelf, but the baby dolphin was always gently handed to me to hold. (I took that as a positive sign of self-nurturing, and that Andy was internalizing messages from his adoption story that Carol and he had been working on. I knew that the story conveyed the message, "We chose you out of all the children," and other messages that conveyed that he was "special.") Andy returned to burying the baby dolphin deeply in the sand, but with a different story line this time. For the first time he identified the large dolphin as a mother and then handed it to me as if I knew what I should do.

S: What am I supposed to do? (soft voice).

Andy: Look for baby.

S: Is he going to be hard to find or easy to find?

Andy: Hard (I started to look in the sandbox).

(Continued)

Andy: No—everywhere, not here. (Now, I understood, I was supposed to search for the baby dolphin the way I searched for Andy when we played hide-and-find.)

S: I may need some help if you want me to find him. (After I had spent a long time looking for the baby and not getting a sense of what Andy needed from me. I was not sure who I represented—birth mother, orphanage caregiver, or maybe even Carol; neither did I understand if he wanted me to find the baby or not, so I was careful to let him fully direct this play sequence. Andy never did direct me to find the baby, but he seemed to enjoy that I was methodically looking all over the playroom.)

S: I'm looking everywhere I can think to look, but I can't find him. . . . I wonder where he is? (Andy looked at me and shrugged his shoulders.)

S: I don't know where he is either, but I'm going to keep looking. . . . I'm not giving up.

Andy seemed content that I (as the mother dolphin) looked everywhere and never gave up. He also seemed content or resigned to the fact that in this session the mother never found the baby. Andy seemed to be integrating his previous experiences into a positive memory of being wanted and special, even if his mother had left him. Just before we left the playroom each week, he was always careful to return the dolphin to its place on the shelf. It seemed important to him that the baby was left in its safe and predictable spot. In subsequent sessions Andy's mother–baby animal play continued, but with less focus on the mother dolphin. He no longer buried the baby dolphin and began to include the polar bear, seal, and walrus as more central figures in his play. Although he occasionally continued to place the mother dolphin in the sandbox, the other figures played a more active part in his play. These figures seemed to represent his current family, with the polar bear taking on an increasingly nurturing role. Often, he would make a "home" just for the polar bear and baby dolphin, and the other animals were left out. Consistent with Carol's report, although Andy would now stay with Tom while she went out for a brief period of time, he still preferred to spend time just with her. Although we were making progress, Andy was not at the point with Carol that he had fully internalized the important attachment messages "When you leave me, I know you will come back" and "I can count on you to meet my needs." Andy was clearly working on attachment issues and making sense of his adoption experience; thus Carol and I decided to continue play therapy and reevaluate monthly.

During this phase of therapy, hide-and-find and the spinning game were central to Andy's play activity. He continued to fill the bottle with juice each week, but often simply drank from it more than he sucked. He would often fill it and leave it on the shelf (in case he needed it). He explored the limits of our relationship by purposefully, yet playfully, choosing to break limits that neither hurt the room nor me, such as shooting me in the back with the dart gun and spraying me with water. The only new play that he introduced during this time was related to making sense of his cultural identity. He introduced two puppets, "Shake Your Bootie Guy," a ferocious-looking dragon who spoke English, and "Donga," a cute little girl puppet with a big smile that made baby-like noises that sounded like the Chinese equivalent of "ga-ga-goo-goo." From Carol's report, Andy did not know any Chinese-language words other than a few words he had learned from Dong. Andy incorporated Shake Your Bootie Guy and Donga primarily into our hide-and-find play, varying how he used them. I took it as a positive sign that both puppets were important to him. Toward the end of his therapy, Andy began to choose a similar, but friendlier-looking version of Shake Your Bootie Guy to sometimes represent Donga. I thought this might be a sign that he was beginning to integrate his two cultures.

The fifth measure of treatment outcome was administered after session 42, at the end of the fall semester. Carol reported overall improvement in Andy's behavior, although school continued to place additional stress on Andy, which placed additional stress on Carol. Her scores on the CBCL and the PSI reflected Andy's school stress, as well as her stress related to parenting a more stressed Andy. Although he continued to be much improved from when he started play therapy, his scores were slightly more elevated than they had been prior to the beginning of this school year. Carol and I decided that Andy would continue in play therapy. I encouraged Carol to resume her home play sessions with Andy, at least during the holidays.

Sessions 43 to 45 marked a brief but tumultuous shift in Andy's play, with a marked increase in expression of negative affect. He was clearly feeling conflicted about something. His anger was expressed more directly toward me, although I suspected this was transference of his feelings toward his mother. On two occasions he stated, "I'm gonna make a big mess" and proceeded to follow through with his threat, purposefully knocking toys off the shelves that he knew would not break. (I thought to myself that this was progress: Andy seldom expressed his anger directly and in such a controlled manner.) I reflected that he seemed angry and that he was showing me how mad he was. The second week that this happened, I wondered aloud, "Seems like maybe you're still mad about something." Andy exclaimed, "Yeah—you're mean!" He then proceeded to hammer the nails really hard for several minutes until he seemed spent, and I reflected, "It feels good to hit it really hard when you're mad." Andy spent the rest of the session focusing on our relationship by playing hide-and-find in the dark with the flashlight. During our last 5 minutes, he initiated the spinning game with a new twist; he filled the bottle with juice, took his glasses off, and pushed the chair so it was touching my legs. Then he showed me he how he wanted me to just barely move the chair back and forth (it felt like rocking). He lay across the chair and contentedly sucked while he gazed into my eyes with a glazed look. It was a very intimate moment, the kind he needed to be having with Carol and Tom. I made a mental note to talk with Carol about taking a break from play therapy and beginning filial therapy in the next couple of weeks.

When Andy and I returned to the reception area, Carol was insistent that she needed to talk to me before they left. I knew by her tone of voice that it must be important, and so did Andy. I bent down to let Andy know that his mom and I would be back in 15 minutes (that was all the time I had before another appointment) and that he would stay with Jane (the receptionist) while we were gone. Andy grabbed his mom around the waist and stated adamantly that he didn't want her to go and was not going to let her go. Although on the surface his words and actions conveyed one message, I had the strongest sense that the real issue was that he did not want me to hear what his mother was planning to say, that he believed that what she had to say would negatively impact my view of him. I did something I have never done before; I knelt down beside Andy and whispered so that only he could hear, "Andy,

(Continued)

there's nothing your mom could say to me that would ever change how I feel about you." Although, in general, I believe that my actions with children speak much louder than my words, I sensed that Andy needed to hear this. I knew that he experienced my acceptance of him as unconditional, but his past experiences told him that things can (and will) change. He looked at me for a few moments as if he was deciding if I was telling the truth, then smiled at me as if to say "Okay" and went over to watch the cartoon playing in the waiting room. Our relationship had passed a test. I was reminded once again of the importance of trusting my intuitive sense of what children need from me.

Andy's academic performance and behavior at school were bothering Carol, and her frustration was carrying over to home, where she felt unsupported. Although Andy seemed to be experiencing more problems at school than he had in a while, Carol's extreme reaction was my main concern. Her escalating level of stress was an indication that I needed to shift my focus to strengthening the relationship between Carol and Andy and at the same time provide Carol with some much-needed parental support. Carol was initially unsure about taking a break from play therapy to focus on filial therapy, but I emphasized to her that right now Andy needed her more than he needed me. Coincidentally, I also sensed at this moment that Carol needed me more than Andy did. We decided that she would begin filial play sessions with Andy in 2 weeks during our regularly scheduled appointment time.

At the beginning of our next session, I explained to Andy that he and I would be taking a break from playing together: "You and I will come to our playroom two more times, and after that, you and Mom will get to play together in the family playroom." (I always use a different playroom for parent-child play sessions if I am concurrently seeing the child in play therapy.) In Andy's next two sessions with me, he showed me that he was secure and confident in our relationship. The spinning game and sucking on the baby bottle were his primary play activities. Instead of just counting fingers and toes, Andy taught me how to sign "I love you" as I spun him around.

For the next 4 weeks, I coached and supervised Carol's play sessions with Andy. I spent time supporting her worries and concerns about Andy and about her being a good enough mother for him. We actively worked on increasing her enjoyment and acceptance of Andy for who he is, school difficulties and all. Andy enjoyed seeing me at the clinic, but was eager to play with his mom. Carol reported feeling much less stressed, and we both agreed that Andy's behavior had improved markedly by the end of the 4 weeks. A return to filial play sessions proved to be just what Carol and Andy needed. With the end of the school year 5 weeks away, Carol and I decided that it would be a good time to end treatment, at least for now.

Planning for the ending of therapy is important for all children, but even more so for children who have had multiple experiences of abandonment and loss. I knew that how I approached the ending of our relationship would be critical so that Andy would not perceive me as yet another important adult (and female) who was leaving him. I explained to Carol that I would meet with her and Andy briefly before Andy's play session in the following week to talk with both of them about termination. I explained to Carol that I would be letting Andy know why I believed that he no longer needed to come, and that I would ask Andy and Carol what they thought about ending our sessions. I encouraged Carol to say to Andy what she had reported to me about the improvements she was seeing. Because Andy and I had such a long-standing relationship, I decided that 4 weeks would be an appropriate termination phase. In our meeting with Andy, Carol did a remarkable job of conveying to Andy all the positive changes that she had seen over the past several months. Although Andy did not say much, he seemed to understand that we would be ending soon. Marking the weeks on a calendar I gave him, I told Andy he would come to the clinic four more times, and that each week he could decide if he wanted to play with his mom or with me. Because he had been playing most recently with his mother, it seemed important to give him the option of play therapy with me or filial play sessions with his mom.

For the first of our termination sessions, Andy decided to have a filial play session with his mother, but afterward he announced, "All the next times, just you and me play." His play over the last three sessions was primarily constructive and showed his mastery over the playroom. He didn't introduce any new play and seemed to be replaying our time together, almost like fast-forwarding a favorite home movie. He briefly played out some of his more destructive, confused, and chaotic play, but without the previous intensity. Mostly, he enjoyed repeatedly playing his favored hide-and-find and spinning game, while making sure he had some time for hammering the log in our last moments together.

When I went to meet Andy in the waiting room for our last time together he showed me the cupcake he had brought. He whispered in my ear that he needed a lighter and showed me the candle he had in his pocket. (I later found out that he wanted Carol to let him bring a lighter and, understandably, she refused.) It seemed very important to Andy, so I retrieved a lighter from my office. He directed me to light the candle on the cupcake and sing "Happy Birthday," after which he blew out the candle and said, "Do it again!" Andy's birthday was 2 months away, but he seemed to have found a perfect way to celebrate our ending and at the same time, his beginning. We repeated the scenario 12 times, with Andy sometimes joining in the singing. He looked into my face with a huge smile the entire time I sang to him. After the 12th round of "Happy Birthday," he said that we could now eat the cupcake and carefully cut it in half with a play knife from the kitchen.

"Spinning game!" Andy announced, which I had long ago learned meant he would sit in the swivel chair and that I would sit in the smaller chair. After a few rounds of playing our traditional spinning game, touching fingers, counting, and signing, he went to get the flashlight and announced with a huge grin, "Hide and find!" At that point in our relationship, we needed few words to communicate meaningfully with each other. Andy spent most of the rest of the session hiding in all the places he had hid over the months we had been together, starting with the oven in the play stove that he was no longer able to fit in and ending with the dress-up clothes trunk that had been such an important part of his play. With each new hiding place he would giggle as he told me without my prompting whether he was going to be "easy to find" or "hard to find."

After I announced that there were 5 minutes left in the session, he came back and sat down by me and began to tell me about going to his grandmother's beach house for the summer (it was very unusual for Andy to sit and talk!). He let me know that he is going to have two birthday parties, one here with his friends and his "real" birthday party at his grandmother's house. Then Andy looked up

(*Continued*)

at me and said, "I won't see you." I assured him that although we wouldn't see each other for a while, he could always call me. I wrote down the clinic phone number and gave it to him. Then he looked up at me for a few moments and said quietly, "You might need to call me." I leaned over and quietly replied, "Sounds like you're worried about us not seeing each other. Anytime you need me or want to come back here, you can call or tell your mom." Then Andy responded with a big smile, "I know! I give you my phone number," as he wrote the number and gave it to me. I smiled in response and exclaimed, "Now we both know how to call each other if we need to." Andy seemed very satisfied that he had figured this out; it was important for him to know that although I would not physically be with him, I was not abandoning him, that I would be available if he needed me. Andy then jumped up and ran behind the puppet theater and yelled, "Guess where I am?" (without turning out the lights). I stood up to begin our usual ritual of hide-and-find, prepared to search all around the room for him, when after just a few moments (not waiting for me to find him, as he had always done in the past), he jumped from behind the puppet theater, threw his arms wide in the air, and with a huge smile on his beautiful face, exclaimed, "HERE I AM!" I could not have summed it up any better! I responded by throwing my arms in the air and exclaimed, "Yes, THERE YOU ARE!"

I am always amazed by how children know what they need to bring closure to the therapeutic relationship if they have proper notice. Just thinking about our last moment together brings a huge smile to my face. Andy was free; he no longer needed me. He was well on his way to fully becoming all that he was meant to be.

In the following week, Carol and I met for a final consultation without Andy to bring closure to our relationship, to review Andy's progress, and to devise a plan that would support Andy's continued progress without therapy. We briefly reviewed Carol's scores on the CBCL and PSI and discussed Andy's progress since the beginning of treatment. Andy's posttreatment CBCL scores indicated normal functioning in 8 of the 10 areas that were initially elevated, with an average mean decrease of 8.5 across all areas. Carol seemed almost surprised at her initial scores on the CBCL and how much differently she now viewed Andy's behavior. Tears came to her eyes (for the first time in our 20 months together) when we reviewed the PSI outcomes and she realized how much her stress related to parenting Andy had been affecting their relationship. She finally seemed to understand that her view of Andy had a considerable influence on Andy's view of himself. We discussed, among other things, his school placement for next year, strategies to minimize Andy's stress related to school, involvement in extracurricular sports that he excelled in, and continuing special family activities at home, including reading Andy's adoption story, "Chinese Night," and weekly filial play sessions. Carol's recent experience with Andy in their play sessions had been particularly rewarding for her, and she seemed highly motivated to continue. But I suspected that without support, she might have difficulty following through once the stress of the new school year began. We discussed the importance of follow-up and agreed to talk after Andy had started second grade in approximately 6 months (or sooner, if Carol saw a need).

Complicating Factors

Children's ability to benefit fully from treatment is dependent on their caregivers and other systemic factors. When parents are unwilling or unable to commit to participating in the therapeutic process or when children remain in an environment that is unsafe or is contributing significantly to the presenting issue, therapy is compromised. In this particular case, neither of these scenarios was an issue. Quite the contrary, the systemic factors related to this case were highly facilitative of Andy's growth in therapy. I noted no significant complications to the successful outcome of Andy's treatment.

Managed Care Considerations

In this particular case, managed care considerations were not an issue. Andy was seen at a community clinic with a sliding-scale fee. For those families that rely on managed care systems, educating third-party payors about the length of time of treatment needed for children with a history of interpersonal trauma is critical to ensure that these children receive the help they need. It is also imperative that the value and necessity of working with parents as part of a child's therapy be acknowledged and reimbursed by third-party payors. Although cases such as the one presented are complicated and require longer term therapy, play therapy research shows this method is effective in only a few sessions (Bratton et al., 2005). More research is needed to examine the efficacy of play therapy with specific populations and to determine optimal length of treatment relative to presenting concern.

Follow-Up Treatment

As a matter of practice, with the termination of all child clients I encourage parents to report back in around 4 to 6 months on how their child is progressing. At the time of this writing, 6 months had passed since termination of this case. During a follow-up phone consultation, Carol reported that school continued to be a challenge for Andy, but he was now better able to cope with school-related stress. His extracurricular involvement in tae kwon do and basketball seemed to be an effective outlet and a source of feeling competent. Andy excelled in both sports and particularly enjoyed his family's cheering him on in basketball. He was receiving educational support services in speech and language, but was on grade level in math and science. Although Andy continued to have occasional anger outbursts, the intensity and duration were greatly reduced. He had been sleeping in his own room for the past 9 months, and it had been well over a year since he had exhibited any stealing at home or school. Thus, according to Carol, there was no need for additional counseling at the time of follow-up. I followed up on the suggestions I had given her in our final consultation. She confessed that since school had started she had not been consistent with any of the family activities we had discussed, but acknowledged their importance and committed to setting aside 30 minutes each week for an activity of Andy's choosing. I encouraged Carol to call if any concerns arose and discussed the possibility that Andy might need additional counseling at certain points in his development.

Implications and Recommendations for Practice

Andy was an amazing child. In the face of overwhelming circumstances, he used play to fully experience all aspects of his life, both positive and negative, and assimilate those experiences into a more integrated self. What a privilege it was to be with him on this journey! Andy illustrates children's remarkable resiliency

(Continued)

and ability to master difficult situations if allowed to do so at their own pace and in their own way. Play provided the way for Andy to express, make sense of, and develop mastery over his confusing experiences. I could never have devised a treatment plan that was as brilliant as Andy's internal plan for what he needed in order to heal and overcome his early experiences.

Just as children have an innate drive for mastery and self-actualization, they also possess a protective tendency to suppress that which is painful until they are strong enough to allow difficult and confusing memories into their experience. Thus, the nonthreatening nature of CCPT was particularly appropriate to allow Andy to choose how, when, and to what to degree he would address his worries. Creating a safe, accepting, and respectful relationship provided Andy with the "good growing ground" (Axline, 1947) he needed to support his movement toward fully becoming the person he was meant to be. With no specific direction from me, he actively used his play to confront difficult issues in his life, including abandonment, loss, self-identity (including cultural identity), adoption, attachment, and belonging. Children who have experienced trauma are often triggered by what would be normal events for most children. Through my understanding of what Andy communicated to me in his play, I was able to help his parents and teachers identify potentially retraumatizing events (bedtime, separation, doctor visits) and devise strategies for altering or minimizing their impact on him.

Through the process of play therapy, Andy discovered new dimensions of himself that resulted in a revised self-image and more congruent and satisfying behavior. Outwardly, he demonstrated marked improvement in targeted behaviors, most notably self-regulation and a secure attachment to his parents, particularly to Carol. Andy was blessed to have a home with such remarkable parents as Carol and Tom. In my view, an invested parent is one of the most important tools in play therapy, or any child therapy. Their active participation in almost anything I suggested and willingness to implement changes were critical factors in Andy's growth. Their involvement in CPRT served as both curative and protective factors. It strengthened their confidence in their parenting and gave them a sense of empowerment as they successfully learned to utilize therapeutic play skills with Andy and saw what a difference they were making. Tom and Carol ended therapy armed with the confidence and skills they needed to continue to help Andy reach his potential. Providing parents with the skills and experiences to build a closer parent-child relationship is an essential element of therapy for a child like Andy, whose early experiences disrupted the formation of a strong bond with a caregiver.

For myself, my experiences with Andy on his complicated journey of growth and healing forced me to confront my own issues around wanting to protect children from difficult and overwhelming experiences. Andy did not need me to protect him from his feelings. He needed me to facilitate and witness the full expression of all of his experiences, both positive and negative. Peer consultations during some of the more difficult periods in Andy's therapy helped ensure that my needs were not interfering with Andy's need to fully convey all aspects of himself. Because children so readily express painful events and related emotions through the symbolism of play, play therapists may be more vulnerable to their own unresolved issues surfacing in the context of the child's playing out difficult experiences.

This case has shown how using a child-centered play therapy approach allows child therapists to join children at their level. The toys and materials provide children with a developmentally sensitive and personal means of expressing feelings, experiences, thoughts, and wishes in a way that child therapists can understand and respond to. The implication of this case is that play therapy is an effective and responsive treatment for young children. Furthermore, this case illustrates the value of involving parents as partners in the play therapy process for optimal treatment effects.

SUMMARY

Play therapy has grown over its over 100-year history to include a variety of treatment methodologies and theoretical schools of thought that embrace the therapeutic powers of play. Play therapy is based on developmental principles, and thus provides, through play, developmentally appropriate means of expression and communication for children. Enjoying a rich history of literature and research dating back to 1942, play therapy is the longest standing modality of psychotherapy developed specifically for children. Through early studies and recent meta-analyses, play therapy demonstrates a base of evidence to support its effectiveness.

This chapter has focused specifically on the principles and procedures of child-centered play therapy. In practice, CCPT offers a clear method of treatment, in which the relationship between child and therapist is the catalyst for all therapeutic change. The child's experience within the counseling relationship is the factor that is most meaningful and helpful in creating lasting, positive change. Hence, the therapist works toward creating an environment of acceptance and understanding that helps the child feel safe to fully express thoughts and feelings, moving toward more positive functioning. Following guiding CCPT principles (Axline, 1947; Landreth, 2002), the therapist develops a warm relationship with the child, accepts the child unconditionally, allows permissiveness within the relationship, reflects the child's feelings, respects the child's ability to solve problems, does not attempt to direct the child's actions, recognizes the gradual nature of the child's process, and establishes minimal limits.

For further effectiveness in play therapy, the play therapist is trained to work within the system that supports the child. Working with parents on understanding and responding to their children's needs is critical to the progress of play therapy. Parent consultation is one method of alignment with parents so that the therapist makes consistent intimate contact with the parents to sustain their commitment to their child's play therapy and to offer brief opportunities for education. Filial therapy is a more in-depth approach and provides extensive education in play therapy procedures and group support to parents so that they are empowered to use therapeutic play skills with their child.

This chapter has served to provide an introduction to the modality of play therapy for child therapists. The rationale and history of play therapy, as well as the research in the field, presented a base for its therapeutic use. The practice of CCPT was enumerated through descriptions of the therapist role, objectives, structure, therapist responses and attitudes, and applications of play therapy concepts. The case study offered a concrete example of how play therapy is applied in a real-life setting, working with a child with a complicated presentation. Play therapy serves as a developmentally responsive intervention for children, allowing therapists to speak the language of the child. Skill in using play therapy is an essential tool for mental health professionals who work with children. Therapeutic play allows children to express themselves fully and at their own pace with the assurance that they will be understood and accepted. Through this experience, children learn to express, accept, respect, and take responsibility for themselves and their feelings, which leads to creative insight, learning, problem solving, coping, and mastery.

REFERENCES

Abidin, R.R. (1995). *Parenting Stress Index: Professional manual*. Lutz, FL: Psychological Assessment Resources.

Achenbach, T.M., & Rescorla, L.A. (2000). *Manual for the ASEBA school age forms & profiles*. Burlington: University of Vermont, Research Center for Children, Youth, and Families.

Allan, J. (1997). Jungian play therapy. In K. O'Connor, & L. Braverman (Eds.), *Play therapy: Theory and practice* (pp. 100–130). New York: Wiley.

American Psychiatric Association (1994). Diagnostic and statistical manual of mental disorders (4th ed.). Washington, DC: American Psychiatric Association.

Association for Play Therapy (2001, June). Play therapy. *Association for Play Therapy Newsletter, 20*, 20.

Association for Play Therapy. (2006). *Membership*. Retrieved November 12, 2006, from www.a4pt.org.

Axline, V. (1947). *Play therapy*. New York: Ballantine Books.

Axline, V. (1964). *Dibs in search of self*. New York: Ballantine Books.

Baggerly, J. (2004). The effects of child-centered group play therapy on self-concept, depression, and anxiety of children who are homeless. *International Journal of Play Therapy, 13*, 31–51.

Brandt, M. (2001). An investigation of the efficacy of play therapy with young children. *Dissertation Abstracts International, 61*, 2603.

Bratton, S., Landreth, G., Kellam, T., & Blackard, S. (2006). *Child Parent Relationship Therapy (CPRT) treatment manual: A 10-session filial therapy model for training parents*. New York: Routledge.

Bratton, S., & Ray, D. (2000). What the research shows about play therapy. *International Journal of Play Therapy, 9*, 47–88.

Bratton, S., & Ray, D. (2002). Humanistic play therapy. In D. Cain & J. Seeman (Eds.), *Humanistic psychotherapies: Handbook of research and practice* (pp. 369–402). Washington, DC: American Psychological Association.

Bratton, S., Ray, D., Rhine, T., & Jones, L. (2005). The efficacy of play therapy with children: A meta-analytic review of treatment outcomes. *Professional Psychology: Research and Practice, 36*(4), 376–390.

Brody, V. (1997). Developmental play therapy. In K. O'Connor, & L. Braverman. *Play therapy: Theory and practice* (pp. 160–183). New York: Wiley.

Casey, R., & Berman, J. (1985). The outcome of psychotherapy with children. *Psychological Bulletin, 98*, 388–400.

Cassell, S. (1965). Effect of brief puppet therapy upon the emotional responses of children undergoing cardiac catheterization. *Journal of Consulting Psychology, 29*, 1–8.

Center for Play Therapy. (2006). *Bibliography*. Retrieved November 12, 2006, from www.centerforplaytherapy.com.

Center for Play Therapy. (1998). *What parents and children need to know about play therapy*. Denton, TX: University of North Texas, Center for Play Therapy Press.

Clatworthy, S. (1981). Therapeutic play: Effects on hospitalized children. *Journal of Association for Care of Children's Health, 9*, 108–113.

Cohen, J. (1988). *Statistical power analysis for the behavioral sciences* (2nd ed.). Hillsdale, NJ: Erlbaum.

Cox, F. (1953). Sociometric status and individual adjustment before and after play therapy. *Journal of Abnormal Social Psychology, 48*, 354–356.

Crow, J. (1990). Play therapy with low achievers in reading. *Dissertation Abstracts International, 50*, 2789.

Danger, S., & Landreth, G. (2005). Child-centered group play therapy with children with speech difficulties. *International Journal of Play Therapy, 14*, 81–102.

Dulsky, S. (1942). Affect and intellect: An experimental study. *Journal of General Psychology, 27*, 199–220.

Fall, M., Balvanz, J., Johnson, L., & Nelson, L. (1999). A play therapy intervention and its relationship to self-efficacy and learning behaviors. *Professional School Counseling, 2*(3), 194–204.

Findling, J., Bratton, S., & Hensen, R. (2006). Development of the Trauma Play Scale: An observation-based assessment of the impact of trauma on the play therapy behaviors of young children. *International Journal of Play Therapy 15*(1), 7–36.

Flahive, M., & Ray, D. (2001). Effect of group sandtray therapy with preadolescents in a school setting. *Journal for Specialists in Group Work.*

Frank, L. (1982). Play in personality development. In G. Landreth (Ed.), *Play therapy: Dynamics of the process of counseling with children* (pp. 19–32). Springfield, IL: Charles C. Thomas.

Freud, A. (1928). *Introduction to the technique of child analysis* (L.P. Clark, Trans.). New York: Nervous and Mental Disease.

Froebel, F. (1903). *Education by development.* New York: Appleton.

Garza, Y., & Bratton, S. (2005). School-based child centered play therapy with Hispanic children: Outcomes and cultural considerations. *International Journal of Play Therapy, 14* (1), 51–80.

Gaulden, G. (1975). Developmental-play group counseling with early primary grade students exhibiting behavioral problems. *Dissertation Abstracts International, 36*, 2628.

Ginott, H. (1961). *Group psychotherapy with children: The theory and practice of play therapy.* New York: McGraw-Hill.

Girard, L. (1989). *We adopted you, Benjamen Koo.* Toronto, Ontario, Canada: General.

Gould, M. (1980). The effect of short-term intervention play therapy on the self-concept of selected elementary pupils. *Dissertation Abstracts International, 41*, 1090.

Guerney, L. (1983). Play therapy with learning disabled children. In C. E. Schaefer & K. L. O'Conner (Eds.), *Handbook of play therapy* (pp. 419–435). New York: Wiley.

Guerney, L. (2000). Filial therapy into the 21st century. *International Journal of Play Therapy, 9*(2), 1–17.

Hambidge, G. (1955). Structured play therapy. *American Journal of Orthopsychiatry, 25*, 601–617.

Hannah, G. (1986). An investigation of play therapy: Process and outcome using interrupted time-series analysis. *Dissertation Abstracts International, 47*, 2615.

House, R. (1970). The effects of nondirective group play therapy upon the sociometric status and self-concept of selected second grade children. *Dissertation Abstracts International, 31*, 2684.

Johnson, P., & Stockdale, D. (1975). Effects of puppet therapy on palmar sweating of hospitalized children. *Johns Hopkins Medical Journal, 137*, 1–5.

Jones, E., & Landreth, G. (2002). The efficacy of intensive individual play therapy for chronically ill children. *International Journal of Play Therapy, 11*, 117–140.

Jones, L., Rhine, T., & Bratton, S. (2002). High school students as therapeutic agents with young children experiencing school adjustment difficulties: The effectiveness of filial therapy training model. *International Journal of Play Therapy, 11*(2), 43–62.

Karcher, M., & Lewis, S. (2002). Pair counseling: The effects of a dyadic developmental play therapy on interpersonal understanding and externalizing behaviors. *International Journal of Play Therapy, 11*, 19–42.

Kirschenbaum, H. (2004). Carl Rogers's life and work: An assessment on the 100th anniversary of his birth. *Journal of Counseling and Development, 82*, 116–124.

Klein, M. (1932). The psychoanalytic play technique. *American Journal of Orthopsychiatry, 25*, 223–237.

Knell, S. (1997). Cognitive-behavioral play therapy. In K. O'Connor & L. Braverman (Eds.), *Play therapy: Theory and practice* (pp. 79–99). New York: Wiley.

Kot, S., Landreth, G., & Giordano, M. (1998). Intensive child-centered play therapy with child witnesses of domestic violence. *International Journal of Play Therapy, 7*, 17–36.

Kottman, T. (1995). *Partners in play: An Adlerian approach to play therapy*. Alexandria, VA: American Counseling Association.

Kottman, T. (2001). Adlerian play therapy. *International Journal of Play Therapy, 10*(2), 1–12.

Lambert, S.F., Le Blanc, M., Mullen, J., Ray, D., Baggerly, J., White, J., et al. (2005). Learning more about those who play in session: The national play therapy in counseling practice project (Phase I). *International Journal of Play Therapy, 14*(2), 7–23.

Landreth, G. (1991). *Play therapy: The art of the relationship*. New York: Brunner-Routledge.

Landreth, G. (2002). *Play therapy: The art of the relationship* (2nd ed.). New York: Brunner-Routledge.

Landreth, G., & Bratton, S. (1998). Play therapy. *Counseling and Human Development, 31*(1), 1–12.

Landreth, G., & Bratton, S. (2005). *Child parent relationship therapy (CPRT): A 10-session filial therapy model*. New York: Routledge.

Landreth, G., & Sweeney, D. (1999). The freedom to be: Child-centered group play therapy. In D. Sweeney, & L. Homeyer (Eds.), *Handbook of group play therapy: How to do it, how it works, whom it's best for* (pp. 39–64). San Francisco: Jossey-Bass.

LeBlanc, M., & Ritchie, M. (1999). Predictors of play therapy outcomes. *International Journal of Play Therapy, 8*, 19–34.

LeBlanc, M., & Ritchie, M. (2001). A meta-analysis of play therapy outcomes. *Counseling Psychology Quarterly, 14*, 149–163.

Levy, D. (1939). Release therapy. *American Journal of Orthopsychiatry, 9*, 713–736.

Morrison, M. (2006). *An early mental health intervention for disadvantaged preschool children with behavior problems: The effectiveness of training Head Start teachers in child teacher relationship training (CTRT)*. Unpublished doctoral dissertation, University of North Texas Denton.

Moustakas, C. (1953). *Children in play therapy*. New York: McGraw-Hill.

Oaklander, V. (1994). Gestalt play therapy. In K. O'Connor & C. E. Schaefer (Eds.), *Handbook of play therapy* (Vol. 2, pp. 144–146). New York: Wiley.

O'Connor, K. (2000). *The play therapy primer* (2nd ed.). New York: Wiley.

O'Connor, K. (2001). Ecosystemic play therapy. *International Journal of Play Therapy, 10*(2), 33–44.

Oualline, B. (1976). Behavioral outcomes of short-term non-directive play therapy with preschool deaf children. *Dissertation Abstracts International, 36*, 7870.

New Freedom Commission on Mental Health. (2003). *Achieving the promise: Transforming mental health care in America: Final report* (DHHS Publication No. SMA-03-3832). Rockville, MD: U.S. Department of Health and Human Services.

Packman, J., & Bratton, S. (2003). A school-based group play/activity therapy intervention with learning disabled preadolescents exhibiting behavior problems. *International Journal of Play Therapy, 12*, 7–29.

Pelham, L. (1972). Self-directive play therapy with socially immature kindergarten students. *Dissertation Abstracts International, 32*, 3798.

Perez, C., (1987). A comparison of group play therapy and individual play therapy for sexually abused children. *Dissertation Abstracts International, 48*, 3079.

Piaget, J. (1962). *Play, dreams and imitation in childhood*. New York: Rutledge.

Post, P. (1999). Impact of child-centered play therapy on the self-esteem, locus of control, and anxiety of at-risk 4th, 5th, and 6th grade students. *International Journal of Play Therapy, 8*, 1–18.

Quayle, R. (1991). The primary mental health project as a school-based approach for prevention of adjustment problems: An evaluation. *Dissertation Abstracts International, 52*, 1268.

Rae, W., Worchel, F., Upchurch, J., Sanner, J., & Daniel, C. (1989). The psychosocial impact of play on hospitalized children. *Journal of Pediatric Psychology, 14*, 617–627.

Raman, V., & Kapur, M. (1999). A study of play therapy in children with emotional disorders. *National Institute of Mental Health and Neuro Sciences Journal, 17*, 93–98.

Raskin, N., & Rogers, C. (2005). Person-centered therapy. In R. Corsini & D. Wedding (Eds.), *Current psychotherapies* (7th ed., pp. 130–165). Belmont, CA: Brooks/Cole.

Ray, D. (2006). Evidence-based play therapy. In C. Schaefer & C. Schaefer (Eds.), *Contemporary play therapy* (pp. 136–157). New York: Guilford Press.

Rousseau, J. (1930). *Emile*. New York: Dent. (Original work published 1762).

Schaefer, C. (2001). Prescriptive play therapy. *International Journal of Play Therapy, 10*(2), 57–73.

Schumann, B. (2005). Effects of child-centered play therapy and curriculum-based small-group guidance on the behaviors of children referred for aggression in an elementary school setting. *Dissertation Abstracts International, 65*(12A), 4476.

Shashi, K., Kapur, M., & Subbakrishna, D. (1999). Evaluation of play therapy in emotionally disturbed children. *NIMHANS Journal, 17*, 99–111.

Shen, Y. (2002). Short-term group play therapy with Chinese earthquake victims: Effects on anxiety, depression, and adjustment. *International Journal of Play Therapy, 11*, 43–63.

Thombs, M., & Muro, J. (1973). Group counseling and the sociometric status of second grade children. *Elementary School Guidance and Counseling, 7*, 194–197.

U.S. Public Health Service, (2000). *Report of the surgeon general's conference on children's mental health: A national action agenda*. Washington, DC: Author.

VanFleet, R. (1994). *Filial therapy: Strengthening parent-child relationships through play*. Sarasota, FL: Professional Resource Press.

Weisz, J., Weiss, B., Han, S., Granger, D., & Morton, T. (1995). Effects of psychotherapy with children and adolescents revisited: A meta-analysis of treatment outcomes studies. *Psychological Bulletin, 117*, 450–468.

White, J., & Flynt, M. (1999). Play groups in elementary school. In D. Sweeney & L. Homeyer (Eds.), *Handbook of group play therapy: How to do it, how it works, and whom it's best for* (pp. 336–358). San Francisco: Jossey-Bass.

White, J., Flynt, M., & Draper, K. (1997). Kindertherapy: Teachers as therapeutic agents. *International Journal of Play Therapy, 6*, 33–49.

CHAPTER 21

Behavior Modification

Raymond G. Miltenberger

Behavior modification is the field of psychology devoted to understanding and changing human behavior. In behavior modification, assessment procedures are used to record the problem behavior and identify the factors that contribute to its occurrence, and intervention procedures are used to help people change their behavior. Behavior modification procedures are based on basic principles of behavior discovered in experimental research with laboratory animals and humans over the past 70 years (e.g., Skinner, 1938; Ullmann & Krasner, 1965; Ulrich, Stachnik, & Mabry, 1966). As behavior modification is currently practiced, it is synonymous with the field of applied behavior analysis (Baer, Wolf, & Risley, 1968; Miltenberger, 2004).

In behavior modification there is an emphasis on observable behaviors, both behavioral excesses and behavioral deficits. Objective definition and measurement of behavior is a hallmark of behavior modification. Behavior change is accomplished by changing environmental events occurring at the time of the behavior, antecedents that evoke the behavior, and consequences that maintain the behavior. Behavior modification is largely based on operant conditioning principles and, to a lesser extent, on respondent conditioning principles (Miltenberger, 2004). Behavior modification has been successful in helping people of all ages and ability levels change a wide variety of socially significant behaviors in a wide variety of natural contexts (J. Carr & Austin, 2001; Gross & Drabman, 2005; Hersen & Rosqvist, 2005; Sugai & Horner, 2005; Vollmer et al., 2000).

This chapter provides an overview of the field of behavior modification, starting with issues in assessment and research design, followed by a review of basic behavioral principles that form the foundation of behavior modification procedures. Next, procedures to establish new behaviors are reviewed, the functional approach to assessing and changing behavior is presented, and various behavioral interventions are described.

USING DATA IN BEHAVIOR MODIFICATION

Observing, recording, and displaying data to evaluate treatment and make treatment decisions are important activities that help define behavior modification.

Observing and Recording Behavior

In behavior modification emphasis is placed on objective measurement of behavior through direct observation procedures. A number of steps are involved in the process of recording behavior (Miltenberger, 2004).

Defining the Behavior

The first step in the process of recording behavior is to define the target behaviors in objective terms. Target behaviors are chosen based on their social importance (Baer et al., 1968; Wolf, 1978) and may include problematic behaviors to be decreased (behavioral excesses) and desirable behaviors to be increased (behavioral deficits). Target behaviors are defined using action verbs so that two independent observers can record their occurrence reliably.

Logistics of Recording

Once the target behaviors are defined, the next steps are to choose an observer and the time and place of observation. The observer may be the person engaging in the behavior (self-monitoring) or a care provider (e.g., parent, teacher, staff member), therapist, or researcher. The observation period will be the time and place in which the behavior is most problematic or in which the behavior has the highest likelihood of occurrence.

Recording Method

The next step in the process of recording behavior is to decide on the use of event recording or a sampling procedure. With event recording, every instance of the behavior is recorded during the observation period. The four dimensions of behavior that can be measured are frequency (number of times the behavior occurred), duration (the time from onset to offset of the behavior), intensity (a measure of the force of the behavior), and latency (the time from some stimulus to the onset of the behavior). One or more dimensions are chosen for recording based on their relevance to the target behavior.

Sampling procedures, including interval and time sample recording, are not designed to record every instance of the behavior but rather to provide an estimate of the occurrence of the behavior. In *interval recording,* the observation period is divided into smaller consecutive intervals of time and the behavior is recorded as occurring or not in each interval. *Time sample recording* involves recording the occurrence of the behavior in brief intervals of time separated by longer intervals of time without observation. The outcome of interval or time sample recording is reported as the percentage of observation intervals in which the behavior occurred.

Recording Instrument

The final step is to choose a recording instrument. The most common recording instrument is a data sheet prepared for the particular client and target behaviors in question. The data sheet, designed to be convenient and easy to use, provides a space for recording each instance of the behavior as it is observed. Other recording instruments are counters or timers, stopwatches, PDAs or other hand-held devices, and laptop computers, to name a few. The recording instrument is designed to be practical, to minimize disruption of ongoing activities during behavior recording, and to facilitate immediate recording of the behavior as it occurs.

Interobserver Agreement

Behavior recording procedures are designed to produce information that is as reliable as possible. One index of reliability commonly used in behavior modification is interobserver agreement. Interobserver agreement is the degree to which two independent observers agree on the occurrence of the behavior during the same observation period. Interobserver agreement is a necessary component of research in behavior modification, although it is used less often in clinical applications of behavior modification. The reader is referred to Miltenberger (2004), Bailey and Burch (2002), and J. Cooper, Heron, and Heward (2007) for details on calculating interobserver agreement.

Indirect Measures

In behavior modification, emphasis is placed on direct observation of behavior. However, in some instances, indirect measures of behavior, including product measures and retrospective reports, are used. Product measures may be used when the target behavior produces permanent changes in the environment (products) that can be measured. Examples of product recording are the number of assignments completed in an educational setting, the number of units assembled in a factory setting, and the number of hairs pulled by a person diagnosed with Trichotillomania. Retrospective reports about the occurrence of behavior can be gathered through interviews or questionnaires. Retrospective reports of behavior are not used as the sole assessment method but are typically used during the initial phase of assessment to plan direct observation procedures.

Data Display and Research Design

In behavior modification, the target behavior is recorded before, during, and after intervention is implemented. By recording before the intervention, a baseline level of the behavior is established and the effects of the intervention can be assessed by looking at changes in the behavior. A graph is the tool used in behavior modification to identify changes in the behavior from baseline to intervention. In a graph, the level of the behavior is plotted on the vertical axis (y axis) and time is plotted on the horizontal axis (x axis) so that changes in behavior over time can be easily discerned.

In most clinical applications of behavior modification the target behavior is recorded and displayed on a graph in two phases: baseline and intervention. However, when research is conducted in behavior modification, more sophisticated graphs are used that demonstrate a functional relationship between environmental

events (the intervention) and the target behavior. To demonstrate a functional relationship between intervention and the target behavior the researcher must:

- Reliably record the target behavior.
- Show that the target behavior changes when (and only when) the intervention is implemented.
- Provide a replication of the effect. In essence, the intervention is implemented two or more times and the behavior changes each time the intervention is implemented, but only when the intervention is implemented.

A number of research designs are used in behavior modification to demonstrate a functional relationship. These include the ABAB reversal design; multiple baseline designs across behaviors, participants, or settings; alternative treatment design; and changing criterion design. See Miltenberger (2004), Bailey and Burch (2002), or J. Cooper et al. (2007) for descriptions of these behavior modification research designs.

BASIC PRINCIPLES

Behavior modification procedures are based on a core set of basic behavioral princi-
ples that describe functional relationships between specific types of environmental events and behavior. These basic behavioral principles are reinforcement, extinction, punishment, stimulus control, and respondent conditioning.

Reinforcement

Reinforcement is a fundamental principle that underlies many behavior modifi-
cation procedures. First studied extensively by Skinner (1938) and Ferster and Skinner (1957), reinforcement is defined as the process in which the consequence of a behavior strengthens the future probability of the behavior. Understanding the principle of reinforcement is important for understanding the causes of behav-
ior and for strengthening appropriate behavior. There are two forms of reinforce-
ment: positive reinforcement, in which behavior is strengthened when it results in the delivery of a positive reinforcer, and negative reinforcement, in which be-
havior is strengthened when it results in escape or avoidance of aversive stimuli. The consequences of the behavior involved in both positive and negative reinforcement may consist of changes in the physical environment or the behavior of others.

Reinforcement is influenced by a number of factors, including immediacy, contingency, establishing operations, individual differences, and magnitude (see Miltenberger, 2004, for discussion of these factors). One important factor that is increasingly utilized in behavior modification procedures is the establishing operation (e.g., Vollmer & Iwata, 1991). An establishing operation is an environmental event that makes a reinforcer more potent and evokes the behavior that produces that reinforcer (Michael, 1982).

Extinction

Extinction occurs when the reinforcing consequence maintaining a behavior is no longer present following the behavior, and as a result, the behavior decreases and eventually stops occurring. For behavior maintained by positive reinforcement, extinction occurs when the positive reinforcer no longer follows the behavior. For behavior maintained by negative reinforcement, extinction occurs when the individual is no longer able to escape or avoid the aversive stimulus following the behavior. In each case, when the behavior is no longer reinforced, it will stop occurring.

One phenomenon frequently seen during extinction is an extinction burst (Lerman & Iwata, 1995). In an extinction burst, there is a temporary increase in the behavior or the occurrence of novel or emotional behaviors when the target behavior no longer produces the reinforcer. The extinction burst is a transient phenomenon, and the target behavior will eventually stop occurring if the reinforcer continues to be withheld following the behavior. Understanding the extinction burst is important for the successful use of extinction in clinical practice.

Punishment

Punishment occurs when the consequence that follows a behavior decreases the future probability of the behavior. There are two variations of punishment. In positive punishment the behavior is followed by the addition of an aversive stimulus (also called a punisher); in negative punishment, the behavior is followed by the removal of a positive reinforcer. In both cases, the behavior is weakened. As with reinforcement, punishment occurs naturally in our contact with the physical environment and in our interactions with others. Some behavior modification procedures are based on the principle of punishment (e.g., time-out and response cost). The same factors that influence reinforcement influence punishment: immediacy, contingency, establishing operations, magnitude, and individual differences (Miltenberger, 2004). See Lerman and Vorndran (2002) for an in-depth discussion of punishment.

Stimulus Control

Although reinforcement, extinction, and punishment are the basic principles that determine whether a behavior will continue to occur, the effects of these operations are relatively situation-specific. Reinforcement strengthens behavior in situations that are similar to the ones in which the behavior was reinforced in the past. Likewise, extinction and punishment weaken behavior in situations that are similar to the ones in which the behavior was subjected to extinction or punishment procedures in the past. The increased probability that behavior will occur in specific situations (in the presence of specific stimuli) is referred to as stimulus control. A behavior is under the stimulus control of a specific stimulus when it is more likely to occur when that stimulus is present.

Stimulus control is developed through stimulus discrimination training. In stimulus discrimination training (also called discrimination training), the behavior is reinforced in the presence of one stimulus (a discriminative stimulus or S^D) and is not reinforced in the presence of other stimuli. As a result, when the S^D is present in the future, the behavior is more likely to occur. The S^D has stimulus control over the behavior. The S^D will continue to have stimulus control over the behavior as long as the behavior continues to be reinforced in its presence.

Although discrimination training makes the behavior more likely to occur in the presence of the S^D, the behavior is also likely to occur in the presence of stimuli that are similar to the S^D. The more similar a stimulus is to the S^D, the more likely the behavior is to occur in its presence (Guttman & Kalish, 1956; Lalli, Mace, Livezey, & Kates, 1998). The occurrence of behavior in the presence of stimuli that are similar to the S^D is called generalization.

Respondent Conditioning

Reinforcement, extinction, punishment, and stimulus control are all operant conditioning principles. In operant conditioning, behavior is controlled by its consequences (reinforcement strengthens behavior, and extinction or punishment weaken behavior). Although operant behavior comes under the stimulus control of antecedent stimuli (the S^D), stimulus control is developed through the differential consequences that are present when the S^D is present. Whereas operant behavior is controlled by its consequences, respondent behavior is controlled by its antecedents. Respondent behavior is elicited by a prior stimulus, either an unconditioned stimulus or a conditioned stimulus.

Respondent conditioning occurs when a neutral stimulus is paired with an unconditioned stimulus (US). The US elicits an unconditioned response (UR) and, as a result of its pairing with the US, the neutral stimulus comes to elicit a response similar to the UR. The neutral stimulus is then called a conditioned stimulus, and the response it elicits is called a conditioned response. Anxiety, anger, and inappropriate sexual arousal are examples of conditioned responses that may be targets of intervention in behavior modification procedures.

Behavior modification procedures, the actual techniques used to help people change their behavior, are based on the basic principles just described. Behavior modification procedures are used to establish new behaviors, to identify the variables contributing to the occurrence of behaviors, and to help people increase or decrease existing behaviors.

PROCEDURES TO ESTABLISH NEW BEHAVIORS

When a desirable behavior is not currently in a person's repertoire, a number of procedures can be used to help the person acquire the behavior. These procedures include shaping, prompting and fading, chaining, and behavioral skills training procedures.

Shaping

Shaping is the differential reinforcement of successive approximations of a target behavior. Shaping is used to help an individual engage in a new behavior (e.g., a child saying a word for the first time), a new dimension of an existing behavior (e.g., a patient speaking with increasing voice volume), or a previously exhibited behavior that is no longer occurring (e.g., a stroke patient walking again; Jackson & Wallace, 1974; Miltenberger, 2004; G. W. O'Neill & Gardner, 1983). To use shaping, the target behavior is defined and then a starting behavior is chosen. The starting behavior (or first approximation), a behavior that already occurs at least occasionally, is reinforced a number of times until it occurs consistently. Then it is no longer reinforced (extinction), and the next approximation to the target behavior is reinforced instead. Once this behavior occurs a number of times, it is no longer reinforced, and a closer approximation to the target behavior is then reinforced. This process continues until the individual engages in the target behavior. Once the target behavior is exhibited it is reinforced consistently to strengthen it and maintain its occurrence over time.

Shaping, a procedure that came from experimental research with laboratory animals (Skinner, 1938, 1951), has been used extensively in animal training (Pryor, 1985) and with humans to help individuals acquire a number of socially significant target behaviors in areas such as education, developmental disabilities, rehabilitation, and sports (Hagopian & Thompson, 1999; Horner, 1971; G. W. O'Neill & Gardner, 1983; Scott, Scott, & Goldwater, 1997). Shaping is used when more efficient behavioral acquisition strategies (e.g., prompting, instructions, modeling) are not possible.

Prompting and Fading

Prompting is used when a desired behavior is not currently occurring or not occurring in the correct circumstances (in the presence of the S^D). Prompting is a procedure in which an antecedent stimulus is delivered to evoke the behavior in the presence of the S^D so that the behavior can get reinforced. Fading is the gradual elimination of the prompt once the behavior is occurring in the presence of the S^D. The prompt gets the correct behavior to occur at the right time, and fading eliminates the prompt to get the behavior under the stimulus control of the S^D.

Prompts can include the behavior of another person (response prompt) or a change in an antecedent stimulus (stimulus prompt). There are four types of response prompts: verbal, gestural, modeling, and physical. A *verbal prompt* is when the verbal behavior of another person is used to get the correct behavior to occur in the presence of the S^D. A *gestural prompt* is when a physical movement or gesture of another person gets the correct behavior to occur. A *modeling prompt* is when a demonstration of the behavior gets the correct response to occur. A *physical prompt* is when another person physically assists or guides a person to engage in the correct behavior. Physical prompting typically consists of hand-over-hand guidance.

When prompting is used to evoke the correct behavior, the trainer first presents the S^D and, if a response does not occur immediately, the trainer provides the prompt. When the prompted response occurs, the trainer provides a reinforcer.

Consider the case of a training program to teach a child with autism to hit a baseball off a tee as part of a recreational program. The S^D is the ball on the tee on home plate on a baseball field in front of the child while she holds the bat. In the presence of the S^D, hitting the ball is the correct response and praise from the coach is the reinforcer. A verbal prompt might be to say "Hit the ball" while the child is standing in position holding the bat. If the child hits the ball after receiving the prompt, the behavior can be reinforced. If the child does not hit the ball after receiving the verbal prompt, a gestural prompt such as pointing to the ball on the tee can be delivered. If the child does not engage in the correct behavior following the gestural prompt, a modeling prompt can be delivered. A modeling prompt might consist of hitting the ball off the tee yourself as the child watches. If the modeling prompt does not evoke the correct behavior, then a physical prompt can be used. A physical prompt might involve holding the child's hands on the bat and swinging the bat with the child to hit the ball. The use of hand-over-hand guidance in this way would result in the correct response and praise from the coach.

In the baseball example, once the child is hitting the ball correctly with the coach's physical guidance, the coach will fade the physical prompt. Over consecutive trials, the coach will provide less and less assistance (e.g., he will help the child start to swing and let her finish with no assistance) until the child swings the bat to hit the ball without any further assistance. Once prompts are no longer needed, the behavior is under the control of the S^D (the ball on the tee). See J. Cooper et al. (2007), Miltenberger (2004), and Sulzer-Azaroff and Mayer (1991) for more information on the use of prompting and fading.

Chaining

A chaining procedure is used to teach the learner to engage in a chain of behaviors. A behavioral chain (also called a stimulus-response chain) consists of a number of behaviors, each consisting of an S^D and a response, that occur together in a sequence. Each response in the chain creates the S^D for the next response in the chain. For example, consider the behavior of getting a drink from a water fountain. There are at least three behaviors in the chain: pushing the handle for water, bending over the stream of water, and drinking the water. In this example, the water fountain is the S^D. The first response is turning on the water. This behavior creates the second S^D (the water stream). The second response is bending over the water stream. This behavior creates the third S^D (the water stream in proximity to or touching your mouth). The third response is drinking the water.

Before using a chaining procedure to teach a chain of behaviors, you must conduct a task analysis. A task analysis identifies every S^D and response in the chain of behaviors (e.g., Bellamy, Horner, & Inman, 1979). Careful observation of someone engaging in the chain of behaviors is used to develop the task analysis.

Three procedures are used to teach a chain of behaviors: forward chaining, backward chaining, and total task presentation (Miltenberger, 2004).

Forward Chaining

In forward chaining you use prompting and fading to teach the first component in the chain. After the learner engages in the first response when the first S^D is presented without any prompts, prompting and fading are used to teach the first two components. At this time, the learner will engage in the first response when the first S^D is presented. When the first response creates the second S^D, the learner is prompted to engage in the second response. Once prompts are faded, the learner can now engage in the first two responses in the chain without prompts. Then prompting and fading are used to teach the first three components, and so on until all of the component behaviors occur together.

Backward Chaining

In backward chaining, the last S^D is presented and prompting and fading are used to get the last response to occur. Once the last response is under the stimulus control of the last S^D, the next to last S^D is presented and the next to last response is prompted. Once the next to last response occurs, it creates the last S^D and the learner will then engage in the last response. After the last two behaviors in the chain occur without prompts, the third to last S^D is presented and prompting and fading are used until the last three responses occur without prompts. This process continues until the learner engages in the whole chain of behaviors without prompts.

Total Task Presentation

In total task presentation, you present the first S^D and physically guide the learner through the entire chain of behaviors from start to finish. Over trials, you fade the physical guidance to shadowing until the physical prompt is eliminated. This fading method, in which physical prompting is faded to shadowing and eventually eliminated, is called graduated guidance. Total task presentation is typically used with more capable learners, and forward or backward chaining is used with learners with significant disabilities.

Behavioral Skills Training

Behavioral skills training (BST) is one final strategy for helping a learner acquire new skills. Behavioral skills training consists of four training components: instructions, modeling, rehearsal, and feedback (e.g., Himle & Miltenberger, 2004). With instructions and modeling, the skills are described and demonstrated for the learner. Rehearsal is an opportunity for the learner to practice the skills in a simulation or role-play situation. Finally, feedback consists of praise for correct performance of the skills and correction or further instruction when the skill is not performed correctly. Typically, BST is used for behaviors that can be demonstrated and practiced in a simulation or role-play format. Various skills have been taught with BST procedures, including social skills, parenting skills, job-related skills, child safety skills, and clinical interviewing skills (Bakken, Miltenberger, & Schauss, 1993; Himle, Miltenberger, Flessner, & Gatheridge, 2004; Johnson et al., 2005; Miltenberger & Fuqua, 1985).

To conduct BST, you first define the target behaviors and all of the situations in which the behaviors are to be performed. In teaching abduction prevention skills, for example, the target behavior consists of saying no, running away, and telling an adult when faced with an abduction lure. All of the different ways an adult might try to lure a child would then be identified and incorporated into training (e.g., offering the child candy or a toy to leave, asking for assistance, invoking authority). Once the target behaviors and S^Ds (situations) are identified, training begins with instructions and modeling. The trainer describes the behavior in detail and the situations in which the behavior is to be performed. The trainer then models the behavior in the context of a role-play of one of the relevant situations.

After receiving instructions and modeling, the learner then has the opportunity to rehearse the behavior. The trainer role-plays the same situation that was just modeled and the child practices the skill in response to the situation. For example, the trainer might tell a child, "Pretend I am a stranger that walks up to you in your front yard and asks you to help me look for my puppy down the street. Show me what you would do if this happened." The trainer then role-plays the situation, delivers the lure, and observes the child's response. Immediately after the child rehearses the behavior, the trainer provides feedback. The trainer provides descriptive praise for any aspect of the behavior the child performed correctly and then tells the child how the behavior could be improved (if needed). The trainer then immediately conducts the same role-play and provides the child the opportunity to rehearse the behavior again after receiving feedback. Once the child demonstrates the correct behavior in the role-play, other situations are incorporated into role-plays so that the full range of situations and responses is trained.

PROCEDURES TO INCREASE OR DECREASE EXISTING BEHAVIORS

A number of behavior modification procedures are used to help individuals decrease undesirable behaviors and increase desirable behaviors. The functional approach to assessment and intervention starts with a functional assessment to identify the antecedents and consequences influencing the behavior (R. E. O'Neill et al., 1997). Functional interventions, designed to address the antecedents and consequences of the behavior, include extinction, differential reinforcement, and antecedent control procedures (Miltenberger, 2004). Changing the antecedents and consequences of the behavior and promoting functionally equivalent alternative behavior alter the conditions that influence the behavior, resulting in the greatest likelihood of change in the behavior.

Functional Assessment

Functional assessment is a process of gathering information on the target behavior and the antecedents and consequences that are functionally related to the occurrence of the behavior (Lennox & Miltenberger, 1989). The outcome of a functional assessment is a hypothesis about the reinforcing consequences maintaining the behavior and the antecedents that evoke the behavior (R. E. O'Neill et al., 1997).

There are four categories of reinforcing consequences that could be maintaining a target behavior: social positive reinforcement (e.g., attention, tangible, or activity reinforcers provided by another person), automatic positive reinforcement (some form of sensory stimulation arising directly from the behavior), social negative reinforcement (escape or avoidance of aversive activities or interactions mediated by another person), and automatic negative reinforcement (escape from aversive stimulation such as pain, discomfort, negative emotional responding; Iwata, Vollmer, Zarcone, & Rodgers, 1993). A functional assessment produces information that enables you to identify the type (or types) of reinforcement maintaining the problem behavior.

Antecedents that are identified in a functional assessment are the events, people, and circumstances that are reliably associated with the occurrence of the behavior. Antecedents can include S^Ds that occur immediately prior to the behavior and establishing operations (EO) whose onset may be proximal or more distal to the occurrence of the behavior. Identifying the S^D and EO associated with the behavior allows you to alter these antecedents to influence the problem behavior and alternative behaviors (Smith & Iwata, 1997).

There are three methods for conducting a functional assessment: indirect assessment, direct assessment, and functional analysis.

Indirect Assessment

An indirect assessment involves interviews, questionnaires, or rating scales in which individuals who have frequent contact with the client (informants) provide information from their recall of antecedents and consequences associated with the behavior (Lennox & Miltenberger, 1989; R. E. O'Neill et al., 1997). R. E. O'Neill et al., for example, developed the Functional Analysis Interview Format to gather detailed functional assessment information. The advantage of an indirect functional assessment is that it is easy and convenient to administer and does not take much time. The limitation is that it does not involve direct observation of the behavior as it occurs but instead relies on the informant's recall of events.

Direct Observation Assessment

A direct observation functional assessment (also called ABC recording) involves direct observation and recording of the behavior and its antecedents and consequences as the behavior occurs (Lennox & Miltenberger, 1989; R. E. O'Neill et al., 1997). Observations occur across a number of instances of the behavior until patterns in the antecedents and consequences are evident in the data. ABC recording can involve descriptive recording or the use of a checklist. In descriptive ABC recording, the observer writes down a description of antecedents, behavior, and consequences as they occur. To be of most value, the descriptions must be detailed and objective. In the checklist method, the observer has a checklist of possible target behaviors, antecedents, and consequences and places a checkmark in the appropriate column to designate the particular antecedents and consequences that were observed at the time of the behavior. The advantage of ABC recording is that the antecedents and consequences are observed as they occur, which results in objective (and likely more accurate) recording of the events. The limitation is that it takes more time to conduct multiple observations of the individual in the natural context (group home, school, etc.).

Functional Analysis

A functional analysis involves direct observation of the target behavior as antecedents and consequences are systematically manipulated to identify their influence on the behavior (e.g., E. G. Carr & Durand, 1985; Iwata, Dorsey, Slifer, Bauman, & Richman, 1982). For example, you could provide attention following each instance of the target behavior to see if the behavior increased, thus demonstrating that attention functioned as a reinforcer. Likewise, you could provide escape from demands contingent on the behavior or tangible reinforcers contingent on the behavior to see whether these events functioned as reinforcers for the behavior.

A functional analysis might be used to test a hypothesis, in which case one reinforcer might be manipulated, or a functional analysis might test a number of possible reinforcers. For example, to test the hypothesis that attention is reinforcing the target behavior, a functional analysis would alternate conditions in which attention is provided contingent on the behavior and conditions in which attention is withheld contingent on the behavior (e.g., Arndorfer, Miltenberger, Woster, Rortvedt, & Gaffaney, 1994). If attention is a reinforcer, the behavior will increase in the first condition relative to the second. To test a number of reinforcers, you might alternate conditions in which attention, escape, or tangible reinforcers are made contingent on the behavior. An alone condition would also be used to see if the behavior persisted in the absence of social consequences (e.g., Iwata et al., 1982). The advantage of a functional analysis is that, because antecedents and consequences are manipulated and resulting changes in the target behavior are recorded, a functional relationship between the antecedents and consequences and the behavior is demonstrated. The limitation of a functional analysis is that it takes substantial time and expertise to conduct and requires temporarily reinforcing the undesirable behavior.

Once a functional assessment is conducted and hypotheses about the antecedents and consequences of the behavior have been developed, functional interventions (described later) are chosen based on the hypotheses.

Extinction

Extinction, described earlier, is a basic principle of behavior. Extinction is also a behavioral procedure when it is used to help an individual eliminate an undesirable behavior (Lerman & Iwata, 1996). To use extinction, you must first conduct a functional assessment to identify the reinforcer maintaining the problem behavior. Once the reinforcer is identified, extinction involves eliminating the reinforcer after each instance of the behavior. If the behavior no longer gets reinforced, it will cease to occur. However, the successful use of extinction in clinical practice requires careful consideration of a number of questions (Miltenberger, 2004):

- Have you identified the reinforcer for the behavior? You cannot assume a particular reinforcer is maintaining a problem behavior; you must identify the reinforcer from a careful functional assessment. Sometimes, multiple reinforcers are maintaining a problem behavior in different contexts.

- Can you eliminate the reinforcer? Eliminating the reinforcer can be a problem when the behavior is reinforced by other people and you do not have influence over those individuals or when the behavior is automatically reinforced.

- Is extinction safe to use? In some cases of aggressive or self-injurious behavior, if the parent or teacher no longer responds to the behavior, it might put individuals at risk for harm. Even though the adult's response to the behavior may be reinforcing the behavior (i.e., attention), during extinction it may be necessary for the adult to respond to interrupt the behavior and assure the individual's safety. In such cases, the reinforcing consequence may be attenuated if it cannot be totally eliminated.

- Will individuals using extinction be able to deal effectively with an extinction burst? In most cases when extinction is used, the problem behavior temporarily worsens (increases in frequency, duration, or intensity) before it decreases. The parents, teachers, or others using extinction must be alerted to the probability of an extinction burst and be prepared to deal with it effectively. If they are not prepared, they might accidentally reinforce a more extreme problem behavior when it emerges during an extinction burst.

- Can consistency be maintained over time with all people? For extinction to be effective, it must be implemented each time the problem behavior occurs. If some instances of the behavior are reinforced only at some times by some individuals, then the behavior will likely persist and possibly worsen due to intermittent reinforcement.

When extinction is used clinically, it must be used in the context of other functional interventions as well. Not only should the problem behavior result in extinction, but differential reinforcement should be used to strengthen more desirable behavior. In addition, antecedent conditions should be altered to prevent the occurrence of the problem and evoke desired behaviors while using extinction.

Differential Reinforcement

Differential reinforcement involves the use of reinforcement to increase desirable behavior and extinction to decrease the occurrence of the problem behavior. There are three variations of differential reinforcement: differential reinforcement of alternative behavior (DRA), differential reinforcement of other behavior (DRO), and differential reinforcement of low rates of behavior (DRL; Miltenberger, 2004).

Differential Reinforcement of Alternative Behavior

In DRA, reinforcement is provided for a desirable alternative behavior, and extinction is used for the problem behavior. The goal of DRA is for the desirable behavior to increase in frequency and replace the problem behavior as it is decreased through extinction. For DRA to be effective it is important to reinforce the desirable behavior each time it occurs while withholding reinforcement for every instance of the problem behavior. In addition, the reinforcer chosen for the desirable behavior should be a known reinforcer. When possible, it is best to reinforce the desirable behavior with the same reinforcer that was maintaining the problem behavior prior to the use of extinction. For example, if the problem behavior was maintained by attention, attention should be provided as a reinforcer for the alternative behavior. In this way, the desirable alternative behavior is functionally equivalent to the problem behavior because it produces the same outcome that used to produce the problem behavior (e.g., E. G. Carr, 1988).

Differential reinforcement of alternative behavior may involve positive reinforcement or negative reinforcement. In the case of positive reinforcement involving attention, attention no longer follows the problem behavior and instead is delivered following each occurrence of a desirable alternative behavior (Durand & Carr, 1991, 1992). In the case of negative reinforcement involving escape from aversive activities, escape is no longer contingent on the problem behavior and is delivered instead contingent on the occurrence of a desirable behavior (Allen & Stokes, 1987; Marcus & Vollmer, 1995). Steege et al. (1990) used DRA to decrease self-injurious behavior that was maintained by escape from grooming activities. In this case, a child with intellectual disabilities bit his wrist while an adult was brushing the child's teeth and the biting was reinforced by the termination of tooth brushing. When DRA was used, wrist biting no longer resulted in termination of tooth brushing (extinction). Instead, the child was prompted to press a switch to activate a tape-recorded message asking for a break. When this alternative behavior occurred, it resulted in a break (termination of tooth brushing for a brief period of time). When pushing the button to activate the taped message was reinforced with escape but wrist biting was not, the child quit biting his wrist and engaged in the alternative behavior instead.

Differential Reinforcement of Other Behavior

Differential reinforcement of other behavior is a procedure that utilizes extinction for the problem behavior and reinforcement for the absence of the problem behavior. If the problem behavior no longer produces a reinforcer and the reinforcer can be acquired only for the absence of the behavior, the behavior will decrease. Before using DRO you must first identify the reinforcer maintaining the problem behavior. Then you identify the reinforcer to be delivered contingent on the absence of the problem behavior. In most cases, the reinforcer delivered for the absence of the problem behavior will be the reinforcer that was maintaining the problem. Next, you identify the interval for the delivery of the reinforcer. The interval will be based on the average time between occurrences of the problem behavior in baseline. For example, if a problem behavior occurs on average 3 times per minute, the average time between responses is 20 seconds and the DRO interval should be set at 20 seconds or less.

To use DRO you provide the reinforcer after each interval of time in which the problem behavior does not occur. If the problem behavior does occur at any time, the reinforcer is withheld and the interval is reset. Again, the problem behavior must be absent for the entire interval for the reinforcer to be delivered. Once the problem behavior begins to decrease in frequency and the reinforcer is being delivered for its absence in the majority of intervals, the interval is gradually lengthened. As the interval is lengthened, the problem behavior must be absent for longer periods of time before the reinforcer is delivered. The goal when lengthening the DRO interval is to end up with an interval length that is practical for the parent or teacher to implement. Although it will require the complete attention of the caregiver to deliver the reinforcer after every 20-second interval with the absence of the problem behavior, once the interval is lengthened to a more manageable time (such as 30 minutes) the caregiver will be able to resume normal activities while implementing DRO (e.g., Cowdery, Iwata, & Pace, 1990; Iwata, Pace, Cowdery, & Miltenberger, 1994; Vollmer & Iwata, 1992).

Differential Reinforcement of Low Rates of Behavior

Differential reinforcement of low rates of behavior is a procedure in which a reinforcer is delivered if a problem behavior happens fewer than a specified number of times in an observation period. The goal is to provide a reinforcer for a lower rate of the behavior. Consider the case of a child with Attention-Deficit/Hyperactivity Disorder who gets up from the dinner table on average more than 10 times per meal. In a DRL procedure, the parent might arrange a contingency in which the child gets dessert (a reinforcer) only if she gets up from the table fewer than 5 times during the meal. Once the child is successful, the number of acceptable responses can be lowered to a more desired level. When using DRL, it is important to provide the child with a way to keep track of the number of responses that have occurred. In this case, the parent might bring to the table a chart with five boxes and place an X in a box each time the behavior of getting up from the table occurs. The child would have to have at least one blank box at the end of the meal to receive the reinforcer.

In another form of DRL, a reinforcer is delivered only if x amount of time has elapsed since the last response. In this form of DRL, the timing of responses is important. As the interresponse time increases, the response rate decreases. An example of this form of DRL is from a study by Lennox, Miltenberger, and Donnelly (1987). The authors worked with adults with mental retardation who engaged in rapid eating at meals. To decrease the rate of eating to make the individuals more socially acceptable, the authors used a DRL procedure in which a bite of food was allowed in the mouth only if 15 seconds had elapsed since the previous bite of food. If 15 seconds had not elapsed since the previous bite, the authors blocked the participants from putting the bite in their mouth. In this way, the time between bites increased to more than 15 seconds (thus, eating rate decreased).

Antecedent Control

Antecedent control procedures involve the manipulation of S^Ds, EOs, or response effort to make the occurrence of a problem behavior less likely or evoke the occurrence of desirable behaviors (Miltenberger, 2004).

To use antecedent control to increase desirable behavior you can present the S^D or an EO for the behavior or decrease response effort for the behavior. Presenting an S^D for a behavior makes the behavior more likely to occur because it has been reinforced in the presence of the S^D in the past. An example might be to send a student to a quiet room with textbooks on a desk to increase the likelihood of studying. Presenting an EO makes a behavior more probable because it increases the reinforcing value of the outcome of the behavior (Vollmer & Iwata, 1991). In the case of a training program with a child with autism in which small edible reinforcers are used (bits of favorite cereal), the trainer can run the training program just before meals, when the child has not eaten in a few hours, as a way to make the edible reinforcers more potent. The trainer can also make sure the child does not have access to the favorite cereal until the training session as a way to make the cereal more reinforcing. Decreasing response effort for a behavior makes the behavior more probable than a functionally equivalent alternative behavior that requires more effort (e.g., Horner & Day, 1991). When a child with tantrum behavior maintained by attention is taught how to ask for attention, the child is more likely to ask for attention if asking takes less effort than engaging in the tantrum behavior and produces an equal amount of attention.

To use antecedent control to decrease a problem behavior, you can remove an S^D or EO for the behavior or increase response effort for the behavior. A behavior is less likely to occur in the absence of the S^D, so removing the S^D is one way to make the behavior less likely. If watching television and playing computer games interfere with doing homework, then turning off the television and computer removes the S^Ds for these competing behaviors to make them less likely (and make doing homework more likely). If the EO for a particular reinforcer is removed, the reinforcer is no longer potent and the behavior producing that reinforcer will be less likely. In the case of the child whose tantrums are reinforced by parent attention, frequent noncontingent attention from the parent will make the tantrums less likely because the reinforcing value of parental attention is decreased through satiation (e.g., Vollmer, Iwata, Zarcone, Smith, & Mazaleski, 1993). Noncontingent reinforcement can make behavior maintained by various forms of reinforcement (attention escape, tangibles) less likely by altering the EO through satiation (Wilder & Carr, 1998). Increasing response effort for a problem behavior makes the behavior less likely because the individual will be more likely to engage in a less effortful, functionally equivalent alternative behavior. For example, when a student with multiple disabilities in a special education classroom slapped students near him, the behavior was reinforced by teacher attention (the teacher came over to him, expressed concern, and explained why the behavior was inappropriate). In this case, the student was moved to a location in the classroom where other children were out of reach. Because it now required more effort to slap another student, the student was more likely to engage in alternative behavior (e.g., raising his hand) for teacher attention.

To use antecedent control procedures successfully, you must identify relevant antecedents through a functional assessment and alter the antecedents that are functionally related to the target behaviors. Numerous studies have demonstrated the effectiveness of antecedent control procedures for problem behaviors maintained by positive reinforcement and negative reinforcement (Luiselli, 2006).

Punishment

In behavior modification problem behaviors are addressed first through a functional approach to assessment and intervention. After conducting a functional assessment,

extinction, differential reinforcement, and antecedent control procedures are utilized, often with success. In cases where problem behaviors are not successfully
treated with these functional interventions, punishment may be considered (Iwata,
1988; Miltenberger, 2004). The most commonly used punishment procedures are
based on the principle of negative punishment and include time-out and response
cost. Although positive punishment procedures involving the delivery of aversive
stimulation (such as the use of contingent shock) have been used in the past, such
procedures are rarely if ever used in contemporary behavior modification.

Time-out

Time-out from positive reinforcement ("time-out" for short) is a procedure in which,
contingent on a problem behavior, a child is removed from a reinforcing environment for a brief period of time. Time-out is a negative punishment procedure because the child is removed from all sources of positive reinforcement contingent
on the problem behavior and the behavior decreases. The child is typically escorted
to a nearby room or an area devoid of any access to reinforcers. Time-out has been
shown to be a successful intervention for a range of childhood problem behaviors (e.g., Mathews, Friman, Barone, Ross, & Christophersen, 1987; Porterfield,
Herbert-Jackson, & Risley, 1976; Rortvedt & Miltenberger, 1994).

For time-out to be effective, a number of factors must be considered
(Miltenberger, 2004):

- First, the environment from which the child is removed (the time-in environment)
  must be reinforcing (must contain positively reinforcing activities, interactions,
  and/or stimuli). If the time-in environment is not reinforcing, time-out will not
  function as negative punishment.
- Second, time-out must be initiated immediately contingent on the problem
  behavior.
- Third, time-out must be brief (a few minutes in duration) to provide minimal
  disruption of ongoing educational or other important activities.
- Fourth, attention or other reinforcers must not be available in the time-out area.
  If the time-out room or area is reinforcing, time-out will not be effective.
- Fifth, the child should not get any attention while being taken to time-out. Con-
  tingent on the problem behavior the parent should simply state the problem
  behavior and that the child has to go to time-out and proceed to escort the child
  to time-out without any further discussion.
- Sixth, the child should not escape from time-out until released by the parent
  when time-out is over.
- Seventh, the time-out room or area must be safe.

Response Cost

Response cost is a procedure in which, contingent on the occurrence of the problem
behavior, a specified amount of a reinforcer is removed to decrease the behavior.

Losing the opportunity to have dessert contingent on problem behavior at supper, or loss of a portion of an allowance contingent on the occurrence of a problem behavior are examples of response cost that might be used by parents. In each case, the loss of the reinforcer makes the problem behavior less likely in the future. Response cost procedures are used frequently by governments and other organizations (e.g., speeding tickets, fines for parking in handicapped parking spaces, fees for bounced checks, late fees from credit card companies). Response cost procedures are used effectively for a variety of child behavior problems as well. For example, Little and Kelley (1989) use response cost to decrease noncompliance to parental requests; Long, Miltenberger, and Rapp (1999) use response cost to decrease thumb sucking; and Rapport, Murphy, and Bailey (1982) used response cost to decrease hyperactive behavior in children.

For response cost to be effective, the loss of the reinforcer (or a statement that the reinforcer will be lost) should occur immediately contingent on each instance of the problem behavior. The magnitude of the reinforcer loss should be sufficient to function as a punisher. Finally, ethical issues must be considered such that the loss of the reinforcer does not harm the child in any way or violate the child's rights (e.g., loss of meals, for example, is not an acceptable form of response cost).

Promoting Generalization

In behavior modification, generalization is defined as the occurrence of target behavior outside of the treatment or training setting in the natural environment. For example, if a child learns social skills in treatment sessions with the school psychologist, generalization occurs when the social skills are used with peers at school or in other natural settings. A number of strategies can be used to promote generalization (e.g., Stokes & Baer, 1977; Stokes & Osnes, 1989):

- Provide reinforcement for the target behavior when it occurs in the natural environment. In the social skills example, the school psychologist could provide praise whenever she observes the child engaging in good social skills with peers.
- Teach skills that will contact natural contingencies of reinforcement. The child should be taught the kind of social skills likely to generate a reinforcing response from peers.
- Modify natural contingencies of reinforcement. The psychologist might talk to the student's teachers and have them provide praise for the student's appropriate use of social skills.
- Incorporate a variety of relevant stimulus situations in training so that the child has practiced and received reinforcement for engaging in the correct behavior in a wide range of situations he might encounter in the natural environment.
- Incorporate stimuli from the natural environment into the training situation (common stimuli). An example would be to have some same-age peers in the social skills training sessions so the student practices with the kinds of peers he is likely to encounter in school.

- Teach self-generated mediators of generalization. This strategy might include teaching the student some simple self-instructions that he could use in social situations to cue himself to use the social skills that he had learned in training sessions.

Another form of generalization occurs when a target behavior that decreased in treatment sessions also decreases in the natural environment. To promote a generalized reduction in problem behavior, it is important to reinforce a functionally equivalent alternative behavior so that the desirable behavior takes the place of the problem and produces the same type and amount of reinforcement that the problem behavior did before treatment (E. G. Carr, 1988). It is also important to maintain extinction or punishment contingencies across situations and over time in case the problem behavior occurs again for some reason (e.g., spontaneous recovery).

Habit Reversal

Habit reversal is a procedure developed by Azrin and Nunn (1973) as a treatment for nervous habits (hair pulling, thumb sucking, nail biting, skin picking, and other repetitive self-directed behaviors) and motor and vocal tics. Habit reversal procedures were also applied successfully to stuttering by Azrin and Nunn (1974). Since the original studies describing these procedures, numerous studies have demonstrated the effectiveness of the procedures or streamlined versions of the procedures (Miltenberger, Fuqua, & Woods, 1998).

Habit reversal is a multicomponent procedure with the following components: (a) motivational procedures involving review of all the inconveniences, embarrassment, or social and personal problems caused by the habit behavior; (b) awareness training in which the client describes the habit behaviors and learns to detect each instance of the habit as it occurs or as it is about to occur; (c) competing response training in which the client learns to engage in a physically incompatible motor response contingent on the occurrence of the habit behavior or in anticipation of the habit behavior; and (d) social support procedures in which a parent or other adult helps the child control the habit behavior by prompting the child to use the competing response when necessary, praising the child for using the competing response at the appropriate time (DRA), and praising the child when the habit behavior is not occurring (DRO).

Habit reversal procedures are taught to the child with the parent present in a few treatment sessions. Booster sessions are then used as needed to help the child continue to use the procedures successfully over time (Rapp, Miltenberger, Long, Elliott, & Lumley, 1998; Romaniuk, Miltenberger, & Deaver, 2003). Although habit reversal has been used successfully for child habit behaviors, research has shown that it may not be effective for younger children (Long, Miltenberger, & Rapp, 1999; Rapp, Miltenberger, Galensky, Roberts, & Ellingson, 1999) or individuals with disabilities (Long, Miltenberger, Ellingson, & Ott, 1999).

Token Economy

A token economy involves the systematic application of conditioned reinforcers called tokens to promote and maintain desirable behaviors (Ayllon & Azrin, 1968). In a token economy, tokens are delivered for desirable behavior and later exchanged for backup reinforcers. Tokens maintain their effectiveness as conditioned reinforcers because they are paired with already established backup reinforcers. The following steps are involved in developing and implementing a token economy (Miltenberger, 2004):

1. Identify and define the target behaviors you want to strengthen through the use of the token economy.
2. Identify the objects that will used as tokens. Tokens must be able to be delivered immediately to the client following the desirable behavior. They can consist of small objects such as poker chips, pennies, or marbles that can be accumulated by the client. They can also include points, checkmarks, hole punches in a card, or anything else that can be delivered and accumulated easily.
3. Identify the backup reinforcers. Because tokens maintain their power as conditioned reinforcers by being paired with backup reinforcers, it is important to choose items or activities that are known to be powerful reinforcers for use in the token economy. Furthermore, it is best to have a variety of backup reinforcers available to help avoid satiation.
4. Identify the number of tokens that will be delivered for each of the target behaviors. Typically, more tokens are delivered for more difficult or more important target behaviors.
5. Identify the exchange rate for backup reinforcers. You need to determine how many tokens are required to exchange for each backup reinforcer. Larger or more valued reinforcers will require more tokens.
6. Identify a time and place for exchanging tokens for backup reinforcers. Clients will be receiving and accumulating tokens each day for engaging in desirable behavior. Unless a time and place is set for exchanging tokens, the clients may seek to purchase backup reinforcers numerous times daily, thus disrupting ongoing activities.

To use a token economy effectively, it must be planned in advance, taking into consideration each of these steps. In addition, staff must be trained and supervised to carry out the program successfully. Finally, it is important to develop the token economy in such a way that the tokens cannot be acquired in any way other than by engaging in the target behaviors and that the backup reinforcers cannot be acquired in any way other than with tokens. If backup reinforcers are freely available, individuals will not work to earn tokens to exchange for them.

Behavioral Contracts

A behavioral contract is a written agreement specifying a desired behavior and a consequence for the behavior (O'Banion & Whaley, 1981). By writing a behavioral contract, a person is making a commitment to engage in a specified behavior in a specified time frame and arranging a consequence as a reinforcer for the behavior. Typically, a contract manager implements the contract with the person seeking behavior change. It is the contract manager's job to verify the occurrence of the behavior and carry out the consequence specified in the contract. For example, a student might agree to a behavioral contract with a school counselor in which the student commits to being on time for school each day for a week. When agreeing to the contract, the student gives the counselor five personal checks for $10 each. Each day the student gets to school on time, she gets one of the checks back. If she is late, the check for that day is sent to charity. Knowing that she will avoid the loss of $10 by arriving on time helps motivate the student to engage in the behavior.

The essential components of a behavioral contract include (a) a clear description of the target behavior to be engaged in or avoided, (b) the time frame in which the target behavior (or its absence) should occur, (c) how the target behavior will be measured, (d) the consequence for engaging in (or not engaging in) the target behavior, and (e) signatures of the individual seeking behavior change and the contract manager (Miltenberger, 2004).

Case Illustration

Christy was a 25-month-old girl referred by her mother for feeding difficulties. She was seen by a psychology graduate student under the supervision of a faculty member in clinical psychology.

Identifying Features of the Client
Christy was 25 months of age at the time of referral. She lived at home with her parents and 5-year-old brother. Due to her feeding problems, she had a gastric tube and received supplemental feedings each night while she was asleep.

Presenting Complaints
The problem for which her mother sought help was a feeding problem involving food refusal. Christy refused to accept bites of food presented to her on a spoon by closing her mouth, turning her head, placing her hands in front of her mouth, and trying to get away from the table. Another problem was gagging and food expulsion, which occurred to a lesser extent than food refusal. Gagging was most likely to occur when coarser foods were eaten or larger bites were attempted. Christy refused most foods except baby foods, pureed foods, soft foods such as ice cream and pudding, and shakes.

History and Developmental Factors
Christy's mother had an uncomplicated pregnancy and delivery. Within 10 days after birth, during which time Christy cried, grimaced, and vomited frequently during bottle feeding, she was diagnosed with gastro-esophageal reflux. She received a medication but the problem continued for the next 4 months. Because Christy did not gain weight at the appropriate rate in the first 6 months of life,

---

a gastric tube was implanted and she received supplemental feedings while asleep in bed. Her medication was also changed and the reflux problem abated. However, Christy exhibited food refusal problems when her mother started feeding her baby food and then table food.

At the time of referral, Christy was developmentally normal in all areas except oral-motor development, where she was slightly delayed. However, she did have the ability to chew and swallow food cut up into small pieces. She was at the 30th percentile for height and the 2nd percentile for weight.

Parental Factors
Both parents were present in the home and committed to solving Christy's feeding problem. Her mother was at home with her while her father worked for the first 2 years of her life, so her mother was the one who usually fed Christy. Christy started day care 2 months before the referral.

Assessment
Assessment was conducted through interviews with the mother, direct observation of meal times by the graduate student therapist, and behavioral recording by her mother. The behaviors recorded during direct observation were (a) number of bites presented, (b) number of bites accepted, (c) type of food, and (d) amount of food consumed. Functional assessment information was gathered through the interview and through direct observation to determine the types of food refused and parental responses to food refusal.

Case Conceptualization
It appeared from history that food refusal was initially negatively reinforced by escape from aversive stimulation arising from reflux. It also appeared that food refusal was reinforced through avoidance of gagging. At the time of referral, both positive and negative reinforcement appeared to play a role in maintaining food refusal. Christy escaped from eating foods that were more coarse or required more chewing by engaging in food refusal behaviors. In addition, when she refused to accept bites of food, her mother provided substantial coaxing and other attention in an attempt to get her to eat. Furthermore, when she refused to eat food being served at the meal, her mother gave her preferred foods instead so that she was consuming some calories. Therefore, the food refusal appeared to be maintained in part by attention and the receipt of preferred foods. Gagging was probably reinforced in part by attention, preferred food, and escape as her mother expressed great concern each time she gagged, let her stop eating, and let her have access to the pureed foods or baby foods instead.

Course of Treatment and Assessment of Progress
Treatment consisted of (a) a shaping program, (b) differential reinforcement involving the use of attention and bites of preferred food for accepting bites of nonpreferred food, and (c) extinction in which attention and preferred foods were no longer given as a consequence for food refusal.

In the shaping procedure, Christy was asked to eat very small portions of nonpreferred foods at the beginning of treatment, and the portion size was gradually increased across days and weeks. In the differential reinforcement procedure, each time she ate the nonpreferred food that was presented to her,

(Continued)

she received her preferred food. She also received enthusiastic praise for each bite of nonpreferred food she accepted. In the extinction component of treatment her mom and dad were taught to withhold their attention for any refusal behaviors or gagging. They were also taught not to provide preferred food following food refusal behaviors.

The graduate student therapist went to the family home and modeled the intervention procedures at a few mealtimes and coached the mom and dad as they used the procedures in subsequent meals. Once the parents were successfully using the procedures and stated that they were comfortable with the procedures, home visits were terminated and office visits were continued to discuss progress and troubleshoot any problems. Initially, mealtimes were videotaped to collect data on Christy's refusals and gagging. When it was evident that refusals were declining greatly and the amount eaten was increasing, videotaping was no longer conducted. Christy's mother continued to record type and amount of food consumed and number of refusals.

Complicating Factors
There were no complicating factors making assessment or intervention more difficult in this case.

Managed Care Considerations
The intensity of the intervention, conducted at supper time in the home a few times per week, would be difficult to carry out in a typical managed care environment. Because a graduate student receiving practicum training was involved in the case, the home visits and increased frequency of sessions could be accomplished.

Follow-up Treatment
Christy continued to make improvements over the course of 3 months, engaging in far fewer food refusal behaviors and eating larger quantities of food. Her weight increased into the 10th percentile after 3 months of treatment. Although she continued to be fed through the gastric tube each evening, the amount of supplementation was gradually decreased.

Implications and Recommendations to Clinicians and Students
This case illustrates how a functional approach to assessment and intervention can effectively address a serious child behavior problem. The intervention procedures were chosen based on the results of the functional assessment, which identified the antecedents and consequences maintaining the problem behavior. The antecedents and consequences were then addressed in treatment to change the variables contributing to the problem. Clinicians and students are encouraged to utilize a functional case conceptualization and a functional approach to treatment as best practice when using behavior modification.

SUMMARY

Behavior modification is a field of clinical psychology that emphasizes objective measurement of behavior before and after intervention to document the effects of the intervention. Intervention involves the application of behavioral principles to help people change socially significant behaviors. Behavior modification procedures are aimed at changing aspects of the physical or social environment to bring about changes in behavior. Behavior modification procedures are used to help people develop new behaviors (to overcome behavior deficits) and to help people stop engaging in undesirable behavior (to decrease behavioral excesses).

When using behavior modification procedures to help people address behavior problems, a functional approach to assessment and intervention is utilized. A functional assessment is conducted first to identify the variables contributing to the problem behavior. Interventions are then developed based on the results of the functional assessment information. Interventions seek to alter the antecedents and consequences that contribute to the problem behavior while promoting functionally equivalent alternative behavior to replace the problem behavior. Behavior modification procedures are successful when they produce desired behavior changes that generalize to the client's everyday environment.

REFERENCES

Allen, K. D., & Stokes, T. F. (1987). Use of escape and reward in the management of young children during dental treatment. *Journal of Applied Behavior Analysis, 20*, 381–390.

Arndorfer, R. E., Miltenberger, R. G., Woster, S. H., Rortvedt, A. K., & Gaffaney, T. (1994). Home-based descriptive and experimental analysis of problem behaviors in children. *Topics in Early Childhood Special Education, 14*, 64–87.

Ayllon, T., & Azrin, N. (1968). *The token economy: A motivational system for therapy and rehabilitation.* New York: Appleton-Century-Crofts.

Azrin, N. H., & Nunn, R. G. (1973). Habit reversal: A method of eliminating nervous habits and tics. *Behaviour Research and Therapy, 11*, 619–628.

Azrin, N. H., & Nunn, R. G. (1974). A rapid method of eliminating stuttering by a regulated breathing approach. *Behaviour Research and Therapy, 12*, 279–286.

Baer, D. M., Wolf, M. M., & Risley, T. R. (1968). Some current dimensions of applied behavior analysis. *Journal of Applied Behavior Analysis, 1*, 91–97.

Bailey, J. S., & Burch, M. R. (2002). *Research methods in applied behavior analysis.* Thousand Oaks, CA: Sage.

Bakken, J., Miltenberger, R., & Schauss, S. (1993). Teaching mentally retarded parents: Knowledge versus skills. *American Journal on Mental Retardation, 97*, 405–417.

Bellamy, G. T., Horner, R. H., & Inman, D. P. (1979). *Vocational habilitation of severely retarded adults.* Austin, TX: ProEd.

Carr, E. G. (1988). Functional equivalence as a means of response generalization. In R. H. Horner, G. Dunlap, & R. L. Koegel (Eds.), *Generalization and maintenance: Lifestyle changes in applied settings* (pp. 221–241). Baltimore: Paul H. Brookes.

Carr, E. G., & Durand, V. M. (1985). Reducing behavior problems through functional communication training. *Journal of Applied Behavior Analysis, 18*, 111–126.

Carr, J., & Austin, J. (Eds.). (2001). *Handbook of applied behavior analysis.* Reno, NV: Context Press.

Cooper, J., Heron, T., & Heward, W. (2007). *Applied behavior analysis.* Upper Saddle River, NJ: Prentice-Hall.

Cowdery, G. E., Iwata, B. A., & Pace, G. M. (1990). Effects and side-effects of DRO as treatment for self-injurious behavior. *Journal of Applied Behavior Analysis, 23*, 497–506.

Durand, V. M., & Carr, E. G. (1991). Functional communication training to reduce challenging behavior: Maintenance and application in new settings. *Journal of Applied Behavior Analysis, 24*, 251–264.

Durand, V. M., & Carr, E. G. (1992). An analysis of maintenance following functional communication training. *Journal of Applied Behavior Analysis, 25*, 777–794.

Ferster, C. B., & Skinner, B. F. (1957). *Schedules of reinforcement.* Upper Saddle River, NJ: Prentice-Hall.

Gross, A. M., & Drabman, R. S. (Eds.). (2005). *Encyclopedia of behavior modification and cognitive behavior therapy: Child clinical applications.* Thousand Oaks, CA: Sage.

Guttman, N., & Kalish, H. I. (1956). Discriminability and stimulus generalization. *Journal of Experimental Psychology, 51*, 79–88.

Hagopian, L. P., & Thompson, R. H. (1999). Reinforcement of compliance with respiratory treatment in a child with cystic fibrosis. *Journal of Applied Behavior Analysis, 32*, 233–236.

Hersen, M., & Rosqvist, J. (Eds.). (2005). *Encyclopedia of behavior modification and cognitive behavior therapy: Adult clinical applications.* Thousand Oaks, CA: Sage.

Himle, M. B., & Miltenberger, R. G. (2004). Preventing unintentional firearm injury in children: The need for behavioral skills training. *Education and Treatment of Children, 27*, 161–177.

Himle, M. B., Miltenberger, R. G., Flessner, C., & Gatheridge, B. (2004). Teaching safety skills to children to prevent gun play. *Journal of Applied Behavior Analysis, 37*, 1–9.

Horner, R. D. (1971). Establishing use of crutches by a mentally retarded spina bifida child. *Journal of Applied Behavior Analysis, 4*, 183–189.

Horner, R. H., & Day, H. M. (1991). The effects of response efficiency on functionally equivalent competing behaviors. *Journal of Applied Behavior Analysis, 24*, 719–732.

Iwata, B. A. (1988). The development and adoption of controversial default technologies. *Behavior Analyst, 11*, 149–157.

Iwata, B. A., Dorsey, M. F., Slifer, K. J., Bauman, K. E., & Richman, G. S. (1982). Toward a functional analysis of self-injury. *Analysis and Intervention in Developmental Disabilities, 2*, 3–20.

Iwata, B. A., Pace, G. M., Cowdery, G. E., & Miltenberger, R. G. (1994). What makes extinction work: Analysis of procedural form and function. *Journal of Applied Behavior Analysis, 27*, 131–144.

Iwata, B. A., Vollmer, T. R., Zarcone, J. R., & Rodgers, T. A. (1993). Treatment classification and selection based on behavioral function. In R. Van Houten & S. Axelrod (Eds.), *Behavior analysis and treatment* (pp. 101–125). New York: Plenum Press.

Jackson, D. A., & Wallace, R. F. (1974). The modification and generalization of voice loudness in a fifteen year old retarded girl. *Journal of Applied Behavior Analysis, 7*, 461–471.

Johnson, B. M., Miltenberger, R. G., Egemo-Helm, K., Jostad, C. M., Flessner, C., & Gatheridge, B. (2005). Evaluation of behavioral skills training for teaching abduction prevention skills to young children. *Journal of Applied Behavior Analysis, 38*, 67–78.

Lalli, J. S., Mace, F. C., Livezey, K., & Kates, K. (1998). Assessment of stimulus generalization gradients in the treatment of self-injurious behavior. *Journal of Applied Behavior Analysis, 31*, 479–483.

Lennox, D. B., & Miltenberger, R. G. (1989). Conducting a functional assessment of problem behavior in applied settings. *Journal of the Association for Persons with Severe Handicaps, 14*, 304–311.

Lennox, D. B., Miltenberger, R. G., & Donnelly, D. (1987). Response interruption and DRL for the reduction of rapid eating. *Journal of Applied Behavior Analysis, 20*, 279–284.

Lerman, D. C., & Iwata, B. A. (1995). Prevalence of the extinction burst and its attenuation during treatment. *Journal of Applied Behavior Analysis, 28*, 93–94.

Lerman, D. C., & Iwata, B. A. (1996). Developing a technology for the use of operant extinction in clinical settings: An examination of basic and applied research. *Journal of Applied Behavior Analysis, 29*, 345–382.

Lerman, D. C., & Vorndran, C. M. (2002). On the status of knowledge for using punishment: Implications for treating behavior disorders. *Journal of Applied Behavior Analysis, 35*, 431–464.

Little, L. M., & Kelley, M. L. (1989). The efficacy of response cost procedures for reducing children's noncompliance to parental instructions. *Behavior Therapy, 20*, 525–534.

Long, E., Miltenberger, R., Ellingson, S., & Ott, S. (1999). Augmenting simplified habit reversal in the treatment of oral-digital habits exhibited by individuals with mental retardation. *Journal of Applied Behavior Analysis, 32*, 353–365.

Long, E., Miltenberger, R., & Rapp, J. (1999). Simplified habit reversal plus adjunct contingencies in the treatment of thumb sucking and hair pulling in a young girl. *Child and Family Behavior Therapy, 21*(4), 45–58.

Luiselli, J. (Ed.). (2006). *Antecedent assessment and intervention: Supporting children and adults with developmental disabilities in community settings*. Baltimore, MA: Brookes.

Marcus, B. A., & Vollmer, T. R. (1995). Effects of differential negative reinforcement on disruption and compliance. *Journal of Applied Behavior Analysis, 28*, 229–230.

Mathews, J. R., Friman, P. C., Barone, V. J., Ross, L. V., & Christophersen, E. R. (1987). Decreasing dangerous infant behavior through parent instruction. *Journal of Applied Behavior Analysis, 20*, 165–169.

Michael, J. (1982). Distinguishing between discriminative and motivational functions of stimuli. *Journal of the Experimental Analysis of Behavior, 37*, 149–155.

Miltenberger, R. G. (2004). *Behavior modification: Principles and procedures*. Belmont, CA: Wadsworth.

Miltenberger, R. G., & Fuqua, R. W. (1985). Evaluation of a training manual for the acquisition of behavioral assessment interviewing skills. *Journal of Applied Behavior Analysis, 18*, 323–328.

Miltenberger, R. G., Fuqua, R. W., & Woods, D. W. (1998). Applying behavior analysis with clinical problems: Review and analysis of habit reversal. *Journal of Applied Behavior Analysis, 31*, 447–469.

O'Banion, D. R., & Whaley, D. L. (1981). *Behavioral contracting: Arranging contingencies of reinforcement*. New York: Springer.

O'Neill, G. W., & Gardner, R. (1983). *Behavioral principles in medical rehabilitation: A practical guide*. Springfield, IL: Charles C. Thomas.

O'Neill, R. E., Horner, R. H., Albin, R. W., Sprague, J. R., Storey, K., & Newton, J. S. (1997). *Functional assessment and program development for problem behavior: A practical handbook*. Pacific Grove, CA: Brooks/Cole.

Porterfield, J. K., Herbert-Jackson, E., & Risley, T. R. (1976). Contingent observation: An effective and acceptable procedure for reducing disruptive behavior of young children in a group setting. *Journal of Applied Behavior Analysis, 9*, 55–64.

Pryor, K. (1985). *Don't shoot the dog: The new art of teaching and training*. New York: Bantam.

Rapp, J., Miltenberger, R., Galensky, T., Roberts, J., & Ellingson, S. (1999). Brief functional analysis and simplified habit reversal treatment for thumb sucking in fraternal twin brothers. *Child and Family Behavior Therapy, 21*(2), 1–17.

Rapp, J., Miltenberger, R., Long, E., Elliott, A., & Lumley, V. (1998). Simplified habit reversal for hair pulling in three adolescents: A clinical replication with direct observation. *Journal of Applied Behavior Analysis, 31*, 299–302.

Rapport, M. D., Murphy, H. A., & Bailey, J. S. (1982). Ritalin vs. response cost in the control of hyperactive children: A within subject comparison. *Journal of Applied Behavior Analysis, 15*, 205–216.

Romaniuk, C., Miltenberger, R., & Deaver, C. (2003). Long term maintenance following habit reversal and adjunct treatment for trichotillomania. *Child and Family Behavior Therapy, 25*(2), 45–59.

Rortvedt, A. K., & Miltenberger, R. G. (1994). Analysis of a high probability instructional sequence and time-out in the treatment of child noncompliance. *Journal of Applied Behavior Analysis, 27*, 327–330.

Scott, D., Scott, L. M., & Goldwater, B. (1997). A performance improvement program for an international-level track and field athlete. *Journal of Applied Behavior Analysis, 30*, 573–575.

Skinner, B. F. (1938). *The behavior of organisms: An experimental analysis*. New York: Appleton-Century-Crofts.

Skinner, B. F. (1951). How to teach animals. *Scientific American, 185*, 26–29.

Smith, R. G., & Iwata, B. A. (1997). Antecedent influences on behavior disorders. *Journal of Applied Behavior Analysis, 30*, 343–375.

Steege, M. W., Wacker, D. P., Cigrand, K. C., Berg, W. K., Novak, C. G., Reimers, T. M., et al. (1990). Use of negative reinforcement in the treatment of self-injurious behavior. *Journal of Applied Behavior Analysis, 23*, 459–467.

Stokes, T. F., & Baer, D. M. (1977). An implicit technology of generalization. *Journal of Applied Behavior Analysis, 10*, 349–367.

Stokes, T. F., & Osnes, P. G. (1989). An operant pursuit of generalization. *Behavior Therapy, 20*, 337–355.

Sugai, G., & Horner, R. (Eds.). (2005). *Encyclopedia of behavior modification and cognitive behavior therapy: Educational applications*. Thousand Oaks, CA: Sage.

Sulzer-Azaroff, B., & Mayer, G. R. (1991). *Behavior analysis for lasting change*. Fort Worth, TX: Holt, Rinehart and Winston.

Ullmann, L. P., & Krasner, L. (Eds.). (1965). *Case studies in behavior modification*. New York: Holt, Rinehart and Winston.

Ulrich, R., Stachnik, T., & Mabry, J. (Eds.). (1966). *Control of human behavior: Expanding the behavioral laboratory*. Glenview, IL: Scott Foresman.

Vollmer, T. R., & Iwata, B. A. (1991). Establishing operations and reinforcement effects. *Journal of Applied Behavior Analysis, 24*, 279–291.

Vollmer, T. R., & Iwata, B. A. (1992). Differential reinforcement as treatment for severe behavior disorders: Procedural and functional variations. *Research in Developmental Disabilities, 13*, 393–417.

Vollmer, T. R., Iwata, B. A., Cuvo, A. J., Heward, W. L., Miltenberger, R. G., & Neef, N. A. (Eds.). (2000). *Behavior analysis: Applications and extensions 1968–1999: Reprint series* (Vol. 5). Lawrence, KS: Society for the Experimental Analysis of Behavior.

Vollmer, T. R., Iwata, B. A., Zarcone, J. R., Smith, R. G., & Mazaleski, J. L. (1993). The role of attention in the treatment of attention-maintained self-injurious behavior: Noncontingent reinforcement and differential reinforcement of other behavior. *Journal of Applied Behavior Analysis, 26*, 9–22.

Wilder, D. A., & Carr, J. E. (1998). Recent advances in the modification of establishing operations to reduce aberrant behavior. *Behavioral Interventions, 13*, 43–59.

Wolf, M. M. (1978). Social validity: The case for subjective measurement, or how applied behavior analysis is finding its heart. *Journal of Applied Behavior Analysis, 11*, 203–214.

CHAPTER 22

Parent Training

Mark W. Roberts

Surely parents were given advice about how to raise their difficult children long before the introduction of parent training to the child clinical literature in the 1960s. McLoughlin (1982) cites explicit American efforts dating back to 1815. What is surprising is that professional therapists attempted to treat emotionally disturbed children during the first 60 years of the twentieth century without involving parents! This chapter traces the therapeutic use of parents to socialize defiant, aggressive children from its humble beginnings at midcentury to the relatively robust protocols of today. The entire parent training literature is too vast to be integrated into a single book, let alone a chapter, so a specific focus must be adopted. First, only articles regarding overt problems of conduct are considered. Specifically excluded are literatures on teaching parents to promote skills in children with disabilities (e.g., S. L. Harris, Wolchick, & Milch, 1982), to facilitate normal adaptive skills such as toileting (e.g., Azrin & Besalel, 1979), or to treat internalizing disorders (e.g., Barmish & Kendall, 2005) or covert problems (e.g., stealing, vandalism). Second, the chapter is limited to children in the preschool and middle childhood periods (roughly 2 to 12 years of age), eliminating publications addressing infants and adolescents. Third, only parent training based on social learning theory is considered (Miller & Prinz, 1990), excluding parent training based on humanistic, dynamic, or family systems theory (Rinn & Markle, 1977). Fourth, the use of parent training as a primary prevention tool (Sanders, 1999) or a secondary prevention strategy (Conduct Problems Prevention Research Group, 2004) is beyond the scope of this chapter. The chapter does presume to accurately represent parent training studies that treat problems of overt social aggression in 2- to 12-year-old children from a social learning perspective.

The chapter is organized into six sections in which the current status and limitations of knowledge are reviewed. A brief history of parent training, its purpose and origins, is presented, which includes references to major review articles and identification and discussion of six ongoing research domains. The theoretical basis for parent training is examined from a historical perspective with an eye toward case conceptualization and treatment selection. The various methods of teaching skills to parents are compared in terms of effectiveness and efficiency. Current parent

Thanks to Stacy B. Shaw for her review and editorial assistance with an earlier version of this manuscript.

training curricula are reviewed, with a focus on treatments for noncompliance and aggression plus brief discussions of negative vocalizations and situational issues. A case illustration and articulation of future challenges conclude the chapter.

A BRIEF HISTORY OF PARENT TRAINING

The Early Years: 1959 to 1973

Children disobey parents and teachers; they fight with other children; they scream and yell at adults who attempt to discipline them or deny their requests; they argue with "uncooperative" parents, siblings, and peers; and they talk rudely to those who attempt to thwart their interests. Essentially, the presenting problems of oppositional and disruptive children are problems of social interaction, including parent-child, teacher-child, sibling-child, and peer-child interaction. It is to the credit of the small set of clinical child researchers who launched parent training research in the 1960s that they recognized the inextricable relationship between child social aggression and the social contexts in which it flourishes.

A case study by Williams (1959) is often cited as the first published account of parent training, in which the parents of a 21-month-old were instructed to ignore his bedtime screaming. The recommended extinction procedure did successfully co-vary with decreased tantrum duration at bedtime. Boardman's (1962) florid account of a conduct disordered 6-year-old is often cited as the second documented parent training case. "Rusty" defied his mother, left home and school without permission, set fires, and destroyed property. Boardman met with the family just once, but followed up with several phone calls. Room time-outs and logical consequences were prescribed. Rusty reacted with violent resistance, running away, and continued defiance until an intense spanking episode appeared to suppress his coercive efforts. Positive reinforcement for cooperation had also been recommended by Boardman, but there was no evidence of its use. Boardman's treatment plan elicited concerned and scholarly comments from Bandura (1962), who noted the limitations of punishment-only strategies and recommended the systematic use of positive reinforcement. Intriguingly, the 1962 Boardman and Bandura exchange foreshadowed some of the basic questions faced every day by clinicians, only some of which have been resolved by research. Can we treat social aggression by reinforcing socially appropriate alternative responses or periods of inhibition? Must we actively teach alternative responses to replace coercion, or might such skills already reside within the youth's repertoire? How might we alter natural contingencies among siblings and peers to support alternatives to social aggression, given the effort and non-reinforcement that often accompanies "social skills"? If discipline is necessary to block reinforcers for aggression, how do we advise parents to manage the child's aversive reaction to the recommended discipline routine?

Neither Williams nor Boardman articulated the case for parent training. The case studies, single-case designs, and uncontrolled group studies that followed in the next decade, however, did offer explicit rationales for using "mothers as behavior therapists" (Wahler, Winkel, Peterson, & Morrison, 1965, p. 113) to "reprogram the social environment" (Patterson, McNeal, Hawkins, & Phelps, 1967, p. 181).

Review articles of published studies from the 1960s and early 1970s summarized the many reasons advanced in these vanguard publications for abandoning individual psychotherapy with socially aggressive youth and replacing it with the new therapeutic modality, parent training. Three good reviews from this period are available: Berkowitz and Graziano (1972), Johnson and Katz (1973), and O'Dell (1974). Each reviewer looked at the same set of studies a bit differently, but induced three rather similar themes.

First, all reviewers noted that traditional therapy (i.e., relationship-based, insight-oriented) occupies a minor amount of time in the life of a child (e.g., 1 hour a week) and is performed in an unusual situation (i.e., an office playroom with an unfamiliar adult). Even if successful, therapeutic gains might not generalize to home, school, or neighborhood settings where the social aggression was manifest, let alone persist in those natural settings. In contrast, parents interact almost continuously with the young child referred for treatment. Generalization of treatment effects to the home setting and across time could be directly programmed by providing parents with guidance on how to perform the therapy themselves at home. The parent would assume the primary therapy role, while the licensed clinician would assume a consulting role. Essentially, the first theme culled by reviewers of the period was one of quantitative advantage and setting relevance for parents over traditional therapists.

Second, Berkowitz and Graziano (1972) and O'Dell (1974), and to a lesser extent, Johnson and Katz (1973), inferred a theoretical rationale for parent training from the initial spate of publications. Because parents are intrinsically involved in the socialization of their own children, and because referred children present as socialization failures (i.e., significant aggression and defiance beyond the age of 4 years), parents with socially aggressive children are likely to be unwitting contributors. Typical parenting errors might include providing attention for misbehavior; succumbing to the relentless drone of crying, arguing, or sultry mood displays by providing previously denied objects or activities; allowing natural reinforcers for aggression to operate by ignoring sibling fighting; or modeling angry, defiant responses with one's adult partner. Whatever the parenting mistakes might be, the therapeutic implications of the new theoretical position were clear. A psychopathogenic home environment could overwhelm any therapeutic change a clinician might achieve in a clinic playroom, since the pattern of child management in the home had not been addressed and would continue to elicit and reinforce social aggression. The extreme case of the new theoretical perspective was that targeting social aggression without changing the behavior of parents would simply fail.

Third, all three reviews called for improved research methodology. Published studies at that time often failed to embrace basic research procedures needed for replication and to establish internal validity. These basics include pretreatment measures of child deviance, objective definitions of parenting skills and the techniques of teaching those skills, measurements of parent acquisition and use of therapeutic skills, measurements of child reactions to changed parent behavior, and adequate experimental controls. The early work clearly set the stage for the very productive science of the next 3 decades, which addressed methodological shortcomings, proposed theoretical models, and expanded the research questions.

Patterson, Wahler, and Hanf

Three early entries into this literature warrant special recognition: Gerald Patterson at the University of Oregon (and later the Oregon Social Learning Center, hereafter OSLC), Robert Wahler at the University of Tennessee, and Constance Hanf at the University of Oregon Medical Center. Each contributed substantially to measurement, treatment, and theory during a sensitive period in the development of parent training based on social learning. A new measurement strategy often leads the way in science, and Patterson, Hanf, and Wahler did just that. Each developed microbehavioral observational systems to record parent-child event sequences. Although Patterson and Wahler focused on home settings under general conditions (Reid, 1978; Wahler, House, & Stambaugh, 1976) and Hanf on clinic settings under specific simulated conditions (Hanf, 1968), each coding system could detect frequencies of child and parent behavior, as well as conditional probabilities that revealed the stimulus control and contingent relationships among the behavioral events. Verifiable, observational data were used to confirm the presence of child deviance, identify likely parenting mistakes, provide treatment outcome data, and contribute to theory development.

Patterson and his colleagues defined 29 behavioral codes that sampled an alternating sequence of child and family member interaction in a general home context. Wahler's observational system is similar. He defined 24 child and parent codes, but used an interval-sampling approach, rather than the event-sequence approach pioneered by Patterson. The Patterson and Wahler observational systems provided data that served as the foundation of theoretical advancements, including the measurement of coercive processes (Patterson, 1982; Patterson, Reid, & Dishion, 1992; Wahler & Dumas, 1987). In contrast, Hanf defined nine standard laboratory situations derived from parent interviews about the conditions associated with preschool children's misbehavior (e.g., a parent denies a child's request). Unlike Patterson and Wahler, Hanf's codes did not apply to all measurement situations, and only some codes operationalized an event sequence (e.g., child compliance given a parent's command). Nevertheless, Hanf's observational system directly influenced the coding systems constructed by Forehand (Forehand & McMahon, 1981, pp. 183–218) at the University of Georgia, Eyberg (Eyberg, Bessmer, Newcomb, Edwards, & Robinson, 1994) at the University of Florida, and Webster-Stratton at the University of Washington, who adopted Eyberg's Dyadic Parent-Child Interaction Coding System. By moving the field of child clinical psychology toward observational methods and away from a reliance on interviews, symptom checklists, and personality measures, Patterson, Wahler, and Hanf created the primary tool needed for the development of parent training as a legitimate alternative to traditional psychotherapy.

Hanf and Patterson also developed influential treatment protocols (Eyberg, 1992), based in part on the earlier work of Wahler. In 1965, Wahler and his colleagues trained two parents of oppositional children to use differential attention, and one parent to use differential attention and a room time-out, based on the time-out procedure first defined by Wolf, Risely, and Mees (1964). Wahler (1969a) subsequently published one of the most widely cited empirical demonstrations of the combined use of social reinforcement and time-out by parents to reduce oppositional behavior. Concurrently, Patterson and his colleagues (Patterson, Reid, Jones, & Conger, 1975) were developing a general set of learning-based strategies to use with parents of socially aggressive 3- to 14-year-old youth. The OSLC introduces parents to social learning principles; specific misbehaviors and prosocial activities are then defined and tracked by the parent in the home; some combination of token reinforcement, token fines, and room time-outs are tailored to the individual child to modify behavior and replace the parenting errors presumed to maintain child misbehavior; the token economy is then extended to address classroom misbehavior as needed; finally, the token economy is gradually replaced by more typical contingencies (e.g., an allowance system). Hanf's (Hanf, 1969; Hanf & Kling, 1973) treatment protocol targeted a narrower developmental range, 2 to 7 years, and focused on noncompliance. It was not Hanf's (Hanf, 1968) intent to focus exclusively on noncompliance. Indeed, she attempted to construct clinic simulations to measure and treat the full range of parent-reported child misbehaviors for this age group. Unfortunately, her outcome measures were limited to noncompliance and parent-child play quality, to the exclusion of other social aggression targets like fighting, tantrums, and negative talk. Hanf's treatment protocol for noncompliance recommended that parents first improve the quality of play with their child in order to enhance the mother's "social desirability" (Hanf & Kling, 1973, p. 7). Parents are taught to discriminate and positively attend to the child's age-appropriate play, to inhibit instructions and questions, and to ignore minor misbehavior. Hanf's first treatment stage is commonly referred to as "the child's game" by the Forehand group (McMahon & Forehand, 2003, *Helping the Noncompliant Child* [HNC]) and "child-directed interaction" by the Eyberg group (Eyberg, 1988, parent-child interaction therapy [PCIT]). Hanf's second stage of therapy taught parents to issue direct commands, praise compliance efforts, warn the child given noncompliance, and use a chair time-out system for continued noncompliance. Hanf's second treatment stage is referred to as "the parent's game" in HNC projects and "parent-directed interaction" in the PCIT tradition. It would be very difficult to find a parent training publication with preadolescent externalizing disordered children that did not include some or all of the Wahler, Patterson, or Hanf treatment protocols. Arguably, Patterson, Wahler, and Hanf, in conjunction with their prominent students (e.g., Chamberlain, Dumas, Eyberg, Forehand, and Webster-Stratton), and the students of their students, have produced much of the knowledge on social learning–based parent training reported in this chapter. Joining these direct descendants is Matthew Sanders (1999) of the University of Queensland in Australia and his many students reporting on the Triple P-Positive Parenting Program.

Discoveries and Reactions

Parent training has been reviewed many times since the early 1970s in peer-reviewed journals, book chapters, and monographs. Journal reviews focusing exclusively on social learning–based parent training are instructive of the maturation of the field across the past 3 decades. The scholarly reader is directed to the work chronologically: Moreland, Schwebel, Beck, and Wells (1982), Griest and Wells (1983), Miller and Prinz (1990), Graziano and Diament (1992), Taylor and Biglan (1998), Brestan and Eyberg (1998), and Nixon (2002). In some cases, parent training reviews are embedded within the larger topic of treatments for antisocial children (Dumas, 1989; Estrada & Pinsof, 1995; Kazdin, 1987, 1997; Kazdin & Weisz, 1998). Journal reviews have also included more focused aspects of the parent training literature, such as noncompliance (Houlihan, Sloane, Jones, & Patten, 1992), father involvement in parent training (Coplin & Houts, 1991), and applications with Attention-Deficit/Hyperactivity Disorder youth (Chronis, Chacko, Fabiano, Wymbs, & Pelham, 2004). Noteworthy book chapters include Forehand's (1977) initial review of the noncompliance literature; O'Dell's (1985) efforts to clarify the different methods of teaching skills to parents; theoretical contributions by Eyberg (Foote, Eyberg, & Schuhmann, 1988), Wahler and Dumas (1987), and Patterson, Dishion, and Chamberlain (1993); and a relatively recent comprehensive parent training chapter by McMahon (1999). Monographs have also contributed to organizing the field, from those presenting PCIT and HNC traditions to clinicians (Hembree-Kigin & McNeil, 1995; McMahon & Forehand, 2003) to more general parenting applications (Briesmeister & Schaefer, 1998; Dangel & Polster, 1984; Mash, Handy, & Hamerlynck, 1976). The OSLC contributions are presented in the five-volume series, *A Social Learning Approach to Family Intervention* (Patterson, 1982; Patterson, Reid, & Dishion, 1992; Patterson et al., 1975; Reid, 1978), which spans 1975 to 1994, plus a more recent collection of invited chapters in Reid, Patterson, and Snyder (2002).

Consolidating the parent training literature to capture its essential themes and historical transitions is a daunting task. McMahon (1999) conceptualized three stages. The first stage witnessed the development of parent training as a viable model of intervention for socially aggressive children, which corresponds nicely to this chapter's previous discussion of the "Early Years: 1959 to 1973." McMahon's second stage was stimulated by Forehand and Atkeson's (1977) clarion call for research to evaluate and promote generalization of parent training effects from clinic to other relevant settings (e.g., home, community), to untreated siblings, to untreated child misbehaviors, and across time. Part of the promise of parent training, relative to individual psychotherapy, was exactly these generalizations. It was hoped that once the parent understood social learning principles and had gained some degree of reinforcement (and associated self-confidence) for the successful application of new skills, the parent would continue to use effective child management skills in the home (promoting generalization from clinic to home and across time) and to apply principles and specific skills to new problems (generalization across responses) and with other family members (sibling generalization). McMahon's third stage emphasized the development and empirical evaluation of methods to enhance and expand basic prescriptive parent training to address newly identified child problems (e.g., cognitive distortions), relevant contexts (e.g., unsupervised postschool periods), and barriers to successful treatment (e.g., maternal depression, marital discord). See the review on enhancements to parent training by Miller and Prinz (1990) and the earlier call to reformulate the field to "behavioral family therapy" (Griest & Wells, 1983).

A complementary model to McMahon's (1999) three stages is offered next. Six distinct and unending waves of research can be conceptualized, each a reaction to discoveries made at different points in time, and each wave a contributor to progress in the others.

Wave I

The initial spate of reviews (e.g., Berkowitz & Graziano, 1972) challenged the field to empirically test the effectiveness of parent training approaches to externalizing disorders. Clear progress has been made. Social learning theory–based parent training now meets APA's Division 12 criteria as an "empirically supported treatment" (Brestan & Eyberg, 1998; Chambless & Ollendick, 2001; Kazdin & Weisz, 1998). Meta-analytic reviews of parent training effects, contrasted primarily with wait-list control conditions, have reported average effect sizes of .86 (Serketich & Dumas, 1996) and .56 (Weisz, Weiss, Han, Granger, & Morton, 1995). Barlow and Stewart-Brown (2000) reported effect sizes from .20 to .68 for observational data following group-based parenting programs (e.g., Webster-Stratton, 1981a). Far less is known about how well social learning–based parent training compares to alternative family-based treatments, such as Parent Effectiveness Training (Gordon, 1970), family systems theory (Minuchin, 1974), or Systematic Training for Effective Parenting (Dinkmeyer & McKay, 1973, 1976). These counseling approaches to parent training were positively reviewed during the 1970s (Reisinger, Ora, & Frangia, 1976; Rinn & Markle, 1977; Tavormina, 1974, 1975), although more recent social learning-oriented reviewers have found little empirical support for such models (McMahon, 1999; Miller & Prinz, 1990). A meta-analytic review of Parent Effectiveness Training (Cedar & Levant, 1990), however, arrived at a different conclusion. Treatment comparisons appear to be hampered by disagreements over participant inclusion criteria and outcome measures. When overt misbehaviors are measured (Patterson, Chamberlain, & Reid, 1982; Wells & Egan, 1988), social learning programs have usually outperformed the alternative models, but not always (Bernal, Klinnert, & Schultz, 1980). A second ongoing task of Wave I research is dismantling the major treatment programs to determine the active components to successful treatment (e.g., Roberts, 1985).

Wave II

Generality of treatment effects constitutes the second ongoing research domain, corresponding to McMahon's second stage. Much knowledge has been gained (e.g., Sanders & James, 1983) since Forehand and Atkeson (1977) articulated the issues. Generalization of parenting skills from clinic to home settings has been documented multiple times by all major research programs (HNC: e.g., Peed, Roberts, & Forehand, 1977; PCIT: e.g., McNeil, Eyberg, Eisenstadt, Newcomb, & Funderburk, 1991; the group discussion videotape modeling [GDVM] protocol developed by Webster-Stratton: e.g., Webster-Stratton, Kolpacoff, & Hollinsworth, 1988; Triple P: e.g., Sanders & Christensen, 1985; and OSLC: e.g., Patterson, 1974). It is reasonable that home data would confirm setting generalization effects, since clinic work is designed explicitly to reprogram the home environment, giving parents new methods to manage child misbehavior. Generalization to school settings, however, has quite understandably yielded mixed results, since the teacher is not involved in the parent training, nor are relevant classroom conditions targeted by parent trainers (e.g., independent seat work, peer conflict on the playground). As early as 1969 Wahler (1969b) demonstrated independence of the home and school settings, which necessitated specific interventions designed for the school. Similarly, HNC researchers have not found generality to school settings, despite positive home setting outcomes (Breiner & Forehand, 1981). In contrast, PCIT scientists, using a very similar Hanf-based protocol, have found positive generalizations to untreated school settings (McNeil et al., 1991). Durability of treatment effects has also been repeatedly demonstrated with young noncompliant children (McMahon, Wells, & Kotler, 2006, pp. 162–172) for periods up to 14 years (Long, Forehand, Wierson, & Morgan, 1994). Wahler's (1980) data, however, documents the clear failure to maintain treatment gains over even brief periods when treatment samples include impoverished or isolated mothers. Some evidence of generality to untreated siblings has been detected by various groups (e.g., Eyberg, Boggs, & Algina, 1995; Humphreys, Forehand, McMahon, & Roberts, 1978), which is reasonable, given shared conditions and treatment procedures when both children are in the same developmental period. In contrast, response generalization seems less likely, since untargeted child misbehaviors are likely to involve different psychosocial conditions (e.g., a sibling conflict versus a parental instruction), different functions (e.g., attention seeking versus task avoidance), and different topographies (e.g., hit versus argue). Nevertheless, it is possible that response classes exist to the degree that conditions and functions overlap, despite differences in response topography (Wahler, 1975). Unfortunately, such overlaps are rare (Sanders & James, 1983), although a few have been reported (Wells, Forehand, & Griest, 1980). It appears that parent trainers are usually required to program change across a child's set of presenting problems, rather than focusing on a narrow band (e.g., noncompliance).

Wave III

Techniques for training parents effectively and efficiently have drawn the attention of many researchers, especially O'Dell (1985) at the University of Mississippi and Webster-Stratton (e.g., 1994) at the University of Washington. Given the centrality of parent training techniques to this chapter, research representative of Wave III is reviewed later in some depth.

Wave IV

Treatment failures and dropout data led Wahler (1980) and his colleagues to study the adverse impact of social disadvantage and social isolation on parenting practices. Specifically, inattention, inadequate monitoring, and indiscriminate responding characterize the child management patterns of poor, uneducated, socially isolated women. Wahler and Dumas (1987, 1989) hypothesized that distal setting events (e.g., an aversive interchange with a relative) disrupt parent attention, monitoring, and recognition of the stimulus events actually associated with coercive child behavior, especially for disadvantaged parents. Subsequently, Wahler, Cartor,

Fleischman, and Lambert (1993) developed and evaluated synthesis training, a supplement to basic parent training that has the look and feel of traditional insight-based psychotherapy, centered on each mother's child care experiences and associated extrafamilial events. Synthesis training combined with basic parent training was found to improve child behavior and reduce indiscriminate parenting, whereas basic parent training alone was ineffective with these socially disadvantaged and isolated parents. Teaching complex parenting skills to multistressed, uneducated parents remains a critical and unsolved problem in the literature.

Wave V

Parent pathology has been found to increase risk for inadequate parenting and poor responses to parent training interventions (Griest & Wells, 1983, pp. 42–46; McMahon, 1999, pp. 168–170; McMahon et al., 2006, pp. 149–152; Miller & Prinz, 1990, pp. 294–295). Specifically, parental depression has been associated with attenuated parental monitoring and inaccurate judgments of child behavior, poorer treatment outcomes, and dropout. Similarly, marital distress may disrupt the parent training process. Meta-analyses performed by Erel and Burman (1995) and by Krishnakumar and Buehler (2000) reported significant average correlations between marital distress and child misbehavior. Although distressed couples may profit from parent training to treat externalizing disorders (Forehand, Griest, Wells, & McMahon, 1982), follow-up data reported by Dadds, Schwartz, and Sanders (1987) indicated that marital distress adversely impacts treatment durability. This fifth research wave implies that interventions addressing parental depression and marital discord should be screened for, and treated if necessary, to render parent training effective. Fortunately, empirically supported treatments exist for both adult depression and marital distress (Chambless & Ollendick, 2001). In addition to depression and marital discord, the OSLC group (e.g., Patterson et al., 1992, pp. 102–112) and developmental psychopathologists (e.g., Frick & Loney, 2002) have repeatedly noted the empirical association between parents' antisocial behavior and child externalizing disorders. It is not difficult to understand the adverse effects of an antisocial parent who models angry, aggressive reactions to normal frustrators and interacts coercively with both society and the developing child. Moreover, antisocial adults may be court-ordered to treatment, bringing little motivation to accommodate to therapist recommendations. Parental substance abuse can also disrupt parenting and appears to be exacerbated by disruptive children, creating an event chain rendering both parent substance abuse and child misbehavior more likely (Pelham & Lang, 1993). Unlike parental depression and marital distress, there are no robust outpatient treatment protocols for Antisocial Personality Disorder or substance abuse, leaving the parent trainer with substantive challenges. For the reader interested in the extensive work on parent pathology and child developmental problems, see the recent volume edited by McMahon and Peters (2002).

Wave VI

Variables that promote or degrade parent engagement in the parent training process are now recognized as quite important. See discussions by Miller and Prinz

1990, pp. 299–300), McMahon (1999, pp. 163–164), and Patterson et al. (1993, pp. 65–67) regarding the relatively small and emerging literature on the therapeutic alliance. Although the child's misbehavior is the precipitating factor for the clinic referral, the parent is the mechanism of change, and hence the individual with whom a therapeutic alliance is central. Chamberlain, Patterson, Reid, Kavanagh, and Forgatch (1984) found that high rates of parent refusal statements ("I can't" and "I won't") during the first two treatment sessions are linked to dropout and are associated with maternal depression, paternal social disadvantage, and high base rates of antisocial child behavior. Erstwhile parent trainers inherently place many demands on parents in sessions (e.g., to role-play a new skill) and between sessions (e.g., to use time-out for noncompliance), some of which are very difficult as a result of complexity, child resistance, and/or associated parent emotionality. Parents may have even attempted some variation of a therapist-recommended routine at some point in the past and met with blatant failure. Consequently, many parents argue with the therapist and/or passively avoid therapeutic activities between sessions, to the great consternation of therapists. The OSLC group has consistently called for therapist support and supervision (e.g., Patterson, 1985) to mitigate the potentially adverse effects of nonresponsive parents on therapists.

Balancing traditional supportive therapeutic processes (e.g., active listening skills, reframing, empathic communications, and genuine regard for family members) with prescriptive parent training is an important goal for all therapists. Balancing, however, does not imply abrogating one's professional responsibility to confront difficult problems for the sake of parent comfort, even if that confrontation requires complex and demanding interventions. Flexibility is recommended. Tailoring interventions to accommodate the idiosyncratic issues of a specific family is always appropriate, given that the recommended procedures are theoretically reasonable and the outcome can be monitored. For example, a therapist might opt for a relatively slow shaping process with an unusual but salient positive reinforcement menu, despite an available, efficient, and socially valid standard treatment strategy. Clearly, much is unknown about the dialectical process between prescriptive therapies like parent training and needed therapeutic alliance building.

THEORETICAL FOUNDATIONS OF PARENT TRAINING

Operant Conditioning

The continuing strength of parent training protocols rests on operant principles. Early clinical interventions were attempts to apply learning principles to the treatment of child misbehavior. Patterson (1982, p. 2) views the seminal publications by Skinner (1953), Bandura and Walters (1963), and Ullmann and Krasner's (1965) edited collection of *Case Studies in Behavior Modification* as setting the stage for applied behavior analysis with parents in a therapist role. Early efforts to positively reinforce prosocial child behavior with parent attention or token reinforcers, to extinguish minor misbehaviors via parent ignoring, and to punish aggression and noncompliance with time-outs, fines, or privilege losses are all operant techniques. After a decade of data collection and clinical trials, the OSLC group articulated a series of conceptual breakthroughs. First, they defined socially aggressive behavior as aversive and contingent (Patterson, 1982, p. 12). An aggressive act is aversive if interacting agents (parents, teachers, siblings, or peers [PTSP]) report it as unpleasant and work to actively escape from it or avoid it. An aggressive act is contingent if its conditional probability is greater that its base rate probability (i.e., demonstrating it is not displayed at random). The OSLC data convinced most scientists that socially aggressive child behavior could coerce interacting agents (PTSP) into changing their own behavior in exchange for temporary cessation of the child's aggression. A "reinforcement trap" (Patterson, 1982, p. 145) was hypothesized to exist, in which the child coerces positive or negative reinforcement from PTSP with aggressive behavior, while PTSP is negatively reinforced by aggression termination. Patterson's widely accepted coercion theory is, therefore, based on rather simple operant processes, but its implications for the psychopathology of childhood social aggression are profound:

1. Aggression is likely to be stable across time, since the child and PTSP are both reinforced, and resistant to extinction, since reinforcement schedules are likely to be intermittent.
2. The child and/or PTSP will escalate to even greater intensities of aggression if either party withholds expected reinforcers (i.e., an extinction burst).

No mechanisms beyond positive reinforcement, negative reinforcement, schedules of reinforcement, and extinction are necessary to appreciate implications 1 and 2. Treatment implications of coercion theory are equally important:

3. Parents and teachers must block reinforcers coerced by social aggression; treatments that do not do so will likely fail.
4. Because most siblings and peers are not sufficiently mature to assume any responsibility to change on behalf of the target child, therapists must teach parents and teachers to guide and protect siblings and peers if the child's aggression is to be successfully treated; otherwise, siblings and peers will continue to unwittingly reinforce child aggression.
5. Parental ignoring will be an ineffectual treatment for child coercion, which is negatively reinforced by parent withdrawal of events aversive to the child (e.g., instructions, denials, discipline efforts), since ignoring allows the negative reinforcement process to operate.
6. Implications 1 through 5 render the successful treatment of socially aggressive children very difficult, especially for middle childhood youth who have experienced thousands of reinforced coercive trials over the course of many years and who can violently oppose parent and teacher efforts to adjust.

Important assessment and case conceptualization strategies are also implicated by coercion theory. Assessments should identify the idiosyncratic set of stimulus events that discriminate the occasion for coercion, as well as guide hypotheses about the parenting errors that are likely to reinforce coercion. The specific stimulus events (e.g., parent "Stop X" instructions) and settings in which they occur (e.g., bedtime, unsupervised sibling play) must be known to construct a comprehensive yet family-specific treatment plan. Because aggressive behavior is partly defined by its contingent quality, coercion theory implies there will be a set of 1 though K events, presented by PTSP, each of which are discriminative for coerced reinforcement. Figure 22.1 is offered as a heuristic device for the practitioner. Common interpersonal events that elicit social aggression are included in the first two columns of the figure. Any given referred youth will display some subset of the many possible event sequences displayed in the figure. Knowing the relevant operant sequences, however, is not an adequate assessment. See the recent chapter by McMahon and Frick (2005) for a full discussion of evidence-based assessment procedures for externalizing disordered youth.

Figure 22.1 requires elaboration. It is based entirely on coercion theory as presented by Patterson and his many colleagues (Patterson, 1982; Patterson et al., 1992, 1993) and Hanf's (1968) identification of common situations provoking child misbehavior. The figure attempts to characterize typical event sequences consisting of

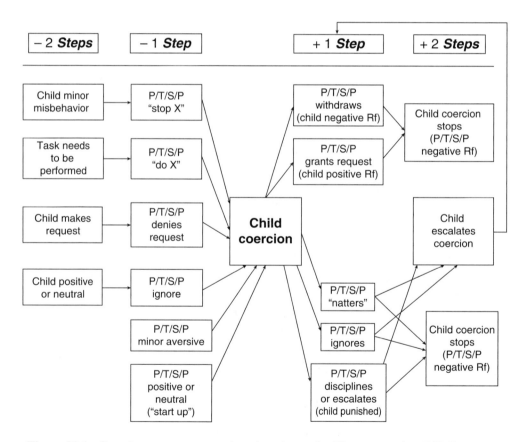

Figure 22.1   Coercive event sequences based on the work of Patterson, other OSLC scientists, and Hanf, designed as a heuristic device for clinicians to conceptualize the specific clinical presentations of referred families. P/T/S/P = Parent/Teacher/Sibling/Peer; Rf = Reinforcement.

six antecedent events ("−1 Step") and five consequent events ("+1 Step"), anchored in the middle by child coercion. Child coercion is defined as overt, contingent, and aversive behavior that is most commonly expressed by the subjects of this chapter as fight, noncomply, negative verbalization, and/or tantrum. Up to two behavioral events that precede coercion ("−2 Steps" & "−1 Step") and two that follow coercion ("+1 Step" & "+2 Steps") are needed to conceptualize the operant mechanisms. At "−2 Steps" an identifiable behavior or condition is present (e.g., child teases his sibling) that increases the likelihood of the "−1 Step" event (e.g., parent instructs child to inhibit teasing). Note that a "−2 Steps" condition has not been identified for all "−1 Step" events. For example, a host of different events probably precede "P/T/S/P minor aversive" (e.g., sibling teases the target child) that are difficult to characterize. Similarly, what precedes the positive or neutral behavior of family members that sometimes evokes child coercion (known as "Start Up"; Patterson et al., 1992, pp. 47–54) is currently unknown. Child coercion is likely to follow "−1 Step" events, especially in clinic-referred youth. At "+1 Step" the child may be reinforced, ignored, or punished for coercion in an indiscriminant manner, resulting in the hypothesized intermittent reinforcement schedule.

The concept of "nattering," introduced by John Reid (Patterson, 1982, p. 69), may be unfamiliar to some and requires discussion. Nattering is interpreted as a hostile, verbal outburst by PTSP (e.g., threatening gestures, angry tone of voice, criticisms, stop instructions, empty threats) that fails to discriminate subsequent discipline but may provide positive reinforcement in the form of contingent attention and certainly provides a hostile verbal model. Figure 22.1 supposes that on some occasions, nattering is followed by child cessation ("+2 Steps"), negatively reinforcing the natterer, but more often than not, nattering simply prolongs the aversive interchange and sets the occasion for escalated intensities of social aggression (Patterson, 1982, pp. 67–84; Patterson et al., 1992, pp. 39–54). The model hypothesized in Figure 22.1 also captures the paradoxical concept of punishment acceleration (Patterson, 1976), in that referred children are much more likely than normal controls to react to discipline efforts ("+1 Step") with escalated intensities of coercion ("+2 Steps"), throwing PTSP back to "+1 Step" options, where the PTSP may finally relent and provide reinforcement, attempt to ignore, or continue the struggle by escalating the intensity of punishment or by nattering.

Patterson's (1976) concept of the aggressive child as both "victim and architect" of his or her own environment is germane within the operant framework. The model provided in Figure 22.1 implicates both PTSP and the child. Certainly the operant model implies that PTSP lack skills. These important socialization agents are reinforcing social aggression on an indiscriminant, intermittent basis. To that extent, the child is a "victim" of dysfunctional child management. On the other hand, the operant model exposes the child's unintended role as "architect" of the very environment that sustains his or her psychopathology. First, aggressive child actions coerce their own reinforcement from the many unwitting interactive agents who seek short-term relief from the child's aversiveness via misguided child management strategies. Second, to avoid the aversive child coercion altogether, PTSP are likely to inhibit presenting "−1 Step" events, thus abrogating their normal socialization roles.

Social Learning Theory

Most parent trainers ascribe to the theoretical framework provided by social learning theory (Bandura, 1977), rather than relying on the more narrow principles of operant learning. Indeed, Patterson's published series is entitled *A Social Learning Approach to Family Intervention*. Social learning theory embraces the full range of biopsychosocial variables that interact continuously during the child's development. Consequently, social learning theory provides a better theoretical home for evidence-based parent trainers than the more limited operant model. For example, it is presumed that biological-based temperaments impact parenting (e.g., Wahler & Dumas, 1987), that models of antisocial behavior promote coercion (Frick & Loney, 2002), that modeling and discussing child management skills can result in parent knowledge and performance acquisitions (e.g., Webster-Stratton, 1994), that social-cognitive processes influence overt social behavior in middle childhood (e.g., Dodge, 1980), and that a family's cultural background is an important consideration in parent training (Forehand & Kotchick, 1996). Each of these biopsychosocial processes are well beyond the confines of operant mechanisms.

Developmental psychopathology is consistent with social learning theory. The relevant examples of this are the child-onset (i.e., "early starter") Conduct Disorder model, nicely summarized in McMahon et al. (2006, pp. 147–152), the Patterson stage model (e.g., Patterson et al., 1992, pp. 115–141), and Frick's (2004) recent review of the developmental psychopathology of severe antisocial behavior. Child-onset Conduct Disorder models are based on the continuous interaction of biopsychosocial variables from a developmental perspective across the changing social contexts of the child's cultural group from infancy to adolescence. Of particular relevance to clinicians are two classes of findings from the child-onset developmental model. First, inept parental discipline and inadequate parental monitoring have been repeatedly found to increase the risk of social aggression (Patterson et al., 1993). Consequently, parent trainers must invariably evaluate and improve parent discipline and monitoring. Second, social (e.g., Dodge, 1980) and academic (e.g., Hinshaw, 1992) skill deficits are very likely to emerge in externalizing disordered youth by middle childhood (Patterson et al., 1992, pp. 120–131). Consequently, parent trainers should assess sibling and peer skills and classroom function and, if needed, intervene or refer to address the identified deficits.

The empirical and theoretical work of Wahler and Dumas with impoverished, socially isolated mothers deserves special comment here. It is consistent with the cognitive elements of social learning theory (Wahler & Dumas, 1987, p. 616) and adds to our theoretical understanding of seemingly intractable dysfunctional parenting. Specifically, Wahler and Dumas (1989) argue that multistressed parents (e.g., impoverished, socially isolated, depressed, abusive) operate with trait-like response classes, such that setting events irrelevant to parent-child interaction adversely impact temporally distal parent monitoring, judgments, and responses to children. Coercion theory cannot explain the apparent overgeneralization of parent responding from a child-irrelevant context (e.g., friend, employer, spouse) to child encounters. Moreover, this parental failure to attend to the differences in social context and respond adaptively may be a significant cognitive barrier to parent training with multistressed parents. All social learning theory–based parent training programs attempt to teach parents to discriminate specific child actions, track those actions in the home, and respond in the prescribed manner. In opposition to these well-intended recommendations, multistressed parents appear to operate with macro-, trait-like cognitive strategies that link seemingly disparate social encounters. It is currently unknown if synthesis training, a very cognitive, insight-based therapeutic process, will reduce this barrier to treatment success.

Attachment Theory

Eyberg and her colleagues (Foote et al., 1998) have oriented the child clinical field to the special importance of parental sensitivity to child signals. Parental sensitivity and the establishment of synchronized turn taking have long been found to facilitate secure attachments and promote general socialization (Maccoby & Martin, 1983, pp. 26–37). Developmental psychologists have repeatedly found specific positive associations between mother-child reciprocity and successful socialization (e.g., Kochanska, 1997; Stayton, Hogan, & Ainsworth, 1971). In contrast, parents of aggressive children are likely to be indiscriminate and aversive (e.g., Dumas & Wahler, 1985) in comparison to normal control parents. Eyberg's child-directed interaction (in Hembree-Kigin & McNeil, 1995) and McMahon and Forehand's (2003) child's game are treatment components in noncompliance programs that actively teach the parent to be sensitive to age-appropriate child signals during free-play conditions. Eyberg argues that by enhancing the responsiveness of parents to appropriate child signals, therapists will strengthen the parent-child relationship in a manner analogous to the development of secure attachments in normal infants. Whaler and Dumas would support this position, since child-directed interaction skills teach the parent to discriminate and attend to age-appropriate child behavior. Even operant devotees would applaud the parental attention to "good" behavior found in child-directed interaction. Because teaching parent responsiveness is a fairly widespread clinical practice, the theoretical linkage to normal child development is important. Indeed, child-directed interaction looks like the nurturance component of Baumrind's (1967) classic conceptualization of the successful authoritative parent, who combines firm control with nurturance and communication skills. A second intriguing linkage is to traditional humanistic-based play therapy (Axline, 1969), with the major procedural exception, of course, that parents are trained to perform the therapist role.

Summary of Theoretical Perspectives

Parent trainers earn their daily living with operant strategies. Coercive processes must be minimized if the child is to gain a normal socialization path. The much broader shoulders of social learning theory, however, are embraced to consider the wider range of biopsychosocial variables needed to assess, conceptualize, and treat externalizing disorders. Finally, attachment theory, stripped of its psychodynamic overtones, provides a basis for the common goal of strengthening the parent-child relationship.

TECHNIQUES FOR TRAINING PARENTS

Training techniques can be dimensionalized in terms of therapist time and degree of contact. At the least intrusive, least expensive level, therapists can impart skills didactically via discussion, handouts, and programmed reading materials, all of which can be used in group formats to add even more efficiency. Modeling is usually conceptualized as more intrusive than didactic approaches, especially in vivo modeling, since it requires an actor in addition to the therapist. Videotaped modeling, however, does not require an actor and is very compatible with group training (e.g., Webster-Stratton, 1994). Because discussion, written materials, and modeling are passively received by parents, the clinician remains uncertain if acquisition has occurred. In contrast, role-playing and guided practice are more intrusive, active, and informative strategies, since the parent must perform overtly. In role-play formats the parent responds to an actor (or therapist) simulating child behavior. During guided practice the therapist provides immediate feedback to the parent while the parent interacts with his or her own child. Guided practice provides direct evidence of both parent acquisition and child reaction to the recommended protocol. Finally, techniques to prompt and motivate home use of newly acquired skills include specific homework assignments (accompanied by written materials for reference), visually posted behavioral tracking systems, and phone contacts.

Psychologists tailor the set of training techniques to the child's presenting problems, developmental level, social-cultural circumstance, and treatment protocol. For example, introducing a home token system for use with aggressive grade-school siblings would likely require discussion, written materials, a home tracking system, modeling, and role-playing. In addition to the parent, both siblings would be actively involved in all facets of the training to gain their input regarding the reinforcement menu, as well as their awareness of the new rules, the reasons behind the rules, and all the changed contingencies. In contrast, introducing differential attention skills to the parents of a defiant 3-year-old would emphasize guided practice using a bug-in-the-ear during free-play conditions. Moreover, the 3-year-old would not be involved in discussion with the therapist about goals, rationales, and choices.

Psychologists also adjust their training techniques, based on parent performance. For example, role-playing might reveal a parent tendency to repeat instructions quickly, despite verbal feedback. Consequently, the therapist might revert to several modeling trials before attempting a second try at the more demanding role-play routine. Conversely, efficiencies can be obtained by sampling a parent's performance following minimal training, for example, brief discussion. If the advice is specific and meaningful, a parent might adjust his or her behavior immediately and with little difficulty (e.g., "Ignore whichever child is crying and play with the other sibling"). The data will inform the clinician if this 3-second intervention worked!

A brief and representative review of empirical findings is offered.

Didactic Strategies

Simple advice giving in the absence of other techniques has been described (Boardman, 1962; Holland, 1969), but not studied with adequate experimental control.

Obviously, verbal instructions are an inherent component of all other training strategies (i.e., "Do X under Y conditions for Z reasons"). The therapist's interpersonal skill in communicating these instructions is likely an important component of engaging (or failing to engage) the parent in the therapeutic process, represented by Wave VI of ongoing research in parent training discussed earlier.

Written materials can be a sufficient intervention under limited circumstances. Clark et al. (1977) used a multiple-baseline design with observational data to test the effects of a written manual of advice for parents on how to shop successfully with preadolescent children. Procedures included providing information about shopping, differential attention, token reinforcement for rule following, and token loss for misbehavior. Child misbehavior and ineffective parenting declined as a function of reading the manual (Green, Clark, & Risley, 1977). Similarly, McMahon and Forehand (1978) used a brochure to instruct parents on a mealtime routine, consisting of differential attention, instruction giving, and brief room time-outs. Again, a multiple-baseline design indicated that children reduced their overt misbehavior and parents displayed new skills. Sloane, Endo, Hawkes, and Jenson (1991) found that written self-instructional materials alone helped most parents provoke some improvement in their child's compliance.

Together, these three multiple-baseline projects reveal the potential contribution of a well-written manual or handout for changing overt parent behavior and subsequent child adjustment. Each project was limited, however, by the use of recruited subjects. Connell, Sanders, and Markie-Dadds (1997) evaluated the effects of written materials on parents of oppositional children relative to a wait-list control group. The positive results, however, were limited to improved questionnaire data. When parents have been randomly assigned to reading-only conditions and compared to those experiencing more active training techniques, reading-only is usually less effective on performance measures (Eyberg & Matarazzo, 1980; Flanagan, Adams, & Forehand, 1979; Nay, 1975; O'Dell et al., 1982), but can be equivalent (O'Dell, Krug, Patterson, & Faustman, 1980; O'Dell, Mahoney, Horton, & Turner, 1979). See McMahon and Forehand (1980) for an early review of self-instructional studies and McMahon and Forehand (1981) for a discussion of the many parameters (e.g., parent reading level) that should be considered when using or researching written instruction techniques.

Modeling

Modeling specific skills has a long history (Mash & Terdal, 1973) and a sound theoretical basis in social learning theory (Bandura, 1977). Several years ago Webster-Stratton (1981b) developed a training protocol in which videotape modeling is the primary technique. Parents in small groups (8 or 9) view vignettes of parents displaying specific skills with children in a variety of normal social contexts. After viewing each vignette (about 2 minutes), a therapist prompts discussion of the critical events, helps the group discuss how to apply the skill at home, and assigns homework. A programmatic series of publications has largely supported the efficacy of Webster-Stratton's GDVM protocol. Performance measures of parental responsiveness during play contexts improved relative to wait-list controls posttreatment (Webster-Stratton, 1981a) and were maintained at 1-year follow-up (Webster-Stratton, 1982). Early conclusions were attenuated, however, by the use of recruited subjects and nonspecific play observation conditions in a clinic (i.e., a condition not likely to provoke coercion). More recently, the GDVM protocol was found to be as effective as an individually administered videotape (IVM) modeling procedure and a group discussion protocol, relative to a wait-list condition (Webster-Stratton et al., 1988). Importantly, participants in these later projects were referred children who met a questionnaire criterion for deviance, and observational data were collected in the home. Consumer satisfaction with GDVM and group discussion protocols has been rated higher than for IVM, suggesting the importance of the therapist contribution (Webster-Stratton, 1989); moreover, parents found that GDVM led to skills that were easier to implement at 1-year follow-up than either IVM or group discussion alone. Therapist consultation appears to improve the effectiveness of IVM (Webster-Stratton, 1990). Because highly stressed families (cf. Wahler & Dumas, 1987) were less likely to profit from IVM (Webster-Stratton, 1992), GDVM can be augmented by parent communication, problem solving, and self-control components (Webster-Stratton, 1994), a nice example of McMahon's Stage 3 in parent training research. The enhanced program yielded increased benefits in consumer satisfaction, child pro-social knowledge, and problem-solving and communication skills not targeted by GDVM.

Recently, Foster and Roberts (2007) replicated the effectiveness of videotape modeling combined with didactics to improve parent skills in both play and clinic task conditions, but also replicated the need for therapist monitoring of initial parent use of time-out (Roberts & Powers, 1990). In addition, technique comparison studies have generally favored more active techniques, which include modeling, over didactic strategies and wait-list on performance measures (Eyberg & Matarazzo, 1980; Flanagan et al., 1979; Nay, 1975), although O'Dell et al. (1982) found that written instructions compared well with videotape modeling and a more intrusive procedure, live modeling plus role-playing.

In summary, modeling, like written instructions, has been demonstrated to be an important technique for parent trainers. Modeling is invariably more effective than no training and competes well with alternative techniques. The effectiveness of Webster-Stratton's GDVM protocol is truly impressive. The opportunity to discuss the modeled event sequence with other parents under the watchful eye of a therapist appears to be an important component of GDVM. If videotapes are self-administered, a therapist consultant is recommended, especially to assist the parent in initial use of potentially emotion-provoking routines such as time-out.

Role-Playing and Guided Practice

Role-playing has three distinct advantages over all other techniques: flexibility, control, and the opportunity to present retrials immediately. A little imagination and a few props allow psychologists to tailor role-play analogues to family-specific problem conditions (e.g., bedtime, shopping, car trips, sibling aggression, toilet training). For example, the trainer might say, "Let's pretend this doll represents your child and these four chairs are the family car. When the doll starts fighting with his pretend brother (another doll), you practice stopping the 'car' just like you saw me do it a moment ago." There is no limit to creative simulations. Second, the therapist has complete control over the doll, enabling task difficulty to be modulated to accommodate the parent's acquisition rate. Third, immediate retrials of exactly the same stimulus array can be presented to practice a skill or to correct an error. For example, given an error, the parent trainer can discuss the error, the targeted response, the reason for the targeted response, and then immediately present the task again. No other training technique allows this intensive, individualized practice. Written materials and videotape models are inflexible; guided practice puts the trainer at the mercy of the child, who often exhibits nongraduated task difficulties, will not pause for discussion, and may not give a second chance at the same misbehavior. Only in vivo modeling with an actor matches the flexibility and control of role-playing, but lacks the retrial component, since performance is not required. Consequently, parent trainers often provide live models followed by a role-play to teach specific event sequences.

Several experiments (Flanagan et al., 1979; Nay, 1975; O'Dell et al., 1982; Webster-Stratton, 1984) have found that live modeling plus role-playing outperformed didactics and no training on performance measures, but sometimes, equivalent acquisition rates are found (O'Dell et al., 1979, 1980). Powers and Roberts (1995) contrasted a standard training protocol, toy cleanup, with an augmented simulation procedure designed to enhance generalization. Parents who rehearsed skills to mastery via modeling and role-playing for wake-up/dressing, mealtime, and cleanup/bedtime conditions performed better during unstructured clinic and home conditions than parents trained solely under toy cleanup conditions, suggesting that multiple, content-valid exemplars should be incorporated into modeling and role-play regimens.

If the parent is provided prompts and feedback during interaction with his or her child, the training technique is considered "guided practice." A bug-in-the-ear device is often used to allow the therapist in an observation room to talk to a parent in an adjacent clinic room without the child's awareness. The "bug" is a small radio receiver worn by the parent like a hearing aid; the radio signal is transmitted locally to the clinic room via an antenna. Hanf (1969) introduced the procedure into the literature, which is now a staple of HNC and PCIT parent training programs that target 2- to 7-year-old disruptive and oppositional children. Note that guided practice loses its applicability in middle childhood, as youth become savvy to one-way windows and clinic simulations lack credibility. The training advantages to guided practice are obvious: immediate social reinforcement, corrections for errors of commission, and prompts for errors of omission. Therapist support via the bug can be gradually faded as the parent displays mastery, allowing the parent to practice with the child under more home-like conditions. Because the target child is providing the behavior display, programming for setting generality is maximized. Unlike all other training techniques, a psychologist using guided practice has the opportunity to observe the child's reaction to the recommended changes in parent behavior, which allows the psychologist to make procedural adjustments as needed. Because young defiant children are especially prone to react to discipline with coercion (Roberts & Powers, 1988), a phenomenon consistent with theory and data (e.g., Patterson, 1982; Roberts, 1982b), it is particularly important to monitor initial time-outs with overtly defiant children (Roberts & Powers, 1990). Guided practice provides that mechanism. Only one thorough test of this position, however, is available. Webster-Stratton (1984) randomly assigned recruited parents to individual therapy, which made use of live modeling, role-playing, and guided practice with a "bug," to GDVM and a no-treatment condition. Both treatment groups performed equally well posttreatment and better than wait-list controls; no behavioral differences were present at 1-year follow-up. Neither treatment group, however, manifested a significant decrease in child noncompliance ratios, which is inconsistent with data from HNC and PCIT outcome studies. It is hypothesized that guided practice fills an important niche in the tools of the parent trainer, but no group comparison data currently support that contention.

Homework, Posted Tracking Systems, and Phone Contacts

To facilitate transfer of training from clinic to home settings, specific homework is routinely assigned (e.g., "Use the compliance program every time you give an instruction at home this week"). In addition, some form of record keeping system is provided to parents to monitor progress at home. These participant-observation devices are usually posted somewhere central (e.g., the refrigerator), thereby serving a prompting role in addition to their use as treatment outcome data. If a therapist anticipates parent difficulty in implementing a recommended child management routine (e.g., initial time-outs, a bedtime program), phone calls can be scheduled to provide support and guidance. Parents are invariably invited to contact the therapist during working hours if problems arise at home and can be provided after-hours emergency contact systems if needed.

Although homework, participant observation, and phone support are well integrated into parent training programs, only participant observation has been studied systematically. The parent daily report (PDR; Chamberlain & Reid, 1987) is the best example. Parents are contacted by phone and report on the occurrence or nonoccurrence of specific misbehaviors during the prior 24 hours. Test-retest reliability of PDR data has been adequate in clinic samples ($r = .60$) and excellent in recruited samples ($r = .82$); interparental agreement has been modest ($r = .56$), but given differential daily interaction with the child, would not be expected to be a sensitive index of accuracy. Importantly, PDR data have converged well with total aversive behavior rates collected by professional observers in three samples ($.46 < r < .69$). Moreover, normative data are available, indicating an average of 5.3 misbehaviors per day ($SD = 3.1$) in 4- to 10-year-olds. Unfortunately, the PDR system is more of a research tool than a practical clinical instrument at this point, and does not serve the prompting role of posted tracking systems. Most clinicians cannot make daily phone calls, even for brief periods, and most clinicians want daily frequency counts rather than binary data. Parent-collected daily frequency counts of targeted sibling aggression (Olson & Roberts, 1987) have yielded good evidence of internal consistency (i.e., the odd/even day correlation for sibling aggression was $r = .88$), but nothing is known about the accuracy or concurrent validity of such parent-collected frequency data.

CHILD MANAGEMENT SKILLS

The core curricula of all modern social learning–based parenting programs were established by the early work of Patterson, Wahler, and Hanf. Six generic parenting skills can be identified. First, parents are introduced to the social learning principles that underlie the acquisition and maintenance of externalizing disorders (see Figure 22.1) and the use of operant, cognitive, and developmental principles to treat the child's coercive patterns. Patterson and Gullion's (1968) *Living with Children,* a programmed textbook, served as the prototype for all future efforts (e.g., McMahon, Forehand, & Griest, 1981; Patterson, 1975) to help parents understand why their child misbehaves and how they could be part of the solution. Second, parents are taught to define, observe, and record the presence of targeted misbehaviors and prosocial accomplishments in the home setting. Participant observation provides more than assessment and treatment outcome data; it enhances the parent's awareness of child acts that will become discriminative for implementing therapist-recommended interventions and could help multistressed parents with the cognitive appraisal problems identified by Wahler and Dumas (discussed earlier). Third, parents are trained to attend to age-appropriate child behavior while ignoring coercive behavior maintained by parent attention. There are two distinct and different purposes behind differential attention skills. First, clinic-referred parents commonly provide attention to misbehavior in the form of reprimands, "Don't" instructions, and/or nattering in general (e.g., Patterson, 1976), which at worst positively reinforces coercion and at least models arguing. Teaching parents to withhold attention for specific misbehaviors can effectively extinguish some coercive acts, such as negative verbalizations (Herbert & Baer, 1972), tantrums during time-out administrations (Hobbs & Forehand, 1975), and defiant talk during compliance training (Roberts & Hatzenbuehler, 1981). Note, however, that differential attention can make some misbehaviors worse (Herbert et al., 1973). Moreover, differential attention does not play a substantive role in treating noncompliance (Roberts, 1985), since noncompliance appears to be reinforced by task avoidance rather than misguided parental attention. For an early discussion of differential attention, see Sajwaj and Dillon (1977), and for a modern procedural description of the effective use of differential attention, see McMahon and Forehand (2003, pp. 106–129). The second purpose of differential attention skills is to improve the parent-child relationship via responsiveness during play. Eyberg and her many students (e.g., Foote et al., (1998) emphasize parental responsiveness during play contexts as a mechanism to enhance the parent-child bond, as discussed earlier under attachment theory. Fourth, because noncompliance is a foundational problem in externalizing disorders (Loeber & Schmaling, 1985; Patterson et al., 1992), parenting programs invariably teach parents to use verbal instructions that provoke child attention and provide precise information. Verbal instructions that specify a specific motor task, followed by a 5-second pause, elevate compliance ratios of 3- to 7-year-olds relative to experimental control subjects (Roberts, McMahon, Forehand, & Humphreys, 1978). In addition, eye contact has been experimentally shown to increase compliance ratios in middle childhood (Hamlet, Axelrod, & Kuerschner, 1984), a finding supported by a group comparison project with 3- to 7-year-olds (Hudson & Blane, 1985). Specifically, nonclinic parents used more eye contact than parents of referred children. In addition, Hudson and Blane found that instructions issued in close proximity, at the child's eye level, while orienting toward the relevant objects and using a pleasant tone of voice were more likely in parents of normal children than clinic-referred children. Wruble, Sheeber, Sorensen, Boggs, and Eyberg (1991) demonstrated that direct commands (e.g., "Come here") were more effective than indirect commands (e.g., "Would you come here?") in a recruited sample of 3- to 5-year-olds. These data are consistent with the common recommendation to use an imperative grammatical form of verbal instruction rather than the interrogative form in which choice is implied. Fifth, most parenting programs introduce some form of discipline to block the reinforcers previously coerced by the child. Time-outs, token fines, privilege losses, or work chores are routinely recommended for noncompliance and aggression, if not for other targets. Sixth, token reinforcement systems are introduced to provide a mechanism to deliver activity and material reinforcers for prosocial behavior on the assumption that social reinforcers (e.g., praise) are relatively weak compared to coerced reinforcers (e.g., task avoidance), especially for referred middle childhood youth (e.g., Patterson et al., 1975; Wahler, 1969a). Successful applications of token systems are not limited to middle childhood, however, and can be used successfully with children as young as 3 years (Christophersen & Mortweet, 2001, pp. 223–239).

Noncompliance Programs

The classic Hanf protocol for teaching noncompliant 2- to 7-year-olds to obey parent instructions has been repeatedly evaluated and come through 35 years of empirical scrutiny relatively unscathed. Figure 22.2 presents the often displayed familiar event sequence (e.g., McMahon & Forehand, 2003, p. 131). Parents are first taught to present effective instructions as discussed earlier. If the child makes any motoric

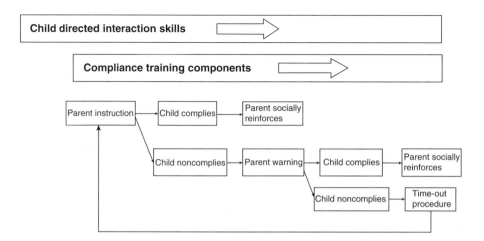

Figure 22.2 Recommended compliance training protocol for 2- to 7-year-olds based on the sequential strategy of current HNC and PCIT programs.

effort to comply within 5 seconds, social reinforcement is provided. If the child makes no effort within 5 seconds of the termination of the instruction, a warning is issued. Child effort within 5 seconds of the warning is socially reinforced, whereas a lack of effort results in a time-out administration. Upon completion of time-out, the original instruction is re-presented and the process is recycled as needed until the child complies. It sounds simple, but there are endless complexities. Fortunately, some empirical guidance is available.

Because the parent's game and cleanup conditions frequently provide the context for teaching compliance-eliciting skills in both HCN and PCIT traditions, the many successful demonstrations of compliance acquisition focus on child initiations to perform discrete acts (e.g., "Put the toy on the shelf"). Less is known about motivating children to display sustained effort to complete a substantial task (e.g., "Clean your room") or to cease an ongoing response (e.g., "Stop yelling"). The ability to sustain effort in the absence of an adult requires complex self-regulatory skills that emerge gradually (e.g., Maccoby & Martin, 1983, pp. 35–37), highlighting the need for parents to discriminate noncompliance from normal developmental errors. For example, parents might instruct an 8-year-old to clean his or her room, but not a 3-year-old for whom parent proximity, modeling, and repeated instructions would be needed. A different set of issues involves "Don't" instructions. We know that even 2-year-olds can inhibit actions given an instruction (Minton, Kagan, & Levine, 1971), but the immediate cessation is less relevant than the resultant frequency of the targeted misbehavior. For example, does the child's base rate of teasing his sibling decline, given compliance to the adult instruction "Stop teasing"? That is currently an empirical question, addressed at the level of the individual child. For physical aggression, however, some general knowledge exists. Jones, Sloane, and Roberts (1992) found clear evidence that parent "Stop fighting" instructions can function like nattering, socially reinforcing misbehavior and allowing coerced reinforcers from siblings to operate. Because the child stops fighting briefly, the parent is negatively reinforced for issuing "Stop fighting" instructions, as predicted by coercion theory (Figure 22.1), despite an unchanged or worsened fight frequency. Similarly, Kendall, Nay, and Jeffers (1975) observed that adolescent peer aggression in a residential facility increased when an instruction or warning procedure preceded time-out. Therefore, parent trainers are advised to consider the type of instruction used by the parent and adjust the treatment plan according to developmental variables and empirical evidence. Using a noncompliance protocol to reduce physical aggression is contraindicated.

Hanf recommended a 5-second interval as the window for child initiation of effort to instructions and warnings, which intriguingly has some observational support (Wruble et al., 1991), despite its clearly arbitrary roots. If the child does display effort during the 5-second window, social reinforcement is recommended. Interestingly, social reinforcement is not necessary for compliance acquisition or maintenance (Roberts, 1985; Roberts, Hatzenbuehler, & Bean, 1981) in overtly noncompliant referred preschoolers, failing to augment instruction and time-out effects. Noncompliance appears to be negatively reinforced by task avoidance rather than misguided parental attention, and compliance acquisition, at least in previously noncompliant 2- to 7-year-olds, appears to be negatively reinforced by active avoidance of time-out. Compliance acquisition in normally developing toddlers may be quite a different process, however, and involve such variables as infant temperament and parental responsivity, as discussed earlier. Hopefully, all children, including previously noncompliant ones, eventually internalize a standard of conduct to obey legitimate authority and, subsequently, regulate their own behavior rather than obey simply to avoid discipline. Nothing in these empirical findings and theoretical speculations indicates that parents should not be taught to praise child compliance. Theoretically, every opportunity to respond positively to prosocial child behavior is an opportunity to promote the parent-child relationship. The high consumer satisfaction (McMahon, Tiedemann, Forehand, & Griest, 1984) and social validity (Forehand, Wells, & Griest, 1980) of HNC protocols suggest that the Hanf two-stage protocol, which includes social reinforcement for compliance and mastery skills in child-directed interaction (PCIT) or the child's game (HNC), is thoroughly justified. Consequently, child-directed interaction is included in Figure 22.2 as the first step in compliance training. Nevertheless, the scholarly skeptic is not yet convinced that parent social reinforcement of child compliance is important, given the current limited set of dependent variables. See Forehand (1986) for a more thorough look at this issue, and the ensuing rejoinder by Lutzker, Touchette, and Campbell (1988) and the Forehand reply (1988).

Warnings to obey instructions (or be sent to time-out) have proven useful when the instruction is to initiate a discrete task (Roberts, 1982a). The warning component has reduced the number of time-outs needed to elicit compliance criterion responding and has not attenuated compliance acquisition rates relative to no-warning control conditions. The concern has always been that warnings will function like nattering, which appears not to be the case for instructions to initiate behavior. As noted earlier, however, fighting is not well served by "Don't" instructions and warnings, suggesting that the type of instruction interacts with the utility of warnings. If parent trainers are trying to manage a misbehavior other than noncompliance (e.g., tease, yell, dangerous climbing) with "Don't" instructions, the base rate of the misbehavior should be used to evaluate the protocol, rather than compliance to the instruction or warning.

The time-out component of Hanf-based programs has been repeatedly shown to be a critical treatment component (Roberts et al., 1981), yet one plagued with difficulty (Roberts, 1982b, 1984). Time-out procedures are complex. Early reviews (K. R. Harris, 1985; MacDonough & Forehand, 1973) explicated the many parameters of time-out (e.g., duration, location, release rules), some of which are now understood. Decades ago Leitenberg (1965) queried whether time-out is an aversive condition. It is. Overtly noncompliant children will fiercely resist initial time-outs (Roberts, 1982b), and successfully treated referred children will persistently comply to avoid them (Roberts, 1985). The more noncompliant the child at baseline, the more intense the time-out resistance (Roberts & Powers, 1988, table 2). If parent trainers allow children to successfully escape from time-out, compliance acquisition is significantly degraded (Bean & Roberts, 1981; Roberts & Powers, 1990). Moreover, contingency awareness does not mitigate the defiant child's behavioral insistence on testing the limits of the newly imposed contingencies (Roberts, 1984).

Fortunately, the spanking component of Hanf's original time-out maintenance procedure proved unnecessary (Day & Roberts, 1982; Roberts, 1988). Brief room time-outs maintained by a barrier suppress chair time-out escape efforts just as well as spanking, while avoiding corporal punishment and modeling aggression. That finding does not imply that putting a barrier or door between the parent and an angry child is a pleasant process. For just that reason, Roberts and Powers (1990) and Foster and Roberts (2007) have called for clinicians to monitor initial time-outs, support parents and children through the process, and adjust the procedures as needed. A legitimate and unanswered question focuses on time-out location. Why not use the prototype room time-out (Wolf et al., 1964) and avoid the escape problems of chair time-outs? The early work of Wahler and the OSLC group did just that. The argument voiced by HNC and PCIT programs is that 2- to 7-year-olds are better served by chair time-out conditions that can be visually monitored for safety and readily adapted to community settings. This argument, however, is rational rather than empirical. For a recent discussion of time-out parameters, see Roberts (2005).

Aggression Programs

The OSLC database has yielded some important empirical insights into the interrelationships of aggressive boys, their siblings, and their mothers. All parties appear to elicit, model, and reinforce physical aggression, yielding about one fight per hour, with the most likely victim a male sibling (Patterson, 1984, 1986). Years ago O'Leary, O'Leary, and Becker (1967) established the basic intervention for sibling aggression: immediate chair time-out combined with reinforcement for cooperative sibling interaction. An important distinction between treatments for noncompliance and aggression was anticipated by the O'Learys. The noncompliance protocol promotes its prosocial replacement skill (i.e., compliance) via an instruction and two reinforcement mechanisms: time-out avoidance and social reinforcement. In contrast, suppressing aggression with time-out or other strategies (e.g., token fines) does not directly provoke an acceptable replacement skill. Indeed, siblings might actually avoid each other, as was observed by O'Leary et al. The immense social skill training literature is designed specifically to teach a repertoire of nonaggressive strategies to solve myriad interpersonal sibling and peer conflicts (see McMahon et al., 2006, pp. 178–186), and, although well beyond the scope of this chapter, needs attention from parent trainers working with sibling aggression. The social skill assessment and training issues are complex and unresolved. For example, does the child know how to "share," or "take turns," or "ask nicely," or "take 'no' for an answer," or "be verbally assertive," given a specific and complex social condition (Roberts, Arnold, & Mangum, 1992)? What is the best way to teach those skills (Thomas & Roberts, 2006), let alone motivate performance of those skills in relatively unmonitored home settings?

Immediate time-out is effective at suppressing sibling aggression in 2- to 7-year-olds (Allison & Allison, 1971; Jones et al., 1992; O'Leary et al., 1967; Olson & Roberts, 1987). Referred to as a "standing rule" by HNC theorists (McMahon & Forehand, 2003, pp. 150–155), both children are immediately sent to time-out for fighting, effectively blocking all reinforcers that might be coerced by the aggressive act and simultaneously calming down both children via the quiet release contingency inherent in time-out routines. Following time-out, parents are taught to discuss the event-sequence leading up to the fight to enhance awareness of the conflict situation and alternative solutions. Does the parent trainer also need to program reinforcement for aggression inhibition or prosocial alternatives? Leitenberg, Burchard, Burchard, Fuller, and Lysaght (1977) have done so successfully with recruited families. Moreover, there is a huge literature on peer aggression that indicates success with various combinations of discipline, reinforcement, and skill building (e.g., Fehrenbach & Thelen, 1982). Therefore, a comprehensive and sequential approach to sibling aggression is recommended and is displayed in Figure 22.3: reinforcement for inhibition, immediate time-out, and skill building, in that order. Each component can be added as needed, based on parent records of sibling aggression at home. Developmental limitations, however, preclude most 2- and 3-year-olds from the skill-building and reinforcement components, given cognitive and attentional limitations. Aggressive siblings under age 4 might profit from immediate material reinforcement for cooperative play if a therapist could be inserted into the home (O'Leary et al., 1967), but such a routine seems impractical for parents and would lack social validity. Reducing sibling aggression without an immediate time-out seems especially unlikely in children under age 4. It is true that one can find theoretical arguments and some empirical support from developmental psychology (e.g., Brody & Stoneman, 1987) and family systems therapy (e.g., Dinkmeyer & McKay, 1973) to ignore sibling aggression. Others vehemently disagree (Bennett, 1990; Ihinger, 1975), noting that a quiet tyranny of the mighty could emerge, consistent with coercion theory (Figure 22.1). It is difficult to imagine how a delayed reinforcer for inhibition and/or skill building role-played in a clinic could override the immediately coerced reinforcers for sibling aggression in children under 4. In contrast, middle childhood youth (7 to 12 years old) might be effectively discouraged from sibling aggression by reinforced inhibition and/or social skill building alone (see the peer aggression literature reviewed by

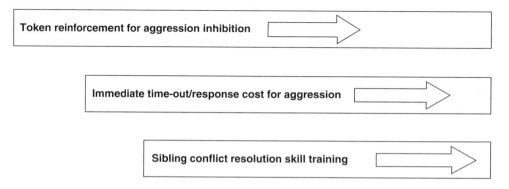

Figure 22.3   Recommended sibling aggression protocol for 2- to 12-year-olds based on a sequential strategy. Immediate time-out or response cost is needed if reinforcing inhibition is insufficient; skill training is needed if the combined reinforcement and time-out/response cost programs are insufficient.

McMahon et al., 2006, pp. 178–186). If sibling aggression still persists, then immediate time-outs, token fines, privilege losses, or work chores are indicated.

Other Programs and Situational Variables

Unlike noncompliance and aggression, which are motoric actions, tantrums and negative verbalizations are both vocal, suggesting extinction processes might be successful. If the function of coercive vocalizations is to provoke adult attention (e.g., nattering), differential attention procedures can effectively extinguish verbal coercion (e.g., Herbert & Baer, 1972). If the function is to terminate time-out conditions, a quiet release rule is effective (Hobbs & Forehand, 1975). If the coercive verbalizations covary with instruction presentations, simply persisting with the instruction routine can extinguish the negative verbal output despite socially reinforcing compliance in the presence of negative talk (Roberts & Hatzenbuehler, 1981). Therefore, teaching parents to persist with the stimulus conditions (Figure 22.1, "–1 Step") that provoke the negative vocal outburst is just as important as ignoring negative vocalizations (Figure 22.1, "+1 Step") in other contexts (e.g., sibling tease, disagree, bossy talk). Extinction, however, can be an aversive routine for many adults, given an extinction burst, and is sometimes impossible to implement (e.g., the child may climb on parent and scream). Teaching the parent to assume a physical posture and activity (e.g., turn one's back, leave the area, stand up) that makes ignoring viable is one option. Some unignorable emotionally aroused preschoolers, however, may need a time-out to successfully structure the extinction procedure for the parent. Only the quiet contingency of the time-out needs to be met to terminate time-out conditions for unignorable tantrums. In middle childhood, specific negative verbalizations (e.g., cursing) might be targeted within a larger token system by reinforcing inhibition and fining specified negative talk with tokens, backed up by activity or material reinforcers. Contingent chores (Fischer & Nehs, 1978) have also been used to suppress negative verbalizations in middle childhood.

Three social contexts require accommodations and are briefly discussed: bedtime, community, and car. Defiance, aggression, and tantrums at bedtime can befuddle the parent trainer if standard daytime treatments are applied. Time-out on a chair in the living room may function like "time-in"; differential attention may lead to reinforcing the child for refusing to go to bed, since staying up is ignored and attention for remaining in bed cannot compete with unrestricted access to the common rooms; token reinforcers for successful bedtime behavior are often delayed until morning. Traditional routines targeting bedtime crying, such as ignoring and graduated extinction (i.e., a gradual and systematic increase in parent response latency to crying), are effective (Kuhn & Elliot, 2003) but aversive to parents and presume that the child will remain in bed. Repeated "walk-backs" to bed or ultimately a shut door may prove necessary. Edwards and Christophersen (1994) recommend a sequential strategy, in which daytime self-quieting is targeted prior to attempting a bedtime extinction procedure (which requires children to calm themselves). Daytime ignoring and/or time-outs with quiet contingencies for tantrum and negative verbalizations provide practice opportunities for successful self-quieting. Recently,

Burke, Kuhn, and Peterson (2004) tested a clever positive reinforcement system (a prize under the pillow, left by the Sleep Fairy) that warrants replication with an oppositional sample. See Christophersen and Mortweet (2001, pp. 99–122) for a recent review of the psychopathology and empirically supported interventions for managing sleep problems.

Car and community situations often fail to provide the rich array of play options found at home (e.g., a long car trip, watching mother shop, sitting through big sister's piano recital), increasing the chance of coercion to provoke reinforcers. Further, community settings may be discriminative for misbehavior, since some parents actively mollify the child in public to avoid the embarrassment of child tantrums. For those two reasons, planned activity training combined with modified time-out routines are recommended. Sanders and Dadds (1982) helped parents identify and promote age-appropriate activities in specific community settings (e.g., quiet toys and games for the car; reinforced shopping participation; outdoor toys for a teenage sister's soccer match) that significantly enhanced generalization of parent training effects to community settings. Time-out locations can be defined in any specific, low-traffic area, backed up by the two private locations found in the community: bathrooms and the parent's car (Christophersen & Rapoff, 1979, p. 371; McMahon & Forehand, 2003, pp. 155–157). Sibling aggression in the car or seat belt refusal may necessitate stopping the car in a safe location and declaring time-out until all children are sitting quietly.

Some children may not adjust to community or car settings despite good planned positive activities and appropriately modified time-out routines. Consequently, parent trainers should consider inserting more powerful token systems tailored to the community setting (e.g., Barnard, Christophersen, & Wolf, 1977) to reinforce rule following and participation in planned positive activities. In addition, parent trainers can shape community skills by initially assigning brief, repetitive exposures under rich reinforcement conditions combined with simulation practice in the clinic. Data collected by the parent in the target setting can be used to adjust the treatment protocol.

Case Illustration

Ms. Smith and her three children, ages 7, 5, and 2, were referred to the clinic by their pediatrician for evaluation of conduct problems and possible therapy. During the standard interview, Ms. Smith reported that the 5-year-old, Zachary, was her main concern. Zach had been asked to leave a day care facility that summer for repeatedly fighting with peers and was now "in trouble" in kindergarten. Ms. Smith reported that Zach had always been "difficult" to raise. He argued, disobeyed, tantrummed, and was even aggressive with her when he didn't get his way, his requests were denied, or when she attempted to spank him or send him to his room. Zach was very bossy with his 2-year-old brother, which led to angry outbursts and aggression. In contrast, the 7-year-old sister had been "very easy" to raise and seemed to disregard the two boys. Ms. Smith voiced worry that her 2-year-old was learning "bad habits" from Zach. Questionnaire data from the Child Behavior Checklist (Achenbach & Rescorla, 2000) and the Eyberg Child Behavior Inventory (Eyberg & Pincus, 1999) both yielded elevated scores on Social Aggression scales for Zach, but not for either sibling. The Slosson Intelligence Test Revised 3 (Slosson, 2002) was administered to screen for delays in Zach's cognitive/verbal development. He was normal (SS = 92). Maternal depression was also screened and fortunately absent (Beck Depression Inventory II = 9, "minimal"; Beck, Steer, & Brown, 1996). Since Ms. Smith was a single parent, a marital adjustment scale was not administered, but an instrument like the Marital Satisfaction Inventory R (Snyder, 1997) is recommended to screen for marital conflict. Because neither depression nor marital conflict was present, referrals to address these issues were not needed. A phone call to Zach's kindergarten teacher revealed disruptive behavior and occasional aggression, but no teacher interest in assistance from an outside professional at that time. The school had its own system for managing misconduct (an escalating response-cost system). His teacher did request (and was eventually mailed) a copy of his psychological evaluation, findings, and recommendations.

Home record data collected by the mother during the 2-week evaluation period yielded 3.6 fights per day (usually with the 2-year-old brother) and over 5 tantrums per day. In addition, Zach ran away from the house twice when confronted by his mother over conflict with his brother, provoking necessary but distressing "chase" episodes. Clinic observations under child's game conditions showed a responsive mother (64% positive or neutral reactivity, given a signal from Zach or the 2-year-old), but a very high rate of questions plus instructions (8.3 per minute) and a virtual absence of positive maternal signals (praise + descriptions + imitations = 0.2 per minute). The 7-year-old was not available for the observational measures since she was in school when the family attended clinic sessions. Under cleanup task analogue conditions, Zach's compliance ratio was 22%. Ms. Smith, however, repeated her instructions so quickly that her beta instruction ratio was almost 75% (i.e., repeated + vague instructions divided by the total number of instructions issued); her praise ratio was 0%. A compliance test was administered to ensure that Zach's defiance was not simply an artifact of maternal instruction style. It was not; his compliance ratio, given well-presented instructions to pick up toys, was 3%. He also became quite angry during the compliance test, yielding cry and back-talk ratios over 50%.

Given the interview, questionnaire data, home record data, clinic observations, and school information, Zach met criteria for Oppositional Defiant Disorder. Using Figure 22.1, it could be seen that several paths were relevant to help conceptualize the case. Coercion was very likely, given maternal or sibling instructions to "Do X" or "Stop Y," as well as denials of Zach's requests. Fortunately, there was no evidence that minor aversive events (e.g., disagree with siblings), ignoring, or positive or neutral events set the occasion for Zach's misbehavior. Zach played alone quite well. Discipline efforts, however, were ineffectual and provoked escalating intensities of coercion (e.g., he had physically hurt his mother on more than one occasion when she attempted to guide him to his room). Common parenting errors (i.e., Figure 22.1, "+1 Step"), although not observed, presumably reinforced Zach's coercion on a partial reinforcement schedule. Social learning–based parent training was recommended.

(Continued)

In addition, Zach's school progress was to be monitored to ensure that programs implemented in that setting were successful.

Child-directed interaction skills were targeted first. Within three sessions Ms. Smith became rather skillful at giving attention to age-appropriate play when interacting with Zach and his 2-year-old brother in the clinic playroom. Her responsiveness index remained high (over 70%), while the quality of her responses became more positive (praise + descriptions + imitations exceeded 4 per minute). It was difficult for her to learn to inhibit question asking, since she seemed to want to "teach" skills via this route, but she eventually adopted a more child-centered strategy, limiting questions plus instructions to under one per minute. She also had difficulty learning to ignore the boys when they became bossy, angry, or disruptive with each other, but finally learned to turn her back and play with the other sibling or simply model quiet toy play until one or both siblings began to play more appropriately. Ms. Smith was asked to set aside some morning time (e.g., 15 to 20 minutes) to use child-centered play with her 2-year-old and a similar time after school with all three children. In addition, she was instructed to look for opportunities throughout the day to socially reinforce child initiations with her new listening skills. Handouts on responsive play skills and the principles of shaping and positive reinforcement were provided for review and future discussion.

Compliance training, which began during the third treatment session, was more difficult. During modeling and role-playing of instruction, social reinforcement, warning, and time-out skills, Zach displayed interest in his mother's reactions to the doll, but when queried about why the doll went to time-out, Zach refused to talk to the therapist. During the initial guided practice with Zach, his mother, wearing a bug-in-the-ear, met with immediate defiance and time-out resistance. Zach refused to go to the time-out chair and physically fought his mother when she guided him to the backup room. He banged on the door and yelled angrily for the entire 60-second period; when escorted back to time-out for his second opportunity at chair time-out conditions, he repeated the entire sequence of escape, a furious 1-minute room backup, and subsequent replacement on the time-out chair. During his third experience with chair time-out conditions, he inhibited escape for about 5 seconds before arising and throwing the chair against the wall. He was immediately escorted to the backup room for a third and final time; there to remain until a 5-second quiet rule was met. Ten minutes later he finally extinguished his crying and yelling sufficiently for the therapist to instruct the mother to open the door and say, "Since you're quiet, you can come out now." Zach immediately reinitiated screaming and refused to leave the time-out room. Pouting after initial time-outs is not unusual, but Zach was extreme. The therapist had to enter the playroom, prop the time-out backup room door open (because Zach kept slamming it), and prompt the mother to play positively with the 2-year-old out of Zach's visual field. This process also allowed the therapist to provide social support and compassion for the mother beyond what could be done over the radio device. Zach was ignored. Four minutes later he emerged from the time-out room. Rather than re-present the disobeyed instruction immediately (as in Figure 22.2), the therapist and mother continued in a responsive play mode with the younger sibling and Zach until Zach began to play and talk normally. The therapist then left the room and resumed compliance training via the bug. Zach immediately disobeyed the same cleanup instruction and was sent to time-out again. The entire coercive cycle repeated itself, although greatly toned down. Zach remained on the time-out chair after just one 60-second trip to the backup room and became quiet within 3 minutes. He again refused to leave time-out when told he could, but when the mother began playing with his little brother, Zach left the chair and began playing (the therapist did not have to enter the playroom this time). Once Zach began playing, the therapist instructed the mother to say (via the bug), "Okay Zach, we still need to put the stuffed animals back in the toy box." Zach started yelling, but when given the warning, he picked up one toy despite continued verbal protests. His mother praised his efforts and continued to use the basic Figure 22.2 system under guidance via the bug. Zach met the criterion of 10 compliant responses in a row (despite the necessity of three warnings, which he obeyed). Ms. Smith was instructed to give him a big hug and inform Zach that he could play the way he wanted to now. Responsive play was resumed until both boys were playing and talking appropriately. The 2-year-old was then issued similar, but very simple motor tasks (e.g., "Come here"; "Take this (toy)"; or "Put it (location)," always accompanied by close proximity, eye contact, and a gesture. The 2-year-old met compliance criterion with only one time-out and virtually no time-out resistance. A record card was sent home to monitor chair time-outs for disobeyed warnings and needed room backups (using the child's bedroom). Because Zach had been extremely resistant to time-out, phone contacts were scheduled during the next few days and until the mother was confident she could administer the Figure 22.2 program. Handouts on the compliance program and the principles of extinction and punishment were sent home and reviewed at a later session.

During the fifth clinic visit, the home record data indicated that Zach had required from one to four chair time-outs per day for disobeyed warnings and room backup procedures about half the time. His mother did report that Zach often obeyed warnings, which pleased her, and the younger brother obeyed almost all the time if she "made it simple" as instructed. The mother had clearly gained some confidence in the compliance routine, but felt helpless about the boys' fighting. A no-fighting rule (Figure 22.3) was instituted in addition to reviewing responsive play and compliance protocols. Zach sat beside his mother while the therapist sent two dolls to time-out for fighting over a toy. An effort was made to discuss the conditions, mistake, and optional responses, but Zach would have none of it. Ms. Smith, however, role-played the post-time-out effort at incidental training regarding the conflict conditions (e.g., brother 1 had taken brother 2's toy), the mistake (i.e., fighting), and the optional responses (e.g., using an assertive instruction or seeking maternal help). During the responsive play sample, Zach pushed his brother intentionally; the mother was prompted to implement the no-fight rule, marching Zach immediately to the time-out chair while labeling the contingency in an authoritative manner (i.e., "Since you hit your brother, you must go to time-out"). Zach actually stayed on the time-out chair, but refused to talk to the mother during the incidental learning procedure after time-out. There was no more fighting during that clinic session. Time-out for fighting was added to that week's home record card and monitored thereafter. A token system was also initiated. Zach was shown spaces on the home card where stickers would be entered for remembering his no-fight rule; he could earn up to two on school

(Continued)

days and three on the weekends. Both Zach and his brother were shown the clinic store where stickers could buy prizes the next week. His mother was instructed to insert stickers for specified periods of aggression inhibition and lavish praise for rule following.

During the sixth through eighth clinic sessions home cards were reviewed, stickers were rewarded with clinic prizes, responsive play and clinic task conditions were observed, and rule protocols were reviewed. Zach's little brother always received a prize, despite not participating in the token system. A set of planned positive activities and adaptations for time-out, if needed, were modeled and role-played for shopping and car situations. Both boys watched with great interest as Ms. Smith role-played with the dolls. Shopping and car opportunities were monitored on the home record card and discussed with Ms. Smith during follow-up sessions. During the eighth session an allowance system was established for Zach and his older sister to substitute for the token system. Both older siblings earned a set amount of money each week (10 cents per day for Zach) for completing at least one household chore each day. In addition, Zach was fined 5 cents for every time-out, which had dropped to about four per week at that point. The token reinforcement system for aggression inhibition was then discontinued. Because fighting rates had declined dramatically, sibling conflict resolution skill training (Figure 22.3) was not considered necessary. Zach was, however, still having trouble in school. A school psychologist had been called in by the principal to address continued classroom disruption and occasional fighting. Following phone consultation and one lengthy meeting, a program was jointly evolved that included a token reinforcement system for rule following and classroom productivity, token fines and privilege losses for fighting, and a weekly social skill session with two other boys and two "peer helpers" led by the school psychologist.

After eight treatment sessions, two follow-up sessions, and 3 months, Zach's home data finally looked normal for a 5-year-old (i.e., 1 to 2 time-outs per week, no room backups), but school problems persisted. Long-term follow-up was planned to provide continued support and educational services to the mother, as well as consultation services for the school district as needed.

FUTURE CHALLENGES

Current parent training treatment modalities have limitations. In particular, effective discipline procedures for middle childhood have not been identified. Theoretically (Figure 22.1), the coerced reinforcers of violence must be blocked to make progress with oppositional and conduct disordered grade-schoolers. Unfortunately, parent trainers lack an effective procedure to enforce time-outs, token fines, privilege losses, or work chores with those 8- to 12-year-olds who fiercely resist discipline efforts. Their 2- to 7-year-old counterparts can be safely escorted to time-out as needed. In contrast, older children can intensify the level of violence toward the parent, thwart the implementation of the discipline, coerce denied reinforcers, and/or run out of the house! Increasing the level of care to psychiatric facilities, therapeutic foster care, community residential programs, or juvenile detention centers is the current solution, but it is not satisfactory.

Similarly, some middle childhood referrals continue to display unacceptably high rates of aggression and defiance, despite the establishment of a seemingly good set of treatment procedures. Frick (2004) has identified a subset of externalizing disordered children he calls "callous-unemotional" who may not respond to family-based interventions. Specifically, family dysfunction may be less important than temperamental and physiological differences for this minority of violent clinic referrals, suggesting a need for supplemental treatment modalities. Unfortunately, there are no specific and effective interventions for instilling guilt for transgressions, acceptance of responsibility for mistakes, empathy for victims, or identification with mainstream social activities. These important self-regulatory processes emerge gradually in normal children during socialization. Parent trainers often observe phenomena that suggest improvement in these important covert processes by many of our child clients, but not all. The discussion of "child effects" is not new in our field (Lytton, 1990), nor resolved (Dodge, 1990; Wahler, 1990). There is, however, no doubt that some young males seem untreatable. Relentless and remorseless appear apt descriptors to this author. Psychiatric medication and higher levels of care appear to be their current destination.

SUMMARY

Parent training is based on the recognition that externalizing disorders of childhood are rooted in coercive patterns of social interaction. Intentional, aversive child behavior is very likely to coerce parents, teachers, siblings, and peers into unwittingly reinforcing common referral symptoms, such as disobedience, fighting, negative talk, and tantrums. Parent training evolved as a new treatment modality to address the reinforcement traps perpetuating the child's social aggression. The pioneering work of Patterson, Wahler, and Hanf led the way toward the sophisticated theoretical models, assessment strategies, and treatment protocols of today. Social learning–based parent training is now widely recognized as an empirically supported treatment. Parents can learn child management skills, use those skills at home, and reduce socially aggressive child behavior. Improvements observed in clinic settings generalize to home settings and persist over time. Basic child management skills include knowledge and use of social learning principles, observation, differential attention, responsiveness, instruction giving, discipline, and token systems. Basic methods of teaching skills to parents include didactic strategies, modeling, role-playing, guided practice, and homework. Both parent group and individual family approaches have been effective.

Problems not initially considered became evident as clinical scientists pursued the dropouts and treatment failures from parent training programs: poverty, social isolation, parent pathology, and therapeutic disengagement head the list. Moreover, there are some child presentations we still cannot manage on an outpatient family therapy basis (e.g., violence in middle childhood), let alone successfully treat. Parent training is a work in progress, as witnessed by the ongoing waves of clinical research discussed in the chapter. Nevertheless, routine defiance, aggression, negative talk, and tantrums, especially for oppositional and disruptive children under 8 years of age, can be successfully treated at home and in other relevant situations via parent training. Under those conditions, parent training is the empirically supported treatment of choice.

REFERENCES

Achenbach, T. M., & Rescorla, L. A. (2000). *Manual for the ASEBA preschool forms and profiles*. Burlington: University of Vermont, Department of Psychiatry.

Allison, T. S., & Allison, S. L. (1971). Time-out from reinforcement: Effect on sibling aggression. *Psychological Record, 21*, 81–86.

Axline, U. (1969). *Play therapy*. New York: Ballantine Books.

Azrin, N. H., & Besalel, V. A. (1979). *A parent's guide to bedwetting control: A step-by-step method*. New York: Simon & Schuster.

Bandura, A. (1962). Punishment revisited. *Journal of Consulting Psychology, 26*, 298–301.

Bandura, A. (1977). *Social learning theory*. Englewood Cliffs, NJ: Prentice-Hall.

Bandura, A., & Walters, R. H. (1963). *Social learning theory and personality development*. New York: Holt, Rinehart and Winston.

Barlow, J., & Stewart-Brown, S. (2000). Behavior problems and group-based parent education programs. *Developmental and Behavioral Pediatrics, 21*, 356–370.

Barmish, A. J., & Kendall, P. C. (2005). Should parents be co-clients in cognitive-behavioral therapy for anxious youth? *Journal of Clinical Child and Adolescent Psychology, 34*, 569–581.

Barnard, J. D., Christophersen, E. R., & Wolf, M. M. (1977). Teaching children appropriate shopping behavior through parent training in the supermarket setting. *Journal of Applied Behavior Analysis, 1*, 49–59.

Baumrind, D. (1967). Child care practices anteceding three patterns of preschool behavior. *Genetic Psychology Monographs, 75*, 43–88.

Bean, A. W., & Roberts, M. W. (1981). The effect of time-out release contingencies on changes in child noncompliance. *Journal of Abnormal Child Psychology, 9*, 95–105.

Beck, A. T., Steer, R. A., & Brown, G. K. (1996). *Beck Depression Inventory: II*. San Antonio, TX: Psychological Corporation.

Bennett, J. C. (1990). Nonintervention into siblings' fighting as a catalyst for learned helplessness. *Psychological Reports, 66*, 139–145.

Berkowitz, B. P., & Graziano, A. M. (1972). Training parents as behavior therapists: A review. *Behavior Research and Therapy, 10*, 297–317.

Bernal, M. E., Klinnert, M. D., & Schultz, L. A. (1980). Outcome evaluation of behavioral parent training and client-centered parent counseling for children with conduct problems. *Journal of Applied Behavior Analysis, 13*, 677–691.

Boardman, W. K. (1962). Rusty: A brief behavior disorder. *Journal of Consulting Psychology, 26*, 293–297.

Breiner, J. L., & Forehand, R. (1981). As assessment of the effects of parent training on clinic-referred children's school behavior. *Behavioral Assessment, 3*, 31–42.

Brestan, E. V., & Eyberg, S. M. (1998). Effective psychosocial treatments of conduct-disordered children and adolescents: 29 years, 82 studies, and 5,272 kids. *Journal of Clinical Child Psychology, 27*, 180–189.

Briesmeister, J. M., & Schaefer, D. E. (Eds.). (1998). *Handbook of parent training: Parents as co-therapists for children's behavior problems* (2nd ed.). New York: Wiley.

Brody, G. H., & Stoneman, Z. (1987). Sibling conflict: Contributions of the siblings themselves, the parent-sibling relationship, and the broader family system. *Journal of Children in Contemporary Society, 19*, 39–53.

Burke, R. V., Kuhn, B. R., & Peterson, J. L. (2004). Brief report: A "storybook" ending to children's bedtime problems: The use of a rewarding social story to reduce bedtime resistance and frequent night waking. *Journal of Pediatric Psychology, 29*, 389–396.

Cedar, B., & Levant, R. F. (1990). A meta-analysis of the effects of parent effectiveness training. *American Journal of Family Therapy, 18*, 373–384.

Chamberlain, P., Patterson, G., Reid, J., Kavanagh, K., & Forgatch, M. (1984). Observation of client resistance. *Behavior Therapy, 15*, 144–155.

Chamberlain, P., & Reid, J. B. (1987). Parent observation and report of child symptoms. *Behavioral Assessment, 9*, 97–109.

Chambless, D. L., & Ollendick, T. H. (2001). Empirically supported psychological interventions: Controversies and evidence. *Annual Review of Psychology, 52*, 685–716.

Christophersen, E. R., & Mortweet, S. L. (2001). *Treatments that work with children: Empirically supported strategies for managing childhood problems*. Washington, DC: American Psychological Association.

Christophersen, E. R., & Rapoff, M. A. (1979). Behavioral problems in children. In G. M. Scipien, M. U. Barnard, M. A. Chard, J. Howe, & P. J. Phillips (Eds.), *Comprehensive pediatric nursing* (2nd ed., pp. 361–383). New York: McGraw-Hill.

Chronis, A. M., Chacko, A., Fabiano, G. A., Wymbs, B. T., & Pelham, W. E. (2004). Enhancements to the behavioral parent training paradigm for families of children with ADHD: Review and future directions. *Clinical Child and Family Psychology Review, 7*, 1–27.

Clark, H. B., Greene, G. F., Macrae, J. W., McNees, M. P., Davis, J. L., & Risley, T. R. (1977). A parent advice package for family shopping trips: Development and evaluation. *Journal of Applied Behavioral Analysis, 10*, 605–624.

Conduct Problems Prevention Research Group. (2004). The effects of the Fast Track Program on serious problem outcomes at the end of elementary school. *Journal of Clinical Child and Adolescent Psychology, 33*, 650–661.

Coplin, J. W., & Houts, A. E. (1991). Father involvement in parent training for oppositional child behavior: Progress or stagnation? *Child and Family Behavior Therapy, 13*, 29–51.

Dadds, M. R., Schwartz, S., & Sanders, M. R. (1987). Marital discord and treatment outcome in behavioral treatment of child conduct disorders. *Journal of Consulting and Clinical Psychology, 55*, 396–403.

Dangel, R. F., & Polster, R. A. (1984). *Parent training: Foundations of research and practice*. New York: Guilford Press.

Day, D. E., & Roberts, M. W. (1982). An analysis of the physical punishment component of a parent training program. *Journal of Abnormal Child Psychology, 11*, 141–152.

Dinkmeyer, D., & McKay, G. D. (1973). *Raising a responsible child: Practical steps to successful family relationships*. New York: Simon & Schuster.

Dinkmeyer, D., & McKay, G. D. (1976). *Systematic training for effective parenting*. Circle Pines, MN: American Guidance Service.

Dodge, K. A. (1980). Social cognition and children's aggressive behavior. *Child Development, 51*, 162–170.

Dodge, K. A. (1990). Nature versus nurture in childhood conduct disorder: It is time to ask a different question. *Developmental Psychology, 26*, 698–701.

Dumas, J. E. (1989). Treating antisocial behavior in children: Child and family approaches. *Clinical Psychology Review, 9*, 197–222.

Dumas, J. E., & Wahler, R. G. (1985). Indiscriminant mothering as a contextual factor in aggressive-oppositional child behavior: Damned if you do and damned if you don't. *Journal of Abnormal Child Psychology, 13*, 1–17.

Edwards, K. J., & Christophersen, E. R. (1994). Treating common sleep problems of young children. *Journal of Developmental and Behavioral Pediatrics, 15*, 207–213.

Erel, O., & Burman, B. (1995). Interrelatedness of marital relationships and parent-child relations: A meta-analytic review. *Psychological Bulletin, 118*, 108–132.

Estrada, A. U., & Pinsof, W. M. (1995). The effectiveness of family therapies for selected behavioral disorders of childhood. *Journal of Marital and Family Therapy, 21*, 403–440.

Eyberg, S. M. (1988). Parent-child interaction therapy: Integration of traditional and behavioral concerns. *Child and Family Behavior Therapy, 10*, 33–46.

Eyberg, S. M. (1992). Assessing therapy outcome with preschool children: Progress and problems. *Journal of Clinical Child Psychology, 21*, 306–311.

Eyberg, S. M., Bessmer, J., Newcomb, K., Edwards, D., & Robinson, E. (1994). Manual for the Dyadic Parent-Child Interaction Coding System, II. *Social and Behavioral Sciences Documents* (MS No. 2897). San Rafael, CA: Select Press.

Eyberg, S. M., Boggs, S. R., & Algina, J. (1995). Parent-child interaction therapy: A psychosocial model for the treatment of young children with conduct problem behavior and their families. *Psychopharmacology Bulletin, 31*, 83–91.

Eyberg, S. M., & Matarazzo, R. G. (1980). Training parents as therapists: A comparison between individual parent-child interaction training and parent group didactic training. *Journal of Clinical Psychology, 36*, 492–499.

Eyberg, S. M., & Pincus, D. (1999). *The Eyberg Child Behavior Inventory and Sutter-Eyberg Student Behavior Inventory: Professional manual*. Lutz, FL: Psychological Assessment Resources.

Fehrenbach, P. A., & Thelen, M. H. (1982). Behavioral approaches to the treatment of aggressive disorders. *Behavior Modification, 6,* 465–497.

Fischer, J., & Nehs, R. (1978). Use of a commonly available chore to reduce a boy's rate of swearing. *Journal of Behavior Therapy and Experimental Psychiatry, 9,* 81–83.

Flanagan, S., Adams, H. E., & Forehand, R. (1979). A comparison of four instructional techniques for teaching parents to use time-out. *Behavior Therapy, 10,* 94–102.

Foote, R., Eyberg, S., & Schuhmann, E. (1998). Parent-child interaction approaches to the treatment of child behavior problems. In T. H. Ollendick & R. J. Prinz (Eds.), *Advances in clinical child psychology* (Vol. 20, pp. 125–151). New York: Plenum Press.

Forehand, R. L. (1977). Child noncompliance to parental requests: Behavioral analysis and treatment. In M. Hersen, R. M. Eisler, & P. M. Miller (Eds.), *Progress in behavior modification* (Vol. 5, pp. 111–147). New York: Academic Press.

Forehand, R. L. (1986). Parental positive reinforcement with deviant children: Does it make a difference? *Child and Family Behavior Therapy, 8,* 19–25.

Forehand, R. L. (1988). Reinventing the wheel and attacking strawmen: A reply to Lutzker et al.'s rejoinder. *Child and Family Behavior Therapy, 10,* 35–39.

Forehand, R. L., & Atkeson, B. M. (1977). Generality of treatment effects with parents as therapists: A review of assessment and implementation procedures. *Behavior Therapy, 8,* 575–593.

Forehand, R. L., Griest, D. L., Wells, K., & McMahon, R. J. (1982). Side effects of parent counseling on marital satisfaction. *Journal of Counseling Psychology, 29,* 104–107.

Forehand, R. L., & Kotchick, B. A. (1996). Cultural diversity: A wake-up call for parent training. *Behavior Therapy, 27,* 187–206.

Forehand, R. L., & McMahon, R. J. (1981). *Helping the noncompliant child.* New York: Guilford Press.

Forehand, R. L., Wells, K. C., & Griest, D. L. (1980). An examination of the social validity of a parent training program. *Behavior Therapy, 11,* 488–502.

Foster, B. W., & Roberts, M. W. (2007). Training parents with videotapes: Recognizing limitations. *Child and Family Behavior Therapy, 29,* 21–35.

Frick, P. J. (2004). Developmental pathways to conduct disorder: Implications for serving youth who show severe aggressive and antisocial behavior. *Psychology in the Schools, 41,* 823–834.

Frick, P. J., & Loney, B. R. (2002). Understanding the association between parent and child antisocial behavior. In R. J. McMahon & R. D. Peters (Eds.), *The effects of parental dysfunction on children* (pp. 105–126). New York: Kluwer Academic/Plenum Press.

Gordon, T. (1970). *P.E.T: Parent effectiveness training.* New York: Peter H. Wyden.

Graziano, A. M., & Diament, D. M. (1992). Parent behavioral training: An examination of the paradigm. *Behavior Modification, 16,* 3–38.

Green, G. F., Clark, H. B., & Risley, T. R. (1977). *Shopping with children: Advice for parents.* San Rafael, CA: Academic Therapy Publications.

Griest, D. L., & Wells, K. C. (1983). Behavioral family therapy with conduct disorders in children. *Behavior Therapy, 14,* 37–53.

Hamlet, C. C., Axelrod, S., & Kuerschner, S. (1984). Eye contact as an antecedent to compliant behavior. *Journal of Applied Behavior Analysis, 17,* 553–557.

Hanf, C. (1968). *Modifying problem behaviors in mother-child interaction: Standardized laboratory situations.* Paper presented at the meeting of the Association of Behavior Therapies, Olympia, WA.

Hanf, C. (1969, June). *A two-stage program for modifying maternal controlling during mother-child (M-C) interaction.* Paper presented at the meeting of the Western Psychological Association, Vancouver, BC, Canada.

Hanf, C., & Kling, J. (1973). *Facilitating parent-child interaction: A two-stage training model.* Unpublished manuscript, University of Oregon Medical School.

Harris, K. R. (1985). Definitional, parametric, and procedural considerations in timeout interventions and research. *Exceptional Children, 51,* 279–288.

Harris, S. L., Wolchick, S. A., & Milch, R. E. (1982). Changing the speech of autistic children and their parents. *Child and Family Behavior Therapy, 4,* 151–173.

Hembree-Kigin, T. L., & McNeil, C. B. (1995). *Parent-child interaction therapy.* New York: Plenum Press.

Herbert, E. W., & Baer, D. M. (1972). Training parents as behavior modifiers: Self-recording of contingent attention. *Journal of Applied Behavior Analysis, 5,* 139–149.

Herbert, E. W., Pinkston, E. M., Hayden, M. L., Sajwaj, T. E., Pinkston, S., Cordua, G., et al. (1973). Adverse effects of differential parental attention. *Journal of Applied Behavior Analysis, 6,* 15–30.

Hinshaw, S. P. (1992). Externalizing behavior problems and academic underachievement in childhood an adolescence: Causal relationship and underlying mechanisms. *Psychological Bulletin, 111,* 127–155.

Hobbs, S. A., & Forehand, R. (1975). Effects of differential release from time-out on children's deviant behavior. *Journal of Behavior Therapy and Experimental Psychiatry, 6,* 256–257.

Holland, C. J. (1969). Elimination by the parents of fire-setting behavior in a 7-year-old boy. *Behavior Research and Therapy, 7,* 135–137.

Houlihan, D., Sloane, H. N., Jones, R. N., & Patten, C. (1992). A review of behavioral conceptualizations and treatments of child noncompliance. *Education and Treatment of Children, 15,* 56–77.

Hudson, A., & Blane, M. (1985). The importance of nonverbal behavior in giving instructions to children. *Child and Family Behavior Therapy, 7,* 1–10.

Humphreys, L., Forehand, R., McMahon, R., & Roberts, M. (1978). Parent behavioral training to modify child noncompliance: Effects on untreated siblings. *Journal of Behavior Therapy and Experimental Psychiatry, 9,* 235–238.

Ihinger, M. (1975). The referee role and norms of equity: A contribution toward a theory of sibling conflict. *Journal of Marriage and the Family, 37,* 515–524.

Johnson, C. A., & Katz, R. C. (1973). Using parents as change agents for their children: A review. *Journal of Child Psychology and Psychiatry, 14,* 181–200.

Jones, R. N., Sloane, H. N., & Roberts, M. W. (1992). Limitations of "Don't" instructional control. *Behavior Therapy, 23,* 130–140.

Kazdin, A. E. (1987). Treatment of antisocial behavior in children: Current status and future directions. *Psychological Bulletin, 102,* 187–203.

Kazdin, A. E. (1997). Practitioner review: Psychosocial treatments for conduct disorder in children. *Journal of Child Psychology and Psychiatry, 38,* 161–178.

Kazdin, A. E., & Weisz, J. R. (1998). Identifying and developing empirically supported child and adolescent treatments. *Journal of Consulting and Clinical Psychology, 66,* 19–36.

Kendall, P. C., Nay, W. R., & Jeffers, J. (1975). Timeout duration and contrast effects: A systematic evaluation of a successive treatments design. *Behavior Therapy, 6,* 609–615.

Kochanska, G. (1997). Mutually responsive orientation between mothers and their young children: Implications for early socialization. *Child Development, 68,* 94–112.

Krishnakumar, A., & Buehler, C. (2000). Interparental conflict and parenting behaviors: A meta analytic review. *Family Relations, 49,* 25–44.

Kuhn, B. R., & Elliott, A. J. (2003). Treatment efficacy in behavioral pediatric sleep medicine. *Journal of Psychosomatic Research, 54,* 587–597.

Leitenberg, H. (1965). Is time-out from positive reinforcement an aversive event? A review of the experimental evidence. *Psychological Bulletin, 64,* 428–441.

Leitenberg, H., Burchard, J. D., Burchard, S. N., Fuller, E. J., & Lysaght, T. V. (1977). Using positive reinforcement to suppress behavior: Some experimental comparisons with sibling conflict. *Behavior Therapy, 8,* 168–182.

Loeber, R., & Schmaling, K. B. (1985). Empirical evidence for overt and covert patterns of antisocial conduct problems: A meta-analysis. *Journal of Abnormal Child Psychology, 13,* 337–352.

Long, P., Forehand, R., Wierson, M., & Morgan, A. (1994). Moving into adulthood: Does parent training with young noncompliant children have long term effects? *Behavior Research and Therapy, 32,* 101–107.

Lutzker, J. R., Touchette, P. E., & Campbell, R. V. (1988). Parental positive reinforcement might make a difference: A rejoinder to Forehand. *Child and Family Behavior Therapy, 10,* 25–33.

Lytton, H. (1990). Child and parent effects in boys' conduct disorder: A reinterpretation. *Developmental Psychology, 26,* 683–697.

Maccoby, E. E., & Martin, J. A. (1983). Socialization in the context of the family: Parent-child interaction. In P. H. Mussen (Ed.), *Handbook of child psychology* (4th ed., Vol., 4, pp. 100–101). New York: Wiley.

MacDonough, T. S., & Forehand, R. (1973). Response-contingent time out: Important parameters in behavior modification with children. *Journal of Behavior Therapy and Experimental Psychiatry, 4,* 231–236.

Mash, E. J., Handy, L. C., & Hamerlynck, L. A. (1976). *Behavior modification approaches to parenting.* New York: Brunner/Mazel.

Mash, E. J., & Terdal, L. G. (1973). Modification of mother-child interactions: Playing with children. *Mental Retardation, 11*, 44–49.

McLoughlin, C. S. (1982). Procedures and problems in behavioral training for parents. *Perceptual and Motor Skills, 55*, 827–838.

McMahon, R. J. (1999). Parent training. In S. W. Russ & T. H. Ollendick (Eds.), *Handbook of psychotherapies with children and adolescents* (pp. 153–180). New York: Kluwer Academic/Plenum Press.

McMahon, R. J., & Forehand, R. (1978). Nonprescription behavior therapy: Effectiveness of a brochure in teaching mothers to correct their children's inappropriate mealtime behaviors. *Behavior Therapy, 9*, 814–820.

McMahon, R. J., & Forehand, R. (1980). Self-help behavior therapies in parent training. In B. B. Lahey & A. E. Kazdin (Eds.), *Advances in clinical child psychology* (Vol. 3, pp. 149–176). New York: Plenum Press.

McMahon, R. J., & Forehand, R. (1981). Suggestions for evaluating self-administered materials in parent training. *Child Behavior Therapy, 3*, 65–68.

McMahon, R. J., & Forehand, R. L. (2003). *Helping the noncompliant child* (2nd ed.). New York: Guilford Press.

McMahon, R. J., Forehand, R., & Griest, D. L. (1981). Effects of knowledge of social learning principles on enhancing treatment outcome and generalization in a parent training program. *Journal of Consulting and Clinical Psychology, 49*, 526–532.

McMahon, R. J., & Frick, P. J. (2005). Evidence-based assessment of conduct problems in children and adolescents. *Journal of Clinical Child and Adolescent Psychology, 34*, 477–505.

McMahon, R. J., & Peters, R. D. (2002). *The effects of parental dysfunction on children.* New York: Kluwer Academic/Plenum Press.

McMahon, R. J., Tiedemann, G., Forehand, R., & Griest, D. L. (1984). Parental satisfaction with parent training to modify child noncompliance. *Behavior Therapy, 15*, 295–303.

McMahon, R. J., Wells, K. C., & Kotler, J. S. (2006). Conduct problems. In E. J. Mash & R. A. Barkley (Eds.). *Treatment of childhood disorders* (3rd ed., pp. 137–268). New York: Guilford Press.

McNeil, C. B., Eyberg, S., Eisenstadt, T. H., Newcomb, K., & Funderburk, B. (1991). Parent-child interaction therapy with behavior problem children: Generalization of treatment effects to the school setting. *Journal of Clinical Child Psychology, 20*, 140–151.

Miller, G. E., & Prinz, R. J. (1990). Enhancement of social learning family interventions for childhood conduct disorder. *Psychological Bulletin, 108*, 291–307.

Minton, C., Kagan, J., & Levine, J. A. (1971). Maternal control and obedience in the two-year-old. *Child Development, 15*, 256–268.

Minuchin, W. (1974). *Families and family therapy.* Cambridge, MA: Harvard University Press.

Moreland, J. R., Schwebel, A. I., Beck, S., & Wells, R. (1982). Parents as therapists: A review of the behavior therapy parent training literature—1975–1981. *Behavior Modification, 6*, 250–275.

Nay, W. R. (1975). A systematic comparison of instructional techniques for parents. *Behavior Therapy, 6*, 14–21.

Nixon, R. D. (2002). Treatment of behavior problems in preschoolers: A review of parent training programs. *Clinical Psychology Review, 22*, 525–546.

O'Dell, S. L. (1974). Training parents in behavior modification: A review. *Psychological Bulletin, 81*, 418–433.

O'Dell, S. L. (1985). Progress in parent training. In M. Hersen, R. M. Eisler, & P. M. Miller (Eds.), *Progress in behavior modification* (Vol. 9, pp. 57–108). New York: Academic Press.

O'Dell, S. L., Krug, W. W., Patterson, J. N., & Faustman, W. O. (1980). An assessment of methods for training parents in the use of time-out. *Behavior Therapy and Experimental Psychiatry, 11*, 21–25.

O'Dell, S. L., Mahoney, N. D., Horton, W. G., & Turner, P. E. (1979). Media-assisted parent training: Alternative models. *Behavior Therapy, 10*, 103–110.

O'Dell, S. L., O'Quinn, J., Alford, B. A., O'Briant, A. L., Bradlyn, A. S., & Giebenhain, J. E. (1982). Predicting the acquisition of parenting skills via four training methods. *Behavior Therapy, 13*, 194–208.

O'Leary, K. D., O'Leary, S., & Becker, W. C. (1967). Modification of a deviant sibling interaction pattern in the home. *Behavior Research and Therapy, 5*, 113–120.

Olson, R. L., & Roberts, M. W. (1987). Alternative treatments for sibling aggression. *Behavior Therapy, 18*, 243–250.

Patterson, G. R. (1974). Intervention for boys with conduct problems: Multiple settings, treatments, and criteria. *Journal of Consulting and Clinical Psychology, 42*, 471–481.

Patterson, G. R. (1975). *Families: Applications of social learning to family life* (Rev. ed.). Champaign, IL: Research Press.

Patterson, G. R. (1976). The aggressive child: Victim and architect of a coercive system. In E. J. Mash, L. A. Hamerlynck, & L. C. Handy (Eds.), *Behavior modification and families* (pp. 267–316). New York: Brunner/Mazel.

Patterson, G. R. (1982). *A social learning approach to family intervention: Vol. 3. Coercive family process.* Eugene OR: Castalia.

Patterson, G. R. (1984). Siblings: Fellow travelers in coercive family processes. In R. J. Blanchard & D. C. Blanchard (Eds.), *Advances in the study of aggression* (Vol. 1, pp. 173–215). New York: Academic Press.

Patterson, G. R. (1985). Beyond technology: The next stage in development of an empirical base for parent training. In L. L'Abate (Ed.), *Handbook of family psychology and therapy* (Vol. 2, pp. 1344–1379). Homewood, IL: Dorsey.

Patterson, G. R. (1986). The contribution of siblings to training for fighting: A microsocial analysis. In D. Olweus, J. Block, & M. Radke-Yarrow (Eds.), *Development of antisocial and prosocial behavior: Research theories, and issues* (pp. 235–261). New York: Academic Press.

Patterson, G. R., Chamberlain, P., & Reid, J. B. (1982). A comparative evaluation of a parent training program. *Behavior Therapy, 13*, 638–650.

Patterson, G. R., Dishion, T. J., & Chamberlain, P. (1993). Outcomes and methodological issues relating to treatment of antisocial children. In G. R. Giles (Ed.), *Handbook of effective psychotherapy* (pp. 43–88). New York: Plenum Press.

Patterson, G. R., & Gullion, M. E. (1968). *Living with children*. Champaign, IL: Research Press.

Patterson, G. R., McNeal, S. S., Hawkins, N., & Phelps, R. (1967). Reprogramming the social environment. *Journal of Child Psychology and Personality, 8*, 181–195.

Patterson, G. R., Reid, J. B., & Dishion, T. J. (1992). *A social learning approach to family intervention: Vol. 4. Antisocial boys.* Eugene, OR: Castalia.

Patterson, G. R., Reid, J. B., Jones, R. R., & Conger, R. E. (1975). *A social learning approach to family intervention* (Vol. 1). Eugene, OR: Castalia.

Peed, S., Roberts, M. W., & Forehand, R. (1977). Evaluation of the effectiveness of a standardized parent training program in altering the interaction of mothers and their noncompliant children. *Behavior Modification, 1*, 323–350.

Pelham, W. E., & Lang, A. R. (1993). Parental alcohol consumption and deviant child behavior: Laboratory studies of reciprocal effects. *Clinical Psychology Review, 13*, 763–784.

Powers, S. W., & Roberts, M. W. (1995). Simulation training with parents of oppositional children: Preliminary findings. *Journal of Clinical Child Psychology, 24*, 89–97.

Reid, J. B. (1978). *A social learning approach to family intervention: Vol. 2. Observation in home settings.* Eugene, OR: Castalia.

Reid, J. B., Patterson, G. R., & Snyder, J. (2002). *Antisocial behavior in children and adolescents: A developmental analysis and model for intervention.* Washington, DC: American Psychological Association.

Reisinger, J. J., Ora, J. P., & Frangia, G. W. (1976). Parents as change agents for their children: A review. *Journal of Community Psychology, 4*, 103–123.

Rinn, R. C., & Markle, A. (1977). Parent effectiveness training: A review. *Psychological Reports, 41*, 95–109.

Roberts, M. W. (1982a). The effects of warned versus unwarned time-out procedures on child noncompliance. *Child and Family Behavior Therapy, 4*, 37–53.

Roberts, M. W. (1982b). Resistance to timeout: Some normative data. *Behavioral Assessment, 4*, 239–248.

Roberts, M. W. (1984). An attempt to reduce time out resistance in young children. *Behavior Therapy, 15*, 210–216.

Roberts, M. W. (1985). Praising child compliance: Reinforcement or ritual? *Journal of Abnormal Child Psychology, 13*, 611–629.

Roberts, M. W. (1988). Enforcing chair timeouts with room timeouts. *Behavior Modification, 12*, 353–370.

Roberts, M. W. (2005). Timeout. In M. Hersen, A. M. Gross, & R. S. Drabman (Eds.), *Encyclopedia of behavior modification and cognitive behavior therapy* (Vol. 2, pp. 1070–1075). Thousand Oaks, CA: Sage.

Roberts, M. W., Arnold, S. B., & Mangum, P. F. (1992). The sibling conflict resolution scale. *Behavior Therapist, 15*, 254–255.

Roberts, M. W., & Hatzenbuehler, L. C. (1981). Parent treatment of command-elicited negative verbalizations: A question of persistence. *Journal of Clinical Child Psychology, 10*, 107–113.

Roberts, M. W., Hatzenbuehler, L. C., & Bean, A. W. (1981). The effects of differential attention and time out on child noncompliance. *Behavior Therapy, 12*, 93–99.

Roberts, M. W., McMahon, R. J., Forehand, R., & Humphreys, L. (1978). The effect of parental instruction-giving on child compliance. *Behavior Therapy, 9*, 793–798.

Roberts, M. W., & Powers, S. W. (1988). The compliance test. *Behavioral Assessment, 10*, 375–398.

Roberts, M. W., & Powers, S. W. (1990). Adjusting chair timeout enforcement procedures for oppositional children. *Behavior Therapy, 21*, 257–271.

Sajwaj, T., & Dillon, A. (1977). Complexities of an "elementary" behavior modification procedure: Differential adult attention used for children's behavior disorders. In B. C. Etzel, J. M. LeBlanc, & D. M. Baer (Eds.), *New developments in behavioral research: Theory, method, and application* (pp. 303–315). Hillsdale, NJ: Erlbaum.

Sanders, M. R. (1999). Triple P-Positive Parenting Program: Toward an empirically validated multilevel parenting and family support strategy for the prevention of behavioral and emotional problems in children. *Clinical Child and Family Psychology Review, 2*, 71–90.

Sanders, M. R., & Christensen, A. P. (1985). A comparison of the effects of child management and planned activities training in five parenting environments. *Journal of Abnormal Child Psychology, 13*, 101–117.

Sanders, M. R., & Dadds, M. R. (1982). The effects of planned activities and child management procedures in parent training: An analysis of setting generality. *Behavior Therapy, 13*, 452–461.

Sanders, M. R., & James, J. E. (1983). The modification of parent behavior: A review of generalization and maintenance. *Behavior Modification, 7*, 3–27.

Serketich, W. J., & Dumas, J. E. (1996). The effectiveness of behavioral parent training to modify antisocial behavior in children: A meta-analysis. *Behavior Therapy, 27*, 171–186.

Skinner, B. F. (1953). *Science and human behavior*. New York: Macmillan.

Sloane, H. N., Endo, G. T., Hawkes, T. W., & Jenson, W. R. (1991). Improving child compliance through self-instructional parent training materials. *Child and Family Behavior Therapy, 12*, 39–64.

Slosson, R. L. (2002). *The Slosson Intelligence Test Revised—3*. East Aurora, NY: Slosson Educational Publications.

Snyder, D. K. (1997). *Marital Satisfaction Inventory, Revised*. Los Angeles: Western Psychological Association.

Stayton, D. J., Hogan, R., & Ainsworth, M. D. S. (1971). Infant obedience and maternal behavior: The origins of socialization reconsidered. *Child Development, 42*, 1057–1069.

Tavormina, J. B. (1974). Basic models of parent counseling: A critical review. *Psychological Bulletin, 81*, 827–833.

Tavormina, J. B. (1975). Relative effectiveness of behavioral and reflective group counseling with parents of mentally retarded children. *Journal of Consulting and Clinical Psychology, 43*, 22–31.

Taylor, T. K., & Biglan, A. (1998). Behavioral family interventions for improving child-rearing: A review of the literature for clinicians and policymakers. *Clinical Child and Family Psychology Review, 1*, 41–60.

Thomas, B. W., & Roberts, M. W. (2006, November). *Training siblings to resolve conflicts*. Poster presented at the annual meeting of the Association for Behavioral and Cognitive Therapies, Chicago.

Ullmann, L., & Krasner, L. (1965). *Case studies in behavior modification*. New York: Holt, Rinehart and Winston.

Wahler, R. G. (1969a). Oppositional children: A quest for parental reinforcement control. *Journal of Applied Behavior Analysis, 2*, 159–170.

Wahler, R. G. (1969b). Setting generality: Some specific and general effects of child behavior therapy. *Journal of Applied Behavior Analysis, 2,* 239–246.

Wahler, R. G. (1975). Some structural aspects of deviant child behavior. *Journal of Applied Behavior Analysis, 8,* 27–42.

Wahler, R. G. (1980). The insular mother: Her problems in parent-child treatment. *Journal of Applied Behavior Analysis, 13,* 207–219.

Wahler, R. G. (1990). Who is driving the interactions? A commentary on "Child and Parent Effects in Boys' Conduct Disorder." *Developmental Psychology, 26,* 702–704.

Wahler, R. G., Cartor, P. G., Fleischman, J., & Lambert, W. (1993). The impact of synthesis teaching and parent training with mothers of conduct disordered children. *Journal of Abnormal Child Psychology, 21,* 425–440.

Wahler, R. G., & Dumas, J. E. (1987). Family factors in childhood psychology: Toward a coercion-neglect model. In T. Jacob (Ed.), *Family interaction and psychopathology: Theories, methods, and findings* (pp. 581–627). New York: Plenum Press.

Wahler, R. G., & Dumas, J. E. (1989). Attentional problems in dysfunctional mother-child interactions: An interbehavioral model. *Psychological Bulletin, 105,* 116–130.

Wahler, R. G., House, A. E., & Stambaugh, E. E. (1976). *Ecological assessment of child problem behavior: A clinical package for home, school, and institutional settings.* New York: Pergamon Press.

Wahler, R. G., Winkel, G. H., Peterson, R. F., & Morrison, D. C. (1965). Mothers as behavior therapists for their own children. *Behavior Research and Therapy, 3,* 113–124.

Webster-Stratton, C. (1981a). Modification of mothers' behaviors and attitudes through a videotape modeling group discussion program. *Behavior Therapy, 12,* 634–642.

Webster-Stratton, C. (1981b). Videotape modeling: A method of parent education. *Journal of Clinical Child Psychology, 10,* 93–98.

Webster-Stratton, C. (1982). The long-term effects of a videotape modeling parent-training program: Comparison of immediate and 1-year follow-up results. *Behavior Therapy, 13,* 702–714.

Webster-Stratton, C. (1984). Randomized trial of two parent-training programs for families with conduct-disordered children. *Journal of Consulting and Clinical Psychology, 52,* 666–678.

Webster-Stratton, C. (1989). Systematic comparison of consumer satisfaction of three cost-effective parent training programs for conduct problem children. *Behavior Therapy, 20,* 103–115.

Webster-Stratton, C. (1990). Enhancing the effectiveness of self-administered videotape parent training for families with conduct-problem children. *Journal of Abnormal Child Psychology, 18,* 479–492.

Webster-Stratton, C. (1992). Individually administered videotape parent training: Who benefits? *Cognitive Therapy and Research, 16,* 31–35.

Webster-Stratton, C. (1994). Advancing videotape parent training: A comparison study. *Journal of Consulting and Clinical Psychology, 62,* 583–593.

Webster-Stratton, C., Kolpacoff, M., & Hollinsworth, T. (1988). Self-administered videotape therapy for families with conduct-problem children: Comparison with two cost-effective treatments and a control group. *Journal of Consulting and Clinical Psychology, 56,* 558–566.

Weisz, J. R., Weiss, B., Han, S. S., Granger, D. A., & Morton, T. (1995). Effects of psychotherapy with children and adolescents revisited: A meta-analysis of treatment outcome studies. *Psychological Bulletin, 117,* 450–468.

Wells, K. C., & Egan, J. (1988). Social learning and systems family therapy for childhood oppositional disorder: Comparative treatment outcome. *Comprehensive Psychiatry, 29,* 138–146.

Wells, K. C., Forehand, R., & Griest, D. L. (1980). Generality of treatment effects from treated to untreated behaviors resulting from a parent training program. *Journal of Clinical Child Psychology, 8,* 217–219.

Williams, C. D. (1959). The elimination of tantrum behavior by extinction procedures. *Journal of Abnormal and Social Psychology, 59,* 269.

Wolf, M., Risely, T., & Mees, H. (1964). Application of operant conditioning procedures to the behavior problems of an autistic child. *Behavior Research and Therapy, 1,* 305–312.

Wruble, M. K., Sheeber, L. B., Sorensen, E. K., Boggs, S. R., & Eyberg, S. (1991). Empirical derivation of child compliance time. *Child and Family Behavior Therapy, 13,* 57–68.

CHAPTER 23

Cognitive-Behavioral Treatment

Lisa W. Coyne, Angela M. Burke, and Jennifer B. Freeman

If you have ever observed or listened closely to children in clinical situations, at school, or in a playground, you have most likely heard at least a few of the following:

- "She said no when I asked to sit at her lunch table. I'll never have any friends."
- "I can't do this math problem—I'm a total idiot!"
- "If I don't get this homework done perfectly, it just shows how stupid I am."
- "I'll never hit the ball, not even if I try a million times."

For a century or more, we have known that children aren't little adults (Kingery et al., 2006). However, like adults, they too experience cognitions that reflect irrationality or overgeneralization or catastrophic thinking. They may predict that small upsets in peer relationships will continue "forever"; they may interpret spelling errors as total failure; and they may describe normative fluctuations in mood as making life utterly impossible and overwhelming. Such patterns of thinking, in concert with individual personality characteristics and contextual factors, interact to determine both adaptive and maladaptive psychological functioning. Although prevalence rates vary with methodologies used, recent epidemiological estimates have found that roughly 15% to 22% of youngsters will suffer from psychological issues and their related functional impairment during childhood and adolescence (Costello, 1989; McCracken, 1992).

Cognitive-behavioral models posit that, like adults, children and adolescents have faulty beliefs and automatic thoughts that negatively impact their behaviors and contribute to the development and maintenance of psychopathology. Cognitions refer to beliefs, schemas, attributions, perceptions, or mental representations of events. Cognitive-behavioral theory is phenomenological in that it assumes that behavioral responses are a function of an individual's perception of events, rather than the events themselves. In other words, we imbue our worlds with meaning and respond to them in terms of these meanings. Attributions we make about the world may be more or less accurate and, similarly, more or less helpful in directing our behavior.

Recent approaches argue that cognitions may function as "rules." They suggest that because the behavioral responses associated with such thoughts are thus rule-governed, they may be especially intractable (Hayes, Strosahl, & Wilson, 1999). Very often, we don't have control over environmental contextual factors that maintain maladaptive behaviors. However, we do have access to thoughts and emotions: We can monitor internal psychological events, notice how they appear to be connected to behavioral responses, evaluate them, and, if we choose, engage in attempts to change them. Changes in thoughts are linked with changes in behavior, and thus, cognitive-behavioral theorists ascribe them causal status. As such, cognitive-behavioral approaches contend, our thoughts may be ideal targets for treatment.

Cognitive-behavioral therapy (CBT) has enjoyed a wealth of empirical attention over the past few decades. In the past 10 years or so, these approaches have been adapted for use with children and adolescents. Although originally developed for use with adults, child-focused CBTs are now numerous and have been investigated for youth of varying ages and across a variety of disorders. Whereas early efforts in treatment development involved downward extensions of adult models of CBT (e.g., based on the work of Ellis and Beck), newer approaches reflect more sophisticated thinking about the developmental nature of child psychopathology, representing more bottom-up innovations (e.g., Kendall & Hedtke, 2006; Kendall, Kane, Howard, & Siqueland, 1990). Interventions have been designed in more contextually and developmentally sensitive ways, thus expanding the utility of CBTs in broader domains and with more diverse populations. Recent advances include applications with very young children (Freeman, Garcia, Coyne, Leonard, & Compton, 2007), family-based CBT models (Barrett, Dadds, & Rapee, 1996; Freeman, Garcia, Fucci, Karitani, Miller, & Leonard, 2003), and those incorporating acceptance- and mindfulness-based approaches (Semple, Reid, & Miller, 2005), to mention just a few. Moreover, CBT has been adapted for use across multiple settings, including primary care, behavioral health, and with severely emotionally disturbed youth; for multiple purposes, including prevention and intervention efforts; and with diverse racial-ethnic populations. This chapter provides an overview of contemporary cognitive-behavioral treatments with children, discusses current research in CBT efficacy, with particular focus on childhood depression and anxiety, and illustrates an innovative use of family-based CBT for young children through a case study depicting intervention for a young child with Obsessive-Compulsive Disorder (OCD).

OVERVIEW

Cognitive-behavioral therapy is based on principles of operant and respondent conditioning. Consistent with a social learning perspective, CBT models assume that an individual's behaviors are a function of antecedent and consequent control. Contingencies may be directly experienced or observed. However, perceived environmental contingencies, in concert with individual characteristics such as biological predispositions, temperament, or personality, as well as particular contexts, interact to influence behavioral responses and dynamically developing repertoires. Cognitive-behavioral therapy holds that although distorted or irrational thoughts alone are not sufficient to precipitate psychological difficulties, they are a major contributor to maladaptive behavioral repertoires. As such, unrealistic or unhelpful thoughts and emotions are primary treatment targets in cognitive-behavioral approaches. Clinicians strive to help clients modify or reframe irrational thinking to effect desired changes in behavior. Thus, CBT dually targets client thoughts and behaviors to ameliorate symptoms and improve functioning. This is accomplished through a collaborative relationship between clinician and client that is at times didactic and at times experiential. Often, clinicians use Socratic questioning to call client attention to maladaptive thinking patterns and to challenge the logic of such cognitions. Treatment tends to be structured, goal-oriented, and time-limited and may be delivered in an individual or group format.

Although there is variation across different treatment manuals and clinical issues, CBT consists of three fundamental components: psychoeducation, cognitive restructuring, and behavioral experiments. *Psychoeducation* is perhaps the most didactic element of CBT and serves as an important first step in treatment. Children are educated about the role that cognitions play in their emotions and behavior. Clinicians help children recognize and monitor their response patterns and appraisals of problematic situations. By educating children about how their response patterns work, they may exhibit greater facility in applying their knowledge and new skills after treatment concludes and across different situations. Though psychoeducation is the first step in treatment, the education process continues for the duration of a given intervention.

Cognitive restructuring is the central cognitive feature of CBT and was originally defined by Albert Ellis (1962) and Aaron Beck (1976). Cognitive restructuring requires that children strive to do two things: first, identify their erroneous or distorted thoughts or beliefs, and second, dispute them. This "rational disputation" is the hallmark of this therapeutic approach. Contemporary conceptualizations of cognitive restructuring include a variety of techniques meant to help children and adolescents reframe or challenge their own beliefs, automatic thoughts, and schemas. Techniques include, but are not limited to, perspective taking, problem solving, replacing negative self-evaluations with positive self-statements, revising distorted views of social interactions and relationships, as well as more experiential exercises such as guided imagery and relaxation. Although these strategies may differ somewhat among CBTs, their overarching goal is to assist individuals in modifying the content of their thoughts, reducing their believability, and thus supporting the eventual development of more functionally useful behavioral responses.

Another core component of CBT is a set of skill-building techniques that strive to help children develop behavioral competencies for coping with difficult or feared situations. In this component of treatment, children are asked to try out a variety of responses, including testing their faulty appraisals, automatic thoughts, and beliefs through behavioral experiments. Two examples of this set of techniques are exposure with response prevention (EX/RP) in the treatment of OCD and behavioral activation in the treatment of depression. Exposure with response prevention consists of exposing children to feared stimuli, then preventing their ritualized response. In so doing, children experience their discomfort rise and fall and learn that the situations they have avoided are not catastrophic after all. Behavioral experiments can either be *in vivo*, whereby children practice engaging in the behavior, or *imaginal,* whereby they visualize the behavior and its consequences. In practicing this technique, children learn that they need not engage in rituals to reduce their anxiety and that they may use more adaptive coping skills to address their fears. This technique is most commonly found in treatment for OCD, although exposure is used more broadly across numerous child and adolescent anxiety disorders.

Behavioral activation involves pleasant event scheduling, which assists depressed children and adolescents in more frequently engaging in behaviors that will allow them to experience rewarding consequences. Engaging in behaviors that are either inherently reinforcing or that bring children in contact with naturally occurring rewards helps children to refute their beliefs of hopelessness and the intractability of their negative moods. It may also create behavioral momentum by increasing the density of reinforcers experienced.

Although each of these components is present in some degree in cognitive-behavioral treatments, some approaches rely more heavily on more traditional behavioral techniques (e.g., treatment for child and adolescent OCD), and others use more explicitly cognitive tools (e.g., treatment for depression or Generalized Anxiety Disorder) that emphasize the modification of thoughts, beliefs, and appraisal processes. The degree to which each of these strategies is used is in part a function of the childhood disorder targeted and in part a function of the age of the child or adolescent in treatment. Cognitive-behavioral therapy also incorporates a number of other techniques, such as problem solving and skills training, in the treatment of adolescent depression.

DEVELOPMENTAL CONSIDERATIONS

When using cognitive-behavioral therapy with children and adolescents, it is critical to evaluate the developmental stage of the client. Careful evaluation of the cognitive and emotional functioning of a given child will help guide the selection of therapeutic techniques and strategies: Children 8 and younger may have great difficulty with tactics such as thought monitoring and rational disputation, whereas older children might benefit greatly from these exercises.

Similarly, parents may be helpful as architects of their young children's attempts at behavior change, given that young children are far more dependent on parents for structure and guidance. The purpose of enlisting parents in treatment is twofold: First, they can ensure that behavioral changes and homework are occurring at home; second, the clinician can intervene in any parent behaviors that may inadvertently exacerbate the child's problems. In contrast, adolescents may benefit more if given greater autonomy to effect behavioral changes at their own pace, rather than as dictated by parents.

It is also crucial to consider the contextual factors that may impact a child's or adolescent's behavioral presentation. These include home, school, and peer environments. Depending on a child's age and interests, the relative importance of these factors may vary over time. For adolescents, peer relationships may stand out as a critical treatment issue. Young children, on the other hand, may be more influenced by their parents. Additionally, youngsters' functioning may differ across each of these environments; thus, using multiple informants (e.g., child, teacher, parent) to describe behavior in each of these domains is recommended.

Finally, a developmental perspective is important in helping to determine whether behaviors are timely and normative or reflective of psychopathology. One example of this is the topography of normal fears across childhood and adolescence. Fear of monsters under the bed is quite normative (if distressing) in preschool-age children; however, such a fear in a teenager might represent a hallucinatory event. Conversely, teens are often concerned with violence and unfairness in the world at large, but a 6-year-old overly concerned with terrorism might merit assessment for anxiety or trauma.

EMPIRICAL SUPPORT FOR COGNITIVE-BEHAVIORAL THERAPY WITH YOUTH

Cognitive-behavioral treatments have been used with a variety of child and adolescent disorders, including anxiety disorders (Albano & Kendall, 2002; Berman, Weems, Silverman, & Kurtines, 2000; Flannery-Schroeder, Choudhury, & Kendall, 2005), OCD (Franklin et al., 1998; J. M. March, Mulle, & Herbel, 1994; Piacentini, 1999; Pediatric OCD Treatment Study [POTS], 2004), depression (Compton, Burns, Egger, & Robertson, 2002; Crisp, Gudmundsen, & Shirk, 2006), eating disorders (Lock, 2005; G. T. Wilson & Sysko, 2006), Attention-Deficit/Hyperactivity Disorder (ADHD; Hinshaw, 2005), conduct problems (Southam-Gerow, 2003), substance abuse (Kaminer & Slesnick, 2006; Kaminer & Waldron, 2006), and trauma (Cohen, 2005; Cohen, Mannarino, & Knudsen, 2005). Gains following CBT appear robust over time (Albano & Kendall, 2002; Dadds et al., 1999; Flannery-Schroeder et al., 2005). A thorough review of the treatment outcome literature is beyond the scope of this chapter; however, in the following we describe the relative efficacy of CBT across childhood and adolescent depression and anxiety and briefly describe applications with each, as well as recent innovations in their use.

Cognitive-Behavioral Therapy for Child Depression

Data suggest that prevalence rates of Major Depressive Disorder (MDD) among children and adolescents are increasing (Cross-National Collaborative Group, 1993; Kessler et al., 1994; Kessler & Walters, 1998). Moreover, suicide is the third leading cause of death in children ages 10 to 19 (Centers for Disease Control and Prevention, 2004). Yet, in an overwhelming majority of youngsters, MDD goes undiagnosed for a year or more, and few receive treatment even by the end of adolescence (Jensen, 2006; Kessler, Avenevoli, & Merikangas, 2001; Leaf et al., 1996). Thus, the need for accurate detection, diagnosis, and effective treatment of depression during childhood is critical. Applications of cognitive-behavioral treatments constitute a strong attempt to meet that need.

Cognitive models of MDD highlight the role of maladaptive beliefs in development and maintenance of depression, although there is some variability across conceptualizations. Recent theoretical work has stressed the importance of evaluating cognitive vulnerability in context and has relied on diathesis-stress conceptualizations. As originally described by Beck, Rush, Shaw, and Emory (1979), depressed individuals are thought to have systematic biases in thinking that lead to idiosyncratic interpretations of events. Additionally, individuals who are vulnerable to depression appear to have schemas that guide information processing and may potentiate negative self-attributions that are at the heart of depression. Finally, cognitive models characterize vulnerability to depression in terms of the negative cognitive triad: negative perceptions of the self, the world, and one's future. All these increase an individual's risk for depression. Depression has also been explained in terms of Seligman's (1975) model of learned helplessness and as a function of negative attributional style (Abramson, Seligman, & Teasdale, 1978). This latter term refers to the tendency to attribute poor outcomes to internal, global, and stable factors and to ascribe positive outcomes to external, specific, fleeting, or transient factors. Some data suggest that links between attributional style and depression get stronger as children age (Nolen-Hoeksema, Girgus, & Seligman, 1992) and with the increasing sophistication of abstract thinking (Turner & Cole, 1994).

Research on CBT for adolescent depression has found it to be a promising treatment, although not without shortcomings (Birmaher et al., 1996; Brent, Birmaher, Holder, Johnson, & Kolko, 1995; Kolko, Brent, Baugher, Bridge, & Birmaher, 2000). Very recently, the most comprehensive study ever conducted on the efficacy of CBT for adolescent depression was completed (Jensen, 2006). The Treatment of Adolescent Depression Study (TADS) was an incredibly sophisticated, 6-year-long, multisite, randomized controlled trial comparing cognitive-behavioral therapy alone, fluoxetine + CBT, fluoxetine alone, and a placebo control in a sample of 439 adolescents with moderate to severe levels of depression (March et al., 2004). Results indicated that the combined CBT + fluoxetine treatment led to statistically significant reductions in depression compared to placebo. Data also revealed that neither fluoxetine alone nor CBT alone fared better than placebo, although fluoxetine alone had a slight advantage over CBT (March et al., 2004). However, other studies have shown that CBT and CBT + antidepressant medication were similarly effective in symptom reduction (Melvin et al., 2006). Severity of depression, comorbid anxiety or dysthymia, and family factors, such as parent psychopathology, parent conflict, low socioeconomic status, and exposure to stressors, predict attenuated treatment gains (Birmaher et al., 1996; March et al., 2004). In the TADS trial, age, expectations about treatment, severity, complexity, and chronicity also contributed to poorer outcomes (Brent, 2006; Curry et al., 2006). Further work is needed to better elucidate the efficacy of CBT and to develop more effective interventions. However, initial data are positive.

A meta-analysis of published studies on internalizing disorders indicated the following components as key features of CBT for depression in children: cognitive restructuring, problem-solving skills, decision-making skills, relaxation training, coping strategies, and skill generalization strategies (Compton et al., 2002). These combined strategies get at the main goals of CBT, which are to challenge and change thoughts, and then change behaviors. Recent data examining mediators of treatment response suggest that CBT effects treatment outcome though reducing cognitive distortions (Kolko et al., 2000). However, such data are scarce, and more research is needed (Chorpita, Brown, & Barlow, 1998; Kazdin, 2004).

The treatment of depression via CBT is a common practice for older children and adolescents, although randomized clinical trials are far more rare in younger children. However, one innovative cognitive approach to childhood depression is contextual emotion regulation therapy (CERT; Kovacs et al., 2006). The model on which CERT is based focuses on the emotion regulatory aspects of depression. In particular, youngsters who are unable to regulate their distress or dysphoria are at increased risk of developing symptoms of depression. Thus, treatment focuses on teaching children coping skills to reframe their experiences of compromised mood in terms of coping with accumulating stressors in their daily lives. A small, open trial in 15 children ages 7 to 12 years found that 53% of completers had full remission of dysthymia, and at 1-year follow-up this number grew to 92% (Kovacs et al., 2006).

Cognitive-Behavioral Therapy with Anxiety Disorders

Recent epidemiological data suggest that between 12% and 20% of children and adolescents experience clinically significant anxiety disorders (Achenbach, Howell, McConaughy, & Stanger, 1995; Velting, Setzer, & Albano, 2004). Although anxiety may change in presentation, it tends to be stable over time and if left untreated results in significant functional impairment in social, academic, and vocational domains (Gosch, Flannery-Schroeder, Mauro, & Compton, 2006; Velting et al., 2004). As was the case for depression in childhood, only a small proportion of children who suffer anxiety receive adequate assessment and treatment services. Thus, making effective treatments available is essential.

Anxiety has been conceptualized in terms of respondent, operant, and social learning principles. With regard to respondent conditioning models, the association of a neutral stimulus repeatedly paired with an unconditioned stimulus may lead to an unconditioned anxiety response. Unpleasant internal states, in addition to observable environmental stimuli, can also come to have elicitative properties (Gosch et al., 2006; Watson & Raynor, 1920). Mowrer (1960) argued that a respondent conditioning paradigm was not sufficient in and of itself to explain anxiety. He proposed a two-factor theory, which relies on both respondent and operant models. Operant models suggest that avoidance behaviors arise and are maintained by the reduction of fear and/or positive reinforcement by significant others, such as parents (Gosch et al., 2006; Skinner, 1969). Social learning models of anxiety hold that individuals may begin to doubt their self-efficacy in anxiety-provoking situations and thus learn avoidant repertoires vicariously, through observing others (Bandura, 1977). Cognitive models of anxiety, such as Rachman's (1991) neoconditioning theory, stress the importance of verbal constructions of events.

The use of cognitive-behavioral approaches for the treatment of childhood anxiety disorders has been well-studied. Empirical data suggest the efficacy of CBT across a broad range of anxiety and anxiety-related disorders, including simple phobias, Social Phobia, Generalized Anxiety Disorder, Agoraphobia, and Separation Anxiety Disorder (Albano & Kendall, 2002; Berman et al., 2000; Flannery-Schroeder et al., 2005). Findings are positive, and largely consistent, although some data suggest that children and adolescents who struggle with anxiety and comorbid depression may be less likely to complete or benefit from treatment. For example, in one study of exposure-based treatment for anxiety in children ages 6 to 17, results indicated that children in the treatment failure group were significantly more likely to have comorbid depression (Berman et al., 2000).

With regard to maintenance of treatment gains in anxious children and adolescents, CBT has been found to have significant effects at long-term follow-up (Albano & Kendall, 2002; Flannery-Schroeder et al., 2005). For example, one investigation of how children fared several years out from termination of treatment indicated maintenance of gains from CBT for anxiety at an average of 7.4-year follow-up (Kendall, Safford, Flannery-Schroeder, & Webb, 2004). This may indicate that the skills and patterns learned during CBT for childhood anxiety remain with the child throughout subsequent years and even into different developmental stages. Cognitive-behavioral therapy has been found to be equally efficacious at 1-year follow-up, regardless of whether it was delivered in an individual or group format (Flannery-Schroeder et al., 2005). Delivery of CBT in a group format provides an efficacious yet cost-effective treatment.

Cognitive-behavioral therapy has also been found to be an effective tool for preventing the development of anxiety in at-risk children. A study by Dadds and colleagues (Dadds, Spence, Holland, Barrett, & Laurens, 1997) examined the effects of a school-based cognitive-behavioral intervention program for anxiety disorders in at-risk children ages 7 to 14. Treatment focused on the use of coping strategies in group-based exposure exercises and included child management skills sessions for parents. Results indicate that children in the intervention group had significantly lower rates of anxiety disorders at 6-month follow-up. Intervention also reduced the rates of anxiety in those children who had mild to moderate levels of anxiety at onset. At 2-year follow-up, participants in the intervention group reported significantly lower rates of anxiety when compared to the monitoring group (Dadds et al., 1997).

Cognitive-behavioral approaches to anxiety disorders in children and adolescents contain the same core components common to CBT for other issues. Generally speaking, these include psychoeducation, coping skills training, exposure tasks, and contingency management procedures (Gosch et al., 2006). As in CBT for depression, psychoeducation aims to educate the children and their parents about the cognitive, affective, and physiological components of anxiety. Child behavioral responses to feared situations are typically conceptualized in two ways. Attempts to avoid feared situations or stimuli are described to children as "avoidant coping" and are discouraged. More appropriate replacement behaviors, classed as "coping, or bravery-based responses," are encouraged (Kendall, 1990; Pincus, Eyberg, & Choate, 2005). One well-researched treatment manual targeting younger children uses the analogy of a "scaredy cat" versus a "coping cat" to assist children in understanding and engaging in treatment (Coping Cat; Kendall, 1990).

Cognitive restructuring for child anxiety focuses on teaching children to test their hypotheses about feared situations by engaging in approach rather than avoidance behaviors. For example, socially anxious children often come into treatment believing they "cannot" tolerate their fear in social situations, or with certainty that they will do "something stupid," peers will laugh at them, and they will feel greatly embarrassed. Cognitive restructuring then revolves around approaching these thoughts as hypotheses and testing them via actually placing children in feared social situations and asking children to self-monitor their fear-based cognitions and check the degree of truth of these cognitions. Children may also be coached to use self-instructions, or positive self-statements, as an additional strategy to support the development and generalization of approach-based responses.

Exposure-based treatment components involve approaching feared situations in a hierarchical manner. Children practice "behavioral experiments," which consist of approaching feared stimuli so that they may watch their level of anxiety rise and then fall until habituation is reached. Children then progress through treatment until mastery is reached at each step; in other words, they have learned and effectively used their approach-based, rather than avoidance-based, behaviors.

Many manualized treatments for childhood anxiety have been developed in recent years and reflect innovative uses of CBT for a spectrum of anxiety disorders. For example, the Coping Cat Program (Kendall, 1990) is widely used and has versions for use with adolescents and school-age children. Other novel uses of cognitive principles are Pincus and colleagues (2005) adaptation of parent-child interaction therapy (PCIT), a well-established behavioral training program typically used with parents of young oppositional children, for use with young separation-anxious children. Two treatment phases in PCIT target the development of a warm and responsive relationship between children and caregivers and then focus on imparting appropriate behavior management techniques. To make it more relevant to separation-anxious children, Pincus and colleagues added a "bravery directed interaction" module in which parents are taught how to encourage approach behaviors and set limits around avoidance. This component specifically targets parent cognitions that may impede their encouragement of their children's approach attempts (Pincus et al., 2005). Other innovative uses include recent adaptations of CBT for groups of young separation-anxious children in the context of a summer camp Ehrenreich, Goldstein, Wright, & Barlow, under review) and for young children with OCD (Freeman et al., 2003).

Cognitive-Behavioral Therapy for Obsessive-Compulsive Disorder

Recent data suggest that CBT is a treatment of choice for childhood OCD (Pediatric OCD Treatment Study, 2004). When treating adults and older children, CBT with EX/RP is considered the first-line intervention (Franklin et al., 1998; J. M. March et al., 1994; Piacentini, 1999). Only recently has the efficacy of CBT, and in particular, EX/RP, been carefully reviewed and studied in children and adolescents (J. March, 1995; Piacentini, 1999). The publication of the Pediatric OCD Treatment Study, a multisite, randomized controlled trial, reported that CBT and CBT plus augmentative pharmacotherapy with serotonin reuptake inhibitors were efficacious in treating pediatric OCD. Although CBTs have been developed and effectively used for older children and adolescents, there has been growing interest in adapting this approach to younger children.

Until very recently, there were no cognitive-behavioral treatments available for children 8 and younger with OCD. However, Freeman et al. (2007) formulated a manualized CBT with EX/RP for early childhood OCD in children ages 4 to 8. Initial results from a small randomized clinical trial indicated that this treatment resulted in more positive gains for children in a family-based cognitive-behavioral treatment condition compared to those in a family-based relaxation treatment (Freeman et al., 2007).

Cognitive-Behavioral Therapy for Young Children with Obsessive-Compulsive Disorder

Onset of OCD has been documented in children as young as 3 years and may be more common in younger children than previously believed (Hollingsworth, Tanguay, Grossman, & Pabst, 1980; Swedo, Rapoport, Leonard, Lenane, & Cheslow, 1989). Although the presentation of OCD is similar across child and adult populations, the developmental context of young children complicates how cognitive-behavioral treatment may best be adapted. When using CBT with young children, it is important to consider (a) their developmental level and (b) their dependence on and involvement in their family system. Failure to address these issues would constitute significant treatment obstacles for the use of CBT with younger populations.

Developmental Issues

It is important to consider developmental factors in treating early childhood-onset OCD for numerous reasons. First, cognitive-behavioral treatments for anxiety and related disorders in children often involve the use of client-generated exposure hierarchies both in and between sessions. Young children may be unable to accurately collaborate in creating an exposure hierarchy due to their more limited skills in recognizing and articulating the level of distress or discomfort elicited by particular stimuli. This may lead clinicians or parents who assist with between-session homework assignments to implement exposure hierarchies that are too easy or too difficult. It is also important to note that early-onset OCD cases are more likely to have comorbid tic disorders and "just-right" obsessions (Geller, Biederman, Griffin, Jones, & Lefkowitz, 1996; Geller et al., 1998; Pauls, Alsobrook, Goodman, Rasmussen, & Leckman, 1995). It is difficult for children of any age to describe "just right" urges, but it is considerably harder for very young children to describe these urges. In a related vein, compulsive behavior in young children is not always perceived as ego-dystonic, but rather, as "just what kids do." Thus, it is important to include the observations of parents in developing an appropriate hierarchy. Additionally, it is useful to revisit the hierarchy in a systematic way during each session, to continually assess its level of appropriateness, and to provide opportunities to incorporate new information as young children progress through the treatment.

When treating young children, it is essential to use simple, concrete, child-friendly descriptions of symptoms or exposure tasks. For example, in J. S. March and Mulle's (1998) cognitive-behavioral treatment for older children and teens with

OCD, the disorder is described in psychobiological terms. With young children, it may be more useful to conceptualize OCD symptoms as a "hiccup of the brain." Younger children may be asked to label OCD symptoms with a silly name or to draw a picture of OCD as a "worry monster." Active participation in exposure may be described as "bossing back the worry monster" (e.g., J. S. March & Mulle, 1998, p. 152). Where possible, relying more on experiential tools in treatment is helpful. For example, active modeling of approach behaviors by clinicians and parents is particularly helpful for younger children.

When considering a plan for assessment during cognitive-behavioral treatment, it is helpful to evaluate symptoms and functional impairment not just at the outset of treatment, but throughout treatment, at termination, and, if possible, at follow-up check-in appointments. Systematic assessment assists in accurately and comprehensively describing treatment gains, as well as possible plateaus and exacerbations of symptoms. Before engaging in treatment, it is helpful to perform a structured clinical interview to assess the breadth of possible symptom areas given the high rate of comorbidity in childhood anxiety disorders, but especially due to higher rates and different patterns in young children relative to older children (Geller et al., 1996, 1998; Pauls et al., 1995). In particular, OCD is often comorbid with other anxiety disorders, mood disorders, tic disorders, and ADHD. With older children, the Anxiety Disorders Interview Schedule (both parent and child versions) is useful.

Family Contextual Issues

Consideration of family contextual factors that may impact how young children will respond to cognitive-behavior therapy is also critical. Young children are far more dependent on their parents for assistance and support than are older children. Parents of younger children are more likely to inadvertently reinforce or even actively accommodate their child's rituals (Lenane, 1989, 1991; Pollack & Carter, 1999; Steketee, 1997). Young children are particularly likely to involve family members in rituals, especially in the form of reassurance seeking (Lenane, 1989; Leonard et al., 1989; Rettew, Swedo, Leonard, Lenane, & Rapoport, 1992). Moreover, parents of younger children may have greater difficulty tolerating the distress that OCD symptoms precipitate in their children (Freeman et al., 2003). Thus, parents are often trained as coaches or cotherapists in CBT approaches with younger children. However, children who experience early childhood-onset OCD are far more likely to have parents who may struggle with their own OCD symptoms, other anxiety disorders, or depression (Nestadt et al., 2000; Pauls et al., 1995; Rosario-Campos et al., 2005). This is complicated by the fact that very young children rely on parents for guidance and direction in remembering and practicing exposure skills at home between sessions. This constellation of factors may lead to significant disruption of family routines and emotional distress as families progress through exposure-based treatment.

Parents struggling with their own compromised mental health may be less willing or able to actively support their children in treatment. In addition, they may have more difficulty tolerating their own or their child's negative affect during challenging exposure exercises (Freeman et al., 2003). They may also have difficulty modeling adaptive, approach-oriented coping strategies. Studies of child anxiety have shown an effect of parental anxiety on child outcome (Cobham, Dadds, & Spence, 1998). Whether parents use avoidant- or approach-oriented coping strategies with their own anxiety issues, they may be at risk of undermining treatment, whether intentionally or not. This may occur through overt resistance during sessions, noncompliance with between-session homework tasks, or potentially, more subtle indicators such as providing distraction for children during EX/RP or "bailing out" of EX/RP tasks before habituation occurs.

Family accommodation has been associated with a host of additional negative factors, such as less developed problem solving, higher rates of depression in family members, and more expressed anger (Amir, Freshman, & Foa, 2000; Przeworski et al., 1999). Because EX/RP requires children to resist engaging in rituals, such a treatment approach often causes a great deal of distress and disruption of the family. This, unfortunately, is a typical pattern in families of individuals with OCD and may be especially problematic in families of younger children. Thus, effective use of behavior management strategies is critical to support the effective use of exposure and ritual prevention, especially with regard to between-session homework.

It is not uncommon for parents to disagree about the nature or intensity of symptoms or about their engagement in treatment. Thus, clinicians should carefully consider viewpoints of both parents, in addition to children's own report of their symptoms. It is fairly common to receive discrepant reports about an individual child's symptoms across parents and the anxious child. In particular, children may report more distress than parents, although given young children's less developed ability to appreciate and express complex or intense emotions, the reverse may be true here.

Because of these complex issues, the direct involvement of families in treatment is essential. Direct involvement in planning, exposure, coaching, and psychoeducation may improve the child's treatment outcome, adherence, and motivation. Research has indicated that the addition of a developmentally appropriate family component to CBT leads to more positive outcomes (Waters, Barrett, & March, 2001; Wood, Piacentini, Southam-Gerow, Chu, & Sigman, 2006). This may be especially true for younger children with OCD.

The cognitive-behavioral treatment illustrated in this chapter reflects current clinical treatment outcome research investigating family-based CBT for young children (ages 4 to 8) with OCD. This treatment explicitly addresses young children's cognitive and emotional sophistication, the role of parents or caregivers, and common comorbid conditions (externalizing and internalizing disorders). To date, a preliminary clinical trial has concluded, and a larger multisite replication and extension is under way (e.g., Freeman et al., 2003). Initial results are promising. The following case study illustrates the adaptation of cognitive-behavioral treatment for a young child struggling with OCD and his family. It also describes the use of new advances in cognitive-behavioral treatments, including acceptance and mindfulness techniques.

Case Illustration

Identifying Features of Client

Max was a 5-year-old Latino boy presenting to an outpatient child anxiety treatment center that is part of a Department of Child and Family Psychiatry at a large public hospital in an urban setting. Max was brought in for an initial evaluation by his mother and was accompanied by his older sister, Nina, who was 9, and his infant brother, Carlos, who was 7 months old. Max appeared slightly tall and underweight for his age. He made limited eye contact with his interviewers. He was neatly groomed, although his clothing fit poorly and seemed to be several sizes too large. He was extremely polite during the interview, often replying "Yes, sir" and "No, sir" to the interviewer. He fidgeted and shifted in his chair throughout the evaluation and appeared to make some subtle facial grimaces, lifted his eyebrows, and moved his eyes upward and from side to side. Max spoke quickly and quietly during the interview and at times seemed distracted from what he was saying. This tendency was so pronounced that the interviewer prompted him several times to finish what he had started to say.

Max spoke English quite clearly, without accent, although the family spoke primarily Spanish in the home. Max's mother spoke some English, but often relied on Max or his older sister to translate the interviewer's questions and comments. The family emigrated from the Dominican Republic 2 years ago, when Max was 3. They moved to the United States to join other members of their extended family who live and work here. Max's father worked for an upholstery cleaning company. His mother stayed at home with the children and also cared for Max's maternal grandmother, who was infirm. The family rented a small second-floor apartment in a predominantly Latino neighborhood.

Presenting Complaints

Max's mother and Max himself served as informants. Max was referred for evaluation by his family physician after a visit during which his mother complained that he was often noncompliant and was very anxious about getting sick. Max's mother described him as "stubborn," always wanting things his own way, even if it bothered other members of the family. Her primary complaint was that Max spent a great deal of time in the bathroom, often using up all the soap, shampoo, and toilet paper so that there was none left for the rest of the family. Often, there was no hot water left for showers or baths. This was a particular problem due to the family's limited budget. Max also insisted that his mother wash his toys when he felt they were dirty, and he grew quite distressed if they were not "clean enough" or if she refused to wash them.

In addition to this, Max also was a "picky eater." Max's mother reported that she often cajoled and scolded him to eat his meals, but typically, he would take only a few bites. Max described feeling that there was something "wrong" with his food. According to his mother, he tended to get particularly distressed if different types of food "touched" or got mixed together on the plate. Max's mother also described incidents during which Max would come down to breakfast and refuse to eat anything, and she reported that he would not say why. When asked directly about this by the interviewer, Max simply sat silently. Finally, Max reportedly tended to hoard a number of items that did not appear to have any sentimental value, notably, used tissues, rocks, and twigs. Max threw tantrums if he was prevented from "doing things his way," according to his mother. He also sometimes hit or screamed at his older sister if she tried to "boss him," according to Max.

The amount of time Max spent washing, eating meals, refusing to speak, and hoarding objects had grown over time, and at the time of evaluation, constituted a significant proportion of the day. Max often missed opportunities to play with his older sister and with neighborhood children due to his involvement in ritualized behavior. In addition, his distress had also grown over time. At first, he did not appear to notice how disruptive his symptoms were and simply thought of them as "what I do." However, over the past several weeks, he had become more aware of them, concurrent with their increasing intensity. According to his mother, he described having more "bad days" than good days, and he sometimes cried in frustration at feeling that he "had to" continue engaging in rituals.

Max's mother reported that he was having difficulties at school, in addition to his struggles at home. According to her, his teacher was concerned that he had difficulty sitting still in class, completing tasks and art projects, and practicing holding and using pencils correctly. He also had some difficulty making friends and tended to play by himself on the playground. Occasionally, he got into physical fights with the other children, although he often denied this and would not tell his mother any details about the altercations.

Max's father reportedly did not think there was anything wrong with Max. According to Max's mother, he viewed Max as very similar to how he himself was as a child. Max's father felt strongly that Max's behavior was a "family issue" and that the family should not be seeking special help from another doctor. He believed that Max would "grow out of it" and was not supportive of Max's initial evaluation visit.

Developmental Factors

A number of factors were considered essential to adapting a cognitive-behavioral treatment for Max and his family. These included, first, assessment of Max's rituals as developmentally normative versus clinically significant. Second, it was important to determine Max's ability to recognize and express his anxiety in such a way as to contribute to building an accurate, workable fear hierarchy.

Parental Factors

Given Max's young age and relative dependence on his mother for guidance and limit setting, family accommodation of his rituals constituted a significant obstacle to treatment. In Max's case, there was already some evidence of his mother's acquiescence to his requests that she assist in his rituals. Moreover, other family members, especially his older sister, were considered unwitting participants in helping maintain his OCD-related behaviors.

In addition, several other familial factors stood out as potentially critical factors in using CBT effectively. First, his parents disagreed about the nature of Max's symptoms. His mother appeared concerned, at least enough to follow the advice given her by her family physician. However, Max's father saw his symptoms as more of an adjustment issue that Max would outgrow. Thus, the viewpoints of both parents, in concert with Max's own, were considered. In light of the parents' disagreement, the clinician decided to carefully observe Max's level of anxiety during sessions and to foster his ability to communicate how he felt throughout the treatment. Additionally, psychoeducation provided during CBT

(Continued)

helped to create more consistency in how Max and his parents understood his symptoms, his level of distress, and the functional impairment the symptoms created.

Given that Max often grew oppositional when limits were set on his compulsive behavior, his family may have been involved in subtle or overt accommodation of these symptoms. Again, educating the parents with regard to the nature of Max's noncompliance or distress around thwarted rituals was central to treatment. Highlighting the parents' distress when observing their son's discomfort when he was prevented from engaging in rituals enhanced parent treatment compliance. It was also useful to enlist the help of his older sister to prevent her inadvertent accommodation of his compulsions.

Finally, because Max and his family were Dominican, and perhaps more important, were recent immigrants dependent, at least in part, on an extended family network, the therapist took great care in assessing cultural differences in how young children were treated in both Max's immediate and extended family. It was also important to accurately conceptualize the degree to which the family had acculturated. In less acculturated Latino families, children may be given less autonomy than might be expected in the majority culture in the United States. However, there is such diversity in Latino groups that it is important that clinicians do not make assumptions about cultural differences (Szalacha et al., 2003). Both of these related factors impacted Max and his family's ability to understand, implement, and benefit from cognitive-behavioral treatment. Max's clinicians made every attempt to elicit and welcome discussion of cultural differences and to structure CBT in a culture-specific, culturally acceptable way. Failure to do so might have resulted in treatment resistance or even dropout.

History

Max reached all developmental milestones on time. As an infant, he had difficulties with transitions and novelty, often becoming overwhelmed when experiencing new situations, toys, or people. He stayed at home with his mother until the year of his initial assessment, when he began kindergarten at a local public school. At the beginning of the school year, Max had separation difficulties and often cried inconsolably when his mother dropped him off at school. He often sought reassurance about when his mother would pick him up from school and where he should wait for her when she did so.

Max had engaged in ritualistic behavior since he was 4, but this became more pronounced upon his entry into preschool. At age 5, one of Max's more involved rituals involved complicated sequences of events, which he requested his mother to perform, at bedtime. For example, Max required his mother to lay out his pajamas in a particular way on the bed and help him take off his play clothes in a particular order. After his pajamas were put on in a circumscribed sequence, Max brushed his teeth until they "felt" clean, which often went on for more than 5 minutes. Following that, he required his mother to line up his animals, tuck him in "just so," read three bedtime stories, and kiss him twice on each cheek. She then had to say "I love you" and "Don't let the bedbugs bite." Failure to perform any of these behaviors or doing them out of sequence caused Max great distress. If that happened, Max often cried until they could repeat the sequence correctly. Repeating morning routines resulted in lateness to school as well as general irritability toward his teacher and peers.

Most recently, Max had become concerned with "germs" and often complained to his mother that things were dirty and need to be cleaned. He made frequent attempts to have his mother wash his toys. She acquiesced because this placated him. Max was also very worried about toileting and spent an excessive amount of time cleaning himself after using the bathroom. This often resulted in dry, irritated skin and a great deal of discomfort. Other areas of concern for Max were that his food may be contaminated and that he felt compelled to keep nonsentimental items. His collection of used tissues, for example, constituted two large black garbage bags in his room. He became very distressed when any family member touched or moved the bags.

In general, the frequency and intensity of Max's rituals were exacerbated by stressful events. In addition, Max appeared to tic more during symptom exacerbations. Onset of his symptoms was gradual, rather than acute. As a toddler, he hated sticky or greasy substances on his hands and typically asked his mother or sister to wipe or wash them. He would tantrum until they did so.

Max did not have a history of significant medical problems. His mother had discussed Max's "picky eating" with the family physician, who reported that Max was "on the thin side" but that his weight and growth were within normal limits. Max's mother reported that she suffered from "nervous spells" and that Max's father was "moody." No other history of mental health issues was reported.

Assessment

Because Max was 5 and the Anxiety Disorders Interview Schedule for *DSM-IV* has not been normed in young children, a broader structured clinical interview, the Schedule for Affective Disorders and Schizophrenia for School-Age Children—Present and Lifetime Version (K-SADS-P/L; Chambers et al., 1985; Kaufman et al., 1997) was used to establish his diagnostic status. The K-SADS-P/L is a semi-structured, clinician-rated interview that yields *DSM-IV* diagnoses across the Axis I domains. The interview is administered to the parents (or primary caretakers) regarding the child, and to children 6 years and older. The K-SADS is routinely used to assess psychiatric diagnoses in children as young as 5 years (Hirshfeld-Becker et al., 2004; Youngstrom, Gracious, Danielson, Findling, & Calabrese, 2003).

The Children's Yale-Brown Obsessive Compulsive Scale (CY-BOCS), a 10-item semi-structured clinician-rated interview, was administered to assess OCD symptoms and severity at baseline, at midtreatment, at termination, and at all follow-up check-ins. The CY-BOCS rates obsessions and compulsions on 5-point scales on five dimensions (time, interference, distress, resistance, control) and yields a total obsessions score (0 to 20), a total compulsion score (0 to 20), and a combined total score (0 to 40). This scale has adequate psychometric properties and, more important, has been shown to be sensitive to change in both behavioral therapy and pharmacotherapy treatment studies. The CY-BOCS has been successfully used with children as young as 6 years (J. S. March & Leonard, 1998).

Because Max demonstrated some facial tics, the presence of a tic disorder was assessed with the Yale Global Tic Severity Scale (Leckman et al., 1989). This is a clinician-rated scale used to assess severity of motor or phonic tics, as well as related impairment. Motor and phonic tics are each rated on a 6-point scale

(Continued)

regarding number of tics present, frequency, intensity, complexity, and inter-ference. Motor and phonic tic scores may range from 0 to 25, and the com-bined total score ranges from 0 to 50. There is also an impairment score that provides a score from 0 to 50 that reflects overall burden due to tics. This in-strument has demonstrated excellent psychometric properties (Leckman et al., 1989).

In addition to these measures, more general indexes of functioning in both home and school environments were sought. The Child Behavior Checklist Par-ent and Teacher Report forms (CBCL; Achenbach & Rescorla, 2001) is a widely used scale with well-established psychometric properties used to assess an array of behavioral problems in children ages 1.5 to 18 years.

Max's clinician was interested in both the impact of treatment and the rate at which Max's behaviors changed. The clinician also wanted to provide feedback to Max's mother regarding her son's progress, in the hopes that when treatment hit a rough patch, the feedback would be a motivating factor for the family. Thus, symptoms were assessed at several points throughout the treatment. To assess symptoms at midpoint, termination, and follow-up appointments, the CY-BOCS and CBCL were used, as well as unstructured interviews with Max's mother and teachers. General indexes of functional impairment were used, including Max's self-reported distress and level of satisfaction with school, his peer relationships, and his interactions with his family.

It is important to note that the assessment measures just described have not been used extensively with minority groups. However, they were considered the most appropriate measures available for use in this case. Thus, the scores ascribed to Max from these instruments were interpreted with some caution and were reported to Max's family and teachers with the appropriate caveats.

Case Conceptualization

Max is a 5-year-old Dominican male who, after participating in an extensive assessment procedure, was diagnosed with clinically significant OCD and sec-ondary Tic Disorder. Although the externalizing disorders ADHD and Opposi-tional Defiant Disorder were considered, Max's presentation did not warrant as-signment of these diagnoses.

Obsessive-Compulsive Disorder in children, as well as in adults, is character-ized by recurrent, upsetting obsessions and repetitive, purposeful compulsive behaviors. Max's obsessions involved contamination fears: excessive and irra-tional worry about getting severely ill through exposure to germs and microbes, as well as contaminating others. He exhibited a number of compulsions related to these fears, including excessive hand washing, showering, and wiping after using the toilet. Max also had concerns about germs or poison in his food, al-though these worries included a general sense that "something was wrong" with his food when different food items touched on his plate. His compulsion regarding this was to refuse to eat or request a new plate of food items that did not touch. Max also felt compelled to hoard items that had no sentimental value and did not constitute items that would be considered developmentally normative to save. At school, Max reported that when he made pictures or held his pencil, it did not feel "right." Thus, he avoided coloring and writing altogether. If that was impossible, he would continue to make new pictures until he created one that was "perfect."

Max exhibited a number of motor tics, particularly facial grimaces, eyebrow movements, and shifting his eyes from side to side. Occasionally he did exhibit mild vocal tics, including clearing his throat and sniffing. However, the tics did not tend to co-occur and waxed and waned over time and across situations. They grew more pronounced in stressful situations or when Max felt vulnerable. The frequency and intensity of these tics was mild to moderate, and often Max did not realize that he was engaging in them. His teacher and the other children had begun to notice them at school; however, they did not constitute a significant source of distress for him.

Although Max was described by his mother as oppositional and noncompliant, those behaviors typically occurred in the context of ritual prevention. Rather than reflecting clinically significant oppositionality, they were more a manifestation of Max's frustration and anxiety when he felt compelled to engage in ritualized behavior. For example, Max's refusal to talk, although suggestive of oppositionality, actually represented his compulsive attempt to "protect" his family from contamination by germs Max breathed out. Max was also assessed for ADHD, in part because of a high level of observed activity as well as some symptoms typically attributed to inattention. However, interviews suggested that these were more reflective of his being distracted by obsessive fears. Given the high rate of comorbidity of OCD, ADHD, and Tourette's Disorder, Max would be watched over the course of treatment to remain vigilant for any changes in his symptom presentation.

Max's family had certain strengths on which to draw as they progressed through treatment. Namely, they were part of an extended family network that may be helpful in providing social support. Additionally, the fact that Max's mother sought the help of her family physician, and followed that advice to seek the services of a clinical psychologist suggested that she recognized a problem in her child's behavior and was amenable, at least initially, to participating in treatment.

Max's family was also characterized by what might constitute significant obstacles to treatment. These included many of the developmental factors outlined earlier, including Max's young age, his dependence on his parents, the family's potential difficulty in understanding the rationale of treatment, and issues with emotion regulation around his symptoms. Parental issues, including frank accommodation of Max's symptoms, his mother's level of anxiety and potential difficulty tolerating her own and Max's negative affect, and her lack of support from her husband, were complicating factors.

Course of Treatment and Assessment of Progress

Given Max's symptom presentation, in concert with developmental and familial issues outlined earlier, it was decided that Max would benefit from a family-based cognitive-behavioral approach, specifically adapted to a child of his age. This treatment was developed by researchers at Rhode Island Hospital/Brown Medical School in the Pediatric Anxiety Research Clinic (Freeman et al., 2003). The treatment was designed specifically to treat OCD in young children and, as such, does not directly target Tic Disorder. Treatment of choice for clinically significant tics would be habit reversal. However, given that Max's tics were not as pronounced or distressing as his symptoms of OCD, treatment was designed in a sequential way to address his OCD first.

(Continued)

The family-based cognitive-behavioral treatment was designed to address the unique needs of young children with OCD. In particular, it attends to young children's cognitive and socioemotional issues, the critical role of the family and their beliefs and behaviors around OCD symptoms, and the potential need for training in appropriate behavior management skills. Therapeutic material is tailored to younger children by including simple, concrete, child-friendly metaphors and experiential exercises. A great deal of attention is paid to young children's relatively less sophisticated emotion recognition and expression skills. Thus, a "child tools" section of each therapy session includes strategies to help children understand the treatment rationale and develop skill in acknowledging and expressing their anxiety along a continuum. The treatment also incorporates basic behavioral management strategies that parents may utilize in many situations, including, but not limited to, the child's OCD symptoms. These include overt modeling of approach behaviors, as well as psychoeducation regarding accommodation of symptoms. As an additional measure, the treatment deals with parents' and children's thoughts and feelings about and within their relationship and considers the role these may play in parent responses to child symptoms. Thus, both child and parent behaviors are targets of treatment.

Treatment consists of five main components, which are described next. This particular treatment was designed and its feasibility and efficacy compared to a family-based relaxation treatment (Freeman et al., 2007). It comprises 14 sessions. The first two sessions are with the parent(s) alone and generally last 90 minutes. The remaining 10 sessions include both parents and child and last approximately 60 minutes. Follow-up sessions are added as needed to address any residual OCD symptoms or symptom exacerbations that may occur over time. Because this is a manualized treatment, there is a suggested structure in the sequence of presentation of each element. However, as with most CBT manualized treatments, flexible use tailored to each individual client's needs is encouraged, with the constraint that all treatment components are eventually addressed.

Psychoeducation

During this portion of the treatment, the family is given education about the nature of OCD. Psychoeducation occurs during the first two sessions for the parents and the third for the child, according to the manual. However, in practice, it is also woven throughout sessions as needed. The main goals of this treatment component are to describe OCD as a neurobiological disorder such that it is understandable to the family. Oftentimes, parents who do not understand the nature of a psychological illness such as OCD are likely to blame their child or interpret symptoms as oppositionality or stubbornness. Similarly, they may be likely to require their child to "just cut it out." Providing detailed information conceptualizing OCD as a brain-based behavioral disorder helps to redirect parent change strategies in ways that may be more useful for their child. Thus, a second goal of this therapeutic component is to correct misattributions about OCD.

Children with OCD may blame themselves for their symptoms. They may also see their symptoms as part of themselves and view them as impossible to change. A core goal of psychoeducation is to help children view OCD symptoms as separate from themselves. This is accomplished through a number of strategies, including asking children to draw a picture of their OCD, asking them to think in terms of "bossing back" (see J. S. March & Mulle, 1998) their OCD instead of allowing the OCD to "boss" them, and drawing a map of what parts of their life are under their own control and what parts are under the control of the OCD. The overarching goal of therapy is to increase the domains of the children's life in which they, and not OCD, are in charge.

During this portion of the treatment, it is of utmost importance to describe to parents what they can expect. Treatment is designed to facilitate the child to participate in exposure and response prevention in a graduated way both within and outside of session. Parents are asked to become part of the treatment team and, as such, act as coaches for their child throughout the course of therapy. Because exposure and response prevention are inherently uncomfortable and stressful for children and parents, therapists must take care to address this issue in an honest and realistic way. Parents should be told that the treatment is often stressful and may disrupt family routines. If this is not carefully discussed, parents may have difficulty accepting their child's or their own affect during exposure exercises. This can impede the progress of therapy, lead to setbacks, and, ultimately, to dropout.

The following is a sample clinical transcript of how the therapist approached Max's parents:

> **Therapist:** First and foremost, it is important for you to know how exposure works and what it may be like for your family to go through it. Helping Max participate in exposure will be hard, although we will start with easier exercises, and then move on to harder ones. It will likely be stressful for you as parents to watch Max go through the treatment, and watch him feel anxious. He may get scared, sad, or angry. Those are normal responses, and come from being prevented from engaging in rituals, which he now uses to make himself feel better. Even though he will feel uncomfortable, and it may be hard for you to watch and participate in that, it is important that he continue the treatment, but also that he does his exposure exercises until his level of distress goes down. Through doing this, he will learn that whatever anxiety and distress he feels is simply his OCD bossing him around. And if we as a team help him put his foot down and stand up to his OCD, he will learn that he doesn't have to do his rituals. Eventually, our goal is to help him get more of his life back, so that he can do more of the fun things he wants to do, without being disrupted by his OCD symptoms. So if it gets difficult for you, try to keep that in mind if you feel your resolve weakening.

To increase both parent and child participation, it is important to make the process of psychoeducation as simple and interesting as possible. This not only assists therapists in building rapport with the family, but also sets the tone for therapy. Presenting the information in several modalities and using visual imagery, metaphors, and concrete examples make it more memorable.

The following is an example of how a therapist described the nature of OCD to Max:

> **Therapist:** Sometimes we all get thoughts that pop into our heads over and over again, like when a song gets stuck in your head. The problem is that sometimes those thoughts are *worries* and they scare or upset us. When someone
>
> *(Continued)*

gets lots of worries that keep popping into their head over and over again, and they feel scared or upset a lot, we might call these thoughts (for example) "The Worry Monster." To try to make those worries stop, a person might try doing some different things. Like, if someone felt dirty, they might wash their hands, or if they felt like they said something wrong, they might need to repeat it or apologize for it. These behaviors are called (for example) "re-do's." The problem is that you feel better for a second, but then you worry again and you have to do these things again and again. (Coyne, McVey-Noble, Freeman, & Garcia, 2005, p. 5)

To describe to Max how OCD might impair his functioning, the therapist relied on a comical, child-friendly metaphor:

Therapist: Imagine you bought a hermit crab and it was really cute and cool to play with. Every day you fed it and changed its water and hung out with it. That would be fun, right? Then imagine that it started to grow really big, and it started to follow you everywhere. Sometimes it even ate your lunch and your favorite dessert, and it annoyed you when you were playing with your friends and wouldn't let you watch your favorite TV shows, and it made a lot of noise when you were trying to go to sleep at night, and maybe even tried to sleep in your bed, which would squish you. Pretty silly, but not much fun, right? Then, imagine that it started being a really bratty crab and giving you little pinches unless you paid attention to it and gave it snacks all the time. Not nice. That's what happens when those worries take over and start being the boss of you. So, let's make you the boss of you and your worries! (Coyne et al., 2005, p. 2)

Parent Education

In addition to educating parents and children about the nature of OCD symptoms and distinguishing those symptoms from normative developmental rituals and any comorbid symptoms of other anxiety disorders, therapists also teach parents skills for behavior management. Although parents may enter treatment with their children at various levels of knowledge and performance of appropriate behavior management strategies, it is important to help parents strengthen this skill set and adapt it to their child's OCD symptoms. Tools addressed in this program include differential attention, modeling, and scaffolding. These skills are taught in session and practiced in the home. Therapists are trained to troubleshoot incorrect or inconsistent use of these skills and to help foster better usage, especially with regard to the child's OCD symptoms.

Differential attention refers to removing attention to a child's attempts to resist or refuse to engage in exposure or homework exercises, while attending to the child's approach behaviors. Use of this tool reflects the hypothesis that parent attention is an important motivational factor in CBT for early-onset OCD, as previous research has shown that family members often accommodate children's symptoms.

As previously discussed, parents learn to model approach behaviors for their children. Reasons for teaching this particular skill come from a social learning perspective that assumes that the parents' modeling of approach behaviors will help motivate and support their children in engaging in exposure and exposure-based homework during the course of treatment.

Finally, scaffolding (or coaching) involves parents' assessment (guided by the therapist) of their child's progress through treatment and encouragement of their child to engage in increasingly difficult exposures. It involves empathic encouragement and includes eliciting the child's feelings, use of a brainstorming approach to collaboratively come up with a way to approach rather than avoid the stimulus, choosing a method of approach, and implementation of that method. Clinicians may teach parents by example or in a more didactic way. Approaching the potentially hesitant child in this way helps to engender and maintain the child's positive momentum and may prevent treatment resistance or fallbacks. It also assists the child in learning emotional and behavioral regulation and the internalization of these responses. This is thought to promote generalization of gains made across settings and time.

The following is a sample of how the therapist addressed the brainstorming component of scaffolding with Max's parents:

Therapist: It is often helpful to brainstorm with your child reasons *why* he should do EX/RP. You might remind him about the hermit crab metaphor [see previous example], and say that OCD doesn't go away simply if you ignore it—it just gets bigger! Another way is to use the idea of "bossing back" OCD. You might ask Max who he wants to be the boss—himself, or mean old Mr. Worry.

Externalizing Obsessive-Compulsive Disorder and Exposure/Response Prevention

Exposure and response prevention is a core component of cognitive-behavioral treatment for OCD. This involves graduated exposure to feared stimuli and prevention of discomfort-reducing responses until habituation is reached. Generalization of exposure practice and response prevention is facilitated by the use of a token reward system implemented by parents. To that end, both parents and children learn to externalize, or separate, OCD symptoms from themselves. For young children, this is best accomplished through having them "boss back" OCD. Children also learn how to use a "fear thermometer" to help them report gradations in their experience of discomfort, whether to structure an anxiety hierarchy or to communicate rising and falling levels of anxiety during exposure. Parents are encouraged to use rewards to encourage children to practice EX/RP at home between sessions.

The following is an example of how a clinician educated Max about the use of a fear thermometer:

Therapist: Do you know how a thermometer works? (Child nods.) Well, my feelings thermometer works exactly the same way. When you don't feel scared at all, the red stuff stays down at the bottom. If you are sort of scared, the red is somewhere near the middle. If you are really, really scared, the red is all the way at the top. Can you think of how scared you might be if you were sitting on your couch, watching your favorite show, eating popcorn? Can you show me where the red might be on my thermometer? (Give child a chance to point out fear level, typically at the bottom.) What about if you were really really scared of heights, and you had to parachute out of an airplane? Where would the red be then? (Give child a chance to point out fear level, usually near the top.) Well, we are going to use this thermometer to figure out how much your OCD bugs you when you don't do your re-dos (compulsions).

(Continued)

Family Process Components

Family accommodation of symptoms is addressed very specifically via this component of treatment. This is often a process that continues throughout the course of therapy, as parent insight and ability to discriminate between accommodating and nonaccommodating responses grows. Sometimes parents are angry with or hostile toward their children, given that child symptoms have the potential to significantly disrupt family routines. In a related vein, parents may have great difficulty tolerating their own distress when watching their children struggle with symptoms. Thus, parents are encouraged to discuss these emotions, and in turn, to engage in more adaptive problem solving with regard to their child's symptoms. Finally, in this treatment component, therapists may highlight for parents their own anxious interpretations and behaviors about their child's symptoms.

The following reflects a conversation between the clinician and Max's parents regarding their feelings about his OCD:

Therapist: What is it like for you when you see Max struggling to wash his hands over and over?

Parent: Well, it's really hard. It breaks my heart to see him so anxious. I'd do anything to make him feel better.

Therapist: What are some things you do when you see him like that?

Parent: I try to tell him it's okay, but that doesn't help at all. I plan on extra time getting anywhere, because I know that Max will have to spend some time washing and checking his hands. I buy really gentle soap so that his hands don't get so chapped. I even write notes to his teachers when he is having a bad day, so that they will be more understanding and let him spend extra time in the bathroom, and he won't get in trouble.

Therapist: That sounds like it's pretty distressing for you as well, and that you try to do a lot of things to give Max the space he needs to do his rituals.

Parent: It is hard for me, but it's definitely harder for Max. I do what I can to help.

Therapist: get how important it is for you to help Max. I want you to consider this: What if Max had a medical disorder, like diabetes, and you had to teach him to manage his sugar intake?

Parent: Okay.

Therapist: What if he threw a really big fit one day, because he really wanted a piece of chocolate cake? Say his sugar was fairly high already that day.

Parent: Well, he couldn't have it. I wouldn't let him have it.

Therapist: But what if he got really upset?

Parent: Well, it just wouldn't be an option—it would make him sick.

Therapist: But it would be hard to say no, wouldn't it?

Parent: Sure, but I would know I was doing what was best for him.

Therapist: OCD is exactly like that. If Max is allowed to do his rituals, then he will likely keep having his OCD symptoms. If you help him learn to resist them, even though it will be hard, you will be doing what is best for him.

Contingency Management

In addition to the parenting tools described earlier, therapists also address potential (or actual) resistance to engaging in EX/RP by teaching parents appropriate limit setting. Sometimes young children develop compensatory strategies to cope with their OCD, such as oppositional behavior when required to approach a feared stimulus. If this is the case, clinicians may impart to parents how to effectively use response-cost procedures to address child resistance or token systems to encourage EX/RP practice. Once parents learn this component, their skills in this area may generalize to other domains of their children's behavior that are not specific to their OCD.

Mindfulness, Acceptance, and Values

What have been called "third wave" behavior therapies have developed technologies for addressing thoughts and emotions in a slightly different way than traditionally defined cognitive-behavior therapy. Acceptance and commitment therapy (ACT) is one such treatment paradigm. It may be classed as a cognitive-behavioral therapy in that it addresses the role of cognition in behavior. Thus, individuals progressing through the therapy learn to attend to their internal psychological experiences and the meanings with which they imbue external events. However, whereas traditional cognitive therapies conceptualize maladaptive behavior as the product of faulty cognition and therefore strive to change the content of such mentation, ACT stresses mindful awareness and acceptance of unpleasant or unwanted thoughts. As such, individuals are taught in an experiential way that they may simply notice and detach from their thoughts without evaluation or response. Doing so permits them to engage in valued, personally meaningful activities. Accruing evidence suggests that ACT may work through different mechanisms than CBT (Hayes, 2005).

Core components of ACT include mindfulness or awareness and valuing. Incorporating these components of ACT into CBT approaches may help to address motivational issues in treatment. Mindfulness has been defined in similar ways across the literature and generally means moment-to-moment awareness of one's experience—including thoughts, feelings, and physiological responses—without judgment. With regard to parents, mindful acceptance may help parents identify without response their thoughts and feelings about their child. This may minimize parent reactivity to their child's expression of strong emotion when rituals are prevented, and thus may help parents resist accommodation. For children, learning to be mindfully aware of their own thoughts and feelings in a detached way may augment their approach attempts during exposure exercises. Moreover, it may facilitate children's attending more fully to their actual experience of exposure, rather than their "stories" or expectations about how it will go. In this way, they may be more sensitive to actual environmental contingencies, and thus may benefit from exposure more fully. Finally, teaching mindfulness skills to children may help inoculate against mental rituals or "white knuckling" and engender more willingness to engage in exposure. This may also reduce the possibility of parents' coercion of the child into the exposure.

Here is an example of how mindfulness was used to increase the efficacy of exposure with Max:

(Continued)

Therapist: I am going to show you a way to be what we call "mindful" when you are doing your exposure work. We're going to practice being scientists. Do you know what scientists do?

Max: They find out stuff, I guess.

Therapist: How do you think they do that?

Max: I don't know. Maybe they watch stuff to see what happens?

Therapist: That's exactly right. Scientists watch stuff and see what happens. But here's the trick—they watch stuff without trying to change it.

Max: I don't get it.

Therapist: Think of it this way. When you eat an ice cream cone, what do you think about?

Max: Nothing, I guess. I just eat it.

Therapist: Yup. And you probably notice that it's cold, and that it's sweet, and maybe a little melty if it's hot out, and that the cone is crunchy, like a cracker, but sweet too. Well, that's like what a scientist does—noticing stuff, without trying to change it. That's what we call being mindful. Can we try to practice that right now?

Max: I guess so.

Therapist: Okay. Close your eyes...get comfy in your chair...notice how your body feels...where it touches the chair, where your feet touch the floor...notice all the sounds you hear...see how many different ones you can notice...see if you can notice how warm or cool the room is...see if you can tell what color the light is on your eyelids...see if you can notice your breathing, gently, in and out...notice that the air is cool when you breathe it in, and warmer as you breathe it out. Now notice what you are thinking...if you are seeing pictures in your head, see if you can print them on billboards on a highway...imagine that each thought or picture in your head is on a billboard...and just look at it until it passes and a new image pops in.

The therapist practiced this skill with Max in the context of his neutral thoughts, feelings, and bodily sensations, and then progressed onto distressing thoughts and images in the context of exposure exercises. Because mindful awareness constitutes exposure to feared psychological events (called *defusion* in the ACT literature), it is helpful to encourage children to practice it in a graduated way, just as they would with more traditional modes of exposure.

Mindfulness and acceptance are components that have been used in a number of different cognitive-behavioral therapies, including those targeting reduction of stress, depression, and anxiety (Hayes, 2005; Hoppes, 2006; Levitt & Karekla, 2005; Roemer, Salters-Pedneault, & Orsillo, 2006). *Valuing* is a component unique to ACT. It refers to activities and ideals that are meaningful and vital to an individual (K. G. Wilson & Murrell, 2004). Values are not goals; rather, they are directions in which to move. As such, engaging in a valued activity is inherently reinforcing, and self-renewing, since values cannot be reached, but rather, serve to direct behavior. Clinicians may harness valued action in treatment to help motivate parents and their children to engage and actively participate in treatment. For example, if parents feel that helping children engage in EX/RP is consistent with the value of being a good parent, this may inspire better treatment adherence, as well as dignify their often difficult work in and outside of session.

The following is a sample of how the clinician worked with Max's mother to identify her values with regard to Max:

Therapist: (After a brief, experiential centering exercise, eyes closed) I want you to imagine Max 13 years from now, at his high school graduation. There are many people at the ceremony, graduates, their families and friends. You see Max from where you are sitting. . . . As part of the ceremony, there is an announcement that one of the graduates will give a speech. There is silence, and you see Max slowly rise and walk toward the podium. When he reaches it, he clears his throat, and looks for you in the crowd. Notice his face, his eyes, the way he looks at you. He smiles. Imagine that he begins to speak about his struggle with OCD, and your role in that struggle. I want you to take a few minutes and imagine where you would like for him to be at that moment in his life, and how you would like him to describe your role in his struggle. (Pause.)

Mother: I want him to be happy, to be successful, to have a good life. I want to fight for him. I want him to say I fought for him, and that I helped him. That I didn't give up on him.

Therapist: (Pause) Is that what is most important to you?

Mother: Yes. More than anything. I want to protect him.

Therapist: What if our work here, even when it is at its hardest, is the best way to protect Max? What if it is a step toward Max having a successful, good life? What if this is one way you can fight for him, right now, by helping him to do his exposure work?

Mother: I would do it.

Therapist: Even when it is hard for him, and for you. . . and it will be, if it is to work. . . I want you to keep that picture of him in your mind, and in your heart. That will be our goal—to do the work here, now, that will help Max get to that place in the future, where he is living the life he wants, and doing the things he most cares about. You will help him get there.

Complicating Factors

Many factors that may complicate a family's progress through treatment have been detailed in previous sections. Two broad areas—developmental issues and parenting issues—were identified. Given Max's young age, his developmental stage and skills in emotion recognition and expression, care should be taken by his clinician to ensure that encouragement of these skills is woven into treatment. Similarly, given his developmental level, Max is more embedded within his family and dependent on his parents than an older child might be. This highlights the importance of motivating parents to become involved and to maintain their involvement in Max's treatment. One obvious difficulty is Max's parents' contrasting views of his OCD symptoms. His mother views them as impairing and emblematic of a pathological process; his father views them as a phase that he will outgrow. A clinician working with this family would be well advised to help build consensus between the parents, as well as to be vigilant for any parent behaviors that might undermine Max's treatment.

Parents may have difficulty tolerating their child's distress as the family progresses through treatment. This may lead to parent accommodation of child symptoms in the name of reducing child distress and minimizing disruption to

(Continued)

the family. Clinicians should offer support for parents in this area and take opportunities to notice, empathize with, and normalize perceived parent stress. Additional treatment components, such as motivational interviewing and acceptance and mindfulness-based techniques may be helpful with regard to facilitating treatment adherence in both parents and children, although data on these approaches are limited (Barmish & Kendall, 2005; Gance-Cleveland, 2005; Semple et al., 2005).

Max's Dominican culture may also prove to be a complicating factor in treatment, especially if the clinician is unaware of (or worse, insensitive to) important cultural differences that may impact treatment. Unfortunately, there is very little research involving anxiety in Hispanic and Latino cultures, and less in its particular subgroups (Varela, Vernberg, & Sanchez-Sosa, 2004). There is some evidence, however, that Hispanic Americans of Dominican descent may frame their troubling anxiety symptoms using idioms such as *nervios,* which may reflect a more benign, culturally sanctioned conceptualization (Salman, Diamond, Jusino, Sanchez-LaCay, & Liebowitz, 1997). This could suggest that Dominican families may view mental health issues, and anxiety in particular, as stigmatizing or shameful. This may result in a family's attempts to minimize or conceal anxiety symptoms and their related interference in family function (Salman et al., 1997). This view may be more or less pronounced, depending on differences in the level of acculturation within a particular family and its members. In Max's case, it may in part explain his father's minimization of his son's OCD symptoms.

When faced with families with racial and ethnic origins different from their own, clinicians should remain open and maintain the stance that clients are the experts on their own culture, degree of acculturation, and culturally accepted practices with regard to mental health issues. If issues of shame or stigma are identified, it may be useful to address these with the family in a nonevaluative way. It is important for clinicians not to make assumptions, but rather, to approach those from diverse cultural or ethnic groups with openness and respect throughout the course of treatment.

Treatment resistance constitutes another broad obstacle to treatment progress. For example, one hindrance to cognitive-behavioral treatment for young children with OCD is failure to complete homework tasks between sessions. To address this issue, clinicians should plan and troubleshoot homework assignments with great care. Some parents are more likely than others to comply with homework assignments. Reasons for variability in compliance include level of family disorganization, time constraints, parent accommodation and unwillingness to tolerate distress or disruption of family routines, poor planning, overzealousness, and failure to make treatment a priority. Clinicians should spend time assessing for these issues and making as detailed a homework plan as possible. It is also helpful if the development of such a plan is undertaken collaboratively, with compromises on the part of both family and clinician. Clinical judgment must be wisely used in terms of weighing issues of family skill, commitment to treatment, and logistical problems against the necessity of the child's engaging in sustainable, slightly difficult EX/RP exercises throughout the week. It is also useful to elicit information from the family about what worked and what did not, in the service of better planning future homework assignments.

Within-session resistance, whether from parents or children, may also be a problem. Parent tools, including differential attention, positive verbal praise, scaffolding, use of a token system, and limit setting techniques, have been incorporated into the treatment to address child resistance. Clinician attention to family process issues, such as parents' emotions and attributions about their child's symptoms, parents' role on the treatment team, and how parents cope with their own anxiety around treatment, is essential to treatment success.

Children, young children in particular, may have difficulty generalizing the skills that they learn in session to their lives more broadly, especially as time passes after treatment termination. Between-session homework addresses this issue, to some degree. As Max's family gained mastery over particular rituals, the therapist encouraged them to practice in a wide variety of settings, from home to school, restaurants, movie theaters, and elsewhere. The family was also encouraged to try impromptu practice; in other words, whenever Max's symptoms crept up, his parents were asked to remind him to use his skills to "boss back" his OCD. The therapist also educated the family with regard to the tendency of OCD symptoms to wax and wane, or shift in topography, so that they might be watchful and ready to use their skills as needed. The package of skills taught in therapy is conceptualized as a life change—one that the family must continue to practice as needed should symptoms return in times of stress or transition. Finally, the therapist highlighted major developmental events in Max's life—transition to first grade, increasing demands in school, puberty—that might herald periods when Max might be vulnerable to symptom recurrence or difficulty implementing his EX/RP skills.

Managed Care Considerations

Cognitive-behavioral treatments for children and adolescents are oftentimes constrained by managed care. Psychological practice undertaken in a managed care setting must address careful measurement of client progress and outcomes to justify continued reimbursement by insurance providers. There are many downsides to this situation, including reliance on "quick and dirty" assessment methods that may not capture the full complexity of a family's struggle, the fact that families that do not progress quickly may exhaust their allotted mental health services, and that some families have less access to needed mental health services because they cannot afford insurance. Some may view the increased accountability of health care providers, emphasis on developing more effective treatments, and greater emphasis on careful tracking and measurement of meaningful outcomes as positive consequences of managed care (Fonagy, Target, Cottrell, Phillips, & Kurtz, 2002). For Max's treatment, the clinician included multiple methods of measuring treatment gains, as detailed earlier.

Follow-Up Treatment

Follow-up visits were useful to continue to assess Max's symptom picture. In addition, booster sessions may be offered as his symptoms wax and wane or change in topography over time. Just as it is important to meet Max at his developmental level, it is also important to consider the demands of developmental transitions: progressing from kindergarten to first grade, the beginning of each school year, the onset of puberty, the increasing autonomy that comes with adolescence, and so on. The option of follow-up treatment is especially critical at these junctures, as families may need additional help tailoring their use of EX/RP skills in more developmentally sensitive ways.

(Continued)

Implications of the Case

The case described in this chapter illustrates that cognitive-behavioral therapy can indeed be adapted to younger populations. However, such adaptations must take into account issues such as the phenomenology of different mental health issues in young children, their increased reliance on and embeddedness in the family, and levels of cognitive and socioemotional sophistication.

Despite the increasingly recognized need, there still exists a gap in the treatment literature on the application of CBT to young children with OCD. The majority of the published treatment studies do not include children under the age of 7 or 8, nor do they address early developmental considerations. Though current clinical trials are working to adapt CBT with EX/RP for children ages 4 to 8, there still exists the need to address the unique developmental factors for this younger age group and its possible moderators of treatment. It is for this reason that treatment formulation for young children must be approached by considering all of these factors as well as any other developmental factors unique to a particular child. Comprehensive assessment of a child's developmental attainment and stage will allow for the augmentation of current CBT approaches that have been found to be highly successful in treating OCD.

Recommendations to Clinicians and Students

Increasingly, CBT approaches for children also address parent issues, such as stress, deficits in skills acquisition or performance of appropriate behavior management techniques, and parents' own struggles with mental health issues (Barmish & Kendall, 2005; Barrett et al., 1996; Chronis, Chacko, Fabiano, Wymbs, & Pelham, 2004). Given the increasing diversity of the U.S. population, coupled with disparities in access to and utilization of mental health services to minority populations, it is essential for clinicians to keep apprised of empirical research regarding the use of CBT with these groups. Additionally, the increasing use of acceptance and mindfulness-based techniques and motivational interviewing may open up new ways to improve and broaden outcomes of more traditional CBT approaches. Finally, although we as a field have accrued a good deal of evidence detailing the efficacy of CBT, we need to turn our focus to the mechanisms of treatment, as well as mediators and moderators of treatment outcome (Kazdin & Nock, 2003). Without investigation in this area, we will not be able to make continued advances in the broad goals of helping to ameliorate mental health concerns so that individuals may live more effective, meaningful lives.

SUMMARY

Cognitive-behavioral treatment approaches have been successfully developed and used with a variety of psychological issues in children, adolescents, and their parents. Although empirical data suggest that CBTs are efficacious in many domains and across many disorders, there is still room for growth and refinement in how they are conceived, operationalized, applied, and evaluated. Recent developments include applications with diverse groups, in diverse settings, using different media (e.g., virtual reality, computer-based programs, use of palm devices), and with younger children. In addition, clinical treatment researchers have been increasing their emphasis on mechanisms of action in treatment and mediators and moderators of treatment outcome. Taken together, these new directions promise continued sophistication, efficacy, and, hopefully, effectiveness in CBTs as the empirical literature continues to advance.

REFERENCES

Abramson, L. Y., Seligman, M. E., & Teasdale, J. D. (1978). Learned helplessness in humans: Critique and reformulation. *Journal of Abnormal Psychology, 87*(1), 49–74.

Achenbach, T. M., Howell, C. T., McConaughy, S. H., & Stanger, C. (1995). Six-year predictors of problems in a national sample of children and youth: I. Cross-informant syndromes. *Journal of the American Academy of Child and Adolescent Psychiatry, 34*(3), 336–347.

Achenbach, T. M., & Rescorla, L. (2001). *Manual for ASEBA school-age forms and profiles.* Burlington: University of Vermont, Research Center for Children, Youth and Families.

Albano, A. M., & Kendall, P. C. (2002). Cognitive behavioral therapy for children and adolescents with anxiety disorders: Clinical research findings. *International Review of Psychiatry, 14*(2), 129–134.

Amir, N., Freshman, M., & Foa, E. B. (2000). Family distress and involvement in relatives of obsessive-compulsive disorder patients. *Journal of Anxiety Disorders, 14*(3), 209–217.

Bandura, A. (1977). *Social learning theory.* Oxford: Prentice-Hall.

Barmish, A. J., & Kendall, P. C. (2005). Should parents be co-clients in cognitive-behavioral therapy for anxious youth? *Journal of Clinical Child and Adolescent Psychology, 34*(3), 569–581.

Barrett, P. M., Dadds, M. R., & Rapee, R. M. (1996). Family treatment of childhood anxiety: A controlled trial. *Journal of Consulting and Clinical Psychology, 64*(2), 333–342.

Beck, A. T. (1976). *Cognitive therapy and the emotional disorders.* Oxford: International Universities Press.

Beck, A. T., Rush, A. J., Shaw, B. F., & Emery, G. (1979). *Cognitive theory of depression.* New York: Guilford Press.

Berman, S. L., Weems, C. F., Silverman, W. K., & Kurtines, W. M. (2000). Predictors of outcome in exposure-based cognitive and behavioral treatment for phobic and anxiety disorders in children. *Behavior Therapy, 31*(4), 713–731.

Birmaher, B., Ryan, N. D., Williamson, D. E., Kaufman, J., Brent, D. A., Kaufman, J., et al. (1996). Childhood and adolescent depression: A review of the past 10 years. Part 1. *Journal of the American Academy of Child and Adolescent Psychiatry, 35*, 1427–1439.

Brent, D. A. (2006). Glad for what TADS adds, but many TADS grads still sad. *Journal of the American Academy of Child and Adolescent Psychiatry, 45*(12), 1461–1464.

Brent, D. A., Birmaher, B., Holder, D., Johnson, B., & Kolko, D. J. (1995, October). *A clinical psychotherapy trial for adolescent major depression.* Paper presented at the 42nd annual meeting of the American Academy of Child and Adolescent Psychiatry, New Orleans.

Centers for Disease Control and Prevention (2004). *Unintentional injuries, violence, and the health of young people.* Available at http://www.cdc.gov/HealthyYouth/injury/pdf/facts.pdf.

Chambers, W. J., Puig-Antich, J., Hirsch, M., Paez, P., Ambrosini, P. J., Tabrizi, M. A., et al. (1985). The assessment of affective disorders in children and adolescents by semi-structured interview. *Archives of General Psychiatry, 42*, 696–702.

Chronis, A. M., Chacko, A., Fabiano, G. A., Wymbs, B. T., & Pelham, W. E. (2004). Enhancements to the behavioral parent training paradigm for families of children with ADHD: Review and future directions. *Clinical Child and Family Psychology Review, 7*(1), 1–27.

Chorpita, B. F., Brown, T. A., & Barlow, D. H. (1998). Perceived control as a mediator of family environment in etiological models of childhood anxiety. *Behavior Therapy, 29*, 457–476.

Cobham, V. E., Dadds, M. R., & Spence, S. H. (1998). The role of parental anxiety in the treatment of childhood anxiety. *Journal of Consulting and Clinical Psychology, 66*(6), 893–905.

Cohen, J. A. (2005). Treating traumatized children: Current status and future directions. In E. Cardena & K. Croyle (Eds.), *Acute reactions to trauma and psychotherapy: A multidisciplinary and international perspective* (pp. 109–121). New York: Haworth Press.

Cohen, J. A., Mannarino, A. P., & Knudsen, K. (2005). Treating sexually abused children: 1 year follow-up of a randomized controlled trial. *Child Abuse and Neglect, 29*(2), 135–145.

Compton, S. N., Burns, B. J., Egger, H. L., & Robertson, E. (2002). Review of the evidence base for treatment of childhood psychopathology: Internalizing disorders. *Journal of Consulting and Clinical Psychology, 70*(6), 1240–1266.

Costello, E. J. (1989). Child psychiatric disorders and their correlates: A primary care pediatric sample. *Journal of the American Academy of Child and Adolescent Psychiatry, 28*(6), 851–855.

Coyne, L., McVey-Noble, M., Freeman, J., & Garcia, A. (2005). Using exposure strategies for young children with obsessive compulsive disorder. *Child Anxiety Special Interest Group Newsletter, Association of Behavioral and Cognitive Therapies* (3), 1–5.

Crisp, H. L., Gudmundsen, G. R., & Shirk, S. R. (2006). Transporting evidence-based therapy for adolescent depression to the school setting. *Education and Treatment of Children, 29*(2), 287–309.

Cross-National Collaborative Group. (1993). Major depression on the rise. *Clinician's Research Digest, 11*(3), 2.

Curry, J., Rohde, P., Simons, A., Silva, S., Vitiello, B., Kratochvil, C. et al. (2006). Predictors and Moderators of Acute Outcome in the Treatment for Adolescents With Depression (TADS). *Journal of the American Academy of Child and Adolescent Psychiatry, 45*(12), 1427–1439.

Dadds, M. R., Holland, D. E., Laurens, K. R., Mullins, M., Barrett, P. M., & Spence, S. H. (1999). Early intervention and prevention of anxiety disorders in children: Results at 2-year follow-up. *Journal of Consulting and Clinical Psychology, 67*(1), 145–150.

Dadds, M. R., Spence, S. H., Holland, D. E., Barrett, P. M., & Laurens, K. R. (1997). Prevention and early intervention for anxiety disorders: A controlled trial. *Journal of Consulting and Clinical Psychology, 65*(4), 627–635.

Ehrenreich, J. T., Goldstein, C., Wright, L., & Barlow, D. H. (in press). Toward a unified treatment for emotional disorders in adolescence. *Child & Family Behavior Therapy.*

Ellis, A. (1962). *Reason and emotion in psychotherapy.* Oxford: Lyle Stuart.

Flannery-Schroeder, E., Choudhury, M. S., & Kendall, P. C. (2005). Group and individual cognitive-behavioral treatments for youth with anxiety disorders: 1-year follow-up. *Cognitive Therapy and Research, 29*(2), 253–259.

Fonagy, P., Target, M., Cottrell, D., Phillips, J., & Kurtz, Z. (2002). *What works for whom? A critical review of treatments for children and adolescents.* New York: Guilford Press.

Franklin, M. E., Kozak, M. J., Cashman, L. A., Coles, M. E., Rheingold, A. A., & Foa, E. B. (1998). Cognitive-behavioral treatment of pediatric obsessive-compulsive disorder: An open clinical trial. *Journal of the American Academy of Child and Adolescent Psychiatry, 37*, 412–419.

Freeman, J., Garcia, A. M., Coyne, L. W., Leonard, H. L., & Compton, S. (2007). *Family-based cognitive-behavioral treatment for early childhood OCD: Preliminary findings.* Manuscript submitted for publication.

Freeman, J., Garcia, A., Fucci, C., Karitani, M., Miller, L., & Leonard, H. L. (2003). Family-based treatment of early-onset obsessive-compulsive disorder. *Journal of Child and Adolescent Psychopharmacology, 13* (Suppl. 1), S71–S80.

Gance-Cleveland, B. (2005). Motivational interviewing as a strategy to increase families' adherence to treatment regimens. *Journal for Specialists in Pediatric Nursing, 10*(3), 151–155.

Geller, D., Biederman, J., Griffin, S., Jones, J., & Lefkowitz, T. R. (1996). Comorbidity of juvenile obsessive-compulsive disorder with disruptive behavior disorders. *Journal of the American Academy of Child and Adolescent Psychiatry, 35*, 1637–1646.

Geller, D., Biederman, J., Jones, J., Park, K., Schwartz, S., Shapiro, S., et al. (1998). Is juvenile obsessive-compulsive disorder a developmental subtype of the disorder? A review of the pediatric literature. *Journal of the American Academy of Child and Adolescent Psychiatry, 37*, 420–427.

Gosch, E. A., Flannery-Schroeder, E., Mauro, C. F., & Compton, S. N. (2006). Principles of cognitive-behavioral therapy for anxiety disorders in children. *Journal of Cognitive Psychology, 23*(3), 247–262.

Hayes, S. C. (2005). Stability and change in cognitive behavior therapy: Considering the implications of ACT and RFT. *Journal of Rational-Emotive and Cognitive Behavior Therapy, 23*(2), 131–151.

Hayes, S. C., Strosahl, K. D., & Wilson, K. G. (1999). *Acceptance and commitment therapy: An experiential approach to behavior change.* New York: Guilford Press.

Hinshaw, S. P. (2005). Enhancing social competence in children with attention-deficit/hyperactivity disorder: Challenges for the new millennium. In E. D. Hibbs & P. S. Jensen (Eds.), *Psychosocial treatments for child and adolescent disorders: Empirically based strategies for clinical practice* (pp. 351–376). Washington, DC: American Psychological Association.

Hirshfeld-Becker, D. R., Biederman, J., Faraone, S. V., Robin, J. A., Friedman, D., & Rosenthal, J. M., et al. (2004). Pregnancy complications associated with childhood anxiety disorders. *Depression and Anxiety, 19*, 152–162.

Hollingsworth, C. E., Tanguay, P. E., Grossman, L., & Pabst, P. (1980). Long-term outcome of obsessive-compulsive disorder in childhood. *Journal of the American Academy of Child Psychiatry, 19*, 134–144.

Hoppes, K. (2006). The application of mindfulness-based cognitive interventions in the treatment of co-occurring addictive and mood disorders. *CNS Spectrums, 11*(11), 829–851.

Jensen, P. S. (2006). After TADS, can we measure up, catch up, and ante up? *Journal of the American Academy of Child and Adolescent Psychiatry, 45*(12), 1456–1460.

Kaminer, Y., & Slesnick, N. (2006). Evidence-based cognitive behavioral and family therapies for adolescent alcohol and other substance use disorders, In M. Galanter (Ed.), *Alcohol problems in adolescents and young adults: Epidemiology, neurobiology, prevention, and treatment* (pp. 383–405). New York: Springer Science + Business Media.

Kaminer, Y., & Waldron, H. B. (2006). Evidence-based cognitive-behavioral therapies for adolescent substance use disorders: Applications and challenges, In H. A. Liddle & C. L. Rowe (Eds.), *Adolescent substance abuse: Research and clinical advances* (pp. 396–419). New York: Cambridge University Press.

Kaufman, J., Birmaher, B., Brent, D., Rao, U., Flynn, C., Moreci, P. et al. (1997). Schedule for Affective Disorders and Schizophrenia for School-Age Children: Present and Lifetime Version (K-SADS-PL): Initial reliability and validity data. *Journal of the American Academy of Child and Adolescent Psychiatry, 36*, 980–988.

Kazdin, A. E. (2004). Evidence-based treatments: Challenges and priorities for practice and research. *Child and Adolescent Psychiatric Clinics of North America, 13*(4), 923–940.

Kazdin, A. E., & Nock, M. K. (2003). Delineating mechanisms of change in child and adolescent therapy: Methodological issues and research recommendations. *Journal of Child Psychology and Psychiatry, 44*(8), 1116–1129.

Kendall, P. C. (1990). *The coping cat therapist manual*. Ardmore, PA: Workbook Publishing.

Kendall, P. C., & Hedtke, K. (2006). *Cognitive-behavioral therapy for anxious children: Therapist manual* (3rd ed.) Ardmore, PA: Workbook Publishing.

Kendall, P. C., Kane, M., Howard, B., & Sigueland, L. (1990). *Cognitive-behavioral treatment of anxious children: Treatment manual*. (Available from P. C. Kendall Child and Adolescent Anxiety Disorders Clinic, Temple University, Philadelphia 19122).

Kendall, P. C., Safford, S., Flannery-Schroeder, E., & Webb, A. (2004). Child anxiety treatment: Outcomes in adolescence and impact on substance use and depression at 7.4-year follow-up. *Journal of Consulting and Clinical Psychology, 72*(2), 276–287.

Kessler, R. C., Avenevoli, S., & Merikangas, K. R. (2001). Mood disorders in children and adolescents: An epidemiologic perspective. *Biological Psychiatry, 49*(12), 1002–1014.

Kessler, R. C., McGonagle, K., Zhoa, S., Nelson, C. B., Hughes, M., Eshleman, S., et al. (1994). Lifetime and 12-month prevalence of DSM-III-R psychiatric disorders in the United States. *Archives of General Psychiatry, 51*, 8–19.

Kessler, R. S., & Walters, E. (1998). Epidemiology of DSM-III-R major depression and minor depression among adolescents and young adults in the National Comorbidity Survey. *Depression and Anxiety, 7*, 3–14.

Kingery, J. N., Roblek, T. L., Suveg, C., Grover, R. L., Sherrill, J. T., & Bergman, R. L. (2006). They're not just "little adults": Developmental considerations for implementing cognitive-behavioral therapy with anxious youth. *Journal of Cognitive Psychology, 20*(3), 263–273.

Kolko, D. J., Brent, D. A., Baugher, M., Bridge, J., & Birmaher, B. (2000). Cognitive and family therapies for adolescent depression: Treatment specificity, mediation, and moderation. *Journal of Consulting and Clinical Psychology, 68*(4), 603–614.

Kovacs, M., Sherrill, J., George, C. J., Pollock, M., Tumuluru, R., & Ho, V. (2006). Contextual emotion-regulation therapy for childhood depression: Description and pilot testing of a new intervention. *Journal of the American Academy of Child and Adolescent Psychiatry, 45*(8), 892–903.

Leaf, P. J., Alegria, M., Cohen, P., Goodman, S. H., Horwitz, S. M., Hoven, C. W., et al. (1996). Mental health service use in the community and schools: Results from the four community MECA study. *Journal of the American Academy of Child an Adolescent Psychiatry, 35*, 889–897.

Leckman, J. F., Riddle, M. A., Hardin, M. T., Ort, S. I., Swartz, K. L., Stevenson, J., et al. (1989). The Yale Global Tic Severity Scale: Initial testing of a clinician-rated scale of tic severity. *Journal of the American Academy of Child and Adolescent Psychiatry, 28*, 566–573.

Lenane, M. (1989). Families and obsessive-compulsive disorder. In J. L. Rapoport (Ed.), *Obsessive-compulsive disorder in children and adolescents* (pp. 237–249). Washington, DC: American Psychiatric Press.

Lenane, M. (1991). Family therapy for children with obsessive-compulsive disorder. In M. T. Pato & M. Zohar (Eds.), *Current treatments of obsessive compulsive disorder: Clinical practice* (Vol. 18, pp. 103–113). Washington, DC: American Psychiatric Press.

Leonard, H. L., Swedo, S. E., Rapoport, J. L., Koby, E. V., Lenane, M. C., Cheslow, D. L. et al. (1989). Treatment of obsessive compulsive disorder with clomipramine and desipramine in children and adolescents: A double-blind crossover comparison. *Archives of General Psychiatry, 46*, 1088–1092.

Levitt, J. T., & Karekla, M. (2005). Integrating acceptance and mindfulness with cognitive behavioral treatment for panic disorder, In S. M. Orsillo & L. Roemer (Eds.), *Acceptance and mindfulness-based approaches to anxiety: Conceptualization and treatment* (pp. 165–188). New York: Springer Science + Business Media.

Lock, J. (2005). Adjusting cognitive behavior therapy for adolescents with bulimia nervosa: Results of case series. *American Journal of Psychotherapy, 59*(3), 267–281.

March, J. (1995). Cognitive-behavioral psychotherapy for children and adolescents with OCD: A review and recommendations for treatment. *Journal of the American Academy of Child Adolescent Psychiatry, 34*(1), 7–18.

March, J. M., Mulle, K., & Herbel, B. (1994). Behavioral psychotherapy for children and adolescents with obsessive-compulsive disorder: An open trial of a new protocol-driven treatment package. *Journal of the American Academy of Child and Adolescent Psychiatry, 33*, 333–341.

March, J. S., & Leonard, H. L. (1998). Obsessive-compulsive disorder in children and adolescents. In R. P. Swinson, M. M. Antony, S. Rachman, & Richter M. A. (Eds.), *Obsessive-compulsive disorder: Theory, research, and treatment* (pp. 367–394). New York: Guilford Press.

March, J. S., & Mulle, K. (1998). *OCD in children and adolescents: A cognitive-behavioral treatment manual.* New York: Guilford Press.

March, J., Silva, S., Petrycki, S., Curry, J., Wells, K., Fairbank, J. et al. (2004). Fluoxetine, cognitive-behavioral therapy, and their combination for adolescents with depression. *Journal of the American Medical Association, 292*(7), 807–820.

McCracken, J. T. (1992). The epidemiology of child and adolescent mood disorders. *Child and Adolescent Psychiatry, 1*(1), 53–71.

Melvin, G. A., Tonge, B. J., King, N. J., Heyne, D., Gordon, M. S., & Klimkeit, E. D. (2006). A comparison of cognitive-behavioral therapy, sertraline, and their combination for adolescent depression. *Journal of the American Academy of Child and Adolescent Psychiatry, 45*(10), 1151–1161.

Mowrer, O. H. (1960). *Learning theory and behavior.* Hoboken, NJ: Wiley.

Nestadt, G., Samuels, J., Riddle, M., Bienvenu, O. J., Liang, K. Y., LaBuda, M., et al. (2000). A family study of obsessive-compulsive disorder. *Archives of General Psychiatry, 57*, 358–363.

Nolen-Hoeksema, S., Girgus, J. S., & Seligman, M. E. (1992). Predictors and consequences of childhood depressive symptoms: A 5-year longitudinal study. *Journal of Abnormal Psychology, 101*(3), 405–422.

Pauls, D., Alsobrook, J. P., Goodman, W. K., Rasmussen, S. A., & Leckman, J. F. (1995). A family study of obsessive-compulsive disorder. *American Journal of Psychiatry, 152*(1), 76–84.

Pediatric OCD Treatment Study. (2004). Cognitive-behavior therapy, sertraline, and their combination for children and adolescents with obsessive-compulsive disorder. *Journal of the American Medical Association, 292*(16), 1969–1976.

Piacentini, J. (1999). Cognitive behavioral therapy of childhood OCD. *Child and Adolescent Psychiatric Clinics of North America, 8*, 599–616.

Pincus, D. B., Eyberg, S. M., & Choate, M. L. (2005). Adapting parent-child interaction therapy for young children with separation anxiety disorder. *Education and Treatment of Children, 28*(2), 163–181.

Pollack, R. A., & Carter, A. S. (1999). The familial and developmental context of obsessive-compulsive disorder. *Child and Adolescent Psychiatric Clinics of North America, 8*(3), 461–479.

Przeworski, A., Nelson, A., Zoellner, L., Snyderman, T., Franklin, M. E., March, J., et al. (1999 November). *Expressed emotion and pediatric OCD.* Paper presented at the 33rd annual convention of the Association for Advancement of Behavior Therapy, Toronto, Canada.

Rachman, S. J. (1991). Neoconditioning and the classical theory of fear acquisition. *Clinical Psychology Review, 11*, 155–173.

Rettew, D. C., Swedo, S. E., Leonard, H. L., Lenane, M. C., & Rapoport, J. L. (1992). Obsessions and compulsions across time in 79 children with obsessive compulsive disorder. *Journal of the American Academy of Child and Adolescent Psychiatry, 31*(6), 1050–1056.

Roemer, L., Salters-Pedneault, K., & Orsillo, S. M. (2006). Incorporating mindfulness- and acceptance-based strategies in the treatment of generalized anxiety disorder. In R. A. Baer (Ed.), *Mindfulness-based treatment approaches: Clinician's guide to evidence base and applications* (pp. 51–74). San Diego, CA: Elsevier Academic Press.

Rosario-Campos, M. C., Leckman, J. F., Curi, M., Quatrano, S., Katsovitch, L., & Miguel, E. C., et al. (2005). A family study of early-onset obsessive compulsive disorder. *American Journal of Medical Genetics: Part B, 136*, 92–97.

Salman, E., Diamond, K., Jusino, C., Sanchez-LaCay, A., & Liebowitz, M. R. (1997). Hispanic Americans, In S. Friedman (Ed.), *Cultural issues in the treatment of anxiety* (pp. 59–80). New York: Guilford Press.

Seligman, M. E. P. (1975). *Helplessness: On depression, development, and death.* San Francisco: Freeman.

Semple, R. J., Reid, E. F. G., & Miller, L. (2005). Treating anxiety with mindfulness: An open trial of mindfulness training for anxious children. *Journal of Cognitive Psychotherapy, 19*(4), 379–392.

Skinner, B. F. (1969). *Contingencies of reinforcement.* New York: Appleton-Century-Crofts.

Southam-Gerow, M. A. (2003). Child-focused cognitive-behavioral therapies, In C. A. Essay (Ed.), *Conduct and oppositional defiant disorders: Epidemiology, risk factors, and treatment* (pp. 257–277). Mahwah, NJ: Erlbaum.

Steketee, G. (1997). Disability and family burden in obsessive-compulsive disorder. *Canadian Journal of Psychiatry, 42*, 919–928.

Swedo, S., Rapoport, J., Leonard, H., Lenane, M. C., & Cheslow, D. L. (1989). Obsessive compulsive disorders in children and adolescents: Clinical phenomenology of 70 consecutive cases. *Archives General Psychiatry, 46*, 335–343.

Szalacha, L. A., Erkut, S., Garcia Coll, C., Fields, J., Alarcon, O., & Ceder, I. (2003). Perceived discrimination and resilience. In S. S. Luther (Ed.), *Resilience and vulnerability: Adaptation in the context of childhood adversities* (pp. 414–435). New York: Cambridge University Press.

Turner, J. E., & Cole, D. A. (1994). Developmental differences in cognitive diatheses for child depression. *Journal of Abnormal Child Psychology, 22*(1), 15–32.

Valleni-Basile, L. A., Garrison, C. Z., Jackson, K. L., Walter, J. L., McKeown, R. E., Addy, C. L., et al. (1994). Frequency of obsessive-compulsive disorder in a community sample of young adolescents. *Journal of the American Academy of Child and Adolescent Psychiatry, 33*(6), 782–791.

Varela, R. E., Vernberg, E. M., & Sanchez-Sosa, J. J. (2004). Anxiety reporting and culturally associated interpretation biases and cognitive schemas: A comparison of Mexican, Mexican American, and European American families. *Journal of Clinical Child and Adolescent Psychology, 32*(2), 237–247.

Velting, O. N., Setzer, N. J., & Albano, A. M. (2004). Update on and advances in assessment and cognitive-behavioral treatment of anxiety disorders in children and adolescents. *Professional Psychology: Research and Practice, 35*(1), 42–54.

Waters, T. L., Barrett, P. M., & March, J. S. (2001). Cognitive-behavioral family therapy of childhood obsessive-compulsive disorder: Preliminary findings. *American Journal of Psychotherapy, 55*(3), 372–387.

Watson, J. B., & Raynor, R. (1920). Conditioned emotional reactions. *Journal of Experimental Psychology, 3*(1), 1–14.

Wilson, G. T., & Sysko, R. (2006). Cognitive-behavioural therapy for adolescents with bulimia nervosa. *European Eating Disorders Review, 14*(1), 8–16.

Wilson, K. G., & Murrell, A. R. (2004). Values work in acceptance and commitment therapy: Setting a course for behavioral treatment. In S. C. Hayes, V. M. Follette, & M. M. Linehan (Eds.), *Mindfulness and acceptance: Expanding the cognitive-behavioral tradition* (pp. 120–151). New York: Guilford Press.

Wood, J. J., Piacentini, J. C., Southam-Gerow, M., Chu, B. C., & Sigman, M. (2006). Family cognitive behavioral therapy for child anxiety disorders. *Journal of the American Academy of Child and Adolescent Psychiatry, 43*(3), 314–321.

Youngstrom, E. A., Gracious, B. L., Danielson, C. K., Findling, R. L., & Calabrese, J. (2003). Toward an integration of parent and clinician report on the Young Mania Rating Scale. *Journal of Affective Disorders, 77*, 179–190.

CHAPTER 24

Primary Care Behavioral Pediatrics

Patrick C. Friman

Children are not born civilized and socialized. They do not emerge from the womb predisposed to use the toilet appropriately, sleep through the night on their own, wait their turn, sit still or be quiet when stillness or quiet are called for, or to exhibit any of the myriad behavioral requirements of civilized society. Unfortunately for parents, teachers and other caretakers, some children will resist most, and most children will resist some, critical aspects of the socialization and education processes in this culture, and a vast number and array of child behavior problems are the result (e.g., American Academy of Pediatrics, 2001; Christophersen, 1982; Christophersen & Rapoff, 1979; Costello & Shugart, 1992; Earls, 1980). For example, nutritional and maturational health is predicated on food preferences that include the major food groups, and yet many children, apparently satisfied with milk and pureed food, resist parental attempts to introduce new tastes and textures into the daily diet. Adaptive child performance during the day is dependent on receipt of adequate sleep at night, yet many children resist parental efforts to impose a reasonable bedtime. Most parents, preschools, and many day care programs require full toilet training during the third year of life, yet many children resist parental training efforts. Success in most life situations requires a reasonable amount of instructional control, yet many children resist following important adult instructions. There are many other examples, and they generally emerge in situations that require child adherence to or conformance with the family, school, or societal standards or requirements. There are also a large number of child problems that do not involve child resistance so much as child inability to perform, maintain, reduce, or cease important behavior. Although all of these problems pose risks for the child and family, they mostly represent skill deficits rather than pathologies, especially in young children (e.g., Christophersen, 1982, 1988; Friman, 2002; Earls, 1980; also see Horwitz, 2002). An obstacle for mental health practitioners interested in addressing these problems is that they are much more likely to surface initially in primary medical care (PMC) than in mental health service (MHS) settings (e.g., American Academy of Pediatrics, 2001; Costello, 1988; Costello, Burns, et al., 1988; Costello, Edelbrock, et al., 1988; Costello & Shugart, 1992; Dulcan et al., 1990; Goldberg, Roghmann, McInerny, & Burke, 1984; Hickson, Altemeier, & O'Connor, 1983; Horwitz, Leaf, Leventhal, Forsyth, & Speechley, 1992; Lavigne et al., 1993; Starfield et al., 1980).

Although the skills children need to overcome these problems can emerge through vicarious experiences, most skills have to be trained directly by parents or caregivers. Unfortunately, there is an implicit assumption in this culture that those who provide the training should be able to do so without benefit of MHS. Although there is substantially more cultural permission to seek assistance with child behavior problems in PMC settings, as well as a much greater likelihood of parents doing so, the structure of typical PMC visits imposes substantial limits on the assistance actually made available (e.g., Finney et al., 1990; Wissow et al., 2002). Mental health service is vouchsafed by the culture only when child behavior problems reflect significant deviations from cultural norms (e.g., it meets criteria for a psychiatric diagnosis; American Psychiatric Association, 1994); correspondingly, costs accrued from obtaining MHS for such problems are usually reimbursable through third-party payers. Some assistance for problems that are not considered clinically significant is available outside of MHS and PMC (e.g., websites, books, television shows, lay counseling), which is fortunate for parents because they appear to be mostly on their own when training children whose behavior problems are not considered clinically significant. Unfortunately, the quality of that assistance is hard to determine and impossible to guarantee to any meaningful degree, and reimbursement for it is not available from third-party payers. In addition to that assistance, there are multiple child training methods that are an integral part of the parenting process in this country, and virtually all parents have direct access to them. Prominent examples include praising, scolding, yelling, warning, restrictions, and rewards (e.g., Blum, Williams, Friman, & Christophersen, 1995; Peters, 1998; Regalado, Sereen, Inkelas, Wissow, & Halfon, 2004) and a range of methods collectively referred to as time-out (Friman, 2005c; Friman & Finney, 2003). How well the nonprofessional assistance and freely available training methods work can be estimated through inspection of epidemiological surveys of children whose behavioral concerns meet criteria for diagnostic classification; presumably these are children whose behavior has been exposed to some combination of the assistance and the methods. Major surveys indicate that between 11% and 25% of children in this country have behavioral problems that meet criteria for a psychiatric diagnosis (cf. American Academy of Pediatrics, 2001; Costello, 1988; Costello, Burns, et al., 1988; Costello, Edelbrock, et al., 1988; Costello & Shugart, 1992; Dulcan et al., 1990; Goldberg et al., 1984; Hickson et al., 1983; Lavigne et al., 1993; Starfield et al., 1980). These data suggest that a substantial portion of child behavior problems, although not initially deviant from cultural norms, devolve to something much more serious and that a very large number of parents need more help addressing the problems than is made available to them outside of professional contexts.

The two most logical sources of professional help are PMC (e.g., pediatricians) and MHS (e.g., psychologists). The former source is utilized by virtually all parents, although mostly for medical care. Nonetheless, child behavior problems are much more likely to be initially presented in PMC than MHS. Unfortunately, service seeking for children with behavior problems presenting in PMC is restricted by three challenges: limited time, training, and reimbursement. Regarding limited time, early time-and-motion studies showed that the length of the average visit in

PMC for children was between 8 and 15 minutes, with only a small portion of that time devoted to behavior (Christophersen, 1982; Reisinger & Bires, 1980); more current research shows that these early findings have not changed appreciably in recent times (Cooper, Valleley, Polaha, Begeny, & Evans, 2005). Regarding limited training, the curriculum for physicians planning to work in pediatric settings has historically included very little training for assessing and treating behavior problems (e.g., Friedman, Phillips, & Parrish, 1983; Glasscock, O'Brien, Friman, Christophersen, & MacLean, 1989), although the American Academy of Pediatrics is attempting to remedy this problem by requiring a rotation in developmental-behavioral pediatrics (2001; Hagan, 2001). The average rotation, however, is only a month long, which is certainly better than no training at all but is hardly sufficient to develop the expertise necessary to identify and manage the range and number of behavior problems that present in PMC. Regarding reimbursement, physician provision of behavior assessment and treatment involves services that managed care companies are increasingly reluctant to cover (Kelleher, Scholle, Feldman, & Nace, 1999), resulting in non-revenue-generation time by PMC providers and/or limits on services for child behavior problems supplied by PMC providers.

In MHS, providers typically have both the time and the training to competently assess and treat child behavior problems, and they have a service code and nosological system that can lead more effectively to reimbursement for related services than the system used in PMC. Unfortunately, whereas very few parents have reservations about seeking advice about child behavior problems from providers in PMC, many parents have substantial reservations about seeking advice from providers in MHS. Among the reasons for these reservations are the routine use of psychopathology in the conceptualization of child behavior problems, the related stigma associated with the failure of tactics available outside professional contexts to address the problems, the common reliance on strong medication in treatment, high costs, and fear of permanent labeling by third-party payers. To phrase this point in blunt colloquial terms, most parents are loath to see a shrink about their children's behavior problems unless those problems have become severe (e.g., Friman, 2002; Leinwand, 2006).

As a result of the limited services in PMC and limited service seeking in MHS, a large gap in behavioral health care for children has opened up in this country. In that gap is a large number and array of child behavior problems. By definition, these are addressed only with tactics made available outside of professional contexts, and, as indicated by data from epidemiological research, a large portion worsen over time (cf. American Academy of Pediatrics, 2001; Costello, 1988; Costello, Burns, et al., 1988; Costello, Edelbrock, et al., 1988; Costello & Shugart, 1992; Dulcan et al., 1990; Goldberg et al., 1984; Hickson et al., 1983; Lavigne et al., 1993; Starfield et al., 1980). A professional movement focused on addressing this mounting problem involves primary care behavioral pediatrics (PCBP). Primary care behavioral pediatrics does not currently have a widely accepted technical definition, and yet a seemingly noncontroversial one can be abstracted from various descriptive papers. Specifically, PCBP involves behavioral health care that employs applications drawn from the behavioral and child developmental sciences to address child behavior problems that populate the intersection between child PMC and MHS. Although the problems that present in PCBP can involve secondary (curative) or tertiary (rehabilitative) features, PCBP upholds the long-standing tradition in pediatric medicine of emphasizing prevention over cure or rehabilitation. In the words of Stanford Friedman (1975, p. 515), an early architect of the general field of behavioral pediatrics, "Curative and rehabilitative orientation [is] always second best to preventing the disease or defect in the first place."

DESCRIPTION OF PRIMARY CARE BEHAVIORAL PEDIATRICS TREATMENT

Essentially pragmatic, PCBP treatment is much more concerned with problem resolution than with explication of hypothetical underlying psychogenic causes or constructing elaborate theories about such causes. Additionally, PCBP is concerned mostly with problems that have not devolved sufficiently to fit major diagnostic categories, such as suicidal behavior, Major Depressive Disorder, Conduct Disorder, Bipolar Disorder, Posttraumatic Stress Disorder, or psychosis. These major disorders and conditions are the ones most likely to generate complex theorizing about mental illness, and they are generally outside the domain of PCBP. Nonetheless, it is important that PCBP practitioners be able to recognize major disorders so that they can refer clients to professionals who do specialize in the appropriate evaluation and treatment. The therapy provided for those problems that remain in PCBP typically involves two intersected kinds of therapy: supportive health education and prescriptive behavioral treatment.

Supportive Health Education

Supportive health education involves provision of information about the appropriate classification and developmental, learning, and prognostic context of presenting problems. As an example, there is a widespread cultural ignorance and misunderstanding of the etiology of elimination disorders, and belief in characterological and/or psychopathological defects as major contributing factors has historically been widespread (Friman, 1986, 2002). Relatedly, incontinence is a major contributor to child abuse (Helfer & Kempe, 1976; Kempe, Helfer, & Krugman, 1997; Schmitt, 1987). To address this problem, PCBP supplies health education about elimination processes, ordered and disordered, summarized nicely by the term "demystification" first offered by Levine (1982) and now used by multiple others (e.g., Christophersen & Friman, 2004; Friman, 1986; Friman & Jones, 1998, 2005). As another example, supportive health education often involves the reassurance that many child behaviors reported in primary care are actually developmentally normal and will resolve with the tincture of time. For example, common problems such as thumb sucking, periodic separation anxiety, and crying at bedtime in 3-year-olds, although often of concern to parents and disruptive of the family (Earls, 1980; Costello & Shugart, 1992; Christophersen, 1982, 1988; Christophersen & Rapoff, 1979), are usually benign and not deviant from a developmental perspective. If such problems perpetuate beyond certain age limits, substantially worsen, or begin to cause health concerns, supportive health education is insufficient, and prescriptive behavioral treatment recommendations are provided.

Prescriptive Behavioral Treatment

If a behavior problem does not resolve following the provision of supportive health education and does not involve a major psychiatric condition (e.g., major depression) at the boundary of PCBP, practitioners recommend a series of therapeutic steps for the parents and child to follow at home (or school). The therapeutic recommendations typically emphasize procedure over process, and most procedures used are derived from the more pragmatic parts of the behavioral sciences, particularly those focused on learning and development (Blum & Friman, 2000; Christophersen, 1982; Friman, 2005a; Friman & Blum, 2003; Friman & Piazza, in press). Practitioners of PCBP tend to interpret behavior problems not as representative of pathologies per se, but as representative of skill deficits whose signature behaviors are currently aggravating health and development and that could devolve to actual pathologies if not remedied. Treatments that work are valued for their own sake, and their importance is not diminished because they are at odds with this or that theory. Efficiency, effectiveness, and acceptance are valued over and above theoretical consistency, precision, and scope.

Treatment, although predominantly verbal and thus consistent topographically with traditional child psychotherapy, differs from it in at least two important ways. First and perhaps most fundamental, parents (or primary caregivers) rather than children are often the direct recipients of treatment (i.e., supportive health education and the recommendations that make up the prescriptive behavioral treatment regimens). Children are, of course, the ultimate recipients of PCBP treatment regardless of its form, and they are often present during its delivery and even participate in its preparation. But the fundamental vehicle for PCBP therapy is educational and/or prescriptive advice that pertains to the parent portion of parent-child interactions. Although the comparison is not perfect, it may be helpful to view PCBP therapy as a specialized form of parent training. The critical point, however, is that although child problems are the reason for PCBP therapy, parents are the proximal recipients of the therapeutic advice pertaining to those problems.

Second, because of limitations on time and an emphasis on procedure in pediatric settings, PCBP treatments are often brief and protocol-driven. In this respect they differ substantially from the process-based, time-intensive interventions that characterize traditional child psychotherapy. However, PCBP therapy is consonant with the increasing emphasis on empirically supported treatment and manualized practice in the contemporary practice of psychotherapy (e.g., Christophersen & Mortweet, 2001). The therapeutic armamentarium of the PCBP therapist includes a variety of procedures, each with abundant empirical support, including (but not limited to) time-out, contingency management, home-school notes, simple token economies, and various empirically supported procedures for simple habits, chronic incontinence, bedtime struggles, feeding problems, mild depression, and most of the anxiety disorders.

WHO ARE THE PRACTITIONERS?

Because of its preventive emphasis, clinical expertise in the major psychiatric problems of childhood is not a prerequisite for practitioners in the field. In some respects, such expertise could even handicap practitioners by predisposing them to interpret routine child problems as evidence of a latent or occult pathology (Friman, 2002). For example, hair play, twirling, and pulling in toddlers, although potentially problematic and certainly important enough to address in a behavioral pediatric visit, is not necessarily reflective of psychopathology or indicative of true Trichotillomania (Drews & Friman, 2003; Friman & Hove, 1987). Thumb sucking in preschoolers is more likely a benign source of self-soothing than a malignant sign of oral fixation or regressive personality disorder (Friman, Byrd, & Oksol, 2001). Soiling in young children is much more likely to result from constipation than from psychic mechanisms such as resentment, regression, or anal fixation (Field & Friman, 2006; Friman, 2003). Daytime wetting in first graders is more likely due to incomplete training than insufficient personality (Christophersen & Friman, 2004). Nocturnal wetting is almost always due to developmental variables (e.g., reduced functional bladder capacity) and only rarely to psychological variables suggestive of pathology (Friman, 1986, 1995, in press-a; Friman & Jones, 1998, 2005). There are many other examples.

Because highly specialized psychiatric expertise is unnecessary for effective practice, and because the child problems that occupy the intersection between MHS and PMC are diverse, the field of PCBP is professionally eclectic. Thus primary care physicians (e.g., pediatricians, family practitioners) can specialize in PCBP just as readily as pediatric, school, and clinical child psychologists, and there are specialized training programs for various types of professionals. One essential qualification for all PCBP practitioners is some knowledge of the biological variables that are functionally related to child behavior problems. The primary reason this specialized knowledge is needed is that several behavioral problems that respond well to PCBP intervention involve significant medical (i.e., biological) dimensions. The overall field includes the evaluation and treatment of at least three categories of problems: (1) routine behavior problems, (2) behavior problems with significant medical dimensions, and (3) medical problems with significant behavioral dimensions. Although a fourth category can plausibly be described, one that emphasizes the interaction between medical and behavioral issues more than is typical of categories 2 and 3 (e.g., Blum & Friman, 2000; Friman, 2005a; Friman & Piazza, in press), this chapter focuses only on these three categories, presenting a descriptive PCBP analysis of and therapeutic approach to a representative problem from each area.

COMMON BEHAVIOR PROBLEMS IN PRIMARY CARE SETTINGS

As indicated, a substantial portion of children seen in PMC have symptoms that meet criteria for a behavioral or emotional disorder (e.g., American Academy of Pediatrics, 2001; Costello, 1988; Costello, Burns, et al., 1988; Costello, Edelbrock, et al., 1988; Costello & Shugart, 1992; Dulcan et al., 1990; Goldberg et al., 1984;

Hickson et al., 1983; Lavigne et al., 1993; Starfield et al., 1980), and a much larger percentage exhibit behaviors or emotions that cause their parents concern and/or cause some functional impairment for the child but do not meet criteria for a disorder (American Academy of Pediatrics, 2001; Costello & Shugart, 1992; Earls, 1980; Christophersen, 1982, 1988; Friman, 2002). The problems parents report to PMC providers vary with the age and developmental level of their children. During infancy, parents are most likely to report concerns about their children's excessive crying and problems initiating and maintaining sleep. During the preschool years, parents are most likely to report concerns about their children's oppositional behavior, toileting practices (especially resistance), limited attention span, overly selective eating, and fears or worries (Earls, 1980; Lavigne et al., 1993). During the school years, parents continue to report concerns about problems first encountered during the preschool years that have persisted, as well as new concerns about academics, school behavior, and peer problems (Kanoy & Schroeder, 1985).

Many of these behavior problems will ultimately resolve without the direct intervention of a professional. For this reason, PMC providers often initially describe presenting problems as fitting within the range of normal expectations and recommend that parents let their children grow out of it. The "tincture of time" approach, however, does little to address the substantial stress that behavior problems can place on a family while they are occurring, a fact that is highlighted by the increased risk of child abuse that occurs in association with many problem behaviors (Helfer & Kempe, 1976; Kempe et al., 1997; Schmitt, 1987). Furthermore, children do not always grow out of their behavior problems, and, in most cases, it is very difficult to distinguish those who will from those who will not. Without treatment of problems that persist, children can have serious consequences later in life. For example, untreated, persistent oppositional behavior can devolve into major conduct problems that require extraordinary therapeutic interventions for remission (Caspi & Moffitt, 1995). Unresolved toileting problems can lead to serious medical problems, such as megacolon, urinary tract infection, and the unstable bladder of childhood (Christophersen & Friman, 2004; Friman, 1986, 1995; Friman & Christophersen, 1986; Friman & Jones, 1998). Untreated bedtime problems can lead to habitually disrupted sleep patterns, family discord, and child maltreatment (Blampied & France, 1993; Blum & Carey, 1996; Edwards & Christophersen, 1994; Ferber, 1985). Unresolved school problems can lead to incomplete education, truancy, and school failure, which, in turn, are instrumental in the development of delinquency, drug use, and ultimately criminal behaviors (Friman, 2000). There are many other examples; collectively, they underscore the benefit of brief, problem-specific, effective treatment for children whose behavior problems have persuaded parents to discuss those problems in PMC, even if they involve low-intensity, high-frequency problems such as those just mentioned. The next section discusses one example in detail.

Bedtime Problems

Teaching children to go to bed, go to sleep, and stay asleep throughout the night is difficult for many families in this culture (Blampied & France, 1993; Blum

& Carey, 1996; Edwards & Christophersen, 1994; Ferber, 1985; Friman, 2005c). A representative survey indicated that at least 30% of families contend with this problem three or more nights a week (Lozoff, Wolf, & Davis, 1985). The difficulties reported by parents include bedtime struggles such as resistance to going to bed, fussing and crying while in bed, and night waking with fussing, crying, and unauthorized departures from the bedroom. These problems are important because they disrupt parents' and their children's sleep, which, in turn, decreases the subsequent capacity of both to execute emotional self-control (Teitelbaum, 1977). Although PCBP advice about sleep is needed from the age of 3 months on, its importance is greatly amplified if bedtime struggles continue after 6 months of age. One intervention for child bedtime problems employed by many pediatric providers (and often parents acting on their own) involves medication. Although sometimes effective in the short term, all soporific medication results in unwanted side effects, and sleep-related benefits are usually lost when the medication is withdrawn. Additional information on medication for bedtime problems is available in published reviews of the research on them (e.g., Edwards & Christophersen, 1994).

Treatment for Bedtime Problems

The cardinal component of the most effective behavioral interventions for bedtime problems involves one of the first documented and most frequently used in behavioral psychology: extinction. As children develop sleep habits, they often learn to associate specific environmental factors with self-quieting and the induction of sleep. Misinformed parental efforts to help children sleep often result in problematic sleep associations that mitigate the process of falling asleep. For example, for most children sleep induction is enhanced by the presence of a parent to sooth and cuddle them and thereby ease the transition from wakefulness to sleep. These parental activities can contribute functional status to a constellation of stimuli that influence children's behavior in bed. With the parent present, rapid sleep induction typically occurs. Unfortunately, when the parent is absent at bedtime, the child is left without the stimulus that is most powerfully associated with sleep. The children's response to parental absence typically involves prolonged and intensive crying that resembles an extinction burst (Blampied & France, 1993; Ferber, 1985; Edwards & Christophersen, 1994; Friman, 2005b). This response motivates most parents to intervene either by soothing or disciplining their child, which, unfortunately, usually worsens the problem. Soothing responses to crying can reinforce the crying; disciplinary responses to crying often provokes more crying; and both responses limit the child's learning of self-quieting skills (Blampied & France, 1994; Edwards & Christophersen, 1994; Ferber, 1985; Friman, 2005b; Lozoff et al., 1985). Not surprisingly, after failed attempts to solve the problem themselves, parents whose children exhibit bedtime problems often seek professional advice. The four procedures most likely to be prescribed by PCBP practitioners are described next.

Complete Extinction This approach to bedtime problems involves no visits by the parent to the child's bedroom after the child has gone to bed. In effect, the child is left to cry it out. Generally, complete extinction works more rapidly than other approaches, but it presents problems that mitigate its overall effectiveness (Adams & Rickert, 1989; Edwards & Christophersen, 1994; Rickert & Johnson, 1988). For example, the child's crying can be highly aversive during the first nights of implementation. If the family lives in an apartment complex, or the treatment is implemented during a season when windows are open, the crying and screaming can draw attention from the neighbors, with predictably problematic consequences. Additionally, extended crying and screaming differentially affects parents. Discord is possible (probable) when crying is substantially more aversive for one parent than the other (Adams & Rickert, 1989; Ferber, 1985). Thus, complete extinction is a straightforward behavioral approach to bedtime problems in children but has limited social validity. In an attempt to improve social validity, sleep researchers have developed other, multicomponent methods that employ extinction but decrease its intensity and aversiveness for parents through the inclusion of other procedures.

Graduated Extinction   This procedure involves advising parents to ignore bedtime problem behavior for specific time intervals that gradually increase. The optimal length of the intervals has not been established empirically, but expert advice (Ferber, 1985) and related research studies (e.g., Adams & Rickert, 1989) recommend beginning with a 5-minute interval on the first episode, 10 at the second, and 15 minutes for subsequent episodes on night 1. These intervals increase over the course of a week, ending with 35 minutes for the first episode on night 7, 40 for the second, and 45 minutes for all subsequent episodes and nights. Although children can tantrum for longer than 45 minutes at night, published data (Adam & Rickert, 1989; see also Edwards & Christophersen, 1994) and a large amount of clinical experience described by Ferber (1985) suggests that very few do.

An important question about graduated extinction is why it works. At first glance, it would seem to be the perfect procedure for teaching children to cry gradually longer and longer, culminating in a reliable 45-minute bout reproducible throughout the night. This, however, is not what happens. No research has yet addressed why, and the following explanation is speculation. The procedure is perhaps more appropriately labeled a differential reinforcement schedule than scheduled extinction. The parents visit the room only if their child is crying; thus, visits are contingent. However, increasing the response requirement to 45 minutes of crying may stretch the schedule so much that the reinforcing effects of sleep supersede the reinforcing effects of parental visitation.

Positive Routines   This procedure involves a hybrid of extinction and a rewarding bedtime ritual. In the procedure, parents determine when they would like their child to go to sleep and when the child typically falls asleep. Beginning shortly before the time the child typically falls asleep, parents engage the child in several quiet activities lasting no longer than 20 minutes total. During the activities, the parents issue easily followed instructions and richly supply rewarding responses for compliance. In this respect, the procedure resembles a widely studied procedure for increasing instructional control called behavioral momentum (Mace et al., 1988). In positive routines, as in behavioral momentum, the child is given a series of instructions with a high probability of compliance, followed by a terminal instruction whose probability of compliance is low. In this case, the terminal instruction is "Now stay in bed and go to sleep," or something equivalent. If at any time after the completion of the routines and the terminal instruction the child leaves the bed, the parent places the child back in bed, telling him or her that the routine is over and it is time for bed. Crying and verbalizations are ignored. At specified intervals (e.g., 1 week) the parents move the positive routine back in time 5 to 10 minutes. They continue this backward movement until they arrive at the bedtime they prefer for their child. For example, the child may typically fall asleep at 9:15, and the parent's preferred bedtime might be 8:15. Thus, it could take between 6 and 8 weeks for parents to arrive at the preferred bedtime. Experimental comparison of the positive routines procedure with scheduled extinction showed that both produced substantially improved bedtime behavior for children, but that the parents using positive routines reported significantly improved marital relations, suggesting a more socially valid procedure (Adams & Rickert, 1989).

The Bedtime Pass   The bedtime pass program involves (a) requiring that children get into bed; (b) providing them with a small, laminated note card exchangeable for one free trip out of the bedroom or one visit to them by the parent after being put to bed in order to have a small request satisfied (e.g., for a drink, hug, or visit to the bathroom); (c) surrender of the pass after it is used; and (d) extinction thereafter. In the initial study, the program eliminated the high rates of crying out, calling out, and coming out of the bedroom after bedtime exhibited by two children, ages 3 and 10 years. Additionally, these successful results were achieved without an accompanying extinction burst during initial intervention periods, and a large group of sample parents rated the intervention as more acceptable than extinction alone (Friman et al., 1999). The pass program was subsequently replicated in a single-subject analysis of four 3-year-old children (Freeman, 2006) and a randomized trial involving nineteen 3- to 6-year-old children (Moore, Friman, Fruzetti, & MacAleese, 2007).

Two plausible possibilities for how the pass achieves its effects have been proposed. First, the pass program is analogous to differential reinforcement of alternative behavior (with use of the pass as an alternative to crying, calling, or coming out from the bedroom and the parents' response as reinforcement), which is a well-established method for reducing disruptive behavior (Vollmer & Iwata, 1992). Second, the use of the pass involves the reinforcement of a request made by the child. A small line of recent research shows that reinforcing appropriate behavior in disruptive individuals and subsequently placing disruption on a course of extinction can reduce the disruption without producing an extinction burst (e.g., Bowman, Fisher, Thompson, & Piazza, 1997).

This brief discussion of child bedtime problems and their treatment is by no means complete. It merely describes a PCBP analysis and four representative PCBP interventions that are the most frequently used and have the most empirical support. There are other interventions used by parents (and prescribed by some professionals) but usually avoided in PCBP (e.g., medication, the family bed; see Friman,

2005b, for description) as well as others that almost certainly will become part of the PCBP armamentarium if they generate sufficient empirical support. Examples include the sleep fairy intervention, a variation on the tooth fairy (Burke, Kuhn, & Peterson, 2004), and the teaching of self-quieting skills during the day to promote a better transition to bed at night (Edwards, 1993; Edwards & Christophersen, 1994).

The general premise of this section is that child bedtime concerns represent a very important and common presenting complaint in PMC, one that is not appropriate for conventional medical evaluation and not optimally responsive to conventional medical treatment (e.g., medication). The vast majority of bedtime concerns fit within the category of common behavioral problems: They are high-frequency, low-intensity presenting complaints. As with most common behavior problems, bedtime problems have a fundamental behavioral and learning basis; thus, not surprisingly, they respond well to behavioral- and learning-based evaluation and treatment. Yet conventional pediatric training does not emphasize this type of evaluation and treatment, and even if it did, most pediatricians would not have sufficient time during the average visit to accomplish it (cf. Christophersen, 1982).

As indicated, PCBP research has contributed several behavioral- and learning-based treatments for bedtime problems; however, the research agenda is far from complete, especially in light of the extent of the problems in this culture. For example, little research on the actual function of bedtime problems has been reported and, although the assumption that the primary function is attention seeking has served the field well, there may be other functions. Additionally, although the treatment procedures described here extend the clinical effectiveness of PCBP practitioners, new procedures, especially those with high social validity, are needed. More generally, new effective and socially valid treatments are needed for all of the common behavior problems presenting in pediatric settings, and PCBP is uniquely well positioned to address that need.

BEHAVIOR PROBLEMS WITH SIGNIFICANT MEDICAL DIMENSIONS

A fundamental assumption of PCBP is that behavior occurs mostly as a function of environmental circumstances, but this assumption does not disavow the influence of medical (i.e., physiological) variables. Rather, many physiological variables are indeed seen as determinative, but are themselves the result of environmental behavior contingencies that occurred in a phylogenetic context (Skinner, 1966). Physiological variables often play an initiating role in behavioral problems that present in PMC. For example, an immune response can lead to a rash, a rash to scratching, scratching to tissue abrasions, and tissue abrasions to scratching unrelated to the rash. Child stomach pain brought on by physiological variables (e.g., flu virus) can lead to missed school. While the child is home from school, the child's behavior is influenced by reinforcers involving avoidance of schoolwork as well as contact with sympathetic responses from caregivers. These influences can, in turn, result in complaints of stomach pain that do not involve physiological variables, a condition sometimes referred to as recurrent abdominal pain (Finney, Lemanek, Cataldo, Katz, & Fuqua, 1989). Hair loss caused by medical problems (e.g., alopecia areata) can lead to social avoidance, the extended duration of which can lead to a deterioration of social skills that can, in turn, lead to social avoidance even after hair has grown back. There are many other examples; the one elaborated upon here involves constipation, a physiological variable that can cause common toileting problems, the most serious of which is retentive encopresis.

Retentive Encopresis

Descriptive Features

Definition   Encopresis, a common presenting complaint in pediatrics (3% to 5% of all referrals), is a disorder in which children either voluntarily or involuntarily pass feces into or onto an inappropriate location, usually their clothing (Friman & Jones, 1998; Wright, 1973; Wright, Schaefer, & Solomons, 1979). Encopresis is not diagnosed if the problem is exclusively due to an anatomic or neurologic abnormality that prevents continence. The current criteria from *DSM-IV* (American Psychiatric Association, 1994) are (a) inappropriate passage of feces at least once a month for at least 3 months, (b) chronological or developmentally equivalent age of 4 years, and (c) not due exclusively to the direct physiological effects of a substance (e.g., laxatives) or a general medical condition, except through a mechanism involving constipation. The *DSM-IV* distinguishes two subtypes of encopresis, one with constipation and overflow incontinence (i.e., retentive encopresis) and one without these symptoms (i.e., nonretentive encopresis). For reasons that will be discussed later, this section focuses only on encopresis with constipation.

Relevant Physiology   The large intestine, or colon, is the distal end of the alimentary tract, which is sequentially composed of the esophagus, stomach, small intestine, and colon. A thorough review of the colonic system is beyond the scope of this chapter (for more thorough reviews, see Weinstock & Clouse, 1987, or Whitehead & Schuster, 1985). Some rudimentary description of the system, however, is necessary to understand the physiology that supplies the logic of effective treatment. The colon is a tubular organ with a muscular wall. It connects the small intestine to the rectum and anus. It has three primary functions: fluid absorption, storage, and evacuation. Extended storage and planned evacuation are the defining features of fecal continence. Movement of waste through the colon is achieved through muscular contractions called peristalsis, which produce a wave-like motion of the colon walls. As the waste moves through the colon moisture is absorbed from it, creating semisolid feces. Movement through the colon is potentiated by a variety of external events that instigate muscular contractions in the colonic wall. For example, eating a meal increases colonic contractions (referred to as the gastrocolonic reflex), and moving about will have a similar effect (referred to as the orthocolonic reflex).

Usually the rectum, a hollow receptacle at the distal end of the large colon, contains little or no feces, but prior to defecation muscular contractions in the colonic wall propel feces into the rectum. This results in distension, which stimulates sensory receptors in the rectal mucosa and in the muscles of the pelvic floor, resulting in relaxation of the internal sphincter, which facilitates defecation. This process is involuntary, but the child can constrict the anal canal and inhibit defecation by contracting the external anal sphincter and the functionally related puborectalis muscle. When the urge to defecate is suppressed this way, the rectum accommodates the retained stool through the adaptive pliance of its structure and terminates the reflex relaxation of the internal sphincter. The urge gradually decays, and some of the fecal matter in the rectum is returned to the descending colon by retroperistalsis.

Etiology   Between 80% and 95% of encopresis cases can be traced to a primary causal variable: constipation (Hatch, 1988; Levine, 1975, 1982; Wright et al., 1979). Although definitions for constipation vary, children who frequently go two or more days without a bowel movement are probably prone to constipation. A common complaint by the parents of encopretic children is that they deliberately soil their clothing (Wright et al., 1979), but this accusation is usually false (Levine, 1982). The primary cause of soiling is fecal retention (constipation). In most cases, retention is not caused by characterological or psychopathological problems (Friman, Mathews, Finney, & Christophersen, 1988; Gabel, Hegedus, Wald, Chandra, & Chaponis, 1986). Retention is usually the result of a constellation of factors, many of which are beyond a child's immediate control (Levine, 1982). These factors include a constitutional predisposition (i.e., slow gastrointestinal transit time), diet, insufficient leverage for passage of hard stools, and occasional or frequent painful passage of hard stools, resulting in negative reinforcement for holding stools (Christophersen & Rapoff, 1983). Although retention is frequently attributed to sexual abuse, an association between fecal retention and accidents has not been established (e.g., Mellon, Whiteside, & Friedrich, 2006). For some children, especially those with extreme constipation and/or treatment failure, there is an increased threshold of awareness of rectal distension, a possibly weak internal sphincter, and/or a tendency to contract the external sphincter during the act of defecation (Meunier, Marechal, & De Beaujeu, 1979; Wald, Chandra, Chiponis, & Gabel, 1986). The combined effect of all these factors is a lowered probability of voluntary stool passage and a heightened probability of fecal retention.

Chronic fecal retention results in fecal impaction, which results in enlargement of the colon. Colon enlargement results in decreased motility of the bowel system and, occasionally, in involuntary passage of large stools and frequent soiling due to seepage of soft fecal matter. The seepage is often referred to as paradoxical diarrhea because the children retain large masses of stool and thus are functionally constipated, but their colon allows passage of soft stool around the mass, which results in diarrhea (Christophersen & Rapoff, 1983; Levine, 1982).

That fecal impaction is related to retentive encopresis has been established by several investigators, primary among whom are Davidson (1958), Levine (1975), and Wright (1975). All independently reported that 80% of their patients had fecal impaction accompanying fecal incontinence at the first clinic visit. Subsequent to his 1975 report, Levine and his colleagues developed a simple clinical procedure to identify fecal impaction from an X-ray of the lower abdomen (Barr, Levine, Wilkinson, & Mulvihill, 1979). As a result of the improved diagnostic method, Levine revised his initial 80% estimate of fecal impaction's coexistence with fecal incontinence to 90% (Christophersen & Rapoff, 1979).

Differential Diagnosis There are rare anatomic and neurologic problems that can lead to fecal retention and soiling. Anatomic problems include a variety of malformations and locations of the anus that are detectable on physical exam and require medical management (Hatch, 1988). Hirschsprung's disease or congenital aganglionosis is a disorder in which the nerves that control the muscles in the wall of the colon or in an entire section of the colon are absent, causing severe constipation. Its incidence is approximately 1 in 25,000, and it usually causes severe symptoms in infancy (Levine, 1975). Thus the clinical presentation itself should prevent the astute clinician from mistaking one for the other. The possible exception is ultra-short segment Hirschsprung's disease, which has a more subtle clinical picture. However, the existence of this condition is controversial, and, even if it does exist, proper collaboration between pediatrician and behavior analyst should ensure timely diagnosis.

Evaluation

The initial PCBP evaluation should begin with a physical examination that usually includes a routine check of history, abdominal palpation, rectal examination, and sometimes an X-ray of the abdomen to determine the extent of fecal impaction. A barium enema is rarely necessary unless features of the exam suggest Hirschsprung's disease. The evaluation should also include a behavior assessment that begins with a behavioral interview that involves critical questions related to constipation. These include asking whether there is ever a long period between bowel movements, whether bowel movements are atypically large (stop up the toilet), whether fecal matter ever has an unusually foul odor, whether fecal matter is ever hard, difficult, or painful to pass, and whether the child ever complains of not being able to feel the movement or make it to the toilet on time. An additional question that pertains more to treatment history than to pathogenesis is whether the child ever hides soiled underwear. Affirmative answers to any or all of these questions are highly suggestive of retentive encopresis, and hiding underwear indicates a history that includes some form of punishment.

The encopresis evaluation is usually the first step in treatment because it always includes a substantial amount of supportive health education. Encopresis is not well understood outside of the medical community, and the child's parents are likely to be under the influence of the characterological and psychopathological interpretations that are prevalent in Western culture (e.g., Friman, 2002; Horwitz, 2002). The parents' interpretation of the condition is also likely to influence how the children view their problem. Thus, the encopresis evaluation can actually begin treatment by providing accurate information that demystifies the problem. Last, the evaluation should include questions about diet and timing of meals. Low-fiber diets and irregular meals can be contributing factors in encopresis.

Treatment

During the past 15 years, several descriptive and controlled experimental studies have supported a multicomponent approach to treatment of chronic retentive encopresis partly derived from the pioneering work of Davidson (1958), Christophersen and Rainey (1976), Levine (1975), and Wright (1975). As indicated earlier, the first component can be addressed within the evaluation. Specifically, the entire elimination process, including its disordered manifestations, should be demystified (Christophersen & Rapoff, 1983; Levine, 1982). Generally this means providing information about bowel dynamics and the relationship of the problem to constipation (Levine, 1982). Second, if there is a fecal impaction it should be removed with enemas and/or laxatives (Christophersen & Rapoff, 1983; Levine, 1982; O'Brien, Ross, & Christophersen, 1986). Third, the child should sit on the toilet for about 5 minutes one or two times a day (O'Brien et al., 1986; Wright, 1975). Fourth, the parents should promote proper toileting with encouragement and not with coercion. Additionally, they should not reserve all of their praise and affection for proper elimination; a child should be praised just for sitting on the toilet (Christophersen & Rapoff, 1983; Levine, 1982; Wright, 1975). Fifth, a stool softener such as mineral oil (Davidson, 1958) or glycerin suppositories (O'Brien et al., 1986; Wright & Walker, 1977) should be used to ease the passage of hard stools. Sixth, dietary fiber should be increased in the child's diet (Houts, Mellon, & Whelan, 1988; O'Brien et al., 1986). Seventh, to increase and maintain motility in the child's colon, the child's activity levels and fluid intake should be increased (Levine, 1982). Eighth, during toileting episodes the child's feet should be on a flat surface. Foot placement is crucial to the Valsalva maneuver (grunting push necessary to produce a bowel movement; Levine, 1982; O'Brien et al., 1986). And ninth, the child should be rewarded for all bowel movements in the toilet (Christophersen & Rainey, 1976; Levine, 1982; O'Brien et al., 1986; Wright & Walker, 1977).

The literature on this approach (or variations thereof) has progressed sufficiently to lead to group trials. For example, in a study of 58 children with encopresis, 60% were completely continent after 5 months, and those who did not achieve full continence averaged a 90% decrease in accidents (Lowery, Srour, Whitehead, & Schuster, 1985). There are multiple other examples that document similar levels of success (e.g., Stark et al., 1997). However, not all children succeed with the conventional approach; for these children, augmentative methods have been developed. These methods developed through study of behaviors associated with treatment failure (Stark, Spirito, Lewis, & Hart, 1990). Incorporating behavior management methods relevant to the behaviors, teaching parents to use them, and delivering treatment in a group format resulted in an 83% decrease in accidents in 18 treatment-resistant children with encopresis, and the results were maintained or even improved at 6-month follow-up (Stark, Owens-Stively, Spirito, Lewis, & Guevremont, 1990).

The general premise of this section—that medical variables can influence or cause behavior problems—is not controversial, even in sciences such as behavior analysis that are devoted to the study of environmental cause (e.g., Friman & Piazza, in press). Constipation is one such variable, and it can cause behavior problems ranging from minor toileting resistance to encopresis, and there are many others (e.g., anorexia due to gastroesophogeal reflux, restricted activities due to pain). Because of the medical component of these problems, there are frequently serious health consequences for unsuccessful treatment that compound any psychological or behavioral components. For example, extreme fecal retention can be life-threatening, and even routine cases seriously decrease social standing and increase social distancing in affected children. Because of the behavioral component of these problems, a solely medical intervention is insufficient for effective treatment. Needed are treatments that deliver or aid the delivery of the medical components of treatment while addressing the behavioral components. Thus, PCBP is an appropriate context. Additionally, although there are many types of behavior problems that stem from physiological influences, for the medical dimensions the most frequently occurring problem is some form of noncompliance with a treatment regimen. As an example, cooperation with prescribed treatment for encopresis is so necessary for success that instructional control training is frequently either a component of treatment or a prerequisite for it (Friman, 2003). Furthermore, although reasonable progress has been made in improving pediatric compliance, encopresis remains one of the most chronic problems in all of pediatric medicine.

MEDICAL PROBLEMS WITH SIGNIFICANT BEHAVIORAL DIMENSIONS

The immediately preceding section discussed the influence of medical variables on child behavior problems, with emphasis on constipation and its influence on toileting resistance and retentive encopresis, problems that are frequently seen in PMC. This section discusses the influence of behavior on medical variables with emphasis on the behavioral treatment of physiologically based behavior problems that are also frequently seen in PCBP. For decades health-based sciences have demonstrated relationships between child behavior and health. For example, eating nutritious food and engaging in modest exercise can improve child cardiovascular health. Obtaining sufficient sleep can help sustain immunological responses, emotional resiliency, and adaptability. Maintaining adequate personal hygiene can decrease child susceptibility to infectious disease. There are many other examples. More recently, PCBP has demonstrated a variety of healthful outcomes from changes in behavior (e.g., Finney, Miller, & Adler, 1993; Friman & Christophersen, 1986; Irwin, Cataldo, Matheny, & Peterson, 1992; Stark et al., 1993). A review of this literature is beyond the scope of this chapter, and thus the focus here is on biofeedback, a treatment involving the manipulation of behavioral variables to improve health; treatment of nocturnal enuresis is offered as the primary example.

Nocturnal Enuresis

Biofeedback Perspective

Biofeedback involves the use of electrical or electromechanical equipment to measure and increase the salience of stimuli associated with pertinent physiologic processes and training patients to discriminate and control them in order to improve their own health. The penultimate goal of biofeedback is to train individuals to alter the physiologic processes in healthful directions, and the ultimate goal is to train them to do so without biofeedback (Culbert, Kajander, & Reaney, 1996; Friman, in press-b). Most biofeedback-type treatments require sophisticated instrumentation and specialized training and thus may not be incorporated readily into primary care practices (e.g., anorectal manometry combined with electromyography for treatment of fecal incontinence). However, nocturnal enuresis, a physiologically based behavioral problem that is one of the most frequent presenting behavioral complaints in PMC, is highly responsive to urine alarm treatment, a minimally technical, uncomplicated form of biofeedback that is readily used in PMC (Christophersen & Friman, 2004; Friman, 1986, 1995, in press-a; Friman & Jones, 1998, 2005). In fact, urine alarm treatment is the most empirically supported treatment for nocturnal enuresis, by a wide margin, despite more than 50 years of research devoted to discovery of effective physiologically based treatments (e.g., medication). There are at least two medications (DDAVP and imipramine) that can improve enuresis, but with significantly smaller magnitude and duration of effects than the urine alarm. This section discusses descriptive features of nocturnal enuresis as well as its evaluation and treatment.

Descriptive Features

Definition   The current criteria for enuresis (nocturnal and diurnal) from *DSM-IV* (American Psychiatric Association, 1994) are (a) repeated urination into bed or clothing; (b) at least two occurrences per week for at least 3 months or a sufficient number of occurrences to cause clinically significant distress; (c) chronological age of 5 or, for children with developmental delays, a mental age of at least 5; and (d) not due exclusively to the direct effects of a substance (e.g., diuretics) or a general medical condition (e.g., diabetes). There are three subtypes of enuresis: nocturnal only, diurnal only, and mixed nocturnal and diurnal. There are two courses: The primary course includes children who have never established continence, and the secondary course involves children who, after establishing continence, resume having accidents. This section primarily discusses nocturnal enuresis (although some discussion of diurnal enuresis is supplied), which is estimated to occur in as many as 20% of first-grade children (Christophersen & Friman, 2004; Friman, 1986, 1995, in press-a; Friman & Jones, 1998, 2005).

Relevant Physiology   The bladder (detrusor) is an elastic hollow organ with a muscular wall. Its shape resembles an upside-down balloon with a long narrow neck; it has two, primarily mechanical functions: storage and release of urine (Vincent, 1974). Extended storage and volitional release are the defining properties of urinary continence. In infancy, distension of the bladder leads to contraction of the bladder and automatic (nonvolitional) evacuation of urine. As children mature, the capacity of the central nervous system to inhibit bladder contraction increases, typically coinciding with the development of continence in early childhood (Berk & Friman, 1990; Koff, 1995).

The components of the urogenital system that are under volitional control and that are necessary for continence skills are the muscles of the pelvic floor. Except during imminent or actual urination, these muscles remain in a state of tonus or involuntary partial contraction, which maintains the bladder neck in an elevated and closed position (Vincent, 1974). Even after initiation of urination has begun, contraction of the pelvic floor muscles can abruptly raise the bladder neck and terminate urination.

But for children with nocturnal enuresis, these urinary inhibitory responses are either not present or are sporadic (Friman, 1995; Friman & Jones, 1998; Houts, 1991; Mellon, Scott, Haynes, Schmidt, & Houts, 1997).

Etiology   Although nocturnal enuresis has a strong genetic basis, its exact cause is unknown. For decades there has been a sustained effort to link it to causal psychopathology, but contemporary research (Friman, Handwerk, Swearer, McGinnis, & Warzak, 1998), as well as several reviews of older research (Friman, 1986, 1995, 2002; Friman & Jones, 1998), suggest that most enuretic children do not exhibit clinically significant psychopathology, and when they do, it is more likely to be an outcome than a cause of nocturnal enuresis. Physiologically oriented studies of nocturnal enuresis suggest that some affected children may have difficulty concentrating their urine during the night and, thus, produce more urine nocturnally than their nonenuretic peers (Lackgren, Neveus, & Stenberg, 1997; Rittig, Knudsen, Norgaard, Pedersen, & Djurhuus, 1989). The overall importance of this factor, however, is controversial because the proportion of enuretic children with urine concentration problems may be small (Eggert & Kuhn, 1995). Finally, nocturnal enuresis may be viewed as merely a deficit in the skills necessary to prevent urination while asleep (Houts, 1991).

Evaluation

As with encopresis, the initial stage of an enuresis evaluation should include a physical examination. Once a thorough history has been obtained and preliminary information about enuresis has been shared with the parents and child, PCBP goes no further until all possible pathophysiological causes of enuresis have been ruled out. There are several such causes, some of which are common (e.g., urinary tract infection) and some rare (e.g., diabetes), and they must be ruled out before treatment begins. There are several other elements necessary for a full evaluation of enuresis, and these are well documented in multiple other papers (e.g., Christophersen & Friman, 2004; Friman, 1986, 1995; Friman & Jones, 1998; in press-a).

Treatment

The two most common treatments for nocturnal enuresis are the urine alarm and the medications DDAVP and imipramine. These medications can provide symptomatic relief; approximately 25% to 40% of children will be dry most nights when taking them. However, when the medications are stopped, the enuresis usually returns (Moffatt, 1997). The urine alarm is a moisture-sensitive switching system, the closing of which (when the child wets the bed) rings the alarm. Repeated pairing of awakening by the alarm with episodes of wetting is consistently described in the literature as the single most effective treatment for enuresis (Christophersen & Friman, 2004; Friman, 1986, 1995; Friman & Jones, 1998, in press-a). Its success rate is higher (approximately 75%) and its relapse rate lower (approximately 41%) than any other drug- or skill-based treatment.

The urine alarm is a simple form of biofeedback treatment because its primary function is to provide feedback for a physiological event, urination, which in enuretic episodes occurs beneath awareness. The feedback (ringing of the alarm) increases the salience of the urination and, thus, aids in the ultimate establishment of urinary self-control. The mechanism by which the alarm improves enuresis, however, is still unknown. Changes in secretion of hormones that affect the ability to concentrate urine (Friman, 1995; Friman & Jones, 1998; Houts, 1991) or alterations in the brain's inhibition of bladder contraction are at least theoretically possible, but have not been investigated. Early conceptualizations described the mechanism as classical conditioning, with the alarm as the unconditioned stimulus, bladder distention the conditioned stimulus, and waking the conditioned response, but most children successfully treated with the alarm learn to sleep through the night without wetting (or waking). Subsequent conceptualizations emphasized a negative reinforcement paradigm in which the children repeatedly awakened by the alarm avoided it by urinating in the toilet (initially) and (ultimately) holding their urine until a more convenient time. The current prevailing account involves a combination of the two previous accounts with classical conditioning of pelvic floor muscles and operant conditioning of volitional behaviors related to continence (Houts, 1991). The key distinguishing feature of the current account is that children are not necessarily trained to awaken to the alarm; most merely learn to engage their urinary inhibition system even if they are asleep, a skill that would be difficult to teach without the sensory feedback provided by the alarm.

Alarm-based treatment produces cure slowly, and during the first few weeks of alarm use, waking, if it occurs at all, occurs only after a complete voiding. Recent research using the size of the urine stain on the soiled sheets as the dependent measure showed that prior to accident-free nights, the stain grew increasingly smaller on successive nights, suggesting a graduated process of continence attainment (Ruckstuhl & Friman, 2003). In other words, the feedback properties of the alarm gradually but inexorably strengthened the skills necessary to avoid it. The core skill involves contraction of the pelvic floor muscles, resulting in sustained elevation of the bladder neck, resulting in the cessation or, preferably, prevention of urination. There is also the possibility of increased sensory awareness of urinary need and waking to urinate, but this is a less likely outcome and actually inferior to sustained, accident-free sleep throughout the night.

However, increasing sensory awareness of urinary need prior to daytime accidents is also a key component in the most empirically supported treatment for diurnal enuresis. Only two studies are available (very little research has been conducted on diurnal enuresis), and the first used a much simpler conceptualization (Halliday, Meadow, & Berg, 1987). Specifically, this early study merely suggested that the alarm served as a reminder to urinate. A subsequent study utilizing the biofeedback conceptualization was conducted with a young girl who was initially unresponsive to urinary urge and onset, but who rapidly became responsive with use of the alarm (Friman & Vollmer, 1995). The decreasing latency between alarm onset and appropriate response was characteristic of learning curves resulting from alarm-based treatment for nocturnal enuresis and biofeedback treatments in general.

As indicated earlier, most biofeedback treatments are much more technically complex than the urine alarm, and they are used for a broad range of physiologically based behavioral concerns that often initially present in PMC. Among the physiological processes that can be monitored are muscle tension, skin temperature, respiratory rate, blood pressure, and skin moisture (perspiration). Biofeedback devices sensitive to these processes have been used in treatment of a wide variety of disorders, including headaches, other varieties of chronic pain, asthma, bruxism, anxiety disorders, sleep disorders, and dysfunction of the autonomic nervous system (Culbert et al., 1996). Additionally, evidence is mounting that biofeedback can generate operant responses that, in turn, lead to control over physiologic processes long thought to be outside of volition, such as skin temperature and blood pressure. For example, verbally based awareness-enhancement methods have been shown to alter the level of mediators of the immune system in saliva (Olness, Culbert, & Uden, 1989) and to decrease the recurrence of chronic mouth ulcers (Andrews & Hall, 1990). Collectively, the large body of research documenting the effectiveness of the urine alarm, along with the even larger literature on the effectiveness of biofeedback treatment for a broad range of medical conditions, underscores the research and clinical potential represented by the influence of behavioral variables on physiology.

Case Illustration: A Routine Case of Bedtime Problems

Identifying Features of the Client
Tom was an 8-year-old Caucasian boy who lived at home with his natural parents, his 12-year-old brother, Bill, and his 3-year-old sister, Suzie. His medical, developmental, psychiatric, and educational histories were unremarkable. He attended a local parochial school and was in the third grade. According to his teachers and his parents his grades were excellent and his behavior was very good. For example, the school used a demerit system and he had received only one demerit at the midyear point and that was for misplacing an assignment. At school, he had several good friends, and during his initial clinic session he identified three of them as best friends. When asked what he liked about his best friends, he mentioned that they were nice to him, funny, and shared similar interests.

Presenting Complaint
Tom's presenting complaint included disruptive emotional behavior after bedtime. Approximately 4 weeks prior to the initial visit, Tom began waking up 2 to 3 hours after bedtime and crying out for his parents or coming into their room to summon them if they did not heed his call. When asked about the nature of his distress, he typically used a range of complaints, including nightmares, upset stomach, noises in his bedroom, and worry over school the following day. In response, the parents either allowed him to sleep in their room until the following morning or took him back to his room, at which point one parent would lie with him until he fell asleep. These responses to his distress actually appeared to worsen rather than improve his nighttime concerns, and by the time of the initial appointment, he had begun exhibiting distress at or even prior to bedtime, often refusing to go to bed without being accompanied by a parent.

(Continued)

Parental Factors

The parents described their marriage as good and their relationship with all three of their children as loving and supportive. They did exhibit a difference of opinion about how to manage Tom's bedtime concerns. The father thought that too much attention was being paid to these concerns, whereas the mother thought Tom needed the extra attention. Due to Tom's distress, his mother's concern, and the conflict between the parents, the mother presented the problems to Tom's pediatrician, who initially recommended that the parents ignore Tom's nocturnal distress. The parents found this advice impossible to follow because of Tom's extraordinary emotional response, and subsequently the pediatrician recommended they seek services from my office.

During the interview, the parents revealed several potentiating factors, the most significant of which appeared to be a recent move from a small home in a well-established neighborhood to a large home in a new suburb. Tom had shared a bedroom with his sister in his previous home that was very close to their parents' room. He had his own room in the new home, and it was on the opposite end of the second floor from the parents' room. In addition, Tom's mother disclosed that she was an anxious person who had had trouble with bedtime, sleep onset, and nightmares as a child. She also reported that several of her relatives, including her own mother, had histories of anxiety problems. Thus she empathized with her son and said it was very hard for her to ignore him when he was distressed at night. According to Dad, Mom was overly solicitous with Tom not only at bedtime but in response to any form of distress, physical or emotional. Mom reported feeling that Dad was possibly too emotionally distant when it came to addressing Tom's distress and felt that she needed to do extra to supplement Dad's presumed insufficient response. Thus she was the parent targeted by Tom at night.

History

A typical day interview revealed that bedtime was at 8:30 and included a well-established bedtime routine involving hygiene (e.g., bath), dressing (e.g., pajamas), stories, hugs, and lights out. Immediately prior to the initial episode, the bedtime routine had been nonproblematic. However, the parents reported an early history of resistance to bedtime, resulting in periodic stays by Tom in their room. Although their memory of these events was somewhat hazy, they reported that the peak incidence occurred around the age of 3. Additionally, Mom reported that Tom had been mildly colicky. Neither of Tom's siblings had exhibited bedtime problems, and both had their own room and their own routine, which they followed regularly. However, the intensity of Tom's distress at night had begun distressing his siblings at the time of the referral, especially his younger sister. The parents were fearful that she would begin to mimic his responses in order to obtain their attention.

The remainder of the typical day interview revealed little of clinical significance. For example, Tom's morning routine was regularly completed without disruption or instances of significant countercontrol. There was no resistance to the seatbelt on the car ride to school. Upon returning home from school he routinely had a snack, did about 15 minutes of homework, and then played with friends in the neighborhood or his siblings. The family evening meal was a sit-down version, and there were no reported instances of significant misbehavior during it. He watched approximately 1 hour of television a day and was allowed to play video games for 1/2 hour.

However, he had no household responsibilities that were regularly enforced. For example, the parents had requested that he make his bed on a daily basis and also bring his dishes to the sink after the evening meal, but, on average, he made his bed once a week and it usually had to be redone by his mother. He also rarely brought his dishes to the sink. The parents reported that bedroom time-out was their primary disciplinary method but that they employed it rarely and could not remember a recent instance. As the parents described expectations and discipline, their tone took on a confessional note and they seemed somewhat embarrassed by how easy they had made life for Tom. Nonetheless, behavior screening via the parent version of the Child Behavior Checklist (Achenbach, 1991) did not reveal any significant externalizing problems; the only elevations were in the Anxiety subscale.

Case Conceptualization

My clinical impression of this case was that it involved a form of separation anxiety brought on by problematic adjustment to a recent move, a related dramatically altered bedroom configuration, and nocturnal separation between child and parent. Tom was probably predisposed to anxiety and worry as a function of family history stemming from mother's own history and symptoms that, in turn, had their own family history leading back through a grandparent. The difference of opinion between parents about how best to approach Tom's distress and the limited extent to which household expectations of him had been enforced and discipline had been imposed may have increased his susceptibility to clinically significant experiential avoidance problems such as separation anxiety (Friman, in press-c; Hayes, Wilson, Gifford, Follette, & Strosahl, 1996). In other words, he may not have been prepared to manage the sudden onset of bedtime distress because he had had little experience addressing daytime distress. The progression of his overt distress that was occurring an hour or two after bedtime prior to the referral to distress occurring at, and increasingly before, bedtime at the time of the referral suggests that Tom's condition was worsening and that he was at risk for more generalized problems.

Course of Treatment

The treatment prescribed involved the bedtime pass procedure. In addition, Tom was taught relaxation exercises, to visualize pleasant settings and events when distressed, and controlled breathing. In the bedtime pass portion of treatment, Tom was given a bedtime pass after he had completed his bedtime routine and was in bed. He was informed that he could use the pass to summon his parents to address a simple request or to seek them out for the same purpose. Once the request had been satisfied, he would surrender the pass and spend the remainder of the evening in bed alone. An incentive was added to the program, allowing Tom to turn in unused passes for use in a simple reward program. In that program, Tom identified something that he wanted his parents to purchase for him and that they agreed was appropriate (a video game). Tom and his parents drew a picture of the item using a dot-to-dot format. For each unused pass, Tom was allowed to connect one dot, and when the dots were completely connected, the parents purchased the item for him.

(Continued)

Estimate of Progress

Immediately upon implementation of the program, Tom completed three nights without calling out or coming out of his bedroom, thus earning three dots on his dot-to-dot incentive program. On the fourth night, a strong storm moved through the area and Tom called out for his parents and subsequently joined the entire family in the basement because of a tornado warning. Because of the extraordinary nature of this night, he was allowed to keep his pass and turn it in for a dot. However, the next night he again called out for his parents and used his pass even though the weather was calm. Subsequently, he stopped calling out or coming out and earned 12 continuous days of nonpass use. On the 13th night he had a bad dream and called out for his parents and used his pass. In the 3 weeks since that night, he has not used the pass, has earned his reward, and the parents asked if they could discontinue the pass program and transfer the dot-to-dot reward program to other accomplishments.

Complicating Factors

The only complicating factor in this case involved the disagreement between the parents over how to manage Tom's nocturnal distress, and it was resolved easily with the pass program. Tom's enthusiastic response to the pass program and to the exercises he was taught seemed to reassure the parents that they had pursued the right course of action.

Managed Care Considerations

Primary managed care considerations in cases such as this one involve third-party reimbursement. There were no concerns here, however, because Tom met criteria for a covered condition, specifically Adjustment Disorder with Anxiety Features. Only three visits were needed to resolve the problem, and although a fourth was scheduled, it was canceled by the parents by telephone because there was no apparent need. Therefore, the diagnosable condition along with the short number of visits rendered any managed care concerns moot. After the third and final treatment session, follow-up was accomplished by telephone just prior to the scheduled fourth visit, and during the telephone call, the parents expressed no concern. Tom also participated in the call and expressed his excitement about mastering bedtime and also earning his video game.

Implications of the Case

This case represents a classic example of PCBP treatment for routine behavior problems. The problem initially surfaced in PMC and failed a course of treatment provided there. Subsequently, the PMC provider referred the case to a PCBP clinic, where it was quickly classified and effectively treated with just three clinic visits. Additionally, a generalized anxiety condition did not occur, and thus the brief course of treatment could be characterized as preventive. This last point is important because I suspect Tom was at risk for more generalized conditions given his history and the spread of symptoms that had occurred prior to the first visit. Thus, this case represents the fundamental goal of treatment in primary care behavioral pediatrics: prevention.

RECOMMENDATIONS TO CLINICIANS AND STUDENTS

My primary recommendation is to consider following a similar approach to problems of a routine sort that are referred to practitioners by PMC providers. Specifically, routine problems initially presenting in PMC, as was the case with this one, do not necessarily require a comprehensive psychiatric evaluation before treatment is pursued. A simple behavioral screening in conjunction with a good, verbally based diagnostic interview can direct the clinician to prescribe treatment for the vast majority of referral problems or more evaluation for those problems that appear to involve clinically significant dimensions that extend beyond the initial description of the presenting complaint. In the majority of cases where treatment is pursued, the treatment itself becomes a form of assessment because response to it directs the next course of action. In situations where the problem resolves, such as this one, no further clinical care is needed. In situations where it does not, additional assessment and treatment revision are needed.

A second recommendation is to consider modifying treatment protocols in accord with the presentation of the case, even if an empirically supported treatment is used. The safest way to do this is to include all of the components of the empirically supported treatment and add other components in accord with presumed clinical benefit. In this case, the bedtime pass program was used in a fashion consistent with its description in the two experimental small n studies (Freeman, 2006; Friman et al., 1999) and randomized clinical trial (Moore et al., 1997) mentioned in the section on common behavior problems, and it was augmented by visualization, relaxation, and a breathing exercise, along with an incentive system. Whether these augmentations added to the active ingredients in treatment or merely enhanced its social validity isn't possible to determine from a case report. Nonetheless, the added components did appear to please Tom as well as his parents and may possibly have made the entire treatment protocol more acceptable. Whether this can be demonstrated empirically is a question for future research.

SUMMARY

The three domains of care—common behavior problems, behavior problems with significant medical dimensions, and medical problems with significant behavioral dimensions—the representative problems used to illustrate them, and the case illustration were supplied to provide an overview of PCBP. The main purpose of this chapter was to present PCBP as a partial solution to problems occupying the gap in behavioral health care between PMC and MHS for children with behavior problems. Because many more providers are needed, another purpose of the chapter was to increase interest in PCBP. Generally, the field favors those whose orientation to practice is guided by science more than art, whose claim to expertise is predicated on empiricism more than clinical or ex cathedra authority, and whose methods are typified more by procedure than process. Thus, there are similarities between PCBP providers and those in some branches of psychology (e.g., behavior therapy, applied behavior analysis, pediatric psychology) but not in others (e.g., psychoanalysis, existentialist psychology, human potential psychology).

Although many of the behavior problems addressed in PCBP are clinically un-remarkable, some actually are, resemble, or if unresolved can lead to clinically significant conditions, and thus they require some level of professional assessment prior to intervention. For example, most bedtime problems are functional, but they can chronically resist lay attempts at resolution, resulting in multiple other problems that put not only children at increased risk, but also the parents and family. Furthermore, a small percentage of problems actually involve biologically disordered sleep processes, and these need to be identified and referred to appropriate specialists. As another example, most cases involving child incontinence are also functional, but they can easily be under- or overinterpreted and correspondingly under- or overtreated, resulting in serious health consequences for affected children. Furthermore, a small percentage of cases actually involve pathological processes, and these need to be identified early and referred to appropriate specialists. There are many other examples, generally involving behavior problems resulting from a mismatch between situational requirements for child exhibition of adaptive behavior and/or inhibition of maladaptive behavior and child behavioral skill levels (Blum & Friman, 2000; Christophersen, 1982; Friman, 2005a; Friman & Blum, 2003; Friman & Piazza, in press).

The PCBP perspective on these problems is that most do not involve pathology, many will resolve with time and health education, some will require prescriptive treatment, and all can benefit from some level of professional assessment to determine which is which. As indicated, the problems usually emerge as a function of the friction between child preference and/or skill level and the requirements inherent in socialization and education processes. If unresolved, the problems can devolve into bona fide pathological conditions, but the PCBP perspective is that little scientific or clinical benefit is gained from the assumption that the presence of a behavior problem necessarily occurs as a function of an underlying psychopathology (e.g., Friman, 2002; also see Horwitz, 2002). This perspective, unfortunately, appears to be at odds with the vast majority of psychology and psychiatric literature on child behavior problems, which is focused almost entirely on detection of psychopathology with minimal regard for detection of child health. In fact, very few clinical assessment instruments are even designed to detect healthy child behavior. Behavior assessment instruments used in the research on and practice of child behavior problems ask questions about symptoms or behavior problems, and the typical intent is to determine whether a given child has significantly more symptoms or problems than the children of a similar age in the group used to norm the instruments. The de facto definition of child behavioral health within clinical child psychology and psychiatry appears to involve a composite of symptoms and problems that are below a threshold established for clinical significance, not a composite of healthful behaviors. In other words, appropriate functioning is conventionally viewed as the absence of illness, not necessarily the presence of health.

Because it is much more concerned with prevention than cure or rehabilitation, PCBP provides a health-based alternative to the psychopathological context that pervades mainstream clinical child psychology and psychiatry (Friman, 2002; Horwitz, 2002). This is not to say that PCBP disputes or disregards the possibility of child psychopathology. Standard practice in PCBP involves referral to appropriate specialists when presenting problems are deemed to be beyond the bounds of primary care or when they prove resistant to interventions attempted with PCBP. This referral practice is as much a part of PCBP as it is any other branch of pediatrics. The essential point here, however, is that the conventional assumption in PCBP is one of child behavioral health until proven otherwise.

Perhaps the best way to view the PCBP approaches to behavior problems is as a first line of defense. To use a medical metaphor, the typical intent is to strengthen children's immunity against threats to behavioral health. The problems that pose such threats typically involve mild to moderate child behavior problems, most of which are responsive to changes in practices by parents, other caregivers, and teachers. Although some of the problems may meet diagnostic criteria for clinical conditions (e.g., enuresis, encopresis, simple phobias, Oppositional Defiant Disorder), the problems are usually in their early stages and are much more responsive to changes in teaching or training practices than problems that have been chronic for years. Thus, even though PCBP provides treatment, the context of care is still characterized as preventive rather than curative or rehabilitative. And, as the provision of PCBP services widens, the gap in behavioral health care for children in this country could correspondingly narrow.

REFERENCES

Achenbach, T. (1991). *Manual for the Child Behavior Checklist/4–18 and 1991 profile*. Burlington: University of Vermont, Department of Psychiatry.

Adams, L. A., & Rickert, V. I. (1989). Reducing bedtime tantrums: Comparison between positive routines and graduated extinction. *Pediatrics, 84*, 756–761.

American Academy of Pediatrics, Committee on Psychosocial Aspects of Child Family Health. (2001). The new morbidity revisited: A renewed commitment to the psychosocial aspects of pediatric care. *Pediatrics, 108*, 1227–1230.

American Psychiatric Association. (1994). *Diagnostic and statistical manual of mental disorders* (4th ed.). Washington, DC: Author.

Andrews, V. H., & Hall, H. R. (1990). The effects of relaxation/imagery training on recurrent aphthous stomatitis: A preliminary study. *Psychosomatic Medicine, 52*, 526–535.

Barr, R. G., Levine, M. D., Wilkinson, R. H., & Mulvihill, D. (1979). Chronic and occult stool retention: A clinical tool for its evaluation in school aged children. *Clinical Pediatrics, 18*, 674–686.

Berk, L. B., & Friman, P. C. (1990). Epidemiologic aspects of toilet training. *Clinical Pediatrics, 29*, 278–282.

Blampied, N. M., & France, K. G. (1993). A behavioral model of sleep disturbance. *Journal of Applied Behavior Analysis, 26*, 477–492.

Blum, N. J., & Carey, W. B. (1996). Bedtime problems among infants and young children. *Pediatrics in Review, 17*, 87–93.

Blum, N. J., & Friman, P. C. (2000). Behavioral pediatrics: The confluence of applied behavior analysis and pediatric medicine. In J. Carr & J. Austin (Eds.), *Handbook of applied behavior analysis*. (pp. 161–186.). Reno, NV: Context Press.

Blum, N. J., Williams, G., Friman, P. C., & Christophersen, E. R. (1995). Disciplining young children: The role of verbal instructions and reason. *Pediatrics, 96*, 336–341.

Bowman, L. G., Fisher, W. W., Thompson, R. H., & Piazza, C. C. (1997). On the relation of mands and the function of destructive behavior. *Journal of Applied Behavior Analysis, 30*, 251–265.

Burke, R. V., Kuhn, B. R., & Peterson, J. L. (2004). A "storybook" ending to children's bedtime problems: The use of a rewarding social story to reduce bedtime resistance and frequent night waking. *Journal of Pediatric Psychology, 29*, 389–396.

Caspi, A., & Moffitt, T. (1995). The continuity of maladaptive behavior: From description to understanding in the study of antisocial behavior. In D. Cicchetti & D. Cohen (Eds.), *Developmental psychopathology* (Vol. *2*, pp. 472–511). New York: Wiley.

Christophersen, E. R. (1982). Incorporating behavioral pediatrics into primary care. *Pediatric Clinics of North America, 29*, 261–295.

Christophersen, E. R. (1988). *Little people.* Kansas City, MO. Westport Press.

Christophersen, E. R. (1994). *Pediatric compliance: A guide for the primary care physician,* New York: Plenum Press.

Christophersen, E. R., & Friman, P. C. (2004). Elimination disorders, In R. Brown (Ed.), *Handbook of pediatric psychology in school settings* (pp. 467–488). Mahwah, NJ: Erlbaum.

Christophersen, E. R., & Mortweet, S. (2001). *Treatments that work with children: Empirically supported strategies for managing childhood problems,* Washington, DC: American Psychological Association.

Christophersen, E. R., & Rainey, S. (1976). Management of encopresis through a pediatric outpatient clinic. *Journal of Pediatric Psychology, 1*, 38–41.

Christophersen, E. R., & Rapoff, M. A. (1979). Behavioral pediatrics. In O. F. Pomerleau & J. P. Brady (Eds.), *Behavioral medicine: Theory and practice* (pp. 99–123). Baltimore: Williams & Wilkins.

Christophersen, E. R., & Rapoff, M. A. (1983). Toileting problems of children. In C. E. Walker & M. C. Roberts (Eds.), *Handbook of clinical child psychology* (pp. 583–605). New York: Wiley.

Cooper, S., Valleley, R. J., Polaha, J., Begeny, J., & Evans, J. H. (2005). Running out of time: Physician health concerns in rural pediatric primary care. *Pediatrics, 118*, 132–138.

Costello, E. J. (1988). Primary care pediatrics and child psychopathology: A review of diagnostic, treatment, and referral practices. *Pediatrics, 78*, 1044–1051.

Costello, E. J., Burns, B. J., Costello, A. J., Edelbrock, C., Dulcan, M., & Brent, D. (1988). Service utilization and psychiatric diagnosis in pediatric primary care: The role of the gatekeeper. *Pediatrics, 82*, 435–441.

Costello, E. J., Edelbrock, C., Costello, A. J., Dulcan, M., Burns, B. J., & Brent, D. (1988). Psychopathology in pediatric primary care: The new hidden morbidity. *Pediatrics, 82*, 415–424.

Costello, E. J., & Shugart, M. A. (1992). Above and below the threshold: Severity of psychiatric symptoms and functional impairment in a pediatric sample. *Pediatrics, 90*, 359–368.

Culbert, T. P., Kajander, R. L., & Reaney, J. B. (1996). Biofeedback with children and adolescents: Clinical observations and patient perspectives. *Journal of Developmental and Behavioral Pediatrics, 17*, 342–350.

Davidson, M. (1958). Constipation and fecal incontinence. *Pediatric Clinics of North America, 5*, 749–757.

Drews, A., & Friman, P. C. (2003). Trichotillomania. In T. Ollendick & C. Schroeder (Eds.), *Encyclopedia of pediatric and child psychology* (pp. 685–687). New York: Kluwer Press.

Dulcan, M. K., Costello, E. J., Costello, A. J., Edelbrock, C., Brent, D., & Janiszewski, S. (1990). The pediatrician as gatekeeper to mental healthcare for children: Do parents' concerns open the gate? *Journal of the American Academy of Child and Adolescent Psychiatry, 29*, 453–458.

Earls, F. (1980). Prevalence of behavior problems in 3-year-old children: A cross national replication. *Archives of General Psychiatry, 37*, 1153–1157.

Edwards, K. J. (1993). The use of brief time outs during the day to reduce bedtime struggles. *Dissertation Abstracts International, 54*, 2181.

Edwards, K. J., & Christophersen, E. R. (1994). Treating common bedtime problems of young children. *Journal of Developmental and Behavioral Pediatrics, 15*, 207–213.

Eggert, P., & Kuhn, B. (1995). Antidiuretic hormone regulation in patients with primary nocturnal enuresis. *Archives of Diseases in Childhood, 73*, 508–511.

Ferber, R. (1985). *Solve your child's bedtime problems.* New York: Simon & Schuster.

Field, C., & Friman, P. C. (2006). Encopresis. In J. Fisher & W. O'Donohue (Eds.), *Practitioners' guide to evidence based psychotherapy* (pp. 277–283). New York: Springer.

Finney, J. W., Brophy, C. J., Friman, P. C., Golden, A. S., Richman, G. S., & Ross, A. F. (1990). Promoting parent-provider interaction during child health supervision visits. *Journal of Applied Behavior Analysis, 23*, 207–214.

Finney, J. W., Lemanek, K. L., Cataldo, M. F., Katz, H. P., & Fuqua, R. W. (1989). Pediatric psychology in primary health care: Brief targeted therapy for recurrent abdominal pain. *Behavior Therapy, 20*, 283–291.

Finney, J. W., Miller, K. M., & Adler, S. P. (1993). Changing protective and risky behaviors to prevent child-to-parent transmission of cytomegalovirus. *Journal of Applied Behavior Analysis, 26*, 471–472.

Freeman, K. A. (2006). Treating bedtime resistance with the bedtime pass: A systematic replication and component analysis with 3-year-olds. *Journal of Applied Behavior Analysis, 39*, 423–428.

Friedman, S. B. (1975). Foreword: Symposium on behavioral pediatrics. *Pediatric Clinics of North America, 22*, 555–556.

Friedman, S. B., Phillips, S., & Parrish, J. (1983). Current status of behavioral pediatric training for general pediatric residents: A study of 11 funded programs. *Pediatrics, 71*, 904–908.

Friman, P. C. (1986). A preventive context for enuresis. *Pediatric Clinics of North America, 33*, 871–886.

Friman, P. C. (1995). Nocturnal enuresis in the child. In R. Ferber & M. H. Kryger (Eds.), *Principles and practice of sleep medicine in the child* (pp. 107–114). Philadelphia: Saunders.

Friman, P. C. (2000). Behavioral family-style residential care for troubled out-of-home adolescents: Recent findings. In J. Carr & J. Austin (Eds.), *Handbook of applied behavior analysis* (pp. 187–210). Reno, NV: Context Press.

Friman, P. C. (2002, May). *The psychopathological interpretation of common child behavior problems: A critique and related opportunity for behavior analysis*. Invited address at the 28th annual convention of the Association for Behavior Analysis, Toronto, Canada.

Friman, P. C. (2003). A biobehavioral bowel and toilet training treatment for functional encopresis. In W. Odonohue, S. Hayes, & J. Fisher (Eds.), *Empirically supported techniques of cognitive behavior therapy* (pp. 51–58). Hoboken, NJ: Wiley.

Friman, P. C. (2005a). Behavioral pediatrics. In A. M. Gross & R. S. Drabman (Eds.), *Encyclopedia of behavior modification and therapy* (Vol. 2, pp. 731–739). Thousand Oaks, CA: Sage.

Friman, P. C. (2005b). *Good night, we love you we will miss you, now go to bed and go to sleep: Managing bedtime problems in young children*. Boys Town, NE: Girls and Boys Town Press.

Friman, P. C. (2005c). Time out. In S. Lee (Ed.), *Encyclopedia of school psychology* (pp. 568–570). Thousand Oaks, CA: Sage.

Friman, P. C. (in press-a). Behavioral assessment. In M. Hersen, D. Barlow, & F. Andrasik (Eds.), *Single case experimental designs* (3rd ed.). Boston: Allyn & Bacon.

Friman, P. C. (in press-b). Evidence based therapies for enuresis and encopresis. In R. G. Steele, T. D. Elkin, & M. C. Roberts (Eds.), *Handbook of evidence-based therapies for children and adolescents*. New York: Springer.

Friman, P. C. (in press-c). The fear factor: A functional approach to anxiety. In P. Sturmey (Ed.), *Treatment and intervention in clinical psychology: Functional analytic approaches*. San Diego, CA: Elsevier.

Friman, P. C., & Blum, N. J. (2003). Primary care behavioral pediatrics. In M. Hersen & W. Sledge (Eds.), *Encyclopedia of psychotherapy* (pp. 379–399). New York: Academic Press.

Friman, P. C., Byrd, M. R., & Oksol, E. M. (2001). Oral digital habits: Demographics, phenomenology, causes, functions, and clinical associations. In D. W. Woods & R. Miltenberger (Eds.), *Tic disorders, trichotillomania, and other repetitive behavior disorders: Behavioral approaches to analysis and treatment* (pp. 197–222). New York: Kluwer Academic/Plenum Press.

Friman, P. C., & Christophersen, E. R. (1986) Biobehavioral prevention in primary care. In N. Krasnegor, J. D. Arasteh, & M. F. Cataldo (Eds.), *Child health behavior: A behavioral pediatrics perspective* (pp. 254–280). New York: Wiley.

Friman, P. C., & Finney, J. W. (2003). Teaching parents to use time out (and time in). In W. Odonohue, S. Hayes, & J. Fisher (Eds.), *Empirically supported techniques of cognitive behavior therapy* (pp. 429–435). Hoboken, NJ: Wiley.

Friman, P. C., Handwerk, M. L., Swearer, S. M., McGinnis, C., & Warzak, W. J. (1998). Do children with primary nocturnal enuresis have clinically significant behavior problems? *Archives of Pediatrics and Adolescent Medicine, 152*, 537–539.

Friman, P. C., Hoff, K. E., Schnoes, C., Freeman, K. A., Woods, D. W., & Blum, N. (1999). The bedtime pass: An approach to bedtime crying and leaving the room. *Archives of Pediatric and Adolescent Medicine, 153*, 1027–1029.

Friman, P. C., & Hove, G. (1987). Apparent covariation between child habit disorders: Effects of successful treatment for thumb sucking on untargeted chronic hair pulling. *Journal of Applied Behavior Analysis, 20*, 421–426.

Friman, P. C., & Jones, K. M. (1998). Elimination disorders in children. In S. Watson & F. Gresham (Eds.), *Handbook of child behavior therapy* (pp. 239–260). New York: Plenum Press.

Friman, P. C., & Jones, K. M. (2005). Behavioral treatment for nocturnal enuresis. *Journal of Early and Intensive Behavioral Intervention, 2*, 259–267.

Friman, P. C., Mathews, J. R., Finney, J. W., & Christophersen, E. R. (1988). Do children with encopresis have clinically, significant behavior problems? *Pediatrics, 82*, 407–409.

Friman, P. C., & Piazza, C. (in press). Behavioral pediatrics. In W. Fisher (Ed.), *Handbook of applied behavior analysis*. New York: Guilford Press.

Friman, P. C., & Schmitt, B. D. (1989). Thumb sucking: Guidelines for pediatricians. *Clinical Pediatrics, 28*, 438–440.

Friman, P. C., & Vollmer, D. (1995). Successful use of the nocturnal urine alarm for diurnal enuresis. *Journal of Applied Behavior Analysis, 28*, 89–90.

Gabel, S., Hegedus, A. M., Wald, A., Chandra, R., & Chaponis, D. (1986). Prevalence of behavior problems and mental health utilization among encopretic children. *Journal of Developmental and Behavioral Pediatrics, 7*, 293–297.

Glasscock, S. G., O'Brien, S. O., Friman, P. C., Christophersen, E. R., & MacLean, W. E. (1989). Residency training in behavioral pediatrics. *Journal of Developmental and Behavioral Pediatrics, 10*, 262–263.

Goldberg, I. D., Roghmann, K. J., McInerny, T. K., & Burke, J. D. (1984). Mental health problems among children seen in pediatric practice: Prevalence and management. *Pediatrics, 73*, 278–293.

Hagan, J. F. (2001). The new morbidity: Where the rubber hits the road or the practitioner's guide to the new morbidity. *Pediatrics, 108*, 1206–1210.

Halliday, S., Meadow, S. R., & Berg, I. (1987). Successful management of daytime enuresis using alarm procedures: A randomly controlled trial. *Archives of Disease in Children, 62*, 132–137.

Hatch, T. F. (1988). Encopresis and constipation in children. *Pediatric Clinics of North America, 35*, 257–281.

Hayes, S. C., Wilson, K. G., Gifford, E. V., Follette, V. M., & Strosahl, K. (1996). Experiential avoidance and behavior disorders: A functional dimensional approach to diagnosis and treatment. *Journal of Consulting and Clinical Psychology, 64*, 1152–1168.

Helfer, R. E., & Kempe, C. H. (1976). *Child abuse and neglect*. Cambridge, MA: Ballinger.

Hickson, G. B., Altemeier, W. A., & O'Connor, S. (1983). Concerns of mothers seeking care in private pediatric offices: Opportunities for expanding services. *Pediatrics, 72*, 619–624.

Horwitz, A. V. (2002). *Creating mental illness*. Chicago: University of Chicago Press.

Horwitz, S. M., Leaf, P. J., Leventhal, J. M., Forsyth, B., & Speechley, K. N. (1992). Identification and management of psychosocial and developmental problems in community-based, primary care pediatric practices. *Pediatrics, 89*, 480–485.

Houts, A. C. (1991). Nocturnal enuresis as a biobehavioral problem. *Behavior Therapy, 22*, 133–151.

Houts, A. C., Mellon, M. W., & Whelan, J. P. (1988). Use of dietary fiber and stimulus control to treat retentive encopresis: A multiple baseline investigation. *Journal of Pediatric Psychology, 13*, 435–445.

Irwin, C. E., Cataldo, M. F., Matheny, A. P., & Peterson, L. (1992). Health consequences of behaviors: Injury as a model. *Pediatrics, 90*, 798–807.

Kanoy, K. W., & Schroeder, C. S. (1985). Suggestions to parents about common behavior problems in a pediatric primary care office: Five years of follow-up. *Journal of Pediatric Psychology, 10*, 15–30.

Kelleher, K. J., Scholle, S. H., Feldman, H. M., & Nace, D. (1999). A fork in the road: Decision time for behavioral pediatrics. *Journal of Developmental and Behavioral Pediatrics, 20*, 181–186.

Kempe, C. H., Helfer, R. E., & Krugman, R. D. (1987). *The battered child* (5th ed.). Chicago: University of Chicago Press.

Koff, S. A. (1995). Why is desmopressin sometimes ineffective at curing bedwetting? *Scandinavian Journal of Urology and Nephrology (Suppl.), 173*, 103–108.

Lackgren, G., Neveus, T., & Stenberg, A. (1997). Diurnal plasma vasopressin and urinary output in adolescents with monosymptomatic nocturnal enuresis. *Acta Paediatrica, 86*, 385–390.

Lavigne, J. V., Binns, H. J., Christoffel, K. K., Rosenbaum, D., Arend, R., Smith, K., et al. (1993). Behavioral and emotional problems among preschool children in pediatric primary care: Prevalence and pediatrician's recognition. *Pediatrics, 91*, 649–655.

Leinwand, D. (2006, December 4). Ads target stigma of mental illness among youth. *USA Today*. Retrieved January 3, 2007, from http://www.usatoday.com/news/health/2006–12-3-mental-ad-x.htm.

Levine, M. D. (1975). Children with encopresis: A descriptive analysis. *Pediatrics, 56*, 407–409.

Levine, M. D. (1982). Encopresis: Its potentiation, evaluation, and alleviation. *Pediatric Clinics of North America, 29*, 315–330.

Lowery, S., Srour, J., Whitehead, W. E., & Schuster, M. M. (1985). Habit training as treatment of encopresis secondary to chronic constipation. *Journal of Pediatric Gastroenterology and Nutrition, 4*, 397–401.

Lozoff, B., Wolf, A. W., & Davis, N. S. (1985). Bedtime problems seen in pediatric practice. *Pediatrics, 75*, 477–483.

Mace, F., Hock, M. L., Lalli, J. S., West, B. J., Belfiore, P., & Pinter, E., et al. (1988). Behavioral momentum in the treatment of noncompliance. *Journal of Applied Behavioral Analysis, 21*, 123–142.

Mellon, M. W., Scott, M. A., Haynes, K. B., Schmidt, D. F., & Houts, A. C. (1997, April). *EMG recording of pelvic floor conditioning in nocturnal enuresis during urine alarm treatment: A preliminary study*. Paper presentation at the sixth Florida Conference on Child Health Psychology, University of Florida, Gainesville.

Mellon, M. W., Whiteside, S. P., & Friedrich, W. N. (2006). The relevance of fecal soiling as an indicator of child sexual abuse: A preliminary analysis. *Developmental and Behavioral Pediatrics, 27*, 25–32.

Meunier, P., Marechal, J. M., & De Beaujeu, M. J. (1979). Rectoanal pressures and rectal sensitivity in chronic childhood constipation. *Gastroenterology, 77*, 330–336.

Moffatt, M. E. (1997). Nocturnal enuresis: A review of the efficacy of treatments and practical advice for clinicians. *Journal of Developmental and Behavioral Pediatrics, 18*, 49–56.

Moore, B., Friman, P. C., Fruzetti, A. E., & MacAleese, K. (2007). Brief report. Evaluating the bedtime pass program for child resistance to bedtime: A randomized controlled trial. *Journal of Pediatric Psychology, 33*, 283–287.

O'Brien, S., Ross, L. V., & Christophersen, E. R. (1986). Primary encopresis: Evaluation and treatment. *Journal of Applied Behavior Analysis, 19*, 137–145.

Olness, K., Culbert, T., & Uden, D. (1989). Self-regulation of salivary immunoglobulin A by children. *Pediatrics, 83*, 66–71.

Peters, R. (1998). *It's never too soon to discipline*. New York: St. Martin's Griffin.

Regalado, M., Sereen, H., Inkelas, M., Wissow, L. S., & Halfon, N. (2004). Parents' discipline of young children: Results from the national survey of early childhood health. *Pediatrics, 113*, 1952–1958.

Reisinger, K. S., & Bires, J. A. (1980). Anticipatory guidance in pediatric practice. *Pediatrics, 66*, 889–892.

Rickert, V. I., & Johnson, M. (1988). Reducing nocturnal awaking and crying episodes in infants and young children: A comparison between scheduled awakenings and systematic ignoring. *Pediatrics, 81*, 203–212.

Rittig, S., Knudsen, U. B., Norgaard, J. P., Pedersen, E. B., & Djurhuus, J. C. (1989). Abnormal diurnal rhythm of plasma vasopressin and urinary output in patients with enuresis. *American Journal of Physiology, 256*, F644–671.

Ruckstuhl, L. E., & Friman, P. C. (2003, May). *Evaluating the effectiveness of the vibrating urine alarm: A study of effectiveness and social validity*. Paper presented at the 29th annual convention of the Association for Behavior Analysis, San Francisco, CA.

Schmitt, B. D. (1987). Seven deadly sins of childhood: Advising parents about difficult developmental phases. *Child Abuse and Neglect, 11*, 421–432.

Skinner, B. F. (1966). The phylogeny and ontogeny of behavior. *Science, 153*, 1205–1213.

Starfield, B., Gross, E., Wood, M., Pantell, R., Allen, C., Gordon, I. B., et al. (1980). Psychosocial and psychosomatic diagnoses in primary care of children. *Pediatrics, 66*, 159–167.

Stark, L. J., Knapp, L. G., Bowen, A. M., Powers, S. W., Jelalian, E., Evans, S., et al. (1993). Increasing caloric consumption in children with cystic fibrosis: Replication with 2-year follow-up. *Journal of Applied Behavior Analysis, 26*, 435–450.

Stark, L. J., Opipari, L. C., Donaldson, D. L., Danovsky, M. R., Rasile, D. A., & DelSanto, A. F. (1997). Evaluation of a standard protocol for rententive encopresis: A replication. *Journal of Pediatric Psychology, 22*, 619–633.

Stark, L. J., Owens-Stively, J., Spirito, A., Lewis, A., & Guevremont, D. (1990). Group behavioral treatment of retentive encopresis. *Journal of Pediatric Psychology, 15*, 659–671.

Stark, L. J., Spirito, A., Lewis, A. V., & Hart, K. J. (1990). Encopresis: Behavioral parameters associated with children who fail medical management. *Child Psychiatry and Human Development, 20*, 169–179.

Teitelbaum, P. (1977). Levels of integration of the operant. In W. K. Honig & J. E. R. Staddon (Eds.), *Handbook of operant behavior* (pp. 7–27). Upper Saddle River, NJ: Prentice-Hall.

Vincent, S. A. (1974). Mechanical, electrical and other aspects of enuresis. In J. H. Johnston & W. Goodwin, (Eds.), *Reviews in pediatric urology* (pp. 280–313). New York: Elsevier.

Vollmer, T. R., & Iwata, B. A. (1992). Differential reinforcement as treatment for behavior disorders: Procedural and functional variations. *Research in Developmental Disabilities, 13*, 393–417.

Weinstock, L. B., & Clouse, R. E. (1987). A focused overview of gastrointestinal physiology. *Annals of Behavioral Medicine, 9*, 3–6.

Whitehead, W. E., & Schuster, M. M. (1985). *Gastrointestinal disorders: Behavioral and physiological basis for treatment.* New York: Academic Press.

Wissow, L. S., Roter, D., Larson, S., Wang, M.-C., Hwang, W.-T., & Johnson, R. (2002). Mechanisms behind the failure of longitudinal primary care to promote the disclosure and discussion of psychosocial issues. *Archives of Pediatrics and Adolescent Medicine, 156*, 685–692.

Wright, L. (1973). Handling the encopretic child. *Professional Psychology, 3*, 137–144.

Wright, L. (1975). Outcome of a standardized program for treating psychogenic encopresis. *Professional Psychology, 6*, 453–456.

Wright, L., Schaefer, A. B., & Solomons, G. (1979). *Encyclopedia of pediatric psychology.* Baltimore: University Park Press.

Wright, L., & Walker, E. (1977). Treatment of the child with psychogenic encopresis. *Clinical Pediatrics, 16*, 1042–1045.

CHAPTER 25

Peer Intervention

Michelle S. Rivera and Douglas W. Nangle

Peers are being used as intervention agents with increasing frequency. No doubt, this growth is largely attributable to the many advantages of peer interventions, perhaps the most prominent of which are convenience and cost-effectiveness (Covert & Wangberg, 1992; Fowler, 1988; Topping & Ehly, 1998). Though most often used with elementary-school-age children and adolescents, these interventions have also targeted preschoolers (e.g., Carey, 1997; Kohler, Strain, Hoyson, & Jamieson, 1997) and adults (e.g., Moore, 2005). The wide scope of peer interventions is evidenced not only in their application across developmental levels, but also in the diverse range of targeted clinical problem areas and disorders. By no means an exhaustive list, peers have been used in interventions aimed at improving the social and communication skills of children with autism (e.g., Kohler et al., 1997), reducing medical fears (e.g., Elkins & Roberts, 1986), decreasing delinquency and aggression (e.g., Becker, Hall, Ursic, Jain, & Calhoun, 2004), resolving conflicts (e.g., Johnson & Johnson, 1996), promoting health behaviors (e.g., Agha & Rossem, 2004), and preventing suicide (e.g., Bagley, Tse, & Hoi-Wah, 1994).

This chapter provides an overview of peer interventions as they have been used with children and adolescents. Given the variety of populations, targets, and intervention formats, we begin the chapter with a review of recent categorization efforts and the delineation of specific intervention types. This is followed by coverage of more general issues in intervention implementation. Among these are important considerations regarding the peer interveners themselves, which include selection, training, and often overlooked concerns over the relative benefits and risks of participation. Continued discussion of general implementation issues, including advantages, disadvantages, ethical considerations, and evaluation, is followed by a review of applications targeting specific clinical problem areas. The chapter closes with an illustrative case example.

PEER INTERVENTION FORMS

The frequent and widespread use of peer interventions has given rise to a number of attempts to define and categorize the various approaches. One area of agreement is that such interventions are a method of delivery rather than a specific treatment technique (e.g., Shiner, 1999). Their common element is that a child, rather than a therapist or teacher, implements the intervention (Shiner, 1999). Of course, adult involvement is still needed, but should not include continual prompting of the child's intervention efforts (Fowler, 1988). Common roles for adults are training the interveners, supervising the intervention, maintaining systems to monitor behavior, and arranging for rewards (Fowler, 1988). Some intervention formats may require greater adult supervision to ensure appropriate implementation, and younger children may require more adult support than older children or adolescents. Even with such adult involvement, however, peer interventions are "designed to be by and for young people; they themselves largely determine what is relevant in terms of information and how it is to be delivered" (Backett-Milburn & Wilson, 2000, p. 94).

Researchers have categorized past efforts in a number of different ways. Distinctions have been made between methods emphasizing skill development and those focusing on knowledge acquisition (Topping & Ehly, 1998). Shiner (1999) distinguishes between the constructs of peer development (i.e., a focus on the development of the interveners) and delivery (i.e., the provision of services). Perhaps the most widely discussed and useful distinctions are based on the roles of the children involved. That is, the child can either intervene directly or indirectly and either be the intervener or the target.

Peer interventions can be direct or indirect (Kalfus, 1984; Odom & Strain, 1984). In indirect approaches, an adult implements the intervention and the child is used in a supplementary role (e.g., as a model, employing group reinforcement contingencies). For instance, to reduce fears of medical procedures, children observed the responses of another child going through the same procedures (Elkins & Roberts, 1986; Stokes & Kennedy, 1980). In direct approaches, the peer implements the intervention and works to directly influence the target child's behavior. For example, Krantz, Ramsland, and McClannahan (1989) had one child with autism prompt others with the disorder to engage in conversations about sports. Most peer interventions appear to fall into the latter category. In the review of specific approaches that follows, we therefore include several direct approaches (e.g., education, mentoring, and counseling) and only one indirect approach (i.e., modeling).

The second distinction focuses on the rigidity of roles and whether a child can be both the intervener and the target or can serve only one of those functions (e.g., Fowler, 1988; Johnson & Johnson, 1995). Fowler describes three basic models characterizing the relationship between the target and the intervening child. In the "subject as client" model, the target child receives an intervention implemented by another child who generally exhibits desired behaviors (e.g., good social skills and teacher compliance) and is well-liked by peers. As such, one child or a small group of children are selected, by adults, to perform the role of intervener. In the "subject alternating as client and therapist" model, all group members have the opportunity to be both therapist and client and to switch between these roles. Members of the group may differ in their intervention needs, and some children may not be in need of intervention. Specific criteria may be used to choose the child who will serve as intervener on a particular day. For instance, the child may be required to exhibit a minimum level of a particular behavior. In the "subject as therapist" model, the target child serves as the intervener rather than the "client." This encourages the child to focus on the positive behaviors that he or she is rewarding in another child and may result in new positive interaction patterns between the child and his or her peers. Similarly, Johnson and Johnson described two models of the roles in peer counseling interventions. In the "cadre approach," a small number of children are trained to serve as counselors to aid other children in their problem-solving efforts. In the "student body approach," the entire student population is trained in intervention strategies (e.g., problem solving, conflict resolution) and has the opportunity to serve as counselors. These authors suggest that an advantage to this approach is that all children learn new strategies and can apply them outside of a formal intervention.

Having discussed common elements and distinguishing features, we now turn to a review of specific peer intervention types, including modeling, prompting and reinforcement, initiation, tutoring, education, mentoring, and counseling.

Peer Modeling

In peer modeling approaches, one or more competent children are used to exemplify the desired behaviors (Schunk, 1998). Three features are required: one or more models, one or more observers (learners), and a task to be performed (Schunk, 1998). Generally, a target child is paired with a more competent peer model whose behavior can be imitated. A common distinction is between mastery and coping models. The mastery model engages competently and skillfully in the desired behavior. In contrast, the coping model still needs to improve and learn to overcome problems. Thus, through observing a peer who is a mastery model, the target child can see what the desired behavior should look like. By observing a coping model, the target child can learn how to improve performance and handle difficulties or failures, in addition to the possibility of being comforted by the realization that other children face such challenges. Research has shown that both coping and mastery models can be effective in changing children's behavior (e.g., Schunk and Hansen, 1985). Regardless of whether a mastery or a coping model is used, the model and behavior should be selected carefully to reduce the chance of incorrect modeling or inability to learn the behavior (Schunk, 1998).

Another variant commonly used in social skills interventions is the "peer pairing" approach (e.g., Bierman & Furman, 1984; Prinz, Blechman, & Dumas, 1994). Target children are paired with a more competent peer, who receives no training and very little guidance. For instance, Prinz and colleagues used teacher ratings to select aggressive and nonaggressive socially competent children. These two types of children were then paired and given instructions (e.g., "Find out something that made your partner laugh this week") for performing role-plays. The socially competent peer always enacted the role-play first in an attempt to model appropriate behaviors; however, this peer was not given any prior instructions.

The effectiveness of modeling interventions depends on characteristics of the target child, the model, and the behavior to be learned. The modeled behavior is more likely to be followed if the model is the same sex as the target child and is perceived to have high power and the target child has high self-efficacy for and places importance on performing the action (Bandura, Ross, & Ross, 1963;

Grusec, 1992). When behaviors are rare or difficult to elicit or the model may have an unpredictable response (e.g., coping with medical procedures), video modeling of the desired behavior may be preferable (e.g., Gilbert et al., 1982). Observation of the model may be sufficient for simple behaviors, but further intervention is often required for more complicated actions (Schunk, 1998). When modeling alone is insufficient, the target child will need to practice the observed behavior and receive feedback regarding performance.

Modeling can be used to teach a variety of behaviors, including cognitive strategies, social skills, and coping methods. In modeling cognitive strategies, other children can be asked to verbalize their thought processes in solving problems. For example, Schunk and Hanson (1989) used two types of coping models to exhibit cognitive processes involved in learning math skills. The coping-emotive model initially made negative statements (e.g., exhibiting low self-esteem or the perceived difficulty of the task) and then positive coping statements (e.g., regarding the use of concentration or working hard), and the coping-alone model verbalized only positive coping statements. Peers have also been used to model social skills, such as conversational skills (e.g., Kohler et al., 1997) and play behaviors (e.g., Pierce & Schreibman, 1995). As part of a larger intervention, Pierce and Schreibman taught children to model social skills, including complex play behaviors and appropriate verbalizations during play in an attempt to improve the social behavior of children with autism. Others have used children to model emotional coping with stressful or anxiety-provoking events. For instance, Elkins and Roberts (1986) had children observe the emotional coping responses (e.g., talking about and successfully coping with fear) of a peer model undergoing an operation in an attempt to reduce fear of medical procedures.

With its versatility and potential for teaching novel responses, modeling has been included in interventions targeting quite a variety of clinical problems, such as coping with medical fears (e.g., Elkins & Roberts, 1986; Gilbert et al., 1982; Stokes & Kennedy, 1980), ameliorating academic difficulties (e.g., Schunk, Hanson, & Cox, 1987), and improving language skills (e.g., Kohler et al., 1997) and affective behavior in children with autism (e.g., Gena, Couloura, & Kymissis, 2005). In a particularly interesting application, Gena et al. used video modeling to help preschool-age children with autism better regulate their emotional expressions in reaction to situations eliciting the emotions of sympathy, appreciation, and disapproval. Videotapes exhibited age- and sex-matched peers displaying appropriate verbal and facial responses for each situation. Targeted children evidenced 100% accuracy in emotional responses within 10 sessions of video modeling.

Peer Prompting and Reinforcement

Peers are often used to prompt target children to engage in particular behaviors or to reinforce the appropriate use of behaviors. Prompting includes instruction and reinforcement for appropriately following the instruction (Odom & Strain, 1984). This strategy has been used to increase autistic children's language skills (e.g., Krantz et al., 1989), improve autistic children's social skills (e.g., Odom & Strain, 1986), and improve healthy eating behaviors in obese children (Foster, Wadden,

& Brownell, 1985). For example, Foster and colleagues conducted an intervention to improve health-related behaviors of obese children using behavioral change strategies that included a peer intervention component. In this component, eighth graders were trained to reinforce the eating behaviors of selected second- through fifth-grade students. A few times a week, children met with their peer intervener, who examined their lunchbox and provided verbal praise and stickers based on food choices. When compared to control children, those receiving the intervention lost significantly more weight and evidenced greater improvement in self-concept.

Peer Initiation

In peer initiation interventions, other children are used to initiate or maintain social interactions, such as play or conversation, with the target child (Carey, 1997; Guevremont, MacMillan, Shawchuck, & Hansen, 1989; Odom & Strain, 1984). It is sometimes difficult to ensure consistent implementation by the peer initiators, and adult prompts or rewards may be beneficial (Carey, 1997; Fowler, 1988). All in all, peer initiation interventions are relatively straightforward, and even preschoolers are able to successfully implement them (Carey, 1997).

Peer initiation has been included as a component of social skills training studies targeting children with autism (e.g., Goldstein, Kaczmarek, Pennington, & Shafer, 1992; Sasso, Mundschenck, Melloy, & Casey, 1998) and behaviorally disordered or developmentally delayed preschoolers (Goldstein & Wickstrom, 1986). Goldstein and Wickstrom (1992) taught two nonhandicapped peers to intervene with three target children with behavioral problems and developmental delays. The peer interveners prompted social interaction through actions such as establishing eye contact or a joint focus, responding to the target child's verbalizations, and describing play behaviors. The teacher used rewards (tokens that could be traded in for stickers or toys) and prompts (e.g., suggested new strategies) to ensure the cooperation of the interveners. All three target children exhibited and maintained improvements in the frequency of social interactions.

Peer Tutoring

Kalfus (1984) describes peer tutoring as needing to include any two or more of the following: instructions to the student, prompts for correct responding, praise, corrective feedback, and ignoring of specific student behaviors. Peer tutors are generally thought of as individuals who focus on ameliorating academic problems, and tutoring programs can take a structured or unstructured format (Kalfus, 1984). Structured programs provide formal training and clearly delineate who is the student and who is the tutor, whereas unstructured programs do not. The independence conferred on the tutor can vary across programs (Topping & Ehly, 1998). Tutors may be provided with specific materials or a detailed curriculum. In contrast, other tutors may be expected to design their own materials and curriculum content.

These programs have been applied effectively at the classroom (see Greenwood, Maheady, & Delquadri, 2002, for a review) and individual (Calhoon, 2005; DuPaul, Ervin, Hook, & McGoey, 1998) levels. Though specific academic skills are generally targeted, broader improvements in classroom behavior and on-task performance are often seen. In one example, DuPaul and colleagues used a classroomwide peer tutoring program to help improve the mathematics, spelling, and reading skills of target children diagnosed with Attention-Deficit/Hyperactivity Disorder (ADHD). Children were paired with each individual taking on the role of tutor. The tutor was given academic materials, including correct answers so that he or she could provide praise and reinforcement to the target child. Targeted ADHD children exhibited improvements in their on-task behavior as well as specific academic skills. In an example of a more structured program, Wright and Cleary (2006) implemented a cross-age reading skills tutoring intervention in which one child served exclusively as the tutor and the other as student. The tutor received four sessions of training that included appropriate behavior for tutors, the use of praise and other forms of encouragement, how to manage problem behavior, and instruction in the specific tutoring activity. Overall, children exhibited an increase in reading fluency of one word per week.

Peer Education

Peer education programs serve as a method of dispersing important or sensitive information throughout the peer group (Topping & Ehly, 1998). Children can, and already do, provide information to each other in a shared language (Mathie & Ford, 1998; Topping, 1996). Unlike teachers and other adults, peers can impart knowledge without being perceived as someone with authority. Children and adolescents may be unlikely to speak freely with individuals whom they know in other roles (e.g., teacher, administrator) that carry the weight of authority. Formalizing previously informal methods of knowledge transmission serves to increase the accuracy and credibility of the information communicated (Mathie & Ford, 1998; Topping, 1996; Topping & Ehly, 1998).

Peer education programs have been used to address substance abuse (Botvin, Baker, Filazzola, & Botvin, 1990), bullying (Salmivalli, 2001), and the prevention of HIV/AIDS (Agha & Rossem, 2004) and suicide (Sandoval, Davis, & Wilson, 1987). These educational programs can take a variety of forms. Some are comprehensive and ongoing, whereas others are focused and brief. An example of the former is a bullying prevention program described by Salmivalli. Students gave a schoolwide presentation (including information about bullying, participants' roles in bullying, and dramatic skits demonstrating bullying) and led small group discussions in classes (focusing on classroom climate, bullying problems, and how students could reduce bullying). During a weeklong period, the topic was also integrated in several school activities. Examples included coverage of conflict negotiation topics in the school news and related posters displayed in art classes. Following the intervention, reductions were found in self-reported victimization across all grades and peer-reported bullying for seventh-grade girls. In contrast, an HIV/AIDS prevention program with Zambian adolescents was conducted in single sessions lasting less than 2 hours (Agha & Rossem, 2004). Adolescents attended one discussion-oriented session focused primarily on condom use and abstinence.

The educators provided factual information, performed skits, and provided the adolescents with informational pamphlets. Adolescents exhibited improvements in their beliefs regarding abstinence and condom use.

Peer Mentoring

Unlike other peer interventions where similarity in age is generally preferred, peer mentoring is often characterized by an age discrepancy (Topping & Ehly, 1998). In this relationship, the mentor exhibits more experience, skill, or knowledge in a particular area and fills the role of passing this information on to the target child. Sometimes, peer mentors and their mentees are chosen from different schools in an effort to smooth future school transitions. For instance, in one mentoring program, youth in a secondary school were chosen as mentors for primary school students (Dearden, 1998). The mentors served as resources during the transition to the secondary school.

Mentoring interventions have also been used in efforts to scaffold appropriate behaviors (e.g., Fair, Vandermaas-Peeler, Beaudry, & Dew, 2005), improve school connectedness (e.g., Karcher, 2005), and decrease violent or delinquent behavior (e.g., Becker et al., 2004). In a cross-age mentoring program, high school students served as mentors to fourth- and fifth-grade students (Karcher, 2005). Mentors and mentees were given the opportunity to select their pairs, and the mentees included several children whom teachers had identified as being at high risk for academic failure. Meetings between the dyads occurred in a group setting twice a week for 2 hours. The mentoring program positively improved school and parent connectedness in mentees. In the Caught in the Crossfire intervention, Becker and colleagues employed young adults from backgrounds similar to that of target adolescents as peer mentors and provided them with training in counseling skills, anger management, cultural competency, and resource identification. Target adolescents were individuals who had been hospitalized as the result of a violent injury. For many target adolescents, these young adults served as role models for up to a year following the initial hospitalization. Mentees were less likely to be arrested or have any criminal involvement when compared to youth receiving no intervention, but there was no difference between the groups in injury and death rates.

Peer Counseling

Despite their nonprofessional status, peer counselors serve functions similar to those of professional counselors (Topping & Ehly, 1998). They offer help to other children and adolescents by listening, providing empathy, and using problem-solving skills (D'Andrea & Salovey, 1983; Topping & Ehly, 1998). These services can be offered in groups or individually, in person or over the phone, and can involve the provision of information and resources rather than advice giving.

Most often, peer counselors address typically occurring stressors and life issues, such as conflict resolution, relationship problems, and school transitions (Bell, Coleman, Anderson, Whelan, & Wilder, 2000; Johnson & Johnson, 1995; Morey, Miller, Rosen, & Fulton, 1989). For instance, in one high school peer counseling program, the issues most frequently discussed were relationship problems (Morey et al., 1989). Another peer counseling program addressed conflict resolution (Bell et al., 2000). Teachers and students selected a small group of sixth through eighth graders to serve as peer mediators for the school, which included students in the first through eighth grades. When conflicts arose, teachers had the option of referring children to these counselors or to the principal. Over a 6-week period, 32 of the 34 conflicts mediated by peers were deemed successful; that is, the mediator and disputants came to a written agreement and the conflict was not referred to the principal for follow-up.

Individuals presenting with more serious concerns (e.g., depression and suicide) have also been served by peer counselors (e.g., Bagley et al., 1994; Boehm & Campbell, 1996). When difficult or complicated problems arise, peer counselors should have a method for referring the counselee for professional services or other appropriate resources (Leader, 1996; Topping & Ehly, 1998). This is often the case with hotlines developed for adolescents. Callers to such hotlines present with concerns ranging from family and peer relationship problems to sexuality, academic difficulties, suicide, and drug and alcohol use (Boehm, Schondel, Marlowe, & Manke-Mitchell, 1999). An example is Teen Line, a counseling hotline staffed by adolescents trained to handle a variety of calls, including those from suicidal individuals, and provide appropriate resources as needed (Boehm & Campbell, 1996). Additional supports for the peer counselors included an available adult and the ability to trace the calls of suicidal individuals.

GENERAL ISSUES AND CONSIDERATIONS

Identifying and Selecting Peer Interveners

To start, it is important to delineate who constitutes a "peer." In a very broad definition, peers can include everyone from close friends to virtual strangers involved in a shared activity (Coleman & Hendry, 1990). In peer interventions, peers are often described as nonprofessionals who are similar to the target child in age, status, and knowledge (Ehly & Vasquez, 1998; Leader, 1996). Though using age as the sole factor in establishing similarity is a rather common practice, Shiner (1999) points to other identity characteristics, such as ethnicity, sexual orientation, social class, and sex that may be more salient features.

In addition to ensuring similarity, there are a variety of additional criteria and methods for selecting peer interveners. Many times, children are chosen because they exhibit exemplary behaviors (Fowler, 1988). Similarly, there is evidence that children who are highly respected and socially accepted can have a more significant influence on behavior change (Hamburg, 1989). Exhibiting appropriate behaviors and being socially accepted, however, are not absolute requirements. Kalfus (1984) points out that a variety of children (e.g., mentally retarded, learning disabled, juvenile delinquents) have served as effective peer agents in past interventions. Additional selection criteria might include an interest in performing the role and a consistent ability to follow adult instructions (Fowler, 1988; Kalfus, 1984; Strain, 1981). Others include a specific grade-point average, a certain time commitment, or enrollment in a course designed to provide appropriate skills and training (Covert & Wangberg, 1992).

Although some criteria can be broadly applied, others are specific to the characteristics of the intervention (e.g., fixed versus flexible roles), the amount of adult supervision provided, or the clinical problem being addressed (Fowler, 1988). For instance, good verbal and other communication skills may be desirable in verbally based interventions, but may be unnecessary for a modeling intervention (Hamburg, 1989; Kalfus, 1984). Counseling interventions may require adequate problem-solving abilities and social competence (Leader, 1996), and regular school attendance is an important element for school-based interventions (Fowler, 1988; Odom & Strain, 1984; Strain, 1981).

Selection methods vary considerably as well. The first component of the selection process is choosing potential interveners from a broader population; this has been done in a number of ways. Bell and colleagues (2000) had students choose a pool of potential interveners from which teachers or school administrators then selected appropriate individuals. In another intervention, teachers or school staff provided recommendations, and the potential interveners were given the ultimate decision regarding participation (Kim, McLeod, Rader, & Johnston, 1992). Chapman (1998) suggests using sociometric nominations of social acceptance as a method of identification to ensure that interveners are drawn from various subgroups of the population. Greater diversity of interveners in terms of race, cultural background, interests, personality, or other characteristics improves the chances that a target child will have someone with whom he or she can identify (Chapman, 1998; Covert & Wangberg, 1992). Sociometric measures of acceptance have been the major selection method for social skills interventions (e.g., Fantuzzo et al., 1988).

Selection often includes an effort to determine whether or not the peers meet recommended criteria. Generally, the potential peer interveners and others (e.g., teachers) are included in this process in order to assess the ability to intervene, intellectual and emotional capabilities, commitment, tolerance, and empathy (Chapman, 1998; Leader, 1996). Chapman recommends including the intervention recipients, the potential interveners, school or community personnel, and the program coordinators in this step. Leader described use of a multiple-stage process for selecting adolescents to serve as counselors for a teen hotline. Potential peer counselors were asked to complete a questionnaire and were individually interviewed by a clinician. This was followed by a group interview and an orientation meeting with their parents.

Training Peer Interveners

Once selected, interveners need sufficient instruction to adequately implement the intervention. As mentioned, the selection process often elicits interveners with specific personality characteristics or skills. Although this expertise should be respected, these individuals will benefit from further training (Leader, 1996). The format, duration, and components of training vary across interventions. Training may include lectures on important topics, modeling of techniques, role-playing, pre- and postassessments of skills, and continued monitoring and supervision (e.g., Covert & Wangberg, 1992; Fowler, 1988; Leader, 1996; Martin, Martin, & Barrett, 1987).

A number of peer interventions include instruction on similar topics and skills, such as communication and listening skills; delineation of responsibilities, requirements, and rules; confidentiality; and enumeration of additional community resources or referral sources (Bishop, 2003; Covert & Wangberg, 1992; Fowler, 1988). Bishop recommended that certain core skills (e.g., active listening, empathy) be taught to train individuals in supporting others, regardless of the specific intervention to be used. Of course, most interventions will also necessitate the addition of more tailored instruction topics. For example, training for an adolescent suicide prevention counseling program included topics such as depression and characteristics of individuals who are suicidal (Martin et al., 1987).

The depth and breadth of training needed will depend on the type of intervention. Little or no training might be needed to teach a child to model appropriate behaviors, whereas in-depth training may be needed for peer education or peer counseling formats. In one school intervention, for example, training for peer mediators required sessions held once every 2 weeks over a 2-month period (Bell et al., 2000). To ensure the maintenance of training benefits, two booster sessions were held. For another intervention, adolescent hotline counselors participated in a 13-week training program that included two weekly sessions focusing on listening skills and adolescent psychology (Leader, 1996). Training also involved the observation of others fielding phone calls and participation in monthly supervision sessions.

Studies examining training intensity needs for peer counseling interventions have been inconclusive. For example, Guttman (1987) randomly assigned peer counselors to either a high-training or minimal-training condition. Counselors in the high-training condition participated in a yearlong training and practicum, whereas those in the minimal-training condition participated in three workshops, each 4 hours long. Both groups exhibited improvements; the only group difference was that the minimal-training group used a greater number of statements identifying the group or group process. In another study, Cooker and Cherchia (1976) found that adolescents were able to competently facilitate adolescent groups on drug use after only 8 hours of training. Although there is not agreement regarding the optimal duration or intensity of treatment, there is consensus that supervision or adult monitoring should continue beyond the constraints of formal training (e.g., Covert & Wangberg, 1992; Fowler, 1988; Leader, 1996).

Considering the Peer Interveners Themselves

In addition to the benefits afforded to target children, peer interventions have been shown to have positive effects on the interveners such as improvements in classroom behavior, grade point average (Garner, Martin, & Martin, 1989), mental health (Silver, Coupey, Bauman, Doctors, & Boeck, 1992), and self-esteem (Kim et al., 1992). Indeed, Hamburg (1989, p. 9) suggests that "the long-term effects of peer counseling may be more important for the peer leaders than for the youngsters counseled. By being useful to others, adolescents can build a more durable basis for self-esteem."

Some gains may come from participating in training and gaining the skills necessary to intervene. In an intervention described by Silver and colleagues (1992), inner-city adolescents who participated in a 3-month counselor training and accepted positions as peer counselors exhibited improvements in their mental health. The training, however, did not promote such improvements in all of the adolescents. Those who declined counseling positions or who were not judged to be adequately skilled following training did not exhibit similar gains. In another peer counseling intervention, Kim et al. (1992) reported that trainees in their intervention evidenced improvements in empathic responding and personal growth (i.e., communication skills, emotional control, helping others, and interpersonal relations).

Unfortunately, there is an absence of research examining the potential risks for peer interveners. In the absence of empirical findings, we are left to speculation. For instance, Fowler (1988) suggests the possibility that the target child could retaliate against the peer implementing treatment. Perhaps worthy of some exploration is the potential for risks associated with increased deviant peer affiliation. In well-publicized research, Dishion and his colleagues have demonstrated iatrogenic effects for group interventions that bring together at-risk youth (e.g., Dishion, McCord, & Poulin, 1999). They reviewed evidence from two experiments suggesting that youth participating in group interventions had increased negative behaviors (e.g., smoking, delinquent behavior) in short- and long-term follow-ups. Dishion and colleagues suggest that "deviancy training" may be occurring within adolescent groups and interfering with intervention effects. That is, deviant peers may socialize each other to engage in antisocial behavior. Though it seems plausible that such processes could operate in peer interventions, there are unique elements that are likely to afford some protection. For instance, peer interveners typically pass through selection procedures and are often chosen based on their social competence. As such, they may not be as prone to deviancy training.

Advantages and Disadvantages of Peer Interventions

Using youth as interveners has several advantages relative to more traditional adult-mediated approaches (e.g., teacher-implemented educational strategies, psychotherapy). Their convenience and cost-effectiveness enhances their applicability to school settings (Covert & Wangberg, 1992; Fowler, 1988; Topping & Ehly, 1998). In this way, they have the potential of expanding service provision to larger numbers of children and establishing links between at-risk children and needed professional services (Henriksen, 1991). They also allow adults to focus efforts on other activities and interventions (Kalfus, 1984; Topping & Ehly, 1998). Even if not always meeting the same quality standards as adult-mediated approaches, peers have the advantage of being able to implement without delay (Greenwood, Carta, & Kamps, 1990; Topping & Ehly, 1998). They are in a unique social position that allows them to observe behaviors that may go unnoticed by adults and to effect change on other children's behavior (Carey, 1997; Fowler, 1988). More immediate feedback and consequences are also possible. Another advantage is the facilitation of maintenance and generalization. Typically, the intervention is carried out in the target child's natural environment; thus, the peer intervener, as well as other relevant stimuli, remain in place after treatment and serve as cues for appropriate responding in the future (Stokes & Osnes, 1989).

Given the social milieu in which children operate, peers may be especially important for influencing and changing behavior. This may be particularly true during adolescence, when greater amounts of time are spent with peers, who become a primary source of social support. Also important to consider is that such peer influence can be positive or negative. Well before adolescence, for example, children can unintentionally contribute to unwanted behaviors. Fowler (1988) suggests four main ways in which children reinforce negative behaviors. First, children positively reinforce the negative behavior. For instance, a child who uses aggression to resolve a conflict may be subsequently accepted by the peer group. Second, peers negatively reinforce the behavior. In this case, a child who is being teased might hit the bully, resulting in the cessation of taunting. Third, alternative positive behaviors are ignored or inappropriately reinforced, resulting in their eventual diminishment. Thus, a child may attempt to enter group play appropriately (e.g., asking nicely to play, attempting to take turns with a toy) but be denied access to the group. Over time, the child may cease to use these appropriate behaviors if they do not result in the desired outcome. Fourth, positive behaviors or social attempts are met with negative peer responses. In this case, children may respond to an appropriate social request, such as asking to share a toy, with aggression or by making negative comments (e.g., "I don't want to play with you"; "I don't like you").

Including peers in intervention has other advantages. For instance, having another child model appropriate behavior can be more beneficial than using an adult model (Schunk, 1998). The peer model is likely to be perceived as more similar to the target child and is less likely to demonstrate a perfect performance. As such, the target child may better identify with the child model and perceive himself or herself as able to mimic the model's behavior. In addition, children might be more likely to use services provided by their peers than more traditional services (Covert & Wangberg, 1992). For example, the use of traditional counseling services may carry a greater stigma than meeting with a school's peer counselor. For some topics, youth may be perceived as more expert than adults and better able to understand the child's or adolescent's experience (Mathie & Ford, 1998). When attempting to educate adolescents about sexual behavior or social decision making, for instance, it may be difficult to separate an adult from his or her other roles (e.g., a teacher), increasing discomfort and decreasing willingness to openly engage in discussions. Another adolescent may be perceived as having a better understanding of the youth's real-life struggles with these topics.

Despite these advantages, there are some limitations. Increased adult involvement can undermine efficiency and cost-effectiveness and might suggest that the intervention is no longer truly peer-mediated (Fowler, 1988; Kalfus, 1984). Indeed, the many advantages of using peers notwithstanding, Kalfus suggests that adults may be more efficient and effective in producing behavior change. For example, an adult may be better able to teach new skills or effectively implement rewards. Another disadvantage of using peers relates to the need for informed consent and confidentiality (Ehly & Vasquez, 1998). The peer intervener might need to be privy to sensitive information regarding the target child's behavior and need for treatment. As discussed earlier, there may also be risks for the peer intervener. Finally, as illustrated in our case example, these interventions are often implemented in schools and other nonclinic settings, and their feasibility for clinicians not already working within such environments may be an important concern.

Ethical Considerations

The use of peers as intervention agents raises some unique ethical considerations. One of the major issues is maintaining client confidentiality. The peer intervener may need to be made aware that treatment is occurring and learn private information. The ability of the intervener to understand and protect confidentiality should be carefully considered in the selection process. Such concerns may be greater in some forms of intervention than others. For instance, peer education interventions rely primarily on the dispensation of information and may not include disclosure of personal information. In contrast, peer counseling interventions often involve discussion of sensitive, private matters that would require counselors to have an understanding of and respect for confidentiality. Furthermore, peer counselors should be trained on the limits of confidentiality and when it may be appropriate to seek adult support or intervention (Ehly & Vasquez, 1998).

A second major concern pertains to informed consent. In some interventions, target children may not need to know that they are participating in an intervention. In fact, the intervention may be more successful if the target child does not realize another child has been instructed to help them. For example, in a social skills intervention, the target child may be naive to the fact that other children are being instructed to initiate social interactions (e.g., Middleton, Zollinger, & Keene, 1986). The degree to which the intervener participates voluntarily is also a significant ethical concern. Individuals selected as peer interveners should have the option of whether or not to participate (Greenwood et al., 1990). Some children may feel more comfortable in this role than others. Given the responsibilities placed on the peer intervener, he or she should be informed of all aspects of the role in the intervention and be allowed the choice of whether or not to be involved.

Evaluating Peer Interventions

A variety of approaches have been used to evaluate peer interventions, ranging from assessments of the interveners' abilities to reports of treatment satisfaction and objective measures of behavioral changes (Covert & Wangberg, 1992). Fowler (1988) recommends the use of a number of different methods to assess intervention effects, including consumer satisfaction surveys, daily assessments of effectiveness, assessment of generalization and maintenance of behavior changes, and assessment of behavioral changes in the intervener. Compliance with treatment protocols and the accuracy with which youth implement the intervention or reward systems should also be examined. Although the evaluation of peer interventions is important for many reasons (e.g., determining behavior change, funding, and gaining continued commitment from schools), the quality of program evaluations varies dramatically, and a number of studies do not use any form of objective evaluation (Covert & Wangberg, 1992).

In spite of such variation in outcome assessment quality, there is a fair degree of empirical support for the effectiveness of peer interventions. As indicated in our review thus far, peer interventions have been effective in addressing a wide range of presenting concerns. Published reviews of two of the major forms of peer intervention have also been favorable. In a review of peer education programs, Mellanby, Rees, and Tripp (2000) reported that, in general, peer-mediated programs were at least as effective as adult-led programs in improving knowledge and inducing behavioral changes. Johnson and Johnson (1996) completed a review of school counseling programs evaluating the knowledge gained from training as well as outcomes at the individual and school level. After conflict resolution training, students were found to have made improvements in their management of conflicts and use of resolution skills. In peer mediation programs, high levels (i.e., over 80%) of successful resolutions were generally obtained, although some programs had lower rates (e.g., 58% to 74%) and not all programs resulted in changes to the overall school climate.

CLINICAL APPLICATIONS

Not surprisingly, with their flexibility and many other advantages, peer interventions have been applied to many different clinical problem areas. Our review of peer intervention forms included many example applications. In this section, we provide a selective review highlighting the targeted problem areas.

Communication and Social Skills Deficits

Related interventions for communication and social skills deficits generally take the form of peer modeling, peer social initiations, or peer prompting and reinforcement. Children targeted have included those with autism, developmental delays, and cognitive deficits, as well as those evidencing social withdrawal. In an intervention aimed at improving social and communication skills in children with autism, normally developing preschoolers were used as models of appropriate play behavior (Kohler et al., 1997). Target children's social interactions with other children increased during the peer intervention phase and were maintained at follow-up. Peer modeling, however, is not always successful with autistic children. For instance, Charlop and Walsh (1986) used time delay and modeling procedures to facilitate affection responses in autistic children. The children were quick to learn the behaviors through the time delay technique, but peer modeling was ineffective. The authors suggest that the loosely structured environment of the modeling intervention may have contributed to its failure.

In a unique application, Krantz and colleagues (1989) trained an adolescent with autism to prompt three other autistic children in an effort to increase conversational abilities. Through a series of role-play sessions, the adolescent prompter was trained to talk about sports and ask five questions that could be applied to a variety of topics (e.g., "Do you like basketball/baseball?"). The target children evidenced improved conversational skills in dyadic and group conversations. Moreover, the skills generalized to new situations and were maintained at a 1-month follow-up. Other evidence suggests that peer initiation interventions may be most successful when the target child is paired with one child instead of multiple children. In a study by Sasso and colleagues (1998), children with developmental delays and autism showed greater improvement in social behaviors when paired than in a similar intervention conducted in triads.

Socially withdrawn children have also been the focus of such interventions. Guevremont and colleagues (1989) trained classmates to initiate and maintain interactions with two withdrawn children. Significant improvements in each child's social behavior were observed during and following the intervention. Similar success was observed in an intervention for four blind, socially withdrawn elementary school children (Sisson, Van Hasselt, Hersen, & Strain, 1985). Peers were used to initiate social behaviors in the target children, and increases in social behaviors were maintained at a 4-month follow-up assessment. In a treatment for socially neglected children, Middleton and colleagues (1986) selected accepted or popular peers to act as interveners and provided them with weekly instruction on behaviors to use with the target children (e.g., greeting or sitting next to at lunch). Also included were instruction and modeling components in which the peer modeled proper behavioral responses and offered suggestions for coping with unwanted behaviors. Socially neglected children who received treatment showed increases in peer nominations during posttest assessments.

Academic Problems

Tutoring is the most common form of peer intervention used to address problems of an academic nature, although other approaches (e.g., mentoring, modeling) have been used as well. Intervention targets have included specific academic skills, such as writing, spelling, and reading (e.g., Braaksma, Rijlaarsdam, & van den Bergh, 2002; James, Charlton, Leo, & Indoe, 1991), as well as school behaviors, such as work skills and attention to task (e.g., DuPaul et al., 1998). Formats of these interventions have also varied in terms of who is selected to intervene and the rigidity of roles. Competent peers may be used in the fixed role of intervener (e.g., Topping, Peter, Stephen, & Whale, 2004) or children may alternate between being the target child and the intervener (e.g., Kohler, Schwartz, Cross, & Fowler, 1989).

Several studies have suggested that children learn academic skills from peer models better when the model's competency level is similar to their own (e.g., Schunk et al., 1987). For instance, young teens were assessed on their ability to learn argumentative writing in three different conditions (Braaksma et al., 2002). Two conditions involved observing another child who was either a good or a weak model. The final condition was a control condition in which the children had to write short arguments. Individuals learned better from the model that was more similar to them in competence. Similarly, children had greater self-efficacy for learning and actually learned math skills better when observing a peer of similar competence gradually learn the skill than when observing a child who had already mastered the skill (Schunk et al., 1987). Notably, however, repeated observations of a mastery model resulted in similar effects.

Other interventions have been aimed at improving general academic skills. Kohler and colleagues (1989) selected three low-achieving students to receive a peer intervention aimed at improving independent work skills. Rather than assume solely the client role, these children and their classmates alternated roles daily. Regardless of the role assumed, the target children exhibited improvements in work skills (i.e., on-task behavior); however, task completion and accuracy did not improve.

Bullying, Aggression, and Disruptive Behavior

Peer programs aimed at bullying, aggression, and disruptive behavior have taken on a number of formats, including counseling, mentoring, mediation, and education. In his suggested strategies for preventing school violence, Stephens (1997) encourages the implementation of peer counseling and mediation programs. In his words:

> Students represent some of the best agents for promoting and maintaining a safe and secure campus. An effective peer counseling program can head off many problems before they reach explosive and violent levels. In addition, the students who are trained as counselors become wonderfully influential resources for nonviolent problem solving. (p. 74)

Bullying has been spotlighted recently, and a number of programs focus on providing support services to victims. For example, Boulton (2005) developed one-on-one peer counseling programs for victims in two secondary schools in the United Kingdom. When students were asked about their previous and future use of these programs, 22% stated that they had previously used the program and the majority said they would definitely (37%) or maybe (60%) use the program if needed in the future. In choosing the people they were most likely to go to for help with bullying, students chose close friends over the peer counselor, but the peer counselor was rated higher than a teacher or sibling. There was no difference in the likelihood of seeking help for bullying between the peer counselors and school counselor or parents.

Other programs focus on the aggressors or individuals who exhibit disruptive behaviors. For example, the Caught in the Crossfire program involved peer mentoring in a community setting for adolescents who sustained violent injuries (Becker et al., 2004). This program was developed to reduce the likelihood of reinjury or future involvement in delinquent activities. Recipients were less likely to be arrested or have any criminal involvement when compared to individuals who did not receive the intervention. Rather than target individuals at high risk for violence, other programs use a broader approach by intervening schoolwide. For instance, sixth-grade students received a violence prevention program taught by a teacher with or without a peer leader (Orpinas, Parcel, McAlister, & Frankowski, 1995). Individuals who received the teacher plus peer leader intervention exhibited greater attitude changes toward violent responses.

Peer Mediation and Conflict Resolution

Although in some ways similar to peer counseling, peer mediation is a more focused intervention strategy aimed at resolving conflicts between two individuals. In a schoolwide implementation of a peer mediation program, Bell et al. (2000) observed important changes in student conduct. Thirty students in the sixth through eighth grades were trained to be peer mediators for the entire school population of first through eighth graders. Teachers were given the option of referring students to the program or to the principal. During the 6-week study period, 34 mediations were conducted, and the percentage of suspensions and fighting decreased. Johnson and Johnson (1995) evaluated the effectiveness of conflict resolution training using both student body and cadre approaches. Overall, the results indicated that conflict resolution strategies and problem solving can be learned by the students and used in real-world settings.

Suicide and Depression

Suicide and depression interventions are generally in the form of prevention and detection programs or counseling programs. Some interventions encompass a two-tiered system of primary (curriculum-based prevention program) and secondary (peer counseling) prevention components (Sandoval et al., 1987). Further, a number of peer counseling programs address depression and suicide prevention but do not focus exclusively on these issues (e.g., Boehm et al., 1999). For example, one teen counseling hotline received 441 calls pertaining to depression or suicide over a 5-year period (Boehm & Campbell, 1996). Researchers in Hong Kong developed a schoolwide suicide prevention program that was designed to address concerns with available alternatives (Bagley et al., 1994). The Health Intervention Training—Mutual Aid Network promotes positive social support among students using a "student-body approach" in which all students serve as both intervener and client.

Health Behaviors

Health behaviors have been addressed mainly through peer education programs focusing on topics such as sexual behaviors (Agha & Rossem, 2004), AIDS and HIV prevention (Backett-Milburn & Wilson, 2000), substance abuse (Botvin et al., 1990), and asthma education (Shah et al., 2006). A review of studies comparing youth-led and adult-led health education programs indicated that participants in youth-led programs evinced knowledge gains, attitude changes, and behavioral outcomes that were as positive, or more so, as in adult-led programs (Mellanby et al., 2000).

Backett-Milburn and Wilson (2000) described an HIV/AIDS peer education program in which educators worked together in groups. With this enhanced flexibility, the peer educators could capitalize on individual strengths. In addition, while some members led the groups, others were able to work behind the scenes to plan sessions or search for information and resources. In another intervention focused on sexual health and HIV prevention, peer educators conducted single sessions with groups of Zambian adolescents (Agha & Rossem, 2004). The trained educators used dramatic skits to depict sexual behavior models. At follow-up, the intervention group showed significant improvements in their approval of condom use and intent to use condoms. At the 6-month follow-up, intervention adolescents were more likely to think that it was normal for both women and men to suggest using a condom.

Coping with Illness or Medical Procedures

Acknowledging the negative impact of chronic illness on children's social relations and development, coping interventions have also targeted peer interactions (Harbeck-Weber, Fisher, & Dittner, 2003). For instance, Greco, Shroff Pendley, McDonnell, and Reeves (2001) included the best friends of adolescents with diabetes in a group intervention. In this informal peer intervention, the friends learned diabetes knowledge and ways to better support the adolescent with diabetes. A novel intervention approach, STARBRIGHT, capitalizes on computer technology in a peer intervention for hospitalized children (Holden, Bearison, Rode, Rosenberg, & Fishman, 1999). The STARBRIGHT program connects hospitalized children (ages 9 through 19) through an online community. Less formal than many other peer interventions, it allows children to gain support from others experiencing similar conditions. Children using STARBRIGHT reported less intense pain and reduced anxiety compared to those receiving standard pediatric care alone (Holden et al., 1999).

More conventional modeling approaches have been frequently used to help children with medical fears (e.g., Elkins & Roberts, 1986; Melamed & Siegel, 1975). In a normative population of children, modeling was examined by Elkins and Roberts to see whether medical fears could be reduced. Third- and fifth-grade children were randomly assigned to view one of four videotapes. Peer models were used in two videotapes (either one child alone or two children talking together), an adult was used in another videotape, and the last film was a control video in which a child models coping but outside the hospital setting. Children high in medical anxiety reported reduction in their anxiety after viewing all three medically related films; a similar effect was not seen in children with low medical anxiety. Similar methods have been used with children who have significant medical fears or who are uncooperative with medical treatments. For instance, as part of a larger intervention, highly uncooperative children observed peers undergoing a dental procedure and being reinforced for appropriate behavior just prior to their own treatment (Stokes & Kennedy, 1980). Children's uncooperative behaviors (e.g., body movements, complaints, crying) were reduced following the intervention.

Case Illustration

Identifying Features of the Client
Bobby D. is a 7-year-old boy who was diagnosed with Autistic Disorder at age 3. Bobby attends first grade at a public elementary school and engages in an intensive applied behavioral analysis program for children with autism and other developmental delays approximately 20 hours per week. Currently, Bobby lives with both parents and two siblings (4-year-old sister and 9-year-old brother).

Presenting Complaints
Bobby currently divides his weekdays between a structured applied behavioral analysis program and a regular classroom with the support of a behavioral specialist. He also receives individual speech and language therapy 3 days a week. All of these services are coordinated by his school as part of his individual education plan. At home, Bobby's parents receive

---

additional support from a behavior specialist contracted through a community agency who provides extra instruction on activities such as communication skills (e.g., asking for objects) and daily living skills (e.g., mealtime behaviors).

More recently, Mr. and Mrs. D. sought some adjunctive intervention to help Bobby improve his social behavior. On the advice of school personnel, they contacted a clinical psychologist who was in private practice and had frequently consulted with Bobby's school on cases involving autism spectrum disorders. Although Bobby's social behavior (e.g., eye contact and use of gestures) had improved, it was still of major concern. He is relatively high-functioning and has adequate communication skills, as he is able to speak in simple sentences and occasionally uses nonverbal gestures or sign language to communicate. According to his most recent speech and language evaluation, Bobby has mildly delayed expressive language and moderately delayed receptive language. At the present time, Mr. and Mrs. D. would like to see improvements in Bobby's ability to appropriately respond to and engage with his peers.

Developmental Factors

Like many children with this disorder, Bobby exhibited developmental delays in the communication and social domains. Though he started to walk and crawl on time, his first spoken words came at about 27 months. His parents also noted his frequent resistance to eye contact, lack of response to his name, and failure to reciprocate social initiations. Mrs. D. reported a normal pregnancy and on-time delivery without medical complications. Bobby was a relatively healthy child and had no major illnesses, injuries, or hospitalizations.

Parental Factors

Bobby lives in an intact, two-parent household in which both parents work full time. As such, Bobby spends several hours a day with a behavioral specialist while his parents are at work. Mr. D. has some college education and Mrs. D. completed high school. Both Mr. and Mrs. D. are involved in Bobby's treatment and work with his behavior specialist to provide Bobby with discrete trial training to address daily living skills such as appropriate mealtime and bedtime behaviors.

Bobby's behavior and special needs contribute to Mr. and Mrs. D.'s daily stress. At times their marriage has become strained due to differing opinions regarding Bobby's care. Another concern is that the additional attention given to Bobby will have detrimental effects on their other children. Mr. and Mrs. D. appear to be coping well with this stress and are involved in a support group for parents with children with autism.

History

Prior to intervention efforts starting at age 3, Bobby had very limited language abilities. He exhibited severe delays in both expressive and receptive language. As previously mentioned, Bobby's language skills have improved and he now evidences only mild to moderate delays. At times, Bobby uses jargon and echolalic speech, but he can communicate using simple sentences.

Bobby has also exhibited a number of delays in the acquisition of social skills. When initially diagnosed, Bobby rarely made eye contact and made very few

(Continued)

attempts at social referencing. For instance, he would occasionally grab one of his parent's hands and pull him or her toward a requested item. However, he never made attempts to show his parents completed activities or gain their assistance when injured. When around his siblings or peers, Bobby rarely made any attempts to engage them and often ignored other children's social bids. For instance, in preschool, he would sometimes push other children away when they approached him to engage in a joint activity. At this time, Bobby has made improvements in his eye contact such that he consistently makes eye contact with familiar individuals (e.g., parents, teachers, siblings, familiar peers). He still has difficulty in his peer interactions and does not spontaneously engage in reciprocal play behaviors.

Assessment

The consulting psychologist conducted a clinical interview with Bobby's parents. In addition, Mr. and Mrs. D. each completed the Achenbach Child Behavior Checklist for ages 6 to 18 (CBCL) and his teacher, Ms. Baker, completed the Teacher Report Form (TRF) and Social Skills Rating System (SSRS). Bobby was also observed in his classroom and on the school playground to assess for the frequency and quality of interactions with peers. Based on information obtained from the parental interview and observations of Bobby's behavior, the psychologist completed the Childhood Autism Rating Scale (CARS), a clinician-completed scale assessing abilities or domains that are frequently impaired in children with autism.

On the CBCL, Mr. and Mrs. D.'s responses both resulted in clinical elevations on the Social Problems, Attention Problems, Externalizing, and Total Problems subscales. Mrs. D.'s responses also resulted in an elevation on the Withdrawn/Depressed subscale. On the TRF, Ms. Baker's responses resulted in clinical elevations on the Social Problems, Attention Problems, Aggressive Behavior, Externalizing, and Total Problems subscales. Overall, Ms. Baker endorsed a greater severity of symptoms than either Mr. or Mrs. D. Her SSRS endorsements indicated that Bobby's social skills were well below that of more normative comparison children, and his overall conduct was somewhat more problematic. Frequently occurring behaviors included temper tantrums, whereas behaviors such as making friends easily and giving compliments to peers were endorsed as never occurring.

Behavioral observations in both the classroom and on the playground revealed that Bobby rarely engaged in social interactions with his peers. During a 20-minute play period, Bobby was observed to interact with his peers for less than 5 minutes. All interactions were initiated by peers, but Bobby often ignored such initiations. On two occasions, Bobby was observed to push other children away. In the classroom, he ignored other children even during a group task. While three other children in his group interacted and worked together to complete a puzzle, Bobby was observed to stare off into space and rock in his chair.

On the CARS, Bobby received an overall score that placed him in the mild autism range. Domains in which he exhibited the most significant delays included his relations to others, interactions with objects, nonverbal communication, and emotional responding.

Case Conceptualization

A major characteristic of autism is impairment in social functioning, including difficulties initiating or maintaining social interactions, impaired social relationships, and a lack of reciprocity or sharing of social or emotional experiences. Similar to other children with autism, Bobby has difficulty engaging in social interactions with peers and often refuses or ignores other children's social bids. Bobby exhibits other behaviors characteristic of autism, such as rocking, spinning, and repetitive play behaviors. Unlike other children his age, Bobby's play activities are generally limited to playing with trains or railroad-related toys and pictures. When looking at pictures of trains or playing with trains, he often becomes immersed and has difficulty being redirected to other activities. At this time, the major treatment concern is to increase the frequency of Bobby's social interactions with his peers. Improvements in social and other domains are difficult to achieve, and progress is incremental.

Course of Treatment and Assessment of Progress

The major goals of treatment were to improve Bobby's responses to other children's social initiations. The treatment approach was based on that used by Goldstein and colleagues (1992). Based on Ms. Baker's report, three socially competent peers were selected from Bobby's classroom to facilitate the intervention. The psychologist obtained Mr. and Mrs. D.'s permission to involve these children in intervention efforts. Prior to the start of the intervention, the psychologist discussed the responsibilities and behaviors required with each peer intervener and their parents. Parental consent and child assent were obtained. The parents were informed of the nature of the intervention and the need for confidentiality. The children were told that they had been selected to play with Bobby, but were not explicitly informed of the treatment aspect of this play to minimize responsibility for maintaining confidentiality. Bobby was not informed that he was the target of an intervention. The children were trained in separate steps to use several strategies to promote social interaction. Consistent with Goldstein and colleagues, the steps included (a) establishing joint attention by moving into Bobby's visual space, (b) saying "Bobby," (c) repeating "Bobby" and physically tapping him if he remained unresponsive, (d) starting a conversation and listening to see if Bobby responded, and (e) continuing to speak to Bobby. Each peer had individual play sessions with Bobby in which these steps were practiced. To gain peer intervener compliance, rewards were given following each play session for following the steps and engaging in conversations with Bobby.

Bobby's progress during these sessions was monitored by a teacher or teacher's aide who recorded the number of steps that were required to gain Bobby's attention and whether or not he engaged in conversation with the peer. To assess generalization, the psychologist observed Bobby on a biweekly basis in his regular classroom setting or on the playground. As with the baseline observations, the frequency of Bobby's interactions with peers was tallied. Over a 4-week period, Bobby exhibited substantial improvement in his responses to the three peers during the one-on-one play sessions. However, these improvements failed to generalize to other, less structured settings.

(Continued)

Complicating Factors

Although Bobby's behavior improved in the one-on-one play sessions, it failed to generalize to other situations, such as unstructured play with other peers. During her observations, the psychologist noticed that Bobby's responses to peer initiations had not improved and that peers rarely attempted to initiate such interactions. Even those peers who engaged in the one-on-one play sessions were rarely observed to attempt social interactions outside of these sessions. To address these concerns, the peer prompters were instructed to also initiate social interactions outside of the individual sessions. Teachers took note of these initiations and rewarded interveners for attempts outside of the individual sessions. Over the next 6-week period, Bobby's peers engaged in more frequent initiation attempts. Further, Bobby's responses to these attempts improved such that the frequency of ignoring initiations decreased dramatically and aggressive behavior (e.g., pushing children away) was eliminated completely.

Managed Care Considerations

Receiving compensation for services provided in schools is often a challenge. In this case, only the time spent with the parents in the clinic may be billable according to most managed care guidelines. The time spent training and supervising the peer interveners, as well as coordinating and monitoring the ongoing intervention, would probably not be covered by most insurance companies. Travel to and from the school would likely be an additional unrecoverable expense. Being directly contracted by the school as a consultant is a preferable arrangement in cases such as the one presented here.

Follow-Up Treatment

Once the frequency of Bobby's social interactions and the quality of his responding had improved to reasonable levels, the active peer intervention was terminated. Continued observation and teacher report indicated that Bobby was engaging in more frequent social interactions with his classmates and rarely ignored other children's social bids. Subsequently, a follow-up treatment was started that consisted of attempts to use peers to model more complicated and extended social interactions.

Implications of the Case

Bobby's case highlights several concerns regarding the implementation of peer interventions. In this case, some difficulty in achieving generalization was encountered. Although the peer interveners initiated interactions with Bobby during structured play sessions, they failed to initiate in other situations in which they were not directly reinforced. This emphasizes the need for continued monitoring of progress and supervision of peer interveners. Bobby's situation also illustrates some of the challenges in obtaining consent and maintaining confidentiality. Given the young age of the children involved in this intervention, they were not fully apprised of the therapeutic nature of their involvement. Further, Bobby was not made aware that he was being targeted in these social initiations.

Recommendations to Clinicians and Students

Despite their many advantages and seeming simplicity, peer interventions pose some significant challenges. Given issues relating to reimbursement and availability of peers to intervene, a majority of these interventions take place in a school setting. Even those interventions in community settings occur outside of a typical clinic setting. Added demands include the time required for training the peer interveners, consulting with teachers, and providing ongoing supervision and monitoring. In combination with the unique concerns regarding informed consent and confidentiality, the feasibility of this intervention form is an issue for most practitioners. Such interventions may be best suited to those already working within the school setting.

SUMMARY

With their many inherent advantages, peer interventions have grown in popularity and have been used in efforts to address a wide variety of clinical problem areas and disorders. For many reasons, peer interventions may be preferable to adult-led treatments. Due to their similar social status, children may be perceived as more accessible and can be convenient for implementing treatment. Information may be more readily received when coming from one's peer, and the stigmas associated with treatment seeking may be lessened. The convenience and cost-effectiveness of peer interventions enhances their applicability to school settings, thus potentially expanding service provision to large numbers of children. Using peers as treatment agents and implementation in the natural environment also facilitates maintenance and generalization.

With these advantages come some considerations and potential concerns. Though often touted for their convenience and cost-effectiveness, peer interventions are not as straightforward as they may seem. Clinicians must carefully weigh the pros and cons relative to more traditional adult-mediated approaches. Setting is one consideration, as these interventions are most frequently implemented in the child's natural environment and seem most amenable to school environments. A variety of particular intervention forms are available, and one most suitable to the target child and presenting problem must be chosen. Implementation requires a carefully considered approach to the selection, training, and supervision of the peer interveners, as well as sensitivity to the unique ethical challenges posed by peer interventions. Securing the cooperation of others in the child's environment, such as teachers and other school personnel, and obtaining quality outcome data are additional considerations.

REFERENCES

Agha, S., & Rossem, R. (2004). Impact of a school-based peer sexual health intervention on normative beliefs, risk perceptions, and sexual behavior of Zambian adolescents. *Journal of Adolescent Health, 34*, 441–452.

Backett-Milburn, K., & Wilson, S. (2000). Understanding peer education: Insights from a process evaluation. *Health Education Research, 15*, 85–96.

Bagley, C., Tse, J., & Hoi-Wah, M. (1994). Suicidal adolescents in Hong Kong: Peer counseling strategies. *Journal of Child and Youth Care, 9*, 71–87.

Bandura, A., Ross, D., & Ross, S. A. (1963). A comparative test of the status envy, social power, and secondary reinforcement theories of identificatory learning. *Journal of Abnormal and Social Psychology, 67*, 527–534.

Becker, M. G., Hall, J. S., Ursic, C. M., Jain, S., & Calhoun, D. (2004). Caught in the Crossfire: The effects of a peer-based intervention program for violently injured youth. *Journal of Adolescent Health, 34,* 177–183.

Bell, S. K., Coleman, J. K., Anderson, A., Whelan, J. P., & Wilder, C. (2000). The effectiveness of peer mediation in a low-SES rural elementary school. *Psychology in the Schools, 37,* 505–516.

Bierman, K. L., & Furman, W. (1984). The effects of social skills training and peer involvement on the social adjustment of preadolescents. *Child Development, 55,* 151–162.

Bishop, S. (2003). Young people generating a repertoire of counseling psychology: Talking theory. *Counselling Psychology Quarterly, 16,* 95–102.

Boehm, K. E., & Campbell, N. B. (1996). Suicide: A review of calls to an adolescent peer listening phone service. *Child Psychiatry and Human Development, 26,* 61–66.

Boehm, K. E., Schondel, C. K., Marlowe, A. L., & Manke-Mitchell, L. (1999). Teens' concerns: A national evaluation. *Adolescence, 34,* 523–528.

Botvin, G. J., Baker, E., Filazzola, A. D., & Botvin, E. M. (1990). A cognitive-behavioral approach to substance abuse prevention: One-year follow-up. *Addictive Behaviors, 15,* 47–63.

Boulton, M. J. (2005). School peer counselling for bullying services as a source of social support: A study with secondary school pupils. *British Journal of Guidance and Counselling, 33,* 485–494.

Braaksma, M. A., Rijlaarsdam, G., & van den Bergh, H. (2002). Observational learning and the effects of model-observer similarity. *Journal of Educational Psychology, 94,* 405–415.

Calhoon, M. B. (2005). Effects of a peer-mediated phonological skill and reading comprehension program on reading skill acquisition for middle school students with reading disabilities. *Journal of Learning Disabilities, 38,* 424–433.

Carey, K. T. (1997). Preschool interventions. In A. P. Goldstein & J. C. Conoley (Eds.), *School violence interventions: A practical handbook* (pp. 93–106). New York: Guilford Press.

Chapman, E. S. (1998). Key considerations in the design and implementation of effective peer-assisted learning programs. In K. Topping & S. Ehly (Eds.), *Peer-assisted learning* (pp. 67–84). Mahwah, NJ: Erlbaum.

Charlop, M. H., & Walsh, M. E. (1986). Increasing autistic children's spontaneous verbalizations of affection: An assessment of time delay and peer modeling procedures. *Journal of Applied Behavior Analysis, 19,* 307–314.

Coleman, J. C., & Hendry, L. (1990). *The nature of adolescence.* Florence, KY: Taylor & Frances/Routledge.

Cooker, P. G., & Cherchia, P. J. (1976). Effects of communication skill training on high school students' ability to function as peer group facilitators. *Journal of Counseling Psychology, 23,* 464–467.

Covert, J., & Wangberg, D. (1992). Peer counseling: Positive peer pressure. In G. W. Lawson & A. W. Lawson (Eds.), *Adolescent substance abuse: Etiology, treatment, and prevention* (pp. 131–139). Gaithersburg, MD: Aspen.

D'Andrea, V. J., & Salovey, P. (1983). *Peer counseling: Skills and perspectives.* Palo Alto, CA: Science and Behavior Books.

Dearden, J. (1998). Cross-age peer mentoring in action: The process and outcomes. *Educational Psychology in Practice, 13,* 250–257.

Dishion, T. J., McCord, J., & Poulin, F. (1999). When interventions harm: Peer groups and problem behavior. *American Psychology, 54,* 755–764.

DuPaul, G. J., Ervin, R. A., Hook, C. L., & McGoey, K. E. (1998). Peer tutoring for children with attention deficit hyperactivity disorder: Effects on classroom behavior and academic performance. *Journal of Applied Behavior Analysis, 31,* 579–592.

Ehly, S. W., & Vasquez, E. G. (1998). Peer counseling. In K. Topping & S. Ehly (Eds.), *Peer-assisted learning* (pp. 219–233). Mahwah, NJ: Erlbaum.

Elkins, P. D., & Roberts, M. C. (1986). Reducing medical fears in a general population of children: A comparison of three audiovisual modeling procedures. *Journal of Pediatric Psychology, 10,* 65–75.

Fair, C., Vandermaas-Peeler, M., Beaudry, R., & Dew, J. (2005). I learned how little kids think: Third graders' scaffolding of craft activities with preschoolers. *Early Child Development and Care, 175,* 229–241.

Fantuzzo, J., Jurecic, L., Stovall, A., Hightower, A. D., Goins, C., & Schachtel, D. (1988). Effects of adult and peer social initiations on the social behavior of withdrawn, maltreated preschool children. *Journal of Consulting and Clinical Psychology, 56,* 34–39.

Foster, G. D., Wadden, T. A., & Brownell, K. D. (1985). Peer-led program for the treatment and prevention of obesity in the schools. *Journal of Consulting and Clinical Psychology, 53*, 538–540.

Fowler, S. (1988). The effects of two alternating peer intervention roles on independent work skills. *Education and Treatment of Children, 12*, 205–218.

Garner, R., Martin, D., & Martin, M. (1989). The PALS program: A peer counseling training program for junior high school. Special issue: *Preventive and Developmental Counseling, 24*, 68–76.

Gena, A., Couloura, S., & Kymissis, E. (2005). Modifying the affective behavior of preschoolers with autism using in-vivo or video modeling and reinforcement contingencies. *Journal of Autism and Developmental Disorders, 35*, 545–556.

Gilbert, B. O., Johnson, S. B., Spillar, R., McCallum, M., Silverstein, J. H., & Rosenbloom, A. (1982). The effects of a peer-modeling film on children learning to self-inject insulin. *Behavior Therapy, 13*, 186–193.

Goldstein, H., Kaczmarek, L., Pennington, R., & Shafer, K. (1992). Peer-mediated intervention: Attending to, commenting on, and acknowledging the behavior of preschoolers with autism. *Journal of Applied Behavior Analysis, 25*, 289–305.

Goldstein, H., & Wickstrom, S. (1986). Peer intervention effects on communicative interaction among handicapped and nonhandicapped preschoolers. *Journal of Applied Behavior Analysis, 19*, 209–214.

Greco, P., Shroff Pendley, J., McDonnell, K., & Reeves, G. (2001). A peer group intervention for adolescents with Type 1 diabetes and their best friends. *Journal of Pediatric Psychology, 26*, 485–490.

Greenwood, C. R., Carta, J. J., & Kamps, D. (1990). Teacher-mediated versus peer-mediated instruction: A review of educational advantages and disadvantages. In H. C. Foot, M. J. Morgan, & R. H. Shute (Eds.), *Children helping children* (pp. 177–205). Chichester, England: Wiley.

Greenwood, C. R., Maheady, L., & Delquadri, J. (2002). Classwide peer tutoring programs. In M. R. Shinn, H. M. Walker, & G. Stoner (Eds.), *Interventions for academic and behavior problems II: Preventive and remedial approaches* (pp. 611–649). Washington, DC: National Association of School Psychologists.

Grusec, J. E. (1992). Social learning theory and developmental psychology: The legacies of Robert R. Sears and Albert Bandura. In R. D. Parke, A. P. Ornstein, J. J. Rieser, & C. Zahn-Waxler (Eds.), *A century of developmental psychology* (pp. 473–497). Washington, DC: American Psychological Association.

Guevremont, D., MacMillan, V., Shawchuck, C., & Hansen, D. (1989). A peer-mediated intervention with clinic-referred socially isolated girls: Generalization, maintenance, and social validation. *Behavior Modification, 13*, 32–50.

Guttman, M. A. J. (1987). A peer counselling model: Social outreach. *Canadian Counsellor, 19*, 135–143.

Hamburg, D. (1989). Preparing for life: The critical transition of adolescence. *Crisis: Journal of Crisis Intervention and Suicide Prevention, 10*, 4–15.

Harbeck-Weber, C., Fisher, J. L., & Dittner, C. A. (2003). Promoting coping and enhancing adaptation to illness. In M. C. Roberts (Ed.), *Handbook of pediatric psychology* (3rd ed., pp. 98–118). New York: Guilford Press.

Henriksen, E. M. (1991). A peer helping program for the middle school. *Canadian Journal of Counselling, 25*, 12–18.

Holden, G., Bearison, D. J., Rode, D. C., Rosenberg, G., & Fishman, M. (1999). Evaluating the effects of a virtual environment (STARBRIGHT World) with hospitalized children. *Research on Social Work Practice, 9*, 365–382.

James, J., Charlton, T., Leo, E., & Indoe, D. (1991). Using peer counselors to improve secondary pupils' spelling and reading performance. *Maladjustment and Therapeutic Education, 9*, 33–40.

Johnson, D. W., & Johnson, R. T. (1995). Teaching students to be peacemakers: Results of five years of research. *Peace and Conflict: Journal of Peace Psychology, 1*, 417–438.

Johnson, D. W., & Johnson, R. T. (1996). Conflict resolution and peer mediation programs in elementary and secondary schools: A review of the research. *Review of Educational Research, 66*, 459–506.

Kalfus, G. (1984). Peer mediated intervention: A critical review. *Child and Family Behavior Therapy, 6*, 17–43.

Karcher, M. J. (2005). The effects of developmental mentoring and high school mentors' attendance on their younger mentees' self-esteem, social skills, and connectedness. *Psychology in the School, 42*, 65–77.

Kim, S., McLeod, J. H., Rader, D., & Johnston, G. (1992). An evaluation of prototype school-based peer counseling program. *Journal of Drug Education, 22*, 37–53.

Kohler, F. W., Schwartz, I. S., Cross, J. A., & Fowler, S. A. (1989). The effects of two alternating peer intervention roles on independent work skills. *Education and Treatment of Children, 12*, 205–218.

Kohler, F. W., Strain, P. S., Hoyson, M., & Jamieson, B. (1997). Merging naturalistic teaching and peer-based strategies to address the IEP objectives of preschoolers with autism: An examination of structural and child behavior outcomes. *Focus on Autism and Other Developmental Disabilities, 12*, 196–206.

Krantz, P., Ramsland, S., & McClannahan, L. (1989). Conversational skills for autistic adolescents: An autistic peer as prompter. *Behavioral Residential Treatment, 4*, 171–189.

Leader, E. (1996). Teen line: A listening post for troubled youth. In P. Kymissis & D. A. Halperin (Eds.), *Group therapy with children and adolescents* (pp. 311–328). Washington, DC: American Psychiatric Association.

Martin, D., Martin, M., & Barrett, C. (1987). A peer counselor crisis intervention training program to help prevent adolescent suicide. *Techniques, 3*, 214–218.

Mathie, E., & Ford, N. (1998). Peer education for health. In K. Topping & K. Ehly (Eds.), *Peer-assisted learning* (pp. 203–218). Mahwah, NJ: Erlbaum.

Melamed, B. G., & Siegel, L. J. (1975). Reduction of anxiety in children facing hospitalization and surgery by use of filmed modeling. *Journal of Consulting and Clinical Psychology, 43*, 511–521.

Mellanby, A. R., Rees, J. B., & Tripp, J. H. (2000). Peer-led and adult-led school health education: A critical review of available comparative research. *Health Education Research, 15*, 533–545.

Middleton, H., Zollinger, J., & Keene, R. (1986). Popular peers as change agents for the socially neglected child in the classroom. *Journal of School Psychology, 24*, 343–350.

Moore, B. (2005). Empirically supported family and peer interventions for dual disorders. *Research on Social Work Practice, 15*, 231–245.

Morey, R. E., Miller, C. D., Rosen, L. A., & Fulton, R. (1989). High school peer counseling: The relationship between student satisfaction and peer counselors' style of helping. *School Counselor, 40*, 293–300.

Odom, S. L., & Strain, P. S. (1984). Peer-mediated approaches to promoting children's social interaction: A review. *American Journal of Orthopsychiatry, 54*, 544–557.

Odom, S. L., & Strain, P. S. (1986). A comparison of peer-initiation and teacher-antecedent interventions for promoting reciprocal social interaction of autistic preschoolers. *Journal of Applied Behavior Analysis, 19*, 59–71.

Orpinas, P., Parcel, G. S., McAlister, A., & Frankowski, R. (1995). Violence prevention in middle schools: A pilot evaluation. *Journal of Adolescent Health, 17*, 360–371.

Pierce, K., & Schreibman, L. (1995). Increasing complex social behaviors in children with autism: Effects of peer-implemented pivotal response training. *Journal of Applied Behavior Analysis, 28*, 285–295.

Prinz, R. J., Blechman, E. A., & Dumas, J. E. (1994). An evaluation of peer coping-skills training for childhood aggression. *Journal of Clinical Child Psychology, 23*, 193–203.

Salmivalli, C. (2001). Peer-led intervention campaign against school bullying: Who considered it useful, who benefited? *Educational Research, 43*, 263–278.

Sandoval, J., Davis, J. M., & Wilson, M. P. (1987). An overview of the school-based prevention of adolescent suicide. *Special Services in the Schools, 3*, 103–120.

Sasso, G. M., Mundschenck, N. A., Melloy, K. J., & Casey, S. D. (1998). A comparison of the effects of organismic and setting variables on the social interaction behavior of children with developmental disabilities and autism. *Focus on Autism and Other Developmental Disabilities, 13*, 2–16.

Schunk, D. H. (1998). Peer modeling. In K. Topping & S. Ehly (Eds.), *Peer-assisted learning* (pp. 185–202). Mahwah, NJ: Erlbaum.

Schunk, D. H., & Hanson, A. R. (1985). Peer models: Influence on children's self-efficacy and achievement. *Journal of Educational Psychology, 77*, 313–322.

Schunk, D. H., & Hanson, A. R. (1989). Influence of peer-model attributes on children's beliefs and learning. *Journal of Educational Psychology, 81*, 431–434.

Schunk, D. H., Hanson, A. R., Cox, P. D. (1987). Peer-model attributes and children's achievement behaviors. *Journal of Educational Psychology, 79*, 54–61.

Shah, S., Peat, J. K., Mazurski, E. J., Wang, H., Sindhusake, D., Bruce, C., et al. (2006). Effect of peer led programme for asthma education in adolescents: Cluster randomised controlled trial. *British Medical Journal, 322*, 1–5.

Shiner, M. (1999). Defining peer education. *Journal of Adolescence, 22*, 555–566.

Silver, E. J., Coupey, S. M., Bauman, L. J., Doctors, S. R., & Boeck, M. A. (1992). Effects of a peer counseling training intervention on psychological functioning of adolescents. *Journal of Adolescent Research, 7*, 110–128.

Sisson, L., Van Hasselt, V. B., Hersen, M., & Strain, P. (1985). Peer interventions: Increasing social behaviors in multihandicapped children. *Behavior Modification, 9*, 293–321.

Stephens, R. D. (1997). National trends in school violence: Statistics and prevention strategies. In A. P. Goldstein & J. C. Conoley (Eds.), *School violence intervention: A practical handbook* (pp. 72–90). New York: Guilford Press.

Stokes, T. F., & Kennedy, S. H. (1980). Reducing child uncooperative behavior during dental treatment through modeling and reinforcement. *Journal of Applied Behavior Analysis, 13*, 41–49.

Stokes, T. F., & Osnes, P. G. (1989). An operant pursuit of generalization. *Behavior Therapy, 20*, 337–355.

Strain, P. (1981). Peer-mediated treatment of exceptional children's social withdrawal. *Exceptional Education Quarterly, 1*, 93–105.

Topping, K. (1996). Reaching where adults cannot: Peer education and peer counseling. *Educational Psychology, 11*, 23–29.

Topping, K., & Ehly, S. (1998). Introduction to peer-assisted learning. In K. Topping & S. Ehly (Eds.), *Peer-assisted learning* (pp. 1–23). Mahwah, NJ: Erlbaum.

Topping, K., Peter, C., Stephen, P., Whale, M. (2004). Cross-age peer tutoring of science in the primary school: Influence on scientific language and thinking. *Educational Psychology, 24*, 57–75.

Wright, J., & Cleary, K. S. (2006). Kids in the tutor seat: Building schools' capacity to help struggling readers through a cross-age peer-tutoring program. *Psychology in the Schools, 43*, 99–107.

PART VI

Special Issues

CHAPTER 26

Cultural Issues

Laura Johnson and Christina Tucker

Culture is the lens through which we view children and adolescents. Culture pro-vides the frames we use to label, categorize, and make sense of childhood devel-opment and behaviors. It defines our relationship to children, what is considered normal and desired child behavior, and what is considered pathological. Culture indisputably impacts childhood psychopathology. How disorders are expressed and communicated, whether help is sought for children, treatment processes and desired outcomes are all influenced by culture. Psychologists and other mental health pro-fessionals must have a thorough understanding of culture and the ways it impacts child and adolescent mental health, psychopathology, service utilization, assess-ment, and treatment (American Psychological Association [APA], 2003; Constan-tine & Sue, 2005; Cuellar & Paniagua, 2000).

In this chapter, we first provide an overview of major sociocultural changes oc-curring globally and in the United States that have implications for children. With this contextual frame we highlight the need for cultural competence in the assess-ment and treatment of children. Next we define culture and describe its complexity, outlining the ways that it influences the status of children, child development, so-cialization processes, family and social relationships, and beliefs about child and adolescent psychopathology. We introduce key cultural concepts, such as accul-turation, ethnic identity, and worldview, and provide suggestions for working with culture at each phase of assessment and treatment. Problems related to culture, cultural adaptations to treatment, and unique populations are also discussed.

A CHANGING MULTICULTURAL CONTEXT

Global Perspectives

Worldwide increases in population mobility and economic globalization are bring-ing together people from all cultures at unprecedented rates (Global Commission on International Migration [GCIM], 2005; Population Resource Center [PRC], 2005; N. Kaufman & Rizzini, 2002). Children and adolescents, accounting for 39% of the world's population, are increasingly growing up in a multicultural context (GCIM, 2005). Economic globalization and infrastructure development have resulted in in-creased opportunities for living, working, and studying in other countries. There is an overall increase in voluntary migration, usually from rural to urban areas and from developing countries to economically developed countries (GCIM, 2005; PRC, 2005). There is also an increase in forced migration, resulting in 25 million children uprooted from their home due to natural disasters, ethnic conflict, and war (United Nations High Commission for Refugees, 2001). While the importance of the extended family network remains high on a global level, population mobility breaks up traditional kinship networks and strains family and community supports.

Currently, the global population exceeds 6 billion, and over 1 billion children will be born in the next decade (PRC, 2005). Most of these children will be children of color, many will be poor, and most will live in developing countries (GCIM, 2005; PRC, 2005). Critical challenges facing these children include poverty, violations of human rights (e.g., child trafficking, involvement in armed conflict), and social justice concerns, such as the widening gap between rich and poor and between developed and developing countries (GCIM, 2005; PRC, 2005). A lack of sociopolitical power, racism, environmental threats, health risk behaviors, and global population pressures are other critical concerns facing today's children (GCIM, 2005; N. Kaufman & Rizinni, 2002; Lerner, Fisher, & Weinberg, 2000; PRC, 2005). While population rates are on the rise, natural resources are dwindling, and cultural ideology (based on ethnicity, religion, or social class) often frames the argument over resources and supplies the justification for violent conflict. Trends in population growth and mobility are expected to continue, resulting in more opportunities and demands for intercultural contact and communication (Martin & Nakayama, 2005).

Cultural Diversification of the United States

The United States is becoming an increasingly diverse, multicultural society. Children today are more likely to belong to an ethnic minority group (Hernandez, 2004, 2006). As illustrated in Figure 26.1, ethnic minority children are quickly becoming the new statistical majority. Immigrant families and children account for the greatest growth in the ethnic minority population, and about 84% come from countries in Latin America and Asia (Hernandez, 2004). Current estimates indicate that approximately 35 million foreign-born persons live in the United States, with about 1 in 5 children having at least one foreign-born parent (Hernandez, 2004; PRC, 2005). The top countries of origin are Mexico (30.7%), the Philippines (4.5%), India (4%), Mainland China (3.4%), and Vietnam (3%), with all other countries combined accounting for 45.6% (PRC, 2005).

Implications for Children

The changing multicultural context in the United States and worldwide has implications for how children and adolescents will interface with educational, legal, occupational, and health and mental health care systems (Hernandez, 2004; GCIM, 2005). These institutions were designed from a particular cultural perspective (European American) and, at least historically, were for the benefit of a population with that same cultural perspective (Marsella & Yamada, 2000). Educational, economic, health, and mental health disparities are well documented (U.S. Department of Health and Human Services, 2001). Compared to European Americans, ethnic minorities in the United States face lower educational status, higher unemployment,

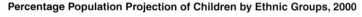

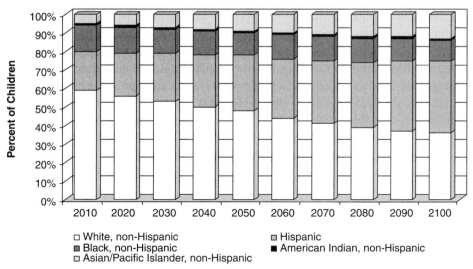

Figure 26.1   Changing ethnic profile of children in the United States. *Source:* "Demographic Change and Life Circumstances of Immigrant Families," by D. J. Hernandez, April 2004, *Future of Children*, pp. 17–47. Reprinted with permission.

higher rates of poverty, a higher risk of health and mental health problems, and increased rates of victimization and incarceration (Cuellar & Paniagua, 2000). Children living in immigrant families have higher poverty rates, are more likely to have poorly educated parents, and are more likely to live in linguistically isolated households than native-born families (Hernandez, 2004).

Despite the cultural and linguistic diversification of the United States, ethnic minority and immigrant populations continue to underutilize outpatient professional psychological services. Those who do seek help are more likely to be misdiagnosed, receive inappropriate treatment, drop out of treatment early, and receive fewer positive benefits overall compared to European Americans (Kurasaki, Sue, Chun, & Gee, 2000; Sue, Chun, & Gee, 1995; Sue, Zane, & Young, 1994). Psychologists have an ethical imperative to understand these disparities and to work toward clinical, scientific, and educational excellence in the applicability and effectiveness of their approaches (APA, 2003; Whol & Aponte, 2000).

Cultural Competence

Cultural competence is a product of general, cross-cultural, and culture-specific competencies that allow for effective functioning in the context of cultural differences (APA, 2003). It applies to individual and organizational practices and spans the areas of education, research, clinical training, and practice in psychology (APA, 2003; Constantine & Sue, 2005; D. Sue, Arredondo, & McDavis, 1992). Operationally, cultural competence is often described as three interrelated components of awareness, knowledge, and skills (Arredondo et al., 1996; D. Sue et al., 1992).

Awareness

Clinician *awareness* is commonly viewed as a prerequisite for the development of cultural competence. This requires clinicians to become aware of themselves as cultural beings. Clinicians are encouraged to intentionally bring their attention to the role of culture in their own life and to consider how it impacts their own values, beliefs, and behaviors, including biases and stereotypes about diverse children and families (APA, 2003). Skills in self-reflection can be developed and awareness enhanced through written reflection assignments, such as journal writing or reaction papers, case studies, small experiential exercises, group discussions, and coaching (Hong, Garcia, & Soriano, 2000; Martin & Nakayama, 2005).

Clinical self-awareness must extend to the profession. It is crucial to understand the sociocultural and historical context in which mainstream (i.e., European and American) theories of psychological assessment and treatment emerged (Pedersen, 2004). Although individuals of European or North American ancestry account for only one sixth of the world's population, a Western worldview and cultural perspective dominates modern psychological therapies and practices (Marsella & Yamada, 2000). Psychologists are gaining increased awareness of the cultural embeddedness of their approaches to defining, assessing, and treating childhood psychological problems.

Knowledge

Beyond awareness, clinicians must enhance their *knowledge* and understanding of culture and how it impacts children, adolescents, and the assessment and treatment process. This includes general cultural concepts applicable across many cultural groups and culture-specific information related to a particular cultural group (APA, 2003; Constantine & Sue, 2005). General knowledge includes a clear understanding of the nature of culture and how it impacts the expression of pathology, beliefs, and attitudes about childhood problems, expectations for the assessment and treatment process, and the clinician's relationship with the family.

Specific knowledge about one's *own culture* and *other cultures* is also necessary. Clinicians can enhance their cultural knowledge by reading literature, attending continuing education conferences or workshops, watching films, and reading professional books and journals as well as popular books or magazines. Experiential-based activities, such as visits to ethnic neighborhoods, international travel, second-language learning, interviews with diverse others, volunteer work, and practicum experiences, are additional ways of enhancing one's knowledge of other cultural groups.

Clinicians should undertake particular efforts to educate themselves about the major cultural groups with whom they are likely to come in contact. Additionally, when children or their family members come from cultural backgrounds with which the clinician is unfamiliar, clinicians should learn about relevant culture-specific group norms, including, but not limited to, sociopolitical history or history of oppression, cultural beliefs and values, communication styles, and attitudes toward mental health and illness (Pedersen, 2004; D. Sue & Sue, 2003). Although it is important to be knowledgeable about group norms, there is vast within-group variability.

Skills

Clinician *skills* for cultural competence include reflective thinking, establishing rapport, bridging cultural differences, intercultural communication, and accurate and culturally appropriate assessment, diagnosis, conceptualization, and treatment (APA, 2003; Arredondo et al., 1996; Constantine & Sue, 2005; Hays, 2001). In the following sections, we provide information to further clinician awareness and knowledge about the nature of culture and how it impacts the lives of children and adolescents.

THE NATURE AND COMPLEXITY OF CULTURE

A better understanding of culture and its role in shaping beliefs and behaviors is essential for clinicians working in a multicultural environment. Although there are well over 150 definitions of culture, most describe culture as being learned and shared among a group of people and passed on through the generations (Kluckholm & Kroeber, 1952). Culture includes external factors, such as style of dress, language, food, traditions, kinship structures, and social patterns, and behavioral norms, including norms for expression of psychological problems (Draguns, 2000; Paniagua, 2000). Culture can be considered a macro-template for predicting and explaining child and adolescent behavior. However, this view of culture is deceivingly simple. Culture is quite complex and has a number of features that present challenges in the clinical setting. A failure to understand the complexity of culture can result in an over- or underemphasis on culture, stereotyping, misdiagnosis, misuse or misinterpretation of tests, or culturally incompatible treatment (Canino, Canino, & Arroyo, 1998; Canino & Spurlock, 2000).

Culture Is Pervasive and Subjective

Culture has a pervasive influence in the lives of children. It encompasses a wide range of human behaviors and activities and ways of seeing, understanding, and interacting with the world. It influences our sense of time and time consciousness, relational styles, patterns of communication, sense of personal space, family structures, worldview, and ways of thinking, categorizing, and problem solving. Culture includes overt aspects, which are driven by internal features, such as beliefs, attitudes, norms, and values, that are largely unobservable and subjective. These are the unwritten rules of culture. An iceberg analogy is often used to illustrate that the observable aspects of culture are just the tip of the iceberg. Not only are most cultural factors unobservable, but they are also out of our awareness. Like fish in water we go about our daily lives, behaving and interpreting from a particular cultural frame without the awareness that we are doing so. Intentionally bringing culture into one's awareness (and keeping it there) can help clinicians recognize cultural influences and biases (Pedersen, 2000).

Culture Is Multidimensional and Dynamic

Culture is multidimensional, and children and families may describe their culture in relation to one or more dimensions or sociocultural reference groups, such as sociorace, ethnicity, tribal or clan affiliation, language group, religion, socioeconomic status, age or generational status, gender, sexual orientation, disability, geographic or regional location, nationality, and political affiliation (D. Sue & Sue, 2003; Hays, 2001). Although these groups have common features that are shared with others, the importance of different dimensions of culture (and therefore their relative importance in assessment and treatment) is in a state of flux as children develop and move in and out of various cultural milieus.

What cultural dimensions are salient will vary from child to child and family to family across time and contexts. The importance of various cultural factors and identity dimensions may change as a function of developmental stage. For example, ethnic identity and sexual orientation may be more relevant for adolescents than for young children. Relevance may also be spurred by an event, such as experiencing an act of racism. Many ethnic minority children and adolescents report that they were unaware of their race until they were called a racist name. Other events that require a child or adolescent to recognize and adapt to another culture, such as moving to a new country, a new school, or even a different state or region, can highlight the importance of different aspects of culture and identity.

Culture Is Uniquely Expressed

Cultural influences interact with individual and environmental factors to manifest idiographically in each child. The relative importance of different dimensions will vary based on a child's learning history, life experiences, and context. For example, in the United States, where there is a history of slavery, segregation, and oppression and no shortage of racial discrimination today, "being Black" is often a salient feature in determining the worldview and identity of African American children, adolescents, and their parents (Helms, 1990). In other countries, religion, social class, or tribal affiliation may be more contextually salient. Status as a member of the majority or minority may also influence a child or family's worldview or identity. Sexual identity may be more salient for gay and lesbian youth than heterosexual youth, and religious identity may be more salient for Muslim youth growing up in a majority Christian environment. It is important to note that cultural contexts change as well, bringing to the forefront different dimensions. For example, prior to the Belgian colonization of Rwanda, one's ethnicity (e.g., Hutu or Tutsi) was largely irrelevant, but from 1993 to 1994 it became the basis for who would kill or be killed.

Culture Is Interactive

Children and their families are involved in multiple cultural systems and interactions. Children and youth move in and out of different cultural contexts and social environments in their day-to-day lives (Akiba & Garcia-Coll, 2004; Bronfenbrenner, 1979, 1989; Cuellar, 2000). As illustrated in Figure 26.2, culture

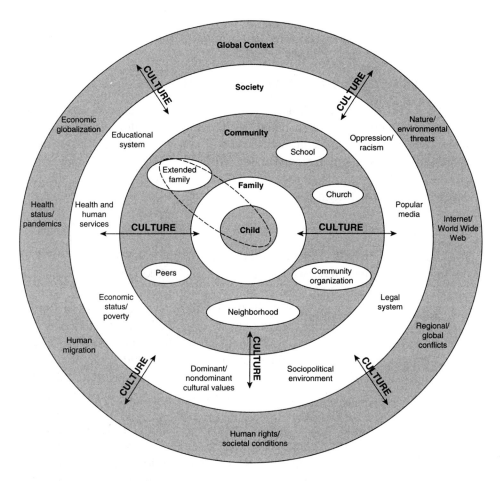

Figure 26.2   Interactive and reciprocal influence of culture across ecological contexts.

has a multilevel and reciprocal influence across children's contexts, at the proximal, microsystem level as well as at the more distal, macrosocial level. Family and community cultures interact with larger societal cultural systems and global influences. There may be drastic differences in communication, accepted norms, rules, and behaviors in the various microsystems of home, community, and school, or between the child's community and the larger society. Clinicians should consider how culture impacts the child's functioning and fit within his or her range of daily experiences. This includes the cultures of the home, school, neighborhood, and community and how they interact with each other (Bronfenbrenner, 1979, 1989).

Macrosystem factors include globalization, sociopolitical atmosphere (e.g., human rights, degree of democracy and freedom), socioeconomic conditions (e.g., poverty, educational opportunities), environmental threats related to industrialization and urbanization (pollution, safety concerns, overcrowding, noise, connection to natural environment), and overall health status (epidemics, pandemics, health risks). Of key importance is that children and adolescents are engaged in a reciprocal relationship with culture. The ecological model of child development shows that children play an active role in defining, interpreting, and shaping their cultural environment (Brislin, 2000; Bronfenbrenner, 1979, 1989).

THE IMPACT OF CULTURE ON CHILDREN

Cross-cultural research in psychology, anthropology, and sociology has revealed much about cultural variation in the role and status of children, approaches to education and socialization, cultural and social norms for development, family structure, and social relationships (Brislin, 2000; Schmidt, 2006; Tseng, 2003). Clinicians should be aware of these differences, as they have important implications for assessment and treatment.

Role and Status of Children

Around the world there is considerable cultural variation in children's roles and status, influencing how they are viewed and treated (Brislin, 2000; Petersen, Steinmetz, & Wilson, 2005a; Tseng, 2003). For example, children and adolescents living in more individualistic cultures, such as in the United States and Western Europe, may be viewed as separate, equal individuals deserving of respect. They may have considerable choice in their day-to-day lives and are frequently given a voice in family and community matters. In the context of the one-child policy in China, it has been suggested that Chinese children are likely to be pampered and doted on by parents and grandparents. However, their status as only children in a collectivist society also brings an expectation for filial piety, increased responsibilities for future caretaking, and intense pressure to succeed (Feng, 2002; Tseng, 2003). Other cultures view children as property or as essentially providing a service. In some parts of the world, for example in New Guinea, children as young as 8 may be responsible for growing, harvesting, and cooking food for themselves and their younger siblings.

The responsibilities, role, and status of children can influence risk and protective factors that may enhance or reduce their physical and psychological health. This has implications for a child's overall development; the supports, services, and resources afforded them; and their potential to be neglected or abused (Tseng, 2003). Gender, class, and cultural issues tend to interact in this regard, often conferring male and class privilege though reduced social status and fewer economic and educational opportunities for young girls worldwide (United Nations Children's Fund, 2004).

Education and Socialization

Cultural factors shape the ways that children and adolescents are educated, socialized, enculturated, and disciplined. Major differences in child-rearing practices are found cross-culturally in terms of who is involved in education and socialization of children and also in the methods used to teach children (Brislin, 2000; Petersen et al., 2005a). In a Western setting, teaching styles favor a direct approach emphasizing written history, direct verbal communication, and linear and dialectical thinking. Critical thinking and Socratic questioning are often encouraged, and the uniqueness of each individual is valued. Teaching in the United States, in particular, is considered child-centered, with the responsibility for the child's learning placed with the parent or teacher. In other cultures, approaches to teaching, and often parenting, tend to place more responsibility on the child and have high expectations for obedience and respect for authority (Petersen, Steinmetz, & Wilson, 2005b). Blending in and working for the good of the whole is valued, and personal distinction is frowned upon. Asking questions of persons in authority (teachers or parents) is desirable behavior in one context, whereas in another it brings ridicule and shame.

Cultural differences exist in tolerance for misbehavior and in approaches to punishment (e.g., short or long term, mild or severe) and types of punishment (e.g., physical; suspension of social, material, or activity rewards; emotional response such as shame or embarrassment, or withdrawal of love; Brislin, 2000; Peterson, Steinmetz, & Wilson, 2005c; Tseng, 2003). Families may have different approaches for boys and girls, or for children of different ages. Discipline may be used consistently or haphazardly (Tseng, 2003). In the United States, African American parents often have a more authoritarian approach to child rearing than European American parents. American Indians, on the other hand, may value a natural unfolding of development (Brislin, 2000). Misunderstanding of the cultural norms for parenting may lead one to incorrectly jump to assumptions about abuse or neglect with these and other populations.

Sense of Self, Family, and Social Relationships

How one views the self and an emphasis on different aspects of the self is a fundamental concern to multicultural assessment. The idea of the unique, autonomous, and bounded self and the American ideal of rugged individualism are in contrast with the view of the majority of the world's population, which is more interdependent or sociocentric in nature. In these cultures, the boundaries of the child's sense of self extend to include siblings, parents, grandparents, aunts, uncles, and other extended family members; members of the community, ethnic group or tribe, and nation; ancestors; even the solar system and the universe (Brislin, 2000). The nature of interpersonal relationships that children and adolescents share with others varies from culture to culture, and the differences in closeness of relationships and the kinship structures can be drastic. American ethnic minority groups and immigrants are more likely to have important extended family structures and obligations than Euro-American children and families. Immigrant children are more likely to live with extended family members (Hernandez, 2004). Clinicians should pay careful attention to flexible family roles and assumptions related to the closeness and the importance of significant relationships of children. Ideas about dependence, enmeshment, and differentiation of the self should be examined critically (Hays, 2001; Tseng, 2003).

Normative (and Valued) Development

Definitions about what is healthy and desired child and adolescent development and behavior vary culturally. Different modes of behaving (passive versus active), communication (oral versus written, verbal versus nonverbal), relating to others (independent versus interdependent), and acquisition of different skills (e.g., motor versus language skills) vary culturally (Brislin, 2000). So, too, do the ways that development is shaped by a child's family and society and how poor (or abnormal) development is tolerated and handled. Cultural differences in expectations and valued processes and outcomes are commonly seen between individualist cultures and collectivist cultures (Triandis, 1995). It is useful for clinicians to keep in mind that worldwide, the majority of cultures (including all major ethnic minority groups in the United States) are rooted in collectivism. Individualistic cultures tend to value independence in behavior and relationships, competitiveness, and autonomy. Egalitarianism and fairness are also valued, and individuality and uniqueness are encouraged. On the other hand, traditional collectivist cultures tend to stress an interdependent sense of self, cooperative behaviors, and dependence, and value social responsibility over personal interests.

In collectivist cultures, consideration of children's attachments may be expanded to include attachment and bonding relationships with extended family and other important caregivers. Developmentally, 2- to 4-year-old children in a Eurocentric culture may be encouraged toward autonomy, whereas other cultures may view too much independence as problematic and thus place a greater value on shame. In some sociocultural contexts, child initiative may be expressed as aggression, whereas other cultures may value a "being" over "doing" orientation toward activity (Tseng, 2003). The age at entering adulthood also varies. Instead of moving toward independence, some cultures may emphasize adolescents' understanding and fulfilling their family or societal roles. Gender expectations and roles will interact with both age and cultural differences, and these roles may be more or less defined and rigid.

Variation in Psychopathology

How problems of a psychological nature are defined is determined by culture, and behaviors can be understood only within their cultural context. Culture impacts the incidence of various problems of childhood, symptom expression, help seeking, and treatment process (Aponte & Johnson, 2000; Draguns, 2000). Culture may directly or indirectly contribute to pathology, shaping the clinical picture as a whole or at level of symptom manifestation (Jenkins, 1996).

Some challenges to clinicians include cultural issues related to mind-body dualism, somatic presentation, the role of spirituality, ideas of selfhood, and categories of emotion and related semantics (Angel & Williams, 2000; Draguns, 2000; Good & Good, 1986). This separation of mind and body and the associated symptoms stems from Western dualism and runs contrary to holistic views of the mind and body that dominate non-Western thinking. How one views the self and emphasis on different aspects of the self will impact the cognitive and affective aspects of disorders and their associated meanings. This has implications for the prominence or absence of symptoms and how they are expressed. Statements assessing depression, for example, emphasize the self ("I feel sad"), whereas individuals from non-Western cultures may be more apt to express dysphoria in terms of their relations to others, for example, concerns about disappointing or embarrassing other individuals (Manson, 1995). Symptoms associated with anxiety and the content of phobias also vary greatly across cultures.

Variations in the language of emotion and differential emphasis on particular emotions also present difficulties. *Indeterminacy of meaning* refers to problems that arise in the semantic translation of concepts and symptoms and the assumptions made about emotional categories (Good & Good, 1986). For example, Western-based diagnostic systems (e.g., the *Diagnostic and Statistical Manual of Mental Disorders [DSM]*) may construe guilt, shame, and sinfulness as generally having the same meaning, whereas other cultures may see important differences. In other instances, symptoms or disorders that are conceptually distinct (e.g., anxiety and depression) according to Western nosology may be presented as fused (e.g., feeling "sad and bothered"; Good & Good, 1986).

Another issue of concern for clinicians is how to respond to somatic and spiritual or religious presentations of problems. Somatic symptoms play a more central role in both the experience and expression of mental disorders worldwide. Somatic distress is common in non-Western populations and in American ethnic minority groups (Kleinman, 1987). Similarly, spiritual and religious factors may play a greater role in understanding culturally diverse populations. Spiritual concerns may include concerns related to religious identity, loss of faith, religious beliefs that a child's disorder is a sign from God (blessing or punishment), problems of the soul, angered ancestors or God(s), concerns related to being cursed though witchcraft or sorcery, or problems interacting within a religious community. These symptoms may be puzzling to Western clinicians and are not well integrated into Western conceptions of mental illness. Spiritual or religious beliefs may also come into play as cultural strengths, coping resources, paths to treatment, or the means of treatment.

Cultural Strengths and Resources

Thinking about the complexity of culture and the many ways that it can impact children and their families, it is easy to see how clinicians may become overwhelmed with all that cultural competence requires of them. Culture can also be a great help to clinicians, allowing them to tap natural strengths and coping resources of children and families. Identifying family cultural values and resources can help the clinicians develop treatment plans that are acceptable to the family and also work with their strengths and supports (Hill, 1993). Some of the cultural strengths and values of the major ethnocultural groups in the United States are shown in Table 26.1.

CULTURAL CONCEPTS IN ASSESSMENT AND TREATMENT

Responding to culture effectively in the clinical setting requires that we unpackage culture into its many parts (or cultural factors). Defining and assessing specific cultural concepts can allow for a deeper understanding of culture as it impacts children within and across cultural groups. Included among these, and essential for accurate assessment and treatment, are etic and emic approaches, enculturation, acculturation, cultural identity, worldview, and explanatory models.

Table 26.1   Cultural Strengths and Resources of U.S. Ethnic Minority Groups

African Americans	American Indians	Asian Americans	Latinos/as
Strong desire to achieve in education	Success in learning important cultural values of tribe	Family expects high academic performance from children; Peer support for academics	Academic success supported by family and community
Strong work ethic	Strong work ethic	Intense loyalty to employer	Vigorous work ethic
Flexible family roles; Extended kinship and supports; Connection to other African Americans	Diverse family structures; Communal values of sharing within group and extended family	Family roles are hierarchical and interdependent	Value marriage, importance of immediate, extended family, and friends
Strong spiritual and religious orientation	Sense of connection between nature and self	Strong sense of connection among family members	Importance of interpersonal relationships and sensitivity

Etic and Emic Approaches

Western European and American psychological research and practice traditionally relied on a nomothetic or etic approach aimed at discovering universals (Lewis-Fernandez & Kleinman, 1995). An idiographic, or emic, approach emphasizes the importance of the local cultural context in shaping phenomena (Munroe & Munroe, 1980). Kleinman (1977, 1980) offers a conceptual distinction between the etic construct of "disease/disorder" and the emic construct of "illness." Disorder refers to the malfunctioning of biological or psychological processes. Illness is a cultural construct that refers to the expression and experience of the disorder. It includes the personal and social meanings of the disorder and how it impacts the lives of children and their families (Kleinman, 1977, 1980). Use of the two perspectives is considered essential to adequate assessment and treatment planning (Lewis-Fernandez & Kleinman, 1995). The right balance between etic and emic approaches largely depends on the child's and family's level of enculturation and acculturation.

Enculturation

Enculturation refers to the process of socialization into a particular cultural, ethnic, or social group (Aponte & Johnson, 2000; Brislin, 2000). Enculturation occurs directly and indirectly through teaching, coaching, reinforcing various behaviors, social role modeling, media, and other environmental and contextual influences. Enculturation of children is an ongoing process and is impacted by the parents' enculturation history, ethnic identity, social class, and current living context. Cultural knowledge, awareness, pride, and feelings of connectedness in one's ethnic or cultural group (i.e., a strong ethnic or cultural identity) are possible outcomes of enculturation. Successful enculturation also results in skills for interacting effectively within one's cultural group (Aponte & Johnson, 2000). In some cases, children and adolescents will not be well enculturated. Children of refugees and immigrants may reject parental attempts at enculturation, whereas other children are not exposed to their cultural heritage due to parental and/or societal pressure to assimilate into the majority cultural group. Enculturation processes and outcomes interact with acculturation processes that occur as a result of contact with other cultures.

Acculturation

Acculturation Process

Acculturation refers to changes in values, beliefs, and behaviors that occur as a result of sustained contact with a second culture (Berry, 1997; Berry & Kim, 1988). Due to the increase in cultural contact worldwide, the concept of acculturation has garnered increased attention and application over the past few decades. It is considered crucial in the experiences of refugees, immigrants, indigenous groups, ethnic minorities, and sojourners, such as international students and business travelers (Aponte & Johnson, 2000; Berry, 1997; Roysircar, 2004). Additionally, attention has recently been given to "the other side of acculturation," referring to acculturation processes occurring in dominant majority cultures as a result of immigration and other population trends that cause increased intercultural interactions.

Whereas acculturation generally refers to changes resulting from group-level encounters between two or more cultures, *psychological acculturation* refers to psychological changes occurring at the individual level (Berry, 1998). Psychological acculturation is of key importance in assessing culturally diverse children because it involves changes across a number of domains, including language, cognitive style, attitudes, style of relating, and identity (Berry, 1986).

Acculturative Stress

In the context of acculturation, children and families may experience *acculturative stress*. This refers to mildly pathological and disruptive behaviors and experiences that are commonly generated during acculturation. Symptoms of acculturative stress may include family conflict, academic or behavioral problems, depression, anxiety, physical complaints, anger, identity confusion, and substance abuse (Berry, Kim, Minde, & Mok, 1987). Several group and individual factors interact to impact the amount of acculturative stress experienced by children and families. These include (a) macrosocial influences of the child's environment, such as legal constraints, discrimination, degree of tolerance for cultural diversity; (b) factors associated with the background of the acculturating family, such as worldview, social and familial network structure, cultural distance from American society; and (c) individual factors such as age, sex, language proficiency, personality, coping skills, and cultural knowledge (Aponte & Johnson, 2000; Berry, 1986, 1997). Two other factors affecting acculturative stress are (d) phase of acculturation and (e) acculturation strategy (Berry, 1986, 1997, 1998). Phase of acculturation refers to the pattern of adjustment over time (Berry, 1986). Different patterns of responding to the demands of acculturation have been referred to as acculturation strategies or modes (Berry, 1997).

Modes of Acculturation

Of the many factors impacting acculturation problems in children and families, the mode of acculturation may be the most important in predicting overall adjustment outcomes. Four different modes are assimilation, separation, marginalization, and integration. The modes of acculturation account for the relative degree of cultural contact and participation by families and the amount of value placed on such actions (Berry, 1997). As seen in Table 26.2, those with an *assimilation* strategy try to disengage completely from their culture of origin in hopes of being completely absorbed and accepted into the dominant host culture (LaFromboise, Coleman, & Gerton, 1993). Assimilated children may operate effectively within the new social, cultural, and academic environment, but they may sacrifice their sense of identity, their cultural or familial supports, and groundedness in their culture of origin. Families and children using the *separation* strategy will segregate themselves from mainstream American society and establish relationships primarily with others from their own ethnic or cultural group. Often living in ethnic pockets or neighborhoods, these families may garner much needed social support. However, as these children and their parents face demands to speak English, perform academically, access

Table 26.2   Acculturation Modes and Approaches to Working with Children and Families

Mode of Acculturation	*Positive* Contact, Affiliation, and Effectiveness with *Dominant/Majority* Culture	*Lack of* Contact, Affiliation, and Effectiveness with *Dominant/Majority* Culture
Positive Contact, Affiliation, and Effectiveness with *Own Culture*	**Bicultural** Children and families have an integrated identity; skills to interact across multiple, cultural settings; ability to access services and benefits from heritage culture and majority culture. Consider bicultural approaches; adapt mainstream approaches; integrate culturally related or traditional approaches; use culture as a resource.	**Separated** Children and families are supported in their community but separated from the dominant culture. Conflicts arise in negotiating school, legal, health, or other systems. Mistrust related to racism, oppression, or cultural differences may exist. Consider culturally related and traditional approaches; be aware of biases and miscommunication.
Lack of Contact, Affiliation, and Effectiveness with *Own Culture*	**Assimilated** Children and families function reasonably well in dominant society and systems. May lack cultural identity and traditional supports; internalized racism or inability to fully assimilate may cause conflict. Consider mainstream approaches and culturally adapted approaches.	**Marginalized** Children and families lack effectiveness in both cultures. Without resources, natural coping strengths, and the ability to access help, these families are likely to suffer from multiple hardships, including psychological problems. Consider bicultural approaches.

resources, and/or negotiate school, legal, or health care systems, they are likely to experience high levels of acculturative stress (Berry, 1997; LaFromboise et al., 1993). *Marginalized* families will experience the highest levels of acculturative stress, as they lack the behavioral repertoire needed to interact with members of their own culture and with the dominant society. They have the greatest risk of psychological maladjustment (Berry, 1997; Berry & Kim, 1988).

Children and families with a certain degree of integration into the majority culture will experience the fewest problems (Berry, 1997). The *bicultural* strategy suggests that children can acquire the skills and psychological flexibility to function effectively in both their culture of origin and the majority culture. Achievement of bicultural effectiveness serves as both a coping strategy for and a protective factor against acculturative stress (Berry, 1997, 1998; LaFromboise et al., 1993). In practice, bicultural effectiveness may involve the techniques of *code switching* (completely shifting behavior depending on the context) and *culture blending* (merging aspects of two or more cultures; Garcia Coll & Magnuson, 1997; Szapocznik, Santisteban, Kurtines, Perez-Vidal, & Hervis, 1984).

Acculturation modes are not dichotomous, and families can be at the extremes or in the middle on either dimension. Moreover, children and their families usually do not undergo acculturation at the same rate or approach it in the same way. For example, among immigrant and refugee families, children and youth may tend toward assimilation, while their parents, fearing loss of their traditional heritage, may tend toward separation.

Cultural, Ethnic, and Racial Identity

Cultural identity is a multidimensional construct that results from a dynamic combination of different aspects of social identity, such as ethnic, racial, and gender identity (Aponte & Johnson, 2000; Schmidt, 2006). Theory and research related to cultural, ethnic, and racial identity are prominent contributions to the field of multicultural psychology (Atkinson, Morten, & Sue, 1998). One's cultural identity is usually evolving, but at any point, it represents an outcome of one's age and developmental stage, processes of enculturation and acculturation, and immediate and historical contextual situations. A strong or well-developed sense of one's ethnic or cultural identity is considered to be a protective factor, or developmental asset, among youth (Phinney, 1990).

Numerous models of cultural, ethnic, and racial identity have been developed for various groups, for example, Black racial identity development (Cross, 1971, 1995; Helms, 1990); minority identity development (Atkinson et al., 1998); person of color identity development (Helms, 1995); homosexual identity development (Cass, 1979); biracial identity development (Root, 1990); and White racial identity development (Helms, 1990, 1995). Most of the models describe a process of development from a lack of awareness of oneself as a cultural being and the implications of culture (or race) to an integrated and balanced identity. Along the way, individuals may experience dissonance and confusion about cultural differences (often spurred by an event), and at other times may develop a strong sense of cultural identity and pride coupled with complete immersion into their own cultural heritage and background. In the more advanced stages of identity development, individuals incorporate many identity dimensions and reference groups into their overall self-concept. This includes the ability to respond objectively to members of the dominant cultural group. Integrated identity awareness often extends to advocacy or social action to benefit culturally marginalized or oppressed groups. Although these models often use a stage process to describe identity development, development does not always occur in a linear fashion. Children may have characteristics of more than one stage at any time (Helms, 1995).

Worldview

Worldview refers to psychological and value orientations that influence how people think, behave, and interpret and experience situations, including the assessment and treatment process. Several models draw attention to different aspects or conceptualizations of worldview. Kluckhohn and Strodtbeck's (1952) orientation model (as cited in Mio, Barker-Hackett, & Tumambing, 2006) is based on four dimensions: (1) orientation to time (e.g., past, present, future), time flexibility, and time consciousness; (2) relationship to nature (e.g., harmony or control over nature); (3) view of the self and social relations (e.g., independent or interdependent); and (4) activity orientation (e.g., focus on being or doing). Other concepts of worldview highlight the two dimensions of locus of control and locus of responsibility, suggesting that unique worldviews emerge based on their combination (D. Sue, 1978). A strong belief in fate among parents, or feeling incapable of controlling or changing the behavior of their children or their circumstances, would have major implications for the assessment and treatment process. Other commonly discussed worldviews are collectivism and individualism (Triandis, 1995). Clients from individualistic cultures tend to place the individual's rights and needs before that of the group, whereas clients from collectivistic backgrounds emphasize the rights and gains of the group over the individual. Another concept of worldview, the minority worldview, highlights one's status as a minority (e.g., ethnic, gender, sexual orientation) and related experiences of oppression as influencing worldview (Mio et al., 2006). These aspects of worldview may be extremely important in guiding the behaviors of the client and the clinician.

Explanatory Models

Explanatory models are beliefs about an episode of illness that give meaning to the illness and convey how the illness is understood or conceptualized by the child and the child's family. These beliefs play a key role in understanding the illness experience of the child and family, their treatment choices, patterns of mental health service utilization, and treatment outcomes (Kleinman, 1980; Pelto & Pelto, 1996; Weiss & Kleinman, 1988). Explanatory models contain information about the cause of the illness, its onset, the probable course of the illness, its severity, and level of impairment. Eliciting an explanatory model will provide useful information about fears associated with the illness, the main problems it has caused, and, importantly, what kind of treatment the family is expecting and what they hope the outcomes will be (Chrisman & Johnson, 1996; Kleinman, 1980).

CULTURE AND ASSESSMENT

The influential nature of assessments and their results can dramatically affect the lives of children and their families. All clinical interactions are to some extent intercultural. Therefore, it is safe to assume that culture is always operating in *some* capacity in *every* case, and the need to address culture when conducting assessments is always applicable. When interpreting test results, making diagnoses, and conceptualizing cases clinicians should undertake a cultural formulation of the client. The *DSM-IV* (Appendix I) offers clinicians an outline for things to keep in mind while composing the cultural formulation. This formulation, in addition to other assessment procedures, will assist the examiner in understanding the relative importance of culture and the extent to which procedures, instruments, and interpretations need to be adjusted. In this section, we discuss the cultural formulation along with other cultural aspects of assessment, such as assessing the context, identifying biases of the examiner and the tests, interviewing the family, selecting and administering tests, adapting tests, assessing the child and family's culture, and interpreting the results.

Identify Cultural Bias in Assessment and Testing

The *DSM-IV* Outline for Cultural Formulation stresses that clinicians must identify cultural elements of the relationship between the client and the clinician (APA, 1994). Bias in testing and assessment may be related to the examiner, the approach to assessment, and the testing tools and procedures. Determining which questions to ask and to explore, deciding which instruments to administer, and interpreting the results are all influenced by unique, culture-bound beliefs. Clinician self-awareness is key to accurately observing and interpreting the verbal and nonverbal behaviors of clients. For instance, the Western idea that a high level of eye contact is acceptable and preferred may be contrary to that in other cultures, and a lack of eye contact may be misinterpreted as a negative characteristic. Sullivan (1954, as cited in Takushi & Uomoto, 2001) states that clinicians should continually ask themselves about alternative explanations for behaviors (e.g., "Could this mean something different from what readily comes to mind?" or "What might the client mean by that?").

The cultural formulation also states that clinicians must identify cultural differences between themselves and their clients that may influence the therapeutic relationship. This suggests that clinicians need to identify their personal biases, stereotypes, and assumptions about diverse children and families. Clinicians should be aware of within-group variability. Each family has its own cultural traditions and belief systems and each child should be thought of as coming from his or her own unique amalgam of cultural influences. Failure to account for within-group variability and a reliance on stereotypes or group norms can lead to misdiagnosis or inappropriate treatment (Canino & Spurlock, 2000). It is impossible to learn all of the details of every cultural system, but it is the clinician's responsibility to understand the limits of his or her own cultural knowledge and seek out additional knowledge as needed.

In addition to clinician biases, many standardized tests are biased. In general, assessments favor European American and middle-class children, while disadvantaging ethnic minority children (Kaufman & Lichtenberger, 2002). If interpreted incorrectly, results can be particularly harmful to children in school settings. To provide a culturally responsive assessment to diverse children, the following steps are suggested:

- Research the cultural context of the referral question.
- Conduct a culturally informative and sensitive clinical interview.
- Select and administer tests in a culturally responsive way.
- Use the cultural formulation to guide assessment and interpretation.

Research the Cultural Context of the Referral Question

It is essential that the child's behaviors be considered in multiple contexts (i.e., within the microsystems of home, peer network, school). This gives the examiner information regarding the development of the child's behaviors as well as the responses of parents, siblings, teachers, and extended family. Working with the culturally diverse child, clinicians should try to understand any discrepancies regarding how the behavior is viewed across contexts. It is possible for a behavior to be interpreted as extremely disruptive, offensive, and maladaptive within one context; however, the same behavior may be considered adaptive and culturally appropriate within the child's family system or community. During this process, it is important to consider not only maladaptive behaviors, but also the child's strengths.

The *DSM-IV* Outline for Cultural Formulation states that the clinician must gather information regarding the cultural factors related to the psychosocial environment and levels of functioning for each client. Important cultural and historical information may be gathered from records prior to testing. For instance, knowing the regions a child has lived in prior to the current context, the origin of the child's family and ancestors, and the child's first language could be helpful for better understanding the nature of the question, the family's cultural perspective, and whether an interpreter will be needed. If possible, the examiner should obtain information regarding the client's socioeconomic status, family history, language, and acculturation experiences before the interview. While cultural information gathered prior to the assessment can be helpful as a starting point, a culturally sensitive and informative interview is essential for understanding the unique perspective of each child and family.

Conduct a Culturally Informative Clinical Interview

This portion of the assessment is critical for obtaining culturally valid information. During a parental interview there are a number of goals to be considered. The examiner should first offer information regarding the process of the assessment and answer any questions to help ease possible anxiety or cultural discrepancies. The examiner should be aware that it is considered offensive in some cultures to ask personal questions and should therefore address this possibility in the beginning. Perhaps a cultural broker could be used to facilitate this process in a more culturally responsive manner. The examiner should explain not only confidentiality and its limitations but also the purpose of the questioning. It should be clear to the parents that the intent of the examiner is not to offend but to gather information to gain a full picture of the child's environment. However, the examiner should also explain that if anything is asked that is deemed too personal by the parents, they may choose not to disclose, and they should understand that the examiner means no disrespect.

It is essential to gain the parents' trust to obtain all the information needed regarding the child's history and current functioning. The clinician may also want to ask about any previous experiences with mental health and let the client's parents explain their frustrations or satisfactory experiences. This gives the examiner a better picture of the level of trust the parents have in mental health providers in general and any cultural misunderstandings that may have occurred in the past. In the case of school or court referrals, parents may feel that an evaluation insinuates that there is a deficit or something abnormal with their child; if the "maladaptive" behaviors being assessed are viewed as adaptive within their own culture, the parents may believe an assessment is unnecessary. This may result in defensiveness, and parents may withhold information they consider evidence of such a deficit. It is the examiner's responsibility to inform the parents of the objective and neutral nature of the assessment.

Next, the examiner should obtain a familial and developmental history of the child. It should also be noted what languages are spoken within the home as this may be a factor in language acquisition and development. The examiner should inquire about any incidences reported in the records, such as previous illnesses or developmental milestones, and what the parents' explanatory models are regarding these occurrences. Information to be considered by the clinician includes the following:

- The child's cultural context within all settings.
- Year or time period each developmental stage occurred within the child's life and the correlating events or cultural beliefs.
- Client's language usage and comfort speaking the clinician's language (may require an interpreter or referral).
- Cultural strengths the client may gain from membership in a particular cultural group.
- Cultural information apparent in how the parents and family interact with the child.

Assess Child's Enculturation, Acculturation, and Ethnic Identity

In addition to the issues presented by the clients, psychologists must also keep in mind generational history (how many family members in the country, circumstances of the move, etc.); citizenship or residency status (e.g., number of years in the country); fluency in standard English or other language; extent of family support or disintegration of family; availability of community resources; level of education; change in social status; and work history and level of stress related to acculturation (APA, 2003). According to the *DSM-IV* Outline for Cultural Formation, psychologists must explore these issues and their influence in the progression of treatment. Hays (2001) suggests the following questions for inquiring about the client's enculturation and acculturation:

- On what terms did you or your family arrive here (refugees, students, etc.)?
- How long have you lived here?
- What language did you first learn to speak? What is spoken in your home? What language do you prefer?
- What is your cultural (or ethnic) heritage or background?
- What is your involvement with _____ (Americans and American culture, own ethnic culture)?
- Would you mind telling me about your religious upbringing? Do you have a religious (or spiritual) practice now?
- What is it like to grow up as a boy/girl in your culture and family?
- Would it be okay if I ask you about your family?
- How is your family's economic situation now? Are there ways it impacts your family life or child's problem?
- Are there ways in which discrimination (prejudice, racism) impacts your family or your child's problem?
- Are there ways in which your (or your child's) disability contributes to the problem?

Assess the Family's Explanatory Model

Assessing the explanatory model of the child and family will help the clinician understand the child's and the family's perspectives on the problem. The model will reveal important cultural and/or personal beliefs about the child's problem that have implications for assessing and treating the child. Research suggests that the family's explanatory model may be just as important as, if not more important than the child's in determining help seeking. Kleinman (1980, p. 106) suggests several questions for exploring explanatory models:

- What do you call your child's problem? What name does it have?
- What do you think caused your child's problem?
- Why do you think it started when it did?
- What does your child's illness do to him or her? How does it work?
- How severe is it? Will it have a short or long course?
- What do you fear most about your child's problem?

- What are the problems your child's illness has caused? What is the impact on the family?
- What kind of help (assessment/treatment) do you think your child needs? What are the most important results you hope to get from treatment?

These questions may be asked during the clinical interview, but keep in mind communication norms and sensitivities. Rather than barrage the family with direct questions, questions can be incorporated more naturally into a conversation about the family's concerns. Young children in particular may not have a complete explanatory model; some parts may be missing, vague, or fused together. The beliefs will change over time, and the child's and parents' views may be different from each other. Depending on the age, developmental stage, and cultural background of the child, consideration of the child's perspective may be more or less important in the family's eyes. The clinician needs to consider the family structure when making efforts to elicit or communicate the child's perspective. For example, having the child vocalize a difference or disagreement with a parent, either alone or in front of the parent, could cause a loss of face, shame, or embarrassment for the parent. Moreover, giving equal weight to a child's or adolescent's explanatory model may threaten the parent's authority and jeopardize the examiner's credibility.

Select Appropriate Test Instruments

Clinicians must understand and be knowledgeable about the reliability, validity, standardization, and appropriate use of any procedures or instruments used in an assessment (APA, 2002). The APA Ethics Code urges psychologists to "use assessment instruments whose validity and reliability have been established for use with members of the population tested" (p. 13). The Ethics Code states that "when such validity or reliability has not been established, psychologists must describe the strengths and limitations of test results and interpretation" (p. 13). It is the responsibility of the examiner to understand the instrument's cultural limitations and adapt procedures and interpretations of results as needed.

The number of school-age children coming from minority backgrounds is increasing rapidly; however, assessment instruments normed on nonmajority populations are sparse. Padilla (2001) states that using a test with individuals of cultural or linguistic groups who were not included in the standardization group calls into question the reliability and validity of the results. Instruments appropriate for use with children from diverse cultural backgrounds and varying linguistic abilities are not commonly available in educational and psychological settings. According to Torres (1991, as cited in Padilla, 2001), studies have shown that approximately 5 million students are inappropriately tested each year by standardized assessment instruments. This is of great concern, particularly in special education, where standardized testing is mandatory to give a child a diagnosis and secure appropriate support. Students' results may be deflated, resulting in inappropriate academic labeling and placement, such as being retained in a grade or placed on a low-expectation education track (Padilla, 2001).

Suggestions for Making Standardized Tests More Culturally Responsive

Although no test can be considered culture-free, there are some tests considered to be culturally responsive in testing with minorities. Some of the instruments were developed with a particular ethnicity in mind; there are also many available for use with larger diverse populations. For instance, the Wechsler Intelligence Scale for Children III, Woodcock-Johnson Psychoeducational Battery—Revised, Child Behavior Checklist, and the Kaufman Assessment Battery for Children are all considered appropriate for use with children from diverse populations (Canino & Spurlock, 2000).

In an attempt to lessen the cultural bias toward diverse populations, many clinicians choose to alter the administration of the instrument. For instance, when giving timed tests, it is important to understand that the emphasis in Western culture on quick responding as an indicator of intelligence is culture-based. Some cultures (e.g., Asian) may emphasize careful consideration of a question before responding and may further consider a careful, unrushed, and thoughtful response to be a sign of intelligence (Gopaul-McNicol & Thomas-Presswood, 1998). As a result, some clinicians eliminate (or extend) the time limits for some subtests or items (Canino & Spurlock, 2000).

Gopaul-McNicol and Thomas-Presswood (1998) advocate altering vocabulary portions of instruments to allow the child to use the vocabulary item within a sentence (Canino & Spurlock, 2000). This allows the child to contextualize the word and may give the examiner a better picture of the true knowledge the child has regarding the vocabulary word. Another method used to alter testing administration and minimize cultural bias is to advocate the use of paper and pencil to work out math problems. This not only allows the examiner to see the process the examinee uses but may also help the examinee in the task. It may be beneficial for the examiner to model the required behavior prior to giving actual test items. Doing so may clarify directions that were misunderstood due to a language deficiency or cultural misunderstanding. It also gives the child the opportunity to ask questions regarding the task and minimizes the possibility that the child's behaviors during testing are misinterpreted as low levels of ability rather than a lack of clarity (Paniagua, 1994). Adaptations should be made with awareness and knowledge of the child's acculturation level and language usage and fluency. Some strategies for culturally responsive testing include:

- When using an interpreter or cultural broker, set up a meeting prior to the assessment to discuss the process and possible cultural concerns.
- Explore all possible venues to explain the client's responses, scores, and behaviors during testing.
- If possible, current scores should be compared relative to the client's prior performance instead of against others' scores or the norm.
- Avoid the use of standardized personality tests for diagnostic purposes with clients of minority identities.

Interpretation and Case Conceptualization

The clinician's overall interpretation of the client's situation stems from his or her own way of perceiving the client's presentation of problems. This evaluation is guided by the clinician's professional orientation, sociocultural background, cultural awareness, and experiences. It is the clinician who tailors the interviewing process, test selection and administration, interpretation and perception, and ultimately the understanding and reporting of the problem. Therefore, it is essential that clinicians compose a thorough case conceptualization that takes culture into account and is alert to possible biases. It is through this culturally relativistic prism that test scores and behaviors should be interpreted.

CULTURE AND TREATMENT

Culturally responsive treatment can be developed through collaborative negotiation between the clinician and the family (Hays, 2001). How and what cultural material should be integrated vary with each child and family. According to the *DSM-IV* Outline for Cultural Formation, information about the client and the client's cultural background should be organized into an overall approach for treatment that links the conceptualization to the treatment. Culture frames beliefs of the clinician and of the family about the best route to recovery and the desired result. Therapeutic theories, orientations, and approaches have their own cultural roots and reflect a particular worldview and philosophy (Pedersen, 2004). Whether the goal of therapy is to work for a reduction of psychological symptoms or for an acceptance of them is a value-laden question (Tseng, 2003).

Ideally the treatment plan will flow from two sources: the clinician's conceptualization (based on theoretical orientation and comprehensive assessment) and the perspective and goals of the child and family. Cultural factors should be considered at every phase in the treatment process.

Next we consider culture across the phases of treatment, from before treatment begins to building rapport, establishing roles and boundaries, and planning and adapting treatments.

Establish a Relationship

First, clinicians should take the necessary time to establish rapport, respect, and credibility with the family (Hays, 2001; Hong et al., 2000; Okazaki, 2000). This asks the clinician to develop an appropriate level of intimacy with the child and other family members. What level is appropriate and the expected degree of formality will vary based on cultural, gender, and age-related factors, as well as the nature of the problem. Clinicians should consider the use of titles, differences in communication (e.g., language usage and fluency, paralanguage), and social interaction (formal versus informal, gender roles). With clients from patriarchal and authoritarian cultures, it will be important to pay special attention to establishing respect and credibility with the father; in other cultures it could be a maternal grandmother who deserves special consideration. Necessary family support for treatment may hinge, to some extent, on the support, approval, and cooperation of these individuals. With other groups, such as African Americans, efforts to connect equally with all family members, including the child and other siblings, will be valued.

Therapists should also appreciate that some families will have a need to contextualize the clinician, or otherwise understand something about the clinician or the clinician's background (Hays, 2001). To build trust and engender respect and rapport, a clinician may engage in small talk, use appropriate self-disclosure, and adapt language style by avoiding jargon and using the language of the family members (e.g., idioms, ways of describing) when possible. Providing concrete help to the family or otherwise quickly addressing a family concern can also build trust. Clinicians should be mindful of personal reactions or biases related to race or culture that may result in mistrust, suspicion, hostility, ambivalence, overreliance or overfriendliness, excessive guilt, anger, or denial of ethnicity on the part of the family or the clinician. All of these interfere with the therapeutic relationship (Vaughn, 2004; Wohl, 2000). In all cases, a clinician's skills in conveying warmth, openness, and respect can go a long way in building a working alliance with the child and family members. A certain degree of humility and appropriate use of humor are also considered to be essential to building intercultural relationships (Hays, 2001).

Understand and Address Treatment Barriers

Understanding and addressing obstacles to treatment barriers is essential to equitable service provision. Ethnic and cultural minorities and low-income and other disenfranchised groups face a number of barriers in accessing and benefiting from professional psychological treatment. These barriers include a lack of affordability, accessibility, acceptability, and appropriateness in current services. Efforts to address the psychological needs of children and adolescents should be particularly attuned to culture-based beliefs about psychological problems, such as stigmas and beliefs regarding from whom and what type of help is needed. A lack of familiarity with mental health services or counseling, cultural mistrust due to racism, or previous negative experiences with mental health services are additional factors that prevent psychological help seeking. Instead, families may seek informal help from family and friends; from religious, spiritual, or other community supports; or from medical providers. Psychological services may be sought only as a last resort, when problems have escalated or the family is in a state of crisis. Moreover, service may be sought due to outside pressures (e.g., legal or school referral) rather than family choice. Once help is sought, clients may experience communication barriers or institutional or individual racism and treatment that may be culturally incongruent with their values and beliefs.

The nature and extent of these treatment barriers will need to be assessed and addressed for each child and family. In general, clinicians should be aware of common barriers within their treatment context (location, service population, type of service). Culturally competent responses to such barriers might include sliding fee scales; transportation vouchers; flexible operating hours; community-based or school-based service provision; flexible treatment modalities, such as group, family, and culturally adapted approaches; and culturally sensitive and knowledgeable clinicians.

Primary and secondary prevention approaches to child and adolescent problems should be considered for their nonstigmatizing nature. Likewise, strengths-based approaches that view culture as a resource and aim to build protective factors and resilience in children and adolescents are encouraged (Hays, 2001; Lerner, Brentano, Dowling, & Anderson, 2002). Coordination of services and collaboration among stakeholders, such as community participation in planning and evaluation, can also aid in successful programming.

Determine the Family's Familiarity with the Treatment Setting

It is important to determine, early on, the child's and family's familiarity with psychotherapy and expectations for treatment. This may include discussing their previous experiences with mental health services or other interactions with the health care system. Personal and social meanings and beliefs about seeking psychological help should also be explored. There may be a lack of familiarity with the concept and practice of Western counseling and psychotherapy. Even when psychological treatment is sought, families may continue to have a certain level of cultural mistrust and apprehension entering the therapy setting. Certain routine intake procedures, such as signing consent and confidentiality forms, may increase distrust, especially if the need for such forms is not well explained (Hays, 2001). Additionally, the typical therapy format relies on a direct style of communication to identify and address personal problems in the presence of a professional (the psychologist or clinician), who is usually a stranger. This format may be very foreign to families coming from cultures that rely on familiar social and religious supports, such as community leaders, village elders, family members, priests, religious leaders, or shamans for addressing such problems. Counselors and therapists who lack cultural knowledge can exacerbate the problems and feelings of unease.

Conduct Pretherapy

Families that are unfamiliar with the therapy setting (e.g., ethnic minorities, immigrants, rural populations, and lower income populations) may benefit from pretherapy, which refers to time spent orienting the child and family to the therapist and the treatment setting. The family should be invited into the therapist's culture (Hays, 2001). Pretherapy may include added time for rapport building, education about what to expect in therapy, knowledge about the therapist's credentials and approach, and demystification of the therapy process. At this time, the role of the therapist will be clarified and so will the general expectations of the child and family members. Some cultures do not have a history of keeping regular, scheduled appointments that begin and end at a certain time. Additionally, children and families with no transportation or a lack of child care for siblings may have difficulty keeping appointments.

In many traditional approaches to helping, payment or reciprocity for service is not required on a regular basis, but is offered as a donation after treatment. Expectations regarding payment should be handled in a delicate and sensitive manner. Procedures related to confidentiality should be given careful attention, as parents with strong authoritarian family roles may expect that the clinician will automatically share all information with them (Tseng, 2003). The child's parents will need to be carefully informed of limits to confidentiality, such as child abuse reporting laws. The time spent in pretherapy can also be used to further establish credibility and rapport and to gather cultural information.

Gather Cultural Information

Next, attempts are made to learn about and understand the cultural perspectives of the child and family by crossing into the client's culture (Hays, 2001). That is, the clinician should learn about the child's cultural context and background. The client and the client's family are good sources for relevant cultural information. However, it is not appropriate to rely solely on clients, and the clinician should seek information about a child's cultural background and group-related norms outside of the therapy session. There are a number of excellent books and book chapters, scientific and practice-related journals, and Web-based resources that provide information specific to different cultural and minority groups. Important background information includes sociopolitical and historical events, history of oppression, worldview, communication and language issues, cultural variation in symptom expression, stigmas and related help-seeking patterns, cultural strengths, values, and supports.

In learning about cultural norms and values, clinicians should attempt to suspend judgment about a client's cultural beliefs and remain mindful of their own, culture-based reactions to areas of difference (Martin & Nakayama, 2005). In addition to learning about cultural norms and values, identifying the strengths of children and families and mobilizing them as a resource in treatment is one of the most important skills for effective practice with diverse clients (Hays, 2001).

Clarify Clinician Roles and Boundaries

Working in a multicultural context, careful attention should be given to clarifying the function and roles of the therapist, determining the nature of the therapeutic relationship, and defining the boundaries of the relationship (Constantine & Sue, 2005; Tseng, 2003). The role of clinicians and the nature of the therapist-client relationship should be viewed from a cultural perspective. Practitioners from multicultural, feminist, and humanistic approaches, for example, may encourage enhanced authenticity and genuineness in the client-therapist relationship. Boundaries are not as rigidly defined, but continuous in nature, with shifts readily occurring in areas such as self-disclosure, giving and receiving gifts, multiple roles, bartering, and nonsexual touch and other expressions of care. Indeed, when grounded in one's theoretical approach and well thought out in each case, relaxed boundaries in some of these areas are considered culturally competent service provision. Although research findings are inconclusive, practitioners suggest that appropriately timed self-disclosure by the clinician can engender feelings of trust and respect and facilitate the development of rapport with youth and with some cultural groups. Acceptable practices vary greatly across different treatment settings and populations.

Proponents of multicultural approaches also call on psychologists to take on multiple helping roles beyond traditional individual therapy (Atkinson et al., 1998).

With a host of concerns related to diverse clients' environment or external context, a case management approach is often called for to assess and treat children with awareness of their familial, cultural, and ecological contexts. A task for the clinician may be building parents' skills for successfully advocating for their children and accessing needed resources and services. Other clinician roles may include conducting groups, intervening in systems, serving as a consultant or cultural broker, and implementing community-based preventive interventions (Atkinson et al., 1998).

Involve the Family

Working with the family members of children and adolescents is a common practice generally, and in the context of cultural difference can be a great asset (Wilson, Kohn, & Lee, 2000). Family members, including parents and siblings, grandparents, aunts and uncles, and close others in the child's family network can be valuable resources of collateral and/or corroborating information about the occurrence of various behaviors and how they are interpreted. Family members can provide a base for assessing cultural perspectives and for determining the extent to which various behaviors or other psychological manifestations are culturally acceptable. Family members will also be knowledgeable about culturally appropriate coping choices and ways of responding. It is important that clinicians be aware of culturally diverse family hierarchies, rules for relating among family members, and taboos. For example, it may be inappropriate for a family member to mention the cause of a parent's death (Tseng, 2003).

Address Communication Differences

Even when clinicians and their clients are able to communicate in the same language, cultures vary greatly in their communication styles (whether they are direct or indirect, high or low context), communication patterns, and norms and rules for verbal and nonverbal expressions (Martin & Nakayama, 2005). Clinicians should pay attention to the language used by themselves and the children and families with whom they work. Efforts should be made to use simple and clear language and to minimize the use of psychological jargon, idioms, and colloquialisms. The process of communication and rules for formality and nonverbal communication, such as eye contact, gestures, and body movements, vary widely. Clinicians should clarify the intended meaning of any expression with which they are unfamiliar. An incorrect interpretation can result in minor misunderstandings or serious mistakes, such as misdiagnosis. It is important for clinicians to know that a client who says "Yes, yes" does not necessarily mean "I agree with you." How symptoms are expressed is also a matter of culture, and expressions may be culturally stylized (Tseng, 2003).

Direct communication about emotions or discussions of certain other matters may be taboo, or considered very private. If an indirect style is used, the clinician may need to adjust his or her communication style and seek consultation on specific indirect methods, such as making use of proverbs or stories that reflect cultural wisdom. Clinicians should proceed with caution and determine cultural norms for discussing family matters, sexual or religious practices, money, suicide, and ancestors (alive or dead). Individuals with a collectivist background may consider it improper to discuss family members or family matters, because to do so would bring great shame to the family. Clinicians should explain their need for the information and ask permission first (e.g., "May I ask you about your family?"). Invite clients to share and then pay attention for signs (nonverbal and verbal) that you might have overstepped cultural boundaries (Pedersen, 1997).

Work with Interpreters

Children and their families should have access to treatment in a language that they completely understand and in which they can comfortably express themselves (APA, 2003; Constantine & Sue, 2005). With 19% of families in the United States speaking a language other than English in the home, mental health practitioners will increasingly be providing services to individuals with limited English proficiency (LEP). In all cases in which children, youth, or their families are considered LEP or prefer speaking in their native language, clinicians should arrange for the services of a professional interpreter. Under Title VI of the 1964 Civil Rights Act, institutions and service providers that receive federal funds are required to provide such interpretation services. Professional interpreters are trained to provide direct, simultaneous, or sequential interpretation in a professional and ethical manner. They often have had training in confidentiality, dual roles, and medical or psychological terminology.

Interpretation is provided verbatim and in the first person. Typically, interpreters will sit beside the client and family. During the session, an interpreter often takes a rather technical role, serving as the conduit for communication between the clinician and the patient. Eye contact, to the extent that it occurs, will largely remain between the clinician and the child and family. If the interpreter needs to interject or further explain something, he or she may enter the conversation by saying "The interpreter would like to say. . . . " This may be done to clarify a communication, explain a concept, or provide important cultural information. If trained professionals are not available, for example in rural locations, telephone interpreters can be arranged. Some things to consider when selecting an interpreter are sex and ethnic background, as these may influence client disclosure and trust. Despite their level of training, brief pre- and posttherapy sessions with interpreters can provide a chance to discuss therapeutic concepts that may be difficult to translate, such as relaxation training. Presessions may help prepare the interpreter for a potentially difficult (e.g., crisis) situation.

Use a Cultural Consultant

Cultural brokers may be useful in accessing cultural knowledge or advice. Who is a cultural broker? This role is rather loosely defined, but may include a professional (e.g., anthropologist, sociologist, psychologist, or other mental health professional) with experience or training in a cultural population. A cultural broker could be a person with knowledge and experience in the culture or community in question, such as a community leader, spiritual person, pastor, or other traditional helper.

Cultural brokers can provide background, group-level cultural information, or case-specific consultation. Interpreters can also serve as cultural brokers and have the benefit of providing this service as treatment sessions unfold and directly afterward. Interpreters serving as cultural brokers may be able to further elaborate or explain culturally embedded concepts and recognize and head off cultural clashes. For example, the interpreter may inform the clinician that, if a concept is literally translated, it will offend the client. Cultural brokers may even assist the therapist in coming up with a culturally acceptable way to address a sensitive issue, such as suicidality.

Negotiate a Common Explanatory Model

In selecting and developing a treatment plan, clinicians should begin with what the family presents (their explanatory model) and make appropriate adjustments.

After assessing the family's explanatory model, clinicians can compare it to their own (Chrisman & Johnson, 1996; Lewis-Fernandez & Kleinman, 1995). Studies suggest that, more often than not, the models of clinicians differ from their patients' (Cohen, Tripp-Reimer, Smith, Sorofman, & Lively, 1994; Kleinman, 1980). Disparate beliefs, left unexplored, may result in poor patient-practitioner communication and lead to misdiagnosis, inappropriate treatment, treatment nonadherence, early attrition, and reduced treatment outcomes (Chrisman & Johnson, 1996; Kleinman, 1980; Wohl, 2000). The following steps are suggested to negotiate a common model with children and their families.

- Start with what the family presents.
- Share your own model, using client language when possible.
- Bridge the models by emphasizing similarities and discussing differences.
- Make modifications that are culturally salient for the family.
- Agree on a common model and a treatment plan that emphasizes strengths.
- Continue to monitor and modify as needed.

First, the clinician should summarize the family's view of the problem and expectations and goals for treatment. This will convey an accurate understanding and highlight misunderstandings that the clinician has. Next, the clinician can share his or her conceptualization of the problem and suggested treatment. Next, clinicians should make efforts to engage the family in a collaborative approach to goal setting and treatment planning. Even when there are drastic differences in practitioner and family explanatory models, clinicians can emphasize similarities and work toward shared goals. To the extent that the clinician has built credibility and trust, families may be more receptive to new ideas or methods proposed by the therapist. Reframing or psychoeducational approaches can be used to present treatments in culturally palatable ways. Strengths-based approaches are also suggested, and because they are congruent with cultural and family values may be more likely to engender family support (Hays, 2001).

Adjust the Therapeutic Frame

Efforts to make treatments culturally relevant and meaningful often involve making adjustments to the therapeutic frame. Although some families may not be familiar with formal, Western-based psychological treatments, families all over the world are familiar with the idea of talking to or otherwise seeking help from a caring and concerned person. Keeping this basic similarity in mind, clinicians can make a variety of technical and theoretical adjustments, ranging from minor adjustments to mainstream approaches to drastic changes in the foci, goals, and process of treatment so that treatments are developed largely from cultural (emic) approaches (Koss-Chiono, 2000).

Adaptations should be made with consideration of the family's cultural perspective and available resources and services. Simple adjustments in mainstream approaches can lay the groundwork for effective services. For example, although many therapists are taught not to give advice, families from diverse backgrounds may seek out the therapist's guidance in various dilemmas (Tseng, 2003). Clinicians who can provide concrete help to families in solving problems are adjusting the relational frame to meet the family's expectations and needs.

Other therapeutic adjustments may come into play as treatment foci, goals, and processes are selected. Goals should be culturally congruent and contextually relevant. Which behaviors are targeted for change should be considered in light of the child's multiple contexts. For example, working to increase assertiveness with a Chinese adolescent may be helpful in the school environment, but problematic at home. These issues should be explored thoroughly before treatments are pursued.

Adapt Treatments

Clinicians consider a number of factors when selecting the treatment mode and format, and culture should be among these. Culturally sensitive and adapted treatment programs may garner increased patient support and satisfaction.

Level and Mode of Intervention

Family approaches to treatment are often suggested for ethnic minority and culturally diverse youth, as are small groups and peer-based and systems-level interventions (Aponte & Bracco, 2000; Wilson et al., 2000). Community approaches are considered preferable to individual approaches in meeting the needs of ethnic minorities. Typically, they emphasize ecological validity, a multiproblem focus, commitment to interagency collaboration, employment of bicultural and bilingual staff, development of cultural competency, strengthening social support networks, and use of prevention and consultation strategies (Aponte & Bracco, 2000; Cuellar, 2000).

Culturally Related and Culture-Specific Approaches

Treatments range widely in terms of intensity, focus, modality, and the degree to which cultural material is incorporated. Many clinicians choose to adapt standard European-based strategies such as behavioral, cognitive, interpersonal, or family systems, by incorporating cultural values, strengths, and resources into therapeutic goals and techniques (Hays, 2001). Examples of adjustments in a cognitive-behavioral treatment might include using proverbs, religious verses, or other cultural metaphors to help counter negative thoughts, and using family to help support home-based exposures. Culture-based coping, such as meditation or prayer, could be integrated into a stress reduction program, and other cultural rituals related to healing may be included in an overall treatment plan. For example "having a sweat" (i.e., in a sweat lodge) may be recommended alongside other treatment recommendations for an American Indian adolescent living on an Indian reservation. Alternative approaches to treatment include narrative, testimonial, and bibliotherapy, as well as the use of creative, expressive, and somatically based therapies (Hays, 2001).

Culture-specific approaches are based on specific cultural frameworks. Most of these interventions provide cultural education based on traditional values, and then use these values as the underpinnings of the treatment. For example, clinicians may use concepts of *familismo, simpatia,* and *respeto* as themes when working with Latino/a children and adolescents, and themes related to collective responsibility, self-determination, or spirituality when working with African American youth. Culture-adapted and culture-specific treatments may make use of ethnically similar role models, discussion of cultural attitudes regarding risk behaviors, ethnic identity development, and issues related to racism and discrimination (Belgrave et al., 1994). Traditional cultural customs, stories, songs, and other cultural materials may be used, and treatment should be in accessible locations where families can draw support from community leaders or organizations. Some culture-specific approaches make use of a "rites of passage" paradigm to facilitate, formally recognize, and celebrate the physical and emotional development of youth. Although there has been little controlled research on the therapeutic efficacy of these interventions, cross-sectional research has indicated that a grounding in traditional cultural values is negatively associated with substance abuse, anxiety, hostility, juvenile crime, and depression (Belgrave et al., 1994).

Two culturally related treatments are cuento therapy for Latinos/as (Constantino, Malgady, & Rogler, 1986) and Afrocentric "rights of passage" programs for African American youth (Brookins, 1996; P. Hill, 1992). Cuento therapy draws on the themes in Hispanic cultural stories of heroes, heroines, and moral messages. Afrocentric programs have youth undertake a series of behavioral tasks and related rituals that signify growth, maturity, and a commitment to self and community. These programs aim to educate and empower adolescents and enhance their life skills, cultural identity, self-esteem, and academic performance. One obvious concern is the practicality and costs of designing culture-specific treatments. Moreover, to make treatment decisions based on the ethnic background of the child and family may be considered an ethnic slur and a violation of ethical and clinical rules of practice (Wohl, 2000). Instead, multiple cultural factors will overlap and manifest idiographically, accounting for vast diversity within ethnic groups.

Work with Traditional Healers

Children and families may benefit from traditional approaches, such as in the case of culture-bound syndromes or when families are highly *separated* from mainstream society. Clinicians should develop awareness and understanding of indigenous healing and helping methods so that they can better understand their client's cultural perspective and provide referrals (Koss-Chioino, 2000). Clinicians should recognize that there are several parallels between the functions of traditional healers and those of psychologists. Traditional healers vary greatly in type, level of training, and approaches to treatment, and include shamans, priests or pastors, imams, herbalists, curanderos, and spiritualists. Traditional and indigenous healing approaches are gaining increased attention, and it is suggested that clinicians learn about practicing local healers and develop respectful relationships with them (Koss-Chioino, 2000).

Select a Focus for Treatment

The focus of treatment may or may not be culturally related. Clinicians will assess and treat children referred for common child and adolescent problems involving conduct, social relations, mood, mental retardation or other developmental delays, learning problems, and adjustment difficulties. Although there may be phenomenological variation in the presentation of these disorders, if the presenting problem is directly related to or influenced by cultural factors, then a more direct focus on cultural issues is needed. Some common treatment foci that are culturally related are school adjustment, acculturation-related problems, and identity concerns.

School Adjustment

Children from low socioeconomic backgrounds, ethnic minorities, immigrants, and refugees all face formidable challenges in the school system. The school system in the United Sates, for example, has a pedagogical philosophy valuing written expression, direct verbal communication, student-centered approaches, competitiveness, and individual achievement. To the extent that children live in households or communities with different cultural values, or have a history of schooling in another system, adjusting to school can be quite a challenge. Language problems, cultural differences in learning style or behavioral norms, discrimination, and the inability of parents to help with schoolwork are challenges faced by immigrant and ethnic minority youth.

Among refugees and immigrants, language issues, difficulty making American friends, and differences in educational systems are some of the acculturative problems reported (Vinokurov, Trickett, & Birman, 2002). Other problems are discrimination by peers, such as name-calling and teasing (Bemak & Greenberg, 1994). A lack of previous access to formal education can make the adjustment even more difficult for some immigrant and refugee youth. Self-efficacy will be important for adjustment in the school setting, with some studies suggesting an impact on academic skills and performance, computer skills, and interpersonal skills. A thorough assessment will be needed to determine the appropriate type, target, and level of intervention (e.g., a system- or organizational-level change or child behavior change).

Acculturation Problems

The seriousness of symptoms and the degree of psychological difficulty experienced by children and families in cultural conflict will vary considerably. Berry (1997) breaks symptom severity into three levels of distress: (1) mild to moderate cultural conflict, (2) acculturative stress, and (3) psychopathology. Mild to moderate cultural conflict is explained by the need to learn new ways of behaving (Ward, 1997). These conflicts arise as certain behaviors are unlearned or shed, while being replaced with a new behavioral repertoire. If behavioral shifts are not easily made, the second level of difficulty, acculturative stress, will occur (Berry, 1997). When major conflicts are experienced, a psychopathology perspective is helpful. Children and their family members may be in crisis or otherwise suffering from incapacitating levels of depression, anxiety, and/or other mental disorders needing serious attention (Berry, 1997).

Parent-Child Acculturation Gap

Children of immigrants and refugees often acculturate more rapidly than their parents and older family members. They may adopt new behaviors and values that are incongruent with their parents' expectations. Refugee and immigrant youth may become ashamed of their parents, reject their culture of origin, and rapidly assimilate to America's youth-oriented society. Parents are often fearful that their children will forget their cultural values, and they may become upset as their adolescents adopt new styles of dress, wear makeup, or engage in unacceptable social behaviors, such as dating and attending parties (Sourander, 2003).

Children may learn English before their parents do, and power shifts may occur as children take on new roles interpreting for the family. At the same time, parents may lose their status and effectiveness in the new culture (Tousignant et al., 1999). These shifts in power dynamics can be quite upsetting for children and adults, especially those coming from more traditional, patriarchal families or collectivist cultures. Family conflict may result, which can easily escalate to child or domestic abuse situations that did not exist prior to migration (Bemak & Chung, 2000; Colic-Peisker & Walker, 2003).

Bicultural Effectiveness

In working with mild to moderate acculturation concerns, clinicians may employ strategies for culture learning and social skills acquisition. A bicultural (or multicultural) approach will reinforce the value and importance of maintaining effectiveness in the culture of origin and the new culture. Some suggestions for addressing the acculturation gap between parents and children include the following:

- Reframe family conflict as acculturation differences that normally occur.
- Identify cultural similarities and differences.
- Teach families about the process of cultural adjustment and how it can play out in families.

- Examine the cultural values and demands faced by the child outside the home (e.g., in school, with peers).
- Help youth understand the value in their heritage culture.
- Learn skills needed to be effective in different cultural environments (i.e., bicultural competence).

Bicultural effectiveness programs have been developed to reduce intercultural conflict among Cuban American youth and their parents (Szapocznik et al., 1984) and to reduce substance abuse among American Indian adolescents (Schinke et al., 1988).

Identity Concerns

Questions related to one's personal and social identity, such as "What kind of person am I? Do others like me? Do I belong to a group? What is my ethnic/racial or other cultural group? How do others see me as a part of this group?" and "How do I see myself as a part of this group?" are common beginning with middle-age children and may be especially so for ethnic and cultural minority youth (Schmidt, 2006). Efforts to nurture a positive social and cultural identity can be integrated into standard treatment approaches. Effort to enhance a child's awareness of and sense of belonging to his or her cultural group may include bibliotherapy (including cultural stories, myths, proverbs), attendance at cultural events, cultural and personal values exploration, identification of cultural strengths and resources, learning about the cultural or sociopolitical history of one's cultural group, and appreciation of or participation in creative or expressive arts and artistic traditions of one's group. Approaches that work toward an integrated (e.g., bicultural or multicultural) identity offer maximal benefits across settings.

Mistakes and Modifications

Once the treatment focus and techniques are agreed upon, clinicians need to consider cultural factors and influences throughout treatment. During the entire process, clinicians should make efforts to maintain therapeutic rapport, monitor the child's and family's progress and commitment, be mindful of mistakes that are made, and make modifications as necessary. Maintaining a good working alliance with children and credibility with families requires ongoing attention and effort. Clinician roles, boundaries, and style of interaction may need adjusting as treatment and the level of familiarity increases. Latino families, for example, may expect the clinician to shift from an interactional style favoring *formaliso* to one of *personalismo* (Hays, 2001). Cultural impasses may occur as new material comes up and/or new techniques or interventions are discussed or implemented.

Multicultural psychologists point out that mistakes will be made in treating the culturally diverse. Successfully recognizing and responding to cultural missteps is an important clinical skill (Pedersen, 1997, 2000). Awareness of changes in relating or treatment nonadherence may indicate a potential miscommunication. Mistakes may be addressed directly or indirectly (as culturally appropriate) and modifications made in the technique or approach. Respect, humility, and humor are considered among the most important cross-cultural skills and can be quite effective in maintaining relationships in spite of mistakes (Hays, 2001; Pederson 1997, 2000).

Termination

Cultural expectations of the relationship may impact termination. Families may not understand such an artificial termination and may feel a need to maintain the relationship. Clinicians may help terminating children and families by linking them with community supports and also by scheduling spaced-out sessions and booster sessions or otherwise inviting families to return for additional treatment (Tseng, 2003).

SPECIAL POPULATIONS AND EMERGING TOPICS

Children Living in Poverty

Children and adolescents growing up in poverty are affected on multiple levels by compounding factors. High poverty often goes hand in hand with lack of education or poor education; lack of good nutrition and health care; unsafe, high-crime neighborhoods; lack of supervision; few social supports; poor environmental conditions; and uprooted cultural values (Vargas & Koss-Chiono, 1992). The background of children with low socioeconomic status emphasizes survival. These children's behaviors could be the direct result of living without proper care or sustenance, lack of formal education, and an insecure environment. Clinicians need to keep in mind the influence their own worldview may have when interpreting the behaviors of children from such groups. Flexible clinician roles, case management approaches to treatment, and community-based approaches may be helpful.

Immigrant and Refugee Children and Youth

Challenges faced by immigrant and refugee children and youth include changes in daily living, language, behavior, education system, and socialization practices. Clinicians should facilitate new culture acquisition and also encourage retaining cultural ties (see skills under "Bicultural Effectiveness"). Immigration status, legal or illegal, will have implications for the degree of stress experienced and service available. Immigrant youth who do not have legal status or who have undocumented family members face challenges accessing health and educational resources and are vulnerable to legal retribution, unfair and unsafe labor practices, family separation, and added stress related to their uncertain status and need for secrecy.

Refugee children's adjustment problems are underscored by multiple losses, family separation, refugee camp experiences, and trauma (Bemak & Greenberg, 1994). Resettling refugee children and adolescents report depression, irritability, withdrawal, low self-image, isolation, estrangement, loneliness, a loss of power, feeling out of place, sleep problems, feeling that their old values are useless, and a sense of being devalued (Sourander, 2003). Refugee and immigrant services organizations provide some services for refugees and immigrants, such as language classes, assistance in finding housing and enrolling children in school, accessing health care services, and limited economic support. Clinicians should consider a case management approach to service provision and bicultural effectiveness.

Ethnic Minority Children and Adolescents

Ethnic minority children and adolescents face discrimination, racism, and prejudice related to their minority status (Porter, 2000). Stress associated with racism is one factor accounting for higher rates of stress-related health problems in ethnic minority groups. Overall, ethnic minority youth are at increased risk for developing emotional and behavioral problems. Issues facing ethnic minority youth include physically threatening environments, conflicting messages about appropriate identity development, economic hardship, and limited access to supportive services that may place many ethnic youth at a significant disadvantage when compared to their White counterparts (Hoberman, 1992). Experiences of oppression and racism further impede their healthy psychosocial adjustment and development. Signs of maladjustment associated with these many contextual factors include substance abuse, mood disturbances, academic underachievement, premature sexuality and childbearing, delinquency, underemployment, and instability of family life (Barbarin, 1993).

Biracial Children

Children of biracial or multiethnic backgrounds may have unique concerns related to their personal and social identity. A child's physical appearance may impact his or her self-identity and also influence parental identification. Models of biracial or multiracial identity development can help clinicians get a sense of where biracial children are in their identity development (Root, 1990). For biracial children, cultural conflicts regarding values, family roles, and parenting may arise in multiple contexts. If parents and families successfully negotiate these cultural differences, problems may not arise, but conflict in these areas could result in inconsistency, confusion, and family stress. Depending on the parents' origins, the child could be attempting to understand and negotiate multiple cultural influences. The clinician must assess the child's identification with each culture and the impact this may have across contexts.

Internationally Adopted Children

Rates of international adoption in the United States have increased dramatically in the past decade (Friedlander et al., 2000). More and more children are growing up with parents and siblings from a different language and cultural background from themselves and, importantly, who look different from themselves. These children may face teasing, name-calling, and discrimination, just as ethnic minority children do. White parents may be ill equipped to understand and/or address their adopted child's experiences with racism or struggles with racial or ethnic identity.

Families may also experience conflict with other family members or the community regarding their decision to adopt an ethnically different child.

Children with a history of institutionalization (e.g., living in an orphanage) face health problems, delays in cognitive or socioemotional development, sensorimotor integration difficulties, and problems with attachment and bonding. Additionally, adoptive parents of these children may be dealing with unresolved fertility issues, disappointments related to the child, or problems related to family integration. As young children mature, issues related to ethnic and cultural identity may emerge to an even greater extent. Family activities and routines that promote bonding and relationships among all family members can be encouraged. Families may need assistance resolving cultural conflicts and skills training on how to become a bicultural (or multicultural) family (Friedlander et al., 2000).

Gay, Lesbian, Bisexual, and Transgender Youth

When dealing with children and adolescents who identify themselves as gay, lesbian, bisexual, or transgender (GLBT), the clinician must be aware of not only the client's current functioning within that identity but also the past experiences associated with it. Worldwide, GLBT youth face discrimination and social marginalization related to their sexual or gender orientation. Models of identity development indicate that GLBT individuals may undergo a series of stages of confusion, identification, and acceptance of their sexual orientation (Cass, 1979). When this occurs, how it occurs, and the outcomes will vary from person to person. Individual and contextual factors certainly come into play when assessing each client's experience of this process. In an atmosphere of family support and openness, the client is psychologically equipped to handle outside pressures or discrimination. However, in an environment with strong family, religious, or cultural sanctions against homosexuals, children and adolescents may have to face these societal pressures alone.

Given these factors, it is important to give GLBT youth a safe and open environment to express their experiences, frustrations, and ideas. The worldview of GLBT individuals is one that has developed alongside experiences of discrimination, fear, and possibly danger (Herek, 1995, 2000). It is important for the clinician to recognize the multidimensional nature of the client and address GLBT issues as they relate to the presenting problem.

NEW DIRECTIONS IN CULTURALLY RESPONSIVE TREATMENT

Consistent with an increased global interest in positive psychology and cultural competence, new directions in child and adolescent approaches to treatment view children and culture as resources (Lerner et al., 2002). Positive youth development (PYD) supports the notion that cultivating social, emotional, and cognitive competencies in children and adolescents can head off, or at least ameliorate some emotional and behavioral problems (Larson, 2000). Programs employing PYD promote resilience by helping children and youth to better understand their environment and act in ways that promote healthy development (Dworkin, Larson, & Hansen, 2003; Lerner et al., 2002).

These programs may be particularly appropriate for addressing the mental health needs of culturally diverse youth (Johnson & Johnson-Pynn, 2007). They offer a broad-based approach that is widely culturally acceptable and accessible (i.e., often school- or community-based). Nurturing cultural strengths and community connections is integral to most PYD programs. Program outcomes, such as social competencies, positive bonds with people and institutions, positive self-regard, self-efficacy, positive ethnic identity, and social justice values, have obvious benefits for culturally diverse youth (Catalano, Berglund, Ryan, Lonczak, & Hawkins, 2002; Lerner, 2002).

SUMMARY

In this chapter, we have described the nature and functioning of culture as it impacts children and families and the process of assessment and treatment. First we discussed important contextual factors, such as the changing demographic landscape in the United States and the increasing multicultural nature of society, that highlight the need for cultural competence in child assessment and treatment. We discussed the complex, multifaceted, subjective, and dynamic aspects of culture that must be understood in order to fully appreciate culture's influence and intricacies. Next we outlined some of the ways that culture interacts with other factors to affect child development, socialization, education, values, and norms. We also described how culture results in variations in mental heath functioning and psychopathology in children, shaping symptom expression and communication, help seeking, illness beliefs and expectations, and desired outcomes for assessment and treatment.

Next, we provided an overview of key cultural constructs to consider in assessment and treatment. Acculturation, ethnic identity, worldview, and explanatory models were defined, as was their potential to influence the assessment and treatment process. We then discussed how culture may come into play at each phase in the assessment and treatment process. We integrated suggestions for attending to culture into each section and provided practical ideas, such as how to build a satisfactory relationship with clients, how to ask clients about their culture, how to adapt one's communication style, how to incorporate cultural strengths into treatment, and how to work with interpreters and cultural brokers. Culture-related problems, such as acculturative stress and identity concerns, were discussed, as were culturally responsive interventions.

Finally, we called attention to the unique concerns of certain groups of children, including refugee and immigrant children, gay and lesbian youth, bicultural children, ethnic minorities, children living in poverty, and internationally adopted children. In closing, we point to the promise of positive youth development programs as culturally responsive approaches to meeting the mental health needs of significant numbers of culturally diverse children and adolescents. Although this chapter covered many aspects important for understanding and working with clients from a variety of cultures, it is impossible to sufficiently address cultural issues in assessment and treatment in a single chapter. Clinicians working in the context of cultural differences are encouraged to make ongoing efforts to enhance their cultural competence in assessing and treating children and adolescents.

REFERENCES

Akiba, D., & Garcia Coll, C. (2004). Effective interventions with children of color and their families: A contextual developmental approach. In T. B. Smith (Ed.), *Practicing multiculturalism* (pp. 123–144). Boston: Allyn & Bacon.

American Psychological Association. (1994). *Diagnostic and statistical manual of mental disorders* (4th ed.). Washington, DC: Author.

American Psychological Association. (2002). Rules and procedures: October 1, 2001 [ethics committee rules and procedures]. *American Psychologist, 57*, 626–645.

American Psychological Association. (2003). Multicultural guidelines: Education training, research, practice and organizational change for psychologists. *American Psychologist, 58*, 377–402.

Angel, R. J., & Williams, K. (2000). Cultural models of health and illness. In I. Cuellar & F. A. Paniagua (Eds.), *Handbook of multicultural mental health* (pp. 25–44). San Diego, CA: Academic Press.

Aponte, J. F., & Bracco, H. F. (2000). Community approaches among ethnic minorities. In J. F. Aponte & J. Wohl (Eds.), *Psychological intervention and cultural diversity* (2nd ed., pp. 131–148). Needham Heights, MA: Allyn & Bacon.

Aponte, J. F., & Johnson, L. R. (2000). The impact of culture on intervention and treatment of ethnic populations. In J. F. Aponte & J. Wohl (Eds.), *Psychological intervention and cultural diversity* (2nd ed., pp. 18–39). Needham Heights, MA: Allyn & Bacon.

Arredondo, P., Toporek, R., Brown, S. P., Jones, J., Locke, D. C., Sanchez, J., et al. (1996). Operationalization of the multicultural counseling competencies. *Journal of Multicultural Counseling and Development, 24*, 42–78.

Atkinson, D. R., Morten, G., & Sue, D. W. (1998). Current issues and future directions in minority group/cross-cultural counselling. In D. R. Atkinson, G. Morten, & D. W. Sue (Eds.), *Counseling American minorities: A cross-cultural perspective* (5th ed., pp. 303–359). Boston: McGraw-Hill.

Barbarin, O. (1993). Emotional and social development of African American children. *Journal of Black Psychologists, 19*(4), 381–390.

Belgrave, F. Z., Cherry, V. R., Cunningham, D., Walwyn, S., Letlaka-Rennert, K., & Phillips, F. (1994). The influence of Africentric values, self-esteem, and Black identity on drug attitudes among African American fifth-graders: A preliminary study. *Journal of Black Psychology, 20*(2), 143–156.

Bemak, F., & Chung, R. (2000). Psychological interventions with immigrants and refugees. In J. F. Aponte & J. Wohl (Eds.), *Psychological interventions and cultural diversity* (pp. 200–212). Needham Heights, MA: Allyn & Bacon.

Bemak, F., & Greenberg, B. (1994). Southeast Asian refugee adolescents: Implications for counseling. *Journal of Multicultural Counseling and Development, 22*, 115–125.

Berry, J. W. (1986). The acculturation process and refugee behavior. In C. L. Williams & J. Westermeyer (Eds.), *Refugee mental health in resettlement countries* (pp. 25–37). Washington, DC: Hemisphere.

Berry, J. W. (1997). Immigration, acculturation, and adaptation. *Applied Psychology: An International Review, 46*, 5–68.

Berry, J. W. (1998). Acculturation and health: Theory and research. In S. Kazarian & D. Evans (Eds.), *Cultural clinical psychology: Theory, research, and practice* (pp. 39–60). New York: Oxford University Press.

Berry, J. W., & Kim, U. (1988). Acculturation and mental health. In P. R. Dasen, J. W. Berry, & N. Sartorius (Eds.), *Health and cross-cultural psychology: Toward applications* (pp. 207–236). Newbury Park, CA: Sage.

Berry, J. W., Kim, U., Minde, T., & Mok, D. (1987). Comparative studies of acculturative stress. *International Migration Review, 21*, 490–511.

Brislin, R. (2000). *Understanding culture's influence on behavior* (2nd ed.). Toronto: Thomson Learning.

Bronfenbrenner, U. (1979). *The ecology of human development*. Cambridge, MA: Harvard University Press.

Bronfenbrenner, U. (1989). Ecological systems theory. In R. Vasta (Ed.), *Annals of child development* (6th ed., pp. 187–251). Greenwich, CT: JAI Press.

Brookins, C. C. (1996). Promoting ethnic identity development in African American youth: The role of rites of passage. *Journal of Black Psychology, 22*(3), 388–417.

Canino, I. A., Canino, G., & Arroyo, W. (1998). Cultural considerations for childhood disorders: How much was included in DSM-IV? *Transcultural Psychiatry, 35*(3), 343–355.

Canino, I. A., & Spurlock, J. (2000). *Culturally diverse children and adolescents.* New York: Guilford Press.

Cass, V. C. (1979). Homosexual identity formation: A theoretical model. *Journal of Homosexuality, 4,* 219–235.

Catalano, R. F., Berglund, M. L., Ryan, J. A. M., Lonczak, H. S., & Hawkins, J. D. (2002). Positive youth development in the United States: Research findings on evaluations of positive youth development programs. *Prevention and Treatment, 5*(15), 1–111. Retrieved September 12, 2005, from http://a:/pre0050015a.htm.

Chrisman, N. J., & Johnson, T. M. (1996). Clinically applied anthropology. In C. F. Sargent & T. M. Johnson (Eds.), *Medical anthropology: Contemporary theory and method* (Rev. ed., pp. 88–109). Westport, CT: Praeger.

Cohen, M. Z., Tripp-Reimer, T., Smith, C., Sorofman, B., & Lively, S. (1994). Explanatory models of diabetes: Patient practitioner variation. *Social Science Medicine, 38*(1), 59–66.

Colic-Peisker, V., & Walker, I. (2003). Human capital, acculturation and social identity. *Journal of Community and Applied Social Psychology, 13,* 337–360.

Constantine, M. G., & Sue, D. W. (2005). The American Psychological Association's guidelines on multicultural education, training, research, practice, and organizational psychology: Initial development and summary. In M. G. Constantine & D. W. Sue (Eds.), *Strategies for building multicultural competence* (pp. 3–15). Hoboken, NJ: Wiley.

Constantino, G., Malgady, R. G., & Rogler, L. (1986). Cuento therapy: A culturally sensitive modality for Puerto Rican children. *Journal of Consulting and Clinical Psychology, 54*(4), 639–645.

Cross, W. E., Jr. (1971). The Negro-to-Black conversion experience. *Black World, 20,* 13–27.

Cross, W. E., Jr. (1995). The psychology of nigrescence. In J. G. Ponterotto, J. M., Casas, L. A., Suzuki, & C. M. Alexander (Eds.), *Handbook of multicultural counseling* (pp. 93–122). Thousand Oaks, CA: Sage.

Cuellar, I. (2000). Acculturation and mental health: Ecological transactional relations of adjustment. In I. Cuellar, & F. A. Paniagua (Eds.), *Handbook of multicultural mental health* (pp. 45–62). San Diego, CA: Academic Press.

Cuellar, I., & Paniagua, F. A. (2000). *Handbook of multicultural mental health.* San Diego, CA: Academic Press.

Draguns, J. G. (2000). Psychopathology and ethnicity. In J. F. Aponte & J. Wohl (Eds.), *Psychological intervention and cultural diversity* (2nd ed., pp. 40–58). Needham Heights, MA: Allyn & Bacon.

Dworkin, J. B., Larson, R., & Hansen, D. (2003). Adolescents' accounts of growth experiences in youth activities. *Journal of Youth and Adolescence, 32*(1), 17–26.

Feng, X. (2002). A review of only-child studies in China. *Jianghai Academic Journal, 5,* 90–99.

Friedlander, M. L., Larney, L. C., Skau, M., Hotaling, M., Cutting, M. L., & Schwann, M. (2000). Bicultural identification: Experiences of internationally adopted children and their parents. *Journal of Counseling Psychology, 47*(2), 187–198.

Garcia Coll, C., & Magnuson, K. (1997). The psychological experience of immigration: A developmental perspective. In A. Booth, A. C. Crouter, & A. Langdale (Eds.), *Immigration and the family: Research and policy on U.S. immigrants* (pp. 91–132). Mahwah, NJ: Erlbaum.

Global Commission on International Migration. (2005). *Migration in an interconnected world: New directions for action.* Report of the Global Commission on International Migration (pp. 1–98). Retrieved November 5, 2006, from www.gcim.org/attachments/gcim-cimplete-report-2005.pdf.

Good, B., & Good, M. D. (1986). The cultural context of diagnosis and therapy: A view from medical anthropology. In M. Miranda & H. Kitano (Eds.), *Mental health research and practice in minority communities: Development of culturally sensitive training programs* (pp. 1–28). Rockville, MD: National Institute of Mental Health.

Gopaul-McNicol, S., & Thomas-Presswood, T. (1998). *Working with linguistically and culturally different children: Innovative clinical and educational approaches.* Needham Heights, MA: Allyn & Bacon.

Hays, P. A. (2001). *Addressing cultural complexities in practice: A framework for clinicians and counselors.* Washington, DC: American Psychological Association.

Helms, J. E. (1990). *Black and White racial identity: Theory, research, and practice.* New York: Greenwood.

Helms, J. E. (1995). An update of Helms's White and people of color racial identity models. In J. G. Ponterroto, J. M. Casas, L. A. Suzuki, & C. M. Alexander (Eds.), *Handbook of multicultural counseling* (pp. 181–198). Thousand Oaks, CA: Sage.

Herek, G. (1995). Psychological heterosexism in the United States. In A. D'Augelli & C. Patterson (Eds.), *Lesbian, gay, and bisexual identities over the life span: Psychological perspectives* (pp. 321–346). New York: Oxford University Press.

Herek, G. (2000). The psychology of sexual prejudice. *Current Directions in Psychological Science, 9,* 19–22.

Hernandez, D. J., (2004, April). Demographic change and life circumstances of immigrant families. *Future of Children,* 17–47.

Hernandez, D. J. (2006, August). *Diversity in 21st century America: Children in immigrant and native-born families—Growing up with diversity: The role of psychology in strengthening families.* Symposium presentation at the 2006 annual meeting of the American Psychological Association, New Orleans, LA.

Hill, P. (1992). *Coming of age: African American male rites-of-passage.* Chicago: African American Images.

Hill, R. B. (1993). Dispelling myths and building on strengths: Supporting African American families. *Report, 12*(1), 3–5.

Hoberman, H. (1992). Ethnic minority status and adolescent mental health services utilization. *Journal of Mental Health Administration, 19*(3), 246–267.

Hong, G. K., Garcia, M., & Soriano, M. (2000). Responding to the challenge: Preparing mental health professionals for the new millennium. In I. Cuellar & F. A. Paniagua (Eds.), *Handbook of multicultural mental health* (pp. 455–476). San Diego, CA: Academic Press.

Jenkins, J. H. (1996). Culture, emotion, and psychiatric disorder. In C. F. Sargent & T. M. Johnson (Eds.), *Medical anthropology: Contemporary theory and method* (Rev. ed., pp. 71–87). Westport, CT: Praeger.

Johnson, L. R., Johnson-Pynn, J. S., & Pynn, T. (2007). Youth civic engagement in China: Results from a program promoting environmental activism. *Journal of Adolescent Research, 22*(4), 355–386.

Kaufman, A. S., & Lichtenberger, E. O. (2002). *Assessing adolescent and adult intelligence* (3rd ed.). Hoboken, NJ: Wiley.

Kaufman, N. H., & Rizzini, I. (2002). *Globalization and children: Exploring potentials for enhancing opportunities in the live of children and youth.* New York: Kluwer Academic/Plenum Press.

Kleinman, A. (1977). Depression, somatization, and the "new cross-cultural psychiatry." *Social Science Medicine, 11,* 3–10.

Kleinman, A. (1980). *Patients and healers in the context of culture.* Berkeley: University of California Press.

Kleinman, A. (1987). Anthropology and psychiatry: The role of culture in cross-cultural research on illness. *British Journal of Psychiatry, 151,* 447–454.

Kluckholm, C., & Kroeber, A. (1952). *Culture: A critical review of concepts and definitions.* Cambridge, MA: Peabody Museum.

Koss-Chioino, J. D. (2000). Traditional and folk approaches among ethnic minorities. In J. F. Aponte & J. Wohl (Eds.), *Psychological intervention and cultural diversity* (2nd ed., pp. 149–166). Needham Heights, MA: Allyn & Bacon.

Kurasaki, K. S., Sue, S., Chun, C., & Gee, K. (2000). Ethnic minority intervention and treatment research. In J. F. Aponte & J. Wohl (Eds.), *Psychological intervention and cultural diversity* (2nd ed., pp. 234–249). Needham Heights, MA: Allyn & Bacon.

LaFromboise, T., Coleman, H. L., & Gerton, J. (1993). Psychological impact of biculturalism: Evidence and theory. *Psychological Bulletin, 114*(3), 395–412.

Larson, R. (2000). Towards a psychology of positive youth development. *American Psychologist, 55,* 170–183.

Lerner, R. M. (2002). *Concepts and theories in human development* (3rd ed.). Hillsdale, NJ: Erlbaum.

Lerner, R. M., Brentano, C., Dowling, E. M., & Anderson, P. M. (2002). Positive youth development: Thriving as the basis of personhood and civil society. In R. M. Lerner, M. C. S. Taylor, & A. von Eye (Eds.), *New directions for youth development: Pathways to positive development among diverse youth* (pp. 11–34). San Francisco: Jossey-Bass.

Lerner, R. M., Fisher, C. B., & Weinberg, R. A. (2000). Toward a science for and of the people: Promoting civil society through the application of developmental science. *Child Development, 71*(1), 11–20.

Lewis-Fernandez, R., & Kleinman, A. (1995). Cultural psychiatry: Theoretical, clinical, and research issues. *Psychiatric Clinics of North America, 18*(3), 433–447.

Manson, S. M. (1995). Culture and major depression: Current challenges in the diagnosis of mood disorders. *Psychiatric Clinics of North America, 18*(3), 487–501.

Marsella, A. J., & Yamada, A. M. (2000). Culture and mental health: An introduction and overview of foundations, concepts, and issues. In I. Cuellar & F. A. Paniagua (Eds.), *Handbook of multicultural mental health* (pp. 3–24). San Diego, CA: Academic Press.

Martin, J. N., & Nakayama, T. K. (2005). *Experiencing intercultural communication* (2nd ed.). New York: McGraw-Hill.

Mio, J. S., Barker-Hackett, L. B., & Tumambing, J. (2006). *Multicultural psychology: Understanding our diverse communities*. Boston: McGraw-Hill.

Munroe, R. L., & Munroe, R. H. (1980). Perspectives suggested by anthropological data. In H. C. Triandis & J. W. Berry (Eds.), *Handbook of cross-cultural psychiatry: Vol. 2. Methodology* (pp. 253–318). Boston: Allyn & Bacon.

Okazaki, S. (2000). Assessing and treating Asian Americans: Recent advances. In I. Cuellar & F. A. Paniagua (Eds.), *Handbook of multicultural mental health* (pp. 171–193). San Diego, CA: Academic Press.

Padilla, A. M. (2001). Issues in culturally appropriate assessment. In L. A. Suzuki, J. G. Ponterotto, & P. J. Meller (Eds.), *Handbook of multicultural assessment: Clinical, psychological, and educational application* (pp. 5–28). San Francisco: Jossey-Bass.

Paniagua, F. A. (1994). *Assessing and treating culturally diverse clients*. Thousand Oaks, CA: Sage.

Paniagua, F. A. (2000). Culture-bound syndromes, cultural variations, and psychopathology. In I. Cuellar & F. A. Paniagua (Eds.), *Handbook of multicultural mental health* (pp. 139–169). San Diego, CA: Academic Press.

Pedersen, P. (1997). *Culture-centered counseling interventions: Striving for accuracy*. Thousand Oaks, CA: Sage.

Pedersen, P. (2000). *A handbook for developing multicultural awareness* (3rd ed.). Alexandria, VA: American Counseling Association.

Pedersen, P. (2004). The multicultural context of mental health. In T. B. Smith (Ed.), *Practicing multiculturalism* (pp. 17–32). Boston: Allyn & Bacon.

Pelto, P. J., & Pelto, G. H. (1996). Research designs in medical anthropology. In C. F. Sargent & T. M. Johnson (Eds.), *Medical anthropology: Contemporary theory and method* (pp. 293–324). Westport, CT: Praeger.

Peterson, G. W., Steinmetz, S. K., & Wilson, S. M. (2005). Introduction: Macro-level influences on parent-youth relations. In G. W. Peterson, S. K. Steinmetz, & S. M. Wilson (Eds.), *Parent-youth relations: Cultural and cross-cultural perspectives* (pp. 3–20). Birmingham, NY: Haworth Press.

Peterson, G. W., Steinmetz, S. K., & Wilson, S. M. (2005b). Introduction: Parenting styles in diverse perspectives. In G. W. Peterson, S. K. Steinmetz, & S. M. Wilson (Eds.), *Parent-youth relations: Cultural and cross-cultural perspectives* (pp. 3–20). Birmingham, NY: Haworth Press.

Peterson, G. W., Steinmetz, S. K., & Wilson, S. M. (2005c). Persisting issues in cultural and cross-cultural parent-youth relations. In G. W. Peterson, S. K. Steinmetz, & S. M. Wilson (Eds.), *Parent-youth relations: Cultural and cross-cultural perspectives* (pp. 3–20). Birmingham, NY: Haworth Press.

Phinney, J. S. (1990). Ethnic identity in adolescents and adults: Review of research. *Psychological Bulletin, 108*(3), 499–514.

Population Resource Center. (2005). *Providing the demographic dimension of public policy, 2005 annual report (pp. 1–32)*. Retrieved November 5, 2006, from www.prcd.org/html/annual-reports.html.

Porter, R. Y. (2000). Understanding and treating ethnic minority youth. In J. F. Aponte & J. Wohl (Eds.), *Psychological intervention and cultural diversity* (2nd ed., pp. 167–182). Needham Heights, MA: Allyn & Bacon.

Root, M. P. P. (1990). Resolving the "other" status: Identity development of biracial individuals. In L. Brown & M. P. P. Root (Eds.), *Diversity and complexity in feminist theory and therapy* (pp. 181–189). Newbury Park, CA: Sage.

Roysircar, G. (2004). Counseling and psychotherapy for acculturation and ethnic identity concerns with immigrant and international student clients. In T. B. Smith (Ed.), *Practicing multiculturalism* (pp. 255–275). Boston: Allyn & Bacon.

Schinke, S. P., Botvin, G. J., Trimble, J. E., Orlandi, M. A., Gilchrist, L. D., & Locklear, V. S. (1988). Preventing substance abuse among American-Indian adolescents: A bicultural competence skills approach. *Journal of Counseling Psychology, 35*, 87–90.

Schmidt, J. J. (2006). *Social and cultural foundations of counseling and human services.* Boston: Allyn & Bacon.

Sourander, A. (2003). Refugee families during asylum seeking. *Nordic Journal of Psychiatry, 57*, 203–207.

Sue, D. W. (1978). Eliminating cultural oppression in counseling: Toward a general theory. *Journal of Counseling Psychology, 25*, 419–428.

Sue, D. W., Arrendondo, P., & McDavis, R. J. (1992). Multicultural competencies/standards: A pressing need. *Journal of Counseling and Development, 70*(4), 477–486.

Sue, D. W., & Sue, D. (2003). *Counseling the culturally diverse: Theory and practice* (4th ed.). Hoboken, NJ: Wiley.

Sue, S., Chun, C., & Gee, K. (1995). Ethnic minority intervention and treatment research In J. F. Aponte, R. Young Rivers, & J. Wohl (Eds.), *Psychological interventions and cultural diversity* (pp. 266–282). Boston: Allyn & Bacon.

Sue, S., Zane, N., & Young, K. (1994). Individualism-collectivism, social-network orientation, and acculturation as predictors of attitudes toward seeking professional psychological help among Chinese Americans. *Journal of Counseling Psychology, 41*(3), 280–287.

Szapocznik, J., Santisteban, D., Kurtines, W., Perez-Vidal, A., & Hervis, O. (1984). Bicultural effectiveness training: A treatment intervention for enhancing intercultural adjustment in Cuban American families. *Hispanic Journal of Behavioral Sciences, 6*, 317–344.

Takushi, R., & Uomoto, J. M. (2001). The clinical interview from a multicultural perspective. In L. A. Suzuki, J. G. Ponterotto, & P. J. Meller (Eds.), *Handbook of multicultural assessment: Clinical, psychological, and educational application* (pp. 47–66). San Francisco: Jossey-Bass.

Tousignant, M., Habimana, E., Biron, C., Malo, C., Sidoli-LeBlanc, E., & Bendris, N. (1999). The Quebec adolescent refugee project: Psychopathology and family variables in a sample from 35 nations. *Journal of the American Academy of Child and Adolescent Psychiatry, 38*(11), 1426–1432.

Triandis, H. (1995). *Individualism and collectivism.* Boulder, CO: Westview.

Tseng, W. (2003). *Clinician's guide to cultural psychiatry.* San Diego, CA: Academic Press.

United Nations Children's Fund. (2004). *State of the world's children 2004.* Retrieved February 20, 2004, from http://www.UNICEF.org/sowc04/15579_contents.html.

United Nations High Commission for Refugees. (2001). *The world of children at a glance.* Retrieved April 2, 2006, from http://www.unhcr.ch/children/glance.html.

U.S. Department of Health and Human Services. (2001). *Mental health: Culture, race and ethnicity—A supplement to mental health: A report of the surgeon general.* Rockville, MD: U.S. Department of Health and Human Services, Public Health Office, Office of the Surgeon General.

Vargas, L. A., & Koss-Chioino, J. D. (1992). *Working with culture: Psychotherapeutic interventions with ethnic minority children and adolescents.* San Francisco: Jossey-Bass.

Vaughn, B. E. (2004). Intercultural communication as contexts for mindful achievement. In T. B. Smith (Ed.), *Practicing multiculturalism* (pp. 57–75). Boston: Allyn & Bacon.

Vinokurov, A., Trickett, J., & Birman, D. (2002). Acculturative hassles and immigrant adolescents: A life-domain assessment for Soviet Jewish refugees. *Journal of Social Psychology, 142*, 425–246.

Ward, C. (1997). Culture learning, acculturative stress, and psychopathology: Three perspectives on acculturation. *Applied Psychology: An International Review, 46*, 58–62.

Weiss, M. G., & Kleinman, A. (1988). Depression in cross-cultural perspective: Developing a culturally informed model. In P. R. Dasen, J. W. Berry, & N. Sartorius (Eds.), *Health and cross-cultural psychology* (pp. 179–205). Thousand Oaks, CA: Sage.

Wilson, M. N., Kohn, L. P., & Lee, T. S. (2000). Cultural relativistic approach towards ethnic minorities in family therapy. In J. F. Aponte & J. Wohl (Eds.), *Psychological intervention and cultural diversity* (2nd ed., pp. 92–109). Needham Heights, MA: Allyn & Bacon.

Wohl, J. (2000). Psychotherapy and cultural diversity. In J. F. Aponte & J. Wohl (Eds.), *Psychological intervention and cultural diversity* (2nd ed., pp. 75–91). Needham Heights, MA: Allyn & Bacon.

Wohl, J. & Aponte, J. F. (2000). Common themes and future prospects for the twenty-first century. In J. F. Aponte & J. Wohl (Eds.), *Psychological intervention and cultural diversity* (2nd ed., pp. 286–300). Needham Heights, MA: Allyn & Bacon.

CHAPTER 27

Divorce and Custody

Shannon M. Greene, Kate Sullivan, and Edward R. Anderson

Divorce is a common transition for growing numbers of parents and children in the United States. Each year over a million American children experience their parents' divorce (U.S. Census Bureau, 2000). As part of the divorce, families encounter the legal system as they attempt to make plans for how children will be raised in the new family structure. Clinical psychologists may become involved in several ways, such as by providing mediation and custody evaluations that influence the way family life will proceed after divorce. Thus, clinical psychologists may benefit from information on divorce and custody issues for these litigating families.

This chapter provides an overview of divorce and custody issues relevant for clinical psychologists. It introduces a general model of divorce adjustment, followed by a review of critical factors affecting child outcome for divorcing families. Then it presents three areas that affect postdivorce legal decisions: guiding legal principles, custody and visitation arrangements, and child support. Finally, it focuses on mediation and custody evaluations as mechanisms for assisting families through the divorce transition.

A GENERAL MODEL OF DIVORCE ADJUSTMENT

Perhaps the most widely accepted theoretical model of divorce involves a process perspective. Specifically, divorce is viewed not as a single isolated event, but as a complex chain of marital transitions and family reorganizations that alter roles and relationships and affect individual and family adjustment (Hetherington, Bridges, & Insabella, 1998). Prior to divorce, conflict within the family may increase, accompanied by periods of physical separation between spouses and attempts at reconciliation. Divorce itself may lead to additional disruptions in daily routines, roles, activities, and social relationships, including continued shifts in living arrangements and visitation, such as physical separation, accompanied by changes in contact between the child and the nonresidential parent. Even after the divorce occurs, changes may continue, brought about by parental efforts to establish new partnerships, including dating and nonmarital cohabitation. These changes present children and

Work on this chapter was supported by Grant #1 R01 HD41463-01A1 from the National Institute of Child Health and Human Development, awarded to Edward R. Anderson and Shannon M. Greene.

families with adaptive challenges. The response to these challenges is influenced by previous functioning and experiences and subsequent stresses and resources (Amato, 2000; Hetherington et al., 1998).

Converging research indicates that parenting practices mediate many of the contextual changes that occur during and after divorce (e.g., Simons & Associates, 1996). Thus, divorce precipitates changes in family life that have the potential to disrupt effective parenting practices. These practices include monitoring children's whereabouts, providing consistent discipline, using constructive problem-solving strategies, and engaging in positive involvement. Disruption in parenting subsequently increases the likelihood of children's exhibiting behavioral and emotional difficulties.

Empirical sources suggest there are four key factors that have implications for how children and families adapt: economic hardship, interparental conflict, parental distress, and cumulative transitions and related life stress. These factors are related (e.g., parents experience distress when conflict is high and economic resources are low), but each has potential challenges and implications for child adjustment.

Economic Hardship

With divorce, families often encounter dramatic reductions in income, with per capita declines averaging between 13% and 35% in national samples (R. Peterson, 1996). Economic pressure may mean that families are unable to meet material needs, fall behind on debt payments, and have to cut back on everyday expenses to live within available means (Conger, Ge, Elder, Lorenz, & Simons, 1994). Economic hardship, when combined with high levels of life stress, is associated with increased psychological distress and decreased parenting skills. Not surprisingly, some parents become distracted and emotionally or physically unavailable to their children (Simons et al., 1996). Such disruptions in parenting lead to problematic behavior in children (Forgatch, Patterson, & Ray, 1996). With sufficient time, stress usually abates, although families with lower income may continue to experience disruptive events. The increase in economic hardship following divorce is a potent factor in the emergence of problematic outcomes for children and thus a key reason why courts attempt to determine and enforce child custody payments.

Interparental Conflict

Research indicates that the frequency and intensity of conflict, as well as more overt forms of conflict (e.g., verbal and physical aggression), are related to problematic adjustment in children, regardless of marital status of the parents (Amato, 1999). In fact, interparental conflict has been shown to be a better predictor of child maladjustment than changes in the parents' marital status (Davies, Harold, Goeke-Morey, & Cummings, 2002). Interparental conflict appears to increase children's emotional distress, disrupt peer relations and academic performance, and lead to physical health difficulties. Children who have a family history of exposure to interparental conflict (particularly if conflict is unresolved) show increasing sensitivity or reactivity over time, with reactions ranging from fear and sadness to anger and aggressiveness. Children may be particularly sensitive when conflict concerns child-related issues such as child rearing and custody arrangements. Conflict over these topics may cause children to feel shameful, to blame themselves for the divorce, or to fear becoming involved in the conflict (Grych, Harold, & Miles, 2003). Some theorize that exposure to highly conflictual situations undermines children's sense of emotional security, as evidenced by emotional and behavioral problems (Davies et al., 2002). Others show that high levels of conflict disrupt parenting practices, so that mothers show more negativity and inconsistent discipline, and fathers become less involved with their children, in contrast to counterparts in low-conflict marriages (Gonzales, Pitts, Hill, & Roosa, 2000).

Parental Distress

Divorce is one of the most stressful experiences that an individual may experience. Many individuals experience a variety of adjustment problems, such as increased risk of psychopathology, higher incidence of motor vehicle accidents, elevated drinking and drug use, alcoholism, suicide, and even death (see review by Amato, 2000). More recently separated and more emotionally attached divorcing individuals have poorer immune functioning, greater levels of depression, and other health problems (Kiecolt-Glaser, McGuire, Robles, & Glaser, 2002). For some, divorce may bring about positive effects, such as increased personal autonomy, overall happiness, social involvement, and career development (Hetherington & Kelly, 2002).

Adults who experience difficulties in adapting to stressful postdivorce changes may have problematic relationships with their children (Tein, Sandler, & Zautra, 2000). These problematic relationships interfere with adjustment in children (e.g., Martinez & Forgatch, 2002). In the context of the divorced family, parental adjustment assumes a critical role, given that child adjustment typically follows from how well adults in the household fare. Children's own adjustment difficulties also contribute to the custodial parent's level of stress and quality of parenting (Forgatch et al., 1996). So processes that operate within the parent-child relationship appear to contribute to the long-term adjustment of each family member.

Cumulative Transitions and Related Life Stress

Adjustment problems also arise from transitions that surround relationship dissolutions and consequent repartnering in both formal and informal unions (e.g., Martinez & Forgatch, 2002). After divorce, most adults enter into new relationships; one study found that at the time of the divorce filing, half of the parents already had begun to date, and over one quarter were in a serious romantic relationship (Anderson et al., 2004). Within 10 years of separation, about two thirds of families with two or more children have experienced a nonmarital cohabitation (Bramlett & Mosher, 2002). Parents who remarried had dated an average of three to five people prior to meeting the person they would eventually remarry (Montgomery, Anderson, Hetherington, & Clingempeel, 1992). These relationships introduce additional transitions and reorganizations within the family (Raley & Wildsmith, 2004). Echoing findings discussed earlier, the effect of repartnering transitions on child adjustment is mediated by parenting practices (DeGarmo & Forgatch, 1997).

Short-Term and Long-Term Adjustment to Divorce

Children's adaptation to divorce depends on the particular combination of stress and resources in their lives (Amato, 1993). As stresses begin to decrease and resources become more plentiful, many children who had exhibited problematic adjustment will improve. However, problems with adjustment may persist when stressors such as financial hardship, interparental conflict, and disrupted parenting continue.

POSTDIVORCE DECISIONS

Divorce calls for a restructuring of parental rights and responsibilities along two broad areas relating to child rearing: custody and visitation, and child support. Before discussing each area, we present information on the overarching or guiding legal principles in decisions related to child custody.

Guiding Legal Principles in Child Custody Decision Making

Divorce law and the determination of child custody are established through state statutes. The most prevalent criterion for determining placement of children after divorce is the Best Interest of the Child standard, which emerged in the 1960s and 1970s as an alternative to the Tender Years Doctrine, an earlier standard favoring placement with mothers. The Tender Years Doctrine itself supplanted a custody preference for fathers, when children were considered legal property. Most jurisdictions now explicitly state a gender-neutral preference for custody decisions (see O'Donohue & Bradley, 1999, for more details).

The Best Interest of the Child standard set forth a list of factors to be used in determining child placement after divorce, although states vary in their relative consideration and weighting of these factors. Judges too have great latitude in applying the standard for making determinations in custody cases. Buehler and Gerard (1995) provide a compilation of all Best Interest factors used throughout the United States (see Table 27.1).

Before considering Table 27.1 in detail, note that a critical distinction should be made with respect to legal custody versus physical custody. Legal custody refers to the relative level of continuing responsibility and involvement each parent will have in decisions about the child, ranging from joint, where custody is shared, to sole, where custody is assigned to one parent. Physical custody refers to the daily residential and supervisory arrangements for the child. In practice, these two decisions are independent; for example, parents may be awarded joint legal custody, but one parent may receive physical custody (i.e., the child resides primarily within that parent's household and sees the other parent at established times). Or there may be some form of joint physical custody awarded. Although less clearly defined than sole physical custody (Buchanan & Williams, 2006), a minimum criterion in use for joint physical custody is that children spend at least 25% of the time with each parent (Bauserman, 2002).

With respect to Table 27.1, factors 1 to 5 correspond to the criteria outlined in the Uniform Marriage and Divorce Act (1970); the remaining factors consist of

Table 27.1   "Best Interest of the Child" Factors

Criteria Described in the Uniform Marriage and Divorce Act (1970)
1. Wishes of the child's parent or parents as to his/her custody
2. Wishes of the child as to his/her custodian
3. Interaction and interrelationship of the child with his/her parents, his/her siblings, and any other persons who may significantly affect the child's best interest
4. Child's adjustment to his/her home, school, community
5. Mental and physical health of all individuals involved

Criteria Related to the Primary Caretaker Standard
6. If one parent, both parents, or neither parent has provided primary care of the child
7. Capacity and interest of each parent to provide for the emotional, social, moral, material, and educational needs of the child
8. Capacity and disposition of each party to provide the child with food, clothing, medical care, and other material needs

Criteria Related to Safety and Well-being of Children
9. Evidence of domestic violence, abuse, or neglect
10. Evidence that substance use affects the child's well-being
11. Moral fitness of the parents

Criteria Related to the Cooperative Parent Factor
12. Which parent is more likely to allow the child frequent and continuing contact with the noncustodial parent
13. Nature and extent of coercion or duress used by a parent in obtaining an agreement regarding custody
14. Ability of both parties to cooperate and make decisions jointly
15. Child support noncompliance

Other Criteria
16. Out-of-state residence
17. Length of time the child has lived in a stable, satisfactory environment and the desirability of maintaining continuity
18. Permanence of custodial home
19. Nature and amount of contact with both parents
20. Love and affection existing between the child and each parent
21. Age and sex of the child
22. Parents' respective home environments
23. Physical, emotional, mental, religious, and social needs of the child
24. Health, safety, and welfare of the child
25. Child's cultural background

Source: "Divorce Law in the United States: A Focus on Child Custody," by C. Buehler and J. M. Gerard, 1995, *Family Relations, 44,* pp. 439–458.

outgrowths or restatements of these basic criteria. It is noteworthy that the first two factors involve the direct wishes of the parties involved, although the preference for the child's wishes typically is reserved for older children. Standards are emerging for representing these and other child interests in custody cases (e.g., Ackerman, 2006; American Bar Association [ABA], 2003; American Law Institute, 2002; American Psychological Association [APA], 2002; Elrod, 2003).

Factors 6 to 8 in Table 27.1 address the preference for placing the child with the primary caretaker, the individual who has provided the daily pattern of care.

In principle, this preference appears determinative and relatively easy to establish (Buehler & Gerard, 1995). In actual practice, however, it may lead to inequitable physical custody arrangements, such as granting sole physical custody to a parent who has performed only marginally more than the other with respect to caretaking. An alternative standard has evolved, called the approximation rule, with custody arrangements attempting to resemble what had been in place prior to the divorce. Emery (1999) has advocated for this preference because it combines the best aspects of the primary caretaker and joint custody standards. The determinate standard of time spent caring for the child is used to establish the custody arrangement, thereby accommodating a wide variety of potential predivorce parenting situations.

Factors 9 to 10 in Table 27.1, domestic violence and substance abuse, arguably may override other factors as they directly impact the safety of the child (Buehler & Gerard, 1995). Most states prohibit custody for a parent with verified domestic violence. Factor 11 mentions "moral fitness," a vague term often equated with sexual promiscuity. Seven states, for example, outlaw cohabitation between unmarried partners, which may indirectly affect awards of child custody.

Factors 12 to 15 in Table 27.1 relate to the "cooperative or friendly parent," such that parents who act to restrict access to the child in the absence of compelling reasons of safety may face greater challenges in obtaining custody and visitation. Relatedly, efforts to restrict access (along with other behaviors such as efforts to "brainwash" the child from wanting to have a relationship with the other parent and unfounded accusations of abuse) have been the focus of a controversial proposed psychiatric disorder for understanding children who become resistant to contact with the noncustodial parent, called Parental Alienation Syndrome (Gardner, 1998). More recent views, however, have recast the situation of the child who is resistant to visitation more broadly, now called the *alienated child;* sources of resistance now include the behaviors of both parents, along with developmental preferences and reactions to the divorce. In support of this reformulation, results of two cross-sectional studies show child resistance to visitation arising from multiple determinants, such as prolonged litigation, parental lack of warmth, and the child's own emotional and social problems. Johnston (2005) has integrated this work into Figure 27.1.

Finally, as listed in Table 27.1, Buehler and Gerard (1995) provide factors relating to contact and continuity. Out-of-state residence, for example, is likely to affect practical access to the child. Clearly, the information in Table 27.1 shows that no single approach will fit all potential situations. In the case of incarcerated fathers, for example, judges must weigh the desire of the parties to maintain contact, along with a consideration of whether the visit itself may be difficult for the child, or whether written or phone contact may be more appropriate (Menno, 2003). Moreover, issues such as the nature of the offense, length of prison stay, and past history may affect the form that custody will take.

Thus, in practice, there is wide latitude given to the courts in determining the nature of custody and visitation arrangements. Buehler and Gerard (1995) propose a presumption of favoring parental agreements, such that parents forward their preference for custody and visitation to the court, which the court will honor. In the absence of an established parental agreement, these authors propose a presumption

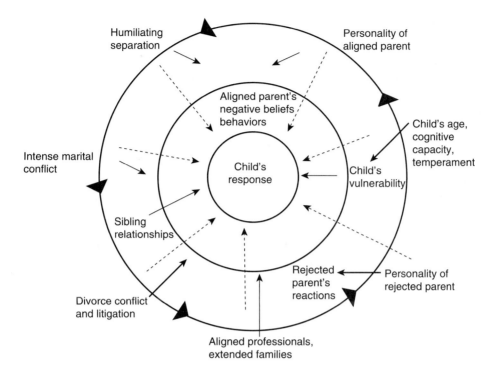

Figure 27.1   A model of factors predicting child alienation. *Source:* "Children of Divorce Who Reject a Parent and Refuse Visitation: Recent Research and Social Policy Implications for the Alienated Child," by J. R. Johnston, 2005, *Family Life Quarterly, 38*(4), pp. 757–775. Reprinted with permission.

of shared legal custody, sole physical custody to the primary caretaker, and substantial access by the nonresidential parent.

Custody and Visitation Arrangements

In this section, we consider differences across custody arrangements identified in previous research, issues related to maintaining contact with the nonresidential parent, and special considerations that impact custody and visitation arrangements.

Common Practices and Comparisons across Custody Arrangements

Following divorce, up to 80% of children are in the sole physical custody of their mother (Emery, 1999). The prevalence of sole father custody, however, is increasing rapidly, with fathers more likely to be awarded custody when children are adolescent (Maccoby & Mnookin, 1992). Buchanan, Maccoby, and Dornbusch (1996) note that mother and father sole custody arrangements were similar on a wide variety of dimensions. Differences were noted in emotional closeness and monitoring, which favored mother custody households; this can be explained in part by the lower rate of behavior problems for children in mother custody households. It also should be noted that fathers essentially may be taking on more challenging situations to begin with, given that they gain custody under more difficult family circumstances than mothers (Emery, 1999). Sole custodial father families are less likely to be granted child support awards, and nonresidential mothers are less likely to comply with the child support awards given (Meyer & Garasky, 2003).

In response to social and economic changes beginning in the 1970s, there has been an increased preference for parents to share custody, with the hope of maximizing involvement of both parents in their children's lives. There has been a call for current legal practices to recognize the child's need to have both parents actively involved in his or her life (Menno, 2003). The movement toward recognizing the importance of both parents has coincided with the tendency for states to deregulate custody arrangements, allowing parents to establish individualized arrangements (Buehler & Gerard, 1995). Additionally, developmental research has stressed the role that both parents play in children's lives as well as the need for custody arrangements to be flexible (J. B. Kelly & Lamb, 2000). When awarded, joint custody is more common for children in middle childhood and for families with higher income (Cancian & Meyer, 1998; Maccoby & Mnookin, 1992).

As opposed to comparisons across different kinds of sole custody homes, meta-analytic evidence suggests that children in joint custody arrangements fare better across a variety of indexes; in fact, they showed comparable levels of adjustment with children from never-divorced households (Bauserman, 2002). Better adjustment appears to be accounted for by greater closeness between the child and both parents. In addition, interparental conflict is lower in joint custody homes. Finally, children from joint custody families were more likely to see their father weekly, have more overnight stays, and benefit from more child support (Seltzer, 1998). However, the families that enter into joint custody arrangements may themselves be different from those that enter into sole custody arrangements; as described earlier, states likely award joint custody to families that demonstrate that they can get along well enough to manage the close contact and coordination between parents that such arrangements may require. So better outcomes may be due, in part, to selection effects.

What factors are associated with acquiring sole custody? Several studies have shown that parents are more likely to receive custody when they are the plaintiffs and have higher income and education levels compared to their spouse, but not when they have prior marriages, children from prior marriages, or marital infidelity (Cancian & Meyer, 1998; Fox & Kelly, 1995; R. F. Kelly, Redenbach, & Rinaman, 2005; Seltzer, 1998). Fathers are more likely to receive sole custody if ending a long-term marriage; they are less likely to receive custody when they are unemployed or owe child support arrears or when the family is eligible for welfare support (Cancian & Meyer, 1998; Fox & Kelly, 1995). Mothers are more likely to receive custody when they are older, when the oldest child in the family is female, or when there are high levels of conflict (Cancian & Meyers, 1998; Fox & Kelly, 1995; R. F. Kelly, et al., 2005). Joint custody is more likely when all the children are male, both parents work and own homes (Cancian & Meyer, 1998), and when fathers are more educated (R. F. Kelly et al., 2005).

In addition to sole and joint custody, split custody is available to families with more than one child. In this individualized custody arrangement, some of the children may live with the father while other children may live with the mother (Ellis, 2000).

Continuing Contact with the Nonresidential Parent

A critical issue with sole custody arrangements concerns continued contact with the nonresidential parent, typically fathers, given prevailing custody arrangements. Adults who experienced parental divorce in childhood report a sense of loss due to the lack of contact with their father (Laumann-Billings & Emery, 2000) and a wish to have been more involved with him while growing up (Fabricius & Hall, 2000). Some level of contact is necessary for closeness (Fabricius, 2003), especially for younger children (Leventhal, Kelman, Galatzer-Levy, & Hraus, 1999; Pruett & Johnston, 2004), though contact alone is not always a sufficient determinant for relationship quality (Berscheid & Peplau, 1983; Buchanan & Williams, 2006).

When fathers were able to maintain strong emotional ties with their nonresidential children, their children had greater psychological and behavioral adjustment during adolescence (Buchanan et al., 1996; McLanahan & Sandefur, 1994; Seltzer, 1994; Whiteside & Becker, 2000). Sheer contact with the nonresidential father may not be directly tied to children's adjustment (Amato & Gilbreth, 1999; Hetherington & Kelly, 2002; Marsiglio, Amato, Day, & Lamb, 2000; McLanahan & Sandefur, 1994; Seltzer, 1994; Whiteside & Becker, 2000), although its absence is certainly reflected in other ways, such as adult children's sense of loss mentioned earlier. Rather than a direct effect on children's adjustment, the impact of contact between the noncustodial parent and the child on the child's well-being may depend on other factors, most notably the amount of conflict between the divorced parents (e.g., Buchanan & Williams, 2006; Lamb et al., 1997). High interparental conflict may undermine the closeness between the nonresidential father and child, or involve children directly in marital disputes. Relatedly, conflictual parents are less likely to carry out visitation plans, even when court-imposed (Pruett, Williams, Insabella, & Little, 2003; Whiteside & Becker, 2000). Conflict over visitation is one of the primary reasons for the courts to determine that supervised visits should occur. In a multisite study of supervised visitation, over three-quarters of the families reported that anger toward the other parent was the primary reason for the court determination of supervised visitation (Pearson & Thoennes, 2000). Those most satisfied with supervised visits were the families who had reported fighting at drop-off and pickup times.

Special Considerations

There is a considerable controversy over whether to encourage or discourage overnight stays when children are infants and toddlers. Much of this controversy concerns a study by Solomon and George (1999a, 1999b) in which overnight stays were linked to problems in infant-mother attachment. However, infant adjustment to the overnight stays could be promoted with parental cooperation and maternal support. Results highlight the need to consider more than simply the child's age when making decisions about overnight contact.

There also is legal recognition that high-conflict custody cases represent a substantial risk factor for the involved children and families (High-Conflict Custody Cases, 2001). The Family Law section of the ABA, in conjunction with the Johnson

Foundation (2001), developed standards of practice to recognize and address the challenges that these children and families face.

Given high rates of geographic mobility in the United States, parental relocation following separation and divorce is increasingly problematic as joint custody has become the preferred custody arrangement (J. B. Kelly & Lamb, 2003). Joint physical and/or legal custody assumes that both parents maintain geographically close residences to enable contact between children and parents. Relocation by one or both parents makes this difficult to maintain (Austin, 2000). Relocation of one parent also may reduce financial support and lead to a more distant relationship between that parent and the child (Braver, Ellman, & Fabricius, 2003). Relocation may depend on the children's own developmental status (J. B. Kelly & Lamb, 2003) or, as Warshak (2000) suggests, on unique considerations that require a case-by-case analysis.

Child Support

Though the emotional upheaval that typifies divorce is most commonly at the forefront of issues for families experiencing this transition, financial problems also present challenges to child well-being. Single-parent families are more likely to be poor (Bartfeld, 2000). Thus, children have a greater chance of living in poverty after divorce.

Public policy in the United States has increasingly sought to address this issue by establishing the financial responsibility of both the custodial and the noncustodial parent for their children. As early as the nineteenth century, public policy began to enforce parental financial responsibility for dependent children. More sweeping changes to child support policy appeared during the twentieth century, coinciding with the dramatic increase in separation and divorce in American families. Beginning with the Social Security Act of 1935, government support was granted to women and their dependent children based on need, specifically in cases where one parent was not providing any financial support. Additional policies since then have addressed the need for parents to assume greater parental responsibility for their children, such as the Uniform Interstate Family Support Act in 1992 and the Personal Responsibility and Work Opportunity Reconciliation Act in 1996. Currently, child support is regulated by the Child Support Enforcement Program, a partnership of federal, state, and local authorities to collect child support (U.S. Department of Health and Human Services, 2005). Current policy efforts to enforce child support have yielded benefits: Children are less likely to live in poverty (Edin, 1995), their families are less reliant on government support, and their parents take on greater financial responsibility for their children (Altman, 2003).

More generally, child support represents an important resource on which children rely (Amato & Gilbreth, 1999). Increases in their standard of living likely improve children's health and educational attainment (Furstenberg, Morgan, & Allison, 1987; King, 1994; McLanahan, Seltzer, Hanson, & Thompson, 1994). There is evidence, for example, that child support shows positive effects on children's school achievement (Argys, Peters, Brooks-Gunn, & Smith, 1998; Knox, 1996). A meta-analysis of 14 studies shows child support related to greater academic success and fewer externalizing problems in children (Amato & Gilbreth, 1999).

Developmental gains from child support may be more important for younger children (King & Soboleski, 2006) and for involuntary types of payments (Argys et al., 1998; Hernandez, Beller, & Graham, 1995).

Though the general consensus favors child support enforcement, establishing guidelines for child support awards is a more complex issue. Before legislative changes in the 1980s, child support was typically awarded on a case-by-case basis (Rogers, 1999). However, policy changes with the Family Support Act sought to ensure a more equitable system that made use of economic data to estimate the financial costs associated with raising children (Beld & Biernant, 2003). Within these federal guidelines, individual states were free to establish their own formulas; the more common formulas are described next. More detailed reviews of these and other formulas can be found elsewhere (Beld & Biernant, 2003; Blumberg, 1999; Morgan, 2004).

> *Income Shares.* Developed by the U.S. Department of Health and Human Services, the basis for this formula is to provide children with the same proportion of financial resources and support that would have been available to them had their parents remained married.
>
> *Percentage of Obligor Income.* Developed by the state of Wisconsin, this formula takes into account the parent's income, the amount of time the child spends with each parent, and whether the parent is supporting other children. Formulas may differ based on the complexity of the family arrangement, although the basic support guidelines assume that the noncustodial parent is responsible for providing 17% of gross income for 1 child, 25% for 2, 29% for 3, 31% for 4, and 34% for 5 or more children.
>
> *Cost Shares.* The cost shares formula takes into account the costs of raising children, as well as tax benefits associated with dependent children.
>
> *Hybrid Models.* Evolving out of some of the limitations with previous formulas, various hybrid models have emerged, such as one proposed by the ALI [American Law Institute] that allows for greater discretion in deciding costs associated with living arrangements. (Bartlett, 2001; Czapanskiy, 2001; Harris, 2001)

As with any public policy, the various formulas for determining child support have come under fire. Some charge that states do not raise award standards often enough to fairly reflect the actual cost of raising children, given federal legislation that requires updates only every 4 years (Venohr & Griffith, 2005; Venohr & Williams, 1999). Others criticize specifics of the formulas, charging that the income shares and the percentage of obligor income models allow custodial parents to achieve a higher standard of living than nonresidential parents (Rogers, 1999). In fact, formulas such as income shares were designed to protect the primary custodial parent and residential children from a precipitous drop in standard of living after the divorce, although Braver and colleagues (2003) counter that the drop may not be as drastic as once thought. Criticism also is levied because many of the formulas assume that one parent will have sole custody, rather than acknowledging the growing numbers of shared custody arrangements and situations in which visitation and residence vary over time (Melli & Brown, 1994). In fact, child support awards typically do not factor in costs of rearing children for the nonresidential parent until time spent in that household approaches the level of joint custody. Fabricius and Braver (2003) provide evidence for a linear relationship between household expenses and amount of contact, suggesting that nonresidential expenses are being underestimated. Findings by Garfinkel, McLanahan, and Wallerstein (2004) differ, perhaps because of sample characteristics. The use of a nationally representative, multi-informant sample may be required to address this issue further.

There also is disagreement with whether child support should end when children achieve majority status or after receiving additional post–high school education and training. Current formulas and legislation typically do not consider expenses incurred after children turn 18 years old. New state laws are beginning to address this issue, although there is evidence that some divorced parents are voluntarily providing equal proportions of support to their college-age children (Fabricius, Braver, & Deneau, 2003).

Finally, difficulties surround international child support enforcement. There is currently no global legislation regarding child support, although the United States has reached agreement with several nations on a case-by-case basis (Duncan, 2004). Efforts have been made to develop international policy, but there is no obligation to adhere to the legislation.

A recent report published by the U.S. Census Bureau provides a report card of sorts on child support awards, actual receipts, and enforcement, based on the Current Population Survey reports from 1994 to 2004 (Grall, 2006). It showed that the proportion of children living in poverty after divorce has dropped, from one third in 1993 to less than one fourth in 2003. However, only half of custodial parents had received all their child support award due; the average amount of child support in arrears was $5,100, for a combined total of $37 billion past due. Many custodial parents acknowledge receiving noncash support, such as gifts and coverage of expenses, and over half of child support awards included health insurance provisions from the nonresidential parent.

What would help the parents without primary custody maintain their child support payments? With respect to policy, Freeman and Waldfogel (2001) found that compliance with child support was greatest when paired with stronger enforcement laws. Additionally, greater compliance occurs when child support awards explicitly state the amount to be paid (J. Peterson & Nord, 1990). With respect to individual considerations, greater compliance is linked to access to children, as measured by actual contact (Argys, Peters, & Waldman, 2001; Seltzer, Schaeffer, & Charng, 1989) or geographic proximity (Teachman, 1991). Greater compliance occurs when the award is perceived as fair (Lin, 2000) and when mediation has been used (Emery, Matthews, & Kitzmann, 1994). Greater compliance also occurs when noncustodial parents believe they have some say in the child's life and how the money will be used (Braver et al., 1993; Weiss & Willis, 1985). Perceptions of control influence the likelihood of child support payments indirectly through visitation. Payment of child support is more likely among nonresidential parents who see their child frequently (Seltzer et al., 1989).

Other factors also may decrease the likelihood of child support receipt. Noncompliance is associated with more marginalized groups, such as the less educated and the poor (J. Peterson & Nord, 1990). It also is associated with families with greater interparental conflict (Hetherington & Stanley-Hagen, 1999) and domestic violence, although victims of domestic violence are less likely to seek and receive child support awards (Menard & Turetsky, 1999). Though recent policy efforts have been made to ensure the safety of those seeking child support, greater advances need to be made in securing the safety of victims of domestic abuse in seeking child support.

Finally, there are few established policies or laws that dictate how child support should be handled among divorces involving stepparents. Few states have laws requiring continuing support from the stepparent following divorce (Hans, 2002; Fine & Fine, 1992).

ASSISTING FAMILIES WITH THE DIVORCE TRANSITION

When assisting parents with the divorce transition, clinical psychologists may make use of various strategies, some of which place them in an advisory role to the family or legal community. This section discusses two such strategies: mediation and custody evaluation.

Mediation

Reflective of dissatisfaction with litigation, mediation has evolved as an alternative. Mediation is essentially cooperative in nature, having originated from the field of negotiation. Thus, mediation is based on the fundamental premise of self-determination: Each parent makes a voluntary effort to reach mutually agreed upon decisions about a parenting plan.

Mediators are typically attorneys, psychologists, or social workers who assist with identifying needs and interests and facilitating an agreement between the parents. The format used is goal-oriented and short term, usually lasting from 1 to 5 sessions. The mediator acts as an advocate for both parents in attempting to create a mutually agreeable solution. Emery and Wyer (1987) outline four aims for mediation, otherwise known as the four "Cs": to reduce *conflict,* to increase *cooperation,* to allow individuals *control* over key decisions affecting their lives, and to reduce *costs* associated with divorce and litigation.

There has been rapid growth in the use of mediation in divorce over the past 2 decades, with some states mandating an attempt at mediation in custody disputes. When mandated, parents must attend one or more meetings with a mediator in an attempt to reach an agreement, but they are not required to reach an agreement. Additionally, some states have implemented programs to educate parents about the impact of divorce and related transitions on children's well-being.

Typically, mediators seek to generate a mutually agreed upon, workable coparenting plan that defines the respective boundaries of each parent and, in doing so, minimizes the need for future contact. The process of mediation helps to model how the coparenting relationship should operate in future interactions, with communication that is less emotional and more businesslike in tone. A distinct advantage with mediation is the evolution of a detailed, uniquely tailored parenting plan. Such plans may generate greater satisfaction, thereby yielding better adherence.

Reviewers of related research have concluded that mediation appears to have moderate success (J. B. Kelly, 1996; Saposnek, 1998). Benefits are cost savings incurred when litigation can be avoided, improved parental satisfaction, and increased compliance for mediated agreements compared to those reached through adjudication. Perhaps because of the increases in parental satisfaction, parents tend to report lower levels of conflict at 1 year after the divorce, although such results are less consistently seen over the long term. Mediation does not appear to garner benefits to parent and child psychological adjustment. Also, court-mandated mediation appears to be less successful at producing an agreed upon parenting plan. Finally, mediation may be less appropriate in situations involving domestic violence and child abuse, where there are substantial discrepancies in bargaining power, or when parents are severely disturbed.

Custody Evaluation

When collaborative efforts such as mediation fail, families may turn to the courts for adjudication. Maccoby and Mnookin (1992) note that about 50% of families settle out of court, with custody uncontested; about 30% contest custody but settle through attorney negotiations out of court; another 11% resolve custody issues with mediation; the remaining are given mandatory custody evaluations consistent with the local courts, with about half of those settling out of court after the evaluation is conducted. Thus, approximately 4% of the sample proceeded to trial, and about half of those cases settled during the course of the trial. Only 1.5% of the sample completed a custody trial and received a final determination by the judge. The authors conclude that about 25% of the sample had entrenched legal battles over their children. These families were not distinguished from the larger sample with respect to race, education, and income; discriminating factors were children younger than 3 and mothers not engaged in paid employment.

Custody evaluations have become a routine part of litigation, either sponsored by the parties themselves or initiated by the courts. The custody evaluation comprises an assessment of the child, the parents, and the family by a psychologist. Because the stakes are high—an evaluation carries weight in determining parental rights relative to the child—custody evaluations are often difficult and demanding work. Adding to the difficulty are evaluations that involve accusations of child abuse, negligence, and family violence. Either parent may retain the psychologist, but generally most psychologists prefer to be retained by the court or jointly by the attorneys of both sides (Ackerman & Ackerman, 1997).

Although state statutes differ, generally the evaluation assesses "parenting capacity" and its fit with the psychological and developmental needs of the child: (a) parental capacity of the prospective custodians: their knowledge, skills, and abilities; (b) psychological functioning and developmental needs of the child (can also include the wishes of the child in some cases); and (c) functional ability of each parent to meet the child's needs. Thus the assessment includes the mental and physical health of all family members involved; the child's adjustment at home, school, and community settings; and the interaction of the child with parents and siblings. The APA (1994) directs evaluations to focus on three issues: (1) the needs of the child, (2) the abilities and capacities of the parents, and (3) the best fit between the two.

Custody evaluations can be extensive, as the psychologist conducts clinical interviews with each parent and child (and any cohabiting romantic partner), reviews all relevant documents, conducts parent-child observations, conducts psychological testing on parents and children, and talks with teachers, attorneys, and therapists. The total time to conduct a custody evaluation (excluding court testimony time) ranges from 18 to 28 hours, and fees average $3,000 (Bow & Quinnell, 2001). As such, custody evaluations are often a critical part of the divorce proceedings, and may have a pivotal effect on the determination of the so-called ultimate issues of a case: custody and visitation rights.

In this legal setting, the custody evaluator is a professional expert who is called on to inform and advise the court in a balanced and impartial way, in contrast to a judge, who renders a final decision, or an advocating attorney, who represents the interest of one party. More recently, this role of imputed impartiality has come under increased scrutiny. Tippins and Wittmann (2005) state that custody evaluations are most valuable (and potentially least biased) when focused on facts and observations rather than clinical inference or judgments. The authors propose a four-level model for directing clinical involvement in custody cases, with the levels reflecting the degree of clinical inference involved (see Figure 27.2). At Level I, the lowest level of clinical inference, custody evaluators make observations about actual behaviors and test outcomes and processes occurring as part of the evaluation. Examples the authors provide include "She hung her head low and was often tearful" and "There is an elevation on scale two of the MMPI-2 [Minnesota Multiphasic Personality Inventory-2]."

At Level II, the custody evaluator begins to make simple inferences about Level I data. Examples the authors provide include "The father's style of parenting is very authoritarian" and "The mother's blue mood, the child's report of her chronic sadness, and her MMPI-2 elevations suggest that she is moderately depressed." In contrast, at Level III, the evaluator makes reference to custody-specific constructs, such as "parenting capacity" and "potential psychological risks of primary custody with this parent." The authors provide this example: "Multiple days away from the mother, this child's primary psychological parent, will be emotionally stressful." Finally, Level IV comprises the evaluator's custody-related recommendations about the ultimate issues, such as a proposed access schedule and physical custody. The authors direct evaluators to be circumspect in their evaluation, charging that specific empirical support may be lacking in making recommendations at Level IV. They and others (Karras & Berry, 1985; Melton, Petriala, Poythress, & Slobogin, 1997) recommend that custody evaluators avoid making specific recommendations about what a court "should" do. Ironically, specific recommendations are often viewed as what is most valuable about custody evaluations (Bow & Quinnell, 2004). Some argue instead that custody evaluators should provide recommendations, but that judges should view them as advisory in nature (Stahl, 2005).

If custody evaluators cannot be impartial, they should attempt to withdraw from a case, or at a minimum provide information to the court about factors that affect their impartiality. Custody evaluators also should avoid multiple relationships. In

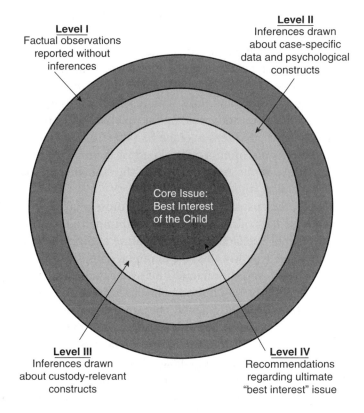

Figure 27.2 A model for directing clinical involvement in custody cases. *Source:* "Empirical and Ethical Problems with Custody Recommendations: A Call for Clinical Humility and Judicial Vigilance," by T. M. Tippins and J. P. Wittmann, 2005, *Family Court Review, 43*(2), pp. 193–222. Reprinted with permission.

cases where they have served in a therapeutic role, they should avoid providing custody evaluations. They may testify as a witness, although recommendations are generally to decline such a role unless ordered by the court to do so. During the custody evaluation, they should refrain from accepting any of the involved parties as therapy clients, and even after the evaluation is complete, they are urged to be cautious in agreeing to treat former participants of the custody evaluation.

Custody evaluators should have a thorough understanding of ethical guidelines for conducting custody evaluations. For example, APA guidelines specify that the custody evaluator obtain informed consent from each adult participant, including identifying the assessment tools and techniques that will be used. Informed consent also specifies fees, who will pay, and the limits of confidentiality, including what information will be disclosed. In conducting the evaluation, the psychologist should refrain from inappropriately interpreting the data and should use multiple methods of data collection.

The APA standards do not address many of the issues involved in child custody evaluations, and thus are considered aspirational in nature. Additionally, custody evaluations have a high risk for malpractice suits and ethical complaints (Kirkland &

Kirkland, 2001). Thus, the psychologist should follow closely the ethical guidelines and other risk management procedures. See Craig (2005) for other guidelines that may apply for custody evaluations.

Because of the nature of the work, custody evaluators should have competency in psychological assessment of adults, children, and families. They should be knowledgeable in child development, family development, adult and child psychopathology, and research on children and divorce. Further, they should be familiar with applicable legal standards, especially for their state or jurisdiction. Their work should reflect acceptable clinical and scientific methods. Their evaluation should be based on multiple methods, with important facts or opinions based on at least two sources of information.

Additionally, the psychologist should use standard and commonly used assessment techniques in custody evaluations. Measures that have been frequently used can be found in Bow and Quinnell (2001) and Hagen and Castagna (2001). The measure most frequently used by psychologists in evaluating child custody issues is the MMPI. This test is often used to assess parenting capacity and emotional adjustment of each party. It also allows for detecting impression management, or the degree to which individuals are consciously inflating or concealing various aspects of themselves. This test has been normed on child custody litigants (e.g., Strong, Greene, Hoppe, Johnston, & Olesin, 1999) and has been used to identify parents who attempt to alienate the child from the other parent (Siegel & Langford, 1998). Craig (2005) recommends that evidence from the MMPI should be explored further as part of the workup. However, Bradley (2004) warns of potential cultural biases in this instrument and others. The Millon Clinical Multiaxial Inventory (MCMI) is being used increasingly in child custody evaluations. There is some controversy over the use of the MCMI because it lacks established norms for differentiating clinical from nonclinical respondents (Butcher & Miller, 1999) and there are issues with scale interpretation. Craig recommends caution when using the MCMI for custody evaluations. Hysjulien, Wood, and Benjamin (1994) report the use of various instruments, including the Achenbach Child Behavior Checklist (McConaughy & Achenbach, 1996), FACES III (Edmon, Cole, & Howard, 1990), and the Parent Attachment Structured Interview (Roll, Lockwood, & Roll, 1981). Bradley recommends the Child Perception of Parent and Parent Awareness Skills Survey (Bricklin, 1995) and the Parental Discipline Techniques Self Report Instrument (Gardner, 1997).

SUMMARY

Parental divorce has the potential to create considerable risk for children, but there is large variation in how children respond to the experience. Key risk factors for maladjustment after divorce are economic hardship, interparental conflict, parental distress, and cumulative transitions and related life stress. Clinical psychologists may provide mediation or custody evaluation, both of which require a sophisticated knowledge of legal, ethical, and clinical issues. The work is painstaking and difficult, but offers help to families attempting to make plans for how children will be raised in the new family structure.

REFERENCES

Ackerman, M. J. (2006). The APA code of ethics and child custody work. *American Journal of Family Law, 20*, 102–111.

Ackerman, M., & Ackerman, M. (1997). Custody evaluation practices: A survey of experienced professionals (revisited). *Professional Psychology: Research and Practice, 28*, 137–145.

Altman, S. (2003). A theory of child support. *International Journal of Law, Policy, and the Family, 17*, 175–210.

Amato, P. R. (1993). Children's adjustment to divorce: Theories, hypotheses, and empirical support. *Journal of Marriage and the Family, 55*, 23–38.

Amato, P. R. (1999). Children of divorced parents as young adults. In E. M. Hetherington (Ed.), *Coping with divorce, single parenting, and remarriage: A risk and resiliency perspective* (pp. 147–163). Mahwah, NJ: Erlbaum.

Amato, P. R. (2000). The consequences of divorce for adults and children. *Journal of Marriage and the Family, 62*, 1269–1287.

Amato, P. R., & Gilbreth, J. G. (1999). Nonresident fathers and children's well-being: A meta-analysis. *Journal of Marriage and the Family, 61*, 557–573.

American Bar Association. (2003). Standards of practice for lawyers representing children in custody cases. *Family Law Quarterly, 37*, 131–160.

American Law Institute (2002). *Principles of the law of family dissolution: Analysis and recommendations.* Dayton, OH: LexisNexis.

American Psychological Association (1994). Guidelines for custody evaluations in divorce proceedings. *American Psychologist, 49*, 677–680.

American Psychological Association. (2002). *Ethical principles of psychologists and code of conduct.* Retrieved August 4, 2006, from http://www.apa.org/ethics/homepage.html.

Anderson, E. R., Greene, S. M., Walker, L., Malerba, C. A., Forgatch, M. S., & DeGarmo, D. S. (2004). Ready to take a chance again: Transitions into dating among divorcing parents. *Journal of Divorce and Remarriage, 40*, 61–75.

Argys, L. M., Peters, H. E., Brooks-Gunn, J., & Smith, J. R. (1998). The impact of child support on cognitive outcomes of young children. *Demography, 35*, 159–173.

Argys, L. M., Peters, H. E., & Waldman, D. M. (2001). Can the Family Support Act put some life back into deadbeat dads? An analysis of child-support guidelines, award rates, and levels. *Journal of Human Resources, 36*, 226–252.

Austin, W. G. (2000). A forensic psychology model of risk assessment for child custody relocation law. *Family and Conciliation Courts Review, 38*, 192–207.

Bartfeld, J. (2000). Child support and the postdivorce economic well-being of mothers, fathers, and children. *Demography, 37*, 203–213.

Bartlett, K. T. (2001). Principles of the law of family dissolution: Analyses and recommendations. *Duke Journal of Gender Law and Policy, 8*, 1–85.

Bauserman, R. (2002). Child adjustment in joint-custody versus sole-custody arrangements: A meta-analytic review. *Journal of Family Psychology, 16*, 91–102.

Beld, J. M., & Biernant, L. (2003). Federal intent for state child support guidelines: Income shares, cost shares, and the realities of shared parenting. *Family Law Quarterly, 37*, 165–202.

Berscheid, E., & Peplau, L. A. (1983). The emerging science of relationships. In H. H. Kelley, E. Berscheid, A. Christensen, J. Harvey, T. Huston, & G. Levinger, et al. (Eds.), *Close relationships* (pp. 1–19). New York: Freeman.

Blumberg, G. G. (1999). Balancing the interests: The American Law Institute's treatment of child support. *Family Law Quarterly, 33*, 39–110.

Bow, J. N., & Quinnell, F. A. (2001). Psychologists' current practices and procedures in child custody evaluations: Five years after American Psychological Association guidelines. *Professional Psychology: Research and Practice, 32*, 261–268.

Bow, J. N., & Quinnell, F. A. (2004). Critique of child custody evaluations by the legal profession. *Family Court Review, 42*, 115–127.

Bradley, A. R. (2004). Child custody evaluations. In W. T. O'Donohue & E. R. Levensky (Eds.), *Handbook of forensic psychology: Resource for mental health and legal professionals* (pp. 233–243). Amsterdam: Elsevier.

Bramlett, M., & Mosher, W. (2002). Cohabitation, marriage and divorce and remarriage in the United States (DHHS Pub. No. PHS 2002–1998). *National Center for Health Statistics: Vital Health Statistics, 23*(22).

Braver, S. L., Ellman, I. M., & Fabricius, W. V. (2003). Relocation of children after divorce and children's best interests: New evidence and legal considerations. *Journal of Family Psychology, 17*, 206–219.

Braver, S. L., Wolchik, S. A., Sandler, I. N., Sheets, V. L., Fogas, B., & Bay, R. C. (1993). A longitudinal study of noncustodial parents: Parents without children. *Journal of Family Psychology, 7*, 9–23.

Bricklin, B. (1995). *The custody evaluation handbook*. New York: Brunner/Mazel.

Buchanan, C. M., Maccoby, E. E., & Dornbusch, S. M. (1996). *Adolescents after divorce*. Cambridge, MA: Harvard University Press.

Buchanan, C. M., & Williams, A. K. (2006). Custody issues. In G. G. Bear & K. M. Minke (Eds.), *Children's needs III: Development, prevention, and intervention* (pp. 759–770). Bethesda, MD: National Association of School Psychologists.

Buehler, C., & Gerard, J. M. (1995). Divorce law in the United States: A focus on child custody. *Family Relations, 44*, 439–458.

Butcher, J. N., & Miller, K. (1999). Personality assessment in personal injury litigation. In A. Hess & I. B. Weiner (Eds.), *Handbook of forensic psychology* (2nd ed., pp. 104–126). New York: Wiley.

Cancian, M., & Meyer, D. R. (1998). Who gets custody? *Demography, 35*, 147–157.

Conger, R. D., Ge, X., Elder, G. H., Lorenz, F. O., & Simons, R. L. (1994). Economic stress, coercive family process, and developmental problems of adolescents. *Child Development, 65*, 541–561.

Craig, R. J. (2005). *Personality-guided forensic psychology*. Washington, DC: American Psychological Association.

Czapanskiy, K. S. (2001). ALI child support principles: A lesson in public policy and truth-telling. *Duke Journal of Gender Law and Policy, 8*, 259–267.

Davies, P. T., Harold, G. T., Goeke-Morey, M. C., & Cummings, E. M. (2002). Child emotional security and interparental conflict. *Monographs of the Society for Research in Child Development, 67* (Serial No. 270).

DeGarmo, D. S., & Forgatch, M. S. (1997). Determinants of observed confidant support. *Journal of Personality and Social Psychology, 72*, 336–345.

Duncan, W. (2004). The development of the new Hague convention on the international recovery of child support and other forms of family maintenance. *Family Law Quarterly, 38*, 663–687.

Edin, K. (1995). Single mothers and child support: The possibilities and limits of child support policy. *Children and Youth Services Review, 17*, 203–230.

Edmon, S., Cole, D. A., & Howard, G. S. (1990). Convergent and discriminant validity of FACES-III: Family adaptability and cohesion. *Family Process, 29*, 95–103.

Ellis, E. M. (2000). *Divorce wars: Interventions with families in conflict*. Washington, DC: American Psychological Association.

Elrod, L. D. (2003). Raising the bar for lawyers who represent children: ABA standards of practice for custody cases. *Family Law Quarterly, 37*, 105–125.

Emery, R. E. (1999). Postdivorce family life for children: An overview of research and some implications for policy. In R. A. Thompson & P. R. Amato (Eds.), *The postdivorce family: Children, parenting, and society* (pp. 3–27). Thousand Oaks, CA: Sage.

Emery, R. E., Matthews, S. G., & Kitzmann, K. M. (1994). Child custody mediation and litigation: Parents' satisfaction and functioning one year after settlement. *Journal of Consulting and Clinical Psychology, 62*, 124–129.

Emery, R. E., & Wyer, M. M. (1987). Child custody mediation and litigation: An experimental evaluation of the experience of parents. *Journal of Consulting and Clinical Psychology, 55*, 179–186.

Fabricius, W. V. (2003). Listening to children of divorce: New findings that diverge from Wallerstein, Lewis, and Blakeslee. *Family Relations, 52*, 385–396.

Fabricius, W. V., & Braver, S. L. (2003). Non-child support expenditures on children by nonresidential divorced fathers: Results of a study. *Family Court Review, 41*, 321–336.

Fabricius, W. V., Braver, S. L., & Deneau, K. (2003). Divorced parents' financial support of their children's college expenses. *Family Court Review, 41*, 224–241.

Fabricius, W. V., & Hall, J. A. (2000). Young adults' perspectives on divorce. *Family and Conciliation Courts Review, 38*, 446–461.

Fine, M. A., & Fine, D. R. (1992). Recent changes in law affecting stepfamilies: Suggestions for legal reform. *Family Relations, 41*, 334–340.

Forgatch, M. S., Patterson, G. R., & Ray, J. A. (1996). Divorce and boys' adjustment problems: Two paths with a single model. In E. M. Hetherington & E. A. Blechman (Eds.), *Stress, coping, and resiliency in children and the family* (pp. 67–105). Mahwah, NJ: Erlbaum.

Fox, G. L., & Kelly, R. F. (1995). Determinants of child custody arrangements at divorce. *Journal of Marriage and the Family, 57*, 693–708.

Freeman, R. B., & Waldfogel, J. (2001). Dunning delinquent dads: The effects of child support enforcement policy on child support receipt by never married women. *Journal of Human Resources, 36*, 207–225.

Furstenberg, F. F., Jr., Morgan, S. P., & Allison, P. D. (1987). Paternal participation and children's wellbeing after marital dissolution. *American Sociological Review, 52*, 695–701.

Gardner, R. A. (1997). An instrument for objectivity comparing parent disciplinary capacity in child-custody disputes. *Journal of Divorce and Remarriage, 27*, 1–15.

Gardner, R. A. (1998). *The parental alienation syndrome* (2nd ed.). Creskill, NJ: Creative Therapeutics.

Garfinkel, I., McLanahan, S., & Wallerstein, J. (2004). Visitation and child support guidelines: A comment on Fabricius and Braver. *Family Court Review, 42*, 342–349.

Gonzales, N. A., Pitts, S. C., Hill, N. E., & Roosa, M. W. (2000). A mediational model of the impact of interparental conflict on child adjustment in a multi-ethnic, low-income sample. *Journal of Family Psychology, 14*, 365–379.

Grall, T. S. (2006). *Custodial mothers and fathers and their child support: 2003* (Current Population Reports, P60–230). Washington, DC: U.S. Census Bureau.

Grych, J. H., Harold, G. T., & Miles, C. J. (2003). A prospective investigation of appraisals as mediators of the link between interparental conflict and child adjustment. *Child Development, 74*, 1176–1193.

Hagen, M. A., & Castagna, N. (2001). The real numbers: Psychological testing in custody evaluations. *Professional Psychology: Research and Practice, 32*, 269–271.

Hans, J. D. (2002). Step-parenting after divorce: Stepparents' legal position regarding custody, access, and support. *Family Relations, 51*, 301–307.

Harris, L. J. (2001). The ALI child support principles: Incremental changes to improve the lot of children and residential parents. *Duke Journal of Gender Law and Policy, 8*, 245–257.

Hernandez, P. M., Beller, A. H., & Graham, J. W. (1995). Changes in the relationship between child support payments and educational attainment of offspring, 1979–1988. *Demography, 32*, 249–260.

Hetherington, E. M., Bridges, M., & Insabella, G. M. (1998). What matters? What does not? Five perspectives on the association between marital transitions and children's adjustment. *American Psychologist, 53*, 167–184.

Hetherington, E. M., & Kelly, J. (2002). *For better or for worse: Divorce reconsidered*. New York: Norton.

Hetherington, E. M., & Stanley-Hagen, M. (1999). The adjustment of children with divorced parents: A risk and resiliency perspective. *Journal of Child Psychology and Psychiatry, 40*, 129–140.

High-conflict custody cases: Reforming the system for children. *Family Court Review 39*, 146–157.

Hysjulien, C., Wood, B., & Benjamin, G. A. H. (1994). Child custody evaluations: A review of methods used in litigation and alternative dispute resolution. *Family and Conciliation Courts Review, 32*(4), 466–489.

Johnston, J. R. (2005). Children of divorce who reject a parent and refuse visitation: Recent research and social policy implications for the alienated child. *Family Life Quarterly, 38*(4), 757–775.

Karras, D., & Berry, K. K. (1985). Custody evaluations: A critical review. *Professional Psychology: Research and Practice, 16*, 76–85.

Kelly, J. B. (1996). A decade of divorce mediation research: Some answers and questions. *Family and Conciliation Courts Review, 31*, 373–385.

Kelly, J. B., & Lamb, M. E. (2000). Using child development research to make appropriate custody and access decisions for young children. *Family and Conciliation Courts Review, 38*, 297–311.

Kelly, J. B., & Lamb, M. E. (2003). Developmental issues in relocation cases involving young children: When, whether, and how? *Journal of Family Psychology, 17*, 193–205.

Kelly, R. F., Redenbach, L., & Rinaman, W. C. (2005). Determinants of sole and joint physical custody arrangements in a national sample of divorces. *Journal of Family Law, 19*, 25–43.

Kiecolt-Glaser, J. K., McGuire, L., Robles, T. F., & Glaser, R. (2002). Psychoneuroimmunology: Psychological influences on immune functioning and health. *Journal of Consulting and Clinical Psychology, 70*, 537–547.

King, V. (1994). Nonresident father involvement and child well-being: Can dads make a difference? *Journal of Family Issues, 15*, 78–96.

King, V., & Soboleski, J. M. (2006). Nonresident fathers' contributions to adolescent well-being. *Journal of Marriage and the Family, 68*, 537–557.

Kirkland, K. D., & Kirkland, K. D. (2001). Frequency of child custody evaluation complaints and related disciplinary action: A survey of state and professional psychology boards. *Professional Psychology: Research and Practice, 32*, 171–174.

Knox, V. W. (1996). The effects of child support payments on developmental outcomes for elementary school-age children. *Journal of Human Resources, 31*, 816–840.

Lamb, M. E., Sternberg, K., & Thompson, R. A. (1997). The effects of divorce and custody arrangements on children's behavior, development, and adjustment. *Family and Conciliation Courts Review, 35*, 393–404.

Laumann-Billings, L., & Emery, R. E. (2000). Distress among young adults from divorced families. *Journal of Family Psychology, 14*, 671–687.

Leventhal, B., Kelman, J., Galatzer-Levy, R. M., & Hraus, L. (1999). Divorce, custody, and visitation in mid-childhood. In R. M. Galatzer-Levy & L. Kraus (Eds.), *The scientific basis of child custody decisions* (pp. 205–225). New York: Wiley.

Lin, I. (2000). Perceived fairness and compliance with child support obligations. *Journal of Marriage and the Family, 62*, 388–398.

Maccoby, E., & Mnookin, R. H. (1992). *Dividing the child: Social and legal dilemmas of custody.* Cambridge, MA: Harvard University Press.

Marsiglio, W., Amato, P., Day, R. D., & Lamb, M. E. (2000). Scholarship on fatherhood in the 1990s and beyond. *Journal of Marriage and the Family, 62*, 1173–1191.

Martinez, C. R., Jr., & Forgatch, M. S. (2002). Adjusting to change: Linking family structure transitions to parenting and boys' adjustment. *Journal of Family Psychology, 16*, 107–117.

McConaughy, S. H., & Achenbach, T. M. (1996). Contributions of a child interview to multimethod assessment of children with EBD and LD. *School Psychology Review, 25*(1), 24–39.

McLanahan, S. S., & Sandefur, G. (1994). *Growing up with a single parent.* Cambridge, MA: Harvard University Press.

McLanahan, S. S., Seltzer, J. A., Hanson, T. L., & Thompson, E. (1994). Child support enforcement and child well-being: Greater security or greater conflict. In I. Garfinkel, S. S. McLanahan, & P. K. Robins (Eds.), *Child support and child well-being* (pp. 239–256). Washington, DC: Urban Institute Press.

Melli, M. S., & Brown, P. R. (1994). The economics of shared custody: Developing an equitable formula for dual residence. *Houston Law Review, 31*, 543–584.

Melton, G., Petriala, J., Poythress, N., & Slobogin, C. (1997). *Psychological evaluations for the courts* (2nd ed.). New York: Guilford Press.

Menard, A., & Turetsky, V. (1999). Child support enforcement and domestic violence. *Juvenile and Family Court Journal, 50*, 27–38.

Menno, J. V. (2003). View from the bench. *Family Court Review, 41*, 362–366.

Meyer, D. R., & Garasky, S. (2003). Custodial fathers: Myths, realities, and child support policy. *Journal of Marriage and the Family, 55*, 73–89.

Montgomery, M. J., Anderson, E. R., Hetherington, E. M., & Clingempeel, W. G. (1992). Patterns of courtship for remarriage: Implications for child adjustment and parent-child relationships. *Journal of Marriage and the Family, 54*, 686–698.

Morgan, L. W. (2004). The economics of child support guidelines: A short examination of the "cost shares" model. *American Journal of Family Law, 18*, 149–154.

O'Donohue, W., & Bradley, A. R. (1999). Conceptual and empirical issues in child custody evaluations. *Clinical Psychology: Science and Practice, 6*, 313.

Pearson, J., & Thoennes, N. (2000). Supervised visitation: The families and their experiences. *Family and Conciliation Courts Review, 38*(1), 123–142.

Personal Responsibility and Work Opportunity Reconciliation Act of 1996, Pub. L. 104–193, 110 Stat. 2105.

Peterson, J., & Nord, C. W. (1990). The regular receipt of child support: A multistep process. *Journal of Marriage and the Family, 52,* 539–551.

Peterson, R. R. (1996). A re-evaluation of the economic consequences of divorce. *American Sociological Review, 61,* 528–536.

Pruett, M. K., & Johnston, J. R. (2004). Therapeutic mediation with high conflict parents: Effective models and strategies. In J. Folberg, A. Milne, & P. Salem (Eds.), *Divorce and family mediation: Models, techniques, and applications* (pp. 92–111). New York: Guilford Press.

Pruett, M. K., Williams, T. Y., Insabella, G., & Little, T. D. (2003). Family and legal indicators of child adjustment to divorce among families with young children. *Journal of Family Psychology, 17,* 169–180.

Raley, R. K., & Wildsmith, E. (2004). Cohabitation and children's family instability. *Journal of Marriage and the Family, 66,* 210–219.

Rogers, R. M. (1999). Wisconsin-style and income shares child support guidelines: Excessive burdens and flawed economic foundation. *Family Law Quarterly, 33,* 135–156.

Roll, S., Lockwood, J., & Roll, E. (1981). *Preliminary manual: Parent attachment structured interview.* Albuquerque, NM: Author.

Saposnek, D. (1998). *Mediating child custody disputes.* San Francisco: Jossey-Bass.

Seltzer, J. A. (1994). Consequences of marital dissolution for children. *Annual Review of Sociology, 20,* 235–358.

Seltzer, J. A. (1998). Father by law: Effects of joint legal custody on nonresident fathers' involvement with children. *Demography, 35,* 135–146.

Seltzer, J. A., Schaeffer, N. C., & Charng, H. (1989). Family ties after divorce: The relationship between visiting and paying child support. *Journal of Marriage and the Family, 51,* 1013–1031.

Siegel, J. C., & Langford, J. S. (1998). MMPI-2 validity indicators and suspected parental alienation syndrome. *American Journal of Forensic Psychology, 14,* 55–63.

Simons, R. L. (Eds.). (1996). *Understanding differences between divorced and intact families: Stress, interaction, and child outcome.* Thousand Oaks, CA: Sage.

Social Security Act (1935). ch. 531, 49 Stat. 620.

Solomon, J., & George, C. (1999a). The development of attachment in separated and divorced families: Effects of overnight visitation, parent and couple variables. *Attachment and Human Development, 1,* 2–33.

Solomon, J., & George, C. (1999b). The effects of attachment of overnight visitation in divorced and separated families: A longitudinal follow-up. In S. Soloman & C. George (Eds.), *Attachment disorganization* (pp. 243–264). New York: Guilford Press.

Stahl, P. M. (2005). The benefits and risks of child custody evaluations making recommendations to the court: A response to Tippins and Wittmann. *Family Court Review, 43,* 260–265.

Strong, D. R., Greene, R. L., Hoppe, C., Johnston, T., & Olesin, N. (1999). Taxometric analysis of impression management and self-deception on the MMPI-2 in child custody litigations. *Journal of Personality Assessment, 73,* 1–18.

Teachman, J. D. (1991). Who pays? Receipt of child support in the United States. *Journal of Marriage and the Family, 53,* 759–772.

Tein, J.-Y., Sandler, I. N., & Zautra, A. J. (2000). Stressful life events, psychological distress, coping, and parenting of divorced mothers: A longitudinal study. *Journal of Family Psychology, 14,* 27–41.

Tippins, T. M., & Wittmann, J. P. (2005). Empirical and ethical problems with custody recommendations: A call for clinical humility and judicial vigilance. *Family Court Review, 43*(2), 193–222.

Uniform Interstate Family Support Act. (1992). 9 Part 1 U.L.A 77.

Uniform Marriage and Divorce Act. (1970). 9A U.L.A. 205 5 405.

U.S. Census Bureau. (2000). *Statistical abstract of the United States.* Washington, DC: U.S. Government Printing Office.

U.S. Department of Health and Human Services. (2005). *Handbook on child support enforcement.* Washington, DC: Author.

Venohr, J. C., & Griffith, T. E. (2005). Child support guidelines: Issues and reviews. *Family Court Review, 43*, 415–428.

Venohr, J. C., & Williams, R. G. (1999). The implementation and periodic review of state child support guidelines. *Family Law Quarterly, 33*, 7–37.

Warshak, R. A. (2000). Blanket restrictions: Overnight contact between parents and young children. *Family and Conciliation Courts Review, 38*, 422–445.

Weiss, Y., & Willis, R. J. (1985). Children as collective goods and divorce settlements. *Journal of Labor Economics, 3*, 268–292.

Whiteside, M. F., & Becker, B. J. (2000). Parental factors and the young child's postdivorce adjustment: A meta-analysis with implications for parenting arrangements. *Journal of Family Psychology, 14*, 5–26.

CHAPTER 28

Child Maltreatment

Christine Wekerle, Harriet L. MacMillan, Eman Leung, and Ellen Jamieson

It was a sunny day in a popular vacation spot, crowded with children and adults in the pool area, some swimming, some lying about on chairs, and some in conversation. A mom, lying face down, was oblivious to the world. A dad, sitting in a nearby chair, seemed quite uncomfortable. Perhaps he did not favor the heat. His daughter, about 12 years old, was restlessly standing in front of him. She approached and sat on his knee, moving from side to side. Finally, she got up, turned around and straddled him. The frankness of that straddle, his delay in responding to this movement, and my audible response of shock put this man in motion and he roughly pushed her off him. The child's face registered no emotional reaction, just a watchful blankness. The child left her dad and came in the pool beside me. I tried to make friendly conversation—"Hi." "The pool water is really warm!" "Do you like to swim?" The total lack of response from the child in any dimension indicating registering the prior event or registering my communication efforts led me to entertain several hypotheses: non-English speaker, hearing-impaired, cognitively delayed, or fearful of connecting to another (the first three could later be ruled out). After a little while, the father said words to the mother. He called his daughter. Child and father walked away together, leaving the mother behind who had remained frozen in her ideal tanning position.

Child maltreatment disturbs your peace. If it is clear, it sets you in motion. If it is unclear, it may nag, percolate, and unsettle you in the background workings of your mind. You struggle because the pieces of information do not align well and, likely, the child is not talking. For the safety of the child, you move carefully through ruling out more hypotheses than is typical. In child clinics, the assessment question may come as broadly as "What is going on?" and in person, your colleague seems at a loss. The clinician may observe or have reported such behaviors as public self-stimulation, "daydreaming" during a conversation, back arching from a light touch, aggression or emotional overreactivity at the slightest provocation, or selective mutism. As hyperactivity is a nonspecific symptom, relevant to Attention-Deficit/Hyperactivity Disorder, genetic syndrome disorders, children of newly clinically depressed mothers, and so on, maltreatment leaves scant symptom

The authors wish to acknowledge research funding from the Canadian Institutes of Health Research, the Center of Excellence in Child and Youth Mental Health @ CHEO, the Ontario Women's Health Council, and the Ontario Ministry of Child and Youth Services. For their great support on this chapter, we thank Jennifer Fong and Maria Chen.

profiles. This is due to the possibility of maltreatment affecting every developmental domain—difficulties sustaining attention and learning, behavioral hyperactivity and aggression, depression, anxious clinging to or overreaching with friendly adults, nonnormative fears, and bizarre or nonnormative behaviors—potentially layered on top of preexisting problems.

Childhood maltreatment is no disorder. It is the result of adult action serving adult purposes or stemming from adult deficits. People who interact regularly with maltreated children may note that things seem "off." Clinical examples include a kindergarten child repeatedly referring to himself as "having the devil inside him," and teachers describing a child sibling pair as "weird" given their unusual behaviors (e.g., licking a classmate's hand) and another child as "Dr. Jekyll/Mr. Hyde" given his extreme behavioral and affective changes. For other children, their adaptation may not include individual signs, but may take on compulsive caregiving of younger siblings, sublimating their own distress. Other children may find avenues for more positive development by becoming essentially members of another family, be it via other family members, school and work relations, or in their neighborhood. Finally, for some children, symptomatology is not evident or may be delayed or very restricted in its expression, even in the context of high-impact trauma (e.g., witnessing one parent's murder by the other parent) or chronic maltreatment. Regardless of symptom expression, we have child protection laws acknowledging that it is not the child's responsibility to fend off violence from adults.

Professionals wrestle with the legal requirement to report suspected maltreatment and the ethical requirement to intervene and document concerns. Documentation is one way to establish a pattern of concerns, even if the initial report is not investigated or substantiated by child protective services (CPS). With clear injury patterns, indications of patterned behavior, and verbal disclosures, the clarity of reasonable *suspicion* of abuse, neglect, or risk increases. Professional hesitation regarding reporting and quantifying confidently "reasonable suspicion" in less than clear situations has reasonable grounds. These include concern about civil litigation challenging "good faith" reporting; the fact that the short-term and long-term child effects of CPS involvement have received little research in its 30 years of existence; the concern that the only CPS service offered will be investigation; and the puzzlement, given current clinic wait-lists, that most children are returned to the home within 6 months. Further, there is a community threshold for reportable abuse or neglect within the practical reality of limited resources.

Erring on the side of caution is a prudent approach when considering that U.S. figures of mortality from child abuse are likely underestimates (Herman-Giddens et al., 1999). Using North Carolina medical examiner data over a 10-year period, nearly 60% of fatal cases were recorded as due to battery, not child abuse specifically. The probable assailant was male (66%) and a biological parent (63%). It is generally accepted that much serious abuse and neglect go undetected by formal systems. The World Health Organization (WHO) estimates that 57,000 children die yearly from maltreatment fatalities (Krug, Mercy, Dahlberg, & Zwi, 2002). In the United States, falling is the most common reason given initially, with the child being found unresponsive as the next most prevalent (Collins & Nichols, 1999).

Most deaths occur when the mother and her unrelated boyfriend live in the home (Stiffman et al., 2002). Another large category is neglect deaths from starvation, exposure to heat or cold, and failure to safeguard. As a risk factor for childhood death, any protection system involvement for neglect or physical and/or sexual abuse dramatically increases mortality, especially for children under 1 year of age (Sabotta & Davis, 1992).

When maltreatment is repeated, we can only acknowledge all of our system failures, from public monitoring to front-line professionals (community recreation, faith-based institutions, education, health, substance abuse, mental health, hospital emergency, police, domestic violence shelters, etc.) to child protective services. Part of our citizenry social contract is to provide a safety net for expectant and at-risk parents, and government is the ultimate partner in providing leadership in this.

Most United Nations member states have committed to an action plan to uphold the child's human rights to be protected from abuse and to have the basic necessities of life provided. The U.S. surgeon general's "Healthy People 2010" targets specific reductions in rates of child abuse and related fatalities and research goals of understanding the magnitude of new cases and evaluating the impact of existing interventions. Child maltreatment is properly regarded as an issue of human rights, public health, mental and physical illness prevention, and economics. The remainder of this chapter addresses the definition and scope of the problem of maltreatment, using brief case descriptions to illustrate these. An overview of theoretical models and current knowledge on outcomes is presented. Finally, current gold standards in intervention are highlighted. We end with thoughts on future directions for research and practice and provide a summary for this chapter.

DEFINITION AND SCOPE OF THE PROBLEM OF CHILD MALTREATMENT

Barber and Sibert (2000, p. 743) note, "The initial recognition of the possibility of abuse is in some ways the most important step . . . and one should never walk alone" in the child protection process. Thus, the first step is to have maltreatment in mind as an active possible hypothesis to rule out, as well as to know local applicable laws and key consultation experts. U.S. figures (Federal Fiscal Year, October 2004–September 2005) place the annual substantiated rate of abuse or neglect at about 12.10/1,000 children. Most (75%) are first-time victims. The recurrence rate for substantiated abuse over 6 months is about 6% (U.S. Department of Health and Human Services [USDHHS], 2007). Canadian rates of entries into child protection, which may reflect substantiated high risk as well as substantiated discrete events, are about 22/1,000 children (Canadian Incidence Study; Trocmé et al., 2005). Consistent over recent years, neglect is the most common form presenting to CPS (62.8%), with psychological abuse the least frequent in the United States (7.1%) and sexual abuse the least frequent in Canada (3%). With the exception of sexual abuse, parents are the vast majority of perpetrators, with mothers somewhat higher than fathers (83.4% abuse by a parent acting alone or with another person; USDHHS, 2007). Dramatic gender differences exist only with sexual abuse, the majority being female victims and the majority of perpetrators being male. Younger children show the highest victimization rate (16.1/1,000 children, birth to age 3), with decreasing rates across ages to teens. However, substantial levels of maltreatment do occur in adolescence (12–15 year-olds: rate of 10.2/1,000; 16–17 year-olds: rate of 6.2/1,000; USDHHS, 2007). It should be noted that victims in CPS have an estimated 6-month maltreatment recurrent rate of 94.6%, as determined by the 2006 Child and Family Services Reviews (USDHHS, 2007). Further, community survey data suggest that physical abuse is more than 40 times more prevalent and sexual abuse is more than 15 times more prevalent than official rates (Wekerle, Miller, Wolfe, & Spindel, 2006).

Neglect

Neglect is challenging to define as it covers a wide range of failure-to-care events. Neglect can be willful disregard of child needs or more passive acts of omission. Neglect examples include abandonment or desertion; failure to provide a home or a safe, sanitary shelter; supervisory neglect; neglect of personal hygiene; refusal or delay in providing normative health care (e.g., specific concern visits, such as ear infection, maintaining recommended immunization schedule, routine dental care); nutritional neglect; failure to meet standards for education (e.g., high absenteeism); and failure to meet special needs (e.g., failure to treat asthma from secondary smoke, failure to treat learning disorders with educational support). Exposure to physical hazards (e.g., exposed wiring, broken glass, nonsecured and loaded guns, illegal drugs, dangerous or unhygienic pets, asking child to perform dangerous activities, driving with child while intoxicated) is another area of concern. Neglect is a chronic condition with high recidivism, experiencing the greatest rate of placement in out-of-home care. In the United States, parents are perpetrators in 86.6% of cases. Neglect is more prevalent among younger caregivers, households with a primary male caregiver, and families with low socioeconomic status (Trocmé et al., 2005).

The U.S. case-level statistics indicate that neglect accounts for 60% of children receiving clinical services (USDHHS, 2007). The rate of cases of neglect reported to CPS is also around 60%, or 7.4/1,000 children (USDHHS, 2007). The most common form of investigated neglect is "failure to supervise leading to physical harm," where the child suffered or was at substantial risk of suffering physical harm because of the caregiver's failure to monitor and protect the child adequately. This form of neglect constitutes 37% of the substantiated forms of maltreatment (3.06/1,000 children) among new reports to CPS (Trocmé et al., 2005).

Research indicates that caregiver substance abuse is strongly linked to neglect (Takayam, Wolfe, & Coulter, 1998; Wekerle & Wall, 2002; Yampolskaya & Banks, 2006). Among a range of caregiver vulnerability factors, caregiver substance abuse was the single best predictor of neglect, although the composite of vulnerabilities was the best overall predictor (Wekerle, Wall, Leung, & Trocmé, 2006) after controlling for other child and parent characteristics. Other significant single predictors were socioeconomic disadvantage, caregiver history of childhood maltreatment, and caregiver lack of social support. Recent caregiver violent partnership interacted with total caregiver vulnerability, indicating an exacerbating impact, more than doubling the likelihood of a substantiated versus nonsubstantiated neglect finding. Addressing caregiver vulnerabilities early on, when the family first comes to the attention of CPS, seems a critical move.

Some definitions of neglect also include emotional neglect (a marked indifference to children's need for affection, attention, and emotional support), as well as exposure to chronic or extreme spousal abuse or intimate partner violence (IPV). These subtypes can be summarized as involving three major forms of neglect: (1) lack of emotional support, affection, or both; (2) lack of protection from family conflict, violence, or both; and (3) lack of protection from community violence (Wekerle et al., 2006). A recent epidemiological survey of randomly selected teens on the active caseload of an urban center found that the teens reported higher prevalence for emotional neglect items than physical neglect items, as measured by the Childhood Trauma Questionnaire (Bernstein & Fink, 1998). Item examples include often or sometimes "did not have enough to eat" (37%) and often or sometimes "parent too drunk/high to care for them" (27%; Wekerle et al., 2006).

Case Illustration

Robert, age 4, was observed playing on the roof of his house by his neighbors, who called the child protective agency. When the social worker investigated the home situation, she found Robert and two other siblings, Nancy, age 5, and Alice, age 2, living in unsafe and filthy conditions in the care of their mother, age 30, and her boyfriend, who was the children's stepfather. The mother, Carol, reported that her partner, Frank, had a cocaine habit and used much of what she received from social assistance to buy drugs. He was physically and verbally abusive to her and threatened to hurt the children if she told anyone about the abuse that she was experiencing. They had been together for 1 year; previously, Carol had been with another man, the father of two of the three children, who had also been abusive to her. Carol had grown up in a home where she had been sexually abused by a maternal uncle; when she disclosed this to her mother, she was not believed, and so left home at the age of 15 years. She also witnessed violence between her parents. Carol dropped out of school in grade 10 and had hopes of eventually finishing her education, but was struggling to first look after the children. She acknowledged that she occasionally left the children locked in a room together while she went out to buy groceries; it was during one of these occasions that Robert had climbed out the window onto the roof.

Physical Abuse

According to the World Health Organization (WHO, 2006), physical abuse is defined as the intentional use of physical force against a child that results in, or has a high likelihood of resulting in, harm to the child's health, survival, development, or dignity. This includes exposure to such behaviors as hitting, beating, kicking, shaking, biting, strangling, scalding, burning, poisoning, and suffocating. Some physical violence against children in the home occurs in the context of parental discipline attempts in response to normative child behaviors such as constant crying, whining, toilet-training issues, defiance, and sibling fighting. Closed-fisted strikes, striking with a hard object (belt, board, bat), and throwing the child into objects (furniture, wall) are extremes on a continuum of corporal punishment. Public debate continues about whether spanking constitutes a form of maltreatment; however, there is growing consensus that certain types of spanking—for example, of a teenager, or spanking resulting in injury, such as a bruise—is abusive. Multiple bruising is more consistent with abuse, with slap marks being common; evidence of severe physical injury describes a minority of substantiated physical abuse cases. In the United States, 16.6% of cases were physical abuse (about 2/1,000 children; USDHHS, 2007). In Canada, the rate of substantiated physical abuse (or deemed at high risk of) was 5/1,000 children: 41% were hit with a hand; 21% shaken, pushed, or thrown; 19% were hit with objects; and 8% were punched, kicked, or bitten (Trocmé et al., 2005).

The U.S. Developmental Victimization Survey (Finkelhor, Ormrod, Turner, & Hamby, 2005) found that over half of community children (age 2–17) surveyed experienced a physical assault in the past year. Poly-victimization (four or more different types of events) best described 18% of surveyed children (Finkelhor, Ormrod, & Turner, 2007). One state population survey found physical abuse in the form of kicking, slapping, or punching was most common among teenagers (Theodore et al., 2005). Also, shaking of children less than 2 years of age was reported by caregivers more often than previously recognized. It was estimated that for every child who sustains a serious medical injury as a result of shaking, an estimated 150 children may have been shaken yet were undetected. These authors noted that comparing their survey rate to those from the National Child Abuse and Neglect Data System places physical abuse at more than 40 times higher than the official state-level statistic. Bruising is suspicious for abuse when the marks occur are recent, when the bruising is over nonbony areas (ears, abdomen, anterior chest), and when bruise patterns capture the image of an object (e.g., a hand). Considerable force is needed to cause a bone fracture; this type of abuse is seen mostly in children 6 months and under (Barber & Sibert, 2000). Although most bruising is the result of physically abusive discipline, some actions are more sadistic and planful.

One type of physical abuse more likely to present in hospital emergency rooms and to hospital-based abuse and neglect specialty teams is Munchausen by proxy syndrome (MBPS), in which the caregiver (typically the mother) purposefully makes the child ill (e.g., induces vomiting, administers poison), fabricates the medical complaint and/or psychological symptoms, or subjects the child to medical testing repeatedly, including invasive procedures. Moving from expert to expert increases the amount of medical testing. Fabricated and induced illness is also a diagnostic term (Craft & Hall, 2004), as is fictitious disorder by proxy (*DSM-IV-TR;* American Psychological Association, 2004). These conditions are considered uncommon, although their incidence is unknown.

Although there is no clear understanding of parental motivation in these cases, it has been suggested that such behaviors result from a desire to be recognized as a caring parent, to gain positive adult attention from medical professionals, to prevent a partnership breakup, to avoid criminal culpability, and for secondary economic gain. Others may witness the illness crisis but not the initiation of the medical event, yet the MBPS caregiver is present consistently. Girls and boys seem equally targeted. Younger children tend to be the focus, although MBPS can span childhood and include participation of a teenager in self-harm. The symptoms cease or decrease when the child is separated from the MBPS caregiver. In a study on male MPBS caregivers, perpetration of physical abuse (e.g., bone fractures) or sexual abuse emerged in the background data collection (Meadow, 1998). Fathers often themselves had Munchausen syndrome or a somatoform or factitious disorder; no father was in regular employment or had been in long-term employment, and about a third of fathers were receiving a disability allowance. Unlike MBPS mothers, fathers were noted by hospital staff as overbearing, aggressive, and quick-tempered. Other situations more likely to occur in MBPS families included unusual pet deaths, home fires, and formal complaints filed by a parent about the hospital.

In a British study that used covert video recordings of suspected MBPS in a hospital ($N = 39$ children; median age 9 months), evidence of abuse (suffocation, poisoning, arm breaking) was captured in the majority of cases. Risk of abuse extended to other children in these families. About 30% of siblings had died suddenly and unexpectedly (most were previously categorized as sudden infant deaths); abuse was documented in a further 36% (Southall, Plunkett, Banks, Falkov, & Samuels, 1997; see article for case examples of sequential observation notes from recordings). Compared with controls, the abused children were less likely to have been born prematurely and more likely to present with bleeding from the nose or mouth, and more of the abusive parents were diagnosed as having personality disorders. These parents were not deemed psychotic; they were observed to attack their children in the absence of challenging child behavioral conditions (e.g., when child was asleep). Maternal allegations of their own maltreatment or the presence of domestic violence were common. The likelihood of a problematic childhood is strengthened by the finding that over 80% of the mothers in one study showed insecure adult attachment of a dismissing or disorganized type, reflecting an undervaluing of close relationships and a frightened and frightening caregiver (Adshead & Bluglass, 2005). Although only a minority of these mothers scored in the personality disorder range, about half showed clinically elevated scores, mostly on Cluster B personality problems (*DSM-IV-TR;* American Psychiatric Association, 2000). Given the planful and persistent nature of this behavior and the harm to the children, the potential role of antisocial and dissociative parental tendencies and subdisorder level of clinical issues need to be studied.

In one follow-up study of maternal MBPS ($n = 17$) with coordinated intervention for the individual (offending) mother and family, the majority of children were functioning reasonably well in their biological family homes (Berg & Jones, 1999). Parents who persistently denied abuse and culpability or had a severe parental personality disorder were not considered suitable for treatment; in these cases, alternative care (fostering, adoption) was maintained. Despite the severity of the initial abuse, in other cases family reunification was achieved and maintained in the context of treatment with attachment-based psychotherapy, cognitive-behavior therapy, and systemic family therapy, along with in-depth assessments of child outcomes, intensive liaison with key professionals local to the family, and involvement of other family members and friends in the treatment process. One of the

13 treatment cases re-presented with MSBP. As these children ranged from 2.5 to 12 years at the 2-year follow-up mark, what remains unclear is the impact of developmental level on outcome and recidivism assessment. Full assessment of sibling outcomes and longer term follow-up are important research goals. For instance, when all siblings are considered, reabuse rates of 20% have been reported (Davis et al., 1998).

It should be noted that criminal and clinical approaches to MPBS are distinct, with intentionality difficult to confirm and more central to legal objectives (Pankratz, 2006). It is important to consider in MSBP, and indeed in all forms of maltreatment, that positive, appropriate, and affectionate parent behavior is likely to be observed or reported. Observational studies of parenting have clearly shown that aversive parenting and positive affect are independent (Solomon & George, 1999). In the vast majority of substantiated abuse cases, parents do declare that they love their child. Affective switching and reactivity are prominent in problematic personality styles, as well as in personality, mood, and anxiety disorders. Careful attention to context is critical in understanding the range of parental behaviors historically and currently demonstrated. Erring on the side of caution for child safety is a reasonable professional stance.

Case Illustration

Susan, age 9 years, was noted by her teacher to wear long sweaters even in summer. She presented as subdued and rarely interacted with the other children; in class, she seemed distracted at times. During an outdoor track and field day, when the children were in gym clothes with short sleeves, the teacher noted that Susan had two or three bruises brown to red in color on each forearm. When the teacher met with Susan and asked her about the bruises, Susan said that she had fallen off her bicycle. In fact, the injuries were not consistent with such an explanation; they fit the pattern of grab marks. The teacher was alert to the fact that these physical marks did not fit with a fall from a bicycle and contacted the local child protection agency.

Psychological and Emotional Abuse

According to the WHO (2006), emotional abuse involves both isolated incidents and a pattern of failure over time on the part of the caregiver to provide a developmentally appropriate and supportive environment. Acts in this category may have a high probability of damaging the child's physical or mental health, or physical, mental, spiritual, moral, or social development. Acts include the restriction of movement; a pattern of belittling, blaming, threatening, frightening, discriminating against, or ridiculing; and other nonphysical forms of rejection or hostile treatment. In the United States, as a single type, the psychological abuse rate was .9/1,000 children in 2004 (USDHHS, 2005). In Canada, the rate of substantiated emotional abuse was 3/1,000 children in 2003 (Trocmé et al., 2005). Emotional abuse is considered to be an undercurrent to other types of maltreatment.

Case Illustration

Tiffany was a 15-year-old waiting to go to court for her sexual abuse victimization by her biological father. As part of a victim impact statement, she spoke of the severe impact of his emotional abuse and how it was connected to the sexual abuse. She recalled that only two hugs in her life from her dad were nonsexualized. There was an unwritten rule that you were not allowed to close or lock the bathroom door when you were using it. She was given many household jobs, living with a single dad. When she failed to comply according to his view, she was required to eat her dinner from the dog bowl. When younger, she was required to kneel in a corner for long periods of time as a parental sanction. Her father played her compliance off her brother's, referring to who was his "best child" that day. Tiffany viewed her father as part of her biology, but never as a dad.

Exposure to Intimate Partner Violence

One type of child maltreatment that has been recognized only recently is exposure to IPV. Empirical studies examining this type of abuse first appeared in the 1980s (Kitzmann, Gaylord, Holt, & Kenny, 2003). The WHO defines IPV as

> any behaviour within an intimate relationship that causes physical, sexual or psychological harm to those in that relationship. It includes acts of physical aggression (slapping, hitting, kicking or beating), psychological abuse (intimidation, constant belittling or humiliation), forced sexual intercourse or any other controlling behaviour (isolating a person from family and friends, monitoring their movements and restricting access to information or assistance. (WHO Intimate Partner Violence and Alcohol Fact Sheet, page 1)

Most *reported* IPV is committed by men against women (Krug et al., 2002). Some surveys suggest that similar proportions of men and women experience IPV; however, abused women experience more physical and emotional impairment in relation to IPV than men (Archer, 2000; Tjaden & Thoennes, 2000). Violence against men by women and between same-sex partners is important for future research to consider at greater depth.

Two recent reviews underscore the broad range of health problems experienced by children exposed to IPV (Bair-Merritt, Blackstone, & Feudtner, 2006; Kitzmann et al., 2003). In a meta-analysis of 118 original studies, Kitzmann and colleagues examined the psychosocial effects of IPV; child outcomes included psychological, social, emotional and behavioral, and academic measures. About 63% of children who witnessed interparental violence were "doing more poorly" than the average child without such exposure. The authors emphasize that effect size did not depend on outcome type. Children who witnessed violence had levels of adjustment problems that were similar to those exposed to physical abuse. A second review that included 22 research articles examined the physical health outcomes of IPV exposure (Bair-Merritt et al., 2006). Exposure to IPV among children was associated with increased risk-taking behavior, such as alcohol abuse and risky sexual activities, during adolescence and adulthood.

There is substantial overlap between exposure to IPV and other types of maltreatment. In a review focusing on the co-occurrence of these exposures, Osofsky (2003) referred to several studies concluding that in homes where a woman is physically abused, 60% to 75% of children have also experienced physical abuse. Children residing with a mother exposed to physical abuse are at increased risk of sexual abuse, either by the mother's partner or a perpetrator outside the home (McCloskey, Figueredo, & Koss, 1995). Osofsky suggests that the co-occurrence of child maltreatment and IPV is important "from a risk and protective factors framework" since it may be more difficult to ensure adequate safety and protection in these families. As a general rule for all maltreatment concerns, it is essential when one subtype of child maltreatment is identified to consider the co-occurrence of other types of abuse and neglect. Research is clear on the predominance of severe male-to-female battering as opposed to female violence. However, child abuse and neglect is concerned with the negative impact on the child, irrespective of the sex of the primary perpetrator.

Case Illustration

Tyrone was working full time while his wife, Jan, was at home with their five young children. When Tyrone came home from work, he completely took over all child care activities. Jan was always finding fault with Tyrone and put him down in front of the children, calling him "fat," "useless," and "a loser," often within a string of expletives. The children, ranging in age from preschooler to preteen, were typically present during fights that often escalated to Jan's threatening to kill Tyrone and slapping, hitting, scratching, and pulling his hair. On several occasions she gave him a black eye, which was noted at his place of work. Tyrone always gave excuses for his marks, such as that he fell over something or the kids got carried away in rough-housing. The children would reenact these scenarios at school, causing concern among the teachers, and the youngest child would use inappropriate language, including swear words and "sex." Generally, Jan presented well outside the home for short durations, confining most of her explosiveness and inappropriate behaviors to the household, although she had a history of suicidal gestures. She alternated rage with a hopeless, helpless depression and would lock herself in her room for days. She had a history of suicidal gestures and had threatened self-harm in front of her children. She had no friends or social life outside of her family and had cut off all contact with her own and Tyrone's family. Eventually, Tyrone's boss confronted Tyrone on the repeated patterns of his injuries and harassing phone calls from Jan to his place of work. Tyrone's boss initiated intervention for Tyrone, which led to other system involvement.

Sexual Abuse

Sexual abuse is defined by the WHO as the involvement of a child in sexual activity that he or she does not fully comprehend, is unable to give informed consent to, or for which the child is not developmentally prepared, or else that violates the laws or social taboos of the society. Children can be sexually abused by both adults and other children who, by virtue of their age or stage of development, are in a position of responsibility, trust, or power over the victim. Authors of a U.S. community survey study noted that the rate of childhood sexual abuse generated from their self-report data is more than 15 times higher than the official state-level statistic (Theodore et al., 2005). For 2004, 1.2/1,000 children was the official sexual abuse rate (USDHHS, 2005), keeping the same rate over 5 years. Three-quarters of perpetrators were friends or neighbors. Victims are predominantly in the age 12 and up category, although 9% are in the 4- to 7-year category and 2% are in the 3 and under category. In Canada, for 2003, the rate was less than 1/1,000 children (Trocmé et al., 2005).

Case Illustration

Scott, age 9, lived with his mother, Susan, who worked part time as a teacher; his father, Brant, a physician; and his younger brother, Stephen, age 7. The family got along well together with no major stressors, although Brant worked long hours. Scott was an excellent student attending grade 3 and loved all sports. The couple had been married 5 years before Scott was born; both children were planned pregnancies. The family did many activities together; one night a week, Susan attended an art class and Brant worked in the local walk-in clinic. The parents arranged to have a 16-year-old son of close friends, Bruce, as a babysitter. This arrangement appeared to work well for about 6 weeks, until Scott became increasingly resistant to his mother's attending art class. On two occasions, he said that he felt ill and expressed tearfully that he wanted her to stay home. When Susan questioned Scott about his reluctance at her going out, Scott disclosed that on two occasions, Bruce had made him "suck his penis." Bruce had told Scott that this was the latest thing at school, and all teenagers were doing it. Scott became tearful while telling his mother what had happened; he expressed confusion and not wanting to do this, but Bruce was someone that he and all the other kids looked up to, so he thought it must be okay.

MALTREATMENT-ASSOCIATED MALADJUSTMENT

Childhood maltreatment is not a psychiatric disorder but an exposure. It is associated with a range of impairment in areas of basic functioning (eating, sleep), cognition (attention, memory, learning, academic achievement), affective style (modulation, regulation, mood disorders), motivation, and relationships. The challenges in managing tendencies toward both avoidance and overreactivity can create secondary problems in somatization, substance abuse, behavioral risk taking, and aggression toward oneself and others. These problems can persist, yielding implications for partnering and parenting.

The cycle of violence is a clinical reality, particularly when IPV is included with abuse and neglect, but, empirically, is of modest predictive significance in many studies. Across types of maladjustment, a parent's history of maltreatment no more than doubled his or her risk of abusive parenting. This suggests that parental psychiatric status and socioeconomic disadvantage are more weighty, proximal predictors, compared to a parent's own childhood history (Hurley, Chiodo, Leschied, & Whitehead, 2003; Renner & Slack, 2006; Sidebotham & Heron, 2006). In reviewing generational physical abuse (parent and offspring), most studies fell short methodologically, with the strongest study estimating a relative risk of 12.6 (Ertem, Leventhal, & Dobbs, 2000). In a longitudinal study that involved 224 former male victims of sexual abuse, who were identified based on a nationwide search of clinical and social service case records, 26 had subsequently committed sexual offenses, in most cases involving children outside their family (Salter et al., 2003). Thus, it would seem appropriate to consider a cycle of dysfunction and disadvantage, in addition to a cycle of violence.

Maltreatment is linked with lower school achievement (Wekerle & Wolfe, 2003), which has been accounted for by such factors as school engagement and social competence (e.g., Shonk & Cicchetti, 2001). One prospective, longitudinal study of substantiated abused and neglected children found that only 22% were deemed resilient in adulthood (e.g., no period of homelessness, consistent employment, and no juvenile or adult arrests), which significantly differed from matched controls (McGloin & Widom, 2001). As such, maltreatment may be one of the most modifiable barriers to living a "normal" life, including freedom from mental illness (DeBellis, 2001).

Psychiatric Disorders Associated with Childhood Maltreatment

Mood, anxiety, substance use, eating, and personality disorders in youth will be considered. Research in childhood maltreatment is uneven; most studies have focused on the areas of sexual and physical abuse, and on adults, mostly females. To provide an overview of the associated risk of the considered disorders, odds ratios have been compiled into a table on adult female functioning (Table 28.1).

Mood Disorders

Depressive symptoms have commonly been associated with childhood maltreatment (Danielson, de Arellano, Kilpatrick, Saunders, & Resnick, 2005; Gover, 2004; Meyerson, Long, Miranda, & Marx, 2002). As can be seen from Table 28.1, depression and anxiety problems far outstrip other maladjustment for female survivors of childhood maltreatment. In a community-based longitudinal study, individuals with a history of child abuse and neglect reported a two- to threefold increased likelihood of Dysthymic Disorder and Major Depressive Disorder during adolescence and young adulthood, as compared to nonabused individuals, even after statistically controlling for certain confounding variables (Brown, Cohen, Johnson, & Smailes, 1999). In a meta-analysis of child sexual abuse, victims exhibited significantly greater social withdrawal and internalizing symptoms, such as depressed mood, anhedonia (i.e., lack of pleasure in previously reinforcing activities, such as leisure, sex), and feelings of worthlessness and guilt (Kendall-Tackett et al., 1993). Other common emotional effects include guilt (i.e., feeling responsible for the abuse), helplessness and hopelessness, sleep disturbance, appetite disturbance, and low self-esteem. According to the *DSM-IV-TR* (APA, 2004), the symptoms of depression for children and adolescents are the same as those for adults. However, it is suggested that different symptoms may be more prominent at different ages.

Table 28.1   Adult (Female) Maladjustment Based on Childhood History of Maltreatment

Diagnoses/problems	Physical Abuse	Sexual Abuse	Emotional Abuse	Child Neglect
Anxiety	39.4 (33.8–45.1)	42.9 (35.3–50.4)		
Major Depressive Disorder	23.3 (18.2–28.3)	28.5 (20.8–36.2)	2.7 (2.3–3.2)	4.1 (1.9–8.8)
Alcohol abuse	9.9 (7.0–12.8)	10.3 (5.9–14.8)		1.65
Other substance use disorders	4.1 (2.7–5.5)	6.6 (2.5–10.7)		1.7 (1.5–2.0)
Posttraumatic Stress Disorder	1.03 (1.00–1.06)	10.2 (7.1–14.5)	5.67 (2.74–11.74)	3.5 (1.5–7.9)
Antisocial personality	4.1 (2.5–5.7)	4.7 (2.2–7.2)		1.32 (0.6–2.88)
Criminality	1.09 (1.01–1.19)	1.14 (1.02–1.27)	b = 2.06	1.7 (1.2–2.3)
Suicidal ideation	2.77 (1.26–6.12)			
Suicide attempt	1.64 (0.63–4.28)		b = 0.57	3.03 (1.11–8.33)

Note: Odds ratios and confidence intervals are presented unless otherwise specified. *Source:* H. A. Bergen, G. Martin, A. S. Richardson, S. Allison, & L. Roeger (2003); A. C. Boudewyn & J. H. Liem (1995); K. Brewer-Smyth, A. W. Burgess, & J. Shults (2004); J. Brown, P. Cohen, J. G. Johnson, & E. M. Smailes (1999); D. P. Chapman, C. L. Whitfield, V. J. Felitti, S. R. Dube, V. J. Edwards, & R. F. Anda (2003); E. Evans, K. Hawton, & K. Rodham (2005); C. Evren, S. Kural, & D. Cakmak (2005); J. G. Johnson, P. Cohen, J. Brown, E. M. Smailes, & D. P. Bernstein (1999); P. R. Joyce, J. M. McKenzie, S. E. Luty, R. T. Mulder, J. D. Carter, P. F. Sullivan, et al. (2003); S. J. Kaplan, D. P. Covitz, S. Salzinger, F. Mandel, M. Weiner, & V. Labruna (1999); D. G. Kilpatrick, K. J. Ruggiero, R. Acierno, B. E. Saunders, H. S. Resnick, C. L. Best, et al. (2000); D. G. Kilpatrick, K. J. Ruggiero, R. Acierno, B. E. Saunders, H. S. Resnick, & C. L. Best (2003); J. B. Kingree, D. Phan, & M. Thomson (2003); D. E. Nelson, G. K. Higginson, & J. A. Grant-Worley (1995); C. S. Widom (1999).

For example, somatic complaints and irritable mood are especially common during childhood and adolescence. Sleep and appetite disturbances in children and adolescents, as in adults, may vary, with some patients oversleeping and/or overeating (hypersomnia and hyperphagia, respectively), while others present with difficulty falling or staying asleep and/or having no appetite.

Anxiety Disorders

General symptoms of anxiety, nightmares, inappropriate fears of certain places, and clinging to parents are commonly found among maltreated children (Giardino & Giardino, 2002; Kendall-Tackett et al., 1993). Child inpatients with histories of exposure to abuse were described by their parents as being significantly more afraid of being left alone with others, exhibiting more suspicion, and getting more upset when touched, as compared to nonabused inpatients (Kolko, Moser, & Weldy, 1988). Based on self-report, sexually abused children were significantly more anxious than both clinical and normal controls (Mannarino, Cohen, & Gregor, 1989). Physical abuse has been shown to increase the likelihood for any anxiety disorder, as well as for Generalized Anxiety Disorder (GAD), indicating excessive worries (Flisher et al., 1997).

The initial response to single-event trauma may be hyperarousal, notably, hyperactivity, disorganization, and disruption in maintaining routines. However, as trauma is repeated, the adaptation response can become more complicated by dissociation, affective disturbance, and prolonged gaps in historical memory. With a single-event trauma, there is an emphasis on pathological fear and erroneous associations (people, object) with danger (Tolin & Foa, 2002). Most of the focus has been on the Posttraumatic Stress Disorder (PTSD) diagnosis, although subclinical symptom levels are important as they have been linked to significant functional impairment in youth (Carrion, Weems, Ray, & Reiss, 2002; Putnam, 1998). From age 8 to 10 years, PTSD reactions are more in line with adult diagnostic criteria, with females more likely to show PTSD-like responses and males to show aggression responses (Dyregrov & Yule, 2006).

Beyond the presence of a traumatic stressor, there are three main symptom clusters, with the *DSM* diagnostic requirement that criteria be met in each of the clusters. The three-cluster symptom model consists of (1) reexperiencing the trauma (e.g., flashbacks, nightmares); (2) avoidance of trauma-related cues and emotional numbing; and (3) problems with arousal (e.g., sleep onset, maintenance; exaggerated or diminished startle response). Some of these symptoms may manifest in other ways, including somatic symptoms (e.g., stomachache, headache to support escape or avoidance), self-destructiveness (e.g., cutting to support release from numbing), and hostility (e.g., lashing out under hyperarousal; sexual play as trauma-based reenactment).

In a clinical sample (most had multiple traumas and prior child protective services involvement), PTSD was commonly comorbid with other anxiety and mood disorders (Carrion et al., 2002). The most intense PTSD symptoms were irritability and anger, distressing dreams, and feelings of detachment from others. The most frequent symptoms were avoidance of trauma-related thoughts, feelings, and cues; distressing recollections; inability to recall important aspects of the trauma; distressing dreams; and difficulty concentrating. Full diagnosis for PTSD was predicted by severe and frequent hypervigilance, exaggerated startle, and detachment from others. The most common symptom cluster was reexperiencing or intrusions about the trauma. Clearly this symptom pattern of sleep and concentration difficulties must challenge the PTSD child and youth in school.

Similarly, in a study of randomly selected teens involved with the child protection system, reexperiencing was among the most common self-reported PTSD symptoms ("bad dreams or nightmares"; "remembering things that happened that I didn't like"). As is consistent with developmental level and abstract thinking about a shortened future, teens reported feeling a vague sense of impending doom ("feeling afraid something bad might happen"; Wekerle et al., 2006). In a study of teen inpatients, emotional abuse was the only consistent predictor of PTSD symptoms across all three clusters when considering all types of abuse and neglect simultaneously. Sexual abuse history also predicted the reexperiencing symptom cluster (Sullivan, Fehon, Andrew-Hyman, Lipschitz, & Grilo, 2006). Taken together, PTSD symptomatology may be as important to consider as the issue of meeting full criteria for the disorder. Given that the likelihood of meeting all three cluster criteria is greater in older children, current *DSM* criteria for PTSD may not be sensitive to the developmental manifestation in younger children. Symptomatology of PTSD has been shown empirically to mediate maltreatment and negative outcome (e.g., Risser, Hetzel-Riggin, Thomsen, & McCanne, 2006; Wekerle et al., 2001); therefore, targeting PTSD symptomatology is a fruitful intervention avenue.

Research has suggested that those with PTSD tend to have lengthier histories of maltreatment and/or broader exposure to violence (Deblinger, Steer, & Lippman, 1999; Linning & Kearney, 2004; Wood, Foy, Layne, Pynoos, & James, 2002). This may be why sexual abuse tends to predict PTSD diagnosis better than physical abuse, if both are present. Symptoms of PTSD may be associated with behavior inhibition problems (Ruchkin, Schwab-Stone, Koposov, Vermeiren, & Steiner, 2002). One study of youth from shelter facilities found that PTSD was comorbid with other mood or anxiety disorders, most notably dysthymia, major depression, GAD, panic with and without agoraphobia, and specific phobias (Linning & Kearney, 2004). In studies of adult PTSD, the majority of PTSD diagnoses occurred among females and in the context of other diagnoses, notably depression, where PTSD contributes to functional impairment across social, physical, emotional, and general health domains (Cloitre, Koenen, Gratz, & Jakupcak, 2002). The adult literature is investigating the tenet that chronic maltreatment is more likely to manifest as PTSD "personality" or complex PTSD, with characterological symptoms (impulsivity, aggression, self-destructiveness), pervasive despair and hopelessness, somatization symptoms, transient dissociative episodes, and difficulties in maintaining close relationships. In this way, PTSD has become a central organizing construct for personal and interpersonal style for the maltreated individual.

Overall, PTSD may be a relatively underassessed condition, whereas depression or anxiety may be noted rather than the more complex symptom picture. However, given that studies suggest reexperiencing is a frequent outcome, sleep patterns and distressing or intrusive dreams and thoughts should be considered in the context of coping with maltreatment. Further, with adolescence and young adulthood, the issue of personality involvement is raised.

Behavioral Problems and Disorders

Children exposed to maltreatment, especially those who are physically abused, show problems with aggression (Joshi, Daniolos, & Salpekar, 2004a, 2004b; Kendall-Tackett et al., 1993), and it is a problem that continues to emerge in adulthood (see Table 28.2); Also, see Botash and Ricci (2006). Social competence is further challenged by the tendency for aggression to co-occur with withdrawing behaviors in maltreated samples (e.g., Rogosch & Cicchetti, 1994). Physically abused youth show greater sensitivity to anger displays and threat cues (Pollak & Kistler, 2002, Pollak & Tolley-Schell, 2003) and more hostile attributions toward others (Dodge, Pettit, Bates, & Valente, 1995). During adolescence, physical abuse victims are more likely to engage in delinquency and risk-taking behaviors (Giardino & Giardino, 2002). Prevalence studies of disruptive behavior disorders among physically abused youth, as compared to those who are nonabused, reveal high rates of Conduct Disorder (CD) and Oppositional Defiant Disorder (Flisher et al., 1997; Pelcovitz et al., 2000; Pelcovitz, Kaplan, Goldenberg, Mandel, Lehane, & Guarrera, 1994). Both physically abused males and females are 9 times as likely to meet criteria for CD, even after controlling for potential mediating factors (e.g., parental psychopathology, lack of family cohesion, and lack of parental support; Kaplan et al., 1998). However, other research suggests that *females,* rather than

Table 28.2   Signs of Maltreatment

Type of Abuse	Signs
Physical Abuse	*Bruising of soft tissue (e.g., head, neck, trunk, arms):* → Pattern bruising in the shape of objects or hand marks. → Imprint of large, multiple, clustered bruises; bruises at different stages of healing (multiple color bruising). *Burns:* → Normally occur on hands, feet, and genitalia. → Burn patterns: • Inflicted burns are symmetrical when forced. • Accidental burns are irregularly shaped. → Cigarette burns: • Inflicted cigarette burns appear 7 to 10 mm round and have deep central crater. • Accidental cigarette burns appear oval in shape. → Scald burn (with hot liquid) is a common cause of childhood burns, both accidental and inflicted: • Accidental burns with hot liquids are irregularly shaped, with patches and splash marks. • Immersion burn injury occurs when a child is dunked in hot liquid; it can leave a stocking- or glove-like burn pattern found on the hands or feet. *Bites:* → Human bites cover a larger surface area than animal bites and tend to tear or crush (3 cm or greater space between canines indicates the bite was most likely by an adult). *Other:* → Inadequately explained bone fractures (X-ray evidence of history of multiple fractures). → Brain injuries from blunt head trauma: • Shaken baby syndrome: cerebral contusions, subdural hemorrhages, injury to cervical spinal cord, rib fractures; may present with seizures, decreased consciousness, respiratory difficulty, irritability, lethargy, vomiting, and sleep apnea.
Emotional Abuse	Unexplained physical symptoms/complaints with no medical basis. Sleep disturbances. Extreme dependence. Inability to trust. Feelings of shame and guilt. Child's own sense of his or her potential is limited. Child fails to thrive. Withdrawal. Poor self-esteem.
Neglect	Child's inability to adequately grow and develop to or above the 3rd percentile in height and weight, with no organic reason. Malnutrition, poor growth, consistent hunger, distended stomach. Untidy appearance, inappropriate dress, poor hygiene. Pale or listless appearance. Repeated or unattended lice. Recurring and unexplained patterns of minor injuries. Aches, pains, migraine, gastrointestinal problems.

(continued)

Table 28.2   (*Continued*)

Type of Abuse	Signs
Sexual abuse	Trauma to genital or anal area:
	→Abrasions or bruising of the genitalia.
	→Abdominal, genital, or rectal pain.
	→Genital or rectal discharge; unexplained sexually transmitted infection.
	Findings sometimes seen following sexual abuse but also other causes: History and other investigation is important in diagnosing abuse.
	→ Frequent urinary tract or yeast infections.
Exposure to Intimate Partner Violence	Increased risk of physical harm or injury due to proximity to an act of family violence. Headaches.
	Stomach pains (e.g., ulcers).
	Difficulty sleeping/insomnia.
	Difficulty with memory.
	Hearing and articulation problems.
	Anxiety-related increases of physical issues (asthma, tics, eczema, epileptic fits, enuresis/encopresis).

Note: This table is an expanded version of Cheng, Munn, Jack, & MacMillan, 2006 based on American Academy of Pediatrics (n.d.); American Humane Association (2006); E. D. Bariciak, A. C. Plint, I. Gaboury, & S. Bennett (2003); J. Bays & D. Chadwick (1993); W. Bernet, W. Ayres, J. E. Dunne, E. Benedek, G. A. Bernstein, E. Bryant, et al. (1997); S. E. Chaney (2000); C. Doyle (1997); K. M. Drach, J. Wientzen, & L. R. Ricci (2001); J. Emans, E. Woods, N. Flagg, & A. Freeman (May 1987); E. Evans, K. Hawton, & K. Rodham (2005); J. Fantuzzo, R. Boruch, A. Beriama, M. Atkins, & S. Marcus (1997); J. W. Fantuzzo & C. U. Lindquist (1989); M. E. Herman-Giddens, G. Brown, S. Verbiest, P. J. Carlson, E. G. Hooten, E. Howell, et al. (1999); V. M. Herrera & L. McCloskey (2003); G. Hornor (2005); N. Kellogg & The Committee on Child Abuse & Neglect (2005, August); W. J. King, M. MacKay, & A. Sirnick (2003); J. R. Kolbo, E. H. Blakely, & D. Engleman (1996); L. Kos & T. Shwayder (2006); G. W. Lambie (2005); S. Maguire, M. K. Mann, J. Sibert, & A. Kemp (2005); B. W. Mayer & P. Burns (2000); S. S. Mudd & J. S. Findlay (2004); K. Nimkink & P. K. Kleinman (2001); *Ontario Association of Children's Aid Societies* (n.d.); V. J. Palusci, E. O. Cox, T. A. Cyrus, S. W. Heartwell, F. E. Vandervort, & E. S. Pott (1999); M. D. Peck & D. Priolo-Kapel (2002); C. Powell (2003); A. Slep & R. Heyman (2006, August); R. Wright, H. Mitchell, C. M. Visness, S. Cohen, J. Stout, R. Evans, et al. (2004, April).

males, are at high risk for CD when physically abused (MacMillan et al., 1999) or when experiencing multiple forms of maltreatment (Romano, Zoccolillo, & Paquette, 2006). Similarly, E. Nelson and colleagues (2002) found an increased risk for the development of CD and Antisocial Personality Disorder among women who report histories of childhood sexual abuse. When compared to physical abuse and exposure to marital violence, childhood sexual abuse appeared to be the strongest predictor of self-reported violent and nonviolent criminal behavior among females (Herrera & McCloskey, 2003). Epidemiological work suggests that type of maltreatment exposure is not specific in explaining the increased risk of conduct problems (MacMillan et al., 2001).

Substance Use Disorders

There has been greater recognition of the overlap between substance abuse and maltreatment, both in terms of childhood history and in perpetrators of maltreatment (Wekerle & Wall, 2002). Both physical and sexual abuse are linked with a greater likelihood of early-onset smoking, drinking, illicit drug use, and injection drug use and nonmedical prescription drug abuse compared to nonmaltreated children and adolescents (De Marco & Phelan, 2004; Kessler et al., 1996; National Clearinghouse on Child Abuse and Neglect, 2004; Raghavan & Kingston, 2006; Vermeiren, Schwab-Stone, Deboutte, Leckman, & Ruchkin, 2003). In a study using a nationally representative probability sample, investigators found that having a history of physical or sexual abuse doubled the risk of alcohol, marijuana, or other hard drug abuse or dependence in the past year. The victimizations reported by this sample occurred prior to nonexperimental drug use, suggesting that victimization is a risk factor for later abuse or dependence (Kilpatrick et al., 2000). Further, sexual abuse history directly predicts both earlier age of substance abuse and higher reported rates of lifetime traumatic events among adults, raising the issue of an interplay between substance use and revictimization (Raghavan & Kingston, 2006).

Drug and alcohol use may function as a coping mechanism for increased stress brought on by childhood abuse. Alcohol and other illegal drug use may reduce symptoms of hyperarousal and unpleasant emotions and produce emotional numbing or euphoria (Cohen, Mannarino, Zhitova, & Capone, 2003; Kilpatrick et al., 2000). The frequent comorbidity between PTSD and substance use is consistent with a self-medication hypothesis (Cohen et al., 2003; Stewart & Israeli, 2002).

Youth with a history of maltreatment may enter service systems through a number of doors. Aarons et al. (2001) found high rates of lifetime prevalence of substance use disorders (SUDs) among youth from child welfare (19%), mental health (24%), and juvenile justice (41%) systems, whereas comparable community rates are less than 10%. Although child welfare youth seemed to be less vulnerable than those from other entry points, this study did not investigate the association between child maltreatment across service site and SUDs. This study is important, however, as child welfare youth are not often included as a population for epidemiological study.

Eating Disorders

Elevated risk for eating disorders or weight problems among teens reporting sexual abuse or physical neglect has been noted, above and beyond the risk from parental psychopathology, childhood eating disorders, and difficult temperaments (Johnson, Cohen, Kasen, & Brook, 2002). Sexually abused teens also appear to report significantly higher levels of distress about their weight more often than nonabused adolescents (Wonderlich et al., 2000). Women diagnosed with Bulimia Nervosa and those who have recovered for at least 1 year reported significantly higher levels of physical and psychological abuse (Rorty, Yeager, & Rossotto, 1994).

Personality Disorders

An interesting prelude to personality research is the finding based on story retelling tasks that maltreated children display from an early age (e.g., 3.5 years) affective splitting, and that greater negative emotionality is evidenced thereafter. Most nonmaltreated individuals would develop a positivity bias, being able to see the positives in themselves, others, and situations (Ayoub et al., 2006). Thus, it is not a surprise that childhood abuse has been linked with an increased risk of personality disorders (Battle et al., 2004). Specifically, documented and self-reported physical abuse is significantly associated with Antisocial Personality Disorder, even after controlling for previous sexual abuse, neglect, and characteristics of other personality disorders. When controlling for these mediating factors, childhood sexual abuse was significantly associated with Borderline Personality Disorder (Johnson, Cohen, Brown, Smailes, & Bernstein, 1999). Borderline Personality Disorder has been frequently cited as the personality disorder most commonly associated with sexual abuse (Battle et al., 2004; Zanarini et al., 1997).

Suicidal and Self-Harm Behaviors

A history of childhood maltreatment is a significant risk factor for suicide (Giardino & Giardino, 2002; Wozencraft, Wagner, & Pellegrin, 1991). For instance, a Turkish study of teenagers revealed that the rate of suicide attempt for those with a history of childhood maltreatment was 7.6 times higher than for those without such a history (Zoroglu et al., 2003). Autopsy studies of youth have found an association between physical abuse and suicide (Kaplan, Pelcovitz, Salzinger, Mendel, & Wiener, 1997; Riggs, Alario, & McHorney, 1990). These findings are consistent with prospective longitudinal community studies (Brown et al., 1999; Johnson et al., 2002). Johnson and colleagues (2002) found an increased risk of suicide attempts in early adulthood with a history of maltreatment, even after adjusting for demographic characteristics and psychiatric symptoms and disorders in childhood and early adolescence. It is suggested that interpersonal skills may be the linking factor, with the maltreated individual experiencing greater social isolation and/or antagonistic interactions with others, which in turn adds risk for suicidal behavior. A study reviewing the risk factors for youth suicide reported that youth with a history of childhood sexual abuse had an increased risk for suicide up to about 12 times that of youth with no reported history of abuse (Beautrais, 2000). Individuals with histories of sexual abuse who report suicidal ideation tended to be older at the time of abuse and to have remained in their home after abuse was detected (Wozencraft et al., 1991). The relationship between childhood sexual abuse and suicidality was greatly reduced, but not eliminated, after controlling for a wide range of potentially confounding factors (Fergusson & Mullen, 1999). Thus, the increased risk for suicide from maltreatment may be partly accounted for by other factors.

A significant portion of the empirical literature demonstrating the association between maltreatment and *nonsuicidal* self-injurious behavior has focused on adults (e.g., van der Kolk, Perry, & Herman, 1991; Wiederman, Sansone, & Sansone, 1999). For example, 62% of subjects who self-mutilate reported being sexually or physically abused at a young age (Favazza & Conterio, 1989). However, a number of studies specifically focusing on childhood maltreatment and adolescent self-injurious behavior exist as well. In one inpatient adolescent sample, those in the self-mutilation group reported histories of physical and sexual abuse more often than those in the control group. However, when all types of maltreatment were controlled simultaneously, only sexual abuse and emotional neglect appeared to be significant predictors of self-mutilation (Lipschitz et al., 1999). Similarly, more sexually abused adolescents reported deliberate self-harm, as compared to the non-sexually abused adolescents. In this study, 30% of the abused teenagers reported deliberately harming themselves five or more times (Martin, Bergen, Richardson, Roeger, & Allison, 2004). Zoroglu and colleagues (2003) found a 27-fold increase in self-mutilation in adolescents reporting a history of maltreatment compared to those who did not. It is advised that clinicians working with maltreated populations be mindful of, and regularly assess, potential risk for self-injurious behavior.

Dissociation

Dissociation is considered a psychological avoidance strategy, or an unconscious attempt to become emotionally numb via altering one's level of conscious self-awareness. To accomplish an emotionally disconnected state, one's emotions, thoughts, and behavioral experiences are separated from one another (Giardino & Giardino, 2002). In children and adolescents, dissociation can take the form of a trance-like state (e.g., abruptly distracted, sudden change in head orientation in midconversation) or manifest as a sudden change in behavior (e.g., one moment cooperative and the next moment oppositional or aggressive). Typically, activities during the dissociative episode are not remembered during nondissociative states. Dissociation may manifest as functional amnesias for sets of behaviors, a sense of depersonalization or derealization (e.g., problems with tracking of own activities in real time; sense of detachment from others; sense of being outside of oneself; repressing pain sensations in parts of the body), and experiences in identity alterations (e.g., true self versus projected, public self; chameleon-like personality with different interactants, pretending to be someone else; Putnam, 1996). Dissociation is thought to be a key contributor to the maltreated child's fragmented sense of self. As early as the preschool years, physically and sexually abused children exhibit signs of dissociation, although this is not as apparent for neglected children (e.g., Macfie, Cicchetti, & Toth, 2001). There is evidence for differential relationships between dissociation and physical and sexual abuse (Joshi et al., 2004a, 2004b; Giardino & Giardino, 2002). Using a longitudinal, prospective design, Kisiel and Lyons (2001) evaluated the prevalence of dissociation among physically and sexually abused youth using self-report and parent report questionnaires. Whereas sexually abused children reported significantly higher levels of dissociation compared to nonabused subjects, physically abused children did not. However, parental report of child dissociative symptoms indicated a significant association with both physical and sexual abuse histories. Dissociation may be more likely when maltreatment involves physical violence and multiple perpetrators (Trickett, Noll, Reiffman, & Putnam, 2001).

Asymptomatic Victims

Maltreatment covers a wide range of behaviors, from single events to chronic exposure. Within types there is also substantial variability; for example, fondling is the most frequently substantiated form of sexual abuse, as compared to penetration acts (Trocmé et al., 2005). The impact of maltreatment can manifest in myriad ways, suggesting that there is no single symptom profile associated with maltreatment (Kendall-Tackett et al., 1993).

A meta-analysis of sexual abuse studies found that between 21% and 49% of the subjects appeared asymptomatic at the time of assessment (Kendall-Tackett et al., 1993). McLeer and colleagues (McLeer, Deblinger, Atkins, Foa, & Rolphe, 1988) suggest that psychiatric sequelae can develop well after the time of the actual abuse (McLeer et al., 1988). Such a "sleeper effect" (Fergusson & Mullen, 1999) may emerge at developmentally sensitive times; for example, in teen dating, maltreatment-relevant threat cues may be heightened (e.g., physical proximity, physical contact, push-pull affect, sexual response; Wekerle et al., 2001). Maltreatment characteristics predict symptomatology, such as child age at onset, the type of abuse, the frequency and severity of abuse, the relationship between the victim and the perpetrator, the family environment, and family psychiatric history (Boney-McCoy & Finkelhor, 1995; Flisher et al., 1997; National Clearinghouse on Child Abuse and Neglect, 2004). The likelihood of having adjustment problems after experiencing abuse increases if the abuse is severe, violent, and lengthy in duration, and if limited family support is available (Boney-McCoy & Finkelhor, 1995; Fergusson & Mullen, 1999). Elements such as coping style, attachment status, and perceptions of self-identification as abused may influence distress and adjustment levels (Wekerle & Wolfe, 2003; Wekerle et al., 2001). For assessment of adjustment and trauma-related issues, see Cohen, Mannarino, Murray, and Igelman (2006), Kolko (1996), Wekerle et al. (2006), and V. Wolfe (in press).

Continued research on child and adolescent adjustment postmaltreatment is needed; the majority of work to date has been conducted on adults, mostly with retrospective reporting on maltreatment, with some important twin and prospective longitudinal studies. As Table 28.1 demonstrates, the importance of childhood maltreatment is underscored when considering adult disorders and impairment. As with adults, a similar pattern in impairment domains is shown for youth: substance abuse, antisociality and aggression, anxiety, depression, PTSD, and suicidality. We are forced to acknowledge that it is hard for many abused individuals to cope and to stay alive.

THEORETICAL MODELS OF MALTREATMENT-ASSOCIATED MALADJUSTMENT

Social Learning and Attachment Theories

Caregiver vulnerabilities of various kinds have been linked to compromised parenting, for example, anxiety and depression, substance abuse, aggression and antisociality, social support, and poor physical health (e.g., Egeland, Yates, Appleyard, & van Dulmen, 2002; Eiden & Leonard, 2000; Lyons-Ruth, Lyubchik, Wolfe, & Bronfman, 2002; MacMillan & Munn, 2001; Pine et al., 2005; Rogosch, Cicchetti, & Toth, 2004; Shea, Walsh, MacMillan, & Steiner, 2005). Developmental research shows that inadequately responsive parenting increases children's risk for problems with future relationships, managing emotions, self-efficacy, and violence (Dube et al., 2001; Kim & Cicchetti, 2003; National Institute of Child Health and Human Development Early Child Care Research Network, 2004).

According to social learning theory, children form a schema for how stress is regulated in a close relationship through their experience of interacting with their caregivers. Longitudinal research has shown, for example, that maternal depression typically precedes child aggression and hyperactivity, as well as affective disturbances (Elgar, Curtis, McGrath, Waschbusch, & Stewart, 2003). Early abusive relationships inform relationship schema, wherein maladaptive stress–maladaptive coping is learned via modeling and experience with reinforcement schedules. For example, attack can end the stress from the interactant by causing harm and shutting down conflict or interaction, promoting the interactant to acquiesce, appease, and remove himself or herself from the immediate environment. Maltreated individuals may maintain developed dysfunctional coping partly as the result of their dysfunctional relationship strategy.

According to attachment theory, the end goal of the early caregiving relationship is to protect us from harm and enhance our exploratory behavior. The confidence in the protection that subsequently develops serves as both the source for stress regulation and a model of stress regulation to be internalized. This internal model is carried into future situations as a central means to regulate stress (Goldberg, 2001). An abusive relationship turns the source of predictable comfort and first choice for support into a source of fear, confusion, and hesitancy, thereby compromising the development and practice of stress-regulating strategy (Lyons-Ruth & Jacobvitz, 1999). Thus, from both social learning and attachment perspectives, relationship functioning represents a key ongoing area of adaptational challenge for maltreated children (Rutter & Sroufe, 2000). This heightened vulnerability has been tied, theoretically, to holding a conceptualization of relationships that are organized along power abusive, victim-victimizer dimensions (e.g., Crittenden & Ainsworth, 1989; Crittenden & Claussen, 2002), as attachment theory (Bowlby, 1970, 1972, 1980, 1982) advances that both sides of a relationship are learned.

Maltreated victims may, by implication, have a more developed (and more generally applied) conceptualization of their victimizer. Defensive processes (e.g., including perceptual information that is consistent with one's relationship schema and excluding perceptual information that is inconsistent with the relationship schema) are thought to interfere with being open to new input, thereby increasing the likelihood of schema maintenance. Maltreated teens would be expected to select partners who would contribute to the maintenance of distressed relationships (Crittenden & Ainsworth, 1989).

Much recent evidence has accumulated to show that maltreated youth, relative to their nonmaltreated counterparts, exhibit indicators of self-system dysfunction, including poorer self-representations, self-esteem, and ego control (e.g., Cicchetti & Rogosch, 1997; Toth, Cicchetti, Macfie, & Emde, 1997). Such disorganization has been linked with higher trauma-related symptoms, specifically dissociation, in adolescents who had childhood histories of maltreatment and other trauma (Carlson, 1998). The PTSD trauma symptomatology is also functionally related to relationship disturbance, including adolescent dating violence (Wolfe, 1999; Wekerle et al., 2001). Dissociation, for example, may contribute to asynchrony in and abrupt withdrawal from interacting. Hypervigilance may lead to an agitated, highly reactive response in interactions.

Developmental Traumatology Theory

According to the theory of developmental traumatology, early exposure to the intense traumatic stress of maltreatment, compounded by the underdevelopment of an optimally functioning stress-regulating system, will result in an overreactive stress system (Cicchetti & Walker, 2001; DeBellis, 2001; DeBellis & Putnam, 1994). Such a long-term effect of maltreatment experience on stress and adverse health outcomes has been linked to the impairment of the hypothalamic-pituitary-adrenal axis, the psychobiological stress system that is sensitive to the effect of early environment. In turn, this compromises other stress-related systems, including the immune, neurotransmitter, and sympathetic nervous systems, and may be associated with structural changes to the brain (DeBellis, 2001). Nowhere is this convergence of malfunctions across difference stress systems more apparent than in PTSD.

In the developmental traumatology model, PTSD symptomatology is seen as the key mediator of negative outcomes. Such symptoms may persist and overwhelm youth who are disadvantaged by their stress response mechanisms, thereby interfering with their sense of self-continuity and ability to cope, leading to maladjustment (Bradley, 2000; Chandler & Lalonde, 1998). Due to maltreatment-related cues directly leading to aversive experience, escape-avoidance mechanisms may be reinforced. Substance abuse and self-harming may be efforts to self-medicate in response to PTSD symptoms via reducing negative affect, numbness, dissociation, tension, and hypervigilance or enhancing positive affect. However, progression to more harmful behaviors (e.g., abuse of cocaine, opiates) may exacerbate affect problems and increase victimization risk (e.g., Ginzler, Cochran, Comenech-Rodriguez, Cauce, & Whitbeck, 2003).

Personality Trait Model

Personality research posits that people differ on a set of underlying hypothetical dimensions, and these represent stable dispositions that are inherent in the individual, manifest early in life, and generalize across a variety of situations. Research on maltreating caregivers has highlighted the role of the caregiver's personality in limiting his or her ability to cope with stress associated with parenting, thus predisposing the individual to abusive behavior (Marziali, Damianakis, & Trocmé, 2003). To further understand the role of the caregiver's personality in the perpetration of child maltreatment and spousal violence, the model suggests that certain personality traits are a risk factor for child and partner abuse, operating singly or in conjunction with other risk factors such as substance abuse (Flett & Hewitt, 2002). In addition, it has been shown that personality may serve as a mediator in the relation between the individual's own history of childhood maltreatment and the perpetration of partner violence (Ornduff, Kelsey, & O'Leary, 2001). This indicates that the development of personality is shaped by the abusive experience during early childhood and consolidated into a stable behavioral and cognitive tendency that individuals bring to close relationships, perpetuating the cycle of violence and abuse (see also Pickering, Farmer, & McGuffin, 2004).

It has also been suggested that childhood maltreatment and individual personality traits contribute synergistically to adverse behavioral and health outcomes. For example, Blackson, Tarter, and Mezzich (1996) showed that the adverse effect of parental discipline by substance-abusing fathers on their child's behavioral adjustment is exacerbated by the child's difficult temperament, an indicator of poor affect regulation. Similarly, Trocki and Caetano (2003) have shown that children who were exposed to family violence were more likely to develop depressive symptoms and abuse substances during adulthood if they also have a difficult temperament. Child response to trauma may be moderated by preexisting psychopathology, attributional or coping style, and temperament (Feiring, Taska, & Lewis, 2002). The mechanism underlying such interaction between personality and maltreatment can be conceptualized along gene-environment interaction effects. Because of its effect on the monoamine (e.g., serotonin, norepinephrine, and dopamine) level at the prefrontal cortex, different polymorphisms of genes associated with the monoamine system have been linked to individual differences in temperamental affect regulation, measured in terms of maternal report as well as behavioral observation (Benjamin, Ebstein, & Belmaker, 2002). In a now classic study, Caspi and colleagues (2002) found that male children who were maltreated were more likely to exhibit externalizing behavior if they had the low monoamine oxidase A activity genotype. Similarly, Kaufman et al. (2004) demonstrated that maltreated children who receive low social support and carry the short allele of the serotonin transporter gene promoter polymorphism were twice as likely to develop depression, even compared to their nonmaltreated counterparts who carry the same polymorphism. Maltreated children who carry the short allele but receive high social support had only minimal increase in the depression score, indicating the buffering effect of a positive environment. Recently, in validating the gene-environment interaction effect observed among maltreated children, Kim-Cohen and colleagues (2006) examined two different types of gene-environment correlation that may have potentially confounded the interaction effect: (1) The abusive parent may have transmitted to the child both an adverse environment and a genetic susceptibility for behavioral maladjustment, and (2) children who carry the risk genotype may behave in ways that are more challenging to an underskilled, stress-vulnerable parent. To address these issues, the researchers tested for the former by controlling for maternal antisocial personality and for the latter by assessing whether exposure to child maltreatment is predicted by the child's genetic polymorphism. Results indicate that even after controlling for the two types of gene-environment correlation, the interaction effect remains significant, indicating that children who carry the polymorphism that calls for low monoamine oxidase A activity were more vulnerable to the exposure to physical abuse.

One point to consider in reviewing these studies of gene-environment interaction in maltreated samples is the potential difference in maltreatment experience even between genetically identical twins. The shared environment may not be shared in a chronically chaotic and dysfunctional household. Such family dynamics as role reversals (e.g., parentification), scapegoating (e.g., targeting one child), and changing household rules with changing caregivers, adults, and siblings may lead to very different daily realities, as well as different maltreatment events, when considered in detail. Further, rather than the actual event, it may be the perception of the experience of maltreatment that differs, even when children are similarly maltreated by the same perpetrator. For example, one child may view himself or herself as a victim, whereas the other embraces spirituality, such as forgiveness of the perpetrator, seeing a greater value in individual suffering, believing he or she has a special relationship with God, and so on. In our clinical experience, one mother identified that God had allowed such substantial abuse when she was a child since he knew she was "strong enough" to "take it" and survive. In research, youth differed in their acknowledgment of exposure to physical abuse even when endorsing physical abuse items with clear injury outcomes (Wekerle et al., 2001). Capturing the maltreatment event, the perception of the maltreatment, and the "theory" or story (or lack thereof) created to understand the maltreatment may be important aspects of a shared environment.

SCREENING FOR CHILD MALTREATMENT

During the 1980s and 1990s, attempts were made to screen individuals to determine risk for committing child maltreatment (Brayden, MacLean, Bonfiglio, & Altemeier, 1993; Caldwell, Bogat, & Davidson, 1988; Center on Child Abuse Prevention Research, 1996; Kotelchuck, 1982; McCurdy, 1995). One study examined the association between staff assessment of a participant's risk for committing abuse based on personal and familial characteristics such as economic difficulties, and scores on the Child Abuse Potential Inventory, a self-report measure (McCurdy, 1995). The predictive validity of this strategy for subsequent abuse, however, was not determined. Two investigations followed families prospectively and measured risk of future maltreatment (Brayden et al., 1993; Center on Child Abuse Prevention Research, 1996). Such risk approaches have shown only limited ability to predict future maltreatment. For example, the interview used by Brayden and colleagues had a positive predictive value of 6.6% and a sensitivity of 55.6% for physical abuse. The main factor that precludes use of child maltreatment screening approaches continues to be the unacceptably high false-positive rate (Caldwell et al., 1988; Kotelchuck, 1982); individuals are identified as potentially at risk for abusing a child and yet do not go on to do so. Certain child, parental, and social factors are important to consider in any assessment of child maltreatment, including evaluations of parents or caregivers to determine their ability to care for a child (often referred to as a parenting capacity assessment).

Table 28.2 outlines physical and other signs linked with an increased risk for occurrence of child maltreatment. Although the presence of these variables increases the risk of maltreatment, it is important to recognize that abuse or neglect can occur without any risk indicators present. At the same time, many individuals and families with one or more of these indicators present are not experiencing child maltreatment. Adverse events for children in the home tend to cluster together (multiple forms of maltreatment, parental alcohol and drug abuse, IPV, parental marital discord, divorce or separation, parental criminality; Dong et al., 2004) and may also be reflected in the community context (e.g., safe, affordable, low crime, high in parenting resource areas).

There is a strong tendency among both researchers and child protection agencies to focus exclusively on mothers when considering issues of child neglect. Yet some research suggests that the involvement of a father (biological or the mother's partner) protects against abuse and neglect (Biller & Solomon, 1986; Dubowitz et al., 2000; Egeland, Jacobvitz, & Sroufe, 1988; Quinton, Rutter, & Liddle, 1984; Turcotte, Dubeau, Bolté, & Paquette, 2001). Other research, however, found that male partners were rarely a significant source of support to neglecting mothers (Polansky, Chamlers, Buttenwieser, & Williams, 1981). The research suggests that an analysis of the family type leads to a better understanding of the problem of neglect (Mayer, Dufour, Lavergne, Girard, & Trocmé, 2003). This underscores both the challenge and the importance of conducting a careful history with all family members. The assessment of the child in multiple locales (at home during family routine times, such as meals; at school; in service centers) and in multiple contexts (separating and returning to parent, response to strange adults, bonding with teacher and school staff) may be helpful. It is essential that all forms of maltreatment be considered as simultaneous working hypotheses for the clinician in order to capture possible polyvictimization (Finkelhor et al., 2007).

Another issue that has arisen more recently is screening women for exposure to IPV. Citing the prevalence, consequences, and costs associated with IPV (Campbell et al., 2002; Ulrich et al., 2003), some organizations advocate screening as a key aspect of identification and response; the American Medical Association (1992), the Family Violence Prevention Fund, and the American Academy of Pediatrics, among others, have recommended universal screening to their members (Bair-Merritt, Mollen, Yau, & Fein, 2006). Taket and colleagues (2003, p. 674) have asserted that "routine inquiry is the only way to increase the proportion of women who disclose abuse and who may benefit from intervention." These recommendations disregard the fact that no evidence exists regarding the possible harm associated with universal screening.

Those relying on evidence-based approaches favor caution. Systematic reviews by the Canadian Task Force on Preventive Health Care, the U.S. Preventive Services Task Force, and Ramsay and colleagues (MacMillan & Wathen, 2003; Nelson, Nygren, McInerney, & Klein, 2004; Ramsay, Richardson, Carter, Davidson, & Feder, 2002; U.S. Preventive Services Task Force, 2004; Wathen & MacMillan, 2003) have concluded that there is insufficient evidence to recommend universal screening for IPV. Efforts have been made to assist health care providers to use the best available evidence to address the issue of IPV with their clients (Ferris, 2004; Liebschutz, Frayne, & Saxe, 2003; MacMillan & Wathen, 2003a, 2003b; Rhodes & Levinson, 2003). The key question, however, is not whether to screen universally; the issue is the lack of evidence for the effectiveness of interventions for IPV. Identification is only the first step.

ASSESSMENT OF CHILD MALTREATMENT

In most regions in North America, it is the responsibility of child protection agencies to carry out investigative interviews with children and family members when child maltreatment is suspected. Although there is no evidence to support general screening of children for child maltreatment, it is important to include questions about exposure to the four main types of child abuse and neglect (physical, sexual, and emotional abuse and neglect) in any diagnostic assessment of a child that involves emotional or behavioral problems (some clinicians separate exposure to IPV as a type of maltreatment, while others include it as a form of emotional abuse).

Clinicians must ask clients directly whether they have been abused. A history of victimization form that focuses on the behavioral aspects of maltreatment may be an appropriate prelude to the clinical interview for age-appropriate children. Examples of appropriate forms are the Juvenile Victimization Questionnaire (Hamby & Finkelhor, 2004), Childhood Trauma Questionnaire (Bernstein & Fink, 1998), and Childhood Experience of Violence Questionnaire (Walsh, MacMillan, Trocmé, Dudziuk, & Boyle, 2000). The use of behavioral referents and the avoidance of labels are critical and need to be contextualized (e.g., discipline, relationships). Such paper-and-pencil or computer-administered questionnaires may be helpful because they do not require individuals to self-label and conceptualize their experiences as abuse or neglect. An initial family interview is a good time to explain the goals, perceptions of concerns, expected procedures, and ethical issues (i.e., harm to self, harm to others, child abuse and neglect) of assessment. In maltreating families, it is important to understand who in the family is the person in power so that the clinician can support child empowerment. Going directly to the child may lead to more conflict for the child if the perception is that a child broke an adult's rule. Research shows that most children do not tell.

Children will most typically indicate their maltreatment behaviorally rather than in terms of verbal disclosures. Children will not respond with disclosures readily to the caregiver unless there is a "talking" and warm relationship with a reliable caregiver. For example, in one case, a child did not disclose sexual abuse when directly queried by an older sibling witnessing the child's distress after an incident had occurred with a neighbor. In another example, three male siblings did not disclose bizarre punishment (i.e., hanging a child upside down over an apartment balcony to elicit compliance) by their mother's boyfriend. In this case, the mother herself reported in a family session with the boyfriend present that she was physically abusive to her children (e.g., punching child in the face, knocking out child's teeth). Also present in the family assessment session was the maternal grandmother, who declared a "no tears" rule for this extended family. In all the discussions of violence, no distress was expressed by any family member. Thus, it is important for the clinician to maintain openness to disclosures of violence from a variety of family members and in a variety of presentational forms.

In the event of a disclosure, the maltreatment utterances and clinician questions and responses should be recorded verbatim in writing, in real time, and dated and signed. Clinicians need to be prepared to relay their concerns in terms of observed and reported behavior or signs, the sequential actions leading to the discovery, incongruence and improbabilities in explaining physical signs (see Table 28.2), the presence of risk indicators, as well as the basic facts (alleged perpetrator name, relationship, address, child level of fear of current danger or risk of victimization, knowledge of other victims and/or contact with other children, whether others were told about the abuse or neglect). The person who receives the information directly should act on the report or suspicion forthwith and should not engage the alleged perpetrator or other caregiver in the report. Such limits to confidentiality should be clearly conveyed prior to clinical intervention.

All clinicians involved in the care of children should be alert to entertaining a hypothesis of maltreatment. A general principle to assist in identifying abuse injuries is when the history is not consistent with the physical findings. Even when the client is an adult or a couple, the best interests of the child remain the first priority. As a helping professional, the clinician has entered into the social contract that makes protection of children a priority over family privacy and unification or adult treatment goals. Discipline-specific codes of ethics and legal statutes exist to ensure child health and safety. The duty to report overrides most privileged information, including with police and religious authorities. Beyond familiarity with applicable laws, clinicians may consult local CPS to discuss the situation and obtain guidance anonymously. Abuse or neglect does not have to be proven for a report to be made; "reasonable" or "probable" grounds for suspicion are required. With the best interests of the child in mind, reports are made in "good faith," and malicious reporting is rare. Failure to report carries with it penalties such as fines, disciplinary action from the professional licensing body, civil suits, and prosecution by authorities. For further details, see texts by Wekerle et al. (2006), Reese & Ludwig (2001), and an article by Sirotnak, Grigsby, and Krugman (2004).

A helpful approach to understanding the context of symptomatology is to query caregivers and youths about a typical day. This allows the clinician to understand who does what generally and how the day proceeds, including levels of child self-care and sibling responsibilities, eating times, hygiene, affection displays, and discipline routines. It may be helpful to compare the child's perspective with that of siblings and caregivers. Examples of broad questions that provide opportunities to ask about child maltreatment are: What things do you worry about? What happens in your family when someone gets in trouble? Has anyone ever touched you in a way that made you feel uncomfortable or upset? Has anyone ever made you do something sexually you did not want to do? It is generally not appropriate to ask detailed questions about a disclosure of maltreatment because in many jurisdictions, a child protection agency worker needs to obtain the disclosure. Children should not be subjected to investigative interviews by clinicians without specialized training in this area. Maltreatment victims hope for an empathic response, reassuring them that telling was the right thing to do, allowing them to express their feelings and thoughts about the disclosure; the clinician should convey positive messages but not promises that cannot be kept. Helpful messages include conveying that the children did not do anything to provoke or deserve their maltreatment, that abuse and neglect are against the law, that you are sorry that they have had to go through this or suffer so, that they are not alone, and that other children have experienced it. The child should be monitored and supported postdisclosure with a known professional (i.e., CPS staff, family doctor). In cases where abuse is suspected but not substantiated by CPS investigation, the risk of subsequent reports and substantiation is high. As with many clinical phenomena, a good predictor of future behavior is past behavior.

TREATMENT AND PREVENTION OF CHILD MALTREATMENT

There are several promising and effective interventions on different aspects of mal-treatment effects and violence prevention (for a review of the evidence base and available interventions, see J. Cohen et al., 2006). Recent infant-parent psychotherapy reports indicate success in altering the insecure attachment status of infants (about 66% were abused and/or neglected in the first year of life), as compared to low-income normative controls. There were substantial increases in secure attachment, and disorganized attachment was prevalent among the treatment-as-usual community maltreated infants (Cicchetti, Rogosch, & Toth, 2006). Certain interventions appear to hold promise for neglected children and families: Group play training and resilient peer-mediated treatment for withdrawn preschoolers may improve social behavior; therapeutic day treatment may improve self-esteem; and multisystemic therapy and parent training may improve parent-child relations, reduce parenting problems, and decrease family social problems (National Clearinghouse on Family Violence, 2006).

Currently, the two most researched and supported interventions are home visitation models (HVM) for younger children and trauma-focused cognitive-behavioral therapy (TF-CBT) for preschool and school-age children and adolescents. Research studies are under way to assess effectiveness in community settings, including child protection populations. Further research is needed in terms of entry into these interventions. Both HVM and TF-CBT are very promising approaches to support child protection services work in the area of referring families whom CPS does not serve but who are reported to the system, if families are interested and deemed appropriate. For example, a dating violence prevention program, the Youth Relationships Project, was found to significantly reduce the self-reported trauma symptomatology and dating violence among CPS and at-risk youth over a 2-year postintervention, as compared to youth receiving typical agency service (Wolfe et al., 1996).

Home Visitation Models

The prevalence and consequences of maltreatment have prompted many efforts in primary prevention in the past 2 decades. The U.S. Advisory Board on Child Abuse and Neglect identified child maltreatment as a national emergency in 1991 and promoted an expansion of Hawaii Healthy Start, a program of paraprofessional home visitation that had shown some evidence of effectiveness in nonrandomized trials (Duggan et al., 1999). Healthy Families America (Daro & Harding, 1999) was modeled after Hawaii Healthy Start and disseminated nationally. Currently, Health Families America programs are running in 430 locations in the United States and Canada.

In the past 10 years, randomized controlled trials have been conducted on Hawaii Healthy Start and Healthy Families America in New York State, San Diego, and Alaska. The trials have found significant effects on some domains of self-reported parenting behaviors (including abusive behaviors) and beliefs. The Alaskan study showed positive effects on some aspects of the child's environment, child development, and parent-reported child behavior at age 2, but the San Diego trial showed that the effect on child development was not sustained. The programs showed no effect on official reports of child abuse or neglect, childhood injuries, or other objective measures that are proxies for maltreatment (Olds, 2006). In 2004, the Washington State Institute for Public Policy estimated that Healthy Families America has incurred a $4,500 (U.S.) per family loss in investment.

The 1991 home visitation recommendations of the Advisory Board were based on evidence from research on the Nurse-Family Partnership Program (NFP; Olds, Henderson, Chamberlin, & Tatelbaum, 1986), a substantively different program from that offered by Hawaii Healthy Start and Healthy Families America. The NFP is a program of prenatal and infancy home visiting by nurses (not paraprofessionals) for low-income mothers having their first child. Nurses follow detailed visit-by-visit guidelines in their efforts to (a) help women improve the outcomes of pregnancy by promoting healthy prenatal behaviors, (b) improve child health and development by promoting parents' competent care of their children, and (c) enhance parents' life-course development by encouraging pregnancy planning and parents' education and work. The nurses help families make use of needed health and human services and attempt to involve other family members and friends in the pregnancy, birth, and early care of the child. The NFP has a schedule of visits beginning before the end of the second trimester in pregnancy, as follows: weekly for the first four visits, every 2 weeks for the remainder of the pregnancy, every week for 6 weeks in the postpartum period, every 2 weeks until the infant is 21 months old, then once a month for the next 3 months until the child is 2 years old.

The NFP has been tested in three randomized controlled trials over 3 decades. The first trial was conducted in Elmira, New York ($N = 400$, 89% White). The second, conducted in Memphis, Tennessee ($N = 1139$, 92% Black), was designed to determine if the results from Elmira could be replicated when a health department delivered the NFP and when it served low-income Blacks in an urban area (Kitzman, Cole, Yoos, & Olds, 1997). The Denver trial ($N = 735$, 45% Hispanic) was designed to determine whether the NFP might be delivered effectively by paraprofessionals who shared many of the characteristics of the families they visited (Olds et al., 2002). The Denver trial also included a randomly assigned group visited by nurses and a control group. At randomization and in subsequent assessments, treatment and control groups were essentially equivalent in terms of demographics, and high rates of sample retention were maintained in each trial.

In each of the trials, women were randomized to receive either home visiting during pregnancy and in the first 2 years of their children's lives or comparison services that consisted of some combination of free transportation for prenatal and well child care and sensory and developmental screening and referral of the child for potential problems. All three studies employed a variety of data sources, including maternal interviews, developmental tests of the child, and medical and administrative data. The randomized controlled trials fell somewhere between efficacy and effectiveness trials, in that the samples had few restrictions, nearly entire populations of low-income first-time mothers were registered in the communities where the trials were conducted, and the interventions were conducted in collaboration with local agencies (Olds, 2002).

In Elmira, the intervention reduced rates of state-verified reports of child abuse and neglect. A 15-year follow-up showed that this effect was increased: the nurse-visited group had 48% fewer verified reports of maltreatment than did the control group, and among mothers who were at higher risk, 77% fewer verified reports compared to control group counterparts (Olds et al., 1997). However, rates of maltreatment found in official records in Memphis and Denver were too low in the first 2 years of children's lives to be reliable outcomes. Rates in Elmira were about 3 times higher than in Memphis and Denver, and 6 to 7 times greater for high-risk families. Child protection service records typically pick up only a fraction of actual maltreatment; therefore, the results in Elmira may be an underestimate of the effect. As well, a surveillance bias could have been operating in the study; maltreatment could be detected at a greater rate in nurse-visited families because the nurses are mandated reporters.

Because of the low rates of substantiated reports of maltreatment in Memphis, the research used childhood injuries reported in the medical record as a proxy (Kitzman et al., 1997). Program effects on injuries were similar to the pattern in Elmira; program effects were enhanced among children born to mothers with low psychological resources. In Denver, the health care delivery system made it impossible to trace children's utilization patterns reliably, so infants' early emotional expressions (which are associated with child abuse and neglect) were measured. Nurse-visited 6-month-olds born to mothers with low psychological resources had higher rates of observed emotional vitality and lower rates of emotional vulnerability than their control group counterparts. As the children matured, the program produced effects on language and executive functioning consistent with better prenatal and caregivng environments.

The Elmira follow-up showed that the program effect on child maltreatment decreased as the level of IPV increased, although the program had no impact on the incidence of IPV in this trial. The moderating effect of IPV was specific to child maltreatment and did not attenuate program effects on any other outcomes (Eckenrode et al., 2000).

It is noteworthy that nurse-visited women in the Denver trial reported significantly less IPV from partners during the 6-month interval prior to the 4-year interview than those in the control group (6.9% versus 13.6%, $p = .05$; Olds et al., 2004). Future research should be focused on this interplay between IPV and child maltreatment and efforts made to enhance IPV-effective components for these families.

The best evidence for prevention of physical abuse and neglect in high-risk groups comes from the nurse home visitation program developed by Olds and colleagues in 2007. MacMillan and colleagues examined the effectiveness of an intensive program of nurse home visitation in preventing recidivism of physical abuse and neglect among CPS-involved families referred because of at least one child in the family experiencing either physical abuse or neglect. Families were randomly assigned to a control group, which received CPS standard service such as risk assessment, parenting education, or referral, or the intervention group, which was provided standard CPS service plus a 2-year program of nurse home visitation. Both the control and the intervention group were followed up annually over 3 years. Results showed no statistically significant reduction in recurrence of either child physical abuse or neglect; the recidivism rate for both intervention and control groups was high. The only promising finding was that among those families whose involvement with child protection lasted less than 3 months, there was a reduction in recurrence of physical abuse but not neglect. This suggests the possibility that early intervention with families involved with CPS might lead to less recurrence of child physical abuse. While the NFP has been shown to be effective in preventing maltreatment and associated outcomes, the trials by Olds and colleagues and MacMillan et al. (2005) have substantial differences. The NFP (Olds et al., 2007) targeted high-risk first-time mothers and began prenatally, whereas the study by MacMillan and colleagues (2005) involved a much broader range of families. In the NFP, the nurses assisted mothers prenatally, and then after the birth of the infant worked closely with mothers in helping them understand the needs of their infants. Although the original rationale for assessing a program of nurse home visitation with a sample of families involved with the CPS was based on the positive findings of the NFP, it was structured very differently from the NFP. The trial was designed to evaluate an intervention that paralleled the in-home services being offered by CPS in general, but at a more intensive level than was available in the community. The negative findings, though disappointing, emphasize that randomized, controlled clinical trials in the CPS population should be a priority for research. Disseminating findings from strong methodological studies should be a priority for CPS practice and policy, regardless of whether the outcome was positive or negative. Further, there remains an urgent need for rigorous evaluation of the effectiveness of parenting programs that are specifically designed to treat physical abuse and neglect, either independently or as part of broader packages of care. Studies need to measure outcome broadly to assess effects on child abuse and neglect per the legal definitions (CPS reports) as well as objective measures of parenting (e.g., home behavioral observations). A recent systematic review indicates treatment effectiveness of some programs on associated aspects of parenting; currently, the evidence on reduced maltreatment rates is limited for treatment compared to prevention with at-risk samples (Barlow, Johnston, Kendrick, Polnay, & Stewart-Brown, 2006).

Clearly, the effects seen in the NFP were not observed in the paraprofessional visiting model of Hawaii Healthy Start and Healthy Families America. The Denver trial of the NFP showed that nurses produce a larger and broader range of beneficial effects in, among others, infant caregivng and language development versus paraprofessionals. However, a one-size-fits-all model is not effective. The NFP model showed substantial limitations when interparental violence was present; the positive findings in reduction of child maltreatment were not maintained under such conditions (Eckenrode et al., 2000). This may be the best option for high-risk, young mothers prenatally or beginning their parenting career. Program implementation and fidelity are critical. In 1996, the U.S. Justice Department recommended replication of the NFP in community settings. This led to the creation of the NFP National Service, which develops and maintains procedures for ensuring faithful reproduction of the program's essential elements as it is replicated in new communities. The NFP is currently operating in over 170 sites, serving 20,000 families per year in 250 counties in the United States. The Washington State Institute and the RAND Corporation estimate that the NFP saves $17,000 (U.S.) for every family served.

Trauma-Focused Cognitive Behavior Therapy

When the diagnosis of PTSD was first formulated in 1980, it was not believed to be relevant to children and adolescents. Child stress reactions were considered short-lived (Masten, Best, & Garmezy, 1990). The empirical basis for such views, however, consisted mostly of reports from parents and teachers, who may underreport child distress (Handford, Mayes, Mattison, & Humphrey, 1986). As the assessment moved to asking children and adolescents themselves about their thoughts, feelings, memories, and emotions following trauma, debilitating and long-lasting PTSD symptoms were noted (Dalgleish, Meiser-Stedman, & Smith, 2005). Pediatric PTSD symptomatology is consistent with children behaviorally enacting their emotional reaction to trauma (Dyregrov & Yule, 2006). For example, it was observed that young children show less emotional numbing and have more problems in reporting avoidance; they require rather complex cognitive introspection.

Consequently, the need for a thorough assessment following exposure to trauma is crucial to the implementation of age-appropriate and developmentally sensitive interventions to capture the intense feelings of shock, threat, terror, horror, or helplessness. In a recent review (Strand, Sarmiento, & Pasquale, 2005), assessment and screening tools currently available to researchers and practitioners were divided into four categories in terms of how trauma is constructed: those that screen for (1) both a history of exposure to traumatic events and the presence of symptoms of trauma, (2) only a history of exposure, (3) symptoms of PTSD or dissociation, and (4) symptoms other than or in addition to PTSD. Alternately, Perrin, Smith, and Yule (2000) categorize these instruments into four different modes: (1) *DSM*-criteria-based semi-structured interview, (2) parental interview, (3) unstructured child interview, and (4) child self-report. In evaluating these instruments, Strand et al. argued that most instruments are not designed to be age-specific, raising questions about the influence of age on outcome. Specifically, only 8 of the 33 measures available are designed for children 10 years or younger, and fewer of these are geared for the very young child. In addition, Perrin et al. point out that since many of the *DSM* PTSD criteria are not developmentally sensitive, existing semi-structured interviews may have only limited usefulness for young children. Further, because children are better reporters of internalizing symptoms and parents are more accurate reporters of externalizing or behavioral symptoms (Greenwald & Rubin, 1999), only instruments that collect information from both sources can provide a balanced account. Very few self-report measures were developed specifically to assess child PTSD. Instead, the majority of these instruments are adapted from adult questionnaires with little normative child data available (see McNally, 1991; Nader, 1997). Clearly, there is a need to develop instruments that measure more developmentally sensitive child PTSD.

The treatment, however, has centered on Trauma-Focused Cognitive Behavior Therapy (TF-CBT), which can be used to target trauma deriving from all types of maltreatment, although it was initially developed for sexually abused children (Berliner, 2005; Cohen & Mannarino, 1996, 1998; Cohen, Mannarino, & Deblinger, 2006; Cohen, Mannarino, & Knudsen, 2005; Deblinger, Stauffer, & Steer, 2001; Stovall-McClough & Dozier, 2004). A systematic review of outcome studies on sexually abused children concludes that some outcomes have been more successfully demonstrated than others (e.g., decreases in child depression, improvements in parenting practices), and some outcomes have yet to be assessed. Overall, more controlled outcomes studies on various populations are encouraged (Macdonald, Higgins, & Ramchandani, 2006).

Treatment proceeds along 12 to 16 weekly sessions. In addition to the recently published manual (Cohen et al., 2006), free Web-based training is available (www.musc.edu/tfcbt/). TF-CBT has demonstrated efficacy for multiply traumatized children, maintaining treatment gains at 1-year follow-up (Cohen, Deblinger, Mannarino, & Steer, 2004; Deblinger, Mannarino, Cohen, & Steer, 2006). While not direct targets of treatment, parental PTSD and depression symptoms have been reduced with TF-CBT, further enhancing the likelihood of adaptive parental support. As is the case with most protocols, where additional intervention is deemed necessary, referral is provided. This is seen as particularly important when parental psychiatric issues are interfering with parenting capacity.

A key issue with TF-CBT is to engage a nonoffending caregiver as an active agent of change, providing the daily continuity needed to support the child's new learning (relaxation, leisure skills) and ability to talk openly about the maltreatment (emotions vocabulary, assertive communication) and to give the child confidence in the caregiver as a protector (caregiver affect management, parent training for child behavior management). Further, relaxation skills can be widely applied by the child and supported by the parent to address sleep, hyperarousal, and somatic issues. For the child, graduated exposure to the traumatizing maltreatment, addressing the phobic response to trauma memories and cues, is addressed in the creation of a narrative. This achieves the goal of decoupling maltreatment cues from debilitating anxiety. The child's story of the maltreatment can be in pictorial, audio, written, or typed form and is developed over time and at the child's pace. The practice of the cognitive components, addressing cognitive errors (e.g., dwelling on the worst possibilities, self-blame for maltreatment) via thought-stopping, positive self-talk, and practice applying the cognitive triangle (linking feeling, thoughts, behaviors), is achieved in therapist-child discussions during rereading and reworking of the narrative in a manner consistent with the CBT gains. Opportunities for corrective relationship experiences are available in individual sessions with the therapist and ongoing supportive work with respect to parenting. In this way, TF-CBT addresses the common relationship issues in maltreatment: impaired trust, social incompetence, poor relationship problem-solving skills, problems in sustaining relationships, and hypersensitivity in interactions. Another key maltreatment issue, affect regulation, is addressed via skill development in self-soothing, distress tolerance, and managing negative affect (sadness, fear, anger, anxiety). Risk behaviors (sexualized, aggressive, unsafe) are addressed in skill-building components.

The flow of TF-CBT sessions moves from assessment to assessment feedback, parallel child and adult individual sessions, and conjoint child-parent sessions.

During assessment, the central aspect of TF-CBT (i.e., the trauma narrative) as a skill is evaluated and practiced in a nonthreatening context. Children share their feelings, thoughts, and bodily sensations about a positive experience or favorite activity. The TF-CBT components form the acronym PRACTICE, reflecting the specific session goals across time: Psychoeducation and parenting skills, Relaxation, Affective modulation, Cognitive coping and processing, Trauma narrative, In vivo mastery of trauma reminders, Conjoint parent-child sessions, Enhancing future safety and development. Although caregiver involvement is optimal, significant PTSD symptom improvement has been documented with child-only work. Clinicians are advised to utilize their clinical judgment in determining the initial focus of treatment, which may need to be crisis management, reinstitution of the child's routine, and child behavior stabilization. Clinicians should assess for fragile states, as creating the trauma narrative could worsen any suicidal ideation or substance abuse. An alternative treatment strategy based on dialectical behavior therapy (Linehan, 1993) that targets suicidal risk and other multiproblem situations, particularly for adolescents, developed by Miller, Rathus, and Linehan (2007), is described in Wekerle et al. (2006).

SUMMARY

Child maltreatment is a serious challenge to adaptation and development across domains and across the life span. Children who experience multiple and/or chronic exposure to maltreatment events adapt less well to normative challenges in life. When maltreatment effects are evident, development is compromised as misses in early skills weaken the foundation for more complex skill attainment. In particular, maltreatment appears to carry an additional cognitive load for the individual such that academic performance is compromised, information integration is slower, affective splitting is more likely, emotion-laden and self-referential communication is more difficult, and negative biases in emotionality, attributions, and behavior (harm to self, harm to others) are more likely. Particular disorder vulnerabilities occur in the domains of mood, anxiety, substance abuse, aggression, eating, and personality. Further, survival is challenged with suicidal ideation and attempts, and suicide is a real possibility. Relationship functioning and self-preservation are consistent themes, with greater insecurities and disorganization in attachment, more problematic peer relationships, and greater likelihood of dating and intimate partner violence. Consistent with theoretical formulations, PTSD symptomatology appears to be central, at least for female victims. TF-CBT is a first line of treatment for those with impairing levels of symptomatology. The bulk of the data on maltreatment, though, continues to urge us toward violence prevention and early intervention. The NFP for first-time socially disadvantaged mothers shows the best evidence for prevention of maltreatment and associated outcomes such as injuries. However, once the line of abuse and official system involvement has been crossed, developing and testing approaches for parents continue to be pressing research questions.

Abuse and neglect of children are entirely unnecessary adult actions that can leave much damage to address in their wake. Even so, most maltreated individuals do not go on to maltreat their partners and children. Many maltreated individuals achieve high functionality in some domains, but may continue to struggle in others (e.g., romantic relationships). Given the social contract that children's human rights be ensured and protected, research must continue to be productive in understanding the full experience of maltreatment for the victim, support the broad uptake of effective programs while continuing to rigorously test them in their field settings, and thank those maltreated individuals and their families for participating in research to intervene, treat, and, most of all, prevent abuse and neglect.

REFERENCES

Aarons, G. A., Brown, S. A., Hough, R. L., Garland, A. F., & Wood, P. A. (2001). Prevalence of adolescent substance use disorders across five sectors of care. *Journal of the American Academy of Child and Adolescent Psychiatry, 40*(4), 419–426.

Adshead, G., & Bluglass, K. (2005). Attachment representations in mothers with abnormal illness behavior by proxy. *British Journal of Psychiatry, 187*, 328–333.

American Academy of Pediatrics (n.d.). *Some more things you should know about physical and emotional abuse.* Retrieved December 14, 2006, from www.aap.org/advocacy/childhealthmonth/ABUSE2.htm.

American Humane Association. (2006). *Emotional abuse: Factsheet.* Retrieved December 14, 2006, from http://www.americanhumane.org/site/PageServer?pagename=nr_fact_sheets_childemotionalabuse.

American Medical Association. (1992). Physicians and domestic violence: Ethical considerations. *Journal of the American Medical Association, 267*(23), 3190–3193.

American Psychiatric Association. (1994). *Diagnostic and statistical manual of mental disorders,* 4th ed. Washington, DC: Author.

American Psychiatric Association. (2000). *Diagnostic and statistical manual of mental disorders* (4th ed., text rev.) Washington, DC: Author.

American Psychiatric Association. (2004). *Diagnostic and statistical manual of mental disorders,* (4th ed. text rev.) Washington, DC: Author.

Archer, J. (2000). Sex differences in aggression between heterosexual partners: A meta-analytic review. *Psychological Bulletin, 126*(5), 651–680.

Ayoub, C. C., O'Connor, E., Rappolt-Schichtmann, G., Fischer, K. W., Rogosh, F., Toth, S., et al. (2006). Cognitive and emotional differences in young maltreated children: A translational application of dynamic skill theory. *Development and Psychopathology, 18*(3), 679–706.

Bair-Merritt, M. H., Blackstone, M., & Feudtner, C. (2006). Physical health outcomes of childhood exposure to intimate partner violence: A systematic review. *Pediatrics, 117*(2), 278–290.

Bair-Merritt, M. H., Mollen, C. J., Yau, P. L., & Fein, J. A. (2006). Impact of domestic violence posters on female caregivers' opinions about domestic violence screening and disclosure in a pediatric emergency department. *Pediatric Emergency Care, 22*(11), 689–693.

Barber, M. A., & Sibert, J. R. (2000). Diagnosing physical child abuse: The way forward. *Postgraduate Medical Journal, 76*, 743–749.

Bariciak, E. D., Plint, A. C., Gaboury, I., & Bennett, S. (2003). Dating bruises in children: An assessment of physician accuracy. *Pediatrics, 112*(4), 804–807.

Barlow, J., Johnston, I., Kendrick, D., Polnay, L., & Stewart-Brown, S. (2006). Individual and group-based parenting programmes for the treatment of physical child abuse and neglect (DOI:10.1002/14651858.CD005463. pub2). *Cochrane Database of Systematic Reviews, 3*(3), article CD005463.

Battle, C. L., Shea, M. T., Johnson, J. M., Yen, S., Zlotnick, C., & Zanarini, M. C., et al. (2004). Childhood maltreatment associated with adult personality disorders: Findings from the collaborative longitudinal personality disorders study. *Journal of Personality Disorders, 18*(2), 193–211.

Bays, J., & Chadwick, D. (1993). Medical diagnosis of the sexually abused child. *Child Abuse and Neglect, 17*(1), 91–110.

Beautrais, A. L. (2000). Risk factors for suicide and attempted suicide among young people. *Australian and New Zealand Journal of Psychiatry, 34*(3), 420–436.

Benjamin J., Ebstein R. P., & Belmaker R. H. (Eds.) (2002). *Molecular genetics and the human personality.* Washington, DC: American Psychiatric Publishing.

Berg, B., & Jones, D. P. H. (1999). Outcome of psychiatric intervention in factitious illness by proxy (Munchausen's syndrome by proxy). *Archives of Diseases in Childhood, 81,* 465–472.

Bergen, H. A., Martin, G., Richardson, A. S., Allison, S., & Roeger, L. (2003). Sexual abuse and suicidal behavior: A model constructed from a large community sample of adolescents. *Journal of the American Academy of Child Adolescent Psychiatry, 42*(11), 1301–1309.

Berliner, L. (2005). The results of randomized clinical trials move the field forward. *Child Abuse and Neglect, 29*(2), 103–105.

Bernet, W., Ayres, W., Dunne, J. E., Benedek, E., Bernstein, G. A., Bryant, E., et al. (1997). Practice parameters for the forensic evaluation of children and adolescents who may have been physically or sexually abused. *Journal of the American Academy of Child and Adolescent Psychiatry, 36*(10), 1–40.

Bernstein, D. P., & Fink, L. (1998). *Childhood Trauma Questionnaire.* San Antonio, TX: Psychological Corporation.

Biller, H. B., & Soloman, R. S. (1986). *Child maltreatment and paternal deprivation: A manifesto for research, prevention, and treatment.* Lexington, MA: Lexington Books.

Blackson, T. C., Tarter, R. E., & Mezzich, A. C. (1996). Interaction between childhood temperament and parental discipline practices on behavioral adjustment in preadolescent sons of substance abuse and normal fathers. *American Journal of Drug and Alcohol Abuse, 22*(3), 335–348.

Boney-McCoy, S., & Finkelhor, D. (1995). Psychosocial sequelae of violent victimization in a national youth sample. *Journal of Consulting and Clinical Psychology, 63*(5), 726–736.

Botash, A. S., & Ricci, L. R. (February 20, 2006). Pediatrics, Child Abuse. *e-Medicine.*

Boudewyn, A. C., & Liem, J. H. (1995). Childhood sexual abuse as a precursor to depression and self-destructive behavior in adulthood. *Journal of Traumatic Stress, 8*(3), 445–459.

Bowlby, J. (1970). Attachment and loss: Pt. 1. Attachment. *Contemporary Psychology, 15*(8), 493–494.

Bowlby, J. (1972). *Attachment.* Middlesex, England: Penguin Books.

Bowlby, J. (1980). *Attachment and loss.* New York: Basic Books.

Bowlby, J. (1982). Attachment and loss: Retrospect and prospect. *American Journal of Orthopsychiatry, 52*(4), 664–678.

Bradley, S. J. (2000). *Affect regulation and the development of psychopathology,* New York: Guilford Press.

Brayden, R. M., MacLean, W. E., Bonfiglio, J. F., & Altemeier, W. (1993). Behavioral antecedents of pediatric poisonings. *Clinical Pediatrics, 32*(1), 30–35.

Brewer-Smyth, K., Burgess, A. W., & Shults, J. (2004). Physical and sexual abuse, salivary cortisol, and neurologic correlates of violent criminal behavior in female prison inmates. *Biological Psychiatry, 55,* 21–31.

Brown, J., Cohen, P., Johnson, J. G., & Smailes, E. M. (1999). Childhood abuse and neglect: Specificity of effects on adolescents and young adult depression and suicidality. *Journal of the American Academy of Child and Adolescent Psychiatry, 38*(12), 1490–1496.

Caldwell, R. A., Bogat, G. A., & Davidson, W. S. (1988). The assessment of child abuse potential and the prevention of child abuse and neglect: A policy analysis. *American Journal of Community Psychology, 16*(5), 609–624.

Campbell, J., Jones, A. S., Dienemann, J., Kub, J., Schollenberger, J., O'Campo, P., et al. (2002). Intimate partner violence and physical health consequences. *Archives of Internal Medicine, 162*(10), 1157–1163.

Carlson, E. A. (1998). A prospective longitudinal study of disorganized/disoriented attachment. *Child Development, 6,* 1107–1128.

Carrion, V. G., Weems, C. F., Ray, R., & Reiss, A. L. (2002). Toward an empirical definition of pediatric PTSD: The phenomenology of PTSD symptoms in youth. *Journal of the American Academy of Child and Adolescent Psychiatry, 41*(2), 166–173.

Caspi, A., McClay, J., Moffitt, T., Mill, J., Martin, J., Craig, I. W., Taylor, A., & Poulton, R. (2002). Role of genotype in the cycle of violence in maltreated children. *Science, 297*(5582), 851–854.

Centers for Disease Control and Prevention (n.d.). *Healthy people 2010: Maternal, infant, and child health.* Retrieved January 31, 2007, from www.healthypeople.gov/Document/HTML/Volume2/16MICH.htm.

Center on Child Abuse Prevention Research. (1996). *Intensive home visitation: a randomized trial, follow-up and risk assessment study of Hawaii's Healthy Start Program: Final report.* (NCCAN Grant No 90-CA-1511). Washington, DC: U.S. Department of Health and Human Services.

Chandler, M. J., & Lalonde, C. (1998). Cultural continuity as a hedge against suicide in Canada's first nations. *Transcultural Psychiatry, 35*(2), 191–219.

Chaney, S. E. (2000). Child abuse: Clinical findings and management. *Journal of the American Academy of Nurse Practitioners, 12*, 467–471.

Chapman, D. P., Whitfield, C. L., Felitti, V. J., Dube, S. R., Edwards, V. J., & Anda, R. F. (2003). Adverse childhood experiences and the risk of depressive disorders in adulthood. *Journal of Affective Disorders, 82*, 217–225.

Cheng, C., Munn, C., Jack, S., & MacMillan, H. L. (2006). *Child maltreatment: A "What to do" guide for professionals who work with children,* Ottawa, ON: Public Health Agency of Canada.

Cicchetti, D., & Rogosch, F. A. (1997). The role of self-organization in the promotion of resilience in maltreated children. *Development and Psychopathology, 9*(4).

Cicchetti, D., Rogosch, F. A., & Toth, S. L. (2006). Fostering secure attachment in infants in maltreating families through preventive interventions. *Development and Psychopathology, 18*(3), 623–649.

Cicchetti, D., & Walker, E. F. (2001). Stress and development: Biological and psychological consequences. *Development and Psychopathology, 13*(3), 413–418.

Cloitre, M., Koenen, K. C., Gratz, K. L., & Jakupcak, M. (2002). Differential diagnosis of PTSD in women. In R. Kimerling & P. Ouimette. *Gender and PTSD* (pp. 117–149). New York: Guilford Press.

Cohen, J. A., Deblinger, E., Mannarino, A. P., & Steer, R. A. (2004). A multisite, randomized controlled trial for children with sexual abuse-related PTSD symptoms. *Journal of the American Academy of Child and Adolescent Psychiatry, 43*(4), 393–402.

Cohen, J. A., & Mannarino, A. P. (1996). A treatment outcome study for sexually abused preschool children: Initial findings. *Journal of the American Academy of Child and Adolescent Psychiatry, 35*, 42–50.

Cohen, J. A., & Mannarino, A. P. (1998). Factors that mediate treatment outcome of sexually abused preschool children: Six- and 12-month follow-up. *Journal of the American Academy of Child and Adolescent Psychiatry, 37*(1), 44–51.

Cohen, J. A., Mannarino, A. P., & Deblinger, E. (2006). *Treating trauma and traumatic grief in children and adolescents.* New York: Guilford Press.

Cohen, J. A., Mannarino, A. P., & Knudsen, K. (2005). Treating sexually abused children: 1 year follow-up of a randomized controlled trial. *Child Abuse and Neglect, 29*, 135–145.

Cohen, J. A., Mannarino, A. P., Murray, L. K., & Igelman, R. (2006). Psychosocial interventions for mal-treated and violence-exposed children. *Journal of Social Issues, 62*(4), 737–766.

Cohen, J. A., Mannarino, A. P., Zhitova, A. C., & Capone, M. E. (2003). Treating child abuse-related posttraumatic stress and comorbid substance abuse in adolescents. *Child Abuse and Neglect, 27*(12), 1345–1365.

Collins, K. A., & Nichols, C. A. (1999). A decade of pediatric homicide: A retrospective study at the Medical University of South Carolina. *American Journal of Forensic Medical Pathology, 20*, 169–172.

Craft, A. W., & Hall, D. M. B. (2004). Munchausen syndrome by proxy and sudden infant death. *British Medical Journal, 328*(7451), 1309–1312.

Crittenden, P. M., & Ainsworth, M. D. S. (1989). Child maltreatment and attachment theory. In D. Cicchetti & V. Carlson (Eds.), *Child maltreatment: Theory and research on the causes and consequences of child abuse and neglect* (pp. 432–463). New York: Cambridge University Press.

Crittenden, P. M., & Claussen, A. H. (2002). *Developmental psychopathology perspectives on substance abuse and relationship violence,* New York: Brunner-Routledge.

Dalgleish, T., Meiser-Stedman, R., & Smith, P. (2005). Cognitive aspects of posttraumatic stress reactions and their treatment in children and adolescents: An empirical review and some recommendations. *Behavioral and Cognitive Psychotherapy, 33*(4), 459–486.

Danielson, C. K., de Arellano, M. A., Kilpatrick, D. G., Saunders, B. E., & Resnick, H. S. (2005). Child maltreatment in depressed adolescents: Differences in symptomatology based on history of abuse. *Child Maltreatment, 10*(1), 37–48.

Daro, D. A., & Harding, K. A. (1999). Healthy Families America: Using research to enhance practice. *Future of Children, 9*(1), 152–176.

Davis, P., McClure, R. J., Rolfe, K., Chessman, N., Pearson, S., Sibert, J. R., et al. (1998). Procedures, placement, and risks of further abuse following Munchausen syndrome by proxy, non-accidental poisoning, and non-accidental suffocation. *Archives of Diseases in Childhood, 78*, 217–221.

DeBellis, M. D. (2001). Developmental traumatology: The psychobiological development of maltreated children and its implications for research, treatment, and policy. *Development and Psychopathology, 13*(3), 539–564.

DeBellis, M. D., & Putnam, F. W. (1994). The psychobiology of childhood maltreatment. *Child and Adolescent Psychiatric Clinics of North America, 3*, 663–677.

Deblinger, E., Mannarino, A. P., Cohen, J. A., & Steer, R. A. (2006). A follow-up study of multisite, randomized, controlled trial for children with sexual abuse-related PTSD symptoms. *Journal of the American Academy of Child and Adolescent Psychiatry, 45*(12), 1474–1484.

Deblinger, E., Stauffer, L. B., & Steer, R. A. (2001). Comparative efficacies of supportive and cognitive behavioral group therapies for young children who have been sexually abused and their nonoffending mothers. *Child Maltreatment, 6*(4), 332–343.

Deblinger, E., Steer, R. A., & Lippman, J. (1999). Maternal factors associated with sexually abused children's psychosocial adjustment. *Child Maltreatment, 4*(1), 13–20.

DeMarco, R., & Phelan, J. (2004). *Maltreatment outcomes.* Ottawa, Ontario, Canada: Public Health Agency of Canada.

Dodge, K. A., Pettit, G. S., Bates, J. E., & Valente, E. (1995). Social information-processing patterns partially mediate the effect of early physical abuse on later conduct problems. *Journal of Abnormal Psychology, 104*(4), 632–643.

Dong, M., Anda, R. F., Felitti, V. J., Dube, S. R., Williamson, D. F., Thompson, T. J., et al. (2004). The interrelatedness of multiple forms of childhood abuse, neglect, and household dysfunction. *Child Abuse and Neglect, 28*, 771–784.

Doyle, C. (1997). Emotional abuse of children: Issues for intervention. *Child Abuse Review, 6*(5), 330–342.

Drach, K. M., Wientzen, J., & Ricci, L. R. (2001). The diagnostic utility of sexual behavior problems in diagnosing sexual abuse in a forensic child abuse evaluation clinic. *Child Abuse and Neglect, 25*(4), 489–503.

Dube, S. R., Anda, R. F., Felitti, V. J., Chapman, D. P., Williamson, D. F., & Giles, W. H. (2001). Childhood abuse, household dysfunction, and the risk of attempted suicide throughout the life span: Findings from the adverse childhood experiences study. *Journal of the American Medical Association, 286*, 3089–3096.

Dubowitz, H., Kerr, M., Cox, C., Radhakrishna, A., English, D., Runyon, D., et al. (2000). Father involvement and children's functioning at age 6: Pt. 2. A multi-site study. *Pediatric Research, 47*(4), A25–A125.

Duggan, A. K., McFarlane, E. C., Windham, A. M., Rohde, C. A., Salkever, D. S., Fuddy, L., et al. (1999). Evaluation of Hawaii's Healthy Start program. *Future of Children, 9*(1), 66–90.

Dyregrov, A., & Yule, W. (2006). A review of PTSD in children. *Child and Adolescent Mental Health, 11*(4), 176–184.

Eckenrode, J., Ganzel, B., Henderson, C. R., Jr., Smith, E., Olds, D. L., Powers, J., et al. (2000). Preventing child abuse and neglect with a program of nurse home visitation: The limiting effects of domestic violence. *Journal of the American Medical Association, 284*(11), 1385–1391.

Egeland, B., Jacobvitz, D., & Sroufe, L. A. (1988). Breaking the cycle of abuse. *Child Development, 59*(4), 1080–1088.

Egeland, B., Yates, T., Appleyard, K., & van Dulmen, M. (2002). The long-term consequences of maltreatment in the early years: A developmental pathway model to antisocial behavior. *Children's Services: Social Policy, Research, and Practice, 5*(4), 249–260.

Eiden, R. D., & Leonard, K. E. (2000). Paternal alcoholism, parental psychopathology, and aggravation with infants. *Journal of Substance Abuse, 11*(1), 17–29.

Elgar, F. J., Curtis, L. J., McGrath, P. J., Waschbusch, D. A., & Stewart, S. H. (2003). Antecedent-consequence conditions in maternal mood and child adjustment: A 4-year cross-lagged study. *Journal of Consulting Child and Adolescent Psychology, 32*, 362–374.

Emans, J., Woods, E., Flagg, N., & Freeman, A. (1987, May). Genital findings in sexually abused, symptomatic, and asymptomatic girls. *Pediatrics, 79*(5), 778–785.

Ertem, I. O., Leventhal, J. M., & Dobbs, S. (2000). Intergenerational continuity of child physical abuse: How good is the evidence? *Lancet, 356*, 814–819.

Evans, E., Hawton, K., & Rodham, K. (2005). Suicidal phenomena and abuse in adolescents: A review of epidemiological studies. *Child Abuse and Neglect, 29*(1), 45–58.

Evren, C., Kural, S., & Cakmak, D. (2005). Clinical correlates of childhood abuse and neglect in substance dependents. *Addictive Behaviors, 31*, 475–485.

Family Violence Prevention Fund. (2004). *National consensus guidelines on identifying and responding to domestic violence victimization in health care settings.* San Francisco: Family Violence Prevention Fund. Available from http://endabuse.org/programs/healthcare/files/Consensus.pdf.

Fantuzzo, J., Boruch, R., Beriama, A., Atkins, M., & Marcus, S. (1997). Domestic violence and children: Prevalence and risk in five major U.S. cities. *Journal of the American Academy of Child and Adolescent Psychiatry, 36*(1), 116–122.

Fantuzzo, J., & Lindquist, C. U. (1989). Effects of observing conjugal violence on children: A review and analysis of research methodology. *Journal of Family Violence, 4*(1), 77–94.

Favazza, A. R., & Conterio, K. (1989). Female habitual self-mutilators. *Acta Psychiatrica Scandinavia, 79*, 238–289.

Feiring, C., Taska, L., Lewis, M. (2002). Adjustment following sexual discovery: The role of shame and attributional style. *Developmental Psychology, 38*(1), 79–92.

Fergusson, D. M., & Mullen, P. E. (1999). *Childhood sexual abuse: An evidence based perspective.* Thousand Oaks, CA: Sage.

Ferris, L. E. (2004). Intimate partner violence: Doctors should offer referral to existing interventions while better evidence is awaited. *British Medical Journal, 328*(7440), 595–596.

Finkelhor, D., Ormrod, R., & Turner, H. (2007). Polyvictimization and trauma in a national longitudinal cohort. *Development and Psychopathology, 19*, 149–166.

Finkelhor, D., Ormrod, R., Turner, H., & Hamby, S. L. (2005). The victimization of children and youth: A comprehensive, national survey. *Child Maltreatment, 10*(1), 5–25.

Flett, G. L., & Hewitt, P. L. (2002). *Personality factors and substance abuse in relationship violence and child abuse: A review and theoretical analysis.* New York: Brunner-Routledge.

Flisher, A. J., Dramer, R. A., Hoven, C. W., Greenwald, S., Alegria, M., Bird, H. R., et al. (1997). Psychosocial characteristics of physically abused children and adolescents. *Journal of the American Academy of Child and Adolescent Psychiatry, 36*(1), 123–131.

Giardino, A. P., & Giardino, E. R. (2002). *Recognition of child abuse for the mandated reporter* (3rd ed.). St. Louis, MO: G. W. Medical.

Ginzler, J. A., Cochran, B. N., Comenech-Rodriguez, M., Cauce, A. M., & Whitbeck, L. B. (2003). Sequential progression of substance use among homeless youth: An empirical investigation of the gateway theory. *Substance Use and Misuse: Special Homelessness and Substance Use, 38*(3–6), 725–758.

Goldberg, S. (2001). Infant-mother attachment and cortisol stress responses. *Psychosomatic Medicine, 63*(1), 154–155.

Gover, A. R. (2004). Childhood sexual abuse, gender, and depression among incarcerated youth. *International Journal of Offender Therapy and Comparative Criminology, 48*(6), 683–696.

Greenwald, R., & Rubin, A. (1999). Assessment of posttraumatic symptoms in children: Development and preliminary validation of parent and child scales. *Research on Social Work Practice, 9*(1), 61–75.

Hamby, S., & Finkelhor, D. (2004). *Comprehensive Juvenile Victimization Questionnaire.* Durham: University of New Hampshire Press.

Handford, H. A., Mayes, S. D., Mattison, R. E., & Humphrey, F. J. (1986). Child and parent reactions to the Three Mile Island nuclear accident. *Journal of the American Academy of Child Psychiatry, 25*(3), 346–356.

Herman-Giddens, M. E., Brown, G., Verbiest, S., Carlson, P. J., Hooten, E. G., Howell, E., et al. (1999). Underascertainment of child abuse mortality in the United States. *Journal of the American Medical Association, 282*(5), 463–467.

Herrera, V. M., & McCloskey, L. (2003). Sexual abuse, family violence and female delinquency: Findings from a longitudinal study. *Violence and Victims, 18*(3), 319–334.

Hornor, G. (2005). Physical abuse: Recognition and reporting. *Journal of Pediatric Health Care, 19*(1), 4–11.

Hurley, D. J., Chiodo, D., Leschied, A., & Whitehead, P. C. (2003). *Intergenerational continuity and life course trajectory in a child protection sample: Implications for social work practice*. London, Ontario, Canada: University of Western Ontario.

Johnson, J. G., Cohen, P., Brown, J., Smailes, E. M., & Bernstein, D. P. (1999). Childhood maltreatment increases risk for personality disorders during early adulthood. *Archives of General Psychiatry, 56*, 600–606.

Johnson, J. G., Cohen, P., Kasen, S., & Brook, J. S. (2002). Childhood adversities associated with risk for eating disorders or weight problems during early adolescence or early adulthood. *American Journal of Psychiatry, 159*(3), 394–400.

Joshi, P. T., Daniolos, P. T., & Salpekar, J. A. (2004a). *Physical abuse of children*. Washington, DC: American Psychiatric Publishing.

Joshi, P. T., Daniolos, P. T., & Salpekar, J. A. (2004b). *Sexual abuse of children*. Washington, DC: American Psychiatric Publishing.

Joyce, P. R., McKenzie, J. M., Luty, S. E., Mulder, R. T., Carter, J. D., Sullivan, P. F., et al. (2003). Temperament, childhood environment, and psychopathology as risk factors for avoidant and borderline personality disorders. *Australian and New Zealand Journal of Psychiatry, 37*, 756–764.

Kaplan, S. J., Covitz, D. P., Salzinger, S., Mandel, F., Weiner, M., & Labruna, V. (1999). Adolescent physical abuse and risk for suicidal behaviors. *Journal of Interpersonal Violence, 14*(9), 976–988.

Kaplan, S. J., Pelcovitz, D., Salzinger, S., Mandel, F. S., & Wiener, M. (1997). Adolescent physical abuse and suicide attempts. *Journal of the Academy of Child and Adolescent Psychiatry, 36*(6), 799–808.

Kaplan, S. J., Pelcovitz, D., Salzinger, S., Weiner, M., Mandel, F. S., Lesser, M. L., et al. (1998). Adolescent physical abuse: Risk for adolescent psychiatric disorders. *American Journal of Psychiatry, 155*(7), 954–959.

Kaufman, J., Yang, B.-Z., Douglas-Palumberi, H., Houshyar, S., Lipschitz, D., Krystal, J. H., et al. (2004). Social supports and serotonin transporter gene moderate depression in maltreated children. *Proceedings of the National Academy of Sciences, 101*(49), 17316–17321.

Kellogg, N., & Committee on Child Abuse and Neglect. (2005). The evaluation of sexual abuse in children. *Pediatrics, 116*(2), 506–512.

Kendall-Tackett, K. A., Williams, L. M., & Finkelhor, D. (1993). Impact of sexual abuse on children: A review and synthesis of recent empirical studies. *Psychological Bulletin, 113*(1), 164–180.

Kessler, R. C., Nelson, C. B., McGonagle, K. A., Edlund, M. J., Frank, R. G., & Leaf, P. J. (1996). The epidemiology of co-occurring addictive and mental disorders: Implications for prevention and service utilization. *American Journal of Orthopsychiatry, 66*, 17–31.

Kilpatrick, D. G., Acierno, R., Saunders, B. E., Resnick, H. S., Best, C. L., et al. (2000). Risk factors for adolescent substance abuse and dependence: Data from a national sample. *Journal of Consulting and Clinical Psychology, 68*(1), 19–30.

Kilpatrick, D. G., Ruggiero, K. J., Acierno, R., Saunders, B. E., Resnick, H. S., & Best, C. L. (2003). Violence and risk of PTSD, major depression, substance abuse/dependence, and comorbidity: Results from the National Survey of Adolescents. *Journal of Consulting and Clinical Psychology, 71*(4), 692–700.

Kim, J., & Cicchetti, D. (2003). Social self-efficacy and behavior problems in maltreated children. *Journal of Clinical Child and Adolescent Psychology, 32*(1), 106–117.

Kim-Cohen, J., Caspi, A., Taylor, A., Williams, B., Newcombe, R., Craig, I. W., et al. (2006). MAOA, maltreatment and gene environment interaction predicting children's mental health: New evidence and meta-analysis. *Molecular Psychiatry, 11*(10), 903–913.

King, W. J., MacKay, M., & Sirnick, A. (2003). Shaken baby syndrome in Canada: Clinical characteristics and outcomes of hospital cases. *Canadian Medical Association Journal, 168*(2), 155–159.

Kingree, J. B., Phan, D., & Thomson, M. (2003). Child maltreatment and recidivism among adolescent detainees. *Criminal Justice and Behavior, 30*(6), 623–643.

Kisiel, C. L., & Lyons, J. S. (2001). Dissociation as a mediator of psychopathology among sexually abused children and adolescents. *American Journal of Psychiatry, 158*(7), 1034–1039.

Kitzman, H., Cole, R., Yoos, L., & Olds, D. (1997). Challenges experienced by home visitors: A qualitative study program implementation. *Journal of Community Psychology, 25*(1), 95–109.

Kitzmann, K. M., Gaylord, N. K., Holt, A. R., & Kenny, E. D. (2003). Child witnesses to domestic violence: A meta-analytic review. *Journal of Consulting and Clinical Psychology, 71*(2), 339–352.

Kolbo, J. R., Blakely, E. H., & Engleman, D. (1996). Children who witness domestic violence: A review of empirical literature. *Journal of Interpersonal Violence, 11*(2), 281–293.

Kolko, D. J. (1996). Clinical monitoring of treatment course in child physical abuse: Psychometric characteristics and treatment comparisons. *Child Abuse and Neglect, 20*(1), 23–43.

Kolko, D. J., Moser, J. T., & Weldy, S. R. (1988). Behavioral/emotional indicators of sexual abuse in child psychiatric inpatients: A controlled comparison with physical abuse. *Child Abuse and Neglect, 12*(4), 529–541.

Kos, L., & Shwayder, T. (2006). Cutaneous manifestations of child abuse. *Pediatric Dermatology, 23*(4), 311–320.

Kotelchuck, M. (1982). Child abuse and neglect: Prediction and misclassification. In R. Starr (Ed.), *Child abuse prediction* (pp. 67–104). Cambridge, MA: Ballinger.

Krug, E. G., Mercy, J., Dahlberg, L. L., & Zwi, A. B. (2002). The world report on violence and health. *Lancet, 360*(9339), 1083–1088.

Lambie, G. W. (2005). Child abuse and neglect: A practical guide for paraprofessional school counselors. *Professional School of Counselling, 8*(3), 249–258.

Liebschutz, J. M., Frayne, S. M., & Saxe, G. N., (Eds.). (2003). *Violence against women: A physician's guide to identification and management.* Philadelphia: American College of Physicians Press.

Linehan, M. M. (1993b). *Skills training manual for treating borderline personality disorder.* New York: Guilford Press.

Linehan, M. M., Dimeff, L. A., Reynolds, S. K., Comtois, K. A., Welch, S. S., Heagerty, P., et al. (in press). Dialectical behavior therapy versus comprehensive validation plus 12-step for the treatment of opioid dependent women meeting criteria for borderline personality disorder. *Drug and Alcohol Dependence.*

Linning, L. M., & Kearney, C. A. (2004). Post-traumatic stress disorder in maltreated youth: A study of diagnostic comorbidity and child factors. *Journal of Interpersonal Violence, 19*(10), 1087–1101.

Lipschitz, D. S., Winegar, R. K., Nicolaou, A. L., Hartnick, E., Wolfson, M., & Southwick, S. (1999). Perceived abuse and neglect as risk factors for suicidal behavior in adolescent inpatients. *Journal of Nervous and Mental Diseases, 187*(1), 32–39.

Lyons-Ruth, K., & Jacobvitz, D. (1999). Attachment disorganization: Unresolved loss, relational violence, and lapses in behavioral and attentional strategies. In P. Shaver & J. Cassidy (Eds.). *Handbook of attachment: Theory, research, and clinical applications* (pp. 520–554). New York: Guilford Press.

Lyons-Ruth, K., Lyubchik, A., Wolfe, R., & Bronfman, E. (2002). Parental depression and child attachment: Hostile and helpless profiles of parent and child behavior among families at risk. In I. H. Gotlib & S. H. Goodman (Eds.), *Children of depressed parents: Mechanisms of risk and implications for treatment* (pp. 89–120). Washington, DC: American Psychological Association.

Macdonald, G. M., Higgins, J. P. T., & Ramchandani, P. (2006). Cognitive-behavioural interventions for children who have been sexually abused. *Cochrane Database of Systematic Reviews, 4*, 295–309.

Macfie, J., Cicchetti, D., & Toth, S. L. (2001). Dissociation in maltreated versus nonmaltreated preschool-aged children. *Child Abuse and Neglect, 25*(9), 1253–1267.

MacMillan, H. L., Boyle, M. H., Wong, M.Y.-Y., Duku, E. K., Fleming, J. E., & Walsh, C. (1999). Slapping and spanking in childhood and its association with lifetime prevalence of psychiatric disorders in a general population sample. *Canadian Medical Association Journal, 161*(7), 805–809.

MacMillan, H. L., Fleming, J. E., Streiner, D. L., Lin, E., Boyle, M. H., Jamieson, E., et al. (2001). Childhood abuse and lifetime psychopathology in a community sample. *American Journal of Psychiatry, 158*(11), 1878–1883.

MacMillan, H. L., & Munn, C. (2001). The sequelae of child maltreatment. *Current Opinion in Psychiatry, 14*, 325–331.

MacMillan, H. L., Thomas, B. H., Jamieson, E., Walsh, C. A., Boyle, M. H., Shannon, H. S., et al. (2005). Effectiveness of home visitation by public-health nurses in prevention of the recurrence of child physical abuse and neglect: A randomized controlled trial. *Lancet, 365*(9473), 1786–1793.

MacMillan, H. L., & Wathen, C. N. (2001). *Prevention and treatment of violence against women: Systematic review and recommendations.* London, Ontario, Canada: Canadian Task Force on Preventive Health Care. Available from www.ctfphc.org/Full_Text/CTF_DV_TR_final.pdf.

MacMillan, H. L., & Wathen, C. N. (2003). Violence against women: Integrating the evidence into clinical practice. *Canadian Medical Association Journal, 169*(6), 570–571.

Maguire, S., Mann, M. K., Sibert, J., & Kemp, A. (2005). Are there patterns of bruising in childhood which are diagnostic or suggestive of abuse? *Archives of Disease in Childhood, 90*, 182–186.

Mannarino, A. P., Cohen, J. A., & Gregor, M. (1989). Emotional and behavioral difficulties in sexually abused girls. *Journal of Interpersonal Violence, 4*(4), 437–451.

Martin, G., Bergen, H. A., Richardson, A. S., Roeger, L., & Allison, S. (2004). Sexual abuse and suicidality: Gender differences in a large community sample of adolescents. *Child Abuse and Neglect, 28*(5), 491–503.

Marziali, E., Damianakis, T., & Trocmé, N. (2003). Nature and consequences of personality problems in maltreating caregivers. *Families in Society, 84*(4), 530–538.

Masten, A. S., Best, K. M., & Garmezy, N. (1990). Resilience and development: Contributions from the study of children who overcome adversity. *Development and Psychopathology, 2*(4), 425–444.

Mayer, B. W., & Burns, P. (2000). Differential diagnosis of abuse injuries in infants and young children. *Nurse Practitioner, 25*(10), 15–37.

Mayer, M., Dufour, S., Lavergne, C., Girard, M., & Trocmé, N. (2003). *Comparing parental characteristics regarding child neglect: An analysis of cases retained by child protective services in Quebec.* Poster presented at the Child and Youth Health 3rd World Congress, Vancouver, British Columbia.

McCloskey, L. A., Figueredo, A. J., & Koss, M. P. (1995). The effects of systemic family violence on children's mental health. *Child Development, 66*(5), 1239–1261.

McCurdy, K. (1995). Risk assessment in child abuse prevention programs. *Social Work Research, 19*(2), 77–87.

McGloin, J. M., & Widom, C. S. (2001). Resilience among abused and neglected children growing up. *Development and Psychopathology, 13*(4), 1021–1038.

McLeer, S. V., Deblinger, E., Atkins, M. S., Foa, E. B., & Rolphe, O. L. (1988). Post-traumatic stress disorder in sexually abused children. *Journal of the American Academy of Child and Adolescent Psychiatry, 27*, 650–654.

McNally, R. J. (1991). Assessment of posttraumatic stress disorder in children. *Psychological Assessment, 3*(4), 531–537.

Meadow, R. (1998). Munchausen syndrome by proxy abuse perpetrated by men. *Archives of Disease in Childhood, 78*, 210–216.

Meyerson, L. A., Long, P. L., Miranda, R. Z., & Marx, B. P. (2002). The influence of childhood sexual abuse, physical abuse, family environment, and gender on the psychological adjustment of adolescents. *Child Abuse and Neglect, 26*(4), 387–405.

Miller, A. L., Rathus, J. H., & Linehan, M. M. (2007). *Dialectical behavior therapy for suicidal multi-problem adolescents.* New York: Guilford Press.

Mudd, S. S., & Findlay, J. S. (2004). The cutaneous manifestations and common mimickers of physical child abuse. *Journal of Pediatric Health Care, 18*(3), 123–129.

Nader, K. O. (1997). *Assessing traumatic experiences in children.* New York: Guilford Press.

National Center on Child Abuse and Neglect. (1996). *Intensive home visitation: a randomized trial, follow-up and risk assessment study of Hawaii's Healthy Start Program.* Chicago, IL: Center on Child Abuse Prevention Research.

National Clearinghouse on Child Abuse and Neglect. (2004, March). *Long-term consequences of child abuse and neglect* [Electronic version]. Retrieved February 8, 2007, from www.childwelfare.gov/pubs/factsheets/long_term_consequences.cfm.

National Clearinghouse on Family Violence. (2006). *Factsheet: Child maltreatment: A "What to do" guide for professionals who work with children.* Ottawa, Ontario, Canada: Public Health Agency of Canada.

National Institute of Child Health and Human Development Early Child Care Research Network. (2004). Affect dysregulation in the mother-child relationship in the toddler years: Antecedents and consequences. *Development and Psychopathology, 16*(1), 43–68.

Nelson, D. E., Higginson, G. K., & Grant-Worley, J. A. (1995). Physical abuse among high school students: Prevalence and correlation with other health behaviors. *Archives of Pediatrics and Adolescent Medicine, 149*(11), 1254–1258.

Nelson, E. C., Heath, A. C., Madden, P., Cooper, L., Dinwiddle, S. H., Bucholz, K. K., et al. (2002). Association between self-reported childhood sexual abuse and adverse psychosocial outcomes: Results from a twin study. *Archives of General Psychiatry, 59*, 139–145.

Nelson, H. D., Nygren, P., McInerney, Y., & Klein, J. (2004). Screening women and elderly adults for family and intimate partner violence: A review of the evidence for the U.S. Preventive Services Task Force. *Annals of Internal Medicine, 140*(5), 387–396.

Nimkink, K., & Kleinman, P. K. (2001). Imaging child abuse. *Radiologic Clinics of North America, 39*(4), 843–864.

Olds, D. L. (2002). Prenatal and infancy home visiting by nurses: From randomized trials to community replication. *Prevention Science, 3*(3), 153–172.

Olds, D. L. (2006). Preventing child abuse and neglect with home visiting. Where are we today? *SCAN: American Academy of Pediatrics Newsletter of the Section on Child Abuse and Neglect, 18*(3), 2–3, 5.

Olds, D. L., Eckenrode, J., Henderson, C. R., Jr., Kitzman, H., Powers, J., Cole, R., et al. (1997). Long-term effects of home visitation on maternal life course and child abuse and neglect: Fifteen-year follow-up of a randomized trial. *Journal of the American Medical Association, 278*(8), 637–643.

Olds, D. L., Henderson, C. R., Jr., Chamberlin, R., & Tatelbaum, R. (1986). Preventing child abuse and neglect: A randomized trial of nurse home visitation. *Pediatrics, 78*(1), 65–78.

Olds, D. L., Robinson, J., O'Brien, R., Luckey, D. W., Pettitt, L. M., Henderson, C. R., Jr., et al. (2002). Home visiting by paraprofessionals and by nurses: A randomized, controlled trial. *Pediatrics, 110*(3), 486–496.

Olds, D. L., Robinson, J., Pettitt, L., Luckey, D. W., Holmberg, J., Ng, R. K., Isacks, K., Sheff, K., & Henderson, C. R., Jr. (2004). Effects of home visits by paraprofessionals and by nurses: Age 4 follow-up results of a randomized trial. *Pediatrics, 114*, 1560–1568.

Olds, D. L., Sadler, L., & Kitzman, H. (2007). Programs for parents of infants and toddlers: recent evidence from randomized trials. *Journal of Child Psychology and Psychiatry, 48*, 355–391.

Ontario Association of Children's Aid Societies, (n.d.). *Signs of abuse and neglect.* Retrieved December 14, 2006, from www.oacas.org/resources/signsofabuse.htm#Emotional.

Ornduff, S. R., Kelsey, R. M., O'Leary, K. D. (2001). Childhood physical abuse, personality and adult relationship violence: A model of vulnerability to victimization. *American Journal of Orthopsychiatry, 71*(3), 322–331.

Osofsky, J. D. (2003). Prevalence of children's exposure to domestic violence and child maltreatment: Implications for prevention and intervention. *Clinical Child and Family Psychology Review, 6*(3), 161–170.

Palusci, V. J., Cox, E. O., Cyrus, T. A., Heartwell, S. W., Vandervort, F. E., & Pott, E. S. (1999). Medical assessment and legal outcome in child sexual abuse. *Archives of Pediatrics and Adolescent Medicine, 153*(4), 388–392.

Pankratz, L. (2006). Persistent problems with the Munchausen syndrome by proxy label. *Journal of the American Academy of Psychiatry and the Law, 34*, 90–95.

Peck, M. D., & Priolo-Kapel, D. (2002). Child abuse by burning: A review of the literature and an algorithm for medical investigations. *Journal of the Trauma-Injury, Infection and Critical Care, 53*(5), 1013–1022.

Pelcovitz, D., Kaplan, S. J., DeRosa, R. R., Mandel, F. S., & Salzinger, S. (2000). Psychiatric disorders in adolescents exposed to domestic violence and physical abuse. *American Journal of Orthopsychiatry, 70*(3), 360–369.

Pelcovitz, D., Kaplan, S., Goldenberg, B., Mandel, F. S., Lehane, J., & Guarrera, J. (1994). Post-traumatic stress disorder in physically abused adolescents. *Journal of the American Academy of Child and Adolescent Psychiatry, 33*(3), 305–312.

Perrin, S., Smith, P., & Yule, W. (2000). The assessment and treatment of post-traumatic stress disorder in children and adolescents. *Journal of Child Psychology and Psychiatry, 41*(3), 277–289.

Pickering, A., Farmer, A., & McGuffin, P. (2004). The role of personality in childhood sexual abuse. *Personality and Individual Differences, 36*(6), 1295–1303.

Pine, D. S., Mogg, K., Bradley, B. P., Montgomery, L., Monk, C. S., McClure, E., et al. (2005). Attention bias to threat in maltreated children: Implications for vulnerability to stress-related psychopathology. *American Journal of Psychiatry, 162*(2), 291–296.

Polansky, N. A., Chamlers, A., Buttenwieser, E., & Williams, P. (1981). *Damaged parents,* Chicago: University of Chicago Press.

Pollak, S. D., & Kistler, D. J. (2002). Early experience is associated with the development of categorical representations for facial expressions of emotion. *Proceedings of the National Academy of Sciences, 99*(13), 9072–9076.

Pollak, S. D., & Tolley-Schell, S. A. (2003). Selective attention to facial emotion in physically abused children. *Journal of Abnormal Psychology, 112*(3), 323–328.

Powell, C. (2003). Early indicators of child abuse and neglect: A multi-professional Delphi study. *Child Abuse Review, 12*(1), 25–40.

Putnam, F. W. (1996). Child development and dissociation. *Child and Adolescent Psychiatry Clinics of North America, 5*, 285–301.

Putnam, F. W. (1998). Trauma models of the effects of childhood maltreatment. *Journal of Aggression, Maltreatment and Trauma, 2*, 51–66.

Quinton, D., Rutter, M., & Liddle, C. (1984). Institutional rearing, parenting difficulties and marital support. *Psychological Medicine, 14*(1), 107–124.

Raghavan, C., & Kingston, S. (2006). Child sexual abuse and posttraumatic stress disorder: The role of age at first use of substances and lifetime traumatic events. *Journal of Traumatic Stress, 19*(2), 269–278.

Ramsay, J., Richardson, J., Carter, Y. H., Davidson, L. L., & Feder, G. (2002). Should health professionals screen women for domestic violence? Systematic review. *British Medical Journal, 325*(7359), 1–13.

Reece, R. M., & Ludwig, S. (Eds.). (2001). *Child Abuse: Medical Diagnosis and Management*. Baltimore: Lippincott, Williams and Wilkins.

Reese, L. E., Vera, E. M., Thompson, K., & Reyes, R. (2001). A qualitative investigation of perceptions of violence risk factors in low-income African American children. *Journal of Clinical Child Psychology, 30*, 161–171.

Renner, L. M., & Slack, K. S. (2006). Intimate partner violence and child maltreatment: Understanding intra- and intergenerational connections. *Child Abuse and Neglect, 30*, 599–617.

Rhodes, K. V., & Levinson, W. (2003). Interventions for intimate partner violence against women. *Journal of the American Medical Association, 289*(5), 601–605.

Riggs, S., Alario, A. J., & McHorney, C. (1990). Health risk behaviors and attempted suicide in adolescents who report prior maltreatment. *Journal of Pediatrics, 116*, 815–821.

Risser, H. J., Hetzel-Riggin, M. D., Thomsen, C. J., & McCanne, T. R. (2006). PTSD as a mediator of sexual revictimization: The role of reexperiencing, avoidance, and arousal symptoms. *Journal of Traumatic Stress, 19*(5), 687–698.

Rogosch, F. A., & Cicchetti, D. (1994). Illustrating the inter-face of family and peer relations through the study of child maltreatment. *Social Development, 3*(3), 291–308.

Rogosch, F. A., Cicchetti, D., & Toth, S. L. (2004). Expressed emotion in multiple subsystems of the families of toddlers with depressed mothers. *Development and Psychopathology, 16*(3), 689–706.

Romano, E., Zoccolillo, M., & Paquette, D. (2006). Histories of child maltreatment and psychiatric disorder in pregnant adolescents. *Journal of the American Academy of Child and Adolescent Psychiatry, 45*(3), 329–336.

Rorty, M., Yeager, J., & Rossotto, E. (1994). Childhood sexual, physical, and psychological abuse in bulimia nervosa. *American Journal of Psychiatry, 151*(8), 1122–1126.

Ruchkin, V. V., Schwab-Stone, M., Koposov, R., Vermeiren, R., & Steiner, H. (2002). Violence exposure, posttraumatic stress, and personality in juvenile delinquents. *Journal of the American Academy of Child and Adolescent Psychiatry, 41*(3), 322–329.

Rutter, M., & Sroufe, L. A. (2000). Developmental psychopathology: Concepts and challenges. *Development and Psychopathology, 12*(3), 265–296.

Sabotta, E. E., & Davis, R. L. (1992). Fatality after reports to a child abuse registry in Washington state, 1973–1986. *Child Abuse and Neglect, 16*, 627–635.

Salter, D., McMillan, D., Richards, M., Talbot, T., Hodges, J., Bentovim, A., Hastings, R., Stevenson, J., & Skuse, D. (2003). Development of sexually abusive behavior in sexually victimized males: A longitudinal study. *Lancet, 361*(9356), 471–476.

Shea, A., Walsh, C., MacMillan, H., & Steiner, M. (2005). Child maltreatment and HPA axis dysregulation: Relationship to major depressive disorder and post traumatic stress disorder in females. *Psychoneuroendocrinology, 30*(2), 162–178.

Shonk, S. M., & Cicchetti, D. (2001). Maltreatment, competency deficits, and risk for academic and behavioral maladjustment. *Developmental Psychology, 37*, 3–14.

Sidebotham, P., & Heron, J. (2006). Child maltreatment in the "children of the nineties": A cohort study of risk factors. *Child Abuse and Neglect, 30*, 497–522.

Sirotnak, A. P., Grigsby, T., & Krugman, R. D. (2004). Physical abuse of children. *Pediatrics in Review,* *25*(8), 264–277.

Slep, A., & Heyman, R. (2006, August). Creating and field-testing child maltreatment definitions: Improving the reliability of substantiation determinations. *Child Maltreatment, 11*(3), 217–236.

Solomon J., & George C. (Eds.). (1999). *Attachment disorganization.* New York: Guilford Press.

Southall, D. P., Plunkett, M. C. B., Banks, M. W., Falkov, A. F., & Samuels, M. P. (1997). Covert video recordings of life-threatening child abuse: Lessons for child protection. *Pediatrics, 100*(5), 735–760.

Stewart, S. H., & Israeli, A. L. (2002). Substance abuse and co-occurring psychiatric disorders in victims of intimate violence. In C. Wekerle & A. M. Wall (Eds.), *The violence and addiction equation: Theoretical and clinical issues in substance abuse and relationship violence* (pp. 98–122). New York: Brunner-Routledge.

Stiffman, M. N., Schnitzer, P. G., Adam, P., Kruse, R. L., & Ewigman, B. G. (2002). Household composition and risk of fatal child maltreatment. *Pediatrics, 109*, 615–621.

Stovall-McClough, K. C., & Dozier, M. (2004). Forming attachments in foster care: Infant attachment behaviors during the first 2 months of placement. *Development and Psychopathology, 16*(2), 253–271.

Strand, V. C., Sarmiento, T. L., & Pasquale, L. E. (2005). Assessment and screening tools for trauma in children and adolescents. *Trauma, Violence, and Abuse, 6*(1), 55–78.

Sullivan, T. P., Fehon, D. C., Andrew-Hyman, R. C., Lipschitz, D. S., & Grilo, C. M. (2006). Differential relationships of childhood abuse and neglect subtypes to PTSD symptom clusters among adolescent inpatients. *Journal of Traumatic Stress, 19*(2), 229–239.

Takayama, J. I., Wolfe, E., & Coulter, K. P. (1998). Relationship between reason for placement and medical findings among children in foster care. *Pediatrics, 101*(2), 201–207.

Taket, A., Nurse, J., Smith, K., Watson, J., Shakespeare, J., Lavis, V., et al. (2003). Routinely asking women about domestic violence in health settings. *British Medical Journal, 327*(7416), 673–676.

Theodore, A. D., Chang, J. J., Runyan, D. K., Hunter, W. M., Bangdiwala, S. I., & Agans, R. (2005). Epidemiologic features of the physical and sexual maltreatment of children in the Carolinas. *Pediatrics, 115*, 331–337.

Tjaden, P., & Thoennes, N. (2000). Prevalence and consequences of male-to-female and female-to-male intimate partner violence as measured by the National Violence Against Women Survey. *Violence Against Women, 6*(2), 142–161.

Tolin, D. F., & Foa, E. B. (2002). Gender and PTSD: A cognitive model. In R. Kimerling, P. Ouimette, & J. Wolfe (Eds.), *Gender and PTSD* (pp. 76–97). New York: Guilford Press.

Toth, S. L., Cicchetti, D., Macfie, J., & Emde, R. N. (1997). Representations of self and other in narratives of neglected, physically abused, and sexually abused preschoolers. *Development and Psychopathology, 9*(4), 781–796.

Trickett, P., Noll, J., Reiffman, A., & Putnam, F. (2001). Variants of intrafamilial sexual abuse experience: Implications for short- and long-term development. *Development and Psychopathology, 13*, 1001–1019.

Trocki, K. F., & Caetano, R. (2003). Exposure to family violence and temperament factors as predictors of adult psychopathology and substance use outcomes. *Journal of Addictions Nursing, 14*(4), 183–192.

Trocmé, N., Fallon, B., MacLaurin, B., Daciuk, J., Felstiner, C., Black, T., et al. (2005). *Canadian incidence study of reported child abuse and neglect: 2003 major findings,* Ottawa, ON: Minister of Public Works and Government Services Canada.

Turcotte, G., Dubeau, D., Bolté, C., & Paquette, D. (2001). Pourquoi certain peres sont-ils plus engages que d'autres aupres de leurs enfants? Une revue des determinants de l'engagement paternal [Why are some fathers more involved than others? Review of father involvement influences]. *Revue Canadienne de Psycho-Education, 30*(1), 65–91.

Ulrich, Y. C., Cain, K. C., Sugg, N. K., Rivara, F. P., Rubanowice, D. M., & Thompson, R. S. (2003). Medical care utilization patterns in women with diagnosed domestic violence. *American Journal of Preventive Medicine, 24*(1), 9–15.

U.S. Department of Health and Human Services. (2007). *Child maltreatment 2005: Reports from the states to the National Center on Child Abuse and Neglect (NCANDS).* Washington, DC: U.S. Government Printing Office. Available from www.acf.hhs.gov/programs/cb/pubs/cm05/cm05.pdf.

U.S. Preventive Services Task Force. (2004). Screening for family and intimate partner violence: Recommendation statement. *Annals of Internal Medicine, 140*(5), 382–386.

Van der Kolk, B. A., Perry, J. C., & Herman, J. L. (1991). Childhood origins of self-destructive behaviour. *American Journal of Psychiatry, 148*, 1665–1676.

Vermeiren, R., Schwab-Stone, M., Deboutte, D., Leckman, P. E., & Ruchkin, V. (2003). Violence exposure and substance use in adolescents: Findings from three countries. *Pediatrics, 111*, 535–540.

Walsh, C. A., MacMillan, H. L., Trocmé, N., Dudziuk, J., & Boyle, M., (June, 2000). *Psychometric properties of the Childhood Experiences of Violence Questionnaire.* Victimization of Children and Youth: An International Research Conference, Durham, NH.

Wathen, C. N., & MacMillan, H. L. (2003a). Interventions for violence against women: Scientific review. *Journal of the American Medical Association, 289*, 589–600.

Wathen, C. N., & MacMillan, H. L. (2003b). Prevention of violence against women: Recommendation statement from the Canadian task force on preventive health care. *Canadian Medical Association Journal, 169*(6), 582–584.

Wekerle, C., Miller, A. L., Wolfe, D. A., & Spindel, C. B. (2006). *Childhood maltreatment.* Ashland, OH: Hogrefe & Huber.

Wekerle, C., & Wall, A.-M. (2002). *The violence and addiction equation.* New York: Brunner-Routledge.

Wekerle, C., Wall, A.-M., Leung, E., & Trocmé, N. (2006). Cumulative stress and substantiated maltreatment: The importance of caregiver vulnerability and adult partner violence. *International Journal of Child Abuse and Neglect, 31*, 427–443.

Wekerle, C., & Wolfe, D. A. (2003). Child maltreatment. In E. J. Mash & R. A. Barkley (Eds.), *Child psychopathology* (2nd ed., pp. 632–686). New York: Guilford Press.

Wekerle, C., Wolfe, D. A., Hawkins, D. L., Pittman, A.-L., Glickman, A., & Lovald, B. E. (2001). The value and contribution of youth self-reported maltreatment history to adolescent dating violence: Testing a trauma mediational model. *Development and Psychopathology, 13*, 847–871.

Widom, C. S. (1999). Posttraumatic stress disorder in abused and neglected children grown up. *American Journal of Psychiatry, 156*, 1223–1229.

Wiederman, M. W., Sansone, R. A., & Sansone, L. A. (1999). Bodily self-harm and its relationship to childhood abuse among women in a primary care setting. *Violence Against Women, 5*, 155–163.

Wolfe, D. A. (1999). *Child abuse: Implications for child development and psychopathology* (2nd ed.). Thousand Oaks, CA: Sage.

Wolfe, D. A., Wekerle, C., Gough, R., Reitzel-Jaffe, D., Grasley, C., Pittman, A. L., et al. (1996). *The youth relationships manual: A group approach with adolescents for the prevention of woman abuse and the promotion of healthy relationships.* Thousand Oaks, CA: Sage.

Wolfe, V. (in press). Child sexual abuse. In E. J. Mash & R. A. Barkley (Eds.), *Assessment of childhood disorders.* New York, Guilford Press.

Wonderlich, S. A., Crosby, R. D., Mitchell, J. E., Roberts, J. A., Haseltine, B., DeMuth, G., et al. (2000). Relationship of childhood sexual abuse and eating disturbance in children. *Journal of the American Academy of Child and Adolescent Psychiatry, 39*(10), 1277–1283.

Wood, J., Foy, D., Layne, C., Pynoos, R., & James, C. B. (2002). An examination of the relationships between violence exposure, posttraumatic stress symptomatology, and delinquent activity: An ecopathological model of delinquent behavior among incarcerated adolescents. *Journal of Aggression, Maltreatment and Trauma, 6*(1), 127–147.

World Health Organization. (n.d.). *World Health Organization Intimate Partner Violence and Alcohol Fact Sheet.* Available from www.who.int/violence_injury_prevention/violence/world_report/factsheets/ft_intimate.pdf.

World Health Organization. (2006). *Preventing child maltreatment: A guide to taking action and generating evidence.* Retrieved October 7, 2007, from http://whqlibdoc.who.int/publications/2006/9241594365_eng.pdf.

Wozencraft, T., Wagner, W., & Pellegrin, A. (1991). Depression and suicidal ideation in sexually abused children. *Child Abuse and Neglect, 15*, 505–511.

Wright, R., Mitchell, H., Visness, C. M., Cohen, S., Stout, J., Evans, R., et al. (2004, April). Community violence and asthma morbidity: The inner-city asthma study. *American Journal of Public Health, 94*(4), 625–632.

Yampolskaya, S., & Banks, S. M. (2006). An assessment of the extent of child maltreatment using administrative databases. *Assessment, 13*(3), 342–355.

Zanarini, M. C., Williams, A. A., Lewis, R. E., Reich, R. B., Vera, S. C., Marino, M. F., et al. (1997). Reported pathological childhood experiences associated with the development of borderline personality disorder. *American Journal of Psychiatry, 154*(8), 1101–1106.

Zoroglu, S. S., Tuzun, U., Sar, V., Tutkun, H., Savas, H. A., Ozturk, M., et al. (2003). Suicide attempt and self-mutilation among Turkish high school students in relation with abuse, neglect, and dissociation. *Psychiatry and Clinical Neurosciences, 57*, 119–126.

CHAPTER 29

Autism Spectrum Disorders and Related Developmental Disabilities

Jennifer M. Gillis and Raymond G. Romanczyk

This chapter addresses the pervasive developmental disorders (PDD) included in the *Diagnostic and Statistical Manual of Mental Disorders*, fourth edition, text revision (*DSM-IV-TR;* American Psychiatric Association, 2000). These disorders include Autistic Disorder (autism), Asperger's Disorder, Pervasive Developmental Disorder—Not Otherwise Specified (PDD-NOS), Rett's Disorder, and Childhood Disintegrative Disorder. Given the sheer amount of information currently available on all of the PDDs, we highlight aspects of the disorders that are particularly pertinent to clinical psychologists.

This chapter first addresses terminology related to the PDDs. In particular, the increased attention to specific PDDs by diverse groups, such as consumers, educators, legislators, and basic researchers, has produced an imprecise umbrella term, autism spectrum disorder (ASD). The lack of clarity in terminology has produced, and continues to produce, significant confusion and miscommunication. Second, we address the three factors common across Autistic Disorder, Asperger's Disorder, and PDD-NOS: social impairment, language and communication impairments, and restricted, repetitive, and/or stereotyped behaviors. This discussion is important because these three areas vary greatly within and across each of these disorders. Issues related to assessment and diagnosis are discussed next. This section introduces the reader to commonly used assessments as well as the issues surrounding diagnostic evaluations for individuals with an ASD. A discussion of intellectual functioning and mental retardation follows. Comorbidity, trends in prevalence, early intervention, and etiology of ASD are covered next. Rett's Disorder and Childhood Disintegrative Disorder are discussed afterward, as these disorders are rare in occurrence and have distinct differences from the other three disorders. Next, treatment for the core symptoms of the PDDs is discussed. A brief section on family issues is last.

TERMINOLOGY

A review of the terminology over the past decade shows that the term pervasive developmental disorder as defined by the *DSM-IV-TR* (American Psychiatric Association, 2000) is often used synonymously with autism spectrum disorder.

Unfortunately, many studies applying either term to describe participants, samples, or population fail to specifically denote which disorders, if any, are included in these categories. Moreover, there is no standard operational definition of ASD, as the term is not in the *DSM-IV-TR,* nor have other attempts to adequately and consistently define this term been made. For consistency purposes, we suggest conceptualizing ASD as a spectrum including Autistic Disorder, Asperger's Disorder, and PDD-NOS. When referring to ASD, Rett's Disorder and Childhood Disintegrative Disorder are not included, mostly due to the low occurrence of each disorder and their specific course.

An additional problem is the use of descriptive labels for presumed subcategories of Autistic Disorder that also have yet to be adequately defined (Volkmar & Klin, 2005). For example, the term "high-functioning autism" is widely used yet has no reference in the *DSM-IV-TR* (American Psychiatric Association, 2000). The term typically refers to individuals with a diagnosis of Autistic Disorder who have adequate verbal language abilities and an average or above average level of cognitive ability (Baron-Cohen, O'Riordan, Stone, Jones, & Plaisted, 1999; Escalante-Mead, Minshew, & Sweeney, 2003; Klin & Jones, 2006). Individuals described as having high-functioning autism present clinically similar to individuals with Asperger's Disorder. However, researchers debate whether there are meaningful differences between individuals diagnosed with Asperger's Disorder and those described as having high-functioning autism (Lincoln, Courchesne, Kilman, Elmasian, & Allen, 1998; Miller & Ozonoff, 2000). This is an important area that has begun to receive more attention, as it might have implications for the study of etiology, response to treatment, type of treatment recommended, and prognosis. Using the term high-functioning autism as a specifier that is not always consistently defined creates potential diagnostic overlap. This can lead to problems when conducting research and when attempting to diagnose an individual with a PDD using the current *DSM* classification system.

Clearly, more precise definitions for Autistic Disorder, Asperger's Disorder, and PDD-NOS are needed. An examination of the *DSM-IV-TR* (American Psychiatric Association, 2000) diagnostic criteria for the PDDs might be helpful in understanding how similar these disorders are to each other. Table 29.1 lists the major diagnostic criteria in the areas of social skills, communication, and behavior for each PDD. Notice that the social skills and behavior criteria are the same for both Autistic Disorder and Asperger's Disorder. Under the PDD-NOS category, the criteria define a less severe impairment than in Autistic Disorder and Asperger's Disorder for social and behavior areas. Given the overlap of symptoms and characteristics of these disorders, the next sections describe the main impairments (social, communication, and behavioral) in turn.

As indicated in Table 29.1, describing the characteristics in the social, communication, and behavioral domains of Autistic Disorder, Asperger's Disorder, and PDD-NOS involves discussion of many similar and overlapping characteristics. We describe these characteristics under the term ASD, given the current trend in the literature. However, characteristics and symptoms specific to a particular disorder are noted.

Table 29.1 Major *DSM-IV TR* Criteria for Pervasive Developmental Disorders

Impairments	Autistic Disorder	Asperger's Disorder	PDD-NOS	Rett's Disorder	Childhood Disintegrative Disorder
Social	Qualitative impairment in social interaction (at least two specific impairments needed)	Same as Autistic Disorder	"A severe and pervasive impairment in development of reciprocal social interaction" (p. 84)	Loss of social engagement early in the course (although often social interaction develops later)	Clinically significant loss in social skills; abnormalities of functioning in qualitative impairments in social interaction
Communication	Qualitative impairment in communication (at least one specific impairment needed)	No clinically significant general delay in language	Impairment in verbal or nonverbal communication skills	Severely impaired expressive and receptive language development (after a period of normal development)	Clinically significant loss in expressive/receptive language; abnormalities of functioning in qualitative impairments in communication
Behavior	Restricted, repetitive, and stereotyped patterns of behavior, interests, and activities (at least one specific impairment needed)	Same as Autistic Disorder	Presence of stereotyped behavior, interests, and activities	Loss of previously acquired purposeful hand skills between 5 to 30 months of age with subsequent development of stereotyped hand movements	Clinically significant loss in adaptive behavior/motor skills; abnormalities of functioning in restricted, repetitive, and stereotyped patterns of behavior, interests, and activities, including motor stereotypes and mannerisms

Adapted from *Diagnostic and Statistical Manual of Mental Disorders*, Fourth Edition, Revised, by the American Psychiatric Association, 2000, Washington DC: Author.

SOCIAL IMPAIRMENT

The impairment in social skills, social interactions, social reciprocity, and social competence in individuals with Autistic Disorder, Asperger's Disorder, or PDD-NOS is central to the diagnosis. In this section we describe the specific impairments associated with each of the disorders in turn.

Autistic Disorder

Leo Kanner (1971) identified social impairment as the primary hallmark of autism (his term was "early infantile autism"). That is, the children's "inability to relate themselves in the ordinary way to people and situations from the beginning of life" (p. 140). Indeed, developmental research supports this claim. For example, infants show preferential attention toward social stimuli (i.e., faces) over other types of stimuli within the first few months of life (Sigman, Dijamco, Gratier, & Rozga, 2004), with initial social development occurring between the infant and caregiver. As children grow, social behavior begins to become increasingly differentiated; children develop peer relationships, pro-social skills, and an increasing capacity for self-regulation (Singer, 1996). In children with Autistic Disorder, however, retrospective studies suggest that aberrant social development starts within the first few months after birth (Goin & Myers, 2004; Osterling, Dawson, & Munson, 2002).

One profound social impairment in individuals with Autistic Disorder is a lack of eye contact. Unlike children with mental retardation or other developmental disabilities (but not a PDD), children with Autistic Disorder may not engage in consistent, predictable eye contact with parents, caretakers, and others (Carter, Davis, Klin, & Volkmar, 2005). Similarly, individuals with Autistic Disorder do not readily initiate other social behavior involving eye contact, such as joint attention, which in typically developing children develops in infancy (Mundy & Burnette, 2005).

Social impairment is not only considered to be the core deficit, but is also complex, as it varies with chronological age and developmental level. Considered a primary deficit, social impairment has been implicated in the aberrant development of other areas, such as language abilities, emotion regulation, and behavioral patterns of rigidity, stereotypies, or self-stimulatory behavior (Bachevalier & Merjanian, 1994; Happe & Frith, 1995). For example, some children have difficulty using nonverbal cues to modulate their social interaction (e.g., continuing a conversation when the listener is looking at his or her watch repeatedly and yawning; Lord, 1990).

Typically, social competence is markedly below the cognitive ability of an individual with Autistic Disorder (and more broadly ASD). For example, a 7-year-old child with Autistic Disorder with cognitive ability in the mental retardation range may neither display eye contact nor respond to the greeting of another person, whereas a same-age child with Autistic Disorder but of average intelligence may display partial eye contact and may have a limited repertoire in responding to a greeting. Both children show deficits in social interaction and social skills when compared to their typically developing peers.

Social skills vary by age as well. By adulthood individuals may develop some social skills that are typical in childhood, while other social skills important in adulthood remain deficient (e.g., relating to others on an intimate level). In addition, some individuals will have more diverse and advanced social abilities than others.

Play skills are also impaired (Kasari, Freeman, & Paparella, 2006). By the end of 2 years of age, most typically developing children demonstrate functional and symbolic play skills. The play skills of children with Autistic Disorder are severely diminished compared to typically developing children. Children with Autistic Disorder may seek out play items but use them in a self-stimulatory manner. Most children with Autistic Disorder show difficulty using a toy or object in a more social, playful manner (Thomasa & Smith, 2004). A preference to play alone and with only a few specific toys is usually observed, whereas the typically developing child would more likely prefer to play with others, explore a variety of toys, and engage in other social interactions with his or her environment.

Deficits in expressive social communication (e.g., gestures) and engaging in eye contact, joint attention, and social reciprocity (Lord, 1990) are observed. It is also the case that abilities to initiate social behavior and understand the rules governing social interaction are impaired (Wing, 1981). Further, individuals with Autistic Disorder are typically not responsive when others are in distress (Travis, Sigman, & Ruskin, 2001). There may also be difficulty with perception of affective content (Hobson & Lee, 1989). One study showed that adolescents with Asperger's Disorder are significantly impaired in their ability to detect the emotional content of videotaped scenes that lack speech content cues as compared to typically developing adolescents (Koning & Magill-Evans, 2001). A series of studies using the Vineland Adaptive Behavior Scales, which is a norm-referenced assessment, found that socialization deficits are greater than expected based on overall developmental level (Sparrow, Balla, & Cichetti, 1984; Volkmar et al., 1987). Additionally, these studies demonstrated that children with Autistic Disorder exhibit significantly lower socialization scores than children with mental retardation.

Decoding of emotions from facial expressions is also impaired relative to typically developing children. It appears that individuals with ASD do not rely on facial expressions for emotional information. In addition, they may have difficulty relying on other situational cues to determine a person's emotional state (Egan, Brown, Goonan, Goonan, & Celano, 1998).

Asperger's Disorder

Individuals with Asperger's Disorder may exhibit all or many of the social impairments just described. The socioemotional and social communicative deficits in Asperger's Disorder are primary deficits. Individuals with Asperger's Disorder usually have significant difficulties identifying ("reading") and understanding social cues. It appears that individuals with Asperger's can learn cues and facial expressions to correctly identify emotions, but do not show generalization of these skills to spontaneous use (Grossman, Klin, Carter, & Volkmar, 2000; Serra, Minderaa, van Geert, & Jackson, 1999). Egan et al. (1998) found that individuals with ASD were unable to use prosody (tone of voice) and facial expression to identify emotions. A more recent study by Lidner and Rosén (2006) supported these results. These authors found that children with Asperger's Disorder are able to utilize verbal content to assist them with identifying emotions. Grossman et al. found that this is not the case for individuals with Autistic Disorder; individuals with Autistic Disorder are unable to compensate using verbal ability to identify emotions.

Individuals with Asperger's Disorder typically desire friendships and want to make connections with others. However, they lack social skills to do so in a meaningful manner. Because individuals with Asperger's Disorder are intellectually typical with regard to their cognitive and verbal language abilities, they are aware that they are "socially different" from others. These individuals, therefore, are at a higher risk for developing depression or anxiety as a result, especially in adolescence and adulthood. Because of the compromised ability of individuals with Asperger's Disorder to understand and interpret social behavior appropriately, forming sustainable relationships is a challenge

Pervasive Developmental Disorder—Not Otherwise Specified

Individuals with PDD-NOS share many of the characteristics of both Autistic Disorder and Asperger's Disorder. However, the severity of this impairment may not be to the same degree. Thus, a separate section that covers PDD-NOS is redundant, even though this is not a reflection of a less important diagnosis.

COMMUNICATION

Children with Autistic Disorder either develop verbal language later than typically developing children or do not develop functional language at all. Fifty percent of children with Autistic Disorder do not develop spoken communication (Sigman & Capps, 1997). For individuals who do develop spoken language, abnormal features are typically present (Sheinkopf, Mundy, Oller, & Steffens, 2000; Sigman & Capps, 1997). For example, Sheinkopf et al. noted that preschool children with Autistic Disorder showed a rate of verbalization similar to normally developing children for their developmental level. However, the types of verbalizations and vocal quality were noticeably abnormal (e.g., growling, squeals).

Echolalia is a characteristic of speech patterns in approximately 75% of individuals with Autistic Disorder (Prizant, 1983). Echolalia is defined as the repetition of the speech of another person or oneself and is often present in typically developing infants. Echolalia can be immediate (i.e., repeating a word, phrase, or sentence immediately after it is spoken by someone else), delayed (i.e., repeating speech heard in the past), or mitigated (e.g., imperfectly repeating speech heard in the past). Echolalia is not unique to Autistic Disorder, as it is an abnormal speech quality observed in other psychiatric disorders and sometimes as a result of brain damage (Sigman & Capps, 1997). There is some question in the field as to whether there is a communicative function of echolalia for individuals with ASD (Tager-Flusberg, Paul, & Lord, 2005). Some researchers suggest that children with ASD use echolalia to engage in a conversation because they do not understand how to use speech to communicate (Loveland & Tunali-Kotoski, 2005).

Prosody is impaired in individuals with ASD. Prosody is the rhythm of spoken language; it helps the speaker add specific meaning to a phrase or sentence. For example, when asking a question, most individuals raise their voice slightly at the end of the sentence. This helps the conversational partner understand that the intent of the sentence is to ask a question. Individuals with ASD typically have abnormal intonation and use of rhythm and stress in speech production. Other characteristic speech abnormalities are pronoun reversals, articulation difficulties, and idiosyncratic use of speech, including the development and use of neologisms (Paul, Augustyn, Klin, & Volkmar, 2005). By age 5 or 6, most children with Autistic Disorder still show a delay in spoken language. If speech is present by this age, it is typically an indicator of better prognosis for the child (Tager-Flusberg et al., 2005).

In typically developing children who have not acquired speech, for example, due to a specific speech delay, the use of nonverbal communication is usually intact. A child who is deaf, for instance, is able to acquire nonverbal forms of communication (e.g., including sign language or other communication methods) and will compensate through the use of physical gestures, eye contact, pointing, and body language to communicate with others. For individuals with Autistic Disorder, these areas of nonverbal communication are either absent or noticeably impaired (Buffington, Krantz, McClannahan, & Poulson, 1998; Kasari, Sigman, Mundy, & Yirmiya, 1990; Tager-Flusberg et al., 2005).

Communicative intent is the planned purpose of a specific communication interaction. There are many purposes or goals for communicating with others; for instance, communicating that one is feeling sad, hungry, or that one would like to read a book located in an unreachable location, are all different yet important reasons to communicate to another person. Communicating with another person is categorized as either declarative (e.g., asking a friend what he received for his birthday) or regulatory (e.g., asking a friend to pass a piece of birthday cake; Landa, 2005; also known in behavior analysis terms as tact and mand, respectively). One of the significant characteristics of communicative intent in individuals with Autistic Disorder is that the intent is typically toward gaining access to an object or activity, not an interaction or conversation with a person. Thus children will use communicative gestures to gain access to an object, but not use such gestures in a social way.

There has recently been much attention devoted to joint attention deficits in ASD. Joint attention is a form of communicative intent that typically develops in infancy. Joint attention involves gestures such as pointing and use of eye contact that serve to focus another person's attention on an object or event for the purpose of shared enjoyment (Landa, 2005). Joint attention begins to emerge between 9 and 18 months (Bakeman & Adamson, 1984). Deficits in joint attention in children with ASD are noticed at an early age and have been well documented in the literature. These deficits include failure to orient to social stimuli, speak sounds, follow eye gaze, and follow pointing in conjunction with eye gaze (Leekam, Hunnisett, & Moore, 1998; Mundy, Sigman, & Kasari, 1994). Children with ASD also exhibit deficits in the initiation of joint attention, including a lack of showing objects of interest and failure to use declarative pointing and referential looking (MacDonald et al., 2006). Deficits in responding to joint attention appear to be less severe than the initiation to joint attention (MacDonald et al., 2006).

Interestingly, it does not appear that joint attention skills are delayed per se, as they sometimes fail to develop after more advanced social skills, such as nonverbal pointing to request an item (Mundy et al., 1994). MacDonald et al. (2006) reported relatively no differences in the use of joint attention behaviors between 2-, 3-, and 4-year-olds with autism. Carpenter, Pennington, and Rogers (2002) reported that the development of joint attention skills in children with autism does not follow the same pattern of development of these skills in typically developing children. These authors suggested that there might be a direct relationship between language ability and joint attention skills. Joint attention has also been shown to be related to social development (Schertz & Odom, 2004) with regard to emotion regulation and the ability to develop connections with other individuals, given that joint attention is related to the ability to share enjoyment and other forms of affect with others (Schertz & Odom, 2004; Wetherby, Prizant, & Schuler, 2000).

Most communication is used in the context of a social interaction. Given that individuals with ASD have pronounced difficulties in the area of social interaction, it follows that these individuals also have difficulties in aspects of communication that require interaction with others. Presuppositional skills represent the ability to produce the necessary quality and quantity of communication given different contexts. This skill emerges in preschool-age children and improves as the child's working memory, social cognitive skills, and metacognitive and linguistic skills develop. Discourse management, which typically develops by age 4, includes conversational skills, such as turn taking, starting and ending conversations, and staying on the topic of conversation (Landa, 2005).

Pragmatic language skills include the ability to adapt communication to listeners and situations. Although typical children become adept at pragmatic language skills as early as the preschool years, individuals with ASD show a wide variety of skill deficits in this area. Specific pragmatic language deficits include asking inappropriate questions (that may result in embarrassment or discomfort to the conversational partner), inappropriately interrupting others, inability to start or end conversations, and perseverating on a topic of interest. When neologisms are used in conversation, confusion may occur, especially when the individual with ASD does not acknowledge that the conversational partner does not understand the neologism. Individuals with ASD have difficulty understanding sarcasm, jokes, and puns. They tend to interpret the meaning of a joke, for example, at face value, or literally (Emerich, Creaghead, Grether, Murray, & Grasha, 2003; Van Bourgondien & Mesibov, 1987).

To converse with another person requires numerous skills in addition to the ability to produce and understand spoken language. A high percentage of children with Autistic Disorder do not acquire verbal skills but do use augmentative or alternative ways to communicate. Thus, these children should be encouraged to engage in conversations with others (Loveland & Tunali-Kotoski, 2005).

Asperger's Disorder

Characteristics similar to those just described are present in Asperger's Disorder. Although there is no delay in the acquisition of language in Asperger's Disorder, the way individuals with this disorder communicate to others, particularly in the social context, is noticeably impaired. For instance, the topic of conversation with someone with Asperger's Disorder may be narrow in scope and idiosyncratic. The individual will typically attempt to keep the conversation focused on a specific topic of interest to him or her, be indifferent to requests to change topics, have considerable difficulty taking turns in the conversation (i.e., social reciprocity), and have difficulty ending the conversation.

Receptive language difficulties include making inferences from others' nonverbal behavior and with certain elements of speech. For example, perspective taking can be difficult, as well as recognizing indirect social cues. Other elements of receptive language that are difficult for individuals with Asperger's Disorder are nonverbal (e.g., eye contact, facial expressions) and paralinguistic (e.g., tone of voice, prosody) cues and discriminating the meaning of a phrase, joke, or pun (i.e., they might have difficulty distinguishing something that has a literal versus a sarcastic meaning). Individuals with Asperger's Disorder tend to have a pedantic style of speech and prefer factual information.

BEHAVIOR

The broad category of restricted and repetitive behaviors in individuals with Autistic Disorder and Asperger's Disorder includes self-stimulatory behavior (e.g., repetitive finger movements, gazing at lights, rocking, toe-walking), stereotypical motor behavior (e.g., posturing), preoccupation with objects and activities, insistence on sameness or inflexibility in routines, and restrictive interest in objects or activities (South, Ozonoff, & McMahon, 2005; M. Turner, 1999). Children with ASD tend to have a narrow range of interests and activities, whereas adults have a somewhat wider range of interests but continue to be more resistant to change. Depending on routine and familiarity, the rigid or stereotyped thinking processes characteristic of ASD make abstraction and comprehension difficult. These clusters of behaviors are not unique to ASD. In fact, they may be seen in individuals with psychiatric conditions (e.g., Obsessive-Compulsive Disorder) and neurological conditions (e.g., Tourette's Disorder).

Recent studies are beginning to identify types or categories of atypical behaviors in ASD (Bishop, Richler, & Lord, 2006; Carcani-Rathwell, Rabe-Hasketh, & Santosh, 2006). In the current literature, the atypical behaviors within the category of restricted and repetitive behaviors are classified as either "lower order" or "higher order" behaviors. Lower order behaviors include stereotypical motor movements (e.g., hand and finger mannerisms) and preoccupations with parts of objects. Higher order behaviors include circumscribed interests, adherence to routines, and resistance to change (Bishop et al., 2006). In addition, Cuccaro et al. (2003) and Bishop et al. reported that younger children more readily engage in lower order behaviors (i.e., sensory-motor behaviors), whereas older children with ASD engage in higher order behaviors (i.e., insistence on sameness).

Bishop et al. (2006) point out that identifying specific atypical behaviors with different subtypes of ASD may be helpful in locating underlying genetic components and pathology among the ASDs. For instance, M. Turner (1999) and Lord, Rutter, and Le Couteur (1994) found that certain atypical behaviors (e.g., repetitive sensory-motor behaviors) were associated with lower levels of adaptive functioning as measured by the Vineland Adaptive Behavior Scales (Sparrow et al., 1984). However, both studies indicated that other atypical behaviors, such as difficulty with or resistance to change, were not associated with adaptive functioning. In addition, there have been advances in research linking repetitive behaviors to specific neurobiological regions (Lewis & Bodfish, 1998; Pierce & Courchesne, 2001) as well as chromosomal regions (Alarcón, Cantor, Liu, Gilliam, & Geschwind, 2001; Cuccaro et al., 2003). Certainly, though more research needs to be conducted, the field is coming to understand the behavioral aspects of ASD much better now than in the past.

Disruptive behaviors are common in children and adolescents with ASD. Common aggressive behaviors observed and reported in individuals with ASD and other developmental disabilities include physical aggression (e.g., hitting, kicking, biting, shoving, pinching), verbal aggression (e.g., yelling, calling names), and destructive behavior (e.g., throwing objects, breaking objects of others). Assessment and interventions for aggression are discussed in the treatment section of this chapter. Other types of disruptive behaviors commonly observed in children with ASD are sleeping and eating problems.

It has been noted that individuals with ASD have significant feeding and sleeping issues. These two problems are serious given the impact they have on parental, family, and child functioning. However, these problems are not part of the *DSM-IV-TR* diagnostic criteria. In the context of this chapter, feeding problems are maladaptive feeding behaviors not due to a medical condition and/or without a medical explanation. They include aversion to food, refusal to eat, gagging or choking responses to food, and restrictive eating patterns (i.e., eating only certain very specific types of food).

Ahearn, Castine, Nault, and Green (2001) suggest that feeding problems in children with ASD may be categorized under the restrictive patterns of interests and activities characteristic of ASD. The *DSM-IV-TR* (American Psychiatric Association, 2000) includes a diagnostic category of feeding problems, which includes failure to thrive. Many children with ASD eat enough to not meet this criterion; however, their restrictive eating patterns might lead to significant nutritional deficiencies that will cause developmental problems later in life. Ledford and Gast (2006) reported that even though children with ASD may not be considered at risk for an eating disorder, the long-term health-related consequences of having a restricted diet should be taken into consideration and treatment of feeding problems in young children with ASD should be a priority.

Ledford and Gast (2006) conducted a comprehensive review of the literature on descriptive studies of feeding problems in ASD and also on interventions for feeding problems. Based on their review, these authors concluded that 46% to 89% of children with ASD have feeding problems. The authors reviewed nine intervention studies, all of which demonstrated positive outcomes of the interventions. It should be noted that the interventions were behavioral and included differential reinforcement, stimulus fading, escape extinction, and appetite manipulation (simultaneous and sequential presentation of a nonpreferred food with a preferred food).

Children with ASD have significantly more sleep problems than typically developing children (Hoffman, Sweeney, Gilliam, & Lopez-Wagner, 2006). Parents reported that these sleep problems include bedtime resistance, parasomnias, night wakings, sleep anxiety, sleep disordered breathing, and sleep-onset delay. However, children with autism are not observed to be sleepier during the daytime than children who do not have sleep problems. Sleep problems tend to decrease as children age, according to the study by Hoffman et al.

Empirically supported treatment of sleep difficulties in ASD has not been documented. However, traditional behavioral methods for sleep intervention do show some promise for children with ASD. It is necessary to understand the etiology of sleep disorders in ASD to provide more efficacious treatments for these individuals. Many parents of children with ASD report that their children have sleep difficulties that exceed those of typically developing children.

Hoffman et al. (2006) surveyed parents of children with ASD and parents of typically developing children and found that children with ASD have significantly more sleep problems in the following areas: (a) bedtime resistance, (b) sleep-onset delay, (c) sleep duration, (d) sleep anxiety, (e) night wakings, (f) parasomnia, and (g) sleep disordered breathing. These authors also found that as children with ASD age, the severity of some sleep problems decreases. A previous paper by Hoffman et al. (2005) demonstrated a positive correlation between sleep difficulties and autism symptomatology. Research is needed to evaluate sleep interventions for children with ASD and the impact that these interventions might have on learning, family and parental stress, and other symptoms of ASD.

ASSESSMENT AND DIAGNOSIS

Autistic Disorder is typically diagnosed before the age of 3. It is quite common for a diagnosis to be given around the age of 18 to 24 months (Robins, Fein, Barton, & Green, 2001). However, the diagnosis of young children with ASD can be quite difficult. There are no reliable biological markers for ASD; thus diagnosis relies on the use of instruments designed specifically for the diagnosis of ASD. These include the Autism Diagnostic Observation Schedule—Generic (ADOS-G; Lord, Rutter, DiLavore, & Risi, 2000), the Autism Diagnostic Interview—Revised (ADI-R; Rutter, LeCouteur, & Lord, 1995), and the Childhood Autism Rating Scale (CARS; Schopler, Reichler, & Renner, 1980). A recent study by Ventola et al. (2006) indicated that the use of the ADOS-G, CARS, and clinical judgment based on the *DSM-IV* (American Psychiatric Association, 1994) criteria demonstrated strong agreement with each other. Even though these results are encouraging, as they suggest that clinicians might be able to use different assessment instruments, more research needs to be conducted to determine which method for diagnosing ASD has the highest sensitivity and specificity.

Autism spectrum disorders are heterogeneous, and each individual with an ASD will present differently in certain areas. In fact, a diagnosis of Autistic Disorder is sometimes more straightforward than a diagnosis of high-functioning autism, Asperger's Disorder, or PDD-NOS. This is because some of the characteristics of these other disorders are more subtle and may not appear to be severe enough according to a measurement instrument. Distinguishing between the boundaries of PDD-NOS, Asperger's Disorder, and high-functioning Autistic Disorder remains a challenge to both researchers and clinicians. As more research is conducted on diagnostic instruments, the symptom clusters and developmental trajectories specific to different ASDs should be illuminated.

The psychological assessment of an individual with ASD should include, but not be limited to, an understanding of the individual's current developmental level, his or her verbal and nonverbal strengths and weaknesses, and adaptive functioning (i.e., daily living skills). Because children with ASD have deficits in other areas than those listed in the *DSM-IV-TR,* the use of instruments that assess cognitive, language, motor, and adaptive skills are important to include in a diagnostic assessment battery. Standardized assessment instruments that can be utilized to assess standard intellectual functioning include the Wechsler Scales (the specific scale depends on the age of the individual); to assess mental processing and acquired language, the Kaufman Autism Behavior Checklist II; to assess developmental abilities, the Differential Ability Scales; and for children with severely limited language abilities, the Leiter-R. For developmental assessment, the Mullen Scales measure nonverbal, language, and motor skills. The Vineland Adaptive Behavior Scales measure adaptive functioning. Speech, language, and communication assessments should evaluate basic speech and language skills (including receptive and expressive language, prosody, paralinguistics, metalinguistics, and narrative skills) as well as social communication skills (such as joint attention, reciprocal social and communicative interactions, and self-regulation).

Importantly, when providing assessment, consultation, or intervention services to an individual with ASD, there will be numerous other professionals with whom a clinical psychologist is likely to interact for a variety of reasons (i.e., assessment, treatment, referral). Professionals range from early intervention service coordinators, special education teachers, and certified behavior analysts to a variety of family members, vocational skills training professionals, and psychiatrists. Of course, this is a short list, as the number and type of professionals depend on a host of factors, such as the client's age and level of functioning and the services available.

Above all, it is important to understand the child's functional skills, that is, skills the child can use on a day-to-day basis to communicate, interact socially, and accomplish tasks. Clinically it may not be important for a person with ASD to be able to do complex math problems consistent with his or her chronological age, but it may be far more important for that person to tell time on a digital clock in order to participate in an environment where schedules must be kept.

INTELLECTUAL FUNCTIONING AND MENTAL RETARDATION

Mental retardation (MR) is diagnosed when an individual's cognitive ability is assessed as an IQ of 70 or less, with adaptive skills deficits, and the age of onset is before 18 years (American Psychiatric Association, 2000). Given the criteria required for a diagnosis of Autistic Disorder, the criteria for impaired adaptive skills and age of onset overlaps. Thus, the critical aspect of diagnostic importance for MR is strictly the cognitive skills deficit (Edelson, 2006). For years, reports of a rate of 70% to 80% of children with Autistic Disorder with comorbid MR have been suggested (Bohman, Bohman, Björck, & Sjöholm, 1983; Chung, Luk, & Lee, 1990; Gillberg & Coleman, 2000). A recent report suggests that between 40% and 55% of children with Autistic Disorder have comorbid MR (Chakrabarti & Fombonne, 2001).

Edelson (2006) examined retroactively the statistics in previous reports and studies to ascertain the nature of support for the claim of the incidence of MR in Autistic Disorder. Edelson provided an excellent and critical review of over 215 studies. For articles in which the methodology for determining MR was described (only 15.7%), the incidence of MR was 71.89%. Interestingly, Edelson found that 157 of the 215 articles reported the diagnosis of MR with autism, but did not provide a methodology for diagnosing MR.

Instruments used to assess cognitive ability are limited because when assessing the cognitive ability of children with ASD, poor motivation in particular may significantly attenuate performance. Given the variability of behavior in some children with ASD, it is difficult to say whether additional factors (e.g., attention, language comprehension, unfamiliarity with structured interactions) negatively influence performance on cognitive tests. Ritvo and Ritvo (2006) insist that whether a child with autism has MR does not really matter; what matters is whether the child can carry out daily activities, including academic ones. These authors suggest that the focus of treatment should be on social and communication deficits, not on cognitive and academic deficits. Future prevalence surveys should include the whole spectrum of Autistic Disorder and other ASDs to ascertain a more accurate estimate of the prevalence of MR (Freeman & Van Dyke, 2006).

COMORBIDITY OF PSYCHIATRIC DISORDERS

Comorbidity refers to the co-occurrence of two disorders where the occurrence of one disorder does not exclude the occurrence of the other (Krishnan et al., 2002). Over the past 10 years, comorbidity issues in ASD have appeared increasingly in the literature, especially with regard to anxiety disorders in ASD.

A recent study by Leyfer et al. (2006) piloted an instrument called the Autism Comorbidity Interview—Present and Lifetime Version (ACI-PL), which was modified from the Schedule for Affective Disorders and Schizophrenia for School-Age Children (K-SADS; Chambers et al., 1985). The ACI-PL is a semi-structured interview and is similar in format and scoring to the K-SADS. In the two pilot samples, the ACI-PL demonstrated adequate specificity, sensitivity, and reliability for three *DSM* diagnoses: (1) Major Depressive Disorder, (2) Obsessive-Compulsive Disorder, and (3) Attention-Deficit Hyperactivity Disorder. This study found that the most frequent disorder comorbid with Autistic Disorder was Specific Phobia, with a comorbidity rate of 44%. Obsessive-Compulsive Disorder was the second most common (37%), and the most common type of compulsion was performing a ritual in a certain way. The full diagnosis of Attention-Deficit/Hyperactivity Disorder (ADHD) is the third most common comorbid disorder (31%). Interestingly, 55% of individuals with Autistic Disorder also had subsyndromal ADHD. The authors note that the inattentive type was more common in individuals with Autistic Disorder (whereas the hyperactive type is most common in the typically developing population). Ten percent of individuals with Autistic Disorder had experienced at least one episode of depression.

Overall, this study found that approximately 30% of the pilot sample had on average two comorbid diagnoses along with Autistic Disorder. The pilot sample tended to represent children with Autistic Disorder who would be described as high functioning, as 67.71% of children tested had Full-Scale IQ scores greater than 70, with a mean age of 9 years.

Comorbidity is an important area in ASD, given that the diagnostic criteria for ASD appear to be broadening (despite no change in the *DSM-IV-TR;* American Psychiatric Association, 2000) and the field is beginning to learn more about these comorbid disorders. The data Leyfer et al. (2006) provided should be accepted cautiously, given that this was a pilot study. However, the results do confirm an increased comorbidity of ASD with other *DSM* diagnoses reported by other investigators (Gillot, Furniss, & Walter, 2001; Kim, Szatmari, Bryson, Streiner, & Wilson, 2000; Towbin, Pradella, Gorrindo, Pine, & Leibenluft, 2005).

CURRENT TRENDS IN THE PREVALENCE OF AUTISTIC SPECTRUM DISORDERS

Historically, autism has been considered a very rare disorder. The *DSM-IV-TR* (American Psychiatric Association, 2000) reports the prevalence of Autistic Disorder to be 5 per 10,000, ranging from 2 to 20 per 10, 000. At the time of publication of the *DSM-IV-TR,* prevalence data were lacking for Asperger's Disorder, PDD-NOS, Rett's Disorder, and Childhood Disintegrative Disorder. Over the past 6 years, since the latest revision to the *DSM,* epidemiological research has been published providing new estimates of the prevalence, not only of Autistic Disorder, but also for Asperger's Disorder, PDD-NOS, and ASD (Fombonne, 2005). Thus, information about the prevalence of ASD in the *DSM-IV-TR* is no longer accurate.

In a recent review of prevalence studies from 1966 through 2004, Fombonne (2005) suggested that the current prevalence of Autistic Disorder is 13 per 10,000, of PDD-NOS is 21 per 10,000, of Asperger's Disorder is 2.6 per 10,000, with a prevalence of 60 per 10,000 for all PDDs. Croen, Grether, Hoogstrate, and Selvin (2002) conducted a study that investigated the change in prevalence of ASD in California from 1987 to 1994. The prevalence of ASD rose from 5.8 per 10,000 in 1987 to 14.9 per 10,000 in 1994. Interestingly, the prevalence of mental retardation showed the opposite trend; in 1987, the prevalence was 28.8 per 10,000 compared to 19.5 per 10,000 in 1994.

The male-to-female ratio of Asperger's Disorder, Autistic Disorder, and PDD-NOS is 4:1. Notably, when a female is diagnosed with Autistic Disorder, she typically has a more severe form (i.e., lower cognitive abilities, increased behavioral problems, and more severe social and communicative impairments).

Questions loom as to why there has been an increase in the prevalence of ASD. Croen et al. (2002) propose that factors accounting for the increase in prevalence rate may include improvements in identification of ASD and changes in the criteria for a diagnosis of ASD in the *DSM-IV-TR* (American Psychiatric Association, 2000) compared to the *DSM-III* (American Psychiatric Association, 1980). Children diagnosed with Autistic Disorder in the *DSM-IV-TR* may represent a broader phenotype than if they were diagnosed using the *DSM-III*. Even though the precise answer to this question is not available, it is the case that we now have assessment tools to identify ASD at a younger age and more accurately, increased awareness and knowledge in communities and among practitioners, and increased services available for ASD (Croen et al., 2002; Fombonne, 2005). Regardless of the reasons for the increase in prevalence of ASD, early identification of the disorder is crucial for early intervention services to begin (Romanczyk et al., 2005).

EARLY IDENTIFICATION

Early identification and early intervention are necessary to provide positive outcomes for children with autism. Of the 3.75 million infants born each year in the United States, 20% are at risk for developmental disabilities due to pre- and postnatal factors (Haber, 1991).

Two federal laws that mandate service provision to children in the early intervention years (birth to 3 years) are Public Law 99-457 and Public Law 105-17. Public Law 99-457 was enacted in 1986 to provide early intervention services for at-risk infants and children (Haber, 1991). In addition, Public Law 105-17 allows eligible infants, toddlers, and children with disabilities to receive both appropriate and free early intervention services (birth to 35 months) and public education (starting at 36 months). Public awareness of the importance of early intervention services for children with autism has also increased. Several studies have shown both the short-term and long-term benefits for children receiving appropriate early intervention services (Anderson & Romanczyk, 1999; Guralnick, 1996; Lovaas, 1987; Smith, Eikeseth, Klevstrand, & Lovaas, 1997). These services are required to be free and it is mandatory for all states to follow the statutes in both public laws. Early identification, which leads to early intervention, is extremely important for individuals with ASD. Numerous studies have demonstrated impressive gains in language, cognition, and social development when individuals received early intervention services (Bondy & Frost, 1995; Harris & Handleman, 2000; National Research Council, 2001; L. Turner, Stone, Pozdol, & Coonrod, 2006).

The importance of early identification and intervention has spurred the development and validation of many screening measures. Given research on early signs of ASD, a diagnosis of ASD can be made before 24 months of age. Screening instruments are not substitutes for a diagnostic assessment, but do allow for the higher probability of identification of children who may be at risk for a developmental disability, such as ASD, in order to receive a more comprehensive diagnostic evaluation. Multiple screening measures are available, including the Checklist for Autism in Toddlers (Baird et al., 2000), the Modified Checklist for Autism in Toddlers (Robins et al., 2001), the Social Communication Questionnaire (Rutter, Bailey, Berument, Lord, & Pickles, 2003), and the Screening for Autism in 2-Year-Olds (Stone & Ousley, 1997).

Table 29.2   Clinical Clues for Autism

Delay or absence of spoken language
Looks through people; not aware of others
Not responsive to other people's facial expressions or feelings
Lack of pretend play; little or no imagination
Does not show typical interest in or play near peers purposefully
Lack of turn taking
Unable to share pleasure
Qualitative impairment in nonverbal communication
Not pointing at an object to direct another person to look at it
Lack of gaze monitoring
Lack of initiation of activity or social play
Unusual or repetitive hand and finger mannerisms
Unusual reactions, or lack of reaction, to sensory stimuli

Excerpted from *Clinical Practice Guideline for Autism/Pervasive Developmental Disorders: Assessment and Intervention for Young Children Ages 0–3 Years* (Guideline Technical Report. no. 4217), Table III-4, by the New York State Department of Health, Early Intervention Program, 1999, Albany, New York: Author.

The New York State Department of Health published *The Clinical Practice Guideline for Autism/Pervasive Developmental Disorders* in 1999. There are three versions of the guideline: *The Guideline Technical Report, Quick Reference Guide,* and *Report of the Recommendations.* Common to each version are basic recommendations for assessment and intervention methods for children with autism or other PDD. Within the assessment content area is a table listing 13 clinical clues recommended for the purpose of screening children for autism or other PDD. These clinical clues were taken from empirical studies that listed diagnostic criteria for autism according to the *DSM-III-R* and *DSM-IV-TR.* Each clue has been validated by empirical studies; has been shown to have a sensitivity or specificity of greater than 50%; is relevant to the *DSM-IV-TR* for the diagnosis of autism; and may be found in other screening and diagnostic instruments for autism. These clinical clues are presented in Table 29.2.

ETIOLOGY

The specific causes of ASD are unknown. As is the case for many disorders, the interaction of a biological predisposition (e.g., genetic mutations) with environmental factors most likely underlies the etiology of ASD, but hypotheses regarding etiology along these lines continue to be investigated (Polleux & Lauder, 2004). Research on the genetic basis and neurobiology of ASD are two important fields that are illuminating possible contributions to the etiology of ASD, but research is still in the early stages.

Familial recurrence of autism is 100 times higher than in the general population. In addition, there are reported concordance rates of 70% to 90% in monozygotic twins, which is not found in dizygotic twins. In fact, most studies show near 0% concordance rates in dizygotic twins, which provides strong support for the genetic component of autism (Veenstra-VanderWeele & Cook, 2003). However, we are far from identifying a definitive etiology for autism.

Approximately 10% of cases of autism have comorbid genetic conditions, such as Fragile X, tuberous sclerosis, and Rett's Disorder (Polleux & Lauder, 2004). One-third of individuals with autism develop seizures, and over half have abnormal sleep patterns. Recently, researchers have developed a working hypothesis characterizing the cortex as having an imbalance of excitation and inhibition, which leads to hyperexcitability in the cortex (Polleux & Lauder, 2004). The imbalance in the cortex could have consequences "on the function of neuronal networks underlying perception and attention" (Polleux & Lauder, 2004, p. 304). Other neuroanatomical features that have been hypothesized to be linked to ASD are abnormal functioning of the brain stem, cerebellum, hippocampus, and amygdala. There is also evidence suggesting that the brain is enlarged in children with autism and that this enlargement occurs during the postnatal period, but there is no further enlargement in adulthood and studies show no differences in brain size in adulthood between adults with Autistic Disorder and typically developing adults. The exact specifications and implications of brain enlargement have yet to be determined.

Multiple genes are hypothesized to be linked to autism, but more research is needed and is currently ongoing to address this. Neurotransmitter abnormalities are also hypothesized to be implicated in autism. Serotonin and GABA are two that have the most evidence suggesting abnormalities in ASD. See Polleux and Lauder (2004) for a review of neurobiological evidence.

A major difficulty in drawing conclusions from the current research evidence from the neurobiology and neuroimaging fields is that the sample size of most studies is still small and is typically biased toward individuals with autism who are considered higher functioning. Thus, generalizing results from these studies is difficult. However, this is an important area of research, as Autistic Disorder is a neurobiological disorder and the genetics, specific brain areas affected, and other biological and neurological characteristics of Autistic Disorder need to be more fully understood. These same concepts hold true for determining biological etiologies or predispositions for Asperger's Disorder and PDD-NOS.

RELATED DEVELOPMENTAL DISORDERS: RETT'S DISORDER AND CHILDHOOD DISINTEGRATIVE DISORDER

Rett's Disorder

Rett's Disorder was discovered by Andreas Rett and (at a later time) Bengt Hagberg. Rett's Disorder is an X-linked, dominant disorder that occurs almost exclusively in females. It has been identified as the second leading disorder that causes MR in females (Down syndrome is the primary). Much is known about the genetic etiology of Rett's and the course of the disorder, which is described next. It is hoped that eventual understanding of this disorder will help with the understanding of related disorders.

The most prominent symptom in Rett's Disorder is stereotypic hand movements. These are often an early warning sign; that is, these types of stereotypies are often present before other associated symptoms of Rett's are noticed. For children with Rett's Disorder, the first 6 to 8 months of life are characterized by normal development. About 50% of cases begin to show a delay in and/or deterioration of skills around 15 months of age. By age 3, a significant deterioration of development is noted, especially loss of language, increased stereotyped hand movements, and decreased interest in objects and social interaction. The deterioration of skills is rapid (i.e., after a 1-year period, severe to profound disabilities are noted). Additional motor difficulties and delays are also present. The characteristic stereotyped hand movements include hand-to-mouth movements, hand wringing, and hand clasping. By the early school years, the pace of deterioration has decreased and children are able to acquire and maintain skills. However, through adolescence there is a decrease in physical growth and problems with ambulation are noted; in addition, many children develop scoliosis (Van Acker, Loncola, & Van Acker, 2005).

In 1986, Hagberg and Witt-Engerstrom (Van Acker et al., 2005) provided a four-stage developmental model of Rett's Disorder, then called Rett syndrome. This model is generally accepted today. Between 6 and 18 months, Stage 1 begins. This stage is characterized by a noted deviation from normal development, particularly in motor abilities. Stage 2 begins between 1 year and 4 years of age. In this stage, a significant loss of previously acquired skills occurs; many symptoms are present that resemble those in individuals with autism. Thus, social, speech, cognitive, and motor skills are deteriorated or lost during this stage. The stereotypic hand movements tend to be continuous, without clear antecedents or triggers. Children with Rett's Disorder are diagnosed with severe to profound MR, and parents characterize their mood as labile and irritable. During this stage abnormal breathing patterns are noticed; 25% of children have clinically significant seizure activity and 75% present with sleep abnormalities. Stage 3 begins between ages 2 and 10. The symptoms characteristic of autism tend to decrease during this stage. In fact, an increase in social interaction, awareness of and interest in the environment, communication skills, and use and acquisition of functional skills occurs. Up to 80% of children have seizures and the motor difficulties become more prominent. Stage 4 begins when a child is 10 or older. During this stage motor deterioration continues, with decreased mobility and frequently need of assistance to move about (e.g., using a wheelchair). Individuals' cognitive functioning is stable, and social skills and attention improves. In addition, a decrease in seizure activity is observed.

Childhood Disintegrative Disorder

Childhood Disintegrative Disorder (CDD) is characterized by typical, age-appropriate development in the areas of language, social, cognition, and other skills, with a regression of skills occurring between the ages of 2 and 10. Some authors suggest that there may be a mild delay in development prior to age 2 (Kurita, Kita, & Miyake, 1992). However, the most common report of age of onset is between ages 3 and 5, with a mean of 3.4 years. With regard to differential diagnostic characteristics, in Autistic Disorder it is not uncommon to observe language regression; however, in CDD there are multiple areas of regression.

The onset of CDD is typically abrupt, with symptoms being noticed within days to weeks. Many cases report a psychosocial stress or medical event, but the etiology is unclear. Prevalence is estimated to be 1 to 9 cases per 100,000 children, according to Fombonne (2002). Because this condition is so rare, it is likely that most clinicians have little familiarity with it, and thus the actual prevalence of CDD is uncertain. Similar to other developmental disabilities, CDD predominantly affects males. It is differentiated from Rett's Disorder by the longer period of normal development before regression begins.

For the most part, the regression and deterioration of skills typically plateaus. Most cases of CDD do not continue to regress to the point of mortality. However, Volkmar, Koenig, and State (2005) reviewed several case studies suggesting an increased mortality rate after a child is diagnosed with CDD. Most of the deaths are related to neuropathology and/or medical diseases. A comorbidity rate of seizures similar to that found in Autistic Disorder has also been suggested in CDD. However, there are no conclusive data suggesting a specific medical etiology for CDD nor a predictive relationship of CDD with other medical disorders or pathologies. The genetic mechanisms in CDD are also not understood, and further research needs to be conducted (Volkmar et al., 2005).

TREATMENT

The field of PDD has experienced notable advances in research and clinical intervention over the past 10 years. However, there is no one treatment that has been shown to be universally effective in the full remediation of ASD. Treatments for ASD are described as either comprehensive interventions that include elements of behavioral, educational, and psychotherapeutic approaches or specific interventions, most of which are behavioral or psychopharmacological, that focus on the treatment of specific behaviors.

In general, learning is quite challenging for individuals with Autistic Disorder, whose difficulties range from overselectivity (i.e., disproportionate attention to irrelevant aspects of a stimulus) to lack of generalization of skills. Most children with ASD tend to lack multiple foundational learning skills; thus, sensitivity to the sequence in typical development is important when designing interventions. It is important to consider the individual's age-equivalent or developmental level when providing interventions and determining expectations. This is important at all levels and ages of intervention. In a recent study by L. Turner et al. (2006), a relatively stable diagnosis was demonstrated in children diagnosed with ASD at age 2 and reassessed at age 9. Thus, it is important that children receive services throughout childhood.

In 2002, the National Institutes of Health sponsored a meeting on the current science of the treatment for children with ASD (Lord et al., 2005). There is no medical or biological treatment for the *core* features of ASD. However, there is medication that ameliorates some of the mood and behavioral problems associated with ASD. Given the heterogeneity of ASD, the specific language difficulties, and the comorbidity of mental retardation, it is not possible to say that a specific type and dosage of treatment is recommended. Interventions should begin as soon as the child is identified. Currently, behavioral interventions have the most empirical support (U.S. Public Health Service, 2001) for the treatment of ASD. Behavioral interventions for ASD have provided an impressive amount of empirical support. Applied behavior analysis, cognitive-behavioral therapy, and psychopharmacology interventions are all discussed in turn. In addition, a selection of interventions specific to the social, communication, and behavioral impairments are also briefly discussed.

Applied Behavior Analysis

Applied behavior analysis (ABA) is a discipline that seeks to understand and improve human behavior and is grounded in principles of operant and respondent learning and conditioning. This approach has the strongest demonstrated research support for efficacy and has been widely acknowledged by independent reviews as a critical part of a child's treatment program (e.g., the report of the surgeon general; U.S. Public Health Service, 2001). There are guidelines for selecting qualified behavior analysts that provide interventions for individuals with ASD (Autism Special Interest Group of the Association for Behavioral Analysis, 2007). In addition, the Behavior Analyst Certification Board provides certification for behavior analysis practitioners.

In intervention programs that use ABA as a framework, operational definitions of behavior are utilized to objectively measure complex behavior patterns. Baseline data are collected on these behaviors, and interventions based on principles of behavior are implemented. Data collection occurs throughout the intervention. This process allows for the evaluation of the intervention on an ongoing basis, and modifications are made depending on the child's performance. Some of the instructional techniques used in ABA programs include discrete trial training, pivotal response training, incidental teaching, and generalization training.

An important component of ABA interventions for ASD is the use of functional behavioral assessments. Functional behavioral assessments assist in determining the functions of specific behaviors (e.g., self-stimulatory behavior, noncompliance, self-injurious behavior, aggressive behavior). A functional behavioral assessment may include interviews, direct behavioral observations, checklists, and manipulating the antecedents and consequences of a behavior. These methods assist in generating hypotheses of the function of a behavior and guide intervention. Common functions of disruptive behaviors are positive reinforcement, negative reinforcement, and nonsocial reinforcement, sometimes referred to as automatic reinforcement or sensory reinforcement (Iwata, Dorsey, Slifer, Bauman, & Richman, 1994; Reese, Richman, Belmont, & Morse, 2005).

Psychopharmacological Treatments

Psychopharmacological treatments for ASD target specific problematic behaviors. In addition, psychopharmacological treatment may be provided to treat comorbid disorders (such as anxiety or depression). A recent report of the American Psychological Association Working Group on Psychotropic Medications (2006) estimates that between 33% and 47% of individuals with ASD have been prescribed at least one psychotropic medication over the course of a 1-year period. The Working Group indicated that the evidence of the effectiveness of psychotropic medications is limited and variable, and that medication should be considered on an individual basis with careful consideration of the risks and benefits of the medication, expected behavior change, and side effects. Recently, the Food and Drug Administration approved Risperdal (risperidone) for the treatment of severe irritability in children and adolescents with Autistic Disorder (U.S. Food and Drug Administration, 2006). Table 29.3 summarizes the information provided in the Working Group's report.

Cognitive-Behavioral Therapy

Cognitive-behavioral therapy (CBT) has garnered recent attention for treatment of anxiety for individuals with high-functioning autism and Asperger's Disorder. Sofronoff, Attwood, and Hinton (2005) implemented a 6-week brief CBT intervention for individuals with Asperger's Disorder and anxiety symptoms. These authors found that having the family (i.e., parents) involved led to the best outcomes (i.e., reduction in anxiety symptoms). However, these authors did rely on parent report to demonstrate the change in symptom frequency and severity, which is a limitation of the study.

Cardaciotto and Herbert (2004) modified a CBT intervention to treat social anxiety disorder (Social Phobia) for an individual with ASD who presented with fear of social situations, specifically assertiveness, talking in front of others, and initiating conversations with those he is familiar with. The authors provided 14 weeks of CBT. The outcome was successful and the client showed maintenance of gains. The recent research examining how to effectively modify traditional CBT interventions is a new and exciting area for the field of ASD.

Social Skills Training

There are many different social skills interventions for ASD. Research has shown that individuals with ASD do not learn social skills in the same way as typically developing children (Gresham, 1981). Developmental level and chronological age should be taken into consideration when teaching social skills. For example, social skills interventions during the early intervention years (i.e., 0 to 3 years old) focus on improving social behavior and interactions with an adult (e.g., parent). In the preschool years, the focus is on play skills and peer interactions. More advanced social skills are taught when a child reaches school age, such as initiation of play and conversations and developing friendships (Guralnick & Neville, 1997; Schreibman, 1996).

A review of social skills interventions for preschool-age children by Vaughn et al. (2003) revealed the following common features: prompting and rehearsal of target behaviors, play-related activities, free-play generalization, reinforcement of appropriate behaviors, modeling of specific skills, storytelling, direct instruction, and imitation of appropriate behaviors. The authors' review indicated that the interventions with the highest effect sizes were those that contained features of modeling, play-related activities, rehearsal and practice, and prompting. Based on their review of components of interventions that yielded improvements in social behavior, the authors suggest the following (pp. 12–13):

- Social skills programs that are embedded into regular class programs by teachers (Antia, Kreimeyer, & Eldredge, 1993; Ferentino, 1991; Fewell & Vadasy, 1989; Jenkins, Odom, & Speltz, 1989; Koenigs & Oppenheimer, 1985)

Table 29.3 Psychotropic Drugs Commonly Used in the Treatment of Symptoms of ASD

Drug Class	Specific Drug Studied	Target Behaviors/ Symptoms	Side Effects	Conclusions of APA Work Group
Stimulants	Methylphenidate (Ritalin)	Hyperactivity, inattention, impulsivity	Agitation, irritability, insomnia	48% to 50% experienced positive response; 18% experienced adverse effects.
Atypical antipsychotics	Risperidone*	Aggression, severe tantrum behavior	Drowsiness, fatigue, constipation, weight gain, may increase risk for diabetes and hyperlipidemia	Approximately 66% experienced improvement in symptoms. However, symptoms recur after medication is discontinued.
Selective serotonin reuptake inhibitors	Clomipramine, fluoxetine	Perseverative behaviors (e.g., compulsions, self-injury, stereotypies)		Limited evidence. Fluoxetine appears to be better tolerated than other SSRIs. Most studies are with adults; little is known about effects on children and adolescents.
Mood stabilizers	Lithium, divalproate	Explosive aggression, severe tantrum behavior		No conclusive evidence for children and adolescents. Only small studies have been conducted with adults, showing preliminary support.
Alpha agonists	Clonidine, guanfacine	Hyperactivity, aggression, severe tantrum behavior		Limited support in open-label, uncontrolled reports.

*Risperdone is now (as of October 6, 2006) FDA approved for the treatment of irritability associated with children and adolescents with Autistic Disorder (http://www.fda.gov/bbs/topics/NEWS/2006/NEW01485.html).
Adapted from *Psychopharmacological, Psychosocial, and Combined Interventions for Childhood Disorders: Evidence Base, Contextual Factors, and Future Directions*, by the American Psychological Association Working Group on Psychotropic Medications for Children and Adolescents, 2006, Washington, DC: Author.

- Interventions that include both instruction in social skills and behavioral contingencies for appropriate and inappropriate behaviors (LeBlanc & Matson, 1995; Matson, Fee, Coe, & Smith, 1991)
- Interventions that provide integrated or social interaction groups for children with and without disabilities (Jenkins et al., 1989)
- Interventions that train parents or peers as models to promote appropriate social behaviors (Dawson & Galpert, 1990; Strain, 1985)
- Interventions that involve an intensive social skills program (Rogers, Herbison, Lewis, Pantone, & Reiss, 1986)

Social skills interventions for individuals with ASD described as higher functioning have included group interventions (Howlin & Yates, 1999; Krasny, Williams, Provencal, & Ozonoff, 2003; Solomon, Goodlin-Jones, & Anders, 2004). Skills typically taught within the context of group interventions include awareness of emotions, face processing and nonverbal communication, theory of mind and perspective taking, conversations, problem solving, stress management, and beginning conversation skills (Solomon et al., 2004).

Communication

It has been observed that approximately 70% of children between the ages of 3 and 5 years with a disability have a delay in language development (Wetherby & Prizant, 1992). Thus, discovering new, innovative ways to teach individuals with ASD to communicate more effectively has been a priority in ASD treatment research. Most comprehensive treatment and educational programs for individuals with ASD include a communication acquisition component. Depending on the strengths and weaknesses of the individual, verbal language, nonverbal language, and social communication acquisition might be emphasized. Successful verbal language acquisition has been documented using interventions such as discrete trial training, incidental teaching, natural language teaching procedures, mand training (Peterson, 2004), and pivotal response training (Koegel, O'Dell, & Koegel, 1987).

The use of visual supports has been recommended and is frequently present in research studies and clinical settings. One such visual support is an activity schedule (McClannahan & Krantz, 1999). An activity schedule provides visual information (in the form of pictures, symbols, or text) to an individual with ASD. This information can be utilized to teach a skill (skills can range from daily living skills to academic skills, self-management skills, social skills) and to help individuals with ASD predict and plan a sequence of events (e.g., daily classroom activities). Research suggests that integrating multimedia components into teaching children with ASD shows initial positive results. However, the mechanism of multimedia effects is unknown. Future research should systematically examine whether and how the use of multimedia components is effective.

Even with available interventions, more than 50% of children with autism are nonverbal or mute (Sigman & Capps, 1997). Thus, language interventions are of great importance to enable these children to use alternative means of communicating with others. Bondy and Frost (1994) developed the Picture Exchange Communication System (PECS) program for children with social communication deficits. This program is appealing to the ASD field for many reasons: (a) The PECS program requires simple motor movements; (b) PECS is portable and can be used across a wide variety of settings; (c) PECS is taught relatively quickly using behavioral principles of shaping, transfer of stimulus control, and differential reinforcement; (d) PECS facilitates child imitations of interactions with others; and (e) PECS has been demonstrated to facilitate verbal language (Charlop-Christy, Carpenter, Le, LeBlanc, & Kellet, 2002). The structured context and use of pictures in the PECS program is appealing because of the visual modality strength in children with ASD. The program enables a functional relation between the environment and the student to develop.

Behavior

Treatment for aggression is commonly requested from families of individuals with ASD. Because of the multiple functions that aggression can serve, no one specific treatment method is suggested. Behavioral and psychopharmacological treatments are typically used to treat aggression. Matson, Dixon, and Matson (2005) reviewed common behavioral interventions that have shown effectiveness for decreasing aggression, such as positive reinforcement, functional communication training (FCT; Carr & Durand, 1985), time-out, social skills training, and differential reinforcement procedures. The most commonly used interventions are FCT and differential reinforcement of other behavior. The authors emphasize the importance of conducting a functional analysis to understand factors influencing the behavior in order to treat aggression effectively.

Functional communication training (Durand, 1990) is an empirically validated procedure shown to be helpful in the management of challenging behaviors in individuals with ASD (Durand, 1990; Durand & Carr, 1991). This approach incorporates a functional behavior assessment to develop intervention plans to teach individuals with ASD to use alternative skills that decrease disruptive behaviors (Iwata et al., 1994). Thus, based on the functions of a behavior hypothesized from the functional behavior assessment, an individual is taught a more adaptive skill that serves the same function as the behavior. For example, if a child engaged in head-banging to escape a task, the child might be taught to use a Stop sign to signal a request to end a task. Treatment for the behavioral deficits in ASD continues to be an important area for future research.

FAMILY ISSUES

Having a child and/or family member with an ASD imposes a tremendous amount of stress on all family members. Family members may cope and manage stress differently. Because ASD is a lifelong disorder, there are challenges a family faces that vary from year to year, from coping with the diagnosis of an ASD to seeking appropriate educational treatment, dealing with adolescence issues, and changing living situations when adult children become more challenging for parents. Families also appear to benefit from early intervention services for their children with ASD. The majority of parents indicated that early intervention services decreased the overall stress in the family (Glasberg, Martins, & Harris, 2005).

Lockshin, Gillis, and Romanczyk (2004) identify five general factors that shape family dynamics. The first is a need for continuous supervision of the child with ASD. This can limit the efficiency of completing other tasks. In addition, it requires family members to coordinate who is responsible for the child with ASD at specified times. Second, the inability or limited ability of the child with ASD to communicate the full range of his or her needs and wants can make the family feel that they are in a constant guessing game as to what they need to do to meet the child's needs. Third, atypical relationships with family members sometimes develop given the increased strain on each family member; this can lead to increased family conflict. Fourth, atypical relationships with peers can develop, in which the family members have limited peer and social support outside of the family. Fifth, atypical, difficult-to-manage behavior (e.g., aggression, rigidity, self-injury, lack of social boundaries) may require extraordinary resources for a family and increased stress if these behaviors are not under control in the family and public settings. Assisting families to identify resources in the community is important as a first step in decreasing family stress. It is then helpful to teach family members possible coping strategies. Helping families prioritize their needs so that all members are considered equally is important to decrease conflict and increase support within the family, as well as with friends and peers.

Research in the area of adolescents and adults with ASD is impoverished and is a critical area for growth. For the majority of individuals diagnosed with ASD in childhood, there is consensus that ASD is a lifelong disorder. However, several studies (Byrd, 2002; Mesibov, Schopler, Schaffer, & Michal, 1989; Piven, Harper, Palmer, & Arndt, 1996) have indicated that the core symptoms of ASD do improve with age. That is, the majority of individuals studied had noted improvements in communication, socialization, and behavior in adolescence and adulthood when compared to their functioning in these areas during childhood. Seltzer et al. (2003) found improvement in ADI-R scores in adolescence and adulthood, meaning that these individuals showed a reduction in the number of ASD-related symptoms. Despite these encouraging results, it remains clear that adolescents and adults with ASD continue to need extensive, but different types of, services.

SUMMARY

In the past 2 decades there have been substantial changes in diagnostic criteria and a broadening of the historically limited conceptualization of autism. Pervasive developmental disorders is the current *DSM-IV-TR* terminology which is used in parallel with the more recent and common umbrella term autism spectrum disorders. The ASD conceptualization emphasizes a focus on the social deficits that form the core deficit. There have been many advances in the field of ASD, and there are many exciting areas for future research. Increased availability and utility of technology, from functional magnetic resonance imaging to PDAs, will assist in measurement that provides information that was not available to researchers 10 (even 5) years ago. Conceptualizing the pervasive developmental disorders as disorders that are on a continuous spectrum changes how we ask questions, think about these disorders, and define the population, and in the future will most likely eventually lead to a further delineation of specific subtypes of ASD.

In the area of intervention, although effective intervention procedures have been identified, more limited efficacy of the generalization of skills acquired is often observed. In addition, more detailed understanding of specific characteristics of individuals with ASD may guide choice of treatment for practitioners, parents, clinicians, therapists, and teachers. We do not yet understand the mediators that affect treatment outcome. There are well over 250 treatments available to individuals with ASD, with the vast majority not effective and wasteful of time and resources. But efficacy information often is overshadowed by marketing efforts by proponents of this vast array of treatments, and thus the treatment choice process is often stressful and difficult for parents and advocates for individuals with ASD. Demonstrating empirical evidence for available treatments and the ethical and responsible dissemination of the evidence is key to helping individuals with ASD and their families.

REFERENCES

Ahearn, W. H., Castine, T., Nault, K., & Green, G. (2001). An assessment of food acceptance for pervasive developmental disorder—not otherwise specified. *Journal of Autism and Developmental Disorders, 31*, 505–511.

Alarcón, M., Cantor, R. M., Liu, J., Gilliam, T. C., & Geschwind, D. H. (2001). Evidence for a language quantitative trait locus on chromosome 7q in multiplex autism families. *American Journal of Human Genetics, 70*, 60–71.

American Psychiatric Association. (1980). *Diagnostic and statistical manual of mental disorders* (3rd ed.). Washington, DC: Author.

American Psychiatric Association. (1994). *Diagnostic and statistical manual of mental disorders* (4th ed.). Washington, DC: Author.

American Psychiatric Association. (2000). *Diagnostic and statistical manual of mental disorders* (4th ed., text rev.). Washington, DC: Author.

American Psychological Association Working Group on Psychotropic Medications for Children and Adolescents. (2006). *Psychopharmacological, psychosocial, and combined interventions for childhood disorders: Evidence base, contextual factors, and future directions.* Washington, DC: Author.

Anderson, S. R., & Romanczyk, R. G. (1999). Early intervention for young children with autism: Continuum-based behavioral models. *Journal of the Association for Persons with Severe Handicaps, 24*, 162–173.

Antia, S. D., Kreimeyer, K. H., & Eldredge, N. (1993). Promoting social interaction between young children with hearing impairments and their peers. *Exceptional Children, 60*, 262–275.

Autism Special Interest Group of the Association for Behavior Analysis. (2007). *Consumer guidelines for identifying, selecting, and evaluating behavior analysts working with individuals with autism spectrum disorders.* Retrieved September 28, 2007, from http://abainternational.org/Special_Interests/AutGuidelines.pdf.

Bachevalier, J., & Merjanian, P. (1994). The contribution of medial temporal lobe structures in infantile autism: A neurobehavioral study in primates. In M. L. Bauman & T. L. Kemper (Eds.), *The neurobiology of autism* (pp. 146–169). Baltimore: Johns Hopkins University Press.

Baird, G., Charman, T., Baron-Cohen, S., Cox, A., Swettenham, J., & Wheelwright, S., et al. (2000). Screening instrument for autism at 18 months of age: A 6-year follow-up study. *Journal of the American Academy of Child and Adolescent Psychiatry, 39*(6), 694–702.

Bakeman, R., & Adamson, L. (1984). Coordinating attention to people and objects in mother-infant and peer infant interaction. *Child Development, 55,* 1278–1289.

Baron-Cohen, S., O'Riordan, M., Stone, V., Jones, R., & Plaisted, K. (1999). Recognition of faux pas by normally developing children and children with Asperger syndrome or high-functioning autism. *Journal of Autism and Developmental Disorders, 29,* 407–418.

Bishop, S. L., Richler, J., & Lord, C. (2006). Association between restricted and repetitive behaviors and nonverbal IQ in children with autism spectrum disorders. *Child Neuropsychology, 12,* 247–267.

Bohman, M., Bohman, I. L., Björck, P. O., & Sjöholm, E. (1983). Childhood psychosis in a northern Swedish county: Some preliminary findings from an epidemiological survey. In M. H. Schmidt & H. Remschmidt (Eds.), *Epidemiological approaches in child psychiatry II* (pp. 164–173). New York: George Thieme Verlag Stuttgart.

Bondy, A. S., & Frost, L. A. (1994). The picture exchange communication system. *Focus on Autistic Behavior, 9,* 1–19.

Bondy, A. S., & Frost, L. A. (1995). Educational approaches in preschool: Behavior techniques in a public school setting. In E. Schopler & G. B. Mesibov (Eds.), *Learning and cognition in autism: Current issues in autism* (pp. 311–333). New York: Plenum Press.

Buffington, D. M., Krantz, P. J., McClannahan, L. E., & Poulson, C. L. (1998). Procedures for teaching appropriate gestural communication skills to children with autism. *Journal of Autism and Developmental Disorders, 28,* 535–545.

Byrd, R. (2002). *Report to the legislature on the principal findings from the epidemiology of autism in California: A comprehensive pilot study.* Retrieved September 10, 2006, from http://www .dds.ca.gov/autism/pdf/study_final.pdf.

Carcani-Rathwell, I., Rabe-Hasketh, S., & Santosh, P. J. (2006). Repetitive and stereotyped behaviours in pervasive developmental disorders. *Journal of Child Psychology and Psychiatry, 47,* 573–581.

Cardaciotto, L., & Herbert, J. D. (2004). Cognitive behavior therapy for social anxiety disorder in the context of Asperger's syndrome: A single-subject report. *Cognitive and Behavioral Practice, 11,* 75–81.

Carpenter, M., Pennington, B. F., & Rogers, S. J. (2002). Interrelations among social-cognitive skills in young children with autism. *Journal of Autism and Developmental Disorders, 32,* 91–106.

Carr, E. G., & Durand, V. M. (1985). Reducing behavior problems through functional communication training. *Journal of Applied Behavior Analysis, 16,* 297–314.

Carter, A. S., Davis, N. O., Klin, A., & Volkmar, F. R. (2005). Social development in autism. In F. R. Volkmar, R. Paul, A. Klin, & D. Cohen (Eds.), *Handbook of autism and pervasive developmental disorders* (3rd ed., pp. 312–334). Hoboken, NJ: Wiley.

Chakrabarti, S., & Fombonne, E. (2001). Pervasive developmental disorders in preschool children. *Journal of the American Medical Association, 285,* 3093–3099.

Chambers, W. J., Puig-Antich, J., Hirsch, M., Paez, P., Ambrosini, P. J., & Tabrizi, M. A., et al. (1985). The assessment of disorders in children and adolescents by semistructured test-retest reliability of the Schedule for Affective Disorders and Schizophrenia for School-Age Children, present episode. *Archives of General Psychiatry, 42,* 696–702.

Charlop-Christy, M. H., Carpenter, M., Le, L., LeBlanc, L. A., & Kellet, K. (2002). Using the Picture Exchange Communication System (PECS) with children with autism: Assessment of PECS acquisition, speech, social-communicative behavior, and problem behavior. *Journal of Applied Behavior Analysis, 35,* 213–231.

Chung, S. Y., Luk, S. L., & Lee, P. W. H. (1990). A follow-up study of infantile autism in Hong Kong. *Journal of Autism and Developmental Disorders, 20,* 221–232.

Croen, L. A., Grether, J. K., Hoogstrate J., & Selvin S. (2002). The changing prevalence of autism in California. *Journal of Autism and Developmental Disorders, 32,* 207–215.

Cuccaro, M. L., Shao, Y., Grubber, J., Slifer, M., Wolpert, C. M., & Donnelly, S. L., et al. (2003). Factor analysis of restricted and repetitive behaviors in autism using the Autism Diagnostic Interview—Revised. *Child Psychiatry and Human Development, 34,* 3–17.

Dawson, G., & Galpert, L. (1990). Mothers' use of imitative play for facilitating social responsiveness and toy play in young autistic children. *Development and Psychopathology, 2,* 151–162.

Durand, V. M. (1990). *Severe behavior problems: A functional communication training approach.* New York: Guilford Press.

Durand, V. M., & Carr, E. G. (1991). Functional communication training to reduce challenging behavior: Maintenance and application in new settings. *Journal of Applied Behavior Analysis, 24*, 251–264.

Edelson, M. G. (2006). Are the majority of children with autism mentally retarded? *Focus on Autism and Other Developmental Disabilities, 21*, 66–83.

Egan, G. J., Brown, R. T., Goonan, L., Goonan, B. T., & Celano, M. (1998). The development of decoding of emotions in children with externalizing behavioral disturbances and their normally developing peers. *Archives of Child Neurology, 13*, 383–396.

Emerich, D. M., Creaghead, N. A., Grether, S. M., Murray, D., & Grasha, C. (2003). The comprehension of humorous materials by adolescents with high-functioning autism and Asperger's syndrome. *Journal of Autism and Developmental Disorders, 33*, 253–257.

Escalante-Mead, P. R., Minshew, N. J., & Sweeney, J. A. (2003). Abnormal brain lateralization in high-functioning autism. *Journal of Autism and Developmental Disorders, 33*, 539–543.

Ferentino, S. C. (1991). Teaching social skills to preschool children in a special education program (Doctoral dissertation, Hofstra University, 1991). *Dissertation Abstracts International, 52*, 4490.

Fewell, R., & Vadasy, P. (1989). Play as an intervention strategy with young children with deaf-blindness. In M. Bullis (Ed.), *Research on the communication development of young children with deaf-blindness* (pp. 105–122). Monmouth, OR: Oregon State System of Higher Education, Teaching Research Division.

Fombonne, E. (2002). Prevalence of childhood disintegrative disorder. *Autism: International Journal of Research and Practice, 6*, 149–157.

Fombonne, E. (2005). The changing epidemiology of autism. *Journal of Applied Research in Intellectual Disabilities, 18*, 281–294.

Freeman, B. J., & Van Dyke, M. (2006). Invited commentary: "Are the majority of children with autism mentally retarded?" *Focus on Autism and Other Developmental Disabilities, 21*, 86–88.

Gillberg, C., & Coleman, M. (2000). *The biology of the autistic syndromes* (3rd ed.). London: Mac Keith Press.

Gillot, A., Furniss, F., & Walter, A. (2001). Anxiety in high-functioning children with autism. *Autism, 5*, 277–286.

Glasberg, B. A., Martins, M., & Harris, S. L. (2005). Stress and coping among family members of individuals with autism. In M. G. Baron, J. Groden, G. Groden, & L. Lipsitt (Eds.), *Stress and coping in autism* (pp. 277–301). New York: Oxford University Press.

Goin, R. P., & Myers, B. J. (2004). Characteristics of infantile autism: Moving toward earlier detection. *Focus on Autism and Other Developmental Disabilities, 19*, 5–12.

Gresham, F. M. (1981). Social skills training with handicapped children: A review. *Review of Educational Research, 51*(1), 139–176.

Grossman, J. B., Klin, A., Carter, A. S., & Volkmar, F. R. (2000). Verbal bias in recognition of facial emotions in children with Asperger's syndrome. *Journal of Child Psychology and Psychiatry, 41*, 369–379.

Guralnick, M. J. (1996). Second-generation research in the field of early intervention. In M. J. Guralnick (Ed.), *The effectiveness of early intervention* (pp. 3–22). Baltimore: Paul H. Brookes.

Guralnick, M. J., & Neville, B. (1997). Designing early intervention programs to promote children's social competence. In M. J. Guralnick (Ed.), *The effectiveness of early intervention* (pp. 579–610). Baltimore: Paul H. Brookes.

Haber, J. S. (1991). Early diagnosis and referral of children with developmental disabilities. *American Family Physician, 43*, 132–140.

Hagberg, B., & Witt-Engerstrom, I. (1986). Rett syndrome: A suggested staging system for describing impairment profile with increasing age towards adolescence. *American Journal of Medical Genetics, 24*(Suppl. 1), 47–59.

Happe, F., & Frith, U. (1995). Theory of mind in autism. In E. Schopler & G. Mesibov (Eds.), *Learning and cognition in autism* (pp. 177–197). New York: Plenum Press.

Harris, S. L., & Handleman, J. S. (2000). Age and IQ at intake as predictors of placement for young children with autism: A 4- to 6-year follow-up. *Journal of Autism and Developmental Disorders, 30*, 137–142.

Hobson, R. P., & Lee, A. (1989). Emotion-related and abstract concepts in autistic people: Evidence from the British Picture Vocabulary Scale. *Journal of Autism and Developmental Disorders, 19*, 601–623.

Hoffman, C. D., Sweeney, D. P., Gilliam, J. E., Apodaca, D. D., Lopez-Wagner, M. C., & Castillo, M. M. (2005). Sleep problems and symptomalogy in children with autism. *Focus on Autism and Other Developmental Disabilities, 20*, 194–200.

Hoffman, C. D., Sweeney, D. P., Gilliam, J. E., & Lopez-Wagner, M. C. (2006). Sleep problems in children with autism and in typically developing children. *Focus on Autism and Other Developmental Disabilities, 21*, 146–152.

Howlin, P., & Yates, P. (1999). The potential effectiveness of social skills groups for adults with autism. *Autism, 3*, 299–307.

Iwata, B. A., Dorsey, M. F., Slifer, K. J., Bauman, K. E., & Richman, G. S. (1994). Toward a functional analysis of self-injury. *Journal of Applied Behavior Analysis, 27*, 197–209. (Reprinted from *Analysis and Intervention in Developmental Disabilities, 2, 3–20, 1982.*)

Jenkins, J., Odom, S., & Speltz, M. (1989). Effects of social integration on preschool children with handicaps. *Exceptional Children, 55*, 420–428.

Kanner, L. (1971). Follow-up of 11 autistic children originally seen in 1943. *Journal of Autism and Childhood Schizophrenia, 1*, 119–145.

Kasari, C., Freeman, S., & Paparella, T. (2006). Joint attention and symbolic play in young children with autism: A randomized controlled intervention study. *Journal of Child Psychology and Psychiatry, 47*, 611–620.

Kasari, C., Sigman, M., Mundy, R., & Yirmiya, N. (1990). Affective sharing in the context of joint attention interactions of normal, autistic, and mentally retarded children. *Journal of Autism and Developmental Disorders, 20*, 87–100.

Kim, J. A., Szatmari, P., Bryson, S. E., Streiner, D. L., & Wilson, F. J. (2000). The prevalence of anxiety and mood problems among children with autism and Asperger syndrome. *Autism: Journal of Research and Practice, 4*, 117–132.

Klin, A., & Jones, W. (2006). Attributing social and physical meaning to ambiguous visual displays in individuals with higher-functioning autism spectrum disorders. *Brain and Cognition, 61*, 40–53.

Koegel, R. L., O'Dell, M. C., & Koegel, L. K. (1987). A natural language teaching paradigm for nonverbal autistic children. *Journal of Autism and Developmental Disorders, 17*, 187–200.

Koenigs, A., & Oppenheimer, L. (1985). Development and training of roletaking abilities with emotionally disturbed preschoolers: A pilot study. *Journal of Applied Developmental Psychology, 6*, 313–320.

Koning, C., & Magill-Evans, J. (2001). Social and language skills in adolescent boys with Asperger syndrome. *Autism: Journal of Research and Practice, 5*, 23–36.

Krasny, L., Williams, B. J., Provencal, S., & Ozonoff, S. (2003). Social skills interventions for the autism spectrum: Essential ingredients and a model curriculum. *Child and Adolescent Psychiatry Clinics of North America, 12*, 107–122.

Krishnan, K., Ranga, R., Delong, M., Kraemer, H., Carney, R., Spiegel, D., et al. (2002). Comorbidity of depression with other medical diseases in the elderly. *Biological Psychiatry, 52*, 559–588.

Kurita, H., Kita, M., & Miyake, Y. (1992). A comparative study of development and symptoms among disintegrative psychosis and infantile autism with and without speech loss. *Journal of Autism and Developmental Disorders, 22*, 175–188.

Landa, R. J. (2005). Assessment of social communication skills in preschoolers. *Mental Retardation and Developmental Disabilities Research Reviews, 11*, 247–252.

LeBlanc, L. A., & Matson, J. L. (1995). A social skills training program for preschoolers with developmental delays: Generalization and social validity. *Behavior Modification, 19*, 234–246.

Ledford, J. R., & Gast., D. L. (2006). Feeding problems in children with autism spectrum disorders: A review. *Focus on Autism and Other Developmental Disabilities, 21*, 153–166.

Leekam, S., Hunnisett, E., & Moore, C. (1998). Targets and cues: Gaze following in children with autism. *Journal of Child Psychology and Psychiatry, 39*, 951–962.

Lewis, M. H., & Bodfish, B. W. (1998). Repetitive behavior disorders in autism. *Mental Retardation and Developmental Disabilities Research Reviews, 4*, 80–89.

Leyfer, O. T., Folstein, S. E., Bacalman, S., Davis, N. O., Dinh, E., Morgan, J., et al. (2006). Comorbid psychiatric disorders in children with autism: Interview development and rates of disorders. *Journal of Autism and Developmental Disorders, 36*, 849–861.

Lidner, J. L., & Rosén, L. A. (2006). Decoding of emotion through facial expression, prosody and verbal content in children and adolescents with Asperger's syndrome. *Journal of Autism and Developmental Disorders, 36*, 769–777.

Lincoln, A. E., Courchesne, E., Kilman, B. A., Elmasian, R., & Allen, M. (1998). Neurobiology of Asperger syndrome: Seven case studies and quantitative magnetic resonance imaging findings. In E. Schopler

G. B. Mesibov, & L. J. Kunc (Eds.), *Asperger syndrome or high functioning autism?* (pp. 145–166). New York: Plenum Press.

Lockshin, S. B., Gillis, J. M., & Romanczyk, R. G. (2004). *Defying autism: Keeping your sanity and taking control.* New York: DRL Books.

Lord, C. (1990). A cognitive behavioral model for the treatments of social-communicative deficits in adolescents with autism. In R. J. McMahon & R. D. Peters (Eds.), *Behavior disorders of adolescence: Research, intervention, and policy in clinical and school setting* (pp. 155–174). New York: Plenum Press.

Lord, C., Rutter, M., DiLavore, P., & Risi, S. (2000). *Autism Diagnostic Observation Schedule—WPS edition.* Los Angeles: Western Psychological Services.

Lord, C., Rutter, M., & Le Couteur, A. (1994). Autism Diagnostic Interview—Revised: A revised version of a diagnostic interview for caregivers of individuals with possible pervasive developmental disorders. *Journal of Autism and Developmental Disorders, 24,* 659–685.

Lord, C., Wagner, A., Rogers, S., Szatmari, P., Aman, M., Charman, T., et al. (2005). Challenges in evaluating psychosocial interventions for autistic spectrum disorders. *Journal of Autism and Developmental Disorders, 35,* 695–708.

Lovaas, O. I. (1987). Behavioral treatment and normal educational and intellectual functioning in young autistic children. *Journal of Consulting and Clinical Psychology, 55,* 3–9.

Loveland, K. A., & Tunali-Kotoski, B. (2005). The school-age child with an autistic spectrum disorder. In F. R. Volkmar, R. Paul, A. Klin, & D. Cohen (Eds.), *Handbook of autism and pervasive developmental disorders* (3rd ed., pp. 247–287). Hoboken, NJ: Wiley.

MacDonald, R., Anderson, J., Dube, W. V., Geckeler, A., Green, G., Holcomb, W., et al. (2006). Behavioral assessment of joint attention: A methodological report. *Research in Developmental Disabilities, 27,* 138–150.

Matson, J. L., Dixon, D. R., & Matson, M. L. (2005). Assessing and treating aggression in children and adolescents with developmental disabilities: A 20-year overview. *Educational Psychology, 25,* 51–181.

Matson, J. L., Fee, V., Coe, D. A., & Smith, D. (1991). A social skills training program for developmentally delayed preschoolers. *Journal of Clinical Child Psychology, 20,* 428–433.

McClannahan, L. E., & Krantz, P. J. (1999). *Activity schedules for children with autism: Teaching independent behavior.* Bethesda, MD: Woodbine House.

Mesibov, G. B., Schopler, E., Schaffer, B., & Michal, N. (1989). Use of the Childhood Autism Rating Scale with autistic adolescents and adults. *Journal of the American Academy of Child and Adolescent Psychiatry, 28,* 538–541.

Miller, J. N., & Ozonoff, S. (2000). The external validity of Asperger disorder: Lack of evidence from the domain of neuropsychology. *Journal of Abnormal Psychology, 109,* 227–238.

Mundy, P., & Burnette, C. (2005). Joint attention and neurodevelopment. In F. Volkmar, A. Klin, & R. Paul (Eds.), *Handbook of autism and pervasive developmental disorders* (3rd ed., pp. 650–681). Hoboken, NJ: Wiley.

Mundy, P., Sigman, S., & Kasari, C. (1994). Joint attention, developmental level, and symptom presentation in autism. *Development and Psychopathology, 6,* 389–401.

National Research Council. (2001). *Educating children with autism* (C. Lord & J. A. McGee, Eds.). Washington, DC: National Academy Press.

New York State Department of Health, Early Intervention Program. (1999). *Clinical practice guideline for autism/pervasive developmental disorders: Assessment and intervention for young children ages 0–3 years* (Guideline Technical Report No. 4217). Albany, NY: Author.

Osterling, J. A., Dawson, G., & Munson, J. A. (2002). Early recognition of 1-year-old infants with autism spectrum disorder versus mental retardation. *Development and Psychopathology, 14,* 239–251.

Paul, R., Augustyn, A., Klin, A., & Volkmar, F. R. (2005). Perception and production of prosody by speakers with autism spectrum disorders. *Journal of Autism and Developmental Disorders, 35,* 205–220.

Peterson, P. (2004). Naturalistic language teaching procedures for children at risk for language delays. *Behavior Analyst Today, 5,* 404–424.

Pierce, K., & Courchesne, E. (2001). Evidence for a cerebellar role in reduced exploration and stereotyped behavior in autism. *Biological Psychiatry, 49,* 655–664.

Piven, J., Harper, J., Palmer, P., & Arndt, S. (1996). Course of behavioural change in autism: A retrospective study of high-IQ adolescents and adults. *Journal of the American Academy of Child and Adolescent Psychiatry, 35*, 523–529.

Polleux, F., & Lauder, J. M. (2004). Toward a developmental neurobiology of autism. *Mental Retardation and Developmental Disabilities Research Reviews, 10*, 303–317.

Prizant, B. (1983). Echolalia in autism: Assessment and intervention. *Seminars in Speech and Language, 4*, 63–77.

Reese, R. M., Richman, D. M., Belmont, J. M., & Morse, P. (2005). Functional characteristics of disruptive behavior in developmentally disabled children with and without autism. *Journal of Autism and Developmental Disorders, 35*, 419–428.

Ritvo, E. R., & Ritvo, R. A. (2006). Invited commentary: "Are the majority of children with autism mentally retarded?" *Focus on Autism and Other Developmental Disabilities, 21*, 84–85.

Robins, D. L., Fein, D., Barton, M. L., & Green, J. A. (2001). The Modified Checklist for Autism in Toddlers: An initial study investigating the early detection of autism and pervasive developmental disorders. *Journal of Autism and Developmental Disorders, 31*, 131–144.

Rogers, S. J., Herbison, J. M., Lewis, H. C., Pantone, J., & Reiss, K. (1986). An approach for enhancing the symbolic, communicative, and interpersonal functioning of young children with autism or severe emotional handicaps. *Journal of the Division for Early Childhood, 10*, 135–145.

Romanczyk, R. G., Gillis, J. M., Noyes-Grosser, D. M., Holland, J. P., Holland, C. L., & Lyons, D. (2005). Clinical clues, developmental milestones, and early identification/assessment of children with disabilities: Practical applications and conceptual considerations. *Infants and Young Children, 18*, 212–221.

Rutter, M., Bailey, A., Berument, S. K., Lord, C., & Pickles, A. (2003). *Social Communication Questionnaire (SCQ)*. Los Angeles: Western Psychological Services.

Rutter, M., Le Couteur, A., & Lord, C. (1995). *Autism Diagnostic Interview, revised WPS edition*. Los Angeles: Western Psychological Services.

Schertz, H. H., & Odom, S. L. (2004). Joint attention and early intervention in autism: A conceptual framework and promising approaches. *Journal of Early Intervention, 27*, 42–54.

Schopler, E., Reichler, R. J., & Renner, B. R. (1980). *The Childhood Autism Rating Scale*. Los Angeles: Western Psychological Services.

Schreibman, L. (1996). Brief report: The case for social and behavioral intervention research. *Journal of Autism and Developmental Disorders, 26*, 247–250.

Seltzer, M. M., Krauss, M. W., Shattuck, P. T., Orsmond, G., Swe, A., & Lord, C. (2003). The symptoms of autism spectrum disorders in adolescence and adulthood. *Journal of Autism and Developmental Disorders, 33*, 565–581.

Serra, M., Minderaa, R. B., van Geert, P. L. C., & Jackson, A. E. (1999). Social-cognitive abilities in children with lesser variants of autism: Skill deficits or failure to apply skills? *European Child and Adolescent Psychiatry, 8*, 301–311.

Sheinkopf, S. J., Mundy, P., Oller, K. D., & Steffens, M. (2000). Vocal atypicalities of preverbal autistic children. *Journal of Autism and Developmental Disorders, 30*, 345–354.

Sigman, M., & Capps, L. (1997). *Children with autism: A developmental perspective*. Cambridge, MA: Harvard University Press.

Sigman, M., Dijamco, A., Gratier, M., & Rozga, A. (2004). Early detection of core deficits in autism. *Mental Retardation and Developmental Disabilities Research Reviews, 10*, 221–233.

Singer, J. (1996). Cognitive and affective implications of imaginative play in childhood. In M. Lewis (Ed.), *Child and adolescent psychiatry: A comprehensive textbook* (2nd ed., pp. 202–210). Baltimore: Williams & Wilkins.

Smith, T., Eikeseth, S., Klevstrand, M., & Lovaas, O. I. (1997). Intensive behavioral treatment for preschoolers with severe mental retardation and pervasive developmental disorder. *American Journal on Mental Retardation, 102*, 238–249.

Sofronoff, K., Attwood, T., & Hinton, S. (2005). A randomized controlled trial of a CBT intervention for anxiety in children with Asperger syndrome. *Journal of Child Psychology and Psychiatry, 46*, 1152–1160.

Solomon, M., Goodlin-Jones, B. L., & Anders, T. F. (2004). A social adjustment enhancement intervention for high functioning autism, Asperger's syndrome, and PDD-NOS. *Journal of Autism and Developmental Disorders, 34*, 649–668.

South, M., Ozonoff, S., & McMahon, W. M. (2005). Repetitive behavior profiles in Asperger syndrome and high-functioning autism. *Journal of Autism and Developmental Disorders, 35*, 145–158.

Sparrow, S., Balla, D., & Cicchetti, D. (1984). *Vineland Adaptive Behaviour Scales (survey norms).* Circles Pines, MN: American Guidance Service.

Stone, W. L., & Ousley, O. Y. (1997). *STAT manual: Screening Tool for Autism in 2-year-olds.* Unpublished manuscript, Vanderbilt University.

Strain, P. S. (1985). Programmatic research on peers as intervention agents for socially isolated classmates. *Pointer, 29*, 22–29.

Tager-Flusberg, H., Paul, R., & Lord, C. (2005). Language and communication in autism. In F. R. Volkmar, R. Paul, A. Klin, & D. Cohen (Eds.), *Handbook of autism and pervasive developmental disorders* (3rd ed., pp. 335–364). Hoboken, NJ: Wiley.

Thomasa, N., & Smith, C. (2004). Developing play skills in children with autistic spectrum disorders. *Educational Psychology in Practice, 20*, 195–206.

Towbin, K. E., Pradella, A., Gorrindo, T., Pine, D. S., & Leibenluft, E. (2005). Autism spectrum traits in children with mood and anxiety disorders. *Journal of Child and Adolescent Psychopharmacology, 15*, 452–464.

Travis, L., Sigman, M., & Ruskin, E. (2001). Links between social understanding and social behavior in verbally able children with autism. *Journal of Autism and Developmental Disorders, 31*, 119–130.

Turner, L. M., Stone, W. L., Pozdol, S. L., & Coonrod, E. E. (2006). Follow-up of children with autism spectrum disorders from age 2 to age 9. *Autism: The International Journal of Research and Practice, 10*, 243–265.

Turner, M. A. (1999). Annotation: Repetitive behaviour in autism: A review of psychological research. *Journal of Child Psychology and Psychiatry, 40*, 839–849.

U.S. Food and Drug Administration. (2006). *FDA approves the first drug to treat irritability associated with autism, Risperdal.* Retrieved October 15, 2006, from www.fda.gov/bbs/topics/NEWS/2006/NEW01485.html.

U.S. Public Health Service. (2001). *Mental health: A report of the surgeon general.* Retrieved October 15, 2006, www.surgeongeneral.gov/library/mentalhealth/toc.html.

Van Acker, R., Loncola, J. A., & Van Acker, E. Y. (2005). Rett syndrome: A pervasive developmental disorder. In F. R. Volkmar, R. Paul, A. Klin, & D. Cohen (Eds.), *Handbook of autism and pervasive developmental disorders* (3rd ed., pp. 126–164). Hoboken, NJ: Wiley.

Van Bourgondien, M. E. & Mesibov, G. B. (1987) Humor in high-functioning autistic adults. *Journal of Autism and Developmental Disorders, 17*, 417–424.

Vaughn, S., Kim, A., Morris Sloan, C. V., Tejero Hughes, M., Elbaum, B., & Sridhar, D. (2003). Social skills interventions for young children with disabilities: A synthesis of group design studies. *Remedial and Special Education, 24*, 2–15.

Veenstra-VanderWeele, J., & Cook, E. (2003). Genetics of childhood disorders: Autism. *Journal of the American Academy of Child and Adolescent Psychiatry, 42*, 116–118.

Ventola, P. E., Kleinman, J., Pandey, J., Barton, M., Allen, S., Green, J., et al. (2006). Agreement among four diagnostic instruments for autism spectrum disorders in toddlers. *Journal of Autism and Developmental Disorders, 36*, 839–847.

Volkmar, F. R., & Klin, A. (2005). Issues in the classification of autism and related conditions. In F. R. Volkmar, R. Paul, A. Klin, & D. Cohen (Eds.), *Handbook of autism and pervasive developmental disorders* (pp. 5–41). Hoboken, NJ: Wiley.

Volkmar, F. R., Koenig, K., & State, M. (2005). Childhood disintegrative disorder. In F. R. Volkmar, R. Paul, A. Klin, & D. Cohen (Eds.), *Handbook of autism and pervasive developmental disorders* (pp. 70–87). Hoboken, NJ: Wiley.

Volkmar, F. R., Sparrow, S. A., Goudreau, D., Cichetti, D. V., Paul, R., & Cohen, D. J. (1987). Social deficits in autism: An operational approach using the Vineland Adaptive Behavior Scales. *Journal of the American Academy of Child and Adolescent Psychiatry, 26*, 156–161.

Wetherby, A. M., & Prizant, B. M. (1992). Profiling young children's communicative competence. In S. F. Warren & J. Reichle (Eds.), *Causes and effects in communication and language intervention* (pp. 217–253). Baltimore: Paul H. Brookes.

Wetherby, A. M., Prizant, B., & Schuler, A. (2000). Understanding the nature of the communication and language impairments. In A. Wetherby & B. Prizant (Eds.), *Autism spectrum disorders: A transactional developmental perspective* (pp. 109–141). Baltimore: Paul H. Brookes.

Wing, L. (1981). Asperger's syndrome: A clinical account. *Journal of Autism and Developmental Disorders, 9*, 11–29.

CHAPTER 30

Parental Psychopathology and Its Relation to Child Psychopathology

Sherryl H. Goodman and Sarah R. Brand

Regardless of one's theoretical perspective, psychopathology in parents raises many concerns about children's psychological well-being. In this chapter, we focus on two of the most prevalent disorders in parents, depression in mothers and alcohol disorders in fathers, and examine the evidence for their effects on various aspects of children's psychological functioning. We also review the mechanisms or processes that best explain those outcomes: the mediators. Because not all children of parents with psychopathology develop psychopathology themselves, we also review the findings on the moderators: characteristics and circumstances that influence the strength of those associations. Finally, we suggest some areas for further research and some implications for clinical practice and policy. Throughout this chapter, we take a developmental psychopathology perspective.

Several sets of findings guided our decision to focus on depression in mothers and alcohol disorders in fathers. With regard to depression, it is common, especially among women of childbearing and child-rearing ages, severe and impairing, and recurrent or persistent. It is not surprising that its presence in mothers has fueled concern for its potential to disrupt aspects of caretaking known to be critical for healthy child development. Knowledge of the heritability of depression adds further concern for the children of depressed parents. More recently, emerging knowledge of the neuroendocrine correlates of depression during pregnancy has raised concern about possible adverse influences even on fetal development. Many of these issues also pertain to the study of paternal alcoholism and the effect on child development. Although mothers have been the dominant focus of high-risk studies, research on parental alcohol abuse has tended to focus more heavily on fathers, likely because of the greater prevalence of such disorders in men (Phares, 1992; Phares & Compas, 1992). Advances in genetics research have also shown a high genetic risk of alcoholism, especially in men passing on the genes to their sons. Also, although mothers remain the primary caregivers for children in the United States, fathers are becoming more involved and taking on greater caregivng roles. Thus, the impact of the environmental correlates of alcoholism in fathers on the development of psychopathology in children will only grow.

Data are consistent with the suggestion that depression in women may be more of a concern than depression in men. That is, although depression in both mothers and fathers has been shown to affect children's psychological functioning, a meta-analysis of 134 samples, with a total of over 60,000 parent-child dyads, showed that both internalizing and externalizing problems in children are more strongly associated with depression in mothers relative to depression in fathers (Connell & Goodman, 2002). On the other hand, the meta-analysis found that alcoholism and substance abuse disorders in mothers were more closely related to externalizing (but not internalizing) problems in children than were such disorders in fathers. This finding is contrary to our premise that paternal alcoholism would be more strongly linked to children's (especially boys') behavior problems, based on both genetic mechanisms of transmission and greater prevalence of alcoholism in men than women. However, the magnitude of the differences was small, and the meta-analysis findings may reflect the adverse influence of maternal substance use during pregnancy on prenatal development, which is later reflected in psychopathology in the children.

PREVALENCE

One reason to focus on depression in mothers is its prevalence in women of child-bearing and child-rearing age. Depression is one of the most common psychiatric disorders in all adults. Among women, between 6% and 17% experience an episode of major depression at some point in their lifetime, a rate that is between 1.5 and 3 times higher than in men (Kessler, 2006). Moreover, depression is the leading cause of both economic and social disability in early to middle adulthood (Wilhelm, 2006), the primary childbearing and child-rearing years. The aspect of disability that has particular implications for depression in children of depressed mothers is depression's interference with quality of parenting, which has been the subject of a large body of research that will be reviewed later in this chapter and was the subject of a recent meta-analysis (Lovejoy, Graczyk, O'Hare, & Neuman, 2000).

Alcoholism is also highly prevalent in the U.S. population, with an estimated 8.45% (17.6 million) adult Americans meeting *Diagnostic and Statistical Manual of Mental Disorders* (*DSM-IV*; American Psychiatric Association, 1994) criteria for alcohol abuse or dependence during a 12-month period (Grant, Stinson, Dawson, Chou, Dufour, et al., 2004). As many as one in four children under 18 are exposed to alcohol abuse or dependency within their family (Grant, 2000). Because men show much higher rates of alcohol-related disorders than women, it is likely that a majority of those children are living in households with an alcoholic father.

THE NATURE OF THE DISORDERS

Researchers define clinically significant depression as either the set of symptoms, duration, and impairment by which an individual meets *DSM-IV* (American Psychiatric Association, 1994) criteria for a mood disorder or gets a high score on a self-report symptom rating scale of depression. The *DSM-IV* divides mood disorders into depressive disorders (sometimes referred to as unipolar depression) and Bipolar Disorders. Bipolar Disorder, which requires the presence of one or more manic or hypomanic episodes, although a concern for its impact on children, has less often been the focus of studies of maternal depression and will not be discussed in this chapter.

The *DSM-IV* divides alcohol-related disorders into two separate categories: alcohol dependence and alcohol abuse. Like other substance abuse disorders in the *DSM-IV,* alcohol abuse requires fewer symptoms and therefore may be less severe than dependence. Alcohol abuse is diagnosed only once the absence of dependence has been established (American Psychiatric Association, 1994). We include studies of both disorders in this chapter.

In the research literature on alcoholism, the issue arises about how to best characterize alcoholics who also have antisocial personality traits. Data from the National Epidemiologic Survey on Alcohol and Related Conditions showed about 28% co-occurrence between personality disorders and alcohol disorders. Antisocial Personality Disorder occurred in 12.3% of alcoholics, both men and women (Grant, Stinson, Dawson, Chou, Raun, et al., 2004). When these traits were examined for their contribution to child outcomes independent of the influence of alcoholism, they were usually found to contribute more to negative child outcomes than the alcoholism. However, many studies do not assess for these traits or do not make it clear if fathers were excluded based on high antisocial personality characteristics. In this chapter, studies that also examine antisocial personality traits are noted. Caution is needed in interpreting findings from studies when measures of such traits were not included.

THEORIZED MECHANISMS/MEDIATORS

Goodman and Gotlib (1999) proposed a model to explain how depression in mothers might contribute to the development of psychopathology in children (see Figure 30.1). We use that model to structure our summary of the current status of evidence for the most likely mechanisms for the effects of maternal depression on children. We also begin with that model for examining evidence for various mechanisms of transmission in the effects of paternal alcoholism on children and modify the model in theory- and data-guided manners.

When reviewing the literature regarding the influence of paternal alcoholism on child development, some issues arose that are important for readers to keep in mind. First, in many cases, only sons of alcoholics were studied. This is most likely due to the strong findings of the genetic contribution to the development of alcoholism in men (Tyndale, 2004). Second, more often than in the parental depression literature, many studies of parental alcoholism failed to distinguish whether the alcoholism was in the father or the mother. We included such studies, but they clearly dilute the potential to inform the literature on paternal alcoholism specifically.

Biological Mechanisms for Effects of Depression in Mothers

Work on biological mechanisms that might explain the development of psychopathology in children of depressed mothers has focused on two lines of research. First, much research has centered on genetic influences, not only of depression as a disorder but also of vulnerabilities to depression and to other disorders. A

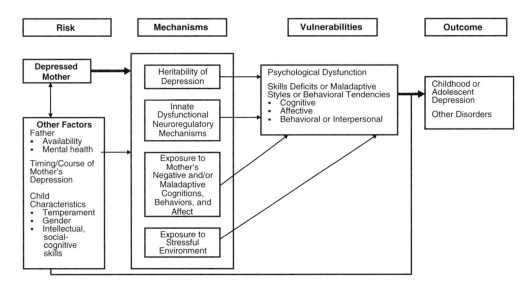

Figure 30.1 Integrative model for the transmission of risk to children of depressed mothers. *Source:* "Risk for Psychopathology in the Children of Depressed Mothers: A Developmental Model for Understanding Mechanisms of Transmission," by S. H. Goodman and I. H. Gotlib, 1999, *Psychological Review, 106,* pp. 458–490. Reprinted with permission.

second line of research has investigated the idea that fetal or postnatal exposures or experiences among children with depressed mothers might adversely influence brain development or hormonal functioning related to neuroregulatory mechanisms, thereby increasing risk for the later development of psychopathology. Support for both of those lines of research is reviewed in the following sections.

Genetic Influences

Research based on family studies, quantitative genetic studies (twin and adoption designs), and molecular genetic studies all provide strong support for heritability of depression in adults, although some evidence suggests that the specific genes related to risk for depression may differ for men compared to women (Caspi et al., 2003; Kendler, Gardner, Neale, & Prescott, 2001). Evidence for the heritability of depression in children and adolescents, however, is mixed. Based on family studies, strictly defined depression in children and adolescents is associated with increased rates of depression in relatives (Harrington, 1996; Harrington et al., 1997). Based on twin studies, heritability is higher in those whose levels of symptoms were below rather than above clinical cutoffs (Rende, Plomin, Reiss, & Hetherington, 1993), for depression in adolescents rather than in children (Eley & Stevenson, 1999; Murray & Sines, 1996; Scourfield et al., 2003; Silberg et al., 2001; Thapar & McGuffin, 1994), for parent-reported rather than child-reported symptoms (Eaves et al., 1997), and for parent-reported symptoms in girls relative to boys (Murray & Sines, 1996; Scourfield et al., 2003). In addition, because heritability of depression is probably not specific to depression, heritability likely contributes to risk for other disorders that are identified in higher rates in children of depressed mothers relative to controls (Moldin, 1999; Tsuang & Faraone, 1990). Thus, heritability likely contributes to the risk for the development of psychopathology in children and adolescents with depressed mothers, although more research is needed to clarify the nature, extent, and specificity of the contribution.

An alternative to the notion that children with depressed mothers inherit a like-lihood for depression per se is the idea that heritability contributes significantly to vulnerabilities to depression and other disorders, such as those proposed in the Goodman and Gotlib (1999) model. In particular, based on behavior genet-ics studies, high levels of heritability are found for behavioral inhibition and shy-ness (Cherny, Fulker, Corley, Plomin, & DeFries, 1994), low self-esteem (Loehlin & Nichols, 1976), neuroticism (Tellegen et al., 1988), sociability (Plomin et al., 1993), subjective well-being (Lykken & Tellegen, 1996), and expression of nega-tive emotion (Plomin et al., 1993). This body of research suggests possible genetic transmission of affective, cognitive, and interpersonal vulnerabilities for the devel-opment of psychopathology.

Neuroregulatory Mechanisms

Biology may also play a role in the development of psychopathology in offspring of depressed mothers in that both prenatal and postnatal experiences might influence aspects of hormonal functioning and brain development, each of which may increase vulnerability to depression and other stress-related disorders in particular (Ashman & Dawson, 2002). Much of the evidence for this premise is based on research exam-ining the role of early (neonatal) life stress in the development of psychopathology, emphasizing neuroregulatory processes and especially hypothalamic-pituitary-adrenocortical (HPA) axis functioning (Graham, Heim, Goodman, Miller, & Nemeroff, 1999). Typically measured in terms of abnormal cortisol responses to stress but sometimes as a baseline cortisol measure, HPA functioning has been associated with depression in adults (Ressler & Nemeroff, 2000) and may suggest vulnerability mechanisms for the development of depression and other disorders in children of depressed mothers. Stress-related physiological dysregulation in children may be a marker of children's sensitivity to stress, suggesting a particular pathway through which maternal depression during pregnancy and the postpartum may increase children's later development of depression (Sanchez, Ladd, & Plotsky, 2001).

Studies from Field's (2002) lab show that depression during pregnancy increases women's levels of cortisol. Other relevant findings are that pregnant women's levels of cortisol account for 50% of the variance in the fetus's levels of cortisol (Glover, 1999), that mothers' prenatal levels of cortisol predict newborns' cortisol levels (Lundy et al., 1999), and that number of months depressed during pregnancy pre-dict preschool-age children's baseline cortisol levels (Ashman & Dawson, 2002). Elevated stress hormone levels, such as cortisol, in pregnant women are of concern because they have been associated with impaired neurodevelopment in the fetus (Wadhwa et al., 2002).

Postnatal exposure to stressors associated with maternal depression may also disrupt HPA processes (Ashman & Dawson, 2002). In particular, depressed moth-ers' insensitive or unresponsive behavior, discussed in a later section of this chapter, may mediate the association between maternal depression and children's emotion regulation abilities, which in turn increases risk for the later development of psychopathology.

Along with disruptions in hormonal functioning, abnormal brain development (in frontal lobe activity) is another aspect of neuroregulatory functioning that may play a role in the development of psychopathology in children of depressed mothers. Researchers have been particularly interested in the abnormal EEG pattern of relatively greater baseline right (compared to left) frontal activation. This pattern is a stable individual difference at least by adolescence (Tomarken, Davidson, Wheeler, & Kinney, 1992) and has been associated with the tendency in children to experience withdrawal emotions such as sadness and fear (Davidson & Fox, 1989) and with depression in adolescents and adults (Davidson, Ekman, Saron, Senulis, & Friesen, 1990). Dawson and colleagues showed associations between frontal lobe activity and affective expressions in infants of depressed mothers (Dawson, Grofer Klinger, Panagiotides, Hill, & Spieker, 1992) and, further, that 3-year-olds' frontal brain activation mediated the relation between maternal depression and children's level of behavior problems (Dawson et al., 2003). That study was not designed to explain the relative (and likely interacting) influences of genetics and fetal and early postnatal experiences on the abnormal brain activation patterns. That is an especially important question given that the frontal lobe develops rapidly during the first 2 years of life (Chugani & Phelps, 1986), suggesting sensitivity to early adverse experiences such as exposure to a mother whose depression interferes with her providing the sensitive and responsive parenting required by infants. Also needed is more research on the extent to which the same or different predictors explain children's stress hormone functioning relative to their brain activation patterns. In 6-month-old infants, these two aspects of neuroregulatory functioning were found to be related; higher basal and stressor reactive cortisol levels were associated with relatively greater right EEG asymmetry (Buss et al., 2003).

Biological Mechanisms for Effects of Alcohol-Related Disorders in Fathers

Work on biological mechanisms that might explain the development of psychopathology in children of alcoholic fathers has focused primarily on genetics but also on electricortical arousal. Support for both of those lines of research is reviewed next.

Genetic Influences

Alcohol dependence is known to be highly heritable, with twin and adoption studies demonstrating that between 50% and 60% of phenotypic variations can be accounted for by a genetic component (Higuchi, Matsushita, & Kashima, 2006; McGue, 1999). Classic twin study estimates of the heritability of alcoholism in men are higher but also more variable (48% to 73%) than in women (51% to 65%; Tyndale, 2004). The variability is likely explained by differences in the classification of alcoholism subtypes. Cloninger and colleagues (Cloninger, Bohmann, & Sigvardsson, 1981) classified alcoholism into two subtypes associated with variations in gender-specific heritability. Type I alcoholism (milieu-limited) is moderately heritable for both males and females, whereas Type II alcoholism (male-limited) is strongly associated with genetic factors in male offspring and is associated with an early age of onset and with elevated rates of externalizing behavior problems in fathers (Sigvardsson, Bohman, & Cloninger, 1996). Overall, the genetic contribution to alcohol dependence in males has been very well established (for review, see Higuchi et al., 2006) and is likely to be a particularly important mechanism in the transmission of alcoholism from fathers to sons. Genetic factors are also likely to bear primary responsibility for the association between paternal alcoholism and child Conduct Disorder (Haber, Jacob, & Heath, 2005).

Although traditional twin and adoption studies are particularly valuable for estimating heritability, they also play an essential role in revealing the relative contributions of shared and nonshared environment (Hopfer, Crowley, & Hewitt, 2003). Of particular interest from a psychosocial research perspective is altered family environments associated with paternal alcoholism and their role, independent of or in interaction with genes, in explaining the development of alcoholism (Jacob et al., 2003). In an effort to address this broader question, Jacob and colleagues used an offspring-of-twins design and assessed adult male monozygotic and dizygotic twins concordant or discordant for alcohol dependence and their biological offspring, examining both genetic and familial influences. Consistent with other genetics studies, offspring of alcoholic fathers were at a significantly higher risk for the development of an alcohol use disorder than were offspring of controls. Interestingly, however, the researchers found that the complete absence of family environmental correlates of alcoholism, even when high genetic risk is present, resulted in offspring alcoholism levels not significantly different from those of controls. If these findings are replicated, it could show that a genetic risk for alcoholism is not sufficient for offspring alcoholism to develop in the absence of significant environmental sequelae (Jacob et al., 2003). The relative contribution of heritability and environment may also vary depending on the particular outcome of interest and on developmental considerations. For example, in a large study of 16-year-old twins, shared environmental effects best explained drinking initiation, whereas genetic effects better explained frequency of drinking among subjects who had already started drinking (Viken, Kaprio, Koskenvuo, & Rose, 1999).

Despite the strong evidence for a genetic contribution to alcohol dependence in males, specific genes that alter the risk have been difficult to identify. This is partially due to the additional influence of environmental components as well as the understanding that multiple genes that have moderate effects are involved in alcoholism, and these different sets of genes may contribute to the disorder in different people (Higuchi et al., 2006). Thus more research is needed not only on the nature and extent of genetic contributions but also on the likely complex interplay between genes and environments.

Other Biological Mechanisms

Much of the research examining possible psychobiological risk factors for the development of alcoholism has focused on individual differences in electrocortical arousal, most often using the P300 responses. P300 is a positive event-related potential response wave that in itself is known to be highly heritable. The electri-cortical research has been focused on the P300 response because of its identification in working memory and attentional resource allocation and its reduced amplitude in recovering alcoholics (Windle & Tubman, 1999). To determine whether this re-duced amplitude is a consequence of frequent inebriation or could be considered a risk factor for the development of alcoholism, children of alcoholics have been studied prior to their onset of drinking. Numerous such studies (see Windle & Tubman, 1999, for review) have found significant differences between children of alcoholics and children of nonalcoholics, with the children of alcoholics showing a reduced P300 response in visual task paradigms, which may generalize across the visual and auditory sensory modalities. Benegal and colleagues (Benegal, Jain, Subbukrishna, & Channabasavanna, 1995) took this a step further by showing that the P300 component was even smaller in children with multiple alcoholic relatives in comparison with children with only a single relative. These findings are consis-tent with the idea that reduced P300 amplitude is a risk factor for the development of an alcohol-related disorder.

Anecdotal reports from alcohol dependent children of alcoholics led researchers to consider one other possible biological mechanism for the development of alco-holism in children of alcoholic fathers. These narratives frequently describe chil-dren of alcoholics' abilities from a young age to consume large amounts of alcohol with few effects. Schuckit and colleagues (1996) examined the possible role of differences in alcohol tolerance by assessing time-to-peak alcohol concentration and the rate of disappearance of ethanol from the blood following the challenge in 453 sons of alcoholics and controls. Because of the confounding effect of fetal alcohol syndrome, the authors placed an emphasis on examining offspring of alco-holic fathers. There were no significant differences in blood alcohol concentration in the two groups, yet about 40% of the sons of alcoholics, but fewer than 10% of controls, reported low subjective feelings of intoxication (Schuckit & Smith, 1996). This finding has been replicated in many studies as well as confirmed by a meta-analysis (Pollock, 1992) and gives weight to the theory that sons of alcoholics possess less subjective (self-rated) sensitivity to alcohol effects than do controls. These findings have been interpreted to suggest that these individuals are more vulnerable to developing an alcohol-related disorder because they are less sensitive to alcohol effects and therefore find it more difficult to regulate their alcohol con-sumption because they are receiving less internal feedback. Thus, they may be more likely to consume more alcohol than those without a family history of alcoholism, which may contribute to their development of dependence or abuse (Pollock, 1992). The data do not allow us to conclude whether the findings are specific to sons or might generalize to daughters.

Quality of Care Mechanisms for the Effects of Maternal Depression

Social Learning Processes

Exposure to depressed mothers' negative affect, behavior, and cognitions is an-other potential mechanism for transmission of the risk of depression from parents to offspring (see Figure 30.1). Through the social learning processes of modeling, observational learning, and reinforcement, children of depressed mothers may acquire cognitions, behaviors, and affect that resemble those of the depressed parent. These acquired depressotypic cognitions, behaviors, and affect may place the children at elevated risk for developing depression in particular, but also potentially other disorders.

Children have ample opportunities to be exposed to negative cognitions, behaviors, and affect associated with depression in their mothers. In terms of affect and behavior, a meta-analysis of 46 observation studies revealed that maternal depression is strongly associated with negative (hostile or coercive) parenting behavior, is moderately associated with parenting characterized as disengaged, and shows a small association with lower levels of positive behavior (Lovejoy et al., 2000). In terms of cognitions, the negatively biased cognitions associated with depression in adults (Gotlib, Gilboa, & Sommerfeld, 2000) emerge in parenting in depressed mothers' (a) more negative views of themselves as parents (Gelfand & Teti, 1990; Goodman, Sewell, Cooley, & Leavitt, 1993), (b) lower confidence in being able to positively influence their children (Kochanska, Radke-Yarrow, Kuczynski, & Friedman, 1987), and (c) more negative, critical perceptions of their children (Goodman, Adamson, Riniti, & Cole, 1994) relative to controls.

Researchers have linked these specific aspects of depression in mothers with the development of psychopathology in children and adolescents. Depressed mothers' negative, critical perceptions of their children are associated with children's self-blaming attributions for negative events and with lowered perceived self-worth (Goodman et al., 1994; Jaenicke et al., 1987; Kochanska et al., 1987; Radke-Yarrow, Belmont, Nottelman, & Bottomly, 1990). Children seem to internalize their depressed mother's negative views of them, thereby acquiring a cognitive vulnerability to depression (Beck, Rush, Shaw, & Emery, 1979). Depressed mothers' greater criticism and hostility (Frye & Garber, 2005; Webster-Stratton & Hammond, 1988) may also contribute to the emergence of coercive processes similar to those implicated primarily in the development of externalizing behavior problems but also of depression (Davis, Sheeber, & Hops, 2002; Hops, Sherman, & Biglan, 1990).

Inadequate Parenting

In addition to social learning processes, other mechanisms that may explain how qualities of parenting contribute to the development of problems in children focus on inadequate parenting (especially if early in life) as a stressor. Although not incompatible with social learning processes, these studies stem from a different tradition of research, emphasizing interpersonal processes such as the depressed mother being an inadequate social partner for the child and the mother being unable to meet the child's stage-salient social and emotional needs (Cicchetti & Toth, 1998). This inadequate parenting would, in turn, negatively affect the child's development of social and cognitive skills and beliefs and leave him or her vulnerable to the development of psychopathology.

In this line of research, inadequate parenting refers to the mother being unable to meet the needs associated with healthy psychological development specific to different phases of child development. Researchers have particularly emphasized infancy given infants' dependence on their caregivers to meet their basic needs (Sroufe, Egeland, Carlson, & Collins, 2005). This research is consistent with the idea that depression in mothers is a stressor for their infants, and thus is related to the literature on HPA activity and EEG asymmetries reviewed earlier. Mothers may be stressors as a function of being unresponsive or inconsistent (unpredictable in their responsiveness) in relating to their infants, thereby interfering with infants' development of emotion regulation skills (Fox, 1994) and secure attachment relationships (Cicchetti, Rogosch, & Toth, 1998; Sroufe & Waters, 1977). Both of the latter are known to increase risk for the development of psychopathology in childhood or adolescence (Southam-Gerow & Kendall, 2002; Thompson, 2006).

Stress

In addition to the notion of parenting as a stressor, especially for infants, maternal depression increases children's exposure to stress in several other ways, which also may mediate associations between maternal depression and the development of psychopathology in offspring (Hammen, 2002). These include the stressfulness for children of the symptoms and episodic course of depression in their mothers (Compas, Langrock, Keller, Merchant, & Copeland, 2002), the chronic and episodic stressors that are often the context for depression (Monroe & Hadjiyannakis, 2002), and the stress-generating quality associated with depression (Hammen, 1991). Although these findings are consistent with the notion of stress as a mechanism, few studies have actually tested stress as a mediator in associations between depression in mothers and outcomes in children. One of the few such studies found support for the role of stressors as a mediator of the association between maternal depression and children's depression (Brennan, Hammen, Katz, & Le Brocque, 2002).

Quality of Care Mechanisms for the Effects of Alcoholism in Fathers

Because mothers are still the primary caregivers in most families, much of the research about alcoholism and parenting focuses specifically on the effects of maternal alcoholism or on familial alcoholism. Although we emphasize studies focusing solely on paternal alcoholism, we included studies involving familial alcoholism to illustrate the effect of alcohol-related disorders on quality of care given to the child.

Although there is a large range in quality of caregivng in families with an alcoholic parent, on average researchers find significantly poorer quality compared to controls. In the few studies involving observations of father-child interaction, paternal alcoholism was found to be associated with problematic parenting behaviors during unstructured free play with an infant, with alcoholic fathers showing higher negative affect, less sensitivity, lower positive engagement, and lower amount and quality of verbalizations relative to controls (Eiden, Edwards, & Leonard, 2002; Leonard & Eiden, 2002). Children of alcoholic parents are also exposed to significantly greater adverse circumstances. Similar to the studies of the role of stress as a mechanism in children of depressed mothers, one model in alcoholism studies is that the problems in family functioning associated with alcoholism in a parent influence the expression of internalizing and externalizing problems among children of alcoholics by acting as a significant stressor for the child (Windle & Tubman, 1999). In homes where one or both parents are alcoholic, both child and parent reports reveal significantly poorer quality of home environment and more household dysfunction as well as exposure to more marital conflict, parent-child conflict, abuse (verbal, physical, and sexual), and domestic violence than in homes where neither parent is an alcoholic (Anda et al., 2002; Reich, Earls, & Powell, 1988). Among these adversities, much research has focused on the role of marital conflict as one of the mechanisms through which children of alcoholic parents are harmed. Marital conflict is related to ineffective parenting (including inconsistent discipline and psychological control), which in turn is associated with children's internalizing and externalizing problems (Cummings, Keller, & Davies, 2005). Thus parents' problematic drinking may be associated with children's behavior problems indirectly, through mediating variables such as marital conflict (Christensen & Bilenberg, 2000; Snow Jones, Miller, & Salkever, 1999).

Patterson and colleagues' (Patterson, Reid, & Dishion, 1992) well-established coercion model, which explains the relationship between parenting influences and childhood conduct disorders, is a useful theoretical model in that children's conduct problems increase the likelihood of alcohol or drug abuse. In this model, the most relevant force in determining a child's development of psychopathology is disturbances in the control dimension of parenting, especially a coercive parent-child interactional style, similar to the pattern that has been identified in studies of parenting in homes with an alcoholic parent. This style is marked by unclear behavioral expectations from the parent and lack of compliance by the child. The continuation of this coercive relational style results in inadequate parental monitoring, supervision, and discipline, which can lead to antisocial behavior in the child, which, in turn, increases the likelihood of the child's alcohol abuse (Patterson et al., 1992).

EVIDENCE FOR EFFECTS OF MATERNAL DEPRESSION AND PATERNAL ALCOHOLISM ON CHILDREN

Given the size and complexity of the literature, we begin with evidence for the effects of maternal depression and then separately review evidence of the effects of paternal alcoholism. Within each of these sections, we present data on effects on children's social, emotional, and cognitive development, which may be vulnerabilities for the later development of psychopathology, and then on psychopathology per se.

Evidence for Effects of Maternal Depression

Effects on Children's Social, Emotional, and Cognitive Development

Children of depressed mothers show problems in each of these aspects of functioning relative to controls. On social and interpersonal functioning, infants show less secure attachment relationships (van IJzendoorn, Goldberg, Kroonenberg, & Frenkel, 1992); preschool-age children engage in excessive compliance with their depressed mothers (Zahn-Waxler, Radke-Yarrow, Wagner, & Chapman, 1992); kindergarten-age children are more often excluded by peers (Cummings et al., 2005); and sons, but not daughters, display more aggressive behavior during interactions with friends (note that the last effect was mediated by the children's exposure to interparental conflict; Hipwell, Murray, Ducournau, & Stein, 2005).

On emotional development, infants imitate their depressed mothers' negative affect (Field, 1994). Infants of depressed mothers show more negative affect and more self-directed regulatory behaviors (Field, 1992; Tronick & Gianino, 1986); toddlers show more dysregulated aggression and heightened emotionality (Zahn-Waxler, Cummings, Iannotti, & Radke-Yarrow, 1984); and adolescents (particularly girls) display more dysphoric and less happy affect (Hops et al., 1990). Infants interacting with their depressed mothers also engage in more gaze and head aversion, consistent with the idea that the infants were using self-regulatory behaviors to minimize the negative affect associated with maternal unresponsiveness (Pickens & Field, 1993).

Children of depressed mothers score lower on measures of intelligence and also have poorer academic performance overall (Anderson & Hammen, 1993; Hammen & Brennan, 2001; Hay & Kumar, 1995; Jaenicke et al., 1987). On other aspects of cognitive functioning, children of depressed mothers show early signs of cognitive vulnerability to depression, including being more likely than controls to blame themselves for negative outcomes, having a more negative attributional style, being less likely to recall positive self-descriptive adjectives, and having a lower self-concept (Garber & Martin, 2002).

Effects on the Development of Psychopathology

Beginning at the earliest ages when it is possible to reliably measure psychopathology in children, children and adolescents with depressed mothers show higher rates of depression relative to a variety of controls (Beardslee et al., 1988; Billings & Moos, 1985; Goodman et al., 1994; Lee & Gotlib, 1989; Malcarne, Hamilton, Ingram, & Taylor, 2000; Orvaschel, Walsh-Allis, & Ye, 1988; Weissman et al., 1984; Welner, Welner, McCrary, & Leonard, 1977). Rates of depression in the school-age children of depressed mothers vary from 20% to 41%, depending on the severity or impairment of the parent's depression, whether both parents are depressed, and a number of other sociodemographic variables (Gotlib & Goodman, 1999). Moreover, depression in offspring of depressed parents, compared with same-age offspring of nondepressed parents, has an earlier age of onset and longer duration and is associated with greater functional impairment and higher likelihood of recurrence (Hammen & Brennan, 2001; Hammen, Burge, Burney, & Adrian, 1990; Hammen, Shih, Altman, & Brennan, 2003; Keller et al., 1986; Lieb, Isensee, Hofler, Pfister, & Wittchen, 2002; Warner, Weissman, Fendrich, Wickramaratne, & Moreau, 1992).

Psychopathology in children with depressed mothers is not limited to depression. Researchers have also found higher rates of Social Phobia, Separation Anxiety Disorder and other anxiety disorders, attention deficit disorders, disruptive behavior disorders, overall levels of behavior problems, and poorer social functioning relative to controls (Anderson & Hammen, 1993; Biederman et al., 2001; Luoma et al., 2001;

Orvaschel et al., 1988; Weissman et al., 1984). In addition, levels of internalizing and externalizing behavior problems are higher in children with depressed mothers relative to controls (Brennan et al., 2002; Fergusson, Lynskey, & Horwood, 1993; Forehand, Brody, Slotkin, Fauber, & McCombs, 1988).

Evidence for Effects of Paternal Alcoholism

Effects on Children's Social, Emotional, and Cognitive Development

Similar to the findings from maternal depression, paternal alcoholism is associated with problematic patterns of father-infant attachment: infant avoidance and infant disorganization as assessed by the Strange Situation paradigm (Eiden et al., 2002; Leonard & Eiden, 2002; Leonard et al., 2000). Teenagers (18 years old) whose fathers were alcoholics rated their attachment to their fathers as significantly more negative than teenagers of nonalcoholic fathers (Cavell, Jones, Runyan, Constantin-Page, & Velasquez, 1993).

In terms of cognitive development, while there is strong empirical support for the severe cognitive deficiencies caused by maternal drinking during pregnancy (Steinhausen, Willms, & Spohr, 1993), the literature surrounding the impact of paternal alcoholism on a child's cognitive functioning is varied. Leonard and Eiden (2002) found no significant difference in the cognitive functioning of toddlers of alcoholic fathers, assessed at 12, 18, and 24 months, relative to toddlers in control families who were matched on maternal education, ethnicity, child sex, and marital status. However, children of alcoholics had poorer intellectual functioning than control children during the elementary school years, although still within the normal range (Poon, Ellis, Fitzgerald, & Zucker, 2000).

When Ozkaragoz, Satz, and Noble (1997) examined differences in neuropsychological functioning of sons of alcoholic fathers, recovering alcoholics, and social drinkers, they found that sons of active alcoholics performed worse on visuospatial, memory, and attention tasks as well as general intellectual functioning. However, no difference in neuropsychological functioning was found between the sons of the recovering alcoholics and those of social drinkers (Ozkaragoz et al., 1997). The latter finding is relevant to moderators, discussed later.

Effects on the Development of Psychopathology

Many studies have shown the link between paternal alcoholism and alcohol-related outcomes in children (Cavell et al., 1993; Chassin, Rogosch, & Barrera, 1991). Paternal alcoholism predicted initial alcohol and drug use in younger adolescents (Chassin et al., 1991) as well as greater alcohol involvement in older adolescents (Cavell et al., 1993). Overall, family alcoholism is associated with a threefold increase in risk for alcohol abuse in young adults (Schuckit & Smith, 1996).

Beyond an increased risk for developing an alcohol-related disorder, a family history of alcoholism put children at a higher risk for developing other psychopathologies, including Conduct Disorder, affective disorder, and Attention-Deficit/Hyperactivity Disorder (ADHD). Edwards, Eiden, and Leonard (2006) found that both male and female 18-month-old toddlers with alcoholic fathers had higher levels of not only externalizing behaviors but also of internalizing behaviors relative to children of nonalcoholic fathers. Early adult (mean age 19) sons of alcoholic-dependent fathers were also significantly more likely to receive a diagnosis of Conduct Disorder than were matched controls from families without a history of alcoholism, indicating a diagnostic crossover in family transmission (Haber et al., 2005).

Many researchers have hypothesized that one potential pathway for the transmission of the risk of alcoholism from parent to child is the likelihood of early conduct problems among children of alcoholics, which has been linked to greater antisocial behavior in adolescence and adulthood, which, in turn, has been linked to a greater risk of substance abuse (Eiden, Leonard, & Morrisey, 2001). In a study examining toddler compliance at 18 and 24 months and comparing children of alcoholics and children of nonalcoholics, Eiden et al. showed that fathers' alcoholism was significantly associated with the development of compliance problems among boys, an effect more pronounced in the presence of maternal alcohol problems. These boys showed increased levels of resistance to parental requests (during a cleaning-up task) at 18 months and continued to show a higher level of resistance at 24 months. Contrary to expected results, daughters of alcoholic fathers showed the opposite pattern, even when the mother was also an alcoholic. The authors pointed out that the mothers with alcoholism were also more antisocial and aggressive than controls, and therefore the daughters could be displaying compulsive compliance. In general, frequencies of disruptive behavior problems in young children tend to decrease over time, most likely due to increases in self-regulatory capacities, which are developed during the preschool years. However, this decrease can be offset by the presence of paternal alcoholism, as Loukas and colleagues (Loukas, Zucker, Fitzgerald, & Krull, 2003) showed that paternal alcoholism was associated with higher levels of disruptive behavior problems across all time points.

MODERATORS

The processes underlying the developmental pathways that lead to psychological problems in children of depressed mothers or alcoholic fathers are likely to be affected by multiple moderating variables, which not only create individual pathways unique to each child but also more generally exacerbate or lessen the extent of risk associated with the psychopathology in the parent (Kraemer, Stice, Kazdin, Offord, & Kupfer, 2001). A transactional perspective suggests that through a process of continuous reciprocation, characteristics and traits of the child influence how the child experiences the environment, which, in turn, influences the child's characteristics and traits and so forth (Sameroff, 1975). Thus, from the perspective of transactional models, various factors may moderate the associations between psychopathology in a parent and children's development and account for some children functioning well and others developing psychopathology and other problems. These factors may include (a) qualities of the children, such as temperament, sex, and various cognitive variables; (b) the broader context of the children's environment, such as the presence and mental health of the other parent or another adult and the quality of the marital relationship; and (c) characteristics of the parent's psychopathology, such as timing, course, and chronicity. Much heterogeneity has been noted in studies of children of depressed mothers and of alcoholic fathers. Moderating variables promise to explain much of that heterogeneity. Empirical support for each of these potential moderators is reviewed next, first for children of depressed mothers and then for children of alcoholic fathers.

Moderators of Associations between Maternal Depression and Children's Development

Qualities of the Children

The sex of the offspring of depressed mothers is one characteristic of the child that has been shown to moderate the association between mothers and limited aspects of children's development. Specifically, sex moderates associations between maternal depression and depression in adolescents (Sheeber, Davis, & Hops, 2002). Adolescent daughters of depressed mothers have more dysphoric and less happy affect than adolescent daughters of nondepressed mothers, whereas no significant difference in affect was found for adolescent boys of depressed mothers compared to sons of nondepressed mothers (Allgood-Merten, Lewinsohn, & Hops, 1990). Among the smaller body of support for sex differences among younger children, depressed mothers and their daughters, but not depressed mothers and their sons, have been shown to have synchronous bouts of depression (Radke-Yarrow, Nottelman, Belmont, & Welsch, 1993). Similarly, in community samples, levels of depression in mothers and daughters are interrelated, but levels of depression in mothers and sons are not related (Davies & Windle, 1997; Fergusson, Horwood, & Lynskey, 1995). Increased risk for depression in daughters compared to sons of depressed mothers is likely to be explained by the same mechanisms that explain risk for depression in adolescent girls compared to adolescent boys in general populations: gender-stereotyped socialization processes, especially early socialization of emotion expression, coping styles, and relationship orientation and possibly greater exposure of girls to family discord (Goodman & Tully, 2006; Sheeber et al., 2002).

Children's age is likely a complex moderator, perhaps most likely interacting with other moderators such as sex, as illustrated in Sheeber et al. (2002). In a meta-analysis, we found a negative correlation between children's age and effect size such that maternal depression was more strongly associated with younger children's internalizing and externalizing problems (Connell & Goodman, 2002). Age is also further complicated by the course of maternal depression in that older children are likely to have been more often exposed.

Researchers have studied children's cognitive abilities, such as IQ, and cognitive vulnerabilities, such as depressogenic attributions, as child qualities that may moderate the link between depression in mothers and children's psychological functioning. Children of depressed parents may be protected against adverse outcome concurrently and prospectively if they are more intelligent (Radke-Yarrow et al., 1990) or have better social-cognitive skills (Beardslee, Schultz, & Selman, 1987). Cognitive theories of depression suggest other potential moderating variables, such as children's perceptions and beliefs about their parents' depression, which may guide children's emotional and coping responses and, then, influence the impact of the mother's depression on the children's development (Beardslee, 1989; Beardslee & Podorefsky, 1988; Compas et al., 2002; Garber & Martin, 2002; Klimes-Dougan & Bolger, 1998; Solantaus-Simula, Punamaki, & Beardslee, 2002).

Although studies have rarely directly tested the moderating role of temperament in associations between depression in mothers and their offspring, research suggests that children with difficult temperaments are more vulnerable to the effects of inadequate parenting, such as that shown by depressed mothers (Goldsmith, Buss, & Lemery, 1997). Other indirect support is that mothers' higher levels of depressive symptoms have been associated with their perceptions of more infant negativity (Pesonen, Raikkonen, Strandberg, Keltikangas-Jarvinen, & Jarvenpaa, 2004) and difficulty (Cutrona & Troutman, 1986; Edhborg, Seimyr, Lundh, & Widstrom, 2000) and with observational measures of infant difficulty (Cutrona & Troutman, 1986). Mothers of more difficult infants also perceive their parenting to be less efficacious, which in turn is linked to depression in mothers (Cutrona & Troutman, 1986; Porter & Hsu, 2003).

The Broader Context of the Children's Environment

Studies of depression are increasingly taking into account the broader context in which depression occurs (Keyes & Goodman, 2006). Researchers sensitive to the importance of context are beginning to find that fathers (their quantity and quality of involvement and their mental health) and marital conflict play important roles as moderators of associations between maternal depression and child outcomes (Goodman & Gotlib, 1999). Assortative mating, the tendency for adults with similar phenotypes to mate more frequently than expected by chance, is pertinent here. This type of mating practice can produce a double jeopardy situation for the children: Not only are the children inheriting a greater genetic predisposition toward psychopathology, but they are also being raised in a home environment that is likely to be highly compromised and have high levels of unpredictability and low levels of parental monitoring (Merikangas, Weissman, Prusoff, & John, 1988; Windle & Tubman, 1999). Assortative mating, in particular the selection of a mate who also has a mood disorder, is known to be a significant factor in mate selection for women with affective disorders (although not as much as for men; Matthews & Reus, 2001). In studies of maternal depression there is some evidence for the ameliorating effect of fathers' mental health (Thomas & Forehand, 1991), although other studies suggest a more complex model may be needed, such as one that takes into account transactional relationships over time (Hops et al., 1990). In addition, an adequate conceptualization of the role of fathers needs to take into account quality and quantity of involvement.

Marital discord is essential to consider in that it is a common contextual factor for depression in women and by itself is related to increased risk for psychopathology in children (Whisman, Weinstock, & Tolejko, 2006). Davies and Windle (1997) found that marital discord significantly mediated the association between histories of maternal depression symptoms and symptoms of depression in children at middle adolescence, but only in girls. Later, Davies and Dumenci (1999) found support for a pathway from marital distress through maternal depression (rather than vice versa) to adolescents' depression. Moreover, particular conflict strategies that parents use (those involving depressive behaviors such as physical distress, withdrawal, sadness, and fear in contrast to destructive or constructive marital conflict strategies) mediate associations between maternal depression and children's depression (Du Rocher Schudlich & Cummings, 2003). These findings strongly support the importance of context and the need to develop and test models that consider its potentially moderating and mediating roles.

Parental Characteristics as Moderators

Timing and course of mothers' depression may also account for differences in risk among children of depressed mothers. The exact role of timing is likely to be complicated and may vary by child sex (Essex, Klein, Miech, & Smider, 2001). Timing and course are interrelated given that children who are exposed earlier in their lives are also likely to be exposed more often, not only to the depression but also to the stress correlates of depression, such as marital difficulty, all of which place the child at greater risk for psychopathology. Given changes in children's stage-salient needs, the timing of depression episodes in mothers may have implications for the development of specific vulnerabilities in their children. Finally, we know little about the effect on children of the unpredictable course of their mother's depression.

Moderators of Associations between Paternal Alcoholism and Children's Development

Qualities of the Children

As in studies of maternal depression, children's sex, age, and temperament have been studied as moderators of associations between paternal alcoholism and child outcomes. With regard to sex, the literature is limited by the majority of studies on the effect of paternal alcoholism on children having excluded daughters. Although it is commonly concluded that sons of alcoholics have a higher risk for the development of an alcohol-related disorder (Assaad et al., 2003), some studies have shown greater family history effects for women than for men (Sher, Walitzer, Wood, & Brent, 1991). Studies that included both sons and daughters of alcoholics have found support for a moderating role of child sex on the effect of paternal alcoholism. Paternal alcoholism had a greater effect on sons' relative to daughters' risk of developing ADHD depressive symptoms and substance use during adolescence (daughters of alcoholic mothers were more at risk for depression than sons; Chassin, Curran, Hussong, & Colder, 1996; Christensen & Bilenberg, 2000). These findings are consistent with both social-modeling theory, in that alcoholism in the parent of the same sex may have the most negative influences, and genetics in terms of male-specific inheritance.

In terms of age, Connell and Goodman's (2002) meta-analysis of the effect of parental psychopathology on children found that paternal alcoholism was more closely related to emotional and behavior problems in samples of older children, a finding opposite to that for maternal depression. This finding is difficult to interpret given the chronicity of alcoholism in that the older children were likely to have been exposed for much or all of their lives; the finding may reflect cumulative effects of exposure.

As with maternal depression, we found few studies directly testing temperament as a moderator of the effect of parental alcoholism. In one study, among children of substance abusing fathers, those who had a difficult temperament, relative to others, were at higher risk for the development of a substance abuse disorder (Tarter, Kabene, Escallier, Laird, & Jacobs, 1990).

The Broader Context of the Children's Environment

Assortative mating is at least as relevant to studies of children of alcoholic fathers as with children of depressed mothers (Windle & Tubman, 1999). When studies have examined children raised in families with two alcoholic parents versus one or no alcoholic parents, children of two alcoholic parents were found to have far more behavior problems and earlier age of alcohol intoxication than children raised in families with only one alcoholic parent (McKenna & Pickens, 1983). In one study, for example, in households where both parents met criteria for current alcoholism or at least one parent had an antisocial alcoholic diagnosis, the children were more reactive and showed more externalizing behaviors relative to the children who only had one alcoholic parent or those with no parent with an antisocial alcoholic diagnosis (Wong, Zucker, Puttler, & Fitzgerald, 1999). As well as assortative mating with other alcoholics, partner pairings may occur between alcoholics and partners with another psychiatric disorder such as depression. Conversely, as with maternal depression, a child with an alcoholic father may benefit from an involved, mentally healthy mother. Edwards and colleagues (2006) found that 18-month-old toddlers with alcoholic fathers who had a secure infant-mother attachment at 12 months had fewer externalizing behavior problems at 24 months and fewer externalizing and internalizing problems at 36 months of age, showing a protective factor against the risk of paternal alcoholism.

Parental Characteristics as Moderators

Much of the variability in the literature on associations between paternal alcoholism and child outcomes could be due to authors either failing to identify or failing to test for differences within samples among types of alcoholics, frequency and quantity of drinking, presence of comorbid Antisocial Personality Disorder, and inclusion of recovering alcoholics. In one study of severity of alcoholism, Malone and colleagues (Malone, Iacono, & McGue, 2002) examined the effect of paternal alcoholism on child behavior using a measure of the maximum number of drinks the father had ever consumed in a 24-hour period. The authors suggest that individuals who consume a high number of alcoholic beverages may have developed a significant tolerance to the effects or possess an unusual insensitivity to the negative effects of alcohol. The maximum number of drinks consumed could be related to loss-of-control drinking, a distinguishing feature in Type 1 alcoholism using Cloninger's (1987) classification. Malone et al. found that a father's maximum number of drinks predicted children's externalizing disorders, especially Conduct Disorder and early substance use.

Other researchers studied the effect of severity or chronicity of parental alcoholism on child functioning by comparing children of active alcoholics to those of recovered alcoholics and social drinkers (DeLucia, Belz, & Chassin, 2001; Ozkaragoz et al., 1997). Ozkaragoz et al. compared children who had parents in these three groups and found that only children of active alcoholics showed neuropsychological deficits and reduced intellectual functioning compared to children of recovered alcoholics and social drinkers. On the other hand, when behavioral and emotional problems were compared, there were no group differences between active and recovered alcoholics' children, but these children had significantly more emotional problems than did the children of the social drinkers. DeLucia et al. found that adolescents of recovered alcoholics continued to show more emotional and behavioral problems than children of nonalcoholic parents. Because alcohol abuse and dependence are chronic conditions that can span decades, more studies are needed of the effects of chronicity.

Because many men with alcoholism also display antisocial personality traits, it is essential, though difficult, to tease apart the effect of paternal alcoholism from the effect of the antisocial traits on parental caregivng. For example, Eiden and Leonard (2000) found a significant impact of paternal alcoholism on fathers' aggravation toward their infants; however, this finding was found to be attributable to the antisocial behavior and depressive symptoms. In research on cognitive-intellectual functioning of children of alcoholic fathers, the children of antisocial alcoholics had significantly lower Full-Scale IQ scores (although still within the normal range) than children of nonantisocial alcoholics and controls (Poon et al., 2000). Further, the child's IQ was directly related to the severity of comorbid paternal pathology.

SUMMARY

The field of clinical psychology has increasingly recognized the importance of psychopathology in both mothers and fathers in relation to the development of psychopathology in children (Connell & Goodman, 2002; Phares & Compas, 1992). The goal of this chapter was to examine the effect of parental psychopathology on the development of psychopathology in children, specifically focusing on depression in mothers and alcohol disorders in fathers, as they are two of the most prevalent disorders in adults who are bearing and rearing children. This chapter adds to the emerging literature about the risks to the children, and while providing many answers also raises multiple questions needing to be addressed.

In bringing attention to this literature, we encourage researchers, clinicians, and public policy makers to consider the centrality of sex in all aspects of the issues raised here. First among those issues is the fact that depression is twice as common in women as men, whereas alcohol dependence and the often accompanying Antisocial Personality Disorder are at least twice as common in men as women. These epidemiological patterns suggest that important work needs to be done to balance efforts to minimize sex bias in the recognition, diagnosis, treatment, and study of these disorders, while at the same time recognizing sex-specific aspects of the disorders such as risk factors, symptom patterns, approaches to help seeking, treatment options offered, barriers, and response to treatment. In this regard, as one example, sex specificity of genetic risks for depression (Kendler & Prescott, 1999) and alcohol abuse (Sigvardsson et al., 1996) are intriguing. Second, sex biases prevail in the studies of these high-risk children, as exemplified by the minimal attention to daughters of alcoholic fathers. Researchers may eventually conclude that sex specificity characterizes some risk and protective factors and pathways in the development of psychopathology in children of parents with psychopathology and identify others that characterize all children. An interesting likelihood is mul-tifinality, the idea that similar risk factors, for example, uncontrollable life events, may increase the likelihood of different outcomes: depression emerging in women and alcohol abuse in men (Cicchetti & Rogosch, 1996). Third, even with the strong evidence of sex-specific prevalence patterns for depression and alcohol abuse in men and women, it is essential that models of the transmission of risk to the children take into account the fact that depression in mothers also affects the husbands and fathers, just as alcohol abuse in men affects the wives and mothers (El-Sheikh & Flanagan, 2001; Whisman et al., 2006). Fourth, researchers and practitioners need to be attentive to the emergence of changing epidemiological patterns such as the possibility that rates of depression worldwide are increasing more rapidly in men than in women (Klerman & Weissman, 1989), and women's rates of alcohol abuse, conversely, may increase worldwide as gender norms shift.

The newest work on identification of specific genes and other biological markers for psychiatric disorders offers promise for fresh insights into both alcoholism and depression research, especially if the work is developed in the context of biopsy-chosocial models and with sensitivity to developmental issues. Throughout the literature on maternal depression and paternal alcoholism, transactional models have emerged as a valuable tool in examining both the mediators for the effect of the parental psychopathology as well as evaluating potential moderators of risk. More research examining transactional effects has tremendous promise for reveal-ing developmental pathways to disorder in children at risk and can benefit from increasing sophistication in longitudinal research design and approaches to data analysis. The findings reviewed here reveal the value of identifying the earliest emerging problems in children of parents with depression or alcohol abuse. Work based on the gateway hypothesis is useful in this regard (Kandel, Yamaguchi, & Klein, 2006). Both risk factor research and evidence-based preventive interventions will also benefit from the appreciation of interactions among risk factors as well as transactional patterns in pathways to disorder.

Research on the effect of paternal alcoholism on child development is not a new line, yet recently has not garnered as much attention as depression in mothers. By using the structure of the integrative model for the transmission of risk (Goodman & Gotlib, 1999; Figure 30.1), we have shown that many of the mechanisms and mod-erators found in the transmission of risk to children of depressed mothers also hold true for the transmission of risk to children of alcoholic fathers. The model bears strong resemblance to Windle and Tubman's (1999) model for the transmission of alcoholism, with several coinciding mechanisms and moderators, further suggest-ing that these two areas of research can learn from each other. The overlap between these two models and the empirical support reviewed here for common mechanisms for the transmission of risk to children as well as moderators of the risk gives credibility to the potential for an overarching general model of the transmission of risk to children, regardless of the specific psychopathology of the parent. Such an approach has the benefit of recognizing common comorbidities with other disorders (including alcoholism with depression in both men and women), the tendency for risk factors to accumulate, and the essential role of context. While research will undoubtedly benefit from continued emphasis on each specific disorder, preventive mental health efforts may well also benefit from a focus on commonalities across disorders. An overarching model of risk would have practical screening, prevention, and treatment implications for children who are at risk for the development of psychopathology due to parental psychopathology. This model would facilitate the development of general approaches to prevention and treatment aimed at reducing the child's likelihood of the development of psychopathology and could be a cost-effective method of identifying and treating the children most at risk.

An essential message to clinical psychologists from the work reviewed in this chapter is that both maternal depression and paternal alcoholism confer not only specific risk for the transmission of the same disorder in offspring but also risk for the development of other forms of psychopathology, many of which show signs much earlier in development then when one typically first diagnoses depression or alcohol abuse. Although abstinence, if one could count on adherence, is an effective approach to the prevention of alcoholism in children of alcoholic fathers, there is no single such solution for children of depressed mothers. Neither does abstinence address the early emerging problems in youth or the other disorders for which children of alcoholic fathers are also at risk. At minimum, the findings in this chapter clearly support screening and prevention targeting risk factors for the development of the respective disorders, such as problems with emotion regulation abilities in both groups of offspring, a low response to alcoholism in children of alcoholic fathers, and cognitive vulnerabilities to depression in children of depressed mothers. Continued research on mechanisms holds promise for the design of specific effective interventions at the same time that ongoing work on moderators will help identify the individuals most likely to benefit from preventive interventions.

REFERENCES

Allgood-Merten, B., Lewinsohn, P., & Hops, H. (1990). Sex differences and adolescent depression. *Journal of Abnormal Psychology, 99,* 55–63.

American Psychiatric Association. (1994). *Diagnostic and statistical manual of mental disorders.* (4th ed.) Washington, DC: Author.

Anda, R. F., Whitefield, C. L., Felitti, V. J., Chapman, D., Edwards, V. J., Dube, S. R., et al. (2002). Adverse childhood experiences, alcoholic parents, and later risk of alcoholism and depression. *Psychiatric Services, 53*(8), 1001–1008.

Anderson, C. A., & Hammen, C. L. (1993). Psychosocial outcomes of children of unipolar depressed, bipolar, medically ill, and normal women: A longitudinal study. *Journal of Consulting and Clinical Psychology, 61*(3), 448–454.

Ashman, S. B., & Dawson, G. (2002). Maternal depression, infant psychobiological development, and risk for depression. In S. H. Goodman & I. H. Gotlib (Eds.), *Children of depressed parents: Mechanisms of risk and implications for treatment* (pp. 37–58). Washington, DC: American Psychological Association.

Assaad, J.-M., Pihl, R. O., Seguin, J. R., Nagin, D., Vitaro, F., Carbonneau, R., et al. (2003). Aggressiveness, family history of alcoholism, and the heart rate response to alcohol intoxication. *Experimental and Clinical Psychopharmacology, 11*, 158–166.

Beardslee, W. R. (1989). The role of self-understanding in resilient individuals: The development of a perspective. *American Journal of Orthopsychiatry, 59*(2), 266–278.

Beardslee, W. R., Keller, M. B., Lavori, P. W., Klerman, G. K., Dorer, D. J., & Samuelson, H. (1988). Psychiatric disorder in adolescent offspring of parents with affective disorder in a non-referred sample. *Journal of Affective Disorders, 15*, 313–322.

Beardslee, W. R., & Podorefsky, D. (1988). Resilient adolescents whose parents have serious affective and other psychiatric disorders: Importance of self-understanding and relationships. *American Journal of Psychiatry, 145*(1), 63–69.

Beardslee, W. R., Schultz, L. H., & Selman, R. L. (1987). Level of social-cognitive development, adaptive functioning, and DSM-III diagnoses in adolescent offspring of parents with affective disorders: Implications for the development of the capacity for mutuality. *Developmental Psychology, 23*, 807–815.

Beck, A. T., Rush, A. J., Shaw, B. F., & Emery, G. (1979). *Cognitive therapy of depression.* New York: Guilford Press.

Benegal, V., Jain, S., Subbukrishna, D. K., & Channabasavanna, S. M. (1995). P300 amplitudes vary inversely with continuum of risk in first degree male relatives of alcoholics. *Psychiatric Genetics, 4*, 149–156.

Biederman, J., Rosenbaum, J. F., Faraone, S. V., Hirshfeld-Becker, D. R., Friedman, D., Robin, J. A., et al. (2001). Patterns of psychopathology and dysfunction in high-risk children of parents with panic disorder and major depression. *American Journal of Psychiatry, 158*, 49–57.

Billings, A. G., & Moos, R. H. (1985). Children of parents with unipolar depression: A controlled 1-year follow-up. *Journal of Abnormal Child Psychology, 14*(1), 149–166.

Brennan, P. A., Hammen, C., Katz, A. R., & Le Brocque, R. M. (2002). Maternal depression, paternal psychopathology, and adolescent diagnostic outcomes. *Journal of Consulting and Clinical Psychology, 70*(5), 1075–1085.

Buss, K. A., Malmstadt, J. R., Dolski, I., Kalin, N. H., Goldsmith, H. H., & Davidson, R. J. (2003). Right frontal brain activity, cortisol, and withdrawal behavior in 6-month-old infants. *Behavioral Neuroscience, 117*, 11–20.

Caspi, A., Sugden, K., Moffitt, T. E., Taylor, A., Craig, I. W., Harrington, H., et al. (2003). Influence of life stress on depression: Moderation by a polymorphism in the 5-HTT gene. *Science, 301*, 386–389.

Cavell, T. A., Jones, D. C., Runyan, R., Constantin-Page, L. P., & Velasquez, J. M. (1993). Perceptions of attachment and the adjustment of adolescents with alcoholic fathers. *Journal of Family Psychology, 7*, 204–212.

Chassin, L., Curran, P. J., Hussong, A. M., & Colder, C. R. (1996). The relation of parent alcoholism to adolescent substance use: A longitudinal follow-up study. *Journal of Abnormal Psychology, 105*, 70–80.

Chassin, L., Rogosch, F., & Barrera, M. (1991). Substance use and symptomatology among adolescent children of alcoholics. *Journal of Abnormal Psychology, 100*, 449–463.

Cherny, S. S., Fulker, D. W., Corley, R. P., Plomin, R., & DeFries, J. C. (1994). Continuity and change in infant shyness from 14 to 20 months. *Behavior Genetics, 24*, 365–379.

Christensen, H., & Bilenberg, N. (2000). Behavioural and emotional problems in children of alcoholic mothers and fathers. *European Child and Adolescent Psychiatry, 9*, 219–226.

Chugani, H. T., & Phelps, M. E. (1986). Maturational changes in cerebral function in infants determined by 18FDG positron emission tomography. *Science, 231*, 840–843.

Cicchetti, D., & Rogosch, F. A. (1996). Equifinality and multifinality in developmental psychopathology. *Development and Psychopathology, 8*, 597–600.

Cicchetti, D., Rogosch, F. A., & Toth, S. L. (1998). Maternal depressive disorder and contextual risk: Contributions to the development of attachment insecurity and behavior problems in toddlerhood. *Development and Psychopathology, 10*, 283–300.

Cicchetti, D., & Toth, S. (1998). The development of depression in children and adolescents. *American Psychologist, 53*, 221–241.

Cloninger, C. R. (1987). Neurogenetic adaptive mechanisms in alcoholism. *Science, 236*, 410–416.

Cloninger, C. R., Bohmann, M., & Sigvardsson, S. (1981). Inheritance of alcohol abuse: Cross fostering analysis of adopted men. *Archives of General Psychiatry, 38*, 861–867.

Compas, B. E., Langrock, A. M., Keller, G., Merchant, M. J., & Copeland, M. E. (2002). Children coping with parental depression: Processes of adaptation to family stress. In S. H. Goodman & I. H. Gotlib (Eds.), *Children of depressed parents: Mechanisms of risk and implications for treatment* (pp. 227–252). Washington, DC: American Psychological Association.

Connell, A. M., & Goodman, S. H. (2002). The association between psychopathology in fathers versus mothers and children's internalizing and externalizing behavior problems: A meta-analysis. *Psychological Bulletin, 128*, 746–773.

Cummings, E. M., Keller, P. S., & Davies, P. T. (2005). Towards a family process model of maternal and paternal depressive symptoms: Exploring multiple relations with child and family functioning. *Journal of Child Psychology and Psychiatry, 46*, 479–489.

Cutrona, D. E., & Troutman, B. R. (1986). Social support, infant temperament, and parenting self-efficacy: A mediational model of postpartum depression. *Child Development, 57*, 1507–1518.

Davidson, R. J., Ekman, P., Saron, C., Senulis, R., & Friesen, W. V. (1990). Approach-withdrawal and cerebral asymmetry: Pt. I. Emotional expression and brain physiology. *Journal of Personality and Social Psychology, 58*, 330–341.

Davidson, R. J., & Fox, N. A. (1989). Frontal brain asymmetry predicts infants' response to maternal separation. *Journal of Abnormal Psychology, 98*, 127–131.

Davies, P. T., & Dumenci, L. (1999). The interplay between maternal depressive symptoms and marital distress in the prediction of adolescent adjustment. *Journal of Marriage and the Family, 61*, 238–254.

Davies, P. T., & Windle, M. (1997). Gender-specific pathways between maternal depressive symptoms, family discord, and adolescent adjustment. *Developmental Psychology, 33*, 657–668.

Davis, B., Sheeber, L., & Hops, H. (2002). Coercive family processes and adolescent depression. In J. B. Reid, G. R. Patterson, J. J. Snyder (Eds.), *Antisocial behavior in children and adolescents: Developmental analysis and the Oregon model for intervention* (pp. 173–194). Washington, DC: American Psychological Association.

Dawson, G., Ashman, S. B., Panagiotides, H., Hessl, D., Self, J., Yamada, E., et al. (2003). Preschool outcomes of children of depressed mothers: Role of maternal behavior, contextual risk, and children's brain activity. *Child Development, 74*, 1158–1175.

Dawson, G., Grofer Klinger, L., Panagiotides, H., Hill, D., & Spieker, S. (1992). Frontal lobe activity and affective behavior of infants of mothers with depressive symptoms. *Child Development, 63*, 725–737.

DeLucia, C., Belz, A., & Chassin, L. (2001). Do adolescent symptomatology and family environment vary over time with fluctuations in paternal alcohol impairment? *Developmental Psychology, 37*, 207–216.

DuRocher Schudlich, T. D., & Cummings, E. M. (2003). Parental dysphoria and children's internalizing symptoms: Marital conflict styles as mediators of risk. *Child Development, 74*, 1663–1681.

Eaves, L. J., Silberg, J. L., Meyer, J. M., Maes, H. H., Simonoff, E., Pickles, A., et al. (1997). Genetics and developmental psychopathology: Pt. II. The main effects of genes and environment on behavioral problems in the Virginia twin study of adolescent behavioral development. *Journal of Child Psychology and Psychiatry, 38*, 965–980.

Edhborg, M., Seimyr, L., Lundh, W., & Widstrom, A. M. (2000). Fussy child: Difficult parenthood? Comparisons between families with a "depressed" mother and non-depressed mother 2 months postpartum. *Journal of Reproductive and Infant Psychology, 18*(3), 225–238.

Edwards, E. P., Eiden, R. D., & Leonard, K. E. (2006). Behavior problems in 18- to 36-month-old children of alcoholic fathers: Secure mother-infant attachment as a protective factor. *Development and Psychopathology, 18*, 395–407.

Eiden, R. D., Edwards, E. P., & Leonard, K. E. (2002). Mother-infant and father-infant attachment among alcoholic families. *Development and Psychopathology, 14*, 253–278.

Eiden, R. D., & Leonard, K. E. (2000). Paternal alcoholism, parental psychopathology, and aggravation with infants. *Journal of Substance Abuse, 11*, 17–29.

Eiden, R. D., Leonard, K. E., & Morrisey, S. (2001). Paternal alcoholism and toddler noncompliance. *Alcoholism: Clinical and Experimental Research, 25*, 1621–1633.

Eley, T. C., & Stevenson, J. (1999). Exploring the covariation between anxiety and depression symptoms: A genetic analysis of the effect of age and sex. *Journal of Child Psychology and Psychiatry, 40*, 1273–1284.

El-Sheikh, M., & Flanagan, E. (2001). Parental problem drinking and children's adjustment: Family conflict and parental depression as mediators and moderators of risk. *Journal of Abnormal Child Psychology, 29*, 417–432.

Essex, M. J., Klein, M. H., Miech, R., & Smider, N. A. (2001). Timing of initial exposure to maternal major depression and children's mental health symptoms in kindergarten. *British Journal of Psychiatry, 179*, 151–156.

Fergusson, D. M., Horwood, L. J., & Lynskey, M. T. (1995). Maternal depressive symptoms and depressive symptoms in adolescents. *Journal of Child Psychology and Psychiatry, 36*(7), 1161–1178.

Fergusson, D. M., Lynskey, M. T., & Horwood, L. J. (1993). The effect of maternal depression on maternal ratings of child behavior. *Journal of Abnormal Child Psychology, 21*(3), 245–269.

Field, T. (1992). Infants of depressed mothers. *Development and Psychopathology, 4*, 49–66.

Field, T. (1994). The effects of mother's physical and emotional unavailability on emotion regulation. *Monographs of the Society for Research in Child Development, 59*(2/3), 250–283.

Field, T. (2002). Prenatal effects of maternal depression. In S. H. Goodman & I. H. Gotlib (Eds.), *Children of depressed parents: Mechanisms of risk and implications for treatment* (pp. 59–88). Washington, DC: APA Books.

Forehand, R., Brody, G., Slotkin, J., Fauber, R., & McCombs, A. (1988). Young adolescent and maternal depression: Assessment, interrelations, and family predictors. *Journal of Consulting and Clinical Psychology, 56*(3), 422–426.

Fox, N. A. (1994). The development of emotion regulation. Vol. 59. *Biological and behavioral considerations*. Chicago: University of Chicago Press.

Frye, A., & Garber, J. (2005). The relations among maternal depression, maternal criticism, and adolescents' externalizing and internalizing symptoms. *Journal of Abnormal Child Psychology, 33*, 1–11.

Garber, J., & Martin, N. C. (2002). Negative cognitions in offspring of depressed parents: Mechanisms of risk. In S. H. Goodman & I. H. Gotlib (Eds.), *Children of depressed parents: Mechanisms of risk and implications for treatment* (pp. 121–154). Washington, DC: American Psychological Association.

Gelfand, D. M., & Teti, D. M. (1990). The effects of maternal depression on children. *Clinical Psychology Review, 10*, 329–353.

Glover, V. (1999). Mechanisms by which maternal mood in pregnancy may affect the fetus. *Contemporary Reviews in Obstetrics and Gynecology, 11*, 155–160.

Goldsmith, H. H., Buss, K. A., & Lemery, K. S. (1997). Toddler and childhood temperament: Expanded content, stronger genetic evidence, new evidence for the importance of environment. *Developmental Psychology, 33*, 891–905.

Goodman, S. H., Adamson, L. B., Riniti, J., & Cole, S. (1994). Mothers' expressed attitudes: Associations with maternal depression and children's self-esteem and psychopathology. *Journal of the American Academy of Child and Adolescent Psychiatry, 33*, 1265–1274.

Goodman, S. H., & Gotlib, I. H. (1999). Risk for psychopathology in the children of depressed mothers: A developmental model for understanding mechanisms of transmission. *Psychological Review, 106*, 458–490.

Goodman, S. H., Sewell, D. R., Cooley, E. L., & Leavitt, N. (1993). Assessing levels of adaptive functioning: The Role Functioning Scale. *Community Mental Health Journal, 29*, 119–131.

Goodman, S. H., & Tully, E. C. (2006). Depression in women who are mothers: An integrative model of risk for the development of psychopathology in their sons and daughters. In C. L. M. Keyes & S. H. Goodman (Eds.), *Women and depression: A handbook for the social, behavioral, and biomedical sciences* (pp. 241–282). New York: Cambridge University Press.

Gotlib, I. H., Gilboa, E., & Sommerfeld, B. K. (2000). Cognitive functioning in depression: Nature and origins. R. J. Davidson (Eds.), *Wisconsin Symposium on Emotion* (Vol. 1, pp. 133–163). New York: Oxford University Press.

Gotlib, I. H., & Goodman, S. H. (1999). Children of parents with depression. In W. K. Silverman & T. H. Ollendick (Eds.), *Developmental issues in the clinical treatment of children and adolescents* (pp. 415–432). New York: Allyn & Bacon.

Graham, Y. P., Heim, C., Goodman, S. H., Miller, A. H., & Nemeroff, C. B. (1999). The effects of neonatal stress on brain development: Implications for psychopathology. *Development and Psychopathology, 11*, 545–565.

Grant, B. F. (2000). Estimates of US children exposed to alcohol abuse and dependence in the family. *American Journal of Public Health, 90*, 112–115.

Grant, B. F., Stinson, F. S., Dawson, D. A., Chou, P., Dufour, M. C., Compton, W., et al. (2004). Prevalence and co-occurrences of substance use disorders and independent mood and anxiety disorders. *Archives of General Psychiatry, 61*, 807–816.

Grant, B. F., Stinson, F. S., Dawson, D. A., Chou, P., Raun, J., & Pickering, M. S. (2004). Results from the national epidemiologic survey on alcohol and related conditions. *Archives of General Psychiatry, 61*, 361–368.

Haber, J. R., Jacob, T., & Heath, A. C. (2005, April). Paternal alcoholism and offspring conduct disorder: Evidence for the "common genes" hypothesis. *Twin Research and Human Genetics, 8*(2), 120–131.

Hammen, C. (1991). Generation of stress in the course of unipolar depression. *Journal of Abnormal Psychology, 100*, 555–561.

Hammen, C. (2002). Context of stress in families of children with depressed parents. In S. H. Goodman & I. H. Gotlib (Eds.), *Children of depressed parents: Mechanisms of risk and implications for treatment* (pp. 175–202). Washington, DC: American Psychological Association.

Hammen, C., & Brennan, P. A. (2001). Depressed adolescents of depressed and nondepressed mothers: Tests of an interpersonal impairment hypothesis. *Journal of Consulting and Clinical Psychology, 69*, 284–294.

Hammen, C., Burge, D., Burney, E., & Adrian, C. (1990). Longitudinal study of diagnoses in children of women with unipolar and bipolar affective disorder. *Archives of General Psychiatry, 47*(12), 1112–1117.

Hammen, C., Shih, J., Altman, T., & Brennan, P. A. (2003). Interpersonal impairment and the prediction of depressive symptoms in adolescent children of depressed and nondepressed mothers. *Journal of the American Academy of Child and Adolescent Psychiatry, 42*, 571–577.

Harrington, R. (1996). Family-genetic findings in child and adolescent depressive disorders. *International Review of Psychiatry, 8*, 355–368.

Harrington, R., Rutter, M., Weissman, M. M., Fudge, H., Groothues, C., Bredenkamp, D., et al. (1997). Psychiatric disorders in the relatives of depressed probands: Pt. I. Comparison of prepubertal, adolescent and early adult onset cases. *Journal of Affective Disorders, 42*, 9–22.

Hay, D. F., & Kumar, R. (1995). Interpreting the effects of mothers' postnatal depression on children's intelligence: A critique and re-analysis. *Child Psychiatry and Human Development, 25*, 165–181.

Higuchi, S., Matsushita, S., & Kashima, H. (2006). New findings on the genetic influences on alcohol use and dependence. *Current Opinions in Psychiatry, 19*(3), 253–265.

Hipwell, A. E., Murray, L., Ducournau, P., & Stein, A. (2005). The effects of maternal depression and parental conflict on children's peer play. *Child: Care, Health and Development, 31*(1), 11–23.

Hopfer, C. J., Crowley, M. D., & Hewitt, J. K. (2003). Review of twin and adoption studies of adolescent substance use. *Journal of the American Academy of Children and Adolescent Psychiatry, 42*(6), 710–719.

Hops, H., Sherman, L., & Biglan, A. (1990). Maternal depression, marital discord, and children's behavior: A developmental perspective. In G. R. Patterson (Eds.), *Depression and aggression in family interaction* (pp. 185–208). Hillsdale, NJ: Erlbaum.

Jacob, T., Waterman, B., Heath, A., True, W., Bucholz, K. K., Haber, R., et al. (2003). Genetic and environmental effects on offspring alcoholism: New insights using an offspring-of-twins design. *Archives of General Psychiatry, 60*, 1265–1272.

Jaenicke, C., Hammen, C. L., Zupan, B., Hiroto, D., Gordon, D., Adrian, C., et al., (1987). Cognitive vulnerability in children at risk for depression. *Journal of Abnormal Child Psychology, 15*, 559–572.

Kandel, D. B., Yamaguchi, K., & Klein, L. C. (2006). Testing the gateway hypothesis. *Addiction, 101*, 470–472.

Keller, M. B., Beardslee, W. R., Dorer, D. J., Lavori, P. W., Samuelson, H., & Klerman, G. R. (1986). Impact of severity and chronicity of parental affective illness on adaptive functioning and psychopathology in children. *Archives of General Psychiatry, 43*, 930–937.

Kendler, K. S., Gardner, C. O., Neale, M. C., & Prescott, C. A. (2001). Genetic risk factors for major depression in men and women: Similar or different heritabilities and same or partly distinct genes? *Psychological Medicine, 31*, 605–616.

Kendler, K. S., & Prescott, C. A. (1999). A population-based twin study of lifetime major depression in men and women. *Archives of General Psychiatry, 56*, 39–44.

Kessler, R. C. (2006). The epidemiology of depression among women. In C. L. M. Keyes & S. H. Goodman (Eds.), *Women and depression: A handbook for the social, behavior, and biomedical sciences* (pp. 22–40). New York: Cambridge University Press.

Keyes, C. L. M., & Goodman S. H. (Eds.). (2006). *Women and depression: A handbook for the social, behavioral, and biomedical sciences.* New York: Cambridge University Press.

Klerman, G. L., & Weissman, M. M. (1989). Increasing rates of depression. *Journal of the American Medical Association, 261*(15), 2229–2235.

Klimes-Dougan, B., & Bolger, A. K. (1998). Coping with maternal depressed affect and depression: Adolescent children of depressed and well mothers. *Journal of Youth and Adolescence, 27*, 1–15.

Kochanska, G., Radke-Yarrow, M., Kuczynski, L., & Friedman, S. (1987). Normal and affectively ill mothers' beliefs about their children. *American Journal of Orthopsychiatry, 57*, 345–350.

Kraemer, H. C., Stice, E., Kazdin, A., Offord, D., & Kupfer, D. J. (2001). How do risk factors work together? Mediators, moderators, and independent, overlapping, and proxy risk factors. *American Journal of Psychiatry, 158*, 848–856.

Lee, C. M., & Gotlib, I. H. (1989). Clinical status and emotional adjustment of children of depressed mothers. *American Journal of Psychiatry, 146*, 478–483.

Leonard, K. E., & Eiden, R. D. (2002). Cognitive functioning among infants of alcoholic fathers. *Drug and Alcohol Dependence, 67*, 139–147.

Leonard, K. E., Eiden, R. D., Wong, M. M., Zucker, R. A., Puttler, L. I., Fitzgerald, H. E., et al. (2000, February). Developmental perspectives on risk and vulnerability in alcoholic families. *Alcoholism: Clinical and Experimental Research 24*(2), 238–240.

Lieb, R., Isensee, B., Hofler, M., Pfister, H., & Wittchen, H.-U. (2002). Parental major depression and the risk of depression and other mental disorders in offspring. *Archives of General Psychiatry, 59*, 365–374.

Loehlin, J. C., & Nichols, R. C. (1976). *Heredity, environment, and personality.* Austin: University of Texas Press.

Loukas, A., Zucker, R. A., Fitzgerald, H. E., & Krull, J. L. (2003, February). Developmental trajectories of disruptive behavior problems among sons of alcoholics: Effects of parent psychopathology, family conflict, and child undercontrol. *Journal of Abnormal Psychology, 112*(1), 119–131.

Lovejoy, M. C., Graczyk, P. A., O'Hare, E., Neuman, G. (2000). Maternal depression and parenting behavior: A meta-analytic review. *Clinical Psychology Review, 20*, 561–592.

Lundy, B., Jones, N., Field, T., Pietro, P., Nearing, G., Davalos, M., et al. (1999). Prenatal depression effects on neonates. *Infant Behavior and Development, 22*, 119–129.

Luoma, I., Tamminen, T., Kaukonen, P., Laippala, P., Puura, K., Salmelin, R., et al. (2001). Longitudinal study of maternal depressive symptoms and child well-being. *Journal of the American Academy of Child and Adolescent Psychiatry, 40*(12), 1367–1374.

Lykken, D. T., & Tellegen, A. (1996). Happiness is a stochatic phenomenon. *Psychological Science, 7*, 186–189.

Malcarne, V. L., Hamilton, N. A., Ingram, R. E., & Taylor, L. (2000). Correlates of distress in children at risk for affective disorder: Exploring predictors in the offspring of depressed and nondepressed mothers. *Journal of Affective Disorders, 59*(3), 243–251.

Malone, S. M., Iacono, W. G., & McGue, M. (2002). Drinks of the father: Father's maximum number of drinks consumed predicts externalizing disorders, substance use, and substance use disorders in preadolescent and adolescent offspring. *Alcoholism: Clinical and Experimental Research, 26*, 1823–1832.

Matthews, C. A., & Reus, V. I. (2001). Assortative mating in the affective disorders: A systematic review and meta-analysis. *Comprehensive Psychiatry, 42*, 257–262.

McGue, M. (1999). The behavioral genetics of alcoholism. *Current Directions in Psychological Science, 8*, 109–115.

McKenna, T., & Pickens, R. (1983). Personality characteristics of alcoholic children of alcoholics. *Journal of Studies on Alcohol, 44*, 688–700.

Merikangas, K. R., Weissman, M. M., Prusoff, B. A., & John, K. (1988). Assortative mating and affective disorders: Psychopathology in offspring. *Psychiatry, 51*, 48–57.

Moldin, S. O. (1999). Report of the NIMH's genetic workgroups: Summary of research. *Biological Psychiatry, 45*, 559–602.

Monroe, S. M., & Hadjiyannakis, K. (2002). The social environment and depression: Focusing on severe life stress. In I. H. Gotlib & C. L. Hammen (Eds.), *Handbook of depression* (pp. 314–340). New York: Guilford Press.

Murray, K. T., & Sines, J. O. (1996). Parsing the genetic and nongenetic variance in children's depressive behavior. *Journal of Affective Disorders, 38,* 23–34.

Orvaschel, H., Walsh-Allis, G., & Ye, W. (1988). Psychopathology in children of parents with recurrent depression. *Journal of Abnormal Child Psychology, 16*(1), 17–28.

Ozkaragoz, T., Satz, P., & Noble, E. P. (1997, January/February). Neuropsychological functioning in sons of active alcoholic, recovering alcoholic, and social drinking fathers. *Alcohol, 14*(1), 31–37.

Patterson, G. R., Reid, J., & Dishion, T. (1992). *Antisocial boys.* Eugene, OR: Castalia.

Pesonen, A. K., Raikkonen, K., Strandberg, T., Keltikangas-Jarvinen, L., & Jarvenpaa, A. L. (2004). Insecure adult attachment style and depressive symptoms: Implications for parental perceptions of infant temperament. *Infant Mental Health Journal, 25,* 99–116.

Phares, V. (1992). Where's Poppa? The relative lack of attention to the role of fathers in child and adolescent psychopathology. *American Psychologist, 47,* 656–664.

Phares, V., & Compas, B. E. (1992). The role of fathers in child and adolescent psychopathology: Make room for Daddy. *Psychological Bulletin, 111,* 387–412.

Pickens, J., & Field, T. (1993). Facial expressivity in infants of "depressed" mothers. *Developmental Psychology, 29,* 986–988.

Plomin, R., Emde, R. N., Braungart, J. M., Campos, J., Corley, R. P., Fulker, D. W., et al. (1993). Genetic change and continuity from 14 to 20 months: The MacArthur Longitudinal Twin Study. *Child Development, 64,* 1354–1376.

Pollock, V. E. (1992). Meta-analysis of subjective sensitivity to alcohol in sons of alcoholics. *American Journal of Psychiatry, 149*(11), 1534–1538.

Poon, E., Ellis, D. A., Fitzgerald, H. E., & Zucker, R. A. (2000, July). Intellectual, cognitive, and academic performance among sons of alcoholics during the early school years: Differences related to subtypes of familial alcoholism. *Alcoholism: Clinical and Experimental Research, 24*(7), 1020–1027.

Porter, C. L., & Hsu, H.-C. (2003). First-time mothers' perceptions of efficacy during the transition to motherhood: Links to infant temperament. *Journal of Family Psychology, 17,* 54–64.

Radke-Yarrow, M., Belmont, B., Nottelman, E., & Bottomly, L. (1990). Young children's self-conceptions: Origins in the natural discourse of depressed and normal mothers and their children. In D. Cicchetti & M. Beeghly (Eds.), *The self in transition: Infancy to childhood* (pp. 345–361). Chicago: University of Chicago Press.

Radke-Yarrow, M., Nottelman, E., Belmont, B., & Welsch, J. D. (1993). Affective interactions of depressed and nondepressed mothers and their children. *Journal of Abnormal Child Psychology, 21,* 683–695.

Reich, W., Earls, F., & Powell, J. (1988). A comparison of the home and social environment of children of alcoholic and non-alcoholic parents. *British Journal of Addiction, 83,* 831–839.

Rende, R. D., Plomin, R., Reiss, D., & Hetherington, E. M. (1993). Genetic and environmental influences on depressive symptomatology in adolescence: Individual differences and extreme scores. *Journal of Child Psychology and Psychiatry, 34,* 1387–1398.

Ressler, K. J., & Nemeroff, C. B. (2000). Role of serotonergic and noradrenergic systems in the pathophysiology of depression and anxiety disorders. *Depression and Anxiety, 12*(Suppl. 1), 2–19.

Sameroff, A. J. (1975). Transactional models in early social relations. *Human Development, 18,* 65–79.

Sanchez, M. M., Ladd, C. O., & Plotsky, P. M. (2001). Early adverse experience as a developmental risk factor for later psychopathology: Evidence from rodent and primate models. *Development and Psychopathology, 13,* 419–449.

Schuckit, M. A., & Smith, T. L. (1996). An 8-year follow-up of 450 sons of alcoholic and control subjects. *Archives of General Psychiatry, 53*(3), 202–210.

Scourfield, J., Rice, F., Thapar, A., Harold, G. T., Martin, N. C., & McGuffin, P. (2003). Depressive symptoms in children and adolescents: Changing aetiological influences with development. *Journal of Child Psychology and Psychiatry and Allied Disciplines, 44,* 968–976.

Sheeber, L., Davis, B., & Hops, H. (2002). Gender-specific vulnerability to depression in children of depressed mothers. In S. H. Goodman & I. H. Gotlib (Eds.), *Children of depressed parents: Mechanisms of risk and implications for treatment* (pp. 253–274). Washington, DC: American Psychological Association.

Sher, K. J., Walitzer, K. S., Wood, P. K., & Brent, E. E. (1991). Characteristics of children of alcoholics: Putative risk factors, substance use and abuse, and psychopathology. *Journal of Abnormal Psychology, 100*, 427–448.

Sigvardsson, S., Bohman, M., & Cloninger, C. R. (1996). Replication of the Stockholm Adoption Study of alcoholism: Confirmatory cross-fostering analysis. *Archives of General Psychiatry, 53*, 681–687.

Silberg, J., Pickles, A., Rutter, M., Hewitt, J., Simonoff, E., Maes, H., et al. (2001). The influence of genetic factors and life stress on depression among adolescent girls. *Archives of General Psychiatry, 56*, 225–232.

Snow Jones, A., Miller, D. J., & Salkever, D. S. (1999). Parental use of alcohol and children's behavioural health: A household production analysis. *Health Economics, 8*(8), 661–683.

Solantaus-Simula, T., Punamaki, R.-L., & Beardslee, W. R. (2002). Children's responses to low parental mood: Pt. I. Balancing between active empathy, overinvolvement, indifference and avoidance. *Journal of the American Academy of Child and Adolescent Psychiatry, 41*, 278–286.

Southam-Gerow, M. A., & Kendall, P. C. (2002). Emotion regulation and understanding: Implications for child psychopathology and therapy. *Clinical Psychology Review, 22*, 189–222.

Sroufe, L. A., Egeland, B., Carlson, E. A., & Collins, W. A. (2005). *The development of the person: The Minnesota study of risk and adaptation from birth to adulthood*. New York: Guilford Press.

Sroufe, L. A., & Waters, E. (1977). Attachment as an organizational construct. *Child Development, 48*, 1184–1199.

Steinhausen, H. C., Willms, J., & Spohr, H. L. (1993). Long-term psychopathological and cognitive outcome of children with fetal alcohol syndrome. *Journal of the American Academy of Child and Adolescent Psychiatry, 32*(5), 990–994.

Tarter, R., Kabene, M., Escallier, E., Laird, S., & Jacobs, T. (1990). Temperament deviations and risk for alcoholism. *Alcoholism: Clinical and Experimental Research, 14*, 380–382.

Tellegen, A., Lykken, D. T., Bouchard, T. J., Wilcox, K. J., Segal, N. L., & Rich, S. (1988). Personality similarity in twins reared apart and together. *Journal of Personality and Social Psychology, 54*, 1031–1039.

Thapar, A., & McGuffin, P. (1994). A twin study of depressive symptoms in childhood. *British Journal of Psychiatry, 165*, 259–265.

Thomas, A. M., & Forehand, R. (1991). The relationship between paternal depressive mood and early adolescent functioning. *Journal of Family Psychology, 4*, 43–52.

Thompson, R. A. (2006). The development of the person: Social understanding, relationships, conscience, self. In W. Damon, R. M. Lerner, & N. Eisenberg (Eds.), *Handbook of child psychology: Vol. 3. Social, emotional, and personality development* (6th ed., pp. 24–98). Hoboken, NJ: Wiley.

Tomarken, A. J., Davidson, R. J., Wheeler, R. E., & Kinney, L. (1992). Psychometric properties of resting anterior EEG asymmetry: Temporal stability and internal consistency. *Psychophysiology, 29*, 576–592.

Tronick, E. Z. & Gianino, A. F., Jr. (1986). The transmission of maternal disturbance to the infant. In E. Z. Tronick, & T. Field (Eds.), *Maternal depression and infant disturbance* (pp. 5–11). San Francisco: Jossey-Bass.

Tsuang, M. T., & Faraone, S. V. (1990). *The genetics of mood disorders*. Baltimore: Johns Hopkins University Press.

Tyndale, R. F. (2004). Genetics of alcohol and tobacco use in humans. *Annals of Medicine, 35*, 94–121.

van IJzendoorn, M. H., Goldberg, S., Kroonenberg, P. M., & Frenkel, O. J. (1992). The relative effects of maternal and child problems on the quality of attachment: A meta-analysis of attachment in clinical samples. *Child Development, 63*, 840–858.

Viken, R. J., Kaprio, J., Koskenvuo, M., & Rose, R. J. (1999). Longitudinal analyses of the determinants of drinking and of drinking to intoxication in adolescent twins. *Behavior Genetics, 29*, 455–461.

Wadhwa, P. D., Glynn, L., Hobel, C. J., Garite, T. J., Porto, M., Chicz-DeMet, A., et al. (2002). Behavioral perinatology: Biobehavioral processes in human fetal development. *Regulatory Peptides, 108*, 149–157.

Warner, V., Weissman, M. M., Fendrich, M., Wickramaratne, P., & Moreau, D. (1992). The course of major depression in the offspring of depressed parents: Incidence, recurrence, and recovery. *Archives of General Psychiatry, 49*, 795–801.

Webster-Stratton, C., & Hammond, M. (1988). Maternal depression and its relationship to life stress, perceptions of child behavior problems, parenting behaviors, and child conduct problems. *Journal of Abnormal Child Psychology, 16*, 299–315.

Weissman, M. M., Prusoff, B., Gammon, G. D., Merikangagas, K. R., Leckman, J. F., & Kidd, K. K. (1984). Psychopathology in the children (ages 6–18) of depressed and normal parents. *Journal of the American Academy of Child and Adolescent Psychiatry, 23*(1), 78–84.

Welner, Z., Welner, A., McCrary, M., & Leonard, M. A. (1977). Psychopathology in children of inpatients with depression: A controlled study. *Journal of Nervous and Mental Diseases, 164*, 408–413.

Whisman, M. A., Weinstock, L. M., & Tolejko, N. (2006). Marriage and depression. In C. L. M. Keyes & S. H. Goodman (Eds.), *Women and depression: A handbook for the social, behavioral, and biomedical sciences* (pp. 219–240). New York: Cambridge University Press.

Wilhelm, K. (2006). Depression: From nosology to global burden. In C. L. M. Keyes & S. H. Goodman (Eds.), *Women and depression: A handbook for the social, behavior, and biomedical sciences* (pp. 3–21). New York: Cambridge University Press.

Windle, M., & Tubman, J. G. (1999). Children of alcoholics. In W. K. Silverman & T. H. Ollendick (Eds.), *Developmental issues in the clinical treatment of children* (pp. 393–414). Boston: Allyn & Bacon.

Wong, M. M., Zucker, R. A., Puttler, L. I., & Fitzgerald, H. E. (1999). Heterogeneity of risk aggregation for alcohol problems between early and middle childhood: Nesting structure variations. *Development and Psychopathology, 11*, 727–744.

Woodside, M. (1991). Policy issues and action: An agenda for children of substance abusers. In T. M. Rivinus (Ed.), *Children of chemically dependent parents: Perspectives from the cutting edge* (pp. 330–345). New York: Brunner/Mazel.

Zahn-Waxler, C., Cummings, E. M., Iannotti, R. J., & Radke-Yarrow, M. (1984). Young children of depressed parents: A population at risk for affective problems. In D. Cicchetti (Ed.), *Childhood depression: Vol. 26. New directions for child development* (pp. 81–105). San Francisco: Jossey-Bass.

Zahn-Waxler, C., Radke-Yarrow, M., Wagner, E., & Chapman, M. (1992). Development of concern for others. *Developmental Psychology, 28*, 126–136.

CHAPTER 31

Problems in Infancy

Tiffany Field

The problems in infancy can be categorized as both the frustrations and challenges of the developmental milestones that occur and the problems they pose for the parent facilitating development and giving care along the way. This chapter reviews some of those problems under the headings of developmental milestones, developing emotions, behavior problems, and caregiving. Under each of these headings, the problems are given in an order that approximates their development or the order in which they may become concerns to parents.

DEVELOPMENTAL MILESTONES

Taste

Although most parents today realize that newborns can see and hear, many are surprised that they can also smell and taste and imitate facial expressions. Newborns are born with very sophisticated abilities to discriminate different tastes, probably because the amniotic fluid comprises all tastes, including sweet, salt, and bitter (Mennella, Jagnow, & Beauchamp, 2001). This has been observed in many studies based on newborns' facial expressions in response to different tastes. For example, disgust faces follow the baby tasting quinine and other bitter tastes, whereas contented faces follow a sweet taste (Liem & Mennella, 2002). Compared to older infants, however, newborns do not seem to reject salty and bitter substances, perhaps because those were familiar in utero. Slightly older infants seem to prefer novel tastes. For example, in one study, infants spent more time breastfeeding after their mothers ate garlic as compared to those infants whose mothers repeatedly consumed garlic. Clearly, though, the sweetest substances are preferred from the first day of life. In fact, sucrose has been used as an analgesic during painful procedures in the newborn nursery. Newborns who were given sucrose solutions to suck on during blood draws, for example, cried less following the procedure and had lower heart rate and more positive brain waves (Fernandez et al., 2003). Children

This research was supported by a merit award (MH No. 46586), Senior Research Scientist Awards (MH No. 00331 and AT No. 001585), and a March of Dimes Grant (No. 12-FYO3-48) to Tiffany Field and funding from Johnson & Johnson Pediatric Institute to the Touch Research Institutes.

who are introduced to new tastes and new foods in early childhood tend to enjoy a variety of different foods later, whereas those with a limited diet tend to have negative reactions to new foods.

Imitation

Until very recently people thought that imitation did not occur until around the end of the first year of life. This concept of imitation was advanced by the famous child psychologist Jean Piaget, who based his ideas on observations of his own two children. More recently several researchers have shown that even a newborn can imitate exaggerated facial expressions made by adults. These expressions include sticking out the tongue, an exaggerated smile, a surprised face, and a sad face. Of course, not all children show imitative behaviors as early as the newborn stage. In fact, some newborns have been described as "poker-faced" and merely stare inquiringly as you model these faces. In a study I conducted on newborn imitation, I first made sure that the newborn was awake and bright-eyed (Field, Guy, & Umbel, 1985). Then I held the baby in front of my face and bobbed up and down with a couple of knee bends to make sure the newborn's eyes were open, and then made a couple of tongue clicks to make sure the newborn was looking directly at my face. I then made an exaggerated facial expression, leaving it there until the infant looked away. I then repeated the action with the same or a different expression. When a baby was in a very alert state and in the mood for this game, we saw very interesting imitative behavior. Later, at around 3 months, mothers almost invariably imitate their baby's cooing sounds during face-to-face games, and the baby in turn imitates the mother. This game goes back and forth for many rounds. A little while later infants imitate gestures and fine motor behaviors. Although much of what infants show us they can do seems to be hardwired and occurs on some predetermined developmental schedule, imitation, like other skills, improves with experience (Learmonth, Lamberth, & Rovee-Collier, 2005).

Eye Contact

Eye contact is present as early as birth and is one of the most important features of social interactions (Farroni, Csibra, Simion, & Johnson, 2002). Without eye contact, it is extremely difficult to communicate with people. Infants and older children will sometimes turn off their eye contact or show gaze aversion when they are being overstimulated and need to process the information, much like taking a break from a conversation (Brooks & Meltzoff, 2002). However, excessive gaze aversion or the absence of eye contact early in infancy is often considered a sign of autism and should be further evaluated if this problem persists (Zwaigenbaum et al., 2005). A recent study of children ages 2 to 6 noted that children who averted their gaze from their parents in the first month of life (a) developed a maladaptive relationship in terms of their interactions by 2 years, (b) showed behavior problems and developmental delays for up to 6 years, and (c) had less favorable development during the preschool years.

Conversation Skills

Conversation skills start developing as early as birth, when babies have face-to-face interactions with their parents. These are particularly frequent and become exciting interactions at around 3 to 6 months, when babies not only have frequent eye contact but also smile, make a lot of funny faces, coo, and make funny sounds. Early conversations have been analyzed in detail by psychologists, who note that these conversations have many prespeech sounds (vowels and consonants), all the universal facial expressions (which occur as early as 5 months in utero), and many expressive hand gestures. When the timing of speech and pauses in speech and looking and looking away are studied, the baby's behavior is very much like an adult's. For example, babies look at their interaction partner when listening and look away when talking, as if to concentrate on what they are saying. Occasionally both speak at the same time, and occasionally there are interruptions, just as in adult conversation. But the turn-taking and the turn-taking signals are already fairly well developed.

Much of the infant's learning of these skills appears to come from imitation, which frequently happens during parent-infant interactions. Like a game, the parent imitates the infant and the infant imitates the parent. In fact, one of the easiest ways to get an infant to stop crying is to imitate that crying. The infant stops crying and pays close attention to the ridiculous-sounding adult. Another game parents often play is providing the words for the infant (Field, 1979). The mother says "I like your hat," and the baby coos; then the mother says "Oh, you like your hat too," as if providing the words for the baby. An important rule the parents learn immediately is to respect the infant's looking away. This indicates (as it does in adult conversations) that the infant is either bored, tired, or has had enough of that conversation. Repeating children's speech sounds and adding to their words helps as the infants become older. By toddlerhood children have conversations with the world, with themselves, and with their imaginary playmates. At that stage the silence at bedtime is a welcome relief.

Babbling

Babbling is the child's first attempt at conversation and consists of long strings of sounds formed with the lips and tongue, including *baba* and *dada* and arias of cooing that make the child seem musically talented (Goldstein, King, & West, 2003). These sounds are universal and gradually become differentiated into, say, American versus Japanese sounds as the child is further exposed to his or her unique speech environment. Importantly, babbling reinforces the parent's attempts to talk to the child. In the first conversations the parent says something, the child babbles, and the parent says "Oh, is that so?" as if the child has truly participated in the conversation.

Exploration

This is usually the precursor to playful behavior. The child explores objects to learn what the object can do and what the child can do to the object. One of the earliest forms of exploration is the newborn sucking on the mother's breast.

For the next 6 months everything gets explored by mouth, and much is learned (e.g., the shapes of things) in this way. The hands take over, and then exploration seems almost an obsession as infants make messes with their finger foods, throw objects on the ground for adults to retrieve, and take everything out of drawers and put them back in again (container behavior) as they explore and learn the properties of things. As exploration proceeds the child's behavior becomes more playful, repeating actions over and over, usually to the sounds and facial expressions of sheer joy. Stifling exploration should be avoided at all costs, as it would in turn stifle curiosity, creativity, and the entire learning process. Extremes of baby-proofing or childproofing the house can seriously interfere with exploration.

Handedness

Handedness, or right or left hand preference, develops very early in infancy and can be determined by placing a desirable object in front of the infant and determining which hand leads to grasp the object. The dominant hand will invariably be preferred for fine motor, dexterity activities (Hinojosa, Sheu, & Michel, 2003). However, a recent study highlights the important staging and guiding function of the nondominant hand from very early in infancy. Left-handedness is more frequent in twins (Derom, Theiry, Vlietinck, Loos, & Derom, 1996) than in single children and in males than in females.

The literature is very mixed about the association between handedness and problems. For example, in one study handedness and dyslexia (a learning disability) were significantly related, but handedness was only weakly associated with immune problems. In another study autoimmune disorders were more prevalent in left-handers. In a third study left-handers had nearly 3 times as many immune disorders as right-handers; the relatives of the left-handers suffered from the same conditions; there was a higher frequency of learning disabilities such as dyslexia, stuttering, and autism in the left-handers; and left-handers had migraine headaches more often (Eglinton & Annett, 1994). One of the theories for left-handedness, aside from the genetic theory, is that during fetal development testosterone (the predominant male hormone) slows the growth of the left hemisphere. When testosterone is elevated, it is more likely to produce left-handedness and, in extreme cases, to lead to alterations in the left hemisphere that may be responsible for learning disorders such as dyslexia. Excessive testosterone levels can also alter immune function, which can then lead to immune problems such as eczema, psoriasis, and asthma.

In earlier days attempts were made to shift children from being left-handed to being right-handed so that penmanship and scissors and virtually all hand-held devices (which are designed for right-handed people) would be more easily mastered. Today, parents and teachers do not attempt to alter handedness because of the undocumented theory that shifting handedness in itself may lead to learning disabilities.

Teething

Teething, or the breaking through of new teeth, can be uncomfortable for infants and distressful for parents. Parents' favorite treatment is probably rubbing the infant's gums with a bit of liquor. Both the rubbing action and the liquor have analgesic effects.

Ear Infections

Ears are vulnerable sense organs because it is difficult to close them to unwanted noise. Ears are also a source of major discomfort to many young children because they experience earaches from inner and middle ear infections. Excessive pulling on the ears, irritability, and signs of difficulty hearing can mean another ear infection. After dozens of these infections and antibiotic treatments, pediatricians often refer the child for a myringotomy (Vaile, Williamson, Waddell, & Taylor, 2006). This procedure involves piercing holes in the eardrums to enable the fluid to drain and is considered a minor procedure, although anesthesia is typically required, and that is certainly not minor. Treatment is critical because data show that repeated, prolonged ear infections contribute to delays in language development and learning difficulties at school. For example, children with inner ear infections (otitis media) have significantly lower expressive language scores, suggesting impairments in language expression (Thomas, Simpson, Butler, & van der Voort, 2006). They also have deficits in processing auditory information and spelling skills and receive more special education services. Despite these problems, their academic achievement tests do not appear to suffer, and by later childhood their early language delays are no longer present.

Immunizations

Immunizations are thought to be critical for preventing disease in early childhood. The most common immunizations are for diphtheria, pertussis, and tetanus and are given at set intervals across the first few years of life (Cohen, 2002). Unfortunately, large numbers of children still are not receiving immunizations. For example, in a large U.S. midwestern city, a study recently revealed low immunization rates (31%), which were said to be due to cost, lack of insurance coverage, and long office visits. Not mentioned was the stressfulness of the immunization procedure on parents and children. Many studies have explored the effects of varying the conditions during immunizations to reduce the stress associated with them. In an attempt to reduce the fussiness and crying and elevated cortisol levels accompanying immunizations, researchers have varied the person accompanying the child for immunizations and varied different directions to the parents. For example, when parents accompany the child there is notably more distress in some studies, and in others there is notably less. That seems to depend on what the parent does during the immunization period. Reassurance, for example, reinforces crying, whereas distraction techniques are much more effective in reducing stress. Other calming interventions help, including music.

Crawling (or Creeping)

Crawling tends to occur at around 6 to 9 months, although some babies never crawl, and those babies sometimes walk at an earlier age (WHO Multicentre Growth

Reference Study Group, 2006). Every baby seems to have his or her own style of crawling, with some tending to crawl backward, some sideways, and some straight ahead. Some crawl on their hands and knees, while others do it on their hands with bended legs. Generally speaking, it seems an awkward way to get from one place to another, and it looks like hard work, so it is perhaps not surprising that there has to be something the baby really wants to reach for crawling to occur. A recent study was conducted on motor skill development in crawlers and noncrawlers during early infancy. The noncrawlers showed slower motor skill development, suggesting that those who do not crawl may develop motor skills more slowly, but crawling and other motor milestones do not seem to be related to later IQ (Capute, Shapiro, Palmer, Ross, & Wachtel, 1985).

A parent recently expressed concern that her child was retarded because she was not crawling at 9 months. After reminding the parent that some babies never crawl, I placed my keys on the carpet, and the baby proceeded to crawl directly to them. The mother, who typically carried her infant on her hip around the house for hours at a time, expressed amazement that all it took was placing her child on the floor with something desirable in view, and her child was no longer "retarded."

Walking

Children typically start walking at around 10 months of age and are pretty proficient by the time they are toddlers at around 16 to 18 months. Temperament differences affect the time of onset, so that one often sees children who are risk takers and exploratory starting earlier than children who are shy and slow to warm up. Although scientists have shown that walking can occur very early if it is practiced, there has been some concern that early walking may slow down the development of other skills, such as talking. Typically, children are focusing on one skill at a time, and those seem to be prewired developmentally to occur at specific times. Crawling and walking, of course, give a child more freedom to explore and get into trouble when the environment isn't childproof. Although walkers seem to be very effective in helping children get around, they are coming under increasing criticism because of their use as babysitters, because some serious falls have been reported, and because they delay the onset of walking (Burrows & Griffiths, 2002; Siegel & Burton, 1999). Hanging harnesses from door frames are very helpful for learning balance and walking movements. Whether walkers or jolly jumpers are used, all children seem to walk at about the same time. If walking is delayed, other functions may also be delayed. In one study, slow walking and slow talking were predictive of lower IQ scores and reading difficulties, but this was true only for children who started walking after 18 months, and only half those children later had low IQs and reading difficulties.

Terrible Twos

The 2-year-old stage has become so notorious for its difficulties that it is now classified as the terrible twos. This is the first of many autonomy-setting stages of the child's life, and it may be the worst (next to adolescence) because it is the first. Parents have come to totally enjoy their lovely child when all of a sudden they find themselves faced with a little monster. Every other word is "no" and every other action is forbidden and accompanied by looks toward the parent of "I dare you." Language has emerged, and with that children act as if they're smarter than their parents. That might be true, as the child repeatedly outwits them. Because of the autonomy-establishing ways of the child at this age, it's important that parents not get into power struggles with their child over the child's behavior. For example, many children who have not been toilet trained by age 2 use toilet training as grounds for power struggles with their parents. Waiting until 2 virtually means waiting until at least 3, when autonomy issues are not as great. Thus, toilet training can dramatically exacerbate the problems of the terrible twos.

Aside from trying not to save important developmental milestones such as toilet training for this stage, parents are probably best advised not to get into verbal power struggles, but to simply move the child from the source of altercation (e.g., an electric socket or a restaurant where the child has resorted to temper tantrums) or to attempt to distract by activities that the child can clearly dominate. Parents' attempts to explain their "unpopular" position typically fall on deaf ears and accelerate the conflict. It is not surprising that this is an increasingly popular age for parents to send their children to school. There the children can have their terrible two struggles with teachers and other terrible-2-year-olds.

Autonomy

Autonomy is probably the primary goal of childhood. It is generally achieved by the end of childhood, just before the long struggle begins for adolescents to have complete autonomy. Teaching children how to take care of themselves, how to monitor and control their own behavior, how to relate to other people in a socially effective way, how to express their emotions, and how to achieve their potential is what has been called "the package of parenting." The developmental course of autonomy proceeds from the infant who cries at 6 months when you stifle his or her crawling attempts or remove a desired object, to the child who wants to walk unassisted, to the terrible twos when the child wants to have everything plus power over parents (LeCuyer-Maus & Houck, 2002). Developing all those skills—motor, cognitive, and social—are all in the service of achieving autonomy.

Problems that get in the way of developing autonomy include deficits in the child; temperament problems, such as inhibition and unwillingness to have commerce with the world; limited time and patience of parents, who might find it easier to do things for the child; and inability on the parents' part to allow the child to fail in trial-and-error learning. The frustration is felt on all sides, but ultimately the child will be autonomous and the parent will be proud. Even the terrible twos are a small price to pay. Actually, this is a time when parents can have fun, enjoying the slapstick humor of their child's clumsiness as he or she achieves the milestones of autonomy.

Play

Play and pretend play are critical to a child's development. Playfulness is measured by physical, social, and cognitive (mental) spontaneity, by joy and a sense of humor. Much of this develops in the child through experience playing, starting in preschool, when a child's entire agenda is play, and tapering off as children get older and have less time for play. In one study on individual differences in young children's pretend play, early social pretend play was significantly related to the child's developing understanding of other people's feelings and beliefs (Keren, Feldman, Namdari-Weinbaum, Spitzer, & Tyano, 2005). These data provide strong support for the notion that early experience in pretend play is associated with mastery of relations between mental life and real life. Parents need to orchestrate some of the play of their children, inasmuch as the natural opportunities for play, such as neighborhood playgrounds, have become more rare in very busy and unsafe cities. Often all it takes is arranging for a child's friend to visit, gathering together the props, and getting the pretend play started. Once they get started, children are very good at pretend play.

Friends

Friendships develop at a very early stage in life, which we never knew until children started attending infant day care. In the nursery school my research group runs, we can no longer graduate infants at 12 months to the toddler nursery without also transferring their best friend with them. Parents told us very early on that they wanted their children to wait until they could move with their best friend, but it was only after studying this phenomenon that we appreciated that even infants experience anxiety and depression when separated from their best friends. In our study the infants who were transferred without their friends experienced sleep problems, eating problems (either more or less), toileting problems (constipation or diarrhea), and sometimes even illness (typically upper respiratory infections; Field, Vega-Lahr, & Jagadish, 1984). Thus, friendship starts at a very early age.

In our studies, when parents were absent for a meeting or for the birth of another child, the preschoolers who remained in day care with their friends were less depressed (Field & Reite, 1984). In the early stages, because of a child's shyness and less-developed social skills, parents may need to set the stage for developing relationships. This can be arranged through shared babysitting, inviting a peer along for special activities, and trying to facilitate cooperative play between the children by giving them the same opportunities to engage in the same activity and by having play materials in twos, ensuring that each child has a play object or a book, so that fighting is less likely to occur.

Sex Differences

Sex differences are present from birth. Research suggests that for most assessments, whether it is responding to social stimulation, discriminating faces and voices, or simple learning tasks, females are more skilled. This sexual advantage for girls persists until at least school age. Although it is widely known that boys are physically at a disadvantage at birth, often being smaller and having more perinatal complications, very little is known about the origins of boys' slower development. This is particularly a problem when parents compare their boy child to their girl child and conclude that the boy's slower language development, for example, is suggestive of developmental delay or retardation. Parents need to have more moderate expectations of their male children, particularly in the early preschool years.

Sometime later in children's schooling, female children lose their gains, often as they develop diffidence and experience more limited expectations for academic performance from adults.

There are, of course, many other sex differences that emerge, for example, in the expression of empathy and social interests. Although most people like to believe that these are socially determined, such as the introduction of dolls to girls and guns to boys, many of these preferences are apparent before the socializing experiences. For example, in a recent study on 12-month-old infants, girl infants presented with the choice of a toy airplane or a doll more often reached for the doll, while boy infants more often reached for the airplane (Servin, Bohlin, & Berlin, 1999). An anecdote highlights a similar response. When a teacher carried her baby into the preschool, the boy children rushed to the block corner and the girl children rushed to the teacher's baby, much to the chagrin of the teacher, who had tried very hard to encourage unisex activities and behavior in her preschool classroom.

Twins

Twins can come as a shock to any family, even though they seem to run in families. Senior family members try to prepare first-time parents for that possibility. Because ultrasound and other prenatal tests typically reveal twins sometime during pregnancy, most parents also have that time to prepare themselves. The downside is that you need two of everything and it is twice as much work, but the upside is that you can have twice the joy in half the time. Identical twins have quite amazing similarities as early as birth. For example, in a study we conducted on newborns, identical twins were almost identical in the amount of time they looked at faces and mimicked faces, whereas fraternal twins were very different in their facial expressions and their attentiveness. Fraternal twins are often perplexing because they seem no more alike than nontwins in the same family (Field, 1982). Despite their similar experiences at the same time in development, they can behave and develop very differently.

Intelligence Tests

Intelligence is still a hotly debated issue, particularly for infants and young children. Although there are now scales that are considered infant IQ tests, such as the Brazelton Scale and the Bayley Scales for Infant Development, these have very little stability over time (Lowman, Stone, & Cole, 2006). For example, some children score high early in infancy because of their precocious motor development, but then score poorly at a later age because of their limited language environment. The scales seem to focus more on motor skills in early infancy and language skills in early childhood. Also, scores are significantly affected by many environmental conditions, suggesting that performance is not strictly determined by genetic factors.

Bayley Scales

The Bayley Scales were created by Nancy Bayley in 1963 (and revised in 1993) to assess infants' mental and motor development (Lichtenberger, 2005). They can be given to children from about 3 months of age to about 4 years. Typically the child is seated on the parent's lap while the Bayley Scales are given, and they last approximately 40 minutes. Developmental age-appropriate items are given, such as a red ring dangled in front of a 3-month-old infant's face, and pegs and peg boards are given at a slightly older toddler age. Motor skills are assessed by watching the child's natural motor behavior and offering more challenging tests at a later age, such as climbing stairs and walking on a rail. These scales yield a score, with an average at about 100. They are used simply to give the pediatrician or developmental professional a sense of how the child's mental and motor development are progressing and whether there are any areas that need work.

Prematurity

Infants who are born prematurely have a number of problems in infancy suggesting delayed growth and development (Vintzileos, Ananth, Smulian, Scorza, & Knuppel, 2002). Long-term follow-ups suggest that children born prematurely have more sleep-related problems and more accidents, inferior eye-hand coordination, delayed language development, more visual and hearing disorders, and more hospital care. Environmental factors account for more variation in their cognitive development than perinatal factors. Preterm children exhibit a self-righting tendency during early childhood, so that eventually environmental influence overshadows biological influences.

DEVELOPING EMOTIONS

Emotional Expressions

The necessary muscles for the universal emotional expressions are present very early in fetal development (3 months gestation). These universal expressions are happy, interest, surprise, sad, angry, fearful, and ashamed. Although the expressions seem exaggerated during early development, when children laugh without restraint as well as sometimes cry incessantly, the expressions become socialized with development, and we begin to see blends of expressions such as a combination of surprise and sadness when feelings are hurt. Some children display their emotions, as in the expression "wearing their heart on their sleeve," and others tend to be more "poker-faced" and show very little emotion. These extremes, sometimes labeled extraversion and introversion, appear in children as early as the newborn stage. In a study we conducted on newborns' imitations of facial expressions, about 20% of infants showed very exaggerated facial expressions and very little heart rate change, while the other 20% extreme showed emotional responses in their heart rate changes but were poker-faced (Field, 1982). Most children (like most adults) show their emotions not only on their face but in their physiological responses, for example in a racing heart, sweaty hands, or blushing.

Anger

Expressions of anger can be seen as early as the newborn period in crying outbursts by an uncomfortable newborn whose needs are not being met. The temper tantrums of a 2-year-old occur for the same reasons: discomfort and not getting what is wanted or needed (Potegal & Davidson, 2003; Potegal, Kosorok, & Davidson, 2003). In the preschool years, transgressions against children either for their possessions or against their person, as in shoving, pushing, hitting, and kicking, sometimes cause anger at having been made uncomfortable or having their feelings hurt.

Anxiety

Children, like adults, have a host of stresses and anxieties that make their lives uncomfortable. Anxiety can cause sleep disturbances and illness as well as learning problems. The anxieties are different at different developmental stages. Infants and toddlers, for example, experience the stress of separation anxiety and stranger anxiety (Kochanska & Coy, 2002). Infants also experience frustration during developmental milestone periods such as crawling and walking, although anxiety is difficult to measure at those ages. Preschooler anxieties are more likely related to being hospitalized or starting school.

Children who are particularly prone to anxiety are those who are temperamentally shy and have difficulty making transitions. To help with the transitions, various comfort objects such as pacifiers at the younger age and blankies and stuffed animals at the older age are helpful (Donate-Bartfield & Passman, 2004). Other solutions are unique to the different types of anxiety. For example, for separation anxiety, which is typically related to the infant not realizing that the parents are going to come back, parents can reassure their infant that they are just going to get something and will return shortly. For stranger anxiety, a goodbye ritual helps, particularly if it is brief and upbeat (Field, 1995; Field, Gewirtz, et al., 1984). Sometimes play-acting these leave-takings with the child by using dolls and making the babysitter come and go in fantasy play helps. Allowing the child time to become familiar with the babysitter before the parents leave helps a great deal.

Most anxieties are normal and pass with the developmental stage, except for separation anxiety, which seems to persist. Most children do not particularly like their parents leaving them (until they reach adolescence and want to leave their parents). Separation anxiety in its extreme form, when the child will not leave the parent and develops symptoms such as headaches and stomach aches, may be a serious form of anxiety, labeled Separation Anxiety Disorder.

Massage therapy invariably helps. A 10-minute back rub on a daily basis invariably reduces anxiety (Field, 1995). This can be observed as reduced agitation and nervous behavior, and it can be measured as decreased stress hormones such as cortisol taken from saliva samples.

Stranger Anxiety

Stranger anxiety starts at approximately 9 months of age, after a rather extended period of infants loving to be held and played with by strangers. It is not clear why it emerges at this time, because even newborns have been shown to recognize the difference between their own mother and women who are strangers. In a study we conducted, newborns showed that they preferred their mothers by looking longer at them than at women who were strangers (Field, Cohen, Garcia, & Greenberg, 1984). This was surprising because they had had only 4 hours of contact with their mothers. Equally surprising is their ability to identify their mother by her smell. Recognition of mother by her voice is probably less surprising since newborns would have had experience with the mother's voice in utero.

Nonetheless, even though infants recognize their mothers as early as the newborn stage, they do not appear to show stranger anxiety until approximately 9 months. This takes the form of fussing and showing fearful faces in the presence of the stranger, whether at a distance or when being handed to a stranger. This persists for anywhere between 3 months and a couple of years, in part depending on whether the infant remains at home with the mother or attends an infant nursery school. When an infant has experience with several adults, the infant shows less stranger fear and sometimes no fear. It is not clear what function the stranger fear serves. It certainly would not prevent kidnapping at this early helpless stage of life, and were it to happen any earlier it might even interfere with parents returning to work or hiring babysitters. Fortunately, it is a stage that disappears as quickly as it appears.

Separation Anxiety

Temporary separations from parents during hospitalizations of the parent or child or during parents' conference trips, and more permanent separation from peers associated with moves to other schools, are relatively stressful for young children (Field, 1984). In a study that we conducted on toddlers' and preschool children's responses to separation from the mother during the birth of another child, the children were agitated during the mother's hospitalization and then depressed after the mother's return (Field & Reite, 1984). During her hospitalization the children were irritable, hyperactive, and unable to sleep. When the mother returned the children showed depressed emotion, changes in eating and toileting, continuing sleep disturbances, and illnesses, including constipation and upper respiratory problems (all characteristic of adult depression). The children were clearly agitated by separation from the mother, even though they visited her at the hospital during this period and their father cared for them. The depression following her return from the hospital may have related to the mother's depression or exhaustion. This decreased animation of the mother, together with the arrival of a new sibling, seemed to alter the relationship the mother and child had previously experienced. Examples of the child's disturbance over this altered relationship were provided by the parents, who commented that their child "remained close" to them, "wanted to be rocked and held," "reverted to baby talk, whining, and screaming for attention," "destroyed his playroom," and "threatened to run a truck across the baby's head." In addition, increased fantasy play in the children was characterized by a number of scenes that involved aggression against the new sibling. For example, children built Lego constructions to "fall on the baby," "run over the baby," or "drive the baby to a high bridge and throw the baby in the water."

Some children did not seem to suffer separation stress as much as others. Those who seemed to suffer least were those who continued attending preschool while the mothers were hospitalized, as opposed to those who stayed at home with the grandmother or babysitter during the mother's hospitalization. Maintaining the child's daily routine seemed to help buffer the effect of children's separation from their mothers.

In a subsequent study we observed children's responses to repeated separations from their mothers, who were attending conferences throughout the year (Field, 1991). Although we were concerned that there may be cumulative effects that made each separation worse than the last, we found that children became accustomed to these separations, and after a few of them were no longer showing the extreme behavioral and physiological changes or illness that accompanied the first and second separations.

Although most parents (and psychologists alike) had assumed that separation stress occurs only when parents are missing (because parents are supposedly the primary attachment figures), separation stress is also experienced over the loss of a teacher or favorite peer. Parents in our nursery school used to tell us that they wanted their infant or toddler to wait to graduate to the next class when their best friend was also ready to graduate. Sometimes parents actually transferred schools when their child's best friend transferred. In a recent study, preschool children who were transferring to new schools were observed during the 2 weeks prior to their leaving (Field, 1984). The children showed increased fantasy play, physical contact, negative statements, fussiness, hyperactivity, and illness, as well as changes in eating and sleeping patterns. Shortly after the children left, those who left the school showed less agitated behavior, but those who remained behind showed increased agitated behavior. Apparently the remaining children were being reminded of their lost friends by staying in the same environment. As in a divorced couple, the person remaining in the old house often has more difficulty because of reminders of the old relationship.

In another study we explored infants' and toddlers' reactions to being graduated to the next classroom with and without their best friends. Infants and toddlers who transferred without their best friend showed increased activity (Field, Vega-Lahr, et al., 1984), negative emotion, fussiness, and changes in eating and sleep patterns. Some children ate too much and some children ate too little; some children slept all the time and others slept not at all. Those who transferred with close friends did not experience the stressful effects of the transition period.

It is clear from these studies that children have difficulty with loss from a very early age, so that the loss of the old relationship with mother after a new sibling arrives or the loss of friends can be the most stressful. At those times, consistency in routine (e.g., remaining in school versus staying at home) can alleviate some of the stress. Having a familiar routine may help not only because it is familiar but also because it provides distraction and opportunities for the child to actively cope with the stress. Otherwise, parents simply need to ride it out and recognize that these are normal responses to loss and change.

Depression

Infants can have symptoms that mimic adult depression, including withdrawal and listlessness around other children, sad facial expressions, a monotone voice, and whining and complaining (Field, Gewirtz, et al., 1984). The child might also show eating problems, such as overeating or undereating, and toileting regressions, difficulty going to sleep, frequent night wakings, and difficulty getting up in the morning. Symptoms of illness include respiratory problems, constipation, and diarrhea. Illness probably occurs because the immune system is negatively affected by high stress levels accompanying depression.

Empathy

Some form of empathy is apparent as early as birth, when newborns cry at the sound of other babies crying (Field, Hernandez-Reif, & Diego, 2006). A typical situation that is used to study empathy in toddlers and preschoolers is asking a mother to pretend she is crying. Almost always the child will show some signs of attempting to comfort the mother. However, some children, who, for example, have depressed mothers or have been prenatally exposed to drugs, show no empathy (Jones, Field, & Davalos, 2000). Some recent research in our lab suggests that there are different forms of nonempathetic behavior, including sad and angry responses. In the mother pretend-crying situation, for example, some preschoolers showed nonempathetic angry behavior, including kicking their crying mother or yelling at her, and other children showed nonempathetic sad behavior by simply ignoring the mother's crying.

Temperament

For most of history parents have blamed themselves for their children's temperaments. More recently considerable research suggests that infants come into the world with a temperament that is only then slightly modified by parents' temperament and things that happen in the environment. Parents will still blame themselves, but now they will do so for transmitting temperament traits through their genes rather than their childrearing. Temperament researchers have described babies, for example, as easy or difficult from the start, and they have based their conclusions on parents' reports and on observations of several characteristics they call temperament traits. These include the child's activity level, adaptability, distractibility, intensity, mood, persistence, regularity or rhythmicity, sensitivity, and weariness. Different temperament traits combine to determine whether a child is easy or difficult. In one of our studies, we noted that newborns in the first hours of life could be placed somewhere on a continuum between being extraverted and being introverted (Field & Greenberg, 1982). The extraverted newborns showed very expressive faces and were not very reactive when we measured heart rate. At the other extreme, the introverted newborns were poker-faced but showed considerable physiological reactivity as recorded by their heart rate. Most newborns (approximately 60%) fell in between these two extremes, being both facially expressive and physiologically reactive. When we looked at these behaviors in identical and nonidentical twins we found that there was more similarity in the personality types of identical than nonidentical twins, suggesting again that there was some genetic component to these personality profiles. Observing these infants over the first few years of life, we noted that if an extraverted infant was born to introverted parents, the extraverted infant moved toward the middle of the continuum, whereas if the extraverted infant was born to extraverted parents, he or she more likely continued to be extraverted. Thus the interplay between genetics and environmental influences became clear.

Extraverted and introverted children have very different ways of interacting with the world. Extraverted children are more exploratory and risk taking and therefore likely to excel in development. On the other hand, if the parent is aware of the temperament traits of the introverted child and tries to match parenting strategies to that style, the child may end up being exploratory in spite of his or her introversion. Several researchers have tracked the development of temperament traits to determine whether they are stable over time and which traits seem to contribute to superior development. Dimensions of temperament that have been closely associated with less difficult responses to stress, fewer behavior problems, and lower stress include predictability, positive mood, adaptability, higher approach, lower intensity reaction, and lower responsiveness threshold (Huttunen & Nyman, 1982).

Because of the stability of temperament traits over development, psychiatrists have been concerned about the relation between those traits and behavioral syndromes in later childhood (Maziade, Cote, Thivierge, Boutin, & Bernier, 1989). In one study, for example, both high emotionality and low sociability predicted high scores on an anxiety/depression scale. In another study, high activity and low rhythmicity was associated with a high degree of psychopathology.

BEHAVIOR PROBLEMS

Crying

The most common causes of crying in infants and young children are fatigue, hunger, indigestion, soiling, wetness, and pain. The most common psychological reason is a parent's leaving. Very soon after birth, parents come to recognize the cry sounds of their infant. The frequency, intensity, and intonation of cry sounds are different for all of these problems. For example, fussy cries are less intense than hungry or pain-induced cries. Parents will often assure themselves that all of these problems are taken care of before letting the child cry it out. Sometimes when a child is overstimulated and, thus, overexhausted, crying serves as a kind of stimulus barrier to ward off all other sounds in the environment.

The parent may be able to stop the crying by rocking or walking or driving the infant around, but often the crying will start again when the infant is put to bed. This could become a pattern of crying for the parent to come and comfort (Räihä, Lehtonen, Huhtala, Saleva, & Korvenranta, 2002). The simplest method for solving this problem seems to be letting the infant cry it out. For the first night, the crying may persist for 20 to 30 minutes, and when there is no rescue from the parents, the infant finally falls asleep. The second night the crying may last only 10 minutes, and by the third night there usually is no crying. Getting up for every cry not only overstimulates and ultimately tires the infant but certainly tires the parent.

Colic

Colic is a syndrome of persistent crying in young infants. Colic is one of the most common problems in infancy (incidence ranges from 10% to 35%; Savino &

Oggero, 1996). Researchers disagree about the definition and clinical criteria for colic; some pediatricians even suggest that colic does not exist. This presents a very confusing picture to parents.

The word "colic" is derived from the Greek word *kolikos,* the adjective of *kolon,* meaning the large intestine. Colic also goes by the labels "infantile colic" and "paroxysmal fussing." Colic has been described as intermittent and unexplained crying during the first 3 months of life by infants who are otherwise well-fed and healthy. Colic usually starts during the second or third week of life and spontaneously disappears at around 3 months. The crying is generally intense and typically lasts from 30 minutes to 3 hours, often occurring in the late afternoon or evening, followed by difficulty falling asleep. The crying may also occur intermittently and last for several hours at any time of the day or night, although the crying episodes tend to recur at the same time of day.

In most cases, crying is considered normal infant behavior and can be treated with reassurance and counseling about appropriate parental responses. In a minority of cases, the crying pattern and other infant behaviors may suggest a gastrointestinal problem that may require treatment. Fussiness and crying are not easy to tolerate by most adults, which probably explains why colic is the most frequent problem presented to pediatricians. Although colic ends almost abruptly at 3 months, irritability and excessive crying have been known to recur during frustrating developmental milestones such as sitting, crawling, walking, and virtually any learning stage.

Some clinicians accept the definition of colic as full-force crying for at least 3 hours per day, for 3 or more days per week, for 3 weeks. Colic begins with a sudden onset of crying. The cry is often high pitched and accompanied by facial grimacing, suggesting that the infant is experiencing severe pain. The crying is accompanied by increased motor activity, flexion of the elbows, clenched fists, and hypertonicity (e.g., the knees are drawn up or the legs are stiff and extended), and the abdomen is tense and distended. The infant's eyes are either tightly closed or wide open, the back is arched, the feet are often cold, bowel sounds can be heard, infants may hold their breath for brief periods of time, and they may resist soothing.

Several factors may be involved in infant colic, including biological factors such as temperament and sleep-state organization and environmental factors, for example, overstimulation by parents. Biological factors include hypertonicity, gastrointestinal and allergic factors, and an immature central nervous system. Although gastrointestinal factors have typically been described for colic, serial radiographs suggest a normal amount of gas in the GI tracts of colic infants. Breast milk, cow's milk, and soy milk have also been implicated in colic. Digestion of milk and soy protein produces excessive intestinal gas and peristalsis, which can result in colic. However, colic occurs as commonly in breastfed as in formula-fed infants.

Feeding patterns have been implicated as a potential contributor to colic. Short interfeed intervals resulted in less crying. Infants who were carried more frequently did not cry at the usual 6-week crying peak, and the crying and fussing that tended to occur in the early evenings decreased. Overstimulation also contributes to colic. This became clear when infants who were hospitalized for colic cried less once they were hospitalized. Other overstimulating factors are excessive noise, bright lights, and irritating blankets or clothing. Colic may cease around 3 months because

infants can now use self-comforting techniques such as gaze aversion, thumb sucking, turning over, reaching, and grasping to avoid or remove the annoying stimulation. Having feeding, bathing, and sleeping routines is very effective. In addition,
providing soothing stimulation such as massaging the infant, rocking or swinging,
and playing classical music or white noise can also be extremely effective (Huhtala,
Lehtonen, Heinonen, & Korvenranta, 2000). The most effective treatment is time,
as colic usually disappears by 6 months (Crotteau, Wright, & Eglash, 2006).

Bedtime Problems

Bedtime is one of those quality times for parents and children. It needs to be a happy
time even though children can fret or procrastinate. Having a bedtime ritual that
the child looks forward to is often helpful. The teddy bear gets tucked in, the child
hears a story, and then a back rub helps a child get to sleep. A recent study in our
lab suggested that back rubs were more effective than rocking from early infancy
through early toddlerhood (Field, Grizzle, et al., 1996). In the case of rocking, the
child goes to sleep during the rocking but awakens as soon as he or she is carried
to bed. In the case of back rubs, the child is awake during the back rub and goes to
sleep in that position shortly thereafter.

Sleep Disturbances

Sleeplessness, in the form of difficulty falling asleep and/or nighttime waking,
is a very common pediatric problem, affecting some 15% to 35% of infants and
toddlers. Sleep problems as early as infancy may relate to physiological factors,
temperament of the infant, and parents' responses to difficult sleep patterns. In recent years the rate of sleep disorders has reportedly increased, possibly because
parents are increasingly less tolerant or more worried about sleep disturbances and
how disruptive they are to the dual-career family, or possibly due to more sophisticated methods of monitoring sleep and knowledge about the development of sleep
patterns. Various methods have been developed to study infant sleep, including
measuring facial muscle activity, EEG, heart rate, and respiration. In addition, diaries are frequently kept by parents to record information on duration of sleep and
crying and other activities.

Infants' wakeful time gradually increases from an average of 8 hours at birth to
12 hours at 6 months (Acebo et al., 2005). By the time the infant is 3 months old,
sleep predominantly occurs during the nighttime hours, with the infant tending to
remain awake during the later afternoon and early evening hours. By 6 months, the
time awake has increased from a mean of 2 hours at 3 months to about 3.5 hours,
and the longest waking period is about one-third of the total awake time. Although
a diurnal (normal) sleep-wake pattern is established by this time and the infant is
capable of sustaining sleep during the nighttime hours, many infants continue to
wake during the night. At this time, the amount of time the infant takes to fall asleep
increases, and parents begin to establish bedtime routines and the use of blankies
and other self-comforting objects to facilitate earlier sleeping.

Once infants are put to bed, there is a large variation in the amount of time
required for sleep onset, depending on age. For example, 2-month-olds are thought

to require approximately 28 minutes and 9-month-olds only 6 minutes to fall asleep. Night wakings occur in approximately 29% of infants during the third month, 17% by the sixth month, and 10% at the end of the first year. Once asleep, newborns typically sleep approximately 17 hours per day, and by the sixth month they are sleeping only approximately 14 hours (including naps), which remains the same across the first 2 years.

Temperament characteristics reported for sleep disturbances include low sensory threshold, difficulty establishing regular routines, and reluctance to move from one activity to another. Given that infants who are stimulated less seem to organize their sleep states sooner, overstimulation by parents may be disruptive to infant sleep. A study of healthy infants suggests that most children need something to assist them to fall asleep. In this study, regular use of a transitional object such as a blanket or toy was described for 44% of the children, bedtime sucking for 22%, and both for 14%, leaving only 20% of the children who fell asleep without assistance.

Parents use a number of comforting techniques to induce sleep in young infants, including swaddling, rocking, and sounds such as white noise or classical music. Others advocate letting the child cry or taking the child into the parents' bed or supplying toys. In addition, infants use their own body to self-comfort, including sucking on hands and rocking or head banging in a rhythmic way.

More formal procedures have been tried in studies giving parents instructions (Skuladottir, Thome, & Ramel, 2005). These have mostly involved having the parents find a consistent sleeping place, a regular bedtime, and a bedtime ritual. In one study parents were asked to try a quiet play routine before bed in which they used soothing and relaxing techniques such as massage and pleasant music. They were asked to refrain from using a light, changing diapers, and talking during their nighttime interactions. The majority of infants showed improvement during the first few weeks of treatment. Whenever parents are present at the time of sleep onset, there are more frequent night wakings.

We recently used massage therapy to help infants sleep (Field et al., 1996). The infants who experienced massage therapy compared to infants who were rocked cried less and had lower stress hormones (salivary cortisol levels), suggesting lower stress. After the massage versus the rocking sessions, the infants spent less time in an active awake state, suggesting that massage may be more effective than rocking for inducing sleep. Over the 6-week period the massage therapy infants gained more weight, showed greater improvement on emotionality, sociability, and soothability temperament dimensions, and had greater decreases in stress hormones.

Food Preferences

As early as birth infants appear to have food preferences. Studies on newborns show that they make different faces to different tastes, with sweet flavors being accompanied by happy faces and quinine or rotten egg flavors being accompanied by grimacing. This seems to happen whether the food is tasted or simply smelled. Of course, the amniotic fluid that engulfs the fetus contains all of the basic flavors, especially the more salty and bitter taste. Newborns will readily take glucose but tend to reject salty water. Taste preferences then shift across age. Very little is known about young children's food texture preferences, although foods prepared for infants and young children tend to be pureed at first and only later have considerable texture. Their preferences for hot and cold foods is also relatively unknown.

Studies show that monozygotic (identical) twins have more similar food preferences than dizygotic (nonidentical) twins, suggesting a strong genetic determination of food preferences. Many children will follow parental likes and dislikes, particularly dislikes after seeing an adult grimace at the thought of eating a particular food. On the other hand, parents who expose their children to wide varieties of foods have children who are not fussy eaters and who are willing to try new foods.

Eating Problems

Eating problems can range from food refusals and minor conflicts with parents to eating disorders (Carruth & Skinner, 2000). The minor food refusals are sometimes just the child being finicky about food preferences, although very little is known about children's food preferences because all the nutritious foods are bottled in baby food form, with very little choice being given the children until they can select from their own lunch box or the school cafeteria menu. In addition to very little being known about taste preferences, very little is known about food textures that children prefer. In a recent study we were surprised to find that very young infants preferred chunky applesauce if they are given the choice before the designated age for chunky applesauce (Lundy et al., 1998). Infants also like vegetable flavors like broccoli and cauliflower (Mennella, Kennedy, & Beauchamp, 2006).

Other reasons for food refusals are the child's own power struggles that happen as early as the terrible twos, when children simply want to be autonomous and do what they want to do when they want to do it. These power struggles can continue into preschool and grade school, when children do not have the good models of their parents for food preferences but the fads of what other children are eating. At this time full lunch boxes might simply mean the child has eaten someone else's more desirable lunch.

Although playing with food is a good way to learn the art of eating at the infancy and toddler stage, by preschool the child should be learning appropriate restaurant eating habits. Around this time the child learns that mealtimes are a social time for the family, not a time for reading or watching TV. Unfortunately, because this is often the family's only time together, mealtimes can become times for conflict and conflict resolution. This can contribute to digestive problems and the association between food and anxiety or sadness. The association of food with joy is perhaps also not good, as it may come to be used as a way of solving problems and warding off depression.

Attention Seeking

Attention seeking is probably one of the most important motivating factors behind child behavior, second only to curiosity, exploration, and learning. From the time infants discover that they can make something happen, at around 3 months, when they can reach, grab on to something, and pull it toward them, to the time that they can crawl from one side of the room to the other, to the time they can walk by holding on to furniture, they are discovering that they can do things. Typically the infant looks to whoever is in the near vicinity to see their reaction. The infant is innately a social being, and social interactions from the beginning of life involve getting attention and paying attention (Hobson, Patrick, Crandell, Garcia Perez, & Lee, 2004).

The problem is that as the world becomes busier and parents are juggling a thousand things, it is simply hard to pay attention to all the positive behaviors and all the accomplishments of the child. Doling out hugs and praise is time-consuming, can sometimes lead to dependency if given too often, and therefore is at odds with our cultural childrearing agenda, which is to facilitate autonomy (self-reliance). But children will inevitably get attention from someone by some behavior; often that is negative behavior, such as temper tantrums, interrupting, complaining, whining, breaking things, or having accidents. The child is impatient and wants attention when he or she wants it.

If possible, diverting the child's attention, mimicking the whining (babies stop crying when you imitate their crying), or attempting to ignore it and trying to engage the child in your activity (talking on the phone or laying out the lunches), will sometimes suffice. Escalations into full-blown temper tantrums, particularly when children are in public places such as restaurants, call for moving the child from the situation and having a time-out.

Clinging

Clinging is a fairly normal activity for young children when they are hesitant about new places and people. Clinging, or "holding on to the mother's apron strings," as they once called it, gives the child a sense of reassurance about the situation. Clinging is also fairly common during developmental milestone periods, for example, around 1 year, when the child is learning to walk and separation and stranger anxiety are occurring, and again during the time of the terrible twos. Situations during which children may cling are leave-takings at preschool and following special events like the birth of a sibling. This behavior occurs most frequently in temperamentally shy, slow-to-warm-up children who have difficulty making transitions to new situations.

Not showing your own anxiety about your child's anxious behavior will help. In addition, engaging children in play may help them adjust to the new situation. For example, when leaving children off at preschool, letting them have their stuffed animal or whatever makes them comfortable should help reduce clinging.

Thumb Sucking

Thumb sucking in newborns and young infants is considered a very sophisticated self-soothing behavior. Except for unusually shy children, most stop thumb sucking at around the preschool stage. After that, thumb sucking typically occurs only during times of stress and going to sleep. If this behavior continues into grade school, it is problematic because of peer rejection. In a study of 7-year-olds, for example, children viewed photos of boys and girls in thumb-sucking and non-thumb-sucking poses and rated the pictures (Friman, McPherson, Warzak, & Evans, 1993). The results indicated that children in a thumb-sucking pose were rated as less intelligent, happy, attractive, likable, and fun and less desirable as a friend, playmate, seat mate, classmate, and neighbor than when they were in the non-thumb-sucking pose. Thus the risk of losing social acceptance is real at this stage. Typically thumb sucking subsides unless it is negatively reinforced. A parent's simple expression of concern that the child will be teased by his or her friends is enough warning for the child. Simply having distracters or substitute activities that are more interesting than thumb sucking can solve the problem.

Aggression

Aggression in young children is considered fairly normal. Usually it is their way of trying to get what they want, a toy or attention. Toddlers and preschoolers engage in pushing, shoving, hitting, kicking, yelling, and biting, and infants pull each other's hair and jab fingers in faces, which is not a problem until it is harmful to another child, a parent, or a teacher. Lots of the aggressive behaviors happen in the natural course of simply being active on the playground or in the classroom. Typically children pick themselves up or go on their way after being assaulted by another child in the course of rough-and-tumble play. Ultimately, with modeling from older children and adults, they learn to express their feelings verbally instead of physically (Tremblay et al., 2004).

Biting

Biting is perhaps the most difficult problem parents and teachers have with toddlers. Unfortunately, very little is known about how to prevent it because it is not a favorite topic for research. Generally children use biting when other behaviors do not manage to get them what they want from their playmates. Pushing another child often escalates into slapping, which escalates into biting. Biting attracts more attention from teachers because teeth marks are generally more alarming and potentially more dangerous than scrapes and bruises. Unfortunately, one child's biting often leads to an epidemic of biting, in which several children follow the lead and the problem becomes unmanageable. Biting occurs most often in the midmorning, randomly throughout the week, probably because children are more active in the midmorning, and most often in September, probably because this is a back-to-school period, which is a frustrating transition for children (Solomons & Elardo, 1989)

Generally teachers will pay additional attention to the biting child and try to predict when the child will bite. The teachers will typically intervene when they think the child is about to bite and attempt to distract the child with toys before the biting occurs. Other situations in which children might resort to biting are when they are extremely tired, frustrated, or overexcited. If children learn that they do not have to resort to biting to get what they want (teacher provides the wanted object before the biting occurs), they will probably no longer resort to biting. If the child appears to be compulsively biting, then more extreme measures may be necessary, such as providing a stuffed animal as a substitute for biting another child (it is less dangerous to bite the stuffed animal than another child). Another measure that may be used is time-out. Usually a minute per year of the child's age is sufficient. Often children will see what they are missing during the time-out and will learn to control their behavior. Another effective measure is giving the child lemon juice. Most bites are minor and can be treated by washing, applying cold compresses, and comforting the child.

The advice of a child psychologist is that the best thing for an adult to do when one child bites another is to remain calm, take the child to a time-out area, tell the child "No biting" and that he or she should remain there until you return, and console the bitten child but without making a big deal of the injury. If the bite has broken the skin, administer a topical antibiotic and call a pediatrician. Then, without appearing that you are on the alert for another incident, be aware of signals that the child is working himself or herself up to a bite, move in, and either remove the child from the playing field or distract him or her. Research suggests that there is no connection between parenting style and biting, nor is biting indicative of psychological problems or predictive of later problems getting along with other children.

Because this behavior problem, more than virtually any other behavior problem, distresses parents, it needs special attention immediately. Parents become extremely emotional about this problem. For example, a thoracic surgeon parent was recently so hysterical about his child being bitten that he claimed the biting child could have pierced his child's lung (if he were being objective he would have remembered that he was a thoracic surgeon and knew very well that the rib cage stands outside the lung and would protect the lung from biting).

Head Banging

Head banging was once considered a pathological activity that only handicapped or emotionally disturbed children showed. However, recent studies on rhythmic be-haviors of infants and toddlers suggest that many children engage in these rhythmic activities as part of normal development. Other behaviors are rocking, lip biting, and thumb sucking. They generally happen when the infant or toddler is otherwise unoccupied and appears to be bored. In this case, these rhythmic activities may be a source of substitute stimulation. At other times they occur when the child is ex-tremely tired, and then they seem to pacify and quiet the child. Generally they will disappear after a short period of time, so they are probably best ignored. Children who show any of these behaviors excessively and are actually hurting themselves may need a professional evaluation (Berkson, 2002).

Stuttering

Approximately 8% of children stutter at some time, most usually between about 1.5 and 6 years of age, when the child is learning to talk, and later when the child begins school. Approximately 3 times as many boys as girls stutter, and stutterers are more often left-handed and have blond hair and blue eyes. Approximately 75% of children who stutter stop stuttering at around 12 or 13 years of age (Kalinowski, Saltuklaroglu, Dayalu, & Guntupalli, 2005).

Typically stutterers are delayed in their expressive language skills, not their re-ceptive language skills, lending support to the hypothesis that language deficits observed in stuttering children result at least in part from their attempts to simplify verbal responses as a means of coping with their stuttering. A recent study suggested that stutterers also show more nonspeech behavior during stuttered words than nonstutterers show during similar words (Bajaj, Hodson, & Westby, 2005). For example, they turn their head to the left, blink, and raise their upper lip excessively. Some evidence suggests a genetic predisposition for stuttering, and some researchers have found that the EEG of stutterers differs from those of nonstutterers, suggesting a disturbance of interhemispheric relationships. This may be a significant factor in the development of stuttering. Stressful events like the birth of siblings or transitions to new schools or new places can exaggerate the stuttering. The most difficult aspect of this problem is the embarrassment it causes the child and the delay it causes in language development.

Parents can help by not drawing attention to the stuttering, trying to ignore it, and certainly not speaking for the child. When children stutter, the tendency is to provide words for them rather than let the child complete the sentences. If the problem becomes so serious that the child cannot be understood, a speech therapist might be helpful. Often the therapist will work with the child to speak more slowly and to practice various breathing techniques that help the child become less stressed.

Temper Tantrums

Temper tantrums occur at frustrating stages in development. They are considered a mark of the child's attempts to become independent, for example around the terrible twos, when the child has power struggles with parents and because of limited language development has difficulty expressing his or her frustration except by tantrums. Temper tantrums typically arise from children's thwarted efforts to exercise mastery and autonomy. They occur more frequently in the active, determined child who has abundant energy. They may also occur in children who are hypersensitive to sounds, lights, and other stimulating features of the environment. Although these are considered normal behaviors, it is also clear that for a number of children temper tantrums turn into more difficult behavior problems (Leung & Fagan, 1991).

In one study, tantrums were reported in about 25% of children, most commonly at 2 to 5 years, becoming less common at 6 to 8 years. Children showing tantrums had a higher incidence of postnatal trauma. Parental overprotection and marital discord were stress factors in a greater number of boys than girls, and parental negligence was a significant stress factor for girls. Behavior problems that accompanied temper tantrums included thumb sucking, bedwetting, tics, head banging, and sleep disturbances. In another study, 52% of those who showed temper tantrums had multiple behavior problems. Factors independently associated with the tantrums included maternal depression and irritability, use of physical punishment, marital stress, child care provided exclusively by the mother, and poor child health (Potegal et al., 2003).

After having established that the child's temper tantrum is not simply related to discomfort, it's important to look at how the tantrum is being treated. Parenting practices that may encourage tantrums include inconsistency, unreasonable expectations, excessive strictness, overprotectiveness, and overindulgence. The child might also be bored, fatigued, hungry, or ill, thus reducing his or her tolerance for frustration. In those situations it would obviously be important to distract the child or interest him or her in something less boring. Beyond these attempts, temper tantrums are probably best handled by ignoring the outburst and saving attention for the posttantrum, as well as helping the child learn to express negative feelings in less annoying ways.

Shyness

A significant body of research suggests that shyness is one of the strongest temperament traits in children (Stein, Chavira, & Jang, 2001). Research from our lab shows that even newborns show behaviors that look like shyness. Approximately 20% of newborns show shy, introverted behavior such as limited responses to social stimulation. We have called this being poker-faced (Field, 1982). At the other extreme, approximately 20% of children are extremely extraverted, or wear their heart on their sleeve. Approximately 60% of newborns and children lie somewhere in the middle of those extremes. In our study we found that when a child seemed to be born with a shy temperament but had extraverted parents, there was often a shift toward being somewhere in the middle. Thus, although this seems to be an inborn trait (particularly because we saw shyness more often being shared by identical than nonidentical twins), the environmental influences (such as shyness or no shyness in the parents) are also very strong (Gerhold, Laucht, Texdorf, Schmidt, & Esser, 2002).

Data also show that children who tend to be shy have unique physiological characteristics such as greater reactivity of heart rate and different brain waves. Sometimes they have very strong physiological responses to emotional situations, and their shyness or social withdrawal might be a way of providing a barrier to the excessive stimulation. If a child is socially withdrawn, there is often a tendency for people to respect the child's shyness and let the child take the initiative. Often the shy, slow-to-warm-up child will be most comfortable making his or her own overtures and contacts.

Researchers at Harvard found that children who were timid during infancy and as toddlers tended to be socially inhibited at age 7. They estimated that 15% of children, significantly more girls than boys, are born shy (Kagan, 2005), although they found that many outgrew their shyness.

Autism

Autism has a variety of genetic and nongenetic causes, although the etiology (development) is unknown in the majority of children. Boys are more frequently affected than girls, and autism first becomes apparent in the preschool years. It always affects sociability, communication, and the child's repertoire of activities and interests. Autism encompasses a broad range of severities and a variety of other signs of brain dysfunction. These include motor signs, notably stereotypes such as head banging and flapping of hands. Abnormal responses to a variety of sensory stimuli occur, and the children have very severe attention problems and problems showing their emotions. A significant number of autistic children experience epileptic seizures and have abnormal EEGs. Magnetic resonance imaging has revealed abnormalities of brain development in some autistic children. The level of intelligence may range from profound mental deficiencies to giftedness. The pattern of cognitive skills is likely to be uneven, typically with better nonverbal than verbal skills (Mitchell et al., 2006). In the preschool years, autistic children have a language disorder. Verbal expression may range from total lack of language to being extremely verbose (some even have echolalia, which is endless talking). Comprehension and language use are invariably impaired. There are no specific drugs that can reduce the symptoms of attention disorder and seizures, but the autistic features can change with maturation and appropriate intervention. Communication skills and sociability remain deficient but improved for all but the most severely affected children. The children can be positively affected by early interventions focused on the development of appropriate social skills and meaningful communication.

Autism is a particularly difficult problem because the child is unresponsive. As early as infancy, autistic children are noted to arch their back when held, to make very little eye contact, and to simply dislike physical affection. At the preschool stage or as young children they prefer to play by themselves and often sit and do nothing, staring into space. Their difficulty staying on task and their autistic behaviors, such as flapping their hands and whirling around, spinning things, or rocking and banging their heads, is very disruptive behavior and often wins them no friends at school.

The number of autistic children has increased dramatically over the past several years, probably because screening techniques are more sensitive but less specific so that more children are labeled autistic (many of whom are not really autistic; Yeargin-Allsopp et al., 2003). Thus this is a "waste-basket" diagnosis, as some clinicians call it. Many schools are now providing special classes for autistic children, and some schools serve only autistic children. Statistically, approximately 1 in every 1,000 children is affected, with males being affected 4 times as often as females (Merrick, Kandel, & Morad, 2004). Generally the disorder is thought to be inherited. However, so many theories have been advanced about neurological and neurotransmitter causes that an entire journal is now devoted to autism. Medical conditions associated with autism include epilepsy, hearing deficits, speech and language impairments, and eyesight problems. A comprehensive medical workup is required in all cases of pervasive autistic symptomatology.

Children with autism have very little language and tend to repeat words, sometimes memorizing and repeating paragraphs of from magazines and in general speaking inappropriately. One study showed that using baby-talk-like language ("motherese") was more effective in gaining the attention of autistic children than using simple conversational tones. Many therapy attempts have focused on physical interactions such as wrapping the children in blankets and holding them to enhance their attentiveness. Although these children are also thought to have an aversion to touch, we were able to successfully perform a massage therapy study with them (Field et al., 1997). In our first study, the children who received massage therapy a couple of times a week for a month showed less off-task behavior, had fewer autistic mannerisms, and related more positively to their teachers, suggesting at least that they did not find touch aversive. In our second study the parents served as the therapists and the children had fewer sleep disturbances and less off-task behavior in the classroom (Escalona, Field, Singer-Strunk, Cullen, & Hartshorn, 2001). This may be a technique that parents could use as a way of being physically more intimate with their typically rejecting autistic children and as a way of enhancing the children's attentiveness. In addition, we have used imitation therapy to help the parents and children interact. The parents imitate the child's behaviors, and the child becomes more social.

CAREGIVING

Touching

In a recent study on the touching behavior of mothers and fathers with their newborn infants, both mothers and fathers touched their infant for an equal amount of time and frequency, but mothers touched or stroked their infants more than they patted or moved them (Prodromidis et al., 1995). Fathers did not show a preference for either type of touching. Mothers preferentially touched their infant's hand and face more than the body, and fathers preferred to touch their infant's hand. The authors suggest that this is consistent with mothers' inclination to care for their infants and fathers' tendency to play with their infants. Another study conducted on touching premature newborns in intensive care suggested that touching occurs 63% of the observation time; 69% of the touching was treatment-oriented, 15% was caregiving-oriented, and 16% was simply comforting touch. The majority of touching was done by the nurses (Modrcin-Talbott, Harrison, Groer, & Younger, 2003).

Massage Therapy

Massage therapy has been noted to help infants and children in many ways. When we gave hospitalized premature infants three 15-minute massages a day for 10 days they gained 47% more weight, were hospitalized for 6 fewer days (at a hospital cost savings of approximately $10,000), and were more responsive to social stimulation (Field et al., 1986). Eight months later they still showed a growth advantage, and their performance on mental and motor developmental tests was superior (Field, Scafidi, & Schanberg, 1987). Massage therapy used with normal infants led to less irritability, more alertness, and better sleep patterns (Field, Grizzle, et al., 1996). Normal infants also gained weight following 5 weeks of massage. When compared to a group of infants who were rocked, the massaged infants were awake while they were being massaged and quickly went to sleep following the massage, whereas the rocked infants slept during the rocking but awakened as the rocking ended. This suggests that massage is a more effective way for parents to help their infants go to sleep.

Although the underlying mechanisms for the effectiveness of massage are not clear, massage seems to put infants and children in a more relaxed state. In that state their stress hormones (cortisol levels) are reduced and they are more alert. The reduction in stress hormones improves the functioning of the immune system.

Infant massage classes are being started in many places in the United States to teach parents how to massage their children. In at least one study we have shown that the person giving the massage benefits as much as the person receiving the massage (Field, Hernandez-Reif, Quintino, Schanberg, & Kung, 1998). In that study we trained grandparent volunteers to massage babies, and after a month of massaging babies they showed several changes: fewer trips to the doctor, more social calls, fewer cups of coffee, less depression, and greater self-esteem. Although mothers are typically given the training, researchers have also trained fathers as massage therapists. For example, in one study Australian fathers were taught to give massages during bath time for 4 weeks after the infants were born (Scholz & Samuels, 1992). In another study by our group, by 3 months the infants were greeting their fathers with more eye contact, smiling, vocalizing, reaching, and orienting responses, and showed less avoidance behavior (Cullen, Field, Escalona, & Hartshorn, 2000). At this time the fathers who had been in the massage group also showed greater involvement with their infants. Thus, massage therapy has many benefits for both parents and their children.

Bathing

Bathing is typically one of those end-of-the-day activities when the parent has prime time with the child. From very early in infancy bath time is a favorite activity of the child. It becomes a family ritual and is intended not only for cleaning but also for relaxing the child at bedtime (Bryanton, Walsh, Barrett, & Gaudet, 2004). Children love the kicking and splashing, sliding under the water, exploring the taste of the shampoo, and even turning on the hot water without realizing it can burn. The most critical thing to remember is not only to have fun playing with the child and the bathtub toys but that the child should never be left unattended in the bathtub. The one inch of water in the bottom of the bathtub is the leading cause of drownings in the United States (Byard & Donald, 2004).

Swaddling

Swaddling, or the tight wrapping of babies (typically with a blanket), is done for a very limited period of time in the United States. Usually parents swaddle their babies to calm them down or help them go to sleep, and sometimes to make it easier to carry them (Franco et al., 2005). Although swaddling is more common in other cultures, such as American Indians wrapping infants tightly to carrying boards, it is discouraged in our country as a baby care practice because it is considered limiting to the development of hand-eye motor coordination.

Rocking

Rocking is a classic technique used by parents to calm their children and probably themselves as well (White-Traut, 2004). Recent studies suggest that pacifiers and massage are more effective at calming children and getting them to sleep, although rocking may very well serve the purpose of calming the parents. For that reason alone, its popularity may well continue.

Carriers

Carriers come in many varieties for various kinds of carrying positions. For example, in a recent study we observed that carrying the baby in a front-to-front position led to infant sleep, whereas carrying the infant facing outward led to more wakeful and exploratory behavior (Field, Malphurs, Carraway, & Pelaez-Nogueras, 1996). The optimal carrier might allow for both positions. Being carried by the parent has a long history in evolution and is popular in many cultures, probably because it provides additional stimulation for the baby, enables the mother to closely monitor the baby, and lets her work unencumbered with hands free. This arrangement might also allow for less heat loss and the conservation of energy.

Music

Music has profound effects as early as birth. Studies on premature infants, for example, show that following repeated exposure to music, infants have reduced heart rate and deeper sleep and grow and develop better (Arnon et al., 2006; Standley, 1998; Standley & Moore, 1995). In a study on preschoolers, performance on cognitive tasks was superior following exposure to music. Much of these effects may be attributed to music's ability to relax infants and young children. When heart rate and blood pressure are recorded, for example, they are lower following music. When infants and children are distressed, they typically show greater EEG activity in the right frontal area of the brain (activity in this region is typically associated with negative emotions and mood states). Exposure to music can actually shift EEG activity from the right to the left side of the brain (Field et al., 1998).

Stimulation

Optimal parenting is often discussed in the context of providing the right amount of stimulation. This is particularly true for the infancy and toddler stages, when children need some help monitoring and regulating the amount of stimulation they receive. By virtue of having different temperaments, different children have different thresholds for the amount and kind of stimulation they desire. Matching the kind of stimulation to the child's personality is critical because either too much or too little stimulation will not enhance growth and development. Sometimes parents provide too little stimulation because they are tired, depressed, or preoccupied by their own problems. At other times, for example when children are unresponsive or slow in doing things, parents will be overstimulating and they try to get a response or an action.

Finding the optimal amount and kind of stimulation a child needs is one of the most difficult tasks of parenting. Probably the most effective approach is to take the cues from the child. When interacting with infants, it is easy to tell whether they are getting the kind of stimulation they want or need. Infants will avert their gaze, turn their head, arch their back, and, at the extreme, fuss and cry when they are either getting too little or too much stimulation. Slightly older children may go into a shell and ignore their parents' attempts to engage them. From very early infancy, children have conversation skills such as turn-taking and paying attention or ignoring. These skills can be used as signals that the parent is doing the right thing and the child is interested. Just like adults, children need breaks to not only process information from the conversation and formulate a response, but also to take rests and have some quiet periods for thinking and imagining things.

Game Playing

Game playing punctuates early interactions between parents and their infants (Field, 1979). Infant games such as pat-a-cake and peek-a-boo appear with such frequency that they are universally recognized as infant games. The importance of early game playing has been underscored by a number of early interaction researchers, who suggest that game playing provides a context for learning one of the most important rules of conversation, that of turn-taking. Infant games are highly repetitive with simple and stereotyped roles for both participants. As such they exemplify the structure of conversational give and take or turn-taking. Even when the infant is yet too young to assume an active role, the structure of these repetitive games may enable the infant to assimilate the turn-taking nature of interaction.

Other important features of early games include the "contingency experience" they provide (i.e., learning to react to and innovate in changing situations) and the facilitation of positive emotion. An illustration of the contingent responsivity provided by a game can be seen in one of the most popular early games, called "Tell Me a Story." The words are provided by the parent, who treats the infants' vocalizations as if they too were words. The parent asks, "Do you want to tell me a story?" The infant coos, the parent responds, "Oh yeah? And then what happened?" The infant coos again and the parent replies, "Oh, that's funny." The infant contingently responds to the parent's words by cooing, and the parent contingently responds to infant cooing by further elaborations of the game.

The game "I'm Gonna Get You" is an illustration of the way in which games facilitate positive emotion. The parent repeatedly looms toward the infant, rubbing his or her head into the lap of the infant, tickling and jostling the infant, and accompanying each repetition with verbalizations such as "Ah, boom!" or "I'm gonna get you." These repetitious behaviors elicit infant smiles, vocalizations, and sometimes laughter. The parents contingently respond to these infant behaviors by playing more of the same game. The game ceases at the point at which it no longer elicits contented responses, and the parent moves on to another game.

Thus, early game playing provides an affective, contingency experience during which infants may learn important rules of communication such as turn-taking. When games are missing from the interaction or age-inappropriate games are played, the interaction appears to be badly timed, disorganized, or disturbed. When a mother plays age-inappropriate games or games that are too complex for a given age of infant, for example peek-a-boo with a 6-week-old infant, the interaction lacks positive emotion and is not sustained.

The early interactions of developmentally delayed, atypical, or failure-to-thrive infants and mothers feature very few games. These mothers do not appear to enjoy playing games and do not as frequently play games, particularly age-appropriate games, with their infants, probably because their infants are less responsive.

In one of our studies, the types and frequency of widely recognized infant games were observed during face-to-face interactions of normal and high-risk infants and parents when the infants were 4 months old (Field, 1979). Approximately six different games were played for approximately one-third of the interaction time. Fathers played with normal male infants more often, and the high-risk infants and parents played games less frequently than the normal infants and parents.

Interaction Coaching

When parents, most typically mothers, are having difficulty interacting with their infants, they can be given interaction coaching, which helps modify the behavior of the parent, and, in turn, the behavior of the infant (Field, 1983b). Typically mothers and infants are seated in a face-to-face position, with the infant in an infant seat. The mothers are given instructions to slow down their behavior. For example, they slow down when they are asked to imitate their infants' behaviors and they provide more stimulation when they are asked to keep their infants' attention. Having to imitate the baby's behaviors slows down the mother's behavior simply because infant behaviors are slower than adults'. The infants usually delight at being imitated, and before long, mothers and infants are engaging in a back-and-forth imitation game. Another way that mothers learn to modify their behavior is by watching video feedback on their interactions. Mothers can usually see the immediate effects of their behaviors and will show change almost immediately.

Schedules

The importance of a schedule cannot be overrated. From the time of birth, newborns need to be on sleeping and feeding schedules so that they can organize their own internal clock and have sustained periods of sleeping and ultimately sustained periods of playfulness (Field, 1978). Having periods of consolidated sleep, including deep sleep, is critical for children to sustain their activities, attentiveness, and interest in their play. Without having a schedule when they are growing up, children can have serious difficulties organizing themselves and often will become hyperactive and develop learning disabilities.

I remember one of our laid back nursery school teachers who believed that every infant should have his or her own schedule, and she operated her infant nursery class on that premise. The infants were extremely fussy, often spitting up and not being able to focus their attention on any activities. Being on 16 different schedules, the four teachers also became exhausted and irritable. The teacher who replaced her ran the infant nursery like an army sergeant and had all the infants on the same schedule within a week. Parents were at first resistant but came to appreciate that their infants were much less irritable. The need for a schedule continues through childhood, which is why children typically do much better in a school setting than they do on weekends, when everyone is on a different schedule.

Quality Time

In today's world of dual-career families parents are concerned about snatching as much time as they can with their children (Broom, 1998). Often this leads to children staying up late and sacrificing the quality time they spend in day care. Quality time, the time parents give their undivided attention to their children, is key—not quantity of time (Brooks-Gunn, Han, & Waldfogel, 2002).

Discipline

Affection and discipline are two of the most important aspects of parenting. Children growing up in the wild without parents become like wild animals because they are missing affection and discipline. In addition to needing affection for growth and development, children need discipline for their behavior to be organized and self-regulated (Socolar, Savage, Keyes-Elstein, & Evans, 2005). While some choices can be left to the child, for example, what the child wishes to wear, other matters that are critical to survival, such as not playing in the street and not being cruel to other children, require very firm limits. A parent should not ask a child if the child wants to hold the parent's hand while crossing the street; this is not a safe choice for a child to make. Having an intellectual discussion on the reasons why hurting someone is bad is also not effective. I recall a teacher in a model preschool quietly leaving the room after having been hurt by a flying block only to return several minutes later to have an intellectual discussion with the children about the "negative aspects of flying blocks." A better lesson would have been reacting normally to being hurt so the children would know the consequences of their actions.

Another problem with discipline is its frequent inconsistency. Recent reviews of the literature on behavior problems and on child abuse suggest that the most predictive factor for both is inconsistent discipline, such as parents being inconsistent from one time to the next or from one parent to the other (Field, 1983a). In societies where discipline is consistent within and across parents and between parents and teachers, such as in France and China, children have fewer behavior problems, and the incidence of child abuse is very low. Socially accepted forms of discipline are practiced by parents and teachers alike. Thus, the child is never seen driving the parent up the wall and the parent doesn't lose control.

A recent study revealed that verbal and physical forms of discipline are not substitutes but, instead, are commonly used together. Parents who yelled frequently were the ones most likely to hit frequently (Wade & Kendler, 2001). Respondents who were spanked (yelled at) frequently as children were more prone to frequently spank (yell at) their own children. Harsh parental discipline occurring early in life was associated with later aggression in children. The good news was that most people were able to break out of the cross-generational cycle of punitive childrearing, although physical punishment is still quite common. In a recent survey, 19% of mothers believed that there are times when it is appropriate to spank a child less than 1 year old, and 74% believed this about children 1 to 3 years old (Vittrup, Holden, & Buck, 2006); 42% reported that they had spanked their own child in the past week. Mothers believed more strongly in spanking for dangerous misbehaviors than for annoying ones. Other traditional disciplinary methods include rewards for good behavior and punishment for unacceptable behavior. The most common rewards are verbal praise, a smile, special attention or activities, or physical affection. Usual kinds of punishment include verbal disapproval, an unhappy look, ignoring the behavior (extinction), or temporary isolation (time-out). Rewards are typically cited as being more effective than punishment.

Childproofing

Childproofing offers the opportunity to simplify your environment. It can even be fun to convert your living room to a playroom where the whole family can enjoy playing together. The obvious safety precautions are removing sharp objects, poisonous substances, plastic bags, and anything that can injure or anything small that can lead to choking or suffocation; placing guards on stairs, safety latches on cupboards, plugs on electric outlets, and locks on doors; and certainly locking up guns. For many years children do not know the difference between reality and fantasy, and for that reason alone guns should be under lock and key. Choking on foreign bodies is the cause of death for more than 300 children each year in the United States. A review of the records of 548 children (ages 4 months to 18 years) was undertaken to identify factors important in diagnosis. A wide variety of objects was recovered, the most common being peanuts, organic material, other nuts, popcorn, seeds, plastic objects, and pins (LeBlanc et al., 2006).

Airway obstruction from aspiration of a foreign body should be suspected in all infants and children who have swallowing or respiratory difficulties (Agran et al., 2003). If the patient is unable to clear the airway by coughing, the Heimlich maneuver should be attempted. Parents can help to prevent airway obstruction by keeping small objects away from infants and children and by teaching them to chew food thoroughly. Whenever the child is approaching a forbidden object or something dangerous, it is best to simply remove the child or distract him or her with a similar object or activity rather than saying no and expecting the child to leave the area. Saying no for most young children is simply a challenge and escalates into a struggle. Simply carrying or taking children by the hand and moving them to another area where they can be distracted is more effective (Glick, Greaves, Kronenfield, & Jackson, 1993).

Leave-takings

Leave-takings are increasingly common, given the increasing numbers of infants, toddlers, and preschoolers attending nursery schools. Research suggests that different children have different leave-taking styles. In one study, children who cried during the early morning separations showed either a slow approach or no response except looking at the mother when she returned from her day's work (Field, Gewirtz, et al., 1984). Those children who left their mothers quickly in the mornings typically continued playing and showed things to the mother when she returned in the afternoon. The mothers of children who cried during separations more often slipped out of the room. The authors of this study suggested that much of the separation and reunion behavior is determined by the child, with the mother merely being in a responding mode at these times, mainly waiting to receive and act on signals from her child. However, in a study we conducted, we thought that the parents were very influential in the leave-takings.

We studied the leave-taking and the reunion behaviors of the infants, toddlers, preschoolers, and their parents as the children were dropped off and picked up at their nursery school each day (Field, Gewirtz, et al., 1984). On arrival at their classroom, infants and toddlers related primarily to their parents, whereas preschoolers related to their teachers. Girls more frequently engaged in interaction with their teachers, and boys more frequently approached the children's play activities. Toddlers showed the most distress behavior during the parents' departures, and the toddlers' parents hovered about them and sneaked out of the room more frequently. When mothers dropped off the children, the children showed more attention-getting behavior and crying than when the children were dropped off by their fathers. Mothers engaged in more behaviors to distract the child and took a longer time to leave the classroom than fathers did. Giving a verbal explanation, distracting the child, lingering in the classroom, and sneaking out of the room were accompanied by more crying. We noted that some children had difficulty making transitions, and those children showed difficulty not only leaving their parents in the morning but leaving their classroom in the afternoon. In addition we noted that fathers were much more nonchalant in their behavior, and the children were less distressed when they were dropped off by their fathers. Thus, the rather business-like style of leave-taking by the fathers seems to work better if parents want to avoid the stress of seeing their children's distress.

Moving

Moving is one of the most stress-producing and growth-producing experiences in childhood. Whether the move is from classroom to classroom, neighborhood to neighborhood, city to city, or country to country, the source of stress is losing one's friends. Separation from peers leads to symptoms very much like those that occur following separation from parents. The child becomes agitated and then depressed. Sleep is most affected by moving, with night wakings and night terrors frequently happening. The child's behavior fluctuates between being aggressive and withdrawn, and like depression in adults, eating habits change (overeating or undereating). The children experience constipation or diarrhea, and sometimes they get sick because of immune problems. We have observed these changes in studies on moves to new classrooms and moves to new schools (Field, Gewirtz, et al., 1984; Field, Vega-Lahr, et al., 1984). Even as young as 1 year of age, we are having to move children's best friends with them when they graduate from infancy classes to toddler classes so that they will not experience these symptoms. The children left behind often experience more severe symptoms, perhaps because they are remaining in the same environment where they are reminded of their long-lost friends.

Maternal Depression

Mothers who are depressed or who have symptoms of depression such as flat affect (showing little emotion) and listless behavior tend to have a difficult time interacting and being responsive to their infants (McLearn, Minkovitz, Strobino, Marks, & Hou, 2006a, 2006b; Paulson, Dauber, & Leiferman, 2006). The infants in turn develop flat affect and low activity levels. If the mother remains depressed over the first 6 months of life, the infant will begin to show growth and developmental delays by 1 year. By 3 years children of depressed mothers develop behavior problems such as depression and conduct problems. If mothers are simply depressed postpartum and the depression does not continue, the infants do not experience long-term effects.

Fathers and substitute caregivers such as infant nursery teachers can buffer some of these effects (Hossain et al., 1994; Pelaez-Nogueras, Field, Cigales, Gonzalez, & Clasky, 1994). Infants of depressed mothers often appear normal when interacting with their nondepressed fathers and teachers. Other effective interventions are the use of mood inductions with the mothers, such as music therapy and massage therapy (Jones & Field, 1999). Interaction coaching to help mothers be more active and responsive to their infants, such as playing peek-a-boo and imitation games, helps them improve their interactions. Teaching depressed mothers to massage their infants also helps improve the mothers' mood and reduce stress in the infants (Field, Grizzle, et al., 1996).

Fathers

In most studies people have found fathers to be more playful and stimulating and mothers to provide more caregiving and comforting. We found an exception to this when we studied fathers who were primary caregivers (Field, 1978). The stay-at-home fathers turned out to be more like mothers than fathers, and the mothers who were the breadwinners were more like the stereotypical father. We suggested that this meant that more caregiving is provided by the person who knows the infant better and more playfulness by the parent who knows the infant less well.

In a sense, the more stimulating, rough-and-tumble play of the fathers is complementary to the more soothing, comforting behavior of mothers. In a similar light, mothers tend to view their infants as being more difficult (perhaps because they are in a comforting role), and fathers are reported to enjoy their infants more (again because they engage in more play with them). Across the first several years, fathers are more involved in social interaction than in caregiving, and mothers continue to provide more of the caregiving. Although the differences between mothers and fathers has lessened over the years as more mothers have joined the workforce, some differences have continued, showing the mother providing more caregiving and the father more playful stimulation (St John, Cameron, & McVeigh, 2005).

Despite the differences in their parents' behaviors, infants and young children are noted to be equally attached to both parents. It may not appear that way, as infants and young children often protest their mothers leaving them at preschool and barely notice their fathers leaving (Field, Gewirtz, et al., 1984). This is probably because fathers matter-of-factly leave, saying they will see their child later, whereas mothers make a greater fuss about leaving their children and express more reassurance about their returning, which seems to draw out this fussing behavior. The children's ambivalence about leaving their mothers is also displayed upon her return, whereas infants greet fathers as they return with intense, brief displays of positive emotion.

Grandparents

Grandparents have a number of positive effects on child development (Harwood, 2001). Children are often more able to explore and try their skills around grandparents when not around their own parents. They seem to recognize a certain autonomy around grandparents, in contrast to their dependence around parents. This may be a two-sided process, as grandparents appear more relaxed and less overprotective around their grandchildren than parents do. They apparently also have less need to set limits than parents, as typically children seem more self-regulated in their presence. Part of this phenomenon may relate to grandparents giving children their undivided attention, whereas parents are often busy trying to juggle children and other activities at the same time. It could be that the child's more demanding and less compliant behavior in the parents' presence is attention-getting behavior. It could also be that the children sense greater demands being placed on them by their parents and higher expectations for performance. Combined experience with parents and grandparents, in any case, would appear to be optimal for any child.

Babysitters

Having a babysitter even for a newborn is a great break for parents and provides them needed time together. Finding someone who has experience, who loves taking care of babies, and who comes with good references from people you know is generally the best way to choose. On the first few occasions it is important to be there for a while until the babysitter becomes comfortable in the environment and familiar with the baby. Watching how the babysitter relates to your child and cares for your child in those few hours of getting acquainted is one way to develop confidence in the babysitter.

Day Care

Early day care helps develop a child's social and intellectual skills, but only if it is quality care. Penelope Leach, in her book *Children First,* and others have claimed that full-time day care can have harmful effects. However, their concerns relate to poor-quality day care (Geoffroy, Côté, Parent, & Seguin, 2006; Schwebel, Brezausek, & Belsky, 2006). In contrast, the average day care that most middle-class kids get is considered helpful for cognitive and social development, according to the National Research Council.

Quality care can be hard to define, but knowing what to look for in a day care center helps. State and federal governments have licensing requirements that ensure the provision of adequate space and safety features (e.g., smoke alarms and sprinkler jets). These requirements also ensure optimal teacher-student ratios and class sizes. For example, quality programs in Florida have no fewer than 1 teacher for every 4 infants, 1 teacher for every 6 toddlers, and 1 teacher for every 10 preschoolers in classrooms with no more than 20 infants, 30 toddlers, and 40 preschoolers. These figures, however, are meaningless if sufficient space is not provided (approximately 35 sq. ft. for indoor space and 50 sq. ft. for outdoor space per child).

Most parents know when they have discovered a quality day care setting. It will be immediately apparent that the teachers are nurturant and the children are happy. Children will be involved in creative activities and the environment will be organized, colorful, and rich with interesting materials and play opportunities. A class schedule with designated times for show and tell, snacks, naps, free play, and expressive arts, along with free time for fantasy play and gross motor play (play that uses muscles) is also an important part of quality day care. Outdoor play areas will include moving vehicles, sand play, and structures for climbing. Parents should ask questions about how long the teachers have been with the center (stability of the teachers is very important) and how much experience they have.

Some of the highest quality centers are found in university lab schools because they are partially subsidized by the universities. Some of the benefits of a laboratory school include active research and teacher training programs affiliated with their early childhood education and psychology departments. Religious centers (e.g., churches and synagogues), hospitals, corporate centers, and Montessori schools also provide quality day care. Specific listings are often provided by early childhood education departments at universities.

In a study on skills needed by preschool children for success in day care, teachers assigned the highest ratings to communication and independence. More specifically, these included children's ability to respond to their names, ask for help from an adult, stay out of restricted areas and respond to adults' questions. The teachers rated skills in the area of preacademics (including sitting cross-legged in a circle and cutting with scissors) the lowest.

In a study we conducted, the longer infants were in quality day care, the greater their emotional well-being and academic performance at grade school (Field, 1991). Similar data have been reported for quality day care in Sweden.

Pacifiers

Pacifiers are often viewed with disdain, and they are discouraged to the extent that premature infants in some hospitals require a physician's prescription for a pacifier. Yet documented and anecdotal reports show that sucking pacifiers helps calm infants during uncomfortable procedures, and toddlers are made more comfortable when adapting to unfamiliar situations (Stevens, Yamada, & Ohlsson, 2004). Pacifiers provide comfort, promote physiological tranquillity, and help in growth and development. In one study, we used pacifiers during painful hospital procedures (Field & Goldson, 1984). The infants who were allowed to suck on pacifiers cried significantly less, and their heart rate and respiration were slower. Pacifiers used during circumcisions reduced crying by 40%. It is not clear whether pacifier use reduces pain associated with invasive procedures or if the sucking is just incompatible with crying and therefore crying occurs less often. It is also possible that sucking on pacifiers releases pain-alleviating chemicals like serotonin. Sucking on pacifiers has also been used for weight gain, particularly with premature babies. In a study we conducted on premies, those who were allowed to use pacifiers gained weight more rapidly and were discharged from the hospital 6 days earlier than those not using pacifiers, at savings of approximately $3,000 per infant

(Field et al., 1982). These infants also performed better on a newborn assessment scale.

Given the positive effects of sucking, it is very fortunate that infants are inclined instinctively to engage in sucking behavior. That predisposition emerges very early in gestation, with fetuses as young as 5 months appearing to suck on their own hands in utero. During the first day of life, infants have been observed sucking as often as 30 minutes per hour. This does not appear to vary with the feeding experience. One survey found that 89% of parents introduced pacifiers to soothe their infants. Most studies in the literature concur that sucking is the most common method for soothing an infant. In another study pacifiers were compared with rocking. Pacifiers produced sleep states, and rocking produced alert states. Pacifiers also reduced heart rate levels significantly more than rocking. Thus pacifiers seem to be more soothing than rocking.

Sucking is also used for exploration and learning. Babies in one study sucked harder to hear their mother's voice than their father's voice, probably because they were more familiar with the vibrations of their mother's voice in utero (DeCasper & Prescott, 1984). Sucking is used in this and many studies to determine whether infants hear, see, make discriminations, and demonstrate sophisticated skills such as performing small math problems, discriminating different colors, and learning musical scales as early as the newborn period. Other investigators have noted how much learning occurs during infants' exploration by mouth. For example, infants are able to show that they can differentiate two different nipples (one with a knobby surface and one with a smooth surface) simply by having experienced sucking on the nipple and then looking longer at the picture of the nipple they had sucked, showing their preference for that familiar nipple (Hernandez-Reif, Field, & Diego, 2004).

Even if infants do not have nipples to suck on, they frequently suck on their hands or other objects. As early as 5 months gestation, fetuses explore their hands with their mouths. This persists through early infancy, when the mouth explores the hands, fist, and fingers. Similarly, for at least the first 6 months of life, everything the infant grasps goes into the mouth. In a recent court hearing I was asked how a 5-month-old infant could stuff a rather unpleasant-tasting alcohol wipe in his or her mouth. Invariably every 5-month-old I filmed for the hearing did exactly that. When babies have something more interesting to suck on, such as a nipple or rattle, they do not choose alcohol wipes. Infants prefer toys because of their interesting textures of softness, hardness, and firmness. Toys also give the infant information about features such as shape. Infants have individual preferences as well. Some infants enjoy sucking their soft toes, and others enjoy hard, firm plastic toys. Thus, sucking is a predominant activity during the first 6 months of life, just as walking is at 1 year, and it clearly provides a very basic learning function.

If sucking is so critical for reducing stress and facilitating growth and development, most especially cognitive (mental) development, and if sucking does not appear to have any negative effects, why should anyone want to eventually discourage the habit? One reason is that as a child develops, sucking on a pacifier or thumb may be incompatible with vocalizing and talking, just as it is incompatible with crying during the newborn stage. When infants become preschoolers they may experience rejection by peers for engaging in "baby behavior." Thus pacifier use at preschool is probably not desirable. In one study pacifier use declined in a voluntary way between 3 and 24 months, suggesting that for most children, the attachment to a pacifier declines naturally. However, for others, sucking is a type of security blanket that becomes difficult to relinquish.

To prevent pacifier overuse parents should not get into the habit of popping pacifiers into their babies' mouth when the baby doesn't need pacifying. It is important to learn to tune in and appropriately respond to your baby's cues and prevent pacifier overuse. Older babies should be given a pacifier only for true pacifying, soothing, and calming.

As an aside, parents often ask whether sucking on a pacifier or thumb can mean that the child will need to wear braces. For most children this is not a problem. Pacifier and thumb sucking have very little effect on a child's oral-facial development and on the primary teeth and position of the jaw when it is done periodically (Adair, 2003). If the child continues to suck when the permanent teeth are coming in, pacifier or thumb sucking could cause movement of the teeth and bones, and orthodontic treatment might be needed.

Security Blankets

Security blankets have their place in infancy and toddlerhood, as they allow children to more securely leave their mother (father leave-takings are typically less difficult). However, beyond the toddler stage, security blankets may be a source of embarrassment for the children when their peers make fun of their security objects. Bringing toys to school may provoke less embarrassment, but that often leads to little wars over possession of each other's toys. For that reason most teachers prefer that children leave their toys at home.

Toilet Training

Toilet training is typically treated by pediatricians as an individual readiness phenomenon, although most children are toilet-trained (according to recent study) by 2.5 years, with physicians beginning to discuss toilet training with parents at around 12 to 18 months of age (Horn, Brenner, Rao, & Cheng, 2006). Although parents are initiating toilet training at later ages, around 3 years (Blum, Taubman, & Nemeth, 2004), waiting to start toilet training at age 2 is particularly problematic because the terrible twos involve power struggles between parents and children that make toilet training extremely difficult (Blum et al., 2004; Schum et al., 2001).

Placing a child in training pants and trying not to use diapers except during nighttime sleep is an effective introduction to toilet training. Buying children their own toilet seat gives them a sense of control over their own activity. Children seem to learn faster when they are attending preschool, probably because the older children model more mature toileting behavior. Taking children to the toilet frequently will give them the idea, whether at home or at school, that there are designated periods when all kids have bathroom time.

Flashcards

The flashcard method was designed by a "better baby" school in Philadelphia to teach children music, language, science, and virtually anything that can be taught on flashcards to infants and toddlers. The school has repeatedly made great claims that 2-year-olds can learn physics, violin, and the classification of insects, for example. This is done by repeated drilling with flashcards, typically at home by the parent. None of these claims, however, has been supported by research, and the directors of the school are reluctant to have their methods tested. It is also not clear why a parent would want their child to know all this by the time the child enters school, only to present the potential problem that the child will be rejected as "weird" by his or her peers. The child who is busily learning flashcard skills has very little time to learn social skills and how to get along with peers, which is certainly a more important priority at the preschool stage.

Television

The American Academy of Pediatrics recommends that children under the age of 2 not watch any television. Yet, several surveys indicate high numbers of infants routinely watching TV, including 17% of 0- to 11-month-old infants and 48% of 12- to 23-month-old toddlers in a large U.S. study, and even larger numbers in a Japanese study (30% of 3-month-olds and 90% of 12-month-olds). Exposure is also high, at an average 44 minutes per day among American 4-month-old infants, increasing to 62 minutes per day in 12-month-old infants; and again, there is higher exposure in Japan. In one study, 92% of exposure of 4-month-olds was to adult TV. Some view TV exposure as a cognitive learning experience, but others are concerned that infants are imitating TV models, both immediately and days later, remembering and mimicking the model's actors. They also are taking directions from TV. For example, in one study, 10- to 12-month-old infants who watched an actress respond to a toy with fear later avoided playing with it themselves, and they were more likely to appear worried and cry. In another study, food-related advertising on TV was associated with brand recognition in toddlers (Connor, 2006). Other studies suggest that television viewing in infants is associated with irregular sleep schedules (Thompson & Christakis, 2005) and with a risk of becoming overweight (Dennison, Erb, & Jenkins, 2002).

Children are first exposed to the audio and video stimulation of TV shortly after birth to the age of 2 months. They then begin to have an interest in and glance at or watch the TV screen at 4 to 5 months of age. When they are able to crawl at around 6 months, they approach and investigate the TV set. At 7 to 8 months they enjoy switching channels, and then they become interested in and speak to the on-screen characters at 10 to 11 months. At 12 to 14 months of age they have favorite TV characters and programs and enjoy TV as ordinary TV viewers. They move their bodies with the music, mimic the actors on-screen, smile, and ask questions of parents. They fix the information from TV in their memory, and they are pleased to see the things they like on TV. Even the fetus is affected by TV, showing heart rate acceleration or deceleration and fetal movement when the mother is watching

TV. Disruption of sleep patterns due to TV may also occur to fetuses. For some, though—for example, infants of depressed mothers—selected children's TV may provide more adequate stimulation.

Accidents

Approximately 80,000 children are killed and another 50,000 disabled by unnecessary accidents, according to the U.S. National Safe Kids Campaign. This makes accidents the number 1 killer of American children. Accidents are now the cause of more deaths in children than the next six most frequent causes combined. The leading causes of these accidents are traffic injury, drownings, burns, choking, poisoning, and falls.

Minor accidents such as scrapes and bruises are inevitable as infants, toddlers, and young preschool children learn to wend their way through the world. Both children and parents overreact to these minor injuries. Accident-prone behavior has been related to hyperactivity, clumsiness, and antisocial behavior in children and lack of parental discipline in the home. Injury-prone behavior is most common, for example, in active boys with irregular sleep and eating problems. Often, though, accidents happen to children who are simply adventuresome.

Solutions for accidents are making the environment safe, including using seat belts and child safety seats to avoid traffic injuries, teaching the infant how to swim, using pool detectors, never leaving an infant alone in the bathtub to avoid drownings, monitoring hot water in the bathtub to avoid burns, making certain that back burners are used on the stove and smoke detectors are in working order, and locking up all medications, liquor, and cleaning substances to avoid poisoning. Children's homes need to be childproofed at least until the early grade school years, including using electric socket covers and safety latches on cupboards and covers on sharp corners of furniture.

Automobile accidents are the number 1 killer of children (Rimsza, Schackner, Bowen, & Marshall, 2002). Until children are 5 years of age (or more than 45 pounds) they need to be in a car seat that protects them from head-on as well as side crashes and meets the U.S. federal motor vehicle safety standards. Every state has laws requiring that children younger than 5 must be strapped into car seats in cars in motion. Children under 5 are most commonly killed in cars. Children under 10 should not be allowed to cross streets without adult supervision. An immediate need following a car accident is, of course, an emergency rescue.

Death from *fires* is the second most common cause of death, with 75% of these being caused by smoke inhalation and 80% occurring in house fires (Istre, McCoy, Carlin, & McClain, 2002). Approximately 50% of house fires are caused by cigarettes. Smoke detectors should be installed in areas just outside bedrooms, and a fire extinguisher placed in the kitchen and on each floor of the house. Scalding is the most common cause of nonfatal burns; 20% of these result from tap water and 80% from spilled food. The average age of children with burns is 32 months. Hot water heaters should be regulated at 120 degrees Fahrenheit. Because coffee burns are most common, infants should not be seated on any adult's lap during a coffee break. For the treatment of burns, cold water should be dribbled on the burn, sterile gauze squares held in place by gauze roll bandaging, and the doctor called or the child taken to the hospital. Other precautionary measures include not heating an infant's bottle in the microwave, dressing the child in fire-retardant sleep wear, and avoiding place mats and table cloths that can be pulled off the table.

The most common cause of *drowning* (the third most common cause of death to children) is leaving the child alone in the bathtub in a few inches of water in a minute's time. Even with swimming lessons, children less than 5 typically have less strength and coordination to swim out of danger, and their parents have a false sense of security from the swimming lessons, which often leads to minimal supervision. A safe rule of thumb is that any child under 10 should be supervised whenever near the water. An increasing percentage of drownings (44%) occur in nominally fenced-in pools in which the gate is open or the fence is in disrepair.

Approximately one-third of *poisonings* by medicine are due to children taking their grandparents' prescription drugs. Thus, not only your own home but the grandparents' home should be made child-safe. Cosmetics, shampoos, detergents, plant poisons, paint materials, and substances associated with automobiles need to be out of reach. Because different poisons require different actions—for example, for some it is important to induce vomiting, whereas others should not be treated that way—it is important to have a poison control center card and to call the poison control center, the doctor, or an emergency room.

An information card is also important in responding to *choking* situations. Parents should take cardiopulmonary resuscitation (CPR) classes in case artificial respiration is needed. And parents should certainly learn the Heimlich maneuver. *Miscellaneous dangers* in the home are stairs, windows, small objects, sharp objects, toilets, matches, tools, plastic bags, telephone cords, and, of course, guns. Most children do not know the difference between real and fantasy guns.

SUMMARY

The problems of infancy can be categorized as both the frustrations and challenges of the developmental milestones that occur and the problems they pose for the parents facilitating development and giving care along the way. The research on these problems is sparse and highlights the need for further studies on the problems of infancy.

REFERENCES

Acebo, C., Sadeh, A., Seifer, R., Tzischinsky, O., Hafer, A., & Carskadon, M. A. (2005). Sleep/wake patterns derived from activity monitoring and maternal report for healthy 1- to 5-year-old children. *Sleep, 28*, 1568–1577.

Adair, S. M. (2003). Pacifier use in children: A review of recent literature. *Pediatric Dentistry, 25*, 449–458.

Agran, P., Anderson, C., Winn, D., Trent, R., Walton-Haynes, L., & Thayer, S. (2003). Rates of pediatric injuries by 3-month intervals for children 0 to 3 years of age. *Pediatrics, 111*, 683–692.

Arnon, S., Shapsa, A., Forman, L., Regev, R., Bauer, S., Litmanovitz, I., *et al.* (2006). Live music is beneficial to preterm infants in the neonatal intensive care unit environment. *Birth, 33*, 131–136.

Bajaj, A., Hodson, B., & Westby, C. (2005). Communication ability conceptions among children who stutter and their fluent peers: A qualitative exploration. *Journal of Fluency Disorders, 30*, 41–64.

Berkson, G. (2002). Early development of stereotyped and self-injurious behaviors: Pt. II. Age trends. *American Journal of Mental Retardation, 107*, 468–477.

Blum, N. J., Taubman, B., & Nemeth, N. (2004). Why is toilet training occurring at older ages? A study of factors associated with later training. *Journal of Pediatrics, 145*, 107–111.

Brooks, R., & Meltzoff, A. (2002). The importance of eyes: How infants interpret adult looking behavior. *Developmental Psychology, 38*, 958–966.

Brooks-Gunn, J., Han, W., & Waldfogel, J. (2002). Maternal employment and child outcomes in the first three years of life: The NICHD study of early child care. *Child Development, 73*, 1052–1072.

Broom, B. L. (1998). Parental sensitivity to infants and toddlers in dual-earner and single-earner families. *Nursing Research, 47*, 162–169.

Bryanton, J., Walsh, D., Barrett, M., & Gaudet, D. (2004). Tub bathing versus traditional sponge bathing for the newborn. *Journal of Obstetric, Gynecologic and Neonatal Nursing, 33*, 704–712.

Burrows, P., & Griffiths, P. (2002). Do baby walkers delay onset of walking in young children? *British Journal of Community Nursing, 7*, 581–586.

Byard, R. W., & Donald, T. (2004). Infant bath seats, drowning and near-drowning. *Journal of Paediatrics and Child Health, 40*, 305–307.

Capute, A. J., Shapiro, B. K., Palmer, F. B., Ross, A., & Wachtel, R. C. (1985). Cognitive-motor interactions: The relationship of infant gross motor attainment to IQ at 3 years. *Clinical Pediatrics, 12*, 671–675.

Carruth, B. R., & Skinner, J. D. (2000). Revisiting the picky eater phenomenon: Neophobic behaviors of young children. *Journal of the American College of Nutrition, 19*, 771–780.

Cohen, L. (2002). Reducing infant immunization distress through distraction. *Health Psychology, 21*, 207–211.

Connor, S. M. (2006). Food-related advertising on preschool television: Building brand recognition in young viewers. *Pediatrics, 118*, 1478–1485.

Crotteau, C. A., Wright, S. T., & Eglash, A. (2006). Clinical inquiries: What is the best treatment for infants with colic? *Journal of Family Practice, 55*, 634–636.

Cullen, C., Field, T., Escalona, A., & Hartshorn, K. (2000). Father infant interactions are enhanced by massage therapy. *Early Child Development and Care, 164*, 41–47.

Dawson, G., Panagiotides, H., Klinger, L. G., & Spieker, S. (1997). Infants of depressed and nondepressed mothers exhibit differences in frontal brain electrical activity during the expression of negative emotions. *Developmental Psychology, 33*, 650–656.

DeCasper, A. J., & Prescott, P. (1984). Human newborns' perception of male voices: Preference, discrimination and reinforcing value. *Developmental Psychobiology, 17*, 481–491.

Dennison, B. A., Erb, T. A., & Jenkins, P. L. (2002). Television viewing and television in bedroom associated with overweight risk among low-income preschool children. *Pediatrics, 109*, 1028–1035.

Derom, C., Theiry, E., Vlietinck, R., Loos, R., & Derom, R. (1996). Handedness in twins according to zygosity and chorion type: A preliminary report. *Behavior Genetics, 26*, 407–408.

Donate-Bartfield, E., & Passman, R. H. (2004). Relations between children's attachments to their mothers and to security blankets. *Journal of Family Psychology, 3*, 453–458.

Eglinton, E., & Annett, M. (1994). Handedness and dyslexia: A meta-analysis. *Perceptual and Motor Skills, 79*, 1611–1616.

Escalona, A., Field, T., Singer-Strunk, R., Cullen, C., & Hartshorn, K. (2001). Brief report: Improvements in the behavior of children with autism following massage therapy. *Journal of Autism and Developmental Disorders, 31*, 513–516.

Farroni, T., Csibra, G., Simion, F., & Johnson, M. H. (2002). Eye contact detection in humans from birth. *Proceedings of the National Academy of Sciences, USA, 99*, 9602–9605.

Fernandez, M., Blass, E. M., Hernandez-Reif, M., Field, T., Diego, M., & Sanders, C. (2003). Sucrose attenuates a negative electroencephalographic response to an aversive stimulus for newborns. *Journal of Development and Behavioral Pediatrics, 24*, 261–266.

Field, T. (1978). The three Rs of infant adult interactions: Rhythms, repertoires, and responsivity. *Journal of Pediatric Psychology, 3*, 131–136.

Field, T. (1979). Games parents play with normal and high-risk infants. *Child Psychiatry and Human Development, 10*, 41–48.

Field, T. (1982). Individual differences in the expressivity of neonates and young infants. In R. Feldman (Ed.), *Development of nonverbal behavior in children* (pp. 279–289). New York: Springer-Verlag.

Field, T. (1983a). Child abuse in monkeys and humans: A comparative perspective. In M. Reite & N. Caine (Eds.), *Child abuse in primates* (pp. 151–174). New York: Liss.

Field, T. (1983b). Early interactions and interaction coaching of high-risk infants and parents. In M. Perlmutter (Ed.), *Minnesota symposia on child psychology* (pp. 1–40). Hillsdale, NJ: Erlbaum.

Field, T. (1984). Separation stress of young children transferring to new schools. *Developmental Psychology, 20*(5), 786–792.

Field, T. (1991). Young children's adaptations to repeated separations from their mothers. *Child Development, 62*, 539–547.

Field, T. (1995). Infant massage therapy. In T. Field (Ed.), *Touch in early development* (pp. 105–114). Northvale, NJ: Erlbaum.

Field, T., Cohen, D., Garcia, R., & Greenberg, R. (1984). Mother-stranger face discrimination by the newborn. *Infant Behavior and Development, 7*, 19–25.

Field, T., Gewirtz, J. L., Cohen, D., Garcia, R., Greenberg, R., & Collins, K. (1984). Leave-takings and reunions of infants, toddlers, preschoolers, and their parents. *Child Development, 55*, 628–635.

Field, T., & Goldson, E. (1984). Pacifying effects of nonnutritive sucking on term and preterm neonates during heelstick procedures. *Pediatrics, 74*(6), 1012–1015.

Field, T., Grizzle, N., Scafidi, F., Abrams, S., Richardson, S., Kuhn, C., et al. (1996). Massage therapy for infants of depressed mothers. *Infant Behavior and Development, 19*, 109–114.

Field, T., Guy, L., & Umbel, V. (1985). Infants' responses to mothers' imitative behaviors. *Infant Mental Health Journal, 6*, 40–44.

Field, T., Hernandez-Reif, M., & Diego, M. (2006). Stability of mood states and biochemistry across pregnancy. *Infant Behavior and Development, 29*, 262–267.

Field, T., Hernandez-Reif, M., Quintino, O., Schanberg, S., & Kuhn, C. (1998). Elder retired volunteers benefit from giving massage therapy to infants. *Journal of Applied Gerontology, 17*, 229–239.

Field, T., Ignatoff, E., Stringer, S., Brennan, J., Greenberg, R., Widmayer, S., et al. (1982). Nonnutritive sucking during tube feedings: Effects on preterm neonates in an intensive care unit. *Pediatrics, 70*(3), 381–384.

Field, T., Lasko, D., Mundy, P., Henteleff, T., Kabot, S., Talpins, S., et al. (1997). Brief report: Autistic children's attentiveness and responsivity improved after touch therapy. *Journal of Autism and Developmental Disorders, 27*(3), 333–338.

Field, T., Malphurs, J., Carraway, K., & Pelaez-Nogueras, M. (1996). Carrying position influences infant behavior. *Early Child Development and Care, 121*, 49–54.

Field, T., Martinez, A., Nawrocki, T., Pickens, J., Fox, N. A., Schanberg, S. (1998). Music shifts frontal EEG in depressed adolescents. *Adolescence, 33*, 109–116.

Field, T., & Reite, M. (1984). Children's responses to separation from mother during the birth of another child. *Child Development, 55*, 1308–1316.

Field, T., Scafidi, F., & Schanberg, S. (1987). Massage of preterm newborns to improve growth and development. *Pediatric Nursing, 13*, 385–387.

Field, T., Schanberg, S. M., Scafidi, F., Bauer, C. R., Vega-Lahr, N., Garcia, R., et al. (1986). Tactile/kinesthetic stimulation effects on preterm neonates. *Pediatrics, 77*, 654–658.

Field, T., Vega-Lahr, N., & Jagadish, S. (1984). Separation stress of nursery infants and toddlers graduating to new classes. *Infant Behavior and Development 7*, 277–284.

Franco, P., Seret, N., Van Hees, J. N., Scaillet, S., Vermeulen, F., Groswasser, J., et al. (2005). Influence of swaddling on sleep and arousal characteristics of healthy infants. *Pediatrics, 115*, 1307–1311.

Friman, P. C., McPherson, K. M., Warzak, W. J., & Evans, J. (1993). Influence of thumb sucking on peer social acceptance in first-grade children. *Pediatrics, 91*, 784–786.

Geoffroy, M., Côté, S. M., Parent, S., & Seguin, J. R. (2006). Daycare attendance, stress, and mental health. *Canadian Journal of Psychiatry, 51*, 607–615.

Gerhold, M., Laucht, M., Texdorf, C., Schmidt, M. H., & Esser, G. (2002). Early mother-infant interaction as a precursor to childhood social withdrawal. *Child Psychiatry and Human Development, 32*, 277–293.

Glick, D. C., Greaves, P., Kronenfield, U. J., & Jackson, K. (1993). Safety hazards in households with young children. *Journal of Pediatric Psychology, 18*, 115–131.

Goldstein, M. H., King, A. P., & West, M. J. (2003). Social interaction shapes babbling: Testing parallels between birdsong and speech. *Proceedings of the National Academy of Sciences, USA, 100*, 8030–8035.

Harwood, J. (2001). Comparing grandchildren's and grandparent's stake in their relationship. *International Journal of Aging and Human Development, 53*, 195–210.

Hernandez-Reif, M., Field, T., & Diego, M. (2004). Differential sucking by neonates of depressed versus non-depressed mothers. *Infant Behavior and Development, 27*, 465–476.

Hinojosa, T., Sheu, C.-F., & Michel, G. F. (2003). Infant hand-use preferences for grasping objects contributes to the development of a hand-use preference for manipulating objects. *Developmental Psychobiology, 43*, 328–334.

Hobson, R. P., Patrick, M. P., Crandell, L. E., Garcia Perez, R. M., & Lee, A. (2004). Maternal sensitivity and infant triadic communication. *Journal of Child Psychology and Psychiatry, 45*, 470–480.

Horn, I. B., Brenner, R., Rao, M., & Cheng, T. L. (2006). Beliefs about the appropriate age for initiating toilet training: Are there racial and socioeconomic differences? *Journal of Pediatrics, 149*, 165–168.

Hossain, Z., Field, T., Gonzalez, J., Malphurs, J., DelValle, C., & Pickens, J. (1994). Infants of depressed mothers interact better with their nondepressed fathers. *Infant Mental Health Journal, 15*, 348–357.

Huhtala, V., Lehtonen, L., Heinonen, R., & Korvenranta, H. (2000). Infant massage compared with crib vibrator in the treatment of colicky infants. *Pediatrics, 105*, e84.

Huttunen, M., & Nyman, G. (1982). On the continuity, change and clinical value of infant temperament in a prospective epidemiological study. *Ciba Foundation Symposium, 89*, 240–251.

Istre, G. R., McCoy, M., Carlin, D. K., & McClain, J. (2002). Residential fire related deaths and injuries among children: Fireplay, smoke alarms, and prevention. *Injury Prevention, 8*, 128–132.

Jones, N., & Field, T. (1999). Right frontal EEG asymmetry is attenuated by massage and music therapy. *Adolescence, 34*, 529–534.

Jones, N., Field, T., & Davalos, M. (2000). Right frontal EEG asymmetry and lack of empathy in preschool children of depressed mothers. *Child Psychiatry and Human Development, 30*, 189–204.

Kagan, J. (2005). Human morality and temperament. *Nebraska Symposium on Motivation, 51*, 1–32.

Kalinowski, J., Saltuklaroglu, T., Dayalu, V., & Guntupalli, V. K. (2005). Is it possible for speech therapy to improve upon natural recovery rates in children who stutter? *International Journal of Language and Communication Disorders, 40*, 349–358.

Keren, M., Feldman, R., Namdari-Weinbaum, I., Spitzer, S., & Tyano, S. (2005). Relations between parents' interactive style in dyadic and triadic play and toddlers' symbolic capacity. *American Journal of Orthopsychiatry, 44*, 599–607.

Kochanska, G., & Coy, K. C. (2002). Child emotionality and maternal responsiveness as predictors of reunion behaviors in the Strange Situation: Links mediated and unmediated by separation distress. *Child Development, 73*, 228–240.

Learmonth, A. E., Lamberth, R., & Rovee-Collier, C. (2005). The social context of imitation in infancy. *Journal of Experimental Child Psychology, 91*, 297–314.

LeBlanc, J. C., Pless, I. B., King, W. J., Bawden, H., Bernard-Bonnin, A., Klassen, T., et al. (2006). Home safety measures and the risk of unintentional injury among young children: A multicentre case-control study. *Canadian Medical Association Journal, 175*, 883–887.

LeCuyer-Maus, E. A., & Houck, G. M. (2002). Mother-toddler interaction and the development of self-regulation in a limit-setting context. *Journal of Pediatric Nursing, 17*, 184–200.

Leung, A. K. C., & Fagan, J. E. (1991). Temper tantrums. *American Family Practitioner, 44*, 559–563.

Lichtenberger, E. O. (2005). General measures of cognition for the preschool child. *Mental Retardation and Developmental Disabilities Research Reviews, 11*, 197–208.

Liem, D. G., & Mennella, J. A. (2002). Sweet and sour preferences in young children and adults: Role of repeated exposure. *Developmental Psychobiology, 41*(4), 388–395.

Lowman, L. B., Stone, L. L., & Cole, J. G. (2006). Using developmental assessments in the NICU to empower families. *Neonatal Network, 3*, 177–816.

Lundy, B., Field, T., Carraway, K., Hart, S., Malphurs, J., Rosenstein, M., et al. (1998). Food texture preferences in infants. *Early Child Development and Care, 146*, 69–85.

Maziade, M., Cote, R., Thivierge, J., Boutin, P., & Bernier, H. (1989). Significance of extreme temperament in infancy for clinical status in preschool years: Pt. II. Patterns of temperament change and implications for the appearance of disorders. *British Journal of Psychiatry, 154*, 551–554.

McLearn, K. T., Minkovitz, C. S., Strobino, D. M., Marks, E., & Hou, W. (2006a). Maternal depressive symptoms at 2 to 4 months post partum and early parenting. *Practices, 160*, 279–284.

McLearn, K. T., Minkovitz, C. S., Strobino, D. M., Marks, E., & Hou, W. (2006b). The timing of maternal depressive symptoms and mothers' parenting practices with young children: Implications for pediatric practice. *Pediatrics, 118*, 174–182.

Mennella, J. A., Jagnow, C. P., & Beauchamp, G. K. (2001). Prenatal and postnatal flavor learning by human infants. *Pediatrics, 107*, e88.

Mennella, J. A., Kennedy, J. M., & Beauchamp, G. K. (2006). Vegetable acceptance by infants: Effects of formula flavors. *Early Human Development, 82*, 463–468.

Merrick, J., Kandel, I., & Morad, M. (2004). Trends in autism. *International Journal of Adolescent Medical Health, 16*, 75–78.

Mitchell, S., Brian, J., Zwaigenbaum, L., Roberts, W., Szatmari, P., Smith, I., et al. (2006). Early language and communication development of infants later diagnosed with autism spectrum disorder. *Journal of Development and Behavioral Pediatrics, 27*, S69–S78.

Modrcin-Talbott, M. A., Harrison, L. L., Groer, M. W., & Younger, M. S. (2003). The biobehavioral effects of gentle human touch on preterm infants. *Nursing Science Quarterly, 16*, 60–67.

Paulson, J. F., Dauber, S., & Leiferman, J. A. (2006). Individual and combined effects of postpartum depression in mothers and fathers on parenting behavior. *Pediatrics, 118*, 659–668.

Pelaez-Nogueras, M., Field, T., Cigales, M., Gonzalez, A., & Clasky, S. (1994). Infants of depressed mothers show less "depressed" behavior with their nursery teachers. *Infant Mental Health Journal, 15*, 358–367.

Potegal, M., & Davidson, R. J. (2003). Temper tantrums in young children: Pt. 1. Behavioral composition. *Developmental and Behavioral Pediatrics, 24*, 140–147.

Potegal, M., Kosorok, M., & Davidson, R. J. (2003). Temper tantrums in young children: Pt. 2. Tantrum duration and temporal organization. *Developmental and Behavioral Pediatrics, 24*, 148–154.

Prodromidis, M., Field, T., Arendt, R., Singer, L., Yando, P., & Bendell, D. (1995). Mothers touching newborns: A comparison of rooming-in versus minimal contact. *Birth, 22*, 196–200.

Räihä, H., Lehtonen, L., Huhtala, V., Saleva, K., & Korvenranta, H. (2002). Excessively crying infant in the family: Mother-infant, father-infant and mother-father interaction. *Child Care Health and Development, 28*, 419–429.

Rimsza, M. E., Schackner, R. A., Bowen, K. A., & Marshall, W. (2002). Can child death be prevented? *Pediatrics, 110*, e11.

Savino, F., & Oggero, R. (1996). Management of infantile colic. *Minerva Pediatrica, 48*, 313–319.

Scholz, K., & Samuels, C. A. (1992). Neonatal bathing and massage intervention with fathers: Behavioral effects 12 weeks after birth of the first baby (The Sunraysia Australia Intervention Project). *International Journal of Behavioral Development, 15*, 67–81.

Schum, T. R., McAuliffe, T. L., Simms, M. D., Walter, J. A., Lewis, M., & Pupp, R. (2001). Factors associated with toilet training in the 1990s. *Ambulatory Pediatrics, 1*, 79–86.

Schwebel, D. C., Brezausek, C. M., & Belsky, J. (2006). Does time spent in child care influence risk for unintentional injury? *Journal of Pediatric Psychology, 31*, 184–193.

Servin, A., Bohlin, G., & Berlin, L. (1999). Sex differences in 1-, 3-, and 5-year-olds' toy-choice in a structured play-session. *Scandinavian Journal of Psychology, 40*, 43–48.

Siegel, A. C., & Burton, R. V. (1999). Effects of baby walkers on motor and mental development in human infants. *Journal of Developmental and Behavioral Pediatrics, 5*, 355–361.

Skuladottir, A., Thome, M., & Ramel, A. (2005). Improving day and night sleep problems in infants by changing day time sleep rhythm: A single group before and after study. *International Journal of Nursing Studies, 42*, 843–850.

Socolar, R. R. S., Savage, E., Keyes-Elstein, L., & Evans, H. (2005). Factors that affect parental disciplinary practices of children aged 12–19 months. *Southern Medical Journal, 98*, 1181–1191.

Solomons, H. C., & Elardo, R. (1989). Biting injuries at a day care center. *Early Childhood Research Quarterly, 4*, 89–96.

Standley, J. M. (1998). The effects of music and multimodal stimulation on responses of premature infants in neonatal intensive care. *Pediatric Nursing, 24*, 532–538.

Standley, J. M., & Moore, R. S. (1995). Therapeutic effects of music and mother's voice on premature infants. *Pediatric Nursing, 21*, 509–512.

Stein, M. B., Chavira, D. A., & Jang, K. L. (2001). Bringing up a bashful baby: Developmental pathways to social phobia. *Psychiatric Clinics of North America, 24*, 661–675.

Stevens, B., Yamada, J., & Ohlsson, A. (2004). Sucrose analgesia in newborn infants undergoing painful procedures. *Cochrane Database of Systematic Reviews, 3*, CD001069.

St. John, W., Cameron, C., & McVeigh, C. (2005). Meeting the challenge of new fatherhood: The early weeks. *Journal of Obstetric, Gynecologic and Neonatal Nursing, 34*, 180–190.

Thomas, C. L., Simpson, S., Butler, C. C., & van der Voort, J. H. (2006). Oral or topical nasal steroids for hearing loss associated with otitis media with effusion in children (Cochrane review). *Cochrane Database of Systematic Reviews, 3*, CD001935.

Thompson, D. A., & Christakis, D. A. (2005). The association between television viewing and irregular sleep schedules among children less than 3 years of age. *Pediatrics, 116*, 851–856.

Tremblay, R. E., Nagin, D. S., Séguin, J. R., Zoccolillo, M., Zelazo, P. D., Boivin, M., et al. (2004). Physical aggression during early childhood: Trajectories and predictors. *Pediatrics, 114*(1), 43–50.

Vaile, L., Williamson, T., Waddell, A., & Taylor, G. (2006). Interventions for ear discharge associated with grommets (ventilation tubes). *Cochrane Database of Systematic Reviews, 2*, CD001933.

Vintzileos, A., Ananth, C., Smulian, J., Scorza, W., & Knuppel, R. (2002). The impact of prenatal care in the United States on preterm births in the presence and absence of antenatal high-risk conditions. *American Journal of Obstetrics and Gynecology, 187*, 1254–1257.

Vittrup, B., Holden, G. W., & Buck, J. (2006). Attitudes predict the use of physical punishment: A prospective study of the emergence of disciplinary practices. *Pediatrics, 117*, 2055–2064.

Wade, T., & Kendler, K. S. (2001). Parent, child, and social correlates of parental discipline style: A retrospective, multi-informant investigation with female twins. *Social Psychiatry and Psychiatric Epidemiology, 36*, 177–185.

White-Traut, R. (2004). Providing a nurturing environment for infants in adverse situations: Multisensory strategies for newborn care. *Journal of Midwifery and Women's Health, 49*, 36–41.

WHO Multicentre Growth Reference Study Group. (2006). Relationship between physical growth and motor development in the WHO child growth standards. *Acta Paediatrica, 49*(5), 96–101.

Yeargin-Allsopp, M., Rice, C., Karapurkar, T., Doernberg, N., Boyle, C., & Murphy, C. (2003). Prevalence of autism in a U.S. metropolitan area. *Journal of the American Medical Association, 289*, 49–55.

Zwaigenbaum, L., Bryson, S., Rogers, T., Roberts, W., Brian, J., & Szatmari, P. (2005). Behavioral manifestations of autism in the first year of life. *International Journal of Developmental Neuroscience, 2–3*, 143–152.

CHAPTER 32

Psychopharmacology as Practiced by Psychologists

Alan Poling, Kristal Ehrhardt, and Matthew Porritt

According to the *Oxford English Dictionary* (*OED*), the term "psychopharmacology" was first used in print by Mora in 1920 to refer to a yet to be developed science dealing with the behavioral effects of drugs (Macht & Mora, 1921). This meaning persists to the present, as indicated by the current *OED* definition: "Psychopharmacology: The branch of science concerned with the way drugs affect the mind and behavior." The mind, of course, cannot be directly assessed, but is studied indirectly by examining behavior, that is, what individuals say and do.

All drugs that affect behavior—broadly construed to include mood, cognitive status, and overt actions—are termed "psychoactive." Drugs that are prescribed with the purpose of improving behavior are called "psychotropic." All psychotropic drugs are psychoactive, but not all psychoactive drugs are psychotropic. The introduction of the first generally effective psychotropic drug, chlorpromazine (Thorazine), in the early 1950s revolutionized psychiatry and changed forever the practice of mental health.

Historically, only physicians prescribed psychotropic drugs. Over the past 20 years, however, the possibility of granting the privilege of prescribing psychotropic drugs to properly trained psychologists has become a highly visible, and hugely important, issue. The American Psychological Associations (APA) supports prescription privileges for psychologists, as do many state-level psychological associations. Two states recently enacted legislation allowing properly trained psychologists to prescribe these drugs, but there is continuing debate among psychologists as to whether or not prescription privileges are generally desirable. The issue is complex and we will examine it in a later section. But quite apart from the prescription privileges issue, psychologists have made and are making major contributions to the study of psychoactive drugs. We first examine some of those contributions.

PSYCHOLOGY AND THE STUDY OF DRUGS

Psychologists are expert in dividing the ongoing stream of behavior into meaningful units, in quantifying those units, in explaining why they occur, and in predicting and (sometimes) influencing future behavior. Their expertise in each of these areas has contributed to understanding the effects of psychoactive drugs.

Explanations of Behavior and Psychopharmacology: Mechanisms of Drug Action

Many important behaviors of humans and other animals are learned. That is, they occur through the processes of operant and classical conditioning. Operant conditioning is a form of learning in which the likelihood of occurrence of a particular response in a given situation is controlled primarily by its historical consequences in similar situations. If the consequences increase the likelihood of occurrence of the response, the process is termed reinforcement and the consequences are called reinforcers. If the consequences decrease the likelihood of occurrence of the response, the process is termed punishment and the consequences are called punishers.

Features of the environment that are present when consequences occur and subsequently exercise antecedent control over behavior are termed discriminative stimuli. Technically, a discriminative stimulus for reinforcement is a stimulus that evokes a response because in the past that kind of response has been more successful in producing reinforcement in the presence of that stimulus than in its absence. The classic example of operant conditioning involves Skinner's mildly food-deprived rats, which press a bar in the presence of a tone but not in its absence, because historically the bar-press response produced food (a reinforcer) in the presence of the tone but not in its absence. Regardless of whether or not the tone is present, substantial levels of bar pressing occur only when the rats are food-deprived. Food deprivation here is a motivational variable, specifically an establishing operation that increases the reinforcing capacity of food and increases the likelihood of occurrence of responses that historically produced food.

Unlike operant conditioning, classical (or respondent) conditioning is a form of learning in which behavior is controlled not by its consequences but by stimulus-stimulus pairings. Classical conditioning begins with a reflex, that is, an unlearned relation in which an unconditional stimulus elicits an unconditional response. By arranging conditions such that a previously neutral stimulus is repeatedly predictive of an unconditional stimulus, that neutral stimulus becomes established as a conditional stimulus, which reliably elicits a conditional response. The classic example involves Pavlov's mildly food-deprived dogs, in which food (unconditional stimulus) reflexively elicits salivation (unconditional response). By repeatedly presenting a sound (neutral stimulus) just before food (unconditional stimulus), the sound comes to elicit salivation (unconditional response) and is established as a conditional stimulus.

Understanding the processes of operant and classical conditioning provides a conceptual framework for examining behavioral mechanisms of drug action. "Mechanism of action" refers to a general drug effect at one level of analysis that produces (or at least, covaries with) another, usually more specific effect at another level of analysis. In lay terms, a drug's mechanism of action refers to how the drug "causes" or "works to produce" whatever effects are of interest. For example, chlorpromazine generally is effective in reducing what are referred to as the positive symptoms of Schizophrenia (hallucinations, thought disorders, bizarre behavior), which is one of the drug's most noteworthy effects (e.g., Baldessarini & Tarazi, 2006). The drug also produces adverse motor effects (rigidity, tremors, slowed movement, restlessness). These effects, which can be observed directly, covary with events at another level of analysis, specifically, antagonism of the neurotransmitter actions of dopamine by competitively blocking dopamine receptors (Julien, 2001).

Early observations indicated that effective antipsychotic medications reduced dopaminergic activity in the brain and reduced positive symptoms of Schizophrenia. In addition, researchers observed that chronic exposure to high doses of drugs that increased dopaminergic activity, such as amphetamine, produced changes in behavior closely resembling those characteristic of Schizophrenia. These findings led to the speculation that Schizophrenia resulted from metabolic errors leading to either (a) overproduction of dopamine in the limbic system or cortex of the brain, or (b) production of an endogenous amphetamine-like compound. Similarly, the finding that drugs useful in treating depression increased monoaminergic activity suggested that depression results from a deficit in serotonergic and/or noradrenergic activity (Baldessarini, 2000). Studies of family resemblance suggested that genetics played some role in both Schizophrenia and depression, and it was soon widely believed that both conditions resulted from inherited diseases of the brain that produced abnormal neurochemical activity, which in turn produced abnormal behavior.

These early biological models of mental illness were crude, even primitive, and ran into problems from the start. For example, antidepressant drugs begin increasing serotonergic activity as soon as they are administered, but clinical benefits take weeks to appear. Also, no one has succeeded in demonstrating consistent neurochemical differences between people who are and are not diagnosed with depression or Schizophrenia. Finally, the role of inheritance in depression and Schizophrenia is rather weak, and the environment clearly plays a role in their genesis. How this occurs was not considered in the early models. In response to these problems, more sophisticated models have been proposed. They, too, are inadequate to explain mental illness (e.g., Baldessarini, 2000; Julien, 2001). Neuroscientists are making dramatic progress in understanding the human brain, however, and it is possible—perhaps even probable—than reasonably comprehensive, testable, and confirmed biological models of particular behavior disorders will soon appear.

Be that as it may, biological models developed to this point have had an enormous influence on how physicians, psychologists, and laypeople conceptualize mental illness. For many people, the signs (occurrence of undesired behaviors or absence of desired behavior) and symptoms (patient-reported affect and cognitive status) that lead to a clinical diagnosis are a manifestation of underlying pathophysiology. Effective treatment, regardless of its nature, corrects the underlying pathology, leading to alleviation of signs and symptoms. Under this model, drugs correct the pathology directly, whereas psychological interventions do so indirectly.

Although it has been criticized as not being supported by compelling evidence and focusing attention away from environmental variables that strongly affect the genesis, course, and treatment of mental illness (e.g., Malott, in press; Whitaker, 2002), this general view is widely held. Referred to variously as the medical, biological, or disease model of mental illness, this view at the extreme supports the notion that each condition listed in the *Diagnostic and Statistical Manual of Mental*

Disorders, fourth edition (*DSM-IV,* American Psychiatric Association, 1994) is a discrete disease with known signs and symptoms and a potentially specifiable neurochemical cause. This conception, however popular, is difficult to defend scientifically. There is, nonetheless, good evidence that particular disorders are fundamentally biological with strong genetic components, even if the specific structural and functional differences between people with and without the disorder cannot presently be specified precisely, if at all. For example, Russell Barkley, a psychologist well known for his research involving children with Attention-Deficit/Hyperactivity Disorder (ADHD), responded as follows when asked by a reporter for PBS's *Frontline* (2006), "So this [ADHD] is a biological disorder?"

> It's largely a biological disorder. It has many causes, but all of the known causes fall within the realm of neurology and genetics. We can rule out the social environment, such as bad parenting, intolerant teachers, the breakdown of the American family, a decline in family values, excess amount of TV viewing or video games. These have all been proposed as causes of ADHD. But there's no evidence that we can find that will substantiate them.
>
> All of the evidence that keeps turning up in our research points to genetics and neurology as being largely responsible for the excessive behavior and the poor self-control that we see in these children. So I think we can safely say that what we've learned in the past 10 years is that environmental causes of ADHD are not credible. They do not account for the substantial amount of scientific findings that exist on this disorder today.

Regardless of whether the drug in question is or is not a psychotropic medication, most of the interest in mechanisms of drug action has focused on the relation between neuropharmacological and behavioral events, and receptor models of drug action have proven invaluable in predicting and explaining drug effects. Some behavioral psychologists, however, have emphasized behavioral, not neuropharmacological, mechanisms of drug action. Behavioral mechanisms of drug action involve the stimulus properties of drugs in the context of operant and classical conditioning and the manner in which drugs modulate the actions of nondrug stimuli (Thompson, 1981; Thompson & Schuster, 1968). More specifically:

> By behavioral mechanism of drug action, we refer to a description of a drug's effect on a given behavioral system (locus) in terms of some more general set of environmental principles regulating behavior. Specifying the behavioral mechanism(s) responsible for an observed effect involves: (a) identifying the environmental variables which typically regulate the behavior in question, and (b) characterizing the manner in which the influence of these variables is altered by the drug. In some instances, the drug assumes the status of a behavioral variable per se, rather than modulating an existing environmental variable. (Thompson, 1981, p. 3)

In passing, it should be noted that the concept of behavioral mechanisms of drug action was developed and popularized by a psychologist, Travis Thompson, and his colleagues. This concept is abundantly supported by demonstrations that certain drugs inherently have, or can acquire through learning, the capacity to function as unconditional, conditional, discriminative, reinforcing, and punishing stimuli and as motivational operations (Poling & Byrne, 2000; Thompson & Pickens, 1971).

Especially significant is the demonstration that drug self-administration involves learned behavior that is maintained, in substantial part, by the short-term reinforcing effects of the drug in question (Laraway, Snycerski, Byrne, & Poling, 2000). Harmful patterns of self-administration, that is, drug abuse and drug addiction, are controlled by the same classes of variables that affect other kinds of excessive learned behavior, such as overeating. This conception of drug abuse suggests strategies for treatment, which often involve arranging the environment such that (a) the client's drug use is consistently monitored, (b) abstinence is consistently reinforced, (c) drug use results in loss of reinforcers, and (d) the density of nondrug reinforcers is sufficient to compete with the reinforcing effects of the drug (Higgins et al., 1991).

A study by Higgins et al. (1993) illustrates the potential value of this approach. They randomly assigned 38 cocaine-abusing clients to a 12-step counseling program or to a program that involved community-based reinforcement and vouchers, earned by producing drug-free urine samples, that could be exchanged for appropriate reinforcers. As part of the community-based reinforcement program, the clients attended behavior therapy sessions that involved employment counseling, assertiveness training, relaxation training, and counseling that targets participation in non-drug-related social and recreational activities. These therapy sessions were intended to increase drug users' participation in activities incompatible with drug use, which, given that they were sufficiently reinforcing, should compete effectively against drug-related activities.

They appeared to do so in many cases, in that only 5% of the clients in the 12-step program achieved 16 weeks of continuous abstinence, whereas 42% of clients in the behavioral program did so. Moreover, the former program appeared to be less acceptable to clients, insofar as only 11% of them completed 24 weeks of treatment, whereas 58% of those in the behavioral treatment did so.

Behavioral Mechanisms of Clinical Drug Effects

In principle, it should be possible to isolate the behavioral mechanisms involved in the beneficial effects produced by psychotropic drugs. For example, objects and events that previously were effective positive reinforcers (i.e., their delivery strengthened the behaviors that produced them) for a given person appear to lose their reinforcing capacity when she or he becomes depressed. Effective psychotropic medications might work, at least in part, by reestablishing reinforcing capacity, and they appear to do so.

With many disorders, however, no one has successfully categorized the characteristic changes in behavior in terms of behavioral processes. Consider, for example, how a person changes with the onset of Schizophrenia. Overt verbalizations become impoverished in terms of amount and content; they reflect delusional thoughts and auditory hallucinations. Anhedonia—a general lack of interest in once important objects and events (i.e., stimuli)—appears and self-care diminishes. Stimulus control, that is, the ability of objects and events to engender or suppress particular responses, clearly has changed, as has the capacity of certain objects and events to serve as reinforcers. But the generation and following of rules—verbal descriptions of relations among stimuli and responses—also changes. Human behavior is unique in that it can be affected by descriptions of relations, such as the consequences of a particular response (e.g., "If you turn left at the second light, the diner will be two miles ahead on your right"), as well as by actual exposure to those relations. Delusions involve counterfactual rules (e.g., "They listen through the TV; if you turn it on they'll know what I'm thinking and hurt me"). It is unclear why people eventually diagnosed with Schizophrenia come to generate and follow counterfactual rules, or how psychotropic drugs reverse the process. The absence of viable, comprehensive behavioral models of mental illness makes it impossible to relate therapeutic drug effects to behavioral mechanisms of drug action. Moreover, the absence of such models appears to increase the appeal of biological models.

Nonetheless, researchers have had some success in relating the effects of psychotropic drugs to behavioral mechanisms of action. For example, Northup, Fusilier, Swanson, Roane, and Borrero (1997) examined the possibility that methylphenidate (Ritalin) functions as a motivational operation (MO) when administered to children diagnosed with ADHD. In brief, an MO is a stimulus that alters the reinforcing (or punishing) effectiveness of another stimulus. Establishing operations (EOs) increase reinforcing (or punishing) effectiveness; abolishing operations (AOs) decrease it (Laraway, Snycerski, Michael, & Poling, 2003).

Northup and his colleagues (1997) studied the behavior of three children diagnosed with ADHD who were receiving methylphenidate each day and attending a summer day treatment program. One of their activities at the camp was solving math problems. Solving a specified number of problems was reinforced with coupons that could be exchanged, depending on the color of the coupon selected, for edible items, other tangible items, activities, teacher attention, peer attention, and escape from academic programs. The effectiveness of each type of reinforcer was determined based on the number of coupons representing that class of reinforcer that a child selected.

The distribution of choices across reinforcer types was examined for each child when methylphenidate and placebo were administered. For all three children, methylphenidate changed the value of at least one type of reinforcer. For example, in the placebo condition, one boy's most preferred reinforcer type was edible items. At 20 mg methylphenidate, however, both activities and tangible nonfood items were preferred over food. Similar results were obtained with the other two children. In all three, activities functioned as more potent reinforcers following methylphenidate than following placebo. In contrast, edible items were more effective reinforcers following placebo than following methylphenidate. In technical terms, the drug served as an EO for activities as a reinforcer, and as an AO for food as a reinforcer.

The capacity of methylphenidate to act as an MO is important with respect to one of the potential side effects of the drug: its capacity to alter the effectiveness of behavioral interventions. That is, the effectiveness of behavior change programs that utilize reinforcement—and most behavioral interventions used to treat children diagnosed with ADHD do so—will differ in the presence and absence of methylphenidate if the drug alters the reinforcing capacity of the objects and events arranged to strengthen appropriate behavior. In addition, reinforcer assessment conducted in the absence of the drug may yield information that is inaccurate in the presence of the drug, and vice versa. Clearly, the demonstration that methylphenidate acts as an MO in applied situations helps to explain how the drug may influence clinically significant behavior in children diagnosed with ADHD.

Methods for Assessing Drug Effects: Basic Research

Quantifying behavior is an important aspect of psychology. Many of the procedures developed by psychologists to quantify behavior and to examine the effects of nonpharmacological variables thereon were subsequently adopted for the study of drug effects. Substantial early impetus for doing so came from a 1956 conference sponsored by the New York Academy of Sciences. The conference, called "Techniques for the Study of the Behavioral Effects of Drugs," featured prominent behavioral psychologists, including Herrnstein, Miller, Morse, Sidman, and Skinner. They forcefully made the case that the methods characteristic of the experimental analysis of behavior were well suited for studying drugs.

The conference occurred shortly after chlorpromazine was introduced into psychiatric practice, and the remarkable success of the drug galvanized interest in basic and applied studies of its effects. Moreover, that success generated a heated quest to develop animal models that effectively screened other drugs for antipsychotic actions. Pickens (1977) reported that between 1917 and 1954 only 28 studies examining drug effects on learned behavior were published in English-language journals, whereas 274 such studies appeared from 1955 to 1963. The vast majority of these studies involved basic research. That is, their intent was to disclose the effects of particular drugs, the mechanisms responsible for those effects, and/or the variables that modulated them, not to help people directly.

Many early studies examined drug effects on learning and performance in mazes. Others were concerned with how drugs affected responding under various schedules of reinforcement. Research in both areas has continued to the present day, but scientists have developed many additional strategies for examining specific aspects of drug action. These strategies are discussed at length by Buccafusco (2001) and van Haaren (1993). Although most basic research has involved nonhuman subjects, a substantial number of studies with humans have appeared. Table 32.1, adapted from Snycerski, Laraway, and Poling (2000), provides examples of some of the behavioral domains examined in these studies and the procedures used to quantify those domains. Psychologists have made substantial contributions to the development and use of these procedures and thereby have played a quintessential role in basic psychopharmacological research.

Methods for Assessing Drug Effects: Applied Research

Psychotropic drugs have some special characteristics (e.g., slow onset of clinical effects) that must be considered in their evaluation. In addition, there are established conventions for clinical drug studies, such as the use of placebo-controlled and double-blind conditions, and determination of dose-response relations (see Gadow & Poling, 1988). Nonetheless, the value of a medication for treating a particular disorder can be determined via the same general tactics and strategies that are used to

Table 32.1 Procedures Commonly Used in Basic Psychopharmacological Research

Domain	Examples of Procedures
Arousal, mood, and activity	Profile of mood states
	Addiction research center inventory
	Visual analogue scale
	Beck Depression Inventory
	Electroencephalogram
	Skin temperature
	Skin resistance
	Heart rate
Perceptual performance	Critical frequency of fusion
	Signal detection
Cognitive performance	Repeated acquisition
	Delayed matching to sample
	Digit-symbol-substitution test
	Vigilance tasks
Motor performance	Reaction time
	Tapping rate
	Hand steadiness
	Pursuit rotor
	Driving simulations
Self-administration	Progressive-ratio schedules
	Concurrent schedules
	Discrete trials
	Single-access procedures
Motivation	Progressive-ratio schedules
	Contingent activity procedures
Drug discrimination	Two-choice procedures
	Three-choice procedures
	Stimulus equivalence procedures

From "Assessing Drug Effects in Humans: Basic Research" (pp. 111–140), by S. Snycerski, S. Laraway, and A. Poling, 2000, in A. Poling and T. Byrne (Eds.), *Introduction to Behavioral Pharmacology,* Reno, NV: Context Press. Adapted with Permission.

evaluate other behavior-change interventions (e.g., cognitive-behavioral therapy). There is no mystery to designing a clinical drug study: One determines whether any independent variable (including medication) affects a behavior of interest by comparing levels of behavior (the dependent variable) when the independent variable is and is not operative, or is operative at different levels (e.g., doses). Factors other than the independent variable that might affect the dependent variable (extraneous variables) are held constant across conditions or rendered inoperative. If appropriate data analysis reveals that levels of the dependent variable differ significantly when treatment is and is not present (or is present at different levels), it is logical to assume that behavior changed as a function of treatment, which is therefore deemed effective.

Many psychologists are truly expert in evaluating the effects of behavior-change interventions, and a substantial number of these experts have done extensive and excellent work in clinical drug assessment. As a case in point, consider Russell

Barkley (1998), who, as noted previously, is a leading ADHD researcher. For more than two decades, he has studied the pharmacological and nonpharmacological management of ADHD and translated the findings of his and others' research into practical, effective strategies for everyday use (e.g., Barkley, 2000). As the case of Barkley illustrates, psychologists can make a major contribution to clinical drug evaluation, even under circumstances in which they do not prescribe drugs themselves.

Several authors have proposed that the tactics and strategies of applied behavior analysis can be especially valuable in clinical psychopharmacology (e.g., Barlow & Hersen, 1984; Kollins, Ehrhardt, & Poling, 2000; Schroeder, 1985). In brief, this approach is underpinned by five beliefs (Poling & Ehrhardt, 1999; Poling & LeSage, 1995):

1. Intensive study of a few participants through the use of within-subject research designs (e.g., multiple-baseline, withdrawal) is a fruitful research strategy.
2. Behaviors targeted for change by a drug should be measured accurately and repeatedly in individual participants.
3. Variable data are best dealt with by isolating the responsible extraneous variables, not by statistical manipulations.
4. Visual (graphic) analysis of data for individual participants is a viable alternative, or adjunct, to statistical analysis.
5. Social validity data, evaluating the acceptability of the goals, methods, and outcomes of treatment to consumers, is desirable.

As Dermer and Hoch (1999) point out, it is common for authors of research methods texts to assert that the within-subject experiments characteristic of applied behavior analysis involve what Campbell and Stanley (1963) termed "quasi-experimental designs" with "low external validity." That is, their findings cannot be widely generalized. Certain between-subjects designs, in contrast, are described as producing results with much greater generalizability. The usual, and reasonable, argument is that between-subjects experiments characteristically involve the study of a clearly defined sample of subjects who are selected to be representative of a larger population with defined characteristics. If this is the case, then inferential statistics provide a basis for describing the true state of affairs in the population, given the results obtained in the sample selected for study.

Although this logic is sound, clinical drug evaluations that involve protected populations (e.g., children with autism) often are limited to small convenience samples; therefore, conventional between-subjects research designs (e.g., randomized between-groups) are inappropriate. Within-subjects designs, such as the multiple-baseline and withdrawal, appear to be the best alternative, even though their findings cannot be generalized with confidence to the population of ultimate concern (e.g., all children with autism). They should, however, extend to people who are very similar to the individuals who were studied. Whether or not this is true is determined by systematically replicating the study. Eventually, the range of conditions under which the drug is useful is established, and valuable prescription guidelines can be established. Although some research in this vein has appeared, it seems that psychologists have had little success in convincing the medical profession that the strategy is useful. Should they eventually do so, there is potential to expand the literature in areas where further research is badly needed.

Everyday Drug Assessment

Psychotropic drugs are unique among medications in that they are used to deal with problems that are defined by, measured in terms of, and best understood at the level of overt behavior. The effects of these drugs on the biological processes responsible for the signs and symptoms characteristic of particular disorders are incompletely understood, and clinical effectiveness cannot be evaluated at this level of analysis. Therefore, clinical evaluations of psychotropic drugs must assess whether medication significantly improves some targeted aspect(s) of the participant's behavior without producing intolerable adverse reactions (side effects). To determine whether a pharmacological intervention is successful in treating a behavior disorder, three questions must be answered: (1) What were the desired effects of the medication? (2) Were those effects obtained? (3) Were there any significant adverse reactions? These are easy questions to ask but not to answer, whether in the context of formal research or in practical everyday drug evaluations (Kollins et al., 2000).

As Sprague and Werry (1971) pointed out 35 years ago, every prescription of a psychotropic medication is in essence an experiment in which the physician and other care providers hypothesize that administering a specific drug will produce a desired change in one or more aspects of a client's behavior. In the context of controlled research, the essential four features of a sound drug evaluation are that (1) treatment effects must be adequately measured, (2) medication must be administered according to the experimental regimen, (3) experimental conditions and their sequencing must allow observed changes in behavior to be attributed with confidence to the drug, and (4) data analysis must be adequate for detecting clinically important changes in client behavior. If these conditions are met, the evaluation is, in principle, sound.

These same characteristics are important in the practical evaluation of medications, although assessment procedures employed outside research settings rarely meet the rigorous standards advocated by scientists. When, for instance, a child diagnosed with ADHD receives methylphenidate for the first time, the child's parents, teachers, and physician are not interested in conducting a study worthy of presentation, but only in determining whether the drug is an appropriate treatment. An abundant scientific literature suggests that it is likely to be effective in a given individual who displays the behaviors that lead to a diagnosis of ADHD (restlessness, impulsivity, short attention span, excessive motor activity), but exceptions have been reported (some children show little or no positive response to the drug), and the most effective dose can vary. Therefore, the response of each young person with ADHD to methylphenidate needs to be monitored.

When competent adults contract for treatment by a physician, the evaluation process is relatively simple: The client and physician agree on treatment goals and a medication, and the treatment is successful, at least to some extent, if the client deems it so and the physician agrees and also detects no serious side effects. Evaluation is complicated, however, when the client, by virtue of age or disability, is not able to decide whether to initiate or continue drug treatment. As Greiner (1958) pointed out soon after chlorpromazine was introduced:

> Sensible adult patients will usually balk when a drug is causing symptoms, but the very young and the very old are forced to take drugs, can't complain or stop on experiencing toxic symptoms, may not even connect them with the drug. The mentally deficient of any size or age cannot protect themselves either, and they also merit special care to avoid toxic doses.

The need for special care in assessing drug effects in people with mental retardation (and other developmental disabilities) is especially important in view of the lack of persuasive evidence of effectiveness in this population. In summarizing the most comprehensive recent review of psychopharmacology and mental retardation, Matson et al. (2000) concluded:

> Our findings were startling and consistent with Baumeister and Sevin's findings in 1990 [Baumeister and Sevin conducted a similarly comprehensive prior review]. Professionals continue to medicate individuals in their care despite a lack of a sound research base to support their treatment decisions. While a small amount of research does exist, it is seriously flawed from a research design perspective. The studies routinely lack appropriate experimental control, and lack reliable measures of drug effect, collateral behaviors, and side effects. Methodological controls are far short of psychological treatment in the field with little improvement over precious decades. This trend is extremely disappointing given the dangerous and restrictive nature of these treatment options.

Johnny Matson is one of a substantial number of psychologists whose conceptual and empirical work has major implications for the everyday use of psychotropic drugs. As regards drug effects in people with developmental disabilities, Matson et al. (2000) are not alone in their skepticism. For example, in reviewing studies examining the effects of antipsychotic medications for challenging behavior in people with intellectual disorder, Brylewski and Duggan (1999, p. 360) reported that they could find only three studies that could be classified as randomized controlled trials: "These trials provided no evidence as to whether antipsychotic medication does or does not help adults with [intellectual disorder] and challenging behavior."

Similar results have been found for persons receiving dual diagnoses of intellectual disability and Schizophrenia. In a review of studies that examined the effectiveness of antipsychotic medication in people dually diagnosed, Duggan and Brylewski (1999) found only one relevant randomized controlled trial, which was published over 40 years ago (i.e., Foote, 1958). These authors found that there is no empirical evidence that antipsychotic medications are, or are not, effective in individuals with developmental disabilities and Schizophrenia. Until methodologically sound trials are conducted, practitioners will have to rely on personal experience as well as extrapolations from studies with individuals with Schizophrenia and "normal" intelligence. These extrapolations may or may not be valid (Duggan & Brylewski, 1999).

Since 1949, when the "Boulder Conference on Graduate Education in Clinical Psychology" was held, the scientist-practitioner model has powerfully influenced clinical psychology, as well as other applied subdisciplines, such as school psychology and organizational behavior management. Three key provisions of this model, discussed in detail by others (e.g., Hayes, Barlow, & Nelson-Gray, 1999; Soldz & McCullough, 1999), are these:

1. Psychologists should use assessment and treatment procedures that have been scientifically validated. That is, whenever possible, applied psychologists are expected to stay abreast of the scientific literature relevant to the areas in which they conduct assessments and arrange treatments, and to use only those techniques supported by the results of methodologically rigorous research.

2. Psychologists should monitor the response of each individual who is assessed and treated to ensure that she or he actually benefits from these processes. Even empirically validated techniques may be ineffective or even harmful for some seemingly appropriate clients.

3. Psychologists should work with other health professions to improve the quality of care provided. This involves contributing the psychologists' expertise to health care teams and ensuring that those teams function in a manner consistent with the scientist-practitioner model.

We have contended elsewhere that these provisions, if widely upheld, would dramatically improve how psychotropic drugs are used in people with developmental disabilities (Poling, 1994; Poling & Ehrhardt, 1998; Poling, Laraway, Ehrhardt, Jennings, & Turner, 2004). Of course, the virtues of the scientist practitioner model are not limited to psychologists; psychiatrists and other physicians who rely on psychotropic medications of proven worth and monitor the effects of those medications carefully can provide excellent care with no involvement from psychologists. However, given that psychologists typically receive extensive training in behavioral assessment, we have advocated for a team approach in which well-trained psychologists and physicians work with other concerned individuals to provide high-quality drug treatments. Such treatments ensure that:

- The goals of treatment are clear, quantitative, and in the patient's best interest.
- The choice of a drug and dose for initially treating a particular patient are consistent with the best available scientific literature.
- Subsequent treatment decisions are made in view of meaningful information regarding the patient's response to the drug.
- Drug therapy is flexible and integrated with nonpharmacological interventions.
- Properly trained psychologists can do much to enhance the quality of drug treatment, regardless of whether or not they actually prescribe.

PRESCRIPTION PRIVILEGES FOR PSYCHOLOGISTS

Up to this point, we have endeavored to show that psychologists who do not pre-scribe drugs have made major contributions to many areas of psychopharmacology and potentially could do even more. One thing that we have not considered is the possibility that they could prescribe psychotropic drugs. Since 1990, 14 states have considered legislation to grant psychologists limited prescription privileges. Alaska, California, Florida, Georgia, Hawaii, Illinois, Missouri, Montana, Tennessee, and Texas rejected the legislation. In 2002, New Mexico became the first state allowing psychologists to prescribe drugs. It was followed in 2004 by Louisiana. Both states allow psychologists who meet certain criteria to prescribe psychotropic drugs inde-pendently. Too little time has passed to allow for meaningful evaluation of the effects of allowing psychologists to prescribe in New Mexico and Louisiana; whether or not psychologists should be allowed to prescribe drugs is a contentious issue, as it has been for the past 15 years.

A recent search of the PsychInfo database using "prescription privileges" as the keyword revealed 163 entries. Of them, 160 appeared from 1986 to 2006. Their distribution across years is shown in Figure 32.1. Clearly, there is a substantial literature relevant to whether or not psychologists should be allowed to prescribe drugs, and it is growing rapidly. This section summarizes that literature. In doing so, we provide an overview of past and current events relevant to psychologists' prescribing drugs and summarize arguments for and against their doing so. More detailed coverage is available elsewhere (e.g., Hayes & Heiby, 1998b; Lavoie & Barone, 2006; Sammons, Page, & Levant, 2003).

Historical Overview

In the United States, the Federal Food, Drug and Cosmetic Act, passed in 1938, determines which medications can be sold over the counter and which are available

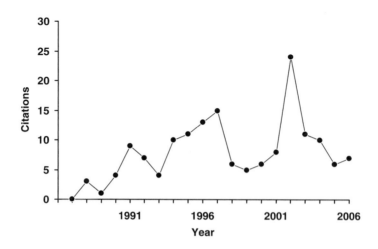

Figure 32.1   Number of publications listed in PsychInfo that used "prescription privileges" as a key word.

only by prescription (U.S. Food and Drug Administration, 2007). State laws, however, determine the professions that are allowed to prescribe, as well as (a) whether they can do so with or without physician supervision and (b) whether they can prescribe all classes of medication or only those relevant to their discipline. In every state, physicians can prescribe all medications independently. Other professions are more limited. Dentists, for example, can prescribe independently, but only those medications relevant to their practice (e.g., antibiotics, analgesics).

From its inception in the late nineteenth century until the onset of World War II, psychology was primarily an academic discipline concerned with understanding human behavior. Freudian psychoanalysis was the predominant treatment, and it was available to relatively few people. There were not sufficient psychiatrists available to serve the mental health needs of personnel returning from the war, and the Veterans Administration (VA) was severely taxed in trying to treat those people. In response, the VA dramatically extended the range of services they allowed psychologists to provide, including the delivery of psychotherapy under the supervision of psychiatrists (Lavoie & Fleet, 2002). Psychiatrists objected, claming that psychologists were not properly trained to provide psychotherapy, but an ever-increasing number of psychologists disagreed. In large part due to effective lobbying by APA and affiliated organizations, by the end of the 1950s psychologists were widely recognized as legitimate providers of clinical services. This recognition was codified in state licensure legislation, which specifies the range of activities in which properly trained and duly licensed (or, in some cases, certified) psychologists can legally engage. For example, in our home state of Michigan, Public Act 368 (Michigan Legislature, 2007):

> Defines the practice of psychology as the rendering to individuals, groups, organizations, or the public of services involving the application of principles, methods, and procedures of understanding, predicting, and influencing behavior for the purposes of the diagnosis, assessment related to diagnosis, prevention, amelioration, or treatment of mental or emotional disorders, disabilities or behavioral adjustment problems by means of psychotherapy, counseling, behavior modification, hypnosis, biofeedback techniques, psychological tests, or other verbal or behavioral means. The practice of psychology does not include the practice of medicine such as prescribing drugs, performing surgery, or administering electro-convulsive therapy.

Psychology flourished in the 1960s and 1970s and into the 1980s. Major conceptual advances, including those associated with behavior analysis and cognitive psychology, were accompanied by the development of effective interventions for various behavioral disorders. Cognitive-behavioral treatment for depression is an obvious case in point. Effective behavior-change interventions were developed and used not only by clinical psychologists, but by organizational and industrial, educational, and school psychologists as well. By 1980, several areas of psychology were well established and providing invaluable services to a wide range of individuals and organizations.

By that same year, the use of psychotropic drugs to treat a wide range of behavior disorders was firmly established. The success of chlorpromazine was soon followed by the introduction of several other antipsychotic drugs, as well as antidepressants (monoamine oxidase inhibitors such as phenelzine [Nardil] and tranylcypromine [Parnate], tricyclics such as amitriptyline [Elavil, Endep] and imipramine [Tofranil]), and anxiolytics (primarily benzodiazepines such as diazepam [Valium]). The use of stimulants (such as methylphenidate [Ritalin]) to treat children diagnosed with hyperactivity (or Attention-Deficit Disorder) became more prevalent, and lithium became popular for the treatment of Bipolar Disorder. A bit later, in the early 1980s, the serotonin-specific reuptake inhibitors, beginning with fluoxetine (Prozac), were introduced for the treatment of depression. They soon became the most prescribed psychotropic medications.

Later still, a new group of antipsychotic drugs, labeled "atypical" because they produced fewer motor disturbances, was introduced. This group includes risperidone (Risperdal) and clozapine (Clozaril). A large number of studies in addition to the initial clinical trials required by the FDA prior to marketing have demonstrated that various psychotropic drugs are reasonably safe and at least somewhat effective (although the evidence in some cases is not overwhelming). The availability of effective psychotropic medications literally revolutionized psychiatry in terms of (a) increasing the effectiveness of available interventions, (b) fostering broad acceptance of a biological model of mental illness, and (c) generating widespread demand for the pharmacological management of behavior disorders.

More than 50 different drugs currently are FDA-approved as psychotropic medications. In 2005, over 10 million prescriptions were written in the United States for each of nine such drugs. The names of those drugs, the number of prescriptions written, and the overall ranking of each are shown in Table 32.2. These data make it clear that psychotropic medications play a central role in the current treatment of behavior disorders. As further evidence, a sample of practicing psychologists recently reported that 43% of their current patients were using psychotropic medication (VandenBos & Williams, 2000). Moreover, 94% of those psychologists indicated that they had consulted with physicians about changing the medications of joint clients.

As the pharmacological management of behavior disorders flourished, two major forces came into play that eventually led some psychologists to push for

Table 32.2   Psychotropic Drugs with >10 Million Prescriptions in 2005

Nonproprietary Name	Proprietary Name	Overall Rank	Number of Prescriptions
Alprazolam	Xanax	9	34,230,000
Sertraline	Zoloft	16	26,976,000
Fluoxetine	Prozac	29	21,403,000
Lorazepam	Ativan	30	19,002,000
Paroxetine	Paxil	38	18,889,000
Trazodone	Desyrel	48	14,505,000
Amitriptyline	Elavil	50	14,385,000
Diazepam	Valium	60	12,093,000
Bupropion	Wellbutrin	66	11,044,000

Source: The Top 300 Prescriptions for 2005 by Number of U.S. Prescriptions Dispensed, by RxList, 2005. Available from www.rxlist.com/top300/.

prescription privileges (Frank, Conti, & Goldman, 2005; Lavoie & Barone, 2006; Sanua, 1998). One, discussed previously, was conceptual, and took the form of growing acceptance among laypeople and health care providers alike of biological models of mental illness and of the logic and effectiveness of pharmacological management of those disorders.

A second was economic, leading ultimately to diminished job prospects for doctoral-level clinical psychologists. In brief, graduate schools had saturated the market with such psychologists, even as it was being demonstrated (e.g., Christiansen & Jacobson, 1994; Dawes, 1994) that non-doctoral-level professionals from a number of disciplines (e.g., psychology, nursing, social work) could provide effective, and relatively inexpensive, treatment for many psychological problems (Lavoie & Barone, 2006). As managed health care came to dominate the provision of mental health services, there was increased reliance on non-doctoral-level professionals and fewer lucrative positions for doctoral-level psychologists (Chiefetz & Salloway, 1984; Cummings, 1995). Concurrently, there was more money available for pharmacological treatments (Frank et al., 2005).

According to Frank et al. (2005), expenditures on psychotropic drugs in the United States in 1987, 1992, 1997, and 2001 were, in billions, $2.77, $3.83, $9.04, and $17.83, respectively. Expenditures on psychotropic drugs increased more than sixfold over this period, and the percentage of mental health spending devoted to them increased from 7.7% to 21% (Frank et al., 2005). Much of this money went to large pharmaceutical companies, which were growing enormously and exerting increasing—and sometimes harmful—influence on the medical profession (Antonuccio & Danton, 2003), but a substantial sum went to physicians who prescribed psychotropic drugs. Perhaps surprisingly, most of them were not psychiatrists, but general practitioners.

In what was in hindsight a predictable reaction to emerging financial and conceptual changes in the field of mental health, during the 1980s some influential psychologists and their allies in government began to advocate for prescription privileges. The APA, which currently has over 150,000 members, played a crucial role in the advocacy, with much of the impetus coming from members of Divisions 12 (Society of Clinical Psychology) and 42 (Psychologists in Independent Practice). Since 2000, a strong push for prescription privileges has come from Division 55, the American Society for the Advancement of Pharmacotherapy, which, according to the APA web site (APA, n.d., para 2), was created specifically "to enhance psychological treatments combined with psychopharmacological medications." Sanua (1998) details the contentious political history of the prescription movement within and outside APA.

As he relates, in 1981 APA convened the Psychologists' Use of Physical Intervention Committee to consider prescription privileges. The committee completed a report in 1981, with a revision in 1986 (see Sanua, 1998). Those reports did not specifically endorse prescription privileges, but instead suggested that psychologists should play a role in pharmacotherapy as dictated by consumer demand (Hayes, Walser, & Bach, 2002). In 1989, APA established an Ad Hoc Task Force on Psychopharmacology to study the issue of pharmacotherapy further; its report appeared in 1992 (APA, 1992). The report outlined three levels of training in psychopharmacology, with the appropriate level determined by a psychologist's degree of involvement in the prescribing practice. Level 3, which has generated the most interest, is for psychologists who actually will prescribe. Level 2 is for collaborative practice, in which the psychologist would partner with a physician to determine the need for and monitor the effects of psychotropic drugs. Level 1 is for any psychologist providing mental health services and essentially provides an overview of psychopharmacology.

In 1995, in response to a request for support of a bill establishing prescription privileges in California, APA's Council of Representatives approved a resolution making prescription privileges for psychologists a major policy directive for the association. From this time forward, APA formally supported prescription privileges (Cullen and Newman, 1997). In 1996, the organization adopted a model prescription bill and training curriculum, and in 2000 it announced that APA-supplied insurance will cover prescription-related activities in any state where such activities are legal. Many APA-affiliated state organizations also have supported prescription privileges.

Many psychologists, however, have not. As Sanua (1998) relates, early on most APA members (and other psychologists) had little knowledge of or interest in the prescription privileges issue. Interest was galvanized by the APA's activities, by the 1985 introduction in Hawaii of legislation to study prescription privileges for psychologists, and by Congress directing the U.S. Department of Defense (DOD) in 1988 to establish a pilot project, called the Psychopharmacology Demonstration Project (PDP), to train psychologists to prescribe psychotropic medications. It became operational in 1991; 10 military psychologists completed training between 1991 and 1997 and were granted the right to prescribe psychotropic medications. Each received a total of 660 hours of academic training and 1,900 hours of clinical training.

By 1996, three national psychology associations, the Society for a Science of Clinical Psychology, the Council of University Directors of Clinical Psychology Programs, and the American Association of Applied and Preventative Psychology (AAAPP), had formally opposed prescription privileges for psychologists (Hayes & Heiby, 1996). For example, following a 1996 conference, AAAPP members generally agreed on three conclusions (Hayes & Heiby, 1998, p. vi):

1. The prescriptions privileges proposal is polarizing the discipline.

2. Psychology's resources should be focused on advocating the profession to managed care. Doing so will involve the development of treatment standards and the promotion of integrated care.

3. Psychologists wishing to obtain prescription privileges at this time are encouraged to obtained an advanced degree in nursing, a physician's assistant degree, or the like in order to develop more experience with the psychology/prescription privilege without first having to alter the discipline and its training focus.

Attendees also generally agreed that the push for prescription privileges was premature and that further reasoned discussion among psychologists should occur before any introduction of legislation seeking such privileges. This did not occur.

The move to secure prescription privileges continued unabated, and at present, psychologists wishing to obtain prescription privileges have options not available in 1996: They can obtain proper training and licensure and work in New Mexico or Louisiana. Whether or not this is good continues to be debated heatedly.

A recent meta-analysis of opinion data from 16 studies concerned with the prescription privileges debate (Walters, 2001) examined responses (agree, disagree) to three statements: (1) Properly trained psychologists should be allowed to prescribe psychotropic drugs; (2) APA should advocate in favor of prescription privileges for psychologists; and (3) I would personally seek prescription privileges should they become available. Collectively, these statements were taken to constitute the "prescription privilege agenda." Results indicated that "there was minimal consensus and a general split of opinion on the advisability of pursuing the prescription agenda" (p. 119). When data for all three statements were summed, there was no statistically significant difference in the number of respondents who agreed (52%; i.e., who supported the agenda) and the number who disagreed (35%; i.e., who opposed the agenda). Only statement 1 engendered significantly higher levels of agreement than disagreement.

The Department of Defense Psychopharmacology Demonstration Project

Good arguments can be made for and against prescription privileges, and data adequate for choosing between them are not currently available. As indicated, 10 psychologists were trained and allowed to prescribe drugs under DOD's PDP. Some information is available concerning the success of the program (Laskow & Grill, 2003; Newman, Phelps, Sammons, Dunivin, & Cullen, 2000). In general, the psychologists who participated demonstrated high levels of competency and achievement prior to entering the 2-year program. They primarily prescribed drugs in outpatient clinics, typically to deal with depressive disorders, anxiety disorders, or adjustment disorders. Psychiatrists who provided clinical supervision rated the quality of care provided by the psychologists as good to excellent and reported no adverse patient outcomes. Moreover, although some conflicts between psychologists and psychiatrists appeared early on, relations became generally harmonious; allowing psychologists to prescribe drugs did not degrade staff morale.

The General Accounting Office (GAO) estimated that the DOD would spend 7% more on its 10 prescribing psychologists than it would have spent to provide equivalent services using a traditional mix of psychiatrists and psychologists. The GAO noted that the PDP did not increase the wartime readiness of the DOD, primarily because psychotropic drugs are rarely a priority in combat, but that it might modestly enhance peacetime readiness. The PDP was successful, and a survey by Klusman (1998) indicated that most military primary care physicians, psychologists, and social workers strongly supported the program and the overall initiative to grant psychologists the authority to prescribe. Military psychiatrists, in contrast, were strongly negative regarding both the PDP and the overall initiative.

Save for demonstrating that psychologists can be trained to prescribe drugs in a safe and competent manner, the PDP's relevance for the prescription privileges debate at large appears to be minimal. A relatively small number of highly competent people were trained, and they practiced in close association with psychiatrists in a highly structured setting. Opinions regarding the PDP's value differed across professions, and, more important, whatever virtues it possessed were not sufficient to lead to widespread DOD adoption of prescription privileges for psychologists. This outcome suggests an absence of social validity for the program. That is, one of its consumers—the DOD—was not satisfied with its goals, methods, or outcomes. Unfortunately, no data are available concerning the satisfaction of the military personnel who actually received medication at the hands of psychologists or, perhaps more important, the actual effectiveness of those medications in solving the mental health problems of those personnel.

Arguments for Granting Prescription Privileges

Advocates of prescription privileges make a number of solid arguments in support of their position. For example, Robert Sternberg (2003) wrote in the president's column of the *APA Monitor* that psychologists ought to be allowed prescription privileges because this would allow them to treat the whole person, provide full service, offer medications to patients who need them but are not presently being served, and reduce psychologists' dependence on medical practitioners. Moreover, he indicated that the success of the PDP program and the passage of a prescription authority bill in New Mexico demonstrate, respectively, the potential value and the political feasibility of obtaining prescription privileges. Other advocates have made similar points. In general, it appears that most of the arguments in favor of prescription privileges fall into two general categories.

1. Allowing Psychologists to Prescribe Drugs Will Help to Meet the Needs of People Not Currently Receiving Adequate Mental Health Services

This argument assumes that (a) psychotropic drugs are valuable treatments, (b) there are substantial numbers of people who currently need but do not have access to those drugs, and (c) allowing psychologists to prescribe would meet the needs of those people. Overall, a good case can be made for the value of psychotropic drugs, although they are not panaceas and, as discussed previously with respect to people with mental retardation, they historically have been misused in some populations. The relevant literature is gargantuan and cannot be addressed here. Perhaps a quote from the World Health Organization (WHO; 2005, p. 8) is sufficient:

> A large number of treatments are available for the pharmacological management of mental disorders. Many of these treatments have been shown to be effective in acute stages and in preventing relapses, but much remains unclear about their effectiveness in long-term treatment and in managing everyday mental disorders.

Despite the reservations expressed in the last sentence, the WHO considers some psychotropic drugs as "essential" medications (see Table 32.3), which should be cheaply and widely available worldwide.

Table 32.3 Psychotropic Drugs on the World Health Organization Model List of Essential Drugs

Drugs used in psychotic disorders	Chlorpromazine, fluphenazine, haloperidol
Drugs used in depressive disorders	Amitriptyline
Drugs used in bipolar disorders	Carbamazepine, lithium carbonate, valproic acid
Drugs used in generalized anxiety and sleep disorders	Diazepam
Drugs used in obsessive-compulsive disorders and panic attacks	Clomipramine

Source: Improving Access and Use of Psychotropic Medicines, by the World Health Organization, 2005, Geneva, Switzerland: Author.

Support for the view that there are many people with significant, untreated mental health needs comes from several sources. Among them is a 1999 report from the surgeon general (U.S. Department of Health and Human Services, 1999) indicating that fewer than one-third of all people in the United States with a diagnosable mental disorder receive treatment in a given year. Also commonly cited are data indicating that there is a shortage of psychiatrists, especially in rural areas.

Support for the view that allowing psychologists to prescribe drugs would meet currently unmet needs is conjecture. Presumably, at least some currently unmet mental health needs would respond to nonpharmacological interventions that could be, but are not, currently provided by psychologists. Why would allowing psychologists to prescribe substantially increase the number of people they serve or change patient demographics? Interestingly, a major argument leading to the acceptance of physician assistant as a profession was that physician assistants would provide medical care for rural and other historically underserved populations. In fact, very few (3%) of them do so (Lavoie & Barone, 2006). Complex interactions of sociocultural, geographic, and fiscal variables that influence patients as well as care providers determine who does and who does not receive treatment; creation of a new profession (psychologists who prescribe) will not alter these interactions.

Moreover, even if psychologists who prescribe will be able to increase access to mental health care, this does not mean that there is public demand for them to do so. Professionals from other disciplines (e.g., nurse practitioners, physician assistants), perhaps working in conjunction with psychologists, may well be in higher demand. Some critics suggest, in fact, that the push for prescription privileges has been driven primarily by financial considerations, as a limited number of influential psychologists work to secure continued access to a substantial share of the health care market, a share that is created by their lobbying efforts, not by legitimate need or public demand.

2. Allowing Psychologists to Prescribe Drugs Will Lead to High-Quality Care

This argument begins with the contention that it is possible to train psychologists to competently prescribe psychotropic medications. As noted previously, the success of the PDP generally supports this view. Compared to New Mexico and Louisiana, however, the PDP training was more extensive. For example, the PDP required 660 hours of academic training and 1,900 hours of clinical training, whereas New Mexico requires 450 hours of academic training and 400 hours of clinical training (for a conditional prescribing certificate; further clinical training is required for a general prescription certificate).

Supporters contend that the specialized training required for psychologists to prescribe, coupled with the training they normally receive, is adequate to allow them to prescribe medications safely and effectively. As we have discussed previously, their training in behavioral assessment and commitment to the scientist-practitioner model could be especially useful in diagnosing behavior disorders, in selecting empirically validated interventions, and in monitoring the effects of psychotropic medications. In addition, competent psychologists with expertise in dealing with particular kinds of patients (e.g., people with developmental disabilities, elderly people, or children and adolescents) would be able to offer state-of-the-art nonpharmacological alternatives to psychotropic drugs when appropriate and to provide combined pharmacological and pharmacological interventions. Whether they would do so, or would instead come to rely on pharmacological interventions alone, is unclear. As time passes, data from Louisiana and New Mexico may bear on the issue.

Critics argue that medical training beyond that required to earn prescription privileges is required to use psychotropic medications safely. Expertise in monitoring the therapeutic and adverse effects in other medications is needed, given that many people treated with psychotropic medications receive other kinds of drugs.

If there is in fact a strong need for psychologists who prescribe drugs, and if they can be readily trained to do so without sacrificing other important activities, such as offering nonpharmacological treatments, then granting widespread prescription privileges for psychologists will benefit the profession and society at large.

Arguments against Granting Prescription Privileges

Like the advocates of prescription privileges, the critics have made a number of good arguments (e.g., Heiby, 1998; Lavoie & Barone, 2006). One common argument, mentioned previously, is that the proposed level of training is not adequate to allow psychologists to prescribe psychotropic drugs safely and effectively. Another argument, also mentioned previously, is that the push for prescription privileges is motivated primarily by potential financial gain for psychologists, which is not a legitimate reason for dramatically altering professional boundaries. Two other arguments, both very general, are discussed next.

1. There Is No Legitimate Need for Psychologists to Prescribe

This argument takes three forms. One rests on the simple contention that there is a strong and persistent demand for effective psychological interventions; competent and innovative clinical psychologists have more than enough to do without prescribing drugs (Hayes et al., 2002). Managed care has changed and will continue to change the role of doctorate psychologists, but the field of clinical psychology will remain viable for the foreseeable future. Rather than advocating for prescription privileges, psychologists would be better served by advocating for enhanced acceptance of empirically validated psychological treatments of all mental disorders and by developing new and effective interventions.

A second form of the argument, alluded to in the preceding section, rests on the contention that the alleged demand for prescription privileges was created by a handful of influential psychologists, such as Pat DeLeon (e.g., DeLeon, Dunivin, & Newman, 2002; DeLeon & Wiggins, 1996) and their political allies, not by requests from mental health agencies, people with mental illness, or their advocates. In actuality, the argument goes, the demand for additional professionals who can prescribe is small and, even if prescription privileges are granted to psychologists, is likely to be filled from other professions (physician assistants, registered nurses). Services provided by doctoral-level psychologists are relatively expensive, and wherever possible managed care will seek to replace them with similar services obtained from less expensive professions.

A third form of the argument rests on the contention that psychotropic drugs are restrictive, largely ineffective treatments that are widely overused, at least in part due to questionable practices by the pharmaceutical industry (e.g., Malott, in press; Whitaker, 2002). Therefore, physicians should curb their willingness to prescribe such drugs and certainly no new profession should prescribe them.

All of these arguments have been countered. For example, many studies can be cited to show the clinical effectiveness of psychotropic drugs, including their value in managing conditions typically not responsive to psychological interventions alone (Schizophrenia). The practices of those who currently write most prescriptions for psychotropic drugs, general practitioners, are demonstrably far below optimal (Lavoie & Barone, 2006); therefore, psychologists who competently prescribe drugs can compete effectively against them. In addition, it is claimed, they can provide outreach to currently underserved patient groups. The truth of this contention, like that of all of the claims and counterclaims mentioned in this section, depends on one's source of information and how that information is interpreted.

2. Allowing Psychologists to Prescribe Drugs Will Harm the Profession

One part of this argument is the contention that the prescription privileges debate has eroded the discipline's cohesiveness and may lead to a split similar to that observed in the late 1980s, when the American Psychological Association, emphasizing basic science and the scientist-practitioner model, broke away from APA. Another part emphasizes dissolution of disciplinary boundaries, with a resulting erosion of focus and values. Allowing psychologists to prescribe drugs, the argument goes, would blur the distinction between psychology and medicine and create an unhealthy competition between the disciplines. Moreover, it would direct attention away from studying the variables historically emphasized by psychologists and on developing and employing new treatments based on those variables. Finally, it would shift emphasis away from advocating for and using psychological treatments. All of these happenings would be harmful for psychology.

Further harm would come in the form of altered training requirements. Although training to prescribe in New Mexico and Louisiana is at the postdoctoral level, widespread adoption of prescription privileges legislation might well create a demand for training at the graduate, or even undergraduate, level. Providing this training would seriously reduce opportunities for training in other important areas. Moreover, extensive training in psychopharmacology would be prohibitively expensive. Finally, allowing psychologists to prescribe drugs would open them to insidious influence from the pharmaceutical industry.

Advocates of prescription privileges have countered these arguments by contending that disciplines constantly evolve and, as we have discussed at some length, psychologists have long been involved in psychopharmacology, albeit not as direct treatment providers. For them, moving to the status of treatment providers is a small, logical, and beneficial step. They suggest that the necessary training can be provided at reasonable cost, without seriously compromising opportunities to develop competency in traditional areas. Psychologists competent in pharmacological and nonpharmacological treatments could provide a full range of services and would be in high demand. With careful planning, untoward influence from industry could be avoided (e.g., Antonuccio & Danton, 2003).

Our Position

In weighing arguments for and against prescription privileges, we find it noteworthy that most of the support comes from practice-based organizations, whereas most of the opposition comes from scientist-practitioner groups, with basic science organizations being largely indifferent (Hayes et al., 2002). Our view, expressed earlier, is that optimal use of psychotropic drugs demands acceptance of the scientist-practitioner perspective. The fact that those groups that are avowedly committed to this perspective argue against prescription privileges is noteworthy.

Although proponents have made a number of compelling arguments, our views parallel those of Lavoie and Barone (2006, p. 63), who end their extensive coverage of the prescription debate by noting, "There does not appear to be compelling evidence of the desirability of granting prescription privileges for psychologists." They go on to suggest that, instead of arguing for prescription privileges, psychologists would be better served by improving the dissemination of nonpharmacological services and working with general practitioners and psychiatrists to improve how psychotropic drugs are used. We agree on both counts.

In our view, it is particularly unfortunate that debate has focused almost entirely on psychologists being granted independent drug prescription privileges and has ignored the possibility of psychologists teaming with physicians and other medical personnel who are currently allowed to prescribe. As emphasized in the first section, many psychologists have skills that would allow them to play an invaluable role in assessing drug effects and in providing nonpharmacological alternatives and adjuncts to psychotropic drugs. Combining these skills with those of women and men specifically trained in medicine would go far in improving mental health care, without necessitating a dramatic change in the activities of either psychologists or medical doctors. Although psychologists have much to contribute to psychopharmacology, our opinion at present, as it was in 1998 (Poling, Christian, & Ehrhardt, 1998), is that the move to obtain prescription privileges is premature, unwarranted, and unwise. Nonetheless, it is sure to continue.

SUMMARY

Psychologists have made (and are continuing to make) many significant contributions to the study of psychotropic and other psychoactive drugs. Their expertise in quantifying behavior has been invaluable in determining how drugs affect mood, cognitive status, and overt actions. Moreover, their conceptual models have been useful in explaining drug effects. Finally, their knowledge of the variables that control behavior has yielded effective strategies for treating drug abuse.

In recent years, some psychologists and their affiliates have argued that properly trained psychologists should be allowed to prescribe psychotropic medications, and New Mexico and Louisiana have recently allowed them to do so. Too little time has passed to allow the outcome of doing so to be determined. There are legitimate arguments for and against granting prescription privileges to psychologists; those arguments are summarized in the present chapter and elsewhere (e.g., Hayes & Heiby, 1998a; Lavoie & Barone, 2006; Sammons et al., 2003). After considering those arguments, our view is that psychologists can best serve mental health needs not by prescribing drugs, but by delivering nonpharmacological interventions and serving as members of multidisciplinary teams that arrange and evaluate pharmacological interventions.

REFERENCES

American Psychiatric Association. (1994). *Diagnostic and statistical manual of mental disorders* (4th ed.). Washington, DC: Author.

American Psychological Association. (1992). *Report of the Ad Hoc Task Force on Psychopharmacology.* Washington, DC: Author.

American Psychological Association. (n.d.). *Division 55: American Society for the Advancement of Pharmacotherapy.* Retrieved from www.apa.org/about/division/div55.html.

Antonuccio, D. O., & Danton, W. G. (2003). Psychology in the prescription era: Building a firewall between marketing and science. *American Psychologist, 58,* 1028–1043.

Baldessarini, R. J. (2000). Fifty years of biomedical psychiatry and psychopharmacology in America. In R. Menninger & J. Nemiah (Eds.), *American psychiatry after World War II (1944–1994)* (pp. 371–421). Washington, DC: American Psychiatric Press.

Baldessarini, R. J., & Tarazi, F. I. (2006). Pharmacotherapy of psychosis and mania. In L. L. Brunton, J. S. Lazo, & K. L. Parker (Eds.), *Goodman and Gilman's the pharmacological basis of therapeutics* (pp. 461–500). New York: McGraw-Hill.

Barkley, R. A. (1998). *Attention-deficit/hyperactivity disorder: A handbook for diagnosis and treatment.* New York: Guilford Press.

Barkley, R. A. (2000). Taking charge of ADHD: *The complete, authoritative guide for parents.* New York: Guilford Press.

Barlow, D. H., & Hersen, M. (1984). *Single case experimental designs: Strategies for studying behavior change.* Elmsford, NY: Pergamon Press.

Baumeister, A. A., & Sein, J. A. (1990). Pharmacological control of aberrant behavior in the mentally retarded: Towards a more rational approach. *Neuroscience and Biobehavioral Reviews, 14,* 253–262.

Brylewski, J., & Duggan, L. (1999). Antipsychotic medication for challenging behaviour in people with intellectual disability: A systematic review of randomized controlled trials. *Journal of Intellectual Disability Research, 43*, 360–371.

Buccafusco, J. J. (2001). *Methods of behavior analysis in neuroscience.* New York: CRC Press.

Campbell, D. T., & Stanley, J. C. (1963). *Experimental and quasi-experimental designs for research.* Chicago: Rand McNally.

Chiefetz, D. I., & Salloway, J. C. (1984). Patterns of mental health services provided by HMOs. *American Psychologist, 39*, 495–502.

Christiansen, A., & Jacobson, N. S. (1994). Who (or what) can do psychotherapy: The status (and challenge) of nonprofessional therapies. *Psychological Science, 5*, 8–14.

Cullen, E. A., & Newman, R. (1977). In pursuit of prescription privileges. *Professional Psychology: Research and Practice, 28*, 101–106.

Cummings, N. A. (1995). Impact of managed care on employment and training: A primer for survival. *Professional Psychology: Research and Practice, 26*, 10–15.

Dawes, R. M. (1994). *House of cards.* New York: Free Press.

DeLeon, P., Dunivin, D. L., & Newman, R. (2002). The tide rises. *Clinical Psychology: Science and Practice, 9*, 249–255.

DeLeon, P., & Wiggins, J. G., Jr. (1996). Prescription privileges for psychologists. *American Psychologist, 51*, 225–229.

Dermer, M. L., & Hoch, T. A. (1999). Improving descriptions of single-experiments in research texts written for undergraduates. *Psychological Record, 49*, 49–66.

Duggan, L., & Brylewski, J. (1999). Effectiveness of antipsychotic medication in people with intellectual disability and schizophrenia: A systematic review. *Journal of Intellectual Disability Research, 43*, 94–104.

Foote, E. S. (1958). Combined chlorpromazine and reserpine in the treatment of chronic psychotics. *Journal of Mental Science, 58*, 201–205.

Frank, R. G., Conti, R. M., & Goldman, H. H. (2005). Mental health policy and psychotropic drugs. *Milbank Quarterly, 83*, 271–298.

Gadow, K., & Poling, A. (1988). *Pharmacotherapy and mental retardation.* San Diego, CA: College-Hill Press.

Greiner, T. (1958). Problems of methodology in research with drugs. *American Journal on Mental Deficiency, 64*, 346–352.

Hayes, S. C., Barlow, D. H., & Nelson-Gray, R. O. (1999). *The scientist practitioner: Research and accountability in the age of managed care.* Boston: Allyn & Bacon.

Hayes, S. C., & Heiby, E. M. (1996). Psychology's drug problem: Do we need a fix or should we just say no? *American Psychologist, 51*, 198–206.

Hayes, S. C., & Heiby, E. M. (1998a). Preface. In S. C. Hayes & E. M. Heiby (Eds.), *Prescription privileges for psychologists: A critical appraisal* (pp. v–vi). Reno, NV: Context Press.

Hayes, S. C., & Heiby, E. M. (1998b). *Prescription privileges for psychologists: A critical appraisal.* Reno, NV: Context Press.

Hayes, S. C., Walser, R. D., & Bach, P. (2002). Prescription privileges for psychologists: Constituencies and conflicts. *Journal of Clinical Psychology, 58*, 697–708.

Heiby, E. M. (1998). The case against prescription privileges for psychologists: An overview. In S. C. Hayes & E. M. Heiby (Eds.), *Prescription privileges for psychologists: A critical appraisal* (pp. 51–73). Reno, NV: Context Press.

Higgins, S. T., Budney, A. J., Bickel, W. K., Hughes, J. R., Feorg, F. E., & Badger, G. J. (1993). Achieving cocaine abstinence with a behavioral approach. *American Journal of Psychiatry, 150*, 763–769.

Higgins, S. T., Delaney, D. D., Budney, A. J., Bickel, W. K., Hughes, J. R., Feorg, F., et al. (1991). A behavioral approach to achieving initial cocaine abstinence. *American Journal of Psychiatry, 148*, 1218–1224.

Julien, R. M. (2001). *A primer of drug action.* New York: Henry Holt.

Klusman, L. E. (1998). Military health care providers' view on prescribing privileges for psychologists. *Professional Psychology: Research and Practice, 29*, 223–229.

Kollins, S., Ehrhardt, K., & Poling, A. (2000). Clinical drug assessment. In A. Poling & T. Byrne (Eds.), *Introduction to behavioral pharmacology* (pp. 191–218). Reno, NV: Context Press.

Laraway, S., Snycerski, S., Byrne, T., & Poling, A. (2000). Drug abuse. In A. Poling & T. Byrne (Eds.), *Behavioral pharmacology* (pp. 219–248). Reno, NV: Context Press.

Laraway, S., Snycerski, S., Michael, J., & Poling, A. (2003). Motivating operations and terms to describe them: Some further refinements. *Journal of Applied Behavior Analysis, 36,* 407–414.

Laskow, G. B., & Grill, D. J. (2003). The Department of Defense experiment: The Psychopharmacology Demonstration Project. In M. T. Sammons, R. U. Page, & R. F. Levant (Eds.), *Prescription privileges for psychologists: A history and guide* (pp. 77–101). Washington, DC: American Psychological Association.

Lavoie, K. L., & Barone, S. (2006). Prescription privileges for psychologists: A comprehensive review and critical analysis of current issues and controversies. *CNS Drugs, 20,* 51–66.

Lavoie, K. L., & Fleet, R. P. (2002). Should psychologists be granted prescription privileges? A review of the prescription privileges debate for psychiatrists. *Canadian Journal of Psychiatry, 47,* 443–448.

Macht, D. L., & Mora, C. F. (1921). Effects of opium alkaloids on the behavior of rats on the circular maze. *Journal of Pharmacology and Experimental Therapeutics, 16,* 219–235.

Malott, D. (in press). Are women, people of color, Asians, and southern Europeans inherently inferior to north-European males? A history of biological determinism: A cultural, spiritual and intellectual disgrace and the implications for our current understanding of "mental illness." *Behavior and Social Issues.*

Matson, J. L., Bamburg, J. W., Mayville, E. A., Pinkston, J., Bielecki, J., Kuhn, D., et al. (2000). Psychopharmacology and mental retardation: A 10 year review (1990–1999). *Research in Developmental Disabilities, 21,* 263–296.

Michigan Legislature. (2007). *Michigan compiled laws.* Available from www.legislature.mi.gov/ (S(gcttdoae4be3f555jmn34e2h))/mileg.aspx?page=getobject&objectname=mcl-act-368-of-1978/.

New York Academy of Sciences. (1956). Techniques for the study of the behavioral effects. *Annals of the New York Academy of Sciences, 65.*

Newman, R., Phelps, R., Sammons, M. T., Dunivin, D. L., & Cullen, E. A. (2000). Evaluation of the psychopharmacology demonstration project: A retrospective analysis. *Professional Psychology: Research and Practice, 31,* 598–603.

Northup, J., Fusilier, I., Swanson, V., Roane, H., & Borrero, J. (1997). An evaluation of methylphenidate as a potential establishing operation for some common classroom reinforcers. *Journal of Applied Behavior Analysis, 30,* 615–625.

PBS-Frontline. (2006). *Interview with Russell Barkley.* Available from www.pbs.org/wgbh/pages/frontline/ shows/medicating/interviews/barkley.html.

Pickens, R. (1977). Behavioral pharmacology: A brief history. In T. Thompson & P. B. Dews (Eds.), *Advances in behavioral pharmacology* (Vol. 1, pp. 230–261). New York: Academic Press.

Poling, A. (1994). Pharmacological treatment of behavioral problems in people with mental retardation: Some ethical considerations. In L. J. Hayes, G. J. Hayes, S. C. Moore, & P. M. Ghezzi (Eds.), *Ethical issues in developmental disabilities* (pp. 149–177). Reno, NV: Context Press.

Poling, A., & Byrne, T. (2000). *Introduction to behavioral pharmacology.* Reno, NV: Context Press.

Poling, A., Christian, L., & Ehrhardt, K. (1998). The implications of basic research in psychopharmacology for prescription privileges for psychologists. In S. C. Hayes & E. M. Heiby (Eds.), *Prescription privileges for psychologists: A critical appraisal* (pp. 133–159). Reno, NV: Context Press.

Poling, A., & Ehrhardt, K. (1999). Applied behavior analysis, social validation, and the psychopharmacology of mental retardation. *Mental Retardation and Developmental Disabilities Research Reviews, 5,* 342–347.

Poling, A., Laraway, S., Ehrhardt, K., Jennings, L., & Turner, L. (2004). Pharmaceutical interventions and developmental disabilities. In W. L. Williams (Ed.), *Developmental disabilities: Etiology, assessment, intervention, and integration* (pp. 105–124). Reno, NV: Context Press.

Poling, A., & LeSage, M. L. (1995). Evaluating psychotropic drugs in people with mental retardation: Where are the social validity data? *American Journal on Mental Retardation, 100,* 193–200.

RxList. (2005). *The top 300 prescriptions for 2005 by number of U.S. prescriptions dispensed.* Available from www.rxlist.com/top300/.

Sammons, M. T., Page, R. U., & Levant, R. F. (2003). *Prescription privileges for psychologists: A history and guide.* Washington, DC: American Psychological Association.

Sanua, V. D. (1998). The political history of the prescription privilege movement within the American Psychological Association. In S. C. Hayes & E. M. Heiby (Eds.), *Prescription privileges for psychologists: A critical appraisal* (pp. 79–95). Reno, NV: Context Press.

Schroeder, S. R. (1985). Issues and future direction of psychopharmacology in mental retardation. *Psychopharmacology Bulletin, 21*, 323–326.

Snycerski, S., Laraway, S., & Poling, A. (2000). Assessing drug effects in humans: Basic research. In A. Poling & T. Byrne (Eds.), *Introduction to behavioral pharmacology* (pp. 111–140). Reno, NV: Context Press.

Soldz, S., & McCullough, L. (1999). *Reconciling empirical knowledge and clinical experience: The art and science of psychotherapy.* Washington, DC: American Psychological Association.

Sprague, R. L., & Werry, J. L. (1971). Methodology of psychopharmacological studies with the retarded. In N. R. Ellis (Ed.), *International review of research in mental retardation* (Vol. 5, pp. 147–219). New York: Academic Press.

Sternberg, R., J. (2003). President's column: It's time for prescription privileges. *American Psychological Association Monitor, 34*, 5.

Thompson, T. (1981). Behavioral mechanisms and loci of drug action: An overview. In T. Thompson & C. Johanson (Eds.), *Behavioral pharmacology of human drug dependence* (pp. 1–10). Washington, DC: U.S. Government Printing Office.

Thompson, T., & Pickens, R. (1971). *Stimulus properties of drugs.* New York: Appleton-Century-Crofts.

Thompson, T., & Schuster, C. R. (1968). *Behavioral pharmacology.* Englewood Cliffs, NJ: Prentice-Hall.

U.S. Department of Health and Human Services. (1999). *Mental health: A report of the surgeon general.* Rockville, MD: Author.

U.S. Food and Drug Administration. (2007). Federal Food, Drug, and Cosmetic Act. Available from www.fda.gov/opacom/laws/fdcact/fdcact1.htm.

VandenBos, G. R., & Williams, S. (2000). Is psychologists' involvement in the prescribing of psychotropic medication really a new activity? *Professional Psychology: Research and Practice, 31*, 615–618.

van Haaren, F. (1993). *Methods in behavioral pharmacology.* New York: Elsevier.

Walters, G. D. (2001). A meta-analysis of opinion data on the prescription privilege debate. *Canadian Psychology, 42*, 119–125.

Whitaker, R. (2002). *Bad science, bad medicine, and the enduring mistreatment of the mentally ill.* Cambridge, MA: Perseus Press.

World Health Organization. (2005). *Improving access and use of psychotropic medicines.* Geneva, Switzerland: Author.

Author Index

Subject Index